Dividing Lines

Dividing Lines

Municipal Politics and the Struggle for Civil
Rights in Montgomery, Birmingham, and Selma

J. MILLS THORNTON III

THE UNIVERSITY OF ALABAMA PRESS

Tuscaloosa and London

Library of Congress Cataloging-in-Publication Data

Thornton, J. Mills, 1943–
Dividing lines : municipal politics and the struggle for civil rights in
Montgomery, Birmingham, and Selma / J. Mills Thornton, III.
p.   cm.
Includes index.
ISBN 0-8173-1170-X (cloth : alk. paper)

1. Civil rights movements—Alabama—History—20th century. 2. African
Americans—Civil rights—Alabama. 3. Political culture—Alabama—History—
20th century. 4. Montgomery (Ala.)—Politics and government—20th century.
5. Birmingham (Ala.)—Politics and government—20th century. 6. Selma
(Ala.)—Politics and government—20th century. I. Title.
E185.93.A3 T48 2002
323.1'1960730761'09045—dc21
2002004774

British Library Cataloguing-in-Publication Data available

For Brenda
opus omniaque

Contents

Acknowledgments

This book had its origins during the academic year 1987–88, when I was a fellow of the University of Virginia's Carter G. Woodson Institute. I had gone to Virginia to prepare a monograph on the 1955–56 Montgomery bus boycott, an event I had been studying for some time, but an invitation to participate in a conference the Woodson Institute had organized that spring on the civil rights movement got me thinking about the seemingly anomalous place of the bus boycott in the larger pattern of events that it had in significant part initiated. The paper I prepared for this conference—subsequently published in the volume of conference proceedings, Armstead L. Robinson and Patricia Sullivan, eds., *New Directions in Civil Rights Studies* (University Press of Virginia, 1991)—and the response of the conference participants to it persuaded me that my ideas were sufficiently out of the mainstream to require a full-scale statement if they were to be entirely convincing to other students of the period, or for that matter, even to me. I therefore undertook the preparation of the present volume, though had I known at the time exactly what I was taking on I might have reconsidered the decision. At any rate, I am now deeply grateful to Paul Gaston and the late Armstead Robinson for having arranged the fellowship and conference that gave rise to these thoughts, and to Jeff Norrell, Bill Chafe, Charles Eagles, Phil Ethington, and others who urged me to develop them. Much of the writing of this study occurred during 1994–95, when I was a fellow at the Woodrow Wilson International Center for Scholars in Washington, D.C. I am equally grateful to the late Charles Blitzer and the staff of the Wilson Center for having created so welcoming an environment for me to begin the process of transforming my ideas into words.

My understanding of this subject rests upon the invariably kind and helpful efforts of numerous archivists. In particular, the rich resources of the Alabama Department of Archives and History, in Montgomery, are the principal foundation not merely of this book but of nearly everything I have ever written. Ed Bridges was always ready to listen to my thoughts and to read drafts of my chapters. Joe Caver and Norwood Kerr often roamed the stacks to locate the documents I needed. But there is not, I think, a single employee of the archives who has not at one time or another gone beyond the call of duty to assist me. Equally obliging were Marvin Whiting and the staff of the Archives and Manuscripts Division of the Birmingham Public Library. The staff of the Archives of the Church of the Brethren in Elgin, Illinois, were especially kind, keeping the archives open for me over a weekend so that I could complete my work there. The staffs of the University of Chicago Library and the Chicago Historical Society were also very helpful. The staffs of the Peace Collection at the Swarthmore College Library, the Amistad Center at Tulane University, the Oral History Collection at Howard University, the Archives Division of the Duke University Library, the Archives Division of the University of Alabama Library, the Oral History Collection of the Alabama State University Library, and the James Madison Library of the Library of Congress did everything possible to assist me. And the staff of the Southeastern Regional Federal Records Center in East Point, Georgia, were particularly accommodating. Finally, I have worked many hours in the quiet and beautiful Library of the Alabama Supreme Court, and I am profoundly thankful for that excellent facility. Three undergraduate research assistants, Jason Cowart, Aaron Kanter, and Joocheol Nam, helped me at various stages of this project, and it is a great pleasure for me to acknowledge their contributions to this final product.

Among my fellow historians, no one has done more to improve this book than Phil Ethington. Always enthusiastic and sympathetic, always ready to give me a swift kick where it hurts, Phil has waded through the manuscript in two different forms with painstaking attention and, what is far more important, with extraordinary intelligence and insight. The structure of the book is much clearer, the prose more graceful, and the argument a great deal more carefully considered thanks to his efforts. Equally supportive for just as long has been Dave Garrow, whose encyclopedic knowledge of this subject and whose faith in this project have stood me in good stead through the years. Sheldon Hackney I have known since my undergraduate days at Princeton. His reading of this manuscript, despite his enormously busy schedule, was especially kind. And my colleague Matt Lassiter, who read this manuscript in the midst of preparing his own excellent new book for the press, was just as gracious. Sheldon's and Matt's suggestions for the restructuring of the chapters were decisive in giving the book its final form. Ed and Martha Bridges have believed in the usefulness of this analysis even when I myself had doubts. Ed's many intellectual contributions to the book I have already mentioned, but his friendship and our many long conversations have mattered even more. Martha typed the manuscript in its next-to-last version, and her interest in it never faltered. Leah Atkins and Glenn Eskew read the Birmingham portions of the book and reassured me that I had not too badly misunderstood their city, alien though it may be to my Black Belt sensibilities. I presented a draft of the Montgomery material to the Cumberland Legal History Seminar at Samford University, thanks to the suggestion of Bryn Roberts, and am appreciative of the advice the participants gave me about it.

I turn finally to what is infinitely my greatest debt. Brenda waited patiently while my research slogged along and my ideas slowly matured, listened to all my qualms and complaints, reassured me and pushed me on. I could not possibly have asked for more. The dedication of this volume is paltry recompense, but it is offered with profoundest gratitude and love.

Ann Arbor, Michigan
September 2001

Dividing Lines

Introduction

1

In October 1954, Professor C. Vann Woodward delivered at the University of Virginia the lectures on the origins of southern racial segregation that the following year would be published under the title *The Strange Career of Jim Crow.* In the years just after Reconstruction, he said, the patterns of race relations in the region were strikingly diverse, varying from town to town and from institution to institution, and the opinions of white southerners about the optimal structure of racial adjustment were correspondingly in flux. It was not until the end of the nineteenth century and the beginning of the twentieth that the governmental enforcement of statutorily defined racial boundaries and the elimination of blacks from the southern electorate by constitutional requirements became the universal regional standard. The source of this development was political. In the early 1890s, Democratic Party politicians had aggressively denounced their Populist adversaries as advocates of racial equality, and therefore as enemies of white security, and the polarization of racial alternatives that had emerged from these campaigns had driven the more moderate, paternalist wing of the Democrats into an acceptance of the leadership of the popular racist demagogues who had made legal segregation and constitutional disfranchisement Democratic Party doctrine. Out of the Populist elections, therefore, had emerged a politically expedient orthodoxy that, because of the demands of political competition, had hardened after the turn of the century into an inflexible regionwide set of legal mandates, embodied in legislative acts and municipal ordinances.

Woodward's portrait of these events began almost at once to provoke objections. An uncompromising commitment to white supremacy had been general among white southerners since colonial times, his opponents observed; the militant defense of slavery established this fact beyond cavil. Segregated institutions, and in particular segregated churches and schools, had already begun to appear during Reconstruction. Moreover, black leaders seeking the advancement of their race had often initiated their establishment. The new statutory and constitutional commands of the 1890s had merely codified and generalized practices already widespread. But the codification and generalization of these practices formed precisely the point, Woodward replied. During the 1880s alternative patterns of racial contact were to be found throughout the region. There were even prominent white spokesmen, usually radical Populists, who questioned white supremacy. And among the white supremacists there was as yet no single accepted institutional expression of the prejudice. By the 1900s, however, the alternatives had been eliminated and dissent had effectively been criminalized. This momentous transformation had been imposed by governmental authorities as a result of explicitly political calculations.[1]

While the controversy about Woodward's argument was engulfing a portion of the academy, the nation was being engulfed by the conflict surrounding the attempt to extirpate the very ordinances, statutes, and constitutional provisions that had been Woodward's subject. Indeed, Woodward's lectures themselves had grown directly out of his efforts during 1953 to assist the NAACP Legal Defense Fund in the preparation of its historical brief to be submitted to the U.S. Supreme Court as a part of the argument of the school segregation cases, which had been decided just five months before he addressed the Virginia audience. But it was the escalating civil rights movement in the decade following the school desegregation decision that, rather ironically, underlay much of the skepticism in subsequent years about his ideas. The black demonstrations seemed so deeply rooted in the most fundamental ethical convictions of Western civilization, and the white resistance seemed so fully to represent the immemorial evil of which that civilization was capable, that Woodward's depiction of southern segregation as a relatively recent and distinctly contingent historical development came to seem to many observers to be belied by the reality surrounding them. How could a system that incarnated a bigotry as old as the region itself, that was so unmistakably a transmutation of the slavery that had preceded it, that was defended so tenaciously by what appeared to be so nearly unbroken a white phalanx, be properly conceived as a product of a few largely forgotten local elections that had occurred within a six-year period some seventy years before?

In truth, however, if the civil rights movement had been correctly understood at the time, it would have had very different lessons to teach. Three aspects of those lessons began to emerge relatively quickly. In the first place, it became clear that white southerners' doubts about segregation were both more extensive and more complex than either zealous segregationists or civil rights advocates initially appreciated. In the second place, it became clear that blacks' desire for civil rights and their enthusiasm for integration were by no means identical sentiments. And thirdly, and most significantly, it became clear that segregation was merely one institutional manifestation of white supremacy, that white supremacy had taken other forms in other parts of the nation, and that the elimination of segregation was not therefore the equivalent of the establishment of racial justice. All three of these discoveries were hard-bought for most disciples of the civil rights movement, and all three worked to diminish the reservations about Woodward's arguments that the movement had aroused. A fourth aspect of the movement's lessons relevant to the historiographical controversy, however, still is not typically comprehended today, and it is the subject of this book: just as local politics was essential to the creation of southern segregation, so local politics was the crucial factor in creating the circumstances that ended it. Woodward's insights into segregation's origins actually could have clarified the nature of the events that were preparing its destruction. Unfortunately, the whirlwind that the civil rights movement generated obscured this element of its lessons at the time. It is the intention of the following pages to illuminate the essential connection between the intensely local concerns of municipal politics and the vast national and international changes in race relations they wrought during the 1950s and 1960s.[2]

The key to appreciating the role of municipal politics in the civil rights movement is to ask ourselves twin questions. Why did the civil rights movement manifest itself as mass direct-action campaigns in certain southern cities and towns, and not in others in which social conditions were apparently so closely comparable? Why were there sustained demonstrations in Birmingham rather than in Mobile, in Montgomery rather than in Columbus or Meridian, in Selma rather than in Valdosta, Bainbridge, or Dothan? And too, why did the direct-action campaigns happen in these places when they did, rather than earlier or later in the period? The history of the civil rights movement as it is customarily told, as an episode in the history of the United States, has not been able to deal effectively with such questions. Indeed, they are usually not even broached. The implication in many popular accounts is that the cities in which confrontations would be staged were consciously selected by national civil rights organizations. It is true that the Southern Christian Leadership Conference (SCLC) frequently selected cities in which it would organize demonstrations with an eye to whether or not the city was likely to gain favorable national publicity for the cause. In every case, however, there was an existing local civil rights organization in the city already engaged in protests; the SCLC was always invited to give its help by the local leaders, though it accepted or rejected the invitation for its own reasons. And this explanation is still less applicable to the activities of other components of the movement. The National Association for the Advancement of Colored People (NAACP) had local branches throughout the nation and ordinarily became involved in litigation when a case came to the attention of local branch officials; it almost never lent its support to demonstrations or direct action. The Student Non-violent Coordinating Committee (SNCC) was committed to long-term community organizing at the local level throughout the region; and except for the Freedom Rides, the Congress of Racial Equality (CORE) attempted, less successfully, to follow the same pattern. The National Urban League was not generally active in the South. The reality about the civil rights confrontations in southern towns during the period, then, is that they were everywhere local in origin, even when they received assistance from sympathetic outside forces.

I suspect that all careful students of these events would grant that much. At any rate, the three direct-action efforts on which this investigation will focus—those in Montgomery, Birmingham, and Selma—were beyond question indigenous in their origins. Though all three received significant assistance from national organizations, and the campaigns in Birmingham and Selma would undoubtedly have been considerably less successful without it, the campaigns were not produced by the national organizations. Rather, the national organizations—the NAACP in Montgomery, the SCLC in Birmingham and Selma—built upon movements initiated locally; indeed, they used the local movements for their own purposes, which in each of the three cases were not entirely consonant with local intentions.

It remains nevertheless much too easy for historians of the civil rights movement to think of its several local collisions as having built upon each other, in a mounting crescendo from Montgomery to Selma. Indeed, the very concept of a civil rights movement, when viewed from the perspective of its impact upon national history, encourages us to do so. And a focus upon the movement's regional and national leaders seems to confirm it; the SCLC did attempt, for instance, to use lessons derived from Montgomery to understand the challenge of Albany, did worry about the errors committed in Albany when it undertook to assist in Birmingham, and did employ in Selma the strategies it had developed earlier in Birmingham. Students of a maturing "movement culture," moreover, are necessarily compelled by the concept itself to emphasize the linkages from one incident to another. In fact, the abstraction is sufficiently powerful that it sometimes betrays its enthusiasts into assuming the importance of prior influences without bothering to establish that they were really at work. Some investigators, for instance, have erroneously attributed to the Baton Rouge bus boycott of 1953 a causative role in the Montgomery bus boycott of 1955–56—in part, it would appear, simply on the basis of *post hoc ergo propter hoc* reasoning.[3]

The notion that the various direct-action efforts in the South after 1955 were particular manifestations of a coherent black protest movement against the southern social system—generated in large part by the U.S. Supreme Court's 1954 decision declaring school segregation unconstitutional, and southern white resistance to that decision—was pervasive among northern journalists and observers at the time. Moreover, in the eyes of most commentators, it was precisely this belief that lent the various local demonstrations broader social significance. And it was what came therefore to seem, in the press reports on it, a swelling regionwide tide of protest that in great part eventually compelled national political institutions to take the movement seriously. Nor, of course, was this perspective devoid of truth. Certainly black hostility to racial discrimination was virtually universal, and the Supreme Court's decisions that the Constitution forbade any governmental enforcement of such discrimination had for the first time in many years placed this long-standing hostility into a powerfully national context. Yet a sensitive examination of the local movements themselves allows us to see them from a different, and no less valid, point of view.

The black Selma attorney J. L. Chestnut, Jr., gives us in his memoirs, for instance, this description of attitudes among his black fellow townsfolk at the time of George Wallace's election as governor of Alabama in 1962:

> Wallace reinvigorated white Alabama's resistance. Each September since [1958] . . . another school system in the South had been forced to desegregate—Little Rock, Richmond, New Orleans. Wallace was elected the fall the courts ordered the University of Mississippi to admit James Meredith, when riots broke out and the Kennedys sent in the National Guard. The walls of Jericho were beginning to crumble and up stepped Wallace saying, "Don't worry, folks. We'll hold the line. I am the man to do it." These claims stiffened white resolve. . . . In Selma, the Wallace phenomenon was clearly in evidence. . . . From my vantage point, the white community in Selma was reacting to phantoms and in every way oversensitive because there was no counter-development I could see in the black community. It seemed to me they were engaged in a paranoid obsession similar to their belief that white women were in danger from black men. When I looked at the black community, I didn't detect any threat to white women or to segregation. [Sheriff Clark's] posse was organized to head off an assault that wasn't developing in black Selma any damn way.
>
> In Selma in 1962, no black institution or organization, with the exception of the little Dallas County Voters League, was promoting civil rights or organizing black people around any goal except going to heaven, providing a decent education, or having a good time— not the clubs or fraternities, not the churches, not Selma University, not the black teachers' association. The NAACP was banned statewide, and the local chapter already was demoralized by the fallout from the unsuccessful petition to integrate the schools.
>
> At the bootleg houses, the clubs, the Elks, Selma University, we

would occasionally discuss the public issues of the day. It was frustrating to listen to the pessimistic theme song: "These [black] folk here won't get together. They won't take a chance." In a way, it was more difficult arguing about oppression with black people than it was with white people—and a whole lot more discouraging. . . . I would be trying to prove that while some particular case—like those that outlawed the all-white Democratic primary in Texas—had been decided elsewhere, the court's decision opened a door nationally. "I don't know about Texas, but I don't see any doors opening in Selma. Do you?" That's what I'd hear. Many black people in Selma thought and talked only in terms of what George Wallace or white people in Selma were going to permit. They thought the state of Alabama was more powerful than the federal government.

And even though Chestnut was fully informed about the rapidly developing body of national civil rights law, he was actually not much more sanguine himself than were his more parochial neighbors. "My concern was whether federal power would be exercised against Southern whites on behalf of blacks, and on this score, in 1962, I was only slightly less pessimistic than the people I was arguing with. . . . I didn't think anything of great consequence would come out of the White House or the Justice Department."[4]

As we shall see, the principal source of the White Citizens' Council's strength in Montgomery and Selma at this period was its confident conviction that, by preventing local white dissent, it was on the verge of winning the battle with the civil rights forces and their federal allies. Nor did black leaders at the heart of the local struggles therefore possess any greater sense of the vast changes that were just about to sweep through their communities. In the summer of 1963, nearly three months after the end of the demonstrations of that spring, Birmingham city councilman Alan Drennen, while campaigning for merger with the city's suburbs, commented that without it, "Birmingham by 1980 could be politically controlled and operated by members of the colored race." Emory O. Jackson, the editor of the *Birmingham World,* the voice of the black community and one of black Birmingham's best-informed spokesmen, greeted this assertion with astonishment and ridicule: "Mr. Drennen knows better than this. At the present rate of Negro voting [registration], it would take over 40 years for the Negro group to get its potential vote on the poll lists." And even when it had done so, "The Negro population is only 38 per cent of the total." In the end, of course, Drennen's prediction proved quite accurate; Birmingham elected its first black mayor in 1979. But the notion seemed so outlandish to Jackson in 1963 that Drennen's mere expression of it caused Jackson to rage, "The issue of merger is now enmeshed with racial bigotry, it seems to us." Jackson simply could not imagine at that time the capacity of the civil rights movement to sweep aside Alabama's restrictions on registration completely within two more years, and the social transformations that the achievement would shortly thereafter engender in his city.[5]

It is precisely this aspect of the events of the period that the assumption of a coherent regionwide civil rights movement obscures: the capacity of what seemed always to have been to limit understandings of what could be. Very few participants in the civil rights movement were able to conceive the shape of thoroughgoing reform. The movement actually proceeded through tiny revelations of possible change. The Montgomery bus boycott initially sought only to obtain the pattern of seating segregation in use in Mobile; the Albany movement was inaugurated simply in an effort to compel the city's bus and train stations to abide by the Interstate Commerce Commission's nondiscrimination order, issued in response to the Freedom Rides; the Birmingham demonstrations had as their goal just the desegregation of the lunch counters in the five downtown department and five-and-ten-cent stores; the Dallas County Voters League asked merely for an evenhanded administration of the state's literacy standard for registration, not its elimination. It is not that blacks in these cities would not ideally have wished for more. It is that even the belief that this much was attainable was itself a momentous achievement—an achievement that may not be presumed, but instead requires an explanation.

If we abandon—as we must—the notion that the cities in which direct-action campaigns occurred were consciously selected for them by national civil rights leaders and organizations, then the conception of a civil rights movement in which each episode leads to the next at once reveals a fatal logical flaw. It is certainly true that black resentment of discriminatory treatment was ubiquitous, and black exultation at civil rights victories elsewhere, whether in the courts or in the streets, was general, if usually tempered profoundly by generations of disappointment. But exactly for that reason, the conception offers no real way of understanding why the accomplishments in Birmingham should have generated a response in Selma, rather than, as I have said, in Dothan, Meridian, or Valdosta. The explanation we seek must be able to distinguish one southern town from all the others and must allow us to comprehend how the black citizens of that town—or at any rate, a significant element among them—came to conclude that the reality all around them, that formed the very substance of their daily existence, was in fact capable of being changed.

Part of the answer, of course, is that the South in the decades after World War II was caught up in an immense economic transformation, one that brought new prosperity and new opportunities and institutions to black communities as well as—if on a rather more modest scale than— white. Viewed from this long-term perspective, the civil rights movement was unquestionably a revolution of rising expectations; blacks were able to believe that reality could change for them because it actually was changing, and very rapidly too, throughout these years. But again, this observation, however accurate, is no less true for towns in which direct-action campaigns did not develop than for those in which they did. Another part of the answer is that integration in other places, once it occurred, proved that it was possible; there is no doubt, for instance, that Fred Shuttlesworth was moved to seek the integration of Birmingham's buses because of the successful integration of the buses in Montgomery. But no such answer can be fundamental, because in that case it would obviously be circular. And probably of even greater significance than the logical objection is the historical one: as a matter of fact, an achievement by blacks in any one town was ordinarily taken up by blacks in other towns, if at all, only very slowly, haltingly, and with enormous hesitation and difficulty.

Another possible explanation, and one that doubtless contains more than a grain of truth, would turn on the quality of local leadership. It would seem reasonable to maintain that racial conflict was more likely to arise in a community when it contained particularly forceful or militant black leaders, or particularly insensitive or brutal white leaders, or both. And the characters around whom the municipal encounters of the decade tended to organize themselves do very often seem to fall into the one or the other category. But the historian who investigates these collisions closely is likely to come to a rather different conclusion. In the first place, before the outbreak of racial strife in a town, black leadership was frequently divided and weak. There might be a small group of energetic leaders, but there was a much larger group of eviscerated figureheads speaking for a timorous and quiescent mass. It was ordinarily the events of the crisis themselves that concentrated the passions of the black population upon the programs of the few dynamic black notables in the community, turned these individuals into spokesmen, and pushed them to the fore. Indeed, the examination of southern municipalities in which open racial conflict failed to appear may well disclose the presence in them of leaders even more vigorous than those to be found heading demonstrations elsewhere. It would seem plausible to suggest that a community that had managed to develop active and effective black leaders, whose remonstrances were at least sometimes heeded by those in power, was less, rather than more, likely to be a community in which blacks would feel compelled to turn to direct action. One clear example of this process at work is Mobile, where the indefatigable president of the NAACP branch, postman John L. LeFlore, together with the powerful dockworkers' union leader Isom Clemon and others, cooperated with the liberal white city commissioner Joseph Langan to transform the patterns of race relations in the city without significant public confrontations.[6]

In the second place, the study of local racial clashes will reveal that the white socioeconomic and political power structures in the towns in which the explosions occurred were not at all uniformly intransigent and oppressive in their racial attitudes. On the contrary, the common denominator that links the white leadership groups in all these cities is that they put out mixed signals, some elements of them offending blacks with their undisguised racism, other elements frustrating blacks with their oblivious indifference to black residents' plight, but still other elements giving clear indications of an openness to reform and a willingness to seek some new modus vivendi within the community. In such circumstances, black spokesmen could be led to conclude that if they could just succeed in communicating to whites how seriously they took matters of particular concern to them, they would find many whites willing to cooperate. Blacks could come to believe, therefore, that the time to press their demands had arrived.[7]

In sum, then, if we are to understand why specific towns developed direct-action movements when others that were apparently similarly situated did not, our explanation must attend to local perceptions, assumptions, and interests. Something in one city must have given a crucial number of blacks there a sense that blacks elsewhere did not share, of the immediate malleability of their world. That something, I argue, was the structures of municipal politics. The following three chapters will offer detailed analyses of the events surrounding the significant direct-action movements in three Alabama cities. Before turning to these narratives, however, I have thought that some summary remarks might prove useful to emphasize the common traits that the stories seem to me to exhibit. These remarks inevitably include allusions to incidents and personalities that the reader will not yet have encountered. The temporary suspension of a degree of puzzlement will therefore be necessary. In the next several pages, the goal is to clarify the governing patterns; the clarification of the particulars will come later. Let me begin with a simple statement of the causes of the three direct-action movements, as I understand them.

In Montgomery, the disintegration of the Gunter machine after World War II in response to the rising political consciousness of lower-middle-class whites in the eastern precincts, the election of the stridently anti-machine east Montgomerian Dave Birmingham with black support in 1953, Commissioner Birmingham's hiring of black policemen, and his resultant defeat in the racially charged city election of 1955 form the essential background to the decision of black leaders to call for a boycott of the buses following the arrest of Rosa Parks. In Birmingham, the increasing doubts among business progressives after World War II about the very significant economic and social costs of the stable municipal political order that the business community had itself played a principal role in putting in place in 1937 culminated, after the Freedom Rider riot of May 1961 and the decision to close the city's parks and playgrounds at the end of that year, in a direct assault on the city commission form of government. The business progressives' attack on the city commission led to interracial contacts that exacerbated the deep rivalries between black activist and moderate leaders and triggered the specific events that produced the demonstrations of 1963. In Selma, the dominance of the Burns-Heinz machine and the success of the White Citizens' Council in discouraging any divisions among whites were both challenged in the fall of 1962 by the creation of the Committee of 100 Plus and its attempt to gain control of the board of the chamber of commerce. The insurgent business progressives carried their campaign into politics in 1964, when they united behind the candidacy of Joe Smitherman to defeat Mayor Heinz. In the meantime, the emerging division among prominent whites had already encouraged Edwin Moss and his allies in the Dallas County Improvement Association to seek in August 1963 to use the Retail Merchants Association to outflank Heinz's adamant refusal to consider alterations in the status quo. And the willingness of the new Smitherman administration to discuss racial reform so emboldened black leaders that their impressive courage and enthusiasm was able to convince the SCLC to agree to assist them in renewing voter registration demonstrations.

The role that race relations played in the three sets of events was not at all similar. In Selma, the young businessmen who formed the Committee of 100 Plus had no particular interest in improving the community's racial climate; the committee's goal was simply to attract new industry to their city. The fact that their efforts had an adventitious racial impact proceeded, quite ironically, from the achievement of the Citizens' Council in imposing so rigid an orthodoxy upon the white citizenry that the appearance of any discord among them had the most startling implications for the community at large. In Birmingham, the comparable group of business progressives was similarly primarily interested in industrial expansion, but despite their common acceptance of white supremacist assumptions, they understood that their city's notoriety for execrable race relations formed a barrier to attaining their economic goals. Thus they eventually overcame their fears and initiated biracial consultations. In Montgomery, the nearly equiponderant electoral rivalry between whites in the eastern and southern sections in the early 1950s had allowed black voters, though few, to exercise a measure of political influence. But Clyde Sellers's use of the race issue to defeat Dave Birmingham in the spring of 1955 compelled black leaders to search for a mechanism beyond the electoral process to force white politicians to take blacks' principal concerns seriously. The bus boycott was the result of this quest.

Nor were the three cities any more uniform in the general style of the white supremacy that characterized them. The Gunter machine had left Montgomery with a heritage of a comparatively gentle and protective paternalism, marred however by a police force rendered quite callous by the machine's persistent tolerance of social corruption. Industrial conflict and a long tradition of Klan influence stained Birmingham's race relations repeatedly with episodes of brutality and violence. Paternalism in Selma was marked by a distinctly hard edge of white contempt and fear, derived in large part from the keen white awareness that they were greatly outnumbered in Dallas County by poor and poorly educated blacks.

It is not, then, the precise shape of race relations in the community that proved crucial to producing the resort to direct action, but rather the existence of a historic moment of political transition. The essence of the psychological inertia that had to be overcome if the black community were to abandon passivity was the widespread, largely unspoken assumption that the community had always fundamentally been as it was and was not likely ever really to change. In the three communities that we will examine, the drama of municipal politics had long worked powerfully to reinforce this belief. The stability that had come to characterize Birmingham's political culture following the city elections of 1937, after two decades of constant conflict and a rapid turnover of officials, and the intimate connection between the achievement of that stability and the triumph of white supremacy in the area's mills, mines, and unions played the same role in the Magic City that the dominance of the Gunter and Burns-Heinz machines did in Montgomery and Selma. And then, quite suddenly, the white political, economic, and social leadership, which had for a generation or more seemed to be essentially monolithic—especially to community residents who were not themselves among the leaders, as was the case with the black population—commenced to display vulnerability, to reveal sharp internal divisions, to send out, as I have said, quite mixed signals. Precisely because the community had for so long appeared immobile, these developments seemed to have extraordinary significance, to disclose a malleability in the social order of which few before had even dreamed. In a town whose political life had traditionally been more dynamic, the outcome of a mayoral election or a referendum on the form of municipal government would doubtless have appeared to have had implications limited chiefly to politics. But for politically aware blacks in towns theretofore apparently confined to a protracted political and social stasis, the revelation of genuine change—the commissionership of Dave Birmingham in Montgomery, the campaign to abolish the city commission in Birmingham, the creation of the Committee of 100 Plus and the defeat of Chris Heinz in Selma—caused them to believe that their world, which had seemed incapable of being altered, was in fact undergoing a fundamental transformation and was therefore subject at this moment to being molded by pressure.

A community is, perhaps above all, defined by its capacity to shape beliefs and aspirations. It might seem, given the fact that the vast majority of blacks in the three cities were excluded from the franchise in these years, that they would have been mere passive observers of the local political scene. Certainly—despite the influence of what whites called the "bloc vote" on the outcome of elections, in Birmingham and Montgomery at least—municipal officeholders at this period almost always proceeded as if politics were exclusively white man's work. And it is true as well that a great many blacks, particularly poorer ones, remained highly dubious of the notion that political activity could eventually bring genuine change to their world. Nevertheless, the community's political culture reached below white supremacist obtuseness and wounded black cynicism to bind virtually all of the community's residents with its implications. In the first place, of course, the officials chosen in the municipal elections, even if most blacks had no voice in selecting them, made decisions that directly influenced the daily lives of all citizens, black and white. Black residents therefore were quite likely to be fully aware of and concerned about the identity and attitudes of local officeholders—and indeed, more likely to be familiar with local than with state, and far more likely than with faraway federal, officials. Hence the local face of power, which blacks knew intimately, would ordinarily seem to them the reality of power, whatever they may have heard about unrealized national or judicial policy pronouncements or social practices in other states or cities. It is this fact that is reflected in J. L. Chestnut's frustrations with the resignation of his Selma neighbors, quoted earlier.

But even more significantly, the community's political culture created, for residents of both races, the limits in their minds of what seemed possible. It is not that they were anesthetized against all reform, of course. Change might—indeed, often did—seem highly desirable. White businessmen could dream of industrial development. Blacks in Montgomery could press for the adoption of the pattern of bus segregation in use in Mobile, and blacks in Selma could believe the evenhanded administration of the voting registration laws a matter of simple fairness. But below such concerns was a level of assumption that would at once have defined truly thoroughgoing reform as impractical and absurd, as proceeding from utopian fascinations or quixotic crusades. And even deeper were the assumptions about social and institutional arrangements and power relationships within the community that, because they were so subtle and so seldom consciously examined, seemed simply to be natural. All of these assumptions were in fact subject to evolution; as changes came to the community, the frontiers of what appeared achievable in the future were gradually moved. But at any historical moment, the limits created by the local political culture were real and powerful.

It is precisely for this reason that the handful of black leaders in the three cities whose experiences and personality permitted them to some degree, at least, to transcend these limits and to envision alternatives not discernible in the imaginations of their fellow townsfolk—Edgar D. Nixon and Jo Ann Robinson in Montgomery, Fred L. Shuttlesworth in Birmingham, and S. William and Amelia P. Boynton in Selma—are such striking figures. But however remarkable these men and women and the few other leaders like them may have been, if circumstances had not created the union of a substantial part of the black citizenry behind their views, their insights by themselves could have had no social consequences. The ability of a tiny number of outstanding residents at a given time to see beyond the limitations imposed by local conditions therefore requires less explanation from history than does the infinitely rarer capacity of thousands not so gifted suddenly to find the impulse to use such perceptions. It is to this latter problem that our observations are intended to speak. An authentic alteration in what had long seemed the fixed structure of local political power—because such an alteration necessarily drew into question also the deeper, and apparently natural, assumptions that had been founded upon that structure—therefore had liberating implications far beyond the ordinary bounds of politics.

In Montgomery, the long-standing hatreds between Edgar Nixon and the working-class blacks of west Montgomery on the one hand and Rufus Lewis and the middle-class blacks generally connected with Alabama State College on the other had for more than a decade before the beginning of the bus boycott made black unity exceedingly difficult to achieve. Yet the boycott was marked by an unprecedented degree of solidarity, across deep divisions of class, sex, denominational affiliation, and personal jealousy and loathing. Of course, the shared antipathy to the insulting treatment that blacks too often received on Montgomery's buses in part accounts for this unification, but it was largely poorer blacks whose experience of such indignities was frequent; middle-class blacks who owned an automobile had sometimes not even been aboard a bus since World War II, when gas rationing had made the use of public transit more general. Yet the extent of the solidarity that the middle class and working class manifested was the source of much of the good feeling that the boycott generated in the black community, and it caused considerable comment at the time. It would seem clear—indeed, the resolutions adopted by the black mass meeting on the first evening of the boycott virtually say as much—that the background of repeated frustrations in attempting to get the municipal authorities to take blacks' bus seating grievance seriously, culminating in the prominent role that the seating proposal had played in the city commission candidates' forum at the Ben Moore Hotel and in the meetings that followed Claudette Colvin's arrest, formed a large part of the middle-class black anger that surrounded this issue. Thus the events of city politics and the attitudes of city politicians—and in particular, the municipal elections of March 1955—led directly to the prompt and ardent mobilization of the middle-class black leadership after Rosa Parks's arrest. For them the boycott was, as Clausewitz says of war, political relations carried out by other means.

In Selma there was only a handful of black voters, and before 1964 city elections had in any case not been competitive for thirty years. But municipal politics nonetheless played an essential role in generating the unwonted black solidarity during the demonstrations of 1963 and 1965. Amelia Boynton's initial contacts with the Southern Regional Council, SNCC, and the SCLC had all proceeded primarily from intensely personal considerations: her anguished attempts to sustain the decades-long but now faltering efforts of her dying husband to ameliorate the conditions under which Dallas County's blacks were compelled to live. With the rise of the White Citizens' Council, S. W. Boynton had adopted the strategy of trying to outflank local authorities by securing outside aid, and Amelia Boynton therefore sought to pursue this tactic. The arrival of SNCC's Bernard Lafayette in the fall of 1962 was, however, coincident with the organization of the Committee of 100 Plus by white advocates of industrial development and the committee's public endeavor to take control of the board of directors of the chamber of commerce. This first revelation of genuine white opposition to the leadership associated with the Burns-Heinz organization apparently strengthened the conservative black belief that it would be possible to procure progress through negotiation with sympathetic Selma whites, reinforced by federal court action when necessary. At any rate, Amelia Boynton's and Frederick Reese's enthusiasm for cooperating with Lafayette provoked initial opposition from the more moderate element within the Voters League, eventuating in the resignation first of Robert Reagin and later of Jackson C. Lawson from the league's leadership, and produced, once the moderates in the league had been reconciled, the organization of the alternative Improvement Association by more conservative blacks led by Edwin Moss, Claude Brown, Marshall Cleveland, and others of like mind. The Improvement Association actively sought to forestall the 1963 demonstrations by inducing either the city government or the Retail Merchants Association to enter discussions. The complete solidarity that characterized black Selma during the demonstrations of late September and early October 1963 derived from twin sources: Judge Daniel Thomas's refusal to see the conduct of the board of registrars for what it was, which seemed to have foreclosed a judicial remedy for the blacks' plight; and the zealous insistence of the White Citizens' Council and the Burns-Heinz machine upon preserving absolute and uncompromising white unity, which made negotiations with blacks a step too dangerous, both socially and economically, for white moderates to take. This situation drove the black moderates, against their preferences, into the arms of the activists.

After Heinz's defeat and the consequent opening of consultations between black leaders and white moderates and, later, with the new Smitherman administration as well, the united white phalanx which the machine and the Citizens' Council had enforced so relentlessly for a decade began to break down. But the remnants of the earlier intransigence were themselves sufficient to generate equal black solidarity behind the 1965 demonstrations. Smitherman's victory and the tentative steps toward concessions to blacks that followed it proved that internal change was not impossible, but they also revealed clearly the vast gulf that now separated the attitudes of the city and county authorities and at the same time made it seem reasonable to believe that the policies of the county government could be transformed as those of the city had been. Events in the summer and fall of 1964 made the new differences between the city and county seem particularly sharp; Sheriff James Clark's intemperate conduct during the brief demonstrations in early July, along with Judge James Hare's indiscriminate injunction that ended them, were immediately followed in August and September by the white moderates' first efforts to establish interracial amity. The extraordinary transition in municipal affairs represented by the outcome of the spring city election and the actions of Smitherman and his supporters in the fall thus made the recalcitrance that lingered at the county courthouse all the more infuriating for blacks, because for the first time it genuinely appeared to be behavior that was subject to being altered. It is for that reason, primarily, that once Mrs. Boynton had succeeded in persuading the SCLC to assist the Voters League in its registration efforts, virtually all of Selma's black leadership, across the entire ideological spectrum, united in support of the renewed demonstrations. Even the black public school teachers—elsewhere notoriously the black community's most thoroughly cowed occupational group—joined to march on the courthouse. Smitherman's triumph over Heinz had made electoral actions seem to be the key to progress. Because the changes at city hall had convinced doubters that the polling booth really could produce change; because the policies of the county authorities now appeared to reflect not a universally implacable white will, but merely the beliefs of one faction within the white community; and because voter registration had thus been revealed to local blacks, in a way that actually spoke to their own local situation, to be crucial to realizing black aspirations—for all these reasons, breaking the resistance of the board of registrars became a goal about whose priority all black Selmians suddenly could agree. Heinz's defeat succeeded in giving blacks a new optimism and a new willingness to commit themselves to the struggle because it seemed to establish that the final elimination of the white supremacist hegemony was no mere chimera, that with sufficient boldness it could, in fact, be even now within their grasp.

The situation in Birmingham was somewhat more complicated because the demonstrations of 1963 generated a solidarity among blacks that was in reality only paper thin. Arthur Gaston, Arthur Shores, and the other blacks allied with the Inter-Citizens Committee were committed to awaiting the new city council's assumption of power before pressing for racial reforms, having been assured that reforms would be forthcoming shortly thereafter. Had it not been for the willingness of Martin Luther King, Jr., at his meeting with them of April 8 to cede to the black moderates a very substantial role in any future negotiations with whites, it seems certain that Gaston and Shores would have sought to suppress the spring demonstrations, just as they succeeded in doing the following October. Shuttlesworth's rivals for black leadership cooperated with the Alabama Christian Movement for Human Rights and the SCLC, therefore, only because by doing so they would be able to shape to their liking any agreement that the Christian Movement's efforts might produce. If no such agreement were forthcoming, they would still be the blacks to whom the new city administration would turn once the demonstrations had played themselves out. In either case, they expected that they could thus emerge on top in their competition with Shuttlesworth himself. Equally crucial to the achievement of black unity in the 1963 demonstrations was eliminating the hopelessness of the vast numbers of poor blacks who were not involved with the Christian Movement. When black bystanders responded to Eugene "Bull" Connor's police and firemen by hurling bottles and bricks, it was a blow to nonviolence, but it was also proof that the mass of the city's ordinary blacks had been aroused to identification with the marchers. This response was elicited by the drama of the demonstrations themselves, and particularly by the SCLC's use of schoolchildren and the violence of Connor's countermeasures. By the beginning of May 1963, then, the black community of Birmingham had indeed achieved a kind of solidarity, but it was a solidarity composed in significant measure of calculated maneuvers for advantage on the part of the black business and professional interests and emotional communication with the impassioned events in the streets on the part of the black masses; the demonstrations' formal goals inspired chiefly the Christian Movement's own authentic membership.

Despite the quite fragile nature of the unity that Birmingham's blacks finally attained, municipal politics was nevertheless at the heart of the events that produced the demonstrations. The fervid white supremacist pronouncements during the municipal elections of May 1961, and particularly the nature of Arthur Hanes's runoff campaign against Thomas King, made inevitable the decision to close the city's parks when Judge Hobart Grooms ordered them integrated in October. The insouciance of the police in the Freedom Rider riot in May 1961, along with the city commission's decision to close the parks in October, united the sentiment of most of the business community behind the chamber of commerce's plan to replace the commission with a mayor and council. The search for a compromise on the closure of the parks that might be acceptable to the commissioners led business interests to begin consultations with the black moderates. The failure of these negotiations induced black college students, with the support of both the black moderates and Shuttlesworth's Christian Movement, to call for a boycott of the downtown merchants, and the boycott's eventual collapse intensified the competition between the moderates and the Christian Movement for the students' allegiance. Shuttlesworth's determination to launch street demonstrations in conjunction with the SCLC convention in September 1962, in order to prove to the students, and to blacks in general, the efficacy of his theory of agitation, threatened to defeat the white business progressives' campaign to abolish the city commission. Merchants therefore agreed to an unannounced removal of the segregation signs from facilities in the downtown department stores in order to preserve calm in advance of the change-of-government referendum. When this agreement became known to city authorities in mid-November, however, the merchants backed out of the arrangement. Shuttlesworth felt betrayed; he had forfeited his most promising means of coercing concessions from the whites, and it seemed likely that once the new city government took office the very concessions he sought would be delivered instead to his black moderate rivals. In an effort to recapture the initiative, he persuaded his friend Martin Luther King to join him in organizing demonstrations—timed to follow the election of the first mayor and council, in order to avoid delivering the mayoralty to "Bull" Connor, but to precede the new city administration's inauguration, in order to ensure that credit for any subsequent reforms would flow to the Christian Movement rather than to the Inter-Citizens Committee. The settlement negotiated by the black moderates and white business leaders, however, was careful to condition all advances on Albert Boutwell's and the council's final assumption of power. Shuttlesworth initially vehemently objected to these accords, but he was persuaded to accept them, though quite reluctantly, by King and agents of the Kennedy Justice Department. Thus local political considerations shaped these events at every stage of their development. As was the case also in Montgomery and Selma, a fundamental alteration in the existing municipal political culture was crucial to generating the black community's resort to direct action in Birmingham.

Local politics was not only an essential factor in the calculations of black leaders; it was also frequently an important, and sometimes a decisive, motive in the actions of segregationist officials. Clyde Sellers's adamant opposition at the beginning of the boycott to the Montgomery Improvement Association's proposal that the bus company adopt the Mobile seating plan certainly was influenced by his rejection of the plan during the municipal election campaign of the preceding spring, when it had been included on the questionnaire distributed at the Ben Moore Hotel meeting. L. B. Sullivan's reluctance to extend police protection to the Montgomery Freedom Riders in May 1961 almost beyond question derived from his relentless attacks upon Sellers during the campaign of 1959 for having paid Martin Luther King's loitering fine. "Bull" Connor's agreement to allow Klansmen to assault the Freedom Riders in his city was demonstrably a product of his efforts to attract Klan support in his race for reelection against T. E. Lindsey. Sheriff Jim Clark's intransigence during the 1965 demonstrations was to a substantial extent determined by considerations derived from what seemed virtually certain to be a renewal of his old and bitter rivalry with Wilson Baker for the shrievalty in the May 1966 Democratic primary: his electoral dependence upon the support of James Hare, Blanchard McLeod, and Bernard Reynolds and his desire to prove to voters the superiority of his forceful methods of dealing with dissent, as opposed to Baker's and Smitherman's more temperate ones.

Such examples could be multiplied; the point doubtless is already clear. Both political competition and the local civil rights movements reflected the rival efforts of elements of the community to shape the community's destiny, to define the structure of policies and power within it. It cannot be surprising, therefore, that they were intimately and inevitably intertwined. Politics in great measure created the limits upon the citizenry's sense of social possibilities. Politics created those limits whether or not—indeed, in important part, precisely *through* whether or not—individual citizens felt themselves permitted to influence the course of political developments. A moment of historic transition in the community's political culture therefore could unleash—had almost inescapably to unleash—a powerful new understanding of what the community could become. It was this circumstance that underlay the willingness of blacks in Montgomery, Selma, and, through a bit more convoluted process, also in Birmingham to attempt to compel concessions through direct action; the cities were in the midst of transforming the politics that had characterized them for decades, and blacks from all sorts of backgrounds and attitudes were thus enabled to believe that firm demands could force a suddenly malleable situation to take account of their aspirations. Politics, as well, codified the structure of power in the community. Because segregationist officials understood themselves at a fundamental level to be defenders of the legitimacy of existing power relationships, it is certainly no wonder that they were intensely sensitive to all evidence of the electorate's approval and sought constantly to depict themselves as spokesmen for a community consensus. It was precisely their allegiance to the established structure of power, indeed, that so often betrayed them in a time of transition, when past experience was losing its validity as a guide to present action. Politics, then, provides a key to understanding the actions of all participants in the local civil rights movements, whether black or white, integrationist, moderate, or white supremacist, because both politics and the civil rights movements formed aspects of the community's contests for power.

Montgomery

2

I. The City before the Boycott

At the beginning of the Montgomery bus boycott in 1955, Montgomery's municipal politics was in the midst of a fundamental transformation—a transformation that, as we shall see, played an essential role in shaping the course of race relations in the city.[1] For essentially the preceding half century, Montgomery had been ruled by the Gunter machine, headed for most of that time by William A. Gunter, Jr., the city's mayor from 1910 to 1915 and from 1919 to his death in 1940. Mayor Gunter had come to power after more than a dozen years of bitter factional warfare between a group of wealthy families headed by the Gunters, who had been leaders in the area since the antebellum period, and the Hill family, whose local prominence dated only from the postbellum years. The abolition of the city council form of government in 1911 and its replacement by the city commission was a central incident in this struggle. After Gunter returned to the mayoralty in 1919, he managed to turn back all challenges to his rule. He could always rely upon the unwavering support of the city's morning newspaper, the *Montgomery Advertiser,* whose editor, Grover C. Hall, Sr., was one of his closest advisers. He had the allegiance of the majority of Montgomery's older families. And in the final two decades of his life, he also commanded the unanimous support of city employees, whom—as a result of an act which he pushed through the state legislature during a term as state senator—he could in effect hire and fire at will.[2]

If there were no successful challenges to the machine after 1919, however, the unsuccessful challenges were many. The Hills continued as Gunter's uncompromising opponents, allying themselves in the various elections with whatever other elements were dissatisfied with the machine's rule. Though they never won city office, the Hills were frequently more fortunate at the county level. Gunter's repeated expressions of disapproval for the prohibition experiment placed the Anti-Saloon League in the ranks

Montgomery

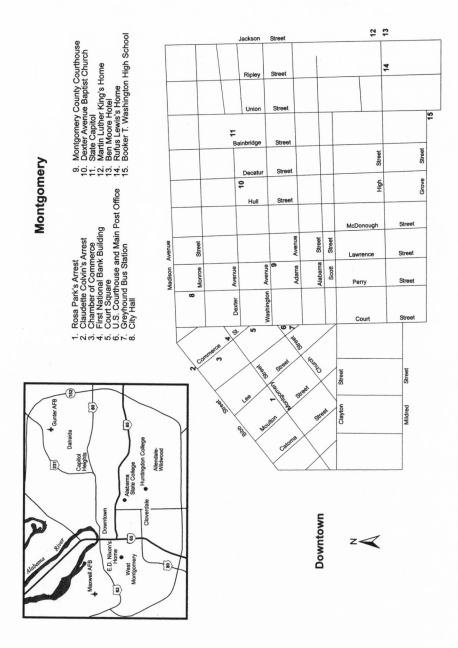

1. Rosa Park's Arrest
2. Claudette Colvin's Arrest
3. Chamber of Commerce
4. First National Bank Building
5. Court Square
6. U.S. Courthouse and Main Post Office
7. Greyhound Bus Station
8. City Hall
9. Montgomery County Courthouse
10. Dexter Avenue Baptist Church
11. State Capitol
12. Martin Luther King's Home
13. Ben Moore Hotel
14. Rufus Lewis's Home
15. Booker T. Washington High School

Downtown

of his enemies, and religious fundamentalists—led by Robert R. Jones, the Montgomery Baptist minister who would later found Bob Jones University—condemned Gunter for his generally lax enforcement of public morality. On the other hand, these encounters acquired for the machine the quite considerable financial support of the city's bootleggers and gambling club operators. In the 1920s, Gunter's energetic and courageous condemnations of the Ku Klux Klan, both for its religious bigotry and for its advocacy of prohibition, made him a special object of Klan hatred. In 1927 a Montgomery druggist and Klan leader J. Johnston Moore made a strong effort to defeat Gunter at the polls. Grover Hall's editorial attacks on the Klan during this period, in large part an outgrowth of his effort to defend the machine on the local level, gained him national admiration and a Pulitzer Prize in 1928. During the Depression, Gunter turned the city government into something of a relief operation, earning the bitter hostility of fiscal conservatives for the substantial city debt that his efforts soon created. By the time of his death in 1940, he was admired by much of Montgomery's upper class and idolized by large numbers of the city's poor and unemployed, but he was also detested by many owners of small businesses, lower-middle-class and conservative citizens, strict Baptists and Methodists, and others to whom his values—rooted in the easygoing tolerance and aristocratic paternalism of his planter and Episcopalian background—were anathema.[3]

After Gunter's death, the machine spent the next decade searching for a leader. The mayor was immediately succeeded by Cyrus B. Brown, who had long been one of Gunter's most powerful lieutenants and was at the time the president of the governing body of Montgomery County, the board of revenue. But Brown, an elderly man, followed Gunter in death in 1944. David Dunn, who had earlier been a political protégé of former governor Bibb Graves, obtained machine endorsement to succeed Brown, but he resigned in 1946 to go into private business. The mayoralty then passed to City Attorney John L. Goodwyn, a cousin of Gunter's wife whom Gunter had appointed city attorney in 1930. Goodwyn resigned in 1951 to accept a position in the state government which soon led to his being appointed to the state supreme court. Goodwyn was succeeded by William A. "Tacky" Gayle, a machine stalwart who had been a member of the city commission since 1935.[4]

During this decade of rapid changes in leadership, the machine grew steadily weaker, a process to which the rapidity of change itself contributed. Another factor in the machine's decline was Gunter's penchant for surrounding himself with colorless, if quite competent, administrators. Montgomery was governed by a commission consisting of three members. In addition to the mayor, there was a commissioner of public affairs, who administered the police and fire departments, and a commissioner of public works, who had charge of parks, libraries, street maintenance, and garbage collection. During the 1930s, Gunter turned to two retired military men to fill these posts. Gayle, a veteran of World War I, had subsequently served as Alabama's adjutant general and had returned to active duty in World War II. In 1943, while serving in Britain as an air force colonel, he was elected to his third term on the city commission in absentia. The other commissioner, General William P. Screws, had been the commander of the Alabama contingent in the famed Rainbow Division during World War I. This tradition continued when George L. Cleere, another former state adjutant general, was selected to succeed Gayle as commissioner of public works when Gayle became mayor in 1951. These men, for all their efficiency, were by no means Gunter's equals as politicians, and without him they had trouble in holding the voters' affection.

By far the most important reason for the machine's decline, however, was the changing character of the city's population and residence patterns. During the first half of the twentieth century Montgomery grew rapidly, at an average of 30 percent a decade. This steady growth concealed after 1940 an important change in the city's racial composition. In 1910, as Gunter was first taking office as mayor, Montgomery's white population for the first time achieved parity in numbers with blacks. During the remainder of the Gunter years, the relative proportion of the two races remained stable at 55 percent white and 45 percent black. But after Gunter's death the proportions began to change, under the impact both of increased black immigration to the North and of increased rural white movement into the city. In 1950 Montgomery was 60 percent white and 40 percent black; during the 1940s the white population grew by 47 percent and the black by only 23 percent. By the outbreak of the bus boycott in 1955, Montgomery contained about 120,000 people, of whom some 63 percent were white and 37 percent were black.

The increasing white population meant, of course, that the number of residents in the city who could vote was growing even faster than was the population at large. The machine had no hold upon either the gratitude or the affection of many of these new voters. Moreover, changing residence patterns reinforced this development. Resentments of Gunter's policies on the part of the lower middle class had existed in the 1920s and 1930s, but the resentment had found little institutional support. The town was small and could sustain few institutions alternative to the ones controlled by the well-to-do. During the 1940s and early 1950s, the development of housing subdivisions, particularly on the eastern edges of the city, with small homes intended for the white lower middle class, effectively separated that group from the institutional control of the upper and upper middle classes.

In the eastern sections of Montgomery—Oak Park, Capitol Heights, Dalraida, and Chisholm—there developed, for instance, churches whose congregations did not contain a mix of classes, and within which leadership could therefore fall to the lower middle class. In 1931 there were only seven white Baptist churches in the city, and in 1940 there were still only eleven, but by 1952 there were twenty. The number of white churches belonging to the Pentecostal sects, always a refuge for poorer elements of the population, also advanced rapidly. In 1931, white Pentecostal congregations constituted less than a fourth of the city's white churches, but by 1940 they were a third of the total, and by 1952 almost 40 percent of it.[5] Similarly, east Montgomery developed alternative men's clubs; the Lions Club, the Civitans Club, and the Exchange Club, for instance, all established separate east Montgomery units during these years, leaving the downtown clubs in the hands of the businessmen who had dominated them. The growth to the east also demanded new schools, and with them came Parent-Teacher Associations to be run by men and women unlikely to have been leaders in a PTA in which the various classes were commingled, as had been the case with the PTAs of the few schools in the earlier, smaller city. Power in these earlier organizations had gravitated toward the city's social leaders. East Montgomery also developed separate shopping and entertainment areas. In these and countless other ways, the simple growth of the city gave the white lower middle class a separate community life and allowed it an increased measure of self-consciousness as a unit.[6]

Meanwhile, this institutional "de-intermixture" of white classes was proceeding from the other side as well, as subdivisions for wealthier residents were developed in south Montgomery, particularly in the Cloverdale section. Between 1951 and 1954 no less than sixty new subdivisions were completed in east and in south Montgomery, and in 1955 another thirty-three were reported to be in the planning stages.[7]

A telling index to the emergence of a greater self-consciousness among Montgomery's upper class was the growing organization of the city's social season. By the final years of the twentieth century, the social season had come to revolve around a series of formal balls given by fourteen "mystic societies," at which the season's debutantes were presented. The membership of the mystic societies was secret, and election to one of them was considered a great honor. Attendance at the balls was by invitation only. Each featured elaborate and expensive tableaux from which the various debutantes emerged. At the end of World War II, however, only two of the fourteen societies existed. Seven were formed between 1948 and 1953, and four more were added later in the 1950s. The fourteenth and last was formed in 1962. The movement to create this highly structured season, through which those who were in and those who were outside "polite society" could be clearly defined, seems almost certainly to have been, at least unconsciously, a response to the rapid growth of the city's white population and to the increasing tendency of many less prosperous whites to deny to Montgomery's traditional social leaders the deference to which they had formerly been accustomed.

The final blow to the machine's political control of Montgomery during these years came in the form of the legislative act of 1949 which established a civil service system for city and county employees.[8] Mayor Gunter had retained complete authority over the jobs of city workers throughout his tenure, and at election time he had exacted absolute fealty from them. The implications of the new system came home to his successors in the legislative election of 1950. Vaughn Hill Robison, a young attorney and scion of the Hill family, ran for state senator against Charles A. Stakely, a former state senator who had the endorsement both of Mayor Goodwyn and of former mayor David Dunn, now the president of the county board of revenue. Despite the new law, Dunn moved vigorously to ensure that county employees voted for Stakely. Robison nevertheless won a narrow victory, primarily on his strength in the city's eastern precincts, by strongly attacking machine rule. He thereupon arranged for county employees who had been pressured into supporting his opponent to file formal complaints with the new personnel board. After a lengthy and emotional public hearing, the board dismissed the complaints by a vote of two to one, but the spectacle had proven so intensely embarrassing to the machine that its leaders apparently felt compelled to abandon thereafter all efforts to use public workers as a voting bloc.[9]

The first real hint of what these alterations in the city's social foundations portended for the machine had come, however, in the city elections of 1947, when General Screws, a member of the city commission since 1931, was challenged by a young east Montgomery schoolteacher and football coach, Earl D. James. James's connection with physical education at Capitol Heights Junior High School placed him in an excellent position to capitalize upon the emerging sense of community solidarity in that section of the city. Screws beat James in Cloverdale, while James swamped all of his opponents in Capitol Heights and also ran well in the older lower-middle-class ward of Oak Park. James thus erected a majority upon a basis not previously seen in Montgomery politics. The division between south Montgomery and east Montgomery that was demonstrated in these returns, which was apparent as well in Robison's victory over Stakely three years later, was to become characteristic of municipal elections for the next three decades.[10]

Nevertheless, the machine did not yet anticipate its doom, since it still controlled two of the city commission's three seats. James proved an able and relatively tractable official. Though elected to a second term in 1951, he resigned in 1953 to enter business. It was in the special election to choose James's successor that the newly emerging shape of city politics first became completely clear. State representative Joe M. Dawkins gathered endorsements for his candidacy from Montgomery's most prominent citizens. In the first-round primary he carried every precinct in the city and missed winning without a runoff by only 523 votes. In the second primary Dawkins faced Dave Birmingham, a man whose candidacy was regarded by the city's upper class as a bad joke. Birmingham had been an early and zealous supporter of former governor James E. Folsom, and he shared much of Folsom's aggressive hostility to the wealthy. Birmingham was a classic demagogue. During his campaign he suggested that the chlorination of the city's drinking water had caused the preceding summer's devastating polio epidemic. He charged, contrary to well-documented fact, that the red color that sometimes appeared in the water was not iron but mud. The burden of Birmingham's appeal, however, was a strident attack on the machine. Dawkins was, Birmingham said, "hogtied to the old ring masters. . . . It is never good for a city to let one 'click' [sic] completely dominate it. Progress would stagnate." He opposed appointive municipal boards: "The ring masters through the board masters are strangling you to death with taxes without any responsibility to you as to how they will spend this tax money." He particularly decried the fees that had been levied to finance the extension of services to new areas of the rapidly growing city. Any action by "that cesspool of gangsters at City Hall," he said, was sure to be corrupt and self-serving.

Birmingham beat Dawkins in the runoff by a margin of 53 percent to 47 percent. Dawkins carried the wealthier precincts; his best ward was Cloverdale. Birmingham swept the lower-middle-class and lower-class white precincts; he ran best in Capitol Heights. He also did well in precincts in which a substantial minority of the voters was black. The meaning of this election for the fortunes of the disintegrating machine was unmistakable. The *Advertiser's* editor, Grover C. Hall, Jr., commented that with Birmingham a member of the commission, "The City Hall is going to be notably different for the foreseeable future." Doubtless, though, Hall had no real conception of just how right he was.[11]

The principal reason for the machine's demise seems unquestionably to have been the growing independence of the white lower middle class. Politicians called this phenomenon "the silent vote." In a 1955 article, the *Advertiser's* city editor, Joe Azbell, explained the meaning of the term. In a city dominated by personal acquaintance, as Montgomery had been in the 1920s and 1930s, family alliances and personal favors, rather than questions of policy, decided the outcome of elections. But the growth of the city had added many voters to the rolls who were not members of the family alliances. The abolition of the city spoils system in favor of appointment by civil service examination, moreover, had deprived the machine of much of its power to bind voters to it by favors. By 1955, Azbell noted, voters lacked personal knowledge of the candidates and had thus begun to make voting decisions on the basis of issues, as filtered through the mass media. Politicians therefore lacked any real sense of where the voters were moving until the election returns were counted. In 1953, 1954, and 1955, knowledgeable observers had repeatedly guessed wrong about the election outcome because so many of the voters were no longer members of cousinries or other blocs whose behavior could be predicted. Of the 1955 municipal elections Azbell commented, "No one seemed to care how the Hills were moving. No one seemed concerned about the po-litical blocs. But twenty years ago a political observer would not dare com-ment on an election without first determining how the blocs were go-ing. For the first time in city political history, ring politics played no important part in the local election, because the old ring politics had been overshadowed by a growing city where there is no control or method of determining how the voters will cast their ballot." As a result, city admin-istrators were coming to fear their new constituents.[12]

If the growing independence of the white lower middle class was the principal factor that had altered the structure of municipal politics, how-ever, another factor of almost equal significance was the newly impor-tant black vote. The white lower middle class might be unfamiliar to the politicians, but the black community was virtual terra incognita. And yet developments within it during the preceding decade had been at least as revolutionary and as portentous as those within its blue-collar white counterpart.

The state Democratic primary of 1946 represented the first primary in which blacks could legally vote. Earlier Democratic elections had been conducted under the white primary rule, which the U.S. Supreme Court had forbidden in a decision rendered in April of 1944.[13] Because they could now participate in the only elections that mattered in Alabama, blacks sought to register in increasing numbers in the years after World War II. The Alabama legislature moved to meet the abolition of the white primary by amending the state constitution to compel applicants for reg-istration to satisfy the county boards of voting registrars that they under-stood any article of the U.S. Constitution presented them by the board. This amendment was in effect from November 1946 to March 1949, when it was declared unconstitutional by the U.S. Supreme Court. Thereafter, the original qualifications provided in the Constitution of 1901, which had required either literacy or ownership of property worth at least five hundred dollars, returned to force. But in December 1951 the state's elec-torate, by a very narrow margin, again amended the constitution, this time to provide for the preparation of a general voter qualification ques-tionnaire by the Alabama Supreme Court, to be administered to applicants by the various boards of registrars. This requirement remained in effect until the passage of the Voting Rights Act of 1965, and it was removed from the constitution by the voters in November of that year.[14]

Despite the legislature's efforts to slow the process, the number of blacks registered in Alabama, and particularly in the larger cities of the state, grew slowly but steadily during the late 1940s and early 1950s. In Montgomery, the first efforts to organize a voter registration drive among blacks date from the summer of 1943, even before the Supreme Court's decision in the white primary case. One of Montgomery's largest and most prominent black families was the Madisons, who had developed the Madison Park community to the northeast of the city. Family members in the early 1940s wished to incorporate Madison Park as an all-black town, but they were unable to do so because state law required the petition of a prescribed number of registered voters in order to obtain a municipal charter. The Madisons, therefore, decided to try to register to vote. A family member, Arthur A. Madison, had obtained a law degree from Columbia University in 1923 and was practicing law in New York City. One of his brothers persuaded him to return to Montgomery to advise them in their registration attempt. The effort spread beyond the Madison family when Edgar D. Nixon, a black labor leader, learned of it and obtained Madison's cooperation in an effort to register a number of other blacks, including Nixon himself, at the same time. Nixon organized the Alabama Voters League to oversee the project. The group made its first applications in September 1943, and when the applications were rejected by the registrars, Madison filed appeals of the decisions to circuit court, as the state constitution provided.

Astonished white authorities struck back hard. One of the applicants was Arthur Madison's niece Sarah Pearl Madison, a schoolteacher. Sarah Madison had prevailed on a number of other teachers at her school to join her in the registration attempt. All now fell under heavy pressure from school administrators, who evidently threatened them with nonrenewal of their teaching contracts, and so in February 1944 they appeared before Circuit Judge Walter B. Jones and swore that they had never given Arthur Madison permission to appeal their rejection. Madison was thereupon arrested for representing clients without authorization. In April he was convicted—in large part on the apparently perjured testimony of his niece—and was fined and disbarred. He appealed his disbarment, but without success. And in the meantime, the state supreme court threw out the appeals of those of the rejected applicants who had not withdrawn them, on the ground that they had not been filed within the time limit prescribed in the constitution.[15]

It would appear at first blush that this initial effort at black registration in Montgomery had resulted in a general debacle. In fact, however, it seems to have had rather positive results for the cause of black voting. It acquainted black leaders with the mechanics for achieving registration and mobilized many in the black community to make the attempt. Even after Madison's disbarment, the registration efforts continued almost unabated. Moreover, it appears to have served to warn the registrars that in the future they might need to be able to justify their decisions to the courts. For that reason, presumably, they began registering the most obviously qualified black applicants. Edgar Nixon was registered in 1945, as was his middle-class rival for the leadership of black Montgomery, funeral director Rufus A. Lewis. By 1950 Montgomery had 813 black voters, or 3.7 percent of the persons registered in the city. By 1955 the number had doubled, to 1,678 of the city's 22,210 voters, or 7.55 percent. Moreover, by 1955 black voters represented a quite substantial proportion of the electorate in some wards: 31 percent in Beat 7W, around the city's black Alabama State College; almost 25 percent in Beat 2, in the working-class black neighborhoods of west Montgomery; and 20 percent in Beat 6, which served the city's poorest black areas of north Montgomery.[16]

Seven and one-half percent remained quite a small figure, of course, especially since blacks constituted 37 percent of the city's residents, but given the near equiponderance in the political rivalry between south Montgomery and east Montgomery during these years, blacks could easily represent the balance of power in a particular election. The returns in the special election of November 1953 in particular appeared to black leaders to demonstrate that Dave Birmingham owed his margin of victory over Joe Dawkins to blacks, and they prepared to press the new commissioner for interest on this debt. And Birmingham stood ready to respond, both because he needed to hold the political allegiance of black voters and because his racial views seem to have been genuinely and remarkably liberal.[17] The inauguration of Dave Birmingham as a city commissioner, therefore, marked the beginning of a heady period for the black leadership, during which it found itself with genuine access to the city government for the first time in living memory.

On the other hand, there was a relatively small number of issues upon which the black leadership spoke with a completely united voice. Blacks in the city were as clearly divided along socioeconomic and geographical lines as were their white fellow townsmen. The symbol of this division was the presence in the city of Alabama State College. Alabama State had been founded in Marion, in the western Black Belt, at first, in 1866, as a private school; in 1874 it had become a state-supported institution, emphasizing the training of black schoolteachers. Following incidents of racial conflict between its students and those of the white Howard College, also in Marion, the legislature moved Alabama State to Montgomery in 1887, establishing it on a campus just south of the downtown area. There grew up around the campus a black residential area in which the school's faculty members and most of the city's relatively small number of black professionals and businessmen lived. The great majority of Montgomery's blacks, however, lived in west Montgomery, a working-class area whose residents were, in general, neither so prosperous nor so well educated as those in the Alabama State community.[18]

Throughout the late nineteenth and early twentieth centuries, most prominent spokesmen for Montgomery's blacks had been connected in one way or another with Alabama State or had lived in its vicinity. By the early 1950s the most active leader of this community was Rufus Lewis. Born in 1907, Lewis had graduated from Fisk University in Nashville, Tennessee, and had moved to Montgomery in 1935 to become the coach of Alabama State's football team. For the next decade he had served as the college's football coach and its assistant librarian. In 1940 he married Jewel Clayton, the daughter of Mr. and Mrs. William M. Clayton, the well-to-do owners of the Ross-Clayton Funeral Home. After the Claytons' deaths, Lewis in 1947 inherited their interest in the mortuary and soon became one of black Montgomery's best-known businessmen.[19]

Shortly after the end of World War II, Montgomery's public schools, in cooperation with the U.S. Veterans Administration, established a program to permit returning veterans to obtain training in job skills. The outbreak of the Korean War in 1950 and the simultaneous racial integration of the armed forces soon created a substantial pool of black veterans who wished to take advantage of this training. In 1949 Lewis was hired to administer the black section of the program. Without abandoning his ownership of the funeral home, he directed the veterans' education effort from 1949 through 1954, incorporating into it a strong emphasis on black pride and community participation. Lewis also owned a nightclub, the Citizens Club, where the veterans often gathered after classes. As an outgrowth of these gatherings, Lewis organized the Citizens' Coordinating Committee to assist the veterans in becoming registered voters. Through the committee, the classes, and the fellowship he encouraged their sense—derived also in part from their experiences in the newly integrated armed services —that they were entitled to full citizenship in Montgomery. One of the Coordinating Committee's most public protests occurred when, in February 1951, a teenaged black baby-sitter accused a white grocer, Sam E. Green, of having raped her as he was driving her home after she had sat with his children. Lewis and his veterans organized demonstrations against Green's grocery, which was located in the black neighborhood near Alabama State, eventually driving it out of business, and even succeeded in pushing white authorities into bringing Green to trial. Though an all-white jury took only five minutes to acquit Green, the mere fact that a white man had been indicted and tried for the rape of a black woman was itself a triumph in 1951.[20]

While Lewis, in encouraging a refusal to accept second-class citizenship in the Alabama State community, was following in an established tradition, Edgar Nixon was himself primarily responsible for arousing and energizing the poorer blacks of west Montgomery. Nixon had been born just outside Montgomery in 1899. Essentially lacking any formal education, he had nevertheless managed in 1923 to obtain a position as a sleeping car porter on passenger trains. As a porter he soon encountered, and was deeply influenced by, A. Philip Randolph, the militant black labor leader who was then attempting to organize the porters into a union. Nixon embraced this effort wholeheartedly, and with the recognition of the union in 1938 he became the president of the union's Montgomery local. From this position he undertook increasingly vocal and public efforts to obtain full civil rights for the city's black citizens. As we have seen, by 1943 he was actively involved in Arthur Madison's voter registration efforts.

The failure of the Montgomery branch of the National Association for the Advancement of Colored People to embrace Madison's registration crusade with what Nixon considered sufficient enthusiasm seems to have angered him. Therefore, in 1944 he determined to try to take over the branch. The branch had long been a middle-class preserve, headed by black insurance agents; in 1944 its president was Robert L. Matthews. After a bitter and divisive contest, Matthews defeated Nixon. But Nixon spent 1945 gathering new members for the branch who would vote for him, and in December 1945, after an even more acrimonious election, he defeated Matthews. Then, in perhaps the most heated of all these rancorous campaigns, Nixon was reelected over former president T. T. Allen in November 1946. After this victory, Nixon cast his eye on statewide office in the organization. In October 1947, in a sort of surprise coup, Nixon was chosen by the state NAACP convention, meeting in Montgomery, to replace the NAACP's first state president, Emory Jackson, the editor of the *Birmingham World*. But the NAACP's national headquarters in New York became increasingly unhappy with Nixon, believing that, because of his lack of education, he was unable to supply the chapters with effective direction; national officials therefore commenced quiet maneuvers to have him superseded by someone of a more conventional middle-class background. In November 1949 the state convention chose Birmingham insurance agent W. C. Patton to succeed Nixon as state president. And the following year, the Montgomery branch replaced Nixon with the man Nixon had defeated in 1945, insurance agent Robert Matthews.[21]

These machinations deeply embittered Nixon, who had always been sensitive about his poor education and resentful of blacks who were better-to-do. After 1950 these attitudes ripened into a genuine hostility toward the middle-class blacks who usually looked to Rufus Lewis for leadership. Despite the loss of his NAACP positions, however, Nixon continued to serve as a vigorous spokesman for the west Montgomery community. In August 1952 he was chosen president of the Montgomery chapter of the Progressive Democratic Association, the voice of black Democrats in the state, to succeed one of Lewis's protégés, Ronald R. Young. And throughout these years he continued to hold the presidency of his union local. In 1954 he created a great stir in Montgomery by becoming a candidate to represent his precinct on the county Democratic Executive Committee, the first black to seek elective office in the city in the twentieth century. Though he lost to a white candidate, Joseph W. Carroll, he won more than 42 percent of the vote in the precinct, only a fourth of whose voters were black. In 1955 Nixon sought unsuccessfully to purchase a ticket to a Jefferson-Jackson Day Democratic Party dinner in Birmingham; the evening's principal speaker, Governor G. Mennen Williams of Michigan, abruptly canceled his appearance in protest against Nixon's exclusion. Such highly visible efforts made Nixon the best-known activist in Montgomery and earned him a considerable and devoted following.[22]

While Nixon bickered with Lewis and his associates, and as the two black communities struggled for control of the various local organizations, one association, the Women's Political Council, increasingly gained recognition as black citizens' most militant and uncompromising voice in the city. The council had grown out of the exclusion of blacks from the Montgomery League of Women Voters, which had been formed in December 1947. The rejected black women had written to the national League of Women Voters asking to establish a separate black chapter, but the league's headquarters had replied that it could permit only one affiliate in each town. The result of this rebuff had been the creation of the Women's Political Council in the spring of 1949. The council had few members, and they consisted almost entirely of women associated with Alabama State College. Mrs. Mary Fair Burks, an English professor at Alabama State, and Rufus Lewis's wife, Jewel, were its first two presidents. They were succeeded by Mrs. Jo Ann Robinson, also a member of Alabama State's English faculty. Other particularly active members were Mrs. Thelma Glass, an Alabama State geography teacher, and Mrs. Irene West, the widow of a prominent dentist.[23]

The council thus was neither large nor representative. The sources of its authority nevertheless seem fairly clear. In the first place, though its members were certainly allied with Lewis rather than with Nixon, the council in general did not waste its energies on these squabbles. Instead, it focused its attention on dealing with the city government. Throughout the early 1950s, with rare exceptions, it was the Women's Political Council that spoke for Montgomery's black residents before the city commission. And it spoke invariably in the most unequivocal and fearless terms. This willingness of the council to speak out boldly for the interests of blacks probably stems in part from the fact that, in the environment created by segregation, black women were under somewhat fewer strictures in dealing with whites than were black men. Whites were more likely to find black men threatening, and hence more likely to take offense at aggressive comments from them.[24] There were, of course, black men—Nixon and Lewis very prominent among them—who refused to be intimidated by this situation, but many others were not so audacious. Another factor in the power of the council within the community surely was the personality of Mrs. Robinson. A native of Georgia and a graduate of Fort Valley State College there, she had obtained a master's degree from Atlanta University and had joined the faculty of Alabama State in the fall of 1949. Once she became the council's president, apparently in 1952, she proved a particularly determined and strong-willed advocate of the council's positions.[25]

Though there were deep divisions among Montgomery's blacks, there were also unifying elements. The city possessed a weekly black newspaper, the *Alabama Tribune,* established about 1940. In 1953 a black radio station, WRMA, began broadcasting, reaching many more people than did the *Tribune.* These media served to increase the sense of community among black Montgomerians. And even more useful in bringing blacks together was the common experience of the insults of segregation and segregationists. As a result of daily experience, certain goals were widely shared among all black leaders. On one of these, voter registration, modest progress had been made. Next to voter registration in importance to most blacks—and probably even exceeding it in the minds of many—was persistent police brutality.

The Montgomery police department entered the era after World War II with an unfortunate heritage. Ralph B. King became the city's police chief in 1910, at the beginning of Mayor Gunter's first term, and continued as chief until 1948. Though Gunter's toleration of illegal liquor during prohibition, of prostitution, and of gambling, particularly in private clubs, had in general given to Montgomery an atmosphere of relaxed broadmindedness, its effect upon the police force seems to have been quite a negative one. Police were constantly called upon to wink at violations of the law by some citizens, while accepting selective prosecutions against others. This regrettable situation was compounded by the expectation, common to all southern cities, that police would maintain among urban blacks the subservience which in rural areas was usually enforced directly by the nature of blacks' relationships with white landowners. And all police officers were, until 1949, subject to being dismissed at the will of the mayor. The result was a legacy within the department of corruption, political favoritism, and unpunished violence.

Chief King, who had presided over this dark tradition, became its victim as a result of public outrage at an incident which occurred on the evening of September 26, 1947. Officers Charles F. Goolsby and John R. Ingram, acting on the word of a police informant, stopped a car containing two blacks, Robert Felder, a service station employee, and his elderly father, B. G. Felder. The officers expected the car to contain moonshine whiskey. When they could find none, Officer Goolsby demanded that Robert Felder reveal the whiskey's hiding place, and when Felder denied possessing any, Officer Goolsby beat him into unconsciousness with a blackjack, leaving him with a fractured skull and his body paralyzed on the right side. One of Felder's white employers visited him in the hospital, and when he saw Felder's condition he complained to the press. The ensuing scandal led to the dismissal of Goolsby and Ingram from the force. A grand jury was empaneled to investigate; at this point, however, Felder's employers fell under pressure and withdrew their support, and the Felders thereupon wrote the grand jury that they wished to drop their charges. For Mayor Goodwyn, who as the former city attorney had long been unhappy with the situation in the police department, the Felder affair proved the last straw. Because of it he compelled Chief King to retire and commenced a search for a replacement who would end such abuses of power.[26]

At the beginning of March 1948, King was succeeded by Carlisle E. Johnstone, whom Goodwyn brought to Montgomery from Hopewell, Virginia. Johnstone at once commenced a general reformation of the police. He established a police academy and compelled all officers to attend it, reorganized the department's command, and, among other personnel changes, jumped one officer whom he respected, Goodwyn J. Ruppenthal, from second-in-command of the detective division to assistant chief. And he took firm disciplinary actions against any policemen who violated regulations. In all these actions he initially had Goodwyn's strong support.[27]

About a year after Johnstone's arrival in Montgomery, however, an incident occurred that put his reform program to the test. In the early-morning hours of March 27, 1949, two policemen arrested a young black woman, Gertrude Perkins, for public drunkenness, placed her in their patrol car, drove her to a secluded area, and there raped her. They then released her, and Miss Perkins reported the rapes to police. Later that morning, the two rapists came to her house and offered her presents if she would withdraw the charges. Instead, she contacted black community leaders. A committee of the black Interdenominational Ministerial Alliance was formed, headed by the Reverend Solomon S. Seay, Sr., and it retained two young white attorneys, the brothers John and Virgil McGee, to represent her. The McGees' vigorous pursuit of the case transformed it into a sensational scandal. The McGees were threatened with disbarment, and a funeral wreath was delivered to their father. Solomon Seay was arrested for resisting arrest, though the charge was later thrown out of court. Miss Perkins swore out anonymous warrants for the arrest of the two officers, but the sheriff refused to execute them. The McGees sued to compel him to do so, but Circuit Judge Eugene Carter ruled them defective because they did not name the guilty parties. Eventually a grand jury was empaneled to investigate the entire matter.

Though Mayor Goodwyn had supported Chief Johnstone's efforts to end police abuses, the idea of prosecuting white police officers for the rape of a black woman seems to have been more reform than he could stomach. He blamed the entire uproar on the NAACP and pronounced Miss Perkins's charges false. Apparently, police records were altered to conceal the rapists' identities. The grand jury announced that Miss Perkins's descriptions of her assaulters did not match those of the only two officers who could have been involved, and her complaint was thereupon dismissed. A few months later Chief Johnstone accepted a position as director of public safety in Raleigh, North Carolina, and left Montgomery for good.[28]

Despite this setback, however, the effort to reform the police department continued, though less publicly. Johnstone's choice as assistant chief, Goodwyn Ruppenthal, was selected to succeed Johnstone, and he pressed ahead with Johnstone's program. He received the firm support of Commissioner Earl James, who, under the provisions of a state legislative act, took administrative control of the police and fire departments in September 1950; and James's successor, Dave Birmingham, was equally unwavering in his backing. But for the city's black leaders, these events elevated one very public reform to a level of importance far above any of the others. As a direct result, it would appear, of the Perkins affair and of Johnstone's resignation, Montgomery's black organizations united, in December 1949, to request the hiring of black police.[29]

Two additional incidents lent this crusade much emotional force. On August 12, 1950, police officer M. E. Mills shot and killed a young black veteran, Hilliard Brooks, and wounded a black and a white bystander in the midst of a large crowd of shoppers on Montgomery's main street. Brooks, who was drunk and cursing, had been refused admission to a bus by the driver, C. L. Hood. Brooks protested, and Officer Mills was summoned. Mills pushed Brooks to the sidewalk and shot him to death after he struggled back to his feet; Mills stated that Brooks was advancing on him, but other witnesses reported that Brooks was standing with his arms at his side. Brooks had been one of the veterans attending Rufus Lewis's classes, and his fellow students, led by Ronald R. Young, strongly protested the killing. But a police board found Mills's action justified, and Mayor Goodwyn accepted its ruling.[30] At the beginning of June 1951, George Freeman, an athletics coach at the black George Washington Carver High School, was arrested for disorderly conduct. He had been reprimanded by sanitation inspectors for the condition of the garbage cans at the apartment complex in which he lived, and was alleged to have responded by cursing the inspectors. They summoned police. After the arresting officers had handcuffed Freeman, they beat him severely. At the jail he was denied any medical attention and was refused permission to contact anyone. Later the principal of his school posted bail for him and took him to a doctor. In court he was eventually fined for disorderly conduct and resisting arrest.[31] After both of these affairs, black leaders renewed the plea for the hiring of blacks as policemen.

The beating of George Freeman in 1951 was the last of the public scandals that had given the Montgomery police department such an unenviable reputation in the years before the bus boycott. As the reforms instituted by Carlisle Johnstone began to take hold in the early 1950s, the department increasingly assumed a more professional character. But its long tradition of execrable conduct was quite sufficient to permit the campaign for black officers to retain vigorous support in the black community despite the evidence of change. Indeed, the tradition was so offensive that the campaign gained support among whites as well. The first whites to endorse the cause were members of Montgomery's relatively small but quite active group of liberal Democrats. Their voice was the weekly *Montgomery Examiner,* edited by Charles Dobbins. Perhaps the best-known member of this group was Aubrey Williams, the former head of the National Youth Administration under Franklin Roosevelt.[32] He was joined by Clifford Durr, an attorney and former member of the Federal Communications Commission, when Durr returned to Montgomery in 1951. Additional leaders included, among others, Gould Beech, a journalist who became an adviser of Governor Folsom's; Will Sheehan, an *Examiner* columnist; the Reverend Andrew Turnipseed, a Methodist minister; the Reverend Thomas Thrasher, an Episcopalian; attorneys Nesbitt Elmore and Virgil and John McGee; architect Moreland G. Smith; and labor leader John G. Ward.

These men were joined by an equally active group of women. Their leader was Mrs. Clara H. Rutledge, the wife of a state highway engineer. Her associates included Miss Juliette Morgan, a librarian; Mrs. Olive Andrews, the wife of an insurance agent; Mrs. Bea Kaufman, the wife of a wholesale grocery executive; Mrs. Frances P. McLeod, the wife of a Methodist minister; and after 1951, Mrs. Virginia F. Durr, the wife of the attorney. As was the case in the black community, the women among the white liberals seem often to have been more open and aggressive in their dealings with city authorities than were their male counterparts.[33]

Enthusiasm for the cause of black policemen, however, spread beyond the confines of black leaders and white liberals to gain support as well among white moderates and business progressives. A number of southern cities had hired black police in the years after World War II—sixty-two of them by the end of 1949—and the action appeared to many businessmen to mark a town as possessing forward-looking attitudes. In August 1949 Dothan became the first Alabama city to employ black officers, and in October 1951 it was joined by Talladega. In May 1952 the Montgomery Grand Jury adopted a formal recommendation that Montgomery take the same step "as soon as it may practicably be done," and in November 1953 a second grand jury reiterated the suggestion. The *Montgomery Advertiser,* an ally for four decades of the Gunter machine and a journal whose editorials generally reflected business progressive attitudes, vigorously supported the proposal.[34]

Black leaders and white liberals clearly regarded the hiring of black officers as a step toward the elimination of racial prejudice in law enforcement, but the proposal was able to gather more general white support because it could also be presented as increasing whites' own safety. Black policemen would have greater knowledge of miscreants in the black community than white policemen did, and they would be able to obtain greater cooperation and elicit more information from black witnesses, white citizens were told. The black officers would patrol only in black neighborhoods and would be authorized to arrest a white person only in an emergency, whites were assured. Under these circumstances, white moderates could join blacks and white liberals in favoring the new policy without joining them in regarding it as undermining the hegemony of white supremacist doctrines. Nevertheless, as we shall see, committed segregationists were under no such illusion. For them, placing blacks in any position of social authority represented the profoundest threat to the standing order, and the adoption of this reform—coincident as it was with the U.S. Supreme Court's decision against the racial segregation of public schools—would sharply increase their anxiety.

In the special election of 1953, Dave Birmingham gave black leaders firm assurances that, if elected, he would press for the hiring of black policemen. Birmingham was inaugurated on December 8, and he immediately arranged a meeting between the city commission and black business and professional representatives to discuss the matter. Birmingham's machine colleagues, Gayle and Cleere, did not oppose the idea, but they did point to budgetary constraints. Nevertheless, Birmingham persisted, and as he was now the commissioner who administered the police department, they agreed to accept the black officers as soon as funds could be found. On December 17, Birmingham told the press that black police would be hired, he hoped, in the near future. In late February 1954, the Montgomery Personnel Board announced civil service examinations to create a register of potential black officers, and in mid-March it reported that ten of the twenty-nine black applicants who took the test had passed and were now eligible for employment. Finally, on April 14, the city commission unanimously adopted a resolution authorizing the hiring of four black officers. Eight candidates began training for the positions on April 26, and the four selected commenced active duty on May 3—two weeks before the U.S. Supreme Court announced its decision declaring the racial segregation of public schools a violation of the U.S. Constitution.

In the meantime, on February 1, Mobile had stolen a march on Montgomery, becoming Alabama's third city, and its first major one, to hire black officers. But Montgomery in September became the first of Alabama's cities to hire black policewomen when it added three female black officers to the force. By the fall of the year, Montgomery's seven black officers allowed it to boast of the largest contingent of black police anywhere in the state.[35]

The reform and desegregation of the police force represented a remarkable triumph for black leaders, particularly in the light of the department's quite brutal past, but that victory was only the most important in a series of significant advances which the city's black residents achieved during these years. Next to the hiring of black policemen, the most encouraging gains were in the field of education. Until just before World War II, Montgomery's public schools did not offer a high school program for black children; the black public schools ended with the ninth grade. Alabama State College did offer blacks a high school diploma, because it conducted a laboratory school as a part of its training of teachers, but the Alabama State laboratory high school had limited space and required a substantial tuition. In October 1934 the federal government, through the Works Progress Administration, began funding a pilot program to offer free high school classes to blacks, using Alabama State's facilities. When the federal funding ended in 1937, the local school board agreed to take over the program, opening the tenth grade to blacks in 1937, the eleventh in 1938, and the twelfth in 1939. In 1938 there were only 66 black students in public high school classes in Montgomery, as opposed to 1,424 whites. By 1940 more than 700 blacks, representing about 55 percent of their age group, were attending high school classes. But the landmark in this educational transformation occurred in 1946, when the school board opened its first black high school facility, Booker T. Washington, and also introduced school bus transportation for blacks, allowing many black children of all ages, particularly from more rural areas, to go to school for the first time. About the same time, it developed, under an agreement with the Veterans Administration, the program of job training classes for black veterans which Rufus Lewis was hired to lead in 1949. And in 1949 it opened its second black high school, George Washington Carver. In 1946, as well, Roman Catholics had opened their first parochial high school for blacks, Saint Jude's. In the dozen years from 1937 to 1949, the percentage of black schoolteachers who were college graduates rose from only 4 percent to 70 percent. By 1948 all "shack schools"—black schools not held in actual school buildings—had been eliminated from the system. In 1940 only 6 percent of adult blacks in the city had obtained at least a high school education. By 1950 more than 10 percent had achieved that level, and by 1960, 20 percent had done so. Though black educational opportunities unquestionably remained inferior to those afforded whites, the progress in these years had been marked.[36]

The area of health care, too, saw a significant advance with the completion in 1951 of Saint Jude's Hospital. This fully equipped 158-bed facility was the city's first genuine hospital for blacks, and the first institution in which black doctors were permitted to practice. Montgomery had six black doctors at this time, two of whom were surgeons. Saint Jude's Hospital, opened in 1951, Saint Jude's School, opened in 1946, and the lovely Saint Jude's Church, which they flanked, were all the work of Father Harold Purcell, a remarkable white Roman Catholic priest who came to Montgomery in 1934 to devote himself to service to the city's black citizens. Until his death in 1952, Father Purcell continued to be one of the black community's most vigorous, outspoken, and effective defenders.[37]

Beginning with the construction of its first two public housing projects—one for each race—in 1937, Montgomery had been one of the state's leaders in the provision of public housing for the poor. Mayor Gunter had been a particularly enthusiastic proponent of this program. By the early 1950s, the city's housing authority, headed by Gunter's son-in-law Charles P. Rogers, administered five sprawling developments, four of them for blacks. All of these projects had been constructed over the determined opposition of white realtors. They were not an unalloyed benefit, of course; many blacks resented the demolition of their small homes, however dilapidated, and their removal into crowded apartment complexes. Nevertheless, the projects did provide large numbers of the poorest black families affordable shelter, including modern cooking and plumbing facilities not otherwise available to them.[38]

In addition to the real advances in the areas of law enforcement, education, health, and housing, there were other, somewhat more modest achievements. In May 1947, with the assistance of the Montgomery Junior Chamber of Commerce, a farmers' market for black cultivators was opened in the rear of the Saint Jude's property. This facility allowed black farmers to sell their produce directly to city dwellers. In September 1948 a black branch of the YMCA was established, and three months later a black branch of the city's public library was created. In September 1951 the city's first black hotel was opened. And as we have seen, the city's first black radio station began broadcasting in 1953.[39]

Finally, in the winter of 1953–54 one small but symbolically significant step toward racial integration occurred when Montgomery's professional baseball team added two blacks to its roster. The hiring of the black players seems to have been prompted by the team's financial difficulties; its management apparently hoped that the integration would increase the attendance of area blacks at its games. Evidently wishing to guard against a segregationist backlash at the same time, the management also changed the team's name from the Montgomery Grays to the Montgomery Rebels. However hesitant may have been the decision, however mixed the management's motives, though, this integration gained an enthusiastic response from the city's black community.[40]

It would doubtless be easy to denigrate the advances Montgomery's blacks had achieved in the decade after World War II. Certainly they represented no more than a tentative beginning toward the goal of disestablishing white supremacy. But we must avoid judging them by the standard of the future. As the black citizen of the early 1950s would have experienced them, against the background of earlier conditions, they represented exciting evidence of genuine progress. The century's first real participation of black voters in the political process; the reform of the police department and the hiring of black officers; the opening of high school education to black students; the establishment of an authentic hospital and a variety of other new institutions for blacks; the integration of a professional sports team—all of these things appeared to black observers to give proof that their situation was rapidly improving and that, with the application of a little concerted pressure, they could achieve much more. Not only were these advances building the institutional strength of the black community, moreover, but their success seemed to be bolstering the authority of white moderates and liberals in municipal life. Looking on in 1953 from the neighboring city of Birmingham, where the situation of black residents was vastly less hopeful, a black editor commented enviously, "Montgomery is fast taking the lead as Alabama's most enlightened city." It was this sense of movement that explains the considerable confidence with which black leaders approached city authorities in this period.

II. The Background of the Boycott

Such was the degree of this confidence, indeed, that in the months immediately following the U.S. Supreme Court's school desegregation decision in May 1954, various Montgomery blacks moved to try to avail themselves of it. On June 10, in a speech at Alabama State College, the NAACP's chief attorney, Thurgood Marshall, had urged the state's black citizens to press local boards of education to put the Court's ruling into practice. In July, one of the city's leading civil rights activists, the Reverend Solomon Seay, had appeared at a public meeting of the state board of education to call for the immediate integration of the University of Alabama. As the new school year opened in September, Montgomery's NAACP chapter submitted a formal desegregation petition to the city-county board of education, and on the first day of classes twenty-three black children, shepherded by white liberals Aubrey Williams, Jr., and Nesbitt Elmore and black leader Horace G. Bell, had presented themselves for admission to a newly constructed white elementary school near their homes on the city's southern edge. Initially many whites feared that this action portended the filing of a desegregation suit in federal court, but as time passed it became clear that the blacks involved were unwilling to serve as plaintiffs in such an action. A year later, in August 1955, the city's NAACP chapter again petitioned the board of education for the adoption of a plan to integrate the schools, but like the earlier petition, this one too was simply ignored.[41]

After the integration of the police force had been accomplished, however, the two black proposals that most occupied the attention of the city commission were the Women's Political Council's requests for the development of new parks and playgrounds in black areas of the city and for the adoption in Montgomery of the plan of seating segregation on city buses that was in use in Mobile. The question of parks in black areas escalated to a new level of public controversy in January 1955 when a delegation from the council appeared at a city commission meeting to urge the appointment of a black member to the city's parks and recreation board and to suggest council member Mrs. Irene West for the position. Dave Birmingham immediately offered a motion that the next vacancy go to a black, but Mayor Gayle persuaded him to withdraw the motion until a vacancy actually occurred. Ever since Birmingham's election, the mayor had been seeking to define a centrist position that would make him appear open to black petitions without at the same time seeming, as Birmingham did, an active proponent of the black cause. He had strongly supported a city program under which three new playgrounds for blacks had been recently built, and now he assured the council delegation that its request would be given every consideration when there was a vacancy on the board. The mayor continued this public relations effort later in the same week when, in an appearance before a large group of blacks gathered to celebrate the second inauguration of Governor Folsom, he praised the work of the city's new black policemen and policewomen. But the question of black representation on the parks and recreation board could not be dismissed so easily. It was to become a principal issue in the city elections in March. In August, Commissioner Birmingham, now a lame duck, offered a motion to expand the parks and recreation board from five to seven members and to designate the two new places for blacks, but Gayle and Cleere voted the resolution down. However, the mayor at a heated meeting in July, as well as the parks and recreation board at an angry encounter in September, assured black delegations that if the city's voters would approve the proposed issuance of a million dollars in parks bonds, significant improvements in black parks would immediately be forthcoming. At a meeting of his Citizens' Coordinating Committee in August, Rufus Lewis sought to persuade the committee to sponsor a federal court suit to seek the integration of the parks, but the majority of the committee voted instead merely to continue efforts to equalize the park facilities within the framework of segregation.[42]

While public attention was focused upon the issues first of black policemen and then of tentative black efforts to secure school integration and to obtain black membership on the parks and recreation board, tension over an issue generally unnoticed by whites, racial relations on the city's buses, had quietly been mounting toward a crisis. Montgomery's buses contained thirty-six seats. Under the bus company's policy, the first ten seats—two bench seats facing each other at the front of the bus and the first row of parallel seats—were reserved irrevocably for whites; they were kept reserved even if there were no white passengers on the bus. In theory the ten seats at the rear—the bench seat across the rear of the bus and two bench seats facing each other just forward of it—were similarly reserved for blacks, though this reservation seems to have been much less vigorously enforced. It was the responsibility of the bus driver to adjust the racial designation of the middle sixteen seats to accord with the changing racial composition of his ridership along the route; he was to shift the racial line in order to provide a number of seats roughly proportionate to the racial division of the riders at any given time. In practice, the racial line almost always shifted backward; it could move forward as white passengers left the bus, and occasionally when there was a vacant forward seat to which a white could move, but seated whites were never forced to stand in order to create additional seating for boarding blacks. On the other hand, bus drivers reseated blacks rather frequently, whenever the bus was not already completely filled and whites waiting to board could not be accommodated unless additional seating for them was made available. The embarrassment and humiliation to blacks of being thus publicly forced to acknowledge and accept legal discrimination was exacerbated by the fact that the harried drivers usually adjusted the seating simply by shouting peremptory commands over their shoulders, sometimes in insulting terms.[43]

Racial segregation had first been required on public transportation in Montgomery by a city ordinance adopted in August of 1900. Alderman John G. Finley, an attorney, had introduced in May, in response to a racial incident on a streetcar in Augusta, Georgia, an ordinance requiring the reservation of half the seats on each streetcar for whites and the other half for blacks. But the proposal had proven quite controversial, primarily because of the practical difficulties its enforcement would pose for the trolley lines, and on July 9 the city council had rejected the ordinance by a vote of five to six. Under the prodding of the *Montgomery Advertiser,* an enthusiastic proponent of the idea, however, Finley revised the ordinance and reintroduced it. The new version eliminated the racial reservation of seats and instead obliged streetcar conductors to assign passengers to seats in such a way as to separate the races. It made a refusal of any passenger to sit in the area assigned to his race a misdemeanor, but it provided that the passenger could be prosecuted for this refusal only if there was a vacant seat in the area which the passenger could have taken. These compromises satisfied the trolley companies' objections. The council passed Finley's new proposal unanimously on August 6, and Mayor Edwin B. Joseph, an insurance agent, signed it into law on August 10, to take effect on August 13.

On August 12, 1900, a Sunday, essentially every black clergyman in the city denounced the segregation ordinance from his pulpit and called on all blacks to decline in the future to ride on the trolleys. Thus, on August 13 the racial segregation of the streetcars and a black boycott of the streetcar lines began together. On August 16 the companies reported their receipts down by 60 percent over the preceding three days, and on September 20 they said that their receipts had been down by more than one-fourth during the boycott's first month. The boycott seems to have continued throughout 1901 and into 1902, by which time the companies had apparently passed quiet instructions to their personnel to turn a blind eye to violations of the regulation. Under these circumstances, blacks slowly drifted back to riding, and the boycott gradually ended.

The lack of any vigorous enforcement of the new segregation ordinance did not go unnoticed among some of the city's whites, however. At the end of 1905, when a firm headquartered in Lynchburg, Virginia, acquired control of all three of Montgomery's competing trolley lines and petitioned the city council for an exclusive franchise, the issue was revived. The council agreed to the consolidation of the trolley companies and the grant of the franchise in April 1906, but in return it extracted from the Lynchburg proprietors a number of commitments, among them that the company would begin insisting upon seating segregation. When no changes in the company's practices were in fact forthcoming, however, in August Alderman John F. Jones, the member who seems to have been the council's most vitriolic white supremacist and who, rather ironically, worked as a clerk at the same department store by which, a half century later, Rosa Parks would be employed as a seamstress, introduced an ordinance to require entirely separate trolley cars for whites and blacks. Further negotiations with the trolley company reached an impasse, and in October the council adopted Jones's ordinance. Mayor William M. Teague, a wholesale hardware merchant, vetoed the ordinance, saying that it would impose an excessive burden on the company, but the council overrode the veto with but a single dissent. The company thereupon sent a formal letter to the mayor announcing that it could not and would not comply with the ordinance, and the mayor, determined to embarrass his council opponents, ordered the police to arrest any trolley employees who assisted in their employer's defiance. The ordinance went into effect on the morning of November 23, and by noon fifty-four arrests had been made and the operation of the city's trolley system had been brought to a complete halt. That afternoon, with the city in an uproar, City Court Judge Anthony D. Sayre—the future father-in-law of F. Scott Fitzgerald—granted the company a temporary injunction against the further enforcement of the ordinance, and trolley operations resumed.

This farcical collision brought the firm's Lynchburg president, R. D. Apperson, and its general counsel, John D. Horsley, scurrying to Montgomery to open further negotiations with the aldermen. At Apperson's suggestion, Alderman William J. Ryan, a dry goods store clerk, drafted a compromise ordinance repealing Jones's proposal for separate trolley cars and substituting a plan which Apperson said had worked well in Lynchburg: the reservation of the front four seats on each car for whites and the back four for blacks, with each race when necessary occupying the middle seats nearest to the seats reserved for it; the reserved seats were to be kept free even if there were no passengers of the appropriate race to use them, and when the cars were crowded, conductors were to have police power to reseat passengers to preserve segregation. The Ryan ordinance was adopted on January 7, 1907, but at the next council meeting, on January 12, Alderman Jones sought its reconsideration. Railing that the ordinance gave special preference to blacks, he denounced it as discriminatory to white people. Alderman J. Lee Holloway, an attorney, replied with the equally remarkable argument that Jones's proposal for racially separate cars would violate the Fourteenth Amendment; only separate seats within the same car, Holloway asserted, could pass constitutional muster. After a lengthy battle, both Ryan's ordinance and Jones's earlier one were repealed, and the council abandoned further attempts to legislate on the matter.

Nevertheless, the affair had had its effect. Though the city was left with the Finley ordinance of 1900 as the only municipal legislation on the subject, the trolley company, in an effort to quiet the controversy, now accepted the Lynchburg pattern of segregation, as embodied in the Ryan ordinance, as its own policy, and its employees began enforcing the front and rear seating reservations and the reseating of passengers in the middle section. By 1955 the 1906–7 squabble had long since faded into a dim local memory, but the bus company that succeeded the trolley line in 1936 continued to rely upon the practices that had become customary on the trolleys as a result of it. On at least two crucial points, the city ordinance of 1900 differed from the inherited bus company policy. The ordinance provided that the driver was to assign seats to the two races only when there were members of each race on the bus, but the bus company in fact kept the first ten seats reserved for whites even when there were no whites aboard. And the ordinance provided that a passenger's refusal to move when ordered by the driver was unlawful only if there was a vacant seat to which the passenger could have moved, but the bus drivers in fact often compelled black passengers to stand in order to accommodate boarding whites. In both of these practices the bus company appeared to be violating the ordinance's provisions.

In 1945 the state legislature had passed a statute compelling all bus companies to provide segregated seating, terminals, ticket windows, and other facilities and instructing the Alabama Public Service Commission to administer this requirement in the same manner that it administered the provisions of the Alabama Motor Carrier Act of 1939. The statute contained none of the exceptions of Montgomery's city ordinance; the bus driver had to seat every passenger, and every passenger had to sit wherever, and move whenever, the bus driver ordered. But the Alabama Motor Carrier Act of 1939 specifically provided that it did not apply to municipal bus lines, the public service commission did not regulate municipal bus lines, and the terms of the 1945 act certainly seemed to refer to intercity buses. In 1947 the legislature passed another act authorizing, but not requiring, bus companies to segregate seating and facilities. This act contained no reference to the Motor Carrier Act, as the 1945 act had, but like the earlier act it referred to ticket windows, terminals, and other facilities relevant only to intercity bus operations. It, too, however, required passengers to obey the bus driver's seating instructions without exception. Both the 1945 statute and the 1947 statute were later carried into the state code as subsections of a single section. The text of each subsection stated that the segregation provisions applied to all bus companies, but the context of each seemed not to include municipal buses. If the state laws did apply to Montgomery's bus company, then they had superseded the city ordinance, and the ordinance's exceptions had become inoperative. But if the state laws were not applicable, then the provisions of the city ordinance were still in force, and important aspects of the company's practices were in conflict with them. Thus the precise legal powers of the city's bus drivers in the early 1950s were quite obscure.[44]

A different and much less complicated pattern of segregation prevailed on buses in Mobile. Segregation had come to public transportation in Mobile on November 2, 1902, after the adoption by the city council on October 15 of an ordinance modeled on Montgomery's. As had been the case in Montgomery, the ordinance at once provoked a black boycott of the trolley line. In Mobile, however, the ordinance also produced sharp protests from white passengers, who resented being reseated by the conductors. On December 1, only a month after the ordinance had taken effect, the management of the streetcar company announced that the complaints had been so numerous that it had told its employees to stop enforcing the new law. The city thereupon began arresting the streetcar conductors for dereliction of duty. The Mobile ordinance, unlike the Montgomery one, had from the beginning contained a proviso that if its enforcement would require the reseating of passengers already seated, the conductor could use his discretion, but this provision apparently was insufficient to meet Mobilians' objections. Finally, in April 1917, the city commission repealed the 1902 ordinance and substituted one that eliminated the racial reservation of seats, reseating, and the role of the conductor altogether. Under the 1917 ordinance, whites seated from the front and blacks from the back, and the racial dividing line was wherever they met; it was readjusted only by the departure of passengers as they reached their destinations. This ordinance was the one that governed public transportation in Mobile in the 1950s. The plan was used also in a number of other southern cities, including Atlanta. But its use in Mobile was particularly significant for blacks in Montgomery because when trolleys were replaced by buses in both cities in the late 1930s, the Montgomery and Mobile bus companies became subsidiaries of the same Chicago-based corporation, National City Lines. It was, therefore, the example of Mobile that Montgomery's black leaders constantly cited in their efforts to obtain the reform of bus seating segregation in their city.[45]

Black leaders first raised with white authorities the possibility of adopting the Mobile plan of seating segregation on October 28, 1952. On that date the city commission held a public hearing on the bus company's petition to increase its fares. Mrs. Zolena J. Pierce, the wife of Alabama State political science professor James Pierce, and Mrs. Sadie Brooks, the wife of Joseph Brooks, assistant to Alabama State's president, Councill Trenholm, headed a delegation of black women who seized this opportunity to appear before the commission and discuss the seating problem. Speaking for the Women's Political Council, Mrs. Pierce and Mrs. Brooks sharply criticized the company's policy of reserving the first ten seats for whites even when there were no whites on the bus. They explained the Mobile pattern and urged that it be used in Montgomery. The bus company's attorney, Jack Crenshaw, assured the women that the commission was familiar with the problem. He said that the company was unable to furnish separate buses for the two races, and added, incorrectly, "I think we've followed as closely as possible the city ordinances in the matter." News accounts reported that the commission took the council's proposal under advisement.[46]

At the end of 1953, encouraged by Dave Birmingham's recent election, the Women's Political Council again met with the city commission to condemn the bus situation. At this meeting the women lodged three specific complaints: that because of the reservation of the front ten seats for whites, blacks sometimes had to stand even though empty seats were available; that black passengers were compelled to get on at the front door to pay their fare and then get off and reboard at the back door to take a seat, rather than being permitted simply to walk down the aisle of the bus; and that buses stopped, when requested, at every corner in white neighborhoods but only at every other corner in black neighborhoods. During the ensuing discussion, allegations were also made of discourtesy by drivers and of buses' passing by waiting black passengers. The meeting was inconclusive, but representatives of the bus line, who were present, evidently offered to investigate any specific charges of discourtesy. Several months later, in March 1954, the council again met with the commission and representatives of the bus company to reiterate its three complaints and to offer the list of specific instances of abuse by bus drivers for which the company had asked in December. At this meeting the council's delegation was reinforced by Rufus Lewis, representing the Citizens' Coordinating Committee, by a delegation from the Federation of Negro Women's Clubs, and by a large group representing black trade union locals. At the

March meeting as at the earlier one, however, the principal black spokesman was the council's new president, Jo Ann Robinson.

As a result of this meeting, the problem of buses' stopping only at every other corner in black areas was remedied, but officials were unwilling to compromise on the seating question. On the advice of City Attorney Walter Knabe and bus company attorney Jack Crenshaw, they informed the black representatives that they were legally powerless to do anything to remedy blacks' grievance. The city ordinance and the state statute on the subject were both read aloud to the petitioners. The meeting was evidently a stormy one. Subsequently, Mayor Gayle testified that several days later Mrs. Robinson called him angrily "and said they would just show me, they were going in the front door and sitting wherever they pleased."

In early April 1954, the Reverend Uriah J. Fields, a militant young black minister who was later to break spectacularly with Martin Luther King, brought the seating complaints before the public with a letter to the *Montgomery Advertiser* demanding that the bus company's seating policy be altered. And on May 21—eighteen days after Montgomery's first black policemen began work, and four days after the U.S. Supreme Court's school desegregation decision—Mrs. Robinson sent Mayor Gayle a letter warning of the possibility of vigorous black protests unless improvements in conditions on the buses were forthcoming. If blacks did not patronize the buses, she noted, "they could not possibly operate. More and more of our people are already arranging with neighbors and friends to ride to keep from being insulted and humiliated by bus drivers. There has been talk from twenty-five or more local organizations of planning a city-wide boycott of buses. We, sir, do not feel that forceful measures are necessary in bargaining for a convenience which is right for all bus passengers. We, the Council, believe that when this matter has been put before you and the Commissioners, that agreeable terms can be met in a quiet and unostensible [*sic*] manner to the satisfaction of all concerned." There, however, the matter rested until the following spring.[47]

Meantime, the elections that could kill the already moribund Gunter machine were approaching. Gayle's only opponent was Harold McGlynn, a candy wholesaler who was a political associate of Commissioner Birmingham's. Cleere's principal opposition came from Frank Parks, an east Montgomery interior decorator who was a former grand master of Alabama's Masons. Parks set out to create an electoral coalition like that which had enabled Birmingham to upset Dawkins a year and a half earlier. Though Gayle and Cleere supported each other, and Birmingham supported McGlynn and Parks, it is unclear whether or not Gayle and Cleere supported one of the candidates opposing Birmingham; at any rate, they did not do so publicly. Birmingham drew two principal opponents. Sam B. Stearns, the owner of a downtown parking garage and a nephew of a former Montgomery County sheriff, ran an energetic and well-financed campaign, but the returns showed him much less popular than observers had thought. The real threat to the incumbent was former state representative Clyde C. Sellers, a resident of south Montgomery and the owner of an exterminating business. Sellers effectively emphasized his extensive experience in law enforcement; he had joined the state highway patrol shortly after its formation, had worked his way up through its ranks, and in 1945 had been appointed director of the department by Governor Chauncey Sparks. His four years in the state legislature also strengthened his credentials. That he had been a star football player for Auburn University in the 1920s gave him additional popularity. But the issue that was to carry him to victory was provided by the events of the canvass.

Birmingham launched a typically demagogic campaign. His two colleagues on the city commission had voted to increase the city sewage fee in order to finance the extension of sewer mains into the Allendale-Wildwood section, a south Montgomery area. Birmingham denounced this decision as class legislation and demanded that the wealthy homeowners in the section pay for the sewers themselves. Frank Parks loudly echoed this argument. Birmingham revived his accusation that chlorination of the water supply was dangerous; he alleged as proof that city water would kill camellia bushes. He also charged that Gayle and Cleere might have favored the construction of a city sewage treatment plant only in order to make a private profit by selling the plant's effluent for fertilizer. With such allegations Birmingham hoped to hold, and Parks to build, constituencies of whites of the lower and lower middle classes. McGlynn refused to stoop to this level, and perhaps for that reason his campaign against Gayle never really gained momentum. McGlynn did join Birmingham and Parks in a strong effort to gain the allegiance of the black vote.[48]

As the campaign of 1955 began, black leaders hoped to use the black balance of power between south Montgomery and east Montgomery to extract real concessions from the candidates. They had just passed through a year in which the city government had shown unprecedented willingness to listen to their proposals. Birmingham, Parks, and McGlynn were eager for black support. One of Birmingham's opponents, Stearns, was equally willing to seek black votes. Nor, indeed, were Gayle and Cleere hostile. Though more reticent than were their opponents about openly campaigning for black ballots, still both men were racial moderates. The remnants of the machine they represented could, moreover, command a certain residue of goodwill in the black community; Mayor Gunter's actions in the 1920s and 1930s had endeared him to many blacks.

All of these circumstances so emboldened the black leaders that they decided in February to hold a public meeting in order to question the various commission candidates about their stands on racial issues. The candidates subsequently also appeared before organized labor and the junior chamber of commerce.[49] But the spectacle of office seekers appearing before blacks to submit to interrogation was a sight for which the white electorate proved entirely unprepared. The meeting, held under the auspices of Edgar Nixon's Progressive Democratic Association, convened in the black Ben Moore Hotel on the evening of February 23. All of the candidates were present. The session commenced with Nixon's distributing to them a questionnaire asking their position on a number of specific black grievances. The first area of complaint on the list was "the present bus situation. Negroes have to stand over empty seats of city buses, because the first ten seats are reserved for whites who sometime[s] never ride. We wish to fill the bus from the back toward the front until all seats are taken. This is done in Atlanta, Georgia, Mobile, Alabama and in most of our larger southern cities." Next came requests that a black be appointed to the parks and recreation board and that blacks be considered for all municipal boards. The third subject mentioned was the lack of middle-class housing subdivisions for relatively well-to-do blacks. The authors of the questionnaire had been upset by the city's decision a week earlier to forbid the development of such an area because of the protests of neighboring whites. The fourth plea was that qualified black applicants be considered for civil service jobs with the city. "Everybody cannot teach," the questionnaire noted, in reference to the limited professional opportunities available to Montgomery's middle-class blacks. The document concluded with three complaints about the inadequacy of city services in black neighborhoods. It asked for the installation of more fireplugs in these sections, the extension of sewer mains to eliminate outdoor privies, and the widening and paving of streets and the addition of curbing.

In their responses, Birmingham, McGlynn, and Parks all agreed to appoint a black member to the parks and recreation board. Stearns, who had adopted the strategy of attempting to defeat Birmingham by outbidding him for the allegiance of the city's various groups, also agreed, and added a proposal for a sixteen-member all-black advisory board as an adjunct of the parks board. The press reported that black leaders were as a result closely divided as to whether they should endorse Birmingham or Stearns. Gayle and Cleere remained noncommittal on the parks board issue. Sellers gave a general talk that did not speak to any of the points in the questionnaire; he said later that he did not see the document until the end of the meeting. Accounts of the session do not indicate any reply by any of the candidates to the questionnaire's proposal on bus seating.[50]

The meeting adjourned after the candidates had completed their presentations, but its repercussions were still being felt years later. Clyde Sellers quickly saw that the black proposals and their deferential handling by his two opponents presented him with the issue that would allow him to win a majority. It appeared that Stearns and Birmingham were going to divide the black vote. Sellers, as a south Montgomerian, could count on a large vote from that section in response to Birmingham's vociferous attacks on its residents. Previously, though, there had seemed to be no way to cut into Birmingham's solid following in east Montgomery. Now, demagogic exploitation of racial tensions promised to counter Birmingham's exploitation of class tensions and thus to capture support in the eastern wards. During March, before the election on the twenty-first, Sellers made the most blatantly and insistently racist addresses heard in Montgomery since disfranchisement in 1901. Sellers converted the Ben Moore Hotel meeting into the principal issue of the canvass. He answered the questionnaire point by point in his speeches and advertisements. He asserted flatly that the blacks' bus seating proposal would violate state law—not bothering to explain how, in that case, the system could be used in Mobile. He pledged himself to oppose the appointment of blacks to city boards. To the request that qualified blacks be allowed to apply for civil service jobs, he said, "If the commission were to comply with this request, it would be only a short time before negroes would be working along side of whites and whites along side of negroes. . . . I have always felt that if a man wanted a job bad enough, he could go where the job, for which he is qualified, is available. There are places in this nation where civil service jobs for negroes in cities are available but not in Montgomery. I will expend every effort to keep it that way."[51] Sellers's campaign was aided by the occurrence of the first serious bus incident in some years, the arrest on March 2 and the trial on March 18 of Claudette Colvin for violation of the segregation ordinance.

Sellers had been correct about the effect of his racial appeal upon the electorate. In the returns he took 43 percent of the poll, to 37 percent for Birmingham, 16 percent for Stearns, and 4 percent for a minor candidate, John T. Weaver. Birmingham carried the wards with substantial black registration and also took the poorest white wards, but the white lower-middle-class areas of east Montgomery that he had swept in 1953 now went to Sellers. Capitol Heights, which had given Birmingham 62 percent of its vote in 1953, making it his banner precinct, now gave him only 31 percent, to 44 percent for Sellers. At the same time, south Montgomery voted heavily against Birmingham; Sellers took 60 percent of the poll in Cloverdale. Despite Sellers's solid lead over Birmingham, a runoff between the two men would have been necessary. However, two days after the election Birmingham collapsed while preparing to give a television speech; his doctor diagnosed his condition as "overexertion and exhaustion" and advised him to withdraw from the race. Birmingham did so, and Sellers was declared elected. We can never know whether Birmingham could have defeated Sellers. Birmingham had come back from an even more substantial deficit to defeat Dawkins in 1953, but his chances of repeating this accomplishment in 1955 would appear to have been poor. Since Stearns, the third important candidate in the race, had made shrill personal attacks on Birmingham, it seems unlikely that a white voter who had cast his ballot for Stearns in the first round would thereafter have moved to the support of Birmingham.

In the mayoral election, McGlynn had seldom indulged in the demagogic appeals of Birmingham and Parks. He may have been hurt by the fact that he was a Roman Catholic, though his religion was certainly not an open issue in the campaign. McGlynn received 40 percent of the vote and carried the wards with substantial black registration and also the city's poorest white ward, West End. Nevertheless, Mayor Gayle won easily.

In the election for commissioner of public works, the incumbent, George Cleere, had refused to follow Sellers in exploiting the racial issue. Instead, he had attempted to answer with reason the strident class-oriented accusations of Parks, particularly with reference to the sewage fee. The result was that Parks was elected on returns whose geographical distribution was virtually identical to the distribution of the support for Birmingham in his race against Dawkins in 1953. Cleere swept the south Montgomery wards, taking more than 75 percent of the vote in Cloverdale, but Parks carried the substantially black precincts and those of the white lower class and lower middle class.[52]

The election's outcome puzzled *Advertiser* editor Grover C. Hall, Jr.; why should the voters have elected Parks, Birmingham's ally, over Cleere, Gayle's ally, but then have repudiated Birmingham himself and returned Gayle?[53] The meaning of the election was probably much clearer to Gayle, now the sole machine survivor in municipal politics, seated between an uncompromising segregationist on his right and an adversary of Montgomery's wealthy on his left. The machine's traditional policies of moderate, paternalistic racial attitudes and a firm alliance with the city's upper class had failed to sustain it, and they held little likelihood of endearing Gayle to the constituencies that had elevated either of his two colleagues. Clearly, Gayle needed a new strategy immediately. The lesson of Parks's victory appeared to be that, given the new social realities produced by the city's rapid postwar growth, an east Montgomerian would always defeat a south Montgomerian when the issues remained class oriented. The lesson of Sellers's victory appeared to be that the vigorous exploitation of racial antipathies could give a south Montgomerian at least a fighting chance of defeating an east Montgomerian. Gayle was, of course, a south Montgomerian. But Gayle's dilemma was much more complicated than this analysis would imply. First, he was not likely to abandon a set of beliefs that he had held sincerely for many decades merely because political strategy seemed to dictate this course. Second, developments within the business community rendered it less than certain that a sound strategy actually dictated such a course. To understand this factor, we must briefly explore the attitude of Montgomery's businessmen toward their city government.

The business community believed that the source of all genuine social ills was the lack of industrialization. Montgomery's economy rested primarily on the presence of the state government and of two air force bases, Maxwell and Gunter. One in every seven families in the city was an air force family in 1955. Aside from income generated by federal and state governmental expenditures, Montgomery relied almost exclusively on its role as a marketing center for the surrounding agricultural area.[54] By 1955, however, businessmen were armed with legislation passed during the preceding decade providing Alabama municipalities with powerful tools for attracting industry to the state, particularly in the form of tax advantages and of public financing of plant construction. Business leaders therefore had high hopes of broadening Montgomery's economic base.

This zealous commitment to industrialization was the source of the tension between businessmen and the city government. Business leaders believed that the city's politicians had been inept in attracting industry. Near the end of October 1953, the *Advertiser* had broken the story that DuPont, the giant chemical company, had purchased 850 acres near Montgomery "as a prospective site for an industrial plant." The article had concluded excitedly, "Announcement is expected soon on the type of plant to be constructed." Months passed, and no such announcement was forthcoming. Reportedly, four other "very large companies" that had considered building factories in Montgomery had been lost to other cities during 1954 and 1955. Worried businessmen sought to discover what they were doing wrong. The chamber of commerce desperately debated ways to attract favorable national publicity for the city. Chamber president James G. Pruett ominously warned the Rotary Club that "industry will come to Montgomery and Alabama only when there is a healthy climate for it and when government on all levels is not hostile to it." In this atmosphere of frustration at the repeated recent failures in the drive for industrialization, forty of the city's most important businessmen met in mid-October 1955 to organize the Men of Montgomery. Adopting the frank motto "We Mean Business," they chose as their first project a campaign to compel the city commission to act on a proposal that had languished in the city hall bureaucracy for years: the construction of a new terminal for the municipal airport to give visitors to the city a more favorable first impression.[55]

Mayor Gayle had always counted on business support. The Gunter machine had been closely allied with business interests, and Gayle himself was a brother-in-law of one of the most influential businessmen in Alabama, Birmingham industrialist Donald Comer of Avondale Mills.[56] Now the mayor faced a business community organized with a new efficiency and motivated by a new hostility. By the fall of 1955 his dilemma was acute. His colleagues on the commission each represented constituencies only recently defined, and Gayle had no real access to either. The black leadership was making militant demands upon the city for the first time and was asking for public responses. The business community was suddenly dubious of Gayle's competence and disposed to press him for positive action. If he moved toward one of the newly emerging constituencies, he risked permanently alienating the elements in the city upon which he had relied ever since he had first entered politics. Against this background, the city moved toward the events of early December.

III. The Initiation of the Boycott

At the Ben Moore Hotel meeting on February 23, bus seating had headed the list of grievances. On the afternoon of March 2 came the arrest of Claudette Colvin, a fifteen-year-old black girl who refused to vacate her seat when ordered to do so by a bus driver, Robert W. Cleere. Miss Colvin, who was returning home from school, was seated far back in the bus, just forward of the rear door, on a seat with another black woman, Mrs. Ruth Hamilton, the wife of a service station attendant. Mrs. Hamilton was pregnant. A white couple sat down in the seats across the aisle from them, the last two vacant seats on the bus. Cleere thereupon ordered the two black women to stand, to preserve segregation. Neither woman moved. Cleere stopped the bus, in the middle of the downtown business district, and summoned police. Officers Thomas J. Ward and Paul Headley answered the call. Discovering Mrs. Hamilton's pregnancy, the officers urged black passengers in the rear seats to allow her to sit. A black man, John Harris, then gave Mrs. Hamilton his seat and left the bus. Miss Colvin now found herself left to face the music alone. She again refused the officers' order to move, and they placed her under arrest. Apparently at this point she became hysterical, and the policemen had to pick her up bodily and carry her weeping to their patrol car. Officer Ward testified that she hit, scratched, and kicked him as he tried to put her in the car. Officer Headley was unable to corroborate this claim, however, and the testimony of other witnesses to the events was divided. Miss Colvin was charged with violation of the city bus segregation ordinance, disorderly conduct, and assault and battery on Officer Ward.

Because of her age, Miss Colvin was docketed for trial before Juvenile Court Judge Wiley C. Hill, Jr., a first cousin of U.S. senator J. Lister Hill and a leader of the Hill faction in local politics. She was very far from being the first person arrested for violating the bus segregation ordinance; as recently as the summer of 1949, Judge Hill had himself tried two black teenagers who, while visiting Montgomery from Newark, New Jersey, had been charged with the same offense. But according to Commissioner Birmingham, Miss Colvin was the first person ever to enter a plea of not guilty to the charge. This plea undoubtedly had much to do with the fact that, six months earlier, Alabama had admitted Fred D. Gray to the bar.

Gray, a native Montgomerian and a licensed minister of the Church of Christ, was an honors graduate of Alabama State College. Taking advantage of a state program to pay the tuition of black students to attend out-of-state professional schools in subjects that Alabama's own black colleges did not teach, Gray obtained a law degree from the Backus Law School of Western Reserve University in Cleveland, Ohio, and passed the Alabama bar examination in August 1954. He thus became the state's twelfth black attorney, and Montgomery's second. His predecessor in Montgomery, however, Charles D. Langford, had essentially limited his practice before Gray's arrival to noncontroversial subjects. Gray, on the other hand, at once embraced a militant crusade for equal rights for his race. Within months, the young man, though only twenty-four years old, became a major leader of the city's black community; the spring of 1955 found him defending Claudette Colvin, and by September he was the principal spokesman for the black delegation in its acrimonious meeting with the parks and recreation board.

On March 18 Miss Colvin came to trial. Gray interposed two defenses to the charge that she had violated the segregation ordinance. The first, that bus segregation violated the Fourteenth Amendment of the U.S. Constitution, Judge Hill overruled in short order. The second was more troublesome. The Montgomery ordinance, as we have seen, provided that it was an offense not to obey a bus driver's order to change seats only if there was another seat available to which the passenger could move. As all witnesses agreed that the bus was completely filled, it followed that Miss Colvin, in refusing to move, had been within her rights. Circuit Solicitor William F. Thetford, who was prosecuting the case, hastened to meet this defense by amending the complaint to allege instead a violation of the state statute of 1945. Gray objected that the statute did not apply to a municipal bus line, but Judge Hill overruled the objection and accepted the amendment. At the conclusion of the hearing, Judge Hill dismissed the charge of disorderly conduct but found Miss Colvin guilty of violating the state bus segregation statute and of assault and battery on Officer Ward, declared her a juvenile delinquent, and placed her on indefinite probation. Gray filed an appeal to circuit court.

On May 2, Circuit Judge Eugene Carter held a hearing on Gray's motion to dismiss the segregation charge against Miss Colvin on the ground that bus segregation was unconstitutional. After hearing arguments, Judge Carter overruled Gray's contention and ordered the case to trial. But at the trial on May 6, Solicitor Thetford announced that the state was dropping the segregation charge and would press only the charge of assault and battery. Judge Carter affirmed Miss Colvin's conviction on that charge, and her sentence of probation. As a result, Gray was deprived of any way to use this case as a means to contest on appeal the various questions that had been raised with regard to the segregation laws. At the suggestion of white liberal attorney Clifford Durr, he considered reintroducing the segregation question by having Miss Colvin sue the bus company in federal court for damages for having enforced the segregation ordinance, a tactic adopted earlier that year by a black woman in Columbia, South Carolina. But before he could file the suit, Miss Colvin became pregnant out of wedlock in June, and her parents, embarrassed to have her appear in public in that condition, withdrew their authorization for the action.[57]

Meanwhile, Miss Colvin's arrest had moved the city's black leaders to make one more effort to deal with the bus problem through the political mechanism. In mid-March, as the municipal election campaign climaxed, blacks arranged two meetings with white officials. At the first one, Commissioner Birmingham and the bus company's manager, James H. Bagley, met in Bagley's office with a delegation that included, among others, the Reverend Martin Luther King, Jr., a twenty-six-year-old Baptist minister who had moved to Montgomery the preceding September to take up his first pastorate, and who in the intervening six months had become active in the city's NAACP chapter. It appears, however, that at this meeting, as at the earlier ones, the principal spokesman for the blacks was a conspicuous member of King's new congregation, Jo Ann Robinson.

This encounter was relatively amicable. Birmingham was eager to conciliate the blacks, and Bagley did not wish to offend his customers gratuitously. The black delegation pointed out that forcing a passenger to stand in order to seat another passenger violated both company policy and the provisions of the city code. Bagley acknowledged that the policy did forbid such action; he promised to investigate and to reprimand the bus driver in the Colvin case if it was warranted. The blacks evidently brought up the seating plan proposed in the questionnaire presented at the Ben Moore Hotel meeting; Birmingham promised to secure a formal opinion from City Attorney Walter Knabe on what seating arrangements were legally permissible. Unfortunately, nothing came of either of these promises.

Birmingham's failure to act is perhaps understandable; within two weeks he was a lame duck, his influence greatly diminished and his health precarious. Bagley's inattention to the matter was simply shortsighted. A principal source of friction on the buses was the company's failure to define carefully for its drivers how the seating policy was to be administered. If Bagley had attempted to specify the terms of the policy more fully and had sought more vigorously to enforce company rules requiring courtesy from drivers, he could have eliminated much of the ill will between the bus line and the black community. If he had simply emphasized to the drivers the company policy against unseating passengers when other seats were unavailable, he would have prevented both the Claudette Colvin and the Rosa Parks incidents.

The second meeting in response to Miss Colvin's arrest appears to have been much angrier than that with Bagley and Birmingham. Bagley arranged this meeting for the blacks. The black delegation included, as usual, members of the black Women's Political Council and the Federation of Negro Women's Clubs. It also included Rufus Lewis of the Citizens' Coordinating Committee and attorney Fred Gray. Mayor Gayle and City Attorney Knabe represented the city. The bus company was represented by its attorney, Jack Crenshaw. The blacks apparently pressed the seating proposal contained in the questionnaire distributed at the Ben Moore Hotel meeting. Gray believed that the proposal violated no existing law. Crenshaw adamantly maintained that the proposal flouted both the city ordinance and the state statute, an opinion in which Knabe concurred.

The importance of Crenshaw's intransigence both in producing and in sustaining the bus boycott can hardly be overstated. He was an excellent lawyer, educated at Harvard. He was a political ally of the racially moderate Governor Folsom. Despite this background, however, he proved incapable of understanding the strategic advantage of accepting a modest compromise in order to forestall a full-scale assault on segregation. He dismissed Gray's arguments out of hand and informed Bagley that the law left the bus company absolutely no room for compromise. The meeting adjourned with the complaints of the blacks still unanswered.[58]

Through the summer and fall of 1955 a series of events kept the bus question before the public. Early in the year, as we have noted, a young black woman, Sarah Mae Flemming, had sued the city bus line of Columbia, South Carolina, for damages for its having enforced the segregation laws against her. In mid-July the U.S. Court of Appeals for the Fourth Circuit ruled in this case that segregated seating on buses was unconstitutional—a decision that received headline treatment in the *Montgomery Advertiser.* Later in July a young black, James M. Ritter, defied the order of a bus driver in Richmond, Virginia—a city under the jurisdiction of the Fourth Circuit—to move to the rear. Despite the *Flemming* decision, he was fined ten dollars for his action. In Montgomery itself another black teenager, Mary Louise Smith, was arrested on October 21 for refusing to yield her seat to a white woman. This case did not become public knowledge at the time, however, because at the insistence of her father, Miss Smith quietly chose to plead guilty; she was fined five dollars.[59]

Equally important in focusing attention on the bus company was the fact that its franchise was about to expire. National City Lines had been granted a twenty-year city franchise in 1936; the franchise would come up for renewal in March of 1956. In late October an official of the company came from Chicago to open negotiations. He and the city commissioners surveyed the city from the air in order to plan revisions in the bus routes, and delegations from a number of the new subdivisions on the city's outskirts appeared before the commission to seek the extension of bus service to their areas. At the same time, the bus company was bargaining with the bus drivers' union for a new two-year contract. Montgomerians who recalled that all bus service had been suspended during a brief strike in December 1953 watched the progress of the negotiations apprehensively.[60]

In August and September of 1955, on instructions from the NAACP's national headquarters, NAACP branches around Alabama—including, as we have already noted, Montgomery's—submitted petitions to their local boards of education asking for the integration of the schools. The petition in Selma (as we shall see in greater detail when we turn our attention to that city) produced the firing of sixteen of its signers from their jobs, at the instance of Selma's White Citizens' Council. Blacks thereupon organized a boycott of a dairy that had cooperated in one of the firings. A kidnapping and an attempt at arson followed, both directed at a black grocer implicated in the boycott; and a police officer charged in the arson attempt committed suicide after his arrest. All of these events received close attention in the Montgomery press.[61]

In early November, black congressman Adam Clayton Powell of New York visited Montgomery to speak to Edgar Nixon's Progressive Democratic Association. The visit aroused intense controversy because Governor Folsom arranged to have his chauffeur meet Powell at the Montgomery airport and bring him to the Governor's Mansion for a drink. But white observers generally missed the real effect of the visit on the black community. Powell had led a successful black boycott of buses in New York City in the spring of 1941 to compel the hiring of black bus drivers and mechanics. In his Montgomery speech on November 5, he warned the White Citizens' Councils that their economic pressure "can be counter met with our own [black] economic pressure." He spent the night at the home of Edgar Nixon.

There can be little doubt that the example of the boycott in Selma and the force of Powell's own precedent and his spirited remarks made a deep impact on Edgar Nixon. Nixon was predisposed in any case to believe in the efficacy of economic action, because of his background in the labor movement and because of his long acquaintance with and intense admiration for his union's president, A. Philip Randolph. Randolph had been associated with Powell in the late 1930s in a series of black boycotts and demonstrations against New York City merchants, to increase black job opportunities. The events of the fall of 1955, therefore, almost certainly strengthened Nixon's growing conviction that a boycott—under discussion among Montgomery's black leaders, as Mrs. Robinson had informed Mayor Gayle, at least since the spring of 1954—might well prove the ideal weapon to force the city and the bus company to deal seriously with black complaints.[62]

The arrest of Mrs. Rosa Parks on the evening of December 1, 1955, was the spark that ignited this tinder. When Mrs. Parks boarded the Cleveland Avenue bus, shortly after getting off from work, she took a seat on the side opposite the driver in the first row of seats in its black section. At the time, the bus was divided into twenty-six seats for blacks and ten for whites. Two blocks farther on, when the bus stopped in front of the Empire Theater, all seats were completely filled and both whites and blacks were standing; all white standing room was taken, but some black standing room remained. The bus driver, J. Fred Blake, therefore undertook to readjust the seating to a more equitable ratio by clearing one row of seats, altering the division to fourteen white and twenty-two black. Three of the blacks rose on Blake's order; one, Mrs. Parks, refused. Since the blacks thus unseated would have to stand, Blake's action clearly violated the city code—though not the state statute, if it was applicable to city buses. On the other hand, if Blake had taken no action, none of the whites waiting to board could have been accommodated, even though there was standing room available in the rear. Blake's order represented a reasonable effort to deal with a practical problem entirely created by the segregation laws, while Mrs. Parks, in ignoring the order, was within her rights even under the terms of Montgomery's segregation ordinance itself. The questions surrounding this encounter were, in short, essentially identical to those created by the arrest of Claudette Colvin nine months earlier.[63]

Mrs. Parks was born Rosa Louise McCauley in February 1913, in Tuskegee. Her father, James McCauley, was a carpenter, the eldest son of Abbeville farmers Anderson and Sue McCauley. Her mother, Leona Edwards, had been a schoolteacher and would resume that profession following the failure of her marriage. In 1915, following the birth of Rosa and her younger brother, Sylvester, Mrs. McCauley and her husband were separated, and Mrs. McCauley and her children returned to live with her parents, Sylvester and Rose Edwards, on a tenant farm near Pine Level in southern Montgomery County. Here Rosa grew up. Mrs. McCauley was ambitious for her only daughter, and in 1924 she arranged for Rosa to move into the city to live with cousins so that she could attend a private school for black girls. This extraordinary institution, called officially the Montgomery Industrial School for Negro Girls, was known universally as Miss White's School, after Alice L. White, the New England Congregationalist missionary who, along with a companion, Margaret Beard, had come to Montgomery in 1886 to devote her life to the work of educating young black women. Under Miss White's tutelage, Rosa McCauley began training for a career as a stenographer and typist. She was also taught considerable skill as a seamstress and, perhaps most important of all, a strong sense of dignity and self-worth.[64]

On completion of Miss White's, which ran through the eighth grade, Rosa decided to seek a high school education. At this time, as we have seen, Montgomery did not provide a public high school for blacks. At some financial sacrifice, Rosa enrolled in Alabama State College's laboratory high school, which required tuition payments from its students. The illness of her mother forced her to leave school in 1930, after the eleventh grade. In December 1932 she married Raymond A. Parks, a barber who was ten years her senior. With Parks's assistance, she resumed her schooling. Finally, in 1933, she received her high school diploma, against considerable odds, at the age of twenty.[65]

Only a tiny percentage of blacks in Montgomery—6 percent of them in 1940, the first year for which the statistic is available—were high school graduates in this period, and even fewer had Rosa Parks's typing and shorthand skills. But she found herself unable to obtain employment commensurate with her education and talent. Secretarial jobs for blacks were virtually nonexistent in the South; there were only 140 black typists or stenographers in Alabama in 1940, as against 8,491 white ones. And employment of any description was scarce in Montgomery at the bottom of the Depression. Mrs. Parks went through a series of menial jobs—as a helper at Saint Margaret's Hospital, as a domestic, as a presser at a tailor shop. She worked at Maxwell Air Force Base for a time during World War II and briefly tried her hand at selling insurance for a black-owned company in 1946. By 1955 she, her husband, and her mother were all living in an apartment in a public housing project, and she was employed altering ready-to-wear clothes at the city's principal department store, the Montgomery Fair.[66]

In the meantime, Mrs. Parks developed an increasing hostility toward the racial barriers which were in part to blame for her plight. In 1934 her husband had joined the Montgomery branch of the NAACP, and in 1943 she joined him as a member. There her secretarial skills were much needed and appreciated. She was elected the branch secretary in the same year, and in 1947 she was put in charge of the NAACP's newly opened office on Monroe Street. These duties she carried on in her spare time; they paid nothing. But through them she became acquainted with Edgar Nixon, and at once she enthusiastically embraced his militant crusade for equal rights. She attended an NAACP leadership training conference in Jacksonville, Florida, in the spring of 1946, at which she met, among others, director of branches Ella J. Baker and assistant special counsel Robert L. Carter; as a result of this conference she professed herself "very much inspired." In October 1947 she served on the three-person nominating committee at the Alabama NAACP convention that arranged to have Nixon replace Emory Jackson of Birmingham as state president. She was a delegate to the state NAACP convention in Mobile in 1948, where she "denounced the stand of some [blacks] for feeling proud of their home or the South when Negroes every day are being molested and maltreated. No one should feel proud of a place as long as Negroes are intimidated," she stated. The convention thereupon elected her as secretary of the statewide conference, in addition to her duties with the Montgomery branch. In May 1949 she was forced by her health and by family responsibilities to resign the two offices, to the distress both of Nixon and of the national NAACP headquarters in New York. But by 1952 she had resumed the position of secretary of the Montgomery branch, and shortly took on as well the responsibility of serving as adult adviser to the branch's youth council, which had been formed in 1953. As adviser, she arranged in the spring of 1955 to have Claudette Colvin describe to the council members the circumstances of her arrest for violation of the bus segregation ordinance. In 1954 she was elected Second Congressional District corresponding secretary of the NAACP's Alabama Coordinating Committee for Registration and Voting; her friend Edgar Nixon was chosen the district chairman. Through Nixon, she became acquainted about 1953 with the white progressive leaders Clifford and Virginia Durr. The Durrs thereafter regularly employed her to do alterations on their daughters' dresses, and in the summer of 1955 Mrs. Durr arranged to have Mrs. Parks invited to attend a two-week-long interracial conference on integration of the public schools held at the Highlander Folk School, a militantly liberal Tennessee institution specializing in the training of union and community organizers. Forty-eight people, including some of the South's most active racial reformers, participated in the gathering. During the early 1950s, too, Mrs. Parks's NAACP position allowed her to be fully informed about the years of quiet negotiations between blacks and city officials regarding the seating regulations on Montgomery buses; indeed, she had herself served, she later stated, on a number of the delegations that met with white authorities to discuss this matter. Thus, the woman who took her seat on the Cleveland Avenue bus that December evening was more actively involved in the struggle against racial discrimination, and more knowledgeable about efforts being made to eliminate it, than all but a tiny handful of the city's forty-five thousand black citizens.[67]

Bus driver Fred Blake was as typical of east Montgomery's blue-collar whites as Mrs. Parks was atypical of west Montgomery's blacks. He was a native of Seman, a rural Elmore County community, located a few miles south of Equality. Born in April 1912, he was some ten months older than Mrs. Parks. He left school after the ninth grade. In 1940 he and his wife, Edna, moved to Montgomery. After living for a brief time in Oak Park, they settled in the Capitol Heights area. Blake worked initially for the Pepsi-Cola Bottling Company, but in 1942 he got a job as a Montgomery City Lines bus driver. Just before Christmas in 1943 he was inducted into the army, and the following July he was sent to Europe, where he saw active duty as a jeep driver in Italy, southern France, and the Rhineland. Blake returned to Montgomery, and to his job as a bus driver, in November 1945. He drove for the bus company until it ended its Montgomery operations in 1972. Thereafter he worked as a deliveryman for an auto parts store until his retirement in 1976.

Mrs. Parks reports that she had had a difficulty with Blake in the winter of 1943, when he had forced her off the bus he was driving for having failed to exit from the front door after paying her fare and reboard at the rear; she says that the rear door was blocked by standing passengers at the time. Mrs. Parks attributed Blake's aggressively rude conduct on that occasion to racial prejudice, and she still remembered and deeply resented it when they had their second fateful encounter twelve years later. But since in December of 1943 Blake would have been preparing to leave his wife and two children within weeks, very probably to enter armed combat, it seems quite likely that his hostility and short temper may actually have proceeded, at least in part, from personal fears of which Mrs. Parks could not have been aware.[68]

When Mrs. Parks refused Fred Blake's order to vacate her seat on December 1, 1955, Blake left the bus and telephoned police. Officers Fletcher B. Day and Dempsey W. Mixon arrived shortly, and when Mrs. Parks again refused to move they placed her under arrest. From the jail, Mrs. Parks telephoned her mother, who contacted Edgar Nixon. Nixon called Clifford Durr, and he and the Durrs drove to the jail, where they arranged for Mrs. Parks's release on bond. They drove Mrs. Parks home, and there they obtained her agreement to allow her case to be used as a test of the constitutionality of municipal bus segregation. Nixon then returned to his own house and began calling the city's black leaders to tell them of Mrs. Parks's arrest and to suggest a meeting to discuss the possibility of a one-day black boycott of the buses on December 5, the day of Mrs. Parks's trial, to emphasize black unhappiness with the bus company's seating policy. Those leaders whom Nixon called, themselves called others, and one of these calls—from attorney Fred Gray to Jo Ann Robinson—essentially took matters out of Nixon's hands. If Mrs. Parks had not been so close a friend of Nixon's and so prominent a figure in black Montgomery, Nixon might well not have made such a bold proposal, and the people whom he contacted might not have responded so readily. Mrs. Robinson, too, was moved by similar considerations. She and her associates in the Women's Political Council saw Rosa Parks as one of their own, a woman of comparable social status and community standing. The council did not await the outcome of Nixon's consultations; it acted. Early the next morning, December 2, Mrs. Robinson mimeographed at her office at Alabama State College a leaflet asking for a bus boycott: "Another Negro woman has been arrested and thrown into jail because she refused to get up out of her seat on the bus and give it to a white person. It is the second time since the Claudette Colbert [sic] case that a Negro has been arrested for the same thing. This must be stopped. . . . Until we do something to stop these arrests, they will continue. The next time it may be you or you or you." Council members busied themselves throughout the afternoon and evening of December 2 distributing these handbills in the black sections of the city.[69]

Meanwhile, Nixon's calls to black civic leaders during the night of December 1 and the morning of December 2 had produced sufficient support for a boycott to warrant summoning a meeting for the night of December 2 at the Dexter Avenue Baptist Church. By the time the seventy-five or so leaders convened, they found themselves faced with a fait accompli; the boycott had already been called by Mrs. Robinson's leaflets. Nevertheless, the meeting was a stormy one because the man who presided, the Reverend L. Roy Bennett, the president of the black Interdenominational Ministerial Alliance, refused to allow any discussion of the question. Bennett's conduct had reduced attendance to about forty people by the time a vote was taken. Eventually, however, after much ill feeling, those remaining accepted the idea of a boycott and appointed committees to attend to various organizational details. They also scheduled a mass meeting for the night of December 5 to consider future action in the light of how successful the boycott that day might prove.[70]

When sixteen black leaders met at Roy Bennett's church, Mount Zion A.M.E.Z., on the afternoon of December 5 to plan the evening's mass meeting, they had two new pieces of information to consider. The boycott had been brilliantly successful, far more so than the leaders had permitted themselves to hope. And Rosa Parks had been convicted and fined ten dollars and costs.

At the trial, City Prosecutor D. Eugene Loe had faced the problem of the city code's prohibition of unseating a passenger unless another seat was available, and he had met it, as had Solicitor Thetford in the Colvin case, by moving to amend the complaint so as to allege a violation of the state statute rather than of the city ordinance. Mrs. Parks's attorney, Fred Gray, had again contended that the state law did not apply to municipal bus lines, but his argument had been overruled by Recorder's Court Judge John B. Scott. Judge Scott, a nephew and appointee of the late Mayor Gunter, had thereupon convicted Mrs. Parks under the terms of the state statute, and Gray had given notice of appeal to the Montgomery circuit court.[71]

The enormous black enthusiasm for the bus protest, which had been demonstrated by the protest's great success on its first day, and the conviction of Mrs. Parks made it clear that the boycott would continue, at least until blacks received conciliatory overtures from the city. The sixteen persons present at the afternoon meeting therefore quickly decided to create a formal organization to run the boycott.[72] At the suggestion of Ralph D. Abernathy, the twenty-nine-year-old pastor of the First Baptist Church (black), they adopted the name Montgomery Improvement Association (MIA). They then constituted themselves the association's executive board and proceeded to choose its officers. Presiding at this meeting, as at the one on December 2, was Bennett, whose high-handed wielding of the gavel had provoked such resentment. When Bennett opened the floor for nominations for president of the new organization, Rufus Lewis of the Citizens' Coordinating Committee saw an opportunity both to depose

Bennett gracefully and, by seizing the initiative, to ensure that his rival Edgar Nixon was not nominated for the office. He suggested the pastor of his church, twenty-six-year-old Martin Luther King, Jr. Lewis, as a member of King's congregation, had some knowledge of King's talents. King had recently submitted a dissertation to Boston University for the Ph.D. degree in systematic theology, which marked him as considerably better educated than most of Montgomery's black clergy. And, though as pastor of the Dexter Avenue Church King was clearly associated with Lewis's constituency in the city rather than with Nixon's, his brief residence in Montgomery meant that he had not yet made the number of enemies that the older leaders had. The selection of King did not proceed, however, from any real recognition of his potential for leadership, but rather from the general hostility to Bennett and from Lewis's own hostility to Nixon. Lewis actually chose King in particular simply because King was Lewis's pastor.

Lewis's nomination was the only one offered. King was quickly and unanimously elected, and Bennett was then unanimously chosen vice-president. King's election determined the element within the MIA that would become dominant in shaping its policy. Bennett was an older man and a Methodist. King's advisers were almost uniformly Baptists and were usually young, often not out of their twenties. It is also worthy of note that, in February, Bennett would become the sole member of the black leadership to urge publicly the acceptance of the business community's proffered compromise.[73]

The executive board next named a committee, headed by Ralph Abernathy, to draft resolutions for the consideration of the mass meeting that evening. The resolutions, adopted at the meeting by acclamation, explicitly attributed the boycott to the events of the preceding March. As the preamble of the resolutions reported:

> Whereas the drivers of [Montgomery City Lines'] busses have never requested a white passenger riding on any of its busses to relinquish his seat and stand so that a Negro may take his seat; however, said drivers have on many occasions, too numerous to mention, requested Negro passengers on said busses to relinquish their seats and stand so that white passengers may take their seats; and . . . Whereas, in March of 1955, a committee of citizens did have a conference with one of the officials of said bus line, at which time said official arranged a meeting between attorneys representing the Negro citizens of this city and attorneys representing the Montgomery City Lines, Incorporated, and the city of Montgomery, and Whereas the official of the bus line promised that as a result of the meeting between said attorneys, he would issue a statement of policy clarifying the law with reference to the seating of Negro passengers on the bus,

and Whereas said attorneys did have a meeting and did discuss the matter of clarifying the law, however the official of said bus lines did not make [a] public statement as to its policy with reference to the seating of passengers on its busses, and Whereas, since that time at least two ladies have been arrested for an alleged violation of the city segregation law with reference to bus travel . . .

As a result, the resolutions called on "every citizen in Montgomery, regardless of race, color or creed, to refrain from riding busses owned and operated" by Montgomery City Lines. They also offered to send a delegation to discuss blacks' grievances with the bus company, and specifically abjured the use of "any unlawful means or any intimidation to persuade persons not to ride" the buses.[74]

On the invitation of these resolutions, the Montgomery chapter of the Alabama Council on Human Relations (ACHR), which was the Alabama branch of the Southern Regional Council, arranged a meeting with the MIA, the city commission, and the bus company on December 8. This success was due primarily to the ironic circumstance that the ACHR's most prominent white member in the city, the Reverend Thomas Thrasher, was the rector of Mayor Gayle's own church. But the task before the meeting was a large one. Both the bus company's manager, James Bagley, and its attorney, Jack Crenshaw, had emphasized in their public statements their belief that the company could not legally alter bus seating arrangements. Crenshaw had maintained that blacks "have no quarrel with our company. If they don't like the law we have to operate under, then they should try to get the law changed, not engage in an attack on our company." To this position King had replied, "We are not asking an end to segregation. That's a matter for the Legislature and the courts. We feel that we have a plan within the law." Thus a principal question before the December 8 meeting, as before all the earlier ones, was whether the law allowed its enforcers any discretion.[75]

The meeting began with King's reading a list of three demands, satisfaction of which was, he said, a prerequisite to the end of the boycott: more courtesy from bus drivers; the hiring of black drivers on the four of the company's fourteen routes that were predominantly black; and the seating of passengers in accordance with the Mobile plan of segregation, blacks seating from the back toward the front and whites from the front toward the back, without any insistence that a section always be kept clear for each race. The demands had been formulated by Edgar Nixon, Ralph Abernathy, and Edgar N. French, the director of the pensions office of the A.M.E. Zion churches, which was located in Montgomery. The three had met at Mrs. Parks's trial on the morning of December 5, and after it concluded they had gone to French's office to discuss the situation. The demands clearly reflect Nixon's thinking; the seating proposal was lifted from the questionnaire of the Ben Moore Hotel meeting, and the request for black drivers was consistent with his long-standing commitment as a labor leader to opening additional occupations to blacks. That afternoon French had read the three demands to the meeting of leaders at the Mount Zion A.M.E.Z. church that formed the MIA, and this group had adopted the proposals as the goals of the newly extended boycott.[76]

Crenshaw replied to the demands by denying that drivers were discourteous, except in the rarest instances; by flatly rejecting the idea of hiring black drivers, at least for the coming decade; and by declaring the seating proposal illegal. On this last point he joined battle with Gray. Gray offered a full-scale legal brief demonstrating that the 1945 and 1947 state statutes did not apply to Montgomery City Lines, and he urged the city commission to seek a formal opinion from the state attorney general on the question. In any case, he noted, both city code and state statute simply required separate but equal accommodations; they made no attempt to specify the precise arrangements by which this goal was to be accomplished. As King put it in a statement issued two days later, based upon a legal memorandum provided him by Clifford Durr, "The Legislature, it seems clear, wisely left it up to the transportation companies to work out the seating problem in a reasonable and practical way. . . . We feel that there is no issue between the Negro citizens and the Montgomery City Lines that cannot be solved by negotiations between people of good will. And we submit that there is no legal barrier to such negotiations." At the meeting, King emphasized that the suggested seating plan was in use in Mobile and other southern cities. Crenshaw did offer to have every other bus on the heavily black Washington Park route designated exclusively for blacks, but beyond this concession he simply reiterated that the company could not "change the law."

After some hours of these exchanges, Mayor Gayle suggested that it might be useful if a smaller group conferred in private. He then withdrew, taking the press, television cameramen, spectators, and peripheral participants with him. King, Gray, and perhaps other blacks remained to talk with Bagley and Crenshaw and the two new commissioners, Sellers and Parks. According to King's account of this session, as soon as the reporters had gone, Parks—who, of course, had defeated Cleere with black votes— ventured, "I don't see why we can't arrange to accept this seating proposal. We can work it within our segregation laws." At once Crenshaw replied, "But Frank, I don't see how we can do it within the law. If it were legal I would be the first to go along with it, but it just isn't legal. The only way that it can be done is to change your segregation laws." Then he added, "If we granted the Negroes these demands, they would go about boasting of a victory that they had won over the white people, and this we will not stand for." Facing this determined opposition from Crenshaw and knowing that Sellers could not be brought to compromise, Parks crumbled. The next day he resignedly informed the press that he regretted that the conference had produced no settlement but that "We cannot break the law."[77]

This sequence of events had been most peculiar. Although all the blacks were integrationists, the thrust of their efforts was to reform the actual practice of segregation so as to make it acceptable and thus to remove the impetus for its elimination. On the other hand, Crenshaw, a firm segregationist, was by implication urging the blacks to seek the complete abolition of segregation in the courts.

Since March the blacks had repeatedly pointed out that their plan for bus seating was in effect in many southern cities, including Mobile. King had reiterated this point at the meeting on December 8. Yet, Bagley subsequently testified that he had been unaware of this fact on December 8 and found it out only later. When the *Advertiser* printed on December 31 an article confirming the accuracy of the blacks' statements, the article was thought worthy of prominent treatment and seems to have caused surprise among whites. Nevertheless, the illogic of maintaining that the state law permitted in Mobile what it forbade in Montgomery escaped the white citizenry; when Bagley was asked about the inconsistency, he replied merely, "I cannot testify what they would do in Mobile, or what they can do, but I know what we can do in Montgomery." It is true, of course, that the Mobile City Code specifically required the seating plan in use in that city, but it is also true that the Montgomery City Code prescribed no specific seating plan.[78]

Similarly, Gray had argued at length at both the Colvin and the Parks hearings that the state statute did not apply to municipal bus lines, and he had submitted a brief to the commission and the bus company expounding this position. No one in authority, except possibly Parks, appears to have paid any attention. Gray had suggested that the commission seek a ruling from the attorney general; the commission toyed with the idea of doing so but in the end took no action. The following spring, however, when Gray joined the Alabama Public Service Commission as a defendant in his federal court suit seeking to invalidate bus segregation, in order to have the state law as well as the city ordinance declared unconstitutional, the state suddenly took up Gray's earlier argument in its entirety. At the trial the president of the public service commission, C. C. "Jack" Owen, flatly denied that his agency had any jurisdiction over municipal bus systems. The court read the state statute of 1945 to Owen and asked him if his construction of the act was that it "does not include common carriers such as busses in the City of Montgomery." Owen, evidently nonplussed by the question, stammered in reply, "I had never thought of it in that particular line of thinking. This is the first time that point has ever been brought up. It seems to me like that means segregation as far as segregation is concerned."[79]

Whites simply did not reflect carefully on the legal points the blacks raised. Indeed, Owen—a Montgomerian whose position ought to have made him more than ordinarily concerned with this aspect of the controversy—did not even know that the question of the applicability of the 1945 and 1947 acts had been at issue throughout the preceding year. These attitudes appear particularly puzzling because what Gray and his associates were actually trying to do was to rationalize the segregation system. Why did segregationists find it so difficult to accept the modest reforms the blacks suggested—reforms whose acceptance would clearly have strengthened segregation itself, by diminishing opposition to it? Consideration of the three efforts to reach a compromise during the boycott's first three months will help provide an answer to this question.

IV. The Failure of Compromise

Mayor Gayle's copy of the resolutions adopted by the black mass meeting on December 5, which King and Abernathy had mailed to the mayor on December 6, was offered in evidence at King's trial for violation of the Anti-Boycott Act. On its back, someone, presumably the mayor, had jotted in pencil, "How about *again* appointing [a] com[mittee of] Retailer[s] *etc.* to meet with [Kenneth E.] Totten [vice-president of National City Lines of Chicago] to bring some recommendations to [the] City Com[mission]?" The reference was to the course which the commissioners had successfully followed in the bus drivers' strike of December 1953. At that time the commission had named a committee of six—the presidents of the chamber of commerce, the Retail Merchants Association, the white Montgomery Ministerial Association, and the PTA; an attorney; and a prominent black businessman, P. McPherson Blair—to mediate the conflict. When the December 8 meeting produced no settlement, the commission evidently decided to make use of this precedent.

Totten returned to Montgomery on December 15 to continue negotiations for the renewal of the company's expiring franchise. After conferring with him, the commission called a meeting of all parties to the controversy on the morning of December 17, and there the mayor suggested the appointment of a ten-member committee—eight whites and two blacks—to act as mediators between the MIA and the bus company. Jo Ann Robinson at once insisted that the number of whites and blacks on the committee be equal. Apparently, the commissioners conceived of the dispute as being between the bus company and the MIA, and of the committee as a neutral mediator, while the MIA thought of the dispute as being between Montgomery's whites and blacks, and of the committee as a sort of collective bargaining arrangement. After some discussion the mayor agreed to add six MIA members to his original ten. These sixteen people met on the afternoon of December 17 and again on December 19, but no agreement was reached.

The blacks included King, Abernathy, and Robinson; attorneys Fred Gray and Charles D. Langford; the Reverend Hillman H. Hubbard, pastor of one of the city's largest black congregations and one of the few older black preachers prominent in the MIA's leadership; and the two well-to-do black businessmen who were Gayle's choices: P. McPherson Blair, who owned a dry cleaners and had served on the mediating committee of 1953, and Dungee "Dee" Caffey, a realtor with diverse interests. The white delegation, balancing the black one, included also three ministers: Dr. Henry Allen Parker of the First Baptist Church (white); the Reverend G. Stanley Frazer of St. James Methodist Church, a strong segregationist; and the Reverend Henry Edward "Jeb" Russell of Trinity Presbyterian Church, a brother of U.S. senator Richard Russell of Georgia. There were two businessmen: James J. Bailey, the manager of a furniture store and president of the Furniture Dealers Association, and William H. Fields, the manager of a local J.C. Penney store and president of the Retail Merchants Association. Mrs. Ernest R. Moore was the wife of a dental technician and the president of the city-county PTA. Mrs. Logan A. Hipp, Jr., the wife of an insurance adjuster, worked as a secretary in the office of the city chamber of commerce. The final white member of the initial delegation was William G. Welch, a bus driver for the Montgomery City Lines and president of the bus drivers' local union. At the committee's second meeting, Luther Ingalls, an attorney who had been principally responsible for the creation of the Montgomery chapter of the White Citizens' Council two months earlier, was added to the white delegation, and Mrs. Hipp became the committee's nonvoting secretary. This alteration in the membership, which was made without any consultation with the blacks, provoked an outraged protest from King.[80]

King charged that the mayor had "not appointed a representative committee of whites." At first glance the allegation would appear unfounded, but an investigation of the committee's deliberations casts the notion into a different light. The blacks advanced their seating proposal, and Gray argued that it could be effected within existing law. At the first session, the white delegation, unlike the black, contained no lawyers. The whites relied for legal advice upon City Attorney Walter Knabe, who attended the meetings. Knabe had been involved in the negotiations stretching back to the preceding spring and was committed to the position that the seating proposal was illegal. He informed the whites that Gray was simply wrong, and the whites adopted this position in their final report, issued on January 18.

King states that Kenneth Totten acknowledged to him privately that the black proposal was used by National City Lines' Mobile affiliate; Totten, King reports, said that he could not see why what worked in Mobile could not work in Montgomery. If Totten made this admission privately, however, he refused to do so publicly. Instead, he declined to become involved in the local negotiations, saying only that National City Lines would abide by any arrangement accepted by Montgomerians. Understandably, a national firm that dealt with cities across the country would wish to avoid becoming entangled in heated municipal controversies. This motive must have been particularly strong in the Montgomery situation because Totten was at this very time attempting to secure a new franchise from the city government. An additional element at work within the company may well have been the fact that Totten's immediate superior, executive vice-president Bernard W. Franklin, came from the South. A native of Anderson, South Carolina, Franklin had received a law degree from the University of Georgia in 1934 and had joined National City Lines in 1938. The company's president, E. Roy Fitzgerald, was a self-made man; a Minnesotan, he had never graduated from college, and had built his bus empire through his own efforts, beginning with one small line in 1920. It would seem likely that Fitzgerald, though confident of his entrepreneurial skills, would have deferred to Franklin in the management of disputes, such as the one in Montgomery, that had complicated legal aspects. In addition, in 1947 the federal government had prosecuted National City Lines, together with General Motors, for criminal conspiracy in connection with the destruction of the trolley system in Los Angeles, California, and the company had been fined five thousand dollars. This experience may well have provided an additional reason for Fitzgerald to defer to Franklin's legal expertise in situations that could result in court actions. And Franklin's southern background and Georgia legal training very possibly made him at least somewhat sympathetic to the segregationists' view of the boycott. Whatever may be the validity of this speculation, it is clear that Totten's refusal to intervene, coupled with the whites' reliance upon Knabe's advice, left the committee captured within the limits of the controversy that had previously been defined, unable to approach the problem from a new perspective.[81]

Of course, the whites on the committee were in general segregationists; had they not been, they would not have reflected accurately the sentiment of the community they represented. However, segregationist attitudes in themselves were no real barrier to a settlement, because the black delegation emphasized that it had no desire to disestablish segregation. Ill will between the two sides on the committee was exacerbated by the inability of Frazer and Russell to resist the urge to lecture the blacks on the morality of segregation and the immorality of ministerial involvement in politics. The black clergymen responded with lectures of their own. Still, the white committee members were not opposed to compromise. Frazer presented what he took to be a compromise: that fixed lines of racial division be marked on every bus, determined by the proportion of the races on each route, but that riders be permitted to sit forward or back of the line until the seats were needed by the other race. The proposal, as Charles Langford noted, ignored the principal black complaint, the unseating of passengers already seated. But at least Frazer's proposal demonstrated a willingness to try to find a solution. Bailey even stated to the committee, "I came here prepared to vote for liberalization of interpretation of the city's laws with certain conditions."[82]

The failure of the committee to recommend an acceptable compromise was not entirely attributable to the racial attitudes of the committee members, though such attitudes doubtless contributed to the impasse. None of the whites on the committee was a member of Montgomery's upper class; Bailey, the member of the white delegation who seems to have been most favorable to compromise, was the only member who was at all prominent in the city's business community. This fact is significant. When King called the whites unrepresentative, what he evidently meant was that they were all too representative. The situation demanded men and women who were sufficiently confident of their social position to allow them to be original in their approach to the problem. The committee contained no such members, and it is primarily for that reason that its deliberations proved sterile.

The mayor, because of his weak political position, had not appointed any of the city's social and economic leaders to the committee. The March elections had emphasized that Gayle could no longer allow himself to appear to be a front man for Montgomery's elite. Rather, he needed to seek the support of other social elements among the whites. He certainly could not permit himself the luxury of an action that flew in the face of white community sentiment. A compromise suggested by the committee that he did appoint would give some promise of generating community consensus. Precisely because the committee was representative, however, its deliberations were doomed without the intervention of some outside figure like Totten. Gayle evidently initially hoped that Totten would help; the pencil notation on the back of the mayor's copy of the MIA's resolutions, as we have seen, had specified that the committee was to meet with Totten and develop recommendations in consultation with him. But when Totten refused to become involved, the committee became an exercise in futility.

The encounter between the city and its black citizens entered a new stage in late January, when attitudes in both camps had hardened considerably. After the December 19 meeting, the biracial committee held no further sessions. On January 18, its white members issued a final report publicly acknowledging the failure of their efforts and urging all parties to accept Stanley Frazer's compromise proposal. On January 6, Clyde Sellers appeared at a meeting of the White Citizens' Council and dramatically announced that he was joining the organization. After this development, the MIA again sought to open negotiations. On January 9, at King's request, the city commission met with a black delegation for two hours. The MIA offered to modify the Mobile seating plan to specify that, as seats became available further to the rear or further to the front, blacks and whites seated nearer the middle of the bus would voluntarily move to the vacant seats. But the commissioners were not satisfied with this concession, and the meeting adjourned in frustration. When the MIA's executive board gathered on January 12, the members gloomily concluded, "It seems that it is now a test as to which side can hold out the longer time, or wear the other down." The point was also made that, unless the MIA abandoned its seating proposal and turned to an attack on segregation, the national NAACP would not lend the boycott its support. Apparently as a result of this meeting, the MIA's leadership began seriously discussing the possibility of filing a federal court suit to seek the integration of the buses.

Initially, the MIA had relied on the criminal proceedings against Rosa Parks to provide a legal test of bus segregation. In addition, its strategists were aware that the *Flemming* suit from Columbia, South Carolina, posing this same question, was then pending before the U.S. Supreme Court. On December 10, Fred Gray had written to Robert L. Carter of the NAACP's legal staff, who was handling the *Flemming* suit, to request Carter's advice on the conduct of the Parks case; Gray feared—and with good reason, as events would prove—that the state courts would attempt to avoid the constitutional issue, and he asked if there were not some way to get the matter into federal court. Carter replied on December 28, suggesting that, in addition to prosecuting Mrs. Parks's state court appeals, Gray consider filing a federal court suit in Mrs. Parks's name asking for a declaratory judgment that bus segregation violated the Fourteenth Amendment. Gray and Clifford Durr began work at once on such a suit, and by mid-January they had drafted the documents necessary for filing it.[83]

In the meantime, city officials had apparently been discussing further among themselves the compromise proposal that the MIA had advanced on January 9, and they seem to have decided to see if a counteroffer might be acceptable. Presumably with his employers' approval, J. Michael Nicrosi, the supervisor of the city's tax assessments office, approached a prominent black acquaintance, merchant and insurance executive Ralph B. Binion, and asked him to propose to the MIA's executive board as a basis for settlement that the number of bus seats reserved for whites be reduced from ten to only two on the three most heavily black routes, and to six (the two front bench seats) on the other routes. Binion did convey this proposal to the executive board, but he was not entirely clear himself on the exact terms of it, and evidently for that reason, no response from the MIA was immediately forthcoming.

While this initiative was still pending, the city commissioners were led into an action that would make continued negotiations vastly more difficult. Throughout the preceding six weeks, discontent had been growing among those black ministers who were not a part of the MIA's directorate. The boycott had so captured the imagination and the loyalties of the city's blacks that the failure of a black minister to be included occasionally as a speaker at the frequent mass meetings that were the movement's backbone demeaned him in the eyes of his congregation. Very probably it was jealousies thus generated that lay behind the decision of three black ministers either to contact white officials with the offer to negotiate a settlement or to reply positively to feelers from officials to them. The Reverend Benjamin F. Mosely, pastor of the First Presbyterian Church (black), Bishop Doc C. Rice, pastor of the Oak Street Holiness Church, and the Reverend William K. Kind, pastor of the Jackson Street Baptist Church, one of the few prominent black preachers in the city who had not been chosen a member of the MIA's executive board, perhaps expected that, if they were able to engineer the creation of a compromise acceptable to the black community, they might gain for themselves a portion of the public attention being focused upon King, Abernathy, Gray, and their associates. The commissioners, who throughout the preceding weeks had repeatedly stressed their conviction that the mass of blacks had merely been frightened or duped into accepting the MIA's control, clearly felt that they had now at last succeeded in tapping into the black community's authentic, temperate leadership. They responded eagerly.

On January 21 the commissioners met with the three ministers, together with Paul B. Fuller, the executive secretary of the chamber of commerce, and the Reverend Thomas Thrasher of the Alabama Council on Human Relations. The meeting produced a compromise under which ten seats in the front would always be reserved for whites, ten seats in the rear would always be reserved for blacks, and the remaining sixteen seats would be filled as the MIA proposed, with blacks seating from the rear and whites from the front; in addition, all-black buses would be provided during rush hours on three predominantly black routes. The proposal did not distinctly specify whether passengers seated in the middle sixteen seats could be unseated, but because the seating in them was to be in accordance with the Mobile seating plan, presumably they could not be. It stated that the city commission had no authority to alter the bus company's hiring policies; the company had repeatedly refused to hire blacks, so this statement implied the rejection of the request for black drivers. This compromise was actually rather less forthcoming than the proposal that Nicrosi had made to Binion earlier.

The MIA promptly denounced the agreement and stated that the three ministers did not speak for the city's blacks. It soon became apparent, moreover, that virtually the entire black community supported the MIA's position in this regard. The three ministers thereupon repudiated the compromise; they told King that they had not understood the proposal and had attended the meeting under the impression that it was to discuss the city's insurance. The commissioners were livid at this turn of events. Mayor Gayle subsequently swore that both Fuller and Thrasher had read the agreement carefully to the ministers, who had fully understood and approved of it. On this basis the commissioners had publicly committed themselves to the compromise. All three commissioners were increasingly in awe of Montgomery's rapidly growing White Citizens' Council, whose membership—which had been 300 when it had been founded in October—was reported by local newspapers to be 6,000 at the beginning of February and 12,000 by the end of that month. By that time it had become the single largest white organization in Montgomery County. Sellers, in a speech to the council on January 6, had pledged to continue fighting the blacks' demands, and he had repeated the promise in even stronger terms on January 17. Gayle and Parks had been somewhat less vocal, but naturally they wished to avoid offending council members unnecessarily. Now all three commissioners found themselves revealed to the voters as willing to compromise but deprived at the same time of any compromise to show for their pains. They felt betrayed.[84]

On January 23 Mayor Gayle announced, "The Negro leaders have proved they will say one thing to a white man and another thing to a Negro." He said, "The City Commission has attempted with sincerity and honesty to end the bus boycott in a businesslike fashion. We have held meetings with the Negroes at which proposals were made that would have been accepted by any fair-minded group of people. But there seems to be a belief on the part of the Negroes that they have the white people hemmed up in a corner and they are not going to give an inch until they can force the white people of our community to submit to their demands—in fact, swallow all of them. . . . We attempted to resolve their reasonable complaints but they proved by their refusal to resolve the reasonable ones that they were not interested in whether the bus service was good or not. What they are after is the destruction of our social fabric." He called the black leadership "a group of Negro radicals" whose only real goal was to "stir up racial strife." He stated, "The white people are firm in their convictions that they do not care whether the Negroes ever ride a city bus again." He concluded, "When and if the Negro people desire to end the boycott, my door is open to them. But until they are ready to end it, there will be no more discussions."

This statement appears to have been the product of a moment of anger, but the astonishing approbation with which whites greeted it transformed it into fixed policy. Appreciative calls swamped the city hall switchboard; hundreds of congratulatory telegrams flooded in, and voters eager for the opportunity to shake Gayle's hand crowded the mayor's office. Commissioner Parks reported himself "amazed with the avalanche" of approval. He concluded with ingenuous relief, "There is no need for us to straddle the fence any longer. I am taking a stand and so are the other commissioners." Both Gayle and Sellers moved at once to identify themselves even more firmly with the "get tough" stand. Gayle called for whites to refuse to drive their domestics to and from work or to pay their taxi fare; "the Negroes are laughing at white people behind their backs" because of the whites' willingness to do so, he warned. Sellers instructed the police to arrest blacks waiting to be picked up by the boycott's car-pool operation and to charge them with loitering. "A person has a perfect right to wait for a ride," he noted, "but the practice of six or eight Negroes huddling together for an hour or more, trampling lawns and making loud noises in white residential districts must cease." On January 24, Gayle and Parks announced that they, too, had joined the White Citizens' Council. Within weeks all members of the county board of revenue also had joined. The Citizens' Council's attorney and leader, Luther Ingalls, proclaimed that the group was now so large that blacks would never again be able to influence candidates for local office by "dangling their bloc votes" before aspirants.[85]

In the face both of this rapidly escalating official intransigence and of the pressure from Fred Gray and the MIA's other legal advisers to file a suit directly attacking segregation, the majority of the MIA's leadership struggled to retain the organization's initial accommodating posture. The MIA's strategy committee met on January 21—at the very time that, unbeknownst to its members, the city commissioners were meeting with the three non-MIA ministers some blocks away—to try to agree on some new approach to the municipal authorities. Attorney Charles Langford urged a court suit seeking an injunction to compel the city to furnish public transportation to nonriders of the buses, but the other members of the committee remained devoted to reaching a negotiated settlement, and once again they declined to recommend legal action. The Reverend William J. Powell of Old Ship A.M.E. Zion Church, representing the other end of the committee's spectrum, suggested that the MIA abandon its efforts to obtain official cooperation and focus its attention simply on improving the efficiency and reliability of its car-pool operation. But the committee was unwilling to give up its hope that the city might be convinced to come to an understanding. Both Langford's desire to rely upon the judiciary and Powell's belief in unaided black self-reliance implied a recognition that further negotiations with the city were futile, and the majority of the committee was at this time only very reluctantly moving toward that conclusion. Jo Ann Robinson finally proposed a way out of the committee's dilemma.

At the beginning of January the MIA's executive board had asked Gray and Langford to prepare an application to the city commission to grant its car-pool operation a franchise as a jitney service. The car-pool operation had rapidly become the boycott's indispensable foundation, moving thousands of black workers between their jobs and homes each day, and often even more conveniently than the bus system had been able to do. The MIA therefore had become fearful that, unless it could gain legal authority to administer the car pool, the city might attack the operation in court and thereby succeed in breaking the boycott itself. The imminent expiration of National City Lines' exclusive Montgomery franchise, however, had offered the MIA an opportunity to avert this threat. But now Mrs. Robinson used the pending submission of the franchise application as a way to draw together advocates of continued attempts to negotiate with the city, advocates of court action, and advocates of black self-reliance. She suggested, and the strategy committee accepted, that the MIA link the franchise application and the suit attacking the constitutionality of bus segregation that Gray and Clifford Durr had prepared, but give priority to the franchise application. If the commissioners would grant the franchise, then in effect Montgomery would acquire an all-black bus line operated by the black citizenry itself, in which the humiliation of white supremacy would cease to be an issue. Only if the application were rejected, and National City Lines' exclusive franchise were renewed, would the MIA then proceed with the federal court challenge to the segregation laws. The MIA's executive board convened on the morning of January 23, at the same time Mayor Gayle was delivering his irate "get tough" statement to the press, and voted to approve the strategy committee's recommendation.

This decision by the executive board was sufficient to satisfy Fred Gray. He was so certain that the commissioners would never grant a franchise to the MIA that he at once left for New York City to confer with the NAACP's Thurgood Marshall and Robert L. Carter to make final preparations for the filing of the federal suit. And King and the MIA's other principal officers evidently shared Gray's enthusiasm for legal action, as is indicated by the fact that, when the franchise application came up for hearing before the commission on January 26, none of them was present to urge its approval. But other executive board members clearly continued to believe that city officials could be brought to see, with the proposal for an all-black jitney service—as they had been unable to see with the proposal for the adoption of the Mobile bus seating plan—the strategic advantage, for the maintenance of segregation, of the elimination from its administration of the constant daily sources of black resentment toward it. That this faith was ill placed was promptly demonstrated. When the MIA submitted the franchise application on January 26, the commissioners united immediately in announcing their intention to reject it; they did so formally at their meeting of January 31. In the meantime, on January 24 the commissioners had voted to extend National City Lines' franchise for an additional ten years.

Given the executive board's resolution of January 23, the city commission's renewal of National City Lines' franchise and its announcement of its intended rejection of the MIA franchise application ought to have meant immediate authorization of the filing of the federal court suit. But when the executive board met on the morning of January 30, the members most opposed to the suit were prepared for a final effort to forestall it. The Reverend William F. Alford, pastor of the Beulah Baptist Church, immediately raised the Nicrosi proposal made earlier to Binion, and urged its acceptance. Binion reiterated its terms, but under questioning from Edgar Nixon he revealed again that he was unclear on its precise provisions. King at this point took firm charge of the discussions and sought to guide them toward the acceptance of the suit. He reminded members that the board had already voted to sue if its franchise application were refused. Gray had now finished preparing the suit, King reported, and was in the process of rounding up plaintiffs; on the advice of Marshall and Carter, he had deleted Mrs. Parks as a plaintiff, for fear that the fact that her appeal was pending in the state courts would introduce unnecessary legal complications, but the two young women who had been arrested earlier in 1955, Claudette Colvin and Mary Louise Smith, had both agreed to serve, and Gray was seeking others. King asserted confidently that the black masses were prepared for further sacrifice and would tolerate nothing less than a genuine victory; he pressed the board to go ahead with the suit. Nevertheless, many board members remained unenthusiastic. When King and Gray asked if one of the twenty-five people present would agree to be listed as an additional plaintiff, ten minutes of pleas from both men failed to elicit a single volunteer. However, the information that the city would have twenty days to respond to the suit once it was filed finally served as the foundation for a compromise. Solomon Seay suggested that, when the suit was filed, the MIA should concurrently give city officials an ultimatum to accept the Mobile plan of seating segregation by the end of the twenty-day period or else face the possibility that the federal court might order complete integration. During the twenty days, Seay proposed, the MIA should begin training black bus riders in how to behave if, as he perhaps expected, the city should comply with the ultimatum. And meanwhile, the boycott should continue. On this basis, Gray was at last authorized to proceed with filing the suit. It seems clear, however, that the decision to do so did not represent, at least for many of the board members, an actual acceptance of the goal of integration, but merely a tactic to put further pressure on the city to agree to modify the practice of segregation.

During the same time, the city commissioners' new "get tough" policy had been having an effect among a segment of the population with which the commissioners were just as unfamiliar as they were with most of Montgomery's black citizenry, the extremist thugs of its racist underworld. Stronger and stronger public statements had followed Mayor Gayle's initial outburst of January 23 as politicians rushed to associate themselves with the commissioners' obviously popular stand. And on January 30, the same day the MIA's executive board approved the filing of the integration suit, these pronouncements bore terrible fruit. That evening a stick of dynamite was thrown onto the porch of Martin Luther King's home; his wife and baby and a visitor, Mrs. Roscoe Williams, narrowly escaped injury. King, who was attending one of the boycott's weekly mass meetings at the time, rushed home and managed to calm a large and very angry crowd that had gathered in the street; only his intervention, all observers agreed, forestalled a riot.

The bombing, it appears, finally united all of the MIA's leadership behind the federal court suit. It had become plain to all of them that merely to continue putting pressure on city officials to accept a negotiated settlement was a strategy now fraught with excessive risk. The suit, on the other hand, held out the prospect of bringing the controversy to a definite conclusion, enforced by judicial authority. Another bomb, thrown at the home of Edgar Nixon early on the morning of February 1, though it did minimal damage, reinforced this realization. Fred Gray filed the suit later that same day, and the MIA's executive board thereafter gave it their full support. The ultimatum that had been an essential part of Seay's compromise resolution of January 30 was never issued. The Reverend William Alford would resign from the board some weeks later, with the failure of the Men of Montgomery's mediation, because of what he felt was the board's growing unwillingness to accept a compromise.[86]

Mayor Gayle denounced the federal court suit as "proof beyond any doubt that Negroes never wanted better bus service as they were claiming, but complete integration." The blacks, he said, stood convicted of double-dealing.[87] In a sense it is true, of course, as the mayor charged, that the MIA's leaders—indeed, that virtually every black person in the United States—actually wanted the abolition of segregation. When the NAACP's Alabama field secretary, W. C. Patton, met with King and Gray at the beginning of the boycott, each emphasized this fact. "Rev. King assured me that the [MIA's] ultimate goals are the same as those of the NAACP," and that it sought the adoption of the Mobile seating plan only "until the present law is changed"; "Attorney Gray made it clear that this [seating proposal] is only a tentative arrangement to meet the immediate crises."[88] But too strong an emphasis upon the general desire among blacks to establish integration would seriously distort the attitudes of most of Montgomery's black leaders during the boycott's first two months. For the majority of them, after a lifetime spent in patient efforts to secure modest improvements in the status of their race within the framework of segregation, the prospect of actually obtaining integration seemed no more than "pie in the sky"; they placed no real confidence in it. Instead, they looked to the boycott as a tool to compel white authorities to engage in serious negotiations about their proposals for reform. In a public statement it arranged to have printed in the local press on January 27, in response to Mayor Gayle's "get tough" remarks of January 23, the MIA characterized the boycott as "a non-violent method of bargaining." Even at this late date, it still asserted, "Negroes want the entire citizenry of Montgomery to know that at no time have we raised the race issue in this movement, nor have we directed our aim at the segregation laws." In reality, the conclusion that Mayor Gayle drew from the filing of the federal integration suit was essentially the exact opposite of the truth. The intransigence of the city commission, along with the rage of the white extremists that it unleashed, virtually drove the city's black leadership, and with considerable reluctance, to recognize the necessity of the suit. Indeed, had it not been for the bombing of King's home, it does not seem at all impossible that the commencement of the Men of Montgomery's mediation effort, to which we shall shortly turn, might well have led the MIA's executive board to vote to withdraw the suit it had just filed if an acceptable compromise could be reached.

A corollary to these observations is that integration itself was never really the central issue in the boycott; the actual question was white supremacy. Black Montgomerians sought not the right to sit with whites, but rather the right not to be unseated in favor of whites, as well as at least a degree of protection from public humiliation at the hands of white bus drivers. These goals could have been achieved just as effectively by the creation of an all-black jitney service, and almost as effectively by the adoption of the Mobile pattern of bus segregation. The MIA turned to an attack on the segregation laws only when it became apparent that white authorities would not accept more modest means to accomplish these objectives. Similarly, though white officials repeatedly asserted that their overriding intention was to preserve segregation, their refusal to consider the chartering of an all-black jitney service belies this claim. Segregation on the initiative of blacks and under black control was unacceptable because authorities' genuine motive, whether consciously or unconsciously, was not the separation of the races but the subordination of blacks to whites. In this connection, it is instructive to observe that, once the integration of the buses had been ordered in December 1956, the same commissioners who had dismissed the MIA's proposal for an all-black jitney service, and who would eventually seek to enjoin the car-pool operation altogether as an infringement on the bus company's franchise, would respond cordially to an application to charter an all-white jitney service and would petition the federal court to allow them to approve it. The tendency of most accounts to depict the boycott as a struggle between segregation and integration, though made virtually inevitable by the filing of the federal court challenge to the constitutionality of the bus segregation statutes, is in fact a conception of it that obscures many of the most fundamental assumptions of Montgomerians of both races.[89]

The events surrounding the false settlement of the boycott and the "get tough" policy that followed it also strikingly illuminate the commission's ignorance of sentiment among both blacks and extremist whites. First, the events emphasize how tenaciously the commissioners and their advisers held the belief that the MIA did not actually speak for the city's blacks. The commissioners had repeatedly urged the masses of blacks, as we have noted, to repudiate King and other spurious leaders who owed their apparent positions as spokesmen for the black community only to the apathy of many blacks and to the intimidation of the remainder by MIA goon squads. Commissioner Sellers estimated that 85 to 90 percent of the city's blacks would immediately resume riding the buses if there were no danger of physical reprisal. "The innocent Negroes should wake up," Commissioner Parks warned. "They don't know what they are doing, but I'm afraid they're going to find out. The white people have been their friends, and still want to be, but we can't sit here and watch them destroy our transportation system." Mayor Gayle accepted both Parks's emphasis on ignorance and Sellers's emphasis on fear, although there is relatively little evidence of intimidation, and none at all linking the intimidation to the MIA. Unfortunately, one of the few instances in which intimidation was indeed alleged involved Mayor Gayle's father-in-law's cook, Beatrice Jackson. The mayor's closeness to this particular incident perhaps increased his sense of the violence surrounding the boycott. Whether because of Sellers's dark, conspiratorial explanation or because of Parks's more benign one, the city's political leaders were convinced that the MIA's claims to represent Montgomery's blacks were false.

This attitude accounts for the commissioners' otherwise inexplicable notion that the three non-MIA black ministers constituted, as the statement of January 21 claimed, a "group representing the Negroes of Montgomery." At the time of the appointment of the biracial committee on December 17, Gayle had insisted on appointing two prominent blacks, Blair and Caffey, who had not been nominated by the MIA, perhaps partly in the hope that he would tap the reservoir of anti-MIA feeling which he thought to exist. This expectation failed; Blair and Caffey proved to be completely committed to the MIA's demands. When the three ministers approached white leaders in late January, the commissioners evidently felt, as we have seen, that they had at last forced from hiding a leadership alternative to King's. Of course, the commissioners knew that no organized group had appointed the three ministers. On the other hand, they regarded the views of the three ministers as more fully consonant with those of the black masses. If the commissioners had been correct in their analysis, it would have been reasonable to suppose that the conclusion of a settlement with the ministers would have given most blacks sufficient encouragement to return to the buses. The compromise produced no such result simply because the commission was wrong; Montgomery's blacks were dedicated to the achievement of the MIA's program. Unfortunately, the repudiation of the settlement by the three ministers obscured this fact for city political leaders.[90]

The commission betrayed similar ignorance in failing to gauge the effect upon the city's racist extremists of the intemperate statements issued in late January. The extremist element evidently took the "get tough" policy and the resulting public ovation as a license for violence. In later months, nevertheless, the belief became general in Citizens' Council circles that blacks themselves had staged the resultant two bombings to gain sympathy and contributions from northerners.[91] The absence of any sense on the part of the city's leaders of the state of sentiment among blacks and among white racial extremists is a complementary phenomenon with a single culprit: these segments of the population were essentially excluded from political life, and the commission had such limited contact with them that it lacked any mechanism for understanding their motives and assumptions. Nothing could be more revealing of the effects of black disfranchisement upon the state's political culture than the fact that in the experience of white municipal leaders, the entire black citizenry was relegated to a position of obscurity comparable to that necessarily occupied by hoodlums.

Contemporary with the events of January, the third and last effort to formulate a compromise acceptable to the MIA emerged from the business community. The Men of Montgomery, already dubious of Montgomery's politicians, were by January persuaded that the commission's mismanagement of the crisis had prevented a settlement and that businessmen might well succeed where politicians had failed. Moreover, the organization had three good reasons to try: the boycott had intensified racial hatred in the city, damaged trade, and directed such unfavorable publicity to the city as to complicate any effort to attract industry to the area. Mayor Gayle's announcement on January 23 that the commission would not negotiate further made the politicians' inability to secure an agreement explicit. The bombing of Dr. King's home clearly announced that the entire affair had gotten out of hand and that unless a compromise could be found quickly, seriously unfavorable reports in the national press would be inevitable.[92] These two events moved the Men of Montgomery to intervene in the boycott. Thus, rather ironically, precisely the same set of circumstances that convinced the black leadership to turn from negotiation to legal action finally moved the city's economic powers to undertake the mediation of the controversy.

During the first three weeks of February a committee of the Men of Montgomery held two full-scale negotiating sessions with MIA leaders and at least one with the city commission. It was also in almost constant informal contact with the two groups in an effort to locate tenable middle ground. The Men of Montgomery members advanced no proposals of their own; they apparently saw themselves as brokers rather than as parties to the conflict. King later wrote of them that they had proved themselves "open-minded enough to listen to another point of view and discuss the problem of race intelligently," and in reference to their arbitration he concluded, "I have no doubt that we would have come to a solution had it not been for the recalcitrance of the city commission." However, the obstacles to any such successful outcome appear to have been genuinely insuperable. The commissioners' statements during the last week of January had made it virtually impossible for them to agree to any substantial concessions, and their receptiveness to compromise was not increased by the fact that on February 10, at a White Citizens' Council rally that filled the state coliseum, a crowd of some twelve thousand gave both Mayor Gayle and Commissioner Sellers sustained, emotional standing ovations.[93]

For its part, the MIA was no longer really in a position to negotiate. At no time would it have been easy for the MIA to have made concessions; as King had noted in mid-January, "We began with a compromise when we didn't ask for complete integration. Now we're asked to compromise on the compromise." The filing of the federal court suit on February 1, however, had eliminated even the small basis for an accord that had been present. The MIA's initial requests had sought only a reform of specific practice within the general framework of segregation; the MIA had repeatedly and strenuously affirmed its view that its proposals were in keeping with city and state law. But the suit sought the elimination of segregation. It so changed the MIA's position that King had evidently given serious consideration to recommending that the boycott be called off. The boycott had been intended to move the city commission and the bus company to action. If the MIA were going to rely on a court order to produce the action, there was no longer any reason for a boycott. Indeed, the only difficulty with this logic was that the MIA could not be certain that the federal courts would declare bus segregation unconstitutional. Despite the MIA's decision to continue with the boycott, the organization could hardly be expected to agree to a compromise perpetuating segregation while it was at the same time asking the courts to compel full integration. The Men of Montgomery's efforts would appear therefore to have been doomed from the outset. Their fatal flaw was their timing.[94] Nevertheless, the businessmen pressed mediation because the city's good reputation could be restored only if Montgomerians solved the boycott themselves. Their task was made especially urgent when some prominent Montgomery lawyers began to advocate a course that would almost certainly destroy whatever respect for the city remained among national opinion leaders: the mass indictment of virtually all the city's most prominent blacks for violation of the Alabama Anti-Boycott Act.

The Anti-Boycott Act had been passed in 1921 as a part of a series of statutes provoked by a bloody strike of Birmingham coal miners in that year. From the beginning of the bus boycott the applicability of this act to the situation had been discussed, but the question was not taken very seriously because, as the *Advertiser* noted editorially on December 8, "As a practical matter, we doubt that either the bus company or the solicitor will attempt to jail 5,000 Negroes." As the hatreds generated by the dispute deepened, however, some Montgomerians came to consider prosecution a realistic weapon. On January 9, Fred S. Ball, an important figure in both legal and social circles in the city, dispatched a letter to the *Advertiser* demanding the boycotters' indictment.

> An individual has the right to ride a bus or not as he or she sees fit and that right should not be interfered with and should be protected by the police, but when certain so-called leaders call a group together and organize a boycott, they are taking the law into their own hands and should be prosecuted. Whether the bus company or its drivers have or have not always themselves obeyed the law and given colored passengers their rights is not the question at all, because two wrongs do not make a right and there is always legal redress against the bus company for anything it does wrong. The question is whether the officials whose duty it is to enforce the law are going to sit idly by and permit the illegal destruction of a transportation system which is most certainly needed by both races.

He added pointedly, "A copy of this letter goes to the county solicitor with the suggestion that he give consideration to presenting this matter to the grand jury."

Grover C. Hall, Jr., the *Advertiser*'s editor, clearly shared the business leaders' view that this course would be sheer folly. Hall attempted to dispose of Ball's argument with gentle ridicule.

> Atty. Ball . . . is against lawlessness. So he has asked Solicitor Thetford to prosecute. What leaves us confused is the question whether Atty. Ball is also opposed to the lawlessness of defying the U.S. Supreme Court, the supreme law. . . . We ask then, is Atty. Ball for law-abiding at the local level and lawlessness at the Supreme Court level? And, as we asked Dec. 8, what if Atty. Ball got some bus boycotters convicted in a Montgomery court? Would not the Supreme Court automatically reverse the convictions? Another perplexity left by Atty. Ball's brief letter is whether he is against all persons who have entered an 'arrangement' to boycott? For example, Police Commissioner Clyde Sellers is a card-carrying member of the White Citizens' Council, an organization dedicated to boycott and economic sanctions against Negroes. Does Atty. Ball want White Councilman Sellers indicted also?

But Ball was not so easily dissuaded. On January 12 he replied:

The question is not, as put in your [editorial], how far to 'cast the net' of law enforcement, or whether we should abide by our own state laws or the most recent ruling of the federal Supreme Court on segregation in public schools. The question is not what the White Citizens' Council stands for. . . . The law against boycotting is not a segregation law. It applies to all instances where people organize to prevent the operation of a lawful business. The single question here is whether certain religious and other misguided leaders who are openly and publicly violating the law against boycotting should be permitted to do so at the expense of the risk of our city losing a much-needed bus system, or whether the law against boycotting should be enforced. I think it should be enforced, and soon, before it is too late.

Hall continued to believe that sensible officials would not pursue Ball's suggestion. On January 15 he referred to "the contradictions and impracticality of Lawyer Ball's vexed demand that the solicitor jug the bus boycott leaders for violation of the anti-boycott law," and noted, "The polite silence of the solicitor substantiates our reservations about the Ball formula." On January 17 an *Advertiser* reader, George C. Poulos, wrote to the paper, "If an organized boycott is against the law, as Mr. Fred Ball states, . . . then why should anyone have to present his letter to the Circuit Solicitor? Doesn't the Solicitor know his job? Why does he have to be reminded of his duty? Maybe he is worried about the Negro vote. He had better start worrying about the white vote."[95] Hall's confidence and Poulos's fear were both misplaced. On January 10, the day after Ball's initial letter appeared, Circuit Solicitor Thetford contacted Commissioner Sellers and asked that two detectives be assigned to the solicitor's office to investigate the boycott. Sellers agreed at once, and the investigation was launched on January 11. That it was being conducted did not become public knowledge during January, but by February 13 it had become clear that officials had determined to seek indictments; on that day Circuit Judge Eugene W. Carter charged the new county grand jury to determine whether the bus boycott violated the Anti-Boycott Act.[96]

The negotiating efforts of the Men of Montgomery now became a race against time to find a settlement before the forces seeking prosecution could obtain the adoption of their strategy. On February 8 the Men of Montgomery published in the newspapers the name and telephone number of their executive secretary, William R. Lynn, and urged anyone having a suggestion for a compromise formula to contact him. In the end the city commission was not in a position politically to offer much more than it had previously conceded to the three non-MIA black ministers: the reservation of ten seats at front and rear, with blacks seating from the rear and whites from the front in an unreserved middle section of sixteen seats from which the drivers could not unseat them. The Men of Montgomery managed to extract from the commissioners, in addition, their agreement that drivers could allow blacks to sit in the reserved white section when there was no probability of additional white passengers' boarding, and also an agreement to abolish the practice of forcing blacks to pay at the front and then exit and reboard at the back. The organization's suggestions sought to make this seating proposal more palatable to blacks by adding other reforms, such as mechanisms for more effectively institutionalizing the right of blacks to enter complaints against drivers; and the proposals included a public promise from the commissioners "that there will be no retaliation whatsoever resulting from the bus boycott"—almost certainly a reference to the grand jury investigation then under way. But the concessions, which might well have satisfied the black leadership a year earlier, came far too late. At an MIA mass meeting on the evening of February 20, the audience shouted the proposals down; only the Reverend L. Roy Bennett, whom King had replaced at the head of the boycott on the protest's first day, and another clerical colleague, presumably the Reverend William F. Alford, who resigned from the MIA's executive board because of the rejection of this compromise, openly supported the proposals. On February 21 the grand jury returned indictments of eighty-nine blacks, twenty-four of whom were ministers, for the misdemeanor of conspiring to boycott.[97]

Thus, by the end of February 1956 both black and white leaders had abandoned the search for compromise, and with it the political process, and had determined to trust their respective causes to the absolute and unconditional judgments of the courts—the blacks depending upon the federal suit to integrate the buses which they had filed at the beginning of the month, and the whites intending to prosecute and punish the boycott's organizers in the state courts. We may pause to reflect upon the dynamic at work in the negotiations during this period. Logic would seem to indicate that whites who desired to forestall integration would have acceded quickly to the blacks' modest demands, whose effect would certainly have been to have strengthened the system of bus segregation itself, by removing the most frequent source of black dissatisfaction with it. The narrative to this point has, I trust, already made clear the complex of political and social forces that worked to prevent white leaders from accepting—indeed, in many cases, even from understanding—this logic. But the other half of the equation deserves further discussion.

As logic would seem to suggest that the whites should have been willing to compromise in order to preserve segregation—if, as I have said, it had really been segregation, and not white supremacy, that they were seeking to protect—so logic would appear to dictate that the blacks should have turned to the federal courts at once to attack the system that they universally despised. Indeed, as the *Montgomery Advertiser* noted editorially at the conclusion of the boycott, "The victory that has been achieved by the colored community is a U.S. Supreme Court decision that bus segregation is illegal. And that decision was achieved in absolute independence of the boycott. Moreover, the court's decision could have been obtained without a single colored citizen walking a single block in boycott."[98]

This riddle is solved in part by the observation that Montgomery's blacks had not yet developed the faith in the federal courts which future years would generate. The city's federal district judge, Frank M. Johnson, Jr., was still an unknown quantity, newly arrived from the northern portion of the state, not the legend that he would become. He had held his position for just three months and had received Senate confirmation only the day before Fred Gray filed the suit seeking to enjoin bus segregation. Montgomery's representative on the Fifth Circuit Court of Appeals, Richard T. Rives, had been allied with the comparatively liberal Hill faction in local politics and had led the unsuccessful effort to defeat the disfranchising Boswell Amendment in 1946. But he had also orchestrated the effort to suppress Arthur Madison's campaign to register black voters in the city in 1943–44 and had represented the Macon County Board of Registrars against the first attempts of Tuskegee's blacks to obtain federal court protection of their right to register in 1945–46. Southern federal judges had in general certainly not proven particular enemies of segregation in previous years. And in fact, in the Montgomery bus suit itself, the third of the federal judges who heard it, Seybourn H. Lynne of Birmingham, a segregationist, dissented strongly from his colleagues' holding that the school integration decision of 1954 was applicable to bus seating.[99]

Yet lack of faith in the federal courts is not the most important explanation for the initial willingness of the black leadership to settle for a compromise within the framework of segregation. The essential reason is that the bus boycott in its origins was much less a social than a political movement. In the years after World War II, and particularly during the year and a half that Dave Birmingham served on the city commission, black leaders developed an increasing sense of the tractability of the system. The size of the black vote continued to grow, and the city government paid new attention to black complaints. The decision to hold a public session to interview the candidates for commissioner in 1955 and to release a list of endorsements reflected this growing confidence that politics could be made to subserve the needs of black citizens. However, the outcome of the election dealt a considerable blow to this optimism. Black leaders had been permitted a brief experience of a happier relationship with their rulers, only to have it snatched away.

Bus seating had been one of the areas in which blacks had genuinely expected that they would be able to make progress. In the conferences that had followed the arrest of Claudette Colvin, they had been promised public clarifications of the seating policy that would have represented a clear acknowledgment of their ability to compel the city to respond to their concerns. But as the months passed, no clarifications were forthcoming; the commission formally rejected Birmingham's motion to add black members to the parks and recreation board; the segregationist Clyde Sellers was inaugurated; and Mrs. Parks was arrested under exactly the same circumstances as Miss Colvin had been. The resolutions adopted by the mass meeting at the Holt Street Baptist Church at the beginning of the boycott emphasize unmistakably the connection between the decision to boycott and the failure of the city and the bus company to define the precise requirements of the segregation ordinance following the Colvin incident. The city elections, which had seemed in the spring so likely to produce an amelioration of black citizens' lot, had produced instead a situation that, if anything, was the worse for having earlier seemed so hopeful.

If government were ever really to benefit blacks, it now seemed, black leaders would have to discover some mechanism other than the electoral process by which to influence politicians. The boycott was intended to be such a mechanism. In the minds of its organizers, at least, it appears to have been analogous to a strike—a way for persons individually weak to bring collective pressure to bear upon the powerful, once negotiating sessions have failed. The boycott was not a revolution; it was merely an extension of the negotiations. Thus the black Birmingham editor Emory Jackson referred to the boycott, shortly after it had begun, as a "riders' strike," and the MIA characterized it as "a non-violent method of bargaining."[100] The black leaders persisted in offering in December and January the seating proposal that they had advanced at the Ben Moore Hotel meeting the preceding February precisely because they initially conceived their movement not so much as a direct action against bus segregation itself as rather a search for a means to manipulate the political process. They genuinely believed that, faced with this proof of how seriously blacks took the seating grievance, the city commission would be compelled to seek a remedy. But for this device to work successfully, the blacks could of course only ask for something that the commissioners might regard themselves as politically and legally able to grant: an amelioration of segregation.[101]

With the benefit of hindsight, one could easily regard both the Ben Moore Hotel meeting and the boycott itself as politically naive. If black leaders had been able to anticipate the extent to which these events would exacerbate racial animosities in the city, they would surely have known that the public endorsement of a candidate by blacks was likely to prove counterproductive. And they would similarly have known that for the commissioners to respond to pressure applied openly through a boycott—

to knuckle under to blackmail, as the segregationists would have seen it—would have infuriated a large part of the electorate. The fact that the black leadership did not understand these things, however, is merely an index to the sense of rapid progress in race relations that was abroad in the community in the decade after World War II. The utter racial polarization in Montgomery in later years was a product of the boycott itself.

At the outset of the boycott, the *Montgomery Advertiser* had stated editorially, "The boycott makes an innocent sufferer of the bus company. Had the company defied city and state laws, its franchise would have been canceled. The quarrel of the Negroes is with the law. It is wrong to hold the company a hostage."[102] The blacks replied over and over again—though the whites never seemed to listen—that their quarrel was not at all with the law, that they had no intention of asking the company to abandon segregation, that they simply wished to have the company apply the law in Montgomery as it did in Mobile. In a peculiar sense, however, the *Advertiser* was right, and the blacks were wrong. As the boycott proceeded, it began to teach many of the city's black leaders that their quarrel actually was—and had to be—with the law. Compromise with segregation was impossible because segregation so forged and underlay social relationships that even the modest reform of its requirements sought by the MIA threatened—just as the white politicians claimed—the entire social fabric. In such a situation reform was impossible; only the fundamental transformation of race relations would do. The white response to the boycott revealed this truth forcefully to many blacks. That revelation was the boycott's supreme achievement, and it was something that no court suit could ever have accomplished.

One of the most interesting aspects of the boycott's early months, however, is that the inflexibility of segregation was something black leaders had to learn. It was so much an essential presumption of the civil rights movement in later years that we find it difficult to believe that there could have been a time when a black—indeed, when anyone—was unaware of this characteristic of the system. It is this difficulty, very probably, that makes the MIA's position in the initial weeks of the boycott seem so peculiar to observers today. But segregation revealed the true extent of its white supremacist intransigence only under the pressure of the civil rights movement itself. For those who had lived all their lives inside segregation, black and white, the pervasiveness of its impact was not always so readily apparent. It is true, of course, that blacks were fully aware of the constant humiliation that segregation entailed. Yet the enormous variety of interracial associations even under segregation made the institution seem less basic to the shaping of attitudes than in fact it was. Particularly in a city like Montgomery, in which the Gunter machine had defeated the Ku Klux Klan and ruled with relative benevolence, it was easy not to know how exceedingly far, into how many unrelated organs, the infection had spread. Black leaders had been too ready to believe that the welcome thaw which Dave Birmingham's tenure had represented for them marked the beginning of spring. They made this mistake, one suspects, because they, in common with most moderate and liberal white southerners, had conceived of their world, though suffused with segregation, as malleable. Segregation as it stood on the statute books appeared to be a set of specific legal provisions that were subject to amendment or reformulation. But the segregation that lived in the hearts of white supremacists was the symbolic representation of black subordination, and its alteration in response to black initiative was therefore at war for them with the very essence of its being. Only after segregation came under assault, and its supporters roused themselves to fight back, were blacks, and later whites, forced to recognize the omnipresence and the obduracy of the system that the embodiment of white supremacist passions in statutory form had inevitably created.

V. The End of the Boycott

Martin Luther King was the first of the indicted boycotters to be brought to trial. The proceedings began on March 20; at King's request, the testimony was heard by Judge Eugene Carter without a jury. On the first day Judge Carter denied a defense motion to dismiss the indictment on the ground that the statute was unconstitutional. Nevertheless, the prosecution was legally quite problematic.

The Alabama Anti-Boycott Act of 1921 had been, as we have said, an outgrowth of a bloody strike by Birmingham coal miners in that year. Governor Thomas E. Kilby had been forced to call out the state militia to restore order during the work stoppage. At its conclusion he had summoned the legislature into special session. In his message to the two houses, he had railed, "Such conditions as existed in the coal mining districts of this State, under the leadership of irresponsible foreign agitators, if not the result or product of socialism, certainly tend to encourage or promote socialism, which often results in anarchy. . . . A conspiracy to starve or freeze the public, or even an agreement to do acts the natural and probable result of which is to cause great suffering or inconvenience to the public, is little less than treason against the government, when the government is like ours—nothing but the public or the people." With this prompting, the legislators, over the determined opposition of pro-labor members, had enacted a law criminalizing many of the tactics employed by unions to bring economic pressure on management. "Two or more persons," read its first section, "who, without a just cause or legal excuse for so doing, enter into any combination, conspiracy, agreement, arrangement or understanding for the purpose of hindering, delaying or preventing any other persons, firm, corporation or association of persons from carrying on any lawful business shall be guilty of a misdemeanor."[103]

From the beginning the act had been a controversial one. In 1940 the U.S. Supreme Court had declared unconstitutional its second section, which forbade the picketing of another person's property for the purpose of hindering or interfering with his or her business. But in 1943 the Alabama Supreme Court had considered and specifically affirmed the constitutionality of the act's first section, under which the boycotters had been indicted. And the U.S. Supreme Court had declined to express any dissatisfaction with this holding by denying *certiorari* in the case. However, the state supreme court had saved the section only by interpreting it very strictly. In a unanimous opinion, Justice William H. Thomas had held that the phrase "without a just cause or legal excuse for so doing" had the effect of limiting the application of the law only to boycotts enforced by violence or other unlawful activities. If the statute were so construed as to permit the state to interfere with protest carried out by lawful means, Justice Thomas clearly implied, it would be unconstitutional. But when limited in its scope simply to conspiracies to hinder a lawful occupation by actions otherwise illegal, the statute was within the state's police power. Under the terms of this opinion, therefore, the prosecution in King's case bore the burden of proving that King had compelled Montgomery's black citizens to abide by the boycott through the use of violence or similar unlawful coercion, rather than the blacks' having done so voluntarily.[104]

Solicitor Thetford and Assistant Solicitors Maury Smith and Robert Stewart offered such evidence as they had to establish King's guilt under this standard. Several bus drivers testified that, during the early weeks of the boycott, shots had been fired at their buses. And two blacks testified that they had been assaulted, and a third that he had been threatened, for continuing to use public transportation. But the prosecutors were unable to produce any evidence whatsoever linking these actions to King or the MIA. The defense called witness after witness to describe unpleasant incidents and maltreatment on the buses, indicating that blacks might well have cooperated with the boycott of their own volition. And at the conclusion of the trial, Judge Carter, though finding King guilty, refused to sentence him to a jail term because, as Carter explicitly stated, King throughout the boycott had discouraged violence. There can simply be no question, therefore, that the state supreme court's 1943 interpretation of the anti-boycott statute entitled King to an acquittal. Judge Carter's decision in King's trial contrasts sharply with Judge Will O. Walton's ruling in a similar proceeding growing out of the Tuskegee boycott the following year. Attorney General John Patterson sought an injunction, predicated on the Anti-Boycott Act, to end a boycott against Tuskegee merchants that had been organized by the black Tuskegee Civic Association. But when Patterson was unable to connect the association to any of the coercive acts by which, as he alleged, the boycott had been maintained, Judge Walton refused to admit the evidence of the coercion and denied the injunction.[105]

After convicting King, Judge Carter fined him five hundred dollars. King's attorneys filed an appeal to the state court of appeals. The trials of the remaining eighty-eight defendants were therefore postponed to await the opinion of the appellate courts on the various constitutional and legal objections that the boycotters had raised to their prosecution. In the end, however, these questions were never answered. The preparation of the voluminous trial transcript in King's case—the longest in a criminal case in the history of Montgomery's circuit court to that time—was not completed until early August. King's lawyers, however, failed to file an application for an extension of time to submit the transcript to the appeals court, so in April 1957 the court dismissed the appeal as untimely, without ever considering its merits.[106]

In the meantime, the federal suit that Fred Gray had filed on February 1 was moving to trial. On the same day that the prosecution of King for violation of the Anti-Boycott Act got under way in state court, the presiding judge of the Fifth Circuit Court of Appeals, Joseph C. Hutcheson, appointed Appeals Court Judge Richard Rives and District Judges Frank Johnson and Seybourn Lynne to constitute the special three-judge court necessary under federal law to hear a constitutional challenge. The hearing was held in Montgomery on May 11. On June 5 the court issued its decision. Judge Lynne in his dissent noted quite correctly that Chief Justice Earl Warren, in *Brown* v. *Board of Education* in 1954, had said that the doctrine of "separate but equal" had no place in the field of public education. It might well be that the Supreme Court by these words intended to imply that the doctrine did have a place in other fields. At any rate, Judge Lynne contended, until the Court ruled otherwise, lower courts in transportation segregation cases were still bound by the "separate but equal" precedent. Writing for the majority, however, Judge Rives pointed to the fact that the Supreme Court had subsequently approved without comment lower court decisions prohibiting segregation in public parks and municipal golf courses. He concluded, as had the Fourth Circuit Court of Appeals in the *Flemming* decision a year earlier, that the *Brown* v. *Board* opinion had actually meant to eliminate legal segregation from every sphere of life. On June 19 the majority entered a permanent injunction forbidding the enforcement of bus seating segregation in Montgomery. But when the defendants gave notice that they intended to appeal this order to the U.S. Supreme Court, Judges Rives and Johnson agreed to suspend the effectiveness of the injunction until the appeal could be decided.[107]

The bus protest dragged on through the summer and fall, accompanied by steadily mounting racial hostility. At the beginning of June, Attorney General Patterson filed suit in Montgomery circuit court seeking an injunction to bar the NAACP from operating in Alabama. To prove that the NAACP posed a threat to the public welfare, Patterson, among other allegations, made the truly preposterous claim that the NAACP had been responsible for organizing and financing the boycott.[108] In August the home of the only white member of the MIA's executive board, the Reverend Robert Graetz, was bombed. Mayor Gayle said of the crime, "We are inclined to wonder if out-of-state contributions to the boycott have been dropping off. Perhaps this is just a publicity stunt to build up interest of the Negroes in their campaign."[109] Racial moderates, who at the beginning of the boycott had been able to voice their opinions freely, now fell victim to telephone harassment and intimidation for merely expressing their views in public. Even whites who provided transportation for their maids received threatening and profane calls.[110] In September, extremists organized a klavern of the Ku Klux Klan, the first in the city for nearly a quarter of a century.[111] As school reopened, Montgomery was engulfed in an acrimonious effort by segregationists to force local Parent-Teacher Associations to withdraw from the National Congress of Parents and Teachers because it had adopted a resolution urging PTAs to seek to facilitate school integration. At a succession of stormy meetings, PTAs in various white schools voted to sever all ties with the national organization.[112] The White Citizens' Council added more bitterness to this controversy when it demanded the dismissal of Montgomery's elderly and distinguished superintendent of education, Dr. Clarence Dannelly, on the ground that he had once served briefly on a Methodist Church commission of which the chairman had been a black. The principal figure in the Citizens' Council chapter, attorney Luther Ingalls, warned the membership of a surreptitious plot to have young children in the nurseries of the city's white churches play with both colored and white dolls so that they would gradually come to favor race mixing.[113]

In the meantime, in late May, after the arrest of two female students at the black Florida A. and M. College for violation of a bus segregation ordinance, a bus boycott had begun in Tallahassee under the leadership of a former Montgomery minister, the Reverend C. Kenzie Steele. Tallahassee's city administration had soon shown itself a great deal more resourceful in dealing with the black challenge than was Montgomery's. With the collapse of negotiations in early July, the city quickly targeted the blacks' car-pool operation; authorities recognized that, without the car pool as an alternative to the buses, black leaders would have great difficulty in persuading the mass of black bus riders to continue the protest. Obtaining opinions from the city attorney and the Florida attorney general that the car-pool operation was subject to the state law governing vehicles for hire, the city began insisting that the car pool's drivers have chauffeur's licenses and that its cars have for-hire license plates. In October, the city induced Municipal Judge John Rudd to levy an $11,000 fine against the blacks' Inter-Civic Council and its officers; Judge Rudd convicted them of operating the car pool in competition with taxicabs and the bus company without first obtaining a permit, and without posting bond, paying the license tax, and having their vehicles inspected. The defendants appealed the convictions and fine to circuit court, but their boycott was badly damaged by the prosecution. On October 22 the Inter-Civic Council was forced to abandon the car pool, though it urged black citizens to continue the protest nevertheless.[114]

These events were closely watched in Montgomery. A group of extreme segregationists headed by Jack D. Brock, the president of the Montgomery local of the printers' union and a former state president of the American Federation of Labor, had been attempting to organize a secession of white union members from the national AFL-CIO because of the sympathy of many national labor officials for the cause of civil rights for blacks.[115] When the Tallahassee authorities' legal tactic proved effective against the car-pool operation in that city, Brock and his associates became enthusiastic about adopting this strategy in Montgomery. They hired County Attorney John P. Kohn to explore the possibility of doing so. Kohn contacted Tallahassee's city solicitor, Edward J. Hill, for details of the Tallahassee offensive. Armed with Hill's response, Kohn and a delegation of labor leaders including Brock met with the city commissioners on October 26. Kohn pointed out that the MIA had twice—on January 26 and again on April 2—petitioned the commission for a franchise to operate a jitney service for blacks, and that the commission had denied each application. The car pool, he said, was accomplishing by subterfuge what the commission had refused the MIA permission to do legally. It was, moreover, supported in part "by people who hate the South and don't understand it," he claimed. He therefore urged the commission to take legal action to suppress the operation. After this meeting, the commissioners issued a statement announcing that the city would seek an injunction to halt the car pool. "We intend to maintain the way of life which has existed here in Montgomery since its origin, so far as we are legally able," the commissioners proclaimed—thereby revealing considerable ignorance of southern history.[116]

On November 1 the *Advertiser* printed an editorial pleading with the commissioners not to pursue this idea. The question of the constitutionality of bus segregation in the city was now before the U.S. Supreme Court, it noted, and a decision would shortly be forthcoming. To attack the car pool at this late date, the editorial concluded, would thus only lead to further negative publicity for the city, while accomplishing nothing practical. But the commissioners, far more interested in retaining the support of their constituents than in avoiding the condemnation of observers elsewhere, ignored the *Advertiser*'s advice on this occasion just as they had its opposition to the Anti-Boycott Act prosecution earlier. Late on the night of that same day, City Attorney Walter Knabe filed the city's petition for an injunction in state circuit court.[117]

The MIA had sought to outflank the city's effort by filing with U.S. District Judge Frank Johnson a request for an injunction to bar the city from interfering with the car pool. Knabe, caught by surprise, had then rushed to file the city's application with the state court's register in chancery that night, so that it would appear that the two petitions had been filed on the same day. Judge Johnson set a hearing on the MIA's petition for November 14. Judge Eugene Carter then quickly set the hearing on the city's petition for November 13, so that the state court proceeding could come first. At this hearing, the city argued that the car pool infringed on the bus company's exclusive franchise. Carter issued an injunction forbidding the car-pool operation as soon as the hearing concluded, and it went into effect at midnight that night. The next day, Judge Johnson refused to intervene, since the matter was now before the state courts. But in the meantime, the *Advertiser*'s prediction in its editorial of November 1 was dramatically fulfilled. While the hearing before Judge Carter was in progress, word arrived in the courtroom that, earlier that morning, the U.S. Supreme Court, in a one-sentence *per curiam* order, had affirmed the decision of Judges Rives and Johnson in the MIA's suit, *Browder* v. *Gayle,* that bus segregation was unconstitutional. The city petitioned the Supreme Court for a rehearing, thereby delaying the final decree in the case until December 20. But on December 21, bus segregation in the city came to an end. The actual effect of Judge Carter's injunction, therefore, was only to impose essentially vindictive discomfort on the boycotters in the boycott's final weeks; from November 14 to December 20, blacks were compelled to walk or to arrange other transportation for themselves.[118]

When bus integration finally came to Montgomery on December 21, 1956, therefore, it came to a city completely polarized. The Montgomery that emerged from the bus boycott at the end of 1956 was virtually unrecognizable as the city that had elected a liberal police commissioner in 1953 and had voluntarily desegregated its police force in 1954. And the sequel was all too predictable.

Violent opposition to the integration of the buses began almost at once. Indeed, in the weeks between the Supreme Court's decision and the actual integration, the first signs of what was to come had already manifested themselves. Some nineteen prominent blacks had acid splashed on their automobiles, damaging the cars' paint. Witnesses to at least two of these incidents swore that the acid had been thrown by uniformed police officers.[119] After the initial integration had occurred, white snipers soon took on the role that the black snipers had played a year earlier, firing at passing buses out of the darkness during the evening hours. These shootings culminated on December 28 with the wounding of a black passenger, Mrs. Rosa Jordan. A young laundry worker who was eight months pregnant, Mrs. Jordan had her left leg shattered by the blast. Doctors were afraid to operate on the leg because of her advanced pregnancy, and she was therefore hospitalized to await her delivery. The city commission ordered the suspension of night bus runs, but the snipers thereupon commenced daylight shootings. Commissioner Sellers stated his suspicion that blacks themselves were responsible for the attacks, presumably to gain sympathy for their cause.[120]

After a total of six sniping incidents and two other assaults, the opponents of integration escalated their campaign to a new level. Early on the morning of January 10, a series of six bombs exploded. Four black churches and the homes of Ralph Abernathy and Robert Graetz sustained substantial damage; for Graetz's home it was, as we have seen, the second such attack. A seventh bombing, of King's Dexter Avenue Baptist Church, was foiled by a night watchman in a neighboring building. The city commission ordered bus service in the city suspended altogether. Violence seemed to subside thereafter, however, and on January 16 the commission allowed daylight bus runs to resume. But the bombers were not through. In the early-morning hours of January 27, a bomb completely destroyed the home of a black hospital orderly, Allen Robertson, located a few hundred yards from Martin Luther King's parsonage. A powerful second bomb was found at the parsonage itself and was disarmed, though the fuse was still smoldering. On the night of January 23, meanwhile, the boycott claimed its first and only life. The same group of Klansmen who would be charged with the bombings received word that a black truck driver was dating a white woman. By mistake they waylaid a delivery truck driven by another black man, Willie Edwards, Jr., and despite his pleas of innocence, forced him to jump to his death from a bridge across the Alabama River just outside the city limits.[121]

As a result of the wave of violence that swept Montgomery during December 1956 and January 1957, racial moderates among the city's businessmen, who had been impelled into silence by the failure of the Men of Montgomery's mediation effort the preceding February, exerted themselves once more. "The responsible citizens of this community look to the officials who are charged with maintaining law and order, namely the Mayor and Commissioners, the Sheriff's office and the Judges of our courts, to see that the guilty are caught and prosecuted," the Men of Montgomery stated pointedly in a newspaper advertisement. "*The future of Montgomery is at stake!!*" And the *Advertiser* asked editorially, "Is the night air of this genteel old city, the capital of a state and once the capital of a nation, to reverberate with dynamite explosions? . . . Is Montgomery to be a city in which a handful of terrorists overawe the police power of city, county and state—squeezing a trigger and abolishing a bus fleet? Are the powers of government of the City of Montgomery to be surrendered to outlaws?" The editorial concluded, "The issue now has passed beyond segregation. The issue *is whether it is safe to live in Montgomery, Ala. . . .* We are already paying a grievous toll. The story of Thursday's dynamiting is already broadcast all over the world, blackening this city's name." Under heavy pressure from business leaders, police launched an intensive investigation. On January 30, they announced the breaking of the bombing cases and the arrest of the culprits.[122]

The violence, police stated, had been centered in the city's Ku Klux Klan klavern, a group the membership of which was closely associated with the segregationist element within the Montgomery Labor Council. A chief conspirator, it appears, was Eugene S. Hall, a printer for the *Alabama Journal,* a leader of the printers' union local, and a close friend of Jack Brock, the local's president and the editor of the *Alabama Labor News,* who had precipitated the legal effort to suppress the MIA's car pool. Until he had been dismissed the preceding November, Hall had been the editor of the White Citizens' Council's newspaper, the *States Rights Advocate;* thereafter he had begun a regularly scheduled series of segregationist talks over radio station WMGY. The other men charged were all laborers.[123]

The arrest of these men, however, was followed by a massive outpouring of white sympathy for them. Segregationists claimed that the prosecutions had been inspired by the NAACP and, incredibly, that they represented Commissioner Sellers's effort to gain the support of the black vote. Two rival campaigns to pay the legal expenses of those indicted were organized, one headed by members of the board of the Montgomery White Citizens' Council and the other headed by Jack Brock and relying for its solicitors upon Klansmen. Volunteers for each campaign went from door to door throughout the white community and set up collection buckets on downtown streets. The defendants retained as their attorney the city's most famous criminal lawyer, John Blue Hill, a first cousin of U.S. senator Lister Hill and a former law partner of U.S. Circuit Judge Richard Rives.[124]

At the trial in May of the first two of the accused bombers to be prosecuted, Raymond Britt and "Sonny" Kyle Livingston, Hill and his associates John Harris and Joseph Pilcher attempted to convince the jurors that the bombings had been the work of the MIA, which was seeking thereby to increase northern donations to its cause. They also implied, though contradictorily, that the bombings had been necessary to defend segregation. The state's evidence was overwhelming. Both defendants had signed detailed confessions, and each had led police to the hiding places of materials which only one of the bombers could have known, Livingston to an unused bomb held in reserve and Britt to the packing materials in which the bombs' components had come. Hill said that the confessions were the product of the "brainwashing tactics of the Communists." He put King and Gray on the stand in an effort to establish the MIA's financial motive for the crimes. In his summation, he attributed the bombings to "Negro goon squads" and warned the jury, "A guilty verdict will be a verdict for Martin Luther King and his imps who seek to destroy our Southern way of life." Hill's partner John Harris proclaimed that an acquittal would "go down in history as saying to the Negroes that you shall not pass," and he concluded, "The time has come in Montgomery for the men to be separated from the boys. Take your choice. I'm going with the men." Solicitor Thetford told the jurors, "If you turn these men loose under the evidence the state has presented, you say to the Ku Klux Klan, 'If you bomb a Negro church or home, it's all right.'" After deliberating for an hour and a half, the jurors returned an acquittal on all counts. As the verdict was read, it was "drowned out by Rebel yells and screams of approval. . . . [S]pectators almost to a person yelled, clapped, shouted and shook hands in agreement."[125]

In the face of this verdict, the state abandoned the attempt to prosecute the other bombing indictments. In April, as we have seen, the state court of appeals had dismissed on technical grounds Martin Luther King's appeal of his conviction under the Anti-Boycott Act. In November, Solicitor Thetford reached an agreement with King's attorneys. King agreed not to press his appeal of the appellate court's ruling to the state supreme court, and on November 26 he paid his fine. In return Thetford dropped the Anti-Boycott Act indictments against all of the remaining eighty-eight defendants. At the same time, Thetford also dropped the remaining bombing cases. "In view of the sentiment of the people of this community," the solicitor said in a public statement, "I see absolutely no possibility of securing a conviction" of the accused Klansmen. In a statement issued in response to this one, Montgomery's two circuit judges, Walter Jones and Eugene Carter, noted that in acquitting the defendants, the jury in the trial of Britt and Livingston had rendered "a verdict which the court would itself have given." And they concluded by expressing the hope that "outside rabble-rousers will not again be brought into the county to denounce our white citizenship, to inflame the feelings of a kindly people and to stir up the just resentment of the white race."[126]

VI. The City in the Wake of the Boycott

The events surrounding the bombings and the trial and acquittal of the first two of the men indicted for them had the effect of completely silencing moderate white opinion in Montgomery. It was not to be heard again for four years. During the years from 1957 to 1961, the city slipped into a surreal dimension in which only extremist views were publicly voiced among whites, and any hint of deviation from white supremacist orthodoxy would incur both active harassment and social ostracism. As the open expression of moderate white opinion disappeared, the apparent uniformity of segregationist convictions encouraged the peculiar notion among segregationist true believers that they were winning—and winning precisely because they were succeeding in preventing any cracks from forming in the solid white phalanx. Citizens' Council doctrine held, as we shall learn in greater detail when we turn our attention to Selma, that without treacherous white assistance, blacks were powerless by themselves to achieve their integrationist goals. The council therefore increasingly focused its efforts in this period on suppressing white, rather than black, opposition. In a resolution adopted by its state leadership, meeting in Montgomery in January 1959, the council proclaimed, "We believe that any person who speaks, writes, or in any way advocates or works for anything short of total and complete segregation will be ostracized, and will earn and will receive the condemnation of the public. . . . We feel sure that an aroused and informed public will make it unprofitable and uncomfortable for any person to remain in our community if he is not willing to support the will of the community in this matter." And the council's success in enforcing this mandate became for its adherents virtually a self-fulfilling prophecy: white dissent had been silenced, and therefore, so they thought, the progress of the black campaign for desegregation had been halted. In the same January 1959 statement, the council asserted its confidence that "When the history of the second reconstruction is written," Montgomery would be recorded as the place where the tide was turned and "integration efforts were stopped cold."[127]

The reign of terror to which white moderates and liberals were subjected was, therefore, very real. In November 1958, for instance, segregationists launched a campaign of public humiliation and private persecution against a group of white women who had attended an interracial prayer group, the Fellowship of the Concerned, at the black Roman Catholic hospital. The prayer group had been formed in the summer of 1955 and had met throughout the boycott without incident. But now extreme white supremacists had gained their own newspaper, the weekly *Montgomery Home News*, established in June 1957 under the strident editorship of apparent Klansman William E. "Senator" Cleghorn. Becoming aware of the fellowship, Cleghorn seems to have employed associates in law enforcement to obtain the names of the persons who owned the cars parked at one of its meetings and then published a list of them on his front page. The resultant abuse and the damage to their husbands' businesses and careers compelled a number of the white women into public recantations and apologies and forced the permanent dissolution of the prayer group itself. One woman earlier associated with the fellowship, librarian Juliette Morgan, who had drawn attention to herself with several powerful letters to the editor of the *Montgomery Advertiser* espousing racially liberal views, was driven to suicide in July 1957, evidently in reaction to constant segregationist torment.

The Episcopal Church of the Ascension, whose rector, Thomas R. Thrasher, was a leading figure in the interracial Alabama Council on Human Relations but whose congregation contained such prominent segregationists as Mayor Gayle and *Alabama Journal* editor Cassius M. Stanley, soon found itself virtually divided into warring camps. After years of resisting segregationist efforts to drive him from his pulpit, Thrasher was eventually compelled to capitulate and leave the city in 1960. The ACHR itself was forced to move its state headquarters from Montgomery to Birmingham when its Montgomery landlord, Jerome Moore, came under segregationist pressure not to renew the lease on its offices in the fall of 1956. Montgomery's small Unitarian congregation, which did not have a church building of its own, was driven from meeting place to meeting place during 1956 and 1957 because of segregationist hostility, based largely upon the visit to the city during the boycott of a racially liberal Unitarian minister from Illinois, Homer A. Jack. Eventually, in 1962, the president of the congregation, Kilby Prison warden Martin J. Wiman, was dismissed from his job by the state board of corrections, in large part because of his religious affiliation.

In two separate incidents in April 1960, when neighbors saw black air force personnel go into the homes of white colleagues, and later observed them inside engaged in casual conversation, police were summoned and the homes' occupants were all arrested for disorderly conduct. In December of the same year, five students from Huntingdon College, the white Methodist liberal arts college in the city, were publicly disciplined for attending a lecture sponsored by the MIA at a black church to commemorate the anniversary of the beginning of the bus boycott. Though the college's dean of students, Charles C. Turner, Jr., admitted that the students' attendance violated no law, he said that it was "in violation of administrative policies of" the institution. "The administration does not feel that activities related to racial agitation are a valid part of its program," he explained. One of the five, Robert Zellner of Mobile, was so offended by the incident that he was led by it into a prominent career as a civil rights worker with the Student Non-violent Coordinating Committee.

The leading figure in Montgomery's chapter of the White Citizens' Council, Luther Ingalls, had spent years—beginning, as we have seen, during the boycott—warning council members of a surreptitious plot to indoctrinate white Sunday school students to accept the morality of miscegenation. His admonitions eventually became council doctrine and influenced state senator E. O. Eddins of Marengo County to launch a crusade against the director of the Alabama Public Library Service, Emily W. Reed, for having permitted the circulation of *The Rabbits' Wedding,* a children's book whose illustrations depicted the marriage of a white and a black rabbit. When later in the year it was revealed that the library service had distributed a list of notable books of 1958 compiled by the American

Library Association that contained among its selections Martin Luther King's account of the bus boycott, *Stride toward Freedom,* Miss Reed's fate was sealed. Under irresistible legislative pressure, she resigned from the directorship at the beginning of 1960 to accept a position in Washington, D.C.

During 1960, the Ku Klux Klan launched a boycott of Montgomery's Pepsi-Cola Bottling Company when the company hired black drivers to replace white ones. The boycott was so successful that the bottler offered a reward of ten thousand dollars to find out who was behind it, and was eventually compelled to return to hiring only white drivers. Another Klan boycott, of a downtown restaurant that had hired black waiters to replace white waitresses, led to gunplay in which the restaurant's owner, James Peek, Jr., a former Klansman, killed an active Klansman in the parking lot of a shopping center in September 1959.[128]

The Klan's most prominent spokesman, retired admiral John Crommelin, a leader as well of the neo-Nazi National States' Rights Party, ran repeatedly for local and state office in order to gain a public platform for his anti-Semitic, anti-black views. And though the anti-Semitism of Crommelin and of the Klan organ the *Home News* failed to gain any substantial following among the white population in general, nevertheless the city's evening daily, the *Alabama Journal,* under its Dixiecrat editor, Cassius Stanley, espoused a racial viewpoint that differed from that of the extremists largely in being more politely expressed. The *Journal's* managing editor, William J. Mahoney, Jr., used his daily column, "As I See It," to press a white supremacist ideology staggering in its fanaticism. Grover Hall, the editor of the morning *Montgomery Advertiser,* held to a moderate position typical of the city's business progressives, as we have seen, but even Hall began to exercise a considerable degree of self-censorship in these years, turning his principal editorial attention from the criticism of local zealots to the denunciation of northern racial hypocrisy.

Some of the episodes to which we have alluded represented direct efforts to intimidate white liberals and moderates, while others were merely reflections of the racial monomania that had come to characterize the city. All of them, however, and others of like character, worked to silence the white businessmen, educators, and church and social leaders who might otherwise have aided in guiding the community toward the tempering of its racial passions. Yet, despite the Citizens' Council's conviction that the absence of moderate white assistance was the chief reason for the lack of further progress toward integration in the years following the boycott, in truth the stalling of the black assault proceeded in greater part from growing disarray and dissension within Montgomery's black leadership.

The first signs of these divisions had already appeared during the boycott itself. Edgar Nixon, the MIA's treasurer, had early become concerned about laxity in the disbursements of the large sums—approximately ten thousand dollars a month—that were being expended to sustain the car-pool operation, administered by Nixon's rival Rufus Lewis. And as the MIA began sending various ministers on fund-raising trips to other cities, Nixon resented the fact that some of the ministers regarded the honoraria paid them for speaking as their own funds. He kept these complaints strictly within the group of MIA officers, but one of the people to whom he evidently made them was the association's young recording secretary, the Reverend Uriah J. Fields of the Bell Street Baptist Church. Angered when he was replaced as recording secretary by the Reverend William J. Powell in mid-June 1956, Fields told the *Montgomery Advertiser* that he had severed his ties with the MIA because its leaders were "using it for their own purposes." Thousands of dollars had been misappropriated, he charged, and "I can no longer identify myself with a movement in which the many are exploited by the few." All of the MIA's financial officers except for Nixon immediately denied these allegations, but Nixon himself merely declined to comment. King, who was out of the city, hurried back to confront Fields. In the meantime, Fields had fallen under enormous pressure from the mass of black Montgomerians, who clearly regarded him as a traitor. His congregation voted to dismiss him as their minister. A chastened Fields therefore appeared with King at the next MIA mass meeting to offer an abject apology and a rather ambiguous retraction of his claims; he had no evidence that would allow him to substantiate them, he said, and had made them because of his resentment at his dismissal. With this statement the initial flurry was papered over—though members of Fields's congregation pressed ahead with the effort to dismiss him, which eventually produced a legal battle and his reinstatement in a bitterly divisive, court-supervised election.

But Nixon's own doubts were not diminished. Shortly after the end of the boycott, in February 1957, he told King that he intended to resign as treasurer, though apparently he was persuaded not to do so immediately. Then in April, an MIA committee headed by the Reverend Benjamin J. Simms recommended that Nixon's compensation as treasurer be reduced and he be required to obtain a bond. On June 3 Nixon dispatched a furious letter of resignation. He had heretofore actually "only been treasurer in name and not in reality," he said. "I resent being treated as a newcomer to the MIA." The organization in fact represented "my dream, hope and hard work since 1932 and I do not expect to be treated as a child." On July 8, King and Abernathy met with Nixon and prevailed on him to relent, with the promise to reform a number of the practices to which he objected. But if any changes were made they were insufficient to satisfy him, and on November 4 Nixon finally in fact resigned. With his departure, the leadership of the organization was left almost entirely in the hands of the middle-class elements who resided in the neighborhood of Alabama State

College, and its genuine contacts with the working-class blacks of west Montgomery were greatly curtailed.[129]

While the dispute with Nixon was mounting to its crisis, the association was floundering as it sought to define its next objectives. It had initially announced in February an initiative to create a credit union for the city's black residents, but after much discussion and effort this project proved a complete failure. In May 1956, Rufus Lewis had surrendered the direction of the car-pool operation to Benjamin Simms in order to devote his full efforts to a program of voter registration. The MIA paid Lewis a salary and paid also for a secretary to assist him, and he labored at this task indefatigably throughout the coming years. But increasing the number of black voters was a very slow and difficult process. There were a few more than two thousand registered blacks at the end of June 1956, and the number had grown only to twenty-five hundred by the time of the municipal elections of March 1959.[130]

The MIA's most public effort during these years, its suit to compel the integration of the city's parks, was no more successful. Black hostility to Montgomery's grossly inadequate provision of recreational facilities for its black citizens had been, as we have seen, a concern that had equaled the antipathy toward the pattern of bus seating in the years just before the boycott. This long-standing antagonism had been revived with fresh intensity, however, in June 1957 when the city commission adopted a new and much more stringent parks segregation ordinance. There followed two well-publicized incidents. A black family from rural Lowndes County was arrested in August for attempting to have a picnic in a park, something that had not previously been illegal; these charges were dismissed because of the family's ignorance of the new prohibition. In October a black teenager, future city councilman Mark Gilmore, was arrested for walking through a park on his way to his job as a porter at a hospital that faced the park; he tried to explain the situation to the arresting officer and was therefore charged with arguing. He alleged that the officer struck him in the process. He was fined fifty dollars for disorderly conduct in Recorder's Court. On appeal to the circuit court the charges against Gilmore were dropped, but in the meantime the hospital had fired him.[131]

These events determined the MIA leadership to sue in federal court, but the decision was surrounded by complications, both personal and legal. In the first place, the Reverend Solomon Seay's son Solomon, Jr., had recently been admitted to the bar, and Seay, Sr., was eager for the association to hire Seay, Jr., to handle the case. But Fred Gray, who had been the MIA's attorney from its creation, hoped to be employed to file the suit himself. Apparently after some considerable acrimony during the spring and early summer of 1958, the MIA's executive board finally voted in July to give the case to Seay, who was offering to do the work for a substantially smaller fee. This choice enraged and hurt Gray, who wrote the board an angry letter of protest, charging Seay in effect with unethical conduct in the affair. This dispute, like the one with Nixon, left a heritage of bitterness with which the association was forced to deal in future years.

And the suit itself had no happier an outcome. On August 25, Seay submitted a petition to the parks and recreation board asking it to order the racial integration of the parks. When the board replied that it had no authority to do so, Seay submitted a petition to the city commission on September 16 asking the commissioners to hold a public hearing on the question. The commissioners promptly refused, warning that if any attempt were made to force the integration of the parks, the city's park system would be abolished. This threat must have given the MIA some pause, because no federal suit was forthcoming for three months. But on December 22, Seay filed suit, in the name of Mark Gilmore and his mother, asking for an injunction to forbid the enforcement of segregation in any recreational facilities. In response, the city commission met on December 30 and ordered all thirteen city parks and the city zoo closed permanently, effective January 1. Seay nevertheless pressed on with the suit. Ruling from the bench immediately after the conclusion of the trial on September 8, 1959, Judge Frank Johnson granted a permanent injunction, but at the same time he informed all parties that he had no power to order the city to reopen the parks; his order, he said, merely meant that if it should ever do so, it would then have to permit all citizens to use them. The parks would remain closed until February 25, 1965, when the commission finally reversed its earlier decision. By that time, however, only seven of the thirteen parks remained, the others having in the meanwhile been sold or put to other uses.[132]

This outcome provided an opening for King's nemesis, Uriah Fields. At the beginning of August 1957, Fields had been invited to give a sermon over the black Montgomery radio station, WRMA, but the storm of protest from the station's listeners caused its management to cut Fields off in the midst of his broadcast. Angered by this action, Fields some days later had joined with construction worker J. J. Israel—who, as we shall see when we turn to Selma, was in fact little more than a confidence man—and some fifty other black Montgomerians to form the Restoration and Amelioration Association, as a rival of the MIA. Fields's group, he said, was opposed to racial strife and would seek to work with city officials for the expansion and improvement of black institutions. There is no evidence that this organization was able to obtain any significant black support during the following months, but with the closure of the parks it evidently saw an opportunity to emphasize the point that it had been attempting to make. In April 1959 the association petitioned the city commission to reopen the parks on a segregated basis. Surely, J. J. Israel told the black community, segregated parks were better than none at all. Judge Johnson's injunction in September rendered the granting of this petition impossible, but Fields at once returned to the attack. He arranged for a vanity press to publish a short book that he had written, *The Montgomery Story: The Unhappy Effects of the Montgomery Bus Boycott,* in which he renewed his allegations of venality and misappropriation of funds on the part of the MIA's leaders and concluded that, as a result, "Negroes of Montgomery who have been misled, exploited and betrayed will never again unite in another bus boycott or similar demonstration." The appearance of the book on September 22 led to an article in the local press and to the commencement of an official audit of King's state income tax returns. In February 1960, Fields testified about his suspicions before the county grand jury, and it thereupon returned an indictment of King for income tax evasion.[133]

The suit to desegregate the parks had thus most certainly not been an unalloyed triumph. Despite having obtained the desired injunction, it had left Montgomerians of both races without public recreational facilities— an outcome substantially harder on blacks and poorer whites because well-to-do whites often had access to such private facilities as country clubs. It had led to the alienation of Fred Gray and the portentous rejuvenation of Uriah Fields's rancor—and would play a major role, as we shall shortly see, in electing the arch-segregationist L. B. Sullivan to the city commission. And even though Fields's criticism did not succeed in drawing any significant number of adherents to his rival organization, he was not wrong in asserting that the events left a growing number of black Montgomerians increasingly dubious of the MIA's leadership. Nevertheless, the MIA pressed ahead with its assault on the segregation laws—in large measure, no doubt, because at this period integration represented, for the MIA as for the great majority of black Americans everywhere, the one clearly available path to liberation from white supremacy. Despite the warnings implicit in the parks suit, therefore, the MIA next turned its attention to school desegregation. That decision would bring an end to Martin Luther King's Montgomery career.

In response to the city commission's decision to close the parks at the end of December 1958, King had defiantly announced that the MIA was already making plans to have a large number of black children apply for transfers to white Montgomery schools under the terms of the recently enacted Alabama Pupil Placement Act, and that if the applications were rejected the organization would then sue in federal court to have the act declared unconstitutional in application. The Pupil Placement Act, as we shall see in greater detail in the next chapter, had established a list of ostensibly nonracial criteria by which school boards were to determine whether to allow a child to transfer from one school to another, and had prescribed a complicated set of procedures through which to make any such transfer request. Birmingham civil rights leader Fred Shuttlesworth had sued to have the act declared unconstitutional on its face, as an obvious attempt to delay desegregation. But a three-judge federal court had ruled, and the U.S. Supreme Court had agreed, that the criteria by themselves were appropriate and that only proof that a particular school board had in practice used them in a racially discriminatory way would render the new statute constitutionally offensive. This decision had erected a substantial barrier for integrationists to overcome—the establishment of a pattern of discrimination in the administration of an act that had only just become law—and it was that barrier which King and the MIA had determined to try to surmount.

King's announcement and the response to it badly frightened a great many white Montgomerians. Incoming governor John Patterson used the occasion of his inaugural address two weeks later to warn black Alabamians ominously to "stand up and speak out now against the agitators of your own race whose aim is to destroy our school system. If you do not do so, and these agitators continue at their present pace, in a short time we will have no public education at all. Our public schools, once destroyed and shut down, may not be reopened in your lifetime and mine." The Ku Klux Klan's grand dragon, Robert Shelton of Tuscaloosa—a man of some influence in the new Patterson administration—promised that the Klan would use violence if necessary to prevent the integration of Montgomery's schools, and the closing of the city's parks at the very same time proved beyond doubt that segregationist officials were prepared to carry through on their threats. The prospect of the total abolition of public schooling, very possibly accompanied by Klan-led riots and bloodshed, therefore seemed very real. A group of white social leaders under the chairmanship of physician Hugh MacGuire scurried to meet the menace of school closure by establishing a private school, limited to "boys and girls of white parentage," the Montgomery Academy; it opened in September. At the same time, Saint James School, a white Methodist parochial school that had been created after the Supreme Court's school desegregation implementation decision of 1955, announced its intention to expand to include the third through the sixth grades, in addition to its existing kindergarten through second grades. The foundations for the educational system that would characterize the city in later decades had thus been laid.

Apparently, after further consultation with its attorneys, the MIA decided that its first action should be to ask the school board to announce a plan to begin the elimination of the dual school system. On August 28, as schools prepared to open for the new year, the MIA's executive committee therefore sent board of education chairman Harold Harris a letter to that effect. Because of events since World War II, they wrote, the United States had "been thrust into the lofty and responsible position of leader and defender of the democratic nations," who were "challenged by a strange philosophy of communism which would relegate the individual to the status of a cog in the wheel of the state, and leave man's sacred destiny in the hands of a small ruling clique." In order to "combat this foreign ideology," it was essential that America provide all youth "with educational opportunities that are non-discriminatory." This obligation was, in addition, required by the Constitution. "We know that there are some problems involved in changing from a segregated to an integrated school system and we realize that mores are not changed without difficulty. Therefore, we are simply calling on you to begin in good faith to study the idea, and then provide a reasonable start. We hope that this problem can be worked out in our community through voluntary goodwill; and that it will not be necessary to carry it into the courts." But the ultimate outcome must be that Montgomery "cease the maintenance of a system which is injurious to both Negro children and white." Governor Patterson responded on September 5, in his weekly radio address to the state. "This fellow here in Montgomery came out the other day and indicated that they were going to start some agitation here about integrating our public schools," he said, in reference to the MIA's letter. Speaking directly to black citizens, he warned, "If you follow a man like Martin Luther King, it is only going to lead to chaos and disorder and violence and the destruction of your public school system. Your children would not receive a public education, and that would be a terrible thing." But the onus to prevent this result rested entirely upon blacks themselves; if desegregation were ordered, the governor reiterated, he would "scrap the whole public school system of this state before I would submit to any integration of our schools."

Patterson's remarks might have been regarded as mere bluster in other parts of the nation, but the statements and actions of all Montgomerians, black and white, make it clear that everyone involved believed that the governor's warning was in deadly earnest. And Judge Johnson's refusal only three days later to compel the city to reopen its parks emphasized that the federal courts were unlikely to be of any help in such a situation. King had said that if the MIA received no response from the school board by January 1, blacks would then file suit. But during the fall, Patterson's admonitions began more and more to take hold among black schoolteachers, who formed a very large part of the city's black middle class— and an even larger part of King's own Dexter Avenue congregation—and who stood to pay with their jobs, of course, if the public schools were abolished. King and the MIA thereupon fell under quiet but urgent and rapidly mounting importunity from the black teachers not to turn to the courts. The parks suit seemed to prove that, though blacks would certainly win the order from Judge Johnson that they wanted, the actual result would only be private schools for well-to-do whites and none at all for poorer whites and blacks. King increasingly despaired of winning the teachers and other middle-class blacks to the support of a school desegregation initiative that appeared so likely to turn out just as the parks suit had. And as himself the pastor of a church in which the teachers' perspective was particularly strong, King was therefore especially troubled by it. At the end of November, he asked the chairman of Dexter Avenue's board of deacons, insurance executive Robert D. Nesbitt, to come to the parsonage, and as they sat together on the porch, an anguished King described to Nesbitt the intense pressure that the teachers in Dexter's congregation had come under from their county and state employers as a result of the MIA's threatened legal action. He was, King said, convinced that he was personally responsible for having placed these parishioners in so desperate a situation, and was certain that if he left Montgomery the pressure on them would decline. He had therefore decided to resign. The following Sunday, November 29, King announced from his pulpit, to a saddened black community and a jubilant white one, that he would move to Atlanta at the beginning of January 1960—the very time that, only three months earlier, he had promised that the school desegregation suit would be filed.

King's speech to the MIA a week later, at the celebration of the fourth anniversary of the beginning of the boycott, thus became a farewell address. He tried as best he could to put a brave front on the surrender. He vigorously denied the allegations of financial improprieties in Uriah Fields's new book—allegations for which just ten weeks later he would be indicted. "Every penny that came to Montgomery to assist in the bus struggle was used wisely and honestly," he insisted. "As president of the MIA I can truthfully say that I do not know of a single instance of mishandling or misappropriation of funds." He defended the parks suit. "All the Negro parks in Montgomery put together could hardly meet the specifications for one good park," he observed, quite correctly, and the city commission had ignored all the black requests through the years to correct the situation. Judge Johnson's injunction forbidding parks segregation "was a significant victory, and one that left every person of goodwill throbbing with inner joy." "Naturally," he confessed, "we want to see the parks opened, for recreation is a vital part of the total welfare of the individual and the community. But we cannot in all good conscience make an agreement to accept a new form of segregation in order to entice the City Commission to open the parks. While compromise is an absolute necessity in any moment of social transition, it must be the creative, honest compromise of a policy, not the negative and cowardly compromise of a principle."

He then turned to school desegregation. "Three months have passed since" the MIA's letter to the school board, "and it has not even given us the courtesy of an answer. It seems now that we have no alternative but to carry this issue into the federal courts." Legal action was only "a last resort. . . . But when the school board absolutely refuses to acknowledge your letter and act on your request, the last resort stage has already emerged." Nor should blacks fear school closing. "In spite of the threats and loud noises, we know that the idea of closing the public schools is a fanatical proposal which is both rationally absurd and practically inexpedient. The absurdity of this approach was clearly seen in the breakdown of massive resistance in Virginia and Arkansas. . . . Two powerful institutions have collided in the South—the institution of segregation and the institution of public schools. And the people, on the whole, have made it palpably clear that when the final moment of choice comes, they will choose public schools rather than segregation. . . . The price to be paid by school closing is much too high. . . . So if our governor is driven to the extreme of closing the public schools, as he has so earnestly promised to do, he will do more to promote integration in Alabama in a few hours than the most powerful integrationist could do in ten years." He then concluded with a plea to the intimidated white moderates of the city, who "are often silent today because of fear of social, political and economic reprisals," to seize the initiative from the "close-minded extremists" and "to speak out, to offer the leadership that is needed."[134]

Despite the logic, the passion, and the bravado of King's farewell address, however, it was apparent that he was merely whistling past the graveyard. Fields's renewed allegations of selfishness and dishonesty; the city's elimination of public recreational facilities; the widespread fear, especially in the black middle class, of the abolition of public schools; the cowering silence of Montgomery's white moderates and the consequent leadership by default of the segregationist zealots—these were the topics upon which King focused because they were the factors that were relentlessly depriving his movement of the momentum it had possessed at the conclusion of the boycott. And his insistence that the black citizenry must not yield to them could not help but lose much of its force as even his most ardent local admirers came to understand that, in leaving Montgomery, he himself just had. Though he had said that the MIA now had no alternative but to sue for school integration, it was obvious that the MIA did in fact have an alternative: the frightened or disillusioned acquiescence in the status quo. And that was the alternative that, at least for a time, the organization in effect chose. The presidency of the association passed initially to Ralph Abernathy, but less than two years later he followed King to Atlanta. It then passed to the considerably more restrained Solomon Seay, who had been the association's executive secretary. Initial school integration was accomplished in Tuskegee, Birmingham, Huntsville, and Mobile, and only then, in May 1964, more than five years after King's announcement of the MIA's intention to do so, was a school desegregation lawsuit finally actually filed. The first black children entered Montgomery's schools the following September.

Disarray within the MIA's leadership, the reappearance of the deep divisions that had long characterized the black community at large, and surreptitious but aggressive intimidation of white moderates and liberals by segregationist extremists, then, account in great part for the arresting of the movement toward black civil rights in Montgomery that at the conclusion of the bus boycott had seemed to be on the verge of creating a breakthrough. But one other element—probably, indeed, the most obvious one—played a significant role as well: the hostility and harassment of state and local government. The bus boycott and, at the same time, the unsuccessful effort to enroll Autherine Lucy at the University of Alabama were responsible for a sharp movement of state politics away from toleration of the racial moderation that had been widespread in the decade after the end of World War II. And the state's young attorney general, John Patterson of Phenix City, had been particularly fortunate in his efforts to ride this dark wave. The suit he had filed in state court in June 1956 had succeeded, as we have seen, in barring the NAACP from operating in Alabama. Legal maneuvers in the case kept the association from reentering the state until October 1964, more than eight years later. The NAACP was in fact the most conservative of all the civil rights organizations, utterly committed to seeking black advancement through the courts rather than through direct action. But segregationists conceived of the NAACP as the true source of all agitation for racial equality; Patterson in his suit had, for instance, alleged—quite absurdly—that the association had been responsible both for staging the boycott and for bribing Lucy to attempt to attend the university. Moreover, the most fanatic segregationists were convinced that the NAACP was a clandestine arm of the Communist Party, cooperating actively in a conspiracy to destroy the racial purity and Anglo-Saxon hegemony that were essential to the preservation of the American republican order. Therefore, Patterson's triumph in excluding the NAACP from Alabama caused many white supremacist true believers to become enthusiastic supporters of the attorney general's gubernatorial ambitions.

In the gubernatorial election of May 1958, to choose a successor to the racially moderate James Folsom, each candidate sought to outdo all the others in the strength of his devotion to segregationist dogma. At the outset of the campaign, almost all observers regarded Circuit Judge George C. Wallace of Clio and state senator James Faulkner of Bay Minette as the two front-runners, and the state's newspapers and traditional courthouse power brokers almost uniformly supported one or the other. Patterson adopted as his campaign motto "Nobody's for Patterson but the People." As soon became apparent, however, the people in question included most prominently the Ku Klux Klan and the leaders of the White Citizens' Council. In a series of startling upsets, Patterson led the initial round of balloting by nearly thirty-five thousand votes and defeated Judge Wallace handily in the runoff, by 56 percent to 44 percent, thus convincing almost all political professionals—including Judge Wallace himself—that Patterson had succeeded in tapping into a newly defined and invincible source of political power in the state. The governor-elect thereupon appointed the White Citizens' Councils' state executive secretary, Sam Martin Engelhardt, both as state highway director and as state Democratic Party chairman. Black Alabamians looked toward the advent of the Patterson administration with the deepest trepidation.[135]

Only two months after Patterson's inauguration, Montgomery's municipal elections took place—in the very midst, as we have seen, of the furor over Martin Luther King's announced intention to seek the integration of the schools and the new governor's pledge in that case to close them. Though the outcome of the municipal voting was somewhat more ambiguous than the state election had been, the results served to give the city's racial extremists further confidence that they were now taking firm control of what had been a volatile situation. In order to understand the municipal election, however, we must briefly retrace our steps and describe one of the consequences of the parks integration suit to which we have not yet alluded.

On August 25, 1958, Solomon Seay, Jr., submitted the MIA's petition to desegregate the parks to the parks and recreation board. Montgomery's law enforcement authorities, who closely monitored the activities of the MIA leaders, evidently responded by quietly informing a young black parishioner of Ralph Abernathy's, Edward Davis, that Abernathy was engaged in an affair with Davis's wife, Vivian McCoy Davis. On August 29, Davis stormed into the offices of Abernathy's church and attacked Abernathy with a hatchet and a pistol. Abernathy fled down the street with Davis close on his heels, waving the hatchet over his head. Police, who had been parked nearby, apparently in anticipation of the incident, quickly took Davis into custody and charged him with assault with intent to murder. On September 3, Abernathy was summoned to Davis's preliminary hearing as the complaining witness. While waiting with the Abernathys on the sidewalk outside city hall for the hearing to begin, Martin Luther King was arrested by police officers and charged with loitering. King was brought to trial on September 5, convicted, and fined ten dollars. He refused to pay, announcing that he preferred to go to jail in order to dramatize what he quite understandably regarded as the extraordinary injustice of these proceedings. Commissioner Sellers thereupon paid King's fine himself in order to deprive King of the considerable publicity that his going to jail would undoubtedly have given him. Sellers told reporters, "I cannot permit him to use the facilities of the City of Montgomery"—by which he meant a cell in the city jail—"for his own selfish purposes."[136]

Sellers's logic proved, however, too subtle for most segregationists, and his payment of King's fine became the principal issue in his campaign for reelection six months later. Sellers's opponent was L. B. Sullivan, like Sellers a former director of the state highway patrol. Though of course himself an outspoken segregationist, Sellers encountered in Sullivan a segregationist even more extreme, a man reported to maintain surreptitious ties to the Ku Klux Klan. In announcing his candidacy, Sullivan had warned, "In dangerous times like these, with our Southern traditions in grave peril, the people of Montgomery need more than the wishy-washy leadership we have had in the past." He had pledged "that I will never pay the fine of a troublemaker to spare him the embarrassment of going to jail." This action, he claimed, convicted Sellers of "using kid gloves in the handling of racial agitators." Nothing more clearly demonstrates the new zealotry of Montgomery's political life than the race that ensued. Sellers—who was in no small measure himself responsible for that zealotry and who was now about to become its victim—reminded voters shrilly of his firm devotion to the White Citizens' Council. But the Klan element regarded the Citizens' Council as little better than the hated racial moderates, a judgment proven in their eyes by the willingness of Sellers's police force to arrest and charge the post-boycott bombers in 1957. The elements who had supported the bombers and raised money for their defense became the backbone of Sullivan's campaign organization. After his victory, indeed, Sullivan's first action would be to remove the head of the police department's detective division, E. P. "Tiny" Brown, who had directed the investigation that had succeeded in breaking the bombing cases, and to replace him with an officer who had the confidence of the most fanatical white supremacists, John B. "Jack" Rucker. Sullivan's east Montgomery residence brought the class resentments of that section of the city into play against the south Montgomerian Sellers, as well. Sellers had been able to use race-baiting to counterbalance those resentments in his campaign against Dave Birmingham in 1955, but no amount of racial demagogy from Sellers could now surpass Sullivan's own. And finally, and more ironically, such was the black hostility to Sellers for his conduct during the boycott that most of the city's twenty-five hundred black voters gave their support to Sullivan also. It appears that blacks were not fully aware of Sullivan's Klan contacts and thus allowed their past resentments to betray them; they succeeded only in jumping from the frying pan into the fire. On this coalition of racial extremists, working-class whites, and blacks, Sullivan erected a victorious margin, 9,123 to 8,150.[137]

The mayoral election also featured elements of the class antagonism between east and south Montgomery, but as with the Sellers-Sullivan election, that antagonism was now, more than at any other time in living memory, refracted through the prism of race. Mayor Gayle's principal opponent was Earl D. James, the former Capitol Heights teacher and football coach whose election to the city commission in 1947 had represented the first clear evidence of the emerging political self-consciousness of the eastern precincts. James reminded voters that this victory had been achieved "in spite of strong opposition from the powers that had ruled our city government for so many years." He vigorously attacked Gayle for the city commission's imposition of a one-cent city sales tax in July 1957, an action that had aroused a storm of protest, particularly in east Montgomery, and had led to a lengthy court battle. But James also repeatedly raised the race issue. James's brother, Ervin "Red" James, had been a protégé, and later a law partner, of the liberal white attorney Clifford Durr in the 1940s and early 1950s, and primarily for that reason, many liberals and moderates had initially hoped that James would adopt a more temperate approach to the racial question. James, however, set out to convince the electorate that he was even more committed to the defense of white supremacy than was the mayor. Under Gayle, he said, the city had "been tormented by outside racial agitators. . . . Our buses are already integrated. Our parks lie idle. Strong leadership is needed to resist these forces that are bent on destroying our Southern way of life." He criticized Gayle for having been willing to negotiate with the MIA in the boycott's early weeks.

Also seeking the mayoralty were the liberal former commissioner Dave Birmingham and the vitriolic anti-Semite and white supremacist fanatic Admiral John Crommelin. Birmingham's paltry 226 votes in the initial round of balloting is an index to how much the city had changed since his victory in 1953. He was booed and hissed when he attempted to speak at a candidates' forum sponsored by the White Citizens' Council. Crommelin's 1,760 votes constitutes a reasonable estimate of the Ku Klux Klan's strength in the city. Gayle led James by a substantial margin—8,563 to 6,789—but the presence of the two other candidates forced a runoff.

In the runoff campaign, the principal issue became the black vote. Blacks, deeply hostile to Gayle as a result of the boycott and evidently convinced that Birmingham could not win, had voted overwhelmingly for James. The mayor therefore seized upon this fact to accuse James of being the candidate of the black bloc vote. The White Citizens' Council joined in this attack. Calling itself "the unquestioned de facto representative voice of white opinion in this city and county," the council proclaimed that a vote for James would "help a candidate who was the choice of a minority of whites, and thus help establish political power in the hands of the negro." James struck back with an assault on Gayle for bungling the white defense during the boycott, for failing to take action against the MIA's car-pool operation sooner than he did, and for agreeing to renew the Montgomery City Lines' exclusive franchise, thus compelling the city to accept integrated buses. As Gayle portrayed James, the former commissioner was practically a tool of Martin Luther King; as James portrayed Gayle, the mayor was virtually the father of bus integration.

In the balloting, James defeated Gayle 9,144 to 8,424. The geographical distribution of the returns in the runoff replicated the distribution in the first round: Gayle took the well-to-do southern wards while James swept the white lower-middle-class eastern wards and the black precincts. More significant, however, was the fact that, despite the White Citizens' Council's strong endorsement of Gayle, the vote of the Klansmen and other racial extremists that had gone to Crommelin in the initial balloting now clearly went to James. Gayle essentially received the same total in both elections, while James added to his original total all of the votes of the two candidates who had been eliminated, and in addition brought out some new voters. Thus James erected his victory on precisely the same odd coalition that also gave Sullivan his triumph over Sellers: black voters, Klansmen, and east Montgomery whites moved by class resentments. In both races, the most fanatical white supremacists parted company from the somewhat more restrained segregationists of the Citizens' Council, whom the Klansmen had come to regard as dangerously moderate. And in both races, ironically, the Klan and the blacks therefore ended up supporting the same candidate.

The blacks' electoral decisions represented an unfortunate level of political naïveté. King, in his farewell address to the MIA on December 3, proudly claimed credit for the defeat of Sellers and Gayle, but in the case of each of the victors, and especially in the case of Sullivan, events would prove that black citizens were no better off under the new leaders. The truth is, as Solomon Seay, Sr., wrote in the MIA's newsletter, that blacks were motivated by hostility to the incumbents rather than by any real familiarity with the challengers: "We will never forget that Mayor Gayle and Commissioner (of police) Sellers were in office during the dark days of the bus protest, when some ninety of our leaders (including 27 preachers) were arrested and later when our churches and homes were bombed. . . . Messers James and Sullivan we do not know. But we are quite familiar with Messers Gayle and Sellers."[138]

Thus the white supremacist who surveyed the situation in Montgomery at the beginning of 1960 could do so with considerable satisfaction. Once we have examined the events in the city in the years just after the end of the boycott, the notion advanced by the Citizens' Councils in January 1959, that history would record Montgomery as the place where the tide in the civil rights battle was turned and "integration efforts were stopped cold," seems a good deal less peculiar.[139] Racial moderation had been eliminated from political discourse at both state and municipal levels, and segregationists with ties to the most uncompromising advocates of these doctrines had taken firm control of both the capitol and the city hall. Wide internal divisions had opened in the city's black leadership. The MIA's effort to bring integration to the parks system had been little short of a disaster for the black community. Judge Johnson had validated the legitimacy of segregationist politicians' strategy of abolishing integrated public facilities. Pressure from white educational authorities on Montgomery's black teachers had played a crucial role in leading Martin Luther King to decide to leave the city and in convincing the MIA to abandon its announced suit to integrate the schools. The NAACP had been barred from operating in the state. The forward march of desegregation, which had appeared at the end of 1956 to be about to create a breakthrough, did indeed seem to have been halted in its tracks. No integration would come to Montgomery during the entire period between the conclusion of the bus boycott in December 1956 and the desegregation of the bus and train terminals in November 1961, the airport terminal in January 1962, and the library and art museum in August 1962, a span of some five years. Moreover, the year 1960, which would give the new order that the white supremacists had now engineered its first genuine test, would seem initially to have produced a general segregationist triumph. The prospects for the ultimate victory of Jim Crow looked bright indeed.

In February 1960, the month after King left the city for Atlanta, and the month in which he was indicted for Alabama income tax evasion, the sit-ins came to Montgomery. Though the sit-ins are often said to have begun with the one in Greensboro, North Carolina, on February 1, the idea for them appears to have come from the Miami, Florida, chapter of the Congress of Racial Equality, headed by a black ophthalmologist, Dr. John O. Brown. Dr. Brown and some forty-five associates staged sit-ins at the lunch counter of a variety store in Miami during June 1959 and succeeded thereby in obtaining the agreement of the store's management to enter into negotiations about its policy of racial segregation. These sit-ins received substantial coverage in the southern press and evidently aroused the enthusiasm of many, particularly younger, blacks. When college classes resumed in the fall, students on a number of black campuses across the region seem to have begun discussing independently the possibility of emulating the Miami example. Students from North Carolina A. and T. in Greensboro were the first to act on this idea, but it spread at once to other cities that were home to black colleges. By the end of February, students in at least a dozen cities had followed the Greensboro precedent.[140]

On February 25, thirty-five students from Alabama State College—led by Bernard Lee, an undergraduate who in later years would become one of King's principal aides and confidants—sought service at the snack bar in the basement of the Montgomery County Courthouse, after conferring with Jo Ann Robinson and Ralph Abernathy. This action produced a genuine crisis in the city. The next day, Governor Patterson demanded the expulsion of all thirty-five from school. On February 27, following a Ku Klux Klan rally at Montgomery's municipally owned baseball stadium, about twenty-five Klansmen armed with baseball bats roamed downtown streets attempting to intimidate blacks. One of these Klansmen hit a young black woman, Christine Stovall, over the head with his bat. This attack went unpunished, despite a photograph of it that was printed in the newspapers, and indeed was actually hailed as a heroic act in extreme segregationist quarters. The organ of the most fanatical white supremacists, the *Montgomery Home News,* exulted, "The crisp crack of a hickory bat on a Negro head snapped the people out of their apathy into the realization that the steady, cold siege against their way of life was now breaking out in an obviously Communist-inspired racial strife."[141]

On March 1 about six hundred Alabama State students marched two by two in a solemn procession from the campus to the capitol to protest the governor's demand for the expulsion of the sit-in participants. But on March 4, the state board of education, which served as Alabama State's governing body, ordered that nine of the sit-in participants be expelled and that twenty others be placed on probation. Those expelled generally were the participants whose homes were out of state, while those placed on probation were Alabamians; apparently the board members assumed that the ringleaders of the protest had to be outsiders. By this time, racial tensions in the city were at a fever pitch. The president of the chamber of commerce, construction executive Carl Bear, denounced the demonstrations on national television as a "coldly deliberate, calculated move on the part of the agitators to goad and provoke the Southern white man to the very limits of his patience and endurance."

On March 6, Montgomery nearly experienced a bloody catastrophe. Blacks had announced their intention to pray on the capitol steps for the expelled students' readmission. As about seven hundred blacks emerged from the Dexter Avenue Baptist Church to walk to the capitol two blocks away, they were met by some five thousand hostile whites. More than four hundred city police, state highway patrolmen, and mounted volunteer sheriff's deputies managed to thrust themselves between the blacks and whites at the last minute, and then they forcibly drove the blacks back up the steps into the sanctuary. After some time the whites were finally dispersed, and blacks were at last able to leave the church in small groups. But everyone involved recognized that a cataclysm had been only very narrowly avoided.[142]

Following this very dangerous incident, Alabama State students began a boycott of classes, and authorities responded with aggressive harassment, both on the campus and in the black community at large. On March 9, Martin Luther King wired President Eisenhower, with only slight exaggeration, that "a reign of terror has broken out in Montgomery, Alabama." King reported his suspicion—the mirror image of the belief expressed by Carl Bear a week earlier—that "police backed by municipal and state authorities . . . are trying to incite a riot in the hope that the responsibility for the injuries and deaths that might result will be fastened on the Negroes." He pleaded for the intervention of the Justice Department. But on March 10, under the most intense official coercion, the boycott of classes collapsed. Governor Patterson and the state board of education thereupon began an investigation of Alabama State that led to a purge of the faculty. In June they ordered the immediate firing of the distinguished historian Lawrence D. Reddick, King's friend and first biographer, on questionable grounds of Communist associations in his youth, and later that summer they forced the resignations of twenty other faculty members sympathetic to civil rights, including the bus boycott leader Jo Ann Robinson. Finally, though he had done everything they had asked, they suspended and then compelled into retirement the college's elderly president, H. Councill Trenholm, who had headed the school since 1925.[143]

In the meantime, the visit to Montgomery at the end of March of a group of ten students from MacMurray College, a small Methodist school in Illinois, on a spring field trip led by a professor of sociology, Richard D. Nesmith, and his wife produced additional official transgressions. On March 31 the Nesmiths and their students were having lunch with two of the students expelled from Alabama State and MIA leaders including Solomon Seay, Sr., in a black restaurant near the Alabama State campus, the Regal Café. Apparently a passing officer saw the biracial group going into the restaurant and notified his superiors. Police fear of the plots of outside agitators, one assumes, caused them to respond in force, and the presence of numerous police officers and vehicles outside the café caused a crowd of curious neighborhood residents to gather. Police then stormed the dining room where the lunch was in progress and arrested all present for conduct calculated to provoke a breach of the peace. Police alleged that the presence of the interracial diners had caused the crowd to gather, though the officers conceded that there had been no crowd at all when they first arrived on the scene. Despite the obvious absurdity of the charge, the entire luncheon was convicted the following day in Recorder's Court and fined, and they all appealed to the next term of circuit court.

In the circuit court the white diners, represented by Clifford Durr, sought a jury trial, while the black diners, represented by Fred Gray, asked to be tried by a judge alone, but challenged the impartiality of both of Montgomery's circuit judges. In the trial of the whites, the jury acquitted all of the defendants except for Professor Nesmith, who the jurors concluded had led the others into their offense. In the trial of the black defendants in a courtroom across the hall, at the same time, however, Special Judge Sam Rice Baker, a white Montgomery attorney appointed to preside because of the challenge to the regular bench, convicted all of them. Immediately following the end of the two trials, one of the white defendants, civil rights activist R. Edwin King, and one of the black ones, Elroy Embry, who was one of the students who had been expelled from Alabama State, left the courthouse, walked to the Jefferson Davis Hotel, where King was staying, and sought to have lunch together in the hotel dining room. The result was their arrest a second time, for trespassing, and a new round of trials and appeals.[144]

Finally, as a result of insignificantly misleading statements about the events of Montgomery's sit-in crisis that were made in the text of a fundraising advertisement printed in the *New York Times* on March 29, Commissioner Sullivan, his two colleagues on the commission, Mayor James and Commissioner Parks, and former commissioner Sellers and Governor Patterson all sued the *Times* and four black Alabama ministers who were listed as endorsing the advertisement (Ralph Abernathy and Solomon Seay of Montgomery, Fred Shuttlesworth of Birmingham, and Joseph E. Lowery of Mobile), alleging that, as responsible public officials, they had been libeled. In the only two of the suits to come to trial, Montgomery circuit court juries awarded Commissioner Sullivan and Mayor James $500,000 each in damages, and the automobiles and land of the four ministers were seized and ordered to be sold at auction to satisfy the judgments.

These verdicts were to be reversed by the U.S. Supreme Court in one of the landmark decisions of American constitutional law, *New York Times* v. *Sullivan.* No public official could ever be libeled, the Court held, unless the libeler acted from demonstrable malice or with reckless disregard for the truth or falsity of the statements. But this reversal did not come until 1964. Six of the nine students whom the state board of education expelled from Alabama State sued in federal court. They were unsuccessful before Judge Frank Johnson at the district court level, but two years later, after a battle that also went to the U.S. Supreme Court, they gained an order forbidding their expulsion without a hearing. The prosecutions of Professor Nesmith and the black diners were reversed by the state court of appeals in March 1961 on the ground that the indictment had failed to specify any conduct by the defendants that could have provoked a breach of the peace; and because the one-year statute of limitations on the offense had by then expired, the city was compelled to drop the case. But Professor and Mrs. Nesmith and two of his students thereupon sued Montgomery police in federal court for damages. The federal jurors initially found for the defendants, but on appeal to the Fifth Circuit, Judge John R. Brown of Texas—joined by Montgomery's Richard Rives, and over a vehement dissent by Judge Ben Cameron of Louisiana—found Judge Frank Johnson's instruction to the jury defective. After reviewing the extraordinary circumstances of the arrests, Judge Brown held that Judge Johnson should have given an instructed verdict for the plaintiffs on their claims of false imprisonment and malicious prosecution, and left to the jurors only the question of the amount of damages. When the city was denied a rehearing in August 1963, it then reluctantly agreed to an out-of-court settlement. Meanwhile, in March 1961, the state court of appeals had also reversed the parallel King and Embry prosecutions because of a technical defect in the indictment. The city had reindicted and retried them, only to have the state court of appeals again reverse in April 1962 because the city had failed to introduce into evidence an ordinance authorizing it to punish the defendants. Undeterred, the city proceeded to try King and Embry a third time, but on the appeal of this third conviction in October 1964, the state court of appeals noted that the U.S. Supreme Court had in the mean-time forbidden trespass prosecutions if the city had an ordinance requir-ing the establishment to maintain racial segregation, as Montgomery did; the appellate court therefore barred any further attempts to try the two young men.[145]

Thus the appellate process would eventually limit some of the tools available to authorities to intimidate and restrain the advocates of integra-tion, and in the course of doing so it would begin to change the landscape of American law as well. But this outcome was still years in the future. As matters stood at the end of the tumultuous year of 1960, it appeared that the various challenges that had flowed from the February 25 sit-in had eventuated in a virtually complete rout for the forces of civil rights. In a conversation with an investigator for the Southern Regional Council, Commissioner Sullivan commented with evident satisfaction, in reference to the Klan element, "The people who might be inclined to take things in their own hands have let us know they now believe we can handle mat-ters." The investigator, his conclusions clearly shaped by his interview with Sullivan, observed that "in Montgomery everybody seems to expect" violence, "to take it for granted as a part of the process of racial relations." White Montgomerians, he said were "openly, candidly, and consciously willing to risk chaos—to preserve the racial status quo." As a result of these attitudes, "no other course is open to police, and to the forces of law and order, but one of *continuous coercion*." Moreover, to see that authorities did not deviate from this course, in October 1960 two additional Montgomery klaverns of the Klan received their charters. Interracial dialogue was un-necessary; as white supremacists understood events, the aggressive appli-cation of force had dealt with the problem.[146]

Even the segregationists' one indisputable defeat during this period only reinforced their sense of the correctness of their tactics. In late May of 1960, Martin Luther King came to trial on his indictment for state in-come tax evasion. The evidence revealed that his income had mounted rapidly in these years. He had reported a taxable income of only $9,150 in 1956 but of $25,348 in 1958, nearly treble the figure from two years ear-lier. This considerable increase in his financial well-being in so short a time undoubtedly fueled the gossip in the black community which the allegations in Uriah Fields's recent book reflected. But the grand jury's in-dictment alleged that King's actual taxable income in 1956 had been $16,162, and in 1958 had been $45,421. As the trial unfolded, it became clear that the Revenue Department's auditor, Lloyd Hale, had arrived at these figures simply by totaling the deposits to King's bank accounts, and thus had incorrectly included in King's income amounts that in fact were nontaxable gifts or reimbursements to him of his travel expenses for speaking to various organizations around the country. King was defended by a prominent Chicago tax attorney, Robert Ming, who thoroughly demolished the state's case. After deliberating for three hours and forty-five minutes, the all-white jury returned an acquittal on May 28.[147]

This vindication only indicated to extreme segregationists, however, that if they could just keep more moderate whites from deviating from the hard white supremacist line, as the jurors had in this case, their region did have ample means with which to crush the integrationist menace. A conviction could have sent King to prison for years and discredited him in the eyes of many supporters. Only the jurors' excessive scruples had prevented this outcome. Southern whites did not lack adequate weapons, the extreme segregationists were convinced. Their cause was endangered simply by the absence of a universally implacable white will. The acquittal therefore merely redoubled the white supremacists' determination to tolerate neither further black advances nor white moderate desertions from the segregationist cause. Their efforts over the preceding four years had virtually succeeded in terminating the civil rights movement's progress, they believed. They now needed only to devote themselves fully to guarding against any hint of weakening. It was into this atmosphere that the Freedom Riders rode in May of 1961.

VII. The Consequences of the Freedom Rides

The idea for the Freedom Rides came from CORE, the Congress of Racial Equality.[148] As we shall see in the next chapter, the two groups of CORE Freedom Riders fell victim to Klan violence in north Alabama on May 14. The group traveling aboard Greyhound was besieged in its bus just outside Anniston, the bus was set afire, and all those aboard narrowly escaped incineration. Later on the same day, the group on Trailways, together with a number of innocent bystanders, was badly mauled at the Birmingham bus terminal. The following day, the demonstrators, bruised and battered, decided to abandon their ride. They continued to New Orleans by airplane.

But one of the original Freedom Riders, future U.S. congressman John Lewis—a twenty-one-year-old black seminarian and native of rural Pike County, near the Banks community—refused to abandon the effort. Lewis had left the Freedom Ride in Rock Hill, South Carolina, to fly to Philadelphia to be interviewed for a position as a missionary; he had been intending to rejoin the Ride in Birmingham. The result was that when the attacks on the Riders occurred, Lewis was in Nashville, where he was a student and had been a leader of the Nashville sit-in movement during 1960. At Lewis's urging, his Nashville acquaintances decided to take up the cause that the original Riders had abandoned. Lewis, along with sixteen other black and three white student volunteers, most of them connected with Tennessee A. and I. College in Nashville and all of them influenced by the

Nashville pacifist leader James Lawson, set out from Nashville for Birmingham, where they intended to launch a new Freedom Ride, south to Montgomery and then on to Mississippi. Birmingham commissioner Eugene "Bull" Connor promptly returned them to the Tennessee line, but within hours they were all back in Birmingham, seeking a bus to Montgomery.

Initially, because of the danger to drivers and buses, neither Greyhound nor Trailways was willing to take the demonstrators. But as a result of negotiations with Attorney General Robert Kennedy and his assistant John Seigenthaler, Governor Patterson eventually agreed to guarantee the safety of the bus as far as the Montgomery city limits, and with this protection, the bus left Birmingham, accompanied by sixteen patrol cars and a state airplane. At the Montgomery city limits, however, the highway patrol escort left the bus. Its security was now the responsibility of Montgomery city police. Montgomery's police commissioner, L. B. Sullivan, had assured the governor that city police would safeguard the bus, but Sullivan, as it later became clear, had given directly contrary assurances to the Klan. Because his political power rested upon the support of the most zealous segregationists, Sullivan could not afford to seem sympathetic to the Freedom Riders. He knew well how easily a segregationist opponent could turn against him any action such as extending police protection to demonstrators. He knew, because he had used just such an issue to defeat Clyde Sellers in 1959.[149]

The bus was met at the Greyhound terminal in downtown Montgomery by an angry mob of whites, which initially numbered two hundred but grew eventually to one thousand. Urged on by Claude V. Henley, the assistant service manager at an automobile dealership and, according to the Justice Department, a Ku Klux Klan member, the mob swarmed around the bus. Henley, a World War II veteran, had grown up in Selma and had joined the state highway patrol in 1947. He became a member of Montgomery's volunteer reserve police force when it was organized in 1956, during the bus boycott, and had continued as a member until just weeks before the riot; in that capacity, he had become close friends with many regular officers. Henley and other rioters initially assaulted Maurice Levy, a cameraman for the National Broadcasting Company. The mob then turned its attention to the only white male among the Freedom Riders, James Zwerg of Appleton, Wisconsin, an exchange student at Nashville's black Fisk University. Some twenty-five or more rioters beat Zwerg into unconsciousness. After he had collapsed, three men held him up so that a woman could kick him in the groin. They then threw him over a railing to the pavement, where he landed on his head. In the meantime, rioters beat John Lewis and other Freedom Riders. Two of the Freedom Riders fled into the post office building next door, with several mob members in hot pursuit.

Police had been called as soon as the violence had begun, but they had consciously delayed responding. About fifteen minutes after the call, several officers, in the words of the *Advertiser*'s account of the events, "sauntered into the loading area" of the station. Shortly thereafter, Commissioner Sullivan, Attorney General MacDonald Gallion, and Assistant Attorney General Willard Livingston—the son of Alabama's chief justice—arrived together. Judge Walter B. Jones, at the attorney general's request, had issued an injunction the day before forbidding any further freedom rides, and the attorney general proceeded to read the entire text of the injunction to John Lewis, who was limping and bleeding from his wounds. Sullivan told newsmen that officers had made no arrests for the violence because no one had sworn out an arrest warrant against any of the rioters. He said that no ambulance had been called for the unconscious Zwerg because Zwerg had not asked for one, and added, falsely, that no one had requested the presence of police officers at the station earlier. Sullivan, Gallion, and Livingston then left. Sullivan later issued a statement saying that police "have no intention of standing guard for a bunch of trouble makers coming into our city and making trouble."

The violence had abated after the initial arrival of police, but when it became clear that they were there only to direct traffic, the riot resumed. The Freedom Riders had sought to leave the station in black taxicabs during the lull, and some of them had succeeded. But one of them, William T. Barbee, Jr., a black ministerial student who had come to Montgomery on May 18 to make arrangements for his colleagues' accommodations in the city, arrived at the station at this moment to collect them and became the focus of the mob's anger. One of the rioters, Thurman E. Ouzts, a Klansman and unemployed glazier and dump-truck operator, knocked Barbee unconscious, and a youth then began beating Barbee's skull with a baseball bat. Just at this point the director of the state highway patrol, Floyd Mann, arrived on the scene. Discovering for the first time that he had been betrayed by Montgomery authorities, Mann waded into the mob and, straddling Barbee's unconscious body, drove the rioters back at gunpoint and personally arrested Ouzts. After extricating James Atkins, a Birmingham television reporter, from the mob, Mann summoned highway patrol reinforcements. A black bystander later testified that, in the midst of the melee, he had overheard Mann ask a Montgomery policeman, "Why didn't you call Sullivan?" and had heard the policeman reply, "The men he would send out probably would have joined the mob." As the riot continued, a white mother was seen holding a black girl so that her young son could hit the girl in the face. White ambulance companies refused to send an ambulance to the bus station to take Zwerg to the hospital, on the claim that all of their ambulances had broken down, and he eventually had to be taken there in Mann's automobile. Black taxis refused to take the two white female Freedom Riders, Susan Wilbur and Susan Herman, and they were left to flee the mob on foot. Attorney General Kennedy's representative, John Seigenthaler, who had arrived with Assistant Attorney General John Doar, was struck from behind and knocked unconscious when he tried to rescue the two women; Seigenthaler lay unattended on the sidewalk for more than a quarter of an hour. City police made only five arrests for any of these incidents, and two of the five were of Mr. and Mrs. Frederick Gach, white passersby who sought to obtain medical assistance for the injured. For their pains, the Gaches were promptly charged with disorderly conduct and failure to obey an officer. In fining them three hundred dollars, Recorder's Court Judge D. Eugene Loe found that Mrs. Gach had caused the rioters to become inflamed when she told them that they should be ashamed of themselves.

About an hour and a quarter after the riot had begun, sixty-five highway patrolmen arrived in response to Floyd Mann's call and began clearing the area. Shortly thereafter the mounted sheriff's posse also arrived, and at that point Montgomery police finally responded in force. Even so, the mob now divided into small gangs and roamed nearby streets attacking black bystanders. One elderly black man was beaten senseless and another bashed in the face with a brick and jumped on for five minutes. Tear gas was used to disperse the mob some three hours after the riot had begun, and five hours after the beginning of the riot, order was finally restored. A total of twenty Freedom Riders, newsmen, and bystanders were injured, at least four of them quite seriously.[150]

Throughout this developing crisis, the Kennedy administration had been extremely reluctant to intervene. Both John and Robert Kennedy felt a strong political obligation to Governor Patterson, and they were loath to do anything that would put him in a bad light. Patterson had been one of the very first public figures in America to endorse Kennedy's campaign for the presidency. And Patterson's endorsement of Kennedy in June 1959— more than a year before the Los Angeles Democratic convention—had been made at considerable political cost, because as a result of it the governor had lost the support of many extreme segregationists, and of strict Baptists and Methodists who objected to Kennedy's Catholicism. In addition, as investigations of the episode subsequently revealed, Patterson had played an important role in assisting the president to stage the ill-fated Bay of Pigs invasion in Cuba only four weeks earlier. Four Alabama Air National Guardsmen had been killed in the operation. Kennedy was himself, moreover, in a rather difficult position because, at the time of the Little Rock crisis in the fall of 1957, the southern congressional leaders of his party had sharply criticized President Eisenhower's use of federal troops, and Kennedy now very much wanted to avoid using them himself so that he could retain these leaders' cooperation with his administration. But the deteriorating situation in Alabama now pushed the president toward action. The attorney general had felt that he had had a commitment from the governor to prevent violence against the Montgomery Freedom

Riders, and he felt betrayed. The attack on his deputy, Seigenthaler, also greatly upset him. Patterson, on the other hand, felt that he had done a great deal to assist the Kennedys, and that they had responded only by putting him in an untenable political position. As his fury grew, he at length refused even to receive President Kennedy's telephone calls. Eventually driven to the initiative by Patterson's refusal to cooperate, the president finally ordered the dispatch of four hundred U.S. marshals to Montgomery on the night of May 20, the day of the bus station riot.[151]

The president's decision, as it turned out, came none too soon. On the morning of May 21, Martin Luther King returned from his new home in Atlanta to his former residence to address a rally at his friend Ralph Abernathy's church, in protest against the bus station violence. As the rally got under way that evening, a mob composed primarily of white teenagers began to gather in a park across the street from the church. The newly arrived U.S. marshals formed a cordon around the church, but their position quickly became precarious. The mob set fire to a car driven by the noted British writer Jessica Mitford, apparently when she and a companion were seen going into the rally. King placed a desperate call to Attorney General Kennedy from the telephone in the church basement to tell him that a violent confrontation appeared imminent. In the meantime, the commandant of the marshals, future U.S. Supreme Court justice Byron White, informed the attorney general that his forces were losing control of the situation. That morning Commissioner Sullivan and City Attorney Calvin Whitesell had met with White and asked him to keep the marshals away from the church and leave the rally to city police. Because White had refused, police now initially left the marshals to fend for themselves. Rioters throwing bricks and rocks pressed forward to test the marshals' cordon, and tear gas fired by the marshals to drive the rioters back drifted into the church, in which some one thousand people were trapped. After about thirty minutes, state highway patrolmen and then city police arrived to assist the beleaguered marshals, and they began to try to clear the area. But the mob thereupon broke into roving bands that scattered through the surrounding streets; they overturned cars, threw rocks and bricks at passersby, and shot into at least four black families' homes. Elsewhere in the city, two homes were firebombed; one of them was the home of the white restaurant owner and former Klansman who, as we have seen, had killed an active Klansman in September 1959 in a dispute over the restaurant owner's hiring of black waiters. A jury's decision that he had acted in self-defense had outraged the city's Klan element.

President Kennedy earlier, while the attorney general was attempting to arrange state protection for the Freedom Riders during their trip from Birmingham, had asked Charles Meriwether to intervene with the governor. Meriwether, an extremely close political associate and friend of Patterson's, had been appointed three months before as one of the five directors of the Export-Import Bank, at Patterson's request. Meriwether had therefore flown to Montgomery the night before the bus station riot and had met with Patterson throughout May 20 and the morning of May 21, trying to persuade the governor to reconsider his intransigence. Meriwether's appeal was lent a personal urgency by the fact that James Atkins, the Birmingham newsman who had been one of the bus station mob's victims, was his son-in-law. These conversations had apparently caused Patterson to temper his position somewhat, and about an hour and a quarter after the second riot had begun he signed a proclamation declaring martial law in the city and calling out the National Guard. Guardsmen began arriving at the church within an hour of this proclamation, and by midnight, four hours after the commencement of the riot, they had succeeded in restoring order. At dawn the besieged congregation was finally permitted to leave the sanctuary. Seventeen white rioters were arrested during the course of the night, six of whom were undergraduates at Huntingdon College, the white Methodist liberal arts institution that had so sternly disciplined five more thoughtful students for having attended an MIA-sponsored lecture only five months earlier. The Freedom Riders, after successfully obtaining service at the white lunch counter of the Trailways terminal on May 24, were able to depart Montgomery for Jackson, Mississippi, where they were arrested and jailed without further violence.[152]

Though among the darkest days in all of Montgomery's history, the final weeks of May 1961 proved to be the great turning point in the city's struggle to emerge from the nightmare of extremist domination into which it had been plunged by the white community's response to the bus boycott. In the first place, the seriously negative national publicity the city received—and quite deservedly—as a result of its handling of the riots forced moderate white opinion back into the open for the first time since the bombings of January 1957. Business progressives voiced their fear that publicity of this kind would make more difficult their efforts to persuade northern industry to locate in the area. And even though they were ordinarily quite unsympathetic to black aspirations for racial equality, many of them showed themselves also genuinely appalled by the rioting, as they had been, as well, by the bombings four years earlier. In the second place, the adventitious succession to the presidency of the Montgomery Improvement Association of Solomon Seay, Sr.—who replaced Ralph Abernathy in December 1961, when Abernathy moved to Atlanta—gave the crucial position of civil rights leadership in the city to a man deeply committed to quiet negotiation and compromise, just as prominent moderate whites were recovering their own willingness to seek a modus vivendi. In the third place, federal authority—both in the form of the Justice Department under Robert Kennedy and in the person of U.S. District Judge Frank M. Johnson—at this same time, and in no small part directly in response to these events, began more and more to discover for itself and to reveal the extent of its capacity for coercion. As it did so, white supremacists' confidence in their power to determine the shape of race relations by themselves began to erode. Their belief that they were winning the battle gave way increasingly to sullen resignation. The interaction of these three phenomena would transform the life of the city.

The business community's response to the violence had already begun to take form on the evening of May 20, following the bus station riot of that morning. Winton M. "Red" Blount, a wealthy construction executive later to be postmaster general in the cabinet of Richard Nixon, summoned more than one hundred of the city's business and professional leaders to a meeting at the chamber of commerce. Blount and the chamber's president, Edgar W. Stuart, a gasoline distributor, attempted to persuade those present to endorse a strong condemnation of the mob's outrages. Their efforts came up against the feeling, general among whites, that the violence had occurred only because of the Freedom Riders' provocation; a heated debate therefore ensued. Eventually, however, T. B. Hill, a segregationist attorney and first cousin of U.S. senator Lister Hill, managed to draw up compromise resolutions that eighty-seven of those attending were willing to sign. The resolutions expressed resentment of the Freedom Riders, "who publicly announced their intention of coming into our community for the avowed purpose of violating our time-honored and respected laws," but continued that, despite this incitement, "we do not under any circumstances approve or condone mob action on the part of any faction, and we do hereby call upon the law enforcement agencies of our city, county and state to take all necessary action and precautions to maintain and preserve law and order in our community."

On the morning of May 22, following the second riot of the night before, the resolutions of May 20 were formally endorsed by the chamber of commerce's board of directors. And at their noon luncheons that day, the Rotary and Kiwanis Clubs also adopted the same statements. At the Rotary Club, the resolutions were offered by Blount, the club's vice-president, and adopted by the unanimous vote of the 185 members present. At the Kiwanis meeting, the resolutions were introduced by the club's president, Richard Compton, the Montgomery County Republican chairman, and their adoption was moved by insurance agent Albert Ashley; here a voice vote was taken, and though the resolutions were passed, there was audible dissent. The same day, the white Montgomery Ministerial Association adopted somewhat stronger resolutions, expressing shock and sorrow at the mob violence and calling on the community to take all steps necessary to prevent any repetition of it. On May 23, the junior chamber of commerce adopted resolutions including the specific statement that "We regret the failure of our law enforcement officials to move against Saturday's mob with sufficient speed and force to prevent violence." And on May 25 the thirty-seven members of the board of directors of the Alabama State

Chamber of Commerce—again at the urging of Blount, who was the state organization's president-elect—adopted the strongest resolutions in this series; they affirmed that all laws and court decisions, "however distasteful to any group, can and must be enforced by lawfully constituted agencies of government," and that mob violence "can never be justified, even in the face of unwarranted and extreme provocation"; they also warned that acts of violence "damage the good name of our state and create an image harmful to its best interests and its business and industrial development" and called "upon all local and state officials to preserve law and order in Alabama under all conditions and at all costs."

The *Montgomery Advertiser* lent vigorous editorial support to these efforts. On May 23, in the face of the widespread white conviction that the riots were only a predictable response to the provocative Freedom Ride, *Advertiser* editor Grover C. Hall, Jr., attacked Patterson's and Sullivan's handling of the disorders. He called Patterson the "chief author" of the city's racial troubles, and he lectured the white community that the mobs "were not duly quelled and that failure is ours alone. In fact, the mobsters were encouraged. . . . The people have got to understand that leaving matters to mobs is calamity." This editorial received the grateful praise of the black Interdenominational Ministerial Alliance. On May 28, Hall hailed the succession of resolutions against violence adopted by white community groups. In the five years since the bus boycott, he noted, "organized originators of public opinions such as civic clubs were silent and passive in the teeth of local violence. This left the field to the loud mouths and pinheads, and Montgomery's name was smutted up to an extent that may take a very long time to wash out. But at last, a week ago, the conditions here degenerated to the point of necessary shock and alarm." Though he acknowledged that the initial resolution "was guarded" because of the hesitation of "timid" and "uncertain" businessmen, "Nevertheless, the resolution was a milestone in the melancholy five-year tale of race relations blunders on the part of white leadership. It was a turning point, an assertion of leadership and intervention in the destinies of this city." And on May 31, Hall lashed out editorially at the city's more conservative social leaders, "Magnificoes of civic clubs and pillars of social rectitude," who, though they would not dream themselves of joining a mob or of letting their children do so, were nevertheless quite happy to have the thug element rough up the Freedom Riders.[153]

Of course, the power of the segregationist social leaders whom Hall thus attacked did not disappear merely because of the reemergence of the moderates from hiding. Prime examples of the sort of influential community figures who were quietly pleased that the Freedom Riders had been beaten were, indeed, Hall's own editorial colleagues at the evening *Alabama Journal,* Cassius M. Stanley and William J. Mahoney, Jr. Stanley characterized the bus station riot editorially as amounting to no more than "a dozen or so bloody noses and blacked eyes . . . inflicted upon a bunch of alien trouble makers." He described the badly mauled James Zwerg as "nutty," a man with "an obsession about associating with Negroes," and "a pariah or outcast among his own people" because of his racial views. And he ridiculed the fears of the business progressives that the riots would make industry less likely to locate in Alabama, asking if the terrible Atlanta race riot of 1906 had inhibited the industrial growth of that city. Mahoney, in his daily column, warned white Montgomerians against focusing their resentment on the rioters, who were merely responding to the Freedom Riders' provocation, rather than on the Freedom Riders themselves, "who came into this state deliberately to foment trouble, to defy the laws of this state, and to further unhinge the emotions of two peoples who had learned to live together in tolerance if not always in harmony. . . . Every decent person hates violence," he affirmed, "but once it has come, be sure of your loyalties. Be sure that, in your hatred of violence, you don't indict your own side and join the ranks of an enemy that has been showing its true colors—red and black—ever since Earl Warren's court started legislating." Both Stanley and Mahoney were enthusiastic apologists for the new John Birch Society. Montgomery became the home of the society's first Alabama chapter, chartered just two days after the riots had occurred.[154]

The view that the riots were attributable to the provocative nature of the Freedom Riders' attempts to make use of their rights was in fact so general among white Montgomerians that it was even held by the city's racially liberal federal judge, Frank Johnson. The Justice Department petitioned his court for an injunction against the Ku Klux Klan, forbidding Klansmen from interfering with interstate travel, and against the Montgomery police department, prohibiting it from failing to extend police protection to travelers through the city. Judge Johnson granted these injunctions but then, on motion of the attorneys for the city commission, added an injunction forbidding civil rights organizations from conducting further Freedom Rides into Montgomery. He lectured black leaders from the bench, telling them that they were as much responsible for the disorders as was the Klan, because they had undertaken the Rides knowing that the action would instigate violence. Though the right of interstate travel "may be one of the legal rights belonging to these individuals as citizens of the United States," he wrote in his formal opinion, "the right of the public to be protected from the evils of their conduct is a greater and more important right." So vigorous was his denunciation of the demonstrators that for a brief time Johnson actually found himself in the entirely unaccustomed position of popular hero in the eyes of white Montgomerians.[155]

Nevertheless, despite the considerable social consequence of many white supremacists and the bluster and bullying of many more, and despite an active hostility to the civil rights demonstrators that spread across the entire spectrum of white opinion, the business progressives, having at last found the courage to launch their moderate project, now vigorously pressed it. On May 22, some thirty business and professional leaders met with Mayor James for more than two hours. From this meeting dates the reintroduction into city politics of a coherent and determined white moderate voice. Thereafter, such meetings apparently continued frequently. And because of both the firm pressure from, and the new support offered by, the business progressive element, first Mayor James and Commissioner Parks, and finally even Commissioner Sullivan, gradually began to move to a less obdurate position.

The urgency felt by the moderate business leaders was rooted in their recognition of the fact that the Freedom Rider riots had focused the Justice Department's attention on the city and that the result would surely be federal suits to compel additional integration. This expectation was not long in being fulfilled. On May 29—the day martial law ended in Montgomery—Attorney General Kennedy filed with the Interstate Commerce Commission (ICC) in Washington a petition asking the commission to compel the integration of all facilities in all bus and train terminals in the United States. The ICC granted this petition on September 22, to take effect on November 1. Meanwhile, John Lewis and the other Freedom Riders who had been assaulted at the Montgomery Greyhound terminal had filed suit to integrate the facilities of the Montgomery stations in particular, and Judge Johnson ordered the integration to take effect at the same time. The Greyhound and Trailways bus stations and the train station were therefore all desegregated peacefully in November. But these stations were the property of private companies; the city's role in this desegregation was merely to keep order during the process. A more direct challenge to the city commission's willingness to cooperate with the business progressives was posed by the Justice Department's concurrent suit, filed in July on behalf of the Civil Aeronautics Board, to integrate the facilities at the Montgomery airport; this terminal was owned by the city itself. Judge Johnson granted the injunction in January 1962. City Attorney Calvin Whitesell responded by announcing initially that all of the terminal's facilities would be eliminated—concrete poured down all the toilets, the water supply shut off to all sinks and drinking fountains, all seats removed from the waiting rooms, and if blacks attempted to use it, the restaurant in the terminal closed as well. The construction of the new airport had been, as we have seen, the very first project of the Men of Montgomery, and business interests regarded it as an extremely important part of their efforts to impress visiting northern industrialists. The city commissioners therefore fell under the most demanding private importunities from the business leadership that they not carry through with

Whitesell's threat; and the next day the commissioners told the press that their attorney had been misinformed. The airport was then desegregated without incident.[156]

The quiet integration of the bus, train, and air terminals convinced one crucial audience of the business progressives' good faith: the Montgomery Improvement Association. Ralph Abernathy had caused a brief flurry in the city in August 1960, when he had renewed the MIA's commitment to sue to integrate the schools; white authorities had convened an emergency meeting to plan their response to this possibility. But then, like King before him, Abernathy had yielded to pressure to do nothing. In the fall of 1961 he had announced his intention to follow King to Atlanta, and in December he was succeeded by the substantially more accommodationist Solomon Seay, Sr. At the end of January 1962, following the business leaders' success in obtaining the desegregation of the airport, Seay dispatched a lengthy letter to prominent figures of both races, outlining the beliefs that would guide his new presidency. Montgomery, he wrote, "is the proving ground for the Christian and democratic ideals of America." It possessed "the potential leadership for peaceful progress in human relations," though in the past that leadership had been "pent-up by fear and mistrust." The path to progress was "positive, respectful, open and unmolested communication." He urged that "all difficult or strained relations in the community should be brought to a conference table for argument and reason," and pledged that he would turn to the courts or to demonstrations "only when peaceful relations have not been attainable through negotiation." Montgomery, he insisted, "is ready for peaceful progress. We have reached the saturation point in bitterness, name-calling, mob violence, and threats of riots. If the voice of the community can be discovered and brought to articulation, there are ears to listen."[157]

These were precisely the sorts of sentiments that the white business progressives wanted to hear. Acting on his faith in quiet approaches made behind the scenes, Seay on April 9 wrote to bus company manager James H. Bagley to ask if the company might now be ready to accede to the MIA's request of 1955 for the hiring of black bus drivers. There then ensued a series of meetings with officials both of the local bus company and of National City Lines, which culminated in an agreement on the part of the company to hire black drivers if the MIA on its part would support a request to the city commission for an increase in bus fares. Only after this understanding had been reached did the sides approach the city commissioners. Commissioner Sullivan vitriolically denounced the hiring of blacks, saying, according to National City Lines' regional director R. A. Hauer, that blood would run in the streets if black drivers were employed; Sullivan went on to lament his inability to revoke the bus company's franchise. Mayor James, Hauer said, joined Sullivan in this attitude. Despite the commissioners' statements, however, the company remained loyal to its agreement, and on July 6, Montgomery's first two black bus drivers, Allen Pierce and Thomas Jackson, commenced work. The commissioners initially rejected the company's petition to increase its fares, but a strike by drivers in late September and early October eventually forced them to yield. Very little of these proceedings leaked out to the public until that time.[158]

In the meantime, the strongest test yet of the white business moderates' resolution was developing. As early as April 1960, as a part of the sit-in crisis in the city, Alabama State College students had sought unsuccessfully to use Montgomery's public library. In March 1962 black high school students renewed the effort, and when they were also refused they filed suit in federal court in April to compel the integration both of the library and of the museum of fine arts, located in the same building. On August 8, Judge Johnson granted an injunction to this effect. The injunction produced a storm of controversy. Segregationist elements, led by the White Citizens' Council, demanded that the library be closed as the parks had been. They insisted, quite reasonably, that there was no logical distinction between the institutions; both were non-essential services voluntarily supplied to citizens by the city which the city could choose to discontinue if it wished. The considerable pressure on the city commission to maintain its consistency in the face of this new integrationist challenge forced the white moderates to move beyond their earlier private arguments to the commissioners and take an open stand. Led by a prominent local surgeon, Dr. T. Brannon Hubbard, Jr.—whose father had been primarily responsible for opening the state medical association to membership by black doctors in 1953—they began coming forward to call publicly for keeping the library and museum in operation. Dr. Hubbard was soon joined by another physician, Dr. Richard A. Harris, and by an official of the Alabama Baptist State Convention, the Reverend Harold L. Anderson. Faced now with equally vigorous but directly opposing appeals from their white constituents, the commissioners struggled to find a middle course. They voted to leave the library and museum open, but ordered that all tables and chairs be removed from the library so that patrons of different races would not be able to sit together. The library was then peacefully desegregated, if on a standing basis, on August 13. The commissioners' compromise made them objects of no little ridicule outside the city, but in truth it represented a substantial achievement. Not only had the moderates found the courage to face down the segregationists in public debate, but the city commissioners, despite their efforts to hide behind the library furniture, had in effect cast their lot with the moderates—and only seven months before they would be up for reelection, at that. There can be no doubt that before the events of the Freedom Rider riots and the resultant reemergence of the business progressives, the commissioners would have closed the library. In the intervening year, the city clearly had embarked upon a new course.[159]

In November, Judge Johnson entered a new order that, over the longer term, would work to guarantee that the commissioners would not retreat from this new commitment: he enjoined the county board of voting registrars from practicing racial discrimination. The Justice Department's endeavors to obtain this injunction dated back to May 1960, when Attorney General William Rogers, acting under the new Civil Rights Act of 1960, first attempted to gain access to the board's records. The board's refusal to allow its records to be examined was fought all the way to the U.S. Supreme Court. When the Justice Department finally gained access to the records in June 1961, a suit alleging the discriminatory treatment of black applicants followed in August. Justice Department figures revealed that between January 1956 and June 1961 the board had accepted 96.6 percent of white applications but had rejected 75.4 percent of black ones. By August 1961 there were 2,885 blacks registered in Montgomery County, constituting a bit less than 9 percent of the county's electorate. The suit came to trial in January 1962. In the meantime, in March 1961, Judge Johnson had granted a sweeping injunction against the board of registrars in Montgomery's eastern neighbor, Macon County, and it was being appealed. He therefore delayed ruling on the Montgomery case to see if the extraordinary terms of his Macon order would be upheld. But when the Macon injunction was affirmed by the U.S. Supreme Court, on November 20 he granted an injunction against the Montgomery board modeled on the Macon one. Thereafter the number of black registered voters began to increase rapidly. When the Alabama Supreme Court, which composed the state's voter qualification questionnaire, greatly toughened it in January 1964, Judge Johnson was compelled to issue a second injunction to forbid the use of the new questions in Montgomery. But he resisted the Justice Department's entreaties to appoint a federal voting referee for the county, and in general the board of registrars repaid his confidence. By January 1965 the number of registered blacks had grown to 7,751, about 40 percent of the total number eligible and nearly 17 percent of the county's electorate, double the percentage at the time of Johnson's initial order just over two years earlier.[160]

Judge Johnson's sweeping injunction against the board of registrars at the end of November 1962 is indicative of a subtle change that begins to be detectable in his approach to civil rights cases about the time of the Freedom Rider riots. As we have seen, Johnson had been appointed to the bench by President Eisenhower in November 1955. During the remaining years of the Eisenhower administration, though no one ever questioned Johnson's sincerity or intelligence, a series of rulings led many to regard him as the same sort of honest but diffident and unadventurous conservative as his fellow Republican, Birmingham U.S. District Judge Hobart Grooms. During the bus boycott, Johnson had refused to intervene in the city's suit to enjoin the MIA's car-pool operation, even though the circumstances of its filing in state court were beyond question a sham intended to forestall his federal court hearing that had already been set. He had affirmed Montgomery's right to close the parks, and by implication other comparable institutions, to avoid their desegregation. He had accepted the legislature's authority to alter Tuskegee's municipal boundaries in order to exclude essentially all black voters from the city, and had ruled the legislators' clear racial motives beyond his power to inquire into. The state board of education's expulsion of the Alabama State College students who had participated in the Montgomery sit-in in 1960 was simply a matter of discipline, as he saw it; no student should be able to defy with impunity academic administrators or college rules. His holding in the federal government's suit against the Macon County Board of Registrars that the Justice Department had no power under the Civil Rights Act of 1957 to sue state officials effectively gutted the act and compelled the passage of the Civil Rights Act of 1960 to restore the earlier act's force. He refused to give a directed verdict in favor of the Regal Café diners in their suit against Montgomery police, even though the charge that their private lunch constituted an action calculated to provoke a breach of the peace was, as the Fifth Circuit subsequently held, simply ludicrous. And in the Freedom Rider trial he had dismissed the Justice Department's allegations —subsequently established—of complicity by "Bull" Connor and the Birmingham police in the Klan's attack there on the CORE group of Freedom Riders; and in granting the injunction against further Montgomery Freedom Rides, he had held that the legal rights of black bus passengers had to yield to the necessity for public order. These and similar rulings in the years before 1961 had left observers substantially less than fully convinced of his commitment to the defense of the civil rights of black citizens.

Coincident with all the other changes that the Freedom Rider riots brought to Montgomery, however, there seems to have been also a change in the general attitudes of Frank Johnson. In part, no doubt, he was merely responding to alterations in the law; Earl Warren's Supreme Court was blazing many new trails in these years, and Johnson gained much new authority and responsibility as a result of the rush of Supreme Court precedents. In part, perhaps, the riots themselves, and the stark light they cast upon the depravity of authority in his city, influenced him. Certainly the violence had a profound effect on many other white moderates and liberals, as the emergence of a vigorous business progressive interest in response to it clearly indicates; and Johnson, who presided at the hearings at which much of the most disturbing evidence about these events emerged, would hardly have been immune to these same reactions. In part, it may be, he simply began to be irritated by the persistence of state and local officials' resistance, defiance, and petty subterfuges. But for whatever reason, it appears that just at this time, Frank Johnson began to move to a much harder line. The extraordinarily broad and specific injunctions that he granted against the boards of registrars in Macon, Montgomery, and surrounding counties proved only the first taste of what was to come. In future years his propensity to order all-embracing remedies and his fierce intolerance of any hint of evasion would become legendary.

It is difficult to overstate how important for the future of Montgomery was the presence of Frank Johnson. As we shall see in succeeding chapters, his conduct was very unlike that of Alabama's three other federal judges. The interminably cautious restraint of Hobart Grooms and the white supremacist paternalism of Seybourn Lynne in Birmingham, as well as the blind commitment of Daniel H. Thomas to the benevolence of the white moderate element in Selma, gradually drove blacks in those cities to a diminished faith in the federal judiciary. As their hope of gaining effective access to equal rights through judicial action within any reasonable span of time declined, their willingness to turn to direct action correspondingly grew. This process played a significant role in the eventual outbreak of demonstrations in both cities. But in Montgomery in precisely the same years, blacks' faith in judicial action was steadily increasing. The black leadership's lack of belief in the reliability of the local federal judiciary—derived in considerable part from their experience with Judge Johnson's segregationist predecessor, Judge Charles B. Kennamer, a "lily-white" Republican appointee of Herbert Hoover—had been one factor in their decision to launch the bus boycott. Just as black residents of the neighboring cities were beginning to accept the necessity for similar direct action, however, black Montgomerians were becoming more and more confident that federal court suits could transform their world. This expanding trust in the judicial process was a direct result of Judge Johnson's increasing sympathy and his growing receptivity to decrees that compelled thoroughgoing reformation.[161]

Thus, by the end of 1962, events had greatly deepened the commitment of Montgomery's black leaders to the emerging new municipal order. The business progressives had kept the airport open. Quiet negotiations with National City Lines had produced the hiring of black bus drivers, despite the opposition of the city commission. White moderates had publicly opposed the closing of the library and the art museum, and their stand had given the commissioners enough boldness to embrace the moderate position, at least in substance. And Judge Johnson had struck down racial discrimination in voter registration, in an order sufficiently forceful that it seemed likely to prove genuinely effective. The business progressives, whose actions in response to the Freedom Rider riots had initiated this train of consequences, were of course committed to the new order as well, and the attitudes Seay had brought to the MIA substantially strengthened their confidence in it. The one element whose loyalty was still rather questionable was the city commission. For bringing the commissioners on board, the municipal elections of March 1963 would prove crucial. All three commissioners had feared that their agreement to leave the library and museum open might draw strong segregationist opposition into the field, but in fact only Commissioner Sullivan ended up with a significant challenger. Mayor James faced a liberal former Folsom administration official on his left and the anti-Semitic racist Admiral Crommelin on his right; he disposed of both of them easily. Commissioner Parks had an equally painless race against a disgruntled former street maintenance supervisor. But Sullivan did indeed have to run against a man much admired in segregationist circles, former assistant police chief John B. "Jack" Rucker. As we have seen, Sullivan had elevated Rucker within the police department, at the urging of white supremacists, when Sullivan had first joined the commission, but had then demoted him as a part of the commissioner's tentative movement toward greater moderation following the Freedom Rider riots. Rucker had therefore resigned from the force in January 1963, and he now launched a vigorous campaign against his former patron—avoiding any direct reference to race, but repeatedly questioning Sullivan's emotional stability. Despite the presence of two minor candidates in the race, however, Sullivan was able, though rather narrowly, to avoid a runoff, taking 51.5 percent of the vote to Rucker's 43.7. In 1962 Sullivan had run for a position on the state public service commission on a strenuously segregationist platform, promising to oppose the implementation of the ICC's order desegregating facilities in the nation's bus stations, but he had failed to get a position in the runoff, receiving only 25 percent of the statewide vote. His lack of success in that election, along with Rucker's failure to unseat him in the municipal election a year later, apparently finally convinced him that a more temperate racial stance would better serve his interests. Therefore, during his second term on the commission he firmly embraced moderate policies and began actively cooperating with the business progressive elements. Ironically, he had overreacted. In 1967 Rucker would succeed in defeating him, erecting an incongruous but victorious coalition of extreme segregationists who resented Sullivan's new moderation and black voters who could not forgive his earlier, aggressively white supremacist positions. But for the time being the city commission now moved to accept full partnership in the new municipal arrangements that the business progressives had engineered.[162]

Immediately following the election, evidently, black leaders and business progressives began pressing the commissioners to reintegrate the police force. In April 1959 the last of the seven black officers hired under Dave Birmingham in 1954 had resigned in the wake of Sullivan's election to the commission, and blacks now wanted the process of desegregating the police department to begin again. The commissioners were at last committed to accommodating reasonable black proposals, but all three of them well remembered that the initial police desegregation had destroyed Birmingham's political career, and this particular request therefore made each of them especially nervous. Nevertheless, in August Commissioner Sullivan announced a first tentative step toward the goal, the hiring of three black policewomen to direct traffic near black public schools. When the white response to this action proved acceptable, at the end of November Sullivan took a second step, the creation of an all-black, thirty-six-member unit of the city's unpaid, volunteer reserve police force. But black leaders were not yet content, and apparently they quietly insisted on further progress. Therefore, at the beginning of December the commissioners let it be known that they were considering the reopening of the municipal park system. And six weeks later, in mid-January 1964, the commission voted to create an official biracial committee as a formal successor to the unofficial discussions that had been initiated by the business progressives at the time of the Freedom Rider riots.

The appointment of the biracial committee was regarded across the entire spectrum of opinion in Montgomery as representing a major breakthrough. Black leaders were delighted. But ironically, the action led to a crisis within the Montgomery Improvement Association. The Reverend James Bevel, an executive in the Atlanta office of the Southern Christian Leadership Conference, had developed a plan for what he called the Alabama Project, a coordinated series of demonstrations, sit-ins, and boycotts in cities and towns throughout the state designed to produce broad-based progress. Martin Luther King had embraced Bevel's proposals, and as early as October 1962 he had announced that Montgomery would serve as the project's headquarters. The substantial movement in race relations that the MIA was witnessing in Montgomery during 1962 as a result of quiet negotiations with the moderate white businessmen made Seay and the MIA leadership quite unenthusiastic about participating in any such direct-action campaign, however, and the SCLC's attention was fully absorbed in any case by the Birmingham demonstrations during the first half of 1963. Late in the year, though, the SCLC resumed pressure on the MIA to cooperate with Bevel's plans. King met with Seay and the MIA leadership in early December to urge them to accept the program. And speaking to the MIA's annual celebration of its founding at the same time, Ralph Abernathy criticized Montgomery's blacks for having become complacent, noting in particular the fact that, unlike blacks in Mobile, Birmingham, Huntsville, and Tuskegee, those in Montgomery had not yet desegregated their schools. In view of the fact that both King and Abernathy himself had ducked this challenge when they had actually headed the MIA, it was an ironic reproof. Nevertheless, Seay and the MIA leadership were indeed vulnerable to attack because, unlike the succession of advances that had characterized 1962, the year 1963 had represented something of a pause, at first because of the municipal elections early in the year and then because of the city commission's hesitation about committing itself to the reintegration of the police force. By December, all Seay really had to show was the hiring of the three black women as traffic patrol officers and the creation of the volunteer reserve police unit, distinctly modest achievements.

Very likely in large part because they recognized Seay's situation, the commissioners responded to Abernathy's speech by making their announcement about the possible reopening of the parks the very next day and pushed on to the creation of the official biracial committee in January. But in the meantime, the prodding from the SCLC had aroused within the MIA a more militant opposition to Seay and the strategy of cooperation with moderate whites that he represented. This conflict came to a head at the beginning of March 1964 as a result of King's decision to summon a meeting in Montgomery of all of the SCLC's Alabama affiliates to give formal endorsement to a redrafted version of Bevel's Alabama Project. Heading the MIA's delegation at this meeting, Seay openly dissented from some of Bevel's ideas. King, speaking directly to the Seay loyalists in the MIA, warned, "This is Montgomery's hour of truth." He favored genuine biracial negotiations, King emphasized, but of municipally appointed bodies such as the one that Montgomery had just acquired, he commented, "Too often they are window dressing committees." And Abernathy added, "Montgomery is one of the most segregated cities in the country." Nevertheless, the MIA cast a lone dissenting vote against the conference resolution which said that Montgomery would be the center of operations for the proposed statewide campaign. Seay said that so far as he knew, no Montgomery black leaders had been consulted about that arrangement; the MIA, he felt, should at least have been represented on the committee that drew up the resolutions.

This public breach between King and Seay produced escalating recriminations within the MIA's membership. In May, doubtless to demonstrate their continued aggressiveness, the MIA's executive board at long last voted to retain Fred Gray to file suit to integrate Montgomery's schools. Gray filed the suit on May 11 on behalf of longtime MIA board member Mrs. Johnnie Carr and her son Arlam. But the attacks on Seay did not diminish. Finally, unwilling to continue to suffer the constant carping, Seay resigned the presidency at the end of June. His opponents then elected as his successor the Reverend Jesse L. Douglas, pastor of the First Colored Methodist Episcopal Church in west Montgomery and the MIA's most enthusiastic advocate of Bevel's Alabama Project. Police considered him "one of the most militant local ministers."[163]

These events of course disturbed the business progressives a good deal, and particularly so because the filing of the school desegregation suit and the imminent passage by Congress of the Civil Rights Act of 1964 both portended the possibility of substantial disorder in the city in the coming months. But as the business leaders soon discovered, Douglas was a man of enormous self-importance whom attention and flattery could very easily bring around. A police report shortly after Douglas's election had actually observed that he was "very egotistical and can be very difficult in conversation where his views are opposed. He feels very strongly about his new position with the MIA. He wants to be thought of as the primary local leader, and treated as such by both whites and negroes." As members of the biracial committee emphasized to him how crucial would be his contribution to facilitating the peaceful desegregation of public accommodations and schools, and as they assured him of how sincerely they supported his desire to see the hiring of black police officers—as indeed they did—Douglas very soon was as fully committed to working with the business progressives as Seay had ever been. The following spring found him denouncing to the SCLC's Randolph Blackwell the personal conduct of SCLC staff members in Montgomery and their lack of deference toward the MIA. Such conflicts soon led Douglas to withdraw the MIA's support from Bevel's efforts, thus dooming them in the city.[164]

As Douglas was being drawn into the new municipal order, the events of the summer and fall of 1964 brought the commencement of genuine desegregation to the city. President Johnson's signing of the Civil Rights Act into law at the beginning of July led to the integration of Montgomery's theaters, restaurants, and hotels during that month. The biracial committee labored mightily to see that the process was uneventful, and it succeeded admirably in achieving that goal. At the end of the month, Judge Johnson granted an order opening the first grade and the three high school grades in white schools to black students seeking to transfer under the terms of the Alabama Pupil Placement Act. In September, three black students entered each of the city's two white high schools, and two black students began classes at one of the elementary schools. Again, the strenuous efforts of the biracial committee, the police, and the ministerial associations enabled this integration to occur entirely without incident, in sharp contrast to the situation in Birmingham and Tuskegee the year before. During July, as well, the MIA found three black applicants willing to take the civil service examination to become a patrolman in the police department. They did so without publicity that summer, and in October Montgomery hired its first black police officer in five and a half years, Hayes L. Gilmore. By that time, too, the appointment of an effective and sincere race relations officer, Lieutenant Paul Dumas, and the friendships that he had been able to develop in the black community had slowly begun to extinguish some of the vast legacy of mistrust that black Montgomerians felt for the police. In October, also, the U.S. Supreme Court at last entered a final order ending the state's lengthy battle with the NAACP, begun by former attorney general Patterson in June 1956, and the next month the Montgomery branch of the organization was reestablished, for the first time in eight and a half years. Following the peaceful desegregation of public accommodations, the schools, and the police force, the biracial committee turned its attention to the last vestige of massive resistance in Montgomery, the closed parks. Despite their announcement of December 1963, the city commissioners had taken no action on this question. But under insistent pressure from black leaders and white business progressives, the commissioners at last, on February 24, 1965, voted unanimously to reopen the seven city parks that remained, of the thirteen that the city originally had operated, for the first time in more than six years. Meanwhile, at the end of January the board of education had submitted to Judge Johnson a plan for the general desegregation of the school system over a five-year period. Much remained to be done in all of these areas, of course, but with these actions there now were no public institutions left in the city that had not commenced integration, at least on a token basis.[165]

Unfortunately for the municipal image of peaceful progress that the white business progressives had struggled so hard to build over the preceding four years, just three weeks after the reopening of the parks had marked the culmination of their efforts to liquidate massive resistance in Montgomery, one final bloody racial encounter would end the story not with cooperation but with violence. Following the brutal suppression by state and Dallas County law enforcement personnel on March 7 of an attempt by black demonstrators to begin a march from Selma to Montgomery to petition the state legislature, then in special session, to alter Alabama's voter registration laws, attorneys for the SCLC had asked Judge Johnson for an injunction to guarantee their right to make such a march. Judge Johnson had begun a hearing on this request on March 11, and while the hearing continued in the Montgomery federal courthouse, the Student Non-violent Coordinating Committee had initiated demonstrations in the city. This entire controversy was extrinsic to the life of the community, but Montgomery authorities in a sense made it their own by insisting on prohibiting any demonstration for which SNCC had failed to obtain a parade permit. SNCC asserted that such an application of the parade permit ordinance rendered it in effect a violation of the First Amendment, and though the organization did obtain permits for some of its marches—marches that police therefore duly guarded—it also staged others without a permit in order to test the city's position. On March 16, the day before Judge Johnson's hearing ended, one of these unpermitted marches, consisting of some 580 demonstrators, about a fourth of whom were out-of-state white college students, was stopped at an intersection three blocks from the capitol. As the demonstrators were standing in the intersection, SNCC's James Forman attempted to lead about eighty of them in an effort to circumvent police lines. The Montgomery County

Sheriff's Mounted Posse, a volunteer reserve group composed largely of area cattle ranchers, was ordered to stop the eighty and return them to the main group. Evidently misunderstanding the order, Sheriff Mac Sim Butler and his possemen spurred their quarter horses forward into the group of five hundred demonstrators still standing in the intersection, and the possemen began beating the demonstrators from horseback with clubs, ropes, and canes. At the end of the melee, eight of the demonstrators had to be hospitalized.

The next day, March 17—the day on which Judge Johnson issued his injunction authorizing the Selma-to-Montgomery march—Martin Luther King led a massive march of three thousand or more demonstrators to the Montgomery County Courthouse to protest the mounted posse's actions. Sheriff Butler met a delegation of the demonstration's leaders, including both King and James Forman, and personally expressed his deep regrets for the previous day's injuries. The black leaders and white authorities then began intensive negotiations in the sheriff's office that lasted until nearly midnight that night; they produced a comprehensive agreement to govern all future demonstrations in the city—an agreement that obtained the assent, albeit grudging, even of the zealous and angry Forman. The incident had revealed the intense bitterness and rancor still seething just below the surface in the city. But the authorities' subsequent handling of the episode showed clearly, too, the new level of maturity that had been forced upon them in the years since the Freedom Rider riots.[166]

The demonstrations that accompanied the Selma-to-Montgomery march constituted the last significant direct-action campaign in the city for several years. The SCLC's James Bevel attempted to prolong the demonstrations into April and May, and he did succeed in arousing the students at Alabama State College to a series of protests, but without the MIA's support his efforts were not successful in extending the demonstrations into the broader black community. That community, indeed, in the years after 1965 turned its attention primarily to an internecine contest within its own leadership. The enmity between Edgar Nixon and the working-class blacks of west Montgomery on the one hand and Rufus Lewis and the residents of the Alabama State College area on the other had always been deep, and the refounding of Montgomery's NAACP branch at the end of 1964 became the event that thrust this antagonism back into the open. Lewis and Nixon commenced a struggle for control of the branch that soon eventuated in its dividing into two completely separate and hostile branches, a west Montgomery one with Nixon as its president and an east Montgomery one dominated by Lewis's allies. Lewis also gained mastery of the city's chapter of the Alabama Democratic Conference, the principal organization of black Democrats. This competition reached its zenith in the presidential election of 1968, when Lewis and Nixon supported rival slates of electors each pledged to Hubert H. Humphrey. The poll served as a sort of referendum on the two men's claims. The electoral slate favored by Lewis, containing his young protégé Joe L. Reed, ran well only in the precinct surrounding Alabama State College, and even there it trailed the slate promoted by Nixon by a few votes. Meanwhile, Nixon's slate, including his longtime friend Virginia F. Durr, swept the west Montgomery beats by enormous margins and led Lewis's in the county at large by two to one. Despite Nixon's triumph in this contest, however, Lewis's control of the Alabama Democratic Conference and his consequent command of party patronage gradually delivered ascendancy to him in the two men's struggle. Nixon drifted into an embittered retirement, while Lewis went on to eventual election to the state legislature. But while it was going on, the engagement so engrossed black Montgomerians that it in considerable part diverted them from the continuing task of placing united pressure on local white authorities for further progress. That such progress was made was in too great a measure thanks simply to federal officials, regulations, and courts.

The relative decline of black pressure on Montgomery authorities in the years just after 1965 was significant, but even more significant was the decline—beginning after 1961, but especially after 1964—of concerted white supremacist pressure on them. And the explanation for this development is unquestionably the erosion of the segregationists' confidence that they could prevail. The Interstate Commerce Commission's order of September 22, 1961, compelling the desegregation of all bus terminals throughout the United States was the very first federal action to seek to bring integration to an entire class of institutions everywhere on a particular date. All of the previous decisions of the Supreme Court, despite their more general implications, had actually integrated only the specific institutions party to the suits; segregationists therefore ordinarily saw no change at all in the patterns of daily life in their communities. The ICC order was by no means universally effective; there was defiance of it in many towns, particularly in the lower South states. Indeed, recalcitrance in Albany, Georgia, generated the next great explosion of the national civil rights movement; when blacks testing whether the Albany bus and train stations were complying with the order were arrested by local authorities in late 1961, civil rights activists began the demonstrations there that would continue throughout much of 1962. Despite such municipal opposition, however, the Justice Department moved aggressively to enforce the directive, and most cities soon complied. The ICC order, therefore, constitutes the first real blow to the segregationists' belief that they were winning the battle; it was the first clear evidence that integration inevitably held the initiative, that the federal government had, if it would but use, the weapons with which to overwhelm the segregationists' defenses. The increasingly widespread entry of federal court injunctions in response to suits proliferating across the South during 1962 and 1963, along with increasingly energetic efforts by federal executive agencies at the same time, encouraged the growth of this realization. And the passage of the Civil Rights Act of 1964, leading to the massive desegregation of the whole range of public accommodations within a period of weeks during July of that year—and with only quite scattered municipal resistance, virtually all of which had crumbled by year's end—made the conclusion almost impossible to avoid.

This process of discovery, which Montgomery's segregationists shared with white supremacists throughout the region, was conjoined in the city with the renewed willingness of Montgomery's white moderates following the Freedom Rider riots of 1961 to speak out and to urge less obdurate attitudes and actions upon the city commissioners. This reemergence of the moderates was so important because it deprived the uncompromising enemies of integration of their essential comforting myth, that they spoke for an undivided white community. The Freedom Rider riots, then, appear in retrospect to have been an authentic turning point in the city's life, because they constituted, both as a result of the revivification of the white moderate constituency and as a result of the breadth of the ICC order, the beginning of the process by which, eventually, the segregationists were convinced that continued resistance was useless. The increasing zeal with which the federal government sought to advance the cause of civil rights, and the growing willingness of the local politicians to respond to the new ad hoc alliance of business progressives and black leaders, began relentlessly to deprive the segregationists of the sense that the tide of events was flowing their way. Divested of its intellectual and perceptual supports, their intransigence turned gradually but ineluctably to resignation.[167]

Birmingham

3

The declining power of the Gunter machine was, as we have just seen, a crucial factor in inducing Montgomery's black leadership to believe that their world was capable of being changed. And as we shall discover when we turn our attention to Selma, the defeat of the intransigent Burns-Heinz machine there played a comparable role in the transformation of that city. Birmingham, however, had no such municipal machine. What it had, instead, was a subtler web of local power that linked together disparate—and formerly, and always potentially, inimical—white elements in a racially based alliance whose increasing contradictions in the early 1960s would have a similar effect among Birmingham's leading blacks.[1] Formed in the municipal election of 1937, this alliance knit together unionized white labor and the corporate executives for whom they worked in support of municipal politicians committed to the defense of various interests that seemed essential to each. The alliance was strictly a marriage of convenience, but for black citizens it was no less malignant for being incongruous. Nevertheless, it was always unstable, and as its instability became increasingly apparent to black observers, the rivalry between two hostile factions of the black leadership over how best to exploit its internal tensions in order to bring it down would eventually plunge the city into crisis. That is the tale which this chapter will tell. But first we must describe the factors that brought the alliance into being.

I. The Origins of the White Alliance

The central figure in initiating the complex historical process that we are about to explore is T. Eugene "Bull" Connor, Birmingham's commissioner of public safety from 1937 to 1953 and again from 1957 to 1963. Born in Selma in 1897, Connor had a rather knockabout childhood. His mother died when he was only eight, and thereafter Connor and his four younger brothers trailed after their father, a railroad dispatcher, as he was trans-

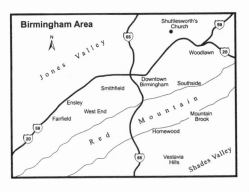

Downtown Birmingham

1. Gaston Motel
2. 16th Street Baptist Church
3. Kelly Ingram Park
4. Greyhound Bus Station
5. Chamber of Commerce
6. City Hall
7. Municipal Auditorium
8. Jefferson County Courthouse
9. Public Library
10. Phillips High School
11. Trailways Bus Station
12. Loveman's Department Store
13. Pizitz Department Store
14. First National Bank Building

ferred from job to job. Connor claimed to have lived in thirty-six states. As a result of the frequent moves, Connor's schooling suffered; he never completed high school, though his father did manage to teach him how to operate a telegraph. During these years his principal source of stability was his late mother's family, whom he would visit in the summers in their hometown of Plantersville, a tiny community in the Black Belt, just to the north of Selma. There in 1916 he met his future wife, and they were married in 1920. In 1922 the young couple moved to Birmingham, Alabama's booming industrial metropolis, where as a result of Connor's knowledge of telegraphy he was hired by a radio station to receive telegraphic reports of the play-by-play action during out-of-town games of the city's white professional baseball team, the Birmingham Barons, and to broadcast them as if he were actually witnessing the contest. Connor, with his booming voice and easy joviality, became an instant celebrity. By 1932 the *Sporting News* called him one of the most popular sportscasters in the South.[2]

In 1934 Connor sought to test his popularity by becoming a candidate for the state legislature, and he was elected without much difficulty as one of Jefferson County's seven state representatives. In the legislature, Connor became a leading opponent of the Bibb Graves administration's ultimately successful efforts to enact Alabama's first general sales tax. This stand gained him the gratitude of many voters reduced to penury by the Depression. And during the referendum campaign in 1935 on the repeal of statewide prohibition and the conversion to a local-option system, he served as the Jefferson County campaign manager for the "wet" forces. But it was a piece of local legislation enacted in that same year which would have the largest implications for his future career. The background of this legislation requires an excursion into the labyrinths of interwar Birmingham politics.

Birmingham's mayor during the Depression, James M. Jones, had begun his career as a protégé of the virulently anti-Catholic mayor Nathaniel Barrett, who owed his election in 1917 to the emerging Ku Klux Klan element in the city. Barrett had appointed Jones as city comptroller, but when Barrett was defeated in 1921 by an alliance of organized labor and the Klan—the latter of whom Barrett had subsequently disappointed by his surprising independence—Jones lost his office. Seeking to return to the public payroll, Jones himself entered the race for mayor in 1925. He received the endorsement of the Klan, whose fifteen thousand or more members in Jefferson County in the mid-1920s made it one of the most significant forces in local politics. But the presence in the race of incumbent city commissioner William L. Harrison, a former state president of the American Federation of Labor, divided the blue-collar vote, and after the first round of balloting the candidate supported by corporate interests, druggist W. J. "Jack" Adams, was far in the lead. In the runoff, however,

Jones consolidated the union and Klan vote and defeated Adams by a narrow margin. He was joined on the commission by John H. Taylor, also a former associate of Barrett's and an active Klansman. But the third commissioner, incumbent William E. Dickson, who had been reelected, had had the support of the corporations.

After its defeat in the presidential election of 1928 the Klan rapidly declined in numbers and influence in Birmingham, leaving the corporations and the unions as the principal rivals in local politics. Forced in effect to choose between these powers, Jones and Taylor increasingly followed Dickson in doing the corporations' bidding. In 1929, therefore, when Adams and Jones again ran against each other for mayor, the endorsements switched; Adams now had the support of the unions and Jones of the corporations, together with the remnant of the Klan. Taylor had the backing of the same alliance that supported Jones, and all three incumbent commissioners were easily returned to office. By 1933, however, as a result of the desperation brought upon the city by the Depression, the hand of the unions had been greatly strengthened. Jones continued to have significant blue-collar support, and with vigorous corporate backing organized by his campaign manager, conservative attorney and future governor Frank M. Dixon, he managed to defeat the labor-endorsed Cleon Rogers. But his commission colleagues Taylor and Dickson were not so fortunate. After a bitter campaign, they were defeated by the unions' candidates, former sheriff and Klan leader William O. Downs and state representative and newspaper reporter Lewey Robinson.

Both Downs and Robinson had had the backing of former and future governor Bibb Graves, a pro-labor New Dealer and former Klan cyclops, and Graves's Jefferson County patronage boss, the vitriolically racist former Klansman Horace Wilkinson. With Wilkinson's active cooperation, Downs and Robinson at once began replacing city officeholders with persons supported by Graves and organized labor. When the two associate commissioners combined their votes to order the firing of Mayor Jones's own appointees in the various city departments under Jones's direct administrative control, however, they had gone too far. Jones at this point appealed to the county's state legislative delegation for the passage of civil service legislation that would end his commission colleagues' raids on his patronage.

Jefferson County's state senator, James A. Simpson, was a wealthy corporate lawyer, reputedly with no fewer than 135 corporations among his clients, and a political opponent of Graves's. Simpson had, moreover, spent a part of his youth in a socialist commune, and the experience had left him with a profound enmity toward anything that smacked of socialism. Deeply hostile to the efforts of Downs and Robinson to give their pro-union allies control of Birmingham's bureaucracy, he readily agreed to support the idea of a civil service system for the county's public employees. At a meeting in his office, he succeeded in arranging the support of his House colleagues as well. But the incoming Graves administration was just as inimical to Jones, Simpson, and the captains of industry with whom Simpson was associated—for whom Governor Graves had coined the derisive label "the Big Mules"—as they were to him. Though opposition in the Alabama legislature to local legislation that had the unanimous support of the members representing the county involved was virtually unheard of, nevertheless when the civil service bill came to the House floor the administration had an amendment offered that would require the approval of the new system by the voters of Jefferson County in a referendum before the bill could take effect. In the effort to defeat this hostile administration maneuver, Senator Simpson had to depend upon the bill's House floor manager, "Bull" Connor. Connor's efforts were successful; the administration amendment was tabled, fifty-one to forty, and the bill was passed.

Out of this encounter grew a devoted, lifelong friendship between Simpson, the rich and cultivated attorney, and Connor, the boorish high school dropout and baseball announcer. Though they moved in very different circles, the two men formed the complementary halves of a political alliance that could draw white Birmingham together across its tense class divisions. With Simpson's guidance and support, Connor at once began to contemplate a race for the city commission in 1937. For Simpson it represented a way to complete the purge of Commissioners Downs and Robinson, whom his civil service bill had now deprived of control of city patronage. For Connor it represented, unlike the part-time position of state representative, a full-time, well-paying job.

The contest for the two associate commissionerships drew eight candidates. Downs and Robinson sought reelection, and one of the Jones allies whom they had defeated in 1933, John H. Taylor, sought to return to power. Connor's opponents denounced the sportscaster, with much justice, as a "jumping jack" of "Jim Simpson, the corporation lawyer," and the favorite candidate of the conservative, anti-Prohibition *Birmingham News* and other business interests. In the meantime, however, Robinson and Downs had been badly damaged when their appointees, whose selection had produced the civil service act, became the targets of a grand jury investigation of graft in the purchase of fire hose. The grand jury's report strongly condemned the two commissioners' conduct in office. Connor, as the ostensible champion of an honest, patronage-free administration of municipal affairs, led the field into the four-man runoff. Commissioner Downs was eliminated in the first round of voting; Commissioner Robinson and former commissioner Taylor faced the two candidates in the race with the least prior contact with city politics, Connor and radio store owner James Morgan. Morgan, a popular young businessman, had finished fifth in the 1933 primary, just behind the four politicians who had contested the runoff in that year, but he had never before held office. In a repudiation of the finagling and squabbling that had characterized Birmingham political life for the preceding two decades, the voters chose Connor and Morgan. Meanwhile, Mayor Jones, depicting himself as the man who had exposed the corruption of his two commission colleagues, was reelected by an overwhelming margin.[3]

The election of 1937 was a turning point in the city's political history. After rather rapid turnover in the personnel of the city commission in the twenty years following 1917, both Morgan and Connor would serve as commissioners for a quarter century. Indeed, the story we are about to tell is framed by two critical municipal elections, those of 1937 and 1963, each of which in retrospect appears to have marked a reorientation of political conflict in Birmingham. The quick sketch of city politics between 1917 and 1937 that we have already offered does not appear at first glance to reflect much in the way of dramatic moral or social conflict: the oscillations in the bestowing and withdrawal of the Klan's, the unions', and industry's endorsements seem sometimes quite fickle; the actual material of electoral controversy, such as the patronage brawl between Jones and his colleagues and the investigation of fire hose graft, has a certain comic-opera quality to it. But if we pause to explore the social bases underlying the political feuds, then the significance of the 1937 readjustment begins to emerge—a significance that will also considerably clarify the parallel readjustment of 1963.

In the Birmingham of the 1880s and 1890s, whose industry was dominated by wrought- and cast-iron foundries, highly skilled craftsmen were at the heart of the production process and their unions were very powerful. The racial division of labor was stark; the skilled craftsmen were all white, and the unskilled workers, with few exceptions, were black and unorganized. But the introduction of steel mills in the city at the turn of the century began to undercut the positions both of the skilled craftsmen and of the unskilled workers. Because the production of steel was more fully mechanized than was the making of cast and wrought iron, there was a greater demand for semiskilled as opposed to unskilled labor, and at the same time workers could more readily be trained in the skills the production process required. With their skills now not nearly so arcane, the craftsmen found themselves replaceable with much less difficulty, and the foundations of their unions' earlier power began rapidly to erode. Beginning in the summer of 1903, Birmingham's steel companies commenced a vigorous concerted effort to eliminate union authority from their mills and to make Birmingham—at least in its heavy industry—an open-shop city. Within a decade this campaign had essentially triumphed in the mills and mines. But its success rested upon an implicit compromise.

The greater demand for semiskilled workers might in large part have been satisfied by training the many black unskilled laborers for the new positions; and with the skills of the craftsmen no longer so difficult to master, black semiskilled workers might similarly have been—indeed, in the normal course of things, would have been—trained to move into the ranks of the skilled. The racial exclusivity of the craftsmen, enforced in the late nineteenth century by the necessity for admission to lengthy apprenticeships and fiercely defended by the craft unions, was therefore threatened by the unions' destruction, at just the time when the skilled positions were in practice more easily accessible than ever before. The companies moved to meet this strong argument for the unions' retention by instituting the racial designation of jobs. By the time of World War I, as a result, Birmingham's heavy industries universally and energetically enforced an explicit policy of racial discrimination in hiring and promotion. With management's personnel policies defending the skilled occupations from the introduction of blacks, the corporations and the craftsmen thus in effect arrived at a modus vivendi that made the unions seem less essential.[4]

Throughout the 1910s and 1920s, Birmingham's heavy industries continued their uncompromising opposition to the unionization of the labor force. But the Depression and the New Deal placed this policy on the defensive. The National Industrial Recovery Act of 1933 (NIRA) and, when it was declared unconstitutional by the Supreme Court, the subsequently enacted National Labor Relations Act of 1935 (NLRA) both contained provisions offering federal auspices to union organizational efforts. Under the aegis of the NIRA, the United Mine Workers made great strides in organizing the coal miners during 1933–34, and the result was a series of strikes in the mines during 1934. After the passage of the NLRA, two unions affiliated with the Congress of Industrial Organizations began encountering success. The Mine, Mill and Smelter Workers' Union sought to organize the iron ore miners, some three-fourths of whom were black, and the Steel Workers' Organizing Committee, later to be called the United Steelworkers, attempted to win the allegiance of workers in the iron and steel mills. The frightened industrialists responded forcefully, and something like a reign of terror settled over Birmingham during 1935 and 1936.[5]

The response of the industrialists coupled physical intimidation of CIO organizers and union members with strenuous warnings of Communist influence within the CIO unions. And the chief threat posed by Communism, in the industrialists' propaganda, was the Communist advocacy of racial equality. The industrialists' case contained many elements of truth. There was indeed a very active Communist organization in Birmingham during this period—the city was the party's southeastern headquarters—and the Communists were militantly committed to civil rights for blacks, just as the industrialists said. Moreover, it is likely that most of the CIO organizers were radicals and, in quite a number of cases, Communists. The locals that the Steelworkers were forming were in fact biracial, if virtually always led by whites. And the direction of the heavily black Mine Mill union was substantially in Communist hands.[6] For the industrialists, of course, the emphasis upon these realities constituted, in considerable measure, a red herring. They were much less concerned with the threat of racial integration than with the threat posed by the rise of industrial unions to their precarious profit margins at a time when they could ill afford increased labor costs. But for a large part of Birmingham's white blue-collar population—in particular, for craftsmen and skilled workers and for whites who wished to become skilled workers—the industrialists' propaganda, and the truth that lay behind it, pointed to very frightening developments.

When it moved to an open shop, heavy industry had not only taken on the task of defending the racial exclusivity of skilled positions but had instituted general social welfare programs and upgraded company housing. In particular, Tennessee Coal and Iron, the Birmingham division of United States Steel, had adopted generous medical, educational and housing benefits.[7] But when the Depression hit, such programs very soon were among its casualties. Company schools were turned over to public authorities. Company housing increasingly became a thing of the past. After 1933, relief became exclusively a governmental function. Despite the energetic efforts of local social workers, dislocation and desperation were widespread.[8] In these circumstances, skilled workers joined semiskilled and unskilled workers of both races in seeking to regain through the new unions the security they had lost. During the organizing drives of the mid-1930s, biracial cooperation was the rule. In a portent of what was to come, however, blacks in virtually all of the Mine Workers' and Mine Mill locals were carefully limited to the subordinate offices of vice-president and recording secretary, and in the Steelworkers' locals they were almost everywhere excluded from office completely. For the truth was that an important element of the security that skilled workers in the mills and mines sought to recover was the racial circumscription of their occupations. In Birmingham's segregated world, the restriction of their jobs to whites represented for them the preservation of a status comparable to that held by AFL craftsmen in other sectors of the city's economy in which the AFL unions had remained powerful throughout these decades, such as the building trades, the railroad yards, and printing. It was a status that company personnel policies had generally accorded workers in heavy industry earlier in the century. But in the 1920s, with the open shop established in the mills and mines, the companies had begun to admit some blacks to semiskilled positions, an action that white skilled workers feared might be an omen of future betrayal. And by the 1930s, in any case, corporate protection had failed workers in all areas of their lives. Workers of every skill level and of both races thus hoped to use the unions to compel their own future protection. One component of that protection in the minds of skilled workers and of white semiskilled workers who aspired to these specialties, however, was racial.

In the late 1930s and early 1940s, therefore, when the organizing drives had ended successfully, the white skilled workers in heavy industry began to exercise their leadership—despite the membership and alleged brotherhood of blacks in the industrial unions, and contrary to the ideals of many of the CIO organizers—to guarantee white supremacy in the workplace. The Steelworkers' locals, usually with white majorities, were particularly aggressive, negotiating contracts that established racially segregated promotion and seniority ladders. In mills where the racial composition of the workforce made the acceptance of such discriminatory contracts unlikely, white skilled workers affiliated with AFL craft unions and closed their positions against the black semiskilled laborers, who were left to the Steelworkers. The leaders of the Mine Workers' locals, less overtly, allowed the introduction of improved technology in the coal mines to eliminate the jobs of a far greater number of black members while arranging for the retraining of many more whites. And among the iron ore miners, the companies, frightened by the radicalism of the Mine Mill union that had organized them, simply stopped hiring blacks until the ratio of white workers had advanced sufficiently that, in 1948, the Steelworkers—assisted by Klan intimidation—were able to replace Mine Mill in a certification election. Thereafter the Steelworkers began to introduce the same sort of segregation in the iron ore locals that they had earlier accepted in the mills.

The unionization of Birmingham's heavy industry—together with the willing cooperation of management—thus gave the city's white skilled workers a powerful new tool to enforce racial privilege. With skilled positions effectively closed to blacks, the development of increasingly sophisticated machinery, which eliminated the unskilled jobs that were in large part filled by blacks while sparing proportionately more of the semiskilled and skilled white classifications, necessarily had the result everywhere that we have already noted in the coal mines: the percentage of blacks in the heavy industrial labor force began an inexorable decline. In the coal mines, 62 percent of the workers were black in 1930 but only 47 percent in 1950. In the iron ore mines, in conjunction with the companies' exclusionary hiring policies intended to weaken the Mine Mill union, the percentage of blacks fell from 70 percent in 1930 to 49 percent in 1950. And in the steel mills, it fell from 47 percent to 37 percent in the same period. It continued to fall through the 1950s, to 32 percent in the steel mills and to 39 percent in the coal mines in 1960.[9]

The attitudes of Birmingham's white workers and employers that underlay the racial practices in the city's shops and factories were embedded within a political culture that constitutes the next step in understanding the significance of the 1937 municipal election.[10] The commitments of blue-collar white Protestants grouped together a distrust of corporations and a hostility to their economic power on the one hand and a profound social conservatism, rooted in fundamentalist religion, on the other. Their social conservatism expressed itself in an enthusiasm for Prohibition and an abhorrence of the moral and sexual emancipation and intellectual cynicism of the post–World War I era; in aggressive anti-Catholicism, exacerbated both by their fundamentalist Protestantism and by their resentment of the competition of southern European immigrants for jobs in the city's factories; in a rather less overt anti-Semitism, which was connected with their enmity toward corporations; and in an uncompromising antipathy toward any manifestation of racial equality. The willingness of workers in the CIO unions to participate in biracial locals did not ordinarily represent a repudiation of this last commitment but merely a toleration of interracial contact in the interests of achieving mutually beneficial economic goals. White Protestant workers' beliefs thus conjoined what outside the South would have been thought economically liberal (verging even on radical) and socially conservative (indeed, distinctly reactionary) convictions. Upper-class whites, similarly, generally linked a commitment to religious toleration, a rejection of Prohibition, and an acceptance of a degree of free-thinking with a deep faith in corporate leadership and a belief in business growth as the great engine of social progress. They condemned the Klan's bigotry and were horrified by its night-rider floggings, but they beheld with near equanimity the comparable violence of corporation thugs directed against union organizers. They abhorred and feared the evidence of workers' economic radicalism. Upper-class whites, nevertheless, did share with their lower-middle-class and working-class white brethren real animosity toward racial integration. They differed on this score only in that some among them, the racially moderate business progressives, did hope to see greater material and institutional improvements in the black community, within the framework of continued segregation. But racial moderation was by no means the general attitude of upper-class whites in the Birmingham district; probably a majority of them were as aggressively committed to white supremacy as were any of their white employees.

The annexation in 1910 of the numerous small company towns surrounding the central city, an action that had more than quadrupled Birmingham's land area and almost quadrupled its population, had transformed municipal politics by giving the city a clear blue-collar electoral majority.[11] The implications of this development first became fully apparent in 1917 when the anti-Catholic nativist Nathaniel Barrett, who had formerly been the mayor of one of the annexed working-class communities, East Lake, defeated the incumbent mayor George B. Ward, patrician investment banker and Episcopalian.[12] Thereafter, as we have seen, political success for the next decade turned upon obtaining the endorsements of the Klan and of the AFL crafts unions that remained dominant in sectors of the economy other than heavy industry, particularly in the building trades; these endorsements spoke to the two halves of blue-collar attitudes, and when they were successfully united, corporate opposition could seldom stand against them. But the decline of the Klan after 1928 and the introduction of CIO competition with the AFL unions after 1933 created a period of instability in the working-class electorate's system of loyalties. The white nativist sentiment organized by the Klan had stretched far beyond the membership of the unions to include non-union workers as well as shopkeepers and professionals. Once the Klan's power had waned, the AFL unions alone could not effectively anoint a particular candidate as the champion of the blue-collar commitments and prejudices that the Klan and the unions together had been able to embody. Corporate influence began to reassert itself. Thus, Mayor James Jones, with his long history of anti-Catholic and anti-black attitudes, was able to achieve reelection in 1929 and 1933 despite the fact that his actions in the late 1920s and early 1930s had offended organized labor; Jones displayed both his accomplishments and his prejudices to the satisfaction of his constituency, and the unions' disapprobation now lacked the broad social authority that their alliance with the Klan earlier would have given it.

The coming of the CIO to Birmingham, similarly, confused labor's political voice for a time. No election showed this difficulty more clearly than did the race for Jefferson County's seat in the U.S. House of Representatives in 1936. George Huddleston, Sr., had represented the county in Congress since 1915 and had long been a favorite of the AFL crafts unions. With the onset of the Depression, he supported much relief legislation, but his opposition to certain New Deal measures, in particular the Guffey Coal Act, drew into the race against him in 1936 Luther Patrick, a personable young attorney who was an ardent New Dealer. Patrick's liberalism was of the sort more common outside the South, because it coupled social with economic progressivism. He received the support of the new CIO unions, under the urging of the United Mine Workers' William Mitch and other labor officials who were in Birmingham as the representatives of national labor organizations. But the leadership of the local AFL craft unions joined the corporate executives and other businessmen in rallying to Huddleston, and AFL spokesmen echoed the corporations in warning that the CIO's biracialism and radicalism, which they associated with Patrick, threatened to bring racial equality to the region. The AFL's Birmingham general counsel, John W. Altman, thundered, "Organized Labor in Alabama will not tolerate social equality between the whites and the blacks as advocated by the Communists. . . . It will be the ruination of Organized Labor if carried into effect." Despite such rhetoric, however, in the runoff between them, Patrick, receiving strong support in all the blue-collar neighborhoods, defeated Huddleston by a margin of 59 percent to 41 percent.[13]

In retrospect, it seems clear that workers' enthusiasm for Patrick proceeded from their economic distress and their faith in the New Deal rather than from any real openness to new social relationships. But at the time, Patrick's victory badly frightened segregationists such as Altman and the many white Birminghamians, whether craftsmen, tradesmen, or professionals, who shared his views. And Patrick's economic policies were quite enough alone to disturb the city's industrialists and their allies, already deeply alarmed by the CIO's organizing drive. It was in this context that "Bull" Connor came to power in 1937, and understanding it allows us to perceive the foundations of Connor's subsequent political success.

Connor's initial election to the city commission did not seem to portend his repeated later electoral triumphs. He was the candidate of the business interests in a city with a blue-collar majority, and his victory rested largely on temporary voter dissatisfaction with a particular episode of municipal corruption. But both Mayor Jones, whom Connor joined on the city commission, and Connor's political patron Senator Simpson offered models in his effort to define a more permanent constituency. Simpson was a thoroughgoing racist who would wage viciously Negrophobic, though unsuccessful, campaigns for the U.S. Senate in 1944 and 1946. Throughout his career, Connor could call upon Simpson to draft, justify, and defend segregation ordinances.[14] But far more importantly, Simpson provided the haphazardly educated Connor the confirmation that a quite intelligent, widely admired attorney and cultivated social leader shared his own prejudices and had no hesitation in affirming their cogency. Simpson's friendship validated and strengthened Connor's white supremacist instincts, and Simpson's advice turned them into municipal policy.

It was James M. Jones, however, whose career indicated the path to Connor's future. Jones's exploitation of religious and racial bigotry had aided him in retaining the loyalty of a blue-collar electorate despite his increasingly pro-business policies. His honest, efficient, and perhaps excessively economical administration of the city departments under his jurisdiction had had general appeal in business circles, but particularly so among small shopkeepers and less well-to-do citizens who could ill afford higher taxes.[15] When Jones died in 1940, Connor in effect inherited his constituency. Efficient administration was utterly beyond Connor; the grand jury that impeached him in 1952 described him accurately as "explosive, vindictive against those employees under his authority who disagree with him, given to jumping at conclusions, dictatorial, immoral, autocratic, and a failure as an executive," who "cracks the whip of authority, but uses no persuasion, logic or reason, if any he has."[16] But though corporate and business interests had unquestionably been behind his initial election to the city commission, from the very outset Connor—a resident of the lower-middle-class east Birmingham neighborhood of Woodlawn and a former member of the Typographical Union—labored to endear himself to blue-collar voters.

Despite his background as a leading advocate of the repeal of Prohibition in 1935, Connor effectively identified himself with fundamentalist righteousness by staging well-publicized crusades against professional gamblers and prostitutes. He thus sought to depict himself as the city's principal champion of public morality. He strongly opposed any tax increases. His campaign against Communists and other radicals among the CIO organizers pleased not only the corporate executives associated with his mentor Simpson, but the AFL crafts unions and many of the skilled workers and white semiskilled workers in the CIO locals themselves. And intertwined in his own mind with his crackdown on Communists was his vigorous and unremitting enforcement of racial segregation.

In November 1938, only a year after he had taken office, Connor gained considerable notoriety for invading the founding convention of the Southern Conference for Human Welfare, attended by Eleanor Roosevelt and many other dignitaries, to compel white and black delegates to sit on opposite sides of the auditorium. A decade later, in the spring of 1948, he ordered the arrest and prosecution of Senator Glen Taylor of Idaho, the Progressive vice-presidential nominee, for entering the convention of the Southern Negro Youth Congress through an entrance that police had marked "colored." These performances gained attention in the national press because their victims were so prominent, but more significant in building his reputation in Birmingham were the constant arrests and harassment that filled the intervening ten years. In response to increasing black ridership on city buses, Connor in the early 1940s forced the installation of "race boards," movable panels that effectively divided the white and black sections into separate compartments. He developed an extensive network of informers to keep him posted on the efforts of black activists and white liberals. And of course his well-known attitudes permeated the police department, as he promoted those policemen whose segregationist zeal and personal subservience satisfied him, and ambitious officers therefore sought to curry his favor by appealing to his prejudices.

In the summer of 1942, shortly after the federal Fair Employment Practices Committee had held hearings in Birmingham, Connor dispatched a letter to President Franklin D. Roosevelt to inform him, "Your N.Y.A. [National Youth Administration] has preached social equality and stirred up strife. The United States Employment Service and the Fair Employment Practices Committee are causing plenty of trouble when there ought to be unity. . . . When the downfall of the doctrine of white supremacy is advocated and taught by agitators and federal officials, who know absolutely nothing about the Negro problem in the South, what happens? Negroes become impudent, unruly, arrogant, law breaking, violent and insolent. Any effort now by any person connected with the federal government officially or socially, to destroy segregation and bring about amalgamation of the races will hinder the Southland in its war efforts, revive organizations like the Ku Klux Klan, which I never joined, and result in lawlessness, disunity and probable bloodshed." Two years later, he again wrote the president with the blunt accusation, "If there is terror, bloodshed and calamity in this state, it will be your fault."

In the summer of 1948, Connor, waving the Confederate battle flag from side to side, led the walkout of the southern delegations from the Democratic National Convention in Philadelphia, in protest against its adoption of an advanced civil rights plank in its platform. And a week later, in the same Birmingham municipal auditorium in which he had disciplined the Southern Conference for Human Welfare in 1938, he played a prominent role in the first and last convention of the Dixiecrats. By that time his hold upon his white blue-collar constituency appeared unshakable. He had been reelected to the city commission twice, in 1941 and 1945, on each occasion by a decisive margin. And the next year he would be returned, equally easily, to his fourth term.[17]

In the meantime, public officials and the white press were for the first time being forced to confront the stirrings of civil rights activism among the city's blacks, primarily because the black community, for the first time in the twentieth century, had gained a lawyer. Arthur D. Shores was born in Birmingham in 1904, the son of a building contractor, and was educated in the black public schools. In 1927 he graduated from Talladega College, the black institution maintained in Alabama as a missionary enterprise by northern white Congregationalists. Thereafter he began a career as a public school teacher, eventually becoming the principal of Dunbar High School in Bessemer. In the meantime, however, he decided to undertake the study of law. Enrolling at the University of Kansas, he attended classes in the summers and finished other courses on a correspondence basis. With considerable struggle he obtained his law degree in 1934, and apparently after several attempts, he was admitted to the Alabama bar in 1937. He thereupon resigned his position as high school principal and commenced law practice on a full-time basis, as the state's only black attorney. The implications of blacks' now for the first time having a lawyer willing to challenge white supremacy were not long in being felt.

In 1939, Shores—in one of the first actions of its kind in the state—sought to use the Alabama Constitution's provision allowing an applicant refused the right to register to vote by a board of registrars to appeal to state circuit court. He filed an appeal in behalf of five rejected Birmingham blacks, and the Jefferson County Board of Registrars, in order to avoid the suit, promptly registered them. The next year, however, when additional applicants were rejected, Shores appealed again. This time the board fought the case to the state supreme court. There, in an ominous defeat for black rights, a closely divided court ruled three to two, with a sixth justice concurring only in the result, that courts were bound to assume the validity of decisions by boards of registrars and that applicants who appealed these decisions therefore bore the full burden of proof. This decision made all subsequent appeals through the state courts extremely difficult. In the fall of 1942, Shores challenged the board's procedures in federal court, but again he was unsuccessful. The preceding spring, Shores himself filed to run in the Democratic primary for the state house of representatives, but the county Democratic Executive Committee refused to permit his candidacy on the grounds that it violated the party's white primary rule. In the meantime, he was arguing in federal court a suit that he had filed in 1941, striking at the very heart of Birmingham blue-collar whites' racial fears. It contested the legality of a railroad labor contract under which the railroad and the union had agreed to exclude blacks from the job of locomotive fireman. In 1944, Shores—opposed by James Simpson—won a landmark ruling from the U.S. Supreme Court that such explicit contractual discrimination was a violation of the Railway Labor Act. Though a great victory, the decision did not forbid the union on its own to deny blacks membership; nevertheless, it badly frightened the city's white skilled workers. In April 1945, Shores won another, comparable victory when the federal district court ordered the Jefferson County Board of Education to equalize the salaries of its black and white teachers, at the time grossly disparate. In the years just after World War II, Shores, with the support of the Birmingham branch of the NAACP, pressed on with these efforts, seeking a contempt citation against the board of education in the salary equalization case; appealing additional registration denials to the state supreme court, again futilely, in 1946; challenging racial zoning ordinances; and in a Mobile case, together with other attorneys, winning from the U.S. Supreme Court in 1949 a ruling that the state's Boswell Amendment—requiring applicants to satisfy the board of registrars that they understood an article of the U.S. Constitution—was a violation of that Constitution. Though Shores was by no means always victorious in these years, his activities did serve constantly to remind the city's whites that blacks were now learning to use the tools with which to undermine the foundations of legal discrimination.[18]

Against this background, the significance of the 1937 municipal election becomes clear. During the twenty years after Nathaniel Barrett's defeat of George B. Ward in 1917, Birmingham's white working class was struggling to find an autonomous political voice. This search underlay the political instability of the two decades. In the 1920s the Ku Klux Klan effectively organized the blue-collar vote, and the Klan's de facto alliance with the craft unions in municipal politics held out the prospect of realizing at least some of white workers' social and economic goals. But though the Klan was quite successful at electing the candidates whom it selected, it was not at all successful at selecting tractable candidates. The aspirations of blue-collar whites for the most part remained unfulfilled. The advent of the Depression for a time elevated economic concerns above social ones in the minds of white workers, permitting the formation of biracial unions. And the resultant triumph of the CIO in unionizing the previously open-shop heavy industries again seemed in the mid-1930s to be about to gain for blue-collar whites the political control of the city. But the success of the industrialists' propaganda in arousing fears of the CIO's biracialism and radicalism, the rivalries between the craft and industrial unions, and the desire of skilled workers in the CIO locals to protect the racial exclusivity of their positions in the end delivered victory in municipal politics to the corporate and business interests. Thereafter, increasing black civil rights activism more and more welded this new white political conjunction together. And the essential figure in consolidating this outcome was "Bull" Connor.

Thus, after two decades of political turmoil in Birmingham, the election of Connor and Morgan in 1937 inaugurated a new period of political calm because it marked, in essence, the abandonment of white workers' efforts to speak autonomously in politics and their acceptance of the leadership of officials allied with business, based on the primacy of racial considerations.[19] Of course virtually no one at the time fully understood the nature of the transition that had taken place—and least of all Connor himself, though he was at the heart of it. But the source of Connor's subsequent political strength was in fact his ability to link white employers' and employees' fears into a single political response.

The late 1930s saw a historic conjunction of forces in the Magic City. The industrialists' shrill warnings against the Communist-integrationist menace found in Connor a fanatic but sincere believer, and their exhortations and his seemed clearly to be succeeding in blunting the industrial unions' initial radicalism. Corporate and business interests therefore regarded Connor, for all his ill-educated buffoonery, as a very useful ally who was assisting effectively in protecting them from perhaps their darkest fears. Meanwhile, the desire of skilled workers in the industrial unions to exclude blacks from their job classifications, and the dedication of the AFL craftsmen to maintaining their racial exclusivity, had the effect of introducing blue-collar whites' social attitudes into the economic sphere of their concerns in a way that functionally merged them. As the number of jobs in the city's heavy industries steadily declined during the 1940s and 1950s, white workers in them especially became increasingly invested in a system that protected them from black competition. For these workers, but also for white organized labor in general, racial justice was an authentic menace. And therefore for them, "Bull" Connor came easily to seem their champion, guarding them from unemployment, destitution, and degradation. By the late 1940s, the hostility between the AFL and the CIO, so apparent a decade earlier, had largely disappeared and had been replaced by cooperation. The foundation for this new common front, however, was the essential acceptance by the CIO in these years of the AFL's long-standing racism—an acceptance facilitated by the CIO's purging from its ranks just at this time of its most radical unions, including Mine Mill. Finally, after decades of slow economic and educational progress, Birmingham's blacks at last had sufficient resources to begin to express their discontent in forums of which whites were compelled to take note. And as they increasingly did so, their efforts served to cement their white opponents' otherwise uneasy alliance, of which Connor was a symbol.

On his death in 1940, James M. Jones was succeeded as mayor by Cooper Green, Birmingham's postmaster, a former Klansman, and a former local official of the National Recovery Administration who, though he was initially opposed by some corporate elements, nevertheless almost immediately established close ties with the city's commercial and industrial elite. The third commissioner, Morgan, also allied himself with business interests. Both men were, in general, racial moderates, at least by Birmingham's standards. Green served until his retirement in 1953 to accept a position as an executive of the Alabama Power Company. Morgan then succeeded him, and he served until his own retirement in 1961. In the elections of the 1940s, though Connor won easily, he always ran behind both Green and Morgan. Indeed, in 1941 and 1945 Green drew no opponent at all. And yet in a sense it was Connor who made it possible for Green, Morgan, and the business forces with which they were associated to continue in power, for it was Connor whose actions and commitments retained the confidence of a sufficient number of blue-collar whites in the commission's leadership so that the class divisions within the white electorate did not demand political expression. Green and Morgan were far less controversial candidates than was Connor, and so without a strong opponent, they received the easy acquiescence of most voters. But the very controversy that surrounded Connor protected both him and his colleagues from the possibility that strong opposition might be drawn into the field against them; he was controversial because he projected the image of an energetic official actively engaged in protecting the interests and enforcing the values of his constituents. And it was this image that gave his constituency continuing confidence in the municipal administration. The result was that Connor's commission colleagues needed and supported him. And so the new conjunction of forces was complete.

Of course the truce among the white classes that settled over Birmingham politics in the late 1930s and 1940s did not extend to every election in the district. In particular, the congressional contests between Luther Patrick on the one hand and John P. Newsome and Laurie C. Battle on the other revealed elements of the historic class divisions.[20] But in general the period saw political calm based upon acceptance of business leadership and protection of racial privilege, especially in the workplace, succeed decades of bitter class conflict within the electorate. "Bull" Connor sustained and reaped the benefit of this settlement. His highly public crusades against gambling, prostitution, vice, and liquor law violations were in fact conducted primarily for the benefit of the press; as later investigations would reveal, the police department's vice squad was the very center of the corruption in this extraordinarily corrupt organization.[21] But the crusades earned him the deep admiration and strong support of fundamentalist blue-collar voters. His relentless enforcement of white supremacy calmed the fears of white workers who felt their jobs threatened by black ambitions, and his cooperation with his colleagues guaranteed municipal policies favorable to business and industrial interests. But by the early 1950s, Connor's actions had begun to create doubts among a portion of the precise segment of the electorate that had initially elevated him to power and that had most profited from the new political order he fortified, the progressive element within the business community. The circumstances that generated this rupture in the core of Connor's constituency may be stated in a single word: Smithfield.

II. The Rise and Fall of the Racial Moderates, 1946–1956

Zoning came to Birmingham in 1915. In 1917 the U.S. Supreme Court declared unconstitutional a 1914 Louisville, Kentucky, ordinance that forbade blacks to purchase property in white sections of the city. New Orleans, Louisiana, then sought to circumvent this decision by adopting an ordinance that permitted blacks to own property in any part of the city, but forbade them to use the property for residential purposes in specified areas. In 1926, Birmingham's newly elected city commission, with its Klan-endorsed majority, amended the city's zoning ordinance to include a racial zoning provision patterned after that of New Orleans. In the meantime, the New Orleans ordinance had come under legal attack, and in 1927 the Supreme Court summarily declared it too unconstitutional. But the Birmingham provision remained on the books. It delineated three small black residential sections, totaling just 15 percent of the city's land area, though blacks were nearly 40 percent of the population. Blacks, however, initially paid little attention to the racial zoning ordinance, because the vast majority of them did not live in residential areas at all; they lived in company housing near the mines and mills, in sections zoned industrial and therefore without racial designation. Few blacks in the late 1920s and 1930s were sufficiently well off to be homeowners. This situation changed rapidly during World War II. In the first place, as we have seen, during the Depression the corporations began to close company housing. Then during the war years, the city's population exploded upward. Between 1940 and 1950 the total population increased by more than 20 percent and the black population by some 30 percent. Birmingham's factories operated at capacity under the stimulus of war production, and the demand for labor in all sectors of the economy was enormous, attracting workers to the city from rural areas. The availability of mortgage financing guarantees from the Federal Housing Administration and the Veterans Administration, added to these other factors, suddenly and sharply increased the demand for black homes.[22]

One of the three sections in which blacks were legally permitted to reside was Smithfield, in northwest Birmingham. Smithfield was a well-to-do black neighborhood, but in 1938 the city had erected a large black public housing project there, absorbing land previously available for private residences and pushing the black middle class toward the northern edge of the enclave. As a result of this decision, and of the more general developments just discussed, by 1945 the pressure on Smithfield's northern racial border had become intense. Smithfield adjoined two middle-class white neighborhoods, Graymont and College Hills. But separating the black and white districts was North Smithfield, an area nominally zoned for whites but in fact very sparsely settled, because its proximity to the black enclave had made whites reluctant to purchase there. In practice, then, North Smithfield served as a buffer zone segregating the races. But its vacant lots infuriated the many blacks who now had the money to buy or build a home but were unable to obtain one zoned for their race when only blocks away, land was going begging. And white realtors, unable to sell to white purchasers, were consequently willing to sell to the eager blacks, who under the city ordinance could legally own but could not live on the land.

Events in early 1946 pushed blacks into action. In the spring the Birmingham Zoning Board recommended that an area near Titusville be rezoned to permit the construction of additional black housing, but in April the city commission refused to permit the change. In July the Birmingham Housing Authority evicted a number of black tenants from its Smithfield and Southtown public housing projects because their incomes were too high to qualify for continued residence, but because of the severe limitations on black housing created by racial zoning, the tenants could find no new accommodations and were left homeless. They appealed to the city commission but found Mayor Green and Commissioner Connor entirely unsympathetic. In August, Birmingham's NAACP branch undertook to sponsor a federal court suit, filed in the name of Mrs. Alice Allen, an administrator at the black Miles College, which sought to have the racial zoning ordinance declared unconstitutional. In September a white real estate developer filed a similar suit against suburban Tarrant City's ordinance that forbade any blacks to buy or own property there. In October, ruling from the bench, U.S. District Judge Clarence Mullins declared the Tarrant City ordinance unconstitutional. At the same time, Arthur Shores, representing the NAACP, filed a companion suit to Mrs. Allen's in behalf of Samuel Matthews, an iron ore miner who had built a home on the edge of North Smithfield, on land he thought was zoned for blacks, but who then was denied an occupancy permit when building inspectors said that it was in fact outside the black area.

In the meantime, these events had led to the revival of the Ku Klux Klan, effectively dormant in the city since the early years of the Depression. In March crosses were burned in various sections of Birmingham, and in July the Klan formally incorporated itself, under the leadership of retired physician Dr. Elihu P. Pruitt, roofing contractor W. Hugh Morris, and salesman Robert S. Gulledge. In January 1947 it sent warning letters to the officers of the NAACP branch, demanding that the suits against the racial zoning ordinance be withdrawn. Later that month, Shores did withdraw Mrs. Allen's suit, on technical grounds, but he pressed Samuel Matthews's. In June Judge Mullins dismissed the Matthews suit when testimony revealed that Matthews had never formally applied for an occupancy permit because building inspectors had told him he could not get one. But in dismissing the suit, Judge Mullins commented that the racial zoning provision was clearly unconstitutional. Matthews thereupon applied for the occupancy permit, it was denied on racial grounds, and Shores refiled the suit. On August 4, 1947, Judge Mullins entered an injunction ordering building inspectors to grant Matthews a certificate of occupancy. On the night of August 18, the Klan responded by bombing Matthews's new home; it was completely destroyed. This was the first of the dozen racial bombings that by 1951 had gained for North Smithfield the unenviable nickname "Dynamite Hill."[23]

Other events in this period intensified the violent emotions surrounding the engagement in Smithfield. The adoption in November 1946 of the Boswell Amendment, strengthening the state constitution's disfranchising provisions, produced, as we have seen, a federal court confrontation that resulted in March 1949 in the U.S. Supreme Court's declaring the amendment unconstitutional. But the state legislature then struck back with a second amendment, ratified by a very narrow margin in December 1951, that introduced a written voter qualification questionnaire; this new questionnaire, in increasingly stringent versions, restricted registration until 1965.[24] These racially charged suffrage debates took place in the midst of the bitter political contests generated by the Dixiecrat revolt of 1948 and the ultimately successful efforts of the national party loyalists, led by U.S. senators Lister Hill and John Sparkman, to recapture control of the state Democratic Executive Committee in 1950.[25] And all of these struggles were reflected in the activities of the newly revivified Ku Klux Klan. In June 1948 a group of hooded Klansmen invaded Camp Fletcher, the black

Girl Scout camp just outside the city, to forbid the continuation of a training session in which two white Scout leaders were instructing a group of black camp counselors. The two white women were ordered to leave Birmingham. A year later, in June 1949, a Klan mob flogged a middle-aged white woman whom they accused of operating a house of ill repute. In a separate incident at the same time, they beat a white restaurant owner and organized a boycott of his restaurant because the establishment served both races, though in segregated sections. In July, whites cut the cables supporting the broadcasting tower of what was to be Birmingham's first black radio station; they thus sent the tower crashing to the ground and delayed the station's debut for a month. In September, Klansmen beat and terrorized two black families in Tuscaloosa who owed money to a white loan shark. By that time the Klan in Jefferson County was estimated to have some sixty-five hundred members, up from only seven hundred at its revival three years before.[26]

It was in this context that the battle of Smithfield escalated. Judge Mullins, in the course of granting Samuel Matthews's injunction, had given his opinion that Birmingham's residential segregation ordinance was unconstitutional, but Matthews's suit was not a class action, the injunction ordered only that Matthews be given an occupancy permit, and the decision was unreported. Nevertheless, armed with Judge Mullins's opinion, blacks now with increasing frequency pressed city officials to open North Smithfield to them. For this purpose they formed the Birmingham Property Owners' Protective Association, headed by the executive secretary of the Negro Tuberculosis Association, Robert F. Coar, and realtor Wilbur H. Hollins. But on the other side, to insist that the races remain divided, their white neighbors rallied to the Graymont–College Hills Civic Association, headed by Colonel Horace B. Hansen, a retired army officer, and Olin H. Horton, personnel manager of an insurance company, who in later years would become a leader of the segregationist American States' Rights Association. Commissioner James Morgan, who supervised the building inspectors and the zoning board, struggled to find a compromise that would satisfy each group. He met with committees of the two residential associations and urged them to accept the creation of a park as a buffer between the neighborhoods. The two groups were open to the plan, but they could not agree on the size and location of the buffer zone. By the spring of 1949, the negotiations reached an impasse and the bombing resumed. On the night of March 25, three North Smithfield homes that had been purchased by blacks were bombed. In May, Klansman Robert Chambliss intimidated a black family into fleeing a home they had just occupied, and other blacks in the area received threatening telephone calls. In July a bomb was found at another black home and disarmed, but in August that home and another one were damaged by bombs thrown from a car.

As the violence continued, Commissioner Morgan rather desperately pressed his compromise plan. At a public hearing on it, both he and Mayor Green essentially conceded that it was unconstitutional, but Mayor Green said, "Sometimes you have to go beyond the letter of the law of man to meet situations like this." In an attempt to persuade the contending forces to reach a settlement, Morgan appointed a committee of blacks led by wealthy insurance executive Arthur G. Gaston, attorney Arthur Shores, and restaurant owner Robert L. Williams and a committee of whites headed by banker A. Key Foster and including former Klansman and Democratic Party leader Ben Ray and United Mine Workers executive William Mitch. Federal authorities privately warned Morgan that he could face prosecution if the city attempted to enforce racial zoning. As a result, though police and building inspectors continued to threaten and harass blacks who moved into North Smithfield, officials took no steps to remove them. Segregationists denounced this timidity. "We want action, even if we lose," former police officer C. E. Henderson told the commission in July. Klansmen seem to have felt that enforcement of segregation was being left up to them. In the meantime, activists in the NAACP denounced the willingness of more moderate blacks to compromise. The branch's most aggressive leader, its executive secretary, Emory O. Jackson, the editor of the *Birmingham World,* resigned his NAACP office in July in protest against the irresolution and conservatism of other prominent blacks. Under this pressure from the militant of both races, Morgan's middle ground gave way. The NAACP refused to renounce the possibility of further legal action, and Commissioner Connor voted against the ordinance creating the buffer zone, thus killing it because changes in zoning required the city commission's unanimous consent. In August Connor proposed a new city ordinance, drafted by his friend James Simpson, that made it a crime for any person to move into an area historically occupied by another race. Simpson believed that what the city could not legally require under its zoning authority, it could nevertheless compel as an exercise of its police power, to keep the public peace. In September the commission enacted the proposal. At the same time, Arthur Shores, finally abandoning the negotiations, turned to the courts to settle the dispute. In August he filed a suit in state court for Mrs. Mary Means Monk, the owner of a lot in North Smithfield, to force the city to issue her a building permit. And when Circuit Judge J. Edgar Bowron dismissed the petition, on the grounds that Mrs. Monk had not yet exhausted all her administrative remedies, in September Shores filed a class action in federal court in behalf of Mrs. Monk and fourteen other black property owners, seeking a formal declaration that both racial zoning and Connor's new criminal ordinance were unconstitutional.[27]

In early December 1949, Commissioner Connor declared his candidacy for governor of Alabama on a platform of saving white supremacy; he denounced the Monk suit as a joint scheme of the NAACP and the national Democratic Party and pledged that, if elected, he would order President Harry Truman "to keep his filthy hands out of our affairs." In mid-December the suit came to trial before Judge Clarence Mullins. To present its case the city had hired the violently Negrophobic former Klan leader Horace Wilkinson, who sought to justify the ordinance by presenting evidence of blacks' moral inferiority and of the economic losses that neighborhood integration could bring to whites. But Judge Mullins would have none of it. Ruling from the bench immediately at the conclusion of the trial, he entered a permanent injunction against the enforcement of residential segregation in Birmingham. The city appealed to the Fifth Circuit.[28]

Following Judge Mullins's ruling, the bombings—which had been suspended in August when Connor offered his tough new ordinance and the city began fighting the black initiative in court—resumed. In mid-April 1950 the recently constructed Smithfield home of black dentist Dr. Joel Boykins was bombed and destroyed. Later that month another black home, which had been bombed in August 1949 and then repaired and resold, was bombed again. Following this bombing, Olin H. Horton of the Graymont–College Hills Civic Association told reporters grimly that the association was determined that North Center Street, where the home was located, would remain a racial dividing line. Robert Chambliss, the Klansman identified in the intimidation of the black family in May 1949, was detained by police in connection with this latest bombing, but he was released at the end of the month. Some weeks thereafter an office building under construction at a point where racial neighborhoods abutted was bombed.

A Fifth Circuit panel heard arguments in the *Monk* case in October, and on December 20, 1950, in an opinion by Judge Wayne G. Borah, it sustained Judge Mullins's decision. Judge Robert L. Russell, a brother of Georgia's U.S. senator Richard Russell, however, filed a bitter dissent. The court, he claimed, was elevating private property rights over the general peace and welfare. On December 21, Mrs. Monk's newly constructed home was bombed and badly damaged. Six persons were in the house at the time of the explosion and narrowly escaped death. The following May the two Center Street homes that had been bombed in August 1949, one of which had been bombed again in April 1950, fell victim to arson and were burned to the ground after a six-hour fire. But thereafter the Smithfield violence ended until 1956, with a single exception in May 1954.[29]

The reasons for the suspension of the Smithfield bombings are twofold. The first of these is that the blacks involved began to take steps to fight back. It had been clear from the beginning that the response of Connor's police to these offenses had been insouciant at best. Officers made virtually no effort to discover the culprits. Later testimony indicated that this inactivity was in accord with Connor's own attitudes. Certainly Connor's adamant hostility to any weakening of racial zoning was well known.[30] Black leaders therefore quickly came to the conclusion that they would have to circumvent the police to end the terror. In their first effort to do so, in the summer of 1949, they hired a white private detective, Herbert Browne, to try to find out the identity of the bombers. But police, learning of this initiative in mid-August, promptly put a stop to it by arresting Browne for doing business without a license. Thereafter blacks turned to the racially moderate Governor James Folsom and the state highway patrol. At the end of August the highway patrol began providing protection in North Smithfield, and as we have seen, the bombing then stopped until the following April. When the violence resumed, Governor Folsom met in May 1950 with a black Smithfield delegation consisting of the Protective Association's Coar and Hollins, attorney Arthur Shores, *World* editor Emory Jackson, and civil rights activist the Reverend James L. Ware. Following this meeting, Folsom offered a reward for information leading to the apprehension of the bombers and ordered his three state investigators to enter the case. And on June 25, Folsom traveled to Birmingham to denounce racial prejudice in an address to more than a thousand blacks at the Sixteenth Street Baptist Church. But without the cooperation of the Birmingham police, the state investigators were unable to make any progress, and the posting of permanent highway patrol guards in the area was impossible given the many demands on the force. However, the cold war, intensified just at this time by the outbreak of fighting in Korea, adventitiously supplied Smithfield's blacks with a more permanent solution. They applied to federal authorities to organize a civil defense unit for their neighborhood. They thus gained helmets, armbands, and badges—and, most importantly, official sanction and justification for maintaining a paramilitary organization. Beginning apparently in early 1951, following the bombing of Mrs. Monk's home, for the next fifteen or more years the fifty-member Smithfield District Civil Defense Reserve Police patrolled every night, initially under the command of letter carrier Robert F. Walker and later of postal maintenance worker James E. Lay. At first their efforts were focused on Smithfield itself, but as Klan violence spread to other areas after 1956 the civil defense unit extended its coverage as well. By 1963 it was assisting in providing security for five black sections of the city.[31]

The second element forcing a suspension of the Klan bombings after May 1951 was just as significant as the black resistance, and for the city's political future even more so. It was the vigorous response to the violence by members of Birmingham's white economic elite who were increasingly anxious to invigorate the area's commercial and industrial growth. As we have already seen in the preceding chapter, and will see again in the next one, these years witnessed the spread among businessmen, particularly younger ones, of a fervent gospel of economic expansion. The attraction of northern industry to Alabama seemed to these enthusiasts the primary challenge facing the state, and the key to eliminating all its genuine difficulties. Their zeal in the cause was very nearly obsessive. The state legislature had facilitated the crusade by the passage of the Cater Act of 1949 and the Wallace Act of 1951, both of which created machinery for the issuance by municipalities of tax-free industrial development revenue bonds to finance the building of factories. And Birmingham had taken the lead among Alabama's cities in pressing the movement when, in December 1949, the chamber of commerce had created the Committee of 100 to search for northern manufacturers willing to locate in Jefferson County.

The business community was not, however, united in its support for economic development. The competitive advantage of Birmingham's established industrial giants, particularly the national steel corporations, U.S. Steel and Republic Steel, derived in part from access to a comparatively low-wage workforce; and though technological advances had eliminated many unskilled positions and unionization had increasingly brought national wage standards to the district, a number of the older industrial executives apparently were not eager for the advent of new employers whose competition for labor seemed likely to drive wages up.

The influence of such men within the chamber of commerce soon led to a widening breach between the chamber and the Committee of 100. The committee more and more came to see the chamber as a reluctant ally. And even more hostile to the chamber was the Young Men's Business Club (YMBC), established in the summer of 1946; the YMBC often thought of the chamber as excessively conservative, while the leaders of the chamber sometimes dismissed the YMBC as a bunch of radicals. Nevertheless, the majority of the city's enterprises embraced the prospect of industrial expansion eagerly. Utilities such as Alabama Power, Alabama Gas, Southern Bell Telephone, and the railroads and trucking companies depended for their own growth on the growth of the area's economy. The same was true of services such as banks, brokerage houses, construction and engineering companies, law firms, insurance agencies, mortgage companies, and realtors, and of mercantile organizations such as the department stores and commercial suppliers. The smaller manufacturers, whose market was primarily local rather than national, also benefited greatly from a more prosperous group of consumers. Increased demand was often more significant for such concerns than were production costs. For many white businessmen connected with these and similar business interests, the diversification of the city's industrial base seemed essential to securing a prosperous future for Birmingham. And for all who shared this viewpoint, the recrudescence of the Klan and the negative publicity that accompanied it posed a serious threat to the attainment of their goal.[32]

Though the advocates of economic development were by no means uniformly racial moderates, many of them were, because the growth of black prosperity was an integral part of the advancement of the general community and would likely diminish social discontent, mark the city as progressive in the eyes of observers in the North, and increase aggregate local demand. And even those enthusiasts for new industry who were nevertheless uncompromising segregationists were sensitive to Birmingham's national image and eager to emphasize what they believed to be the city's harmonious race relations. A principal reason for this concern was the city's long-running competition with Atlanta to become the South's great metropolitan center, a competition to which many of Birmingham's most prominent businessmen were intensely committed. In the face of the renewed Klan violence, such considerations moved the development-oriented business leadership to begin to bring strong pressure on political officials to restore community calm. Donald Comer, the textile magnate who, despite his having been an active Dixiecrat, was also a long-standing racial moderate who had participated in the formation of the Southern Conference for Human Welfare, accepted the chairmanship of a citizens' committee to demand an end to the outrages. And under the urging of white community leaders such as Comer, officialdom did in fact respond.[33]

When the Klan turned its violence on whites in June 1949, with its floggings of the alleged madam and the restaurateur who served both races, the Klansmen thus provided the circuit solicitor's office the opening it needed to obtain an indictment from the county grand jury. In July the grand jury returned indictments of seventeen Klansmen on a total of forty-four counts of flogging while masked, breaking and entering, and conspiring to boycott a lawful business, the restaurant. Among those indicted were Special Deputy Sheriff Colman E. Lollar, who had led the gang that attacked the restaurant owner, and Brookside police chief Elmer B. Brock, accused of intimidating a witness and neglect of duty. In the group indicted for flogging the madam was Robert E. Chambliss, the Klansman who had forced the black family to flee its Smithfield home in May and who would be detained the following April in connection with the bombing of a nearby home. Chambliss was an employee of the city automobile repair shop; he had been suspended from his job for ten days for the incident of intimidation in the spring, and as a result of this indictment Mayor Green and Commissioner Morgan fired him outright in September. Sheriff Holt McDowell dismissed Deputy Sheriff Lollar as well.[34]

When the Klansmen came to trial in March 1950, they were acquitted. The Smithfield bombings, which had ended just after the indictments, resumed a month after the acquittals. But the grand jury had nevertheless begun a process that would eventually lead to the lengthier cessation after May 1951. In the course of its investigation, the grand jury had ordered Birmingham roofing contractor W. Hugh Morris, by that time the Alabama Klan's highest officer, to appear before it and to bring the Klan's complete membership list. When Morris refused, he was jailed for contempt in July 1949. His attorneys appealed to the state supreme court for his release, arguing on First Amendment grounds that the membership list was privileged information. At the end of the month, the supreme court rejected the petition. Morris thereupon claimed that the membership records had all been stolen by Communist leader Sam Hall, in collusion with Arthur Shores. But in September, after sixty-seven days in the county jail, Morris capitulated and gave the grand jury the names of twenty-eight Klansmen. Though this was a tiny percentage of the estimated sixty-five hundred Klansmen in the Birmingham area at the time, Morris's action still was a direct violation of his Klan oath and set off a storm of controversy among his followers. As a result, during 1950 the Klan divided into two competing organizations, the older one headed by Morris and the new one by the Reverend Alvin Horn, a Talladega Baptist minister. Morris apparently thereupon set Horn up for arrest in connection with the night-rider slaying of a Pell City rolling-store operator. Horn was indicted, but prosecutors dropped the charges in 1952 when the Klansmen who had accused him recanted. Throughout the early 1950s, however, the klaverns were preoccupied with the internecine warfare among them. By the mid-1950s Horn had emerged victorious, but by that time Klan membership in the Birmingham area had fallen to approximately thirty-five hundred. And then Horn himself introduced new turmoil into his ranks in the spring of 1957 when, at the age of forty-five, he wed a fifteen-year-old girl. The result was a new schism and the elevation to leadership of Robert Shelton, an employee in a Tuscaloosa tire factory. It was Shelton who finally succeeded in restoring unity of purpose to the state's Klansmen.[35]

As Morris and Horn fought, Birmingham's advocates of industrial development pressed on with their campaign to suppress racial violence. They had already scored a notable victory in June 1949, when in an unusual alliance with Governor Folsom and Attorney General Albert Carmichael, who were usually enemies of business initiatives, they had succeeded in lobbying through the state legislature an anti-masking act directed against the Klan, a law the legislators had repeatedly rejected in earlier years. And their public efforts appear to have chastened even the area's police; the number of blacks killed by law enforcement officers in Jefferson County, fourteen in 1948 and ten in 1949, fell to six in 1950. In these same years business progressives pushed into theretofore unthinkable territory; they began talking to blacks.[36]

In response to the rapid increase of interracial tensions in Birmingham at the end of World War II, the southern regional director of the National Urban League, Nelson C. Jackson, had begun efforts toward the end of 1946 to organize an Urban League chapter in the city. He enlisted the support of Dr. Henry Edmonds, an influential Presbyterian minister and white moderate, and Robert Durr, the editor of the *Birmingham Review,* a conservative black weekly subsidized by the city's industrialists as an alternative to the activist *Birmingham World.* During 1948 and 1949, business progressives and middle-class black leaders undertook exploratory meetings with Jackson. But the Dixiecratic demagogy and Klan bombings of this period, while they emphasized the desperate need for consultations between the races, also greatly intensified the white moderates' fear of being publicly identified with a national civil rights organization. As a result, by the beginning of 1950 business progressives who had been closely involved in the negotiations to establish the Urban League chapter—including particularly Mervyn Sterne, an investment banker who was a leader of the city's Jewish community; Charles Zukoski, a Unitarian freethinker and longtime mayor of the wealthy suburb of Mountain Brook, who headed the First National Bank's trust department; Clarence Hanson, the publisher of the *Birmingham News* and the chairman of the Committee of 100; Crawford Johnson, the president of Birmingham's Coca-Cola Bottling Company; and Bradford Colcord, the president of the Woodward Iron Company—decided instead to form an entirely local, privately sponsored biracial committee. In early May, thirteen of the white moderate leaders met with a group of seven blacks led by insurance agent W. C. Patton, the state president of the NAACP, and attorney Arthur Shores and obtained their endorsement of this proposal. They then turned to the Jefferson County Coordinating Council of Social Forces, an umbrella organization of the area's Red Cross and Community Chest agencies, and in July received the consent of its board to sponsor the new committee. In mid-October the Coordinating Council's president, prominent attorney William J. Cabaniss, summoned selected white moderates and black leaders to an organizational meeting.[37]

These proceedings infuriated the most militant black civil rights advocates. When the proposal for the committee was first publicly announced, following the Coordinating Council board's approval of it in July, Emory Jackson of the *Birmingham World* condemned it in the harshest terms. He suspected, he said, that the whites behind the movement were "those who want the status quo in race relations and education." The blacks who were cooperating with them, he wrote, "have injured their own standing in the community," and he urged black public opinion not to give them any peace. "We must not allow hand-picked, white-folk sponsored leaders to be our spokesmen. Leaders picked by others usually serve those who pick them," he cautioned.

The white moderates seeking to organize the committee saw themselves as striving to find common ground in the midst of an appalling racial crisis. One of the committee's leading white supporters, Baptist minister Dr. John Buchanan, warned, "Our community stands on trial in an attempt to arrive at a solution of problems facing the races." Nevertheless, there was a considerable measure of truth in Emory Jackson's judgment that "There is a concept of vertical race relations and captive Negro leadership at work." The initiative in organizing the committee was not a joint one; it was white. Seven prominent blacks had been asked to consent to the proposal, but only after the first, crucial decisions had been made. And the options that the blacks had been presented essentially were a local committee or none at all. The decision to have an independent committee rather than a chapter of the Urban League proceeded entirely from white fears—fears that a branch of a national organization would not be sufficiently subject to control by white business leaders, and fears that actions taken by a national organization elsewhere might create unnecessary hostility to reform efforts in Birmingham and might even lead to ostracism of or violence against the white members. The connection to a trusted national organization, on the other hand, would have greatly reassured civil rights activists and would have aided in drawing them into the committee's endeavors. In addition, putting the committee under the auspices of the Coordinating Council raised for blacks the fact that as recently as January 1947 the Community Chest had refused, after a heated fight, to elect a black member to its board. But whites were, of course, completely insensitive to these concerns; they acted out of an essentially unexamined assumption of the primacy due their own perspective.

The unconscious arrogance of the white moderates and the deep suspicions of the black activists were not long in bearing fruit. At the end of October, when the NAACP's annual state convention met in Anniston and the nominating committee recommended reelecting W. C. Patton to a second term as state president, Emory Jackson and the AFL's black state vice-president, Cornelius Maiden, launched a floor fight, asserting that Patton's participation in the creation of the Interracial Committee made him unfit to lead the NAACP. During the subsequent debate, Patton was forced in effect to apologize for his actions and to give a public promise that he would immediately notify the committee that he could not serve on it. Only then did the convention agree to his reelection. Dentist E. W. Taggart, the black candidate who had been defeated for election to the Community Chest board in 1947, and two other blacks among the nineteen who had been invited to the committee's organizational meeting at midmonth had already refused to have anything to do with the new organization. And in the end, only nine of the nineteen were among the twenty-five blacks who accepted committee membership the following spring.[38]

The opposition of militants led by the *World* worked to keep strong black voices off the Interracial Committee. Equally significant was the apparent desire of the three white businessmen on the committee to choose the members—Crawford Johnson, Clarence Hanson, and automobile dealer Don H. Maring—to include primarily black moderates, a goal in which the four black committeemen seem in general to have cooperated. The list of black members who were eventually selected contained some leading figures, such as attorney Arthur Shores, who served as the committee's vice-chairman; United Mine Workers official Hartford Knight; Ensley Civic

League president Dillard Scurlark; mortician W. E. Shortridge, who in later years would be a pillar of Fred Shuttlesworth's Alabama Christian Movement for Human Rights; Baptist minister W. Prince Vaughn, a future president of the Birmingham NAACP; and Robert Coar, executive secretary of the Negro Tuberculosis Association, and realtor Wilbur H. Hollins, who together led the Smithfield black homeowners' association. Nevertheless, seven of the twenty-five black members were public school teachers or principals, necessarily fearful for their jobs, and two others held similarly insecure positions. Five were ministers and five businessmen or professionals. It represented, on the whole, a missed opportunity to permit prominent whites fully to confront the extent of black discontent. And it was particularly unfortunate because the twenty-five whites chosen included many of the city's most influential: Arthur V. Weibel, president of Tennessee Coal and Iron, the Birmingham division of U.S. Steel; Claude S. Lawson of Sloss-Sheffield Steel; Joe H. Woodward of Woodward Iron; Lester N. Shannon of Stockham Valves and Fittings; lumber company president Bedford Seale; banker Key Foster; attorney Douglas Arant; investment banker Mervyn Sterne; prominent investor and business leader Allen Rushton; broadcasting executives Thad Holt and Henry P. Johnston; Carey Haigler, state director of the CIO; Ernest Buchi of the AFL; as well as Crawford Johnson and Don Maring. Such men, if enlisted in a cause, had the capacity at least to compel other white leaders to take particular proposals seriously.[39]

The more militant figures in the city's black leadership, such as Emory Jackson, clearly felt that the Interracial Committee would accomplish nothing positive, and worse, would entrap blacks in meaningless negotiations and thus forestall vigorous steps toward genuine equality. More moderate figures, such as Arthur Shores, credited the white business progressives with sincerity and saw the committee as at least likely to produce some amelioration in the harsh circumstances of daily life among the city's black residents. There is strong evidence to support each of these viewpoints. The committee certainly did make positive contributions over the next five years to improving conditions for the community's black citizens, as we shall shortly see, and its white members actively sought to effect even more reforms than those that they were actually able to bring to fruition. On the other hand, there were unmistakable limits beyond which white committee members simply would not go; their goal was amelioration, not equality. Although these were the conflicting terms in which the black leadership conceived, and argued about, the committee, it is probable that they were not the terms in which the white business progressives primarily understood their actions. A few additional reflections on the business progressives' perceptions of the committee's role will clarify its crucial place in the city's history.

In the first place, we should emphasize that, as Birmingham's racial divisions were deeper and more violent in these years than in any other community in Alabama, so the willingness of its white moderates, in response to the Smithfield bombings, to face and to attempt to bridge the divisions in so public a manner was unique. The appointment of such a biracial committee in Montgomery or Selma in 1951, for instance, would simply have been unimaginable. But that is not to say that Birmingham's white moderates and business progressives were more enlightened, and certainly not that they were braver, than elsewhere. Indeed, as we have already discovered, comparable elements were effecting substantial reforms in Montgomery at this same time without the necessity for formal biracial negotiations, and as we have also seen, the same elements would subsequently prove just as pusillanimous in the face of segregationist pressure. Rather, the factor that distinguished the response of Birmingham's business progressives to the Smithfield emergency seems very likely to have been the business community's earlier experience with the district's labor unions. The divisions between labor and management too had been particularly deep and violent in Birmingham in the earlier decades of the century. But during the late 1930s and 1940s, as the business progressives imagined what had happened, the union leadership had been drawn into a constructive community consensus that had brought comparative calm to the district, both in its politics and in labor relations in its mines and mills. Labor spokesmen were now appointed as a matter of course to all important municipal boards and committees—including the Interracial Committee. The business moderates appear to have hoped that the committee would serve to engage those black leaders whom they regarded as "responsible" in the same kind of constructive dialogue, founded on a common commitment to Birmingham's growth, prosperity, and peace. In effect, they took themselves to be seeking grounds upon which to invite moderate blacks into membership in the sort of social alliance that had brought order to white labor-management relations during the preceding decade.

The problem with this design, as more hard-minded industrialists undoubtedly realized, was that the new alliance in the realm of labor relations rested far less upon a mutual commitment to community prosperity, and far more—indeed, fundamentally—upon a mutual acceptance of white supremacy. In fact, the Smithfield bombings that had convinced the white business progressives of the need to create a comparable interracial alliance were if anything a clear reflection of just how much more essential the white labor-management rapprochement had now rendered the maintenance of racial lines of division in the city. The institutionalization of a parallel dialogue between white and black leaders, if it gained any social authority at all, would inevitably destabilize the rival white interclass alliance. And the business progressives' concurrent campaign—independent of the efforts of the Interracial Committee, but interconnected with them, as we shall see—to rid the city commission of "Bull" Connor represented a direct assault on this alliance. The white business progressives were not without a sense of this dark truth, of course; no resident of Birmingham could have been. And so they repeatedly emphasized that the committee must seek no reforms that could threaten segregation. Yet their success in the campaign against Connor and the more modest achievements of the Interracial Committee permitted their optimistic civic boosterism to blind them to the extent to which the life of their city was in reality a function of the racial subordination that utterly permeated it. The institutions of black Birmingham so badly needed improvement; there were so many areas in which the application of goodwill and common sense could diminish the likelihood of racial collisions. Surely, the progressives thought, no one would object to reforms such as these; and in the process of jointly seeking municipal progress, they would at the same time lead like-minded blacks into a shared sense of their common interest in building the community.

These were the aims of the Interracial Committee, as the white business progressives envisioned them. It is impossible, in retrospect, not to consider them virtually doomed from the start. Indeed, the entire enterprise, whether viewed from the perspective of the white business progressives or from that of the black moderates, has a certain quixotic quality to it. The wary distrust between the leaders of the two races—and the fear that the moderate leaders of each race felt of the opinions of the more radical members within their own race—that so damaged the initiative at the outset are an index, if any is needed, to the vast chasm of divisions that needed to be bridged. It is against this background that we must judge the committee's objectively quite limited accomplishments, which I am about to detail. In fact, against this background, the accomplishments may actually appear quite remarkable—as they apparently did to the black moderate participants. These achievements constitute the first of the three ways in which the Interracial Committee contributed to the pattern of events that would culminate in the crisis of 1963. The committee's ability to obtain a number of reforms long sought by blacks—reforms that seemed genuine to black moderates in the context of the time, however tentative they may seem if judged against the enormity of the need—as well as the contemporary humiliation of "Bull" Connor that the white business progressives managed to orchestrate, together vastly strengthened the faith of black moderate leaders in the usefulness of negotiations with their white counterparts. It was a faith that men like Arthur Shores, Arthur Gaston, Wilbur Hollins, and J. L. Ware would continue to hold throughout the years ahead, even when the white business progressives had been intimidated into silence. And it was a faith that would form the very heart of the future rivalry between Ware's Inter-Citizens Committee and Fred Shuttlesworth's Alabama Christian Movement for Human Rights.

The other two contributions of the Interracial Committee to Birmingham's future, however, both proceeded from its failures. The ability of segregationists to force the committee's dissolution in the spring of 1956 drove the white moderate and business progressive forces into a terrified silence from which they would only emerge, with much trepidation, following the Freedom Rider riot of 1961. That period of withdrawal of white moderate voices from community leadership was a second essential element in the movement of the city toward 1963, because it greatly strengthened the hand of militant forces among both blacks and whites. Finally, the committee's unsuccessful effort to induce the city to hire black policemen led directly, as we shall see, to the rise into municipal prominence of Fred Shuttlesworth, whose initial reputation among Birmingham's blacks derived from his aggressive adoption of this crusade. The three crucial steps toward the city's racial crisis were the long silence of the white moderates; the consequent unchallenged authority of the segregationists among whites and therefore the return of "Bull" Connor to city hall; and, once the white business progressives finally reemerged into social activity, the fierce rivalry between Shuttlesworth's Christian Movement, which distrusted the whites' sincerity, and Ware's Inter-Citizens Committee, which did not, for the status of the progressives' black negotiating partners. And each of these steps derives, in a sense, from the earlier efforts of the Interracial Committee. The telling of that larger story requires, therefore, an examination of the committee's aborted endeavors.

The newly appointed Interracial Committee met for the first time in April 1951 and chose Episcopal bishop Charles C. J. Carpenter as its chairman. Over the following summer it constituted seven subcommittees to work on areas of community concern. Three of the subcommittees—those on medical care, housing, and transportation—were evenly divided between the races. Two of them—on day care and recreational facilities—had black majorities. And two—on police and personnel—had white majorities. But all seven had white chairmen. The full membership elected an evenly divided executive committee. The personnel committee, headed by Lester Shannon of Stockham Valves and Fittings, was to choose a black executive secretary. After an extensive search it settled on Clarence O. Brown, an Atlanta social worker, in November 1952. Emory Jackson, who had called the position "a feather-bed job for some social informer," promptly denounced Brown's views as crypto-segregationist; at the same time, "Bull" Connor attacked Brown as an outsider whose employment was a part of the committee's surreptitious campaign to integrate the police and fire departments. Unable to overcome the opposition of the black and white extremes, Brown gave up after less than a year. He was succeeded in January 1954 by Paul R. Jones, an energetic native of Bessemer who would serve until the committee's dissolution in April 1956.[40]

In the meantime, the subcommittees labored in their assigned fields, with varying success. The majority-black subcommittee on day care—which was initially headed by white community volunteer Mrs. Herbert Ryding but which in 1954 became the first of the subcommittees to be chaired by a black, when Mrs. Ryding was succeeded by Mrs. Belzora Ward, the secretary of the black Masonic Lodge and the president of the Birmingham chapter of the National Council of Negro Women—was responsible for one of the committee's most important achievements. After a good deal of effort, it obtained the agreement of the Birmingham Housing Authority to erect a day-care facility in the new black Loveman Village housing project in Titusville, in southwest Birmingham. This nursery opened in 1956.[41] Reflecting the middle-class concerns of most of the committee's black members, the other majority-black subcommittee, that on recreation, devoted most of its early efforts—over the opposition of the city's NAACP—to persuading the city to build a public golf course for blacks. The course opened at the end of 1952. But the subcommittee's other activities were of somewhat more general benefit. It negotiated the terms of black attendance at the state fair; obtained agreement for blacks to use the municipal zoo and Vulcan Park, surrounding the city's famed statue of the god of the forge; arranged for substantial improvements to the black Girl Scouts camp, Camp Fletcher; and assisted in equipping a community center at one of the city's black parks, Memorial Park.[42]

The housing subcommittee faced the question that, more than any other, was responsible for bringing the Interracial Committee into existence; of all the subcommittees, its was the greatest failure. Under the chairmanship of banker A. Key Foster—who had also headed Commissioner Morgan's white Smithfield negotiators—it sought to create an extensive middle-class black subdivision to take some of the pressure off the racially changing North Smithfield and Fountain Heights areas. It managed to locate a 350-acre site owned by Republic Steel near Pratt City. Republic agreed to sell the land for $385,000. But despite vigorous efforts to interest various real estate developers, both local and out-of-state, no developer proved willing to undertake the project.[43]

The subcommittee on hospital care, on the other hand, played a significant role in achieving one of the period's greatest advances, though equal credit for it is due other elements in the community. Both the state and the Birmingham medical associations forbade any nonwhite doctor to join, and all Birmingham hospitals forbade any doctor to practice in them who was not a member of the all-white associations. As a result, it was impossible for Birmingham's thirty-seven black doctors to attend a patient who had to be admitted to a hospital. Black physicians had their own local and state medical societies, but hospitals refused to recognize them. Moreover, the black sections of the city's white hospitals were too small for the existing demand and were often not maintained to the same standards that the white areas were. Only one-sixth of Jefferson County's 2,145 hospital beds were open to blacks in 1950. Immediately after the end of the World War II limitations on new construction, blacks had formed an association headed by A.M.E. Zion bishop B. G. Shaw to seek funds to build a black hospital. By the spring of 1946 they had raised enough money to purchase a site for the facility. With the assistance of the Roman Catholic Sisters of Charity, who had maintained a small clinic for blacks in the area since 1941 and who agreed to take over the operation of the hospital if it could be built, ground was broken on the proposed Holy Name Hospital in the Tuxedo Junction section of Ensley in July 1948. But less than a quarter of the sum necessary to match the federal construction grant was on hand, and fund-raising efforts now failed. At the beginning of 1950, a committee of white business and social leaders—headed by Donald Comer of Avondale Mills, the executive also of the businessmen's anti-Klan campaign—was formed to take up the endeavor. When the Interracial Committee's hospital care subcommittee was created in the summer of 1951, under the chairmanship of investment banker Mervyn Sterne, it at once became an energetic ally of the campaign. Another groundbreaking ceremony was held in September 1952, and the million-dollar sixty-bed facility was opened in January 1954. Holy Name Hospital represented a genuine milestone in improving the health care of Birmingham's blacks.

Nevertheless, civil rights activists such as Emory Jackson suspected that conservative whites were using the construction of the black hospital as an excuse to avoid giving black doctors and patients equality in the existing white hospitals. And indeed, Mayor Green, in urging contributions to the hospital fund, had said that the hospital would "show to the representatives in Congress that the welfare of the Negro can be advanced by local citizens" and would form "a conclusive reply to communism, agitators and socialism." The failure of the hospital care subcommittee's attempts to press beyond the black hospital once it had been built, spoke to the validity of Jackson's concerns. After the hospital opened, Sterne resigned as subcommittee chairman and was succeeded by a Baptist minister, Dr. Lamar Jackson. In the meantime, at its annual convention in April 1953, the Alabama Medical Association had adopted a report by Dr. Brannon Hubbard of Montgomery eliminating any racial bar to association membership and encouraging the county medical societies to admit black doctors. In June the Lauderdale County Medical Society actually admitted Dr. J. L. Hicks of Florence, the first black to join a white medical society in the state's history. And at the same time, the Jefferson County Medical Society voted almost unanimously to amend its membership requirements to eliminate the word "white." As a result of these developments, Dr. Jackson turned the hospital subcommittee's attention to arranging for a black doctor to be admitted to the Jefferson County association. But the final hurdle proved to be one that the subcommittee could not surmount. Candidates for membership required two letters of recommendation from doctors in their area of specialization and could then be blackballed by the negative vote of any two members. As a result, when the Interracial Committee was dissolved more than two years later, the county medical society, and hence the physicians practicing in the white hospitals, remained all white.[44]

The legacy of the transportation subcommittee was a particularly positive one. In its early years, under the chairmanship first of Baptist minister John Buchanan and then of businessman Allen Rushton, the committee accomplished little. But at the beginning of 1954 the chairmanship passed to Lester Shannon of Stockham Valves and Fittings, and under Shannon's leadership, with the active assistance of executive secretary Paul R. Jones, the committee began making progress in several areas. During the preceding decade, the city busses had been notorious as a scene of racial conflict, very often because of the aggressive hostility of the white drivers to black passengers. Quiet intervention with both the bus company and the transit union, together with anonymous monitoring of predominantly black routes to observe drivers' conduct, apparently produced marked improvements; the number of complaints received by the company declined sharply, and black committee members expressed pleasure at the noticeable improvements in service. The committee also urged the bus company to consider hiring black drivers as well as white; and it even explored the possibility of removing the "race boards" from the busses, though it abandoned this idea when it discovered that the boards were specifically required by city ordinance. On another problem, the committee received the effective cooperation of Mayor James Morgan. A single white taxicab company had an exclusive franchise from the city to have its cabs wait for passengers at the Birmingham airport; the cab drivers often refused to take black passengers, forcing blacks to call black taxis to come from the city, which compelled long delays. When the committee brought this situation to the mayor's attention, he intervened forcefully to correct it. Indeed, he instructed the city attorney to tell the company that, if necessary, it was to take black and white passengers in the same cab.

However, the committee left its greatest mark upon a form of transportation not usually associated with that term, elevators. Birmingham's downtown office buildings at this period universally had segregated elevators; often the passenger elevators were limited to whites, and blacks had to use the single freight elevator. However, this practice was one of the very few manifestations of segregation that was not required by law. Because it was entirely customary, the discrimination could be eliminated simply by a decision of the building's owners. The transportation committee therefore commenced a series of patient, confidential negotiations with the owners, seeking to nudge them to action. By the summer of 1954 four buildings had agreed to the integration, including the Jefferson County Courthouse. And by the end of 1955 there were only two buildings in the downtown area—the Massey Building and the Frank Nelson Building—that still had segregated elevators. But these two proved intractable; when the Interracial Committee was dissolved in April 1956, the two remained segregated. In October, a civil rights activist, the Reverend Theodore N. Nelson, decided to force the issue. He boarded one of the white elevators in the Massey Building on the seventh floor and asked to go to the lobby. The building's management thereupon had him arrested. But when he came to trial in Recorder's Court, Orzell Billingsley, the young black attorney defending him, pointed out that the city had no elevator segregation ordinance, and Judge Ralph Parker accordingly dismissed the charges. Nelson then sued the Massey Building for false arrest, and the building agreed to integrate its elevators. But despite this affair, the Frank Nelson Building still refused to abandon segregated elevators, and after 1956 it was left with the only elevator discrimination in downtown Birmingham. The virtual elimination of segregated elevators between 1954 and 1956 constituted Birmingham's first step toward racial integration.[45]

The achievements of the Interracial Committee during its five years of existence were certainly distinctly modest in comparison with the extent of the injustice that Birmingham blacks faced. Nevertheless, its accomplishments—the integration of the elevators; the building of the Holy Name Hospital, the Loveman Village day-care center, the black golf course, and the Memorial Park community center; the opening of the zoo and of Vulcan Park to blacks; and more generally, the willingness of white moderates to work together with black leaders to ameliorate the effects of discrimination—formed a significant element in the list of improvements in the conditions of black life in Birmingham during the years after World War II that gave, particularly to middle-class blacks, a sense of positive momentum, and therefore a growing confidence and insistence. As late as 1943, for instance, there was not a single black park in the city. By 1948 there were seven such parks and a public swimming pool. By 1961 there were thirteen black parks and playgrounds, five community centers, and three municipal pools. A black YMCA was opened in 1951. The city's first black radio station, WEDR, commenced broadcasting—despite, as we have seen, the efforts of the Ku Klux Klan to silence it—in August 1949; together with Birmingham's two black newspapers, it provided an important source of black community consolidation. Black insurance magnate Arthur Gaston constructed a modern motel for black travelers in 1954. In 1959, the Holy Name Hospital added a dental clinic to its facilities.

There had been a black branch of the public library in the downtown area since 1918, and a suburban black branch was added in 1940, but during the 1950s two additional black branches were constructed near two of the city's three black public housing projects. Birmingham had established Alabama's first black high school, initially with a vocational focus, as early as 1899. In 1937 the city added a second high school; by this time, both of them had academic programs as well. But during the 1950s three additional black high schools were constructed and the quality of black secondary education was substantially improved. In 1950 Alabama opened the Lawson State Vocational School, its only trade school for blacks, in Wenonah, near Birmingham. In the same year, Miles College, a four-year black liberal arts college founded by the C.M.E. Church in 1908, achieved accreditation. And in 1955, Daniel Payne junior college, operated by the A.M.E. Church, was accredited.

At the end of World War II, Arthur Shores was Jefferson County's only black attorney. But by 1949 there were four; by 1951, six; by 1959, nine; and by 1961, eleven. The additional lawyers greatly increased blacks' ability to use the court system. In 1945, Shores and Ensley mortician William E. Shortridge organized the Jones Valley Finance Company, which offered both personal loans and home mortgages. In 1956, over fierce opposition from white bankers, Shores, Gaston, insurance executive John J. Drew, dentist Dr. John Nixon, and others organized Alabama's first black savings and loan association, Citizens Federal. Earlier, Shores and Wilbur Hollins had formed a black real estate business. These three organizations vastly expanded black access to the credit and housing markets. And Birmingham, which had always been home to the state's largest and most prosperous black middle class, saw generally rising black incomes. By 1957 more than 20 percent of the city's black families had incomes of over four thousand dollars a year, and two-thirds of them had annual incomes over two thousand dollars. In this context, the achievements of the postwar years seemed earnests of a brightening future. And the forces seeking continued discrimination therefore increasingly lost historical, in addition to moral, legitimacy in the eyes of most Birmingham blacks.[46]

It was, however, the seventh and last of the Interracial Committee's subcommittees, the subcommittee on the police, that would forge the next direct link in the chain of circumstances that eventually would transform Birmingham's race relations. The business progressives' response to the renewal of Klan violence in the late 1940s in effect was three-pronged: the direct response of indictment and prosecution of the culprits, the creation of contacts with moderate black leaders to remedy sources of racial friction, and the reform of the police department that had so signally failed to solve the Smithfield bombings, particularly by the hiring of black policemen. The prosecution of the Klansmen had not succeeded, but the grand jury's investigation had produced sufficient discord within the Klan, at least for a time, to neutralize it. The Interracial Committee's accomplishments were in themselves slender, but the context in which they occurred had the effect of considerably heightening the black middle class's expectations. And the effort to induce the hiring of black policemen would have similarly unintended but momentous consequences.

Under "Bull" Connor, the Birmingham Police Department had become a sink of corruption and racial prejudice. James C. Parsons, who served in the department for a quarter century, eventually as its chief, estimated that 45 percent of the city's policemen were taking payoffs from elements such as bootleggers and operators of the numbers rackets, with another 45 percent eager to do so as soon as they could. Connor was well aware of this fact and used it to control the department. He kept salaries unreasonably low—thus permitting low taxes—and used assignment to the vice and burglary divisions, where opportunities for graft were great, as a reward for those officers who were subservient, while assigning less cooperative officers to relatively less profitable divisions such as traffic. Particular sections of the city (those, for instance, in which saloons and houses of prostitution were more common) and particular shifts (those, perhaps, during which liquor could not legally be sold) were also more lucrative than others. Connor also manipulated the civil service act that he had co-sponsored to keep the police and fire department commanders in awe. Under the act, employees gained civil service protection in a position only after serving in it for a year. Connor therefore constantly shuffled commanders from post to post to prevent any one of them from establishing tenure. His first act after taking office in 1937 was to force the incumbent police chief to accept a demotion, and thereafter the position of chief became virtually a revolving door. Because of these constant personnel changes, office politics within the department was rampant. And of course, adherence to Connor's racial views and support of his political aspirations were prerequisites for promotion.

As early as 1945, a police captain who had quit in disgust and had then run against Connor in the municipal election had sought unsuccessfully to alert the electorate to what was happening to the department. But the utter insouciance of the police response to the Smithfield bombings in 1949, crowned by the uniquely vitriolic racism of Connor's campaign for governor in 1950, convinced many business moderates that if the commissioner continued in power, it would be at the cost of the city's good name. And other business progressives were converted to opposition to Connor's policies by the growing public awareness of police corruption, fed by dismay at the rapid changes in the identity of the chief—and eventually made apparent to everyone by the investigations once Connor had left office, which resulted in the discovery in 1954 that at least twenty-three and perhaps as many as fifty police officers were members of a burglary ring.[47]

In June 1951, at one of its first meetings, the Interracial Committee had established the subcommittee, chaired by prominent attorney Douglas Arant, whose explicit charge was to seek the hiring of black policemen. The committee moved with great speed, and by February 1952 it had formally adopted a report urging the city commission to employ a minimum of six black officers as soon as possible. But events were moving even faster. The drive to hire black policemen was a part of the more general campaign to reform the police department. The need for such a reformation was emphasized less than a month after the subcommittee on police was created, and less than two weeks after Arant accepted its chairmanship, when C. L. Reeves, the principal of Birmingham's newest black high school, who was both a member of the Interracial Committee and a captain of the Smithfield civil defense unit, was fired at and arrested by Detective C. C. Ray while Reeves was patrolling the North Smithfield area. At the request of the Interracial Committee's executive committee, Arant intervened and managed to persuade the city prosecutor to drop the charge that Ray had filed against Reeves following the shooting. In August the executive committee also recorded a strong protest "against the flagrant use of pistols by the police in their attempt to make arrests—particularly in cases of misdemeanors and other minor offenses." This affair added new urgency to the business progressives' sense that the police department was a chief stumbling block to the improvement of the city's racial climate. The chamber of commerce, at the urging of the Interracial Committee, also appointed a committee to seek the hiring of black officers, chaired by realtor and insurance agent John H. Cobbs, and the two committees began to work together toward the goal. But Arant knew that the proposal was very unlikely to get past Commissioner Connor. He had, he told his subcommittee, raised the idea with Connor some three or four years earlier but had gotten nowhere. It was clear, therefore, that just as the police force was a central part of the community's problems, so Connor was the principal element that made it so. A significant part of the business leadership that had for so many years considered Connor a useful politician was about to change its mind.[48]

And as it happened, just at this moment Connor's personal corruption and the venal and perfidious atmosphere he had so assiduously encouraged within the police department were prepared to offer Connor's new business opponents the opportunity they required to attempt to destroy him. Connor determined to arrange an extramarital tryst with his private secretary, Christina Brown, following a police department Christmas party at the Tutwiler Hotel in December 1951, and he instructed one of his flunkies, Captain Charles Pierce, to obtain a hotel room for the purpose. Word of this request evidently spread among the policemen at the party and reached the ears of Detective Henry Darnell, a man whom Connor had for some time been tormenting, in the belief that Darnell was planning to run against him in the next municipal election. Darnell called the police reporter for the *Birmingham Post-Herald,* and together they arrived outside the hotel room about a half an hour after the sexual activities had begun. Connor refused to admit Darnell, and after some twenty minutes of effort, the detective managed to break down the door. By this time both Connor and Miss Brown were fully dressed and wearing overcoats and hats. Darnell arrested the two for violating a city ordinance that forbade any unrelated adults of different sexes to occupy the same hotel room. The *Post-Herald* reporter published a front-page account of the episode.

Connor's subsequent trial in city Recorder's Court revealed details both sordid and sensational. On the opening day of the trial, Detective Darnell discovered that a dynamite bomb had been attached to the starter of his automobile, presumably by one of his fellow police officers. Darnell believed that the action had been taken on Connor's orders. Eventually, Recorder's Court Judge Ralph Parker—whom Connor had been attempting to dismiss—found Connor guilty and gave him a fine of one hundred dollars and a suspended jail sentence of six months. Connor appealed to circuit court, where he asked for a jury trial. In the meantime, the business progressive forces fell upon this affair with almost unseemly gusto. Opposition to vice and immorality had always been an essential element of Connor's portrait of himself, and it was at the heart of his popularity among many white fundamentalists. Also, the testimony at Connor's trial seemed to confirm rumors of police corruption and thus challenged those of Connor's supporters who had believed him an effective and honest administrator. The scandal therefore provided Connor's enemies an ideal means to dismantle the commissioner's electoral constituency. The *Birmingham Post-Herald,* whose editor, James E. Mills, was a close associate of the business progressives, and the *Birmingham News,* whose publisher, Clarence Hanson, was one of their leaders, published exceedingly detailed accounts of the trials, including pages of verbatim extracts from the testimony. The *Post-Herald* urged a thorough investigation of the police department by impartial outsiders: "If complete reorganization of the police department, after necessary firings or resignations, is required to restore public confidence and lift the morale of the honest, hard-working officers remaining, then the sooner that job is done the better." The *News* demanded Connor's resignation. Within days of Connor's conviction in Recorder's Court, Circuit Solicitor Emmett Perry's office had the county grand jury commence hearing witnesses about the state of agencies under the commissioner's jurisdiction. In February 1952, the grand jury returned articles of impeachment against Connor. The jurors reported that "he browbeats his subordinates with whom he does not agree" and "orders his subordinates what to do without clear statements of his policies and with little or no idea of his objectives; . . . he listens to no advice and learns neither from his friends, his enemies nor experience." The impeachment articles charged Connor with incompetence, moral turpitude, and corruption in office. In addition to the Christina Brown affair, they alleged a sexual assault on a switchboard operator, Frances Smith; the private use of city prisoners and city property; and illegal efforts to force the fire chief into retirement. Connor replied that the allegations were merely a continuation of the attempts "of professional gamblers, lottery racketeers, organized criminals and Communists . . . to secure my removal from office."

In the meantime, Connor's colleagues Mayor Green and Commissioner Morgan, under enormous pressure from community leaders, had appointed a four-member committee to propose reforms of the police force. The committee members—its chairman, attorney Greye Tate; investment banker Mervyn Sterne; industrialist Hakon A. Berg, retired president of the Woodward Iron Company; and attorney R. DuPont Thompson—submitted their report later in February. The Tate Committee avoided the inflamed language of the grand jury's indictment, but its lengthy and meticulous documentation of the low morale, inadequate supervision and training, and excessive turnover of the police officers made Connor's administrative failures starkly apparent. The report concluded that he was "deficient in executive ability," "imperious," and given to "taking sudden impulsive and erratic action, without thorough investigation and mature consideration." It went on to offer numerous suggestions for improving the force. Further unsolved bombings, it admonished, "would be evidence of weakness and incompetence in the Department." And, presumably at the urging of Mervyn Sterne, who was also a member of the Interracial Committee and a strong advocate of black officers, it specifically recommended that the city consider hiring eight black policemen. The report was submitted on February 19; the Interracial Committee's subcommittee on black police had submitted its recommendation for at least six black officers on February 18. Thereafter Sterne and Douglas Arant coordinated their efforts to make this proposal a reality.

Connor remained unabashed. He appointed Captain Pierce, who had arranged the hotel room for the commissioner and Miss Brown and who had been the subject of explicit criticism in the Tate Committee report, as the department's new chief. He fired Detective Darnell; the action produced a storm of controversy, but Connor eventually made it stick. He denounced the idea of black policemen. At his impeachment trial in March, all of Birmingham's circuit judges recused themselves and Judge Emmett Hildreth of Greene County was appointed to preside. Judge Hildreth promptly threw out the morals charges on the ground that they did not constitute impeachable offenses, and he limited the jury to considering the allegations of misuse of public property and city prisoners. On these counts the jury deadlocked, and Judge Hildreth declared a mistrial. The impeachment was retried in October, but the outcome was once again a mistrial. In the meantime, a circuit court jury convicted Connor in April on the charge of illegal occupancy of a hotel room with Miss Brown. But in June the state court of appeals held the city's illegal occupancy ordinance unconstitutionally vague and dismissed the prosecution; and in August the state supreme court agreed. As the municipal elections in the spring of 1953 approached, therefore, Connor had surmounted his legal difficulties. He sought strenuously to use his opposition to hiring black officers to revivify his political fortunes, but the scandals had damaged him too badly with too many of his previous supporters. Finally, at the end of February 1953 he announced that he would not be a candidate for reelection. The business moderates appeared to have won the battle.[49]

The reformers among the city's white businessmen could survey their world with some satisfaction in 1953. The bombings in Smithfield had ended; the last incident there had been in May 1951. Their joint efforts with like-minded black leaders seemed to be making progress toward the diminution of racial ill will. Connor was serving his last months in office. The man chosen to succeed him, Robert E. Lindbergh, the chief clerk in the sheriff's office, was a moderate. Commissioner Morgan, also a moderate, had been elected to succeed the retiring Mayor Green. Both Morgan and Lindbergh had been endorsed by blacks' principal political organization, the Progressive Democratic Association, and both had received the virtually solid support of Birmingham's five thousand black voters. And though the Progressive Democrats' choice for the third commissionership, United Steelworkers leader Robert C. Arthur—the man who would head the city school board during the school integration crisis of 1963—had been eliminated, still the winner, Deputy Sheriff Wade Bradley, had had the support of a number of influential black leaders, and blacks had provided his exceedingly narrow margin of victory over former street maintenance supervisor James T. "Jabo" Waggoner. The business moderates felt that they had firm commitments from both Morgan and Lindbergh to hire black policemen, an action which all Birminghamians, of every hue and attitude, regarded as the single most significant racial reform on the city's agenda. Moreover, the new commissioners almost at once began to give evidence that a new day had dawned in the city. In September 1953, the newly inaugurated Mayor Morgan announced that he and Commissioner Lindbergh were considering repealing a city ordinance that forbade blacks and whites from competing against each other in sports, an ordinance that had been introduced by Commissioner Connor in 1950. In January 1954, Commissioner Bradley agreed to the action and the ordinance was repealed unanimously.

Segregationist sentiment remained powerful in the city, however. In February an angry group of whites led by elderly attorney Hugh Locke, who had been the gubernatorial candidate of the Klan and anti-Catholic forces in 1930, appeared before the commission to demand that it restore sports segregation. Though the ordinance had been enacted only a bit more than three years earlier, Locke screamed that the commissioners had ended a form of discrimination in existence for eighty-five years; apparently he identified its introduction with the advent of radical Reconstruction. But the commission held firm; Commissioner Bradley told Locke that the commission "will not be swayed by the wishes of a small dissenting group." The dissenters, though, were more numerous than Bradley supposed. Locke led a petition drive to force a referendum on the question, and by March he had gathered ten thousand signatures. The commission then modified the new ordinance to permit integration only in professional sports. But a referendum was ordered nevertheless. And on June 1, two weeks after the U.S. Supreme Court ruled public school segregation unconstitutional, the electorate voted by a margin of three to one to restore full sports segregation. At almost the same time, in the first incident of Klan violence since 1951, the Smithfield home of wealthy black dentist John Nixon fell victim to an arson attempt.[50]

The outcome of the sports segregation referendum left the new city commission profoundly chastened, but other events of the period encouraged optimists among the business progressives to regard the referendum as the last gasp of a dying order, rather than—as time would demonstrate it actually to have been—the first evidence of an immense white reaction. Earlier in May, "Bull" Connor, who had sought to return to public office by running against Jefferson County sheriff Holt McDowell, had suffered a crushing defeat; Connor received less than a third of the vote. The very next day after the attempted arson against Dr. Nixon's home, police apprehended the culprit, apparent proof that Commissioner Lindbergh's efforts to reform the police department were taking hold. And as the year advanced, Lindbergh pressed ahead with his campaign. He had appointed a retired army officer, Colonel Paul Singer, to administer the force, and Singer undertook extensive personnel changes. His investigations, as we have seen, uncovered the burglary ring within the department. An unfortunate affair at the end of 1954 clearly demonstrated Lindbergh's sincerity.

On the morning of December 11, Charles Patrick, a black ironworker, got into an argument over a parking place with the wife of a police officer, Arthur S. Lynch. Patrick was arrested for disorderly conduct and taken to the city jail. Shortly thereafter, Lynch and his partner James W. Siniard arrived, were admitted to Patrick's cell, and beat him within an inch of his life for his effrontery. On December 17 Patrick was finally taken before Recorder's Court Judge Ralph Parker, who fined him twenty-five dollars on the disorderly conduct charge. By that time, however, word of the incident had reached Lindbergh and his new chief, George L. Pattie. They promptly fired Lynch and Siniard and suspended the jailer who had failed to report the assault. The officers appealed to the full city commission. Mayor Morgan and Commissioner Bradley noted, doubtless correctly, that police had not been subjected to such firm discipline in the past, and therefore believed that it was unfair to begin now without warning. They voted instead merely to suspend the officers for a month and to warn policemen that such actions would result in the future in dismissal. Lindbergh exploded in anger, denouncing the decision as seeming to give "the police department—some 400 men—a blanket permission to go to the jail anytime and beat prisoners because a policeman is personally . . . upset." In the meantime, the publicity surrounding the case had caused Judge Parker to have second thoughts. He allowed Patrick to take a lie-detector test, and when the test indicated that Patrick was telling the truth, Parker dismissed all charges against him. Thereupon Patrick filed a complaint against Lynch and Siniard with the county personnel board. After a two-day hearing in January 1955, the personnel board vacated the city commission's weaker punishment and reinstated Lindbergh's original firm one, adding a prohibition against Lynch's working in law enforcement ever again. In February, a U.S. grand jury indicted the policemen and the jailer for violating Patrick's civil rights. And though a federal trial jury acquitted the three men in June, later that same month a three-judge court of Birmingham circuit judges upheld the personnel board's decision. Never before had Birmingham's institutions been willing to stand so determinedly behind a black man in a dispute with a police officer. It was clear that the principal reason that this incident had not been dismissed, as so many like it had been in the past, was Commissioner Lindbergh.[51]

It was in this context of a newly moderate city political leadership but of a gathering, if not yet fully apparent, white supremacist reaction within the electorate that the Interracial Committee's subcommittee on black police set about effecting its proposed reform. As we have seen, the subcommittee's initial efforts came amidst—and, through the activities of Mervyn Sterne, were connected with—the attempts of business progressive leaders to rid themselves of "Bull" Connor. Beginning in mid-January 1952, as the county grand jury was conducting its investigation of Connor, the subcommittee commenced mobilizing community support for the hiring of black officers. At a meeting on January 17 it voted to ask the *Birmingham News* to send a reporter to southern cities that already had employed black police to prepare a series of articles on the success of the decision. The *News* agreed at once, and correspondent Irving Beiman's reports began appearing in February. The subcommittee itself sent a staff member, Nancy Huddleston, to study the situation in Memphis, which had introduced black policemen in 1948. Her findings, presented in May, were very positive. In the meantime, at the suggestion of Sterne, in April the subcommittee sent a detailed questionnaire to fifteen prominent white community figures in each of thirty southern cities with black police in order to determine their attitudes toward the officers. The results, available by the summer, again were overwhelmingly positive. The subcommittee was so pleased that it determined to assemble Huddleston's and Beiman's investigations and the findings from the questionnaires into a pamphlet to be distributed to Birmingham organizations and leaders of opinion. Advocates of the reform emphasized, as they had in Montgomery, that black officers would patrol only in black neighborhoods and would increase the police department's ability to identify black criminals.

Under those circumstances, many white moderates found the proposal entirely acceptable. Meanwhile, recruitment of support from such sources had already begun when, as we have seen, at the request of subcommittee chairman Arant, the chamber of commerce in May appointed its own committee under realtor and insurance agent John Cobbs to assist the campaign. By October a draft of the proposed pamphlet had been completed, and after approval by the full Interracial Committee and its parent Coordinating Council of Social Forces, it was printed and a thousand copies were distributed during the spring of 1953, in the midst of the municipal election.[52]

All of these events took place while "Bull" Connor was battling for his political life, and as we have seen, Connor seized upon them in an effort to rally segregationist voters to his cause. Because Connor's opposition to black officers was public and vitriolic, after the distribution of the pamphlet and the election of the moderate Lindbergh to succeed Connor in the spring the subcommittee quite reasonably suspended further active steps to await the end of Connor's term as public safety commissioner in mid-October. Subcommittee chairman Arant, with perhaps rather less reason, continued to hesitate thereafter, however; he convinced himself that the committee should take no action until after the December 15 referendum in which Alabamians were to vote on a constitutional amendment to limit the accumulation of back poll taxes to a total of three dollars. And then with the end of the year, he resigned the chairmanship of the subcommittee, though he continued as one of its members. As it happened, Bishop Carpenter declined another term as chairman of the full Interracial Committee at the same time, and because the first three men approached refused the job, it was not until the end of February that a successor to Carpenter, broadcasting executive Henry P. Johnston, was named. Johnston then began the search for a successor to Arant, but he was not able to come up with one until June, when Joe H. Brady, the president of a construction equipment firm, accepted the position. Though these personnel difficulties were probably unavoidable, their effect was quite unfortunate. When Lindbergh had first come into office in October he had been open to racial reform, as his vote to repeal the sports segregation ordinance had demonstrated. Indeed, the Interracial Committee was informed in early December that Colonel Singer, whom Lindbergh had appointed to administer the police, was considering employing black policewomen in connection with a new juvenile bureau that was shortly to be established. And some committee members believed that they had firm assurances from Lindbergh that he favored hiring black officers. But eight months later, when the subcommittee was finally ready to approach Lindbergh about the matter, the Supreme Court's school desegregation decision and the referendum to restore sports segregation had intervened. If the subcommittee had acted in October 1953 it very likely would have gotten a positive response, but by June 1954 Lindbergh had begun to have cold feet.[53]

Nevertheless, with Brady's appointment the subcommittee resumed active lobbying for the reform. Brady received particularly energetic assistance from Henry Johnston (the new committee chairman), Mervyn Sterne, and Arthur V. Wiebel (the president of U.S. Steel's Birmingham subsidiary, who had just been named to the subcommittee). During the late summer and early fall of 1954, the members made contact both with the city commissioners and with the county personnel board and urged them to action. In October they were joined in their efforts by Charles Zukoski, the head of First National Bank's trust department, who was the chairman of the committee's parent Coordinating Council. They continued their quiet but insistent pressure through the winter and into the spring of 1955. But Lindbergh was just at this time involved in the controversy surrounding his firing of Officers Lynch and Siniard and, increasingly concerned about his prospects for reelection in 1957, was fearful of further alienating segregationist voters. The subcommittee remained hopeful of persuading him, but the growing black impatience at the repeated delays was about to eliminate that prospect.

In September 1954 a young black minister, the Reverend George Rudolph, president of the St. Marks Village and Rosewood Voters League, wrote to Lindbergh to urge the hiring of black policemen. Rudolph had announced his candidacy for the presidency of the Jefferson County Progressive Democratic Association, the principal organization of the area's black voters, against the incumbent, attorney Arthur Shores, who was the Interracial Committee's vice-chairman. The fact that the Interracial Committee was actively seeking black policemen was generally known among black leaders, of course, and Rudolph's letter was doubtless intended to establish his own credentials on this question. Lindbergh responded by inviting Rudolph and other prominent blacks to meet with him in his office to discuss the matter, but only Rudolph and Miles College student W. C. Blount showed up at the meeting on September 28. Lindbergh greeted them warmly and told them, "I am surprised and utterly disappointed in Birmingham for not having qualified Negro citizens on the police force. . . . Birmingham should have been the first major city in the south to employ Negro members on the police force," he said, and "it would have greatly helped in bettering racial relations." He assured them that blacks would be hired within the coming year. The only thing holding it up, he said, was opposition from "certain small groups of persons who are not enlightened to the changing times of progress," such as those who had rallied to Hugh Locke's campaign to reject the repeal of the sports segregation ordinance. But he pledged to press the personnel board to eliminate its rule barring blacks from taking civil service examinations and to seek the employment of black policemen despite this resistance.

Rudolph was understandably heartened by these seemingly clear engagements, and thus he was correspondingly frustrated as the coming months showed no signs of their being fulfilled. After having waited almost nine months, during which the Interracial Committee's subcommittee did its best to prod Lindbergh into action, on June 21, 1955, Rudolph appeared before the city commission at one of its public sessions and formally requested immediate steps toward the employment of black policemen. This statement for the first time placed the campaign on the record and drew the first official responses from the commissioners. Mayor Morgan endorsed the proposal and noted the success of black officers elsewhere in the South, but Commissioner Lindbergh's doubts at last took irrevocable form: "In view of the unsettled state of affairs with anxiety expressed by thinking people of both races over the Supreme Court decision, any effort to hire Negro police at this time would pose obstacles that could not be overcome." And Commissioner Bradley echoed the public safety commissioner: "Racial issues have been aggravated by the Supreme Court decision and any attempt to hire Negro police at this time would be unfeasible and dangerous."[54]

The Interracial Committee apparently had been hoping to avoid forcing the commissioners into any such explicit avowal of their opinions so that quiet persuasion could continue. Executive Secretary Paul Jones met with Rudolph to brief him on the subcommittee's efforts, with the intention of securing his cooperation, but it was now too late. With Rudolph's petition and the commissioners' statements in response, the entire matter moved into the public arena, and positions rapidly hardened. By mid-July the Interracial Committee was making plans to gather representatives from all the many community organizations that favored black policemen in order to make a joint approach to the commission in behalf of the proposal. Both the *Birmingham News* and the *Birmingham Post-Herald* endorsed it editorially, and the Young Men's Business Club and the white Birmingham Methodist Ministers Association passed resolutions supporting it. But Commissioner Bradley now opposed the hiring of black policemen under any circumstances, and Commissioner Lindbergh called this the most inopportune time possible to discuss the matter, given the trial of Emmett Till's murderers, the refusal of Michigan governor G. Mennen Williams to speak to the Birmingham Jefferson-Jackson Day Dinner because of its exclusion of Edgar D. Nixon, and the U.S. Supreme Court's decision implementing its earlier school desegregation decision, which had generated petitions from NAACP branches around the state asking local school boards to take action. And then, at the end of July, the cause gained a new advocate, a young black minister even more insistent and ambitious than Rudolph, and vastly more audacious, the Reverend Fred L. Shuttlesworth.[55]

Fred Shuttlesworth was born in Mount Meigs, near Montgomery, in

1922. His name at birth was Fred Robinson. He was the illegitimate son of a young farm woman, Alberta Robinson, by a Montgomery carpenter and future Baptist minister, Vetter E. Green. In 1923 Alberta Robinson moved with her parents to Birmingham, and there in 1926 she married a retired Jefferson County coal miner and bootlegger, William N. Shuttlesworth; the family then moved to Will Shuttlesworth's home in Oxmoor, just south of Birmingham, and young Fred adopted his new stepfather's name. He graduated from high school in 1940, but the following year he became involved in his stepfather's bootlegging operation, was arrested, and was given two years' probation. He married in 1941 and in 1943 moved to Mobile to take a job at the Army Air Corps' Brookley Field. There he was ordained a Baptist minister in the spring of 1944. In 1947 he moved to Selma to enroll in the denomination's Selma University, a junior college. Completing his studies at Selma in 1949, he went on to Alabama State College in Montgomery, from which he received a degree in education in 1952. In the meantime, in 1950 he had become the pastor of Selma's black First Baptist Church. In 1953 he accepted a call to return to Birmingham as the pastor of the Bethel Baptist Church, in the city's Collegeville section.[56]

George Rudolph's appearance before the city commission in June 1955 captured Shuttlesworth's imagination. At a meeting of Birmingham's black Baptist Ministers Conference on July 9, called to discuss the problem of juvenile delinquency, Shuttlesworth argued that the hiring of black policemen would increase black teenagers' respect for law enforcement and urged that the association include an endorsement of the action among its other suggestions. The president of the association was the Reverend James L. Ware, who in later years would become one of Shuttlesworth's principal rivals for leadership of the black community. Ware, a native of Wetumpka, had been ordained in 1929, when Shuttlesworth was only seven, and had come to Birmingham in 1941 to pastor the Trinity Baptist Church. He had been involved in a number of early civil rights campaigns, and in 1949 Emory Jackson had referred to him as the city's most militant minister. But the aggressiveness of the younger generation was now leaving him behind. Ware felt that Shuttlesworth's proposal was too controversial, and at his insistence the conference took no action on it. Shuttlesworth, however, was undeterred. He circulated a draft statement among like-minded conference members, and seventy-seven of them signed it, including a number of his future allies such as Edward Gardner, Robert L. Alford, and Nelson H. Smith. Then on July 25 he presented it to the city commission. He got the same response that Rudolph had received a month earlier. But two weeks later he submitted a petition to the personnel board asking it to create a register of blacks qualified for police vacancies; the board replied that there was no point in doing so unless the city was prepared to hire from it. On August 12, Rudolph appeared before the board to make the same request, presumably in the hope of recapturing the initiative on the questions for himself. But the issue was now Shuttlesworth's. He returned to the city commission on September 1 with the formal endorsement of the black Interdenominational Ministerial Alliance and a petition with thirty-five hundred signatures. He was back on September 30 to renew the request. By January he had been chosen the Interdenominational Ministerial Alliance's president and was named the principal speaker at the installation of the new officers of Birmingham's NAACP branch.[57]

In the meantime the Interracial Committee pressed ahead with its own efforts, but time was now running out not only for this reform but for any reform. In March 1955 the committee had undertaken its most ambitious and public effort; it had staged an integrated, two-day Race Relations Institute on the campus of Birmingham-Southern College, a white Methodist institution. Attendance at all of the institute's sessions had been good, and committee members were initially enthusiastic about the broadening of interracial communication that resulted. But the general attention that the institute drew to the committee's activities proved to be the beginning of the end for the enterprise. During 1954, in response to the business progressives' tentative efforts to introduce modest alterations in the existing racial order, the segregationists among the city's commercial and industrial leadership had started to organize. In March, as a part of attorney Hugh Locke's campaign to restore the sports segregation ordinance, Locke and other prominent businessmen—in particular, William H. Hoover of the Employers Insurance Company, Hugh Morrow of the U.S. Pipe and Foundry Company, construction executive R. Hugh Daniel, F. B. Yielding, Jr., of the Jefferson Federal Savings and Loan, and Sidney Smyer of the Birmingham Realty Company—formed the American States' Rights Association. To head it they chose Olin H. Horton, who together with Hoover was an executive of Employers Insurance and who, as we have seen, had led the white homeowners' opposition during the Smithfield controversy. Its vice-president was realtor William W. Walker. In December, segregationist Methodists established an alliance to defeat their denomination's plan to allow its few black congregations to join its all-white regional jurisdictions. Sidney Smyer was chosen the group's president, and Olin Horton played a significant role in its creation. Horton's States' Rights Association hired the venomous racist Asa Carter to direct its public relations. In September the association began sponsoring a series of radio broadcasts by Carter in which he attacked all evidence of moderation. In February 1955, when he pronounced the National Conference of Christians and Jews a Communist front, the public uproar compelled Carter's dismissal. Nevertheless, during the coming year Carter and Horton cooperated to assist the growth of the White Citizens' Council. Alabama's first chapter of the Citizens' Council had been formed in Selma in October 1954, and its first Jefferson County chapter was created in Tarrant City a year later.[58]

The Race Relations Institute attracted the particular concern of all three of these white supremacist organizations, both because Citizens' Council doctrine warned that blacks could achieve integration only with the co-operation of white moderates and because the institute had taken place on a white Methodist campus. September 1955 found the Interracial Committee confidently planning a second Race Relations Institute for the spring of 1956. It established a new subcommittee to work on employment relations and again urged Commissioner Lindbergh to accept black police officers. In January 1956, the subcommittee on black police gathered leaders of the area's labor unions in Mervyn Sterne's office and obtained their agreement to have their unions adopt resolutions endorsing the hiring of black policemen. But by then the States' Rights Association and the rapidly growing White Citizens' Council were preparing their counterattack.

The Interracial Committee's parent organization, the Coordinating Council of Social Forces, served primarily to synchronize the community efforts of the Red Cross and the Community Chest agencies. Beginning in the last months of 1955, the segregationist publicists therefore started to urge Birmingham whites to withhold contributions to the Red Cross and Community Chest fund drives to protest the Coordinating Council's sponsorship of the Interracial Committee. The committee, which Emory Jackson and other black militants continued to accuse of surreptitious support for segregation, appeared to the obdurate segregationists to be the leading edge of the integrationist campaign. And as the annual fund drives began to get under way, events conspired to lend the white supremacists' apprehensions considerable force even among less rigid segregationists. At the beginning of February, the riots in neighboring Tuscaloosa that accompanied the ultimately unsuccessful attempt of Autherine Lucy to enroll in the University of Alabama's graduate program in library science threw Birmingham into turmoil. Both Lucy and her attorney, Arthur Shores, were Birmingham residents, and the various legal proceedings in the case had taken place in Birmingham's federal district court. Moreover, the Tuscaloosa mob had been in large part composed of Birmingham and Bessemer Klansmen and White Citizens' Council members, led by Asa Carter and Robert Chambliss, the Klansman fired by the city and indicted for the Klan violence surrounding the Smithfield confrontation. And Chambliss, together with other Klansmen, had subsequently sued Lucy and the NAACP for libel for having alleged that they had conspired with the university to prevent Lucy from attending classes. In addition to the Lucy riots, the sense of crisis in Birmingham had been intensified because, as we have seen, at the same time, the Montgomery Improvement Association sued in federal court to force the integration of that city's buses, and the county grand jury there indicted Martin Luther King and other MIA leaders for conspiracy to boycott. Thus by late February, fund-raisers found potential contributors to the local charities suddenly convinced that the Coordinating Council was a controversial organization. Contributions at once dried up.

The Coordinating Council's board of directors—a twenty-six-person body only one of whose members, Arthur Gaston, was black, and five of whose members were also members of the Interracial Committee—initially sought to deal with the crisis by drafting, and asking the Interracial Committee to endorse, a public statement to be issued in the committee's name. Its primary purpose was to emphasize the need for law and order in response to the Tuscaloosa riots, but in the course of doing so it described the intention of the Interracial Committee as "the improvement of interracial understanding and relations in Jefferson County in various specific areas within the prevailing pattern of living in the South." When this text was presented to the committee at a special meeting on March 2, this definition of the committee's goals provoked heated dissent from some of the black members. Two of them—Marguerite W. Stewart, the wife of black physician Dr. Robert C. Stewart, and realtor Wilbur Hollins—led efforts to delete the wording, but white investment banker Mervyn Sterne warned that the deletion "would in effect bring an end to the Committee and the cooperation of many white members." Executive Secretary Paul Jones told the group that this wording had been adopted at his suggestion to avoid the use of the word "segregation," and Coordinating Council chairman Charles Zukoski pointed out that the resolution did not endorse the "prevailing pattern" but merely acknowledged its existence. On this basis the committee rather grudgingly adopted the text prepared for it, and the statement was given to the press. But the action did absolutely nothing to halt the White Citizens' Council's attacks on the committee, which mounted in fury during March.

By the beginning of April, the Red Cross and the Community Chest were in a panic. On April 2 the two organizations' executive committees met in joint emergency session. Segregationists on the two committees, led by William J. Rushton of Protective Life Insurance Company and Claude S. Lawson of Sloss-Sheffield Steel, sought a resolution urging the Coordinating Council to dissolve the Interracial Committee. Banker Charles Zukoski, the chairman of the Coordinating Council, and U.S. Steel's Arthur Weibel, a member of the Interracial Committee and of its subcommittee on black police, urged a more restrained response. Zukoski carried the day with a compromise proposal not to dissolve the committee until a successor organization could be formed. He proposed a new interracial body to be appointed by the city commission; its "work would be more narrowly concentrated on . . . improvements of services and facilities for Negroes, but it would be organized with the clear understanding and agreement that it would not engage, directly or indirectly, in any activity toward desegregation." Mervyn Sterne and *Birmingham Post-Herald* editor James Mills, both apparently influenced by the fight over the text of the "law and order" statement adopted a month earlier, concurred that such limitations were now necessary because "the present climate of thinking has changed, particularly the Negro members concerned."

On April 6, the full board of directors of the Community Chest met to consider the resolution of the joint executive committees' session earlier in the week. Emil Hess of the Parisian department stores led the fight to retain the committee; he warned of the danger of buckling under to the White Citizens' Council. But other community leaders, including Mervyn Sterne, James Mills, Arthur Weibel, and industrial supply executive Paschal G. Shook, argued somewhat paradoxically that Birmingham's racial problems were now so pressing that the committee "had outlived its usefulness." After much debate, the Community Chest was able only to agree "to seek, through the Coordinating Council, a meeting with the Interracial Committee for a discussion of the present problem and a decision through that group, as to whether the committee shall or shall not be dissolved." But when the Interracial Committee convened on April 13, "A statement, prepared and adopted by the board of the Coordinating Council, was read to members by Mr. Zukoski which dissolved the Interracial Committee." It would appear that the Coordinating Council misled the committee by failing to convey the extent of the divisions in the other organizations. The Community Chest board had in fact voted simply to discuss the possibility of dissolution with the committee itself. And the joint executive committees of the Community Chest and Red Cross had voted to retain the committee until a successor organization was in place. But as the matter was presented to the committee, the decision had already been made. "Several members commented on the effectiveness of the Committee's undertakings and expressed disappointment at its being dissolved." A resolution urging the city commission "to discuss the possibility of their establishing" a new interracial body was adopted unanimously. And then, on the afternoon of April 13, 1956, all formal interracial contact in Birmingham came to an end. It would not be resumed for nearly six years.[59]

A number of points about this episode deserve emphasis. In the first place, no set of events could possibly have indicated more clearly the vast gulfs separating the attitudes and perceptions of the rival groups competing to shape Birmingham's future. Black militants always regarded the black members of the Interracial Committee as accommodationists and the white members as crypto-segregationists, intent upon preserving the racial status quo by diminishing discontent with it. Segregationists saw the committee as an agent of the integrationist onslaught, and they were certainly correct in noting, as they did, that the committee shared with the NAACP the desire to desegregate elevators, employ black police officers, and induce the medical association to admit black doctors. And within the committee itself, though its black and white members could cooperate effectively, they approached the effort with very different assumptions. The black members conceived of its modest achievements as initial steps toward the eventual elimination of racial discrimination, while the white moderates thought of the reforms not as elements of a continuing process leading toward fundamental change but as ends in themselves, eliminating vestiges of unfairness and backwardness from an otherwise progressive city.

It is essential to realize that each of these viewpoints contains its own measure of validity. That the white moderates had no thought of eliminating segregation is surely correct, though it was a distortion of their motives to depict them as crafty conspirators. That the black moderates, in comparison with the militants, were accommodationists is clear, but they understood themselves as having adopted a pragmatic strategy in the battle against white supremacy rather than what they took to be the foolish absolutism of their black antagonists. In this sense the committee's vice-chairman, attorney Arthur Shores, was their archetype. He gained an only partially deserved reputation as an integrationist because of his battles in the courts; in fact, he always sought a negotiated compromise first and turned to legal action only as a last resort. As we have seen, for instance, he filed the class action against the residential segregation ordinance only because the negotiations to define an acceptable buffer zone in North Smithfield had failed; he preferred peaceful occupancy of North Smithfield homes to a judicial victory that seemed likely to be followed by violence that would render the neighborhood uninhabitable. It was absurd, of course, to think of the committee, as the segregationists did, as an integral part of a broad-based assault on white supremacy led by the NAACP. But the segregationists were correct, as we have seen, in perceiving the committee as a source of the growing confidence and insistence among the black middle class in these years, because its accomplishments, however slight they may have been when set against the massive injustice under which blacks suffered, nevertheless contributed to a sense of positive momentum among black community leaders.

Recognizing the many elements of truth that underlay the extraordinary divergences in these contending groups' understandings of their situation allows us to assess what exactly was lost when the committee was dissolved. It is impossible to believe that the committee's efforts by themselves could ever have significantly altered Birmingham's race relations. The racial division inhibited the black and white moderates on the committee from appreciating even each other's motives, much less those of the more aggressive segments of their community. Because the rival sets of perceptions were each rooted in considerable part in fact, communication, far from dispelling misconceptions, was much more likely to confirm and emphasize that portion of each group's beliefs that was accurate. We need only observe that within each race, though communication was freer than it was across the racial chasm, the moderates and the militants had no greater respect for each other's views. Birmingham's problems did not derive from a mere failure to communicate. Nevertheless, as the events of the late 1950s and early 1960s deepened those problems, the absence of any mechanism for formal interracial exchanges unquestionably exacerbated the building crisis. Conversation almost certainly would not have limited recrimination. With the dissolution of the committee, however, moderate sentiment ceased to play an active role in public discourse. It seems likely that the hatreds were the more intense for its absence, and the inevitable conflict therefore the more acrimonious. The inexcusable timidity of Birmingham's white moderates, which caused them to quail before the White Citizens' Council's attacks, must bear the blame for this outcome.

This last point brings us to a second observation. In September 1954, Commissioner Lindbergh had characterized those who had supported Hugh Locke in the sports segregation referendum as "certain small groups of persons who are not enlightened to the changing times of progress."[60] The initial failure of the business progressives to appreciate the power of the segregationists tells us something about both groups. The moderates, whose sense of the attributes of progress was derived from the observation of other communities, seem, because of the greater emancipation of their civic ambitions from parochial limitations, to have been at first insufficiently sensitive to the extent of Birmingham's provincialism. They were passionately engaged in their city's fierce competition with Atlanta to become the lower South's great metropolis, and their dreams easily outran reality, especially in the decade immediately following World War II. For that reason, it appears, when events summoned socially respectable segregationists to intensified activity in the middle and late 1950s, the business progressives overreacted. They had tended to identify vehement white supremacist sentiments with the Klan and similar white working-class groups. But segregationists like Hugh Morrow, William Hoover, and Sidney Smyer were among the city's most important business leaders, and it quickly became clear that they had many equally prominent allies. Indeed, it seems quite possible that the business progressives constituted a minority of Birmingham's business community; at the very least, that community was equally divided. The abruptness and force of this revelation may well have been a factor in producing the moderates' craven response to the new white supremacist challenge. At any rate, for whatever reasons, in the years between the reelection of "Bull" Connor in the spring of 1957 and the Freedom Rider riot in the spring of 1961, the white moderates retreated, suddenly and completely, into cowering silence. In Birmingham as in Montgomery, these years saw virtually all white dissent from segregationist orthodoxy disappear, and sentiments once thought extreme became acceptable, indeed usual.

Equally worth noting is the fact that local events played the most significant role in the process by which the non-Klan segregationists were moved to organize. It is easy to attribute these organizations to the Supreme Court's school desegregation decision in May 1954, but it is misleading to do so. The States' Rights Association in fact was formed some three months before the decision and was an outgrowth of the fight over the repeal of the sports segregation ordinance on January 26. The formation of the Association of Methodist Ministers and Laymen in December 1954, though it followed the Supreme Court decision, actually grew out of opposition to the proposal that black Methodist congregations be admitted to the white regional jurisdictions. And though the founding of the White Citizens' Council in Mississippi was a direct response to the Supreme Court decision, the creation of the first Jefferson County chapters during the fall and winter of 1955 was a response initially to the Birmingham NAACP's submission of petitions to the Birmingham and Jefferson County Boards of Education in August 1955, seeking the implementation of the Supreme Court ruling, and the efforts of Rudolph and Shuttlesworth at the same time to obtain the hiring of black policemen, and later to the prospect of Autherine Lucy's admission to the University of Alabama. All of these events were, of course, related at least to the general climate of opinion that produced the school desegregation decision. Nevertheless, it was only when the threat of integration actually manifested itself locally that most segregationists were shaken out of their complacency. So confident was the great mass of segregationists that their social system was immutable that it required the evidence of specific actions in Birmingham itself before most of them could be brought to believe that the menace was real. It was precisely this widespread white complacency that at first deceived the business progressives into supposing that inflexible insistence on absolute white supremacy was not widespread. It not only was indeed widespread, but it was so much an axiom of existence for most segregationists that to imagine the creation of an alternative defeated their capacity for invention. It was as a result of such assumptions that Hugh Locke could claim that the city's sports segregation ordinance, though adopted in 1950, merely codified a system in existence since the Civil War. But what was actually a quiet yet supreme segregationist confidence left the white moderates to be confounded when its force and extent became clear.

These reflections lead us at last to the profoundest of all the ironies surrounding the story of the Interracial Commission: it was the seeming success of the segregationist assault in the spring of 1956 that cleared the way for the creation that summer of a genuinely militant organization among Birmingham's black residents, the Alabama Christian Movement for Human Rights. The founding of the Christian Movement is, indeed, replete with ironies. From 1953 to 1955, the Birmingham branch of the NAACP had focused much of its attention on its struggle to halt the Birmingham Housing Authority's plans to spend $4.5 million to remove some two thousand blacks from their homes in the south-central part of the city in order to create space for the expansion of the University of Alabama's medical school and what eventually became the campus of the University of Alabama at Birmingham. This lengthy, bitter, and expensive battle resulted eventually in total defeat; it left the branch bankrupt and the branch's members at each other's throats. By 1956 the Birmingham NAACP was very nearly moribund.[61] And then, as we have seen, at the beginning of June 1956, Montgomery Circuit Judge Walter B. Jones issued his temporary injunction forbidding the NAACP from operating in Alabama. Attorney Arthur Shores met with the Birmingham branch the following day and warned the members that they could now take no actions without risking punishment for contempt. The older leadership of the chapter, headed by its president, insurance executive E. B. Colvin, acquiesced, but a minority, led by the branch's newly installed membership committee chairman, Fred Shuttlesworth, dissented. On June 4, Shuttlesworth and ten other dissenters met to draft a declaration creating a new organization to carry on the NAACP's fight. The next day more than a thousand blacks attended the new group's organizational session at the Sardis Baptist Church. Two conservative clergymen, the Reverend M. W. Whitt and the Reverend George W. McMurray, who had been a member of the Interracial Committee, pleaded with the crowd to take no action, but the two were shouted down. The enthusiastic gathering then adopted the June 4 draft declaration and, by acclamation, chose the young Fred Shuttlesworth as the rebel confederation's first—and as it turned out, only—president. The Christian Movement was born.[62]

The ironic connections between the segregationists' new militancy and the creation of the Christian Movement are clear in retrospect. Shuttlesworth had been virtually unknown in Birmingham a year earlier. He had been precipitated into prominence in the community in July 1955, when Commissioner Lindbergh, frightened by the segregationists' suddenly evident power, had reneged on his pledges to the Interracial Committee and to George Rudolph to employ black policemen. The segregationists' opposition to this reform doubtless derived in some part from the fact that it was the one with which the white moderates were most publicly identified. But in opposing it, the segregationists at the same time both deprived the black moderates on the committee of the credibility within the black community that would have made them more widely respected voices and also delivered to more militant figures such as Rudolph and Shuttlesworth an issue with which to emphasize the moderates' failure and to portray themselves as truly resolute leaders. The effect on Shuttlesworth's career was immediately evident; within six months he had been accepted into the black community's leadership circles. Then, when segregationist pressure succeeded three months later in producing the dissolution of the

Interracial Committee, the most conservative of the city's prominent blacks were thus deprived of the institutional foundation of their claim to be spokesmen and benefactors of their race. And a mere six weeks after that achievement, Attorney General John Patterson's crusade to destroy the NAACP and to gather segregationist support for his gubernatorial aspirations managed to sweep aside the weak and internally divided NAACP branch and the older, more timid integrationist leadership that dominated it, and thus to leave the path to eminence open to the one black man who had the determination to take it. Therefore, within eleven months, the combination of Shuttlesworth's own audacity and the inability of the segregationists to distinguish between militancy and moderation had contrived to cut the ground entirely from beneath Birmingham's black conservatives and to elevate from obscurity to significance and respectability the single most uncompromising enemy of segregation in the city.

III. Fred Shuttlesworth Goes to Court

From the moment of his election to lead the Christian Movement, Shuttlesworth was, as he later described himself, a caged rat, constantly searching for opportunities to snap at those whom he regarded as his tormentors, persistently challenging the social system he detested.[63] He commenced almost at once. At the beginning of July he appeared before the city commission in his new capacity to renew his request for the employment of black policemen. A week later he dispatched letters to Mayor Morgan and the Birmingham Transit Company, the locally owned bus company, asking for the adoption of the Mobile seating plan that the Montgomery Improvement Association was also seeking. Two weeks later, additional letters demanded a reply to the initial ones. On August 3, Shuttlesworth headed a Christian Movement delegation that met with Transit Company president S. D. James; they apparently agreed to await the outcome of the Montgomery suit then pending before the U.S. Supreme Court. On August 20, Shuttlesworth and George Rudolph escorted two black applicants, Clyde Jones and George Johnson, to the offices of the personnel board, where the two attempted to take the civil service examination to become policemen. Personnel Director Ray Mullins refused to allow them to do so on the grounds that all applicants were required to be white. In October the Christian Movement sponsored a class-action suit filed by Jones and Johnson in state court, seeking to compel the personnel board to allow them to take the test. In November the black Omega Psi Phi fraternity chose Shuttlesworth as Birmingham's Citizen of the Year. On December 20, the Supreme Court having held Montgomery's bus segregation ordinance unconstitutional, Shuttlesworth wrote to the city commission to demand that the commissioners repeal Birmingham's ordinance at their next meeting, December 26. A failure to do so, he warned, would compel blacks to begin defying it.[64]

In the meantime, the dissolution of the Interracial Committee had evidently indicated to the Klan that white community leaders' open disapprobation of Klan violence, which had compelled the suspension of the bombings five years earlier, no longer constituted a hindrance. On April 10, as the crusade against the committee reached its climax, six Klansmen stormed the stage on which black entertainer Nat "King" Cole was performing and assaulted him and a policeman who sought to protect him. On April 26, two weeks after the committee's abolition, the home of a black postman located in a racially changing neighborhood was bombed. There had been an arson attack on the Smithfield home of dentist John Nixon in May 1954, in apparent retaliation for the Supreme Court's school desegregation decision, but the arsonist had been apprehended the next day and the violence had therefore not continued. Aside from this attack, the bombing in April 1956 was the first Klan violence of this sort since May 1951. It apparently demonstrated the Klan's judgment that, with the segregationists' successful silencing of the white moderates, there was once again little danger that the crimes would be actively investigated. When Shuttlesworth delivered his December 20 ultimatum to the city commission, therefore, the Klan did not hesitate to extend its renewed terrorism to him. On Christmas Day, as Shuttlesworth rested in the bedroom of his home, adjoining his church, a bomb consisting of six sticks of dynamite exploded, blowing the frame structure to splinters and causing the roof to collapse. The bomb detonated directly below Shuttlesworth's bedroom, but the blast threw the bed's mattress up in such a way that it cushioned him from the falling timbers. He escaped with only cuts and bruises. All observers considered his survival miraculous. From that moment, Shuttlesworth added to his aggressive self-confidence the unshakable conviction that his actions were the will of God. Far from deterring him, the Klan had succeeded in making an already obstinate man utterly intransigent.

The next day, when the city commission refused to repeal the bus segregation ordinance, Shuttlesworth at once led his followers onto the buses to defy the regulation. Twenty-one of them were arrested. During the next three nights there was a series of incidents of shooting into the buses. On December 31 the home of a black family, purchased a month earlier from a white, was bombed. The city changed the charge against the twenty-one from violation of the bus segregation ordinance to disorderly conduct and breach of the peace in order to prevent the question of the ordinance's constitutionality from being raised in the trials. The twenty-one therefore on January 14 filed an action in federal court seeking a permanent injunction against the ordinance's enforcement. In the meantime, black Birmingham furniture dealer Carl Baldwin and his wife had been arrested in the Birmingham railway terminal on December 22 for sitting in the white waiting room, despite a November 1955 order from the Interstate Commerce Commission forbidding the enforcement of segregation in terminals against interstate passengers, as the Baldwins were. On January 25, with the sponsorship of the Christian Movement, the Baldwins filed suit in federal court for an injunction to compel the enforcement of the ICC order in the Birmingham station. With the filing of the federal court suits against bus and train station segregation and the state court suit against racial discrimination by the personnel board, the legal assault that would occupy the Christian Movement for the next six years had begun. And with the bombings of Shuttlesworth's home on Christmas Day and of the black family on New Year's Eve, the Klan's resurgent campaign of terrorism was likewise under way. During 1957, six homes and a church would be bombed, two homes would be burned to the ground—one of them the house of a black construction worker whom Klansmen had confused with one of the men who had sued to be able to take the police civil service test—and night riders would shoot into the Smithfield residence of Arthur Shores.[65]

The rapidly deteriorating racial climate in Birmingham during 1956 and 1957 created just the sort of dark hatreds and desperate fears necessary to revive the political career of that incarnation of malice, "Bull" Connor. During the preceding four years Connor had been operating a filling station in Avondale and dreaming of a return to power. As we have seen, he had run for sheriff of Jefferson County in 1954 and, in an election that had taken place just two weeks before the Supreme Court's school integration decision, had been trounced by the incumbent. In the spring of 1956 he had been a candidate in a special election to fill the vacancy on the city commission created by the resignation of Wade Bradley as commissioner of public improvements. Exploiting his alliance with the rapidly growing White Citizens' Council, Connor led the field in the initial round of voting, but he was forced into a runoff against the man whom Bradley had only barely defeated in 1953, James "Jabo" Waggoner. In the runoff campaign, Connor descended to the rawest, most vitriolic racism. But Waggoner emphasized that the duties of public improvements commissioner had virtually nothing to do with race relations, and everything to do with a body of technical expertise that Waggoner, a former supervisor in the street maintenance department, possessed and Connor did not. With this appeal, Waggoner managed to hold onto a substantial minority of the white vote, and with the solid support of Birmingham's five thousand black voters he was able to defeat Connor by some twenty-five hundred ballots. The black *Birmingham World* editorialized that it was time for Connor to learn that racial appeals no longer produced inevitable victory in the city. But it was, unfortunately, the *World* that was about to be taught a lesson.

Seven days following Waggoner's defeat of Connor, the mass meeting took place at the Sardis Baptist Church at which the Alabama Christian Movement for Human Rights was formed and Fred Shuttlesworth was chosen its president. During the subsequent summer and fall, as we have seen, Shuttlesworth launched a whirlwind of attacks on white supremacy, culminating in the Klan's bombing of his home and his organization's defiance of bus segregation in December. Shuttlesworth's offensive and the resultant court challenges to discrimination formed the background to the municipal election in the spring of 1957. Connor filed to run against Commissioner Lindbergh for his former position as commissioner of public safety. He could depend upon the support of a now thoroughly aroused segregationist constituency. However, Lindbergh's conduct had by no means endeared him to black voters. They had been angered by the commissioner's refusal to accede to the repeated efforts to persuade him to hire black policemen. And this anger had been further intensified in December when he ordered his men to continue enforcing the unconstitutional bus segregation ordinance; "We will not voluntarily abandon the tradition-honored Southern custom of segregation on buses," he had proclaimed. Doubtless he feared alienating the powerful Citizens' Council element, though they were unlikely to vote for him in any case. But the result was that, as the *World* commented, black leaders found themselves faced with the challenge "to convince the [black] voters that the choice is wide enough for them to have a real stake in the outcome." There is no doubt that the contest was, as another *World* editorial put it, "a choice between moderation and mischief." But the memories of Connor had dimmed somewhat in the intervening four years, and the animosity toward Lindbergh was fresh. Even the presence in the initial primary of the violent racist Asa Carter conspired to aid Connor. Though Carter received just 5 percent of the votes, his campaign made Connor's appeals seem somewhat more respectable by comparison.

Lindbergh led the first round of voting with 46 percent to Connor's 38.5 percent. In the runoff, Connor outdid himself in the vehemence of his white supremacist exhortations. And the result was a victory by a mere 103 votes out of 31,679 cast. Connor's strength was in the white working-class neighborhoods, Woodlawn, East Lake, Roebuck, West End, and Ensley. Lindbergh swept the well-to-do white Southside area and the black boxes. But the crucial factor in his defeat was the light turnout by black voters. Lindbergh's failure was, in a sense, the same failure that had humbled the white moderate group of which he was a part. Terrified of incurring the wrath of the segregationists, whose strength he had once underestimated and now apparently overestimated, he allowed himself to be frightened into immobility. If he had taken even the most modest additional steps to nourish black enthusiasm, as the results proved, he would have won. Instead, his fears became father to his loss. So great was black disaffection from him, indeed, that in the virtually all-black Graymont Armory box, almost a fifth of the votes cast were for Connor. These 111 votes alone could have given Lindbergh the election. Ironically, therefore, Connor's margin of victory demonstrably consisted of black ballots.[66]

Connor's political resurrection, however, rested upon an electoral transformation far more portentous than merely the inclusion among his supporters of a handful of blacks. As we have seen, in Connor's first years on the city commission he had had the firm support of the city's corporate leaders, a support cemented by his close association with James Simpson. But the concern for the city's reputation produced by the Smithfield bombings had created a division in this constituency, and the business progressive forces had then used Connor's sexual indiscretion to bring him down in 1952–53. They remained his enemies throughout the coming decade, as the overwhelming opposition to him in the prosperous Southside precincts in 1957 clearly indicated. But in the years after World War II, well-to-do voters were becoming a continually smaller proportion of Birmingham's electorate, because this period saw increasing numbers of them decide to move to the rapidly growing suburban communities in Shades Valley, to the south of the mountains that formed the city's southern limits. Mountain Brook and Homewood had both been founded in the 1920s, but their growth in the Depression years had been relatively slow. After 1945, however, their populations began a steady expansion, and Vestavia Hills was opened to join them. These municipalities soon became the residences of most of Birmingham's industrial, commercial, and professional elite. The city proper more and more became the home only of the white lower middle and working classes, and of blacks. At this same time, of course, the newly apparent black militancy was increasingly alarming poorer whites, especially unionized white workers whose seniority and promotion arrangements, as we have seen, reserved for them the more highly skilled and better-paying positions in the city's quite evidently declining industries, in which jobs in general were becoming ever scarcer.

Connor had always had substantial support in the white working class, of course. Indeed, his ability to bridge the allegiances of white workers and corporate executives had been the principal source of his political success in earlier times. But now the combination of all these more recent developments—the changing composition of the municipal electorate, the heightened fears of the white working class, and the active hostility of the business progressives—led Connor to cast his lot decisively with his poorer white supporters. James Simpson and some other segregationist ideologues among the professionals and businessmen refused to desert him, but the machinations of the moderates in 1952–53 and the vigorous and enthusiastic backing of the less prosperous white precincts in 1957 convinced him of where his future now lay. After his return to office, he began, essentially for the first time, to indulge in regular denunciations of Birmingham's "over-the-mountain" magnates, of the chamber of commerce they controlled, of the white daily newspapers and their absentee owners. These forces sought to dictate Birmingham's destiny, though they did not even live in the city, he charged with considerable justice. But he would defend the real Birmingham, the hardworking ordinary white people whose champion he was coming to consider himself. Like them, he had been the victim of imperious corporate executives. Like them, he resented increasingly uppity blacks. The Connor who returned to the city commission, therefore, had toughened his class sympathies. If there had been a time when Connor might have listened to the blandishments of business leaders, that time had now passed. Experience had taught him the perils of appeasement, as he would prove.

The essential threat to Birmingham's progress, as white moderates saw it, was not injustice but violence. The statement issued in the name of the Interracial Committee in response to the Autherine Lucy riots had affirmed that "The issue of law and order . . . transcends every other issue before our people. Unless we can maintain law and order, there can be no hope of achieving any of the ends" sought by people of goodwill. "The Committee as a consequence feels impelled to urge upon the people of our entire community, both white and Negro, their solemn obligation as citizens, in the crisis with which we are now faced, to proceed peacefully in all their actions, to avoid violent utterances, and to resort for settlement of their controversies on persuasion and on recourse to the courts." Seven years later, in the midst of the city's gravest racial confrontation, the demonstrations of 1963, a group of moderate clergymen echoed this admonition. "We recognize the natural impatience of people who feel that their hopes are slow in being realized. But we are convinced that these demonstrations are unwise and untimely. . . . Just as we formerly pointed out that 'hatred and violence have no sanction in our religious and political traditions,' we also point out that such actions as incite hatred and violence, however technically peaceful those actions may be, have not contributed to the resolution of our local problems. . . . When rights are consistently denied, a cause should be pressed in the courts and [through] negotiations among local leaders, and not in the streets."[67] This attitude lies at the heart of the white moderates' deep hostility to Shuttlesworth and the Christian Movement. From the moderates' perspective, Shuttlesworth was a sort of black analogue of the Ku Klux Klan. His provocations, as they saw matters, drew the Klan into violent response. The core of the problem, they thought, was Shuttlesworth's use of direct action, rather than peaceful, dispassionate, and, moreover, probably more effective legal proceedings.

This analysis, however, was profoundly misleading. Perhaps because of

Shuttlesworth's association with Martin Luther King and the fact that the Christian Movement was one of the founding organizations of the Southern Christian Leadership Conference in 1957, the moderates seem to have regarded the Christian Movement as committed to direct action from the outset—and many subsequent scholars have adopted this opinion. The Christian Movement did, of course, eventually turn to direct action, but it did so only slowly and reluctantly. Indeed, it is perhaps not too much to say that the Christian Movement was virtually driven into embracing direct action by the willingness of Birmingham's two federal judges, Seybourn H. Lynne and H. Hobart Grooms, to give unusual credence to the arguments of segregationist attorneys. The Christian Movement was created as a successor to the NAACP, and throughout its first years of existence it embraced fully the NAACP's strategy of attacking segregation through the judiciary. In every case, the succession of violent episodes that the moderates considered the product of direct action actually grew out of efforts to induce authorities to enforce the segregation laws in order to obtain a test of them in court. It was necessary to violate a regulation, and to be charged with having done so, in order to get the question of the regulation's constitutionality before a judge. But Shuttlesworth always terminated his actions, in the early years, as soon as a case had been made. The fact that so many of his efforts to create legal tests resulted in disturbances or worse is an index to the belligerence of Birmingham's Klan and the animosity of its police. Shuttlesworth's goal throughout the 1950s was simply to initiate the legal proceedings that the moderates claimed to prefer. In the spring of 1959, a survey of Christian Movement members found that almost 78 percent of them believed that integration could come about only through legislation or court action—a far higher percentage than among comparable activists in the Montgomery Improvement Association and the Tuskegee Civic Association surveyed at the same time.[68] The failure to recognize the extent of this commitment obscured at the time, and has continued to obscure since, an understanding of the process by which the Christian Movement was persuaded to abandon this faith and to turn instead to public demonstrations. But an examination of what happened to the most significant of the court cases filed by the Christian Movement makes this process very clear.

Birmingham's senior federal district judge, Seybourn H. Lynne, was a paternalistic segregationist. His father, Seybourn A. Lynne, a corporate attorney from Decatur, was a former state senator and speaker of the state house of representatives; his grandfather, a Decatur banker, was a former congressman. Judge Lynne graduated from Auburn University in 1927 and received his law degree from the University of Alabama in 1930. In 1934 he was elected judge of the county court in Decatur, and he served there until 1940, when he was elected a state circuit judge, defeating the incumbent William W. Callahan, who had earlier gained considerable notoriety for the prejudice he had displayed in presiding over the Scottsboro rape trials. Lynne continued as circuit judge only until the end of 1942; he then entered the army's judge advocate general corps. Lynne's father had long been a close political associate of Senator John H. Bankhead, Jr., and in 1929 he had played a leading role in obtaining the expulsion of Senator J. Thomas Heflin from the Democratic Party because of Heflin's opposition to Alfred E. Smith in the 1928 presidential election; it was Heflin's expulsion from the party that had opened the way for Bankhead's elevation to the Senate in 1930. In 1945, the death of Judge Thomas A. Murphree presented Senator Bankhead with an opportunity to reward the elder Lynne for his fealty. Over the objection of his colleague Lister Hill, who sought the appointment for his former campaign manager Gordon Madison of Tuscaloosa, Bankhead obtained President Truman's nomination of the junior Lynne to the judgeship. Lynne was thereupon released from the army and took office in January 1946, at thirty-eight. On the bench Lynne quickly established his deep hostility to civil rights initiatives. When he could rule in favor of segregation with some show of logic, he did so; otherwise, he frequently simply left the cases to molder on his docket.[69]

Birmingham's other federal judge, Hobart Grooms, lacked Lynne's distinct racial animus. When the precedents compelled him to uphold black claims and the evidence was clear, he was willing to render judgment accordingly. But like Judge Lynne, Judge Grooms almost invariably held for the segregationists whenever the question was at all close. Grooms, a native of Jeffersonville, Kentucky, was born into that state's mountain Republican tradition. He received his law degree from the University of Kentucky in 1926 and moved to Birmingham to commence legal practice in the same year, arriving just as the Ku Klux Klan was at the height of its influence there. He at once affiliated with Jefferson County's small and impotent group of Republicans, who ran him for the state court of appeals in 1934, for the state house of representatives in 1938, for Congress in 1944, and for the state senate in 1946. The retirement of the racially liberal Judge Clarence Mullins in 1953 presented the Republicans with their first opportunity in twenty years to claim a federal judgeship. The Eisenhower wing of the party, led by state chairman Claude Vardaman, sought the post for Grooms, but they met strong opposition from the Taft wing, led by national committeeman Curtis Adkins, who urged the selection of J. Foy Guin of Russellville. After a considerable intraparty struggle, President Eisenhower gave the nomination to Grooms in July 1953. As soon as he was sworn in, Grooms, taking over from Judge Lynne the hearing of Autherine Lucy's suit for admission to the University of Alabama, promptly dismissed it on the ground that it constituted a suit against the state. The ruling was a portent of things to come.[70]

The first of the Christian Movement's suits to be filed was the state court suit against the personnel board's refusal to allow black applicants to take the civil service examination for policemen. The two rejected examinees' attorneys, future state supreme court justice Oscar Adams and Arthur Shores's young partner Orzell Billingsley, chose to sue in state court because James Simpson's civil service statute of 1935 explicitly forbade the board to discriminate among its applicants, and the board's resolution that kept the examinations all white appeared therefore to be in direct contradiction to the law that had created the body. At the time of the passage of the statute, only two blacks were covered by it. When one of these two placed first on a promotion examination in 1952, Commissioner Morgan had recommended that he get the job; Commissioner Connor had exploded, protesting that the appointment would destroy city workers' morale. But Mayor Green had accepted Morgan's recommendation, and Odis Harris thus became the first and only black person ever employed by Birmingham as a result of a civil service examination; his rank was truck driver I. The petitioners had, to say the least of it, a solid case.

Nevertheless, after a hearing at the end of February 1957, Circuit Judge William A. Jenkins dismissed the complaint. The action had sought a declaratory judgment that the personnel board lacked the power to hold applicants unqualified by reason of their race. But when a board acts to make a judicial determination on a matter within its jurisdiction, Judge Jenkins held, an action for a declaratory judgment is not available. The petitioners appealed to the Alabama Supreme Court, but in January 1958, in an opinion by Supernumerary Justice Arthur B. Foster, the court unanimously affirmed Jenkins's ruling. In the meantime, both of the applicants had been fired from their jobs, and as we have seen, the home of a black construction worker with a name similar to one of them had been burned to the ground, in a case of mistaken identity. Clyde Jones had been convicted of false pretense for writing bad checks, and therefore had forfeited the right to be a policeman in any case. But the other applicant, George Johnson, now turned to the federal courts, filing suit against the personnel board in April 1958. In May, to demonstrate that the board's policies had not changed, Johnson and two other blacks again applied to take the test and again were rejected on racial grounds. But in July, Judge Grooms ruled that, Johnson having sued first in state court and having waited until the Alabama Supreme Court had decided the case, his federal suit was therefore barred by the one-year statute of limitations. At the end of the month, in preparation for filing a new suit, Shuttlesworth led a new group of black applicants to the personnel board's offices to undergo another rejection. But when they arrived, they discovered to their surprise that immediately after Judge Grooms's dismissal of Johnson's suit the board had met and quietly voted to revoke its whites-only rule in order to avoid further federal court scrutiny of its procedures. Five of the astonished blacks took examinations at once, and five more in the following two weeks. The board's action created an uproar in Jefferson County. "Bull" Connor charged that, in view of the threat of war with the Soviet Union, Shuttlesworth's efforts constituted acts of disloyalty to America. At an emergency meeting of the county's municipal officials on August 5, those in attendance dealt with the situation by adding a new and ostensibly nonracial requirement to the existing ones for police; thereafter, all policemen were required to be registered voters. The black challenge to civil service discrimination thus in effect ended in defeat. February 1962 found Shuttlesworth forlornly petitioning the county and city commissioners—from the city jail —for an end to racial barriers to employment by local government. Mayor Arthur Hanes replied that he was throwing the petition in his wastebasket. Birmingham would not hire its first black policemen, as we shall see, until March 31, 1966.[71]

The Christian Movement's suit filed in the names of Carl and Alexinia Baldwin to obtain the enforcement of the Interstate Commerce Commission's 1955 nondiscrimination regulation in the Birmingham train station would appear similarly to have been a straightforward one. But that notion reckons without Judge Seybourn Lynne. The Baldwins had bought tickets to Milwaukee, Wisconsin, in December 1956, and as interstate passengers they were entitled under the ICC ruling to sit in the white waiting room. But when they did so, the ticket agent called the police. They were soon surrounded by five officers, and Lieutenant J. R. Davis gave them twenty seconds to get into the colored waiting room. When they refused, he arrested them for disorderly conduct. While awaiting trial in Recorder's Court, they filed suit in January 1957, in federal district court, asking an injunction forbidding the enforcement of the state waiting room segregation law against interstate passengers. When their case came up in Recorder's Court on February 25, the city announced that they had been arrested in error and dropped the charges. And after their preliminary federal court hearing on March 1, Judge Lynne dismissed their complaint. Their arrest had simply been a mistake, he said, and besides, there was no proof that they had been arrested for violating the segregation statute rather than for a genuine breach of the peace. "This is but another in the growing list of cases wherein both the tutored and the untutored apparently entertain the mistaken notion that the proper function of the federal courts is propaganda rather than judicature," he concluded. The Baldwins appealed.

Immediately after Judge Lynne's opinion was released on March 4, Fred Shuttlesworth called the press to announce that, on Judge Lynne's assurance that interstate passengers were not in fact segregated at the station, he would purchase an interstate ticket on March 6 and take his place in the white waiting room. When he and his wife arrived at the station, accompanied by white racial liberal Lamar Weaver, a candidate for the city commission, they were met by a white mob led by Robert E. Chambliss, the Klansman who had been involved in the Smithfield incidents, had been fired by the city after his indictment for masked flogging, had been arrested during the Autherine Lucy riots, and had sued Lucy and the NAACP for libel. The Shuttlesworths managed to get into the station, but the mob of fifty fell upon Weaver. He fled back to his car, which the mob then tried to overturn. Finally getting the car started, Weaver sped off as the mob threw stones, but in the process he dented a car parked nearby. Police, who had watched this entire proceeding without intervening, now acted to arrest Weaver for reckless driving. Taken before Recorder's Court Judge Oliver B. Hall that same afternoon, Weaver explained that his life was in danger; but Hall fined him twenty-five dollars anyway, and lectured him, "A man cannot fly into the face of tradition and customs and not expect to be burned." Harassment compelled Weaver to drop out of the commission race. In June police forced another black interstate passenger to leave the white waiting room. And in October another black, Dr. Juanita Pitts, was apprehended for sitting in the white waiting room and was fined forty dollars for disorderly conduct and resisting arrest. It was difficult to credit Judge Lynne's notion that integration had already taken place there.

In January 1958, the Fifth Circuit Court of Appeals—in an opinion by Judge John R. Brown joined by Judge Richard Rives, with Judge Warren L. Jones dissenting—reversed Judge Lynne's peremptory dismissal of the Baldwins' complaint and ordered the suit to trial. Nearly two years later, at the end of October 1959, the trial began. A series of witnesses testified that segregation was still being enforced at the terminal, and one testified that she had actually seen the ticket seller call the police to report a black person in the white waiting room. City Attorney John M. Breckenridge objected to her testimony on the ground that her manner was arrogant. Judge Lynne overruled this objection, but he stated from the bench that she was not worthy of belief. On November 24 he dismissed the complaint for the second time. It was true that the white waiting room was required to be open to interstate travelers of all races, he wrote. But in fact, it already was. If segregated seating continued at the terminal, it represented a purely voluntary arrangement for people of goodwill. The Baldwins once again appealed. In February 1961, with Judge John R. Brown again writing, this time joined by Judges Richard Rives and John Minor Wisdom, the Fifth Circuit once more reversed Judge Lynne's decision. Going beyond the ICC's regulation of 1955, Judge Brown held that when the terminal had complied with the Alabama Public Service Commission's 1956 order, in response to the ICC regulation, that required stations to erect signs declaring that segregation was still in effect for intrastate passengers, it had thus converted itself into an agency of Alabama for the execution of state policy; no further evidence of the terminal's complicity in the policy was needed. The Court of Appeals therefore ordered the elimination of any distinction between interstate and intrastate passengers, and the end of all segregation at the terminal. On April 21, Judge Lynne issued the injunction that the Fifth Circuit had required of him. The Baldwins' long struggle to enforce in one Birmingham facility an order that by its terms applied to every such facility in America thus came to an end, more than four years after it had begun. But the stress of the effort had taken its toll; a year later the Baldwins divorced.[72]

The Christian Movement's expensive four-year battle to integrate the waiting room at the Birmingham railroad terminal might have been a more readily justifiable use of the group's very limited financial resources if it had brought with it the integration of the city's other terminals as well, but such was not the case. Birmingham's two bus stations and its airport would necessitate their own separate struggles. The logic of Judge Brown's second opinion in the *Baldwin* case clearly did apply to the two bus stations, because like the railroad station, they were also subject to the 1955 ICC regulation and they had likewise complied with the 1956 public service commission order in response to it. In May 1961, the Christian Movement and attorney Oscar Adams wrote to Greyhound, Trailways, and the public service commission, as well as the Louisville and Nashville Railroad, to demand that they eliminate the segregation signs from all Alabama stations, in compliance with the Fifth Circuit decision. These letters produced no immediate response. However, as we have seen, the Birmingham and Montgomery Freedom Rider riots that occurred at the same time led the Justice Department to apply to the ICC to expand its 1955 order to forbid all racial discrimination in all bus terminal facilities, in accordance with a December 1960 decision of the U.S. Supreme Court. The ICC agreed in September, and its new regulation took effect November 1. The manager of the restaurant in the Greyhound bus station sought to obey. "Bull" Connor at once swung into action; on November 3 he ordered the arrest of the manager for serving a black customer, and he arrested him again on November 5, 7, and 8 and two waitresses at the restaurant on November 5 and 6 for committing the same offense. Greyhound appealed to the Justice Department for assistance, but Birmingham's U.S. attorney, Macon L. Weaver, was reluctant to intervene. Instead, he reached an agreement with City Attorney John M. Breckenridge that the city would halt the arrests, and in return the federal government would leave the question of whether the restaurant could now integrate to be decided by the state courts through the criminal prosecutions of the manager and the waitresses. But this arrangement failed to satisfy Connor. He induced his commission colleagues on December 5 to initiate proceedings to revoke the establishment's restaurant license because of its violation of the city's restaurant segregation ordinance. After a public hearing on December 19, the commissioners voted unanimously to do so. These actions finally forced U.S. Attorney Weaver to file a petition with Judge Lynne for an injunction against the city's interference with the bus stations' efforts to obey the new ICC regulation. Lynne granted a temporary injunction to this effect in January 1962, and he made it permanent in June.[73]

The situation at the airport was a bit less straightforward. It was not subject to the ICC, and the facilities that drew the principal black ire, its restaurant and motel, were both privately operated. Nevertheless, recently decided cases in Georgia and South Carolina had already indicated that airport discrimination was impermissible when, in September 1960, Birmingham's airport restaurant refused to serve Fred Shuttlesworth, his daughter, and his Virginia attorney, Len Holt. They promptly filed suit against the restaurant in federal court. But the initial complaint in the case was poorly drawn, and probably for that reason the case moved slowly. The plaintiffs amended the complaint, improving it somewhat, in February 1961, and at a preliminary hearing in August, Judge Grooms denied a motion to dismiss it. But it was not until February 1962, when prominent civil rights attorneys Jack Greenberg and Derrick Bell agreed to enter the case, that the complaint was placed into a really satisfactory form. In April the Justice Department wrote to Mayor Hanes to demand that the restaurant segregation be terminated, but the city replied that the discrimination was the private action of the restaurant owners and that the city had nothing to do with it. Shuttlesworth's suit came to trial in July, and at the conclusion of the hearing Judge Grooms granted an injunction forbidding continued enforcement of segregation at the restaurant. At the same time, blacks filed suit to integrate the airport motel. In December 1963, Judge Grooms granted an injunction prohibiting racial discrimination in that operation as well. The motel appealed to the Fifth Circuit, and Judge Grooms agreed to suspend the injunction pending the appeal. But in February 1964, by a vote of two to one, a Fifth Circuit panel vacated this stay and ordered the injunction into effect. By then, of course, the Civil Rights Act of 1964, which would outlaw segregation in all such public accommodations, was less than five months away.[74]

The judicial battle against segregation in Birmingham's terminals thus began with the arrest of the Baldwins in December 1956 and ended with the injunction against the airport motel, made effective in February 1964. Almost equally as long, and even more complicated, was the struggle to prohibit segregation on the city buses. As was the case with the Baldwins' suit against discrimination in the railroad terminal, the fundamental legal position of the Christian Movement in the bus cases was impregnable even before the struggle began. And yet the vindication of that position would take five and a half years and a great deal of money. As we have seen, the initial bus suit, *Cherry* v. *Morgan*, was an outgrowth of the U.S. Supreme Court's declaration in November 1956 that bus segregation in Montgomery was unconstitutional. In December, Shuttlesworth wrote to the city commission to demand that Birmingham's now invalid bus segregation ordinance be repealed, and when the commission refused, he and his followers defied the ordinance and were arrested on December 26. On January 14, 1957, they sued in federal court for an injunction to prohibit further enforcement of the ordinance. On February 21, Judge Grooms denied the city's motion to dismiss the suit on grounds of comity, given that the question of the ordinance's constitutionality was already before the state courts in the criminal prosecutions. On March 18 the protesters came up for trial before Recorder's Court Judge Ralph Parker. Citing the Supreme Court's Montgomery decision, their attorney, Arthur Shores, moved to dismiss the charges, but City Attorney James H. "Bep" Willis argued that Judge Parker was not bound by the Supreme Court's decision because the Court had ceased honoring its precedents and had begun basing its judgments on psychology. In a written opinion issued March 21, Judge Parker accepted Willis's argument, and went further. Segregation, he said, had been established by God, and was essential to harmonious race relations, as northern cities with large black populations would very soon discover. The Ninth and Tenth Amendments to the Constitution guaranteed the right of the states and the people to require racial separation. The Supreme Court had claimed that the Fourteenth Amendment had withdrawn that right, but the Fourteenth Amendment had not been ratified by "a valid, constitutional process." Instead, it had been "forced upon the people at the point of the bayonet"; it therefore "is null and void," and so could not be used to justify integration. He acknowledged, "I cannot conceive how any right thinking person who understands the conditions that exist in the South can advocate abandoning our Segregation Laws, when such a course will inevitably lead to racial amalgamation and mongrelization." And to these conclusions he added a plea: "I trust that the leaders of both races will use their good judgment and fight this issue in the Courts of our County." He then fined each of the twenty-one defendants fifty dollars.

The Christian Movement now decided to rely on its federal suit, and rather than appeal Judge Parker's curious ruling, it paid the fines he had assessed. The city maintained at a preliminary hearing the following October that this action foreclosed the defendants from attempting to raise the question of bus segregation again in federal court, but Judge Grooms rejected this contention in February 1958. The suit was then set for trial on October 30, nearly two years after its filing. Two weeks before the scheduled trial at which, it was clear to everyone, the bus segregation ordinance would be invalidated, the city commission turned to a version of the strategy that the personnel board had used successfully in the suit against civil service discrimination. On October 14, the commissioners repealed the ordinance requiring segregation on the buses and substituted one authorizing the bus company to adopt "such rules and regulations for the seating of passengers . . . as are reasonably necessary to assure the speedy, orderly, convenient, safe and peaceful handling of passengers," and constituting "a willful refusal to obey a reasonable request of an operator or driver . . . in relation to the seating of passengers" a breach of the peace. The bus company thereupon removed the "race boards" from the buses, eliminated the requirement that black passengers pay at the front and then exit and reboard at the rear, and adopted a form of segregation modeled on the Mobile plan that had been the initial request of the Montgomery boycott.

Shuttlesworth announced the Christian Movement's rejection of the bus company's new seating plan, and on October 20 a group of Christian Movement members went aboard the buses to create a test of the new ordinance. Thirteen of them were promptly arrested, and the next day "Bull" Connor ordered Shuttlesworth's arrest for having incited them to the action. On October 23, Recorder's Court Judge William Conway convicted the fourteen but then ordered them all jailed without bond while, he said, he pondered their sentences. Their attorney, Orzell Billingsley, thereupon filed a petition for a writ of habeas corpus with Circuit Judge George Lewis Bailes. On October 27, Judge Conway sentenced Shuttlesworth to three months in jail, his associate the Reverend James S. Phifer to two months, and fined each of them one hundred dollars; the other twelve were given suspended sentences. All fourteen appealed to circuit court, and Judge Conway set appeal bonds. But Judge Bailes then ordered them all returned to jail while he considered the habeas corpus petition. On October 28, Bailes ruled the petition now unnecessary, and the fourteen were finally released after five days of essentially vindictive imprisonment. In the meantime, on October 27 police had stormed into a Christian Movement board meeting at Shuttlesworth's home and arrested three Montgomery ministers who had driven up to express their concern about the protesters' jailing; the three were charged with vagrancy, though they were later released.

The point of the black effort had been to demonstrate to Judge Grooms that segregation was actually still in effect on the buses, but Grooms was not impressed. At the previously scheduled hearing on October 30, Grooms refused to permit the existing *Cherry* suit to be amended to challenge the new ordinance, and he granted a motion to dismiss it as now moot. It would be necessary to file a new suit and begin the entire legal process over again. This sequence of events had so angered Christian Movement members that at a mass meeting on October 31 they voted to start a boycott of the buses. The boycott was never very effective, and within a few weeks it had, for all practical purposes, been abandoned. Nevertheless, the city struck back hard. One of Shuttlesworth's associates, the Reverend Calvin Woods, was charged with violation of the Anti-Boycott Act for delivering sermons on November 2 and November 9 urging blacks not to ride the buses, apparently after a member of his congregation reported the sermons to police. And a black employee at the Hayes Aircraft factory, John Harvey Kelly, was given six months at hard labor for distributing boycott literature when he found a flier urging the boycott on the windshield of his car and showed it to a group of his friends. Both of these convictions were later reversed by state appellate courts, but for the time being they further damaged an already weak boycott campaign. On December 2, Circuit Judge George Lewis Bailes ruled the new bus segregation ordinance constitutional and affirmed the Recorder's Court convictions of Shuttlesworth and the other thirteen protesters. These cases now began their long trip through the state appellate process. In the meantime, on November 12 the Christian Movement both appealed Judge Grooms's dismissal of the *Cherry* case and at the same time filed a new suit, *Boman v. Birmingham Transit Co.,* challenging the revised bus ordinance. The city sought to postpone the *Boman* suit until the *Cherry* appeal had been heard, but on January 22, 1959, Judge Grooms ordered the *Boman* case to proceed.

In May the Fifth Circuit affirmed Judge Grooms's ruling that the adoption of the new ordinance had mooted the *Cherry* suit. In September the *Boman* suit came to trial, and on November 23 Judge Grooms delivered his decision. Private discrimination, divorced from state action, did not violate the Fourteenth Amendment, he noted, so the bus company was free to adopt its own plan of segregation, but the arrests of the thirteen plaintiffs by police in October 1958 involved state action and thus had violated their civil rights. A mere refusal of a passenger to move to the rear, unaccompanied by any other action, could not constitute a breach of the peace, he held. If such arrests continued in the future, therefore, they would form the basis for a finding that the new ordinance was being unconstitutionally applied. But as long as the city was willing to leave bus seating entirely up to the bus company, without trying to enforce the company's policy, then the ordinance would be constitutional. Grooms therefore dismissed the bus company as a defendant and denied the injunction that the Christian Movement had sought against the city, but he retained jurisdiction in case renewed arrests should make an injunction necessary. The Christian Movement appealed.

In the meantime, Shuttlesworth and Connor got into a public dispute over the meaning of Judge Grooms's ruling. The Christian Movement passed out circulars saying, correctly, that blacks could now sit wherever they wished on a bus without fear of arrest by the police. But Connor issued a statement saying, equally correctly, that bus drivers retained the right to order passengers to move, and to eject them from the bus if they refused. It was also true that if such a refusal were accompanied by obstreperous behavior, it could then become a breach of the peace for which an arrest was still authorized.

The *Boman* suit now rested with the Fifth Circuit Court of Appeals for nearly two years, but in the fall of 1961 the court reversed Judge Grooms's dismissal of the bus company as a defendant in the case. With its new ordinance, Chief Judge Elbert Tuttle wrote, the city in effect had delegated its power to regulate seating to a franchise holder and thereby had converted the bus company into an agency of the state. The Fourteenth Amendment thus forbade it to discriminate on racial grounds. Judge Grooms was ordered to prohibit the segregation, and he issued the required injunction on November 8.

In January 1962 the struggle entered a new phase. The Alabama Court of Appeals in December 1960 had dismissed the appeals of the fourteen protesters arrested in October 1958 without reaching the merits of their claims, on the ground that the blacks had failed to file the transcripts of their circuit court trials within the time limit imposed by court rules. The Alabama Supreme Court had affirmed this decision, and in January 1962 the U.S. Supreme Court declined to intervene, also without considering the merits of the appeals. "Bull" Connor thereupon ordered the arrest of Shuttlesworth, who had been sentenced to three months, and James Phifer, who had been sentenced to two, and they began serving their terms on January 26. Their attorneys applied to Judge Grooms for writs of habeas corpus, but on February 2, Grooms denied the writs. The circuit court reporter had testified that he had given Arthur Shores a copy of the transcripts of the December 2, 1958, trials on December 27, but then had himself failed to file the transcripts with the Court of Appeals until March 9, 1959, three days after the March 6 deadline. Since the Fifth Circuit had now in effect declared unconstitutional the ordinance that Shuttlesworth and Phifer had been convicted of violating, the result, Shores contended, was that the two men were in jail as punishment for the court reporter's delay in filing the transcripts. But Judge Grooms ruled that Shuttlesworth and Phifer had first to exhaust their avenues of appeal in the state courts by filing an application for a writ of error coram nobis before they could turn to the federal courts for habeas corpus. On February 12, Judge Richard Rives of the Fifth Circuit accepted this contention, though he added that it was quite clear that the two men were being held unconstitutionally, as a result of a good faith error of their attorney. On February 26 the U.S. Supreme Court, reviewing Judge Rives's ruling, ordered Judge Grooms to hold the petitions for habeas corpus for five days to permit the state courts to consider bail; if the state courts refused to act or denied bail, Grooms was then to consider all state avenues of appeal exhausted and proceed to consider granting habeas corpus. As soon as the Supreme Court's order was issued, Circuit Judge George Lewis Bailes refused bail, and both the state appeals court and the state supreme court joined in refusing on March 1. Therefore, on the afternoon of March 1, Grooms granted bail, and Shuttlesworth and Phifer were released after five weeks' imprisonment. In December 1962 the state appeals court refused to review the circuit court habeas corpus proceedings, and the state supreme court later did so as well. In December 1963, Grooms finally accepted jurisdiction and declared the two men's convictions void.

During the first months of 1962, though the bus company had now been forced to revoke its formal rules requiring segregation, drivers continued to reseat black passengers, and police continued to board the buses at the drivers' request and order blacks to comply; officers merely refrained from arresting the recalcitrant. On June 28, therefore, Judge Grooms found the city in violation of his November 23, 1959, order forbidding policemen to assist drivers in enforcing racial seating policies. Thus, at last, Judge Grooms was convinced. He issued a permanent injunction prohibiting either the city or the bus company from doing anything to keep black passengers from choosing any seat. And so, on June 28, 1962, the long legal battle to integrate Birmingham's buses, which had begun with the arrests of December 26, 1956, came to an end.[75]

The struggle to begin the integration of the schools was equally long and even more violent. Despite the 1954 *Brown* v. *Board of Education* decision, the Christian Movement's legal position in this encounter was somewhat less obviously correct because of the Alabama Pupil Placement Act. It was the existence of this act that would bedevil black efforts from the commencement of legal action in 1957 to the eventual admission of the first five black students in 1963. The origin of the Pupil Placement Act is a bit unusual. It was the idea of a Tuscaloosa teenager named Bobby Wood, the son of a hospital nursing attendant. He introduced it into the YMCA Youth Legislature in March 1954, and it passed both houses. Wood was subsequently chosen youth governor of Boys' State. Senator Sam Martin Engelhardt of Macon County, one of the adult legislature's most vociferous segregationists and soon to become the state executive secretary of the White Citizens' Councils, was so impressed with Wood's proposal that he offered a somewhat revised version of it in the regular session of 1955, and it was enacted. A state legislative committee chaired by Senator Albert Boutwell of Birmingham had been appointed in 1953 to study means of avoiding integration and to report to the next regular legislative session. Boutwell's committee received the assistance of a special committee of the state's leading constitutional lawyers, appointed by the state bar association and headed by Birmingham's Joseph Forney Johnston. In 1955 they proposed a constitutional amendment to eliminate the state's obligation to maintain a public school system, along with companion bills permitting both the closing of any school ordered to integrate and the diversion of the public funds involved to aid segregated private schools. These suggestions were adopted at the same time as Engelhardt's Pupil Placement Act. After two further years of study, however, the legislators and lawyers could come up with no other ideas any better than the Tuscaloosa teenager's, and in their final report they therefore contented themselves with suggesting amendments to Engelhardt's act intended to buttress it against probable legal challenges. Adopted in 1957, the amended statute prescribed a list of nonracial psychological and sociological criteria that local boards of education were instructed to use in determining whether or not to approve a student's application to transfer from one public school to another. Among these were the desires of the parents and children of the school to which the student would be transferring. The act also constructed an elaborate process for appealing an adverse decision of a board, to ensure that it would take years before an applicant could exhaust the available administrative remedies and be permitted to turn to the federal courts.[76]

The initial effort to integrate Birmingham's schools had come in August 1955, when the NAACP submitted petitions to the Birmingham, Bessemer, and Jefferson County school boards asking each of them to adopt plans for desegregation. None of the bodies responded, and in August 1957 the Christian Movement renewed the effort. Six black parents of eight children, including Shuttlesworth, submitted a formal request under the new Pupil Placement Act to have their children transferred to white schools. On September 2, Ku Klux Klansmen responded by selecting at random a thirty-four-year-old black man, J. Edward Aaron, taking him by force to a Klan lair and, after they had ordered him to tell Shuttlesworth to withdraw the petition, castrating him with a razor blade and pouring turpentine into the wound. Aaron survived, and the six Klansmen involved were apprehended a week later, when they boasted of their achievement. One of the six had been among those convicted of the assault on Nat "King" Cole a year earlier. Two of the six agreed to testify against the other four, and all four were convicted later that fall and sentenced to twenty years in prison. In fact, however, they were paroled in 1964 and 1965. Three Klansmen, wearing buttons depicting a lynched black person, attended the meeting of the city board of education on September 6 at which the board formally received the transfer applications and set the Pupil Placement Act's ponderous procedures into motion. Shuttlesworth announced that he would attempt to enroll his children at the white Phillips High School on September 9. When he, his wife, their two daughters, and two of the other petitioning children arrived that morning, they were met by a Klan mob and a melee resulted; Shuttlesworth and one of his daughters were injured. They never made it to the school. Police arrested three of the white rioters—one who held Shuttlesworth down, one who beat him with brass knuckles, and one who beat him with a bicycle chain. Shuttlesworth positively identified all three at their preliminary hearing on September 21, but his identification was insufficient evidence for the county grand jury, which refused to indict them. In October, Superintendent L. Frazer Banks had the petitioning students administered achievement and aptitude tests, and in November he surveyed the sentiments of the parents of pupils at the three white schools to which the blacks wished to go. But

Banks had reached no decision by December. Finally, on December 18, Shuttlesworth refused to wait any longer and filed suit to have the federal court declare the Pupil Placement Act unconstitutional.

Because the suit questioned the constitutionality of an act, it required the convening of a special three-judge court. Judges Lynne and Grooms and Judge Richard Rives of the Fifth Circuit were appointed to constitute it. The board of education asked that the suit be dismissed because the children had not exhausted all of the remedies available to them under the act, but the court refused and set arguments for April 3, 1958. At the hearing, Shuttlesworth's attorneys did not allege that the act had been unconstitutionally applied but contended instead simply that it was unconstitutional on its face, as a scheme to perpetuate segregation. Attorney General John Patterson offered the extraordinary opinion that the suit had produced "racial friction where none existed before." Mayor Morgan had earlier voiced the conviction that the effort "is not sponsored by the forward-thinking, civic-minded, loyal citizens of all races in Birmingham." And Commissioner Connor told Shuttlesworth a few weeks later, "You have done more harm to the Negroes in this city than any person I know of and they are your own people." On May 9, the court, in an opinion by Judge Rives, upheld the act's constitutionality. It might later become apparent that the authorities were discriminating in the application of the act, Rives wrote, but there was nothing inherently discriminatory in the various sociological and psychological criteria that the boards were told to use in judging transfer applications. Until the court was presented with evidence to the contrary, he said, it was bound to presume that the boards would administer the act honestly. The Christian Movement appealed to the U.S. Supreme Court, but in late November, the Court, in a brief per curiam order, approved Judge Rives's opinion on the narrow grounds on which it was based. And so it would be necessary for blacks to begin their attempt to integrate the schools, with all its dangers, all over again, and this time they apparently would be bound to satisfy all of the Pupil Placement Act's provisions.[77]

Shuttlesworth, however, remained undeterred. Six weeks after the Supreme Court's decision, he had the eight black children who had earlier sought transfers, including his own three, reapply. This time Superintendent Banks took a firmer line. The eight were again given achievement tests, but following the testing, at the end of February 1959, he rejected all eight applications with the comment that he could see no "special benefits which this child would receive from such a transfer." Shuttlesworth responded that "the struggle is on," but it was an empty threat. As we shall see, Shuttlesworth at this time was caught up in what became known in the black press as the "Birmingham stalemate." He could not obtain a local black lawyer, and federal court rules forbade the out-of-town black attorneys who were willing to assist him—Ernest Jackson of Jacksonville, Florida, and Len Holt of Norfolk, Virginia—from filing suit without associating a Birmingham attorney with them. We shall shortly explore the origins of the stalemate. For the moment, it is enough to say that the difficulty prevented court action on the school question for more than a year. The breaking of the stalemate in the fall of 1959, however, was followed in June 1960 by the initiation of a school desegregation suit in the name of Shuttlesworth's devoted ally, Smithfield barber James Armstrong. The suit sought to avoid the Pupil Placement Act's appeal mechanisms by alleging that they were inadequate to achieve the goal of a unified system. The law in effect operated to perpetuate segregation in the schools, the plaintiffs said, and they asked for an order compelling the board of education to adopt a desegregation plan. In July the school board replied that the suit failed to state any controversy or grounds for relief and asked that it therefore be dismissed. On November 21 the plaintiffs filed an amended complaint. The case was placed on the docket of Judge Seybourn Lynne, and there it sat as 1960 turned to 1961, and 1961 to 1962.

By June 1962, two years after the filing of the *Armstrong* suit, it had become clear that Judge Lynne was not eager to hear it. Blacks decided to try another tactic. On June 13, attorney Orzell Billingsley filed a second school integration suit, in the name of the Reverend Theodore N. Nelson, the black minister whose defiance had eliminated the legal standing of segregation in elevators in 1956. Billingsley hoped that the new petition would be assigned to Judge Grooms, and it was. But Judge Grooms would have none of it. He ruled that the hearing of the second suit should be postponed until the first one had been decided; it could then be entertained if there were still a need. Billingsley then appealed to the Fifth Circuit for an order to compel Grooms to proceed with the case. In August the Court of Appeals panel, consisting of Judges Richard Rives, John Minor Wisdom, and John R. Brown, sustained Judge Grooms's refusal to do so, but in a concurring opinion, Judge Brown denounced Judge Lynne's dawdling with the *Armstrong* suit. In the meantime, however, the initiation of the *Nelson* suit had actually had the desired effect. Contemporaneously with the *Nelson* case, Judge Lynne quickly announced that the *Armstrong* case was now ready for trial. He set a hearing for July 27 on the plaintiffs' motion for summary judgment and at the same time scheduled the hearing on the merits for October 3. At the July 27 hearing Lynne denied the motion for summary judgment, and the Christian Movement appealed this denial to the Fifth Circuit. But the trial went ahead on October 3 despite this appeal.

At the trial, Judge Lynne granted a motion to consolidate the *Armstrong* and *Nelson* suits and proceeded to hear them both. Superintendent Theo R. Wright, who had succeeded L. Frazer Banks in July 1959, testified that no blacks had applied to transfer under the Pupil Placement Act during his tenure; the fact was hardly surprising, however, since the school integration suit had been pending essentially throughout that period. Wright and his staff members also testified that mass integration would bring educational chaos, because the system's black students were so far behind its white in intellectual attainments. But Wright assured the court that the system operated under the terms of the Pupil Placement Act and that the racial segregation in it was merely a custom. However, the school board's chairman, Mrs. Adelia Troxell, the wife of the credit manager for a wholesale drug firm, unhesitatingly confirmed that the board operated a dual system and said that it had no intention of changing the pattern unless ordered to do so. She testified initially that the Pupil Placement Act required the preservation of segregation. After conferring with the board's attorney during a recess, she returned to the stand to report, evidently with astonishment, that the act actually empowered the board to permit interracial transfers. The board offered the testimony of a retired Columbia University psychologist, Henry E. Garrett, that psychological tests had proven blacks mentally inferior to whites. The plaintiff in the second school suit, Nelson, said that he had sent his children to live with their older sister in Detroit, Michigan, so that they could attend integrated schools. But he assured the court that if Birmingham's schools were desegregated, he would at once bring them home.

The trial concluded at the end of October 1962, and Judge Lynne considered his ruling while Birmingham voted to abolish its city commission, elected Albert Boutwell its new mayor, and experienced six weeks of highly charged Christian Movement demonstrations, led by the Reverend Martin Luther King. At the beginning of May, the plaintiffs filed a formal motion requesting a ruling. Finally, on May 28, 1963, five days after the Alabama Supreme Court had confirmed the new Boutwell administration in power, Lynne issued his decision. He dismissed the *Nelson* suit outright because the Nelson children were, he said, no longer Birmingham residents. In the *Armstrong* case, he held that the Pupil Placement Act provided adequate machinery for desegregating Birmingham's schools. Blacks who wished to go to white schools should apply under its terms. Armstrong's four children had failed to exhaust the appeals provided in the act, and they had to do so; the initiative in integrating the schools under the act lay with the students who desired integration, not with the school board. It was true, he acknowledged, that the system remained unconstitutionally segregated, but school officials had assured him that they were now prepared to process the Armstrong children's January 1959 transfer applications in good faith. "This court will not sanction discrimination by them in the name of the placement law, but it is unwilling to grant injunctive relief until their good faith has been tested." In view of the officials' testimony that "indiscriminate mixing" would harm students of both races, it was necessary for the court to use discretion in fashioning its remedy. Lynne was therefore prepared to wait to see how the system handled the Armstrongs' administrative appeals. Shuttlesworth at once announced that the plaintiffs would take the case to the Fifth Circuit.

The suit that had taken Judge Lynne three years to decide took the Fifth Circuit just six weeks to reverse. On July 12, Judges Richard Rives and Elbert Tuttle—over the strong dissent of newly appointed Judge Walter Gewin of Tuscaloosa—granted an immediate injunction to compel the initial integration of Birmingham schools with the start of the new school year in September, even though the court had not yet heard arguments on the merits of the appeal. The admission of the Armstrong children was ordered outright, and the school board was ordered to open at least one grade immediately to any black students who sought transfers under the Pupil Placement Act. On August 19 the district court approved the school board's plan to open the twelfth grade to interracial transfers, and the board then admitted three black applicants to white high schools, as well as Dwight and Floyd Armstrong to the white elementary school located across the street from their house. Eight years after the NAACP's initial petition to the school board, and six years after the first black applications under the Pupil Placement Act, Birmingham at last stood poised for its first school integration. The attempt, as we shall see, would produce three bombings, two full-scale riots, widespread unrest, the death of seven people, and the injuring of at least forty-six others.[78]

The state court challenge to civil service discrimination and the long-running federal court efforts to end segregation in the terminals, on the buses, and in the schools were not the only suits that blacks initiated in these years. In April 1962 they filed suit to end the discriminatory practices of the county board of voting registrars. Proving that these practices formed a pattern of conduct required large resources, however, and the case made little progress until the Justice Department filed its own parallel suit in August 1963. In February 1962, the county Democratic Executive Committee refused to allow blacks to become candidates for party office, on the ground that as blacks they could not possibly believe in the party motto, "White Supremacy for the Right." The committee apparently was not conscious of the contradiction that this position represented to the general white supremacist claim that most blacks were content with segregation. Its action led to still another federal court suit, though in this case the Republican Judge Grooms succeeded in persuading the Democratic officials to relent without the necessity for a formal injunction. In May 1962, blacks sued the county jury commission in an effort to end the exclusion of blacks from juries. At the trial, state Circuit Judges Wallace C. Gibson and J. Edgar Bowron testified that there had been an agreement among white lawyers not to allow a black to serve, and that when the name of a black was drawn, the clerk announced the fact and a new name was selected. This clear evidence of discrimination, however, only convinced Judge Grooms that the fault lay not with the jury commission but with the bar, and he dismissed the complaint, while also criticizing black leaders from the bench for, he said, having failed to supply the jury commissioners with the names of potential black jurors. In July 1962 the Christian Movement sued to integrate the public library and facilities at the city hall and the county courthouse, but Judge Grooms eventually dismissed this case when authorities ceased enforcing segregation in these areas on their own. During the period when he could not obtain a local lawyer, Shuttlesworth, acting as his own attorney, sued "Bull" Connor, unsuccessfully, to bar police from attending all Christian Movement mass meetings. And in addition to these federal suits, there were, of course, the numerous state court criminal cases that were produced by the necessity to create tests of the segregation laws before they could be attacked in the federal courts; all of these criminal prosecutions had to be fought up through the state appellate process, and frequently on to the U.S. Supreme Court. At the end of February 1961, Shuttlesworth was personally a litigant in fourteen lawsuits. In June 1962 he reported that the Christian Movement had paid out almost $75,000 in legal fees since its founding in 1956 and was thousands of dollars in debt, with several major cases pending and others still awaiting filing.[79]

For all the numerous suits that have already been mentioned, we have not yet discussed the one case whose importance for the course of Birmingham's history would eventually prove the greatest, the suit to integrate the city parks. Before turning to this suit, whose implications will carry us forward to the next stage of our story, however, we should pause to reflect on the lessons that this prodigious legal activity taught Shuttlesworth and his associates.

As we have seen, white moderates—and black moderates, too—often stressed the virtues of settling the races' differences in the courts. Readers have been carried through this detailed account of the Christian Movement's efforts to do so in order to enable them to appreciate just what such an attempt actually entailed. At the outset, no one was more convinced of the merits of legal action than was Shuttlesworth. Through the 1950s such action was the central activity of the Christian Movement. It was his experience of the judiciary itself that began to change his mind. In the first place, in Birmingham in this period the bringing of a suit was a good deal more dangerous than most outsiders understood. Both the plaintiffs in the civil service suit lost their jobs, and the Klan directed an arson attack against one of them. Shuttlesworth's home was bombed to prevent any questioning of bus segregation. A mob beat him when he sought to challenge school segregation, and Edward Aaron was castrated in response to the initial applications for transfers under the Pupil Placement Act. A mob similarly assaulted Lamar Weaver in connection with Shuttlesworth's attempt to demonstrate the existence of segregation at the railroad station. Of course, such efforts at intimidation did not faze Shuttlesworth, but they could easily have given a less tenacious man pause. If Klan violence could not deter the adamantine Shuttlesworth, however, what happened to the cases once they were filed could not have been so easy for him and his followers to bear. Seemingly interminable protraction, as Judges Lynne and Grooms gave serious consideration to virtually every segregationist delaying tactic, very often was followed by a dismissal or a weak and highly qualified decree. The result was an almost inevitable appeal, further hearings, additional expense, the passage of more years—and always to sustain a fundamental legal position that had long since been settled by the appellate courts in other cases. In the meantime, the parallel state prosecutions threatened always to land the plaintiffs in jail, while lawyers' fees stretched to the limit—and beyond—the Christian Movement's tiny resources, gathered from the faithful in nickels and dimes at the weekly mass meetings. If we view the situation from this perspective, it becomes easier to understand how the results of Judge Lynne's emotional commitment to segregation, together with Judge Grooms's more benign but only somewhat more easily surmounted devotion to the technicalities of legal craftsmanship, worked increasingly to undermine the Christian Movement members' belief in an exclusive reliance on the courts.

But even if Seybourn Lynne and Hobart Grooms had been more like Montgomery's Frank Johnson, with his ferocious intolerance of segregationist evasions, there was another disadvantage inextricably bound up with legal action that at the same time was also compelling the Christian Movement to have second thoughts about the strategy: it required the use of lawyers. Part of the problem was their cost, given the Christian Movement's very slender treasury, but the difficulty ran deeper than that. It was epitomized by the "Birmingham stalemate," to which we have already alluded. An examination of the stalemate will clarify this point.

Shuttlesworth had long wanted to file a suit to seek the integration of Birmingham's parks. In October 1958, he and more than two hundred of his followers submitted a fruitless petition to the city commission asking for the parks' desegregation. But as local attorneys doubtless warned him, suing was a problematic step. In no area of municipal life did blacks have less leverage to make sure that a victory in court became a practical advance for black residents. The bus line and the terminals were operated by private companies; if they wished to continue their business despite an integration order, the city could do very little about it. Officials constantly threatened to close the public schools if they were integrated, but given the pressure from parents not to do so, it was not unreasonable to believe that authorities would relent, as they generally had in other states. But parks were directly in the control of the municipal government, and their abandonment would represent no truly intolerable loss to the city. There was therefore strong reason to think that the city commissioners might carry through on their pledge to close the parks down if their integration were ever ordered, and if the commissioners decided to do it, blacks really had no way to stop them. Under segregation, blacks at least had their own parks and community centers; it seemed likely, however, that after an integration suit neither race would have any. Such considerations had perplexed a parks integration suit that black attorney David Hood had filed in neighboring Bessemer as early as August 1957. In January 1958 he had withdrawn the suit after the city promised to spend $66,000 to build a park for blacks. Blacks recognized the need for time to allow whites to adjust to integration, Hood had said, and so he had accepted the city's compromise. In fact, it seems likely that Hood and his clients understood that a new park for blacks was, as a practical matter, all they were likely to get. In December 1958, as we have seen, the mere filing of a suit to integrate Montgomery's parks had caused the commission there to order them all closed, and Judge Frank Johnson had subsequently upheld the city's right to take this action. And even Shuttlesworth's own attorney, Ernest Jackson, when he had won an order to integrate the municipal golf courses in his hometown of Jacksonville, Florida, in April 1959, had seen the city promptly close and sell both courses rather than comply. The case for turning a blind eye to the continuation of this particular form of segregation was, therefore, quite compelling. Apparently, Birmingham's black attorneys were nearly unanimous in accepting it.

It was this attitude that generated the stalemate. Federal court rules in Birmingham forbade an out-of-town lawyer to file a suit unless he associated a local attorney with him. Jackson was willing to take Shuttlesworth's case, but he had to find a Birmingham lawyer who would join him. At the beginning of 1959 they believed that they had found one in Demetrius C. Newton of Fairfield, a young black lawyer who had been admitted to the bar in 1953; the Christian Movement paid him fifteen hundred dollars as a retainer. But Newton then fell under intense pressure both from Judge Lynne and from the area's six other black attorneys to withdraw from the case. Judge Lynne apparently wished to use the rule requiring a local associate to halt Shuttlesworth's onslaught of desegregation cases, and he seems to have spoken to Arthur Shores, the city's senior black lawyer, about it. Shores was an associate of David Hood, who had agreed to drop the Bessemer parks suit a year earlier, and as his service on the Interracial Committee and the Smithfield compromise committee had demonstrated, he was a man always eager to accommodate white community leaders, as long as he felt he could do so honorably. In this case, his conviction that a parks integration suit was a strategic error apparently led him to cooperate with Judge Lynne's plan. But he and other black attorneys did not want to be seen as opposing integration. It was very likely for this reason that they hit upon the stratagem of agreeing together that none of them would represent Shuttlesworth unless he could collect enough money to hire them all. Everyone involved understood that the Christian Movement's financial resources were very small and that this demand therefore would effectively deprive Shuttlesworth of access to the federal courts. That, indeed, was precisely the outcome Judge Lynne wished. Not only did the agreement prevent the filing of the parks suit, but as we have seen, it also halted the effort to pursue school integration and forced Shuttlesworth to act as his own attorney in the suit to bar the Birmingham police from the Christian Movement's mass meetings. Quite possibly Newton was not initially a part of this agreement; he practiced law independently in Fairfield and had somewhat more limited contact with the other black attorneys. But when he accepted the Christian Movement's retainer, he very quickly felt the weight of their annoyance and Judge Lynne's displeasure. He at once ceased to cooperate with Ernest Jackson.

This affair came into the open in May 1959, when Jackson filed a formal petition with Judge Lynne asking the court to waive the rule requiring a local associate and to allow the filing of the parks integration suit to proceed. In the petition Jackson described his exasperating dealings with Newton and the rest of the black bar. After a hearing on June 19, Judge Lynne ruled that there were absolutely no circumstances in which the local associate rule could be waived—even though Jackson had in fact argued Shuttlesworth's challenge to the constitutionality of the Pupil Placement Act in 1958 without any local associate, as Emory Jackson of the *Birmingham World* noted. In the meantime, the filing of the waiver petition had generated a bitter controversy in the black community. At a mass meeting on June 5 celebrating the anniversary of the Christian Movement's founding, Shuttlesworth sharply criticized Newton both for his withdrawal from the suit and for his refusal to return the retainer; Shuttlesworth also reported Newton's own statement that he had withdrawn because of the pressure from his fellow black attorneys and from a federal judge. And the evening's principal speaker, acting Southern Christian Leadership Conference executive director Ella Baker, then joined in, lashing out at "accommodating Negro leaders" who were serving as "tools" of white interests.

On June 14 the black lawyers arranged to use the convention of the black Alabama Independent Beauticians Association for a public response to Shuttlesworth and Baker. The young Selma attorney J. L. Chestnut, Jr., who had just been admitted to the bar six weeks earlier, was asked to present their case. Chestnut was introduced by Orzell Billingsley and was thanked at the conclusion of his address by Newton himself. Chestnut assured his audience with extraordinary condescension that "when these learned lawyers refuse to go along with some 'Johnnie Come Lately' who overnight has decided, for reasons best known to him, that his unlearned and unlettered plan is the only means of deliverance for the Negro people, then these lawyers, trained in the law and the constitution, in their refusal have unquestionably adopted the best policy, the best approach, to preserve the dignity [and] security of every Negro in the Jefferson County area." He then launched into a truly slanderous attack on Shuttlesworth, implying that Shuttlesworth's only real goals were to feed his ego and to line his own pocket. "I have no truck for thieves, no matter that they hide behind the pale of integration. . . . Merely because some Negro has learned, of late, to pronounce the word 'integration' and does so quite frequently, is hardly any evidence of itself that this person is a leader. . . . Many people masquerade as leaders for any number of reasons. Some like the feel of money, the sense of personal power. Then some others suffer from a malady best described as 'Newspaperitis.' To see their name in public print sends them off into such ridiculous reveries that reality itself becomes a fiction." And he concluded, "Men who are intent upon becoming rich need to keep their efforts over in the field of business and commerce, and stop trying to show a profit over in the gravely important area of equality before the law." By this time, the dispute threatened to tear the Birmingham black community apart. The *Birmingham World* pleaded editorially for the appointment of a mediation committee to seek common ground between the contending elements. But the *World* at the same time probably added fuel to the fire by lamenting, in obvious reference to Arthur Shores, that since the banning of the NAACP, a number of men who had traditionally been black leaders had "become de-vocalized, impotent and withdrawn."

The immediate crisis was defused in the fall when Birmingham gained its eighth black attorney, Willie L. Williams. Williams, admitted to the bar in September and eager to create a practice for himself, was willing to defy the older lawyers and associate himself with Ernest Jackson. His action broke the cartel. On October 19, Jackson in association with Williams filed the parks integration suit, which had long been prepared. And the following June the two filed an amended parks complaint, correcting technical defects in the original one, and at the same time filed the *Armstrong* school integration suit. In the meantime, the affair had come to the attention of the state bar association. In February 1960, Demetrius Newton was disbarred for having accepted the Christian Movement's retainer and then having refused to act. Newton would not be permitted to resume the practice of law until April 1963.[80]

But the end of the stalemate by no means eliminated the animosities the episode had revealed between Shuttlesworth and Birmingham's better-to-do black leaders. The encounter taught Shuttlesworth and his followers in the Christian Movement that reliance upon legal action placed them at the mercy of the black bar, whose strategic perspectives and social attitudes were often very different from those of the civil rights activists. Just as the behavior of Judges Lynne and Grooms was exposing the truth that the federal judiciary was unlikely to hand blacks their rights without a struggle, the stalemate demonstrated that black professionals could by no means always be regarded as brethren in the cause. Black attorneys, in particular, not only had inescapable ties to the white bench and bar, but even more significantly, depended for their livelihood upon the patronage of the wealthier blacks who were their most important clients. And these wealthier blacks were increasingly disposed to regard Shuttlesworth as a troublemaker. Emory Jackson, the militant editor of the *Birmingham World,* sought repeatedly to defend Shuttlesworth from their attacks. In June 1960, Jackson insisted that Shuttlesworth had now become "a more seasoned leader" who "seems to better understand teamwork leadership and is beginning to adjust his approach to some of the realities of struggle." In December, he conceded, "There are those who question his methods, suspect his motives, and point to flaws in his personality. But none can say with honesty or facts that the Reverend Shuttlesworth has not been on the move in the direction of fuller freedom and whole citizenship." And earlier Jackson had noted that the Christian Movement "has a wider and more devoted following than has been true of any other civil rights organization in this city. It pulls most of its support from the masses who are the salt of the struggle for freedom. It has linked the pulpit leadership to the 'Movement' and given it fervor, idealism and moral vigor." But in these defenses, Jackson plainly identified the nature of the criticisms that middle class black leaders most frequently leveled at Shuttlesworth. He was arrogant, conceited, and utterly unwilling to accept the advice, or even to credit the sincerity, of others, they said—with much justice. He was interested only in self-promotion, they claimed, less persuasively. His confrontational tactics prevented the attainment of advances that amicable negotiations with white moderates could have quietly procured, they asserted, almost certainly wrongly. And they read the "fervor" and "moral vigor" of his followers as unthinking emotionalism and submissive devotion to Shuttlesworth's tutelage. Attorneys like Shores, moreover, had earlier been the leaders of the struggle, and were offended by Shuttlesworth's insistence that they now do his bidding. Though the Birmingham stalemate was broken at the end of 1959, then, it nevertheless confirmed a fundamental parting of the ways between the Christian Movement and the black professional and commercial leaders who, as we shall shortly see, in April 1960 rallied to the banner of the Inter-Citizens Committee.[81]

It is inaccurate to portray the Christian Movement as drawing its members primarily from Birmingham's poorer blacks. Indeed, a survey conducted by a sociologist in the spring of 1959 of a sample of the membership found it reasonably representative of the city's black community. The Christian Movement at that time had about nine hundred to twelve hundred members, of whom about half could be expected to be in attendance at any one of the weekly Monday-night mass meetings that were the group's backbone. Of the sample, 38 percent were men and 62 percent women. The typical member was a middle-aged, married working woman who had lived in Birmingham for more than a quarter of a century. Though almost half of the city's blacks had household incomes between $2,000 and $4,000 a year, the mean annual household income of the Christian Movement sample, $3,715, was on the high side in this group. The typical member's ninth-grade education was identical with that of the city's population at large. In two ways, however, the sample was distinctly atypical. More than two-thirds of them were registered voters, a fact that clearly attests their commitment to civil rights activism. And 88 percent of them were Baptists, doubtless an indication of the extent to which the organization was a reflection of Shuttlesworth's own personality. Though a substantial part of the membership was from the middle class, half of the sample was employed in unskilled or semiskilled jobs, and more than a third of them owned no real property. While it is misleading to depict the Christian Movement as an organization of the poor, then, it is true to say that it drew significant numbers of poorer blacks into its ranks, and allied them with better-to-do activists in a common cause.

It is worth emphasizing again, as well, that at this time—just before the stalemate had become public knowledge and a year before the first sit-ins—the Christian Movement remained committed to court suits rather than direct action. Less than a third of the Christian Movement sample regarded boycotts or mass marches as appropriate means of obtaining civil rights, and a mere 6 percent thought that picketing was. In contrast, 88 percent regarded legislation and court action as the most effective way to get integration, and indeed, 78 percent thought them the only way. On the other hand, the membership also mirrored Shuttlesworth's own deep hostility toward the more conservative blacks who believed in the possibility of progress through cooperation with white moderates. Only a fifth of the Christian Movement sample regarded negotiations as an appropriate means to obtain civil rights, though three-fifths of Montgomery activists and two-thirds of Tuskegee activists thought that they were. And just 7 percent of the Christian Movement members regarded interracial and interfaith pressures as appropriate; five times that percentage thought so in Montgomery and Tuskegee. These strategic differences with the black moderates would interact with the animosities generated by the Birmingham stalemate and the disillusionment produced by the attitudes of Judges Lynne and Grooms to begin moving the Christian Movement, and Shuttlesworth himself, toward a greater openness to direct action. The catalyst that initiated this movement was the sit-ins.[82]

The sit-ins at the lunch counters of department and variety stores that commenced in Greensboro, North Carolina, on February 1, 1960, quickly caught the imagination of students at Miles and Daniel Payne Colleges in Birmingham, in common with students on black campuses all over the South. Student leaders of the two colleges discussed the possibility of staging similar protests with Shuttlesworth and with the Reverend Robert E. Hughes, the white Methodist minister who headed the Southern Regional Council's Alabama branch, the Alabama Council on Human Relations. At Hughes's urging, the students initially decided upon a more restrained action, a public prayer vigil in a black park. But when twelve of them attempted it on March 1, police at once arrested the group; after they had been fingerprinted and photographed, they were released without charge. The result, however, was that eight Klansmen stormed the Bessemer home of one of them, Robert Jones, on March 12, and beat him and his mother and sister. His mother suffered a broken leg and finger and multiple head wounds. This incident served to radicalize the students, and after further discussions with Shuttlesworth, ten of them—nine of whom were students at Daniel Payne—staged sit-ins at five downtown lunch counters on March 31. Police charged the ten, led by Daniel Payne undergraduate Jesse Walker, with trespassing; and when officers learned of Shuttlesworth's role from questioning the students, they charged Shuttlesworth and his Christian Movement associate the Reverend Charles Billups with aiding and abetting a breach of the peace. On April 4, Recorder's Court Judge William Conway sentenced all twelve to six months in jail and fines of one hundred dollars.[83]

The sit-ins served to renew the general black admiration for Shuttlesworth that had been somewhat diminished in the years after 1957 by the slow progress of his many cases through the courts and the failure of his attempted bus boycott in November 1958. But the sit-ins by no means indicated any immediate conversion on his part to direct action. Quite to the contrary, Shuttlesworth seems to have regarded the March 31 protests in exactly the same way that he had looked at the earlier brief defiance of the two bus segregation ordinances and similar episodes: as a limited act of civil disobedience necessary to produce a court test. With the March 31 arrests and the April 4 convictions and appeals, he and his student allies suspended any further actions to await the appellate courts' decisions. And indeed, these cases were destined to produce one of the Christian Movement's most significant legal victories when, in May 1963, the U.S. Supreme Court decided, in the appeals of the Birmingham prosecutions as well as similar ones from Durham, North Carolina, Greenville, South Carolina, and New Orleans, Louisiana, that criminal trespassing ordinances were unenforceable in cities that also had restaurant segregation ordinances, because the trespassing arrests thus in effect became state action to require segregation.[84] It was not the sit-ins themselves, but reactions to them in the black community, that actually moved Shuttlesworth toward direct action.

On April 9, in response to the Recorder's Court sit-in convictions five days before, 318 black civic leaders came together to form the Inter-Citizens Committee, an effort, as they claimed, to forge solidarity among the city's prominent blacks. In fact, the purpose of the new committee was considerably less benign. Shuttlesworth's longtime rival the Reverend James L. Ware was elected the new organization's chairman. Ware had earlier headed another league of black moderates, the Jefferson County Betterment Association, but its reputation for inactivity had forced it to dissolve the year before. The subsequent public controversy over the Birmingham stalemate had greatly embittered the already deep differences between Shuttlesworth and the older civil rights leadership. And now, with the sit-ins, Shuttlesworth's previously somewhat tarnished reputation among the mass of black Birminghamians had quite suddenly recovered its luster. Men like Ware, Arthur Shores, and insurance magnate Arthur Gaston were determined that Shuttlesworth should not be allowed to claim preeminence in the black community's struggle for integration. The committee was intended to provide an institutional focus for the efforts of the older civil rights leaders, alternative to the Christian Movement.

With the backing of greater financial resources than the Christian Movement possessed, the Inter-Citizens Committee was able to open an office and hire an executive secretary, Presbyterian minister C. Herbert Oliver, who had been the president of the Birmingham chapter of the interracial Alabama Council on Human Relations. Though certainly more conservative men than Shuttlesworth was, Ware and Oliver were nevertheless unquestionably sincere in their advocacy of civil rights. Ware's activism stretched back to the 1940s. In 1947 he had chaired the committee whose highly publicized fight against segregated arrangements for viewing the Freedom Train that was touring the country had compelled the cancellation of its stop in Birmingham. Oliver, at that time a pentecostal, had been the pastor of the church that had hosted the convention of the Southern Negro Youth Congress in 1948 at which Senator Glen Taylor had been arrested for violating the segregation laws. Oliver, moreover, had felt the sting of Connor's police in connection with the sit-ins themselves. On April 3, two officers had come to Oliver's home without a warrant, broken open the front door, and arrested him on the utterly absurd charge of vagrancy. Subsequently he had been charged with having intimidated a witness in connection with the sit-in proceedings, but at trial he was immediately acquitted. This experience very probably influenced Oliver's passionate pursuit of one of the committee's most useful activities of future years, the gathering of notarized statements documenting incidents of police brutality. If their sincerity was beyond doubt, however, Ware and Oliver also shared a faith in the efficacy of negotiations with whites that Shuttlesworth strongly rejected. The committee's first action as an organization was to write Mayor Morgan in May to plead with him to appoint a biracial committee to renew the discussions ended when the Interracial Committee was abolished in 1956.

But Ware apparently had learned a lesson from the failure of his Betterment Association: such moderate initiatives would inevitably be taken by the broader black community as accommodationist unless the Inter-Citizens Committee took action to prove its militancy. Ware and Oliver also, therefore, took up the cause of integrating the downtown lunch counters. During the early summer, the committee sought to persuade the two department stores and three five-and-ten-cent stores at which the students had conducted their sit-ins on March 31 to enter into negotiations about the voluntary desegregation of their restaurants. If the merchants agreed, it would demonstrate that negotiations could produce results. And in any case, the request served to emphasize that Shuttlesworth was doing nothing about this problem except awaiting the outcome of the court proceedings. When the merchants proved unyielding, the committee decided to go even further. In July it began to attempt to mobilize the city's blacks to boycott the five stores. As a part of this campaign, it also sponsored a visit to Birmingham by Clyde R. Carter. Carter, a native of Birmingham who had just graduated from Johnson C. Smith University in Charlotte, North Carolina, had led the Charlotte sit-in campaign in February and had participated—along with Birmingham's Jesse Walker—in the organizational meeting of the Student Non-violent Coordinating Committee in April. He addressed the Inter-Citizens Committee and black Birmingham college students on August 6. On August 10, he, Walker, and another SNCC member, Alfonso Crawford, tried to speak with Mayor Morgan, but the mayor refused to see them. The result was a renewal of the sit-ins on August 15 against four of the five stores that had been the objects of the March 31 protests. The August sit-ins were intended to test the constitutionality of the city's newly toughened anti-trespassing ordinance. Police arrested three adults and four juveniles. At the end of the month the three adults were convicted in Recorder's Court, and their cases began what experience indicated would be a long trip through the appellate process.[85]

The Inter-Citizens Committee's exertions to identify itself with the sit-ins, its efforts to organize a boycott of the recalcitrant downtown merchants, and its sponsorship of the SNCC attempts to initiate direct action in the city presented Shuttlesworth with a genuine challenge to his leadership. For the first time since the suspension of the NAACP in 1956, he was not the undisputed champion of militancy. The *World* exulted that at last Birmingham seemed to be developing "civil rights leadership depth." The *World* hoped that the Christian Movement and the committee would coordinate their activities.[86] But teamwork was, to say the least of it, not a part of Shuttlesworth's style. Beginning with the late summer of 1960, the competition between the two organizations became a dominant fact in the life of Birmingham's black community. It would shape every crucial racial encounter over the next three years, and would form the pivot in the interplay of events that dictated the necessity of the mass demonstrations in April and May of 1963. Before we can understand those developments fully, however, we must now retrace our steps and explore the evolution of attitudes among Birmingham's whites in the years since the reelection of "Bull" Connor in 1957.

IV. The Rebirth of White Moderation

In the deep darkness of cowardice and enmity that descended on white Birmingham after the establishment of the White Citizens' Councils and the defeat of Robert Lindbergh, there flickered very few progressive flames. But one of the little lights that segregationist intimidation had not managed to extinguish was the tiny group of white liberals led by the Reverend Robert Hughes who persisted in meeting with a small group of black moderates as the Birmingham chapter of the Alabama Council on Human Relations. Hughes, a Methodist minister who was a native of Gadsden and a graduate of the University of Alabama, had been assigned by the Methodist bishop of northern Alabama, Clare Purcell, to a full-time ministry as the ACHR's executive secretary in 1954. He had initially maintained his office in Montgomery, but in the midst of the bus boycott, the owner of the building in which the office was located, Jerome Moore, fell under such intense pressure from the Citizens' Council that he refused to renew the ACHR's lease. As a result, in the fall of 1956, Hughes moved the state headquarters to Birmingham. With the dissolution of the Interracial Committee the preceding spring, the ACHR's Birmingham chapter was now the only biracial organization left in the city, and Hughes labored to keep it alive. Both segregationists and authorities, however, were dedicated to destroying it. In October 1957, police invaded a meeting of the chapter and took the names and addresses of all present, on the allegation that they were in violation of the city ordinance against racially integrated public meetings. Shortly thereafter, the neighbors and business associates of all the whites who had been at the meeting received anonymous notification of their membership in the group, and each of them began receiving tormenting telephone calls. It seems clear that police officers must have passed the names along to the White Citizens' Councils and perhaps the Klan. The ACHR chapter was compelled to suspend all activities for several months. By September 1958, membership had fallen by half, to only fifty people, and attendance at meetings thereafter averaged no more than five. It was a pathetically small base upon which to try to erect a new life for the community.[87]

Casting about for some other mechanism with which to force moderate white opinion back into the open, Hughes hit upon an expedient that would prove crucial to bringing Birmingham to face its problems. The business progressives, as we have seen, feared almost nothing more than negative national publicity for their city, because their primary goal was the attraction of new industry to the area. It was precisely this fear that had mobilized moderate white business leaders at the beginning of the 1950s to insist upon the suppression of the initial postwar resurgence of Klan violence, to sponsor the creation of the Interracial Committee, and to preside over the political humiliation of "Bull" Connor. This same fear, Hughes came to realize, might now prove the means to move the business progressives to surmount the dread of social ostracism and commercial boycott by which the segregationists bound them into silence—an emancipation through which they could reemerge as a credible opposition to the racial extremists. Hughes therefore commenced a systematic program of providing national publications with information about the extent of Birmingham's dominion of terror.

His first real success came when the December 15, 1958, issue of *Time* magazine carried an extremely uncomplimentary article on Birmingham's racial climate, based largely on material obtained from Hughes. As a direct result, the city's economic powers gave their support to the preparation of a Metropolitan Audit to be conducted by the Southern Institute of Management—a study that its sponsors hoped would refute *Time*'s claim that Birmingham was characterized by a "dearth of leadership, the silence of fear, the bomb blasts of hatred." The audit, when its results began to appear in mid-1960, was frank in its numerous criticisms, particularly of the extraordinary defensiveness and lack of civic stewardship exhibited by the city's social and economic elite. These unexpectedly derogatory findings, widely reported in the local press, contributed to the self-examination in which many moderates were increasingly engaged.

In the meantime, however, Hughes had scored an even more telling triumph with his publicity campaign. In the spring of 1960, the *New York Times* assigned its correspondent Harrison E. Salisbury to develop a report based on the intelligence that Hughes had been providing the paper. Salisbury's articles, which appeared in the newspaper's issues of April 12 and 13, were substantially more detailed, and hence even more devastating, than the *Time* magazine story. The two articles were reprinted in the Birmingham daily papers, and their effect in the city was truly remarkable. White community leaders were virtually unanimous in their denunciations of reporting that the *Birmingham News* called slanderous. But though there were indeed several minor factual misstatements in the articles, Birmingham's elite was not actually distressed by Salisbury's errors, but by his insight. "No New Yorker can readily measure the climate of Birmingham today," he conceded. But he then proceeded to summarize it quite accurately: "Every channel of communication, every medium of mutual interest, every reasoned approach, every inch of middle ground has been fragmented by the emotional dynamite of racism, reinforced by the whip, the razor, the gun, the bomb, the torch, the club, the knife, the mob, the police and many branches of the state's apparatus. . . . The eavesdropper, the informer, the spy have become a fact of life. . . . Birmingham's whites and blacks share a community of fear." And in the second article he noted—prophetically, as the Freedom Rider riot a year later would demonstrate: "The lines between legality and extra-legality are becoming blurred. The police force is not the only power frequently utilized to terrorize the citizenry, both white and Negro. The distinction between exercise of state power and mob power is being eroded."

For Robert Hughes himself, the results of these articles were disastrous. Both the Birmingham and the Bessemer City Commissions promptly filed civil libel actions against Salisbury and the *Times,* and the Jefferson County Grand Jury, meeting in Bessemer, commenced a criminal libel investigation. Hughes was subpoenaed in connection with the grand jury inquiry, and he was ordered to bring with him the ACHR's membership and financial records for the preceding three years. Hughes appeared on the appointed day, but since the U.S. Supreme Court had already ruled in the state's suit against the NAACP that such orders to produce membership lists were unconstitutional, he refused to turn over any such material. Circuit Judge Gardner F. Goodwyn at once ordered him jailed for contempt. His attorneys appealed first to the state supreme court and then to the U.S. Supreme Court for an order to quash the subpoena. Faced with certain reversal by the U.S. Supreme Court, Deputy Solicitor Howard Sullinger then withdrew the subpoena and issued a new one that made no mention of the ACHR records. Hughes thereupon testified before the grand jury for four hours, and was released, having spent four days in jail. The grand jury indicted Salisbury on forty-two counts of criminal libel.

As it happened, however, the North Alabama Conference of the Methodist Church was holding its annual convention in Birmingham just at this time. The segregationist Methodist Laymen's Union, now headed by Birmingham Circuit Judge Whitten M. Windham, had long wanted to rid the church of Hughes, and this confluence of events seemed to be its chance. Hughes's friend Bishop Clare Purcell had retired in 1956, and Purcell's successor, Bishop Bachman Hodge, had proved to be a weak and vacillating man, who by 1960 was near death. In 1958 the conference's cabinet had approved the continuation of Hughes's appointment to the ACHR by only a single vote, and now the public controversy surrounding Hughes's imprisonment for contempt swung some more moderate delegates over to the segregationists' side. On September 6, while Hughes was testifying before the grand jury, the conference was voting to revoke his ministerial license. When he arrived at the convention on September 7, he found himself defrocked. He then commenced a frantic struggle to persuade delegates to change their minds. Finally, just before the convention was to adjourn, a compromise was reached. The conference voted to rescind its action and restore Hughes's credentials, on condition that he would leave immediately to become a missionary to Africa. Hughes agreed and, resigning from the ACHR, moved to Salisbury, Southern Rhodesia. He would find the commitment of white Rhodesians to segregation quite as strong as that of the white Alabamians whom he left behind, and in July 1964 the Rhodesian government would order both him and his bishop deported.[88]

Though Hughes would not be around to see it happen, his actions actually initiated, just as he had hoped, the reemergence of the business progressives' civic leadership. Their first reaction had been to close ranks with the city commissioners. The *New York Times* agreed to publish a statement written by chamber of commerce president Mortimer H. Jordan and Committee of 100 chairman William P. Engel, intended to refute Salisbury's allegations. The two wrote that they "deny vigorously that the image presented by Mr. Salisbury is true, because it distorts and telescopes instances covering many prior years in an effort to provide a picture of the moment—a picture that is not true, even reasonably true." They defended "Bull" Connor as "a firm, effective Police Commissioner" and added that "the record conclusively shows that he does maintain law and order." They complained that "The bridge of communication between Birmingham whites and Negroes, nurtured so carefully for so many years by men of goodwill of both races, is being destroyed by attacks by many of the media of national communication." They then devoted the bulk of their statement to demonstrating statistically—and doubtless correctly—that, over the preceding two decades, "Negro citizens in Birmingham have moved forward rapidly and steadily" in material terms. Their willingness to associate themselves with Connor's bellicose methods of maintaining public order; their extraordinary claim that the national media were destroying interracial communication in the city, in the face of the fact that their fellow business leaders had themselves dissolved Birmingham's only forum devoted to it four years earlier; and perhaps most of all, their conception of black progress as entirely a function of economic advancement—all these revealed how very far they would have to come before they could comprehend the transformation in race relations that was taking shape around them.

And yet their desire to see their city prosper was genuine, and it formed a foundation upon which an understanding of Birmingham's situation could be built, independent of that of the politicians and the more inflexible segregationists. Engel and Jordan had made their central concern about the Salisbury articles explicit: "Your readers could only conclude, on reading these distorted statements, that it is dangerous to live in Birmingham, which is certainly not true." They feared that such publicity would make corporate executives and investors reluctant to locate in Birmingham. But it quickly became clear that the sort of shrill response that greeted the Salisbury articles, far from halting, would only increase such unflattering notice. In October the *Washington Post* published a similar portrait of the city, concerned primarily with the citizenry's reaction to the *Times* pieces. And the following May, the Columbia Broadcasting System telecast a report focused on the city commissioners' libel suits against the *Times*—a program which itself provoked a new round of libel suits, though Judge Lynne dismissed them in August 1962 for lack of jurisdiction. At almost the same time as the CBS program, the Mother's Day Freedom Rider riot, as we shall see, brought the city a new avalanche of criticism. Manifestly, neither the bitter defensiveness that had followed the Salisbury exposé nor the dispassionate but critical Metropolitan Audit that had resulted from the *Time* magazine article could end such attacks. Only real reform could do that. By the end of 1960, this realization was dawning at the chamber of commerce.[89]

The chamber of commerce was dominated by very conservative men. Its president in 1960, Mortimer Jordan, vice-president for public relations of the Southern Natural Gas Company (Sonat), had resigned as the Alabama director of the U.S. Internal Revenue Service in 1948 to protest President Harry Truman's executive order prohibiting racial discrimination in federal employment; he had called the order a threat to peaceful race relations. Jordan's successor as chamber president in 1961, realtor and attorney Sidney W. Smyer, had been a prominent Dixiecrat in 1948 and, as we have seen, was a principal organizer of two segregationist groups, the American States' Rights Association and the Methodist Laymen's Union, in 1954. But the relentlessly negative publicity the city was now receiving, combined with the very nearly messianic status that industrial expansion occupied in the imaginations of business leaders at this period, was bringing even men of this stripe to embrace—if at this stage only tentatively— the business progressive perspective. Though the events of 1961 would complete their conversion, in late 1960 the process had already begun. The chamber joined with the industry-seeking Committee of 100 and the Downtown Improvement Association to appoint a twelve-member study committee to propose means of furthering municipal growth. Named to the committee, in addition to Sonat vice-president Mortimer Jordan, the president of the chamber, and realtor William P. Engel, the chairman of the Committee of 100, was a group of the Birmingham area's most important commercial and industrial figures: U.S. Steel executive Arthur V. Weibel, U.S. Pipe and Foundry president Robert E. Garrett, Chicago Bridge and Iron executive Amasa G. Smith, Vulcan Materials president Bernard A. "Barney" Monaghan, Alabama Gas chairman Joseph N. Greene, Alabama Power president Walter Bouldin, Birmingham Trust National Bank president Frank Plummer, *Birmingham News* publisher Clarence B. Hanson, and department store executives Emil Hess and Isadore Pizitz. An early public indication of the thinking of this committee came in mid-December 1960, when chamber president Jordan addressed the Young Men's Business Club to plead for the annexation to Birmingham of Jefferson County's thirty-two other municipalities. Surely, he said, men of reason and goodwill could work out the problems of control over the schools and zoning regulation and representation on the merged city government that had so far prevented this step. An examination of the implications of this speech will carry us to the next stage of our story.[90]

As the civic courage of the business progressives began slowly to thaw, after the five years during which they had kept it confined in the deep freeze of their fears, it seemed to most of them that the community's essential public relations impediment was political, and that, as in 1951, its personification was "Bull" Connor. A different police administration, intent on halting Klan violence and extending evenhanded protection to all citizens, would go far toward restoring Birmingham's municipal reputation. Thus, at the end of the 1950s as at their beginning, the imperative first step toward progress in the city's race relations, and therefore in improving its national image, appeared to be once again to find some way to get rid of the commissioner of public safety. A direct assault on Connor's white supremacist convictions would, of course, be doomed, for it seemed quite certain that a substantial majority of the white electorate shared the commissioner's faith—as, for that matter, did many of the business progressives themselves. In 1951, Connor had allowed his sordid personal life to provide his opponents with the means to destroy him. But before they had been given this gift, the opposition had been discussing an institutional remedy, the abolition of the city commission form of government and its replacement with the council-manager form. Indeed, rather ironically, Connor himself had endorsed this change in the February 1953 speech in which he announced his decision not to seek reelection. The proposal had gathered sufficient public support to induce Jefferson County's state legislators that summer to sponsor a local bill authorizing the holding of a referendum on the question, if enough voters signed a petition to request one. But in the meantime, Robert Lindbergh had been elected to the commission to replace Connor, and the movement to change the form of government therefore lost steam; no petition campaign was in fact mounted. The city commissioners, however, remained nervous about the existence of the 1953 act, and at their request, the Jefferson County members at the legislature's next session, in 1955, obtained the adoption of two additional statutes, one authorizing a referendum to change instead to the mayor-council form of government and the other providing for a referendum to choose among the three forms, with a runoff to be held among the top two if none received a majority in the initial voting. The commissioners apparently believed that this variety of alternatives would make the success of any one of them less likely. In 1960, all three laws remained on the books.[91]

There was, however, another line of attack available. Connor's victory in 1957 had been by the narrowest of margins, and as both he and the business leaders well understood, central to it had been the fact that upper-middle-class voters were now a significantly smaller element of the city's electorate than had been the case earlier in the century. Lindbergh had swept the well-to-do precincts that remained, but the majority of the county's wealthier voters now lived "over the mountain," particularly in Mountain Brook, Vestavia Hills, and Homewood. It was apparent, therefore, that one immediate way to alter the balance of power in the city was simply to extend its limits southward into Shades Valley. Moreover, there were other very good reasons for doing so, turning on the preservation of the city's tax base and efficiency in the administration of public works and municipal services. Civic boosters had long wished to see a general annexation of the surrounding areas. In 1959, Birmingham business interests and their allies had conducted a vigorous referendum campaign in Mountain Brook and Homewood, seeking their agreement to join the city, but in May of that year the proposal had been decisively defeated. It was to this election that Jordan's speech to the Young Men's Business Club in December 1960 was referring. As Jordan said, the three objections that opponents of annexation had used to defeat it had been that becoming a part of Birmingham meant the loss of their own independent school systems, their subjection to Birmingham's zoning apparatus instead of their own existing ones, and the deprivation of their localities of the immediate concern that their officials now had for their areas' particular problems, since Birmingham's three-member city commission was elected from the city at large. All three of these well-founded arguments turned, in a sense, on the question of representation: whether anyone from Mountain Brook or Homewood was likely to be elected to the city commission; whether, if not, the commission would be sensitive to the annexed municipalities' needs; whether Birmingham's zoning board and board of education, both of which were appointed by the city commission, would be too distant from the new southern sections to sympathize with their special requirements. If the anti-annexationists' challenges were to be met, it would be necessary in some way to reassure Mountain Brook and Homewood residents that they could be confident that Birmingham's institutions would include them and would appreciate their local situation.[92]

It was in the light of the May 1959 annexation elections, then, that business progressives in the winter of 1960–61 surveyed the prospects of Birmingham's surmounting its negative national image. And in this light, the two lines of attack on the problem that had earlier been suggested suddenly merged. The replacement of the city commission with a city council would at one blow both eliminate Connor's autocratic control over the police and also promise the city's disparate geographical areas a genuine possibility of placing a spokesman on the municipal governing body. Even if Connor were himself elected to the new council—even if he were chosen mayor—he would not have in the widely dispersed structure of power under the mayor-council or council-manager forms of government the essentially autonomous authority over the police department that the commission form accorded him. And the fact that the city's various neighborhoods, at any rate the white ones, could all expect to have a voice on the more broadly representative council—and consequently on the various municipal boards appointed by the council, as well—that would reflect their particular viewpoint would work to overcome the objections of the surrounding localities to annexation. Annexation, if it became a reality, would then make the council even more representative in terms of the white social groups of whom its members would need to take account, and hence would even further impair the electoral ascendancy of Connor's east Birmingham lower-middle-class constituency. The change of government and annexation thus came to seem two stages of a single reform program, the result of which would be to deliver the government of the community for the foreseeable future into moderate hands, and therefore to eliminate the attitudes among authorities that had brought the city its negative national publicity. It is perhaps worth emphasizing once again that the aim of these reforms was not to eliminate, or even to harm, racial segregation, a system in which most of the white businessmen believed just as fully as the white working class did. Rather, their goal was to place in power officials who would use discretion and compromise, instead of force, in maintaining the social order. To put the program's intention in the simple terms that its commercial and industrial sponsors would themselves have, what they wanted was a municipal political leadership like Atlanta's.

And so, at the beginning of 1961, the deliberations of the chamber of commerce had settled upon a course of action. There remained the hope that the electoral process would relieve the businessmen of the necessity of pursuing it. It would require a good deal of time to bring the program to fruition, of course, and at every stage there were elements that could easily go wrong. If Connor could be defeated at the polls, as he so very nearly had been in 1957, there would be no need to make the effort. As 1961 began, there was still a possibility that he might be. But by late February, with the close of qualification for the May municipal election, the possibility had disappeared. Connor had drawn three weak and virtually unknown opponents, none of whom seemed capable of giving him a contest. Thus, on February 21, Sidney W. Smyer, who with the new year had succeeded Mortimer Jordan as chamber president, addressed a letter on behalf of the chamber to the president of the Birmingham Bar Association, Walter Mims; the chamber asked that the bar appoint a special committee to examine the advisability of changing the form of Birmingham's municipal government. The bar association's executive committee agreed to the request, and on March 21 Mims and the executive committee appointed a fifteen-member committee to conduct the study. The committee held its organizational meeting on April 6 and agreed to begin meeting biweekly thereafter—significantly, in the conference room of the First National Bank. The business leadership's effort to transform the image of Birmingham had begun.[93]

The bar association appointed no black attorneys to the committee, but its membership otherwise was carefully and fully representative; spokesmen for the full spectrum of attitudes within the white bar were included, from the rigid segregationist J. Kirkman Jackson, who had been a member of the state bar's committee to advise legislators on ways to circumvent the Supreme Court's school desegregation decision, and was later appointed to the Alabama State Sovereignty Commission by Governor George Wallace, to William E. Mitch, son of the socialist former state CIO president who had led the United Mine Workers' Birmingham organizing campaign in the 1930s, and law partner of a son of U.S. Supreme Court Justice Hugo Black. Other members included U.S. District Judge Hobart Grooms; Tarrant City municipal judge and former and future state legislator Paschal P. Vacca; M. Camper O'Neal, a son of the powerful longtime state president of the Farm Bureau Federation and a law partner of Jefferson County's state senator Lawrence Dumas; former circuit judge Leigh M. Clark, the committee's chairman, who was a law partner of Joseph F. Johnston, the arch-segregationist who headed the bar's anti-integration advisory committee on which Kirkman Jackson had served; Waldrop Windham, a leading trial lawyer who was a brother of Circuit Judge Whitten M. Windham, the president of the segregationist Methodist Laymen's Union; Erle Pettus, Jr., a Princeton graduate and former assistant U.S. attorney who was a son of a leading delegate to the disfranchising Constitutional Convention of 1901; Douglas Arant, the prominent corporate attorney who had chaired the Interracial Committee's subcommittee on black police; Abraham Berkowitz, a labor lawyer, Jewish community leader, and vigorous spokesman for Birmingham's liberals; and George Peach Taylor, the young liberal and future Peace Corps official who was the immediate past president of the Young Men's Business Club. That men of such diverse views could reach consensus on so controversial a question must have seemed highly improbable to observers when the committee began its work. But in fact fourteen of the fifteen committee members endorsed the committee's final report; only Chairman Clark dissented. This remarkable outcome was in part a product of the give-and-take during the committee's seven months of deliberations, as we shall shortly see. Very probably even more significant, however, was the impact upon them, as upon most Birminghamians of their class, of the actions of the Ku Klux Klan—and the inaction of the city police—in the Freedom Rider riot that occurred just a month after the committee commenced its meetings.[94]

The idea for the Freedom Ride lay far back in the early history of CORE, the Congress of Racial Equality. In June 1946, the U.S. Supreme Court had ruled in the case of *Morgan* v. *Virginia* that for a state to require racially segregated seating on an interstate bus was an unconstitutional burden on interstate commerce. Though this decision by implication voided all compulsory segregation of seating on interstate buses, the decision was universally ignored throughout the South; indeed, most southerners remained completely unaware of it. As a result, CORE, a small interracial group of northern pacifists founded at the University of Chicago in 1942, decided early in 1947 to undertake an integrated bus journey into the South to call attention to the ruling's practical impotence. Under the leadership of black pacifist Bayard Rustin, sixteen CORE members, eight of each race, left Washington, D.C., in April 1947, traveling in two groups, one aboard Greyhound and the other aboard Trailways. Among the sixteen was James Peck, the New York socialist who would be one of the 1961 Freedom Riders as well. The result was a series of arrests throughout Virginia and North Carolina and a near riot just outside Chapel Hill. The two whites and two blacks arrested at Chapel Hill were convicted in Recorder's Court there in June 1947, and on appeal to Superior Court they were reconvicted by an all-white jury in March 1948 and sentenced to thirty days at hard labor. At this trial, Judge Chester Morris instructed the jury that if it was satisfied that the defendants were interstate travelers, then under the *Morgan* decision the four men were entitled to an acquittal. But the evidence indicated that, on the particular leg of their journey at issue, they were bound only for Greensboro, where they were to attend a previously scheduled rally that night. The jury therefore held that they were in fact intrastate passengers. In January 1949, the North Carolina Supreme Court unanimously agreed. When the NAACP Legal Defense Fund declined to carry the case to the U.S. Supreme Court because of the ambiguity surrounding the interstate status of the demonstrators' trip, Rustin and his two white codefendants dutifully returned to North Carolina that spring and served their sentences.[95]

CORE's 1947 effort had essentially accomplished nothing, but it lived in the organization's institutional memory. In December 1960, the Supreme Court ruled in *Boynton* v. *Virginia* that segregation in bus terminal restaurants violated the nondiscrimination provision of the National Motor Carrier Act of 1935.[96] Just as with the *Morgan* decision fourteen years before, the general implications of this ruling were simply ignored everywhere in the South. And so the leaders of CORE turned once again to the idea of an interracial bus trip through the region to demonstrate that the Supreme Court's decision was not being obeyed. Seven blacks and six whites left Washington, D.C., on May 4, 1961; as in 1947, they traveled in two groups, one aboard Greyhound and the other aboard Trailways. Doubtless not a single one of the thirteen Freedom Riders knew that two days earlier, May 2, had been election day in Birmingham. But that fact would determine their future.

Though none of Connor's three opponents in the May 2 election seemed likely to present him with a significant challenge, Connor himself remained acutely conscious of the tiny margin by which he had been reelected four years earlier and was resolved to leave nothing in this campaign to chance. As early as December 1960, Connor personally telephoned Grand Titan Hubert Page, the leader of Jefferson County's Klansmen, to say that he was distressed that Birmingham police had been compelled to arrest on their own seven black students from Atlanta University who had attempted to stage a sit-in at the Birmingham Greyhound bus station; the police, Connor said, would have welcomed Klan assistance in this effort. As a result of this overture, by January the Klan apparently was planning to support Connor for another term, "even though," as the Klan noted, "they did not see eye to eye all the time." But then T. E. Lindsey, a self-proclaimed "full-time segregationist," resigned from the Birmingham Police Department, after twenty-five years as an officer, to make the race against Connor. The Birmingham office of the FBI thereupon received information that the Klan was now backing Lindsey. Presumably the same intelligence also reached Connor. At any rate, in April, as the election approached, Connor's closest confidant and aide within the police department, Sergeant Thomas H. Cook, suddenly contacted the Klan and offered to meet with Klan leaders and furnish them with police reports on integrationist activities. Meetings took place on April 17 and April 20. Cook turned over reports on Martin Luther King and on the Alabama Council on Human Relations, and he offered to supply any other information he had. He also strongly warned them that the FBI had an informant in the Klan's ranks and said that if they could just identify who the informant was, police would be happy to arrange a charge against him that would send him to the penitentiary. Unbeknownst to Cook, however, one of the Klansmen with whom he was meeting was himself the informant, dairy worker G. Thomas Rowe, Jr., the nighthawk, or sergeant-at-arms, of the Eastview klavern. Rowe, born in Savannah, Georgia, in 1933, had come to Birmingham in 1956. At the FBI's request, he had joined the Klan in June 1960 and had at once begun providing his contact, Special Agent Barrett G. Kemp, a steady stream of information about Klan affairs. In November 1960 the FBI elevated him to the status of full-fledged informant.

Cook emphasized to the Klansmen that Connor did not know that Cook was providing them police intelligence, but the FBI strongly suspected otherwise. The chief of the Birmingham office, Special Agent in Charge Thomas Jenkins, wrote to FBI director J. Edgar Hoover that the Klan's reputed support for Lindsey in the upcoming election might well be behind Cook's actions. "It is possible that [Connor] is using [Cook] to help him line up votes from Klan members by feeding them information which comes to his attention, not only through their own [police] informants but also information received from this [FBI] office, in order to ingratiate himself with members of the Klan. This is particularly significant since it is known by agents of this office that [Cook] takes most of his orders directly from [Connor] and not from [Chief Jamie Moore]. . . . [Connor] in the past has been outspoken to agents of this office as being against the Klan, but it must be realized that he is an extremely strong segregationist, is an opportunist, and it is not believed that he would pass up any opportunity to become re-elected as [city commissioner]." On April 24, FBI headquarters in Washington informed the field offices along the proposed route of the forthcoming CORE Freedom Ride, and on April 27 Special Agent Jenkins called Chief Moore to alert him to the information and to request that the Birmingham police be prepared to deal with any threatened violence. Immediately thereafter, Sergeant Cook, in accordance with his April 17 arrangement with the Klan, called Grand Titan Page to pass on this intelligence. Page at once called Imperial Wizard Robert Shelton in Tuscaloosa to tell him about it. Shelton and Page then contacted Exalted Cyclops Robert Thomas in Eastview, Exalted Cyclops Robert Creel in Bessemer, Exalted Cyclops James "Ace" Williams in Gadsden, Exalted Cyclops Kenneth Adams in Anniston, and other area Klan leaders, and they began planning their response—almost a week before the Freedom Riders had even left Washington.[97]

On election day, May 2, most Birmingham Klansmen demonstrated their gratitude to Connor for his cooperation. In this, the greatest victory of his career, Connor amassed more than 60 percent of the poll. Lindsey, with just 17 percent, ran third, behind Richard R. Andrews, who had the endorsement of Fred Shuttlesworth and received the black vote.[98] But the necessity for conciliating the Klan's favor was not past. After a quarter century on the commission, the moderate Mayor James Morgan had decided to retire, and the bitterly contested race to succeed him would require a runoff, to be held on May 30. In the initial round of voting, the racially moderate attorney J. Thomas King, a son of Circuit Judge Alta L. King and law partner of the prominent young liberal Charles Morgan, led the balloting with 40 percent of the vote. Close behind him, with 36 percent, was Arthur J. Hanes, a graduate of the University of Alabama law school and an uncompromising segregationist who had just completed a term as president of the city board of education. Hanes, a resident of the lower-middle-class East Lake section, had run unsuccessfully for the presidency of the Jefferson County Commission in 1948, and in 1951, abandoning his law practice, he had become an employee of the Hayes Aircraft Corporation, where he had eventually been made assistant sales director. It seems clear that Connor—enthusiastic at the prospect of serving on the commission with a mayor who shared his views, for the first time since the death of James Jones in 1940—was supporting Hanes. On May 9 King paid a courtesy call on Connor to assure the commissioner that, if King were the victor, he would seek to work amicably with his two colleagues. At the meeting, according to King, Connor brought up the impending arrival in the city of the Freedom Riders and stated cryptically, "We will be ready for them, too." As King left city hall, he heard a voice call his name; turning, he found a black man with outstretched hand. King took it, and at once a cameraman stationed at a city hall window snapped. King was convinced that Connor arranged the photograph; he pointed out that only he and Connor knew that he would be at city hall that morning, and only someone with prior knowledge of that fact could have had a photographer there ready to take the picture. At any rate, the photograph—appearing as it did to show King soliciting a black vote—became the principal issue of the runoff campaign. Race had earlier played only a relatively small role in the election, but armed with this picture, Hanes now began emphasizing the segregation issue to the virtual exclusion of all others.[99]

Connor's apparent willingness to assist Hanes's efforts in this instance was likely of a piece with his handling of the Freedom Riders, also much on his mind at this time. Just as he almost certainly had authorized Sergeant Cook's contacts with the Klan in late April in order to ensure the extremists' support for his own candidacy in the May 2 primary, so he very probably now continued the contacts in order to fire the Klan's enthusiasm for Hanes in the runoff. And indeed, the Klan vigorously supported Hanes's campaign, distributing anti-King material at shopping centers even as Klan leaders organized their reply to the CORE demonstrators.

On May 3, the day after Connor's triumphant reelection to the city commission, Grand Titan Page met with the Warrior klavern to discuss the challenge posed by the CORE initiative, and on May 4 he met with the Eastview klavern for the same purpose. Page told them that Imperial Wizard Shelton would issue a statement to the press on May 5, the day after the Freedom Riders' departure from Washington, demanding that state and local officials turn these "professional agitators" back, and warning that if they failed to do so, "he had no choice but to call on the Klansmen all over the state and all other true white people to stop them any way they can." Page informed the klaverns "that this was too big a statement to make not to back it up, so every Klansman is to be alerted to stand by for a call to the cause. That should the Klan fail on something as big as this, it could ruin the organization." Over the next ten days, the Klan shaped its strategy amidst consultations with Sergeant Cook and, apparently, Connor himself. According to the FBI, Page and Exalted Cyclops Thomas told Klansmen that Connor had "indicated when trouble broke out, he would see that fifteen or twenty minutes would elapse before police officers would arrive at the scene. Bull Connor said if Negro members of CORE enter [the] bus depot restaurant, Klansmen are to start an incident and blame the incident on the Negroes, thus allowing a fight to begin. Bull Connor said if they attempt to enter the restrooms in the bus depot, they are to beat them and 'make them look like a bulldog got ahold of them,' then remove the clothes from the person and leave the individual nude in the restroom. If a nude person attempted to leave the restroom, he would be immediately arrested and it would be seen that this person went to the penitentiary. Bull Connor said if any Klansman is arrested, he is to insist that the Negro was at fault, but that if any sentences are given to Klansmen, he would insure that they would be light." Cook advised the Klansmen to purchase tickets at the bus station on their arrival, to give them a legal right to remain there; after the riot, the tickets could then be cashed in for a refund. Connor warned them against carrying any Klan identification or pistols that lacked permits. By May 12 the Klan had delegated some sixty members to stage the assault, and the FBI had been given the names of the Klansmen who were to lead it: informer Thomas Rowe, Lloyd Stone, L. B. Earle, William A. Holt, Jr., Earl Thompson, and H. Eugene Reeves. In order to exculpate the Klansmen, Sergeant Cook apparently planned to blame the assault on CORE itself or on the National States' Rights Party (NSRP), like the Klan a violent white supremacist organization but one that, even though it maintained its national headquarters in Birmingham, was composed of outsiders who had moved to the area and therefore lacked the police department's sympathy.

The receipt of this clear evidence of planned violence threw the Birmingham FBI office into a desperate quandary. It was essential that they alert those local police authorities who were not affiliated with the Klan to the great likelihood of a riot. But it was equally essential that they do so in a way that concealed the identity of the informer Rowe, for there could be no doubt that if he were revealed as the source of the FBI's intelligence, Rowe could be imprisoned or murdered. The FBI believed that it could trust Police Chief Jamie Moore. Moore had been appointed as chief by Commissioner Lindbergh on the basis of a competitive examination, and he had served in the post long enough before Connor's return to the office in 1957 to have gained civil service protection in it. Nevertheless, virtually Connor's first action after his inauguration had been to bring formal charges against Moore before the county personnel board in an effort to obtain his dismissal. Connor claimed both that Moore had quietly campaigned for Lindbergh and, considerably less credibly, that Moore had knowingly tolerated illegal liquor sales. After a bitter hearing, the personnel board in January 1958 had ruled in Moore's favor, and Connor thus found himself stuck permanently with a chief whom he disliked and doubted—and who equally disliked and doubted him. It was for this reason that Connor had undertaken, even more than in his early years, to run the department directly through subordinates and cronies such as Sergeant Cook. And it was for this reason that the FBI hoped it could rely upon Moore. Nevertheless, Moore was not in a position to defy Connor or to withhold any information from him; if he did so, Connor would thus be provided legitimate grounds upon which again to seek the personnel board's agreement to his removal. And since anything the FBI told Moore would therefore be available to Connor and Cook, it was consequently impossible to give Moore the full details of the FBI's information without placing Rowe in the gravest danger. Moreover, though the FBI was certain that Cook was a Klan contact, he had provided the FBI a great deal of useful intelligence on the dangerous neo-Nazi NSRP with which Cook had no truck, and the FBI very much wanted to continue to use Cook for this purpose, if it could be arranged.

Frantic consultations between the Birmingham office and FBI headquarters in Washington during early May produced a plan. Since Imperial Wizard Shelton had issued a public statement on May 5 threatening Klan violence against the Freedom Riders, the bureau concluded that it could safely use this statement as a basis for warning Chief Moore that violence was likely and urging him to take definite steps to prevent it. As a result, Special Agent in Charge Jenkins called Chief Moore on May 8 to tell him of the possibility of violence, on May 11 and May 12 to furnish further details, and on the morning of May 13 to urge him once more to take the threat very seriously. Jenkins called Moore again on the night of May 13, now just hours before the Freedom Riders were to arrive, and in that call, at 9:30 P.M., Moore revealed for the first time that he was leaving the city the next morning and would not return until the evening. Sergeant Cook would be left in charge of this matter. Thus it became apparent that the FBI's hopes of preventing the riot were destined to be dashed. The Klan would have its day.[100]

On the morning of May 14 the Freedom Riders left Atlanta for Birmingham, with one group traveling aboard Greyhound and another aboard Trailways, as they had done throughout the trip. One of the black Freedom Riders, Joseph Perkins, had been arrested in Charlotte, North Carolina, on May 8 and two others, white James Peck and black Henry Thomas, in Winnsboro, South Carolina, on May 10. And on May 9, black John Lewis, the future congressman, and white Albert Bigelow had been assaulted in Rock Hill, South Carolina, though police had rescued them before either was badly hurt. All of these events received prominent attention in the Alabama press. But there had been no other incidents. The Freedom Riders had gained three new recruits in Sumter, South Carolina, as the journey had progressed, and had suffered two losses, so that they now numbered fourteen; there were four black and three white demonstrators aboard each bus. Accompanying the Greyhound group were two reporters, an Alabama state investigator traveling incognito, and the bus company's regional manager. And both buses also carried a number of ordinary passengers, who had boarded with no idea that a demonstration was going on. The Freedom Riders intended to spend the night with Fred Shuttlesworth when they got to Birmingham and then address the regular weekly mass meeting of the Christian Movement the following evening. James D. Peck called Shuttlesworth just before the group left Atlanta to tell him that they were on the way. But Shuttlesworth then told Peck that the Inter-Citizens

Committee's C. Herbert Oliver had informed him that the CBS television newsmen in Birmingham to film the documentary about the city commissioners' libel suit against the *New York Times* had learned from the NSRP leader Dr. Edward Fields that the Freedom Riders would be greeted with violence. Shuttlesworth therefore strongly urged Peck to have his group change its plans, but Peck refused.

The Greyhound bus reached Anniston at 3:20 P.M., and as it pulled into the station it was surrounded by about fifty local Klansmen and an equal number of other whites. Concerned by the mob's angry mood, state investigator Ell M. Cowling barred the bus door and refused to allow either the passengers to disembark or the spectators to get aboard. Bus driver O. P. Jones hastened his departure, and the bus was at the station for only five or six minutes. But during that interval Klansman and burglar Roger D. Couch managed to puncture one of the bus's tires. The original plan had had the Anniston klavern simply making sure that the Freedom Riders were aboard the bus and then sending them on to Birmingham to be assaulted, but when the members of the mob saw that the tire was losing air, they followed the bus in a motorcade of some fifty cars. About four miles west of Anniston, at Forsyth's Store, driver Jones was compelled to pull the bus to the side of the highway. Most of the following mob then gathered on the left side of the bus, in an attempt to turn it over. But while this effort was attracting almost everyone's attention, two of the Klansmen went to the right side. Taxi driver Dalford L. Roberts succeeded in breaking the bus's right rear window, and machinist Cecil L. "Goober" Lewallyn then threw a lighted incendiary device through it into the vehicle. Flower arranger Jerry R. Eason sought to hold the bus door closed to prevent the passengers from escaping, but investigator Cowling drew his pistol and forced Eason back. In the meantime, highway patrolman Millard A. "Buster" Nunnelley had arrived on the scene, in response to a call for help. He summoned additional assistance by radio and then joined Cowling in driving the mob away from the bus, thus allowing the passengers to exit just before the vehicle was engulfed in flame. With the arrival of highway patrol sergeant Timothy O'Flynn, the officers were able to disperse the mob. Thereafter, the passengers were taken to the Anniston hospital. There had been no serious injuries, but it had been a very close call.[101]

While these events were taking place, the Trailways bus, operating on a somewhat later schedule, was also proceeding toward Birmingham. When it reached Anniston, four city policemen met it and informed driver John O. Patterson of what had happened to the Greyhound bus. One of the policemen then told the passengers that while he could not compel segregated seating, he felt that for their own safety, all blacks should move to the rear. Patterson added his own request to the same effect, but the Freedom Riders refused. The police then left the bus. A pregnant white passenger became hysterical, and Patterson took her inside the station to try to calm her. A state investigator then boarded, described how serious the Greyhound incident had been, and urged the Freedom Riders to adopt a policy of discretion. When he left, the frightened non-CORE passengers, saying "We don't want to burn," took matters into their own hands. Eight white males who were among the passengers who had boarded in Atlanta approached black Freedom Riders Isaac Reynolds and Charles A. Person, who were seated near the front, and sought to force them to the rear. White Freedom Riders Dr. Walter Bergman and James D. Peck, who had been seated in the rear, came forward to assist Reynolds and Person. In the ensuing scuffle, Bergman, a retired Wayne State University professor and longtime socialist activist, was struck on the head. No one knew it at the time, but the following September, when Bergman entered a hospital for an appendectomy, he suffered a heart attack, and doctors then discovered that he had sustained massive brain damage from the beating. Following the operation, he was confined to a wheelchair for the rest of his life. Some seven or eight Anniston policemen were standing outside the bus, but none of them intervened to halt the fight. As a result of the violence, the Freedom Riders relented and retired to the rear of the bus. One of the policemen then boarded and asked if any of the passengers wished to swear out a complaint for assault and battery, but—perhaps because they were intimidated, perhaps because they felt that to do so would violate their nonviolent principles—the Freedom Riders all declined. At this point driver Patterson returned and, finding the passengers now segregated, told Anniston police chief J. Lawrence Peck that he was prepared to leave. Peck instructed him to use a route over backroads, and after a stop of about twenty-five minutes, the bus pulled out. During the trip to Birmingham, the male passengers who had forced the demonstrators to observe segregation sat three-quarters turned in their seats, prepared to resume the attack if the CORE members sought to move forward.

The Trailways bus reached the Birmingham terminal at 4:15 P.M. Some eighty Klansmen and NSRP members had been waiting at the Greyhound station, but when word reached them of the destruction of the Greyhound bus, they scurried the four blocks to the Trailways station, carrying their lead pipes, bats, and chains. Police had been in constant contact with the Klansmen through the day; informer Rowe reported that he had talked with Sergeant Cook seven or eight times, and Cook conferred repeatedly with Commissioner Connor, who was in his office even though it was a Sunday. Cook and his associate Detective W. W. "Red" Self checked the terminals on a regular basis; Self was at the Trailways station only five minutes before the bus got there, and Cook had been at the terminal half an hour earlier. But as the bus drew near, they both absented themselves. The Freedom Riders had planned for James Peck and Charles Person to attempt to use the terminal facilities while Dr. Bergman served as a witness in case they were prevented from doing so. As soon as Peck and Person began walking toward the building, Klansman H. Eugene Reeves seized Person, a student at Morehouse College in Atlanta. NSRP leaders Dr. Edward R. Fields and Jesse B. Stoner then shouted to their supporters to come to Reeves's aid. Other Klansmen rushed to attack Peck, and the riot was on. Dr. Bergman ran to get a policeman, but there was none to be found. When Bergman returned, Peck was unconscious on the pavement and the mob had turned its attention to George Webb. Webb, a young Birmingham black, was at the station to collect Mary Spicer, his fiancée. As they went toward the baggage room to claim her luggage, the mob charged and began beating him. But shortly thereafter Klansmen noticed *Birmingham Post-Herald* photographer Thomas Langston taking pictures of the assault. The mob then turned to beating Langston and *Birmingham News* police reporter Thomas Lankford, who was standing with him. Webb was thus able to escape. Langston's camera was taken from him and thrown to the floor, but none of the Klansmen thought to destroy the film in it. In the meantime a third reporter, Clancy Lake of radio station WAPI, when he had witnessed the initial assault on Peck and Person, had run to his car and had begun broadcasting a live account of the riot over a microphone that he had in it. Three Klansmen—the informer Rowe, William Holt, and Ray Graves—saw him and rushed to silence him. Lake locked himself in the car and continued broadcasting. Rowe broke the car's windows and, as Lake pleaded over the air—unsuccessfully—for a listener to call the police, Graves tore the microphone from its connection and smashed it. Lake then ran back inside the terminal and resumed broadcasting over a telephone line. The three Klansmen meanwhile had seen local blacks taking down the automobile tag numbers of Imperial Wizard Robert Shelton, Grand Titan Hubert Page, and Exalted Cyclops Robert S. Thomas and James "Ace" Williams, whose cars were all parked behind the bus station, and ran to prevent them from doing so. A considerable fight ensued, for these local blacks were not committed to a nonviolent philosophy. Rowe received a knife wound in his neck that required eight stitches to close, and Klansman L. B. Earle received severe head wounds that forced his hospitalization. Earle and James Peck were the only two persons who were badly injured in the riot. Police had been summoned at 4:20 P.M., and at least by 4:30 P.M. they had arrived at the station, located across the street from police headquarters; with their arrival, the Klansmen fled. The Freedom Riders bundled into taxis and went to Fred Shuttlesworth's home. Shuttlesworth took Peck to an emergency room for treatment of his injuries and arranged to have the Greyhound Freedom Riders collected in Anniston and brought to Birmingham. Peck's head wound took fifty-seven stitches to close.

That night, Detective "Red" Self called to congratulate the Klan on the job it had done. And though one of the bystanders who had taken down

Grant Titan Page's tag number had given it to police, Sergeant Cook called to reassure Page that nothing would come of it. But the next morning Cook called with the news that the pictures taken by *Post-Herald* photographer Langston had survived and that the newspaper was printing them. Under the circumstances, Cook said, police would have to pursue the identities of the men shown in them. This investigation was turned over to an officer without Klan connections, Detective Melvin Bailey—a future Jefferson County sheriff—and it resulted in the indictment of two men for assault with intent to murder and the arrest of four others for disorderly conduct. Three of those charged with disorderly conduct got thirty-day jail terms. But print shop foreman Harry C. Edwards, indicted for assaulting photographer Langston, apparently was never brought to trial. And Herschel W. Acker of Rome, Georgia, a pulpwood worker and, according to the FBI, a relative of underworld figures, who was indicted for assaulting George Webb, was promptly acquitted; the jury deliberated for just half an hour. The firebombing of the Greyhound bus constituted a federal offense and therefore permitted the FBI to enter this part of the case. Agents quickly rounded up the Anniston Klansmen who had been the ringleaders of that mob, and they came to trial at the beginning of November. But "Goober" Lewallyn, who had actually thrown the firebomb, had been in an automobile accident in August and had suffered a brain injury sufficient to make it legally impossible to prosecute him. Dalford Roberts, who had broken the bus window, became a government witness and testified against the others. However, the Klan had gotten one of its members selected as a juror, and the panel consequently could not reach a verdict. Following the mistrial, a plea bargain resulted in a one-year suspended sentence for everyone except Roger Couch, who had punctured the bus tire. He had in the meantime been sentenced to a ten-year term in state prison for an unrelated burglary, and was given a one-year sentence to be served concurrently with his state one. The Justice Department also sued the Klan and the Birmingham and Montgomery Police Departments in federal court in Montgomery, seeking an injunction against their interfering with interstate bus travel. But the FBI remained unwilling to reveal the identity of the informer Rowe, and for that reason the government's case against the Birmingham police, which would have been virtually ironclad with Rowe's testimony, remained weak and circumstantial. Judge Frank Johnson therefore dismissed this portion of the complaint. There was one final prosecution growing out of these events: the state charged Fred Shuttlesworth with conspiracy to breach the peace, on the extraordinary theory that he had caused the two sets of Freedom Riders—the original ones and the students from Nashville—to come to Birmingham and thus had provoked the white mobs to gather at the bus stations. He was convicted and sentenced to three months at hard labor and a fine of five hundred dollars on each of the two counts. In March 1963, the Alabama Court of Appeals reversed the convictions and the prosecution was then dropped.[102]

The Freedom Rider riots, and particularly the official encouragement that accompanied them and the small number of arrests and very light penalties that flowed from them, played a crucial role in releasing Klan violence in Birmingham once again. As we have seen, the firm measures taken against the Klan had managed to halt the racial bombings that had plagued Birmingham between 1949 and 1951. With the single exception of the attempted arson against the home of Dr. John Nixon in May 1954, there were no such incidents between May 1951 and April 1956. Then, with the mobilization of segregationist sentiment and the beginning of Fred Shuttlesworth's legal assaults on discrimination in 1956, the bombings resumed—very probably because the strident white supremacy of city and state leaders at this time seemed to Klansmen to represent white community sanction for the actions. Beginning with the bombing of Shuttlesworth's home and church on Christmas Day 1956, a near reign of terror enveloped Birmingham. There was another bombing on the last day of 1956, and seven bombings, two acts of arson, and a night-rider shooting during 1957. There were four bombings, a firebombing, and an attempted bombing in the first half of 1958. Many of these acts were directed against the neighborhood of Fountain Heights, which, like Smithfield before it, was undergoing a racial transition; seven of the incidents during 1957 and 1958 occurred there. But the actions of Fountain Heights' black residents also ended them. The Smithfield civil defense unit extended its protection to Fountain Heights and enlisted blacks there in its nightly patrols. In July 1958 the effort paid off. On the night of July 17 the newly purchased home of a black and the home of a white about to be sold to a black were bombed. But black residents on alert for such violence spotted the three Klansmen as they were attempting to leave, gave chase, and beat them. The Klansmen—Herbert E. Wilcutt, Ellis Lee, and Cranford Neal—escaped, but when two of them later sought treatment at the emergency room of the University of Alabama Hospital, police arrested them. In December, Wilcutt was brought to trial and convicted. Even though, upon the jury's recommendation, Judge Wallace Gibson granted Wilcutt probation, and even though Neal and Lee were granted probation on a lesser charge, Wilcutt's conviction was a milestone: the first and, during the civil rights years, the only successful prosecution of a Birmingham Klansman for a racial bombing. And the arrests and trial had an immediate effect upon the Klan. The booking of the three bombers at once produced a halt in all such incidents. There would be none between July 1958 and January 1962.[103]

But the Freedom Rider riots in May 1961 worked to return the Klan to activism after the three years of quiescence. At first, Klan leaders were frightened by the Justice Department's suit against them before Judge Frank Johnson in Montgomery and by the indictment of the Anniston ringleaders in the burning of the Greyhound bus. But when they escaped from the Montgomery hearing with nothing more than an injunction forbidding them to interfere with interstate travel, and when they successfully prevented the imprisonment of the Anniston defendants, they recovered their bravado. On the morning of January 16, 1962, in accordance with the plea bargain, the Anniston defendants entered pleas of nolo contendere and Judge Hobart Grooms gave them one-year suspended sentences. That night the Klan expressed its contempt for this penalty by bombing three black churches in various parts of Birmingham. These three bombings inaugurated a new wave of Klan terrorism. A week later an apartment building for blacks under construction in the downtown area was bombed. In March, night riders shot into the home of Ensley mortician William E. Shortridge, the Christian Movement's treasurer. In December, Fred Shuttlesworth's former church was bombed once again, for the third time, even though Shuttlesworth had in the meantime given up his Birmingham pastorate and moved to Cincinnati, Ohio. These 1962 incidents, however, were a mere prelude to 1963, the climactic, and bloodiest, year of Birmingham's racial conflict, which saw eight bombings, one firebombing, one unsuccessful bombing, three night-rider shootings, a stink bombing, and seven deaths.

The Klan's willingness to renew its campaign of violence was clearly motivated in part by the virtually universal white fury in the city at the Freedom Riders. Of course many whites, in particular the business leadership, were equally angry at the Klan's response to the demonstration. But, especially in view of Commissioner Connor's approval of the response, in addition to that of much of the police force, the Klan quite understandably tended to think of itself as the voice of a white community consensus. And the outcome of the runoff in the election for the city commission on May 30 readily reinforced this attitude. Arthur Hanes, riding the segregationist anger, came from behind to defeat the moderate Thomas King handily, 55 percent to 45 percent. And at the same time, incumbent "Jabo" Waggoner defeated the somewhat more moderate Earl Bruner by 52 percent to 48 percent. For the first time since the establishment of the city commission form of government in Birmingham, all three commissioners would now be racial extremists. It was an outcome that the visit of the Freedom Riders had in no small part, though of course unwittingly, created.[104]

And yet the business progressives' dismay at the Trailways station riot was very real, because the violence had further damaged the city's national reputation and thus had made the location of new industry there even less likely. Chamber of commerce president Sidney Smyer was a case in point. Smyer remained the firm segregationist he had been some seven years before when he was a founder of the American States' Rights Association and the Methodist Laymen's Union. As it happened, however, on the day of the attacks on the Freedom Riders, Smyer was in Tokyo attending the world convention of Rotary International. He was therefore able to observe at first hand the coverage of the violence in the Japanese press and the reactions to it from his fellow Rotarians from around the globe. He returned to Birmingham a few days later determined to attempt to use the chamber as a vehicle for reopening discussions with black moderates in the city. On May 18 he convened the chamber's board of directors, and they adopted a resolution urging the study committee of leading industrial and commercial figures that the chamber, the Committee of 100, and the Downtown Improvement Association (DIA) had earlier appointed— the body from which, it appears, the idea of changing the form of municipal government had originated—to expand its membership and "enlarge their duties to include the study of means of creating better relations with all groups, regardless of their race or religion, to the end of promoting the civic, economic, industrial and social welfare of the people of the Birmingham territory, and to suggest or promote courses of action by civic and governmental agencies to accomplish this end." Smyer evidently hoped that the study committee would become the nucleus of a new version of the Interracial Committee that had been abolished in 1956. The initiative, of course, required the concurrence of the Committee of 100 and the DIA, since they as much as the chamber were the study committee's parent organizations. Presumably for that reason, little immediately came of the idea. By December, however, as we shall see, biracial consultations had begun. In the meantime, the resolution stood as clear evidence of the effect the Freedom Rider episode had had upon the business progressives. So, too, did a resolution adopted at the same time by the junior chamber of commerce and given wide circulation. Because, the Jaycees said, they "are interested in the further economic progress and development of the state of Alabama for the benefit of all its citizens, and recognize that such incidents as have occurred have undermined the effectiveness of all organizations attempting to promote industrial growth of the state," therefore they "call upon all law enforcement officers of the state of Alabama to enforce strictly the laws against agitators and citizens who attempt to take the law into their own hands" and "call upon all of our citizens to work together in a spirit of cooperation to help our law enforcement officers in insuring the safety of all our citizens, for we feel that only in an atmosphere in which we and our families can be confident that law and order will be maintained, is it possible to achieve economic growth to the benefit of all." Such attitudes, with their clearly implied condemnation of Commissioner Connor's handling of the Freedom Riders' demonstration, were widespread among the white business leaders of Birmingham. But for the future of the city, the group whose sympathy to this viewpoint was most significant was that disparate assemblage of fifteen attorneys meeting biweekly in the conference room of the First National Bank, the bar association's committee on changing the form of Birmingham's government.[105]

It appeared in the committee's early deliberations that the members might divide along liberal-conservative lines. Led by labor lawyer Abraham Berkowitz, the liberals pressed for the adoption of the city manager form. They made the turn-of-the-century Progressive case for the "de-politicizing" of city government and for its operation on efficient business principles. They also argued that the manager—if, as they hoped he would be, he was a neutral expert from outside Alabama—would therefore be able to rise above Birmingham's political and social divisions and administer the city justly and dispassionately. The conservatives, led by Princeton and Duke Law School graduate Erle Pettus, Jr.—the son, as we have seen, of a prominent delegate to Alabama's disfranchising Constitutional Convention of 1901—took a considerably more hard-minded approach. "The 'political' and 'business' aspects of city government are so intertwined and intermixed that it is impossible to separate or ignore either" of them, Pettus told his colleagues. "I firmly believe that it is impossible to have a government without an executive political head," he maintained. "Politics is inherent in our governmental institutions and it is a fact which cannot be ignored. The executive head of the municipality must be in theory and in fact both the political and administrative head. The council cannot be a substitute for the essential political leadership in the City Government. The executive head must be political leader of the city." And as to the liberals' desire for an expert non-Alabamian as manager, Pettus replied with a reference to political reality: "I do not go as far as the Chicago Alderman who is reputed to have said: 'Chicago ain't ready for reform,' . . . [but] I do say that Birmingham is definitely not ready for a manager from far away places."

In August, Berkowitz prepared a full-scale draft report endorsing the city manager concept, and rival majority and minority reports seemed likely. Only one of the committee members, Chairman Leigh Clark, appears to have favored retention of the city commission. But the differences between the proponents of the manager and the mayor-council forms seemed irreconcilable. Nevertheless, the widespread revulsion that the Freedom Rider riots had engendered among the city's business and professional leadership stressed for all of the members the desirability of finding common ground, lest the entire reform initiative falter. At the end of the month, Pettus proposed a compromise. He urged the adoption of the mayor-council form of government, essentially as provided in the 1955 local legislative act that had been drafted as an alternative to the 1953 city manager statute; he suggested, however, the addition of a full-time administrative assistant to the mayor, who would be appointed by the mayor and serve at his pleasure, but would otherwise act as a city manager. This idea rapidly gathered support, and when the committee took a final vote on October 20, Judge Clark was alone in his dissent. Thereafter, the members labored on a lengthy and able final report, which they completed and released to the public at the end of February 1962. In addition to the administrative assistant, the report also recommended that the mayor be given the veto power over council legislation and that surrounding areas which voted to be annexed to the city be authorized to retain separate school districts and control over zoning regulations.[106]

In the meantime, the suit to integrate Birmingham's parks and playgrounds, filed by Shuttlesworth in October 1959, at the end of the Birmingham stalemate, had moved with what for Birmingham civil rights litigation was extraordinary speed. At a pretrial hearing in August 1961, Judge Grooms held void on its face the ordinance adopted in 1954, as a result of Hugh Locke's referendum campaign, requiring segregation in sports competitions. On October 20, as a member of the bar association's change-of-government committee, Judge Grooms voted in favor of the adoption of the mayor-council form. And four days later, ruling from the bench immediately at the conclusion of the parks integration trial, he ordered the full integration by January 15, 1962, of all sixty-seven of Birmingham's parks, its thirty-eight playgrounds, four public golf courses, eight public swimming pools, the city zoo, the art museum, and the municipal auditorium. Also in October, the city's new hard-line segregationist mayor, Arthur Hanes, had taken office, and he at once joined Commissioners Connor and Waggoner in announcing that they would appeal Judge Grooms's ruling and would close all of the facilities rather than allow them to be integrated. Grooms refused to stay his order pending the appeal, and the commissioners ordered the facilities closed at the new year. The park and recreation board offered some resistance, but the commission responded by eliminating parks funding from the city budget. One park board member, Mrs. J. H. Berry, resigned in protest. Judge Grooms agreed to stay his order until March 15 in the hope that the city commission could be persuaded to relent, but the commissioners refused all compromise and the facilities closed.[107]

The controversy surrounding the closing of the parks and playgrounds produced, for the first time since the considerable exacerbation of racial tension in the city in the mid-1950s, a willingness on the part of large numbers of white moderates to take a public stand against the intransigent segregationists. The industry-seeking Committee of 100, headed by the racially liberal business supply executive James A. Head, denounced the parks closure, warning, "This is the type of action that will reduce the jobs available in metropolitan Birmingham. It also will cripple our efforts to create new job opportunities for which we must compete with other Southern cities." The chamber of commerce, headed by the segregationist realtor Sidney Smyer, joined in, announcing, "If we follow the course of action to close all the parks and other cultural facilities we believe it will result in irreparable harm to the entire Birmingham district as well as the State of Alabama." The DIA, headed by Sears, Roebuck executive B. Roper Dial and banker and prominent moderate Charles F. Zukoski, told the city commissioners, "It is our strong opinion that no greater mistake could be made than to destroy by closing down the park, recreational and cultural facilities that have contributed so much to our growth and progress. . . . We firmly believe you owe it to all of us, [the] business leadership and the thousands of rank and file workers who must have a healthy business community to earn their daily living, the chance to prove we can work out our problems and live under the restrictive rulings of our Federal courts. Birmingham cannot afford to lose its posture as Alabama's great Metropolitan city without serious business loss to all of us." Even the small businessmen of the North Birmingham Chamber of Commerce and the West Hills Lions Club echoed the same line. The Lions Club emphasized, "The Directors consider themselves strong segregationists, but believe the above recommendations are for the best interest of Birmingham at the present time." More predictably liberal groups such as the Jefferson County Association for Mental Health and the white Methodist and Episcopalian clergy added their voices to the chorus. The mental health association told the commissioners that the closing "would merely penalize ourselves and our children and would leave open the decision we will in any event ultimately have to make, either to go forward making the best of what most of our people consider a bad situation, or to see our community atrophy and go down hill." Both the *Birmingham News* and the *Birmingham Post-Herald* gave editorial endorsement to this consensus. And at the beginning of January, some 1,280 prominent area whites signed a full-page advertisement in the *News* calling for the appointment of a citizens' committee to seek some way to save the parks.

But it was the personal intervention of such influential business leaders as Alabama Power chairman Thomas W. Martin and Vulcan Materials president Bernard Monaghan and the willingness of so many former segregationists to join the moderate ranks on this issue that truly marked the movement as a new departure. Dr. L. Wilkie Collins, a white supremacist East Lake Methodist minister, wrote, "Many of our segregationists, of whom I am one, are violently opposed to this high-handed procedure and are campaigning to groups large and small to realize the far-reaching implications of this drastic move. It is not a matter of segregation or of integration, but of the future of Birmingham and of our children." Emory Jackson of the *Birmingham World* told a mass meeting of Shuttlesworth's Christian Movement, "I never thought I would live to see the day in Birmingham when the Committee of 100 was on one side and the City of Birmingham on the other, and the Chamber of Commerce on one side and the City on the other." The *Wall Street Journal* was certainly correct in concluding that the situation had revealed a "significant realignment of forces."[108]

However, other factors worked to conceal from the city commission the extent of the realignment. Some prominent businessmen, such as industrialist Kirkman O'Neal, the chairman of O'Neal Steel and a cousin of the change-of-government committee member Camper O'Neal, strongly supported the parks closure. Two other businessmen in this group were insurance and real estate agent William B. Houseal and attorney Earl C. Morgan, both of whom had close ties to the nascent gubernatorial campaign of George C. Wallace. Houseal, whose son Walter would become Wallace's first insurance commissioner, wrote to the DIA to denounce its resolution opposing the commissioners' position. It is, he stated, "A well established fact" that many of Birmingham's black leaders "have as their ultimate goal inter-marriage and inter-breeding with the white race. As far as I am concerned there is *no end* to which I am [not] willing to go to hold our ground. . . . Our situation is too far reaching to be treated on an economic basis. If your Association is to continue to dabble in such matters, then the quicker you close shop the better it suits me, and this in view of the fact that I personally have more at risk in proportion to my total income in the future of Downtown Birmingham than many of you have who have made this decision." In addition, the white supremacist organizations rallied to the commissioners' stand. The Jefferson County White Citizens' Council hailed the commissioners as "men of principle, courage, and possessed of a firm and unyielding determination to resist further Federal encroachments on our institutions" and assured them of "our heartfelt appreciation" and "our continuing and unswerving support in the fight to preserve separation of the races, which is part and parcel of the tremendous struggle against the Federal Government to preserve our state and our country in the form intended by the Founding Fathers." And the Ku Klux Klan commenced picketing the downtown Sears store, on the ground that the DIA's parks resolution had revealed the association's president, Sears executive Roper Dial, as an integrationist. But it was the apparently widespread support from Birmingham's blue-collar whites that genuinely steeled the commissioners' resolve against the business leadership's assault. R. J. Bell wrote Mayor Hanes, "I want you to know that all the Christian people are behind you and will never sanction the actions of a group of selfish, half blinded golf-playing preachers and so-called business men, who would sacrifice the future welfare of generations to come just for their own selfish satisfaction." Anthony Bakane assured Commissioner Connor of his support against "the Mt. Brook ruling clique and money-mob": "I know for fact the City Commission is honest because none live 'over the mountain' in expensive mansions and because none have a huge bank account!" The "money moguls . . . hate you because you are an obstacle to their plans for a progressive and 'prosperous' future. There can be no 'prosperity' unless and until the police force can be *deformed* and 'liberalized' and made 'broadminded.'" A lodge of the Brotherhood of Railroad Trainmen denounced the Committee of 100's statement opposing the closure: "We resent the action that was taken by the Committee of 100, for as you know, nearly all of them live outside of our city limits and should not have a say-so as to how our city should be run. We feel that if all the outside interests would let us alone, we could run our city in a manner that all Birminghamians could be proud [of]." Bolstered by such support, the commissioners on January 17 issued a lengthy proclamation of their refusal to cooperate with the federal judiciary's desegregation orders in any way: "If there are those among us who, for another dollar in the till, or for another industry in our city, or for fear of the printed or broadcast tongue-lashings of those who, contrary to Biblical injunction, set themselves up as our judges, would yield to this cacophony of intimidation, bribery, cajolery, economic compulsion, political pressure, clerical suasion and outright threats of fine and imprisonment, let them answer to their consciences." But "we shall, in every lawful way we can, oppose, and urge all patriotic men and women to oppose, and attempt to redress the propagation and spreading of this spurious, false and illegal 1954 Judges' fiat, masquerading in sheep's clothing, as the law of the land." Thus the commissioners summoned their forces to battle, without fully realizing the extent of the desertions that this encounter had created among their troops.[109]

The negative national publicity for Birmingham that had been engineered by Robert Hughes had inspired the business community's reconsideration of its acceptance of Birmingham's racial climate. The Freedom Rider riot had pushed the transformation along by provoking business organizations into condemning the disorder and by creating a unified acceptance of the need for reform out of the great diversity of backgrounds and beliefs on the bar association's change-of-government committee. But it was the closing of the parks that completed the business leadership's metamorphosis. And it was the same event that for the first time attracted a significant number of lower-middle-class and working-class whites who had considered themselves segregationists into the moderate camp, and restored the willingness of the moderates to espouse their position openly. We may pause briefly to consider why the parks closing had such far-reaching implications.

For poorer whites, the elimination of public recreational facilities represented the first time they had been called upon in any obvious way to bear the burden of segregation that blacks for generations had borne. Now segregation would require them, as it frequently had required blacks, to do without institutions they otherwise could have had in the interest of preserving racial separation. Called upon to accept such a sacrifice, some of them were thus led to make their first real examination of their priorities, and they simply placed separation lower on this list than recreation. The overwhelming majority of Birmingham's whites continued to prefer to have both, of course, but when forced to choose, doubtless to the great surprise of the true segregationists, more than a handful of white Birminghamians proved to rank segregation relatively lower in their scale of values.

For wealthier Birminghamians, however, no such choice was necessary. Many of them held country club memberships that insulated them from the impact of the closures. Many, too, resided in the surrounding suburban municipalities that had their own unaffected parks and playgrounds. The threatened closing of the art museum and the city's football stadium, Legion Field, did affect them personally, but after considerable vacillation, the city in the end exempted these two institutions, as well as the city zoo, from the order. For the business leaders, the essential consideration is to be found in their repeated emphasis on the threat the closures posed to industrial development. They worried that corporations were unlikely to locate factories in, and talented managers and engineers were unlikely to accept positions in, a community devoid of recreational and cultural outlets. Moreover, the closing of the parks seemed to portend—and segregationist officials stated explicitly that it did indeed portend—the closing of the public schools once they came under a desegregation order; and a city without public schools was even less likely to seem attractive to new industries. Finally, as to the moderates, the vigorous public statements of opposition to the closures from such important community voices as the chamber of commerce, the Committee of 100, the daily newspapers, and the white ministerial associations, and the broadened base of community support that the statements seemed to encounter, all worked to stiffen the backbones of this pusillanimous element. When the moderates had gone underground following the abolition of the Interracial Committee in 1956, it was because they had feared that Birmingham's apparent white segregationist consensus would lead to their social ostracism and the boycotting, or even the bombing, of their businesses if they spoke out. Such fears were not at all irrational, of course. In fact, the Klan's picketing of Sears in response to Roper Dial's signing of the DIA's resolution on the parks proved that the danger had not passed. And so, the parks episode by no means completely freed the moderates from their anxieties. But the evidence the episode provided that the segregationist consensus was not now so powerful as it had seemed six years earlier did encourage the moderates to begin hesitantly to reemerge from their self-imposed silence.

Nevertheless, when we reflect that the closing of the parks in Montgomery three years before had not had the impact in that city that it had in Birmingham, we are led to look for some additional factor at work in the Magic City. And there does appear to have been one. The mobilization of so much of Birmingham's white community leadership behind retaining the parks, and the willingness of a significant portion of the city's electorate to support the effort, lent a special quality to the commission's adamant and quite vituperative rejection of it. Wilkie Collins had characterized the closure as a "high-handed procedure," we recall. When four community leaders delivered the petition against the closure signed by some 1,280 prominent whites to the city commission on January 9, they were given an hour-long "bombastic and abusive" tongue-lashing by the commissioners. One of the four, Birmingham-Southern College president Henry King Stanford, reported in mortification, "I never had such an experience in my life."[110] For the well-to-do whites who had organized the campaign to preserve the parks, the commissioners' refusal to heed the virtually united voice of the city's economic and social leadership seemed the rankest effrontery, and their aggressive denial of that leadership's legitimacy made the refusal all the more offensive. For the poorer whites who supported the campaign, the commissioners' attitude appeared to reflect insensitivity to the needs of ordinary citizens who depended upon public facilities for recreation. For both groups, the commissioners were thus made to seem unresponsive to their constituents. The commissioners themselves, of course, believed that their action was precisely what the majority of their constituents wished. And many in fact did. But when the votes were counted ten months later in the change-of-government referendum, the commissioners would discover that they had considerably underestimated the extent of the electoral realignment that the parks controversy had wrought.

V. Shuttlesworth versus the Moderates: Round One

Before we can turn to the change-of-government referendum, however, we must explore a final result of the parks controversy—and very likely the most portentous one of all: its effect upon Birmingham's blacks. Since the Inter-Citizens Committee's sponsorship of sit-ins in August 1960, in competition with the sit-ins that had been supported by the Christian Movement at the end of March of that year, the two organizations had indulged in an escalating rivalry for leadership of the city's black community. When the committee in August 1961 released to the press a series of notarized accounts documenting fourteen cases of police brutality in Birmingham, for instance, the Christian Movement in September sought to steal the committee's thunder by wiring the Justice Department to demand that it investigate the conduct of Alabama police. This encounter, and the contest between the two groups in general, formed the background to the bitter conflict that was to ensue as a result of the parks closure.[111]

Following Judge Grooms's decision of October 24 invalidating parks segregation and the city commission's announcement on October 25 that the parks would therefore be closed, the Young Men's Business Club began urging that the commissioners instead seek acceptance of what came to be called the Memphis plan. Memphis, Tennessee, when faced with the prospect of integrating its parks, had secured the agreement of all parties concerned to integrate the facilities slowly over a period of years, starting with the facilities located in areas of the city in which disorders were thought least likely and moving gradually to the facilities located where resistance would probably be greatest. The YMBC believed, and almost certainly correctly, that Judge Grooms would modify his decree to adopt a version of this plan if he were presented a joint request to do so from everyone involved. Indeed, it was in order to facilitate negotiations about this proposal that Grooms agreed to postpone his integration deadline from January 15 to March 15. In the end, the commissioners proved unwilling to consider any integration at all, however much it might be delayed, and so nothing came of the plan. But during November and December, business progressives acted on the conviction that this proposal could be realized. And if it were to be brought to reality, clearly the first step had to be gaining the acquiescence in it of the city's blacks. It was for this reason that, for the first time since the dissolution of the Interracial Committee in 1956, whites initiated formal biracial negotiations.

Immediately after the Freedom Rider riot in May, as we have seen, the directors of the chamber of commerce had proposed expanding the membership of the study committee of prominent businessmen and empowering it to explore means of improving race relations. During the summer the Committee of 100 and the DIA had endorsed the idea, and the study committee had been extended to include "the heads of almost every major business, law firm and professional group in the city." It was this newly reconstituted committee, apparently, that took the lead in arranging the interracial consultations to discuss adopting the Memphis plan in Birmingham. The black insurance magnate Arthur Gaston was asked to gather a group of black leaders to consider the proposal. And Gaston turned to the Inter-Citizens Committee for this purpose.

Toward the end of November, Fred Shuttlesworth wrote to Emory Jackson of the *Birmingham World* and to three other black leaders to say that he had heard that whites were about to contact them to arrange a discussion of the parks compromise. Shuttlesworth wrote that he wanted to be included in any such meeting so that he could insist on full black rights. Jackson printed Shuttlesworth's letter, and he commented that he had heard similar rumors and shared Shuttlesworth's belief that blacks should permit no abandonment of full integration. This exchange was the first volley in the battle between the Christian Movement and the Inter-Citizens Committee over the proper response to the white businessmen's initiative. Shuttlesworth had moved from Birmingham to Cincinnati, Ohio, in August to assume a better-paying pastorate. He had retained the presidency of the Christian Movement, and he continued to fly back to Birmingham frequently to address the group's weekly mass meetings and to confer with his lieutenants. But the day-to-day administration of the organization had passed to its vice-president, the Reverend Edward Gardner. Because Shuttlesworth was no longer a resident of the city, both black and white moderates were reluctant to include him among the black negotiators. But in response to his public demand, the blacks involved did apparently expand their group from its original fifteen to eighteen, adding to it Gardner, Jackson, and the Christian Movement's treasurer, Ensley mortician William E. Shortridge. The first meeting between the black and white delegations took place on December 6 at the Episcopal Church of the Advent.

Other than Gardner, Jackson, and Shortridge, the black negotiators were all connected with the Inter-Citizens Committee. They included the committee's president, the Reverend James L. Ware; its executive secretary, the Reverend C. Herbert Oliver; insurance executive Arthur Gaston, who had organized the delegation; insurance agents John J. Drew, C. J. Greene, and Frederic L. Ellis; attorney Arthur Shores; the Interracial Committee's former executive secretary, Paul R. Jones, who was now a Juvenile Court probation officer; dentists S. E. Welch and E. W. Taggart; Miles College president Lucius H. Pitts; and ministers George W. McMurray, Herman Stone, Joel West Marshall, and C. E. Thomas. All of them were moderates, and many had been associated with the Interracial Committee a decade earlier. McMurray had led the opposition to the creation of the Christian Movement in 1956. The volatile Emory Jackson promptly walked out in protest against what he took to be the initial meeting's prearranged character; his action reduced the black delegation to seventeen and guaranteed that the *World*'s coverage of the negotiations would be hostile.

The day following the negotiators' second meeting on December 13, fourteen of the seventeen blacks issued a statement proclaiming that all of Birmingham's black residents were united in their determination to achieve first-class citizenship, but adding that they welcomed the opportunity to meet with whites to seek solutions to the community's problems. The *World* immediately denounced this statement as seeming to portend a sellout of genuine black aspirations. The fact that the negotiations were being conducted in secret was particularly frightening, the newspaper said, for it threatened to shut the mass of blacks out of determining their own future. The self-appointed black negotiators, the editorial added, were likely to be outsmarted by the whites, thus depriving blacks of the gains they had secured in the courts. Shuttlesworth soon joined in the attack. He had understood, Shuttlesworth said, that the negotiators' statement was to include their determination to implement all federal court civil rights decisions, and he was deeply disappointed that it did not. He demanded a clarification. Ware and Oliver quickly issued a statement in the name of the Inter-Citizens Committee which approved Judge Grooms's parks integration order without reservation and praised Shuttlesworth and the Christian Movement for their courageous fight to obtain it. The statement prayed for community calm. But it was too late.

By early January, black Birmingham was in an uproar. Ware summoned an emergency open meeting of black leaders for the night of January 5 to try to settle the internal dispute. But the student body of Miles College, thoroughly aroused by the controversy, responded with a summons to uncompromising militancy. Led by student government president Frank Dukes, a Korean War veteran and former Detroit automobile assembly line worker, the students issued a manifesto proclaiming their dissatisfaction with the slow pace of racial progress and announcing that they did not intend to wait complacently to receive the rights being denied them. They attacked unequal schools, inadequate housing, the lack of black job opportunities, inadequate hospital, restaurant, and entertainment facilities, voter registration discrimination, and police brutality. And they declared that they intended to use "every legal and non-violent means at our disposal" to rectify these problems. The *World* hailed this document as standing "in sharp, spectacular, dramatic contrast with the almost barren statement issued December 14" by the black moderates of the Inter-Citizens Committee.[112]

The difficulty inherent in the black moderates' efforts is clear in retrospect. The dispute within the black community was in effect an extension of the Birmingham stalemate of 1959. As the black bar had noted at that time, and as was even clearer now, the constraints on politicians' acting on their threat to close institutions that were ordered desegregated were less in the case of the parks than for any other public facilities. The real choice facing Birmingham's blacks in the wake of Judge Grooms's order integrating the parks was to accept some compromise that had a prospect of being sold to the city commissioners, such as the Memphis plan, or to forfeit the use of parks and playgrounds altogether. The immediate integration of the city's recreational system simply was not an alternative, whatever Judge Grooms's decree might say. However, the existence of that decree too easily made any agreement to a gradual and partial integration appear to many blacks to be accommodationist, a surrender of rights to which blacks were constitutionally entitled in order to placate the prejudices of white supremacists. Emory Jackson's denunciations of the negotiations, for instance, were founded on this point of view.

But even the harder-minded blacks, who understood that the practical alternatives were compromise or the closure of the parks, could feel that the latter choice was preferable. In the first place, blacks often took a grim pleasure in being able to force whites for the first time to experience a small measure of the deprivations to which segregation had so long subjected blacks. Edward Gardner, in an address to a Christian Movement mass meeting immediately after the city commissioners' announcement that they would close the parks, "stated we are not worried about the parks here tonight because we will not miss what we have never had. He stated the Negroes had nothing in the way of parks prior to the Supreme Court [sic] decision. . . . If they can't integrate them fair, let them close them."[113] And in addition, blacks who observed that the threat of closure had finally compelled white moderates to reopen biracial contacts, for the first time in nearly six years, and to begin to bring public pressure on the city commissioners to accept at least a measure of integration, for the first time ever, might well have concluded that the actuality of closure would force even further changes in white attitudes. Virtually the first action of the Inter-Citizens Committee following its formation in April 1960 had been to request interracial discussions, but only in December 1961, when the integration struggle had at last affected the lives of whites directly, were the discussions initiated. It was not unreasonable for blacks to conclude, therefore, that as the struggle impinged upon whites' lives more and more, whites would become more and more open to taking blacks' complaints seriously and seeking to remedy them. The logic of this position indicated that allowing the parks to be closed, though it would necessitate some sacrifice in the short run, might in the longer run prove to be a very useful thing. Time would lend this analysis even more force, for there can be little doubt that the discontent among a significant number of whites with the city commission's decision to eliminate public recreation in Birmingham played a crucial role in mobilizing a majority of the electorate behind the campaign in the fall to abolish the commission form of government. Against these considerations, it was very difficult for the black moderates to make their case for compromise—and very easy for their opponents to succeed in depicting them as weaklings.

In the end, the city commissioners' refusal to consider even the gradual desegregation envisioned in the Memphis plan made it unnecessary for the rival elements within the black community to pursue their dispute to a resolution. The failure of the white moderates to get the acceptance of the compromise by the city's political leadership meant that the black moderates did not have to attempt to persuade Shuttlesworth and the other plaintiffs in the parks integration suit. The compromise proposal was dropped, and the parks were closed, though as we shall see, the biracial negotiations continued, now focused upon the desegregation of facilities in downtown stores. Before we turn to this second stage of the negotiations, however, it is important to emphasize a final point about the intense and bitter debate that swept the black community during December 1961 and January 1962. Implicit in this controversy was the dispute that would dominate the coming sixteen months, leading up to the beginning of the demonstrations in April 1963. The essence of this dispute was tactical, even though the rhetoric surrounding it often made it sound as if it were an argument about goals. Shuttlesworth, Emory Jackson, and like-minded black leaders were convinced that no genuine racial progress was possible without a fundamental element of compulsion, whether in the form of a federal court suit or of a black direct-action campaign. Acceptable negotiations for them were consultations about terms of truce or surrender; the notion that a negotiation could in and of itself produce progress they regarded as hopelessly naive. Arthur Gaston, Arthur Shores, and their associates—ordinarily blacks whose professions brought them more frequently into contact with whites, on a level somewhat nearer equality—were more open to the belief that a negotiation could represent an autonomous path to achieving their goals. They fully accepted, of course, that negotiations might become stalemated, thereby necessitating a resort to compulsion. But they were far more likely to assume the sincerity of their white negotiating partners. Or to put the disagreement more succinctly, for Shuttlesworth and Jackson, truly useful negotiations were a product of compulsion, whereas for Shores and Gaston, compulsion was an auxiliary alternative to negotiations. From Shuttlesworth's and Jackson's perspective, Shores, Gaston, and the Inter-Citizens Committee, by accepting the proffered white negotiations, were leading blacks into a trap. From Gaston's and Shores's perspective, Shuttlesworth and Jackson, by rejecting the negotiations, were willfully refusing to explore a promising avenue to progress. As we have already seen, progress for all blacks, militant or moderate, meant movement toward racial equality, whereas for white business progressives it meant primarily commercial and industrial growth. Because of this lack of fully shared assumptions, negotiations necessarily faced substantial barriers to success. But in the flush of optimism at the renewal of interracial contacts, the black moderates did not immediately recognize this problem. Over the coming months, the two rival black groups each sought every opportunity to demonstrate to the mass of Birmingham's black residents—and especially to the black students led by Frank Dukes—the correctness of its analysis.[114]

Though it was obvious by mid-January that no compromise on the closure of the parks would be possible, the biracial negotiations continued. The Inter-Citizens Committee had had its origins in the efforts in the spring and summer of 1960 to obtain the desegregation of facilities in the downtown department and variety stores, and it is therefore not at all surprising that, once further discussion of the parks seemed fruitless, the black negotiators should have turned the deliberations toward that subject. If the Inter-Citizens Committee's leaders could obtain voluntarily, through negotiations with the merchants, the integration of the department store lunch counters that the sit-ins had failed to obtain, it would serve as clear proof of the efficacy of the negotiating strategy. Following the issuance of the Miles College students' manifesto, Miles College president Pitts urged that the students be included in the discussions lest they begin sit-ins or a boycott on their own. The white negotiators agreed, and a student delegation led by Dukes therefore joined the sessions at the end of January. This development produced another attack from Emory Jackson. He had hailed the students' statement at the beginning of the month, but now he denounced the augmented negotiations as a betrayal of the need for strong, open black leadership that was ready to make firm demands and to struggle for full integration. The black negotiators had no right to speak for the mass of black Birmingham, he warned, but "the prestige circles of our community" were prepared to use them as if they did.[115]

In the meantime, Pitts, just as he was seeking the inclusion of his students in the negotiations, also extended his offensive to Shuttlesworth's own Christian Movement. The former executive secretary of the organization of Georgia's black public school teachers, Pitts had come to Birmingham in July to succeed Miles's longtime president William A. Bell, who had died. Since his arrival he had generally allied himself with the black moderates, but he had sought also to avoid alienating the militants; it was typical of him that he had joined Edward Gardner in declining to sign the black negotiators' statement of December 14. On January 22 he gave the principal address at a Christian Movement mass meeting. Blacks, he noted, had said that he would never speak to Shuttlesworth's organization, and he confessed that he had not been anxious to do so. But he agreed to come, he said, because he wanted all blacks in the city to understand that many whites were now putting more pressure on the city commission for reform than Shuttlesworth himself was. He urged Shuttlesworth's followers to investigate the truth of what they were told and to remember that all blacks were proud of the civil rights movement and that many whites were good people. But Pitts did not content himself with advocating reliance on the goodwill of the white businessmen. He came armed with an alternative proposal for compulsion as well. Far more effective in bringing pressure on whites than spending money on court costs and fines, he told the assemblage, would be a program of selective buying. Clearly he intended with this idea to make the allies of the Inter-Citizens Committee seem to be just as militant as was the leadership of the Christian Movement. An observer reported that Shuttlesworth "didn't seem too pleased" with this talk. On February 12, when Martin Luther King was the main speaker, Pitts was again present, this time accompanied by insurance executive Arthur Gaston. Gaston seized the occasion to emphasize his support for Pitts's position. He admonished blacks not to condemn all whites, because, he said, many whites in Birmingham were good.[116]

The negotiations between the white businessmen and the black moderates and students continued through February. The blacks pressed for the integration of the lunch counters, fitting rooms, rest rooms, water fountains, and other facilities in the downtown stores. The whites, led by chamber of commerce president Sidney Smyer, Committee of 100 chairman James A. Head, and DIA president Roper Dial, let this historic opportunity to gain legitimacy for negotiations in the eyes of the black community slip through their fingers. Doubtless they were aware of the dispute that was going on among blacks only dimly, if at all. And they probably would have been incapable of fully appreciating its implications for their own and their city's future in any case. On the other hand, because moderate white opinion had been concealed in Birmingham for so long, they were perhaps excessively conscious of the extent of segregationist hostility to their actions. As a result, they consulted their fears. They told the blacks that merchants did not feel free to eliminate separate facilities in their stores so long as city ordinances required the separation. In fact, as every lawyer could have informed the merchants, and as they almost certainly knew anyway, federal courts had already declared analogous ordinances unconstitutional in other cities. Moreover, in the case of one of the facilities, the fitting rooms, no ordinance actually required the segregation; this discrimination was purely customary. But it was not really a blind obedience to patently void city ordinances that constrained the merchants. They knew from the arrest of the manager and waitresses of the Greyhound bus station restaurant three months before that the city would vigorously enforce the ordinances, even if invalid. And they knew from the Klan picketing of the Sears store two months before, following Roper Dial's statement opposing the closure of the parks, that the resultant publicity would draw segregationist protests and boycotts, and quite possibly bombs, to their stores. They were simply unwilling to take this risk. Their sense of the implications of an agreement for the white world of which they were a part was far stronger than their sense of its implications for the black world that they did not really know. Therefore, just as Shuttlesworth would have predicted, it appeared that the merchants would assent only if blacks could succeed in convincing them that the risk of not agreeing to the black requests was greater than the risk of doing so. If the white negotiators had been wiser and braver men, they could, by accepting the pleas of their black counterparts, have decisively strengthened the case for moderation in Birmingham, and almost certainly thus could have altered the course of their city's history. Instead, their limitations actually left the argument against negotiation to seem all the more compelling.

The white negotiators did not, however, lack a counteroffer. Because what they truly feared was the publicity that would surround the city's attempt to enforce against the stores its void segregation ordinances, from their point of view the real solution lay in the removal of the segregationist city commissioners who would seek to make examples of any merchants who integrated. If the integration could be handled discreetly, then many of the merchants would be far more amenable to introducing it. Therefore, as the white negotiators conceived of the matter, the essential first step to desegregating the facilities in the downtown stores was the adoption of the mayor-council form of municipal government. As we have seen, the bar association's change-of-government committee had voted on

October 20 to recommend converting to a mayor and council, and as the biracial negotiations were proceeding during February, the committee members were in the process of putting the final touches on their elaborate report recommending the reform, a report which they completed and adopted on February 23. The white negotiators apparently acquainted the black ones with the proceedings, theretofore confidential, and urged that they all unite to effectuate the proposal. From the white moderates' perspective, their support for a change in the form of government established the sincerity of their desire for improved race relations; as they saw matters, it was unreasonable to expect merchants to place their businesses, and even their lives, in jeopardy, as steps toward integration under the existing city government would do, but their efforts to change that government established that they were committed to progress as soon as it could be safely accomplished.

A man like Fred Shuttlesworth, who had placed his life on the line so often to achieve racial change, was unlikely to find this argument convincing. Even the black moderates, who had endured the Smithfield bombings and the constant possibility of intimidation or humiliation by the police, were not very easily persuaded. But the white moderates regarded themselves as having adopted a quite forthcoming posture. And the Christian Movement, too, seems at first to have feared that blacks would be satisfied with it. As soon as the final report of the change-of-government committee was issued, Edward Gardner informed a Christian Movement mass meeting—quite correctly—that "the lawyers did not want anyone elected [to the new city council] to be a Negro, so instead of having them elected from each one of the nine precincts, they had recommended that nine be elected at large. He explained to them that if they were elected by precincts, it would be possible to have two or three Negroes elected. The bar association realized this and recommended that nine be elected at large." He added that the form of government was really irrelevant to blacks, because once enough of them were registered to vote, they could get their candidates elected regardless of the form used. Two weeks earlier, the Reverend Abraham L. Woods had told another mass meeting that "they did not need Mr. Connor out of office to succeed, but [only] for all Negroes to stick together." These attacks on the proposal to abolish the city commission did not actually represent opposition to the idea. Indeed, during the referendum campaign in the fall, the Christian Movement strongly supported the mayor-council plan. What they really represented was an attempt by Shuttlesworth's allies to prevent any interracial agreement founded simply on the white business leadership's promise to seek the removal of the segregationist city administration.[117]

In fact, however, the Shuttlesworth forces had much less to worry about at this stage than they feared. In the first place, the proposal to change the form of city government was in the spring merely a suggestion, albeit one with much prominent support; there was no organized drive to effect it, and the petition campaign or new state legislation that would be necessary to do so both seemed daunting challenges which implied that the realization of the reform was at least a couple of years away. Six months later, with a vigorous petition effort actually under way, political action appeared a considerably more realistic alternative, but at the beginning of March it was merely an idea. In addition, the logic of the white negotiators' position indicated strongly that black direct action that had the force to demonstrate that the threat to the merchants from blacks was greater than that from white segregationists would cause them to change their attitude. Moreover, the suggestion for a selective buying crusade had come from within the black moderates' own camp, from Miles College president Pitts. He had urged it on the Christian Movement in January, as we have seen, and we may presume that he would have recommended it to his own students as well. Frank Dukes and his colleagues seem to have been debating the idea of a general downtown boycott at the same time in any case, and they would doubtless have taken this suggestion very seriously. And finally, as we recall, "Bull" Connor had ordered the arrest of Shuttlesworth and his associate James Phifer at the end of January, when the U.S. Supreme Court refused to review the rejection by the Alabama Court of Appeals, on the ground of lack of timeliness, of their appeal of their conviction for having incited the test of Birmingham's second bus segregation ordinance in October 1958; Shuttlesworth and Phifer were jailed on January 26 and remained behind bars until March 1, while their attorneys filed a series of frantic petitions with state and federal courts. The considerable anger aroused in the Birmingham black community by this essentially vengeful imprisonment of the two men for having incited the violation of an ordinance that had in the meantime been declared unconstitutional, an anger that mounted throughout February as the biracial negotiations were taking place, left blacks of all persuasions prepared for emphatic action. As a result of these factors, the black leadership came together unanimously in March behind the launching of a boycott of the downtown stores.

On March 6, Frank Dukes sent a letter to the downtown merchants asking for the prompt integration of facilities in their stores and their consideration of hiring blacks in sales positions. When the merchants had not agreed by March 15, Dukes and his colleagues called for the initiation of a selective buying campaign. Both the Christian Movement and the black moderates of the Inter-Citizens Committee endorsed this response, and at least by the last week of March the downtown boycott was on. The city commissioners struck back in their usual heavy-handed way. On April 3, at the suggestion of "Bull" Connor, who at the time was running for governor on an aggressively segregationist platform, the commission eliminated municipal funding for a program to distribute surplus food to the poor. Mayor Hanes, in a statement issued to the press, commented, with unconscious irony, "The city of Birmingham in cutting off its contributions to the Surplus Food Program is demonstrating to the Negro community who their true friends and benefactors are. If the Negroes are going to heed the irresponsible and militant advice of the NAACP and CORE leaders, then I say let these leaders feed them." On April 6 the commission denied Miles College a permit to conduct a fund-raising campaign, because of the involvement of the college's students in creating the boycott. Police arrested Shuttlesworth and other boycott advocates. Despite these efforts at official retribution, however, the boycott continued almost completely effective throughout April. At midmonth the board of the DIA privately warned that the effort "would have a drastic and far-reaching economic effect on the entire metropolitan area" if it continued many more weeks. But just as the merchants seemed on the verge of seeking a settlement, the boycott began to collapse. It had initially been called an Easter buying campaign, and when Easter had come and gone, blacks with increasing frequency began returning to the stores. At the Christian Movement mass meeting of May 4, a furious Shuttlesworth came as close as possible to urging violence against blacks who did not observe the boycott. But by May 14, Inter-Citizens Committee executive secretary C. Herbert Oliver, who had conducted a survey of the downtown stores, reported that he had wept when he saw the extent of the boycott's decay. By June 11, even Frank Dukes and Lucius Pitts were prepared to concede that the effort had failed. Dukes commented bitterly that blacks "could not refuse the temptation of the all mighty [sic] dollar."[118]

The failure of the downtown boycott in May 1962 seems to have caused all parties involved to draw conclusions that would shape their reactions to future events. Shuttlesworth and his allies were further strengthened in their convictions, first, that whites would offer genuine concessions if and only if they were faced with a black threat sufficient to compel them to do so, and second, that only a court order or a direct-action campaign sufficiently dramatic, aggressive, and well organized to hold the allegiance of the masses of blacks could pose the necessary threat to whites. As a result, at least by May 14, Shuttlesworth was coming to focus his hopes on coupling a black direct-action campaign with the September meeting in Birmingham of the national convention of Martin Luther King's Southern Christian Leadership Conference.[119] The black moderates, on the other hand, were strongly reinforced in their doubts about the practicality of uniting all of black Birmingham into a direct-action effort such as a boycott. They continued to believe in court action, as did Shuttlesworth, but even here they felt that some suits, such as the one to integrate the parks, could be counterproductive. As a result, they were led increasingly to an acceptance of the white business progressives' emphasis on a political solution. If the segregationist city administration could be replaced with a more cooperative one, then the ongoing negotiations seemed quite likely to succeed in producing some voluntary steps toward integration—as had in fact happened in Columbus, Georgia, the preceding January, under the leadership of that city's chamber of commerce.[120] Frank Dukes and his fellow students appear also to have been soured on direct action by their experience of the boycott. As we have seen, Dukes became convinced that too many blacks were too materialistic to sustain a crusade that called upon them to make genuine, immediate sacrifices in pursuit of uncertain future benefits or abstract principles.[121] As a result, the students were as never before open to proof from either the Christian Movement or the Inter-Citizens Committee of the relative effectiveness of the organizations' competing strategies. This fact heightened the rivalry between the two associations, as each sought to demonstrate the superiority of its approach. The white business leadership recognized that the failure of the boycott had represented a very narrow escape for them. They were thus further convinced of the urgent necessity to redouble their efforts to secure racial reform in the city. However, they remained just as frightened of the personal and economic consequences for them of taking any public steps to this end in a context in which white supremacist politicians would attempt to pillory them for doing so. Redoubling their efforts therefore meant to them not acting directly to integrate their businesses, but only increasing their exertions to silence the segregationists who could endanger them once the inevitable integration began. And finally, the city commissioners and their segregationist allies saw the boycott's collapse as proof that, if faced with an uncompromising response, such black initiatives would self-destruct. They had always believed that the blacks of Birmingham lacked the material resources, organizational skills, and unity to be able to mount a successful offensive, and now they were sure of it. All that was necessary to secure victory was sufficient intransigence.

The implications of the quite different morals that these elements of the community had drawn from the failure of the downtown boycott were clearly to be seen in the events of the late summer and fall. Beginning in August, Shuttlesworth's desire to use the SCLC's September national convention to stage a citywide direct-action campaign and the business leadership's plan to abolish the commission form of government in favor of a mayor and council suddenly intertwined to dictate Birmingham's future.

The report of the change-of-government committee had envisioned new legislation that would embody the alterations in the existing 1955 mayor-council act that the committee had recommended and would provide for a referendum on the plan as thus amended; this procedure would eliminate the legal complications that arose, as we shall see, from the conflicts among the provisions of the 1953 act, the two 1955 acts, and a 1959 general act governing the timing of transitions from one form of municipal government to another in all Alabama cities.[122] But the adoption of such a revised statute would require waiting until the next session of the legislature, which would not convene until May 1963. The added urgency that the business progressives now felt led a number of them to decide upon a more direct approach: an immediate petition drive to hold a referendum under the terms of the 1955 act, and the promise of a subsequent local act to make the recommended changes in the new municipal government that, they hoped, would by that time have taken office.

This plan of action originated among a group of young attorneys who had all been active in John F. Kennedy's presidential campaign in Jefferson County in 1960, and who were all members of the Young Men's Business Club. The group included George Peach Taylor, who had been a member of the change-of-government committee; David J. Vann, a future mayor of the city; C. H. Erskine Smith, who would head the War on Poverty in the county for a time during the Lyndon Johnson administration; J. Vernon Patrick, later Vann's law partner; and Charles Morgan, Jr., who would gain prominence as national legislative director of the American Civil Liberties Union. Vann contacted Abraham Berkowitz, who had been the most conspicuous of the liberals on the change-of-government committee, and with Berkowitz's enthusiastic assistance the young attorneys obtained the quiet but vigorous support of both the chamber of commerce and the AFL-CIO leadership for their effort.

In the meantime, this same group of attorneys, under the sponsorship of the Young Men's Business Club, had been pursuing a suit to reapportion the state legislature that would eventually produce the U.S. Supreme Court's landmark "one man, one vote" reapportionment decision, *Reynolds* v. *Sims*. In July they had obtained from the special three-judge U.S. district court handling the suit a stopgap reapportionment to govern the 1962 general election, pending further action in the case.[123] This order increased the number of Jefferson County's state representatives from seven to seventeen, and a special primary had therefore been scheduled for August 28 to nominate the ten additional members. The young lawyers recognized in this special primary a uniquely favorable opportunity to get all at once the required signatures for the change-of-government petition. In the first place, because the petitions would all be gathered on a single day, they could escape the fate of past efforts, in which petitions left at public locations to be signed fell victim to opponents of the proposition, who stole or destroyed them. Second, because the election came at the very end of a long, hot summer during which Birminghamians had for the first time been deprived of all public recreational facilities, it occurred at a moment when the annoyance felt by residents, and particularly by parents, at the commissioners was at a peak. And finally, because signatures could be gathered at polling places in white neighborhoods while black precincts could be excluded, it permitted sponsors to engineer an irrefutable response to the predictable charge by the commissioners and their allies that the signers largely were blacks. The effort secured more than ten thousand signatures, far more than the number necessary, and Probate Judge Paul Meeks therefore ordered the question placed on the ballot for the general election, to be held November 6.

Advocates of the city commission did their very best during September and October to ensure that segregation would dominate the referendum campaign. Mayor Hanes and Commissioner Connor talked of little else. They charged—and not without some justice, of course—that the referendum was a part of a surreptitious plot by the chamber of commerce to bring integration to Birmingham. They sought to emphasize white class resentments by noting that integration in Birmingham would have little effect upon the all-white suburbs in which the chamber of commerce members generally resided. Connor warned that David Vann had been a law clerk for Supreme Court Justice Hugo Black during the term in which the Supreme Court had rendered its *Brown* v. *Board of Education* school desegregation decision. And he reported, quite correctly, that Vann had long-standing ties with the Southern Regional Council and its local affiliate, the Council on Human Relations, of which Vann was a board member. Connor and Hanes both added dark hints that the reformers might have Communist sympathies, even though the allegation fit rather poorly with their persuasive charge that the petition was the work of the business interests. Proponents of mayor-council government sought to emphasize the necessity of the change if the suburbs were to be persuaded to agree to annexation. They insisted that segregation was a completely irrelevant question, that the referendum was about the modernization of the municipal government in order to prepare it for the city's geographical and economic expansion. Nevertheless, the argument with which they sought to refute the commissioners' claim that the reform was integrationist only served to prove, if anyone had actually doubted it, that race was never irrelevant in Birmingham. The council forces maintained that, as more and more blacks gained the right to vote, Birmingham proper would eventually have a black electoral majority unless suburban annexation went forward; and since the suburbs would never agree to be annexed unless the form of city government were changed, in effect therefore the commissioners themselves were the true integrationists. Despite this contention, however, the chamber of commerce also condemned the commissioners for failing to address the city's racial conflicts constructively, and it publicly "urged that there be a line of communication between white and Negro leaders . . . to meet and handle problems." It was clear to all concerned that the reformers' desire for annexation was bound up with the advocacy of racial moderation.

In the voting on November 6, the mayor-council form of government received 52 percent of the poll, to 45.5 percent for the commission form and 2.5 percent for the council-manager form; because the change-of-government committee had proposed to make the mayor's executive assistant effectively a city manager, the council-manager form had never received any separate organized support. The mayor-council form swept the black boxes and the well-to-do south Birmingham white boxes. The commission form generally carried the white lower-middle-class and working-class boxes, but unlike the huge majorities that the council obtained in black and wealthy white areas, the vote in the less-well-off white areas was closely divided. Events of recent months, particularly the closing of the parks and playgrounds, had split the white working class—a fact to which the advocates of the mayor and council had played by naming a white housepainter who was a former officer of the painters' union as the chairman of their campaign organization. This significant minority of blue-collar whites, when added to the overwhelming support among blacks and well-to-do whites, created a majority for the mayor-council proposal. On the other hand, by 1962 Birmingham's black vote had increased to 8,246, a figure much larger than the 2,400 votes by which the mayor-council form led the commission form. It is therefore clear that blacks provided the mayor-council's margin of victory. Consequently, the results also reveal that a majority of the white electorate remained firmly wedded to Birmingham's segregationist past.[124]

Late in the referendum campaign, Mayor Hanes had offered his explanation of the origins of the effort to replace the commission. "The plan to change governments came about because the Negroes went to downtown merchants and said that they would boycott them unless they integrated their stores," he said.[125] While this claim as Hanes stated it is manifestly false, it does correctly point to the intimate interconnection between the referendum and the biracial negotiations that were going on at the same time. Beginning in the late spring and early summer, Shuttlesworth explicitly announced his intention to launch a program of direct action at the time of the SCLC's annual convention, which was to meet in Birmingham from September 25 through September 28. He told a Christian Movement mass meeting on May 21 that when the delegates arrived, "We want to integrate everything we can." And on June 25 he served notice that he would lead blacks in downtown marches. Police attending the mass meetings at once reported these threats to city authorities. Moreover, the national convention of the NAACP, which met in Atlanta at the beginning of July, produced hundreds of picketers who targeted ten segregated hotels and six restaurants in that city, a clear indication of what could await Birmingham in September.[126]

In the meantime, the Miles College students, frustrated by the collapse of negotiations with the white businessmen in March and the failure of the boycott in May, spent the summer gathering 833 signatures on a petition asking the city commission to repeal the ordinances requiring the merchants to maintain segregated facilities in their stores. On August 28—

the day of the special primary at which whites were asked to sign the petition to change the form of municipal government—a student delegation led by outgoing student government president Frank Dukes, his successor Joseph L. Daniels, and freshman Uriah W. Clemon, a future U.S. district judge, appeared before the commissioners to submit their request. The merchants, the students noted, had told them during the negotiations in the spring that the existence of the ordinances prevented the integration of store facilities; the students reported that the store owners had expressed a willingness to remove their segregation signs if the ordinances were repealed, and the petitioners therefore called on the commission "to give freedom to our downtown merchants" to do so. All three commissioners promptly rejected the request, and Connor demanded to know the names of all retailers who had agreed to cooperate.

The students' petition quickly became a bone of contention in the rivalry between the Christian Movement and the Inter-Citizens Committee for leadership of the black struggle. The black moderates had apparently sought to persuade the students not to submit the petition, for fear that it would damage the drive for signatures on the petition for a referendum on changing the form of city government. And indeed, when the students' petition was offered, Connor had at once said of the signatories, "They're all a part of that Vann group." The students evidently had consented to postpone the submission of the petition; though it was dated August 13, it was not offered until the day the change-of-government petition drive took place, August 28. The militant Emory Jackson of the *Birmingham World* hailed the students editorially for their petition; even though its timing was questionable, he said, it was entirely understandable that the students were too impatient for their rights to listen to the restraining counsel of older leaders who advocated other strategies. Meanwhile, Miles College president Lucius Pitts rushed to identify the students with the moderate position. "I personally think this is a better step than mass demonstrations downtown. These students are much more realistic than those who would go downtown and stage mass demonstrations," he said, in obvious reference to Shuttlesworth. "It is a more orderly method. They are asking the city to give merchants an opportunity [to serve blacks] if they want to."[127]

The events only redoubled Shuttlesworth's determination to prove, to the students and to everyone else, that only coercion could produce black progress. And the prospect of demonstrations increasingly moved the moderates, both black and white, toward a state near panic. At the very least, protest marches seemed certain to defeat the change-of-government effort; at the worst, they could lead to many deaths. The distinction that Pitts had sought to draw, between voluntary integration as a result of peaceful petition and negotiation and integration forced by mass action and public disorder, was a distinction without a difference for a segregationist like Connor. Each path ended in integration. Indeed, peaceful integration was, if anything, the more unacceptable of the two, because it implied surrender or, worse, consent. But for the business progressives, for whom very few values ranked higher than social order, and for white liberals, for whom peaceful progress established the South's ability to comprehend and surmount its regional past, the distinction was vital.

During the summer, business leaders prepared to renew the interracial contacts that had been terminated in the spring. The study committee that had been established by the chamber of commerce, the Committee of 100, and the DIA, and which had apparently originated the movement to request the bar association to investigate the possibility of changing the form of the municipal government, had, as we have seen, been expanded the preceding summer and had taken over the negotiations with the black moderates in December, in response to the threatened closing of the parks. But now, on the initiative of the board of directors of the chamber of commerce, it was in effect superseded by an even larger committee, consisting of seventy-seven of the city's most influential business executives and professionals. The new group, christened the Senior Citizens Committee, held its organizational meeting on August 27, the day before the special primary at which the attempt was to be made to gather the signatures necessary to force a referendum on changing the city government. At this meeting the committee named five subcommittees to seek solutions to community problems. One of the subcommittees, chaired by former chamber of commerce president Sidney Smyer, who had played a leading role in the biracial negotiations of the preceding winter and spring, was charged with seeking the preservation of law and order in the face of impending—and to the committee members virtually inevitable—integration. The committee subsequently emphasized that it "is opposed to desegregation and believes wholeheartedly in local self-government." But its members nevertheless "were convinced that lawlessness and violence would be detrimental to all of our citizens."

The subcommittee's first action seems to have been to attempt to persuade the city commission to adopt a more accommodating posture. This effort predictably proved fruitless. The commissioners attended two meetings with the Senior Citizens Committee, at each of which Connor and *Birmingham Post-Herald* editor James Mills got into heated arguments over Mills's desire that Birmingham adopt the plan successfully used in Dallas and Atlanta to prevent school desegregation's resulting in violence. During the second meeting, Commissioners Connor and Waggoner walked out, and Connor thereupon sent the chamber of commerce a letter formally resigning from it. Apparently at the same time, the subcommittee invited a dozen black moderates into discussions that, it was hoped, would aid in ensuring a peaceful racial transition. The black and white moderates soon discovered that they shared growing fears of the possible consequences of Shuttlesworth's contemplated demonstrations.[128]

During the first two weeks of September, the sense of crisis mounted among the relatively few Birminghamians privy to the facts. Miles College's Lucius Pitts and the Reverend Norman C. Jimerson, the white Baptist minister who had succeeded Robert Hughes as executive director of the Alabama Council on Human Relations when Hughes had been forced to leave the state in 1960, undertook a search for common ground. Presumably after an initial consultation with Shuttlesworth, Pitts and Jimerson told Smyer on September 16 that it might be possible to forestall demonstrations if the merchants would now agree to the integration of the rest rooms, fitting rooms, and drinking fountains in their stores, as the black negotiators had asked the preceding winter and as the boycott had sought to compel in the spring. Shuttlesworth would then, of course, be in a position to claim that his threat of demonstrations had been able triumphantly to take up the cause of the boycott and achieve the alteration that the negotiations had not succeeded in effecting. Pitts and Jimerson, reflecting the moderates' own continued faith in negotiations, also sought a commitment from the white business leaders to continue biracial consultations in coming weeks, in the hope of obtaining further concessions from the merchants, particularly as to job opportunities for blacks. Smyer —who, in common with other business progressives, was desperate to prevent demonstrations just as the change-of-government campaign was getting under way, because the exacerbation of racial tensions that demonstrations would cause in the city seemed certain to deliver victory to the commissioners—responded favorably to the suggestions and agreed to broach the ideas with the merchants. But the merchants proved adamant. They had weighed and rejected the proposals just eight months before, because they had concluded that the threat from the segregationists was greater than that from the blacks, and they had then withstood a damaging boycott to make their rejection stick. They were not eager to back down now.

The precariousness of the situation was emphasized for white liberals when they learned that during the weekend of September 15 and 16—at the very time Pitts and Jimerson had been conferring with Smyer—the area's Ku Klux Klan leaders had met in Tuscaloosa with Imperial Wizard Robert Shelton to plan their response to any demonstrations Shuttlesworth might attempt. On the morning of September 18, the Reverend Powers McLeod, the Auburn Methodist minister who was the state president of the Alabama Council on Human Relations, telephoned Assistant Attorney General for Civil Rights Burke Marshall in Washington to warn him that the ACHR's members in Birmingham, "both white and Negroes, are afraid that elements on both sides will not buy the non-violent business. [The moderate] Negro leadership in Birmingham feels that if Dr. King and his group come in up there, there is going to be violence." It was essential, he said, for whites "to make some steps toward giving the Negroes equal treatment." Otherwise, "there are going to be street demonstrations in Birmingham and, frankly, Birmingham is an armed camp. . . . Negroes there are tired of being pushed around and they are carrying pistols." He pleaded for "Washington to get the white community to move and move quickly." The next day, the Alabama Advisory Committee of the U.S. Civil Rights Commission, headed by Father Albert Foley, a Jesuit priest and professor of sociology at Spring Hill College in Mobile, wrote Marshall to urge that the Justice Department seek a federal injunction against the Klan and Birmingham city officials, forbidding them from interfering with demonstrators' constitutional rights of assembly and petition for redress of grievances. It also suggested that a force of U.S. marshals be dispatched to the city. And at the same time, the chamber of commerce sought to deal with the threatened protests in its own, more heavy-handed way. On September 19, Richard A. Puryear, the racially conservative president of the Alabama Gas Corporation who had succeeded Smyer as chamber president, wrote to all chamber members, at the request of the Senior Citizens Committee, to ask them to read a statement to all of their employees warning that any employee who participated in a public demonstration, or who allowed any member of his household to do so, or who committed "any violence, threats, trespasses or breach of peace either singly or in concert with others," could be fired.[129]

The Justice Department officials had begun trying to defuse the situation even before the white liberals had contacted them. On September 17, Burke Marshall had arranged for a delegation of Birmingham black leaders to meet with him and Attorney General Robert F. Kennedy. The delegation contained Shuttlesworth and his second-in-command, Edward Gardner, but it was dominated by the moderates, among them Arthur Gaston, Arthur Shores, Lucius Pitts, C. Herbert Oliver, John Drew, and Oscar Adams. The meeting took place on September 20. Kennedy and Marshall evidently joined in entreating the blacks to avoid demonstrations, the blacks replied with a request for more aggressive federal assistance in their legal attacks on segregation, and they got a promise that an investigation of the discriminatory practices of the Jefferson County Board of Voting Registrars would be launched. Very probably as a result of this meeting, Arthur Gaston told the Senior Citizens Committee on his return that the negotiations, theretofore confined to conversations between the black and white moderates, would now have to include a face-to-face encounter between the merchants and Shuttlesworth. The black moderates had in the past done everything in their power to keep leadership in the biracial discussions in their own hands, for their near monopoly on contacts with prominent whites was the essence of their claim to ascendancy in the black community. But it had become clear that, if demonstrations were to be forestalled as Kennedy and Marshall wished, Shuttlesworth would have to be satisfied. In the meantime, Smyer and his Senior Citizens subcommittee had been pressuring the merchants, who had also been subjected to the pleas of the ACHR's Jimerson. Jimerson reported that he stressed the certainty of demonstrations if there were no discussions, as well as the likelihood of violence if the demonstrations failed to bring progress. The boycott of the preceding spring had greatly soured the merchants on negotiations, for it had seemed to them to indicate a blind and intemperate refusal on the part of the blacks to recognize the difficulty of the merchants' situation. Nevertheless, under the duress created by the imminent arrival of the SCLC convention, they yielded. About September 23, Gaston called Shuttlesworth and invited him to a meeting with the proprietors of the downtown department stores.[130]

This meeting was Shuttlesworth's very first with Birmingham's white businessmen, and it was quite a testy one. The businessmen sought to begin with pleasantries, but Shuttlesworth immediately cut them off; where were their expressions of goodwill when his home and his church had been bombed, he asked. Shuttlesworth did not believe in negotiation, in the sense of give-and-take discussions leading to a compromise, and he lost no time in making the merchants aware of that fact. He was no friend of theirs, nor they of him, he told them, and he had no interest in having a friendly conversation with them. He was there only to decide whether or not the concessions they were prepared to offer were sufficient to meet his demands. Isadore Pizitz, the owner of one of the city's largest retail establishments, responded in kind; he had come to the meeting against his better judgment, and he had no concessions to make, Shuttlesworth reports him as having said. Shuttlesworth at once responded that he, King, and Abernathy would be certain to make Pizitz's store a special target of their protests. After some time spent in these unpleasant and aggressive exchanges, Roper Dial of Sears proposed a modus vivendi. He would be willing to have his maintenance crew remove or paint over the segregation signs at his store's rest rooms, fitting rooms, and water fountains if Shuttlesworth and his associates would agree to say nothing about the change publicly; he wanted, he said, to be able to maintain, if someone subsequently asked, that the omission had simply been a mistake made by the maintenance men, not a conscious action. Despite his aversion to compromise, Shuttlesworth agreed, on condition that the merchants would thereafter continue discussions, looking to the possibility of opening sales and clerical positions to blacks. On this basis, an accord was reached. The SCLC convention, when it met, was a quiet affair, and the change-of-government referendum campaign went forward without any fresh sources of racial recrimination.[131]

But the agreement rested on very shaky foundations. From Shuttlesworth's perspective, the merchants had acted in precisely the way he would have predicted; they had made no concessions until faced with threats that they were convinced were not idle, but then they had immediately accepted the blacks' demands, despite their earlier claim that city ordinances made it impossible for them to do so. As Shuttlesworth saw matters, therefore, the merchants' talk about the city ordinances was a mere pretext to avoid desegregation; they, like all whites, would integrate when they had no other choice, and not before. And so, as the promised additional negotiations with the businessmen on increasing blacks' job opportunities got under way, Shuttlesworth prepared to press his adversaries hard; only thus, he thought, would they accept further advances.

For the merchants, on the other hand, the fear of segregationist retaliation remained paramount. Shuttlesworth's willingness to keep confidential their removal of the segregation signs was the essence of the agreement for them. If the fact that the integration had happened at each of the large downtown stores at the same moment became generally known, the merchants' planned excuse that the omission of the signs had been an innocent error by a maintenance man would cease to be plausible. At once the threat of arrest by the city authorities and boycotts and bombings by the white supremacists that had prevented the merchants from agreeing to the black requests in the spring would again become a likelihood. Under those circumstances, the deal would be off. Shuttlesworth clearly understood that the entire agreement rested on its being kept secret.[132] But apparently he did not appreciate the full implications of the merchants' position. For it meant that the merchants would inevitably reject any integration the knowledge of which seemed certain to become public. If the concession could not remain confidential, it was too dangerous, so long as Connor and Hanes remained in power, ready to arrest any merchant who violated a segregation ordinance, as they had arrested the manager of the Greyhound bus station restaurant the year before, thereby turning the hapless businessman's action into a municipal cause célèbre. From the merchants' perspective, the genuine, long-term solution to the problem remained political.

Given these very different understandings of the situation, it is not surprising that the negotiations during October did not go well. There had been what blacks hoped might prove a breakthrough on the employment question at the beginning of September, when Committee of 100 chairman James A. Head, who was the owner of an office supply business and was one of the city's most prominent white racial liberals, had hired a black salesman, Wilbur Lakey. The Christian Movement hailed this action, and in the October meetings it implored other businessmen to follow Head's example. The blacks also renewed their request for the integration of the downtown stores' lunch counters and dining rooms. But for the merchants, both of these forms of integration seemed too likely to attract attention. The hiring of black sales personnel, they feared, might drive away white customers. And restaurant segregation was, of course, required by a city ordinance that Commissioner Connor was eager to enforce. On the dining facilities, however, the merchants did have a counterproposal. If blacks would again violate the restaurant segregation ordinance, in order to arrange a test case of its constitutionality, the businessmen offered surreptitiously to pay all of the legal expenses involved. For a time a black and a white attorney explored this idea together, but in late October, it appears, Shuttlesworth rejected it. He knew from bitter experience how long a test case would take. And blacks had endured many arrests over the preceding six years to create test cases; why could a merchant not accept the arrest that would follow his agreement to serve blacks, and fight the test case in his own name? The minister, a man who had defied segregationist bombings, assaults, and imprisonment, was not inclined to waste much sympathy on the merchants' desperate fear of publicity.

In the early weeks of October, both Shuttlesworth and Arthur Shores had believed that they were making some progress with the merchants on the matter of hiring black clerks, but by the end of the month no agreement seemed likely. Just after the change-of-government referendum on November 6, Shuttlesworth held a final meeting with the businessmen, at which evidently he gave them an ultimatum. At the Christian Movement mass meeting of November 12, Edward Gardner announced a renewal of the boycott of the downtown stores until black sales personnel were employed. The negotiations clearly had collapsed. And at the same meeting, for the first time, Gardner also violated the confidentiality that the merchants had demanded as the price of their concessions in September, and publicly revealed the achievement to the Christian Movement membership. "You can go in the stores downtown, hardly any of them had any signs up 'colored' or 'white' anymore. Drink at the same water fountains, use the same toilets," he reported proudly, doubtless to prove that the group's efforts had not all been in vain.

Gardner's statements of November 12 were reported to Commissioner Connor the next day. He had known at least since late August, from the statements made by the Miles College students at the time of the submission of their petition, that there were merchants who were willing to accept a measure of desegregation under certain circumstances. And he had learned in mid-October that the merchants were discussing the hiring of black clerks. But now, finding from Gardner's disclosure that actual integration had taken place, he immediately swung into action. As the merchants subsequently reported the event to the moderates, Connor had the fire inspectors, who were under his jurisdiction, contact the merchants and threaten to levy large fines or close their stores for fire code violations; the violations, however, could be overlooked if the segregation signs were returned to their accustomed places. Given that the maintenance of confidentiality had always been essential to the agreement, and that the negotiations with Shuttlesworth had now broken down in any case, the threats of the fire inspectors proved the last straw. The segregation signs went back up in every store except one, Blach's. By mid-November, therefore, the accord that to the moderates had seemed such a hopeful sign in late September was dead.[133]

Just as the agreement with the merchants in September had left Shuttlesworth convinced of the accuracy of his conception of how to obtain concessions, so the disintegration of that agreement in November further convinced the merchants and business progressives of the accuracy of their analysis of Birmingham's problems. It had ended just as they would have predicted. No private arrangement on a matter as sensitive as race relations could be kept secret, and once such an arrangement was known to municipal authorities it would become a political necessity for them to act against it. Effective negotiations on social matters could go forward only after the city's political climate had been changed. That had been their argument in the biracial discussions of the preceding February, and they were made even more certain of it by the events of November. The removal from power of Connor, Hanes, and their allies was the key to all further reform. By November, of course, the businessmen were no longer talking to Shuttlesworth, but they were still talking to the black moderates who had also been their negotiating partners ten months earlier, and for the black moderates the businessmen's case now had new persuasive power. When the merchants had urged in February that the blacks accept that a municipal political transformation had to be a precondition for the integration of facilities in downtown stores, such a transformation had seemed, if not a utopian dream, at least an event quite some years in the future. Now, however, in the wake of the change-of-government referendum, a genuine political revolution seemed possible, even likely, and the test was only four months away, when the first mayor and council were to be elected. Moreover, the business progressives strongly reinforced this nascent optimism by emphasizing privately to the black moderate leaders, in the most explicit terms, that if the white moderates won control of the new city government, the racial reforms that the two groups had been discussing over the past year would at once be put into effect. Under these reassurances, the black moderates and those in the black community who listened to them began more and more to put their trust in the political changes that seemed about to take place, and therefore became increasingly convinced that Shuttlesworth's aggressive strategies were no longer necessary.

On the other hand, following the failure of the negotiations and the merchants' restoration of the segregation signs in their stores, Shuttlesworth and his circle, who had never really trusted the negotiations in any case, were left persuaded that the whites had just been engaged in a confidence game. From Shuttlesworth's perspective, the businessmen had simply wanted to forestall demonstrations in order to defeat the city commission in the referendum, and to achieve their goal they had been willing to prevaricate. They had never really intended to remove the signs on a permanent basis; they had only done so as a temporary ploy, to preserve racial calm until after the referendum was over. Blacks had thus forfeited the principal concern that had made the threat of demonstrations effective, and whites had then immediately reneged on the deal. The business negotiators were dishonest finaglers who would never voluntarily carry through on an agreement to desegregate unless blacks possessed the means to compel them to live up to the commitment. These men had to be taught a lesson. When, at the outset of the demonstrations the following spring, white moderate clergymen sought to reopen discussions, Shuttlesworth's associate the Reverend Abraham Woods thundered, "The white preachers in this city are disturbed. They send us word they want us to negotiate. We did negotiate with the downtown business folks in September of 1962. They lied to us then and they are lying to us now. Talking won't do it for us." And Shuttlesworth directly accused Sidney Smyer of having shaken hands with him on the September 1962 agreement and then having dishonorably double-crossed the black negotiators.

It was in the grip of such resentments that, following the renewal of the downtown boycott on November 12, Shuttlesworth contacted Martin Luther King and asked the SCLC to join the Christian Movement in staging public demonstrations in Birmingham. King had just suffered what had effectively been a defeat for his direct-action tactics that spring and summer in Albany, Georgia, and he was eager to find a venue in which he could prove that direct action could produce real results. But he was not at first convinced that Birmingham was such a place. On December 9, he visited the city to preach at the installation of his associate John Porter as pastor of the Sixth Avenue Baptist Church. While there, he conferred with Shuttlesworth and other officers of the Christian Movement and evidently was persuaded; he appears to have given Shuttlesworth tentative assurances of his cooperation at this time. He took no actual steps toward initiating demonstrations for a month, but on January 10 he convened a two-day meeting of the SCLC staff to begin detailed planning of the Birmingham campaign. By that date, the Magic City's fate was sealed.[134]

In the meantime, however, the city's residents, generally unaware of these events, were proceeding toward the reformation of their political life. Immediately after the change-of-government referendum, the city commissioners' allies had filed suit against it in state circuit court, in the name of Connor's close political associate Joe W. Reid. Reid was represented by Connor's mentor James Simpson and the former Ku Klux Klan leaders and vitriolic segregationists Hugh Locke and Crampton Harris. The city hired to argue the case for the referendum's legality John S. Foster, who rather ironically was the attorney who had defended Connor in 1952 in his trial for occupying the hotel room with his secretary. Reid's lawyers made two different attacks on the change of government, both derived from the conflicts among the various statutes that applied to it. In the first place, as we have seen, the 1955 legislature had passed two different local acts as alternatives to the 1953 council-manager statute. One, signed into law on September 9, 1955, at 11:25 A.M., permitted a special election to change to mayor-council government. The other, signed on September 9 at 10:51 A.M., provided for an election to choose among the city commission, mayor-council, and council-manager forms, with a runoff between the top two finishers if no form received a majority in the initial referendum. Reid's attorneys contended that these two statutes were irreconcilable and that the 11:25 act therefore had effectively repealed the 10:51 act. Because the 1962 change-of-government vote had been held under the terms of the 10:51 act, Reid's argument concluded that it had not been legal. If this claim were overruled, then Reid turned to a second one. The 1955 local act provided for a quick election to choose the officials of the new form of government, if one were adopted in the referendum, and ordered that the officials chosen in this election should take office immediately following the election. But a 1959 general act had provided that when any city changed its form of government, all persons holding office under the existing government had to be permitted to serve out their terms before the new officials could take over. Reid's attorneys argued that the 1959 general law had superseded the provisions of the 1955 local one and that therefore the commissioners would not leave office until October 1965, when their terms expired. These contentions were presented to Circuit Judge J. Edgar Bowron on January 4, but the next day he dismissed them both and ruled the change of government "legal and valid in all respects." Reid at once appealed to the state supreme court.

The supreme court heard arguments in the case on February 26 and issued its ruling on March 1, just four days before the first round of voting for the new mayor and council was to take place. The court had little difficulty with the argument that the 11:25 act repealed the 10:51 act. In an opinion by Justice James Coleman, the court's most uncompromising segregationist, the justices unanimously overruled this contention. The notion that the legislature would have enacted a statute to be in effect for only half an hour was absurd on its face, Coleman wrote, and it was rendered more so by the fact that in 1961, following the census of 1960, the legislature had amended both of the 1955 acts to change the population of the city to which they applied; the legislature would certainly not have amended in 1961 an act that it had repealed in 1955. It was clear, therefore, that the legislators intended both acts to be effective, and it was the duty of the courts to reconcile them. That task was not difficult, Coleman said. The 1953 act and the two 1955 acts provided machinery for posing three different referendum questions; the voters could be asked if they wished the council-manager form or if they wished the mayor-council form, or they could be given a choice among all three forms. Since the referendum that had actually been held in Birmingham had offered voters a choice among the three forms, it had properly followed the procedures prescribed in the 10:51 act. The referendum had been legally held, and its result was binding.

To this point, Coleman's opinion had been without dissent. But when he turned to the question of whether the 1959 general act forbade the new city government to take power until 1965, his reasoning divided the seven justices four to three. The difficulty was not with the substance of the contention. The supreme court's precedents had long since established that the effect of a local act was to carve out an exception to the general system. Alterations in the general system therefore had no effect on the exceptions, which stood unless the legislature explicitly repealed them. When the justices finally reached the question the following May, their answer to it was thus quick and unanimous. But Coleman was unwilling to reach it now. The parties with an interest in the dispute over when the new officials should take office had not all had an opportunity to be heard by the circuit court, Coleman observed; two of the city commissioners were not defendants, and most importantly, the new mayor and council had not yet even been elected, so they necessarily had been unable to present their case. Judge Bowron consequently had erred in agreeing to rule on this matter. A suit for a declaratory judgment before the election had taken place was simply the wrong form of action by which to raise the question. After the new mayor and council had been inaugurated, if the city commissioners refused to vacate their offices, then the mayor and council members should file a petition for a writ of quo warranto against the commissioners; all parties having an interest in the controversy would then be before the court, and the judge could legitimately proceed to a decision.

The court's three more conservative justices, led by Coleman, all accepted this reasoning, and one of the four more liberal justices, Pelham Merrill, was persuaded by it as well. The three remaining liberals were thus left to dissent. Writing for them, Justice Thomas S. Lawson noted that the fact that all the parties to the controversy had not been before the circuit court was not a question that had been argued by either the appellants or the appellees in the *Reid* case; rather, it was a matter that the majority justices were now suddenly raising on their own. The result was to leave the real issue unresolved, even though the rule that local acts stand unless general acts specifically repeal them was absolutely clear. The majority's decision was "highly regrettable," Lawson concluded, because it had quite unnecessarily created "a rather chaotic condition for the City of Birmingham." Martin Luther King and "Bull" Connor were just about to prove Lawson more completely correct than he could possibly have imagined.[135]

Meanwhile, the campaign for mayor and council members was in full swing. Just before the November referendum, "Bull" Connor had stated flatly that, if the new form of government were adopted, he would not run for mayor under it. But in early January, when Judge Bowron ruled the referendum legal, Connor immediately announced his candidacy for the very office that two months before he had said he would not consider. His two principal opponents were Albert Boutwell, whose term as the state's lieutenant governor was just ending, and Thomas King, the liberal whom Arthur Hanes had narrowly defeated in 1961. Seventy-five candidates filed for the nine council seats, among them two blacks, the Reverend James L. Ware, the president of the Inter-Citizens Committee, and W. L. Williams, Jr., the young attorney who had broken the Birmingham stalemate in 1959. King was the overwhelming favorite of the city's approximately 8,300 black voters, and he had the support as well of a number of prominent white liberals such as Committee of 100 chairman James Head. Nevertheless, having been beaten by the race issue two years earlier, King was determined not to suffer the same fate again; he went out of his way to insist that he was a segregationist and indulged in strident attacks upon the national media for their criticism of Birmingham's racial climate. His conduct probably cost him more among white moderates than it gained him among white supremacists. Connor, of course, had the support of the arch-segregationists locked up. Nevertheless, he descended at once to demagogic racism. He also worked to arouse blue-collar resentment of chamber of commerce dictation and of the out-of-state ownership of the city's daily newspapers. And, linking the two appeals, he warned that his opponents were tools of the chamber and the newspapers in their surreptitious offensive to integrate the city. Boutwell placed his chief emphasis on the necessity for industrial expansion and the annexation of the suburbs, and he strongly attacked the municipal budget deficit. On the racial question, he said only that he intended above all to maintain law and order and that he hoped to defend segregation through legal action. But his allies reminded voters that he had chaired the legislative committee that had drafted the state's massive resistance constitutional amendment, and they incorrectly attributed the Pupil Placement Act to him as well. Both daily newspapers and virtually all of the city's business leaders endorsed Boutwell. As between Boutwell and King, business progressives recalled that King had been unable to defeat Hanes in 1961, and they thought it likely that King would suffer the same fate in a runoff against Connor. Boutwell, on the other hand, had proven his popularity with the electorate in his previous races for the state senate, and his segregationist credentials were less vulnerable than were King's to Connor's attacks. For the commercial establishment, the defeat of Connor was the overriding goal. If he were elected mayor, the businessmen's entire lengthy effort to change the form of the municipal government would, in their eyes, have come to naught.

In the initial round of voting, Boutwell received 39 percent to Connor's 31 percent and King's 26 percent; 4 percent went to Commissioner Waggoner, whose campaign had failed to catch fire. King swept the black precincts, and Boutwell did almost as well in the well-to-do white neighborhoods. Connor generally carried the blue-collar white areas, but Boutwell received substantial support there also. As had been the case in the change-of-government referendum, a key to the recent strength of moderation in the city was the inability of racial extremism to unite the white working class as fully as in the past.

If what was wanting was white working-class unity, however, Connor was determined to leave nothing undone in the effort to create it. In the runoff campaign, his demagogy reached new heights. The Mountain Brook moguls were seeking to rule Birmingham, he bellowed; they cared not a whit if the city's blue-collar whites were subjected to integration and mongrelization, so long as the result was a municipal image pleasing to wealthy northern opinion leaders. He reaffirmed the correctness of the decision to close the parks, and extended it to education; if the courts ordered school integration, he would close the schools also. Connor's uncompromising commitments worked to accentuate his differences with Boutwell. Boutwell, too, expressed the hope that the courts could be convinced to permit continued segregation, but when a final decree was entered, he said, it had to be accepted; he would not permit Birmingham "to be a city of unrestrained and unhampered mockery of the law." Boutwell joined the business progressives in ranking the preservation of order above the maintenance of white supremacy. Once the legal defenses of segregation had failed, he was therefore prepared for a quiet surrender.[136]

The distinction between Connor and Boutwell was clear to all Birminghamians, of both races. The fetid atmosphere of Birmingham's municipal politics, indeed, made Boutwell appear more moderate than he would have seemed in a less racially divided city. Shuttlesworth and his associates in the Christian Movement sought to underscore that fact. Early in the runoff campaign, Shuttlesworth told his followers, according to the police officers attending the meeting, "'There isn't a whole lot of difference between Mr. Bull and Mr. Boutwell.' He said the difference as he saw it was that Connor was an undignified Boutwell and Boutwell was a dignified Connor. . . . He further stated that he did not have any use for Mr. Boutwell and he had better not fool with him." A week later officers reported him as claiming, "We don't care about this election coming up. We don't care who wins it. We know that just one of two men will be elected and whichever it is, we will pay him due respect and he will do something for us or he will wish he had." However, on the eve of the balloting, police said that Shuttlesworth "stated that the election tomorrow is one of the most crucial elections to come here in many years. . . . He said, 'Mr. Bout-well is as dignified as Mr. Connor is not.' . . . He stated that if Bull squeezes through, Birmingham would be in a Hell of a place." As early as January 21, Shuttlesworth's vice-president, Edward Gardner, had said that the municipal elections would make history for Birmingham. He had hailed the victory of the mayor-council form in the change-of-government referendum in November, and he was equally exultant at Connor's defeat in April, saying, as officers reported, that it demonstrated that "Many white people living in Birmingham today are sympathetic with our movement but are afraid to come out in the open and say so, but some day soon all good men will come to the front and be heard."[137]

It is clear, then, that the Christian Movement's leaders did recognize that Connor's defeat would significantly advance their cause and that they were appreciative of the white businessmen's efforts to bring it about. Shuttlesworth's assertion of an essential equivalence between Boutwell and Connor did not really proceed from indifference to the outcome of the election, despite his statement to the contrary. It did not even proceed from any genuine belief that the two men's views were indistinguishable. In part, it simply represented exaggeration for the sake of effect. Shuttlesworth wished to emphasize that Boutwell, though a considerably more temperate segregationist than Connor, was a segregationist nevertheless, and that in the end, all segregation, whether enforced with violence or with compassion, was unacceptable. Shuttlesworth shared this opinion of Boutwell with the entire black electorate, as the unanimity of its preference for Thomas King showed. But in part, too, it seems likely, Shuttlesworth was engaged in distinguishing himself from Shores, Gaston, Ware, Oliver, and the other black moderates, in preparation for justifying the demonstrations soon to be launched.

In the competition between the Christian Movement and the Inter-Citizens Committee, it had appeared six months earlier that Shuttlesworth's dismissal of negotiations and his belief in the necessity of coercion were about to be proven correct. The black moderates' attempt to obtain the elimination of segregation in the downtown department and variety stores through negotiations with the business leaders in early 1962 had failed, and the moderates had been compelled to join in endorsing the downtown boycott. The boycott had fallen short as well, of course, but Shuttlesworth's threat of large-scale demonstrations had produced a breakthrough in September, and by early October further concessions had looked imminent. But in November, Shuttlesworth's prescription for advancement also had failed; he was reduced to attempting to renew the downtown boycott, and things seemed to return to square one. At this point, the initiative in the black community's strategic dispute had seemed to shift back to the moderates. The white business progressives were giving Shores, Gaston, and their associates the firmest assurances that, once Connor's intransigence had been dealt with, they would be willing to move quickly to integrate downtown store facilities. And the businessmen's plan for disposing of Connor now appeared quite likely to succeed. If so, it would be the moderates' strategy of negotiations rather than Shuttlesworth's of coercion that would finally have produced the long sought results. Though Shuttlesworth certainly was eager to see the stores integrated, he was exceedingly loath to have the credit for the achievement go to such men as Shores and Ware, and even more to have a part of it shared by Sidney Smyer. He thought it very important for the future of Birmingham's race relations that the integration proceed from the black community's united and resolute demand for its rights rather than from what he took to be servile bootlicking. In truth, therefore, even though the black moderates' immediate goals and Shuttlesworth's were identical, Shuttlesworth did not want the moderates to be successful. It was in the context of these attitudes that he had begun pressing Martin Luther King in November, concurrently with the renewal of the downtown boycott, to join him in leading a direct-action campaign in the city. It was essential, from Shuttlesworth's perspective, that he recapture the initiative from his Inter-Citizens Committee opponents before the municipal elections delivered them the upper hand for good. And it was in this same context that, in the midst of the runoff, Shuttlesworth allowed himself to claim so complete an identity between Connor and Boutwell. In common with all Birminghamians, white and black, Shuttlesworth perfectly well knew that the differences between Connor and Boutwell were considerable; and as the actual voting drew near, he said as much. But he wished also, as completely as he could, to disparage the transition that Boutwell's election would represent, because he wished to belittle the accomplishment of the moderates of both races, and to emphasize the necessity for continued black militancy.[138]

It is important to appreciate Shuttlesworth's perspective on these events, both because it shaped Shuttlesworth's own actions and because it much influenced Martin Luther King. Shuttlesworth had played a leading role in the founding of King's Southern Christian Leadership Conference in 1957, and the two men in succeeding years had developed a firm friendship founded on genuine mutual admiration and respect. Doubtless because Shuttlesworth had King's complete trust, and also because King lacked any very detailed knowledge of the local situation in Birmingham, and so did not fully appreciate the nature and extent of the rivalries that underlay Shuttlesworth's assertions, King appears to have taken Shuttlesworth's claim of a practical equivalence between Connor and Boutwell far more literally than Shuttlesworth himself did. As a result, King unwittingly increasingly arrayed himself against a variety of forces otherwise generally sympathetic to his cause: Birmingham's black moderates, its white liberals, and the Justice Department.

King was not without contacts among the black moderates, of course. Indeed, insurance executive John J. Drew and Drew's wife, Addine, were two of his closest friends. The Drews labored to acquaint King with the moderates' understanding of local affairs, and in particular they pleaded with him to postpone any demonstrations until after the municipal elections for fear that white anger generated by them might deliver the mayoralty to Connor. Shuttlesworth joined in this recommendation—a fact that perhaps ought to have given King second thoughts about accepting at face value Shuttlesworth's declaration that the outcome of the election was unimportant, but apparently did not. In deference to the requests of his Birmingham acquaintances, King agreed to wait, but Addine Drew reports that he remained convinced that there was little difference between Connor and Boutwell and that he postponed the demonstrations only out of regard for the friends who had asked him to do so. He remained essentially insensitive to the black moderates' perspective.

White liberals were as committed to making any racial reforms a product of negotiations between blacks and whites as Shuttlesworth was to making them a product of self-reliant black demands. Just as Shuttlesworth believed that a negotiated compromise would establish an accommodationist pattern for Birmingham's future race relations, so the white liberals believed that it would draw the white moderates and business progressives into a public commitment to change. The liberals were convinced that Birmingham, if left alone, was now at last on the verge of beginning to find solutions to its racial problems through internal dialogue. In addition, they continued to fear, as they had the previous September, that demonstrations injected into Birmingham's highly volatile mixture would inevitably lead to violence. As word that King might be about to target the city began to spread among them, the liberals became increasingly fearful that King would destroy the painfully constructed foundations for biracial cooperation on which, they believed, the initial superstructure was just about to rise. As soon as the direct-action campaign began, Father Albert Foley, the Mobile Jesuit priest and sociologist who chaired the Alabama Advisory Committee of the U.S. Civil Rights Commission, took the lead in criticizing the demonstrations and seeking to persuade King to suspend them and to rely on negotiations with the business progressives instead. He said later that an SCLC staff member had replied that, apart from any other consideration, declining contributions made the publicity surrounding a direct-action effort essential for the survival of the organization.

Finally, the Civil Rights Division of the Justice Department, headed by Assistant Attorney General Burke Marshall, shared completely the Alabama white liberals' conviction that the change of government and the election of Boutwell would render black demonstrations not only unnecessary but, indeed, counterproductive. Marshall and his associates placed great faith in the business progressives and were confident that, with the inauguration of the new municipal authorities, business leaders would at once initiate real efforts to satisfy black aspirations. But demonstrations, coming just at the moment when the businessmen's long struggle to improve the city's political climate was about to prevail, seemed likely to anger the business progressives sufficiently to make them reluctant to exert themselves to benefit people whom they would surely consider ingrates. The Kennedy administration, moreover, was eager to avoid another public racial crisis that would almost certainly lead to further damaging its relations with the largely southern Democratic leadership of the Congress. For these reasons, the Justice Department, too, was distinctly dubious of King's Birmingham campaign. As the demonstrations developed, King would be forced to deal with all three of these elements whom his refusal to accept the significance of the municipal political transition had worked to alienate.[139]

In the runoff election, Boutwell received 58 percent of the vote to Connor's 42 percent. Boutwell swept the wealthiest white areas and received virtually unanimous support in the black precincts. His 7,982-vote majority was smaller than the at least 8,300 blacks eligible to vote, and it therefore seems certain that he owed his victory to them. A narrow majority of the white electorate, consequently, continued to cling to Connor's standard. The backbone of his support was in the areas inhabited by white steelworkers and craft union members. Nevertheless, it is also true that if Boutwell had not been able to obtain a substantial minority of the white working-class vote, he could not have won. Six of the nine members of the new city council had had the endorsement of the black Alabama Democratic Conference, and the body had a clear moderate majority. An exultant *Birmingham News* announced the results with a banner headline proclaiming "New Day Dawns for Birmingham." The next day, the demonstrations began.[140]

VI. Shuttlesworth versus the Moderates: Round Two

Throughout the month of April, "Bull" Connor and the Birmingham police remained on their best behavior. White municipal officials everywhere in the South, including Birmingham, had been much impressed by the achievement of Chief Laurie Pritchett in containing the impact of King's campaign in Albany, Georgia, the year before, through courteous, calm, and evenhanded treatment of the protesters, and Connor apparently had been convinced to give this strategy a try.[141] Connor's only deviation from this tactic in the early weeks of the marches produced such an avalanche of negative publicity that he quickly returned to his more careful conduct. On Sunday, April 7, five days after the demonstrations had begun, a hostile black crowd gathered while police were arresting marchers, and Connor therefore authorized the use of police dogs to hold the spectators back. A young bystander, Leroy Allen, drew a knife to fend off one of the dogs, and the dog, as it had been trained, immediately lunged for the weapon. The resultant news photograph, which seemed to show a dog attacking a demonstrator, caused sharp criticism of the Birmingham police in other parts of the nation. For the time being, at least, Connor had learned his lesson. Other than this single occasion, dogs would not be used at any time during the entire month of April. The following Easter Sunday, April 14, for instance, an angry crowd of black onlookers again assembled as police arrested protesters, but Connor refused to allow officers to call for the dogs. Members of the crowd then began hurling rocks and bottles at the police. Connor's decision doubtless placed officers in some danger, but it obtained the desired public relations dividend: articles in the national press this time emphasized the black aggression. Police behavior in the early weeks of the demonstrations convinced Birmingham's white leadership that the city was about to emulate Albany's achievement. On April 9, the *Birmingham Post-Herald,* Connor's hated nemesis, warmly praised his officers for their restraint.[142]

But if police were exhibiting self-control, they were certainly not remaining passive. Nearly every day from the beginning of the demonstrations on April 3 to their suspension on May 8, officers arrested scores of protesters, usually charging participants in sit-ins with trespassing and marchers with parading without a permit. By late April, arrests totaled more than three hundred. And when demonstrators who were being arrested were slow to cooperate or when spectators turned to violence, police were never hesitant to respond with physical force. The hundreds of arrests during April produced both one of the Birmingham movement's greatest legal victories and one of its most signal defeats. The victory involved the charges of parading without a permit. On the morning the first march had taken place, April 5, Shuttlesworth had sent a telegram to Connor requesting a parade permit, but Connor had wired back that such a permit required approval by a majority of the city commission at one of its regular meetings. Over the coming weeks Shuttlesworth and King had submitted applications for permits both to the commission and, once it was sworn in, to the new city council, but without success. In the meantime, daily marches continued despite the absence of a permit, and daily arrests continued because of its absence. The movement's attorneys initially sought to deal with the situation by seeking to remove the cases to federal court, on the allegation that the city ordinance had the effect of denying the demonstrators their First Amendment rights. But on April 23, U.S. District Judge Clarence Allgood, newly appointed by President Kennedy, ruled that the deprivation of a federal constitutional right was not a sufficient ground for removal of the cases from the state courts, and ordered them returned to city Recorder's Court for trial. On April 12, Shuttlesworth had himself been among those arrested for parading without a permit, and because the evidence was clear that he had actually sought one and been refused, attorneys now chose his case to press before the state appellate tribunals. In November 1965, the state court of appeals surprised many observers by accepting the civil rights lawyers' contentions in their entirety. In an opinion by Judge Aubrey Cates, the court held, two to one, that requiring a parade permit of demonstrators imposed invidious prior restraint on the exercise of free speech, and more, that the Birmingham ordinance was void because it lacked ascertainable constitutional standards by which to determine when a permit should be granted. Judge George Johnson, a segregationist associate of former governor John Patterson, filed a sharp dissent. In November 1967, the state supreme court unanimously reversed this ruling. It was of course true, Justice Thomas S. Lawson wrote for the court, that Birmingham could not deny a permit for improper motives, or in a discriminatory fashion, or solely because the demonstration might provoke disorderly conduct. But if the city fairly applied the procedures by which it determined whether or not to grant the permit, then the ordinance was a reasonable regulation for the city to impose, and certainly not void on its face, as Judge Cates had held. In March 1969, the U.S. Supreme Court equally unanimously reversed the Alabama Supreme Court and accepted the judgment of the state court of appeals. But the U.S. Supreme Court's opinion, by Justice Potter Stewart, did not go as far as Judge Cates had. Cates had held that any such regulation would violate the First Amendment. Stewart wrote that, even though the state supreme court had construed the ordinance narrowly in order to save it, the evidence showed that the city had in fact administered it in a broad and unconstitutional manner. Though Stewart implied that it would be possible to draft an ordinance that would be constitutional, he joined with Cates in finding that Birmingham's ordinance was not. The decision had the effect of vacating all of the thousand or so convictions for parading without a permit that had been a product of the 1963 demonstrations.

The movement's lawyers were far less successful in another appeal to the U.S. Supreme Court that grew out of April's events. On April 10, Commissioner Connor and Chief of Police Jamie Moore sought an injunction forbidding the SCLC and the Christian Movement from continuing the demonstrations, and state Circuit Judge William A. Jenkins granted a restraining order prohibiting King, Shuttlesworth, and a large number of other black leaders "from engaging in, sponsoring, promoting or encouraging mass street parades, marches, picketing, sit-ins and other actions likely to cause a breach of the peace." After they had been served with the order, King, Shuttlesworth, and Ralph Abernathy announced their intention to defy it, and on April 12, Good Friday, they personally led a march and were arrested. Shuttlesworth's arrest on this occasion produced the test of the parade permit ordinance that we have just discussed. King and Abernathy refused bail, and during his detention from April 12 to April 20, King drafted the letter to the moderate white clergy that we shall shortly examine. From April 22 to April 24, Judge Jenkins tried fifteen movement leaders, including King, Abernathy, and Shuttlesworth, for contempt of his restraining order, and on April 26 he found eleven of them guilty; the remaining four he acquitted because of insufficient evidence that they had actually participated in the contempt. The eleven he sentenced to five days in jail and fines of fifty dollars each. They appealed to the Alabama Supreme Court. In December 1965, in a unanimous opinion by the segregationist Justice James Coleman, the court called the defiance of the restraining order clear. It dismissed the convictions of three of the eleven for lack of proof that they had been served with the order, but approved the convictions of the rest. The remaining eight now appealed to the U.S. Supreme Court. In June 1967, a deeply divided Court sustained these convictions, five to four. The dissenters—Chief Justice Earl Warren and Justices William O. Douglas, William Brennan, and Abe Fortas—pronounced the restraining order overbroad and therefore an infringement of freedom of speech. The majority, in an opinion by Justice Potter Stewart, argued that the validity of the restraining order was beside the point. If the defendants thought the injunction a violation of the Constitution, they could fight it in court, but they could not simply ignore it. At the end of October 1967, King and the other SCLC officers dutifully returned to Birmingham, and the eight served their sentences.[143]

Almost as soon as the demonstrations began, an initial attempt was made to negotiate a settlement of them, but the encounter proved a calamitous failure. White liberals Norman Jimerson of the Alabama Council on Human Relations and Albert Foley of the Alabama Advisory Committee of the U.S. Civil Rights Commission arranged to bring movement leaders together with the group of business progressives who had earlier been talking with the black moderates. They gathered on April 9 at the Episcopal Church of the Advent, with Bishop George M. Murray presiding. Foley had attempted to persuade King to attend; King had at first agreed, but later he decided he should leave negotiations to Shuttlesworth and the Christian Movement. He did send Andrew Young, who would represent the SCLC at all future negotiating sessions. Shuttlesworth, Nelson H. Smith, and King's brother, Ensley minister A.D. Williams King, represented the Christian Movement. Shuttlesworth, who had been arrested while leading a march on April 6, had just been released on bail the day before. Sidney Smyer led the businessmen. Among the whites attending was the liberal young attorney Charles Morgan, who had played a prominent role in the change-of-government campaign.

Shuttlesworth deeply distrusted the white negotiators, and he was not particularly eager to reach an agreement in any case. Smyer and the downtown merchants were the very men who, in Shuttlesworth's view, had duped and betrayed him the preceding fall. They had, as he saw it, induced him to abandon demonstrations when the SCLC convention was in the city and effective ones could therefore have been mounted, and then, as soon as they had secured the victory in the change-of-government referendum that had been their real goal, had reneged on the promised reforms by which they had gained his cooperation. He was determined not to be deceived again. His understanding of the way to prevent such an outcome merged with his long-held beliefs about the dangers of negotiations. What the businessmen genuinely feared, it was clear, was the negative publicity for the city that would flow from demonstrations. The speed with which the businessmen had arranged to talk to Shuttlesworth, after five months of ignoring him, as soon as the demonstrations had begun seemed to confirm this truth. If the demonstrations were ended after only a week, during which they had as yet failed to gain much public attention, however, the result would very likely be what it had been in the fall: King would leave town, and with him would go the threat of credible protests; and the whites, reprieved, would at once abandon their commitments. Shuttlesworth was convinced that only demonstrations that became the focus of widespread national publicity and a settlement concluded equally publicly and unequivocally, would compel these whites to keep their word. And the settlement itself, he believed, could not be one that the whites could understand as representing their essentially voluntary concessions to their black fellow townsmen. The core of his disagreement with the black moderates about negotiations, as we have seen, was his recognition that, as long as whites conceived of black advances as benefits that whites had agreed to bestow on blacks, whites could never come truly to see the advances as rights, and the blacks as equal citizens entitled to those rights. Shuttlesworth was therefore convinced that the settlement had to be, and had to be seen to be, a capitulation by whites to black demands, enforced by the capacity of blacks to take away something that whites dearly wanted, Birmingham's good name. As a result, Shuttlesworth, having at last persuaded King and the SCLC to join him in launching demonstrations, was in no hurry to have them end. He did not want an armistice; he wanted a white surrender. At the outset of the meeting, he mentioned the demonstrations' actual goals: the integration of the lunch counters, fitting rooms, and water fountains in the downtown department stores, and the opening of their clerical positions to black applicants. But then he at once went on to add a demand that he knew the businessmen could not possibly grant, the immediate integration of the schools.

The business progressives approached this meeting in a mood only slightly less belligerent than Shuttlesworth's. They had just succeeded in effecting a political revolution in the city, in obtaining the election of a moderate new municipal administration. The entire aim of this considerable effort had been to gain for Birmingham a positive national image, like that enjoyed by the city's great rival, Atlanta. Now, just as these exertions were at the moment of bearing fruit, Shuttlesworth and King had suddenly begun demonstrations that could well sully the city's reputation even more thoroughly than a quarter century of "Bull" Connor's leadership had managed to. And more, the demonstrations presumably sought to achieve reforms that, the moderates believed, would be forthcoming very quickly, without the necessity for any protests at all, as soon as Boutwell secured power. The moderates were dismayed by this turn of events, and furious with Shuttlesworth and King for having created it. They pointed to statements by white liberals such as Father Foley and by Justice Department officials including Attorney General Kennedy that the demonstrations were untimely and unwise, a judgment they themselves passionately shared. Moreover, their opinion of Shuttlesworth had been formed in large part by their contact with the black moderates, and it was therefore very low; they believed that both Shuttlesworth and King were interested only in obtaining national publicity and northern donations and that they had no real concern for the welfare of the citizens of Birmingham.

That Shuttlesworth should demand that the schools be integrated before he would consider ending the marches confirmed all of the business progressives' negative attitudes. In the first place, the businessmen of course had no authority over the school system and hence were in no position to negotiate about this question. Second, Shuttlesworth's own school desegregation suit had been heard by Judge Seybourn Lynne in October, as we have seen, and Lynne's decision in it was now daily expected. Third, the city commission was firmly pledged to close the schools if an attempt were made to integrate them; it was therefore highly desirable, if at all possible, that the integration only take place after the commissioners had been replaced by the new council. Finally, on the assumption that the schools would be ordered to integrate at the start of the new school year in September, the businessmen had in fact made plans to conduct a campaign for community calm over the coming summer, in an effort to forestall violence when schools reopened. They were particularly anxious, therefore, that in this area above all, matters should not be rushed. All of these things Shuttlesworth knew, and the businessmen knew that he knew. Indeed, the day before, Shuttlesworth had told a reporter for the *Birmingham Post-Herald* that Attorney General Kennedy had personally pleaded with the movement leaders not to conduct demonstrations while the school desegregation suit was pending, presumably for fear of the consequences when integration occurred. Under the circumstances, the white negotiators were left with the firm conviction that the minister was heedless of the human costs of his demands and did not want a settlement on any reasonable terms.

In an account apparently written shortly after the end of the demonstrations in May, a leading moderate summarized the outcome of the April 9 encounter. After the election of Boutwell, he wrote, "The way seemed paved for an orderly approach to the finding of solutions to the city's long neglected racial problems." However, "Early communications efforts" with Shuttlesworth and his allies "disclosed a group bent on exploiting the situation." The Christian Movement "claimed that it knew nothing of the previous communications with the Negro community. Although there had been discussions with leaders of most of the major [black] business, ministerial, civic and political groups, it claimed that ACMHR [the Christian Movement] was the only authorized spokesman for the colored community and communications with others were no communications at all. The demands made by ACMHR, which included an immediate school desegregation program, made it clear that no useful negotiation of a settlement would be possible, even if it should be deemed desirable." Because of their fears of ostracism and vengeance by the segregationists, the white moderates had always insisted that interracial contacts remain secret. And because their principal source of authority in the black community proceeded from their contacts with influential whites, the black moderates had jealously guarded such contacts from the inclusion of rival black leaders. Now their past conduct was coming back to haunt the moderates of both races. Based on their negotiations with black moderates, the business progressives believed that their actions had earned them the gratitude and confidence of the black community. In fact, from Shuttlesworth they had earned only the conviction that they were not to be trusted.

The meeting of April 9 had been so disastrous that it is surprising that the participants were even willing to meet again. Nevertheless, they agreed to reconvene two days later. But this meeting of April 11 was a brief one. It concluded with an agreement that further discussions required the broadening of both groups of negotiators to make them more fully representative; the enlarged delegations were then to meet on April 16, the day after Boutwell and the new council were to be inaugurated. It must have been apparent to black negotiators that, if they were to discuss matters beyond the control of the businessmen, it would be necessary for the white delegation to include representatives of the political authorities. And the white businessmen doubtless hoped that the inclusion of black moderate leaders in the opposing delegation would make it more tractable. At any rate, everyone involved understood that the negotiators as presently constituted were not going to agree to anything. But before April 16 arrived, the business progressives informed Norman Jimerson, who was acting as a go-between, that since they did not have authority to bind the new Boutwell administration, and since, if the courts ruled in favor of the city commission, the commissioners would certainly repudiate any agreement that the negotiators concluded anyway, it was therefore pointless to discuss matters further until the Alabama Supreme Court had decided the suit that Boutwell and the council would file immediately after taking their oaths on April 15. It would appear quite likely from this communication that, in their effort to broaden their negotiating group, the white businessmen approached Boutwell and asked him to allow a representative of the new administration to participate, with the power to commit it to a settlement, and that Boutwell must have refused, perhaps fearing that his participation might prejudice the imminent litigation in some way. However that may be, with this message from the white businessmen, all negotiations ceased. The two meetings of April 9 and 11 were the only ones until the first week of May, by which time the introduction of the mass marches of schoolchildren had forced the businessmen to reconsider their position. And at the May meetings, too, Boutwell agreed to allow his executive assistant, William C. Hamilton, to attend.[144]

In the meantime, much of King's efforts during the first weeks of April were devoted to trying to persuade the black moderates to support his campaign. Shuttlesworth had warned him on March 15 that "some few Negroes are not for D.A. [direct action] at this time," but this admission hardly prepared the SCLC staff for the extent of the black opposition they encountered once the demonstrations began. It was, in fact, the first time King had ever faced a situation in which the majority of the black community's most prominent figures were hostile to his leadership, and it appears that he was initially quite taken aback by it. As we have seen, the black moderates generally had very little use for Shuttlesworth, and he for them; King's alliance with the Christian Movement in this campaign would therefore have made his efforts suspect in their eyes in any case. But additional factors exacerbated their antagonism. In the first place, information about the forthcoming demonstrations had remained very closely held, for fear that knowledge that they were being planned would reach Connor and supply him with powerful campaign material. As a result, when the demonstrations began they left most of the black moderate leaders stunned and deeply offended that they had been shut out of the secret. As men who prided themselves on their consequence in the black community, they had had their feelings hurt. Second, the black moderates fully shared with the white moderates, the white liberals, and the Kennedy administration in Washington the conviction that the election of Boutwell and the council had placed Birmingham's racial problems in process toward ultimate solution. They therefore believed, in common with their white counterparts, that the campaign was extraordinarily ill-timed and that, by arousing white Birmingham's ire, it was more likely to retard than to advance black progress. And finally, as we have already seen, the moderates placed great faith in the efficacy of negotiation as the path to creating interracial understanding. Far from wishing to compel whites to concede black rights, as Shuttlesworth did, the moderates wished to persuade whites to recognize and acknowledge the justice of black claims. They were therefore dubious of direct action except when white intransigence clearly compelled the tactic.

It was not only such inveterate moderates as Arthur Shores, Arthur Gaston, J. L. Ware, Lucius Pitts, and Herbert Oliver who were hostile to King's campaign, however. Even the uncompromising militant Emory Jackson, who controlled the black community's principal voice, the *Birmingham World,* astonished observers by opposing the marches. Heretofore, Jackson had never wavered in his defense of Shuttlesworth from the moderates' criticisms, and indeed he had frequently himself attacked the moderates as harshly as Shuttlesworth had. As recently as five months earlier, when prominent black moderates had disapproved of open efforts to force the University of Alabama to accept black applicants, Jackson had derisively labeled them "a group of better-way leaders" and had concluded that actually "the better-way leaders offer no way at all." But now he joined the moderates in their antagonism toward street demonstrations—what he called "the mass-action stunts"—writing that "Much of this direct action seems to be both wasteful and worthless." In part his resistance was simply strategic. "The opposition has scouted, appraised and studied" King's techniques, he warned, and "has caught on and made counter plans. The opposition is better organized, more shrewd, and has more tricks now than in the early days of direct action. The opposition is also resorting to non-violence, escort action and propaganda." Jackson, in short, feared exactly what the white moderates and business progressives hoped, that Birmingham would become another Albany. In addition, he shared the conviction of the moderates of both races that King's intervention was peculiarly ill-timed. "A new mayor and city administration have just been elected. It is in the best interest of all concerned for a certain degree of restraint to be shown on the part of all responsible citizens." And he shared the resentment that the older black spokesmen felt for King, because the minister threatened their authority in the city. He called for "the dependable hometown leadership" to adopt methods and seek goals that are "ours in Birmingham and not outside of us." However, rather ironically, he also deprecated King's association with such middle-class black businessmen as insurance executive John Drew, who had refused in prior years to involve themselves in the civil rights struggle. "Our Birmingham group needs leadership which is responsible to and accountable to the community," he wrote, not "the non-responsible, the non-attached and the non-program 'leader,'" formerly inactive blacks who "cluster around a glossy personality and share in the reflections of his limelight without the obligation of shouldering responsibility or being held accountable." Opposing both the aggressive Shuttlesworth and the previously timorous Drew, he urged that in this crisis the community turn instead to the established leadership associated with the Inter-Citizens Committee, the sort of men who, before it had been banned, had headed the NAACP.

With this last observation, we reach the true core of Jackson's opposition. "Basically, segregation is a legal and constitutional issue," he argued. His many years of dedicated service to the NAACP had left him thoroughly convinced that the one genuinely effective mechanism for achieving black progress was federal court action. Like Shuttlesworth, he placed very little faith in negotiations, especially secret ones, but Shuttlesworth's distrust of negotiations had, as we have seen, been joined since 1961 by a growing distrust of the courts also. He had been forced by degrees to a belief in mass demonstrations. It was a transformation that Jackson had not shared. Direct action, Jackson believed, derived from a quick-fix mentality, a dream that segregation could be defeated with a single knockout punch. In fact, however, segregation was far too powerful and deeply entrenched to yield so quickly. The only real path to black progress was a commitment to the long-term battle in the courts. Direct action to create a test case with which to challenge the constitutionality of a segregation ordinance was one thing. That sort of protest—the sort that Shuttlesworth had used in earlier years—was highly desirable. And as long as Shuttlesworth had had a court suit as his goal, Jackson had supported him against every attack from the moderates. But "when the courts are openly defied on a mass basis, then individual rights, personal freedom and the liberty of the person would seem to be in jeopardy." He could not countenance direct action "when it degenerates into a deliberate disrespect for established law and a snarling defiance of the courts of law." Both Shuttlesworth and Jackson believed that only compulsion, rather than persuasion, could force real reforms from whites. But they parted company now because Jackson continued to believe, as Shuttlesworth formerly had believed, that adequate compulsion could proceed only from the exertion of federal power, whereas Shuttlesworth had come to believe that Birmingham's blacks, by threatening the city's peace and reputation, could themselves compel whites to yield.[145]

Thus King found himself opposed not only by the black moderates, who sought to end segregation through cooperative efforts with whites, but also by black activists previously associated with the NAACP, who emphasized legal attacks on segregation's statutory and constitutional foundations. King publicly lamented the large number of black businessmen and ministers who were not supporting the campaign, and Ralph Abernathy denounced them as "Uncle Toms." An executive of Arthur Gaston's insurance empire was compelled to appear at a movement mass meeting to assure the congregation that, contrary to rumors circulating in the black community, the Gaston interests were not secretly controlled by white money. But behind the scenes, the SCLC leaders were vigorously seeking to close the rifts that the demonstrations had created among

blacks, and their efforts to do so would determine the outcome of the protests a month later. On the morning of April 8, King attended a meeting
of the recently formed black Jefferson County Interdenominational Alliance, of which J. L. Ware was president, in an attempt to gain its support.
He pleaded with the some 125 ministers present to join his crusade. However, though the group was willing to express its general support for desegregation, it declined to endorse the SCLC campaign. Doubtless with
mounting anxiety, King went on that evening to a meeting of one hundred of the city's leading black businessmen and professionals, convened
by Gaston. Again he sought to convince them of the correctness of his
strategy. But now, perhaps because of his earlier failure with the ministers,
he made a momentous concession. He proposed the creation of a tripartite
central committee to direct the protests, to consist of representatives of
the SCLC, the Christian Movement, and the traditional black moderate
leadership, in approximately equal numbers. The twenty-member body, as
finally constituted, contained six members from the SCLC, seven from the
Christian Movement, and seven moderates, led by Gaston.

This idea did indeed begin to break the ice. On April 9—the day, as
well, of Shuttlesworth's disastrous meeting with the white business progressives—Gaston issued a public statement justifying, though not actually supporting, the demonstrations. "I regret the absence of continued
communication between the white and Negro leadership in our city, and
the inability of the white merchants and white power structure of our
community to influence our city's fathers to establish an official line of
communication between the races in our city," he wrote. The absence of
effective interracial negotiations, together with the repeated unsolved
bombings, had made Birmingham a natural target for King's organization,
he said. But he stressed that the city stood on the "threshold of transition,
and I feel it will be a transition to greatness." Clearly Gaston had not abandoned his moderate convictions. But he did explicitly place the blame for
the protests where it in fact belonged, not on King but on the previous
inability of the white moderates to deliver meaningful racial reforms
and on the incompetence or malevolence of Connor's police. This statement by black Birmingham's wealthiest and most influential citizen represented a genuine victory for King's effort to create racial unity. That
night Shuttlesworth happily, if quite misleadingly, informed the mass
meeting that both the ministers and the businessmen the day before had
unanimously endorsed the movement. On April 12, more than sixty of the
city's most prominent black moderates signed a large advertisement published in the *Birmingham News* affirming that "the current struggle in our
community is an expression of the uttered or unexpressed deep yearnings
of the heart of every Negro in this community." They informed white
Birminghamians—almost all of whom, because of the secrecy of the negotiations, were completely unaware of the fact—that "We have had many

conferences with city officials, Chamber of Commerce members, Senior Citizens and individual business and industrial leaders. We have waited with patience and restraint, hoping for a change in attitude and climate in our community. As a result of conferences with leaders in this community, we waited past the gubernatorial election [in May of] last year. We waited in September. We waited in March through the first election. We waited in April through the runoff." They argued that "the rights granted to every citizen are justly ours as contributing and law abiding citizens in this community. We have never asked for any special privileges because of our racial or religious identity. We are not asking for any now. We are appealing to the people of goodwill in this community, people who believe in human rights and dignity, to hear our case and permit us to help make a greater Birmingham. We call upon the City Officials to appoint immediately a biracial committee which will be charged with the responsibility of looking objectively at the problems in this community where race is involved." Both the argument and the recommendation were typical of the black moderates. But like Gaston, the signers were unequivocal in attributing the demonstrations to the timid procrastination of the white business progressives and the hostility of the city commissioners during the earlier negotiations. And even more directly than Gaston, they associated themselves with the SCLC's campaign. By the end of the month, even Emory Jackson had rallied to the cause, and the first week of May found him editorially opposing any suspension of the marches until blacks saw tangible progress in the city. Thus King's efforts to unite the badly fractured black leadership behind him had, at least by late April, succeeded.

But his concessions to achieve this black unity were not without consequences. At the same time that the black moderates were joining the campaign's leadership, the negotiations collapsed as a result of the white businessmen's refusal to meet again after April 11. But when the negotiations did resume on May 4, they were left largely in the hands of the black moderate members of the protest's new central committee. The Christian Movement and SCLC members of the committee were, by and large, not much interested in the negotiating sessions, and they were deeply involved with directing the marches in any case. Andrew Young, representing the SCLC, did attend all of the sessions and played a very active role. And Ensley mortician William E. Shortridge, the Christian Movement's treasurer, also took part in the negotiations. But despite his association with Shuttlesworth, Shortridge was a moderate and longtime participant in talks with the business progressives; he had been a member of the Interracial Committee a decade earlier. Aside from Young and Shortridge, the principal black negotiators were all among the moderates whom King had agreed to add to the leadership: Arthur Gaston, Arthur Shores, Lucius Pitts, and John Drew. These four and two ministers who also joined the committee as a result of King's concessions to Gaston and his allies, the Reverends C. Herbert Oliver and Harold Long, had all been parties to the conferences with the white businessmen over the past year and a half, and all of them fervently shared the moderate faith in compromise and persuasion as the path to racial progress. As a result of King's successful efforts to create a united black front, therefore, he had unintentionally shaped the nature of the agreement that would bring the demonstrations to an end.[146]

This closing of black ranks was not immediately apparent to whites, however, and the initial deep divisions among the city's black leaders were an important influence on white moderates as they pondered their next step. A member of the group reported that not only were the white business progressives alienated by Shuttlesworth's demands following the meetings of April 9 and 11, but "Substantial elements of the Negro community were not sympathetic to the demonstrations and were equally unwilling to see a settlement [on Shuttlesworth's terms]." Faced with the broader black community's failure to enlist in the protests, the Christian Movement's small membership seemed unlikely to be able to sustain the marches for very long. And Connor's continued restraint in dealing with the demonstrators was depriving them of the publicity and emotion upon which the movement could feed. As a result, the same prominent moderate's account states, "Most businessmen felt that the demonstrations would fizzle in time." Generally, therefore, they were content to wait it out.[147]

One group of leading white moderate clergy determined to take a more active approach to the situation, however. In December 1962, at the urging of Auburn Methodist minister Powers McLeod, who was the president of the Alabama Council on Human Relations, Nolan B. Harmon, the Methodist bishop of northern Alabama, had gathered together eleven prominent racially moderate white clerics from Birmingham and Montgomery to discuss what seemed to them all the state's unhealthy racial climate. On January 16, 1963, in the wake of Governor George C. Wallace's extraordinarily provocative first inaugural address—drafted for Wallace in large part by the Birmingham white supremacist agitator Asa Carter, and proclaiming the new governor's commitment to "segregation forever"—the eleven had been moved to issue a public response. They warned that "defiance is neither the right answer nor the solution" and that "inflammatory and rebellious statements can lead only to violence, discord, confusion and disgrace for our beloved state." "Laws may be tested in courts or changed by legislatures, but not ignored by whims of individuals," they declared; "our American way of life depends upon obedience to the decisions of courts of competent jurisdiction." Therefore, "those who strongly oppose desegregation may frankly and fairly pursue their convictions in the courts, [but] in the meantime should peacefully abide by the decisions of those same courts." And they concluded by affirming that "every human being is created in the image of God and is entitled to respect as a fellow human being with all basic rights, privileges and responsibilities which belong to humanity."

This statement had been directed primarily at belligerent segregationists, but as the Birmingham demonstrations developed, it seemed to the members of the Harmon group that the principles they had enunciated were now being threatened from the other end of the spectrum. As a result, on April 12—the day King and Abernathy were arrested for defying Judge Jenkins's restraining order—eight members of the group released a second statement, this time addressed primarily to the city's blacks. "Just as we formerly pointed out [in the January 16 declaration] that 'hatred and violence have no sanction in our religious and political traditions,' we also point out that such actions as incite hatred and violence, however technically peaceful those actions may be, have not contributed to the resolution of our local problems," they lectured. "When rights are consistently denied, a cause should be pressed in the courts and [through] negotiations among local leaders, and not in the streets." However, the essence of the clergymen's argument concerned timing. "We recognize the natural impatience of people who feel that their hopes are slow in being realized. But we are convinced that these demonstrations are unwise and untimely," they said. "In Birmingham, recent public events have given indication that we all have [an] opportunity for a new constructive and realistic approach to racial problems. . . . We do not believe that these days of new hope are days when extreme measures are justified." These white moderates shared most of the assumptions and attitudes of their black moderate counterparts, and they joined the call for biracial talks that had been included in Gaston's statement of April 9 and in the declaration of the sixty black moderates, printed on the same day that the white clergymen prepared their own statement. "We agree . . . with certain local Negro leadership which has called for honest and open negotiation of racial issues in our area. And we believe this kind of facing of issues can best be accomplished by citizens of our own metropolitan area, white and Negro, meeting with their knowledge and experience of the local situation. All of us need to face that responsibility and find proper channels for its accomplishment." They noted that the demonstrations were "directed and led in part by outsiders," and they concluded by "strongly urg[ing] our own Negro community to withdraw support from these demonstrations, and to unite locally in working peacefully for a better Birmingham."

The ministers associated with the Christian Movement, at their mass meeting the next evening, categorically rejected the Harmon group's plea. The Reverend Abraham Woods snapped, as we have already noted, "The white preachers in this city are disturbed. They send us word they want us to negotiate. We did negotiate with the downtown business folks in September of 1962. They lied to us then and they are lying to us now. Talking won't do it for us." And King's brother A.D. Williams King shouted, "Tell the white preachers we ain't going to call it off, we are going to call it on a little bit more." But the most significant reply came from King himself. Having declined bail, he was now in solitary confinement while awaiting his hearing for contempt of Judge Jenkins's injunction. Amidst this enforced idleness, he began to prepare a lengthy response, which he released to the public after the end of his incarceration and subsequently published in a revised version under the title "Letter from Birmingham Jail." This document makes clear the gulf of differing inferences that so inhibited communication between militants and moderates at this time.

King began by acknowledging that the members of the Harmon group "are men of genuine goodwill and your criticisms are sincerely set forth," and he specifically praised one of them, the Reverend Earl Stallings of Birmingham's white First Baptist Church, for having allowed black demonstrators led by Andrew Young seats in his church on Easter, April 14. But he proceeded to a harsh denial of the legitimacy of the moderates' position. "I have almost reached the regrettable conclusion that the Negro's great stumbling block in the stride toward freedom is not the White Citizen's Council-er or the Klu Klux Klanner, but the white moderate who is more devoted to 'order' than to justice; who prefers a negative peace which is the absence of tension to a positive peace which is the presence of justice; who constantly says 'I agree with you in the goal you seek, but I can't agree with your methods of direct action'; who paternalistically feels that he can set the time-table for another man's freedom; who lives by the myth of time and who constantly advises the Negro to wait until a 'more convenient season.' Shallow understanding from people of goodwill is more frustrating than absolute misunderstanding from people of ill will. . . . I had hoped that the white moderate would understand that law and order exist for the purpose of establishing justice." By the "myth of time," he continued, he meant "the strangely irrational notion that there is something in the very flow of time that will inevitably cure all ills. Actually time is neutral. It can be used either destructively or constructively. . . . We must come to see that human progress never rolls in on wheels of inevitability."

This indictment effectively cut to the core of the white moderates' failure. They did indeed too often value order over justice; in fact, much of their openness to racial change proceeded from their desire to forestall unrest rather than from any genuine sense that existing racial practices were unfair. King was surely justified in observing, "I have heard numerous religious leaders of the South call upon their worshippers to comply with a desegregation decision because it is the law, but I have longed to hear white ministers say, follow this decree because integration is morally right and the Negro is your brother." At the same time, while correct as general observations, the criticisms seem insensitive to the specific content of the Harmon group's statement. The moderates' injunction to "'Wait' has almost always meant 'Never,'" King charged. But it is clear that the Harmon group in fact was calling for immediate negotiations and that it envisioned prompt reforms as soon as the Boutwell administration took power. Though he claimed otherwise, King actually credited the moderates with rather little goodwill. As he beheld the churches in which the white clergy preached, King said, "I have found myself asking: . . . 'Where were they when Governor Wallace gave the clarion call for defiance and hatred?'" But of course the Harmon group had publicly and vigorously attacked Wallace for precisely that offense. It is King's distrust of the moderates' sincerity that underlies his response to their plea for negotiations. "You are exactly right in your call for negotiation. Indeed, this is the purpose of direct action. Non-violent direct action seeks to create such a crisis and establish such creative tension that a community that has consistently refused to negotiate is forced to confront the issue." The Harmon group thought of Boutwell's election as having produced "these days of new hope" that "have given indication that we all have [an] opportunity for a new constructive and realistic approach to racial problems." King thought of Birmingham at exactly the same time as "a community that has consistently refused to negotiate" and that therefore had to be "forced to confront the issue." Without demonstrations to compel them to do so, King believed, white Birmingham's leaders would never negotiate in good faith. He shared Shuttlesworth's understanding of what had happened the preceding September. "In these negotiating sessions certain promises were made by the merchants—such as the promise to remove the humiliating racial signs from the stores. . . . As the weeks and months unfolded we realized that we were the victims of a broken promise. The signs remained. . . . So we had no alternative except that of preparing for direct action, whereby we would present our very bodies as a means of laying our case before the conscience of the local and national community." Like Shuttlesworth, King evidently understood the negotiations that he sought to generate, at least at this stage, not so much as a search for a mutually agreeable compromise, as rather a formal acceptance by his opponents of his terms of surrender.

If King quietly distrusted the moderate white clergy and businessmen, his skepticism of Boutwell was explicit and profound. And it was this attitude, more than any other, that accounts for the vast chasm separating his conception of the situation in Birmingham from the Harmon group's. "Some have asked, 'Why didn't you give the new administration time to act?'" King wrote. "The only answer that I can give to this inquiry is that the new administration must be prodded about as much as the outgoing one before it acts. We will be sadly mistaken if we feel that the election of Mr. Boutwell will bring the millenium to Birmingham. While Mr. Boutwell is much more articulate and gentle than Mr. Connor, they are both segregationists, dedicated to the task of maintaining the status quo. The hope I see in Mr. Boutwell is that he will be reasonable enough to see the futility of massive segregation. But he will not see this without pressure from the devotees of civil rights." The moderates may not have expected the millennium from Boutwell's inauguration, but they certainly did believe that he and the council would move at once to initiate racial reforms without the necessity for any coercion from direct action. This disagreement, then, was the very heart of the Harmon group's dispute with King.

The truth of the matter, as one might expect, lies somewhere between King's and the Harmon group's rival certainties. Boutwell was clearly a good deal more temperate in private than King knew. If King had discussed the question seriously with the black moderates who had been talking with the white business leaders in the months before the beginning of the protests, they could have told him of the firm commitments they had been given of the new administration's willingness to cooperate with the merchants in integrating the downtown stores. But the doubts King felt about the moderate whites turned to outright contempt for their black counterparts. He went on to describe them as "a few Negroes in the middle class who, because of a degree of academic and economic security, and because at points they profit by segregation, have unconsciously become insensitive to the problems of the masses." While he had been willing to make concessions to them to create black unity, he was hardly likely voluntarily to seek out their advice. The Harmon group subsequently reported that the "mayor and council . . . had given private assurance that certain desirable changes would be undertaken. The assurances were known to responsible local leaders, both negro and white. . . . [But the] demonstrations began without warning to the local negro leaders with whom we had been working."

On the other hand, the Harmon group and other prominent white moderates and liberals unquestionably had overestimated the extent of Boutwell's flexibility and courage. Weakened by diabetes, the effects of which had forced him to drop out of the gubernatorial campaign a year earlier, Boutwell was both sickly and in any case temperamentally unsuited to the exercise of genuine leadership. A lifelong politician, he dreaded above all things being unpopular; he was therefore by nature a temporizer. But he was also capable of considerable stubbornness, which he too frequently confused with strength. During the coming four years, a time of fundamental transformation in the city, his continuing vacillation and the real limitations of his social vision would combine to alienate virtually all elements of the community. As a result, his attempt to secure reelection in 1967 would meet decisive defeat. Thus there was much truth in King's belief that Boutwell would not embrace reform unless pressured to do so. At the same time, there was equal truth in the moderates' conviction that

Boutwell would resist any demand that made him appear to be knuckling under to coercion.

The remainder of King's letter was devoted to the Harmon group's criticism of his direct-action tactics. To the claim that he was an outsider, he answered that he had been invited to the city by Shuttlesworth and the Christian Movement, and that in any case, "I cannot sit idly by in Atlanta and not be concerned about what happens in Birmingham. Injustice anywhere is a threat to justice everywhere." But the actual thrust of the Harmon group's statement had not been that King had no right to be troubled by Birmingham's problems, but rather that effective solutions were more likely to emerge from negotiations among "citizens of our own metropolitan area, . . . meeting with their knowledge and experience of the local situation." And to the Harmon group's contention that "such actions as incite hatred and violence, however technically peaceful those actions may be," could not be helpful in the search for community reconciliation, King had two replies, the first rather more convincing than the second. In the first place he asked, "Isn't this like condemning the robbed man because his possession of money precipitated the evil act of robbery?" It surely was not the black citizen's fault, King observed, if his peaceful efforts to exercise his rights provoked a criminal response. "Society must protect the robbed and punish the robber." In the second place, King flatly denied that his moral actions could ever be legitimately compared to a racist's immoral ones. "In no sense do I advocate evading or defying law as the rabid segregationist would do. This would lead to anarchy." Rather, the laws that civil rights advocates broke were unjust, and so were not actually laws. "A just law is a man-made code that squares with the moral law or the law of God. An unjust law is a code that is out of harmony with the moral law. . . . So I can urge men to obey the 1954 [school integration] decision of the Supreme Court because it is morally right, and I can urge them to disobey segregation ordinances because they are morally wrong." But for the Harmon group, each of whom knew many thoughtful and devout whites who believed with equal fervor that the segregation ordinances were correct and the Supreme Court decision the moral error, King's certitude could hardly have been very persuasive. In its January 16 statement the Harmon group had written, "We speak in a spirit of humility, and we do not pretend to know all the answers, for the issues are not simple. . . . Many sincere people oppose this change [desegregation] and are deeply troubled by it. As southerners, we understand this. We nevertheless feel that defiance is neither the right answer nor the solution." From their perspective, King's confidence in his capacity to separate the moral from the immoral regulation so definitely must have seemed perilously close to arrogance.

It is clear, at any rate, that the Harmon group was unmoved by King's letter. In a third statement, prepared by six of the group in September but never released to the public, they asserted, "His letter seriously miscon-strued both our statement and our intention." They continued to believe that the "demonstrations stirred into action emotional, uneducated and violent elements in both the negro and the white populations of Birming-ham," and they lamented that, in the wake of the protests, "The lawless minority is so vocal and use such methods that it is hard to get the law abiding majority to come into the open and express itself. Strong continu-ing leadership has not risen up, and no effective umbrella for men of good will has been created." As a result of King's campaign, "there is no atmos-phere in which new trust and confidence between the negro community and the new government of the city can be established." The exchange between King and the white moderates had only one real result. It sharply underscored the profound differences in attitude that would have to be overcome if a compromise settlement were ever to be reached.[148]

In the meantime, on April 15 Boutwell and the council were inaugu-rated and, when the commissioners refused to vacate their offices, the new government, in accordance with the state supreme court's *Reid* decision, immediately filed with the circuit court a petition for a writ of quo war-ranto. On April 23, Circuit Judge J. Edgar Bowron once again ruled, as he had the previous January, that the 1955 local act providing for the change in Birmingham's form of government took precedence over the 1959 gen-eral act that seemed to authorize the commissioners to serve out their full terms. He enjoined Hanes and his colleagues "from further usurpation or intrusion in purporting to act as commissioners of the city of Birming-ham." The next day the commission appealed the decision to the state supreme court, and Judge Bowron suspended the operation of his injunc-tion pending the outcome of the appeal. Hanes and Boutwell had earlier agreed not to make city employees pawns in this contest by issuing them conflicting orders. The commissioners held their meetings in the morn-ings and then vacated the chamber so that the council could meet there in the afternoons. Both bodies approved all routine actions, and Hanes and Boutwell each signed the city's checks. This gentlemanly approach to the rivalry doubtless was necessary to prevent municipal administration from degenerating into chaos. But the accord was about to determine Bir-mingham's destiny.

When Hanes and Boutwell reached their agreement, "Bull" Connor was still treating the demonstrators with restrained professionalism. In their statement of April 12, the Harmon group had reflected the general view of the city's white moderates in commending the police "on the calm man-ner in which these demonstrations have been handled." And even King in his reply had conceded, "It is true that they have been rather disciplined in their public handling of the demonstrators." King, of course, had main-tained, "Maybe Mr. Connor and his policemen have been rather publically non-violent, as Chief Pritchett was in Albany, Georgia, but they have used the moral means of non-violence to maintain the immoral end of flagrant racial injustice." Unlike King, however, most of Birmingham's white moderates hoped for precisely the outcome that Pritchett had achieved in Albany. As long as Connor's actions seemed to be contributing to that result, Boutwell and other moderate leaders were willing to refrain from challenging the commissioner's jurisdiction.[149]

In the first days of May, as we are just about to see, Connor abandoned restraint. But by that time, it would have been very difficult for Boutwell to have attempted to supersede him. After April 23, Connor's command of the police rested solely on the appeal bond that he and his colleagues had filed with Judge Bowron. And with this tenuous remnant of a claim to legitimate authority, he was proceeding to do the city's reputation immeasurable harm. On April 17, the new council had formally transferred all power to themselves and declared any actions by the commissioners without the council's consent illegal. Nevertheless, if Boutwell had sought to countermand Connor's orders—as he surely had a defensible right to do—the new mayor would thus have seemed to be reneging on his promise not to force city employees to choose between the two governments. Moreover, Boutwell hoped to get through this crisis without making any large group of voters angry, and the plea that he did not yet have clear authorization to act allowed him to let the blame for whatever occurred fall on Connor and Hanes. Therefore, Boutwell continued to sit quietly in his office and to ignore what was happening in the streets.

Similarly, the moderate chief of police Jamie Moore opposed Connor's decision to use dogs and fire hoses. After April 15, and certainly after April 23, Moore could justifiably have declined to follow Connor's instructions and begun to look for his directions from the new administration, but Boutwell's quiescence deprived him of the official support he would have needed if he were to pursue such a course. In addition, his own past experience inhibited him. As we have seen, Connor's first action on his return to the commission in 1957 had been to bring formal charges against Moore in an effort to convince the county personnel board to approve Moore's dismissal. Moore had survived this challenge only because Connor's charges against him were so flimsy. But if the state supreme court should rule in favor of the commissioners and permit them to retain office, any open defiance of Connor would then give the commissioner the offense that he had long sought to warrant Moore's firing. It seemed improbable that the personnel board would try to protect him in the face of explicit evidence of insubordination, even though Moore could claim that he had relied in good faith on Judge Bowron's ruling. And even if he convinced the board to support him, it would require an expensive and time-consuming fight. Consequently, Moore too remained silent, and he left Connor to take personal command of the forces facing the demonstrators. Thus Birmingham moved into the climactic stage of the protests with a commissioner whose term in fact had ended but who was nevertheless still in power. Few observers outside the city understood that Connor's continued control of the police derived entirely from the fact that Judge Bowron's decision was under appeal, buttressed by Mayor Boutwell's diffidence and Chief Moore's fears for his civil service status.

By late April, the civil rights campaign in Birmingham was near failure. Just as the white business leaders had hoped, police officers' calm handling of the protests had prevented the marches both from attracting sufficient national publicity and from arousing much anger among the city's black citizenry at large. As a result, the campaign remained confined essentially to the membership of Shuttlesworth's Christian Movement. By April 23 about 350 demonstrators had been arrested, and the ranks of blacks willing to volunteer for this sacrifice had been virtually exhausted. The desperate pleas of leaders at the mass meetings produced mere handfuls of recruits. The boycott of the downtown stores was beginning to crumble. All signs pointed to Birmingham's becoming another Albany for King, as Emory Jackson had predicted it would. At this critical moment, in the final week of April, the SCLC staff hit upon the master stroke that would convert imminent defeat into triumph. At the urging primarily of James Bevel, and over the opposition of the black moderates whom King had added to the movement's central committee, King authorized staff members to investigate the feasibility of using black high school and junior high school students as marchers. By April 29, leaflets were in circulation in all four of the city's black high schools calling on students to join the protests on May 2. The response from the students was overwhelming. By the end of the afternoon of May 2 at least four hundred of them had been arrested, a figure that equaled in a single day the total number of arrests during the entire preceding month. And the next morning, some two thousand young people arrived to renew the crusade. The character of the Birmingham movement had been transformed. This second, effectively brand-new campaign would force fundamental changes first from Connor, then from the white business progressives, and finally from the movement's leaders themselves.[150]

The success of the introduction of the schoolchildren in the first week of May caught "Bull" Connor completely off guard. Essential to the achievement of Laurie Pritchett in Albany had been Pritchett's foresight in arranging ahead of time to lodge any overflow of prisoners in surrounding county and town jails. Connor had made no such plans. During April it appeared that the omission would prove inconsequential. The number of demonstrators in the first four weeks was small, and the capacity of the movement to make bail for them remained ample. But the city simply could not sustain for any extended period the volume of arrests that the beginning of the children's crusade on May 2 had produced. When the park board—still angry over the commission's closure of the parks—refused Connor the right to use the municipal football stadium as a place of incarceration, Connor was compelled to seek a way to disperse the marchers instead of arresting them. The restrained conduct of the police had always represented for Connor a mere strategy, rather than the reflection of personal conviction that it had been for Pritchett. Forced now to alter his tactics, Connor could draw only on his past experience of race relations and his very limited imagination. In this crisis he revealed to the world what Birmingham's blacks already knew, that for men like Connor, the core of white supremacy was violence. He fell back on the past sources of his security. In 1960 he had told the Dallas County White Citizens' Council that Birmingham had trained its firemen to serve with the police in the suppression of racial disturbances. "A fire hose can be a very effective weapon in restoring order, especially on a cold day," he had reported smugly. In 1962, during his unsuccessful gubernatorial campaign, he had told a gathering of supporters, "And these Freedom Riders. All you need to handle them is a few police dogs and a good jail. One trained police dog can handle nine hundred Freedom Riders, and I will train a hundred dogs. I already have twelve of them." He had added, "People say to me, 'Bull, you can't win this segregation thing.' But those people are giving up. I'm not. We are right, and you can't beat right, and they know it."[151] Fire hoses and police dogs had undergirded his confidence before, and now, under intense pressure to meet the movement's unexpected maneuver, it was to fire hoses and police dogs that he turned again.

May 3 saw the first of the fierce encounters between the demonstrators and Birmingham city authorities that would continue for the next five days. They would enrage the local black community, mortify the white moderates, and revolt a national and international audience observing by television. Over the coming weekend of May 4 and 5, Connor was able to arrange to have protesters confined at the state fairgrounds, and on Monday, May 6, he attempted to resume arrests. But by now the black youngsters were committed to the crusade by the thousands. On May 6 more than 2,400 of them were taken into custody, and soon all space again was filled. On May 7, therefore, Connor was compelled to return to the use of the fire hoses and dogs. Birmingham thus had the worst of both worlds. By the end of the demonstrations on May 8 a total of some 3,200 arrests had been made, of which about 2,800 occurred just on the two days of May 2 and May 6. Three-fourths of all the arrests made at any time during the demonstrations occurred on May 6 alone. On May 3, 4, and 7, protesters and bystanders faced the full fury of Connor's minions as the commissioner tried to disperse the marches by force. But neither the arrests nor the dogs and fire hoses diminished in the slightest the enthusiasm of the young participants. What has come to be called the Battle of Kelly Ingram Park therefore continued unabated until movement leaders and white business progressives negotiated a truce.

The introduction of the schoolchildren on May 2 had itself been enough to push the Kennedy administration into action. On May 3, even as Connor's violent response was unfolding, Attorney General Robert Kennedy was already telephoning prominent Birminghamians of both races to urge the renewal of negotiations. That afternoon he issued a statement that showed clearly the extent to which he shared the white moderates' perspective on King's tactics. He sympathized, he said, with the blacks' plight, but he went on to fume that "the timing of the present demonstrations is open to question. School children participating in street demonstrations is a dangerous business. An injured, maimed or dead child is a price that none of us can afford to pay. A new city government has recently been elected and its right to office is now before the courts. The elected mayor, Mr. Boutwell, already has made clear his intention to resolve the difficulties facing the community. The grievances of the Negro residents of Birmingham . . . should be aired and the injustices to them should be removed. But I hope for the sake of everyone that this can be done in meetings, in good faith negotiations, and not in the streets." The administration had very much wished, as had the local moderates, that the election of the new city government would lead to a gradual, quiet working out of Birmingham's racial problems. When the demonstrations had begun, the administration, like the moderates, had been content to wait them out, so long as they remained at a relatively low level and the police remained professional in their handling of the arrests. It was important to the president and other administration leaders that, if they could be avoided, no forceful measures should be taken that would further alienate southern Democratic members of Congress. But it was immediately apparent to Robert Kennedy and his associates in the Justice Department that the enlistment of the schoolchildren as demonstrators threatened to compel the sort of intervention from which the administration wanted to abstain. It was to preclude that outcome that the attorney general began actively seeking to generate negotiations. On the evening of May 3, Kennedy dispatched Burke Marshall, the assistant attorney general for civil rights, and another Justice Department official, Joseph Dolan, to Birmingham to attempt to persuade the parties to resume talking to each other.[152]

In the meantime, the SCLC's new strategy introduced on May 2, and Connor's harsh response on May 3, had worked to disabuse many white business leaders of their belief that Birmingham was on the verge of emulating the success of Albany. As a result, Marshall's arrival in the city on the morning of May 4 found the downtown merchants and business progressives at last disposed to consider renewing contacts with the civil rights activists. On the afternoon of May 3, presumably in response to Robert Kennedy's telephone calls earlier in the day, Sears executive Roper Dial had called David Vann, the liberal young attorney who had headed the change-of-government campaign, and asked Vann on behalf of the merchants' Downtown Improvement Association to represent the organization's membership in any negotiations that might materialize. On the evening of May 4, Vann met with Marshall and the merchants. Marshall "made it clear that he would not advise on what to do, but he would endeavor to be helpful." The committee of the merchants that had met with the black moderates in the past "reported that all chance of open Negro opposition [to King and Shuttlesworth] had gone, and that ACMHR [Christian Movement] control of demonstrations was in danger of breaking down." In addition, "Law enforcement reports [apparently from Jefferson County's moderate sheriff Melvin Bailey] indicated that the situation was growing steadily more dangerous." And the merchants in contact with the black moderates "indicated that the Negroes were willing to substantially reduce their demands." Under these circumstances, the merchants agreed to see if the Senior Citizens Committee would be willing to join in reviving the negotiations.

On the morning of Sunday, May 5, Vann and the DIA committee met with the subcommittee of the Senior Citizens Committee, headed by Sidney Smyer, that had participated in the earlier meetings with the black moderates. "The idea of negotiation was offensive to all present," because the businessmen deeply resented what they regarded as wholly unwarranted demonstrations that were blackening the city's reputation in pursuit of goals that would be immediately forthcoming from the new administration in any case, and because they were loath to appear to be instituting these reforms under compulsion, rather than voluntarily. Nevertheless, the business leaders saw themselves as "the only group in the city that was able to [meet with black spokesmen] without involving a negotiation of public policy matters which should never be subjects of negotiation. The prospect of continued violence . . . was also an unpleasant and even more disastrous alternative." And so the Senior Citizens and DIA committees decided to empower Smyer and Vann to initiate talks with the civil rights activists. The two were, however, "authorized to deal only in the area of privately owned store facilities and employment upgrading." On this basis, Vann contacted Arthur Shores, Shores notified the movement's central committee, and that evening the first negotiating session since the ill-fated meetings of April 9 and 11 took place.[153]

The intervening days of demonstrations, especially those of May 3 and May 4, had begun to prepare the movement's leaders to adopt a more accommodating posture. Professor Robin Kelley is quite right to emphasize the crucial though hitherto perhaps insufficiently stressed importance in these events of the large crowds of black spectators who gathered to watch the demonstrations, particularly in the first days of May. When the Harmon group subsequently complained that "the demonstrations stirred into action emotional, uneducated and violent elements in both the negro and the white populations," it was to these crowds among the blacks that they in large part referred.[154] More fully representative of Birmingham's black population than were the marchers, they were therefore on average substantially poorer and less well educated. They generally were blacks who had heretofore not taken an active part in the civil rights movement, whether because they feared white retaliation, or because they were unable to believe that the social order actually was capable of being transformed, or because the movement's goal of black inclusion in the world of whites failed to attract them or to address their needs. Consequently, they had never accepted the movement's nonviolent faith. Their own lives often were harsh ones, marked by sudden brutality, and they frequently went about armed. Connor's only use of police dogs prior to May 3, on April 7, had provoked a response from just such an onlooker, when Leroy Allen had drawn his knife and the dog had lunged at him. And now the reintroduction of the dogs and the employment of the fire hoses moved the crowd to fury. Provoked by the sight of children being blasted by the high-pressure hoses on May 3, spectators answered by throwing rocks and bottles at the firemen and policemen. Officers then turned on the crowd with their dogs, and the crowd replied with bricks and paving stones. Leaders were forced to call off all demonstrations in midafternoon. At that evening's mass meeting, Andrew Young denounced the rock-throwers and pleaded for a redoubled commitment to nonviolence. But the audience to whom Young was speaking did not in fact include the rock-throwers, and the SCLC staff knew it. The next day, Saturday, May 4, movement leaders, concerned by the ugly mood of the onlookers gathered in the park across from the church, abandoned the mass marches of previous days and instead sent protesters out two by two in the hope that they could slip past the police cordon surreptitiously. But the crowd, some three thousand strong and deprived of the mass demonstrations it had come to see, began angrily taunting the police, daring them to unleash their wrath. When Connor responded with the hoses and dogs, members of the mob replied with bricks. The next day—the day of the initial negotiating session—the movement staged an unannounced march, composed principally of adults, from a different church and along a new route. This action avoided further trouble. But the violence of May 3 and May 4 had taught the SCLC activists that the tactics that had succeeded in exasperating Connor had also inflamed a previously apathetic but potentially very dangerous portion of black Birmingham. The movement clearly was playing with fire. It needed a settlement.[155]

Thus both sides were open to serious negotiations when the talks commenced in Sidney Smyer's office on the evening of May 5. Nevertheless, there was also a bitter past that impeded mutual trust. The meeting opened, we are told, with "a free interchange of counter accusations of bad faith." After this inauspicious beginning, the blacks presented four proposals—a list that represented a considerable retreat from Shuttlesworth's aggressive demands of April 9. The first two proposals were the ones that black negotiators had been seeking since the first talks in December 1961, and that had been the subject of the downtown boycott of April 1962 and the ill-fated negotiations of September and October of that year: first, the desegregation of the lunch counters, rest rooms, fitting rooms, drinking fountains, and other facilities in the downtown stores; and second, the initiation by the stores of a program of nondiscriminatory hiring and of upgrading of the jobs of existing black employees. It was the failure of the earlier talks to achieve these goals that had produced the demonstrations in the first place. The third request was an outgrowth of the demonstrations themselves: that the merchants pressure the city government to drop charges against the arrested demonstrators. Both this request and the fourth one had evidently been modified, presumably in response to the merchants' objections at the April meetings, to ask only what the merchants had the power to grant. The final request incorporated what remained of Shuttlesworth's earlier, more extreme demands. It asked that the merchants pressure the city government to create a biracial committee "to deal with future problems of the community and to develop specific plans for: hiring Negroes to the police force, alleviation of obstacles in voter registration, school desegregation, re-opening all municipal facilities on a desegregated basis [and] desegregation of movies and hotels." Shuttlesworth had initially sought genuine action in these areas, but the blacks' proposal now merely asked the merchants to urge the city to form a committee to study the matters. The demands presented at this meeting constituted, therefore, a very modest group of proposals indeed.[156]

Despite the substantial concessions apparent in this list of requests, however, the whites received them with undisguised hostility. They refused outright to urge the city to drop charges against the demonstrators and to establish a biracial committee. The cases of the protesters were before the courts, they said, and the proceedings now would have to take their normal course. And the creation of a biracial committee was a prerogative of the new city council; the merchants refused to discuss any question within the jurisdiction of the political authorities. Even though the blacks had asked only that the merchants press for these actions, not that the actions actually take place, the merchants believed that such things had nothing to do with private citizens such as themselves, and they declined to involve themselves in what they held to be political and legal matters. As to nondiscriminatory hiring, the merchants claimed that they "already had a program of job upgrading which they were willing to continue, recognizing the ability of employees well-known to them and to their other employees." The blacks might well have replied that if any such program in fact existed, it certainly had yet to produce noticeable results; the stores employed not a single black clerk. The whites' assertion, moreover, said nothing about future hiring policies. Finally, as to the integration of store facilities, the merchants were very little more forthcoming. Some of the stores avowed that they had already removed racial signs from their rest rooms, and the remainder said that they "would be willing to do so if legal." It is clear, however, that many of the whites did not regard the fact that the federal courts had already declared unconstitutional municipal ordinances requiring such segregation to be a sufficient assurance of legality. One of the leading white negotiators subsequently expressed the view that the blacks in reality "wanted the merchants to agree to put pressure on the city to 'wink' at its laws." On the integration of the lunch counters, the merchants professed themselves "willing to under take [*sic*] the type of lunch counter program already in effect in Huntsville and Mobile, commenced on a gradual basis at first, but only after schools had been desegregated, as in the Atlanta pattern"; and in addition, "No store would agree to act until after the city government case had been decided."[157]

The whites' hard-line response, in sum, was not very encouraging, but it did indicate some potential areas of agreement. The principal sources of dispute seemed to be two: the merchants' refusal to discuss political or legal questions, and the timing of those reforms that the merchants did consider within their purview. Ironically, however, though the whites strenuously proclaimed their unwillingness to negotiate on questions they regarded as political or legal, the delays on which they insisted in the desegregation of store facilities rested precisely on political and legal considerations. They would not act until the state courts had seated one of the rival city governments. They wanted assurance that the city would not attempt to enforce its segregation ordinances against them—a fact that indicated that they would likely not proceed unless the victorious government was Boutwell's. And they wished to link the entire matter to Judge Lynne's decision in the pending school integration suit, as well as the outcome of the certain subsequent appeals. Since the beginning of negotiations with black leaders seventeen months before—indeed, since the dissolution of the Interracial Committee in 1956—the businessmen had persistently sought to avoid taking the lead in racial reform. They had always felt that segregation was a problem primarily for the political and judicial authorities, and only the vacuum left by the intransigence or the pusillanimity of the politicians had finally drawn businessmen into a leadership role in this area. But the businessmen continued to feel that it was unfair to ask them to take a public stand for desegregation without the approval and protection of the city government. To do so would leave them open to the loss of clients, ostracism, boycotts, even physical violence against them. It was for that reason that they had earlier insisted on postponing any steps toward integration until after the change of government. And that essentially remained their position now, despite the intervening demonstrations. They therefore adopted the somewhat curious but absolutely adamant position that they would not intervene to urge reform in matters that were within the jurisdiction of the politicians or courts, but at the same time, they would not act on matters within their own jurisdiction unless they had the clear prospect of political and legal support.

The second day of talks served principally to emphasize how unyielding was the merchants' insistence on the question of timing. During the day—while police, as we have seen, were arresting more than twenty-four hundred protesters—the merchants were surveying their membership to gain accurate information about the subjects of the blacks' demands. They discovered five or six black employees who the merchants felt could justifiably be promoted once the demonstrations ended. And they found that only two or three stores maintained separate black fitting rooms, a form of segregation that had never been required by law. The merchants involved expressed a readiness to desegregate these facilities expeditiously. When the negotiators met that evening, the whites reported these findings to their black counterparts and formed the impression that "the Negro committee seemed willing to accept the [five or six] promotions as evidence of good faith." But the merchants remained inflexible on the necessity to delay the desegregation of all facilities other than fitting rooms until Boutwell was in power and the schools had been integrated. And when the blacks—whose request that the merchants urge the dropping of all charges against demonstrators had already been rejected by the merchants—raised the possibility that the merchants might at least oppose the expulsion of student protesters from school, the merchants "immediately refused." The two days of talks had thus produced little significant progress.

The next morning, May 7, the merchants met to discuss the situation. In an effort to get the negotiations moving, they agreed to drop their demand that integration of facilities other than the lunch counters take place after the desegregation of the schools. But they continued to insist that all the desegregation await the settlement of the change-of-government suit and that the desegregation of the lunch counters await both the change of government and school integration. It is possible that some merchants were prepared for additional evidence of flexibility but were forestalled when Smyer and Vann "stated that they would resign before they would even negotiate concerning city laws and law enforcement." After some further discussion, the merchants concluded that they could make no further concessions unless they could gain the full support of the business community at large. Smyer therefore agreed to summon the entire membership of the Senior Citizens Committee to meet later in the day at the offices of the chamber of commerce.

The meeting of the Senior Citizens took place amidst high drama. Having succeeded the day before in filling the jails, the SCLC staff no longer needed the mass marches for that purpose, and they knew that Connor would now have to respond to any such demonstrations with force. Under the leadership of Wyatt Walker, James Bevel, and Dorothy Cotton, and of James Forman of SNCC, staff members divided the young protesters into small groups with instructions to slip quietly past police lines using alleys and side streets and to converge on the downtown business district at the noon lunch hour. This stratagem worked brilliantly, and while the Senior Citizens prepared to gather for their meeting, the downtown was in chaos. The sight of the demonstrators' complete success at outmaneuvering the authorities raised the excitement of the large crowd of black spectators in Kelly Ingram Park to an intense level, and soon something like a pitched battle erupted in the park area. As the Senior Citizens deliberated, sirens could constantly be heard wailing in the distance, and at one point Jefferson County sheriff Melvin Bailey burst in to warn that police were on the verge of losing control of the situation; because there was nowhere to put any additional prisoners, there was little more that authorities could do to restore order. Tension was further heightened by the fact that earlier the same day, in his initial State of the State Address to the opening session of the legislature, Alabama's new governor, George C. Wallace, had vowed to take whatever actions were necessary to end lawlessness in Birmingham. There was genuine reason to fear that Wallace might now order measures that could lead to a cataclysm.

It was in this atmosphere of crisis that the Senior Citizens, Birmingham's seventy or more wealthiest and most influential industrialists and business executives, debated their city's future. And it is quite likely that only such a crisis could have forced from these men the degree of unanimity that was forthcoming in support of a negotiated agreement. Even as it was, "none of the Senior Citizens," a participant tell us, was "anxious to urge a settlement." And indeed, "a few preferred an apparently imminent declaration of martial law" from the governor. Leading this minority was former governor Frank Dixon, who had been a prominent Dixiecrat in 1948 and was a nephew of the racist novelist Thomas Dixon, author of *The Clansman.* Dixon's proposal reached back into Birmingham's dark past. In the late nineteenth and early twentieth centuries, whenever labor union organizing efforts had become strong enough to produce effective strikes, the unions had always been broken because the governor had called out the state militia, in effect to coerce employees back to work. Dixon was confident that the National Guard could serve the same function in the racial unrest of the present day. It had worked against the coal miners in 1921; it would work against the blacks now, more than four decades later. Sidney Smyer patiently answered this argument by explaining that President Kennedy possessed and undoubtedly would use the power to summon the National Guard into federal service and thus place them under his own command; the guard would then cease to be an ally of the segregationists. Very probably the presence of Assistant Attorney General Marshall in the meeting lent force to Smyer's logic. By a very large margin, the Senior Citizens "agreed to share the burden of expected public reaction to a settlement by appointing a public committee on Negro employment. They also agreed to appoint a sub-committee to carry out the actual negotiation of the settlement." And they dropped all reference to linking any desegregation, even that of the lunch counters, to school integration. Their "subcommittee was authorized to work on a time-schedule for delay [in the implementation of the elements of an agreement,] dating from the [state supreme court] order on Birmingham's city government." Smyer, Vann, and Mayor Boutwell's executive assistant, William Hamilton, all of whom had already been participating in the negotiations, were appointed to constitute the subcommittee.[158]

The linkage of the stores' desegregation to the integration of the schools had always been simply a tactical idea. It derived from the plan adopted in Atlanta to avoid a violent response to school integration there. Atlanta's leaders had reasoned that once the highly emotional integration of schools had been peacefully accomplished, segregationists were unlikely to turn to violence over the far less controversial integration of lunch counters. They had therefore decided to put school integration behind them first and then to turn to other forms of integration. Business progressives in Birmingham had been convinced by the success of this pattern and had wished to see it followed in their city, but their desire to wait until the Boutwell administration was firmly in power was of an entirely different order of magnitude. No mere tactic, this delay proceeded from the merchants' fears for their personal safety and economic survival. They well remembered how Connor and Hanes had made a public spectacle of the disciplining of the manager of the Greyhound bus station restaurant when he had tried to integrate it, on orders of the Interstate Commerce Commission, in December 1961. They recalled, of course, the surreptitious pressure Connor had applied to them through the fire inspectors in the fall of 1962, when they had attempted to remove racial signs from their rest rooms. And they were acutely conscious that the White Citizens' Councils stood ready to boycott them, and the Ku Klux Klan and National States' Rights Party to do much worse, if they did not have energetic official protection. The delay to await school integration they could abandon, but the delay for the change of government was a life-or-death matter, particularly to the merchants, and on it they were immovable.

When the negotiators convened on the evening of May 7, therefore, the vote of the Senior Citizens Committee had armed the whites with much greater social authority, but it had also emphasized that black concessions on the question of connecting desegregation to Boutwell's assumption of full authority would be necessary for an agreement to be concluded. Fortunately for the success of the talks, the blacks who were now doing the negotiating were precisely those prepared for concessions. Shuttlesworth had attended the first meeting, on May 5, but had left Andrew Young of the SCLC staff to do most of the talking. Shuttlesworth apparently had not attended on May 6, presumably because he was too involved with coordinating the mass arrests of that day and the demonstrations being planned for the next. And on the afternoon of May 7, as he was leading a group of marchers, he had received a concussion from one of Connor's high-pressure fire hoses and had been admitted to the city's black hospital. Thus he was absent from this third negotiating session as well. The result was that the position of the local black community was left to be represented by Arthur Gaston, Arthur Shores, John Drew, and Lucius Pitts, all moderate, middle-class adherents of the Inter-Citizens Committee whom King had added to the movement's central committee on April 8 in his effort to create black unity. These men disliked Shuttlesworth, and they disagreed with his hostility to negotiations. They had been engaged in discussions with the white business progressives since December 1961, and during that time, and especially as a result of the change-of-government campaign, they had developed a confidence in the whites that Shuttlesworth did not share. Moreover, they had been dubious of the demonstrations from the outset and very much wanted to see them end in order to avoid further inflammation of race relations in the city and to create a more peaceful atmosphere within which, they believed, further progress would now be possible. They were therefore eager to see the talks produce an agreement. The only active black negotiator who was not a member of the Inter-Citizens Committee group was King's aide Andrew Young. But of all the SCLC staff, Young was the most committed to reaching negotiated settlements with white leaders. Indeed, so moderate were his attitudes that they often provoked the ire of his more militant SCLC colleagues. Like King himself, Young instinctively looked for common ground when faced with any contentious situation.

When the white negotiators reported on the meeting of the Senior Citizens Committee earlier in the day, and emphasized that while they were willing to discard any linkage of school desegregation and desegregation of store facilities, the linkage of store integration with the state supreme court's decision on the change-of-government suit was essential, the black negotiators quickly agreed to the connection. This proved to be the crucial compromise. Apparently the blacks did ask what would happen if the court decided for Connor and Hanes. The whites were confident enough of the outcome of the suit, however, to make a further concession on this point. Three of the seven justices, in their dissent in the *Reid* case, had already expressed the opinion that the commissioners' contentions were erroneous, and the court's precedents on the point were clear. The whites therefore agreed to specify that the integration would take place once the suit was decided, regardless of its outcome. At this point the shape of an agreement on the desegregation of the stores rapidly emerged. The merchants had said the night before that fitting rooms could be integrated at once, and therefore no connection between the change-of-government suit and the integration of the fitting rooms was necessary; they were to be desegregated within three days of the end of the demonstrations. Within thirty days of the state supreme court's decision in the change-of-government suit, the stores would remove racial signs from washrooms, rest rooms, and drinking fountains. And within sixty days of the court's decision, a program of lunch counter desegregation would be initiated. The central dispute that had dominated the biracial discussions for the preceding seventeen months—and that indeed had been at issue since the sit-ins of March and August 1960—was thus settled.

The participants then turned their attention to the only other subject on the list of the blacks' demands that the whites considered negotiable, the question of opening clerical and sales positions to black applicants. This problem proved considerably more difficult to solve, and it was the focus of the discussions for the rest of the evening. The talks continued at Sidney Smyer's office until midnight and then adjourned to John Drew's Smithfield home, where they went on until 3 A.M. The disagreements were exacerbated by the fact that each side introduced an additional issue. Because the whites had earlier rejected black requests that white business leaders both urge the city to drop charges against the demonstrators and also urge the school board to refrain from expelling students who had participated in the marches, the blacks now asked the Senior Citizens at least to lend them the money necessary to post bail for the thousands of protesters in jail. And the whites, not wanting to appear to have yielded to black pressure, demanded that the demonstrations be suspended before any public announcement of an agreement was made. The negotiators therefore spent some time haggling over these matters as well. But by the early-morning hours of May 8, the remainder of the pact had begun to take form.

On the employment question, agreement had been inhibited by the merchants' claim that they already had in place a plan to promote blacks to clerical positions. This difficulty was eventually finessed by the adoption of a rather absurd verbal formulation: "When the city government is established by court order, the program of upgrading Negro employment will be continued and there will be meetings with responsible local leadership to consider further steps." This essentially meaningless sentence allowed the merchants to avoid confessing that their asserted plan, if it existed at all, was a sham. At a somewhat more substantive level, the Senior Citizens Committee promised that, within fifteen days from the end of the demonstrations, it would create "a Committee on Racial Problems in Employment . . . with the membership made public and with the publicly announced purpose of establishing liaison with leaders of the Negro community to carry out a program of upgrading and improving employment opportunities for the Negro citizens of the Birmingham community." And finally, the negotiators agreed that by sixty days from the state supreme court's decision in the change-of-government suit, "the employment program will include at least 1 salesperson or cashier."

This part of the agreement would prove completely ineffective. King, Shuttlesworth, and Abernathy interpreted the final stipulation as mandating that each store's program employ at least one black clerk, while the white participants thought that it meant just one black clerk in the city; the whites claimed that one of the local black negotiators, presumably Arthur Shores, was in accord with their understanding of the provision. If the Senior Citizens actually named the employment committee which they had pledged, it never took any prominent role in subsequent events. When the new Community Affairs Committee was appointed in July, as we shall see shortly, the Senior Citizens at once turned all racial matters over to it and withdrew into the background. And the promotion of the one black woman to salesperson, when it did occur, provoked such a storm of complaint and hostility from her new white colleagues that the store was compelled to dismiss her, two or three days later, reportedly on trumped-up charges of theft. Nevertheless, these arrangements, for all their manifest insufficiency, allowed the negotiators to convince themselves that they had dealt with the black demand for increased job opportunities. Thus, by the time the talks broke up at 3 A.M. on May 8, the provisions of a formal settlement were in hand.[159]

However, the matters of bail for the protesters and a suspension of the demonstrations remained outstanding. At some point earlier in the negotiations, Lucius Pitts had prepared a memorandum for presentation to a meeting of the movement's central committee scheduled for that morning. It outlined the general shape of the agreement that seemed to be emerging and urged the central committee to declare a truce on the basis of the modest concessions that the black negotiators had been able to obtain. The debate in the central committee, when it met, seems to have been very heated. Pitts continued to hold out hope that the merchants would agree not to press charges against the demonstrators arrested for trespassing in the stores, and that the Boutwell administration would drop the prosecutions instituted by the city commission for parading without a permit. But the whites had offered no such assurances—indeed, they had explicitly refused them—and in the meantime, demonstrators languished in jail for want of the $250,000 needed to bail them out. There had been some discussion among the white businessmen of raising this money themselves, but they had not as yet actually agreed to do so. And the whites in the meantime were firm in their insistence that, before any final settlement could be concluded, the demonstrations had to stop. Ending the demonstrations could deprive the movement not only of the building enthusiasm and commitment which it was at last receiving among the mass of Birmingham's blacks but also of the pressure that might well prove necessary to move the white businessmen to a public acknowledgement of their agreements and to further concessions in behalf of the jailed demonstrators. A suspension was therefore a very dangerous gamble.

It was at this point that King's desire not to alienate the Kennedy administration played a crucial role. Both Robert Kennedy and Burke Marshall had made their strong sympathy for the perspective of Birmingham's white business progressives a matter of public record, as we have seen. They shared with the businessmen the belief that the demonstrations, given the election of Boutwell, were wholly unnecessary, and indeed had been counterproductive. Marshall had played an active role in arranging the negotiations, had participated in the discussions that had produced the tentative accord, and was convinced of the businessmen's and the new city administration's good faith. Both he and Kennedy strongly disapproved of the use of the schoolchildren as marchers. And each, it appears, had been exerting strong private pressure on King for days to conclude an agreement with the white negotiators expeditiously and end further civil disobedience, lest demonstrations provoke a bloodbath. Now that the terms of a truce had been reached, therefore, it must surely have been clear to King that if he continued to resist halting the marches, he would thereby badly damage his relations with the White House and the Justice Department. And whereas King's local allies in the Christian Movement sought reform principally in the pattern of race relations in Birmingham, King himself also—and primarily—wished for national legislation that would transform race relations throughout the South. And so King brought the central committee's debate to a close by announcing his own support for suspending the demonstrations. He would have his cooperation fully rewarded on June 11, when President Kennedy, in a televised address to the nation, announced his support for a comprehensive civil rights bill, banning among other things all racial discrimination in public accommodations. Once King had accepted the suspension, only a handful of committee members voted to continue. Marshall quickly notified the Senior Citizens' negotiating committee of the black decision to halt the protests, and the leading Senior Citizens and merchants consequently met later that morning and formally accepted the terms of the preceding night's deal. It appeared by midmorning of May 8, therefore, that an agreement was in hand. President Kennedy scheduled a press statement for noon to announce the settlement. There was only one problem. No one had yet asked Fred Shuttlesworth.[160]

Shuttlesworth remained in the hospital, convalescing from the concussion he had received during the march the day before. About the same time the white business leaders were convening to ratify the accord, King sent word to Shuttlesworth that it was imperative that he come at once to

John Drew's home for an emergency meeting. At this point, Shuttlesworth reports, he knew nothing of the agreement, and King did not intimate in any way what the meeting was about; if he had been aware of the terms of the settlement, Shuttlesworth says, he would never have gone. When he arrived, still very weak, he collapsed into a chair, and there followed a lengthy, strained silence, broken when he finally asked what the emergency was. King then told him of the determination to suspend the demonstrations in order to induce the white businessmen to agree to concessions. Shuttlesworth exploded in rage. In the first place, Shuttlesworth's ego, famously large, was offended profoundly. As the conversation continued it became clear that everyone present—King, Abernathy, Marshall, Marshall's aides, Drew, even Drew's wife—knew all about the agreement, while he, ostensibly the movement's co-leader, was hearing about it for the first time. Shuttlesworth thus became progressively more incensed. In the second place, King not only had affronted Shuttlesworth's status as co-leader but seemed to have aligned himself with Shuttlesworth's rivals, the black moderates, thereby perhaps fatally injuring Shuttlesworth's claims to principal authority in the black community. But finally, and most importantly, virtually everything about the settlement, and particularly the suspension of the demonstrations in order to obtain it, represented the antithesis of Shuttlesworth's beliefs about the correct way to deal with the white adversary.

Shuttlesworth did not trust the black moderate leaders who had conducted the negotiations. He could reasonably have suspected that their success in obtaining the merchants' consent to the integration of the store facilities might gain for their negotiating strategy some of the credit he wanted to go to his own tactic of direct action. The moderates could, of course, make a plausible case that only their contacts with the white business progressives and their ability to obtain a reasonable settlement from them had saved the city from the chaos and threatened violence into which Shuttlesworth's obduracy had plunged it. Shuttlesworth placed even less trust in Marshall. Marshall had been working far too closely with the white businessmen for Shuttlesworth's comfort, and Shuttlesworth—quite rightly—suspected him of sympathizing with the business progressives' point of view. And Shuttlesworth had the least trust of all for the white businessmen. These were the very men who had, from his perspective, deceived and betrayed him the preceding fall. He was convinced that they would never live up to an agreement to integrate unless they were held under continuing compulsion to do so. The fact that the black moderates had been willing to agree to put the integration off until a month or two after the state supreme court decision, which would itself occur at some completely indeterminable future date, and had then agreed to suspend the demonstrations that had alone extracted even this limited concession from the merchants, was proof positive, as Shuttlesworth would surely have seen it, that the blacks were mere naive dupes of their white negotiating partners. And the fact that the whites had insisted on both the delay and the suspension would have seemed to him equally clear evidence that they were preparing a repeat of their dishonest ploy of eight months earlier; with the end of the demonstrations, he doubtless suspected, the promised integration would very soon be forgotten, just as it had been when he had agreed to stage no marches in conjunction with the SCLC convention in September. Perhaps most disturbing of all, however, was the black moderates' and the Kennedy administration's apparent success in convincing King to accept the white businessmen's demand for delay. King had repeatedly assured Shuttlesworth that the SCLC would remain in Birmingham for as long as it took to produce the integration of the downtown stores and that no agreement would be concluded without Shuttlesworth's consent. But now King—despite his vigorous rejection in his speeches to the Christian Movement mass meetings and in his letter from the Birmingham jail of the white moderates' plea temporarily to postpone desegregation; despite his condemnations in the same places of too many black middle-class leaders for being insensitive to the problems of the black masses—had endorsed an agreement founded precisely upon the assumptions and commitments of the white and black moderates whom he had so strongly denounced. Shuttlesworth had believed that King shared his convictions about the realities of negotiation, and King's own words indeed had explicitly affirmed that he did. But now King's actions appeared to belie his words. Shuttlesworth had never trusted the white businessmen, the black moderates, or the Justice Department lawyers. Now, however, he was forced for the first time to question whether he could trust King himself. It is not difficult to understand Shuttlesworth's fury.

King and Drew sought to explain to Shuttlesworth why they believed that the suspension of the demonstrations was necessary. Abernathy, kneeling on the floor in front of Shuttlesworth's chair, reminded him of their warm friendship when they had been students together at Alabama State. Marshall added that he had already promised the white business leaders that the marches would be discontinued. But Shuttlesworth would have none of it. His entire understanding of the structure of race relations was at stake. Glaring at King, he insisted, "You and I promised that we would *not* stop demonstrating until we *had* the victory. Now, that's it. That's it. And if you call it off . . . with the last little ounce of strength I got, I'm gonna get back out and lead." Finally, King turned apologetically to Marshall: "We got to have unity, Burke. We've just got to have unity." On that note the meeting soon ended. It appeared that the settlement was in very serious difficulty.[161]

From their encounter with Shuttlesworth, King and Abernathy hurried to Birmingham Recorder's Court, where they were to be tried by Judge

Charles H. Brown for parading without a permit. Brown—only a week away from his death—promptly found them guilty and sentenced them to six months' imprisonment and $300 fines. When they appealed the conviction to circuit court, Brown imposed appeal bonds of $2,500 each, rather than the usual $300. King and Abernathy refused to post this exorbitant bond and were taken to jail. King's associates were enraged; his brother A.D. exploded, "This makes it obvious that City officials are not willing to cooperate. The negotiations are off and plans are being made for the biggest mass demonstration this city has ever seen." It appeared, therefore, that the other civil rights leaders had now joined Shuttlesworth in his desire to renew the protests. In the meantime, the white business leaders, meeting to ratify the settlement, decided not to pursue the idea of themselves providing the bail money for the marchers who remained in custody. By mid-afternoon on May 8, therefore, the agreement seemed all but dead. The fact that the accord that had seemed so firm at midmorning could have come apart so easily as the day progressed was actually a warning for the future; whereas the moderates of both races did honestly want to find common ground, there was so little respect between the races in Birmingham, and there were so many legitimate sources of recrimination, that no compact that required the parties to trust each other could reasonably be expected to hold for very long.

Nevertheless, the advocates of compromise desperately scurried to put the disintegrating deal back together. Black insurance magnate Arthur Gaston, anxious to rid his city of Martin Luther King and the disorder that King had created, personally paid in cash the $5,000 appeal bonds for King and Abernathy; the two ministers were therefore released from jail in late afternoon, and the movement's managers then relented on the threat to resume the marches. In the meantime, Shuttlesworth's determination to lead a demonstration had also been blunted. Alerted by the morning meeting to Shuttlesworth's crucial position in the equation, Robert Kennedy launched an energetic offensive to win him over. Burke Marshall's principal aide in Birmingham, Joseph Dolan, persuaded Shuttlesworth to discuss the situation with Kennedy by telephone, and the attorney general seems at once to have turned on all of his considerable charm. Kennedy had a practical point to make: the suspension of the demonstrations was merely a temporary measure, to prove the blacks' good faith to the businessmen; black leaders certainly could set a deadline by which the whites would have to have announced their acceptance of the accord publicly, or the marches would be renewed. Shuttlesworth was much impressed by this suggestion, and King, on his release from jail that afternoon, jumped at it as a way to paper over the co-leaders' differences. The two men thereupon announced that they would authorize a demonstration the following morning if the businessmen had not formally accepted the agreement by 11 A.M. Very likely, however, the fact of Kennedy's attention was just as significant in gaining Shuttlesworth's cooperation as was the substance of Kennedy's proposal. Shuttlesworth had been deeply flattered by Kennedy's telephone calls two years earlier, at the time of the Freedom Rider riot, and he had used elaborate emphasis upon them to impress his followers with his importance. There is every reason to believe that Shuttlesworth would have been just as pleased now by Kennedy's distinct acknowledgment of Shuttlesworth's consequence. And the attorney general's solicitude had the desired effect. Shuttlesworth now accepted, with the addition of a deadline, the very agreement that earlier that morning he had so strenuously rejected. Thus by nightfall, the agreement that at midafternoon had seemed moribund had been restored to life. Fred Shuttlesworth, against all his initial instincts, had been seduced.[162]

The one remaining stumbling block to a settlement was the businessmen's refusal to assist in raising the $250,000 needed to obtain the release of the still imprisoned demonstrators. The next morning they remained firm in this rejection, and the 11 A.M. deadline came and went. By this time, however, King had fully committed himself to the Kennedy administration's determination to bring the Birmingham demonstrations to an end. The SCLC therefore decided to try to assemble the bail money itself, and with the administration's assistance it arranged during the course of the day to secure the funds from the United Automobile Workers and several other unions. At the Christian Movement mass meeting that night, civil rights leaders proclaimed victory in their struggle. And the following afternoon, May 10, Shuttlesworth, King, and Abernathy held a press conference to announce their formal acceptance of the settlement.

In a final act of resistance, Shuttlesworth read a summary of the agreement that omitted the linkage between the desegregation and the state supreme court decision in the change-of-government suit, thereby making the terms seem rather stronger than they actually were. But announcing even this strengthened formulation represented an intense emotional strain for him; as soon as he had completed reading the statement, he collapsed and had to be returned to the hospital by ambulance. That evening, in an address to the Christian Movement mass meeting, King presented an even more exaggerated account of the businessmen's concessions. He too failed to mention the connection with the pending appeal of the quo warranto proceeding, and he further assured his followers, erroneously, that the settlement provided not only for the hiring of black salesmen and clerks but also for increased black employment in the industrial sector. These misstatements doubtless grew out of Shuttlesworth's and King's desire to emphasize—as much to themselves as to the general public—that the agreement was a substantial accomplishment. Indeed, Sidney Smyer at the same moment was attempting to diminish the agreement by claiming that it contained nothing that the businessmen had not been prepared to grant before the demonstrations had even begun. Nevertheless, the black leaders' distortions very probably contributed to the considerable sense of disillusionment that spread through the black community during the coming summer and fall.[163]

The settlement reached on the night of May 7–8 and announced on the afternoon of May 10 reflected in its every aspect the attitudes of Birmingham's small group of racial moderates. It was, however, presented as a fait accompli to a city whose citizens were, in general, anything but moderate. The destiny of the masses of black and white Birmingham had been determined by a handful of essentially self-appointed negotiators, meeting in secret; the white negotiators represented only the downtown merchants and the industrial magnates, and the black negotiators were drawn exclusively from the black professional and commercial elite. It is hardly surprising that many residents of the city—initially primarily whites, but as time went on, an increasing number of blacks as well—should feel that crucial decisions about their lives had been made without their consent. The dramatic demonstrations of early May had greatly heightened black hopes, and as the limited nature of the demonstrations' achievements became more and more obvious in the coming months, disappointment and bitterness frequently succeeded the initial black euphoria. But among the white segregationists, the resentment both at the promised integration and at the business leaders' dictation was immediate and profound.

The general white ignorance of the negotiations made the segregationist hostility to the agreement, when it was suddenly announced, all the greater. Indeed, very few whites—even those in positions of authority— seem to have known what the goals of the demonstrations were. When Mayor Boutwell was asked at a press conference in early May to specify the blacks' main demands, he could only reply, "I seriously doubt if even the colored people could agree on an answer to that. There are just as many different ambitions, just as many different economic and social problems, just as many different feelings on problems within the colored community as any other. . . . Come back when the pressures have been withdrawn and I think we can not only tell you what the real problems of the colored community are, but we can tell you how they can be worked out."[164] Boutwell, like most whites, apparently thought of the marches as a generalized protest against the conditions of black life. In fact, of course, they were specifically directed toward the integration of the lunch counters, rest rooms, water fountains, and fitting rooms in the five downtown department and variety stores: Loveman's, Pizitz, Newberry's, Woolworth's, and Kress's. But essentially the only whites who were really in a position to understand the pattern of events that had produced the demonstrations were the five stores' executives and their immediate associates among the downtown merchants and professionals.

The proximate cause of the marches was the failure of the agreement of the preceding fall to eliminate the segregation signs from the stores' rest rooms and water fountains. But neither the negotiations of September 1962 nor the subsequent brief removal and then restoration of the signs had become public knowledge, and when black leaders referred to this episode virtually no whites had any idea what the blacks were talking about. The negotiations of September 1962 had been an outgrowth of the downtown boycott of March and April 1962. That, at least, had been a public affair, thanks largely to the city commission's retaliatory cancellation of the surplus food distributions. But the white local press, whose contacts in the black community were quite limited, did a very poor job at the time of reporting on the origins and aims of the boycott, and an even poorer job of reporting on the demonstrations a year later—accounts of which were, as a matter of policy, relegated exclusively to inside pages—so that the connection between the boycott of 1962 and the marches of 1963 never became clear to most whites. The boycott had been produced by the failure of the negotiations between the black and white moderates in the winter of 1961–62. But these talks had remained confidential, except for the one allusion to them by the Miles College students in their appearance before the city commission, so that their existence, and of course therefore their relation to the boycott, were known only to a few of the most prominent whites. And finally, the black moderates' effort to use these negotiations to integrate the store facilities had grown out of the rival sit-ins sponsored by the Christian Movement in March 1960 and the Inter-Citizens Committee in August of that year. But though the sit-ins were public events, virtually no whites—not even the business leaders who participated in the discussions with the blacks—fully appreciated the intensity of the rivalry between the two black organizations, as well as the power of that rivalry to shape black leaders' responses to the unfolding events. Thus the sequence of developments that led ineluctably from the sit-ins of 1960 to the demonstrations of 1963 remained almost entirely hidden from ordinary, and even from quite well-informed, white observers in the city. It was for this reason that so many whites believed that King had simply selected Birmingham for protest marches on his own motion.

Segregationists undoubtedly would have opposed the white businessmen's concessions to the blacks, even if the circumstances surrounding the negotiations had been entirely different. Yet it is clear that the specific circumstances that did in fact surround the negotiations powerfully reinforced the segregationists' resentments. Because so few whites knew anything about the incidents that had produced the demonstrations, or even knew the demonstrations' aims, therefore they could not understand why downtown merchants and businessmen constituted legitimate negotiating partners for the civil rights leaders; what gave them the right to conclude an agreement that seemed to threaten the welfare of all white people? Moreover, because most whites understood the settlement as a response to the demonstrations, rather than the demonstrations as a response to the earlier failure to reach such a settlement, the agreement seemed to most of them a knuckling under to King's coercion. It thus appeared to be an act of cowardice, which stabbed in the back the efforts of hard-pressed law enforcement personnel to hold the line against the illegal marches and widespread disorder that the civil rights forces had unleashed. And finally, the illegitimacy of the business negotiators was further emphasized for white residents by the fact that both of Birmingham's city governments disclaimed any responsibility for the terms of the accord. The commission was entirely sincere in its declaration; the initiation of the negotiations had taken the commissioners completely by surprise. Mayor Hanes denounced the business progressives as "a bunch of quisling, gutless traitors," and the settlement as a "capitulation by certain weak-kneed white people under threats of violence by the rabble rousing Negro, King." The new council was probably almost as sincere; Mayor Boutwell does not appear to have kept the council members apprised of what was going on. But Boutwell's own assertion was disingenuous. As we have seen, his executive assistant, William Hamilton, was one of the three negotiators appointed by the Senior Citizens, along with Smyer and Vann, and Hamilton had taken an active part in the discussions. It is quite inconceivable that Hamilton would have neglected to tell Boutwell about them. Boutwell's refusal to make any public acknowledgment of his connection with the agreement was a portent of things to come; his desperate eagerness to avoid alienating segregationist voters whenever possible would repeatedly inhibit him in the coming years from associating himself openly with efforts to reform race relations. For the present, his position further convinced the segregationists that the settlement had no authentic standing.

The *Birmingham News* both pandered to and validated these attitudes in its editorial comment on the agreement. "Birmingham people want to know: Who was negotiating with Negroes?" Because of the disputed change of government, "Birmingham was in a vacuum. Into this vacuum outside Negroes came and organized demonstrations." Therefore,

A subcommittee of the non-official Senior Citizens Committee met with Negroes. . . . These white citizens voluntarily talked about what local Negroes said they wanted. They established needed communication. They had no authority. They did not speak for *any* elected city officials. They did *not* speak for *any* citizens except themselves. . . . They knew they spoke *only* for themselves. They had no aim of committing, and no illusion they could commit, anyone to anything. They knew they could not agree with Negroes for you-the-citizen to do *anything*. They knew they could not do so for *any* elected city official. They conferred with Negroes on this understanding only. Negroes dealt with them necessarily on this understanding. Negro leaders knew as well as these white leaders that *all* these whites could do was speak *for themselves*. Negroes obviously accepted that basis for the discussion. They obviously knew nothing that anyone "agreed upon" was binding. They knew anything would represent *only* the conclusion and possibly the hopes of that particular white group. Negroes judged this, however, limited as it was, adequate. . . . This group of white citizens did *not* bargain away anything. They did *not* yield to calls from Negroes to drop prosecutions of arrested persons. They did not try to halt school authority action with respect to students in violation of attendance policy. If there are any changes in any conditions in Birmingham, in stores, in employment or otherwise, those remain to be achieved by individual action of private citizens on the one hand, or through court instituted actions for interpretation of existing laws, or by official action of a court-authorized city government which has not yet even come into being.

In the presumptions underlying this account, "you-the-citizen" clearly is white and was not represented in any way by the white negotiators. But "Negroes" evidently are taken to be a unit, and the black negotiators are depicted as accepting terms—and significant limitations on those terms—on behalf of their race. Such premises constituted an exceedingly unstable foundation on which to erect racial harmony.[165]

It took less than thirty-six hours to reveal how difficult it would be for the moderates to shackle the powerful forces that the demonstrations had released in the community. On the evening of May 11, the Ku Klux Klan staged a large protest rally in Bessemer; more than twenty-five hundred sympathizers attended. Imperial Wizard Robert Shelton denounced the businessmen who had accepted the settlement, and he urged all whites to refuse to trade with them. Shortly after the rally broke up, a bomb exploded at the Ensley home of Martin Luther King's brother A. D. Williams King, doing more than $7,400 damage to the $21,000 house, and about an hour later a second bomb exploded at the $200,000 black motel owned by Arthur Gaston, doing some $10,800 damage to the structure and injuring four people. There had been a time when blacks might have responded to such Klan outrages with fear, but the demonstrations had greatly strengthened their resolve not to allow themselves to be intimidated. It was a Saturday night, and the nightclubs and bars surrounding the Gaston Motel were filled with blacks who, at the sound of the blast, poured into the streets. There then ensued a riot that lasted for much of the night. Sixty-nine people were hurt, and property losses amounted to more than $100,000. The toll could well have been even greater had it not been for the efforts of the black Smithfield civil defense unit. Under its captain, postal worker James E. Lay, twenty of its members labored heroically until dawn to contain the violence. One of them, Sylvester Norris, succeeding in driving a city fire truck through the mob to a blazing building after a barrage of stones from rioters had kept white firemen from doing so. Lay personally saved the life of a white cabdriver whom members of the mob had knifed. President Kennedy responded by ordering more than three thousand troops to Alabama in case the violence flared up again, but for the moment it had run its course.[166]

On May 17 the Alabama Supreme Court heard arguments in the city council's quo warranto proceeding against the city commissioners. On May 23, in a unanimous opinion by Justice John L. Goodwyn—the former Montgomery mayor who had initiated the reform of the Montgomery Police Department—the court affirmed Judge Bowron's ruling that the commissioners' terms had ended. As we have seen, the court's precedents had actually long since settled the question at issue: whether the 1959 general act that allowed city officials already in office to serve out their terms in cases of a transition from commission to council or council to commission had by implication repealed the provision in the 1955 local act for an immediate assumption of power by the new city government in Birmingham. The purpose of local acts, Goodwyn wrote, was to carve out exceptions to the general system. If the legislature subsequently made alterations in the general system, those changes had no effect on the exceptions. Only a specific legislative intention to eliminate any exceptions could repeal a local act.

With this decision, the business progressives' long struggle to rid Birmingham of the city commission came to an end. The commissioners cleaned out their offices and left city hall that very afternoon, and the Boutwell administration assumed undisputed authority. For the progressives' original intention of ensuring a positive national image for their city, the decision sadly had come too late. Nevertheless, the final disposition of the case left the progressives facing an urgent new challenge, one that would determine if the city's image would become even worse than it already was. The fitting rooms in the downtown department stores had already been integrated on May 14, but all the other terms of the agreement were tied to the state supreme court's action. And so, against the background of violence and mistrust created by the bombings and riot of May 11–12, the decision of May 23 also had the effect of triggering the settlement's timetable. Within thirty days, the stores' rest rooms and drinking fountains were to be integrated. Within sixty days, the lunch counters were to be integrated and black sales personnel were to be hired. And if those challenges were not sufficient, proceedings in the federal courts shortly provided an additional one. On May 28, as we have seen, Judge Seybourn Lynne at last decided the suit to integrate Birmingham's schools. He refused to order immediate desegregation, and instead re-

quired the plaintiffs to use the mechanisms provided by the Pupil Placement Act. But on July 12—less than two weeks before the lunch counters
were due to be desegregated—the Fifth Circuit reversed Lynne's decision
and ordered that some initial school integration commence with the
opening of school in September. For the white moderates and liberals who
hoped to redeem the Magic City's reputation in the eyes of the world,
therefore, it was clearly going to be a tough summer and fall.[167]

VII. Shuttlesworth versus the Moderates: Round Three

Things seemed at first to be going reasonably well, however. On May 19,
the Birmingham school board, appointed by Connor, voted to expel 1,081
black students for having been arrested in the course of participating in
the demonstrations. The students appealed to federal court, but on the
morning of May 22, Judge Clarence Allgood sustained the school board's
action. However, that same evening, in a truly extraordinary action, Fifth
Circuit Chief Judge Elbert Tuttle, acting alone, reversed Judge Allgood's
decision and ordered the students readmitted. This judgment kept the
settlement on course. On June 5, two weeks after the new city government
gained authority, Birmingham's principal hotel, the Tutwiler, began accepting black guests, the first voluntary integration in the city since that
of the elevators a decade earlier. On May 23, the same day the state supreme court rendered its judgment in the change-of-government suit, the
U.S. Civil Service Commission commenced a vigorous program of recruiting black applicants for positions in the city. Though the federal government employed more than five thousand people in Birmingham, at the
beginning of these efforts blacks constituted less than 1 percent of the
employees in any agency except for the post office and the Veterans Administration hospital. Despite strong and public opposition from Birmingham's congressman, George Huddleston, Jr., by the end of June fifty-
three blacks had been hired, nine of them to executive positions, and
another seven had been promoted. In late June the park and recreation
board voted unanimously to reopen the municipal golf courses at once,
and promised to reopen the parks and playgrounds as well as soon as the
city gave it the funds to do so. During the demonstrations the public library and the art museum had quietly admitted the blacks who had sought
to use them, and with the accession of the new city administration, both
institutions made this policy official. On June 23, in accordance with the
agreement that had ended the demonstrations, the downtown department
stores removed the segregation signs from their rest rooms and water fountains. And on July 23, two months to the day after the state supreme court
decision, the city council formally repealed all city ordinances and regulations that required racial segregation, in preparation for the integration
of the downtown lunch counters. Two segregationist councilmen, John

Golden and Eliazer Overton, had earlier pledged that they would never agree to any such action, but when the city attorney explained that under the U.S. Supreme Court's holding of May 20 in the sit-in cases, the existence of the segregation ordinances made laws against trespass unenforceable, even Golden and Overton acquiesced. The restaurants in the downtown department and variety stores were integrated on July 31. And though they were not bound to do so by the agreement, merchants in the four suburban shopping centers began to follow suit during August. By the end of 1963, rest rooms, drinking fountains, and fitting rooms were desegregated in virtually every retail establishment in the city, and a total of seventeen eating facilities had been opened to black customers. Segregationists attempted to organize a boycott of the integrated stores, and "Bull" Connor initially agreed to head the effort. But Connor's longtime mentor and friend, attorney James Simpson, warned him of the fact that he would thus make himself liable to prosecution under the Anti-Boycott Act of 1921. Connor—yielding, ironically, to the threat posed by precisely the same statute with which segregationists had sought to crush the Montgomery bus boycott in 1956—therefore withdrew his support, and the boycott movement soon collapsed. At a Christian Movement mass meeting on July 15, Martin Luther King jubilantly hailed the summer's developments as having reached substantially beyond the movement's original demands.[168]

Nevertheless, less sanguine observers noted signs of impending trouble. Shuttlesworth, for one, did not share King's optimism, and the enmity between the two men at this time was so apparent that even the police observers at the mass meetings could see it. But Shuttlesworth was by no means alone. On May 28, at its first meeting after gaining undisputed authority, the new city council had adopted an ordinance authorizing the mayor to appoint a broadly based advisory Community Affairs Committee (CAC). The committee had two purposes: first, to serve as a parent organization for a formal biracial subcommittee to continue the consultations commenced during the demonstrations, and second, to mobilize white community support for the unpopular initiatives that the Boutwell administration seemed certain to have to undertake. But the idea of doing anything unpopular greatly distressed the timorous Boutwell, and he postponed the appointment of the CAC throughout the early summer. It was his moderate admirers' first encounter with the mayor's temporizing disposition, a trait with which they were to become all too familiar, and it dismayed many of them. The moderates had intended to use the CAC's proposed subcommittee on the public schools as their principal organ for urging community calm in the face of the assumed necessity for school desegregation in September. But when, on the same day that the council voted to create the CAC, Judge Lynne issued his ruling declining to order anything more than the implementation of the Pupil Placement Act,

Boutwell therefore felt himself relieved of any immediate deadline to appoint the committee, and he at once retreated to his preferred policy of inaction. Only when the Fifth Circuit reversed Lynne's decision on July 12 was Boutwell compelled to move. On July 13 he appointed 212 community leaders, under the chairmanship of Southern Bell Telephone executive Frank Newton, to constitute the new committee; only twenty-seven of the members were black. The committee held its organizational meeting on July 16.

The fainthearted Boutwell could hardly have been encouraged by the reactions to his decision. At their initial meeting, arriving committee members were forced to run a gauntlet of angry Ku Klux Klansmen and National States' Rights Party members, shouting imprecations, under the leadership of Imperial Wizard Robert Shelton, and other segregationists were no less vitriolic, if less violent, in their hostility. The plan had been to divide the committee into an executive committee and ten subcommittees to examine various community problems; one of the subcommittees, with a substantial minority of black members, would focus on race relations, and the other nine, either all-white or with overwhelming white majorities, would look at such matters as the schools, youth, the annexation of the suburbs, municipal finance, economic development, and public health. But the segregationists' antagonism caused Boutwell to pull back. It was essential that the public schools subcommittee be named, in preparation for the schools' integration; indeed, it had been that crisis that had finally precipitated the committee's appointment. And Boutwell also named a nine-member, all-white executive committee, headed by food broker Tom E. Bradford. But the mayor decided to delay the implementation of the rest of the plan. The other subcommittees, including the one on race relations, remained unappointed, and the committee as a whole did not meet again until August 30.

Meanwhile, black activists were no happier with Boutwell's actions than the segregationists were. As soon as the city council had adopted the resolution authorizing the committee, the *Birmingham World*'s Emory Jackson had warned, "Our leaders should weigh with care any setup which might reduce them to puppets or make them merely a buffer leadership which serves the interest which holds the Negro group back." And when Boutwell appointed the committee's members, Jackson denounced the blacks chosen as unrepresentative: "we regard it as a backward step which will lessen the opportunity for the Negro group to move steadily and meaningfully into the mainstreams of the community life. For we suggest that some on the committee selections have participated in closed-door meetings which we believe hurt our cause and misrepresented our aspirations." Nor is it difficult to appreciate the sources of Jackson's fears. Only three of the twenty-seven blacks on the CAC—Edward Gardner, Abraham Woods, and Lucinda Robey—had any connections with Shuttlesworth's

Christian Movement. The rest were moderates, and in many cases they were the same blacks with whom the white businessmen had been negotiating before the change of government: Arthur Gaston, Arthur Shores, Lucius Pitts, J. L. Ware, Harold Long, Oscar Adams, Mason Davis, E. W. Taggart, Leroy S. Gaillard, John J. Drew, Joel S. Boykins, James T. Montgomery, and the like. There were seven educators, five lawyers, five doctors or dentists, four businessmen, and four ministers, along with a labor union official and a housewife. Jackson concluded that, if the twenty-seven wished to prove the black community's suspicions unfounded, they must unite in demanding explicit concessions, which should include at a minimum the appointment of black members to the city's various policy-making boards and the hiring of blacks as policemen, firemen, and other municipal employees. In fact, however, the black moderate CAC members were no more pleased with Boutwell's efforts than were the segregationists or the black activists. When the mayor announced the appointment of the committee's all-white executive committee, all twenty-seven black committee members joined to send him on August 2 a firm protest, warning him that "our position is that without full involvement and membership on all committees, our participation is needless," and requesting a meeting to discuss the matter. When Boutwell did not bother to reply, they sent him a second copy of the letter on August 29, this time by registered mail. But by that date, Boutwell's policy, effectively of passive self-annihilation, had begun to bear its bitter fruit.[169]

The delay in the appointment of the CAC left its new public schools subcommittee—appointed August 9, under the chairmanship of Methodist minister H. Frank Ledford—with less than a month to try to arrange a peaceful integration when school reopened. And the forces prone to violence would require very considerable persuasion. Though there had been no major incidents since the bombings and riot of May 11, the summer's desegregation of store facilities had moved many white supremacists to increased activism. Both the neo-Nazi National States' Rights Party and the Klan had gained additional adherents. The Klan had perhaps eleven thousand members in Alabama, the bulk of them in the Birmingham metropolitan area. The NSRP, under the leadership of its information director, chiropractor Edward R. Fields, and its youth director, Gerald Dutton, made a particular effort to organize support among white high school students in preparation for what they hoped would be a general white boycott of any integrated schools. The party held a number of public rallies during July, and with the integration of the lunch counters it began picketing the downtown stores, passing out mimeographed leaflets urging whites to refuse to patronize them and reportedly urging sympathizers to assault and beat blacks who ate there. Four officials of the party—Fields, Dutton, Albert DeShazo, and James K. Warner—were arrested on July 31 in connection with these activities, but they eventually gained an acquittal. On August 15 a white man whom police suspected of acting for the NSRP detonated a tear-gas bomb in one of the integrated stores, Loveman's; more than twenty customers were overcome by its fumes. In addition, both these more violent segregationists and the more law-abiding ones joined together in a rapidly growing new organization, United Americans for Conservative Government. Founded in August 1962 by a plumber and unsuccessful candidate for the city commission, William A. Morgan, the United Americans at the beginning of 1963 had fewer than five hundred members, but following the May demonstrations they gained the vigorous support of former mayor Arthur Hanes and quickly became an influential force in municipal life. By the end of August their membership had grown to sixty-three hundred. The United Americans, the already active White Citizens' Council, and a third white supremacist group, the Birmingham Regional Association for Information and Needs (BRAIN), under the chairmanship of the Reverend George Fisher, all undertook to rally electoral opposition to any further white concessions. These developments during the course of the summer presaged the disastrous failure of the Ledford subcommittee's efforts.[170]

On August 19, U.S. District Judge Clarence Allgood accepted an exceedingly modest plan for the integration of Birmingham's schools beginning September 4. As the Fifth Circuit had specifically ordered, the plan provided for the admission of plaintiff James Armstrong's two sons, Dwight and Floyd, to the white elementary school located directly across the street from their home. Other than these two students, however, the board agreed, and the court accepted, only that it would consider without racial discrimination the applications of black high school seniors who sought transfers under the Pupil Placement Act. And on this basis, the board eventually admitted two black girls, Patricia Marcus and Josephine Powell, to West End High School and a black boy, Richard A. Walker, to Ramsay High School. But this beginning, though tiny and tentative, was nevertheless too much for the city's segregationists. Klansmen responded to Judge Allgood's acceptance on August 19 of the integration plan by bombing on August 20 the Smithfield home of black attorney Arthur Shores—who, though one of Birmingham's most conservative black leaders, had come to be thought of by white supremacists as among the city's leading integrationists because of his many federal court victories against racial discrimination, stretching back for a quarter of a century. The bombing did more than $7,200 damage to the $40,000 house. After the explosion, a mob of one to two thousand blacks gathered, and a full-scale riot erupted in the area. It lasted for two and a half hours, until the Reverend A. D. King and other black leaders prevailed on the rioters to disperse. Two blacks were jailed for hurling rocks at police and passersby, and a third for possession of a gun.[171]

The court order of August 19 and the bombing and riot of August 20 finally pushed the Ledford subcommittee into action. Eighty-five whites who wished a peaceful integration had met on July 11 to discuss how to prevent the schools' closure. But when the CAC was appointed on July 13, this group apparently had turned the question over to the new committee, and nothing further was done while the CAC was being organized. The Ledford subcommittee was appointed on August 9; it had twenty-three members, three of whom were black. It at once committed itself to keeping the schools open and to preserving public order, but it did little else until the events of August 20 had sufficiently emphasized the danger of the situation. On August 27 the subcommittee appointed three working groups to prepare the public for the coming desegregation. On August 29, Ledford arranged for Police Chief Jamie Moore and Sheriff Melvin Bailey to speak to two hundred ministers at the city auditorium; the law enforcement officials urged the clerics to use their influence with their congregations to preserve obedience to law. And on Sunday, September 1, a great many of them did so, from pulpits throughout the city. On August 30, CAC chairman Frank Newton called the full committee together, and he and Mayor Boutwell pleaded for Birminghamians to maintain calm and good citizenship. On September 1, both of the city's television stations broadcast special programs in which panels of municipal officials and civic leaders echoed these entreaties. The two daily newspapers added their editorial appeals. And on September 2, even Governor George Wallace, speaking to ten thousand at a Labor Day barbecue in Ensley Park, publicly warned against violence.

Unfortunately, this crescendo was matched by an opposing one—one in which other actions of the governor played no small part. Both the United Americans and BRAIN had been holding anti-integration rallies for weeks. They were armed with a state statute, passed in response to the *Brown* decision of 1954, that required a local school board, on petition of the parents of children attending a school ordered to desegregate, to hold a public hearing to consider permanently closing the school. Although the board did not announce until August 29 which schools would be desegregated, the United Americans and BRAIN were actively preparing throughout August to submit closure petitions as soon as the identity of the schools to be integrated became known. In the meantime, as we have seen, the neo-Nazi NSRP was vigorously recruiting high school members in the hope of organizing a white student boycott of the schools, and it had gained significant strength particularly at West End High School, whose student body came entirely from blue-collar households. Following the bombing and riot of August 20, the NSRP announced a series of six rallies over the coming ten days, to culminate on August 31 with a motorcade to Montgomery to present Governor Wallace with a petition to close any desegregated schools.

When, at the end of the month, the NSRP's information director, Dr.

Edward R. Fields, arrived at the state capitol at the head of a motorcade of perhaps one hundred cars, the governor's executive secretary, Earl C. Morgan, and the commandant of the state troopers, Albert Lingo, greeted the anti-Semitic white supremacists at a meeting on the capitol steps and accepted their petition, bearing, Fields claimed, 30,000 names. On the same day, the United Americans submitted a petition to the school board from 595 parents, formally demanding a public hearing on the closure of the three schools to be desegregated. On September 3, BRAIN's George Fisher submitted a similar petition, with 12,000 signatures, to the school superintendent, the mayor, and the governor. At the same time, Fisher addressed an angry segregationist gathering outside the city hall. That evening, Imperial Wizard Robert Shelton spoke to one thousand whites at the Graymont National Guard Armory, near the elementary school to be integrated the next day. And the NSRP staged a large anti-integration rally in connection with its seventh annual convention, which was being held in the city. The day before, former mayor Arthur Hanes had spoken to a gathering in Irondale. Both Hanes and "Bull" Connor had frequently denounced developments in the city since, as Connor put it, they had been "kicked out of City Hall by the niggers." In June, Connor had urgently warned one crowd, "These niggers are on our one-half yard line and they got the ball. We've got to get the ball back."[172]

Such efforts were precisely what the Wallace administration wished. Wallace and his principal advisers—the vehemently segregationist executive secretary Earl Morgan of Birmingham, the shrewd and ambitious legal adviser Cecil Jackson of Selma, the bombastic and unscrupulous finance director Seymour Trammell of Midway; all of them, like Wallace himself, attorneys—seem to have been convinced that if the attempt to integrate the schools produced sufficient public disorder, Wallace could then intervene to close them by virtue of the state's police power, without incurring a federal contempt citation. Their immediate goal was dramatically to demonstrate to the governor's white supremacist constituency that he had done everything in his power to prevent integration. Their ultimate goal was to see the integrated public schools replaced with segregated private ones. And for Wallace himself—who had been deeply scarred by his narrow avoidance of a contempt finding from Judge Frank Johnson in 1958 in connection with his defiance of the U.S. Civil Rights Commission's subpoena of the Barbour County voting registration records—it was equally essential that any efforts to effect these goals be conducted in a way that would not subject him to new contempt proceedings. On September 2, Wallace issued a proclamation invoking the police power to forestall what he claimed to be threatened violence in Tuskegee, whose schools were scheduled to be integrated that day, and dispatched state troopers under Albert Lingo to close all schools in the town for a week. Just after taking this action, Wallace flew to Birmingham to address the Labor Day barbecue. As we have seen, his public message warned against violence, but he also assured the crowd that he had a plan to avert the desegregation crisis in Birmingham, just as he had in Tuskegee, and he urged his listeners to place their faith in him and to follow his leadership—by implication, rather than that of the more moderate municipal authorities—in the coming days. Despite this public condemnation of disorder, however, the prospect of disorder was essential to enable Wallace to act. As a result, the administration—which had always, of course, had extensive ties with the more legitimate segregationist organizations such as the United Americans —appears about this time to have initiated contacts with Birmingham's most violent whites. At any rate, at a meeting on the evening of September 4 attended by the NSRP's Edward Fields, the Klan's Jefferson County grand titan, Hubert Page, and other extreme white supremacists, and surreptitiously recorded for the police, both Fields and a Bessemer Klan leader reported that they had spoken to the governor within the hour and that he had assured them that their efforts to disrupt the integration which was to be attempted the next morning would have state trooper protection. With this initiative, Wallace truly was playing with fire.[173]

Wallace's plan for Birmingham, as subsequent events revealed, had two parts. His preferred alternative was to convince local officials that the situation was too dangerous to proceed. If the city government and the school board would themselves close the schools on an emergency basis and apply to the federal courts for permission to delay integration, the result would be to accomplish Wallace's principal purpose while also eliminating the doubts about the governor's authority in this field, as well as the threat that Wallace might himself become subject to contempt proceedings. But if Birmingham authorities decided to press ahead, Wallace was then ready to have a group of segregationist Birmingham attorneys, headed by three of the men whom he would shortly appoint to the new State Sovereignty Commission—Joseph S. Meade, James H. Faulkner, and J. Kirkman Jackson—file a petition with the Fifth Circuit in the names of parents of white children in the schools to be desegregated, alleging that without a delay in the integration, their children would be placed in imminent danger. Wallace would thereupon use state troopers to close the schools until the Court of Appeals had ruled on this application. Either scheme would make it unlikely that Wallace could be successfully accused of contempt, while at the same time emphasizing to frightened parents the threat to the safety of their children and thus likely causing a substantial number of them to look with favor on the organization of a private school.

Early on the morning of September 3, the day before schools were to open, the United Americans' William Morgan wired the governor to plead for the dispatch of state troopers to Birmingham and the closure of all city schools "until such time that they can be opened with segregated class rooms." Later that morning, Wallace telephoned Mayor Boutwell to attempt to browbeat him into asking the school board to seek court approval to delay integration until January, and into requesting as well that state troopers be sent to the city. Boutwell initially maintained that city police could handle any disorder and that he felt himself bound to support the school board's existing desegregation plan. But when the fainthearted mayor began to fear that Wallace might be questioning his commitment to white supremacy, he beat a hasty retreat and agreed to ask the school board's attorney, Reid Barnes, about submitting the federal court petition that the governor wanted. When Boutwell called Barnes, however, he found the attorney, though a strong segregationist, to be opposed adamantly to seeking a delay. Barnes understood that the school board had been very lucky to have convinced Judge Allgood to accept so modest a plan. Black lawyers had already appealed the plan to the Fifth Circuit, arguing that it was inadequate, but had not pressed for an immediate hearing; Barnes feared that a petition to the Fifth Circuit therefore was likely to produce an immediate hearing and an order for a substantially more general integration. For Wallace, this consideration was unimportant; he had told Boutwell that morning, "It is the idea [of integration], not the number of Negroes entering school. . . . If just one was going in, it would be the same as 101[;] trying to put Negroes into white schools [is the issue]." But the school board attorney's position forced Barnes to look at the question from a less absolutist perspective. Because of Barnes's opposition, the board rejected Wallace's request. And, meeting later in the afternoon, the city council adopted a formal resolution asking the governor not to send state troopers to Birmingham unless the chief of police or the sheriff requested them. By the evening of September 3, therefore, it had become clear that Wallace would not get the cooperation from municipal authorities for which he had hoped. He would have to turn to his alternate plan of action.[174]

The integration the next morning went quite as well as could have been expected. School officials had decided to register just the two Armstrong boys on this first day and to postpone the registration of the three high school students until the following one. Nevertheless, police were out in force at all three schools and took stern measures to maintain order. The NSRP and its allies did their best to disrupt the process. They went in a motorcade from school to school, and at each one they chanted and picketed. But they were only about sixty-five strong. Their initial effort, at West End High, remained peaceful. At Graymont Elementary, where the only actual integration took place, they were joined by some 150 spectators and attempted to rush police lines; this action, however, was unsuccessful and produced only the arrest of an NSRP activist for throwing a rock. Their third demonstration, at Ramsay High, did turn violent; the protesters assaulted a policeman, Lester L. Robinson, and four of them, two of whom were NSRP leaders, were arrested for disorderly conduct. The day's demonstrations ended with a bedraggled rally of sixty of the hard-core segregationists, held in a driving rain outside city hall. Though there had been a beating and five arrests, however, the protests had all been relatively brief and the participants few. The Armstrong children were both registered, and things looked bright for the registration of the high school students the next day.

The disorders, even though comparatively minor, were nevertheless sufficient for Wallace's purposes. He had earlier dispatched some 280 state troopers to the city, despite the city council's resolution asking him not to do so; he now ordered them to take up positions at the three schools the following morning and, presumably, to prevent the schools from integrating. He telephoned NSRP and Klan leaders—or so, as we have seen, they asserted—to assure them that their demonstrations the next day would be protected. At their meeting that evening, the neo-Nazis moaned with unconscious irony that the police during the morning had behaved like storm troopers. But with the governor's reassurances, they resolved to renew their efforts. Meanwhile, Wallace's advisers contacted the segregationist attorneys led by Meade, Faulkner, and Jackson and had them proceed with the filing of the parents' petition asking the Fifth Circuit to delay desegregation because of the threat of violence to their children. The attorneys then submitted the petition to Judge Walter Gewin of Tuscaloosa, who had strongly dissented from his colleagues' decision in July reversing Judge Lynne's refusal to compel immediate integration. Judge Gewin granted the attorneys an immediate hearing that night and took their plea under advisement.

In the meantime, however, extremist Klansmen proceeded to demonstrate how very dangerous were the governor's tactics. Wallace evidently had hoped to stir up just enough disorder, but not too much. But Birmingham's Klan, once unleashed, was not so easily controlled. At the same time that Judge Gewin was entertaining the segregationist attorneys' arguments, the Klan, for the second time in two weeks, bombed black lawyer Arthur Shores's home, still under repair from the September 20 attack. This explosion, more poorly placed than the first one, did less than $1,200 additional damage to the house. But the riot that followed was far bloodier. As before, angry blacks soon filled the streets of the Smithfield section and began hurling rocks, bricks, and bottles at police and passing whites. Four policemen, six other whites, and eleven blacks eventually were injured, and one young black man, John Coley, was killed. Police initially reported that Coley had burst from a nearby house firing a gun; he was shot in the neck, side, and head. But when investigation revealed that Coley had actually been an unarmed spectator, officers changed their story; they now said, and the coroner accepted, that all of Coley's wounds had been produced by stray pellets falling from shotgun shells as police fired over the rioters' heads. After some ninety minutes, authorities finally succeeded in restoring order.

The bombing, Coley's death, and the twenty-one injuries allowed the Wallace administration to return to its preferred strategy. Armed now with convincing evidence that the community might be standing on the verge of chaos, the governor and his aides spent the early-morning hours after the riot telephoning Birmingham school board members and officials. Superintendent Theo Wright initially refused to poll the board, but the board's attorney, Reid Barnes, finally agreed to do so, and the four board members agreed just before dawn to close the schools temporarily and to join the segregationist attorneys' petition to delay integration that had been submitted to Judge Gewin the previous evening. Superintendent Wright was also instructed to wake Gewin with an urgent call and tell him personally of the board's fear that widespread violence might erupt. The administration announced its victory in Montgomery at 4:20 A.M. Wallace had already instructed state troopers on his own authority to take up positions at the desegregated schools, but now he was able to order them to displace the city police and enforce the school board's decree.

The schools remained closed on Thursday, September 5, and Friday, September 6, and would have been closed in any case, of course, over the weekend of September 7 and 8. In the meantime, on September 6, Judge Gewin, joined by Judges John Minor Wisdom and Griffin Bell, rejected the parents' and school board's petition to delay the desegregation. "Law and order cannot be preserved by yielding to violence and disorder," Gewin wrote. And Judge Lynne, on motion of the black attorneys in the integration case, at the same time issued an order to Wallace to show cause why he should not be held in contempt, setting a hearing on the order for September 12. These legal developments were accompanied by numerous telephone calls and telegrams to the school board from more moderate white parents, demanding that the schools be reopened. As a result, board president Robert C. Arthur—a foreman at U.S. Steel's rolling mill and a United Steelworkers leader—announced that schools would reopen on Monday, September 9.

This recovery of their commitment to see the integration through on the part of local authorities, and of their counterparts in Tuskegee and Mobile as well, compelled Wallace to return to unilateral action. On September 7, in a speech at a Birmingham fund-raising banquet, Wallace warmly praised the white supremacists who had opposed officials' efforts to comply with the federal court order, and he publicly congratulated NSRP leaders who were present. On September 8, following a statewide television address, he issued an executive order commanding state troopers to bar the black children from white schools in the three cities, and he directed the detachment of Conservation Department game wardens, the deputizing of several companies of National Guardsmen, and the mobilization of Dallas County's volunteer posse under Sheriff James Clark to assist the troopers in their task. Later that night, the Klan expressed its support for the governor's stand by fire-bombing the home of black insurance magnate Arthur Gaston, though the damage was relatively small. On the morning of September 9 the schools reopened, but trooper commandant Albert Lingo personally barred black students at West End High and Graymont Elementary, and his subordinates did the same around the state.

Wallace apparently still believed that the claim that he was acting to forestall disorder would allow him to escape a contempt citation, but the direct disobedience implicit in this new action moved Alabama's federal judiciary reluctantly toward a confrontation. Judge Lynne had ordered the submission of Birmingham's desegregation plan, and Judge Allgood had approved it; Judge Grooms had ordered the integration in Huntsville, Judge Thomas the integration in Mobile, and Judge Johnson the integration in Tuskegee. Wallace had therefore managed to defy individually every single U.S. district judge in the state. After conferring by telephone on the afternoon of September 9, the five judges jointly entered a temporary restraining order against Wallace, Lingo, and the commanders of the state trooper contingents in Birmingham and the other cities, enjoining them to cease their interference with the desegregation. Federal marshals in Birmingham immediately served Lingo and his subordinates there, while marshals in Montgomery set out for the capitol to serve the governor. A telephone call from Lingo alerted Wallace to the fact that the marshals were on the way. There then ensued a comic-opera encounter. Wallace summoned his state trooper bodyguards and barricaded himself in his office. As long as Wallace had not been formally served, he remained at liberty to take countermeasures against the judges' initiative, which had deprived him of the use of the troopers at the various schools. When the marshals arrived, the bodyguards physically barred them from entering, while the governor inside was taking steps to replace the trooper contingents with three hundred members of the National Guard. At 1:30 in the morning, when Wallace received confirmation that the guardsmen were now prepared to take up positions at the schools, the diminutive chief executive at last emerged from his office, at the center of a circle formed by six burly state troopers, and this escort hurried Wallace home to the Governor's Mansion, where they stood watch against the marshals through the rest of the night.

Wallace evidently believed that the guardsmen could replace the troopers later that morning before federal authorities could learn about it, thus forestalling integration for at least one more day, but in the early-morning hours, word of the guard companies' mobilization reached the Pentagon. President Kennedy consequently was aroused, and just before dawn he signed a proclamation summoning the entire Alabama National Guard into federal service. Secretary of Defense Robert McNamara thereupon ordered the guardsmen to return to their arsenals and restored control of the schools to local police. At 8:30 on September 10, this night of maneuver therefore ended with the admission of the black students to white schools in all four cities. Now clearly outflanked, Wallace at midmorning finally accepted service of the restraining order and abandoned his resistance.[175]

The NSRP's organizing efforts at West End High now bore fruit. As soon as the two black students had registered, virtually the entire white student body of 1,440 walked out and commenced a noisy demonstration in the school parking lot. They were joined by some 200 adults, many of them NSRP members. Some disorders developed, and 10 of the adults were arrested. The next day, about 350 of these students returned to school, but the remainder, under NSRP leadership, rode in a motorcade from high school to high school, urging students to join their boycott. These efforts initially failed, even at the other integrated high school, Ramsay; they produced only another thirteen arrests. But on Thursday, September 12, and Friday, September 13, there were signs that the boycott movement might be gathering some steam. The motorcades continued on both days. On Thursday some students at the still segregated Phillips and Woodlawn High Schools joined the West Enders. That night, segregationists telephoned football players, cheerleaders, and other prominent students at each high school and both importuned and threatened them to join the campaign. The next day the small sympathy boycotts persisted, though it is not clear that they had grown in size, and at West End itself white enrollment had increased to 511. The school day ended with a rally of perhaps 500 young people outside city hall. Many of those present apparently joined in chanting, "Eight, six, four, two; Albert Boutwell is a Jew." BRAIN's George Fisher and the United Americans' Mary Lou Holt, the wife of one of the Klansmen who had led the assault on the Freedom Riders in 1961, addressed the crowd, and about 150 of them then stormed the mayor's office. While a number of the rowdy youths ground out cigarette butts in the mayor's carpet and one young man climbed atop the mayor's desk to wave a Confederate battle flag, a frightened Mayor Boutwell congratulated the intruders on their law-abiding attitudes.[176]

It was against this background of clear evidence that the effort to generate a white boycott of the integrated schools had arrived at a critical juncture that a group of extremist Klansmen reached the conclusion that a decisive public strike to overawe blacks and rally white supremacist sentiment had become essential. And since for the Klan the heart of the segregationist commitment was racial subordination maintained by force, the path to white unity and black submission as they saw it lay through their willingness to turn to violence when the cause demanded it. In this belief, of course, they had their region's past on their side; the quite general white acceptance of lynching as late as the early twentieth century was proof of that fact. That their effort to muster the resistance should actually have produced such widespread disapprobation, even among those who shared their goals, was an indication perhaps of the nature of the genuine progress that had occurred in southern race relations since World War I: white supremacy was seldom willing now to acknowledge its savage foundations. But the Klansmen were not yet fully aware of the extent to which their beliefs had been left behind, and Governor Wallace's active encouragement of militant white defiance in the preceding weeks had further obscured this development for them in any case.

Therefore, in the early-morning hours of Sunday, September 15, several Klansmen placed a bomb with a crude timing device under the side steps of the Sixteenth Street Baptist Church, the church that had served as the headquarters of the black demonstrations during April and early May. The leader of the Klan party was Robert E. Chambliss, the same man who had been involved in the Smithfield bombings of 1949 and 1950; who had been indicted for, but acquitted of, the masked flogging of the madam of a disorderly house at the same time; who had been charged with rioting during Autherine Lucy's attempt to enroll at the University of Alabama in 1956 and had subsequently sued Lucy for libel, asking for a million dollars, because she had accused him of having conspired to prevent her from becoming a student there; and who had been a leader of the assaults on Fred Shuttlesworth and Lamar Weaver at the Birmingham train station in 1957. When the bomb detonated later that morning, there were some two hundred black worshippers, at least eighty of them children, in the church. Four young girls in the basement Sunday school classrooms—Cynthia Wesley, Carole Robertson, Addie Mae Collins, all fourteen, and Denise McNair, eleven—were crushed to death, and twenty other persons were injured. The blast did almost $45,000 in damage to the $100,000 edifice. During the afternoon, widespread disorders began to develop. There were two major fires in black sections, and groups of blacks threw rocks and bricks at passing whites. Officer Jack Parker, the president of the Birmingham chapter of the Fraternal Order of Police, came upon one such incident and ordered sixteen-year-old Johnnie Robinson to halt. When Robinson instead attempted to run away, Officer Parker shot him in the back. The NSRP had scheduled an anti-integration rally for that afternoon, but because of the disorders, party officials told the one thousand people who had gathered to go home. As two of the NSRP's youthful supporters, Eagle Scouts Michael L. Farley and Larry Joe Sims, both sixteen and Phillips High School students, were returning from the rally on a motor scooter, they happened past two black brothers, James Ware, Jr., sixteen, and Virgil Ware, thirteen; James Ware was pedaling a bicycle, and Virgil was riding on the handlebars. Sims—believing, he said, that the Wares would throw rocks at him and Farley—took out a pistol and shot Virgil Ware twice, killing him. The deaths of Robinson and Ware were joined later that afternoon by the wounding of a third black, Charles Lane. The following night there were fires throughout the city.

Ironically, these dark events brought a halt to the protests against school integration in Birmingham. Mayor Boutwell, who had burst into tears when told about the bombing, issued a statement pleading that "the tragedy of this Sunday morning . . . not be compounded by more senseless trouble tonight. Let every citizen who is not required by absolute necessity to be on the streets, to stay at home. Let every one of them pray and think. Tomorrow, I urge as strongly as I know how, for the children of Birmingham to get about the business of their education and leave this fearful task [of dealing with integration] to the School Board and their attorneys, and to our law enforcement officers." And the man who would succeed Boutwell, Councilman George G. Seibels, speaking for the council, the police, and the sheriff, warned at the same time, "Parents of all school children are urged to see that their children refrain from public demonstrations of any kind. Driving around the streets could provoke serious trouble, resulting in possible death or injury. Our police and other law enforcement agencies cannot be responsible for the safety of children if they are allowed to roam the streets, walking or in cars. The members of the Birmingham Board of Education have stated today that all Birmingham schools will be open and the children fully protected." Frightened white parents apparently heeded these admonitions, and parental demands, coupled with stern pressure from the police, forced the abandonment of the segregationists' motorcades and picketing when school reopened. Thereafter, order gradually returned to the city's classrooms.

And so Birmingham's schools had begun the process of integration. Five young blacks were in white schools; seven young blacks had given their lives to make it possible. The balance sheet was hardly encouraging. Nor had the resistance gone away. During the fall a group of segregationists which included the parents of the West End High boycotters organized, with the vigorous support of Governor Wallace, to establish two white private schools, Jefferson Academy and Hoover Academy. But the integration proved irreversible. At the end of May 1964, the three black high school seniors who had been admitted in September were graduated from the two formerly segregated secondary schools. That summer thirty black students applied to transfer to white schools, and the board of education allowed seven of them to do so.[177]

In the meantime, the church bombing and the six deaths on September 15, together with the September 4 death of John Coley, had once again aroused the entire black community's outrage at law enforcement's inability—and too often, reluctance—to protect blacks from racial violence, and had therefore once more renewed the decade-old demands for the hiring of black policemen. Mobile, which had hired its first black officers at the same time that the Interracial Committee had first broached the idea in Birmingham, now had twenty-five of them, as well as a like number of black firemen, seven black traffic patrolwomen, and several black sheriff's deputies, while all of these agencies in Birmingham remained exclusively white. Shuttlesworth, who as we have seen had initially established his civil rights credentials by advocating this reform, stridently took it up again. But his more conservative rivals in the Inter-Citizens Committee, who had from the committee's beginning had a special interest in exposing police misconduct, were no less insistent on the subject. It was the one matter on which all black leaders were completely united.

Despite this unity in support of the policy, however, the actions of the Kennedy administration would shortly produce an open breach between the two black factions. As a part of their call for black policemen, Shuttlesworth, King, and Abernathy had also urged that in the interim federal troops be dispatched to the city. The administration apparently was loath to take an action that would drag it further into Birmingham's tangled affairs, but it did want to indicate its sympathy. Assistant Attorneys General Burke Marshall and Louis F. Oberdorfer therefore prepared a memorandum suggesting that the president appoint a number of nationally prominent individuals as mediators to reestablish talks between blacks and whites in the city. Marshall, of course, had served just this role in brokering the May accords, and Oberdorfer, a Birmingham native whose father had played a significant role in 1946 in the struggle to have Jefferson County's residential segregation ordinances declared unconstitutional, had taken charge of a regionwide Justice Department effort initiated in the summer of 1963 to persuade white business progressives to take the lead in eliminating racial barriers in commercial establishments. Both men believed deeply that the key to peaceful racial progress in the South was the animation of the moderates in its cities. A principal problem in Birmingham, they wrote, was that "white leaders do not seem to sense the urgency of the Negro fears or the validity of their complaints. Many white leaders," they correctly observed, "continue to blame the difficulties on the Reverend Martin Luther King, [the] Reverend Fred Shuttlesworth and federal interference, or focus entirely on the bombers without reflection on the full implications of continued segregation, discrimination and hostility toward federal law." The mediators should critically examine the role of law enforcement in the city, press the investigation of the bombings, and determine if federal troops were actually needed. But beyond those actions, their chief aim should be to "establish and perfect communication between the white and Negro leadership . . . determining what is necessary to cause white and Negro leaders to sit down together and then hold[ing] such a meeting or series of meetings." Later on the same day that Marshall and Oberdorfer submitted their memorandum, President

Kennedy met with a black delegation composed largely of Birminghamians but headed by King and, in reply to their request for troops, announced that he would instead appoint two of the mediators whom Marshall and Oberdorfer had suggested, former West Point football coach Earl H. "Red" Blaik and former secretary of the army Kenneth C. Royall, a law partner of former attorney general and future secretary of state William P. Rogers. Kennedy at the same time invited a group of influential white Birminghamians to meet with him at the White House.[178]

The president, Blaik, and Royall met with the white Birmingham delegation—led by Councilman Don Hawkins and the mayor's executive assistant, William Hamilton—on September 23. The formal statements which each member of the delegation submitted bore out fully the characterization of prominent whites' sentiments that had been contained in the Marshall and Oberdorfer memorandum. They were unanimous in believing that, as Mayor Boutwell himself put it in a statement the next day, "The lines of communication between our local citizens have been hampered largely by professional outsiders who thrive on the fruits of tension and unrest." Despite this unpromising beginning, however, Blaik and Royall, when they flew to Birmingham on September 24, devoted themselves largely to attempting to engage white business leaders and white and black moderates. On the morning of their arrival they met with white industrialists, including U.S. Steel's Arthur V. Wiebel, Hayes Aircraft's Lewis F. Jeffers, Vulcan Materials' Bernard A. "Barney" Monaghan, and former mayor Cooper Green of Alabama Power. That afternoon they conferred with seven blacks associated with the opposition to Shuttlesworth: Arthur Shores, Arthur Gaston, John Drew, Leroy S. Gaillard, the Reverend J. L. Ware, Lucius Pitts, and Orzell Billingsley. Black leaders outside the InterCitizens Committee group were soon complaining about the difficulty of getting to see the emissaries.

Fred Shuttlesworth was not in any case a man to accept quietly actions that threatened to relegate him to the sidelines, but his resentment was rendered considerably more acute by his long-running dispute with the black moderates over the genuine path to racial progress. He was convinced that the sort of private negotiations that Blaik and Royall, at the Kennedy administration's behest, were encouraging would lead only to seduction and betrayal by cunning, insincere whites. Only when blacks were in a position to compel concessions from whites and to force whites to live up to them would an agreement produce real reforms. Even the May accords had not yet been fully implemented—very probably, as Shuttlesworth saw matters, because whites no longer sufficiently feared a resumption of united black pressure. Shuttlesworth's apprehensions therefore mounted as Blaik's and Royall's efforts increasingly seemed to be encountering some success.

The school integration crisis had already moved some white moder ates to brave publicity. In early September, a group of white clergy led by Baptist John Buchanan, a future congressman, and Episcopalian John C. Turner had come together to persuade the city's congregations to pledge funds for a reward to apprehend the culprits in the two bombings of Arthur Shores's home. After the church bombing, this group arranged to have all churches in Birmingham join in a solemn tolling of their bells at noon on each day throughout the following week. And, expanding its membership to include blacks, it undertook to raise funds for the funeral expenses of the murdered girls and the repair of the church. These and similar public acknowledgments of the church bombing's special horror served to bring other moderates and liberals out of the shadows. Quiet pressure from Royall and Blaik, once they arrived, assisted this process. On September 28, fifty-three white Birmingham attorneys published a call for obedience to laws and court decisions, even when they were unpopular, and specifically included decisions of the U.S. Supreme Court in their declaration. At the same time, the Young Men's Business Club, in a statement drafted by David Vann and sent to the *Birmingham News,* went even further, saying that blacks were "entitled, as a matter of simple fairness, to all of the rights and opportunities before the law possessed by any of us," and affirming that "the Supreme Court's decision in the school [segregation] cases was true and just and could not ultimately have been otherwise." And it went on to urge that blacks be hired as police officers and that the planned group relations subcommittee of the Community Affairs Committee finally be activated. On October 3, in a genuine achievement for the Royall-Blaik mediation, the group relations subcommittee held its organizational meeting. Mayor Boutwell and CAC chairman Frank Newton appointed Episcopal bishop C. C. J. Carpenter, one of the city's most prominent moderates and the man who had initially headed the Interracial Committee a decade earlier, as the subcommittee's chairman. The subcommittee's fifteen white and ten black members elected Roman Catholic bishop Joseph A. Durick and the Inter-Citizens Committee's J. L. Ware as vice-chairmen. Of the blacks appointed to the subcommittee, two—the Reverends Edward Gardner and Abraham Woods—were associated with Shuttlesworth's Christian Movement and the remaining seven were moderates allied with Ware. On October 6, in a full-page advertisement in the *Birmingham Post-Herald,* ninety prominent white business, professional, and civic leaders, joined by forty-four of the area's major employers, endorsed the hiring of black policemen. And at its second meeting, on October 11, the group relations subcommittee unanimously adopted a resolution calling on the mayor and council for a public commitment to employ blacks as police officers as soon as they had passed the civil service examination and been certified as eligible by the personnel board. At about the same time, two of the three members of the incoming Jefferson County Board of Voting Registrars, who took office on October 1, privately pledged themselves to register black applicants without discrimination, and over the next three months fewer than 10 percent of the blacks applying were rejected. By October 9, the ever-skeptical Emory Jackson of the *Birmingham World* was willing to venture, "Faint but unmistakable signs of potential progress are beginning to show in Birmingham." The appointment of the group relations subcommittee, he wrote, "could be the turning point in civic relations in our city." Meanwhile, Royall and Blaik, feeling that their work was done, left Birmingham on October 4; on October 10 they met with President Kennedy and assured him that tensions in the city were now easing.[179]

Shuttlesworth responded to these developments by attempting to regain the initiative from the moderates. Martin Luther King initially cooperated with Shuttlesworth in this effort, both because the details of his knowledge of Birmingham's affairs were derived primarily from his conversations with Shuttlesworth and because he shared in any case much of Shuttlesworth's hostility to the Christian Movement's rivals; at a Christian Movement mass meeting following the church bombing, for instance, King, Abernathy, and Shuttlesworth had all blamed Governor Wallace's actions for the outrage, but King had also blamed "Negro business and professional men who think more of their money than they do of their race." Just after Royall and Blaik arrived in Birmingham, King and Shuttlesworth had joined in calling for a resumption of the boycott of downtown merchants to compel them to honor the May agreement to hire blacks in sales and clerical positions. And shortly thereafter, King, interviewed in Richmond, Virginia, was reported to have threatened renewed demonstrations to enforce black Birmingham's united demand for black policemen. Arthur Gaston and Arthur Shores, determined not to find themselves faced with a fait accompli as had happened in April, at once publicly rejected any further demonstrations; the Royall-Blaik mission had to be given time, and an absence of outside interference, to produce results, they said. Concurrently, on September 28, the Inter-Citizens Committee's J. L. Ware and C. Herbert Oliver, attempting once more to prove that black advances could be obtained by negotiation, sent a letter to Mayor Boutwell asking for a meeting to discuss the hiring of black officers. They were shortly joined in this request by the Alabama Democratic Conference, headed by attorneys Orzell Billingsley and Arthur Shores. Chastened, King flew to Birmingham to meet with Shores and Gaston on September 30. That evening a thoroughly aroused Christian Movement mass meeting adopted by acclamation, in response to the statement by Gaston and Shores, a resolution affirming King's and Shuttlesworth's leadership and demanding that Royall and Blaik meet with Christian Movement representatives. And Shuttlesworth assured the enthusiastic crowd that the downtown boycott would begin the next day. But following his meeting with Gaston and Shores, King declared that the press report of his having threatened to resume demonstrations had been only a misquotation; he said that he would wait to evaluate the results of Blaik's and Royall's efforts before concluding whether or not new demonstrations were necessary. Shores and Gaston thereupon proclaimed their support for King's general goals, and King left for Atlanta. At a mass meeting the following night, Shuttlesworth consequently had to announce that the boycott would be delayed, perhaps for a week. The next day, October 2, Shuttlesworth dispatched letters to Royall and Blaik and to the newly appointed group relations subcommittee chairman, Bishop Carpenter, reiterating his call for black policemen and asking for a meeting of his own with city officials. He then hurried off to Atlanta to try, it appears, to reinforce King's backbone. His mission clearly was a success; very possibly, King still felt guilty about having forced the May accords on Shuttlesworth and was therefore quite reluctant to betray him once again. At any rate, King announced on October 8 that if twenty-five black policemen had not been hired by October 22, the SCLC and the Christian Movement would resume demonstrations. And evidently at the same time, Shuttlesworth initiated the downtown boycott that he had been compelled to postpone the week before.[180]

Shuttlesworth's success in inducing King to fix a firm deadline for demonstrations produced a crisis within both the black and the white communities. Mayor Boutwell initially responded carefully, saying only that the authorities' decision on hiring black police "will be based on what is best for the entire City without pressure or outside interference from anyone," but in private he had already been resisting the white business progressives' pressure to take the action, and the outpouring of segregationist hostility to it following King's threat convinced him to issue a somewhat stronger statement on October 14. A "completely impartial study" was already being conducted, he said, "to determine what will best serve the entire city of Birmingham with the best possible law enforcement for all its people. No other interests will be allowed to intervene or defeat that objective. It is obvious to everyone who really wants the problem solved [that] demands, time-tables and deadlines which are both arrogant and unrealistic in view of civil service requirements, serve no purpose that does not hurt rather than help the chances of the very people to whom they render lip service." Boutwell's executive assistant, William Hamilton, added that hiring black policemen within two weeks was actually impossible because the personnel board required a minimum of six weeks to give and grade the civil service examination and to certify the eligibility of the applicants.

The city administrators' toughened stance followed vehement white supremacist opposition to the hiring. The Klan element, of course, was opposed to any concessions at all. Klansmen had greeted Royall and Blaik by staging a particularly vicious bombing in the Smithfield section on the night of the emissaries' arrival. A small bomb had been exploded to draw a crowd of spectators, and fifteen minutes later a large shrapnel bomb, intended to maim and kill many of the onlookers, had been detonated; only the very late hour had prevented the plan from having the desired effect. But such brutal protests had to some degree tended to keep more temperate segregationists quiet for fear that they might be lumped with the most unashamedly violent extremists. The issuance of King's ultimatum completely ended this hesitation. The United Americans resolved that "the hiring of Negro policemen would be directly appeasing outside pressure groups, therefore subjecting this city to future demands that could result in dissension among all peoples," and noted that such hiring would damage police morale and violate the campaign pledges of a number of city officials. A similar organization, the United Protestants, wrote the city council to denounce the business progressives' support for the reform. "The voters of Birmingham elected you to represent the citizens of this city only. . . . It is not your privilege to yield to pressure from people living outside of Birmingham, including men who own or operates [*sic*] business concerns here, even if it means moving their business some place else. We are sick of their threats along with Martin Luther King and Shuttlesworth." Ensley segregationist Robert C. Ward, a design engineer for U.S. Steel, wrote the mayor, "It is my feeling that you are being much more of a Liberal, in [being] much too ready to surrender all to the negros [*sic*]. Of course the money interests of the district favor that, but most of them have no vote in the city. . . . Birmingham's image is not nearly so important as the living conditions of Birmingham's people." And at the same time Ward wrote the *Birmingham News*, "Let [King] order the demonstrations, repel them the instant that they leave the boundaries of Law, in all ways available. If the demonstrations do occur, secure warrants for his arrest for Inciting to Riot. . . . The time has also come for all people who collect at the site of any undue activity to realize that they make themselves a part of a mob and should expect the same treatment as all others in the mob. Our police should not be held in restraint if missels [*sic*] are thrown at them[;] they should be ordered to shoot back[;] some one might get killed but in that case it would be one of the mob and would tend to minimize formation of mobs and their violence." And the West End Civitan Club unanimously resolved that "to employ Negroes, or any other minority groups, in order to appease outside agitators in exchange for peace and calm would accomplish the very opposite; it would mean eventually to accede [to] . . . increasing demands of extremist outside leaders and thus [would] lead to a breakdown of lawful authority." It also observed that "the rules and regulations . . . governing the selection of Civil Service employees would virtually have to be usurped or abrogated in order to comply" with King's demands. The club members announced that "we seriously doubt that the majority of our Negro citizens fear for their lives in our city and hereby refute the charges that the Birmingham Police

Force intimidates or threatens any citizen without a due and just cause." And they noted, with considerable justice, that although "companies, organizations, and institutions, of whom a number are not bona fide resident citizens of the city of Birmingham, have publicly urged or endorsed the employment of Negroes on the Birmingham Police Force," yet the call smacked of some hypocrisy because "they have not employed Negroes for responsible positions in their places of business."

Even more significant for city officials was the reaction of the city's own employees. On October 11, the Association of City Employees presented the mayor and the council with a resolution warning against "the dangerously detrimental affect [sic] which hiring Negroes for the classified service of the City will have on already burdened loyal City employees." It denounced "outside pressures and agitation by those not citizens of our City, who are not directly affected by a breakdown in efficient city services." And it concluded, "We are convinced that the employment of Negroes in any of the classified job positions in the city service will destroy the pride and dedication of the city employees generally." This frank assertion of racial prejudice was followed on October 15 by equally strong opposition from the Fraternal Order of Police, headed by the same officer who had killed Johnnie Robinson four weeks earlier. The FOP sent a thirty-member delegation to a city council meeting to give the councilors a statement proclaiming angrily, "Policemen are professional men and are not pawns to be thrown to the wolves to satisfy the demands of outside agitators. Would the businessmen advocating the hiring of Negroes as policemen be willing to set the example by hiring Negroes as tellers for their banks, sales people for their stores, secretaries for their offices, or other such positions in their businesses?" Clearly the officers thought the idea of employing blacks in such occupations completely preposterous. "With the hiring of Negro policemen, it would make it more difficult to get young qualified career men to apply for the position of patrolmen," they asserted. And in any case, "if you abolish your Civil Service laws to satisfy the demands of outside Negro leaders, your city will likely become a city of corruption and decay in a very short time. This will be absolute blackmail. It may be true that the failure to hire Negro policemen could be the 'excuse' for more demonstrations in Birmingham; however, if they [black leaders] didn't have this for an excuse, they would find another."

The segregationists' adamant response to the idea of black policemen was, of course, rooted deep in their region's history. The exclusion of blacks from all positions of authority over whites was the very essence of white supremacy, and for more than eighty years, police had represented the institution through which the system of racial subordination—usually enforced in rural areas by the direct landlord-tenant relationship—had been maintained in the more anonymous urban environment. But the uncompromising rejection of the reform stemmed also from the great gulf that divided black and segregationist white perceptions of the events of the preceding six months. Blacks tended to think of the demonstrations of the spring as having been suppressed by snarling police dogs and high-pressure fire hoses, though these tactics had been limited to but four days out of more than a month of marches during which arrests had remained quiet and efficient. And as they looked at the school protests of early September, slighting the vigorous police efforts to maintain order and arrest NSRP rowdies, blacks emphasized authorities' sympathetic remarks about the demonstrators and the mayor's willingness to receive them in his office. Thus, for instance, the Miles College student body joined to wire Mayor Boutwell on September 16, "We deplore the racial bias indicated in your allowing white student demonstrators to enter City Hall, stand on your desk, grind cigarette butts on your carpet, and in effect be congratulated for the nobility of their sentiments while you would not allow Negro student demonstrators even to reach City Hall [in May]." At the same time, white segregationists, ignoring the distinction between the almost always orderly marchers and the bystanders who had on a few occasions hurled bricks and bottles at police, thought of the spring demonstrations as violent race riots and the generally professional police response as craven appeasement, while regarding officers' actually quite similar conduct at the schools in September as therefore grossly discriminatory. The white supremacist Business and Professional Men's Association resolved on September 10, for instance, that "the law enforcement officers of the City of Birmingham and of Jefferson County, Alabama have assaulted and inflicted brutal and inhuman blows with loaded clubs on the White citizens of Birmingham, both men and women at the school demonstrations . . . whereas the Birmingham Police Department did these brutal and inhuman acts in contrast and unlike that treatment accorded the Negro people during the riots of Negroes last Spring at which time and place the Negroes used profane and vulgar language, spit into the faces of the officers and assaulted and violently attacked White citizens and officers with brick bats, sticks, bottles, knives and other deadly weapons"; the association denounced "this unusual discrimination of unequal, unjust and unfair treatment of the White citizens by the law enforcement officers." And the next day a segregationist, commenting on a newspaper photograph of a policeman arresting an NSRP protester, wrote the mayor, "When the Negroes were demonstrating in the streets of Birmingham . . . they got completely out of hand, attacked your police, run [sic] through town, shoved old people and pregnant women out of their way, and generally did as they pleased. . . . I understand that the Sheriff and Chief of Police instructed their men not to touch a Negro, even if he spit in their face. . . . Now, we find the shoe on the other foot. A few white people demonstrated at some of the schools recently, and I think the enclosed picture will give you an idea how they were treated. The picture of the officer with his hand around this young boy's neck shows evidence that he was trying to choke him to death. . . . [W]hy does the law not apply equally to both white and colored[?] This is still the South and not the North. I understand up there Negroes are seldom bothered, regardless of the law they violate." Feeling themselves desperately on the defensive, the segregationists regarded what they took to be the bulwark of social order, the power of the police, as having been severely compromised already by moderate commanders. The integration of the force therefore represented for the segregationists not, as blacks and white liberals understood it, a step toward evenhanded law enforcement, but the advent of black supremacy, the final delivery of the city into the hands of the lawless mob.

Given how general and how passionate were the objections to the hiring among white Birminghamians, city politicians had to try once more to convince the electorate that King's threat could not intimidate them. On the day of King's deadline, October 22, the mayor and council joined in explicitly rejecting his demand. Councilman George G. Seibels, who chaired the council's public safety committee, announced, "In the face of the present Civil Service laws, we cannot recommend that anyone be employed as a matter of special privilege only. Excessive demands for hiring any classified employees within a two weeks period were irresponsible, ill-conceived and contrary to existing Civil Service laws." And Mayor Boutwell added that exceptions from the civil service regulations "cannot be dictated by individuals or groups. . . . I have no intention of trying to circumvent those laws for any reason or under any pressure. At no time have I favored special privilege for anyone." But the mayor went on to "restate that there are no restrictions of race upon applications, examinations or qualifications under civil service statutes as they now provide." And Seibels too emphasized that the examinations were "open to anyone wishing to take them" and that the council was actively studying the advisability of employing black officers.[181]

In the meantime, a similar crisis was building among the city's blacks. The Christian Movement began holding meetings around the city and recruiting participants in the planned marches. At the meetings, speakers alleged—very probably with a considerable measure of justice—that many policemen opposed black officers because police were taking payoffs from black operators of gambling clubs and numbers rackets and thus feared that knowledgeable black officers would disrupt these lucrative arrangements. But Gaston, Shores, Ware, and their allies remained determined to prevent the renewal of demonstrations. One Christian Movement adherent, Joseph Williams, was killed in an argument with a black father, Jack Richardson, over Williams's efforts to enlist Richardson's children as potential marchers. On October 14, King and Shuttlesworth returned to Birmingham. The next day, J. L. Ware gathered his Baptist Ministers Association, and at his behest it adopted a resolution calling the employment of black policemen and firemen and the punishment of police brutality Birmingham's most urgent civic needs. But in a direct repudiation of Shuttlesworth and King, the resolution continued that the city's genuine challenge was to accomplish these goals at the conference table rather than in the streets, and it denounced any actions that divided the black leadership.

Faced with the prospect of an open revolt, King and Shuttlesworth summoned a meeting of influential blacks the same day, and the participants spent four and a half hours debating the situation. No agreement was immediately announced, but in the October 18 *Post-Herald* and the October 20 *News* a full-page advertisement appeared, almost certainly as a result of the October 15 conference. The 119 signers included Christian Movement stalwarts such as Edward Gardner, Abraham Woods, James Armstrong, Lucinda Robey, Nelson H. Smith, John T. Porter, and King's brother A. D. Williams King. But far more significant was the inclusion of prominent moderates Arthur Gaston, Arthur Shores, Leroy S. Gaillard, Oscar Adams, the Reverend Harold Long, Dr. James T. Montgomery, John J. Drew, Jessie J. Lewis, Wilbur H. Hollins, Mrs. Ruth Jackson, Orzell Billingsley, Maurice W. Ryles, C. J. Greene, Bishop Elisha P. Murchison, and others of similar sympathies. "We the undersigned," they proclaimed, "are all proud to endorse and support the leadership of our friends Martin Luther King, Jr., and Fred Shuttlesworth, in our common struggle to make Birmingham a better place for all its citizens. We do not consider these men outsiders to our cause." The advertisement warned, "The Negro members of this community believe that we are now in a period of crisis as great as any we have known. . . . Our churches and homes have been bombed, and no one has been charged with one act of bombing. Our children have been wounded and killed, and no murderer has been convicted. Therefore, we fear for our lives and the lives of our families. We are forced to stand guard at our homes. Negro Citizens find it extremely difficult to trust the agents of law enforcement. . . . At this urgent moment we believe that strong, fearless, immediate action on the part of our city government is absolutely necessary. The protection of its citizens and the allaying of their just fears is the responsibility of any government, and the government of Birmingham must not allow threats of reprisal nor unnecessary bureaucratic machinery to stand in the way of its clear and present duty. . . . We are not satisfied with a life of constant intimidation, segregation and fear, nor have we ever been." They demanded as a first step the employment of "a substantial number of Negro policemen for duty in this city" and concluded, "We are certain that the presence of Negro officers will help convince many persons that they no longer need to depend on their own resources for protection, nor turn to violence in search of justice. The morale of Birmingham's Negro citizens is at least as important as the morale of its police force."

This public declaration of unity was undoubtedly intended to convince the city authorities that the threat of renewed demonstrations was real, but the advertisement's emphasis on the actual agreement upon the necessity for black policemen, which had always been present, merely papered over the continued tactical differences. King returned to Birmingham on October 21, the day before the deadline he had imposed on the city council. At the airport, he told reporters firmly that if the council failed to comply with his demand, demonstrations would begin at once. But a detective who was present noted that his other comments seemed to indicate some irresolution. In fact, he was well aware that he probably could not count on the moderates' assistance. The statements by Councilman Seibels and Mayor Boutwell the next morning explicitly rejecting King's ultimatum thus had the effect of calling the advertisement's bluff. Immediately after the city officials' announcement of their negative decision, King went into a meeting with thirty members of Birmingham's black leadership. The debate raged for five hours. But at the end of it, Gaston, Shores, and their friends remained unmoved. King therefore emerged to emphasize to the waiting press that though the city had refused to accept his deadline, it had not actually rejected the idea of hiring of black policemen. In fact, he told them, he had inside information that authorities did intend to add several blacks to the force in the near future. Under these circumstances, he had agreed, he said, to withdraw his ultimatum, simply as a face-saving device for the city council. And with that singularly disingenuous declaration, King left Birmingham. He would not return.

At the Christian Movement mass meeting on October 28, Shuttlesworth was left to put the best face on matters that he could. He urged the continuation of the downtown boycott until the five department and variety stores had each hired a black clerk as, he believed, they had agreed to do in May. But, he said, the Christian Movement would wait through the winter to see if the personnel board would take any action to hire black officers. If no blacks were employed, demonstrations would be renewed in the spring; the "folks down at City Hall are walking a tight rope," he blustered. The following week found him threatening "that he would picket the homes and churches of all Negroes who were against Martin Luther King." But the outcome of the encounter was in fact clear to almost everyone: Gaston and Shores had won.[182]

The long-running philosophical and tactical dispute between the Christian Movement and the Inter-Citizens Committee was, however, never settled with the clarity of this particular episode. The moderates' suppression of the demonstrations did finally earn the committee a meeting with officials on November 13 to discuss allegations of police brutality. The committee's executive secretary, C. Herbert Oliver, and assistant secretary, Harold D. Long, headed a delegation that met with the city council's public safety committee, Chief Jamie Moore, and Inspector W. J. Haley, but the meeting did not go at all well. Oliver and Long attempted to discuss the numerous incidents about which the committee had gathered sworn statements through the years. Chief Moore would have none of it. The department had procedures for full internal investigations of any such complaints, and if a complainant lacked trust in them he could obtain a hearing by the personnel board, take out a warrant for assault and battery, or file a civil suit. The notion that a victim might be afraid to come forward was absurd; what would he have to fear? "We are familiar with Rev. Oliver and his activities for a long period of time around here," he fumed. "I don't intend for the Inter-Citizens Committee or any other organization to hamper the police department. . . . We have been criticized very severely in the last few months for the abuse the police had to take. I do not have any apologies to make. . . . I think it is just an effort to discredit the law enforcement agencies." Such attitudes made it unlikely that the quiet negotiations in which the moderates placed their faith would produce much progress.

Less than a month later, Shuttlesworth scored a real triumph for his theory of agitation. In the weeks after King's desertion the Christian Movement's downtown boycott had sputtered on, and on December 9 three of the five downtown stores—Kress's, Woolworth's, and Newberry's—finally yielded and hired black clerks. Only the two department stores, Loveman's and Pizitz, now retained an all-white sales force. Shuttlesworth jubilantly called off the general downtown boycott, just in time for the Christmas shopping season. He urged that blacks continue to refrain from buying at Loveman's and Pizitz and warned that the boycott would be reimposed in the spring if these two stores remained adamant, and that demonstrations would begin if no black policemen were employed. But for the time being, black pressure on the city was relaxed.[183]

It is clear that the black moderates had expected the hiring of black police officers shortly after the new year. They evidently had been given assurances to this effect by the white moderates, and told King as much at their October 22 meeting. Earlier in October, the city council's public safety committee had commenced a survey of the use of black policemen in other southern cities that essentially duplicated the one undertaken by the Interracial Committee in 1952. The survey's results, published on February 13, 1964, found many more cities employing blacks, and enthusiasm for their performance just as great. Moderates apparently had believed that once this study had been completed, the council would quickly move to adopt a formal policy statement favoring the hiring of black police. But on February 18 the council issued a statement thanking its committee for the report but concluding, "Civil service laws have served Birmingham and Jefferson County well, and no deviation appears either legal or desirable. We are convinced, as both the Mayor and Council have insisted repeatedly, that fair and impartial hiring can be had under civil service procedures and that such has been and is now our practice and policy."

The difficulty with this position was that only authentic encouragement from municipal authorities could overcome blacks' quite understandable hesitation to apply. The salaries of patrolmen were very low, and the initial blacks to join the force could likely expect undisguised hostility from their superiors and colleagues, as the opposition to the reform from the Fraternal Order of Police and the Association of City Employees had made obvious. Only if the new officers could be confident of the support of the mayor and council were they likely to be able to survive the ordeal. Moreover, the civil service examination was a difficult one, and only a large number of black applicants could produce a sufficient pool from which to draw the officers. Experience would establish this fact for any who doubted it. In the eighteen months between July 1963 and December 1964, a total of 382 applicants took the examination for patrolman, of whom 49 were black; 185 whites and 6 blacks were successful. Thus, more than half of the whites but just an eighth of the blacks passed. Of the six blacks who succeeded, three were eliminated by the personnel board for failure to meet other requirements. Of the three who were certified to the police department as eligible, one was initially rejected because he had been convicted of an offense in Recorder's Court, and when he was later cleared on appeal, he then failed the physical examination. Of the two remaining, one, Cicero Hayden, withdrew his name when he decided to move out of the city, and the other, Jonathan McPherson, an employee of Miles College, was eliminated when he failed to appear for a scheduled oral interview. This last occurrence became a matter of some controversy; McPherson claimed that he had not been notified of the interview, but police vigorously denied his assertion. All three of the eligible blacks had already been eliminated even before the council's February 18 statement. Thereafter, no blacks were added to the register, and in January 1965 it remained entirely white. These events surely demonstrated why a passive reliance on the normal operation of the civil service system and the initiative of individual black applicants, in the absence of strong official encouragement, was highly unlikely to produce the expeditious integration of the force.

During January 1964, presumably in anticipation of what it expected would be a positive report from the council's public safety committee, the Community Affairs Committee's group relations subcommittee had been preparing a report of its own. This report called for "employment of qualified Negroes by local government in such positions as police, firemen and in clerical positions and in similar skilled and semi-skilled employment areas." And it went on to suggest that the mayor and council hold a special meeting with "leading merchants and industrial managers" to discuss "hiring and upgrading of qualified Negroes based upon skill, merit and ability" in the private sector; that hospitals, hotels, schools, restaurants, parks, and housing, both public and private, be opened to blacks or provided for them; that the participation of blacks in civic, business, and professional groups be encouraged; that qualified blacks be assured of the opportunity to register to vote; and that blacks be afforded protection and security in their places of residence. This comprehensive and quite forthcoming set of recommendations was approved by the subcommittee and forwarded to the CAC's executive committee before February 12; the executive committee immediately scheduled a meeting for February 19 to consider the report. In the meantime, the council's statement of February 18, in response to its public safety committee's report of February 13, threw considerable cold water on the CAC's efforts. Nevertheless, the executive committee pressed ahead. It decided to make the group relations subcommittee's submission the centerpiece of a general review of the activities of all of the CAC's subcommittees over the preceding nine months. This lengthy report was completed, transmitted to the mayor, and released to the press on March 22. The *Birmingham News* printed it in full. It contained all of the group relations subcommittee's recommendations. And in an obvious response to the council's February 18 statement, it added to the recommendations, "The city government should make, and needs, a firm public statement of policy as to the above matters and [should] assume a leadership beyond the present status."

Mayor Boutwell's reply shattered the moderates' hopes. Waiting a month, he finally summoned the members of the CAC's executive and group relations subcommittees to a meeting on April 29, at which he read them an elaborate prepared statement essentially rejecting all of the recommendations. He had given the city council a statement shortly after the report's release in which he made it clear that he disagreed with its contents, but now he went much further, to a detailed, point-by-point repudiation of each suggestion and a sharp, if indirect, attack on the group relations subcommittee for "exceed[ing] their prerogatives for advising, and stray[ing] beyond the sphere in which they were designed to operate." Schools and parks were already functioning under integration decrees of the federal courts, he pointed out, and the city had no power to alter the decrees in those areas. Public housing and voter registration were both under the jurisdiction of independent governmental agencies, and the city had no authority over either of them. Restaurants, hotels, and hospitals were private enterprises and were free to accept or exclude anyone they wished. "No judgment is required here as to whether this is morally right or wrong. The fact simply spells out that acceptance on either side cannot be legislated or enforced. . . . [W]hile we accept readily and willingly our duty to fully protect all businesses in the exercise of a lawful business, we do not accept a plea that it is our duty to provide or generate them.

This is the privilege of people and business." The same principle applied to civic and professional organizations and to private housing. Clubs and associations were free to admit or reject any members they desired, and people chose to live in particular neighborhoods to be among those whom they liked and with whom they had common interests. "This self-segregation is imposed, not by law, but by choice, and it is inately [sic] the right of those people to so choose—and if they resent intruders . . . this is a matter of their individual consciences and not of law." Coming to the nub of his disagreement with the approach of the group relations subcommittee, he added, "Our job is to provide the public services of this city and to protect its security of person and property—not to prescribe its morals or prompt its conscience. Some there are, who vocally insist that this kind of leadership is the duty of government. I cannot agree. A request by officialdom cannot avoid the effect of compulsion, and compulsion in matters of conscience or personal choice is the very antithesis of freedom, and the impartial and impersonal administration of government." Finally, as to the hiring of black policemen and firemen, he emphasized once again the necessity to allow the civil service laws to operate without any interference. It was true, he said, that the city had occasionally "recruited applicants for highly skilled and tremendously responsible positions, such as the director of finance, certain engineers and planners," but recruitment for "positions less demanding in training or formal education" was out of the question. "I find it profoundly difficult to believe that in a community of approximately 140,000 Negroes, none can meet the requirements of these examinations and investigations. I cannot believe that any thinking Negro citizen would want his race represented in any job by someone for whom the standards had to be lowered, or someone so little dedicated to a civil service career that he had to be sought out, like a needle in the haystack, for special preferment." The mayor simply could not recognize the powerful social and historical forces that inhibited blacks from applying for such posts.

Boutwell's rejection of the subcommittee's recommendations in effect destroyed the Community Affairs Committee. The CAC had already been caught up in a bitter controversy over city taxation. Birmingham desperately needed additional revenue, and the new city council had hoped that a proposal from the CAC to this effect would shield council members from some of the voters' wrath when the new tax was levied. The CAC therefore appointed a subcommittee on finance and revenue, under the chairmanship of accountant Donald C. Brabston, and in December 1963 it forwarded to the CAC executive committee a recommendation that the city sales tax be increased by one cent. But a faction on the executive committee, led by David Vann, evidently feared that this action would persuade the suburbs to oppose annexation to the city, and they succeeded in having the proposal returned to the revenue subcommittee with instructions to study the possibility of imposing a 1 percent tax on the wages of all persons who worked in the city, whether or not they were residents of it. The subcommittee thereupon reversed itself and recommended instead the "occupational tax," as it was called, and at the end of January 1964 a deeply divided city council imposed the levy by a vote of five to four. It was greeted with an outpouring of opposition so extraordinary that at the end of February the council was forced to repeal it and substitute the sales tax increase instead. This debacle had been immediately succeeded by the storm of controversy surrounding the report of the group relations subcommittee. The two disputes taken together so soured the mayor and council on the CAC that they simply ceased referring questions to it and began ignoring its suggestions and requests. The various subcommittees gradually ceased meeting, and by its first anniversary the experiment had for all practical purposes been abandoned.[184]

In the meanwhile, Shuttlesworth had not waited for this drama to play itself out. Even as the group relations subcommittee was debating its recommendations at the end of January, Shuttlesworth had raged to a Christian Movement mass meeting, "The Negroes on the C.A.C. are not going to do anything for the Negroes. They are only going to sit there at the meetings. They are nothing but a brain washed black Negro, and if you can't talk to the Negro, shut up and go home." And in a succinct statement of his most fundamental strategic commitment, he had added, "Birmingham doesn't give anything away[;] what you get you got to fight for." He would never have expected Boutwell or the council to heed the moderates' pleas. Nor, indeed, would he have wished it, for a negotiated accommodation would have delivered a decisive advantage to the very black leaders for whom he had such passionate contempt. He therefore proceeded with plans to renew his own offensive. On March 5 he dispatched letters to Loveman's and Pizitz, saying that though the Christian Movement was "conscious of the untruthful negotiations with you recently on this same matter," it was nevertheless once more renewing its appeal to the stores to hire at least one black clerk. When he got no answer, he announced the resumption of the downtown selective buying campaign on March 9. On March 16, the Christian Movement appointed a committee headed by the Reverend Calvin Woods to contact other stores in the Birmingham area without black sales personnel and request that blacks be hired. This appeal, however, was met with general hostility, and the selective buying campaign was then extended to all the stores that rejected it. On March 19 the Christian Movement began picketing Loveman's and Pizitz, and on March 24 it added the picketing of city hall. In addition to the hiring of black retail clerks, it demanded the employment of black policemen, firemen, and city office workers as well.

But the offensive failed to stir the response in the black community on which Shuttlesworth had counted. City officials remained confident that his efforts posed no threat. On March 16, Mayor Boutwell and city council president M. Edwin Wiggins met in New York City with Kenneth Royall and Earl Blaik and, according to Royall, "told us how wonderfully everything was going in Birmingham, how fair they had been to the Negroes, and how little they feared the Reverend King's recent suggestion of demonstrations." Royall observed acidly that press reports were "not entirely consistent with the views of our visitors," but he and Blaik were unable to convince municipal leaders to adopt more forthcoming attitudes. Shuttlesworth's request on March 21 for a meeting with the president of the chamber of commerce and downtown merchants was not even given a reply. At the Christian Movement mass meeting on March 24, Shuttlesworth denounced blacks who continued to shop in the stores under boycott, and he railed against "these high society Negroes, like [J. L.] Ware and [Arthur] Gaston." He was contemptuous of the CAC report, published on March 22; it had been "written by a White man," he said, and insisted, "if you can't get an answer at the conference table, you have to take it to the battle field." When he called for volunteers to join in the picketing, however, he got only two. He had wanted to initiate mass street marches, but was never able to create sufficient support to do so. By mid-April his campaign had effectively collapsed.[185]

The moderates of the Inter-Citizens Committee and the militants of the Christian Movement had very different explanations for the events of the months from September 1963 to April 1964. From the perspective of Shores, Gaston, Ware, and their friends, the support of white moderate business and civic leaders for the hiring of black policemen in the days immediately following the church bombing had been about to create a breakthrough for this reform, but the public intervention of King and Shuttlesworth in early October, and their impossible demands, had placed city politicians in the position of seeming to yield to extremist intimidations if they endorsed the proposal. Gaston and Shores had sought to save the situation by openly opposing demonstrations, but the reform had been fatally tainted by King's actions; and even by the following spring, officials found it too dangerous politically to act on the idea, despite the CAC's endorsement of it. As a direct result of King's and Shuttlesworth's maladroit demagogy, therefore, only after the passage of many months would it again be possible to edge the city administration toward accepting black policemen. There was much evidence to support this view of things. Councilman George Seibels, for instance, had explicitly told group relations subcommittee member George G. Brownell in late October that "he might have gone along with the hiring of Negro police two or three weeks ago but that there was no chance of hiring them now because of the statements of Martin Luther King."[186]

As Shuttlesworth, Gardner, and their allies saw matters, however, white politicians—who had earlier merely been gulling the moderates—were moved to genuine attention only by King's threat of renewed demonstrations. They might well have been induced to offer concessions to avoid the protests had it not been for Gaston's and Shores's intervention, which convinced officials that the risk that there would actually be marches in fact was small. As soon as black pressure was thus relaxed, all progress ceased. Shuttlesworth's campaign of March 1964 failed because black disunity was now apparent to authorities, and they therefore did not fear him. The city administration would maintain the status quo as long as it faced no necessity to take black anguish seriously. The blame for the fact that there were still no black policemen lay as much upon Shores and Gaston as upon Boutwell and Seibels. The evidence in support of this perspective was equally strong. Three of the five stores that had been parties to the May accords had yielded to the downtown boycott in December and had hired black sales personnel, though months of moderate pleading for them to do so had earlier had no effect. And Boutwell's and Wiggins's statements to Royall and Blaik at their meeting in New York do indeed indicate that the officials were taking a hard line with Shuttlesworth in considerable part because they were confident that his efforts would fail to gather general black support—and correctly confident, as it turned out.

Though there is thus a large measure of truth entwined with the personal animosities that lent the viewpoints of the two black factions such intensity, well-informed observers understood that there actually were other—and to city officials, even more important—sources of the authorities' intransigence at this time. We recall that, for the powerful industrialists and professionals who had originated the idea of the change of government, the goal of inducing the suburbs to accept annexation had ranked just as high as that of improving Birmingham's racial climate. Indeed, from their perspective, the two goals were virtually identical. The consolidation of Birmingham's progress toward obtaining both a healthy civic spirit and a successful racial accommodation—and thus the city's triumph over Atlanta in the competition to become the South's great metropolis—required above all the full incorporation of its economic and social leadership into its municipal life, they believed. The artificial exclusion of this leadership from Birmingham's governance because of the residence of most of its members outside the city limits had to be ended. The changes that annexation would bring to the city's electorate would greatly strengthen the hand of the moderates and the business interests within it, and that strengthening was crucial to attaining for Birmingham the destiny that the business progressives envisioned.

The summer of 1964 would bring the decisive test for their dream. The new city council had immediately appointed a merger committee, headed by Councilman Alan Drennen, to seek the suburbs' consent, and in late 1963 the CAC had created a subcommittee on municipal expansion, chaired by athletic equipment dealer Fred W. Sington, to aid the effort. The chamber of commerce poured its resources into the campaign, and the junior chamber of commerce provided much of the effort's manpower. By the spring these forces had managed to obtain referenda on the question, five of them scheduled for August and one for September, in six surrounding communities: the working-class suburbs of Fairfield and Midfield to the west, Tarrant City to the north, and Irondale to the east, and the wealthy southern suburbs of Homewood and Mountain Brook. The summer months were marked by heated canvasses in all six towns.

In the meantime, as the business progressives struggled to reinforce and extend the transformations they had engineered during the preceding two years, the segregationists were mobilizing to roll them back. In early 1964, supporters of Arthur Hanes and "Bull" Connor, under the leadership of planning commission member Raymond Rowell, who had been an unsuccessful candidate for the council in the 1963 election, seized upon the furor surrounding the enactment of the occupational tax to commence a petition drive to force a referendum on abolishing the mayor-council form of government and returning to the city commission. Rowell began circulating on downtown streets a scurrilous mimeographed newspaper attacking Boutwell and his associates, under the title of the "Birmingham Truth." By mid-October the commission advocates had succeeded in gathering some twenty-one thousand signatures, and a referendum was ordered for December 1.

The twin challenges posed by the annexation referenda of August and September and the second change-of-government referendum at the beginning of December were, it appears, the principal source of the Boutwell administration's refusal to initiate any further racial reforms throughout 1964. During the first half of the year, city leaders feared that any concessions to blacks would anger conservative whites sufficiently to cause them to join the change-of-government movement. And once the referendum had been scheduled, officials desperately dreaded any action or event that might arouse Birmingham voters to take vengeance in the now impending vote. At the same time, race loomed large in the campaigns in the six suburbs. Birmingham was subject to federal court decrees integrating its schools, its buses, its parks, and other institutions, while no such orders had yet reached the suburbs. Opponents of annexation therefore often depicted merger as opening their protected white enclaves to black dominion. It seemed essential to Birmingham's officials to reassure suburban residents that whites remained safely in control of the Magic City's policies and fate. An integrated city police force, in particular, would have formed so clear a contrast with the all-white suburban ones that friends of annexation would likely have found themselves unable to overcome its symbolic value, indicating as it did the capacity of blacks to arrest and jail whites. Alan Drennen, the councilman who was leading the merger effort, attempted to turn the anti-annexationists' argument on its head by maintaining that if the suburbs failed to add their white votes to the city's electorate, Birmingham could well be controlled by blacks politically by 1980; thus it was merger, rather than its defeat, that would actually prevent the subjection of whites to black authority. But Drennen's prescient contention seemed so absurd to so many observers, across the entire ideological spectrum, that it served only to gain for the councilman—one of the most liberal members of the body—denunciation by the black press as a bigot.

The business progressives cared relatively little about the outcome of the referenda in the four working-class suburbs. Indeed, they had really wanted the annexation of these areas only because of their belief that metropolitan planning could be accomplished more efficiently if all the county's municipalities were consolidated under one government. Therefore, they were not excessively distressed by the rejection of the merger proposal in these towns by overwhelming margins of three to one or greater. It was on the two wealthy Shades Valley suburbs that the business leaders actually pinned their hopes. Homewood was the first of the two to vote, on August 11, and there merger was approved by just six votes out of more than forty-eight hundred cast. However, Homewood mayor E. G. "Bud" Walker, faced with the prospect of losing his job, at once commenced court action to block the consolidation on the ground that the legal notice given of the referendum had been inadequate. At the end of September he appealed this question to the state supreme court, and while the court considered the matter the annexation remained in abeyance. But the great blow fell on August 25, when Mountain Brook, the residence of most of the wealthy professionals and industrial magnates who had constituted the Senior Citizens Committee, rejected the merger proposal by 52 to 48 percent. All commentators agreed that the margin of defeat had been provided by young parents, particularly mothers, of school-age children who did not trust Birmingham's pledge that the community could retain control of its own schools and were convinced that the quality of public education would decline after annexation. Without the participation of Mountain Brook, as everyone involved recognized, the progressives' plan was dead. Therefore, when the state supreme court in the spring of 1965 ordered a new referendum in Homewood, the advocates of merger could manage only a weary effort, and annexation this time lost by nearly two to one. Birmingham was to be left on its own.

Faced with this crushing disappointment, the moderates had very little time to brood, as they were quickly plunged into the campaign to prevent the abolition of the city council. This crusade, however, had a very different outcome. The business progressives had deeply feared that, unable to include the vote of Mountain Brook as they had hoped, and with the Homewood vote counted separately and held apart to await the state supreme court's decision on the validity of the area's annexation, supporters of the mayor-council system were quite likely to lose. The system had received the approval of only 19,317 voters in 1962, and more than 21,000 had signed the petition for the new referendum. The December 1 poll produced, however, an irrefutable triumph for the mayor and council; even without the Homewood totals, the council took almost 64 percent of the vote, to just 35 percent for a commission and 1 percent for a city manager. These figures contrasted sharply with the 1962 results, in which the council had received 52 percent and the commission 45.5 percent. A jubilant David Vann called the results "the greatest victory for the people of Birmingham the city has experienced in a long time. It decisively defeated politics." And Boutwell and the council members called the election a clear vote of confidence. An analysis of the returns reveals the origins of the moderates' joy.

The general socioeconomic foundations of the 1962 and 1964 polls did not differ. The mayor-council system swept the black precincts and received equally strong support in the well-to-do white ones; enthusiasm for the commission was centered in working-class white wards, especially in Wylam and Ensley. But the contrasts between the two referenda were nevertheless quite significant. Only about half of the city's registered voters participated in the 1964 referendum, and this fact was itself important because it indicated that the city administration's strategy of taking no actions that would irritate conservative whites into active opposition had been successful. Though more than 21,000 voters had signed the referendum petition, just 15,000 voters actually turned out to support the commission form of government. But despite the fact that half the registered voters did not participate, the total poll in 1964 was some 5,400 larger than it had been in 1962. And this increase appears to have been the source of the council's greater strength. The vote for the commission fell by approximately 1,900 in the two years and the vote for a city manager fell by 450, while the support for the mayor-council system rose by about 7,750. If the decline in the vote for the other two systems represented a transfer of allegiance to the mayor and council, it therefore appears that every single one of the new participants endorsed the council. Who were these new voters? The moderates very probably had a strong suspicion.

As we have seen, it appears that one of the principal achievements of the mission of Royall and Blaik to the city in late September 1963 had been to obtain from two of the three members of the new Jefferson County Board of Voting Registrars that took office in October—the appointees of the state auditor and the commissioner of agriculture and industries—an assurance that they would register all qualified black applicants. A federal suit alleging racial discrimination had been pending against the outgoing board since the preceding July in any case, and the two new registrars, M. L. Bearden and Wellington Gwin, doubtless therefore felt it necessary to be on their best behavior. Between October and December of 1963, as a result, only 9 percent of black applicants were rejected. But with the new year, Governor Wallace's appointee to the board, Mrs. Nell Hunter, complained to the governor about her colleagues' conduct. She herself had never voted to register a single black, she raged to her patron, but Bearden and Gwin had virtually turned the board over to the NAACP. Wallace at once summoned State Auditor Bettye Frink and commanded her to rein in her appointee, Bearden. Mrs. Frink, fearing for her political future, then pleaded with Bearden to reach an accommodation with Mrs. Hunter. Thereafter the black rejection rate rose to 20 percent. But when Bearden was summoned by Justice Department attorneys on February 13 to give a deposition, in connection with the suit filed the preceding summer, he told them the entire story. The resultant federal scrutiny apparently kept the rejection rate from rising any higher. It is not clear exactly how many blacks obtained registration in the city during late 1963 and 1964, but the figures available to us appear to indicate that Birmingham's black electorate had grown by about 5,800, to some 14,000, between the two change-of-government referenda. This growth is greater than the 5,400 votes by which the 1964 poll exceeded that of 1962, and the estimated 14,000 black voters are more than the council's 12,046-vote margin over the commission.

We thus reach the true source of the moderates' relief. They had believed that the annexation of the wealthy suburbs was indispensable to the erection of a stable moderate majority in Birmingham. But the outcome of the December referendum indicated that the changing composition of the city's electorate would accomplish the task without the suburbs' assistance. Mountain Brook had rejected involvement, and the merger with Homewood remained doubtful. But though the vote in Homewood had gone exactly as the moderates would have expected, with support for the mayor and council reaching nearly 80 percent, yet the Homewood returns had proven irrelevant; the 64 percent for the mayor and council in the city proper had been quite enough. It appeared, then, that the newly augmented black vote, combined with the reliably moderate vote of the well-to-do white precincts in the southern part of the city, would be able to create a coalition capable of consistently defeating the segregationists— who still, of course, commanded a majority among Birmingham's white electorate—even if the suburbs would not help. The business progressives continued to wish for annexation, of course, and they would make another unsuccessful effort to obtain it six years later. But for the present, the combination of Mountain Brook's rejection of merger in August and the mayor-council system's decisive victory in December turned the business progressives' attention away from courting the suburbs and toward consolidating their ties with the black moderates who had suddenly emerged as their essential partners in the new anti-segregationist electoral alliance.

The December change-of-government referendum therefore became, very probably to the surprise of everyone involved, the great turning point in the history of Birmingham's race relations.[187]

VIII. The Moderate Alliance Succeeds the White Alliance

To a black or a white liberal who surveyed the status of racial progress in Birmingham in mid-1964, things would undoubtedly have seemed dark indeed. Shortly after Boutwell's rejection in April of the Community Affairs Committee's recommendations to improve the city's racial climate, the May Democratic primaries produced the election of "Bull" Connor as president of the Alabama Public Service Commission and his reelection as Alabama's Democratic National Committeeman. In the public service commission race, Connor came from behind in the first round of voting to win in the runoff over the powerful incumbent C. C. "Jack" Owen, taking 52 percent of the vote to Owen's 48 percent. Owen was as inflexibly segregationist as Connor and surely knew far more about the regulation of utility and freight rates, which was the commission's function, but Connor's conduct during the 1963 demonstrations had given him a vastly greater name recognition and had made him a hero among the state's white supremacists. In January 1965 he was inaugurated at a gala banquet in Birmingham at which Governor Wallace called him "a great citizen of Alabama and this country"; he would serve as public service commission president until a few weeks before his death in 1973. In the same May primary, David Vann was defeated overwhelmingly in a race for Birmingham's congressman by the incumbent George Huddleston, Jr., who in 1961 had joined Connor in actively seeking the support of the Ku Klux Klan. And though Huddleston would go on to lose to the racially moderate Republican nominee, the Reverend John Buchanan, in November, Buchanan's victory rather ironically was a product of the massive landslide in Alabama for the presidential candidacy of Barry Goldwater, a landslide based in large part on white Alabamians' opposition to the civil rights movement.

Weeks after the Democratic primaries, the three Klansmen charged in connection with the church bombing of the preceding September came to trial. The intensive investigation of the bombing by the FBI apparently had convinced Imperial Wizard Robert Shelton and Grand Dragon Hubert Page at the end of September to attempt to foil the federal effort by turning the culprits over to the state troopers. Through the good offices of the United Americans' William Morgan and former mayor Arthur Hanes— whose involvement with the United Americans had forged relationships that would eventually make him for all practical purposes the Klan's attorney—Shelton and Page arranged a secret meeting with trooper commandant Albert Lingo on September 29. At this meeting Page and Donald

E. Luna, a Klansman and Homewood estate planner, identified five fellow Klansmen as having been connected with the bombing, and the five were taken into custody the same evening. But this rapid action actually revealed Lingo's lack of much genuine law enforcement expertise. He presumably expected that he could obtain a confession through vigorous interrogation, but this tactic failed. And because the troopers had not taken the time to build a case against the suspects before their arrest, and prosecutors were required to charge and arraign them quickly once they were in custody, authorities in the end had been reduced to charging three of the five—Robert E. Chambliss, John Wesley Hall, and Charles Cagle—with the misdemeanor of possessing dynamite without a permit. For this violation they had been sentenced in October in Recorder's Court to six months in jail, but all had then appealed to Circuit Court. At their trial in June 1964, Judge Elias C. Watson gave directed verdicts of acquittal for Hall and Cagle, for lack of evidence, and the jury took little time to acquit Chambliss. Since Michael Farley and Larry Joe Sims had already received only probation in the killing of Virgil Ware, it now seemed clear that the violence that had attended the integration of the schools would essentially go unpunished.

Even the one apparent ray of light in this darkness was not unclouded. In July the new president, Lyndon B. Johnson, had signed into law the Civil Rights Act of 1964, the measure initially proposed to Congress by President Kennedy in direct response to the Birmingham demonstrations of May 1963. But later the same month, Birmingham restaurateur Ollie McClung had filed suit in federal court, seeking an injunction to forbid the enforcement of the act against his establishment, Ollie's Barbecue, on the ground that it was not engaged in interstate commerce. In September Birmingham District Judges Seybourn Lynne and Hobart Grooms joined Fifth Circuit Court of Appeals Judge Walter Gewin of Tuscaloosa in unanimously accepting this contention; the restaurant was not engaged in interstate commerce, they held, and in any case the act was not a legitimate regulation of commerce but was in fact an effort by Congress to end racial discrimination. This ruling would eventually be reversed by the U.S. Supreme Court, but that decision would not come until the end of the year.[188]

The situation in Birmingham during 1964, in the months leading up to the December 1 change-of-government referendum, would have seemed so bleak from a moderate or liberal perspective, then, that the sequel must have been quite astonishing. In the wake of Boutwell's rejection of the CAC race relations proposals, Arthur Gaston had already managed quietly to create a personal relationship with the mayor and had begun, with considerable tact, to move him toward a more forthcoming position. Within a few weeks of the victory for the mayor-council system, the city administration publicly revealed its new posture. At the end of December, the council voted five to four to appoint Arthur Shores's business associate, realtor Wilbur H. Hollins, to the Birmingham Planning Commission, making Hollins the first black ever to serve on a policy-making city board. And as 1965 advanced, even more such appointments were made. By the fall there were five blacks serving on municipal commissions, including Hollins on the planning commission; Shores on the board of the housing authority, which supervised the public housing projects; Louis J. Willie, executive vice-president of Gaston's insurance companies, on the pensions and security board, which governed the welfare system; and Mrs. Imogene F. Murchison, the wife of C.M.E. bishop Elisha P. Murchison, on the library board. All were pillars of the black moderate faction, and their selection clearly represented an effort by the white moderates and business progressives to cement the newly emerging electoral alliance whose significance the change-of-government referendum had made obvious. During the same time, Boutwell was actively engaged in creating the machinery to bring President Johnson's recently created war on poverty to Birmingham. Governor Wallace bitterly opposed Boutwell's efforts, but the mayor, aided by business progressive attorney C. H. Erskine Smith and black moderate attorney Orzell Billingsley, nevertheless pressed ahead. By June they had succeeded in organizing a joint city-county Committee for Economic Opportunity to run the program. From the outset blacks were a significant force on this committee—eleven of the city's twenty-one appointees and seven of the county's twenty—though that fact was in large part a response to federal requirements. Despite Wallace's interference, funding for the poverty program was finally approved in October. In the spring, the chamber of commerce opened its membership to blacks. And at this same time there was even movement on the vexed question of black police officers. In May, Sidney Smyer intervened with the mayor on the matter, writing him that though race relations recently had greatly improved, "I find, however, that there is considerable pressure being brought by outside Negroes for a demonstration here in Birmingham. Their excuse for coming is the lack of Negro police. . . . I know that you have publicly announced that if there are qualified applicants that they will be appointed. But I, also, know that you can't convince the public (outside of Birmingham) that in a city the size of Birmingham that there are no qualified Negroes that are willing and want the job as policemen. . . . You can cry to the high heaven's [sic] that you have done all you can to get Negro policemen, but the world opinion will laugh at you and Birmingham. . . . The local Negro leadership is stronger now than ever before. They don't want King to come here because most of these leaders are not in the King camp. My information from these leaders [is] that this is one excuse for him coming that they cannot overcome." Smyer suggested, as a first step to strengthen the black moderates' hand, the hiring of black women as traffic police at schools. The ever cautious Boutwell was at last persuaded, and in the fall he announced the employment of sixteen black and sixteen white women as school crossing guards. They commenced work on October 20.[189]

In the meantime, Fred Shuttlesworth had been deeply involved throughout the late summer and fall of 1965 with a bitter dispute within his Cincinnati church. A majority of his congregation, charging him with dictatorial attitudes and questionable financial dealings, initiated a movement to remove him as pastor. Controversy led to proceedings in the Ohio courts and eventually produced a formal schism in the congregation. But the rapid advances being made by his black moderate adversaries in Birmingham nevertheless forced him to turn his attention once again to the Magic City. It was essential, if his leadership there were not conclusively to be eclipsed, that he recapture the civil rights initiative. To this end, he once again turned to Martin Luther King, whose enormous popularity among blacks of every persuasion had always been Shuttlesworth's trump card in his battles with the allies of the Inter-Citizens Committee. King evidently declined to return to Birmingham, presumably because of the events of October 1963, but he did agree to send members of the Southern Christian Leadership Conference staff, headed by Hosea Williams. Williams and Shuttlesworth arrived in Birmingham in December 1965 and at once began planning demonstrations for the new year, to demand that the federal government send voting examiners to Jefferson County under the terms of the new Voting Rights Act.

The NAACP had been permitted to return to Alabama in October 1964, when the U.S. Supreme Court had at last given a final ruling in the case against it initiated in the state courts by then attorney general John Patterson in the summer of 1956. The newly reconstituted Birmingham chapter had quickly fallen into the hands of the moderates; it was headed by dentist John W. Nixon. The moderates now sought to use the NAACP branch to forestall Shuttlesworth's impending campaign. On December 27, at a meeting organized by the chamber of commerce, Nixon joined Arthur Shores, Arthur Gaston, and Wilbur Hollins to meet with Sidney Smyer, Coca-Cola bottling executive Crawford Johnson, who was the chamber's president; Jefferson County Commission chairman and former mayor Cooper Green; the recently appointed Jefferson County district attorney Earl Morgan, who was Governor Wallace's former executive secretary and a zealous segregationist; and the chairman of the board of registrars, W. M. Owen, who had succeeded the moderate M. L. Bearden. The black moderates and the white business progressives united to extract from the county officials significant additional concessions. The board of registrars had immediately halted the use of the state's voter qualification test when President Johnson had signed the new Voting Rights Act into law the preceding August. It met from eight in the morning to four in the afternoon every Tuesday through Thursday and had registered almost four thousand blacks during the month of December. But at a conference two weeks earlier, Assistant Attorney General John Doar had urged the registrars to add more hours. Therefore, at the meeting with the black moderates, the board agreed to begin holding its sessions on Fridays and Saturdays as well and to increase its staff from six to eleven clerks to speed the processing of applications. In January the board added two more clerks, both of them black, for a total of thirteen. Nixon's participation in what was clearly an effort to deprive Shuttlesworth's demand for federal examiners of a large part of its rationale infuriated Shuttlesworth's supporters within the NAACP branch, however. The resultant explosion compelled Nixon to resign the Birmingham NAACP presidency in mid-January. And though he was permitted to retain the state NAACP presidency, which he had held concurrently, he was forced to pledge that he would not seek reelection when his term expired.

Meanwhile, Shuttlesworth and Williams launched their demonstrations on January 4. Shuttlesworth demanded that the board commence meeting on Mondays and at night and that it leave its quarters in the county courthouse and begin holding its sessions in the various black neighborhoods around the county. Orzell Billingsley and the NAACP's Alabama director of voter registration, W. C. Patton, expressed public doubt about the protests, saying that a campaign to get blacks to apply to register would be far more likely to produce the desired results than marches in the streets. And a furious Arthur Gaston, who owned the building in which the SCLC rented its offices, gave the organization ten days to vacate the premises; the SCLC, responding that Gaston had sold out to the white power structure, refused to go. Williams threatened to organize a black boycott of Gaston's businesses. He attempted to replicate the SCLC's success in 1963 by recruiting black high school students to participate in the daily marches, but white authorities were ready for this tactic. The city and county school boards jointly filed suit in federal court, seeking an injunction to forbid any actions by the SCLC which encouraged truancy. On January 13, all three of Birmingham's federal district judges—Hobart Grooms, Seybourn Lynne, and Clarence Allgood—joined to sign a temporary restraining order to this effect, and following a hearing on January 24, Judge Grooms issued a temporary injunction embodying the same prohibitions on January 26.

The active opposition of the black moderate leaders had prevented the marches from gathering broad support among adult blacks, and the demonstrations, essentially limited after the January 13 restraining order to the Christian Movement's few most committed disciples, soon lost momentum. The SCLC's access to national publicity and its following throughout America gave it the power, however, to reach beyond Birmingham. The new attorney general, Nicholas Katzenbach, was eager to prove his sympathy with the efforts of blacks to become voters and his determination to enforce the Voting Rights Act fully; he was anxious, as well, to see as many blacks registered in Alabama as possible in advance of the state Democratic primaries in May, in which George Wallace's successor as governor would be chosen. On January 20, therefore, despite the faltering local efforts and the substantial concessions made by the board of registrars, Katzenbach agreed to dispatch twenty-three federal voting examiners, nine of them black, to Jefferson County; the examiners began work on January 24. And the result for the number of blacks registered in the county was dramatic. In their first week of operations, the federal examiners registered 7,000 voters, almost all of them black. By March of 1967 the total number of blacks registered in Jefferson had reached 63,000—up from 42,000 when the examiners had been sent in January 1966, and well over half of all blacks of voting age in the county. Thus, though the direct-action campaign initiated by Shuttlesworth and Williams had been virtually a complete failure in terms of mobilizing Birmingham's black community, it nevertheless succeeded in producing a momentous advance for the cause of civil rights in the city.[190]

But the great irony of this achievement for Shuttlesworth's own fortunes was that the rapidly growing number of black voters—made possible in great part by his exertions—necessitated an ever closer and more genuine cooperation between the black and white moderates. As the black vote grew, it became more and more essential for the white business progressives' continued electoral success that they build further bridges to the black moderates; it was a segment of their coalition without which they could not win, and which therefore had to be kept happy. And the growing influence of the black moderates within the black community depended upon their increasingly undeniable access to power; they therefore had every motive to encourage the partnership. Thus the actual effect of Shuttlesworth's success in getting the federal examiners sent to Jefferson County was to guarantee the ultimate triumph of his Inter-Citizens Committee rivals.

On January 20, just before the announcement of Attorney General Katzenbach's decision to send the voting examiners to Birmingham, a Christian Movement delegation including the Reverends Abraham and Calvin Woods, Nelson H. Smith, Mrs. Lucinda Robey, and other Shuttlesworth allies had met with Mayor Boutwell and given him a list of nine requests, headed by their plea for black policemen and additional blacks in policy-making city positions. In a lengthy statement, Boutwell had replied that the requests could not be met at this time. The delegation had been furious at the mayor's response, and the *Birmingham World* had denounced his administration for policies that seemed "to do a better job for business than for human beings." But in fact, Boutwell was already moving toward satisfying the delegation's requests; the council had named five blacks to policy-making boards during the preceding year and had every intention of appointing more, and the administration had hired sixteen black women as school traffic guards only three months earlier. It was just that Boutwell wanted to make certain that any racial progress was seen as having come from cooperation with the black moderates, rather than as a response to the Christian Movement's coercion. To use the *World*'s terms, he wanted to couple together his administration's efforts for business and for human beings so that electoral support for the former would be understood as producing advances for the latter. Shortly after the end of Shuttlesworth's demonstrations following the appointment of the federal voting examiners, Police Chief Jamie Moore appeared before a meeting of the black Interdenominational Ministerial Alliance on February 4 and invited the ministers to help recruit black applicants for the force. He emphasized his eagerness to hire qualified black officers. On February 8, Councilman Alan Drennen circulated among his city government colleagues a memorandum suggesting that "now is the ideal time for the City of Birmingham to take offensive action in an effort to solve some of our racial problems." He organized a meeting of officials to "discuss how to remove points which could later be used to rally the Negro community against us. Things are relatively quiet," he observed; "we cannot be accused of acting under pressure; any action we now take cannot be considered a reaction, and perhaps we will get the entire community's respect—both colored and white."

Unfortunately for the city government's desire to avoid identifying the hiring of black officers with Shuttlesworth's intimidation, a violent incident on February 21 made immediate action imperative. Hosea Williams had been leading demonstrations at a neighborhood food store, the Liberty Supermarket, to protest the actions of a security guard there in allegedly assaulting blacks on February 13. On the night of February 21, an unemployed young white former marine, Emory W. McGowan, attempted to enter the supermarket parking lot. When he blew the horn of his automobile at the demonstrators who were blocking his path, they gathered around his car, shouting. He thereupon drew a pistol and shot into the crowd, wounding five of the blacks. Outraged by this attack, moderate black ministers led by the Inter-Citizens Committee's J. L. Ware and C.M.E. bishop E. P. Murchison joined with Christian Movement activists to march in protest to the supermarket the next day. And at a meeting on February 24 at which Ware and the Christian Movement's Calvin Woods were the leading spirits, the moderates and activists united to attempt to organize a citywide boycott of all white merchants in order to compel the hiring of black police. With its black allies' having now publicly associated themselves with Shuttlesworth's coercive tactics, the Boutwell administration could no longer postpone action. On March 12, Boutwell and council president M. Edwin Wiggins issued a public statement saying that the city had an "immediate need" for black officers; they invited black leaders to help recruit applicants and pledged that the applicants "will be fairly considered for employment, and fairly treated after employment." On March 22 the Christian Movement, Ware's Baptist Ministers Conference, the Interdenominational Ministerial Alliance, and two other organizations joined in a public proclamation of the boycott and summoned "all persons of good will" to march on the city hall on March 26 to enforce the demand for black police. But by then the hiring was already in process. Five blacks had passed the civil service examination for patrolman earlier in the month, and on March 31 two of them, Leroy Stover and Johnny Johnson, were sworn in and began work. That summer a third black was added to the force. And when the NAACP's John Nixon called for even more officers in July, Boutwell at once met with an NAACP delegation and assured them that the city was actively pursuing the matter.[191]

The strategic dispute between the black activists and moderates was never settled in a way that would convince either of the contending groups of the correctness of the other's position. Shuttlesworth, Gardner, and their associates believed that their demonstrations in January 1966 had generated both the newly forthcoming attitudes of the board of registrars and the appointment of the federal examiners, and therefore that without the marches the number of black voters would have remained small for many years to come. And they believed that the hiring of the first black policemen, after years of delay on the part of the city, had been produced only by the unity of the black leadership behind forceful action that had resulted from the Liberty Supermarket incident; if the black leadership had remained divided, with many of them dedicated just to quiet negotiations, the Boutwell administration would have postponed the hiring yet again. Shores, Gaston, and their allies believed that the passage of the Voting Rights Act and their own success in persuading the board of registrars to liberalize its procedures would have produced the same expansion of the black electorate almost as quickly, and without disrupting carefully nurtured interracial ties in the community. And they believed that the events surrounding the Liberty Supermarket incident had merely hastened the employment of black officers, to which the city government was clearly already committed.

But if the dispute was never settled on an intellectual plane, on a practical one it was. The growing electoral dependence of the white business progressives and the black moderates upon each other after the second change-of-government referendum, made stronger by the expansion of the black electorate after the appointment of the federal voting examiners, increasingly delivered into the black moderates' hands a degree of genuine municipal power that the black activists simply could not claim. The activists' influence rested only upon their ability to intimidate those in power, to alter the various policies with which the activists disagreed; the moderates more and more participated in the actual formulation of policy itself. Both Boutwell and his successor, George Seibels, came to consult Arthur Gaston on virtually every question that touched upon race relations. When the death of a councilman created a vacancy on the body in October 1968, the remaining council members chose Arthur Shores to fill it; a year later he was elected to a full term in his own right. And in April 1969, a formal body to coordinate the alliance between black moderates and business progressives was formed. In 1963 the Downtown Improvement Association had created a committee to draw up plans for the economic and physical revitalization of the downtown area. Called Operation New Birmingham, it had announced its blueprint for the project in June 1965, and thereafter, under the leadership of *Birmingham News* vice-president S. Vincent Townsend, it had become an increasingly influential force in the community. When a group of distinguished blacks headed by Miles College president Lucius Pitts and his protégé, the college's dean, Richard Arrington, Jr., sent a telegram to Mayor Seibels in April 1969 asking for the appointment of additional black policemen and city officials and further steps to diminish friction between the police and the black community, it was Operation New Birmingham that took the initiative to respond. Townsend proposed the creation of a new Community Affairs Committee, but under the auspices of the private Operation New Birmingham in order to insulate it from the political pressures to which Boutwell's initial CAC had fallen victim. The resultant body—at first containing twenty-one and after 1974 sixty members—was composed one-third of city officials, one-third of white business leaders, and one-third of prominent black figures. Its weekly meetings became the catalyst for racial reform in Birmingham, and its membership became the breeding ground for the city's emerging black political elite. In 1971, Dean Arrington, a biologist, joined Arthur Shores on the council as its second black member. In 1979, with indispensable white support, Arrington became Birmingham's first black mayor.[192]

The pattern of events in the city must call into question the significance of the 1963 demonstrations in shaping the course of Birmingham's history. Their influence upon the history of the United States is indisputable: they are almost solely responsible for moving the Kennedy administration to propose and endorse what became the Civil Rights Act of 1964. But their influence upon Birmingham is more problematic. In future years they gained heroic status in the collective memory of the black community, and the new black politicians regularly did ritual obeisance to them. Whether or not they greatly accelerated racial progress in any area other than the integration of the lunch counters in the downtown department and variety stores is, however, distinctly debatable. One point, at least, is certain: they failed to have anything like the effect upon the city that Fred Shuttlesworth had expected. It was, rather, the emergence in the second change-of-government election in December 1964 of the inescapable electoral alliance between the white business progressives and the black moderates that truly shaped Birmingham's future. The share of power that Birmingham blacks did eventually achieve flowed in the end, therefore, not to the heirs of Shuttlesworth, but largely to the heirs of Arthur Shores and Lucius Pitts.

Selma

4

I. White Supremacy Joins the Machine

If Birmingham by 1963 had begun tentatively to move beyond the white supremacist past personified by "Bull" Connor, the same could most definitely not be said of Connor's birthplace, Selma. In any ranking of Alabama's cities in the 1950s and 1960s, Selma would very likely have emerged as its single most inflexibly and fervently segregationist. Under the circumstances, it may not be surprising that the little Alabama River town would become the next major focus of the civil rights revolution. Nevertheless, here too the careful examination of the events of municipal history can reveal much about the beliefs, personalities, and institutions that led Selma to play its particular role in the transformation of the region and the nation of which it was a part.[1]

Selma's city charter had been altered in 1852 to provide for the direct election of the town's mayor. During the subsequent three-quarters of a century, only two men—John M. Strong (1852–58) and Victor B. Atkins (1903–10)—served in the office for more than six years.[2] In 1920 the mayor's term was increased from two years to four, and T. J. Rowell, who was elected mayor in 1924 and reelected in 1928, became only the second incumbent to serve for as many as eight years. In 1932, however, after a spirited campaign, wholesale grocer and city council president Lucien P. Burns defeated Rowell handily by emphasizing the city's political tradition that the city council president would succeed the mayor after two terms and by calling for judicious retrenchment in the face of the deepening depression.[3] This election would prove a watershed in Selma's political history; it marked the end of regular and relatively rapid turnover in the mayoralty and the beginning of machine control. Once in office, Burns proceeded to create a powerful electoral organization. The mayoral election of 1932 was to be the city's last genuinely contested one until 1964.

In 1948, without opposition, Burns was elected to his fifth term. The

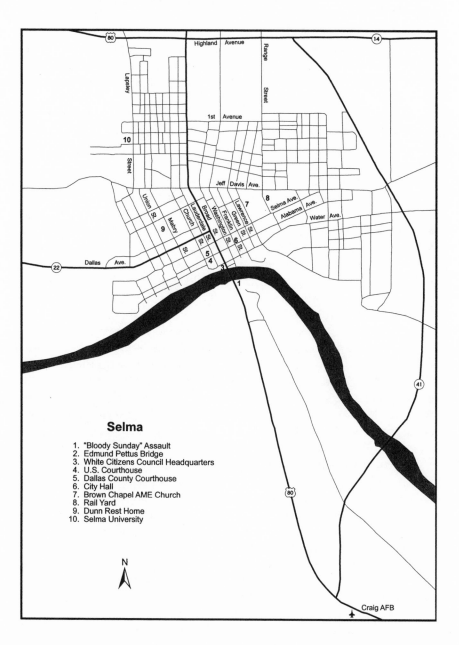

Selma

1. "Bloody Sunday" Assault
2. Edmund Pettus Bridge
3. White Citizens Council Headquarters
4. U.S. Courthouse
5. Dallas County Courthouse
6. City Hall
7. Brown Chapel AME Church
8. Rail Yard
9. Dunn Rest Home
10. Selma University

N

next year, however, he resigned in order to accept the presidency of the City National Bank. The city council president, Ralph D. Nicholson, succeeded him and served out the term. During 1950 and 1951, however, in quiet maneuvering within the Burns organization, the man who had succeeded Nicholson as council president, Councilman Chris B. Heinz, apparently emerged as the choice for mayor. Nicholson announced that he would not seek election to the mayoralty in his own right, and in 1952 Heinz ran unopposed for the office.[4]

Heinz was ideally suited to become Burns's political heir. The city council had initially chosen him to membership on it in 1934, to serve out an unexpired term, and he had been a close associate of Mayor Burns's throughout the succeeding fifteen years. By 1951 he was council president and chairman of the Dallas County Democratic Executive Committee. He was also a former state president of the Exchange Clubs, current state president of the Alabama Association of Insurance Agents, and a director of the Alabama League of Municipalities. Heinz was the son of a Selma furniture store owner. Both of his grandfathers had also been members of the city council. His partners in his insurance agency were Frank Hardy, one of Dallas County's state representatives, and Mallory Privett, who succeeded him as council president. He would be reelected mayor without significant opposition in 1956 and 1960.[5]

The organization Heinz inherited was bound together more by friendship and general outlook than by any clearly defined ideology. Selma was a small city—with about 14,400 whites and 14,000 blacks in 1960—and it was easy for most politically active whites to know each other. Indeed, they had often been friends since childhood. Such, for instance, was the relationship between Mayor Heinz and the county's probate judge, Bernard A. "Babe" Reynolds, who presided over the county governing body, the board of revenue. Reynolds, the son of a Selma dentist and a graduate of Auburn University, had returned to Selma after college and in 1941 had entered the dry cleaning business in partnership with G. Claiborne Blanton, Dallas County's probate judge from 1939 to his death in 1953. Governor Frank Dixon, a political ally of Blanton's, had appointed Reynolds to the position of county coroner, which he held in addition to his job with the dry cleaners, also in 1941. When Blanton died, Reynolds announced his candidacy to succeed his business partner as probate judge, and in a very heated contest he defeated the man whom Governor Gordon Persons had named to the vacancy, former state senator George P. Quarles. Thereafter Heinz and Reynolds, boyhood friends, cooperated closely in administering their respective areas of responsibility.[6]

The organization's control of the city council depended upon these networks of friendship. The council had eleven members—a president and two members from each of the city's five wards. All eleven were elected by all the city's voters, even though the ten council members other than the president had to live in the ward they represented. When a council member decided not to seek reelection, it was the practice for him to resign his seat a year or so before his term expired. The remaining council member from his ward then privately interviewed persons who were interested in joining the council and, after consultation with the other councilors, selected the new member. The person chosen was thus able to run as an incumbent when the election was held. In the late 1950s there was only a single councilor who had initially joined the body through election.[7] This mode of constituting the council ensured that the members would feel a sense of gratitude and regard for each other. And, even more importantly, it ensured that they would ordinarily share common attitudes and perspectives. They were conservative men who could not readily be brought to question the status quo.

Of course, the electorate retained the power every four years to reject the mayor and the councilors, but it was a power they seldom used. In the first place, there were relatively few voters in the city—5,744 of them in 1960[8]—and substantial numbers of the voters had ties of kinship or acquaintance with one or another of the organization's figures. In the second place, the machine's leaders were powerful men, whom the dissatisfied might be hesitant to oppose openly. Their power also extended beyond politics. When Lucien Burns moved from the mayoralty to the presidency of the City National Bank in 1949, he did not abandon his concern for the municipal organization he had created. State representative Frank Hardy, Mayor Heinz's business partner, and Victor Atkins, Mayor Heinz's earliest political mentor, were members of City National's board of directors along with Burns.[9] It might well be in the interest of an ambitious young Selmian to avoid alienating such people.

But more significant than these factors was the operation within the community of forces that made the organization's conservative outlook one that was in fact widely shared. The fifth ward, for instance, was the city's poorest, and the whites who lived in its east Selma precincts had very little in common with Burns, Heinz, or Reynolds in terms of social background. Since the late nineteenth century, however, Selma had been an important rail junction, and the fifth ward was the home of an extensive rail yard and locomotive repair shops. In the years after World War I, and especially after their hand was strengthened by the Railway Labor Act of 1934, the white rail workers' brotherhoods had devoted much of their efforts to excluding blacks from skilled jobs with the railroads. In 1944, in a case that arose in Birmingham, the U.S. Supreme Court had forbidden racially exclusionary labor contracts on the rail lines, but the power of the railroad unions had largely attained unofficially the goal that the Supreme Court had officially barred. This struggle was particularly sharp, and particularly successful, in Selma. In the 1950s and 1960s, the Selma rail yard was declining. The number of people in Dallas County who worked for the railroads, 464 in 1940 and 538 in 1950, had fallen to 223 in 1960 and to 177 in 1970. As the number of railroad jobs began decreasing, the concern of the white railroad unions to see that the available jobs were reserved for their members grew in intensity. In 1956, the financial secretary of the Selma lodge of the Brotherhood of Railway Carmen noted with pride that the entire membership of his local belonged to the Dallas County White Citizens' Council and that they were represented on the Citizens' Council's executive committee. The brotherhoods dominated the fifth ward's electorate, and the machine based its power in the ward upon them. Throughout the Burns-Heinz era, the ward was almost always represented on the city council by railroad workers.[10]

At the other end of the white social spectrum, rather similar social pressures were focused upon another extremely important occupational group in Selma, the wholesale grocers. Until the 1960s, Selma's principal economic role was as the marketing center for the surrounding agricultural area. And throughout the last quarter of the nineteenth century and the first half of the twentieth, that agriculture had rested upon the work of black tenant farmers. The tenants received their food and supplies on credit from the white landowners whose land they farmed, usually through small stores the landowners operated. And the landowners obtained the goods they sold to the tenants from the wholesale grocers. As a result, the economy of Selma in the early twentieth century was dominated by the great wholesale grocery firms that lined Water Avenue, twelve of them in the late 1920s. The firms employed a large number of men as agents to travel the rural Black Belt and sign up the various white landowners as customers. A substantial part of the business of the city's banks came from advancing to the wholesale grocers money with which to purchase the supplies to be sold to the planters; the grocery firms then extended credit to the planters, and the planters to their tenants. Because the business of the wholesale grocers was so completely derived from the agricultural areas, they served as something of a bridge joining rural and urban attitudes; the outlook of the owners and agents of the grocery firms was strongly colored by that of the large white landowners with whom they principally dealt. And because the economy of Selma was so much a function of the grocery firms' activities, the fortunes of many of Selma's leading families were based upon them.

For much of the twentieth century, however, the tenant farming system was in decline. The coming of the boll weevil just before World War I had been the first blow. In every census from 1850 to 1910, Dallas County had been either the first- or the second-largest producer of cotton in Alabama, but in 1920 its rank fell abruptly to thirteenth. The number of bales it produced dropped from 40,000 in 1910 to only 16,400 in 1920, and it remained at about that level for the rest of the twentieth century. The introduction of New Deal crop control and conservation programs in the

1930s, and growing mechanization thereafter, furthered the decline of tenantry. After World War II the county's farmers turned increasingly to cattle ranching. The number of cows in the county, about 28,600 in 1930 and still only 36,000 in 1940, leaped to 54,300 by 1945, reached 61,300 in 1950, and exceeded 79,400 by 1954. The effect of these changes upon black tenant farmers was devastating. Black tenants cultivated more than half of Dallas County's farmland in 1930, but less than a third of it by 1940, less than a fourth of it by 1945, 15 percent of it in 1950, and only 9 percent of it in 1960.

If the effect on the county's black tenants was calamitous, however, it was no less so on Selma's wholesale grocery firms. Of the twelve grocery firms operating in the city in the 1920s, only two were left by 1959. The owners and agents of the grocery firms, scrambling desperately to sign up the fewer and fewer customers available in the decades just before and after World War II, tended to develop an intensely defensive sense that forces far beyond their control—forces bound up with the New Deal federal government's intervention in local affairs, and with increasingly liberated blacks' abandonment of farming to move to northern cities—were threatening to destroy their world. Just as the white rail workers concentrated upon black competitors much of the anxiety they felt because of their tenuous employment situation, so the wholesale grocers often blamed the changing attitudes of blacks in part for the transformation of the rural economy. There is clearly an element of irrationality in each of these reactions, but they were nonetheless powerful. And as it did with the rail workers, so the social situation in which the wholesale grocers found themselves led them to sympathize with the cautious and conservative outlook of the machine, its fear of fundamental change. Thus the electoral success of the Burns-Heinz organization during the thirty years of its existence proceeded in considerable measure from the simple fact that its commitments and policies were representative of large segments of Selma's white electorate.[11]

One man who in the civil rights collisions of the mid-1960s stood at the very center of the conflict summarizes in his career many of the elements that produced the organization's leaders. Victor B. Atkins was a son of one of Selma's mayors from the turn of the century. Mayor Atkins had founded in 1890 one of the city's most successful wholesale grocery firms, and young Victor had been born the following year. The senior Atkins had become mayor in 1903 and had served four terms, resigning in 1910 to become Dallas County's state senator. He died in 1916. His son Victor went to work in the wholesale grocery in 1910. After service in World War I, he returned to manage the grocery firm with his brother. In 1921 he married, and in 1928 he became the firm's head. He was elected to the city council. In 1934, when there was a vacancy in the other seat from his first ward, he selected Chris Heinz from among the five applicants to fill it.

Heinz, who as a young man had been a great admirer of Atkins's father, remained deeply grateful to Atkins for the rest of his life. Also in 1934, Atkins was chosen to head the city's Water Works Commission, a position in which he continued for more than thirty years, winning regular reappointment to successive six-year terms. He served on the city's Democratic Executive Committee, on its first planning board, and during World War II, on the county draft board. He was also a director of the City National Bank. His son Julien succeeded him in active management of the wholesale grocery firm, but in 1958 declining business forced the firm's liquidation, after sixty-eight years. In the meantime, Atkins had converted his own six-thousand-acre plantation into a cattle ranching operation, and after 1958 he devoted himself primarily to its supervision. In the summer of 1961, on recommendation of Dallas County's legislative delegation, Governor John Patterson appointed him as chairman of the county's board of voting registrars, and he was continued in this position by Patterson's successor, George Wallace. Thus Atkins brought to the chairmanship of the Dallas registrars decades of close affiliation with the Burns-Heinz organization and a lifetime shaped by association with the wholesale grocery business. Though his grocery firm had failed three years before he joined the board of registrars, that fact appears only to have strengthened in him the sense of defensiveness against a profoundly threatening, hostile world.[12]

The machine was conservative in its outlook and without question unsympathetic to any reform of the traditional patterns of race relations in the Black Belt, but under Lucien Burns it had no special racial animus. Indeed, its efficient administration of city services and its slow but steady improvement of municipal institutions and infrastructure seem to have earned it the respect of some black leaders. Chris Heinz, moreover, came into the mayoralty with a considerable reputation as an aggressive civic booster. When a young Yale Law School student arrived in Selma in December 1952 to investigate the conditions of black life in Dallas County, a prominent figure in the black community told him that the recently inaugurated Heinz was an "exceptionally good" mayor.[13]

Only a bit more than six months after Heinz had taken office, however, a shadow fell across his administration—a shadow that would darken the entire future history of Selma. On the night of April 24, 1953, the mayor's elder daughter, Mrs. Jean Heinz Rockwell, was asleep in the bedroom of her apartment, with her baby asleep beside her and an older child asleep in an adjoining room; her husband, a pharmacist, was still at work. A fierce storm was raging outside. Mrs. Rockwell was awakened to find a black man with a wet towel over his head approaching her bed. He had gained entrance through a window in the older child's bedroom and had picked up in the kitchen a butcher knife that he now brandished at her. She screamed and ran into the living room, where he caught her and attempted to rape her. In the ensuing struggle she managed to get the knife away from him, whereupon he ran out the apartment's back door. Police arrived almost at once, but they could not pick up his trail because of the storm.

This assault was one of a series of nine such incidents in the city during March, April, and early May, and they produced a virtual reign of terror. Police headquarters received a steady stream of reports of prowlers from frightened residents. The city, the state, and various private organizations —including the black Elks Club—posted a total of thirteen hundred dollars in rewards for the capture of the perpetrator. White males patrolled the streets on their own authority in an effort to apprehend him. Mayor Heinz advised an anxious citizenry, "If you catch a burglar in the house and if you have the proper means of protecting yourself and your family, use them, as I would."

Just before midnight on the night of May 16, a white teenager on foot and a passing motorist, who was an employee of Mayor Heinz's brother, trapped in an alley a black man whom they regarded as suspicious. Police were summoned. After officers had questioned him for five hours on May 17 and two more hours on the morning of May 18, the man, William Earl Fikes, a twenty-seven-year-old service station attendant and paroled convict from Marion, confessed to the entry of Mrs. Rockwell's home and also to entering on May 1 the home of Mrs. Claude C. Binford, the wife of Selma's fire chief. He confessed as well to two similar entries in August 1948, about a year before he was sentenced to the penitentiary for burglary. But he denied the one actual rape among the incidents, that of Mrs. Dolores Stinson, the teenage wife of an air force sergeant, on March 18. Without taking Fikes before a magistrate for a preliminary hearing, police later on May 18 removed Fikes to the state penitentiary in Montgomery, allegedly for his own protection. His questioning continued there, and on May 23, after Mrs. Stinson confronted him, he confessed to raping her, and also to four other entries and numerous "peeping Tom" charges. In his confessions he provided correct details. During Fikes's time at the penitentiary, his father had attempted to see him, but authorities refused to allow him to do so.

On June 2 the Dallas County Grand Jury was summoned into special session. Judge L. S. Moore charged the jurors that they would hear evidence that "things near and dear to our citizens have been violated," and he expressed his confidence that each juror would be able to "visualize your reactions in the matters if you were the party involved." The grand jury indicted Fikes for the rape of Mrs. Stinson and for six counts of burglary with intent to ravish; all were capital offenses.

A special criminal term of circuit court was convened on June 22 to try Fikes for the rape. Judge Walton E. "Jack" Callen appointed Selma attorneys Sam Earle Hobbs and Hugh S. D. Mallory to defend Fikes, and they did so with great vigor. They were able to persuade Judge Callen to refuse to allow either the circuit solicitor, James A. Hare, or the investigating officer, Captain Wilson Baker, to read Fikes's confession to the jury, on the ground that Fikes had not had a preliminary hearing before giving it. But Solicitor Hare then convinced the judge that it would be all right to distribute copies of the confession to the jurors and let them read it to themselves. Mrs. Stinson testified that even though her rapist had worn a mask and a rag over his head, she was able to identify Fikes as the man by his eyes and his voice. The defense called three black psychiatrists from the Tuskegee Veterans Administration Hospital, all of whom testified that Fikes was schizophrenic. And the defense attorneys as well questioned Mrs. Stinson's identification, pointing out that Fikes had been the only suspect shown to her, and maintained that Fikes's confession had been involuntary.

Hobbs was the son of the man who had represented the Selma district in Congress from 1934 to 1950, and Mallory, a city councilman, was the grandson of a Selma mayor. The fact that such prominent white Selmians had mounted so strenuous and aggressive a defense apparently gave the jury pause. After eighteen hours of deliberation, the jurors, all of whom were white, returned a guilty verdict, but refused to sentence Fikes to death; they instead imposed a prison term of ninety-nine years. The failure of the jury to order Fikes's execution was considered an extraordinary triumph for the defense, and it stunned the community. The *Selma Times-Journal* announced editorially its emphatic disagreement with the jury's leniency. The defense declined to appeal. Solicitor Hare thereupon announced his intention to proceed to prosecute Fikes on the charge of burglary with intent to ravish Mrs. Rockwell, in the hope of obtaining a death sentence in this second round.

At this point the NAACP entered the case, and arranged to have black Birmingham attorneys Peter A. Hall and Orzell Billingsley, Jr., defend Fikes. Hall and Billingsley at once entered motions to quash the indictment and the venire (the list of persons who had been summoned for jury duty) on the ground that blacks were systematically excluded from Dallas County juries. In October Judge Callen began a hearing on this charge, and it produced a spectacle that shook Dallas County to its foundations. In the first place, it represented the first time in living memory that black attorneys had practiced in the county, and their combative examination of white officials astounded Selmians of both races. In the second place, local black leaders, in particular S. William Boynton of the Dallas County Voters League and John D. Hunter of the Selma NAACP, demonstrated by their firm testimony their willingness to stand up to the intimidating atmosphere surrounding the trial. And most importantly, the hearing ended, to the consternation perhaps of everyone involved, of both races, in a black victory. After a hearing lasting six days and featuring careful questioning of the county's three jury commissioners and painstaking name-by-name examinations of the three volumes of county jury rolls, dating back to 1931, Hall and Billingsley succeeded in establishing that there were names in the jury box from which the venire was selected that were not on the jury rolls themselves, a violation of state law. Indeed, one of the jury commissioners testified that he had never seen the jury rolls. Hall and Billingsley therefore amended their motion to allege this violation also, Solicitor Hare conceded it, and on that ground Judge Callen quashed the indictment, quashed the venire, and ordered the jury box emptied and refilled. And on the showing that there were only a handful of blacks among the twelve hundred names on the jury rolls, Judge Callen ordered them revised.

The defense's success was, however, short-lived. In response to Judge Callen's order, the jury commissioners added the names of some five hundred individuals to the rolls, perhaps half of whom were black. Fikes was then reindicted, and a new venire of seventy-five men, eight of whom were black, was drawn. Hall and Billingsley renewed their claim of racial exclusion, but Judge Callen ruled that the problem had now been corrected, and in December Fikes came to trial—before an all-white jury, as in June.

The testimony at this trial closely paralleled that given six months earlier. Mrs. Rockwell described the attack, but because her assailant had had a towel over his head, she could not identify Fikes. To corroborate the allegation of an intent to ravish, the state called Mrs. Stinson and Mrs. Claude Binford. Mrs. Binford, alone among all of the victims, had gotten a good look at her intruder. She positively identified Fikes as the man; she had earlier picked him out of a lineup. The defense called the same three black psychiatrists from Tuskegee, who testified once again as to his schizophrenia. Fikes's parole officer testified that Fikes's grandmother and uncle had both been committed to an insane asylum. And Hall and Billingsley opposed the introduction of Fikes's confessions as involuntary, Hall denouncing the "Gestapo-like tactics of an arbitrary police department." They offered to place Fikes on the stand to testify to the circumstances of the confessions if the cross-examination would be limited to that subject, but Judge Callen ruled that, once Fikes agreed to testify, he could be cross-examined on anything relevant to the trial.

The fact that prominent white Selmians Hobbs and Mallory had been willing to defend Fikes so vigorously had apparently caused the jury in June to question the state's case. But Hall and Billingsley's NAACP sponsorship, their aggressive conduct toward white authority, and their attacks on the patterns of white supremacy had caused white Selma to close ranks. Though the testimony at the two trials was quite similar, at this second one the jury debated for only forty minutes before returning with a verdict of guilty and a sentence of death.

Because of the death sentence, Alabama law made appeal to the state supreme court automatic. In the appeal, Hall and Billingsley argued both that blacks continued to be excluded from Dallas County juries and that Fikes's confessions had been involuntary and should not have been permitted in evidence. In May of 1955, the state supreme court affirmed the verdict and sentence. The majority opinion, by Supernumerary Justice Arthur B. Foster, dealt primarily with the question of the number of blacks on the jury rolls. Foster conceded that before Judge Callen had ordered the rolls revised, blacks had been excluded improperly, and that even after the revision the number of blacks on the rolls remained small. But the state statute required jurors to be intelligent and of good moral character, he said, and since in Dallas County "a large majority of the Negroes are ignorant, with little or no education and low moral character, and there is much venereal disease among them and a large percentage of illegitimacy," therefore the number of blacks now on the rolls was not unreasonable. The majority opinion dealt only cursorily with the admission of the confessions. But this question was more troubling for the two dissenters, Justices Thomas S. Lawson and Pelham Merrill, who believed that Judge Callen had erred in ruling that Fikes could not testify to the involuntariness of the confessions without opening himself to general cross-examination on all aspects of the case.

Following the Alabama Supreme Court's ruling, the NAACP appealed to the U.S. Supreme Court. The Supreme Court heard arguments in the case in December 1956, and in January 1957, by a vote of six to three, it reversed Fikes's conviction. The majority opinion, by Chief Justice Earl Warren, focused entirely on the admission of the confessions. Warren noted that when Fikes left school at the age of sixteen, he was still in the third grade. Warren then detailed the circumstances of Wilson Baker's lengthy interrogations of Fikes, both in Selma and at the state penitentiary in Montgomery, and concluded that the methods used to extract the confessions were sufficient to overwhelm the will of a person as weak of mind as Fikes. He held therefore that the confessions failed to meet the standards for being voluntary and thus ought to have been excluded. He failed to make clear in his opinion, however, that Fikes had confessed to the assault on Mrs. Rockwell in Selma, less than thirty-six hours after his arrest and following no more than seven hours of questioning; the confessions at the state penitentiary had been to other offenses, including the rape of Mrs. Stinson. In dissent, Justice John M. Harlan, joined by Justices Stanley Reed and Harold Burton, argued that the facts of the case did not constitute sufficient coercion to justify interference with the verdict.

Because Mrs. Rockwell had been unable to identify Fikes as her assailant, the exclusion of his confessions forced the state to drop the case. James Hare—who had prosecuted the case, and who in 1954, following Judge Callen's death, had succeeded Callen as circuit judge—denounced Warren's opinion as "the sacrifice of the South on the altars of the Supreme

Court's psychological and sociological omniscience." He added bitterly, "The opinion is the voice of the Supreme Court of the United States, but the hand is the hand of the National Association for the Advancement of Colored People." Despite the abandonment of the prosecution in the Rockwell case, however, the ninety-nine-year sentence in the Stinson case, which had not been appealed, still stood. Fikes remained in the penitentiary for more than twenty-one years. In 1975, however, black Selma attorney J. L. Chestnut, Jr., was able to convince a federal district judge that, since the U.S. Supreme Court had ruled Fikes's confessions involuntary in the Rockwell trial, they ought to have been excluded as well in the earlier Stinson trial, and that Fikes had not appealed the Stinson verdict at the time solely because of his well-founded belief that he would receive the death penalty on retrial. Fikes was therefore freed.

It would be difficult to overestimate the importance of the Fikes trials for the future history of Selma. Among the town's blacks, the example of black attorneys' and local leaders' battling on approximately equal terms with white officials, without fear or subservience, was liberating for many observers. And the modest victories the attorneys achieved—the revision of the jury rolls and the reversal of the conviction—formed a significant object lesson that not all power in America was allied with the city and the county, a notion new to most Black Belt blacks. Among white segregationists, this demonstration of the limits of their authority was equally novel. And even more frightening was the evidence provided that blacks, even in Selma, were becoming less resigned to their lot. Speaking to the White Citizens' Council in November 1959, Judge James Hare said that the integrationist attack on Dallas County had begun with the Fikes trial six years earlier. "I remember too vividly the Fikes case, during which we really became fully aware for the first time that the NAACP was organized down to the beat level in every county. Every day for the several weeks which the trial ran, the courtroom was packed with integration leaders from every beat in Dallas County and from several surrounding counties. If we had not stood firm then and on other occasions since that time, I shudder to think where we would be now." The struggle ever since the Fikes trial, he said, had pitted the NAACP's vast financial resources against the White Citizens' Council's superior leadership; he added confidently, "In the end, that leadership will bring us victory."

But perhaps the most portentous result of the trials had a more personal source. Throughout the years from 1953 to 1957, as a result of the Fikes proceedings, Mayor Chris Heinz was faced constantly with the NAACP's energetic and unembarrassed defense of the man whom he regarded as the brutal assailant of his daughter. The individual and family torment, a natural product of the crime, was thus easily transformed in the mayor's mind into a rapidly deepening hostility toward the NAACP, and toward black militancy in general. And the fact that the NAACP's efforts culminated, as the mayor saw it, in allowing this vicious miscreant to escape punishment for his assault further increased Heinz's anger, and added the U.S. Supreme Court as an additional object of it. The mayor's antipathy toward black civil rights activists and the federal courts, consequently, was immediate and intense. In the fall of 1954, Dallas County segregationists organized a Selma chapter of the White Citizens' Councils, an organization whose antagonism toward these same two groups, if less personal, was no less keen. It can be no surprise, therefore, that the mayor at once led his municipal machine into a firm alliance with the new council, an alliance so intimate that it was often hard to tell the two organizations apart. The association established from the outset between the council chapter on the one hand and city and county political leaders on the other appears to have been the principal source of Dallas County whites' unusually aggressive and unanimous commitment to an extremist racial position during the coming decade.[14]

II. The Dominion of White Supremacy

The first chapters of the White Citizens' Council were established in the Mississippi Delta during the summer of 1954. The Citizens' Councils were the idea of Robert B. Patterson, a Leflore County planter and former Mississippi State University football hero.[15] Reflecting the Delta world in which he lived, a world where virtually all blacks depended economically upon whites, Patterson reasoned that, even if the federal courts gave blacks the abstract right to attend white schools or to use other white facilities, integration as a practical matter would be impossible if all whites agreed to deny employment or credit to every black person who sought to exercise these rights. In the Delta, it seemed impossible that blacks could achieve their social goals without the assistance of white people. This analysis made sense to many of Patterson's fellow Mississippians. The first White Citizens' Council, organized to enforce the economic pressure that Patterson advocated, was formed in Indianola in July 1954. By November of that year chapters were reported to exist in fifty-four of Mississippi's eighty-two counties.[16]

Patterson's logic also reflected the experience of those white Alabamians who resided in the western Black Belt. By September 1954, white leaders in that area had begun to discuss the possibility of emulating Mississippi's example. Their deliberations were lent urgency by the unmistakable evidence during the summer and fall that blacks were preparing to use their landmark victory in the Supreme Court's May 17 school desegregation decision. On June 10 the chief attorney of the NAACP, Thurgood Marshall, in a speech at the black Alabama State College in Montgomery, had urged Alabama blacks to press local boards of education to put the Court's ruling into practice. As the new school year opened in September, five

NAACP chapters—in Montgomery, Anniston, Brewton, Roanoke, and Fairfield—had submitted formal desegregation petitions to their boards of education. And as we have seen, on the first day of classes in Montgomery twenty-three black children had presented themselves for admission to a newly constructed white elementary school. Although the school boards in each of these cases had correctly observed to the blacks that the Supreme Court was still in the process of considering how to put its decision into effect and that their efforts were therefore premature, everyone understood that this excuse would justify only a temporary delay.[17]

Selma watched these events with particular concern. Segregationists of a violent disposition apparently turned to terror tactics to prevent Dallas County's blacks from following the examples of the blacks in Montgomery and elsewhere; on September 19 and September 26 arsonists in the county burned to the ground two rural black schools.[18] More temperate white supremacists, however, embraced the gospel of economic intimidation that came from Mississippi. Under the leadership of Selma attorney M. Alston Keith, Dallas County's Democratic Party chairman and the president of the county's bar association, white leaders during October commenced active efforts to form the state's first White Citizens' Council. On November 28 the *Selma Times-Journal* revealed that the chapter existed, with Alston Keith as its first chairman and 200 county residents as members. The newly formed organization first met publicly on November 29; an additional 600 whites then joined. By the following June, Citizens' Council membership had grown to 1,200, and by the time of its first birthday the number had reached 1,500—one-fourth of all adult white males in the county. Keith did not mince words about the chapter's goal. "The white population in this county controls the money and this is an advantage that the Council will use in a fight to legally maintain complete segregation of the races," he told the *Times-Journal*. "We intend to make it difficult, if not impossible, for any Negro who advocates de-segregation to find and hold a job, get credit or renew a mortgage."[19]

In September 1955 the new White Citizens' Council, not yet a year old, faced a challenge that forced it to attempt to use the economic weapon upon which it relied. On May 31 of that year the Supreme Court issued its decree implementing its school desegregation decision of the previous year; it ordered that the new policy be instituted "with all deliberate speed." During the summer, under instructions from NAACP headquarters in New York, NAACP chapters throughout the South submitted petitions to their school boards asking that integration begin. Apparently the NAACP's national officials did not realize the extent of the danger in which they were placing their members in the lower South by making this demand of them, nor did they have a clear sense of the futility of the action. By early September the NAACP chapters had submitted sixteen petitions in Alabama. The petitioners' names and addresses were frequently printed in local papers, and the petitioners found themselves the objects of reprisals. But the harshest reaction came in Selma, the only western Black Belt community in which a petition was offered.[20]

The Selma petition arrived at the city school board's offices on August 30 with the names of twenty-nine black parents subscribed to it. The school board's president, banker Rex J. Morthland, and Superintendent W. Elbert Snuggs announced that school would open on a segregated basis on September 6, as scheduled, and that the board would consider the petition at its next regular meeting, on September 15.[21] Meanwhile, the White Citizens' Council acted. On September 8, Superintendent Snuggs announced that eight of the petitioners had been fired from their jobs and that five others had asked to have their names deleted from the petition.[22]

John D. Hunter, the insurance agent and minister who headed the NAACP's Selma branch, denounced the firings as "unchristian and possibly a violation of the law." He noted that the First Amendment of the U.S. Constitution guaranteed the right to petition governmental bodies. Citizens' Council chairman Alston Keith replied, "Apparently those who signed did so because they were too uninformed to know what they were doing, or just for the purpose of irritating their employers. Whichever of these cases it was, is reason enough to fire them." Calling the petitioners "quite stupid," the attorney assured the public, "The Dallas County Council has operated entirely within its legal rights in whatever action may have been taken in connection with the school petition." He added that although "the Council does not take credit for the discharge of the petitioners who have lost their jobs, I will say this: I don't believe there would have been the unity of action there was in this respect without the educational work we have done. They [the employers] did just what we have been advocating all along." The following day eight additional petitioners were fired, bringing the total to sixteen of the twenty-nine original signers.[23]

White Selma now evidently considered the matter settled. On September 11, the *Times-Journal's* editor, Edward B. Field, an active Citizens' Council member, published a front-page editorial on the encounter. "Ignoring the great advances made by their race in this section, even when compared closely with conditions in Northern states where integration is preached but practiced as a shameful farce," he wrote of the petitioners, "these Negroes have maneuvered the white people of the Black Belt into a defensive action which is unpalatable to them. To defend their own rights and privileges under the Constitution, Black Belters have resorted to economic pressure against the very people to whom they have given economic aid and support in the past." But he ventured, "Now that we know just where we stand, just what we can expect from ceaseless agitation," it ought to be possible to create a permanent compromise between the races. Such a modus vivendi would involve blacks' refraining from attempting to enforce their rights under the *Brown* desegregation decision and whites' recognizing the need to improve black facilities sufficiently that the mass of black people would resist the "extravagant promises by agitators and demagogues seeking to further their own purposes." At its September 15 meeting, the school board referred the blacks' petition to a special committee for study, and there it was buried.[24]

Selma's blacks, however, were not so easily discouraged, and their efforts to fight back pushed the crisis to its next stage. One of the petitioners who had been fired, Joseph Holmes, had been an employee of a Selma dairy, Cloverleaf Creamery. Holmes, who had grown up in Selma, began working for Cloverleaf Creamery shortly after he had finished school in 1946, and over the next decade he had advanced from helper to packer to mixer. About 1949 he had married.[25]

Cloverleaf was one of Selma's most prosperous businesses. Established in 1932, it employed 125 workers, purchased milk from forty-seven dairy farms in the Selma area, and supplied a market in twenty-two Alabama counties. The foundation of its success was a lucrative contract to furnish dairy products to Selma's Craig Air Force Base and Montgomery's Maxwell Air Force Base. Its owner, Edward T. McBride, was an active segregationist who would be elected to the executive committee of the Dallas County White Citizens' Council in September 1956. McBride would serve on that committee until at least 1962, while serving as a vice-chairman of the organization in 1959–60. He was also a close political ally of Mayor Heinz and would be Heinz's campaign manager in the bitterly contested mayoral election of 1964.[26]

The other businesses that had discharged petitioners were not, in general, enterprises that depended to any significant extent upon black customers. One petitioner had been a cook at the Selma Country Club and another a cook at Selma's white junior high school; others were, for instance, employees of a construction company, of a marble works, and of the YMCA. But Cloverleaf Creamery sold its products to both races and was a brand that Selma blacks encountered almost daily. The white supremacist convictions of its owner doubtless also drew blacks' ire. Probably for these reasons, blacks responded to the firings by quietly launching a retaliatory boycott against the Cloverleaf label.[27]

The boycott had been in progress for perhaps three weeks when it entrapped a black grocer, John U. Smitherman. A native of Randolph County, Smitherman had moved to Selma in 1925, obtaining employment as a butler and cook. In the intervening three decades, he had become a prominent figure in the black community. In 1940 he had been elected the superintendent of the Sunday school of one of the city's largest black congregations, Tabernacle Baptist Church; he held this position for the next fifteen years. He was one of Selma's handful of black registered voters. He and his wife, Helena, had three children, a son who was attending college in 1955 and two younger daughters. Smitherman apparently had carefully saved money from his salary, because in 1952 he had fulfilled his dream of purchasing a small grocery store in the black section of town.[28]

Because Smitherman's clientele was almost exclusively black, the surreptitious boycott of Cloverleaf was especially apparent in the sales from his store. At the beginning of October, a white woman who represented a Birmingham dairy, accompanied by a sales promoter from the firm, called at the store and noted that the sales of their brand of milk there had increased by 50 percent in the past few weeks. The sales representative asked to speak with him about the cause. Smitherman asked her to return when he was less busy, and she came back on October 7. Smitherman was again busy, but he wrote his telephone number on a piece of paper torn from his adding machine tape and told her that she could call him later in the day. This action proved to be a serious breach of racial etiquette. Apparently, the woman had been in contact with the White Citizens' Council and was investigating the possibility of a black boycott for the segregationists. The invitation from a black man for a white woman to telephone him implied to Citizens' Council members and other whites—or so they claimed—a desire on Smitherman's part for interracial sexual relations. Within thirty minutes the woman telephoned Smitherman and asked him what he wanted. He told her that he wanted to discuss the milk sales with her, but she clearly did not believe him and pressed him to reveal his ulterior motives. The conversation ended with mutual suspicions. Within an hour, Smitherman received a call ordering him to leave Selma by five that afternoon.[29]

Smitherman phoned the police to report this threatening message and to ask for protection. He also telephoned a former white employer for advice. The employer suggested several steps to calm the situation, and Smitherman took them. Matters remained quiet for a week. Unknown to Smitherman, however, at least two officers in the police force from which Smitherman had sought protection were preparing to enforce the threat made against him.

On October 13, four white men kidnapped an elderly black, John Sturdivant, whom they mistook for Smitherman. Sturdivant, a porter at a Selma jewelry store, had just come out of Smitherman's store and was riding a bicycle home. Smitherman himself often rode a bicycle between his grocery and his home, which was located several blocks farther up the same street. The kidnappers drove Sturdivant about ten miles out into the country, presumably intending to beat him. When Sturdivant established his true identity to them, however, they released him with orders to tell Smitherman to get out of town. This message Sturdivant delivered to Smitherman the following morning. Police would later charge Sergeant Clyde F. Pressley, the department's night desk officer and a member of the force since 1950, with being the leader of the kidnappers. The other three men charged with participating in the crime were C. Benjamin Mitchell, a young owner of a garage and ambulance service, and two students, Lawrence D. Vickers, the son of a foreman at a farmers' cooperative, and Billy Mac Bobo, the son of a state highway department construction foreman.[30]

Despite the kidnapping, Smitherman refused to flee. Therefore, another Selma police officer took up the effort to intimidate him. Officer William D. Bailey had come to Selma in 1951 from his hometown of Ashland, Virginia, near Richmond, with his wife and young son and had taken a position with the Selma police force.[31] On the night of October 17, Officer Bailey was driven to Smitherman's home by Mrs. Maxine Trippe Butler, a machine operator at a cigar factory and the estranged wife of the shop supervisor at the factory.[32] Mrs. Butler evidently believed that she could identify the Smithermans' home, but she instead pointed to the home of Smitherman's next-door neighbor, Mrs. Vera Jones, the widow of a Southern Railway porter who now supported herself by working as a maid. Officer Bailey took a can of gasoline, threw the gasoline on the rear of Mrs. Jones's home, and ignited it. He then threw the empty can in a corner of Mrs. Jones's backyard, and he and Mrs. Butler left. Firemen, who were quickly called, extinguished the blaze before it had done more than relatively minor damage to the house.

The following night, having learned that he had burned the wrong structure, Officer Bailey returned to the Smithermans' home, drove past the house, and fired two shots from his pistol into a front window. One of the bullets, ricocheting from a wall, grazed Helena Smitherman's forehead.[33] By the next morning, Deputy State Fire Marshal Tom Hall of Montgomery, who had been assigned to investigate the October 17 blaze, had informed Selma police that the fire definitely was arson, and police had begun an intensive investigation. On October 20, Police Chief Edward W. Mullen announced the arrests of Officer Bailey for the shooting into the Smithermans' home on October 18 and the arson of October 17, of Mrs. Butler as an accessory to the arson, and of Sergeant Pressley, Mitchell, Vickers, and Bobo for the kidnapping of John Sturdivant on October 13.[34] Later that afternoon all six were brought before Recorder's Court Judge William B. Craig. They waived preliminary hearings, were bound over to the grand jury, and were released on bond.[35]

Racial animosities in the city were now at a fever pitch. Robert E. Hughes, who, as we have seen, was the executive secretary of the Alabama Council on Human Relations, reported to George C. Wallace—at the time still regarded by racial liberals as a firm ally—"Confidentially I happen to know that we almost had a serious incident in Selma as a result of the actions of the two policemen about which you have doubtless read. A group of armed Negroes had gathered to take action against the policemen and were talked out of it by one of their own leaders. Retaliation would have led to retaliation and serious difficulties could have arisen. . . . Please treat this latter event with extreme confidence as it could greatly increase the tension already present in Selma—tension which has not been treated by the press."[36]

After his arrest, Officer Bailey apparently became increasingly distraught about these events. On the afternoon of October 25, he drove his car to the nearby town of Marion, parked it, took out his revolver, and put a bullet into his head. He was buried near Tuscaloosa on October 28.[37] In November the Dallas County Grand Jury convened and the cases against the remaining five people accused were presented. But on November 15, the grand jury adjourned without having returned indictments against any of them. All charges were therefore dropped.[38]

John Smitherman decided, after the refusal of the grand jury to indict the five, that the safety of his wife and two daughters required him to leave town. He sold his grocery to one of Selma's most prominent black businessmen, Edwin L. D. Moss, and moved to Detroit, Michigan. His neighbor Mrs. Jones, though her involvement in the events had been purely accidental, also left Selma; she sold her home to a schoolteacher. And Joseph Holmes, whose dismissal by the Cloverleaf Creamery had begun the episode, now finding himself without work, also left his hometown in search of a new life.[39]

The moral to be drawn from this rather sordid episode depended, of course, upon the observer. At least one prominent black man, John H. Clay, a minister, drew the conclusion that the segregationists intended even before the object lesson of the Smitherman affair had been supplied. In December 1954, Clay sent a letter to Selma's black leaders inviting them to a meeting to form a committee that could come to terms with the Citizens' Council. The council, he assured them, had "promised to work out a solution to all of our problems if we leave off integration and desegregation." But few other blacks found this bargain acceptable, and an aroused black community compelled Clay to cancel his proposed meeting.[40]

Nevertheless, despite the lack of any overt black response, Selma's Citizens' Council members seem to have believed that they had emerged from this first encounter triumphant. It was true that the battle had cost Officer Bailey his life. But on the other hand, Smitherman, Holmes, and Mrs. Jones had been driven from the city, its black civil rights advocates had been badly shaken, and local schools remained completely segregated. The Dallas County White Citizens' Council thus was convinced of the efficacy of its economic weapon. Throughout the late 1950s and early 1960s, as a result, they would attempt aggressively to employ the weapon.

The Citizens' Council was structured with this goal in view. Below the council's county chairman, the city and each of the three rural board of revenue districts had its own board of directors, headed by a vice-chairman. The four district boards were intended to keep each district's residents, whether white or black, under close observation. They passed on the name of any person whose activities they found questionable to the council's executive committee. The executive committee, consisting of the countywide officers and the members of the four district boards, met every two weeks to review the situation in Dallas. Any white who exhibited tendencies toward moderation could expect a visit from friends or business acquaintances in the council; recalcitrance could lead to social ostracism, the withdrawal of patronage by customers, or harassment by co-workers. Council chairman Jim O. Risher, Jr., a wealthy cattle rancher, reported in 1960 that there were "not more than six would-be integrationists in the county, and the council knows what they are doing every minute." A potentially rebellious black could expect an even more draconian response. If he were employed by a white, he might well be discharged; in addition, his photograph would be circulated to prevent other whites from hiring him. Black professionals fell under other sorts of pressure, encountering difficulties with leases, mortgages, credit, insurance, or licenses. All blacks who attempted to register to vote, the council placed on a blacklist.

To facilitate such pressure, the Citizens' Council sought to involve Selma's banks in its activities. City National, with its close ties to the Burns-Heinz organization, cooperated fully in the 1950s. Aubrey Allen, a former county agricultural agent who was in charge of the bank's agricultural loans, was the Citizens' Council's chairman in 1956–57 and its secretary-treasurer from 1957 to 1961. In 1961 he was appointed a member of the Dallas County Board of Voting Registrars, a position in which he served until April 1965. After Lucien Burns was succeeded as the bank's president by William B. Craig in 1959, however, City National seems gradually to have begun to distance itself a bit from the council. Craig, formerly the judge of Selma's Recorder's Court, had resigned his commission as an officer in the Naval Reserve in 1957 to protest President Eisenhower's use of troops to enforce the federal court order integrating Little Rock's Central High School. But during the 1960s Craig had slowly moved to a more moderate stance, though the bank's board continued in the control of council and machine stalwarts. Craig's efforts to restrain his board were by no means always successful, but the bank was now perhaps less a reflex of the council's will than it had earlier been. Selma National Bank, whose president, J. Graham Melvin, was the county Republican Party chairman, also appears to have helped the council in the 1950s. But Melvin, like Burns, retired in 1959, and his successor, Roger ap C. Jones, was a racial moderate who moved the bank to a more centrist position. J. Bruce Pardue, initially vice-president of the Selma Trust and Savings Bank and after 1959 president of the newly established Citizens' Bank, was a strong segregationist who had been the council's secretary in 1956–57. His board of directors was dominated by council leaders. Two officers of the People's Bank also served as officers of the council. Jack P. Tucker was the council's treasurer in 1956–57, and B. Franklin Wilson was a vice-chairman of the council in 1958–59 and a member of its executive committee in 1959–60. But People's Bank president Rex Morthland—a native of California who held a doctorate in economics from the University of Chicago—was one of Selma's leading moderates, and from the outset he refused to assist the council in its efforts. Presumably under Morthland's persuasion, Frank Wilson also embraced more moderate attitudes in the early 1960s. As a result, the council's influence with the banks had declined somewhat by 1963, when the city's civil rights demonstrations commenced. Nevertheless, the council continued to have substantial economic influence in the community.

The political influence of the White Citizens' Council's was even more significant. Its officers and executive committee were selected each year by a nominating committee of which Mayor Heinz and Probate Judge Reynolds were the co-chairmen. The nominating committee's report was presented to the general membership at the annual meeting each October, but it was accepted in a pro forma voice vote. In effect, therefore, the local political organization chose the council's leadership. Judge Reynolds, who presided ex officio over the county's governing body, the board of revenue, appears to have been in charge of selecting the executive committee members from the rural areas, while Mayor Heinz selected the members from Selma. But as we have seen, Reynolds and Heinz were the closest of friends, and they would surely have coordinated their selections. The chairmanship of the council alternated annually between the city and the rural part of the county. Some prominent politicians themselves held council office. Dallas County's state senator, Walter Givhan—who from 1942 had been the president of the county's chapter of the Farm Bureau and was the legislature's principal spokesman for large planting interests—was the chairman of the Dallas County White Citizens' Council in 1957–58 and was state chairman of the Association of Alabama White Citizens' Councils from 1958 to 1962. County board of revenue member L. Seawell Jones was a member of the council's executive committee in 1961–62. Ordinarily, however, politicians left leadership in the council to private citizens. But essentially all politicians actively sought to identify themselves with the council. In the spring of 1958, council founder and county Democratic Party chairman M. Alston Keith noted proudly that since the council's organization, only one nonmember had held elective office in the community.

The Citizens' Council spoke in authoritative tones in the local media, as well. Edward Field, the *Selma Times-Journal's* editor from 1938 to his death in 1963, was a zealous adherent of the council; indeed, he appears to have been one of its organizers. And the *Times-Journal's* city editor, Arthur Capell, was a member of the council's executive committee from 1959 to at least 1962. But after Field's death in November 1963, his successor, Roswell Falkenberry, moved the paper in an increasingly moderate direction. And Capell, promoted to managing editor and assistant editorial page editor at the same time, also adopted more moderate attitudes, primarily because of his growing hostility to the Heinz organization. In the spring of 1961, the council decided to undertake a public information campaign. Two Selma radio stations and the town's only television station, which had begun broadcasting in March 1960, agreed to air without charge, as a public service, weekly programs produced by the council. In September 1963, however, Selma's television station became an affiliate of the American Broadcasting Company's network and thus began offering national news programming. The year before, too, the city granted a cable franchise to bring Selmians clear reception of stations in other cities. The developments at the *Times-Journal* and at the television station therefore meant that the council's influence upon the media, as with the banks, had begun to decline somewhat just as civil rights demonstrations were commencing in the city.[41]

The ideology espoused by the Citizens' Councils emphasized above all the necessity for white unity. The ideology was founded upon racial prejudice, of course. The Reverend E. B. Warren, a Baptist minister in rural Dallas County, lamented the failure of the black citizen to realize that the Constitution "was not written for him or any other colored race" and proclaimed it to be God's intention that whites should lead and blacks should follow. Senator Walter Givhan ranted that the goal of the NAACP "is to open the bedroom doors of our white women to Negro men," and he concluded, "This is a white man's country. It always has been and always will be." Circuit Judge James Hare charged the county grand jury that "integration is a false hope held out to our colored friends by trouble-making elements." The only whites who would accept integration, he told the jurors, were the lesser European stocks. "In all the talk about integration, one important and basic point has been continuously and probably purposely overlooked. That point is that in the entire history of the Anglo-Saxon race, that race has never integrated with any other people." Contradicting—though probably unconsciously—the segregationist ministers who claimed that white supremacy was divinely ordained, Judge Hare told a gathering of white schoolteachers, "I sincerely deplore the efforts of some of our churches to give color of religion or morals to the problem of segregation. To me segregation is solely a social problem and to color it with religious or moral overtones is but to confuse and obscure the issue. Segregation may be defined as a modus vivendi (a way of life), which has been worked out through the centuries in the South whereby two highly divergent races of people may live in the same community in peace and mutual advancement, freed of the daily and constant irritations and conflicts that are inherent in a bi-racial society."[42]

It followed easily in the minds of council members that efforts to destroy so beneficent and necessary an arrangement must proceed from evil and un-American sources. Senator Givhan warned that "we are going to have to face [integration] and meet it in our fashion, or expect [the] ultimate doom of our civilization." And he said of the pending "vicious" civil rights bill of 1964, "It threatens to make all our freedoms null and void and to destroy our present American way of life. It is designed to destroy the America that we love so well." Earlier, Attorney General John Patterson had told Selmians that the pending civil rights bill of 1957 "would be the first step towards creation of a police state." Governor George Wallace told the council that President Kennedy's Defense Department officials "may not be Communists, but they are certainly aiding the Communist cause." The notion that the Kennedy and Johnson administrations were Communist-dominated was widespread, and the belief that the NAACP and other civil rights organizations were controlled by Communists was universal among council adherents. These themes converged in the dark implications of one council advertisement, which asserted that federal officials "know that the Negro level [of intelligence] cannot be raised. Could they possibly want to lower that of the white people? What could be their reason?"[43]

But racial prejudices and fears of subversion formed a ground of assumption for council members. Their active concern focused instead upon the urgency of eliminating all white dissent. Governor-elect Patterson explained part of the problem in an address to the Selma council: "Little Rock's fight has been made more difficult and confusing because the white people there are not united; some of them are agitating for reopening of the schools even if it means integrating them. Situations such as this really puts [sic] a public official on the spot, and that's why we must not have it in our state." Rather, "we must stand together to the man."

Their own observation was equally convincing. Judge Hare believed that because Selma had been marked by "rigidity and cohesion," it had therefore succeeded in preventing any black initiatives, while its Black Belt neighbor Montgomery had shown "indecision and concession," and so had failed the test of the bus boycott. Council chairman Jim Risher urged the public to "check Selma and Dallas County's record of harmony between the races and decide for yourself whether your council has been active and awake." He observed, "Events have proven that integration situations arise in cities and areas where the council is weakest. There has never been an effort to force integration in a city where the council is strong." Council chairman Aubrey Allen said that, though the council had "made considerable progress against the evil forces of integration," nevertheless, "It is only through a united front and a strong organization that we can continue our successful resistance."

The national president of the White Citizens' Councils, Roy Harris of Augusta, Georgia, warned the Selma council, "Integration leaders like Martin Luther King would not have the courage to move into a section if renegade whites didn't lay the groundwork for them." The threat of integration could be defeated, therefore, if white southerners would only unite to "make it so hot the renegades would be afraid to open their mouths." Thus, Governor Wallace's closest adviser, state finance director Seymour Trammell, urged whites to ostracize all federal judges, as well as the judges' families and friends. And for the same reason, the council always understood its principal opponents to be, not black civil rights workers, but white racial moderates and business progressives. In an address to the council, W. J. Simmons of Jackson, Mississippi, the editor of *The Citizen,* the national White Citizens' Councils' official newspaper, denounced the "unholy alliance" among the "country club set, the press and the Negro bloc vote." The country club set, he said, were people "whose children go to private schools and who think that resistance to integration is bad for business." This alliance had produced integration in Atlanta, Dallas, and Memphis, he stated, and it would bring integration to Selma also unless the council there remained vigilant against it.

The emphasis upon the necessity for white unity could make council members very nervous. Council chairman Holt Hamlett, a rural Dallas County planter, feared that a small turnout for a council rally "could result in an immediate deterioration of local race relations." It "would be an open invitation to Negro agitators to increase the tempo and scope of their activities in Selma." He believed that it was essential that whites "show that they are united to fight for their cause." Usually, however, the belief that white unity would necessarily defeat integration was a source of fierce confidence. Indeed, an observer of the present day may find it hard to credit the extent to which council members remained certain of their ultimate triumph.

Because they could not believe that blacks could achieve their goals by themselves, and because they had succeeded in silencing all public advocacy of racial moderation by Selma's whites, council members had little sense that the civil rights movement was making any progress. When token integration came to other states, the council did not perceive it as a portent of defeat. The admission of James Meredith to the University of Mississippi represented no real integration, as the White Citizens' Councils' Alabama state president, C. E. Hornsby, Jr., a Centreville lumberman, understood it. "Ole Miss was not integrated because she never submitted. It can only be said that she has been subjected to integration by overwhelming and unlawful force. Thus Ole Miss' honor remains intact." South Carolina newspaper editor Thomas Waring assured the Selma council in an address, "There is no inevitable outcome of token integration. . . . Even if a few Negro children are forced into scattered white schools, that does not mean they will be there indefinitely." Rather, he said, token integration should be looked upon as a "temporary device to remove immediate pressures" before the winning of the final victory. It was crucial, of course, that white southerners continue to resist all integration firmly, but if they held out long enough, civil rights demands would eventually alienate other Americans. Robert Patterson, the White Citizens' Councils' founder and national executive director, told Selmians that few people had as yet "suffered from this integration which has caused so much trouble. But when they start suffering, there will be a new awakening in this country." He added, therefore, "The fight won't be over in a year or two. So hold what you've got and stubbornly refuse to let anyone integrate you or herd illiterates to the ballot box."

The Montgomery segregationist leader Dr. Henry Lyon, a Baptist minister, told Selmians, "If we think integration is inevitable, it will happen," but actually, "We can do something about it, and we are doing something about it. We are gaining ground in our efforts to maintain our way of life." Senator Givhan, crediting the withdrawal of federal troops from Little Rock to the efforts of the Citizens' Councils, stated confidently, "We will always be on top, and eventually we are going to win a complete victory in our fight to preserve our sacred way of life." Because whites controlled the South's money and could afford to close public facilities and establish private ones in their stead, governor-elect Patterson said, "there is no alternative but defeat for the Negro." Judge Hare thought in 1959 that the 1960 national political conventions would be the last ones at which civil rights would be a major question. "It is my opinion that by 1964 that the entire nation will be so fed up with the civil rights issue that our politicians will be afraid to even whisper the word." Governor Wallace was equally confident in the summer of 1963. "Every day we can hold off and continue our fight, we are gaining thousands of allies across the country," he told the Selma council. "And eventually the reaction we are working for will come with such violent force that it will shake the entire nation to its very foundations. . . . We may lose some more battles and have to make sacrifices, but if we continue to stand, we'll eventually win the war." It was precisely on this basis that Wallace decided in 1964 to enter Democratic presidential primaries in three northern states. Moreover, his reception there only strengthened his conviction. When Congress was about to enact into law the civil rights bill of 1964, Wallace predicted resistance to it throughout the nation, resistance so widespread that it would compel the law's repeal within two to four years.[44]

With such confidence came enthusiasm. Already by the beginning of 1956, the Dallas County Citizens' Council was the largest in the state and was actively involved in founding councils in the surrounding counties. By 1958 the state Citizens' Councils' organization essentially was operated by the leaders of the Dallas County council, and at the Citizens' Councils' national convention in New Orleans in February 1961, the Dallas County council was saluted as the top individual council in the United States.[45]

But this confidence and enthusiasm was founded, of course, upon social blindness. Its fundamental presumption was the white supremacist belief that without white assistance, blacks were powerless to help themselves. Because they so deeply believed that theirs was a white man's country, council members could not conceive of a successful challenge with origins within the black community. Robert Patterson, the movement's creator, understood the Citizens' Councils as a twentieth-century version of the seventeenth-century New England town meeting. The councils, like the town meetings, would maintain community purity and order by institutionalizing and focusing community sentiment. "Neither courts, laws nor pressure groups can change human nature, and public sentiment is the law. It is the duty and obligation of the Councils to mobilize this sentiment." Senator Givhan noted that, since whites were the state's jurors, they could defeat the courts simply by refusing to convict defendants who were resisting integration.[46]

The Dallas County council—and far too often, the juries of Dallas as well—fulfilled completely the challenge given to them by Patterson, Givhan, and the movement's other leaders. Council members drove moderate sentiment so far underground that Selma's officials came to believe that it had ceased to exist. When, in September 1963, three investigators for the National Council of Churches met with Mayor Heinz, Judge Hare, and Judge Reynolds, they had already spoken privately with a number of moderates. "We tried to tell the city officials that many responsible white citizens disagreed with the position of the city government, but were afraid to speak out openly," the investigators reported. "The mayor and the two judges contended, however, that they spoke for a unanimous white community." Judge Hare told the *Times-Journal*, "They said they came here to try to open some lines of communication between the white and Negro communities. I told them that we have quite adequate communication between the two groups, and if there is any breakdown of communication, it is between the white people of the South and Washington. . . . We told them that if their visit was for purposes of social and school integration, that we have nothing to talk about." The investigators concluded, "Under its present leadership, Selma has set itself on a collision course with the United States Constitution and the new Negro who knows his rights and intends to exercise them."[47]

Just as the three investigators were talking with Selma's white political leaders, however, in other parts of the city Selma's blacks and its business progressives were preparing to reveal the fundamental error upon which segregationist strategy was built. Blacks would demonstrate that they did not actually need the assistance of the frightened white moderates in order to strike for full citizenship, and business progressives would show that, however strong the enforced white consensus upon racial questions might appear to be, there were deep divisions within the white community that threatened the power of the machine. By the beginning of 1965, Chris Heinz, now ex-mayor and Citizens' Council chairman, witnessed his city engulfed by the challenge he had labored so long to forestall. He correctly understood the gravity of the moment. "The time of decision is at hand," he warned. But even then he was unable to see that his analysis had proven mistaken. He had only the old solution to offer in the face of the new crisis. "We must lay aside personal differences and stand united as one unbreakable unit," he said.[48]

The strength of the White Citizens' Council in Selma derived, of course, from its close association with the powerful Burns-Heinz political organization, but this strength was, in fact, a weakness as well, and for both groups. As younger businessmen became increasingly hostile in the early 1960s to what they regarded as Mayor Heinz's complacent leadership in the economic sphere, they often came to question the doctrines of the Citizens' Council also, because the council's incessant emphasis on white unity inhibited, as they saw it, a healthy questioning of Heinz's policies. And when the council attempted to take action to enforce white conformity, the objects of such pressure were likely to resent not only the council but the city administration, too. The two groups were so identified with each other that unpopular actions by either one tended to harm them both. The result was that the council's influence in Selma, which had been very great in the last half of the 1950s, began to decline in the first years of the new decade as dissatisfaction with the city machine began to grow.

Throughout the period from 1955 to 1965, the Citizens' Council remained by far the most visible and powerful segregationist organization in Dallas County. However, an even more aggressive element of the segregationist resistance gained institutional form in November 1957, when a klavern of the Ku Klux Klan was established in the city. Initially the klavern had only thirty-nine members, but by the following spring it had grown to at least fifty-five. The Klansmen undertook a variety of public demonstrations to dramatize their existence. In celebration of the founding of the klavern, Klansmen burned five crosses at each of the principal highway entrances to the city. The following summer, when Alabama's black Baptist Sunday School and Training Union Congress held its state convention in Selma, and Martin Luther King delivered the principal address, the group applied for a permit to hold a parade. The city refused. Klansmen, however, responded to this assertion of black self-respect by staging on the night of July 31 a horn-blowing fifteen-car motorcade through black neighborhoods, and on the night of August 26 a sixty-car motorcade, led by a car bearing a four-foot lighted cross, which wound through black neighborhoods for more than two and a half hours. A year later, Selma's klavern, following the example of klaverns in towns all over the state, placed on the highways entering the city signs proclaiming the

Klan's welcome of motorists to Selma; the signs joined several similar ones placed there earlier by civic clubs.

Authorities greeted all of these displays with equanimity. Sheriff James Clark said that the five burning crosses had concerned him only because he feared they might ignite grass fires. Police Chief Edward Mullen, when asked if the motorcades did not constitute violations of the ordinance requiring a parade permit, replied that the ordinance did not apply unless the "parade includes a band and a large number of units for which traffic is halted and traffic signals are turned off, and officers are stationed at street intersections to direct traffic." Only five years later, when the demonstrations were conducted by blacks rather than by Klansmen, officers would decide that even groups of people walking down the sidewalks constituted a parade and would use this very ordinance as the basis for mass arrests. In 1960 the federal Bureau of Public Roads, noting that it permitted the posting of highway welcome signs only by groups that were in the public interest, asked Alabama to remove the Klan's signs from the state's roadways. Governor Patterson, who had received the Klan's support in his victorious gubernatorial campaign, angrily demanded that the bureau reveal the criteria by which it determined that a group was in the public interest and that it send him a list of all groups it considered to be in the public interest.[49]

Such tacit official sanction for the Klan's exhibitions strengthened the organization's hand. But it was not such relatively harmless public manifestations, of course, that made the Klan a threat. Instead, Klan elements engaged in clandestine terror tactics, and these, when added to the Citizens' Council's economic coercion and local authorities' hostility, shaped race relations in Dallas County in the late 1950s and early 1960s.

In 1954, Deputy Sheriff Brantley Lee of Talladega County was involved in an automobile collision in rural Dallas with black well digger Israel Page. Lee was charged with reckless driving and failure to stop at a stop sign. Page's arm was so injured that he became permanently disabled and had to abandon his occupation. He sued Lee for fifteen hundred dollars in damages. The night before the suit was scheduled to come to trial in January 1959, four white men, apparently offended by the effrontery of a black person's suing a law enforcement officer, took Page from his house, beat him into unconsciousness, and dumped his body in a swamp thirty-five miles from his home. The Dallas County Bar Association adopted a resolution calling for the arrest and prosecution of Page's assaulters, but Page seems to have dropped his suit against Lee.

In 1960, when a black man was seen riding with a white woman in an automobile with out-of-state license plates, two carloads of whites beat and abducted him. In 1958 a dynamite explosion at a store owned by a black man in the nearby village of Lowndesboro did some $350 in damage.

In the late spring of 1959, the state Conservation Department opened a public fishing lake just outside Selma. The lake, constructed in part with federal funds, was without a formal racial designation, and the absence of such a designation created trouble from the very beginning. Blacks sought to use it along with whites, and white toughs sought to prevent them from doing so. The lake opened on May 20. On May 23 a number of blacks used the lake without apparent incident, but an elderly black man, Horace Bell of Montgomery, failed to return home that night. The next day, three blacks who attempted to use the lake were severely beaten; one of them suffered a broken arm. These incidents greatly frightened Horace Bell's family, who began to suspect that he had met with foul play. They contacted Chief State Investigator W. L. Allen of the state highway patrol and appealed for a search for Bell. They offered to bring a large group of blacks from Montgomery to assist, but Allen refused. After further discussion, Allen did consent to allow a small group to help, and he contacted Dallas County sheriff James Clark to notify him of the plan. Clark alerted his deputies and Selma police. As a result, according to the *Times-Journal,* "an uneasy public buzzed with widespread unfounded rumors that Gov. Patterson had granted permission for a throng of Negroes to search the lake area." In the meantime, Allen had actually decided to use state highway patrolmen to conduct the search. They succeeded in finding Bell's body; it turned out that he had actually died of a heart attack, unrelated to the racial incidents. But on May 31, three black airmen from Craig Air Force Base who tried to use the lake were set upon by a white mob that seized their fishing permits and then ordered them to leave. In the intervening days a number of other blacks had left—voluntarily, according to the lake's manager—when the manager told them of the earlier attacks. In Montgomery, Martin Luther King and Ralph Abernathy wrote to U.S. Attorney General William Rogers to ask for a federal investigation of the violence. On June 1 the state Conservation Department ordered the new lake closed indefinitely. Racial tension remained high. On June 29, after a fight between three black and five white youths, Selma police chief Edward Mullen placed all Selma teenagers under a midnight curfew. After further fights in August, the curfew was moved forward to 11 P.M.[50]

In December 1959, when a Selma motion picture theater attempted to show *Imitation of Life,* a film that depicted interracial relations, three "stink bombs" were exploded inside, forcing the 125 whites seated on the main floor and the 100 blacks in the balcony to leave. The theater thereupon agreed to cancel the film's run.

The home of Dr. J. H. Williams, a black Selma dentist, was something of a community landmark because, though the house of a black man, it was large and modern, with a picture window. This display of affluence was an intolerable affront to some whites. On four occasions between November 1960 and June 1962 it was attacked by vandals. The picture window was broken by rocks, by timber, and finally by shots from a pellet gun. After the fourth incident, Police Chief Mullen warned that, if the vandals could be caught, they would be prosecuted.[51]

These incidents of private intimidation were coupled with official ones. In 1960 a fifteen-year-old black youth, Willie J. Taylor, was indicted for an alleged assault on Mrs. Smith Howard, Jr., of Safford. Eighteen white Selma women for whom Taylor had done odd jobs signed a petition supporting him and criticizing sheriff's deputies for their handling of Taylor's arrest. Deputies had claimed that Taylor had confessed to the assault, but the women pointed out that Taylor's severe speech impediment made an oral confession impossible. Deputies then admitted that they could not be sure of the confession's reliability, but they insisted that Taylor's mental retardation and his prowling made him a menace to society in any case. When the petition of the white women was submitted, the county grand jury summoned each of the women to appear before it to explain her action. It then formally dismissed the petition's complaints. Because of Taylor's mental condition he could not be tried on the indictment, but he was ordered committed to the state's black mental asylum instead.[52]

The trial of the Reverend Louis L. Anderson in 1959 had almost the impact in the black community that the Fikes trials had had in 1953. Anderson, the minister of one of Selma's largest and most influential congregations, Tabernacle Baptist Church, had been indicted for second-degree murder following an automobile accident. Anderson, who had graduated from the University of Pittsburgh and held a graduate degree from the University of Chicago, was one of Selma's most articulate advocates of black rights. The *Times-Journal,* in reporting his indictment, identified him as a "Negro NAACP leader" even though the NAACP had not operated in Alabama since Judge Walter B. Jones of Montgomery had enjoined it from doing so in 1956. Peter Hall and Orzell Billingsley of Birmingham, who had defended Fikes in 1953, returned to Selma to defend Anderson, and were joined by Fred Gray of Montgomery.

Hall and Billingsley at once entered a motion to quash the indictment and the venire on the ground that blacks were systematically excluded from juries in the county. Since the revision of the jury rolls as a result of the Fikes trial, only one black had actually served on a grand jury, and none had done so on a petit jury. But Sheriff Clark testified that at least one black, and sometimes even as many as six, had been included among the sixty-five to ninety men on each venire since the revision. Judge L. S. Moore therefore denied the motion.

Testimony at the trial was conflicting. It was clear that Anderson had collided with a car driven by another black man, Mike Howard, and that after the collision Anderson's car had proceeded down the street at perhaps seventy miles an hour, striking and killing a third black man, pedestrian Tom Reese. Anderson's car was halted only when it ran into a tree.

Howard and other prosecution witnesses swore that Anderson had been speeding before the collision of the cars, that the collision was Anderson's fault, and that Anderson was upright in his seat when he struck Reese. Anderson and other defense witnesses testified that Anderson was not speeding before the collision and that Howard failed to stop at the intersection and ran into Anderson's car, hitting it on the side. They said that Anderson had been knocked unconscious by the collision and that his body was thrown to the floorboard, depressing the accelerator and thus causing the subsequent events. The defense asserted that Howard's car was damaged in front and Anderson's on the side passenger door.

Judge Moore eliminated the charge of second-degree murder because the state had failed to prove malice on Anderson's part, but he sent the question of manslaughter to the jury. After deliberating for only an hour and twenty minutes, the jury convicted Anderson of voluntary manslaughter and sentenced him to the maximum possible term, ten years in prison.

Even if one credits the prosecution's case rather than the defense's, there can be little question that Anderson's community standing as a black spokesman was responsible for the unusual severity of the jury's verdict and sentence. This fact was brought home to observers a year later when the circuit court tried a very similar case involving two white men. The state's testimony alleged that prominent accountant Clarence "Shorty" Long was going some seventy miles an hour and was weaving on the road when he struck and killed wrecker operator Coley L. Piper, who was attaching his wrecker truck to a previously wrecked car. The only significant difference in the circumstances of the two cases, as the prosecution's witnesses depicted them, was that Anderson's accident had occurred within Selma's city limits, while Long's was on a highway just east of town. Long was convicted only of involuntary manslaughter, however, and was fined five hundred dollars; he received no jail sentence.

Anderson's conviction was affirmed by the Alabama Court of Appeals and the Alabama Supreme Court. The Court of Appeals in its opinion relied in part on the state supreme court's holding in the second Fikes case that the 1953 revision of the jury rolls had been sufficient to eliminate the previous racial discrimination. But in 1961 the U.S. Supreme Court accepted the argument of Anderson's attorneys that blacks were still systematically excluded from Dallas County's juries and reversed the conviction. Despite this decision, however, county authorities refused to take any action to include additional blacks on the jury lists. Not only were they unable to retry Anderson as a result, but they also opened every future conviction of a black person in the county to reversal on the basis of the Anderson precedent whenever a Selma attorney had sufficient temerity to raise the question. Evidently the authorities' hostility to black jurors was so great that they were prepared to run this risk. It hardly needs to be said that all of these proceedings further deepened the distrust and fear that Selma's blacks entertained for their community's courts.[53]

Indeed, many county political leaders remained so aggressively committed to the maintenance of white supremacy that they were prepared to take extraordinarily provocative actions. In May of 1962, U.S. District Judge Daniel Thomas had tried the U.S. Justice Department's suit charging the Dallas County Board of Voting Registrars with racial discrimination. Several of the government's witnesses were schoolteachers who had been denied registration. The following month, the Dallas County Board of Education, which administered the schools in the rural areas of the county, discharged thirty-six black teachers who had testified for the Justice Department or had otherwise cooperated with it. Selma's black leaders made some efforts to help the thirty-six, but only seven of them were willing to fight their dismissals. The rest hoped that, by avoiding publicity and remaining quiet, they might obtain reemployment in the future. Dallas County had earlier obtained local legislation exempting it from the state Teacher Tenure Act so that it would be able to take just such disciplinary action against integrationist educators. In the end, therefore, no legal challenge to the firings was ever filed.[54]

On March 9, 1960, Sheriff Clark led a volunteer force of special deputies to Montgomery to assist in breaking up an anticipated demonstration at Alabama State College in the wake of Montgomery's sit-in crisis. The demonstration did not materialize, but Clark became enthusiastic about turning the volunteer force into a formal organization. On March 11 the sheriff and Circuit Solicitor Blanchard McLeod summoned several hundred white men to the county courthouse and swore them in as members of a sheriff's posse. Solicitor McLeod told the gathering, "We must meet force with force. The day of passive resistance has passed." The posse was divided into a 66-member mounted posse and a 350-member unmounted posse. The mounted posse, composed primarily of cattle ranchers from rural Dallas County, was commanded by Jim Risher, the chairman of the White Citizens' Council. The unmounted posse was commanded by wholesale grocer William M. Agee, who had been the Dallas County campaign chairman for Governor Patterson in 1958. The unmounted posse was divided into units, each of which was assigned to a specific community in the county or to a specific area of Selma. Essentially all of the possemen appear to have been members of the White Citizens' Council. The posse also contained Klan elements. On March 13 the mounted posse, riding four abreast, paraded Selma's streets in what Sheriff Clark described as the first of a series of training sessions. In May, following a flood of the Alabama River, the sheriff organized a water rescue unit of the posse, as well. But at all times the primary focus of the posse remained racial.[55]

Perhaps no event more clearly indicates the militancy and resolve of Selma's white supremacists than their reaction to the attempt to enroll

James Meredith at the University of Mississippi in the fall of 1962. In late September, as the U.S. Fifth Circuit Court of Appeals was beginning contempt proceedings in New Orleans against Mississippi governor Ross Barnett, Mayor Heinz and Probate Judge Reynolds wired Barnett to offer their support and assistance, and the Dallas County Citizens' Council wired Alabama's senators and congressmen to urge that all southern representatives join in withdrawing support from President Kennedy's legislative program until Kennedy agreed to back down on Meredith's registration. At the end of the month, when Kennedy ordered the army to be ready to move into Mississippi if necessary, Mayor Heinz wired the president that such an action "could serve no good purpose and would only result in further dividing this once united nation. The officials and the people of Mississippi have made every effort to avoid bloodshed, and further encroachments of federal power could lead to national disaster." At the same time, the Dallas County Republican Party's executive committee wired Governor Barnett that the issue facing the United States was, "Can we preserve constitutional self-government in America or must we yield to totalitarianism, with supreme authority vested in the president and his appointed officials? Our freedoms would not now be in jeopardy if other southern leaders had possessed your courage, ability and determination," the Republicans believed.

On October 1, following a night of rioting at the University of Mississippi and the dispatch of federal troops to the campus, Alabama state White Citizens' Council chairman Senator Walter Givhan, Dallas County White Citizens' Council chairman Earl Goodwin, a Selma industrialist, and *Selma Times-Journal* city editor and Citizens' Council executive committee member Arthur Capell flew to Oxford in a private plane. The three men constituted an advance party to survey the situation to determine if it would be useful for a large delegation of Dallas County White Citizens' Council members to leave for Oxford by motorcade "to offer moral support." In the meantime, the Citizens' Council assembled its supporters in Selma, under the command of Probate Judge Reynolds, to await the order to move out.

When the advance party landed at the Oxford airport, they found themselves unable to get into the town. Military personnel informed them that in order to block traffic to the campus, trees had been felled across Oxford's streets. They could not even use the telephone to call Selma, as the army had commandeered all lines. But what they saw at the airport was sufficient to infuriate them; they were especially angered to note that about half the troops at the airport were black. The advance party flew on to Tupelo, and from there Earl Goodwin telephoned Judge Reynolds that it would be futile for the Selma Citizens' Council to come to Oxford. But Goodwin and Givhan also wired Alabama's senators and congressmen, "You cannot conceive of the tragedy which has befallen your native land.

Please come immediately to Oxford and see for yourself the gravity of the threat which our democratic form of government now faces." On the flight back to Selma, Senator Givhan observed that the trouble now facing the South stemmed in part from the region's failure to choose a united bloc of unpledged presidential electors in 1960.[56]

There is perhaps a certain comic opera quality to the vision of "Babe" Reynolds at the head of a brigade of middle-aged Citizens' Council members, assembled at the county courthouse to await the summons to speed to the rescue of the University of Mississippi. But the episode in fact well symbolizes the attitudes and commitments of Selma's segregationists. The mental world into which this event gives us a glimpse was the one that would shape the white supremacists' responses when, less than a year later, they faced the initial stirrings of the black revolution in their own city. The council's self-satisfied emphasis upon what Judge Hare had called white Selma's "rigidity and cohesion"; the willingness of political and judicial authorities to use the instrumentalities of government to preserve white racial ascendancy; and the presence of elements—a small minority, but too often an unchecked one—who did not shrink from the use of violence to maintain black fear and subservience: together these defined in great measure the patterns of race relations in Dallas County in the decade after 1954.

The combination of these forces gave the segregationists considerable assurance that they had nothing to fear from the social currents unleashed by the school desegregation decision. In 1959, Selma's white Baptist churches undertook to establish a private school for white children. The churches had made careful inquiries among white parents and had found strong support for such a school. The new school was initially to include only the first three grades. It had places for ninety children and would charge only twenty dollars a month; the remainder of the school's cost would be borne by the Baptist congregations. Yet when the school opened its books for registration, only one child was actually signed up. The school's astonished administrators returned to the parents who had favored its creation and learned that the parents had never actually considered sending their own children to it, but had merely meant that they thought the establishment of a private school was a wise precaution for the future. Chagrined Baptists announced that the public "isn't in the proper frame of mind" as yet to accept private education, and they abandoned their plans.[57] White Selmians simply did not expect that integration would come to their town, at least for many years.

III. Cracks in the Dominion

Profound changes were in fact taking place in the life of Selma and Dallas County, however, and these changes would render the segregationists' confidence illusory. We have already seen that the twentieth century witnessed a constant decline in the numbers of black tenant farmers in Dallas County. There had been nearly 7,000 black tenant farmers in 1910, but by 1964 there were just over 1,000. The number continued to fall in the next decade, and by 1974 there were only 58 black tenant farmers left in the entire county. Black tenants had cultivated more than half of the county's cropland in 1930, but by 1964 they cultivated less than 7 percent of it, and by 1974 only 0.1 percent of it. These figures represent nothing less than a quiet social revolution. And the decline had been particularly concentrated in the fifteen years between 1950 and 1964, when the number of black tenants had fallen from 3,000 to 1,000 as landowners increasingly turned to cattle ranching. In the first half of the twentieth century, these figures had been paralleled by a slow but continual increase in the number of black farm owners, from fewer than 400 in 1900 to more than 600 in 1954. But in the decades after 1954, the general black abandonment of agriculture spread to black farm owners as well. By 1964 the number of black farm owners had fallen below 500, and by 1969 it had returned to the figure of 1900. By 1974, when there were only 169 black farm owners and 58 black tenant farmers in Dallas County, it could fairly be said that, though blacks continued to be employed as farm laborers, agriculture had essentially become a white occupation.

Some of the blacks displaced from farming moved into Selma. The black population of the city grew from about 8,000 in 1920 to 9,000 in 1930, to 11,000 in 1940, and to 14,000 in 1960. The city's white population grew at the same rate, from about 7,400 in 1920 to some 14,500 in 1960, so that Selma's racial division remained approximately half white and half black throughout the period. But a great many rural blacks left the county altogether, either for nearby larger cities such as Birmingham and Mobile or for northern metropolises such as Chicago and Detroit. Thus the increase in Selma's white population was roughly paralleled by the increase in the white population of Dallas County as a whole, from some 12,400 in 1920 to about 24,000 in 1960. But from a peak of about 45,400 in 1900, Dallas County's black population fell steadily throughout the twentieth century. The decline was relatively small at first, to about 40,700 in 1940, but after World War II the trend became conspicuous. The figure decreased to 36,500 in 1950, to 32,700 in 1960, and reached 29,000 in 1970. As a result, the county's racial division moved decade by decade toward parity. In 1900 the population was 83 percent black. It was three-fourths black in 1930, two-thirds black in 1950, and 58 percent black in 1960. By 1970, with about 29,000 blacks and 26,300 whites, it had only a slight black majority—an extraordinary decline from the ratio of better than five to one at the century's beginning.

Finally, as the rural black population decreased and Selma's grew, the county became more and more urban. Throughout the late nineteenth century Selma had represented about 15 percent of the county's total population. By 1910 the town had risen to a fourth of the total and by 1930 to a third of it. By 1950 it had become 40 percent of the county, and by 1960 half of the county's population lived in Selma. Correspondingly, the county's blacks were increasingly city dwellers as well. In 1940 a fourth of Dallas County's blacks resided in Selma, by 1950 a third of them did so, and by 1960 about 43 percent did so; in 1970 the figure stood at 47 percent.

The transformations reflected in these statistics had important implications for the evolution of Selmians' racial attitudes. The declining percentage of Dallas County's blacks who had been acculturated to the attitudes of dependency inherent in the tenant farming relationship meant that ingrained black deference to whites was gradually becoming less widespread. Blacks who resided in the city were considerably more likely than rural blacks to pursue occupations that afforded them at least a measure of freedom from white control. And city life afforded greater ease of communication and greater scope for the efforts of blacks to improve their economic status. Black subservience was still a fact of life in Selma at midcentury, but its material foundations had begun to erode.

One additional important source of the growing black emancipation was an increasing black educational level. Though Selma's black school system was distinctly inferior to the white one, it was also decidedly superior to the black schooling offered in rural Dallas County. A legislative act of December 1890 had separated Selma's schools from those of the county. While the county schools had remained under an elective board of education, the city schools were placed under a self-perpetuating board whose members themselves filled all vacancies on it as they occurred. Immediately before the creation of the independent city school system, Selma's blacks in the fall of 1889 had petitioned the county board for the creation of a school for black children in Selma, and the new school had gone into operation in October 1890. This grammar school, called Clark School, was headed by Richard B. Hudson, who remained its principal until his death in 1931. In 1912 the city school board had created a public high school for whites, and Hudson had soon begun arguing for the establishment of a black high school as well. But the school board had remained deaf to Hudson's pleas. During the first half of the twentieth century, therefore, blacks who desired a high school education were compelled to turn to private institutions.[58]

Fortunately, however, until the Depression, there were four such institutions available. Knox Academy had been established by the Reformed Presbyterian Church in 1874. The state's black Baptists founded Selma University—despite its name, primarily a high school—in 1878. The African Methodist Episcopal Church created Daniel Payne Institute in 1889. And the Lutheran Church, Missouri Synod, founded the Alabama Lutheran

College, also primarily a high school, in 1922. In 1932, however, the A.M.E. Church moved the struggling Payne school to Birmingham, and in 1935 the Reformed Presbyterians announced that they could no longer afford to operate Knox. This crisis led to the revival of the Dallas County Voters League—initially founded by black postal employee and civil rights leader Charles J. Adams a decade earlier, but in the meantime dormant—in an effort to persuade the city school board to take over the operation of Knox. The city board did agree to accept ownership of the Knox property, but it merely used the facility to extend public school classes for blacks through the ninth grade. The small and ill-equipped Selma University and the even smaller Alabama Lutheran College thus were the city's only black senior high schools after 1935. In the meantime, in 1939 the city built a large new high school for whites to replace the 1912 structure.

The Selma school board did not finally undertake public senior high school instruction of blacks until the end of World War II. In 1945 the tenth grade was opened to blacks, in 1946 the eleventh grade, and in 1947 the twelfth. Then, in 1949, the city built a handsome, modern black high school, named for Richard B. Hudson. These developments, which were replicated in many Alabama towns at this same time, were almost certainly a response to the indications in these years that the federal courts were preparing to examine more critically the official claim that black educational institutions, though separate, were equal to those of whites. Thereafter, black educational opportunities began to improve considerably. In 1956 a new black junior high school was erected, and in 1960 a new black elementary school. With high school classes now the responsibility of the taxpayers, Selma University in 1956 abandoned its historic role as a secondary school and transformed itself into a junior college. And Alabama Lutheran College began to focus more attention on its collegiate department as well; in 1958 it moved to an extensive new campus on the edge of the city. In 1950 the Roman Catholics opened a school for the training of black practical nurses, the first one in Alabama. And in 1951, plans for a black branch of the public library were announced.[59]

The fruits of these struggles may be seen in the census statistics. In 1910, illiteracy, though rare among whites, was widespread among blacks. Of Dallas County's blacks age ten and older, 47 percent were illiterate; among black Selmians, the figure was 29 percent. The sharp difference between the city and the rural areas is undoubtedly a tribute to the presence of Clark School in Selma. In the same year, 80 percent of Selma's black children age six to fourteen were in school, while the figure for the county at large was only 51 percent. Though poorly supplied, inadequately funded, and limited to short terms, the black schools in both the city and the county fought on, and the results were salutary. By 1930 the black illiteracy rate in the county had fallen from 47 percent to 34 percent, and in Selma from 29 percent to 18 percent.

By the years after World War II, the battle front had shifted from simple literacy to more refined measures of educational attainment. In 1950 only 13 percent of adult blacks in Dallas County had had no schooling at all, and only 8 percent in Selma. But in the same year, 53 percent of adult blacks in the county had no more than a fourth-grade education, and the figure was 37 percent in Selma. At the same time, only 6 percent of the county's adult blacks, and only 11 percent of Selma's, were at least high school graduates. But the opening of public secondary education to blacks at this time had a marked effect. By 1970 the percentage of Selma's adult blacks who had at least a high school diploma soared from 11 percent to 26 percent, and the figure for the county at large rose from 6 percent to 19 percent. Meanwhile, the percentage who had no more than a fourth-grade education fell from a majority of adult blacks in the county and 37 percent in Selma to about a quarter of them in each jurisdiction.

These changing levels of education carried with them a greater awareness of community affairs and an increasing unwillingness to be excluded from the shaping of public policy. With a fourth of black Selmians and a fifth of blacks in the county now high school graduates, deference to white authority seemed much less a reflection of the natural order of things. Thus advances in the black public schools went hand in hand with the decline of tenant farming and the rise of urbanization to create a new social order in Dallas County.

It is important to emphasize the rapidity of these changes. Older white officials had grown up in a world in which a third or more of the county's blacks were illiterate and thousands were tenant farmers. As recently as 1950, a substantial majority of the county's blacks had had no more than a fourth-grade education. Whites were not unaware of a newly independent temperament—"uppitiness," whites would have called it—among many black residents, especially those living in town, after World War II. But in general, the alterations in the status of the county's blacks had outrun older whites' appreciation of them, and the blacks' new claims seemed to most whites unwarranted by blacks' attainments and profoundly threatening to the community as a whole.[60] As a result, the developments that signified the emergence of the new social order left white segregationists both confused and increasingly frightened.

On the other hand, these same developments left white racial moderates consoled. The steady progress in the status of the county's blacks seemed to moderates to indicate that the gulf between the races would be bridged by an evolutionary process that would require no wrenching dislocations in the life of the community. Like the segregationists, they feared the intervention of ill-informed outside agitators; unlike the segregationists, they feared equally the provocation of white demagogues. But in the absence of either form of rabble-rousing, they felt that goodwill and the economic and social forces evidently at work in the region would eventually lead to the quiet elimination of the remnants of racial repression. Over time, the rising education levels of blacks would permit more and more of them to become voters, and as they did so, government would increasingly respond to their needs—though for most moderates, the response would continue to come within the framework of separate institutions for the two races.

The changing character of the county's racial composition allowed white moderates to accept with a new equanimity the prospect of a gradual increase in the proportion of black voters. As the races moved toward parity in numbers, and as blacks became more prosperous and better educated, the threat of a future vengeful black domination of the county receded in the minds of moderates. Indeed, it was perhaps this very element of their thought that most distinguished moderates from segregationists. And in Selma itself, the fear of any future black majority was made even smaller by an extensive annexation that became effective on May 1, 1956; by taking into the city the new white subdivisions that had grown up on Selma's fringes, the annexation gave whites a numerical majority in its population for the first time in its history. As a result, white moderates—though perhaps for rather different reasons—joined many blacks in the 1950s and early 1960s in regarding the emerging shape of race relations in the community with cautious optimism. Moderates generally felt that, if racial questions were left alone, they would work themselves out naturally.

Black optimism was no less cautious, but considerably more aggressive. Blacks were, of course, more sensitive to the limitations that segregation imposed upon them than whites ordinarily were. They were therefore eager to expand its boundaries by pressing against each barrier as it came to seem safe to do so. By creating the sense that an expansion of opportunities was possible, the opening of additional institutions for blacks was a significant part of the cycle. One organization quite important in this process was the Fathers of St. Edmund.

The Edmundite Fathers first came to Selma in 1937. They established a parochial school for black children in 1940. One grade was added each year until 1948, and thereafter the school, known as St. Elizabeth's, operated with eight grades. But perhaps the Edmundites' greatest contribution was in the area of health care. Inadequate facilities for the hospitalization of black patients had been, along with the inadequate black public schools, a principal community deficiency. Selma's first hospital for blacks was the Burwell Infirmary, founded in 1907, but by the 1960s this ten-bed facility located in a frame house was threatened with closure for fire code violations. The city's white hospital, Vaughan Memorial, permitted blacks to use only ten of its beds. And the third hospital open to blacks, Good Samaritan, founded by the Baptists in 1922, was initially, like Burwell Infirmary, a small facility in a frame structure, the former home of a dentist. The Edmundites purchased Good Samaritan in 1944 and almost at once began trying to improve and expand it. Working with the Sisters of St. Joseph, the Edmundites in 1947 constructed a two-story, thirty-six-bed hospital. In 1950, as we have seen, the two orders established the first school in Alabama to train blacks as practical nurses. In 1943 they had begun a nursing home for elderly blacks, and in 1958 they opened a new twenty-six-bed nursing home to replace the earlier facility. And finally, in 1964, they completed Selma's first genuine, fully equipped hospital for black people. The four-story, sixty-nine-bed new Good Samaritan cost $1.2 million to build. It adjoined the two-story structure of 1947, and the older building was then converted into a home for the school of practical nursing.[61]

In 1947, too, the Edmundites founded the Don Bosco Club, a recreational facility for black youth. This Roman Catholic effort led to a Protestant response. The Reverend Claude C. Brown had been appointed in 1942 as the pastor of Knox Chapel, the only remnant of the Reformed Presbyterians' once extensive presence in the Selma black community after the church had abandoned the operation of Knox Academy in 1935. Brown quickly became a sort of ambassador from the city's blacks to municipal and county authorities. Taking up the challenge of the Don Bosco Club, Brown established a rival Ralph Bunche Club. The two recreational centers thereafter engaged in spirited competitions. Brown's wife, the librarian of the new Hudson High School, was equally dedicated to serving black youth. In 1956, at the urging of a committee headed by white attorney Harry Gamble, a prominent racial moderate, the YMCA adopted Brown's Ralph Bunche Club and converted it into a YMCA branch for blacks.[62]

The opening of public secondary education to black students, the three new black public schools, the new black hospital, nursing home, and school for practical nurses, the black YMCA branch, and other new institutions such as the extensive George Washington Carver public housing project for blacks just north of the downtown that opened in 1952—all were visible evidence of the less tangible but much more important metamorphosis taking place below the surface of daily life in Dallas County in the two decades after World War II in the economic and social positions of blacks. The creation of these new institutions may seem small victories from our perspective today, but the institutions had enormous importance for black Selmians, who could see in them reason to have confidence that blacks' subordination need not be perpetual. They did not indicate, of course, that any great transformation was at hand, but they did seem to prove that things were beginning to change. There was even evidence in the lives of local people. J. L. Chestnut, Jr., was the son of a Selma grocer. He graduated from high school in 1948, in just the second class to finish public high school in the city. He went on to Dillard University and to Howard University law school, and in 1959 he was admitted to the Alabama bar and commenced practice in Selma—the town's first black attorney of the twentieth century, and only the seventeenth in the state. The fact that a local black man was now arguing cases before white judges and juries—even if in the midst of a segregation as pervasive as ever—offered an intimation, at least, that the future would not forever be like the past. And the community contained some blacks who were eager to draw such inferences.[63]

There was one final source of the sense of change that was emerging in Selma in these years, and it was an institution whose influence was as powerful among white residents as among black: Craig Air Force Base. Established in 1940, Craig was a training center for fighter pilots. By the end of World War II it had two thousand military personnel and fourteen hundred civilian employees. The Korean War and cold war tensions kept the base large in later years. In 1952 its monthly cash payroll exceeded a million dollars, and one of every thirty-two residents of the city was employed on the base. The effect of these expenditures on Selma's economy was immense. In addition, the federal government made direct cash payments to the Selma school system to pay for the junior high and high school education of the children of military personnel; after 1950, however, the base provided its own elementary schooling. And the federal government financed as well the construction in 1940 of the Nathan Bedford Forrest public housing project, administered by the city housing authority, for white base employees and airmen.

Blacks stationed at Craig were, of course, subjected to ubiquitous racial discrimination when they ventured into town. Nor was discrimination entirely absent on the base. Nevertheless, the relative lack of racial barriers at Craig was a new experience for many Selmians, white and black. And even in the city, the presence of Craig could be felt. White policemen, for instance, were unaccustomed to being questioned if they mistreated a black man, but if the victim turned out to have been an airman in civilian clothes the police officer might find himself compelled to justify his actions to his superiors. This knowledge perhaps to some degree restrained police actions in the years after 1940. Moreover, contact and conversations with blacks and whites from other areas of the country—and with the foreign officers who were trained at Craig, as well—could influence Selmians' attitudes. Both blacks and whites might be brought to consider the extent to which Selma's patterns of racial contact were normal.[64]

The growing urbanization and increasing prosperity in Dallas County, developments for which Craig was in part responsible, were also significant factors in generating the new level of dissent that gradually became apparent in city and county politics in the late 1950s and early 1960s. The first election in which this new ferment could be clearly seen occurred in 1958 and involved two figures who would play major roles in the civil rights collisions of later years, Wilson Baker and Jim Clark.

Early in November of 1955, less than two weeks after the controversy over the NAACP's school integration petition had climaxed in Officer William Bailey's suicide, Dallas County sheriff William C. McCain died suddenly of a heart attack. Governor James E. Folsom, who had just returned to office the preceding January, appointed to serve out the three years of Sheriff McCain's unexpired term one of the governor's most enthusiastic young followers, James G. Clark, Jr. Clark was a native of Folsom's hometown, Elba, and a nephew of Folsom's brother-in-law and political confidant, J. Ross Clark. Jim Clark graduated from Elba High School in 1940 and enrolled at the University of Alabama. With the outbreak of World War II, however, he enlisted in the air force and saw active duty in the Pacific. In 1945 he returned to the University of Alabama. In 1948 he purchased a farm near the rural community of Browns, in the northwestern corner of Dallas County, and became a cattle rancher. During the gubernatorial campaign of 1954, Clark ardently supported Folsom, and on his inauguration Folsom appointed Clark as executive assistant to the state commissioner of revenue. Clark served in this position for ten months, until his appointment to succeed Sheriff McCain.[65]

Clark was just the sort of person without any experience in law enforcement whose presence in the profession Wilson Baker had come more and more to resent. Baker, a native of South Carolina, had graduated from Newberry College there. He had moved to Selma after marrying a Selma native and had joined the Selma police force the same year Jim Clark graduated from Elba High School, 1940. During the next dozen years he worked his way up to captain. Baker had been the man who had handled the intensive interrogation of William Fikes in 1953; Chief Justice Earl Warren would single him out for criticism of his conduct in the Supreme Court's majority opinion in the Fikes case in 1957. But in the meantime, Officer Bailey's suicide in 1955 seems already to have moved Baker, a charter member of the Selma White Citizens' Council, to begin to reexamine his commitments. Baker had been an honorary pallbearer at Bailey's funeral. The young officer's death and Sergeant Pressley's involvement in the Sturdivant kidnapping very probably were factors in commencing a modification of Baker's sense of the proper limits of police conduct. At any rate, whether or not this episode was an element in the alteration, it is clear that Baker's beliefs did undergo development at this time. He certainly did not become an advocate of civil rights for blacks, of course, but he did become an advocate, and with increasing passion as the years passed, of professionalism in the conduct of law enforcement personnel. Chief Justice Warren's censure of Baker's behavior in the Fikes investigation only added to these concerns. And a particular focus of them was the county's new sheriff. Thus, when Clark announced his candidacy for election to a term in his own right in 1958, Baker resigned from the police force in order to run against him.[66]

The Dallas County sheriff's election of 1958 was one of the most hotly contested races in the county for many years. In addition to Clark and Baker, the contest also included a third candidate, Frank C. Dozier, who had been a deputy sheriff under McCain and Clark. The three men canvassed the county actively. Baker stressed his seventeen years as a policeman and pledged to have all his deputies trained at the Alabama Police Academy. He promised "better police methods and modern enforcement practices, plus a greater understanding of crime prevention techniques," by implication criticizing the standards of conduct that Clark had set in office. Clark rested his appeal primarily on his residence in the rural part of the county; he adopted the motto "A Rural Sheriff for Rural Law Enforcement" and attacked Baker for his urban outlook.

Race played only a minor role in the canvass. Clark in his advertisements asserted that "he has proven he knows how to handle our racial problems" and that he "works in close cooperation with the Citizens Council. There is no racial problem in Dallas County. Jim Clark has had a big hand in handling this problem in a quiet, smooth and efficient manner. Look in the rural areas." Baker replied that he, too, was a Citizens' Council member. Early in the campaign Baker committed a considerable blunder in the eyes of some voters when he and three other candidates allowed themselves to be introduced at a rally near Selma of twenty-five hundred members of the Ku Klux Klan. When the local newspaper reported this appearance, Baker quickly issued a statement that his presence at the rally did not indicate his support of the Klan, that he had merely stated to the Klansmen that he favored segregation. Nevertheless, this incident certainly alienated the county's 180 black voters from Baker, and probably some white moderates as well. But neither it nor Clark's racial appeals appear to have been particularly significant factors in the outcome.

The voting in the initial primary reflected a sharp division between Selma and the countryside. Baker led with 40 percent of the total vote, to 34 percent for Clark and 26 percent for Dozier. But Clark carried fourteen of the sixteen boxes outside the Selma city limits, and Dozier carried one of the other two, as well as four boxes within Selma. Eight of the ten boxes carried by Baker were within the city; he also carried one county box and the absentee box. Excluding the Dozier vote, Clark beat Baker in the rural part of the county by two to one.[67]

The runoff campaign opened with a coup for Clark. The day after the first primary, Clark rehired Dozier as a deputy, and Dozier thereupon endorsed Clark for election. As it turned out, Clark would keep Dozier on his staff only for a short time beyond the end of the canvass, but the endorsement he thus gained was an important one. The distribution of the first primary vote, too, allowed Clark to reemphasize in even stronger terms his contention that Baker's support was essentially limited to the city and that rural residents, who actually depended on the sheriff for law enforcement, were satisfied with Clark's performance. It was in connection with this argument, however, that Clark introduced a new theme into the run-off, one that would dominate the campaign and prove momentous for the future of Selma. He commenced attacking Baker as the candidate of the Burns-Heinz machine, and therefore turned much of his oratorical wrath against the machine itself.

Mayor Heinz was deeply grateful to Baker for his having obtained Fikes's confessions in 1953; at the time, the mayor and Police Chief Ed Mullen had warmly praised Baker's interrogation, Chief Mullen saying, "It is a job that no one else could have done, and without these confessions, Fikes would have been just another suspect." Presumably in considerable part because of the admiration he had developed for Baker as a result of this effort and other similar ones, Heinz had thrown the full weight of his support behind Baker's campaign. Clark now began publishing advertisements urging the voters to stand up to machine intimidation. He alleged that city employees' families had been threatened if they voted for him, and assured them that their ballots were secret. He said that the machine was a "great buga boo [sic]" that "wants you to think it is like a giant octopus with many powerful tentacles reaching into your business, your job, your private life—ever ready to protect you when you 'play ball,' or put the powerful squeeze on you if you try to slip away. It thinks it is your Lord Protector, your Lord Prosecutor, judge and jury." In fact, he said, it consisted only of "5 highly respectabble [sic], secretive, conniving men, branded [sic] together to promote and protect its cause, to keep itself nourished in substance with a Big Bluff." And, he added, the votes of the people can defeat it. As another advertisement asserted, "They say, 'Jim Clark is a good sheriff, but he can't beat the machine.' What machine is so powerful that it can place a sheriff in office against the wishes of the people of Selma and Dallas County?"

These attacks quickly placed Baker on the defensive. Clark even discovered a way to counter Baker's pledge to hire only professionally trained law enforcement officers as deputies. Clark published a large picture of the sheriff with his seven deputies over the caption, "Our job depends on your vote! Help us hold our job!" Toward the end of the campaign, Baker was reduced to running advertisements claiming that he "is not bound to any group, individual or clique" and "will retain every competent individual deputy, clerk or jailer now serving the county efficiently, co-operatively and conscientiously."[68]

In the runoff returns, Clark received about two-thirds of Dozier's voters and defeated Baker by 53 percent to 47 percent. The city-county division persisted; Clark once more led Baker outside Selma by two to one, losing only one county box. But the most important element in the voting was that, though Baker again carried eight of the city's twelve boxes, his margin of victory in them was much slimmer than in the initial primary. It appeared that Clark's attacks on the Selma machine had struck a responsive chord in a substantial segment of the city's electorate, as well as having focused rural resentment. On election night Clark's supporters celebrated, running through the corridors of the county jail shouting, "We've finally busted the old political machine and thrown Dallas County politics wide-open."[69]

The notion that Clark's victory in 1958 had destroyed the machine was distinctly premature. In 1960, without significant opposition, Heinz won his third term as mayor. But the success of Clark's runoff strategy did not go unobserved. Selma political and economic figures who were discontented with the machine's leadership took careful note of it and began to calculate their chances accordingly. This new feeling that the machine was vulnerable proved essential to developments in municipal life over the next six years.

In the meantime, Sheriff Clark settled into his office. He was reelected without opposition in 1962. He continued to be an ardent follower of Governor Folsom and devoted much of the first half of 1962 to assisting in Folsom's unsuccessful gubernatorial campaign against Judge George C. Wallace.[70] But, very naturally, he fell more and more under the influence of the two officials with whom he most closely worked, Judge James Hare and Circuit Solicitor Blanchard McLeod. And his racial views, always strongly segregationist, moved increasingly toward the near paranoia of his two superiors.

Judge Hare, like Sheriff Clark, resided in the Browns community and operated a cattle ranch there. The son of one of Dallas County's most extensive planters, Hare had been elected to the state house of representatives in 1934 and reelected in 1938. He served as an assistant state attorney general and saw active duty as an air force intelligence officer in India during World War II. In 1946, Governor Chauncey Sparks appointed him to fill out an unexpired term as circuit solicitor; he was elected to a full term in the same year, and reelected in 1950. In 1953, at the height of the national hysteria fed by Senator Joseph McCarthy, Solicitor Hare created something of a stir by charging that, while in Karachi as an intelligence officer, he had seen a document indicating that Alabama's Teacher Tenure Act of 1939 was a part of a Communist plot to infiltrate Communist instructors into the state's public school system. He would later easily convince himself that the civil rights movement was a part of the same international conspiracy. In 1953, also, he conducted the two prosecutions of William Fikes. In 1954, Governor Gordon Persons appointed Hare as a circuit judge, to fill the vacancy created by the death of Judge Jack Callen. Hare would serve in this position until his own death in 1969.

On the bench, Hare marked himself as one of the judiciary's most fanatical and inflexible segregationists. As each new county grand jury was empaneled, he made a practice of delivering a lengthy and vitriolic charge warning the jurors of the evils of integration. He was an active member of the White Citizens' Council and frequently addressed its gatherings. And as we shall see, he used the powers of his office to attempt to forestall federal examination of the records of the circuit's boards of voting registrars and to suppress black civil rights demonstrations.[71]

Solicitor McLeod was the son of the single most powerful politician in Wilcox County, Probate Judge Jesse M. McLeod. Wilcox borders Dallas on the south and, like Dallas, is a Black Belt county; unlike Dallas, it was still overwhelmingly rural, with a very large black majority and not a single black voter. Jesse McLeod, born in 1876, had operated a plantation near the Coy community. He was elected to the Wilcox County Commission in 1922 and served until 1938, when he was chosen probate judge and thus ex officio the county commission's president. At that time he moved from Coy to Camden, the county seat. He continued as probate judge until his death in 1958. Blanchard McLeod, born late in his father's life, grew up in an atmosphere of political power. He received a law degree from the University of Alabama and commenced practice in Camden. With his father's strong support, he obtained Governor Persons's nomination to succeed Hare as circuit solicitor when Hare was appointed circuit judge in 1954. He served in this position until his resignation for health reasons in 1969.

Like Judge Hare, McLeod held extreme racial views. The youth of both men had been spent on Black Belt plantations, and each man's attitudes had been shaped by the pattern of white supremacy and black dependency characteristic of tenant farming relationships. McLeod was an active member of the White Citizens' Council. In 1961 he assured a federal judge, "The Negroes of Wilcox County are happy for the white people to rule in peace." But McLeod's passions seem to have been more immediate and violent than Hare's, and in this tendency he encouraged Sheriff Clark. We have already encountered McLeod's strident summons to "meet force with force" when he joined with Clark in creating the Dallas County posse in response to the sit-in crisis in neighboring Montgomery in 1960. During Selma's own demonstrations, McLeod's anger boiled over on several occasions. And his uncompromising hostility to black civil rights underlay the utterly intransigent response by the counties of his circuit to federal efforts to assist in securing those rights.[72]

Sheriff Clark's own attitudes toward questions of civil rights readily fused with those of his admired senior colleagues. He traveled around the state to assist in the suppression of black demonstrations. His posse, formed after he had helped authorities in Montgomery in 1960, was then used in similar encounters in Birmingham, Gadsden, Tuscaloosa, and Tuskegee. He told a civic club audience in 1963 that black marches and sit-ins "are Communist-inspired and led." He continued, "I believe that the Negro does not want equal rights but special treatment. And when the federal government gives them special treatment, they begin to have less respect for local law enforcement." He dismissed the possibility of negotiations: "I would like to say here and now that I do not approve of biracial committees and will not meet with such a group." He concluded, "We will not be bullied." In 1964 he told a similar audience that his experience at demonstrations in Selma and elsewhere had taught him that "force must be used in riot control."[73]

Most of the Dallas County officials with whom Clark served detested Governor Folsom and looked askance at Clark's Folsomite commitments. For instance, the county's state senator, Walter Givhan, who operated a large plantation near Safford in western Dallas and, as we have said, was the legislature's most influential spokesman for the state's great planting interests, had told the Alabama Farm Bureau in an address in 1947 that Folsom's ideals were communistic and posed a threat to white supremacy.[74] Nevertheless, Clark's unqualified adoption of extreme segregationist dogma earned him their acceptance and support as the years passed. And, as a sensational episode in 1959 demonstrated, such patronage could be crucial.

In January 1959, two of Clark's deputies, Martin Williamson and Billy Mac Bobo, resigned and charged the sheriff with permitting illegal liquor sales and gambling in county nightclubs, especially those near Craig Air Force Base. The sheriff, according to the deputies, received substantial kickbacks from the club owners—a fourth of the take in one instance—in return for his toleration of their activities. Drawing the community's racial sensitivities into the allegations, the deputies added, "There are establishments in Dallas County selling beer and whiskey to the tune of juke box music, with Negroes congregated in one end and whites in the other, segregated only by a counter." Neither deputy was a man of unblemished character. Bobo was one of the four young men who had been charged with the kidnapping of John Sturdivant in 1955, in the aftermath of the NAACP's school integration petition. Williamson had been a clerk in the county tax collector's office, and he had been fired after the tax collector had committed suicide in the face of an impending audit. But the two men offered to prove their charges if a county grand jury would agree to investigate, and they provided Solicitor McLeod with a list of 127 potential witnesses.

Clark denied the deputies' claims and stated that he would welcome a grand jury inquiry. As it happened, a special grand jury already existed; it had been summoned in December to take custody of the records of the county board of voting registrars in order to prevent the U.S. Civil Rights Commission from examining them. Its foreman, however, was service station owner Irby Moore, the brother of Clark's chief deputy, Robert A. Moore. Despite this fact, Judge Hare refused to empanel a new grand jury, and Solicitor McLeod announced that the existing grand jury would take up the deputies' allegations on January 27. On the night of January 24, as the two deputies were driving along a road through Mush Creek Swamp, another car pulled alongside theirs and shots were fired into their vehicle, forcing them to swerve off the highway and into a tree. But both deputies survived, and plans for the grand jury investigation proceeded. The white Dallas County Ministerial Association adopted a resolution urging witnesses to come forward, and ministers repeated the plea from their pulpits on Sunday.

When it convened, the grand jury heard a parade of tavern owners and nightclub operators. But a key witness, Leonard Barnes, a distributor of pinball and amusement machines, managed to avoid service of a subpoena and disappeared. Because the sheriff was the object of the investigation, the task of serving the subpoenas had been turned over to the county coroner, and Deputy Martin Williamson charged that Coroner Bailey Green had proven incompetent to the task. After two days of testimony, the grand jury cleared Clark of all charges. The *Selma Times-Journal* put out a special edition to report the jurors' conclusion that there was "no organized vice prevailing in the county of any sort" and that the deputies' accusations were "a libel and slander against the good name of Dallas County."

Seventy-two hours after the grand jury report that the county contained no organized vice, Clark raided a popular nightclub and charged its manager with keeping a gaming table. Ten days later he raided a restaurant that was owned by one of the principal witnesses against him. Deputies managed to find an abandoned pinball machine stored in a back room, and though it clearly had not been used for years and contained no device for paying customers who won, the restaurateur was convicted of possessing gaming equipment. A few weeks later, Clark arrested another of the witnesses against him at a Safford café and, following an altercation, beat him with a blackjack. The victim, Walter L. Bridges, argued in court that Clark's actions were reprisals for Bridges's grand jury testimony, but Bridges nevertheless was convicted of resisting arrest. In 1960 the grand jury foreman, Irby Moore, was elected to the Selma city council. In 1962, Moore's brother, Chief Deputy Sheriff Robert Moore, committed suicide.[75]

Though the grand jury found no basis for the deputies' charges, there are good reasons for crediting them. In the first place, the attempt to murder the deputies, the disappearance of a key witness, and the sheriff's retaliation against those who gave evidence against him all would seem to indicate that an effort was being made to conceal the full truth. In the second place, Clark's later career demonstrates that he was not above involvement in illegal activities. In 1970 he was on three occasions convicted in Montgomery of writing bad checks. In 1972 and again in 1979 he was tried for racketeering in connection with schemes to obtain fees by falsely promising to arrange loans for businesses. And in 1978 he pleaded guilty to complicity in a plot to smuggle more than six thousand pounds of marijuana into the United States from Colombia. He eventually served two years in a federal penitentiary for his crimes.[76] At the very least, the events surrounding the grand jury investigation in 1959 make the fact that Clark was reelected without opposition in 1962 surprising.

The explanation for this circumstance would seem to be the growing confidence that Judge Hare, Solicitor McLeod, Judge Reynolds, Mayor Heinz, and other political leaders had in the soundness of the sheriff's racial attitudes. We know that on Mayor Heinz's instruction, Police Chief Mullen entered into an explicit agreement with Clark at this time to turn the handling of all civil rights cases, whether in the county or in the city, over to the sheriff's department—an order that the mayor gave despite Clark's outspoken attacks on the Heinz organization in 1958.[77]

It appears that the commanding figures of the community may have been willing to tolerate a quiet tendency on Clark's part to accept kickbacks from the county's less reputable elements in return for the assurance that he would use a strong hand to eradicate all black opposition. And Clark, on his part, could retain his quite profitable office by vigorously espousing the extreme segregationist positions that the leadership desired of him. We need not doubt the sincerity of Clark's own white supremacist convictions to see that, given the views of his senior colleagues in the county government, he also would have had every material motive to reject any impulse toward racial moderation.

In the meantime, however, developments were at work in Selma that would create a gulf between the attitudes that characterized the county courthouse and those held at city hall. These developments center on the emergence in municipal politics of a young but ambitious manager of an appliance store, Joe T. Smitherman.

Smitherman was born in Selma in December 1929. He grew up in the poor white section of the city. His father, Thomas, died when young Joe was only two months old, and Smitherman had never even seen a picture of him until 1972, when a political supporter came up with one. Smitherman's mother, Minnie, struggled to support her seven children, but she herself died when Joe was twelve, leaving him an orphan. With the meager financial support of his older siblings—one of whom worked as a clerk in a supermarket, another as a taxi driver, and a third as a waitress—Joe managed to complete high school. College was out of the question. He married in 1948, served in the army, and on his return to Selma he took a job as a salesman in an appliance store.[78] There his diligence and ambition attracted the attention of the store's co-owner, city councilman Walter L. Stoudenmire, a farm equipment dealer. In 1955, Stoudenmire offered to enter a partnership with Smitherman to establish a new appliance store, Home Appliance.[79]

It would be difficult to imagine social origins more unlike those of Mayor Heinz. Smitherman early grew to have a deep resentment of the closed corporation dominated by Selma's upper class that had ruled the city essentially throughout the young man's life. Sheriff Clark's use of attacks on the machine to achieve his victory over Wilson Baker gave Smitherman and those who shared his animosity the sense that the organization might be vulnerable. It was true that Baker had carried the city in both rounds of the election, but his reduced margin in the runoff indicated to the machine's enemies that a carefully planned assault might be able to defeat the city administration even in its citadel. Smitherman's thoughts thus turned toward city politics.

In 1960, when the incumbent president of the city council, Mallory Privett, decided not to seek reelection, Smitherman's partner in the Home Appliance Company, Councilman Stoudenmire, announced his candidacy for the position. Joe Smitherman thereupon filed for the council seat to represent north Selma's second ward, which Stoudenmire was vacating. Observers of city politics predicted that Smitherman, without the support of the organization, would do no better than make it into a runoff. But he in fact was elected in the first round of voting, leading all five second ward candidates, including the other incumbent, and carrying seven of the city's ten boxes. The *Times-Journal* called him "easily the biggest 'surprise' candidate in the election."[80]

On the council, Smitherman at once set out to make a name for himself. In 1956 Mayor Heinz and the council had begun a large project to extend the city's trunk-line sewers into new areas, and at the same time they had decided to undertake the paving of all the unpaved streets remaining in the city through special assessments on the owners of the abutting property. But when they became known, the amounts of the assessments—particularly when added to the sewer costs—had created a storm of protest from the affected residents. After angry public hearings in the spring of 1958, Heinz had been forced to abandon the street project altogether, though the sewer project continued.[81]

When he assumed office, Smitherman immediately took up the question of street paving. Concentrating on his own ward, Smitherman, through patient consultation with the area's property owners, managed to work out an assessment program acceptable to them. When the council adopted it, one member called it "practically a monument to" Smitherman. At the same time, Smitherman addressed widespread discontent with the sewer project. Though the trunk-line extensions had been completed, at considerable cost, ordinary residents saw little benefit because there was no provision for constructing the feeder sewers that would connect individual residences to the mains. Smitherman originated and obtained the adoption of a general program to connect houses to the sewer system on an assessment basis. The results produced the city's first large-scale paving and sewer improvements since 1927. And though Mayor Heinz had been seeking the same goals for many years, Smitherman's efforts seemed to indicate that he could actually deliver on Heinz's empty plans. At the same time, Smitherman aligned himself with other groups discontented with the administration; he spoke out in behalf of those Selmians who feared Heinz's plan to fluoridate the city's water supply, and championed the cause of the owners of black slum property, who opposed Heinz's efforts to strengthen the building and plumbing codes.[82]

As Smitherman was positioning himself as Heinz's principal rival on the council, elements of the city unhappy with the machine's management of affairs were becoming increasingly organized and active. A principal ally of these forces was People's Bank. As we have seen, City National Bank was very closely associated with both the Heinz organization and the chamber of commerce—so much so that the three constituted a sort of iron triangle. People's, on the other hand, had long been considered a maverick enterprise. Under the leadership of W. Henry Plant, who became its president in 1934, the bank had begun making agricultural loans directly to tenant farmers. Up to that time, banks and finance companies had made credit available to the wholesale grocery firms, and the wholesale grocers, through the planters whom they supplied, had been the source of credit for the tenant farmers. Before joining People's, Plant had headed a finance company that serviced the wholesale grocers, and in his dealings with the grocery firms he had discovered that the tenant farmers were often excellent credit risks. Thus when he took over the management of People's, the smallest of Selma's three banks and one in need of new business, he began bypassing the grocers and planters and lending immediately to the tenants. The decision gave the bank a very special character among the area's financial institutions. The grocers regarded the innovation as an infringement on their business, and the planters thought it a threat to their control of their lessees; both grocers and planters therefore were hostile to Plant and his innovative policies. Meanwhile, City National, headed first by Glenn Boyd and then by Lucien Burns, remained firmly allied with the wholesale grocers, many of whom sat on its board of directors; Burns, indeed, had himself been a wholesale grocer before becoming mayor.

Both because of the hostility of many of the county's wealthy citizens to Plant's lending practices and because of the fast friendships between Boyd and Burns and, later, Burns and Heinz, People's was frozen out of any business with the city. All municipal deposits were held by City National. And People's was equally excluded from any financing of new industries enticed to Selma; the executive secretaries of the chamber of commerce during this period, H. Hunt Frazier and M. L. "Jack" Miles, both firm political allies of the Burns-Heinz organization, made a point of directing all such business to City National. As a result of this situation, Plant and his son-in-law Rex Morthland, who moved to Selma in 1946 and succeeded Plant as People's president in 1953, as well as Morthland's vice-president

B. Frank Wilson, were all inveterate enemies of the machine. Thus, in the early 1960s, officers at People's Bank actively encouraged the evident ambitions of young Councilman Smitherman, whose benefactor and business associate Walter Stoudenmire was a member of People's board of directors, and who, the officers had good reason to believe, was disposed to open city business to their bank if he gained the mayoralty.[83]

The factor that moved these enmities beyond the limits of Smitherman's personal desires and the particular business interests of People's Bank, however, was the crusade to attract new industry to the community. As we have seen in earlier chapters, the two decades after World War II witnessed the rise in Alabama of a passionate, almost messianic commitment, particularly among young, white businessmen, to the luring of northern factories into the state. But in Selma this aspiration became a powerful element in the increasing discontent with the municipal machine, especially because of the machine's close association with the chamber of commerce. Though there had been some successes in the search for industry in the 1950s—in particular, the construction of a magnesium smelter, which had initially been announced in 1956 and had finally begun production in 1960—the suspicion grew among younger business leaders that neither the city administration nor the chamber really wanted new industry, because, as the allegation went, the resultant changes in the community might alter existing power relationships. As an outgrowth of this distrust, the young businessmen in the fall of 1962 formed their own organization to seek industry, the Committee of 100 Plus. The committee's chairman, restaurateur Otis "Red" Adams, commented, "What we really mean to do, in just plain language, is to make Selma grow in spite of itself." The committee reported that, in its initial contacts, it "has been amazed to encounter reports from many areas that Selma does not want industry and has turned away payrolls which attempted to come here." Adams said, "There has long been general unrest that Selma, for a number of reasons, has not progressed equal to its potential." But he concluded, "The negative approach which stymied Selma for so long has finally been channeled into a positive action, and the Committee is very optimistic about what it can accomplish."[84]

Within a month the new organization had broken publicly with the chamber of commerce. When the chamber's nominating committee announced its selections to run for the ten vacancies on its board of directors, the Committee of 100 Plus—for the first time in the chamber's history—submitted a rival slate by petition. The committee was, according to the *Selma Times-Journal*, "generally regarded by hard-core chamber supporters and its present governing body as an 'anti' faction." And the chamber nominating committee's list featured many of the stalwarts of the county's political establishment, including Mayor Heinz, Judge Hare, board of revenue member Seawell Jones, *Times-Journal* editor Edward Field,

and White Citizens' Council founder Alston Keith. But the sharply contested election resulted in a general defeat for the Committee of 100 Plus's
insurgent slate, led by People's Bank vice-president Frank Wilson and investment banker Catesby ap C. Jones.[85]

The defeat within the chamber, however, only redoubled the determination of the committee's members to secure the overthrow of the machine at the polls in 1964. With the machine so clearly in control of the
chamber as well as the city government, the young businessmen were now
convinced that only a victory for the machine's political opponents in the
next municipal election could open Selma to the industrial expansion
upon which the businessmen were convinced the community's future
prosperity depended. They thus rallied to the cause of Joe Smitherman. By
way of strengthening the youthful appliance salesman's credentials, they
arranged in December 1963 to have the Selma Junior Chamber of Commerce nominate Smitherman for selection as one of Alabama's outstanding young men. The Jaycees' nomination emphasized that Smitherman
had "sought office as a candidate [for the city council] independent of
political ties, and he has remained outspoken and independent of everything but public need during his entire tenure of office." And in February
1964, the state Jaycees chose Smitherman as one of the four recipients of
the award. Mayor Heinz had flatly said in 1961 that he would not seek
reelection in 1964; indeed, he had earlier said that he would not run in
1960. But in the face of this challenge, Heinz's political associates convinced him that he alone could quell the building rebellion—both from
the young, white businessmen and, as we shall see, from the blacks—and
he reluctantly entered the race.[86]

The mayoral election of 1964 was the first seriously contested one since
1932. Smitherman at once launched a frontal attack on machine rule. He
promised to "represent *all* the people, not *just* the favored few." He warned,
"Selma needs young, positive, and progressive leadership. We have failed
to keep pace with other cities during the past decade. We are today at the
cross-roads of growth or stagnation. We must go *forward* and build a more
prosperous and dynamic community. We dare not fail! I pledge to you that
no clique or group will dictate or control my policies as your Mayor."

Smitherman proclaimed his challenge. "For 30 years, a favored few have
dominated Selma, and have tried to do your thinking for you! Are you
satisfied with Selma's progress under their control? Do you believe their
claims? Or do you agree that, after 30 years, it's time for a change?" He
warned that during the past dozen years, three-fourths of Selma's high
school graduates had chosen to leave the city, and offered this assertion as
proof of the need to recruit additional industry to the area; he added the
allegation that several prospective new factories had been lost to other
cities because of the mishandling of them by the Heinz administration.

And he concluded, "Selma needs to regain her lost position as 4th largest and most influential of Alabama cities."

Heinz fought back energetically, publishing detailed statistics to refute Smitherman's claims about Selma's lack of industrial growth and offering a lengthy catalog of civic improvements during his time as mayor. He called his opponent's charges "the reckless, unfounded rantings of some irresponsible opportunists," and observed caustically, "Knocking and belittling a city has never added one inch to its growth or progress."[87]

Selma's race relations played no overt part in the campaign. Heinz had been closely associated with the Citizens' Council since its very inception, of course, but Smitherman proudly noted that he was at the time a member of the council's board of directors.[88] And yet it seems clear that, as a result of the events of previous years, the city's black leadership was solidly behind Smitherman. The preceding summer and fall in Selma had been dominated, as we shall see, by voting rights demonstrations, and Heinz's response had been wholly intransigent. The election of March 1964 was not only noteworthy for featuring the first seriously contested mayoral race in three decades; it also saw the first black candidates for municipal office since Reconstruction. The three blacks who sought positions on the city council were all prominent in the Dallas County Voters League, the organization that had sponsored the demonstrations: James E. Gildersleeve, a high school teacher at the private Alabama Lutheran Academy; Frederick D. Reese, a minister and instructor at the city's black public high school; and Ernest L. Doyle, a carpenter and insurance agent. All three published advertisements whose appeals closely followed Smitherman's, emphasizing the need for additional industry, more paved streets, better street lighting, and extensions of the sewage system—all themes upon which Smitherman had dwelt at great length.

Mayor Heinz made surreptitious overtures to black leaders. In the weeks just before the election, he ordered the removal of the racial designations from the water fountains in city hall; he instead had dispensers of paper cups installed next to each fountain so that whites would not actually have to drink after blacks. At the same time, the public library, undoubtedly with the mayor's approval, restored the tables and chairs that, as we shall see, it had removed when it had been integrated the preceding May. Heinz also apparently considered, but eventually decided against, the hiring of a small number of black policemen; after the election, he lamented to a friend that if only he had done so, he would have won. In fact, however, those gestures were far too little and too late to gain any significant black allegiance. Wilson Baker—who because of Sheriff Clark's acceptance by the powers of the machine and the Citizens' Council in the intervening years was actively supporting Joe Smitherman—called on the prominent black businessman Edwin Moss with assurances of Smitherman's progressive outlook. Moss, who knew and trusted Baker, began actively canvassing in the black community for Smitherman, and he was joined in these efforts by the Selma field secretary of the Student Non-violent Coordinating Committee, Worth Long. After some discussion, blacks decided not to enter a candidate of their own in the mayoral race, instead staging a rival "mock election" at one of their mass meetings. Only about 250 of Selma's 5,800 to 6,000 registered voters in 1964 were black, but it appears that, with fewer than perhaps a dozen exceptions, essentially every one of them voted for Smitherman.[89]

The 240 or so black votes constituted almost half of Smitherman's 494-vote margin of victory. Smitherman took 55 percent of the poll, to Heinz's 45 percent. Smitherman received heavy support in the poorer precincts of north and east Selma. Heinz's greatest strength was in the older well-to-do neighborhoods of the central city. But the key to Smitherman's success was his ability to divide the vote equally with Heinz in the new upper-middle-class subdivisions of west Selma. Before the election most veteran political observers had conceded west Selma to Heinz, but in fact Smitherman carried the area by sixty-eight votes. Almost certainly the principal factor in determining this outcome was the dissatisfaction of younger, upwardly mobile businessmen with the complacency of the older leaders of the machine, particularly as reflected in what these voters regarded as the city political leaders' lack of aggressiveness in the pursuit of new industry. It had been Smitherman's incessant indictment, and evidently it paid off in the west Selma boxes.

In addition to the defeat of Mayor Heinz, the election produced the victory of four new city council members. In the race for the council presidency, one of the young business leaders, farm equipment dealer Carl Morgan, was elected on a vote almost precisely identical to Smitherman's. Morgan and the three other new councilmen brought to six the number of members who had initially joined the body through election rather than appointment, up from only one in 1960. From 1964, therefore, it may fairly be said that the Burns-Heinz machine's control of city politics had been ended, destroyed in one disastrous defeat. In October, when Mayor Heinz left office, he at once assumed the chairmanship of the White Citizens' Council, a position from which he spent the next year hurling embittered invective against all the changes that were overtaking his city.[90]

Three days after the election, the *Selma Times-Journal*'s new editor, Roswell Falkenberry—a moderate who had been promoted to the position following the death of the segregationist Edward Field five months earlier—wrote, doubtless with far greater prescience than he knew: "Joe Smitherman faces the greatest challenge of his young life. It can make him or break him—and, in either instance, the City of Selma must bear the consequences. Selma stands on the threshold of what is probably the most important era in its history since the Civil War. This is not because Joe T. Smitherman has been duly elected mayor; nor that Chris B. Heinz will no longer serve that office after his term expires. But, simply because the social, economic and industrial complexion of this community has suddenly and simultaneously arrived at a point from which there can be no turning aside."[91] To understand the peculiar conjunction that the editor sensed, we must now retrace our steps and examine developments in black Selma in these years.

IV. The Beginnings of Black Protest

Selma and Montgomery had been, in 1918, the first two cities in Alabama to establish chapters of the NAACP. For most of the next quarter century, the heart and soul of the Selma chapter had been Charles J. Adams. Adams had worked as a railway postal clerk, sorting mail aboard trains. When he retired from this job, he became an insurance agent and obtained appointment as a notary public. Because Selma—indeed, all of south Alabama—had no black lawyers, Adams, through his position as a notary, became a sort of surrogate attorney and legal adviser for the area's black residents. In 1928 he was joined in his efforts by S. William Boynton, a graduate of Tuskegee who came to Selma in that year to become the county's black extension agent. These two men were the city's leading civil rights advocates in the years before and just after World War II.[92]

In the mid-1920s, Adams had founded the Dallas County Voters League in order to supplement the work of the NAACP by focusing on the effort to register blacks as voters. The administration of the disfranchising provisions of the state's Constitution of 1901 had reduced the number of black voters in the county to just 52 by 1904 and to 55 in 1908. The figure was still only 50 in 1946, and it had climbed merely to 112 in 1953, 176 in 1956, and 180 in 1958. The battle to get blacks registered thus was an exceedingly slow and painful one, and it is not surprising that by the early 1930s the Voters League's frustrated members had allowed the organization to languish. But as we have already noted, the attempt to persuade the city school board to take over the operation of Knox Academy moved Adams and Boynton in 1936 to revive the Voters League. Thereafter it met regularly and became a focus of black resistance in the county.[93]

The barriers to registration were many. The Constitution of 1901 required, in addition to age, residence, sanity, and lack of a criminal record, just a lawful employment and either the ability to read and write English or the ownership of property assessed at three hundred dollars or more; registered voters were also required to have paid a poll tax of $1.50 a year to vote, but the poll tax was not a prerequisite to registration. As literacy became increasingly widespread and the value of the dollar diminished, these requirements were within the reach of more and more citizens, of both races. However, it appears that, from the very beginning, the boards of registrars had administered the provisions to black applicants with little or no regard for the actual law. The members of the boards were later reported by one of them to have asked the applicants abstruse, and in some cases even fanciful, questions and to have pronounced their education inadequate when they could not answer, even though the constitution simply required literacy. They refused to register blacks who could not produce white supporters,[94] and sometimes they demanded both literacy and property holding of applicants, even though the constitution made these requirements alternatives.[95]

Before 1946 blacks were barred by party rule from voting in Democratic primaries, and as these were the only elections that mattered in the one-party state, blacks had little incentive to try to register in any case.[96] But perhaps the principal obstacle to registration was not the formal requirements, not official misconduct, not black apathy, but pervasive black fear. The names of blacks who sought to register became part of the public record, of course, and blacks who made the attempt could easily fall victim to harassment or violence.[97] The reluctance of most blacks to seek to become voters was, therefore, founded in an accurate appraisal of the substantial dangers involved. During the years before World War II, very few blacks sought to register, and of those who did, exceedingly few were successful. This situation prevailed throughout the state, but it was especially true of Black Belt counties like Dallas.

During and just after the war this situation began to change, particularly in the cities. We have already encountered the registration effort in Montgomery in 1943. There were similar attempts in Birmingham. In each city, the applications were associated with the availability, for the first time, of a black attorney, Arthur Madison in Montgomery and Arthur Shores in Birmingham. The state constitution had always provided for the right of a person rejected by a board of registrars to appeal the board's decision to the state courts, but until there were black lawyers willing to handle such appeals this right was essentially nugatory. During World War II such appeals started to appear on the circuit court dockets, and at once the Alabama Supreme Court commenced to throw up substantial procedural barriers against the proceedings.[98] Nevertheless, this new necessity for the boards to have to justify their actions to judges caused authorities to pay closer attention to the actual constitutional requirements.

The opening of Democratic primaries to black participation, coupled with the appeals of boards of registrars' decisions, produced a legislative response in the summer of 1945. State representative E. C. "Bud" Boswell proposed a constitutional amendment to require applicants for registration to satisfy the board of registrars that they understood any article of the U.S. Constitution presented them by the board. After a heated campaign, voters ratified the amendment in November 1946. The actual effect of this new requirement was simply to create some legal basis for the sort of oral questioning of black applicants that the boards had in fact been conducting since 1901. But the debate surrounding the adoption of the amendment and the discriminatory conduct of the boards of registrars under its authority had exposed its racial motive so clearly that in January 1949 a three-judge federal court in Mobile declared it unconstitutional. In March the U.S. Supreme Court sustained this ruling.[99]

In the war years, as well, many boards on their own authority began creating additional obstacles to registration. The most effective of these was the voucher system. The statutes authorized the boards both to make their own rules for the expeditious processing of applications and to take testimony to verify the information supplied by the applicants. On the strength of these provisions, many boards, particularly in the Black Belt, started requiring applicants to provide two trustworthy persons already registered who would swear to the applicant's length of residence in the state and county. These vouchers, as they were called, had to appear personally before the board and often had to wait many hours to do so. It was therefore frequently difficult to find acceptable acquaintances who would agree to take on the task. In counties such as Wilcox and Lowndes, in which there were no blacks registered and all whites refused to appear for a black, the voucher system made black registration impossible. Even in a county such as Dallas, in which a handful of registered blacks were available, the board could effectively limit registration through this rule; when board members felt that S. W. Boynton was vouching for too many blacks, for instance, they merely declared him untrustworthy and removed him from the list of persons whose oaths they would believe. Though the requirement of vouchers was completely extra-constitutional, it was validated by both federal and state courts in 1947 and became an important disfranchising device in many counties.[100]

After the Boswell Amendment was declared unconstitutional, the legislature responded in the summer of 1951 with a new amendment, written by the arch-segregationist Senator Miller Bonner of Wilcox and co-sponsored by all the Black Belt senators. Voters ratified the amendment in December by fewer than four hundred votes. It would govern registration in Alabama until 1965, when it was first suspended by the federal Voting Rights Act that summer and then repealed by the electorate in the fall.[101]

The new amendment, unlike the Boswell Amendment, used a standard of simple literacy, not understanding; like the 1901 suffrage article, it required only that applicants be able to read and write in English any article of the U.S. Constitution given them by the board. It eliminated the alternative property qualification and added new requirements that applicants be of good character, embrace the duties and obligations of citizenship, and never have belonged to any group or party that advocated the unlawful overthrow of the American government. Its most important feature, however, was its provision obliging the Alabama Supreme Court to formulate a uniform questionnaire to be filled out by all applicants, "so worded that the answers thereto will place before the Boards of Registrars information necessary or proper to aid them to pass upon the qualification of each applicant. Such questionnaire shall be answered in writing by the applicant, in the presence of the Board, without assistance." The board was further authorized to "receive information respecting the applicant and the truthfulness of any information furnished by him"; the voucher system was thus given a constitutional basis.[102]

In due course, the state supreme court produced a questionnaire.[103] It would remain in use until 1964. Though written in legalistic phraseology that may well have been difficult for the poorly educated to understand, the document was fundamentally straightforward. It asked for the usual personal data, for a list of jobs held over the past five years, when the applicant moved to the state and county, and whether he had "ever been a dope addict or an habitual drunkard" or legally declared insane. It asked for a statement of his educational and business background, if he had a criminal record, if he had served in the armed forces, and if he would bear arms for the country. And it asked if he believed "in free elections and rule by the majority" (something that the amendment's sponsor, Senator Bonner, certainly did not), if he would give aid and comfort to the enemies of the United States, and if he would support and defend the federal and state constitutions. Finally, it asked him to name some of the duties and obligations of citizenship and required him formally to swear his loyalty to the nation and state.

In and of itself, the questionnaire should have posed no substantial barrier to registration, and the fact that it became over the next dozen years the single most important obstacle blacks faced had to do less with the form itself than with the boards' use of it. Increasingly during the 1950s, as the civil rights movement gained momentum, board members came to use the questionnaire not as a document intended to supply them with information on which to base their decision, as the constitutional amendment had said, but as a sort of test. Black applicants—and occasionally white ones—were denied registration for the most minor and insignificant omissions or errors. Any mistake at all in filling out the form could lead to rejection. In addition, the Dallas board, like many others, also questioned registrants orally to determine if they understood the federal and state constitutions—something the state constitution did not require. And members, when in doubt about an applicant's good character, required character references, and they rejected applicants without giving them an opportunity to refute negative allegations.[104] This was the situation the Dallas County Voters League faced in the 1950s and early 1960s as it struggled to increase the number of black voters in the county.

The pattern of increasing white resistance to black registration in Dallas

County during this period is clear. From January 1952, when the new voter qualification amendment took effect, to May 1954, when the U.S. Supreme Court decided the school segregation cases, the board registered seventy-four blacks; between the end of World War II and 1954 the number of black voters in the county had more than trebled. From June 1954 to June 1961, however, the board registered only fourteen blacks. Indeed, from November 1959 to March 1960, and again from December 1960 to June 1961, the county had no functioning board of registrars at all.[105] This recalcitrance is only one aspect of white authorities' efforts to smother the initial indications of a new black assertiveness in these years.

Charles Adams was the first of the black leaders to fall victim to authorities' hostility. He had used his position as a notary public to arrange to get veterans' benefits for blacks returning from World War II and their families. Just after the war, he was charged with notarizing false documents and given a prison term for the offense. After his release from the penitentiary, old and tired, he abandoned Selma in 1948 and went to live with relatives in Detroit.[106] Thereafter the dangerous mantle of leadership fell to S. W. Boynton. Boynton, as a public employee, had been subjected to white harassment for years. In 1953 he retired as the county's black extension agent in the hope that if he were self-employed, whites would have greater difficulty in exerting pressure against him. He joined his wife, Amelia, in the insurance business.

Amelia Platts, like her future husband a graduate of Tuskegee, had come to Selma in 1930 as the black home demonstration agent. In this position she had, of course, worked closely with Boynton, the extension agent, and their professional association had soon ripened into love. In 1936 Boynton had divorced his first wife, and he and Amelia had married. Regulations at the time required home demonstration agents to be single, and the new Mrs. Boynton was therefore compelled to resign. In 1938 she became a collector of insurance premiums, and later she added to this income by establishing an agency to recruit young black women to be sent to northern cities for domestic service. After 1953 the Boyntons formed their own independent insurance agency.[107]

In the 1950s, the Dallas County Voters League met in the Boyntons' office each month. It had only about a dozen members in these early years; some of them had belonged since Adams and Boynton had reorganized it in 1936. The members came faithfully, each person going to the same chair in which he always sat, and they earnestly discussed ways to increase black registration.[108] But as we have seen, after 1954 the board of registrars for all practical purposes halted any further increase in the black electorate. The league's monthly exercises therefore could hardly have been very heartening affairs. White segregationists undoubtedly hoped that the constant persecution, coupled with the evident lack of progress, would eventually lead black activists to become discouraged and to abandon their exertions. What the segregationists did not appreciate, however, was that in a climate as repressive as Selma's, very small advances could be exhilarating and were sufficient to renew the activists' resolve. Thus the new schools, hospital, public housing project, and other improvements that we have discussed convinced at least some Voters League members that amelioration was possible and that the key to advancement in the political arena lay simply in the removal or circumvention of the local white leadership. For that reason, the hopes of those who attended the meetings of the Voters League came increasingly to focus on the possibility of attracting the attention and assistance of sympathetic forces beyond the community.

In 1955, S. W. Boynton traveled to Washington to testify about conditions in Selma before a Senate subcommittee. And when the Congress adopted the measure he had advocated, the Civil Rights Act of 1957, one provision of which established the Civil Rights Commission, both S. W. and Amelia Boynton went to Montgomery in December 1958 to testify before the new commission about the economic pressures and the improper practices of the boards of registrars that inhibited black registration in Dallas and the surrounding counties. They were joined by three prominent blacks: Dr. Sullivan Jackson, a dentist; Ruth K. Lindsey, the wife of Selma University public relations director Pleasant Lindsey, an original member of the Voters League; and Minnie B. Anderson, who with her husband, Marius, operated Burwell Infirmary.[109] Nor were these efforts unavailing, because by this time there were clear signs that federal authorities were concerned about the registration situation in the western Black Belt.

The Civil Rights Act of 1964 and the Voting Rights Act of 1965 proved so much more effective that we may easily forget today the Civil Rights Act of 1957 and its companion Civil Rights Act of 1960. But the Civil Rights Act of 1957 in fact provided the Justice Department with powerful new tools for combating discrimination in voter registration. Both black activists and segregationist leaders were fully aware of the act's importance. Judge Hare called it "a punitive measure directed solely against the southern states" and said that the congressional debates on it had demonstrated "unmistakably that intelligent men in public life are willing to subvert the basic structure of American government and subject all citizens of the United States to a government of injunction issuing from the Federal courts, to compel the South to accept their social objectives." Attorney General John Patterson pronounced the law "the first step towards creation of a police state." Therefore when the Civil Rights Commission came to Alabama to investigate registration practices, authorities reacted with such extraordinary intransigence that it moved President Eisenhower to call their conduct reprehensible.[110]

Dallas and Wilcox were two of the counties whose registration records the commission subpoenaed. At once Judge Hare summoned the counties' grand juries into emergency session, charged them to investigate whether there had been any maladministration of the registration laws, and impounded all the registrars' records while the supposed investigation continued, thus forestalling their production before the commission. Hare emphasized to the jurors that they could take as long as they needed to look into the matter. Thereafter, as grand jury succeeded grand jury, the records remained under impoundment. Solicitor McLeod stated that the jurors would take no action until the federal government presented them with evidence of discrimination, something not very likely since the jurors refused to allow federal investigators to look at any records except ones about which the government had received a specific written complaint from a rejected applicant.

The Civil Rights Commission never did get to examine the records, but in August 1959 its staff reported that the evidence of discrimination in registration in the counties nevertheless was clear. The Justice Department's newly created Civil Rights Division responded at once, and by October the FBI had begun an inquiry into the Dallas board's practices. County officials remained utterly uncooperative, and in May 1960, immediately after President Eisenhower had signed into law the Civil Rights Act of 1960, clarifying and strengthening the 1957 act's provisions, Attorney General William Rogers formally requested the production of the Wilcox records. At once Solicitor McLeod applied for, and Judge Hare granted, an injunction forbidding FBI agents and Justice Department attorneys from seeing the documents. McLeod contended both that sections of the Civil Rights Act of 1960 were unconstitutional and that, since no blacks had applied in Wilcox for well over a decade, the board could not possibly have discriminated against them. The Justice Department thereupon petitioned U.S. District Judge Daniel Thomas to vacate Judge Hare's injunction and grant it access to the records. As was his usual practice, Judge Thomas held no hearing on the petition for more than a year.

In the meantime, in a virtually identical suit that arose in Montgomery at exactly the same time, District Judge Frank Johnson upheld the new civil rights act in August 1960 and ordered the Montgomery board to open its records; in January 1961, the Fifth Circuit Court of Appeals sustained Johnson's ruling. In April, the new Kennedy administration's Justice Department filed a petition with Judge Thomas to permit it to examine the records of the Dallas County registrars as well. In June, Thomas finally heard the Wilcox petition, and on September 28, without an opinion, he denied it, despite the Fifth Circuit's decision in the Montgomery case the preceding January. The Justice Department appealed, and in February 1962 the Fifth Circuit announced itself "unable to find any conceivable justification" for Thomas's ruling. In the meantime, in October 1961, Thomas had heard the Dallas County petition, and when his Wilcox decision was reversed he entered orders compelling the production of the records in both counties at the same time. But even these final orders—more than three years after the grand juries' farcical investigations had theoretically begun—did not end the matter. When FBI agents arrived to examine the Wilcox records in March 1962, the registrars, against whom the order had been directed, maintained that the documents were in the possession of the grand jury. In October, Judge Thomas accepted their contention and ruled that the Justice Department would need to file a new suit, against the grand jurors. The Dallas registrars made a similar argument, and the department did not gain access to the last of the Dallas records until November 1963.[111]

But federal access to the registrars' records, when it finally came, brought with it soon thereafter federal petitions for injunctions to prohibit the boards from engaging in racial discrimination. The complaint against the Dallas board came to trial in May 1962, even while the battle for access played itself out. The United States subpoenaed more than one hundred witnesses and offered more than five thousand exhibits. The government offered testimony from several whites who had been registered with a fifth-grade education or less, while a succession of black doctors, dentists, and teachers told of their rejections. On the hearing's second day, Judge Thomas stunned the government, however, by ruling that evidence about the practices of past boards was irrelevant; only testimony about the sitting board, appointed by the Patterson administration in June 1961, was admissible, he said. This board had taken office after the Justice Department had petitioned to examine the registration records in April 1961, and presumably therefore had been on its best behavior in the intervening ten months. Nevertheless, the chief government attorney, John Doar, was able to present three whites with less than a high school education who had been successful and three black teachers who had not. The registrars confirmed that they interrogated applicants orally about the meaning of the Constitution and that they rejected applicants who friends told them were of questionable character. And they revealed that they had on their own authority adopted a rule that any person who had ever been rejected would never be allowed to reapply. All of this conduct was extra-constitutional.

Judge Thomas's decision, when it came in November, justified the federal attorneys' worst fears. Though he conceded that the boards of the 1950s had been discriminatory, Thomas said that the new board, which in its months in power had registered 71 blacks and rejected 43 while registering 443 whites and rejecting only 37, "has fulfilled its duties in a manner which could well be emulated by all other Boards in the United States." He added that the Justice Department should have been proud of the board's efforts, rather than attacking them. And his opinion lectured the federal attorneys "that there is a terrific sociological problem involved.

Dallas County, Alabama, has problems which other sections do not have. They have problems which other sections do have but do not admit because of political expediency. These problems must be resolved, and should be resolved, by the people and not by the courts."[112]

The government appealed this ruling to the Fifth Circuit, and in October 1963, Thomas was reversed. In the meantime, however, Selma had been plunged into its first round of demonstrations and mass arrests. It would not seem too much to say that one of the causes of the bitter divisions and social turmoil that would so scar the community during the next three years was Judge Daniel H. Thomas.

Dan Thomas was born in 1906 in Prattville, the county seat of Autauga County, which borders Dallas on the east. His father, a leading businessman there, had served as the county's probate judge and the state superintendent of banks and was a longtime trustee of Tuskegee Institute. Thomas received his law degree from the University of Alabama in 1928 and settled in Mobile. He served as an assistant prosecutor from 1932 to 1943, when he joined the navy. On his return from the service, he entered private practice. In the confrontation for control of the state Democratic Executive Committee in 1950 between the Dixiecrats and the national party loyalists, Thomas led the Mobile loyalist faction against the states' rights forces headed by party chairman Gessner McCorvey. He thus gained the deep gratitude of Senators Lister Hill and John Sparkman, Alabama's principal loyalist politicians, and in 1951, on the death of Judge John McDuffie, they recommended Thomas to President Truman for appointment to the southern district's only federal judgeship.[113]

On the bench, Thomas quickly established himself as one of the South's most conservative federal jurists on racial matters. In Alabama, only Seybourn Lynne of Birmingham was more easily persuaded by the arguments of segregationist officials. We have already seen his willingness to accept the delaying tactics of Wilcox and Dallas officials in the Justice Department's efforts to examine the counties' registration records, and his glowing praise for the Dallas registrars' slight retreat from blatant discrimination as a standard to be emulated throughout America. These attitudes were typical of him. When federal authorities finally gained access to the Wilcox records and filed suit for an injunction to bar the registrars from discriminating, Thomas ruled in March 1964 that there was insufficient evidence of discriminatory registration practices, even though there was not one black voter in the county while every single adult white was on the rolls. He enjoined the Perry County registrars from discriminating in November 1962, but within seven weeks the Justice Department had been forced to ask that he declare the board in contempt for its open defiance of his order. Nevertheless, he held no hearing on this request until April 1964, and then refused to consider the 349 letters he had received from rejected blacks complaining of the board's violations of his injunction, because the letters were not in the form of legal petitions. In September 1964 the Fifth Circuit reversed this refusal and strongly suggested that Thomas appoint a federal voting referee, under the terms of the 1960 Civil Rights Act. But the man whom Thomas then appointed, Greensboro attorney O. S. Burke, proved almost as reluctant to register blacks as were the registrars themselves. By the spring of 1965, when Thomas finally entered a general injunction specifying the nondiscriminatory procedures that the Perry board had to follow, Burke had ordered the registration of only thirty-three blacks.

Thomas's delaying tactics, moreover, were legendary. Mobile blacks filed suit in April 1958 seeking the integration of the city's public golf course. The U.S. Supreme Court had ruled such segregation unconstitutional in 1954. Nevertheless, Thomas did not finally hold a hearing in the case until January 1960, and he did not order the integration until March 1961. And even then he filed an apologetic opinion emphasizing in italics that he was constrained to enter the injunction by precedents that *are binding on this court."* Blacks filed suit in April 1959 to end segregation on Mobile city buses—a practice that had been unconstitutional since the Montgomery bus boycott in 1956. But Thomas did not hear the case until November 1961. By the summer of 1963 he had still not ruled, and said at that time that he hoped that the city would eventually repeal its bus segregation ordinance voluntarily so that he could then dismiss the case as moot. He was almost equally dilatory about suits to integrate Mobile's airport terminal and the city's white state trade school. The Justice Department filed suit against the Choctaw County Board of Registrars in the summer of 1962. Thomas heard it in February 1963. In October 1963 the department filed a formal motion requesting a decision, but Thomas did not finally enter his ruling until April 1964.[114]

It is hardly surprising that black civil rights leaders came to regard Judge Thomas as a segregationist.[115] But Thomas was not a segregationist. His was the tragedy of the white moderate. A key to understanding his actions lies in his passionate declaration in his 1962 *Atkins* opinion, already quoted, that his region's racial problems "must be resolved, and should be resolved, by the people and not by the courts." He was explicit and unabashed in his justification for his practice of sitting on civil rights cases. In the summer of 1963, when he agreed to let the initial integration of schools in Mobile be delayed until September 1964, he referred in his opinion to the Mobile golf course suit. "That case had been held under advisement for fourteen months. The opinion was written long prior to its release. The time of release was chosen by the court as being opportune, and evidently it was. There has been no incident on the golf course since its integration," he reported. His failure to rule in the suits seeking the integration of the city's airport and buses had permitted their quiet and voluntary integration, he said, just as he had expected. "The court, close to the community and its problems, believed that this would come about voluntarily and without the necessity of judicial enforcement. Relying upon this belief proved providential. There has not been the first incident." And he added proudly, "Mobile is perhaps the most desegregated city in the South, with no unfortunate" racial clashes. This outcome, he claimed, was a product of his policy of delay, to allow time for genuine and unforced cooperation.[116]

As the son of a politician and business leader in a neighboring county and as a man who had grown up in the area, Thomas had warm relations with a number of prominent Dallas County residents, including Judge Hare.[117] It was difficult for him, therefore, to be suspicious of their motives, and when they provided him with explanations of their conduct that even approached the reasonable, he was at once convinced.[118] He fervently wished to believe that the county's officials were engaged with all goodwill in seeking a voluntary racial accommodation. And because he wanted to believe, over and over again he found the evidence that permitted him to do so. But Selma was not like Mobile—if indeed Mobile was like Judge Thomas's idealization of it. Dallas County's leaders were not gradualists; they were, by and large, uncompromising segregationists. Thus the board of registrars, whose registration of 71 blacks out of 114 between its appointment in June 1961 and Judge Thomas's hearing in May 1962 had moved Thomas to such lavish praise, showed its true colors once the hearing was over. From May 1962 to the Fifth Circuit's reversal of Thomas's ruling in October 1963, it registered only 39 blacks, while rejecting 214, and registered 303 whites out of 399.[119]

Frank Johnson's swift and stern decisions in Montgomery did a great deal to bring that city to an acquiescence in the new patterns of race relations without additional disorders in the years after the Freedom Rider riots of 1961. Montgomery's black leaders came increasingly to feel confidence that segregation could be disestablished through court suits alone, unaccompanied by direct action. When the Southern Christian Leadership Conference proposed in the spring of 1964 that blacks undertake demonstrations in the city, as we have seen, the Montgomery Improvement Association, now headed by the Reverend Solomon S. Seay, Sr., refused to support the campaign, and it failed to materialize.[120] White officials, and even segregationist leaders, meanwhile, came increasingly to accept the futility of further resistance. These parallel developments greatly strengthened the hand of moderates. But in Selma, Judge Thomas's desire to avoid judicial compulsion, in order to allow the community to find its own path to accommodation, ironically had the effect of forcing the city toward just the sort of direct-action movement that Thomas most wanted to avoid. Blacks had no trust in his court at all. When the newly inaugurated Mayor Smitherman sought to forestall Martin Luther King's coming to the city by emphasizing to him, quite correctly, that by that time all of the complaints that King and other blacks had voiced were already under submission in one or another of the many suits pending on Judge Thomas's docket, the point gave neither King nor local black leaders the slightest pause; they had no reason to believe that the suits would afford them any real relief.[121] And among white officials, Thomas's rulings had seemed to them in general to validate the legitimacy of their policies. They therefore saw no reason to make any concessions.

King's demonstrations and the attendant glare of publicity upon them seem to have revealed to Judge Thomas, as they did to many other Americans, the malevolence that underlay many of the actions and attitudes of Dallas County's authorities. Beginning in February 1965, Thomas displayed a growing exasperation with them, and in a series of more and more forceful orders he at last began to rein them in. But if his goal had been, as he said it was, to produce voluntary and quiet desegregation without any "unfortunate incidents," his enlightenment had come much too late.

In the meantime, while Thomas delayed, Selma rushed with gathering momentum toward its collision with history. In 1955, S. W. Boynton suffered the first of a series of slight strokes. Nevertheless, he continued unabated his efforts to secure greater civil rights for Dallas County's blacks and to focus the Justice Department's attention on conditions in his city, and there was increasing evidence over the next five years that the department was preparing to respond. The segregationist pressure on Boynton at this time was unrelenting. On the day Boynton was released from the hospital in January 1956, for instance, a white segregationist competitor in the insurance business, George Tate, came to Boynton's office and attempted to cane him. Boynton suffered three more small strokes during the late 1950s, and finally, in December 1961, a major one. Thereafter, he was confined to the Burwell Infirmary until his death in May 1963.

In the months after Boynton's final hospitalization, Amelia Boynton grew more and more worried about the problem of black leadership in Selma. On her every visit to her husband at the infirmary, Boynton begged her to see that his civil rights work was carried on. But the community's other prominent blacks were extremely reluctant to assume the very public position as activist that Boynton had held. An incident in the early summer of 1962 to which we have already alluded emphasized her concerns. After Judge Thomas tried the federal voter discrimination suit in May, the Dallas County Board of Education terminated thirty-six black teachers who had cooperated with the government and given testimony against the board of registrars. Robert Reagin, the postal employee who, as vice-president of the Dallas County Voters League, was its acting head because of Boynton's illness, declined to become involved in contesting the dismissals. And the black Selma Civic League, headed by Selma University's public relations director, Pleasant Lindsey, seems to have offered only restrained support. The frightened teachers decided that, if they kept the situation quiet, the board of education might agree to rehire them in the future. Therefore, no protest was filed.

In the meantime, in April 1962, Mrs. Boynton attended a meeting of the Alabama Coordinating Association for Registration and Voting, held at Montgomery's black YMCA branch. The Coordinating Association had been formed under the sponsorship of the NAACP in 1954 to bring together all the local black groups interested in increasing black voter registration, and after Judge Walter Jones's injunction in 1956 forbidding the NAACP to operate in Alabama it had taken on much of the NAACP's former role in the state. Amelia Boynton had succeeded her husband as its Fourth Congressional District chairman. At the meeting, in conversation with W. C. Patton, Mrs. Boynton poured out her concerns for what would happen in Selma now that her husband was incapacitated. Patton, a Birmingham insurance agent, had earlier been the NAACP's Alabama field secretary and at this time headed the Coordinating Association. He introduced Mrs. Boynton to an Atlanta attorney, also attending the meeting, who had ties to the Voter Education Project of the Southern Regional Council (SRC), an organization headquartered in Atlanta. The attorney offered to try to obtain financial assistance from the Voter Education Project to assist the Dallas County Voters League in conducting a voter registration drive among black Selmians, if the Voters League would submit a grant application to this effect. A delighted Mrs. Boynton promised to attempt to arrange it. Just a month later, independently, a field secretary of the Student Non-violent Coordinating Committee, Reginald J. Robinson, who was delegated to travel around the South attempting to arouse support for SNCC's efforts on black college campuses, arrived at Selma University. Robinson arranged to meet with a small group of Selma University students, among whom was Selma high school teacher and Voters League member Frederick D. Reese. The students told Robinson that, because classes at Selma University would end for the summer in only a week and most of them would then leave town, they could not consider any protest activities in the city until school began again in the fall. But Robinson reported to SNCC headquarters that they would be interested in working with SNCC to create an organization at that time.

These two unrelated events came together by happenstance in October. SNCC executive secretary James Forman had been attempting during September to obtain financial support from the Southern Conference Educational Fund (SCEF) for SNCC's Bernard Lafayette to spend the year doing fund-raising work for the organization in Chicago, New York, and Boston. Lafayette, a native of Tampa, Florida, was one of the Nashville Fisk students who had participated in the Montgomery Freedom Ride in May 1961 and had been beaten at the Montgomery Greyhound terminal. He had continued on the Freedom Ride from Montgomery to Jackson, Mississippi, had spent more than a month in Mississippi's Parchman Peniten-tiary as a result, and was now doing voter registration work in the Jackson area. At the beginning of October, just as it had become clear that SCEF could not fund this proposal, the Voters League's funding inquiry arrived at the SRC, and the council contacted Forman to ask if he thought an effort in Selma might prove productive. Doubtless recalling Robinson's en-couraging report of the preceding May, and knowing now that Lafayette was available, Forman suggested that Lafayette be dispatched to Selma to evaluate the situation and to advise the SRC on whether or not he believed a grant there would be useful. And thus, at the end of October 1962, Bernard Lafayette arrived in Selma. He remained on this initial occasion only for a short time, leaving in early November to prepare for his forth-coming wedding to Colia Liddell, scheduled for November 29. But his meetings with Mrs. Boynton, Frederick Reese, Alabama Lutheran Academy teacher James Gildersleeve, and others led to a positive report to SNCC and the SRC. As a result, the Voter Education Project approved the grant to the Voters League at the beginning of February 1963, and on February 10 Lafayette, accompanied by his new wife and by SNCC worker Frank Holloway, returned to Selma to commence a full-scale voting registration campaign.[122]

In the meantime, however, Lafayette's initial visit to the city had pro-duced a sharp division within the Voters League. Postal worker Robert Reagin (now the league's president), retired teacher Jackson C. Lawson, Selma University public relations director Pleasant L. Lindsey, and other older members strongly opposed the sort of demonstrations and direct ac-tion that SNCC sought. Younger members, in particular league vice-president James Gildersleeve, his brother-in-law and fellow Lutheran Academy teacher Ulysses Blackman, carpenter and insurance agent Ernest Doyle, insur-ance agent and minister John D. Hunter (former president of the NAACP branch), barber Henry W. Shannon, and Frederick D. Reese—along with Mrs. Boynton SNCC's initial contact in Selma—were enthusiastic. Most of these men were veterans, and their experience in the armed services seems to have prepared them for a more aggressive confrontation. A considerable struggle ensued in the organization during the winter of 1962–63. The activists eventually persuaded the older members at least not to oppose the plan, though Reagin resigned his league office in protest. Reagin was succeeded by Lawson, but Lawson too resigned once the demonstrations began in the fall because he disapproved of the use of schoolchildren in them. Lawson was succeeded by Gildersleeve, who fully supported SNCC's tactics.[123]

In their doubts about the advisability of direct action, however, the older Voters League members actually represented an influential element of the black community at large. Presbyterian minister Claude Brown, business leader Edwin Moss, Selma University president James Owens, and many other prominent blacks shared their misgivings. The fact that the black moderates allowed themselves to be convinced not to oppose the community's cooperation with SNCC openly hence requires an explanation. And the probable source of the moderates' decision helps significantly to clarify the structure of the transformation that Selma was undergoing. No more than three weeks after Lafayette had completed his survey of conditions in the city at the beginning of November 1962, Selmians of all sorts were transfixed, as we have seen, by the spectacle of the challenge filed by the Committee of 100 Plus on November 25 to the slate of establishment nominees for the board of directors of the chamber of commerce; the balloting to choose between the two sets of candidates was taking place from November 30 to December 5, precisely as the league was beginning its debate about sponsoring the SNCC initiative. The young white businessmen who supported the Committee of 100 Plus would have been dismayed, one need hardly say, by the thought that their efforts might hold any implications at all for Selma's race relations. Their concern was solely with the furtherance of the community's, and their own, material advancement. But in fact, and quite ironically, so complete had been the success of the White Citizens' Council and the Burns-Heinz machine up to that time in dragooning whites into what had appeared to be an utterly unified white phalanx on all political, social, and economic questions that this first small revelation of white dissent had—for all concerned, but particularly for black leaders—the most momentous implications. Even though the insurgent slate was roundly trounced by the regular nominees, the discovery that there were fissures in the united white front—that the political organization and its economic and social arms, the chamber of commerce and the Citizens' Council, did not actually speak for all of Selma's consequential white residents—was sufficient to embolden the moderate black leadership to attempt, it seems, a strategic gamble. The threat of demonstrations and boycotts, made credible by a SNCC presence in the city, might well prove enough to draw the young businessmen allied with the Committee of 100 Plus into serious negotiations. And if substantive concessions were thus forthcoming, then no large-scale direct action would be necessary after all. Apparently moved by such calculations as these, a sufficient number of the black moderates eventually agreed to countenance the league activists' cooperation with SNCC, at least for the time being. The moderates did not make their plans public, of course, and we therefore cannot be certain of their thinking. But as we shall shortly see, we do indeed know that this was exactly the course they would pursue once SNCC's campaign had begun to gather momentum.

After Lafayette's visit in October and November, while the activists struggled to gain the league's support, they also took an important step to lay the groundwork for Lafayette's possible return by establishing voter education classes. The classes were the idea of Mrs. Marie Foster, a dental hygienist and the sister of prominent dentist Dr. Sullivan Jackson. She approached Mrs. Boynton with the plan and received her eager approval. By this time, Judge Thomas had rendered his decision finding the conduct of the board of registrars a model for the nation. It seemed clear, therefore, that only those blacks who could fill out the voter questionnaire flawlessly had any hope of being registered. Mrs. Foster proposed to instruct potential applicants in how to answer the questionnaire so that they could avoid the small errors on which the board would pounce. With the backing of the Voters League, she canvassed black churches for students. Her first class, in January 1963, was disappointing; only one person showed up, and he proved to be illiterate. But with the return of Lafayette in February and the beginning of his attempts to organize within the community, attendance began to improve.[124]

The efforts of the Lafayettes and the Voters League's activist members were apparent at once in the number of black applications to the board of registrars. From January 1962 through January 1963, black applications had averaged only 3 a month; in September and October, no blacks had applied at all. But in February 1963, black applications leaped to 14. There were 17 applications in both March and April, and in May, when the mass meetings began, the number mounted to 31. It reached 41 in June, 64 in August, and 215 at the campaign's high point in October. Between the beginning of the mass meetings in May 1963 and their halting by Judge Hare's injunction in July 1964, black applications averaged 47 a month. Thereafter, from August through December 1964, the figure fell back to about 10 a month.[125]

Officials detected the effectiveness of SNCC's exertions at once in these mounting totals, and Sheriff Clark responded with increasing harassment. Local black leaders had expected authorities' hostility, of course, and as a result, very few of them outside the membership of the Voters League had been willing to cooperate openly during the campaign's first six months. Lafayette had great difficulty in locating a site for his proposed fortnightly mass meetings, and when he finally prevailed on the Reverend Louis Anderson to make the Tabernacle Baptist Church available, Anderson had to face down the united opposition of his deacons, who—quite reasonably—feared vandalism against the edifice. At the first mass meeting, on May 14 —the day after S. W. Boynton died—only about 350 blacks summoned the courage to attend, and many of those were teenagers. City police, sheriff's deputies, and fifty possemen surrounded the church. Lafayette and SNCC executive secretary James Forman spoke. Forman did little to calm white fears of black registration when he thundered, "Someday they will have to open up that ballot box, and that will be our day of reckoning." The Reverend Clifton C. Hunter of Clinton Chapel A.M.E.Z. Church, evidently frightened by the presence of white law enforcement officers and reporters, responded to Forman and Lafayette by warning against blaming whites, rather than blacks themselves, for their race's problems.[126]

Despite this rather inauspicious start, the mass meetings became more and more successful as the summer passed. Attendance mounted to 500 in June, 600 in July, and 800 in September. On June 17, the day after the second mass meeting, Sheriff Clark ordered the arrest of Bernard La-fayette for vagrancy. On the day of the mass meeting, Clark himself arrested a teenage SNCC worker, Bosie Reese, for conduct calculated to cause a breach of the peace when Reese, who was assisting voter applicants, failed to leave the courthouse as Clark had ordered. Clark pushed and kicked Reese, and though he failed to tell Reese that he was under arrest, Clark then charged him with resisting arrest. On July 22, during the seventh mass meeting, Clark arrested a young SNCC worker, Alexander L. Brown, for concealing his identity, when the name he used proved not to be the same as the one on his driver's license. At the same time, deputies ticketed twenty-nine cars parked at the mass meeting, including Brown's, for improper lights. On June 26, the Justice Department sued for an injunction to bar these and other similar acts of harassment. On July 25, Judge Thomas began a hearing on the request, but then recessed it to October 15. At the July 25 hearing, Clark's attorneys maintained that Lafayette and Brown "are in Selma for the express purpose of inciting racial disorders, and that they were legally arrested in the interest of preserving the peace," thus apparently conceding the racial motive behind the various charges.[127]

The sheriff's arrests, focused as they were on the mass meetings, were in fact an index to the gathering enthusiasm that the mass meetings were generating in the black community. During July, SNCC and the Voters League increased their frequency to weekly and began preparing to try to use the enthusiasm to launch demonstrations and sit-ins. This prospect now moved moderate black leaders to attempt to put into place their strategy for procuring biracial negotiations. They came together in a new organization, untainted by the Voters League's association with SNCC, the Dallas County Improvement Association (DCIA), that included prominent businessman Edwin L. D. Moss; the Reverend Claude C. Brown, the Presbyterian minister who was the principal spokesman for blacks with white authorities; the Reverend Clifton C. Hunter, the Methodist who had responded to Lafayette and Forman at the first mass meeting; black physician Dr. William B. Dinkins; the Reverend Marshall C. Cleveland, Jr., the son of the conservative Montgomery minister who was the chairman of Selma University's board of trustees; and the Reverend Louis L. Anderson. These men hoped, as we have said, to exert their influence with city and county governments, and especially with white businessmen, to gain concessions that would be sufficient to forestall the contemplated direct action. In May the Selma public library, whose exclusion of blacks had always been only customary rather than required by law, had quietly permitted blacks sent by Lafayette to use the facility. Mayor Heinz had threatened to have the head librarian prosecuted for doing so, and had prevailed on the library board to have all the tables and chairs removed, on the Montgomery model, to limit any further interracial contact. But the librarian, Mrs. Patricia S. Blalock, had then convinced the board that, with the furniture gone, there was no danger in permitting blacks to check out books, and in July several blacks were issued library cards. Though the furniture did not return until the mayoral election the following spring, nevertheless the older black leaders must have regarded this evidence of progress as a very hopeful sign. They apparently were further encouraged, as they had been earlier by the contested chamber of commerce election, to believe that more such openings could be possible.

Bernard Lafayette left Selma at the beginning of August to complete his senior year at Fisk, and his successor, Worth Long, did not arrive to take up the position until mid-September. In the meantime a young Birmingham SNCC worker, Wilson N. Brown, was left in charge of the campaign. Brown seems to have learned of the DCIA's plans, and he and his associates James Austin and Benny L. Tucker, a future city councilman, hit upon a stratagem to outflank their elders. On August 6 the three SNCC workers called at Mayor Heinz's office and asked to speak with him. They were elated when Heinz, presumably unaware of who they were, received them and accepted a petition that they proffered. They asked if they could return soon to discuss the petition's contents, but Heinz said that he would be out of the city until August 16. After leaving the mayor's office, Tucker at once telephoned the *Times-Journal* to report the meeting, to detail the demands in their petition, and to claim that Heinz had promised to meet with them about it on August 16. It asked for the integration of all schools, parks, public swimming pools, movie theaters, drugstores, and other public facilities; the hiring of black policemen and firemen; the hiring of blacks on Alabama Power Company and Southern Bell Telephone Company crews; and the removal of all segregation signs in the downtown area.

The *Times-Journal* called Heinz for comment. By that time he had read the petition and had already called the three SNCC workers to tell them that he was unalterably opposed to integration and would not meet with them or any other blacks to discuss the subject. He assured the newspaper and the public that his devotion to segregation was absolute and said that he would not have admitted the three blacks if he had known that they wished to challenge it.

The outcome was everything for which Brown and his associates could have hoped. When the moderate blacks of the DCIA brought their petition to city hall on August 10, the mayor was already committed publicly to refusing to discuss their proposals. Heinz was not in Selma, so the delegation was reduced to giving the petition to Police Chief Ed Mullen. Considerably more circumspect than the SNCC document, it was nevertheless inevitably associated in the minds of Selma's whites with what they generally regarded as the radicalism of the first petition. And among Selma's blacks, the DCIA's requests, which would under other circumstances have seemed to seek very significant advances, were made to appear fainthearted. The DCIA sought the registration of qualified blacks as voters, the removal of segregation signs from the county courthouse and other public buildings, the end of police brutality and the hiring of black policemen and firemen, an effort on the part of city officials to create a mood among white employers receptive to the hiring and promotion of blacks, and the appointment of a biracial committee.

The DCIA delegation emphasized that it was seeking to head off demonstrations that would lead to increased racial animosity and perhaps violence. Their goal, they said, was to create positive and friendly lines of communication between blacks and the city government. But on his return, Heinz refused to respond to the petition. At a White Citizens' Council rally on August 29 attended by sixty-eight hundred whites, Citizens' Council chairman Holt Hamlett warmly commended Heinz and other city authorities for having rejected negotiations with, as Hamlett put it, two black groups seeking the appointment of a biracial committee; Hamlett said that the Citizens' Council was adamantly opposed to the creation of any committee whose goal was integration. Segregationists apparently were simply unable to see the difference between SNCC and the DCIA.

The Citizens' Council rally, at which Mayor Heinz, Judge Reynolds, and Senator Givhan were seated on the podium, seems to have convinced the DCIA conclusively that it could expect nothing from the city government. Both Heinz's own blindness and the tactical coup of the young SNCC organizers in having forced the DCIA's efforts, which it undoubtedly had hoped to keep confidential, into the open had doomed this first of the moderates' initiatives. But they had another card to play, one for which they had significantly greater hope. At the end of August, the DCIA's chairman, Edwin Moss, dispatched a letter to the Selma Retail Merchants Association urging the merchants to join the DCIA in establishing direct communications, without waiting for governmental sponsorship. The letter asked the merchants to consider promoting black employees to sales and stock clerks; to provide all their black employees a living wage; to open all their facilities to customers of both races and to require their employees to treat all customers courteously; and to remove all segregation signs from their premises. Moss noted that the DCIA was "making special efforts to solve these problems without outside intervention. We see no reason to make demands or to make threats, and we will not do so, but we feel sure that you must know that disregard of basic rights of Negro citizens cannot continue without growing discontent that may lead to discord and possible unnecessary situations that have existed in many other cities." The letter asked for a response by September 15 and said, "Refusal to give an answer will of necessity be concluded to mean that you are not interested."

Merchant Morris Barton and four other Merchants Association members, according to Barton's subsequent account, sought to persuade the group to reply to Moss's letter. The association did agree to summon a general meeting of business and civic leaders to consider the matter, but Citizens' Council adherents turned out for this meeting in force, and their opposition convinced the group to take no action. Despite this decision, however, cotton broker Charles Hohenberg, a well-to-do racial moderate, drafted, as he later reported, a response to Moss's letter on September 16, the day after the bombing of the Sixteenth Street Baptist Church in Birmingham, repudiating the bombing and offering immediate negotiations. Hohenberg intended to ask sixteen of the community's leading whites to co-sign his letter, but when black demonstrations began later that day, all sixteen declined to participate and Hohenberg abandoned the plan. In the meantime, Father Maurice Ouellet, the Roman Catholic priest who was the only white person publicly allied with the black effort, had managed, after weeks of trying, as he stated, to arrange a meeting of the city's white clergy. But the meeting occurred the same day the demonstrations began, and the clergy therefore voted to express no opinion on the blacks' requests. If these statements are accurate, they indicate once again how thoroughly intimidated Selma's moderates were by the Citizens' Council's power. And Hohenberg's delay until September 16 is, as well, an example of whites' general failure to appreciate the urgency of the situation. Moss's letter had been explicit about the September 15 deadline, certainly because he knew that SNCC and the Voters League intended to commence demonstrations immediately after that date. On September 13, SNCC field secretary Wilson Brown filed an application at city hall for a parade permit to authorize a demonstration of three thousand people and ten automobiles on every day from September 16 to October 15. But despite these clear warnings, when the demonstrations began on September 16, evidently surprised authorities speculated that the demonstrations were intended as a response to the Birmingham church bombing of the preceding day.[128]

By mid-September it had thus become obvious even to the moderate blacks in the DCIA that neither segregationists nor white moderates were really taking their pleas for concessions seriously. The result was a degree of unity in the black community that would otherwise have been inconceivable. In a dispatch from Selma, the *Birmingham World*'s Emory Jackson, the first president of the Alabama Conference of NAACP Branches and a tireless advocate of black liberation, reported with some astonishment that SNCC, the Voters League, and the DCIA were all working together cooperatively. The Voters League, he noted, contained Selma's indestructible veterans of civil rights battles, while the DCIA, he alleged, was composed of those blacks never converted to the overall struggle for everyday freedom. But thanks to the enthusiasm of the young SNCC workers, he said, the campaign "has helped to rebuild civic courage" in the city's previously "beaten, frustrated and intimidated group."[129] It is certainly correct that the passion of the SNCC organizers played a role in the demonstrations' success, but of at least equal importance were the intransigence of segregationists and the timidity of white moderates that together drove the moderate blacks into the arms of the activists.

The demonstrations that began on September 16 continued until October 3, amidst rapidly mounting tensions. The demonstrations were accompanied by sit-ins at drugstores and cafés and the picketing of downtown businesses and the county courthouse. During this period about 350 blacks were arrested, of whom about 250 were under the age of sixteen. Much of the strength of the protests was drawn from Hudson High School students, whom SNCC mobilized on the model of SCLC's strategy in Birmingham five months earlier. The Voters League formed a youth auxiliary, headed by student Terry Shaw, and apparently assigned barber Henry W. Shannon, a veteran activist, as the auxiliary's adult adviser. On September 25, Shannon, SNCC field secretary Benny Tucker, and Robert L. Anderson were found guilty by Probate Judge Reynolds of contributing to the delinquency of minors because of these activities, and each was sentenced to a year at hard labor. Anderson's offense had occurred when, on arriving at the county jail to collect his son, who had been placed on probation by Judge Reynolds for participating in a march, Anderson expressed approval for his son's conduct.

The plight of the juveniles arrested was especially acute. Because the county jail was filled with adults, the juveniles were held at state prison road camps near Selma and Camden that were ordinarily used for the temporary housing of convict work crews who were repairing highways. The facilities were poor, and they were especially inadequate for females, because women were not assigned to the work gangs for whom the camps were intended. And the incarceration before trial was relatively lengthy because Probate Judge Reynolds, who served ex officio as Dallas County's Juvenile Court judge, simply worked the hearings of the juvenile offenders in during the course of days already filled with other duties. Eventually, authorities, who were increasingly embarrassed by the delays in processing the juvenile cases, appointed Selma attorney Clay Berry as a special juvenile judge to assist Reynolds, and this action considerably speeded the process. The proceedings, when they finally were held, were secret and lacked the legal safeguards accorded adults. The usual charges were truancy and unlawful assembly. Reynolds ordinarily initially placed the defendants on probation, conditioned on their participating in no more demonstrations. On one occasion, however, according to subsequent testimony, he ordered a girl to jail because she insisted on calling an older black woman "Mrs." Juveniles who were arrested a second time in a subsequent demonstration—as a substantial number apparently were—were then committed to the state reformatory for black juvenile delinquents at Mount Meigs.

But law enforcement was scarcely kinder to adults. Lacking a parade permit, marchers had been careful to remain on the sidewalks; they walked in pairs spaced thirty feet apart and observed all traffic signals. In 1965 the new public safety director, Wilson Baker, would consider this procedure not to violate the parade permit ordinance. And in 1958, as we have seen, Police Chief Mullen had said that a procession did not come under the ordinance unless it had a band and a number of other units and required turning off the traffic signals and stationing officers at intersections to direct traffic. But in 1963, Recorder's Court Judge Edgar Russell held that the pairs of walkers on the sidewalks were indeed a parade and fined all adult participants. Multiple pickets at a business were arrested for violating a city ordinance forbidding more than one picket at an establishment, but when demonstrators therefore limited their pickets to a single person, Solicitor McLeod ordered the arrest of the pickets for unlawful assembly. McLeod justified the unlawful assembly charges at trial on the ground that violence had been advocated at the mass meetings, and the pickets thus constituted an instigation to bystanders to breach the peace. His evidence for the advocacy of violence at the mass meetings rested primarily on a speech by SNCC chairman, former Freedom Rider, and future congressman John Lewis. In the course of a fervent plea for nonviolence, Lewis had said that he hoped that if any blood were spilled in Selma, it would be his own. McLeod contended that Lewis was thus inciting whites to attack him. When a white man, future county commissioner Deans Barber, Jr., brought a large snake into a black rally and tried to thrust it into the face of the black director of the Roman Catholic boys' club, Johnny Creer, who resisted the attempt, police then charged Creer with disturbing the peace.

County Court Judge Hugh S. D. Mallory, who had been one of William Fikes's court-appointed attorneys in 1953, was especially severe in sentencing the demonstrators and civil rights workers who came before him. He regularly imposed jail terms of six months, together with fines and thousand-dollar peace bonds. One of these sentences was imposed on SNCC worker Carver S. "Chico" Neblett, whose offense had been to attempt to distribute sandwiches and water to blacks waiting in a long line to apply to register to vote; Neblett was charged with criminal provocation and resisting arrest. Six blacks appealed the imposition of the peace bonds to Judge Hare. During a brief recess in the hearing on this appeal, Sheriff

Clark charged one of the six, Benny Tucker, with criminal provocation when Tucker sought to use the white rest room. "He just walked right by me and into that rest room. He was just trying to antagonize me," the astonished sheriff reported. Judge Hare upheld the peace bonds, and the six appellants were jailed in lieu of them from October 1963 to March 1964, when in a significant victory, black attorneys persuaded the state court of appeals that requiring peace bonds in these circumstances was illegal.[130]

During these same tense weeks, SNCC and the Voters League tried a new tactic that deeply concerned white authorities. In June, a commission headed by future U.S. district judge Gerhard Gesell had recommended to the Defense Department that the United States close all military bases located near segregated communities. Secretary of Defense Robert McNamara had rejected this proposal as not feasible, but on July 26 he had authorized base commanders to apply to the three service secretaries to have a town declared off-limits to base personnel if the town practiced relentless segregation against black soldiers, sailors, or airmen stationed there. Because of Selma's dependence on Craig Air Force Base, this order placed the city in a delicate situation. In May, SNCC had already asked the Defense Department to investigate the existence of racial discrimination at Craig, but in June the Pentagon had replied that all base facilities were integrated. On September 18, Mrs. Boynton, SNCC field secretary Worth W. Long, and young local SNCC worker Cleophus K. Hobbs called on Craig's commandant, Colonel Richard Ault, and urged him to make use of his new authority against Selma. Ault declined and told the three blacks that they would need to contact Secretary McNamara personally. In fact, Worth Long had filed a formal complaint with the Pentagon on September 16. On September 20, the Defense Department replied that the complaint constituted no grounds for declaring Selma off-limits, because the discrimination that it alleged had been directed against civilians rather than servicemen. SNCC executive secretary James Forman therefore went to work to organize black airmen to demonstrate that they did indeed suffer discrimination in the city. On October 1 a group of black airmen took seats in the front of the bus from the air base into town, and once in Selma they sought service in a white restaurant and tried to enter the white section of a movie theater. In a rare display of tactical intelligence, Selma authorities left them unmolested. The initial black effort to use Craig's importance to the local economy to advance civil rights thus proved unsuccessful. But city officials must certainly have expected other attempts in future months.[131]

In the meantime, another event whose echoes would also be heard in the coming year occurred on September 19. Judge Hare summoned to his office a delegation of sixteen people representing, he said, the "intelligent and responsible Negro leadership in Selma"; he "advised the group that I am certain I would be presented with a petition asking for an injunction against further racial demonstrations and that under the prevailing circumstances in Selma, I would seriously consider granting such an injunction. . . . From all reports, the racial situation is deteriorating in Selma, and rather than be confronted with street mobs and riots, I would invoke any process of law to maintain peace and order in the community." He told the delegation that "It is becoming increasingly difficult to deal with outside interference," and he "excoriated" the blacks, as he reported, for their "disgraceful use of school children as a front for law violations." Judge Hare's threats had no effect on the demonstrations, but he did reveal with them the strategy authorities would actually use the following July.[132]

On October 3, the Fifth Circuit reversed Judge Thomas's decision of November 1962 that had cleared the board of registrars of the charge that it had practiced racial discrimination. In an opinion by Judge Richard Rives of Montgomery, the appellate court ordered Judge Thomas to enter an injunction forbidding the board to use the voter questionnaire as if it were a test unless the board adopted clear, objective, and reasonable standards, approved by Judge Thomas, by which to grade the questionnaire. The injunction also forbade the oral questioning of applicants unless the board kept a written record of the questions and answers, limited the questions to ones about the applicant's qualifications, and applied objective standards in evaluating them; and it forbade the rejection of an applicant for lack of good character unless the applicant were afforded a hearing at which to try to refute the charges against him. With this ruling by the Fifth Circuit, the demonstrations came to an end. It is possible that SNCC, if left to itself, would have wished to continue them in pursuit of a general end to segregation, but the principal goal of both the Voters League and the DCIA was to gain the ballot, and this federal injunction gave them sufficient hope to make them want to focus all of their energies on turning out applicants for registration.

The October sessions of the board of registrars saw the largest number of black applicants of any month for which records are available, as optimistic blacks responded to the promise of the injunction. No less than 215 blacks actually completed the questionnaire, and even more were unable to get into the board's office to do so. But the board accepted only 11 of the 215 applicants. At the same time, the board accepted 219 of 296 white applicants. As the months passed, it became increasingly apparent that the injunction had not altered the board's behavior. From November 1963 through January 1964, a total of 129 blacks applied, and only 22 were registered; in the same months, 407 whites applied and 317 were registered. In February 1964 the board adopted a new and more stringent voter qualification test. On March 5, 1964, the Justice Department petitioned Judge Thomas to declare the board in contempt. But Thomas did not hold a hearing on the petition until October, and then he recessed it to November.[133]

In October 1963, Thomas resumed hearing the Justice Department's suit to enjoin Sheriff Clark and Solicitor McLeod from harassing applicants; Thomas had held an initial hearing in July but then had recessed it. At the October hearing, Thomas excluded any accusations about harassment that had occurred after the first hearing the preceding summer. In November, therefore, the department filed a new complaint so that it could offer testimony about the officials' conduct during the demonstrations. At the same time, it at last hit at the heart of the problem by filing a complaint against the Dallas County White Citizens' Council, charging council members both with using economic sanctions to prevent blacks from seeking to register to vote and with attempting to keep both blacks and whites from answering the questions of federal investigators looking into racial discrimination in the county. But in December, Judge Thomas granted a defense motion to sever the White Citizens' Council case from the suit against McLeod and Clark, and then, true to form, scheduled no hearing on the Citizens' Council complaint, as 1963 turned into 1964 and then into 1965. Meanwhile, in March 1964, Thomas found Clark's and McLeod's actions during 1963 fully justified and dismissed the petition for an injunction against them.[134]

Judge Thomas's injunction against the Dallas County Board of Registrars, which he formally entered on November 1, 1963, was one of a series of very similar injunctions against boards of registrars throughout Alabama that were granted by federal judges during 1962 and 1963. They generally included the prohibition against using the registration questionnaire as if it were a test. As a result, on January 14, 1964, the Alabama Supreme Court, which had made up the questionnaire a decade before, decided to add a genuine test to it. The Dallas County board began using the new test in February.

The test that the board began administering in February continued in use until the end of August. It obliged the applicant to answer four questions on government; the supreme court provided twelve sets of four questions each and instructed the board to change the question set each month. The test also had the applicant read a passage from the U.S. Constitution aloud and then write a passage from dictation given by the board. Again, the supreme court created twelve sets of four constitutional passages, and it ordered the boards to change the sets monthly and to pick one of the four passages at random to give to each applicant. However, the Civil Rights Act of 1964, which took effect in July, contained a provision requiring that voter qualification tests be wholly in writing. In accordance with the new law, the state supreme court on August 24 promulgated a new test. It retained the four general questions on government, with the four-question groups rotated monthly, and provided for copying any one excerpt from the Constitution, chosen from the group of four excerpts changed monthly, but it eliminated the necessity to read the excerpt aloud and to write it from dictation. Instead, the new test contained printed passages from the Constitution, below each of which there were four questions about the passage's contents. There were a total of one hundred passages, and the board chose any one passage, with its four questions, at random for the applicant. Thus each applicant now had to fill out the original questionnaire, copy an excerpt from the Constitution, and answer a total of eight questions, four of them general questions about government and four of them specific questions about a passage from the Constitution that the applicant had just read. An applicant who met all other qualifications was registered if he answered any six of the eight questions correctly.[135]

Boards of registrars began use of the new test in September 1964. Judge Thomas forbade its use in Dallas County on February 4, 1965, when he ruled it a violation of his injunction of November 1, 1963, and its use was suspended everywhere in Alabama in August 1965 by the terms of the Voting Rights Act. But despite its brief life—five months in Selma, less than a year in the state at large—this was the test that gained notoriety throughout the United States. Some of the notoriety was unwarranted. In the first place, opponents of the test often cited examples of the questions used in that portion of it in which the applicant was being asked about a specific passage of the Constitution, without making it clear that the answer to each of the questions was contained in the passage printed immediately above them. If cited alone, the questions could sound quite abstruse, but in the context in which they actually were asked they were intended only to test whether the applicant had been able to understand the excerpt he had been given to read. The general questions on government, in contrast, though much less often cited by opponents, were considerably more straightforward: for instance, the name of the capital of the United States or of Alabama; whether the Supreme Court is a part of the executive, the legislative, or the judicial branch of government; the number of U.S. senators a state has. The questions were very similar, in fact, to those asked of aliens applying for American citizenship.

In the second place, the test itself does not appear to have increased the extent of black disfranchisement a great deal, at least in Dallas County. From the conclusion of Judge Thomas's hearing of the Justice Department's complaint against the board in May 1962 to the Fifth Circuit's reversal of his decision exonerating the board in October 1963, the board registered 76 percent of white applicants and 15 percent of black applicants. From Judge Thomas's injunction forbidding the use of the questionnaire as a test at the beginning of November 1963 to the commencement of the board's use of the Supreme Court's new test at the beginning of February 1964, the board registered 78 percent of white applicants and

17 percent of black applicants. From the adoption of the four-question test in February 1964 to its replacement by the eight-question test at the beginning of September 1964, the board registered 82 percent of white applicants and 11 percent of black applicants. And from the adoption of the eight-question test in September 1964 to its banning by Judge Thomas at the beginning of February 1965, the board registered 66 percent of white applicants and 10 percent of black applicants. The test certainly had some effect, therefore. But the statistics would seem to indicate that the conduct of the board of registrars was in fact vastly more significant than the content of the test in determining the numbers of blacks and whites who were added to the rolls. Throughout the first half of the 1960s, regardless of the changes in the registration requirements, the board always managed to find the overwhelming majority of whites qualified and the overwhelming majority of blacks unqualified.[136]

If the test did not deserve all of the opprobrium heaped upon it, however, it was certainly not the disinterested constitutional necessity that its apologists claimed. It is exceedingly difficult to understand how the state supreme court could have convinced itself that the actual constitutional standard that the boards were supposed to be applying—a simple ability to read and write a section of the U.S. Constitution—could justify the adoption of such a test. The four general questions on government, at least, clearly set up an extra-constitutional standard of knowledge about government, something the state constitution did not in fact require. Moreover, a majority of the white electorate apparently did not even wish that voter qualification tests should be administered impartially. On two different occasions, in 1962 and in 1963, the state legislature proposed a constitutional amendment providing for the machine grading of tests. In May 1962 the amendment received less than 37 percent of the vote and carried only nine of the state's sixty-seven counties, and in December 1963 it did even more poorly, receiving just 27 percent of the vote and carrying only two counties. It was following the second defeat of the amendment that the state supreme court proceeded to devise its own test, to be graded by the boards of registrars.[137]

By July of 1964, the ineffectiveness of Judge Thomas's injunction had become completely clear. In the eight months since he had entered the order, 217 blacks had applied and only 34 had been accepted; in the same period, 490 whites had applied and 385 had been accepted. And the institution of the first version of the new test in February had reduced the black acceptance rate even a bit further. As the months had passed, the frustration of the members of the Voters League and of the SNCC fieldworkers had mounted rapidly. Their mass meetings had continued on a weekly basis throughout this period, and attendance had remained high. Moderate black leaders, equally soured by the official intransigence, had dissolved their DCIA, and moderate prescriptions had become increasingly unacceptable in the black community. The enactment of the Civil Rights Act of 1964 provided the occasion for the public expression of these emotions. President Johnson signed the new law on July 2. On the evening of July 3, blacks who sought service at a drive-in restaurant and a downtown café were refused, in direct defiance of the act's public accommodations section. On July 4, Sheriff Clark personally arrested four blacks who tried to eat at a short-order restaurant. He charged them with trespassing, and charged one of them, Carol Lawson, with carrying a concealed weapon when he found a bicycle chain and its padlock in her purse; Clark called this a "weighted chain." Later that day, disorders were narrowly averted when blacks sought to sit on the main floor of a movie theater; in the past they had been confined to the balcony. Angry whites stormed into the theater, while outside, hostile groups of whites and blacks faced each other on the sidewalk. SNCC worker Alvery Williams of Gadsden was charged with disturbing the peace and conduct calculated to provoke a riot when he encouraged blacks to use their new privileges. Clark's deputies and posse dispersed the crowd and Clark ordered the theater closed, but incidents continued through the night. In one of them, a thirteen-year-old white girl, Roberta Corson, was injured by a bottle thrown by a sixteen-year-old black youth, William Steele; Steele was charged with assault with intent to murder.

At the conclusion of a Voters League mass meeting on the evening of July 5, something approaching a riot erupted. Police said that, as the crowd was emerging from the church, a shower of bricks and bottles suddenly was directed at officers from a dark alley, and that immediately thereafter they heard a shot. Deputies thereupon threw tear gas into the alley, and a melee ensued involving fifty officers and perhaps five hundred blacks. Several deputies were struck by bricks, and two blacks were treated for head wounds. Two white photographers with ties to SNCC were beaten by deputies, and the camera of one was destroyed; Solicitor McLeod, who was present, ordered both photographers to leave town. Earlier, at the mass meeting, Frederick Reese and Louis Anderson had announced that the Voters League planned to begin organized testing of Selma's public accommodations on July 12, and Ralph D. Abernathy, the evening's main speaker, had promised the full support of the Southern Christian Leadership Conference for these efforts.

On July 6 the board of registrars began a five-day special session, and a large group of blacks sought to apply. Sheriff Clark ordered the arrest of fifty-five black demonstrators led by SNCC chairman John Lewis for picketing a building in which a court was in session because, unknown to the demonstrators, the county grand jury was meeting in the courthouse at the time. One of the picketers, Claude Nelson, was a juvenile, and therefore forty-one of the adults in the group were charged also with contributing to his delinquency. The same day, six white youths led by

Richard Turner, the secretary of the extremist Dallas County National States' Rights Party, were arrested for carrying concealed weapons. The next night some fifty whites attended an NSRP rally. On July 8, Frederick Reese was arrested for contributing to the delinquency of minors when he drove two juveniles to the courthouse so that they could join in the demonstrations. On July 9 seven more demonstrators were arrested, bringing the total to seventy, and Alvery Williams was beaten by a jailer in the county jail. On July 10 the session of the board of registrars ended, and the Voters League began preparing for its mass testing of public accommodations, to begin on July 12.

It was in this context of building black insistence and white alarm that Judge Hare took the action that he had threatened the preceding September. On the petition of Sheriff Clark and Mayor Heinz, and without any notice to the affected parties, Judge Hare granted a broad injunction against civil rights organizations and leaders, as well as the Ku Klux Klan and the NSRP; it forbade any three or more persons to assemble in a public place or to block streets or highways, and forbade the organizations to sponsor any meeting at which "violation of the law is suggested, advocated or encouraged." The organizations enjoined included SNCC, CORE, SCLC, the NAACP, and the SRC, together with the Voters League and the now dissolved DCIA. Forty-three blacks were individually named, including the national heads of the civil rights organizations. The list of local blacks included both activists such as Amelia Boynton, Frederick Reese, Marie Foster, and James Gildersleeve and conservatives such as Edwin Moss, Claude Brown, and Clifton C. Hunter.[138]

The injunction brought the mass meetings to an end, and with them the momentum that the movement had regained in the first days of July. During the month a total of ninety-eight blacks applied to register, most of them in the special session of the board between July 6 and July 10, but only six were successful. And with the end of the mass meetings, black applications fell sharply in August, to twelve. Between August and December, they averaged just ten a month; a total of six blacks were registered in the five months. On July 11, attorneys for the civil rights organizations petitioned Judge Thomas to dissolve Judge Hare's injunction as an infringement of the First Amendment, and asked him as well to take jurisdiction of, and dismiss, the cases against the seventy demonstrators arrested during the protests. Thomas held a hearing on the petitions on July 20, but continued it to September 9; however, he ordered all of the demonstrators released on three hundred dollars' bond. After the hearing on September 9, Thomas agreed to take jurisdiction of the cases against the seventy demonstrators, and he scheduled a hearing on whether to dismiss the cases for March 22, 1965. Thomas also took under advisement the petition to dissolve Judge Hare's injunction; he would not rule on this petition until April 16, 1965. In the meantime, Thomas had earlier refused to issue a temporary restraining order to forbid Dallas County authorities to enforce the injunction, and Sheriff Clark therefore continued to do so. Protests in Selma after July 10, as a result, dwindled to a number of efforts, uniformly quiet and unsuccessful, to obtain service at white restaurants.

V. The Origins of the 1965 Demonstrations

At the beginning of September 1964, the Justice Department filed suit seeking an injunction against five Selma restaurants to compel them to obey the new Civil Rights Act. At the same time, it also filed a suit against Judge Hare, Judge Reynolds, Solicitor McLeod, and Sheriff Clark. The suit alleged that the four officials had engaged in a pattern of conduct intended to interfere with blacks' right to vote and their efforts to use public accommodations, and it asked for an injunction to prohibit the conduct. An enraged Judge Hare called the allegations "baseless and libelous" and a part of Attorney General Robert Kennedy's "vendetta against the people of Alabama." Thanks to the 1964 Civil Rights Act, the Justice Department enjoyed a significant new advantage in arguing for these injunctions. The act provided that all suits brought under it were to be heard before three-judge courts. Therefore, Appeals Court Judge Richard Rives and District Judge Frank M. Johnson, both from Montgomery, were assigned to try the cases along with Judge Thomas. For the first time, the department could expect a sympathetic hearing in Selma.

The two suits came to trial in December. In the meantime, on November 12, Judge Thomas completed hearing the government's petition to hold the Dallas County Board of Registrars in contempt of his injunction of November 1, 1963, and to forbid the use of the new voter qualification test, introduced in September. Therefore, by the end of 1964 the three-judge court had under submission the questions of the refusal of Selma's restaurants to integrate and of the various efforts of Dallas County's authorities to preserve white supremacy. And Judge Thomas had under submission the questions of the conduct of the board of registrars, the legality of the voter qualification test, and the constitutionality of Judge Hare's injunction against the civil rights organizations. The cases against the demonstrators arrested that summer had been removed to federal court. And the Justice Department's suit against the Dallas County White Citizens' Council was pending on Judge Thomas's docket, though as yet it was unheard. As a result, as the new year dawned, white moderates were optimistic that all of the outstanding racial issues in Selma were about to receive quiet and authoritative judicial resolution. It seemed to them that, after a long night of reaction, Selma was poised at last to make genuine progress in its race relations.[139]

To understand the viewpoint of the white moderates, we must return briefly to the preceding spring. Joe Smitherman's defeat of Chris Heinz in March had marked the beginning of largely surreptitious but vigorous efforts on the part of moderate leaders to nudge Selma toward acceptance of the inevitability of at least modest change. Their endeavors were much encouraged by the presence in the city of a self-appointed mediator, Ralph E. Smeltzer.

Ralph Smeltzer was a minister of the Church of the Brethren, the radical Protestant sect that came to Pennsylvania in the eighteenth century along with the "Pennsylvania Dutch" immigration. Smeltzer's efforts during World War II to aid the Japanese Americans of California who had been interned in detention camps led him into a lifetime of social service. He came to Selma in November 1963 to assist a group of black women employees of a white nursing home who had been discharged for attempting to register to vote during October's registration campaign. Their employer, Charles E. Dunn, a strong segregationist, had not only fired them but, through the White Citizens' Council, had arranged to have them blacklisted so that they could not obtain any new employment. The extraordinarily polarized community that Smeltzer discovered on his arrival in the city caused him to seek permission from his denominational superiors to return in order to attempt to establish communications across the racial gulf.[140]

In late 1963 and early 1964, Smeltzer labored quietly toward this goal. Much of his initial attention was focused on Craig Air Force Base, where since the demonstration by black airmen the preceding September, blacks had become increasingly unhappy with their situation; they had formally complained to the Senate Armed Services Committee and the Justice Department's Civil Rights Division in January. Smeltzer met on a number of occasions with the base commander, Colonel Ault, and with the black airmen. Two significant steps forward emerged. The Nathan Bedford Forrest Homes, the public housing project operated by the Selma Housing Authority for white base personnel, was quietly opened to blacks, with the assistance of moderate housing authority attorney Edgar Stewart, and at the beginning of May 1964, Airman Enoch Fears, a leader of the black airmen's group, became the first black to receive an apartment. That summer, the classes for white Craig servicemen operated by the extension division of the University of Alabama were opened to black servicemen as well, again without publicity.

In the meantime, Smeltzer had begun to make contacts among Selma's white clergy. Through one of them in particular, Presbyterian minister John Newton, he became aware of the city's circle of white moderates. A group of moderates had begun meeting weekly at the People's Bank in the fall of 1963, just before Smeltzer's arrival in town. Led by the bank's president and vice-president, Rex Morthland and Frank Wilson, the group had focused its attention for the next six months on defeating the intransigent Heinz. But by the spring of 1964, with Smitherman now safely elected, the moderates were ready—in part, it appears, at the quiet urging of Judge Daniel Thomas—to turn to seeking areas in which they might be able to bring about reforms. The group also broadened its membership a bit, from about eight to some fifteen, in order to reach beyond the Smitherman camp. In addition to Morthland and Wilson, it included William B. Craig of City National Bank and Roger ap C. Jones of Selma National Bank. Attorney Edgar Stewart was the president of the Selma school board. Attorney Sam Earle Hobbs had been Stewart's predecessor in that position and was a trustee of the University of Alabama. Harry Gamble was a third prominent attorney, the son of an Episcopal priest. Roswell Falkenberry was the new editor of the *Selma Times-Journal,* and Arthur Capell covered city hall for the paper. Paul M. Grist was the executive secretary of the YMCA. Other moderates included automobile dealer Arthur Lewis, cotton broker Charles M. Hohenberg, and merchants James Gaston and Morris Barton. Lewis and Barton were both members of Selma's small Jewish community; Hohenberg had been born a Jew but had converted to Presbyterianism. As these and a few other whites searched for ways to improve race relations, Smeltzer was in a position to help because he had the trust of a number of the city's black leaders, something the moderates initially lacked.

The moderates proceeded with circumspection because the power of the White Citizens' Council, though not what it had been in the late 1950s, continued to be very great. In December 1963, for instance, the Voters League and SNCC had launched a Christmas boycott of downtown merchants, and though by no means completely effective, it continued into the spring of 1964. In a letter to the Retail Merchants Association, civil rights leaders offered to negotiate an end to the boycott, and a number of merchants, as they had the previous September, sought to have the association send a reply. But Citizens' Council elements were able once again to prevent the association from doing so by threatening a white boycott of any merchants who broke ranks. Nor was the threat an idle one. As we have seen, Citizens' Council ideology identified well-to-do white businessmen as the weak link in the chain of southern resistance. As a result, council members observed with unrelenting suspicion any commercial and professional leaders who were not active white supremacists. During the demonstrations in February of 1965, dark rumors circulated among the segregationists that the president of the chamber of commerce, moderate grocery store executive James M. Gaston, was a secret civil rights sympathizer. The rumors alleged that Gaston had sent sandwiches and fried chicken to the demonstrators, and one man claimed to have seen with his own eyes a check from Gaston contributing a thousand dollars to the NAACP. A white boycott of Gaston's grocery eventually forced him to take out a large newspaper advertisement denying the charges. In April 1965, segregationists launched a boycott of moderate

Arthur Lewis's car dealership, and a campaign of harassment against him, when a letter that he and his wife had written detailing their racial views fell into the council's hands.

But despite their trepidation, the moderates in the spring and summer of 1964 began privately urging county officials to make concessions to blacks. And though nearly all of the officials brushed them off, whether pleasantly or curtly, they discovered, perhaps to their surprise, that Probate Judge "Babe" Reynolds was not entirely unreceptive. In early August, on orders from Judge Reynolds, workers removed segregation signs from the courthouse drinking fountains. Though they followed Mayor Heinz's precedent of the preceding spring in installing dispensers of small paper cups next to each fountain so that whites would not actually have to bend over the same fountains used by blacks, nevertheless this integration was perceived by all concerned as a significant development. In mid-September, the moderates, with Smeltzer's assistance, made their first contacts with black leaders: Morthland met with Edwin Moss, Frank Wilson with Claude Brown, and Paul Grist with Frederick Reese. Blacks were surprised and delighted, and they were even more pleased with the prospect, held out by the moderates, of meetings with Joe Smitherman once he was inaugurated. Shortly thereafter, the moderates met as well with SNCC's Selma field secretary, John A. Love of New York City, who had succeeded Worth Long in June 1964. And at about the same time, they met with Sheriff Clark in an effort to convince him to adopt less aggressive tactics.

On October 5, Smitherman was sworn in as Selma's thirty-second mayor. His inaugural address hardly boded well for improvements in race relations. He used the occasion to denounce the idea of creating a biracial committee. "As mayor I do not believe that there is a place in the community now or in the foreseeable future for a biracial committee, and I will yield to no pressure from either the white or Negro to play a role in the organization of such a group. It is my dedicated opinion that a reasonable Selmian of good conscience, either white or Negro, can of his own knowledge and honest evaluation, recognize areas of racial accomplishment as well as areas of neglect. . . . The attitude, cooperation and good faith of the Negro community will be the key factors in the speed with which the goals we seek can be achieved. As mayor, I will discuss conditions with legitimate representatives of the Selma Negro community who can speak with authority for their race on occasions when it can serve some worthwhile purpose for me to do so." One could hardly imagine a more offensive expression of white supremacist arrogance. It is not surprising that the white moderates as well as the black leaders were disappointed with this start.

There were, however, other, much more positive signs. Very shortly after the inauguration, Smitherman contacted black leaders to arrange a meeting, and the first such session took place on November 6. Moreover, virtually Smitherman's first act as mayor was to ask the city council to create the office of director of public safety, to supervise the police and fire departments. The ordinance creating this position specifically charged the director to "assure the courteous and fair treatment of all persons regardless of race, creed or color." And to the new office Smitherman appointed Wilson Baker.

Since his defeat by Clark in 1958, Baker had been working as an instructor in criminology and law enforcement in the extension division of the University of Alabama. Based in Tuscaloosa, he had traveled all over the state to teach investigative techniques to Alabama's police departments. Earlier in 1964, he had been elected the president of the Alabama Peace Officers Association. But he had not severed his ties with Selma during these years. His family had continued to live there, and he had returned each weekend to be with them. His six years in academia had left him even more committed than he had earlier been to the cause of professionalism in law enforcement. And his detestation of Jim Clark, and of everything for which Clark stood, had grown with each passing year.

Baker at once insisted on reclaiming for the Selma police full authority for every aspect of law enforcement within the city limits. With the support of Smitherman, he informed Clark that the city was abrogating the agreement Clark had earlier made with Mayor Heinz to give the sheriff's department control of all civil rights offenses and arrests in Selma. And soon after he regained authority in this area, he halted the enforcement of Judge Hare's July injunction, on the ground that, when Judge Thomas had removed the injunction to federal court, it had ceased to be within local officials' jurisdiction. In speeches to Selma civic groups, Baker made his new approach clear. In talks to prominent white businessmen on November 1, both Smitherman and Baker called for active municipal business leadership, and Baker promised to try to instill the idea of service to people in the police department. And on December 31, Baker invaded a bastion of the Burns-Heinz organization, the Selma Exchange Club, of which Judge Hare, Judge Reynolds, and former Mayor Heinz were all members, to tell them flatly that Congress and the federal courts had now settled the question of where the United States was going in race relations; the only responsibility of the city administration, he said, was "to lead Selma in dignity through the maze of legal transition" to integration. He asked for their cooperation in this endeavor.

During December, as well, Baker gave proof of these attitudes in his handling of two unfortunate racial incidents. In October, white air force sergeant James O. Burke had defended a group of black teenagers who were assaulted by enraged white parishioners when the blacks attempted to attend mass at a white Roman Catholic church. Sergeant Burke's action marked him for escalating abuse by segregationists that culminated on December 19 when four white toughs lured him from his home and beat him severely. Police responded with vigor, apprehended the four, and charged them with assault with intent to murder and with robbery. On December 21, two white youths attacked a fifteen-year-old black, Fred Scott, for failing to yield the sidewalk to them. Scott had to be hospitalized, and a day later he was still in a coma. Again police immediately arrested and charged the culprits. It was clear that Baker's new spirit had begun to take hold in the department.

During the fall, the initial effects of the programs Smitherman had sponsored as a councilman—those involving laying sewer connections and paving streets on an assessment basis—began to be seen in the black neighborhoods. And the appearance for the first time of paved streets in black areas represented further evidence of the Smitherman administration's sincerity—though, of course, the assessment bills kept black property owners aware of who was actually paying for the improvements.

Finally, the Justice Department suits bore their first fruit at the beginning of the new year. The trial of the suit to compel Selma's restaurants to obey the Civil Rights Act had been held on December 7; on December 14, the U.S. Supreme Court ruled the act's public accommodations section constitutional, thus making the outcome of the Selma case a certainty. As a result, in early January, consultations among the restaurant owners produced an agreement to integrate their establishments voluntarily, without waiting for the inevitable federal injunction. On January 18, therefore, the restaurants began accepting black customers. To their white customers, they distributed handbills emphasizing that they had no choice. "We seek your indulgence and understanding of the unpleasant position into which we have been forced," they said, adding a bit forlornly, "We are confident sanity and good sense will return and that we will be able to revert, in time, to our long-established customs and traditions." In fact, of course, given the number and variety of the suits pending in federal court, the integration of the restaurants seemed likely to be the first of many similar blows to Selma's racial traditions.

These events, then, clarify the viewpoint of the white moderates. From their perspective, the nine months since Smitherman's election had witnessed very considerable progress and hence offered reason enough to expect blacks to be patient for a bit longer. The integration of the Forrest Homes and of the extension classes at Craig; the elimination of the segregation signs from the courthouse drinking fountains, and earlier, those at the city hall; the commencement of interracial meetings, first with the moderate businessmen and then with the new city administration; and the appointment of a director of public safety who gave clear evidence of his commitment to an even-handed administration of justice—taken together, these developments represented a significant forward step for the city. The library had integrated voluntarily in the late spring and summer of 1963 and had restored its tables and chairs in February 1964. The restaurants integrated, if quite grudgingly, in January 1965. And perhaps most importantly, almost all of the most pressing racial issues had by the end of 1964 been submitted to the federal courts, and decisions were expected in the very near future. As the white moderates saw things, blacks were on the verge of obtaining, peacefully and quietly, a degree of progress in race relations that even two years earlier would have seemed completely impossible.

One result of this perspective was the moderates' dedication—very similar to that of Birmingham's moderates in 1962–63—to keeping the lid on things until the federal courts and the Smitherman administration had time to effect reforms. This desire explains the moderates' most disreputable and pathetic effort of these months. Beginning in late August 1964, and continuing through much of the autumn, Frank Wilson and Edgar Stewart, on behalf of the moderates, made substantial payments to a black confidence man from Montgomery, J. J. Israel—the former associate of the Reverend Uriah Fields—under the impression that Israel could influence Selma's black leaders to forgo any public challenge to segregation for a period. The same attitudes led the moderates to regard Martin Luther King's refusal to postpone his Selma campaign in 1965 as primarily an effort on King's part to bilk his northern contributors out of donations. "I feel that his interest in Selma is much more commercial than humanitarian," Mayor Smitherman commented. Moreover, King's refusal to allow the deliberations of the federal courts to settle the outstanding racial issues in the community displayed, according to the mayor, a "dangerous disregard for legal, constitutional processes."[141]

Of course, the moderates' perspective was by no means the only one to be found in the city. Black activists were not unappreciative of the moderates' efforts, but they could be forgiven if the changes struck them as less than momentous. Though the water fountains at the city hall and the courthouse no longer had racial designations, for instance, the bathrooms remained firmly segregated. Though Mayor Smitherman had appointed the moderate Wilson Baker as director of public safety, he had also—over the opposition of at least one of his moderate supporters—appointed the prominent segregationist McLean Pitts as the new city attorney. And though many aspects of the racial conflict were under submission to the federal courts, the past conduct of Judge Thomas left blacks with very little confidence in the justice of his decisions. Thus the leadership of the Voters League was a good deal less convinced than were the white moderates that Selma was witnessing the dawn of a new day.

Equally estranged from the moderates' analysis were the segregationists. In Citizens' Council circles it was generally believed that Selma was the object of a conspiracy orchestrated by the Justice Department, in cooperation with the civil rights organizations; therefore, the efforts of the moderates were thought to be futile and the moderates themselves were regarded as dupes of the conspirators. The principal evidence of the conspiracy dated back to the first weeks of September 1963. A soldier who was stationed at Fort Campbell, Kentucky, and who had ties with Selma reported to local officials that the personnel of the 101st Airborne Division were being briefed for a possible investiture of the city. And then on October 3, a Selmian who was a veteran of this division telephoned Sheriff Clark to say that he had just seen its commanding general and two staff officers, dressed in civilian clothes, driving an unmarked car about the city, apparently to survey its layout. Clark and Judge Hare requested Alabama congressmen George Huddleston and Armistead Selden to ask the Pentagon about these developments. In March 1964, Selden received a reply to his inquiry that, though quite evasive, confirmed that the division had been instructed to prepare a contingency plan for the possible use of paratroopers to suppress civil disturbances in Selma, and that the general and his aides had indeed conducted a reconnaissance of the city as a part of the planning. In the meantime, on October 15, Martin Luther King visited Selma to speak to one of the Voters League's mass meetings, and Sheriff Clark's check of the license plates of the two cars in which he traveled revealed that both had been rented by the Justice Department. When Clark revealed this fact to the press, the department's press spokesman, Edwin Guthman, dismissed the claim on the strength of a denial given the department by future U.S. district judge Thelton Henderson, a black Civil Rights Division lawyer. But two weeks later, Henderson admitted that he had lied to his superiors and confirmed that he had in fact made a car available to King. Henderson was thereupon fired. In Selma, Judge Hare instructed a grand jury headed by county Republican Party chairman Robert D. Wilkinson, Jr., to investigate the affair. The Justice Department sued in federal court for an injunction to bar the grand jury from issuing subpoenas for department attorneys; Judge Thomas denied the injunction, but the Fifth Circuit eventually reversed his decision.[142]

Judge Hare was a man easily convinced of the existence of conspiracies; as we have seen, he had earlier alleged that the state's teacher tenure law was part of a Communist plot. In considering this sequence of events, Hare thought he discerned profoundly sinister implications. How could the Defense Department have known of the impending demonstrations in Selma early in September, when they did not begin until September 16? Why would the Justice Department have paid to bring King from Birmingham to Selma, and then to take him from Selma to Montgomery? In a lengthy charge to the grand jury on November 12, he instructed it to determine who had picked out Selma for the demonstrations, which he called a "hellish nightmare," to determine "who supplied the trained organizers, some of whose principal qualifications were police records of ten years or more," and to determine "who supplied the transportation, the operating funds and the publicity budgets." To Hare, the answer seemed clear. The federal government had selected Selma for a "knock-off," as he later put it. The Justice Department had given SNCC the authorization and the financial resources necessary to create such chaos in the city that it would compel the use of paratroopers to restore order. The purpose was to discredit local government and to push the Congress into passing radical legislation that would transfer control of American race relations to Washington. Only the forceful response of Selma's officials had prevented the demonstrations from taking on their intended dimensions. And that fact explained why the Justice Department had sought repeatedly to enjoin local authorities from suppressing the disorders. As Hare said of the department's September 1964 petition for an injunction against him, McLeod, Clark, and Reynolds, the suit constituted in fact a "political reprisal" by Robert Kennedy, undertaken because the Dallas County officials had "exposed and defeated his efforts" in the city during 1963.[143]

Judge Hare's intellectual and social authority in the community permitted his analysis to gain widespread acceptance in segregationist circles. Citizens' Council members thus generally regarded the efforts of the moderates to bring about reforms in race relations not only as treacherous but as utterly futile. Black activists could not be convinced by modest concessions to await the gradual elimination of white supremacy, precisely because the real goal both of the civil rights organizations and of their Justice Department masters was to generate massive disorder so as to justify the expansion of federal authority. The true interest of the black activists, therefore, was not to see peaceful negotiations succeed, but to have them break down. Black leaders, the segregationists believed, were merely using white moderates to make it appear that blacks had tried to reach a settlement and had been driven reluctantly to the streets. Citizens' Council officers were not unaware of the moderates' actions; J. Bruce Pardue, the president of the Citizens' Bank and a former secretary of the Citizens' Council, often met with the moderates and may well have kept the council informed of the moderates' consultations. But the council apparently was positive that the moderates' overtures to the blacks would fail. There was really only one way to prevent the disorders that the black activists were seeking, as the council members saw it: a vigorous application of force by the authorities.

Thus, in December 1963, in response to the boycott of downtown merchants, Solicitor McLeod and Sheriff Clark led a raid on SNCC's Selma headquarters at which they arrested ten blacks for violations of the Alabama Anti-Boycott Act and seized SNCC's files. In late July 1964, when the black airmen at Craig met at the black Elks Club to discuss their grievances, Sheriff Clark and his deputies burst in to disperse the meeting, on the ground that it was prohibited by Judge Hare's injunction—even though the participants were not assembled in a public place and were not gathered to advocate the violation of the law, the injunction's actual terms. The sheriff also confiscated the Elks Club's liquor license, though he subsequently returned it. And Judge Hare, Solicitor McLeod, and Clark requested a meeting with the base deputy commander, at which they read him the injunction item by item and urged him to enforce it against all base personnel. These and similar constant acts of harassment were essential, from the perspective of segregationists, to prevent the civil rights organizations from producing the anarchy upon which they fed. As Judge Hare wrote to Governor Wallace, the black unrest that threatened northern cities in 1965 would be much worse than that experienced in the South, because it "will be considerably aggravated by the fact that the law enforcement personnel will be continuously drawing back, rather than asserting the force for which they are maintained."[144]

As a consequence of the very different points of view held by the white moderates and the segregationists, with the inauguration of Joe Smitherman and the appointment of Wilson Baker a veritable chasm of distrust and hostility opened between the Selma city hall and the Dallas County courthouse. County officeholders considered the new municipal administration to be dangerously temperate and insufficiently committed to the defense of the social status quo. On the other hand, if viewed from a national perspective, the differences between the white moderates and the segregationists could seem almost insignificant. When two negotiators from the federal government's new Community Relations Service (CRS), Andrew M. Secrest and J. Kenneth Morland, came to Selma at the beginning of 1965, they were dismayed by the extremism of the city's white leaders on racial matters. An initial conference with Baker had left them hopeful, but as they talked to other prominent figures they quickly discovered that Selma's ostensible moderates seemed interested primarily in keeping the peace rather than in change. "We uncovered no white integrationists," they reported to Washington. "There is no real commitment to racial reform, and [white] Selma, moderate or segregationist, will take no steps they are not forced to take." Secrest added, "Once Baker and Mayor Smitherman learned that CRS would not and could not persuade Dr. King to leave Selma, they lost interest in what CRS could do for them," and Smitherman "quite simply told us to go home."[145]

After King and the SCLC came to the city in January 1965, as Secrest and Morland correctly discerned, the moderates' fear of the negative publicity that demonstrations could bring to Selma, along with their desire for a gradual transition to the new order, produced in them a hostility to the black activists fully equal to that of the segregationists. At the same time, King's enormous popularity in the black community caused moderate blacks to unite with the activists behind King's leadership. Thus at one level the initial effect of King's advent was to polarize the town completely along its lines of racial division, by throwing the white moderates into the arms of the segregationists and the black moderates into the arms of the Voters League. Nevertheless, at a deeper level the differences within the racial divisions still persisted. Both moderate blacks and moderate whites continued to be more willing than others of their race to make concessions in order to reach a settlement. And the intense desire of the white moderates to avoid negative national publicity for their community meant that they would wish to see law enforcement agencies adopt a careful and gentle strategy in the handling of the demonstrations, very different from the repressive measures that the segregationists believed necessary.

The white moderates' fear of bad publicity and their acceptance of the necessity of racial reform both stemmed in large measure, of course, from their enthusiasm for industrial expansion. And that fact explains why the division between the intransigent Citizens' Council adherents and the moderates who supported Smitherman in the mayoral election of 1964 tended to parallel a division that must have seemed exceedingly recondite to outsiders like Secrest and Morland: that between the Pattersonites and Wallaceites of 1958. The 1958 gubernatorial election, indeed, had become an issue in the campaign between Smitherman and Heinz. The reason seems to be that in 1958, officials of the Citizens' Councils had, by and large, strongly supported John Patterson. The organization's state executive secretary, Senator Sam Martin Engelhardt of Macon County, had endorsed Patterson in the runoff with Wallace. And in Dallas County, Patterson's campaign co-chairmen were fellow wholesale grocers Walter Craig, perhaps the Citizens' Council's single most uncompromising leader, and William M. Agee, later to be the commandant of Sheriff Clark's unmounted posse. After his election, Patterson had appointed Engelhardt as state highway director and Walter Craig as assistant highway director.

By 1964, however, Patterson was no longer in office, and both Engelhardt and Craig faced legal action in connection with the Patterson administration's most spectacular scandal, in which Hubert Baughn of Birmingham, the publisher of the vehemently segregationist pro-Patterson magazine *South,* and Montgomery contractor Joe Barton had, as the prosecution alleged, obtained the contract to paint the stripes on ten thousand miles of Alabama's highways, subcontracted the work for half of what they were paid, and divided the profits with Craig. Craig's trial was, in fact, in progress in the midst of the Smitherman-Heinz contest. Craig won acquittal when his attorney, John Blue Hill—who had earlier defended "Sonny" Kyle Livingston and Raymond Britt in the Montgomery church bombing cases—turned the trial into an attack on the state's racially liberal attorney general, Richmond Flowers, whose investigation had broken the case. But the entire affair considerably tarnished the Citizens' Council's reputation in the minds of a large number of Alabamians formerly sympathetic to its aims. In 1964, on the other hand, George Wallace had assumed the mantle of segregationist hero, thanks to his "stand in the schoolhouse door" at the University of Alabama in 1963 and his daring entry in the Democratic presidential primaries in Wisconsin, Indiana, and Maryland that spring. Smitherman's campaign thus was eager to paint Heinz's supporters as former Pattersonites.

When Wallace had run for governor in 1958, however, a principal source of his statewide recognition had been his authorship of the Wallace Act of 1951, which had established a mechanism for the issuance of municipal industrial development revenue bonds to attract new industry to the state. Probably a majority of his most ardent supporters in that campaign had been so primarily because they desired industrial development. It is thus no mere coincidence—given Smitherman's heavy emphasis upon the same theme and the strong backing he received from the Committee of 100 Plus—that many of Selma's early Wallaceites should have been attracted to Smitherman's cause as well. Heinz himself, as he rather desperately pointed out, had been a Wallace supporter in both 1958 and 1962, but the same could not be said for most of his Citizens' Council colleagues, and that fact appears to have damaged his reelection effort. After Smitherman assumed office, he further cemented his Wallaceite connections by appointing as city attorney McLean Pitts, who had been the law partner of Governor Wallace's powerful legal adviser and, later, executive secretary, Cecil Jackson. It was thus the new Smitherman administration's profound Wallaceite faith in the redemptive power of industrial expansion, and its consequent desire to avoid unfavorable publicity for the city, that caused it, at least in the fetid atmosphere of political discourse in Selma, to be understood as an embodiment of moderation.[146]

On November 11, 1964, Amelia Boynton spoke to a staff retreat of the SCLC in Birmingham. She had come to try to convince Martin Luther King and his associates to take up the faltering voting rights campaign in Selma. She had sought SCLC's assistance once before, in April 1963, when she had asked King to join in the registration efforts that SNCC was just about to launch. But SCLC was immersed in its Birmingham demonstrations at that time, and declined. After Judge Hare's injunction in July 1964 and the consequent end of the mass meetings, however, SNCC's endeavors no longer seemed to be producing significant results, despite the election of a more moderate city government. The number of applications to register had declined sharply, as we have seen. S. W. Boynton's strategy in the face of local repression had always been to seek to outflank insular power by attracting the attention of the world beyond Dallas County. That had been his hope for his congressional testimony in 1955 and for the Civil Rights Commission's hearings in 1958. Mrs. Boynton had adopted the same tactic in seeking to entice SNCC to Selma in the fall of 1962. And now, with the injunction's having hobbled SNCC's campaign, she turned again to SCLC, with the same goal. She spoke forcefully to the staff retreat, emphasizing how the injunction had trammeled the Selma movement.

Ralph Abernathy, who had been the main speaker at the last mass meeting in July before the injunction had gone into effect, added his support to Mrs. Boynton's plea. For SCLC, a campaign in Selma had two great virtues: it would focus upon precisely the issue that the organization now most wished to emphasize, voting rights, and it would build upon a strong existing local foundation in the Voters League. That afternoon the staff attending the retreat concluded, "Selma should make an effective testing ground since an attitude of defiance has been so strongly demonstrated." Director of Affiliates C. T. Vivian returned to Selma with Mrs. Boynton to meet with the officers of the Voters League, and at midmonth, Frederick Reese, who—in part, apparently, at the urging of the moderate Claude Brown—had succeeded James Gildersleeve as the league's president, issued SCLC a formal invitation. Vivian was impressed with the league's determination. At SCLC's headquarters in Atlanta, planning for the Selma crusade began.[147]

In later years, it appears, white Selma devoted a good deal of effort to puzzling over the question of why Martin Luther King chose the city as the site for his campaign to dramatize the need for federal voting rights legislation. On the one hand, the presumption which seems to underlie such speculation—that King carefully selected Selma as his target city from among many comparable southern towns—is erroneous. King agreed to come to Selma because Mrs. Boynton and the Voters League invited, and urged, him to do so. Indeed, SCLC had some reservations about accepting the invitation, for fear that SNCC would regard an SCLC campaign as an invasion of SNCC territory. And in fact, John Love and the other SNCC field-workers did feel just such resentments.

On the other hand, it is true that King and his associates could have declined to yield to the persuasion of Selma's black activists. And one of their primary reasons for agreeing to come to Selma was, as the Selma speculation seems to imply, actually only broadly connected with the community itself. Voting rights was the one subject with which the Civil Rights Act of 1964 had failed to deal aggressively. The act's voting rights title represented only a very modest advance over the provisions of the Civil Rights Acts of 1957 and 1960. But because of the lengthy and highly emotional fight that the passage of the 1964 Civil Rights Act had generated in Congress, the Johnson administration was exceedingly reluctant to propose additional voting rights legislation the very next year. It was clear to King and his advisers that Washington's politicians would turn their attention to this problem only if there were an irresistible demand for action from their constituents. SCLC thus was intent on creating such a demand. Voting registration lay at the very heart of the racial tensions in Selma, and it had been the main focus of local concern for nearly two years. That fact made Selma a very appealing setting for the SCLC effort. But there were certainly other towns in the South of which the same statements could have been made. And though Selma's blacks had invited King on their own—at least, Mrs. Boynton had done so—doubtless SCLC could have arranged an invitation from some other city if it had wished.

The SCLC's other reason for agreeing to come to Selma, however, was intrinsic to the city itself. The staff at the retreat had believed that Selma would make a particularly effective site for a campaign, "since an attitude of defiance has been so strongly demonstrated" there. And that is the key to understanding the choice of Selma. For the fact is that King did not select Selma nearly so much as Selma managed to select itself. In her talk to the staff retreat, Mrs. Boynton had emphasized the oppressive climate in which the civil rights activists in Selma had to work. And the choice of Selma did derive in part from an appreciation of the dramatic potential of that climate of oppression, created by the intransigent segregationists who remained in charge of the county government. In particular, Selma offered the presence of the bellicose Sheriff Clark, whose political dependence upon the support of extremist elements and whose own hot temper could be counted upon to provide vivid proof of the violent sentiments that formed white supremacy's core.

But even more important than the substance of Mrs. Boynton's address was the fact of it—the fact that she had come to Birmingham of her own volition to seek SCLC's assistance in resisting the oppression. There were many other towns in the South in which such racial oppression existed. There was dramatic potential aplenty. What marked Selma off especially were the dedication, enthusiasm, and optimistic eagerness for the struggle of the local black leaders of the Voters League. And these attitudes derived in large part from the feeling abroad in Dallas County in the latter half of 1964 that things were beginning to change. Judge Hare, Sheriff Clark, Solicitor McLeod, and their allies might bluster as ferociously as ever, but events seemed to show that they no longer spoke for a united white op-position. With the election of Mayor Smitherman and the overtures of the white moderates, the white consensus for segregation appeared to have developed cracks. Thus the mixed signals that the hostility between the city hall and the county courthouse was producing, and the really quite minute changes engineered by the moderates in their effort to buy additional time, became critical elements in determining the Voters League to press its cause with reinvigorated conviction. And the Voters League's fresh determination was essential to the SCLC's decision to give its aid.

It is a rather considerable irony that White Citizens' Council propaganda had repeatedly warned of a closely analogous outcome. The essential exhortation of every council speech was the necessity for white unity. It was only with the assistance of white liberals and moderates, council dogma held, that blacks at the local level would be able to transform their abstract rights into reality. Blacks did not really require white assistance, of course; in that the council was in error. Nevertheless, the willingness of the white moderates to break the previously solid white phalanx in Selma did indeed provide black leaders with vital encouragement. It was not essential, or even important, to blacks' ultimate success, but it was indeed a significant element in convincing Voters League members that forceful action at this time might deliver victory, that with firm resolution it might now be possible to destroy the power of the Citizens' Council that had dominated the county for a decade, precisely as the Burns-Heinz machine had just been destroyed. There proved, therefore, to be more to the Citizens' Council's dread of any white dissent than one might at first have suspected.

In that sense, however, the Citizens' Council may be said to have prepared its own doom. In the first place, the great strength of the council in Selma, because of the uniform adherence to it of all active politicians in Dallas County during the decade from 1955 to 1965, had skewed the center of public discourse in the white community so far to the right that, within the local context, what elsewhere would have seemed modest reforms appeared to Selmians, both black and white, to represent sharp breaks with the past. Thus even the simplest accommodation to black aspirations—permitting blacks to check out books from the public library, removing racial designations from the courthouse drinking fountains, just meeting with black leaders to discuss community needs—had in Selma the profoundest implications. These small steps were in fact genuine attacks on the racial status quo, because the absolute conformity to the patterns of white supremacy that the Citizens' Council had demanded and enforced led everyone concerned to perceive them that way.

But the extraordinarily inflexible structure of race relations in Dallas County meant even more. The White Citizens' Council wished the white citizenry to be a solid phalanx and hence feared every manifestation of white dissent. The result was that any significant discontent among whites, even if it involved nonracial questions, came to be just as threatening to white unity as dissent from white supremacy itself would have been. It was necessary to sustain the Burns-Heinz machine not only in its racial policies but in all its other policies as well, lest the white phalanx be divided. We have already seen that even the unsuccessful and completely nonracial challenge by the Committee of 100 Plus to the regular slate of nominees for the board of directors of the chamber of commerce had apparently been enough to influence black moderates to accept the Voters League's initiative to invite SNCC to the city. In Joe Smitherman's candidacy to defeat Mayor Heinz, race had occupied only a peripheral place. The core of Smitherman's support lay, as we have said, among the younger white businessmen unhappy with the pace of industrial development. And yet a desire for new industry merged easily in the minds of almost all Selmians into a belief in racial moderation, because the Citizens' Council's extremism had managed to equate all open opposition to the community's existing political leadership with a threat to the maintenance of segregation. Thus the council's zeal in insisting on the necessity for white unity had created a situation in which it was forced to try to hold an untenable position. It was simply impossible that, as the years passed, discontent with one or another of the policies of the municipal administration would not develop within various elements of the white electorate. But if white revolt for any cause represented treason to segregation, then the very inflexibility of the demand for white unity had ultimately to condemn the demand to failure.

The SCLC was attracted to Selma as inevitably as the honeybee to the blooming flower. To be sure, SCLC had its own motives—derived from considerations of national policy—for wishing to wage a campaign like the one that Selma's black activists sought. But any such campaign would certainly fail if it could not generate an outpouring of support from the black community in the locality in which it was conducted. That support is what Selma promised. The enthusiastic cooperation offered by the Voters League was essential to the campaign's effectiveness. Both the leaders and the supporters of the Voters League so clearly demonstrated the requisite enthusiasm to the SCLC's staff because local events—events that to the outside observer might appear minor or even irrelevant—seemed to Selmians, interpreting them against the background of their past experience, to indicate that an epochal transition in their community life was occurring. These events suggested to the city's black activists that if they now applied concerted pressure, Selma's segregationist armor might be made to split along its newly visible seams. And among the events that produced this attitude, the crucial one, of course, had been Joe Smitherman's defeat of Chris Heinz for mayor in March.[148]

VI. The 1965 Demonstrations and Their Consequences

Martin Luther King announced the forthcoming demonstrations at a mass meeting on January 2, 1965, and the demonstrations began on January 18. They would continue for more than two months.[149] From the outset, the differences between Wilson Baker and Jim Clark were obvious. Indeed, the demonstrations became almost as much a contest between the Selma police and the county sheriff's office as between the city's whites and blacks. The mass meeting of January 2 was the very first that was not surrounded by scores of possemen. Only a token number of plainclothes police and deputies were present. The night before, police had taken strong action to locate and arrest two young whites who had detonated a tear-gas grenade in a black neighborhood. Earlier, the new city attorney, McLean Pitts, had worked out a formal, written agreement between Baker and Clark in which Clark agreed to leave all law enforcement in the city to the police, except for offenses committed at the county courthouse itself. Smitherman and the moderate business leaders hoped very much that the arrangement would leave the sheriff's role a relatively minor one. In his speech to the initial mass meeting, King acknowledged that Selma was "attempting to change its image," but he added that the attempt could not be successful until all qualified blacks were allowed to vote.

The beginning of the demonstrations coincided with the agreement of the city's restaurants to integrate. King cooperated with Baker in breaking the black processions into small groups in order to avoid violating the city's parade ordinance. Baker went out of his way to indicate his goodwill, vigorously suppressed efforts by the National States' Rights Party and the American Nazi Party to disrupt the protests, and dutifully guarded the marches as they wound through Selma. He studiously avoided arresting the demonstrators except on the few occasions, as on February 1, when King and his associates, by defying the arrangement as to the parade ordinance, consciously sought arrest in order to test the validity of the ordinance itself. On January 21, all members of the city council and the county board of revenue signed a statement pleading, "however strong the provocation," for "calmness and self-restraint by each of us."

But the moderates' hopes were not to be realized. Because the goal of the marches was the office of the board of registrars, located in the county courthouse, the actual result of the agreement between Baker and Clark was simply to deliver the entire group of blacks safely, day after day, to the steps of the building where Clark's jurisdiction began. If anything, therefore, the agreement magnified the sheriff's role, rather than constraining it. Clark was convinced that Baker's way of handling the demonstrations was erroneous, that aggressive arrests and jailings would lead to the collapse of the protests—as, in fact, had been the actual result of that policy the preceding July. And viewing Baker, quite correctly, as a political rival, Clark was intent upon proving to the white voters of Dallas County that his method of meeting the black challenge was more effective than the public safety director's. As a result, when the demonstrators arrived at the courthouse they always found Clark ready for a confrontation, eager to contrast his own approach to the crisis with that of Baker.

The arrests began on January 19, when Clark charged Amelia Boynton and James Gildersleeve with criminal provocation and sixty-two other blacks with unlawful assembly; the charges grew out of Clark's refusal to allow applicants to use the courthouse's front entrance. By the end of January almost 400 blacks had been arrested on various charges, surpassing the total of 350 arrests in the three weeks of demonstrations in 1963. But the sheriff's conduct during January gained Selma's blacks assistance from an exceedingly novel source. On January 22, civil rights attorneys, suing in the name of Mrs. Boynton, filed a petition with Judge Daniel Thomas seeking an injunction to compel Clark, Solicitor McLeod, Probate Judge Reynolds, County Court Judge Hugh Mallory, and County Solicitor Henry

Reese to obey the Civil Rights Act of 1957, which forbade harassment of applicants to register to vote. Acting with a dispatch that must have astonished anyone familiar with his usual practices, Thomas the following morning entered an all-encompassing order forbidding such harassment and regulating in detail the conduct of the registration lines and the procedures at the courthouse. Apparently, Thomas had been watching with mounting disapproval Clark's failure to cooperate with the moderate strategy. His opinion reflected this unhappiness. He observed that most of the early arrests had resulted from "a senseless discussion of which was the front door of the courthouse." He did not need to hold an evidentiary hearing, he said, because the facts were essentially those presented to the three-judge court in the trial of the Justice Department's suit in December. He went on to specify that applicants were to be processed in the order that they appeared, that they were to be given numbers to allow them to hold their places in line, and that nonapplicants were to be permitted to assemble outside the courthouse to encourage the applicants. He said that he would not tolerate interference with registration in the guise of law enforcement. And, as a warning to the board of registrars, he added that he believed the board ought to be able to receive many more than the fifteen or so applications it took during a typical session. His restraining order was to remain in effect until the three-judge court could rule in the suit tried in December; final briefs in that case were not due until February 19.

Despite the clear implications in this opinion that Judge Thomas's patience had at last run out, county officials remained obdurate. Thomas had specified that the numbers to be issued to applicants in line should start with one and run through one hundred. Clark therefore began arresting all applicants beyond the first hundred on the claim that they were violating Thomas's injunction. On January 30 Thomas amended his order to state that he had not meant to limit the number of persons in the registration line. On February 1, at the request of Judge Hare, Clark began arresting anyone picketing the courthouse for contempt of court, on the ground that they were disturbing Hare's court sessions. More than 450 were arrested on this charge on the first day, 505 on February 2, and 331 on February 3; all but 111 of the persons arrested over the three days were juveniles. Late on February 3, Judge Hare issued a blanket injunction forbidding any further demonstrations in, around, or about the courthouse. In the period from February 1 through February 5, the high point of the mass arrests, more than 2,000 people were arrested, bringing the total arrests from the beginning of the demonstrations to more than 2,400. Thereafter, however, during the remainder of February and March, arrests dwindled to fewer than 200.

On February 4, in the face of this behavior, Judge Thomas was finally pushed into ruling on the Justice Department's complaint against the county board of registrars, filed a year earlier and heard the preceding fall. His injunction represented the most sweeping voting rights order that he had ever issued. He found the board members in contempt of the injunction that he had issued in November 1963, on the instruction of the Fifth Circuit. He forbade any further use in Dallas County of the voter qualification test that the state supreme court had promulgated in August 1964; the board was to employ only the original questionnaire. It had to take applications from at least eight registrants at a time, in the order that they appeared, and had to process at least one hundred applications at each session. No applicant could be rejected for a merely technical error in filling out the questionnaire; the board was required to tell any rejected applicant exactly what question he had answered incorrectly and had to inform him that he could have the board's decision reviewed by Judge Thomas himself if he wished. The board had to make monthly reports of its activities to Judge Thomas. If it had failed to process by July 31 every application it had received by the end of June, all the unprocessed applications would be referred to a federal voting referee for decision. Jack Greenberg, chief attorney of the NAACP Legal Defense Fund, commented, "This marks the beginning of the end of voter discrimination in Selma."

Throughout January, Selma's black community had experienced a unity equaled only during the demonstrations in September 1963. There could have been no more impressive proof of this solidarity than the march of some 125 black public school teachers to the courthouse on January 22. Martin Luther King's executive assistant, Andrew Young, jubilantly called this event "the most significant thing that has happened in the racial movement since Birmingham." To an observer unfamiliar with life in a southern town, Young's elation must have seemed puzzling. Teachers were the backbone of the black middle class in the South, because most other middle-class occupations had historically been virtually closed to black residents. But no group of blacks in the region was more easily intimidated, because as public employees they were subject to the discipline and dismissal of white elected officials. The result was that most southern black communities were deprived in any crisis of a large part of their social and intellectual leadership. Frederick Reese, the president of the Voters League, taught science at Selma's black public high school, but among public school teachers his activism was almost unique; most of his colleagues in Dallas County were as frightened as they were elsewhere. In this case, however, Reese had been able to persuade no less than 125 of Selma's black teachers to stand and be counted. He and Selma Teachers Association president Andrew J. Durgan headed the group as it confronted Sheriff Clark, who was joined on the courthouse steps by the school board president, moderate attorney Edgar A. Stewart, and Superintendent of Education Joseph A. Pickard. The teachers fully expected to be arrested, but it was Clark, presumably at the urging of Stewart and Pickard, who backed down; after thirty minutes, the teachers were able to march peacefully away.

Among the mass of poorer blacks and among the youth of the city, the sight of this demonstration was simply electrifying. Nothing else could have more effectively symbolized the emergence of a genuine black militancy in Dallas County. The universal black admiration of King and enthusiasm for his leadership was the principal source of this spirit. It seems quite unlikely, however, that the teachers could have been moved to take so public an action had it not been for the newly evident divisions among Selma's white politicians and businessmen, divisions that left the teachers with the sense that their protest now might not automatically lead to fierce retribution.

The unity evidenced by the teachers' march received a test as a result of Judge Thomas's comprehensive injunction against the board of registrars at the beginning of February. At the suggestion of Ralph Smeltzer, the moderates prevailed upon the board to indicate its good faith by accepting a black proposal to facilitate the administration of the injunction. Thomas had ordered the board to establish a waiting list for applicants. On February 8, the board agreed—quite reluctantly—to begin maintaining at once an appearance book, open every business day; anyone could come in at any time to sign the book, and at its sessions the board would take applications in the order that the registrants' names appeared. The board hoped that, as a result of this arrangement, all demonstrations would cease. But on February 9, James Bevel, the head of the SCLC's direct-action operations, instructed blacks to boycott the appearance book altogether and to continue the marches. Bevel called Thomas's injunction inadequate and demanded registration without any qualification other than age. King himself noted that, since the board met only twice a month, it could take decades to get all eligible blacks registered. And indeed, if the board merely met the minimal terms of the injunction, it would have taken six years to process the applications of the county's fifteen thousand age-eligible blacks, even if the board had acted favorably on every application it received.

The situation, however, was not nearly so bleak as the statements of SCLC implied. In the first place, though boards of registrars normally met only on the first and third Mondays of each month, every board had the right, when the demand justified it, to apply to the secretary of state to hold up to ten special registration days in any six-month period. The Dallas County board had in fact held ten special sessions during January, and it had earlier held the same number in October 1963 and July 1964, as well. Having just offered the special days in January, the board was unable to do so again until July. But there is every reason to believe that Judge Thomas would have ordered the registrars to hold extra sessions later in the fall if the board had not succeeded in exhausting the names in the appearance book by the end of the summer. Secondly, the figure of one hundred applications at each session was merely a required minimum. On March 1, once the new system was fully in place, the board actually processed 266 applications, and 209 on March 15. Thirdly, the board was under great pressure to act immediately on every application it received, because Thomas had said that any application received before July 1 but remaining unprocessed by July 31 would be sent to a federal voting referee. As a result, the board held four extra registration days during July. It processed a record 279 applications on July 8, and by midmonth it had called every name in the appearance book. Fourthly, the board's actions were now subject to close scrutiny. On July 21, Judge Thomas sent the applications of all rejected blacks who had appealed the registrars' decision to O. S. Burke, the Perry County federal voting referee, for review. And finally, an unknown but possibly significant number of the fifteen thousand age-eligible blacks were not especially eager to register in any case. It seems likely, therefore, that under the procedures that Judge Thomas had mandated on February 4, virtually all of the county's blacks who wished to apply could have done so by the injunction's first anniversary; that would certainly have been the case if Judge Thomas had instructed the board to hold the ten extra registration days in as many as three of the twelve months.

In truth, despite King's and Bevel's complaints, the boycott of the appearance book and the continued demonstrations had very little to do with any real dissatisfaction with the terms of Judge Thomas's injunction. The SCLC actually wished to press the Selma campaign in order to avoid losing the national attention to the voting rights cause that the protests had succeeded in procuring. But on this point the SCLC's interest diverged from that of Selma's own black leaders. They had halted the 1963 demonstrations when Judge Thomas had granted his initial injunction, and they were now eager to take advantage of his new one. The SCLC wished to obtain national legislation, but the Voters League wanted to register blacks in Selma; the former goal required continued confrontation, but the latter one would now focus on the less dramatic effort to locate blacks willing to fill out the questionnaire and then to assist them in doing so. The leaders of the Voters League appear to have been quite unhappy with the decision to refuse to utilize the appearance book.

There is no way to know whether the differences between the Voters League and SCLC might have become serious. As he had so often, Sheriff Clark managed to restore black unity. On February 10 he arrested a group of 120 black students who were staging a silent protest outside the courthouse, charged them with truancy, and then took them on a three-mile forced march into the countryside. Riding alongside the group in cars, Clark and his deputies frequently shocked the young people with electric cattle prods to compel them to maintain a rapid pace. Clark had intended to take them to the lodge hall of the Fraternal Order of Police, six miles from Selma, but after three miles the youths broke ranks and managed to escape into black homes along the route. Clark's action seems to have been a spur-of-the-moment decision; he had ignored a similar demonstration earlier in the day, and he ignored another one later that afternoon.

The forced march enraged the black community and appalled white moderates as well. The *Selma Times-Journal* denounced it editorially. As blacks came together in their anger at Clark's conduct, the Voters League and the SCLC managed to compromise their differences. Though the boycott of the appearance book continued until the next meeting of the board of registrars, on February 15, it was ended at that time. And in the meantime, the SCLC devoted most of its efforts to generating a massive turnout for the board session by having black high school students persuade their parents and adult relatives to make the attempt. The result was that more than twelve hundred blacks were in line when the board opened for business.

On February 18, in a front-page editorial, the *Times-Journal* urged the local leaders of the Voters League to ask the SCLC to leave Selma so that the league itself could resume control of the protests. The full installation of the new registration procedures at the February 15 meeting of the board "represented the epitome of any achievement local Negroes can hope to make for themselves in a game which now can be played only with dangerously high stakes," the editorial observed. King and his associates had no real interest in the particular needs of Selma's blacks, the editorial continued; the SCLC's audience was national and congressional. "Any achievements for the local Negro community are but fringe benefits [for SCLC], and their actual worth cannot be determined until a final accounting against all losses, including the loss of good will." Selmians of good conscience should take note of the increasing possibility of violence as frustrations grew in the city. The editorial also urged white moderates to abandon timid anonymity and to begin speaking out firmly and clearly. Only local control in the black community and responsible leadership in the white could avoid tragedy, the newspaper concluded. But by that time the divisions between the Voters League and the SCLC had been successfully papered over.

Nevertheless, with the abandonment of the voter qualification test and the beginning of black use of the appearance book mechanism in mid-February, the resistance of the board of registrars was effectively broken. At the March sessions of the board, registration proceeded rapidly and efficiently. In April, Aubrey C. Allen, the Citizens' Council activist and City National Bank agricultural loan officer, resigned from the board of registrars in disgust and was succeeded by the board's clerk, Robert T. Elder. The SCLC, recognizing that voter registration was no longer really an issue in Selma, announced on February 18 that it would shift its attention in the city to an effort to secure the hiring of black police and sheriff's deputies and of black clerks in downtown stores. The voter registration campaign would now center in the surrounding rural Black Belt counties, initially Perry to the northwest and later Wilcox to the south and Lowndes to the east.

Demonstrations had begun in Marion, the Perry County seat, at the beginning of February under the leadership of Albert Turner, a young bricklayer and the president of the Perry County Civic League, and SCLC field secretary James Orange of Birmingham. The SCLC had been drawn to Marion both because the Civic League was eager and well organized and because Judge Thomas, under orders from the Fifth Circuit, had appointed Alabama's first and only federal voting referee there. Both factors indicated that a campaign in Perry was likely to meet with more success than elsewhere in the Black Belt. On February 1 some 300 blacks sought to register without incident. But the next day, fifteen civil rights workers attempting to desegregate a restaurant were arrested, and on February 3 about 400 black high school students protesting these arrests were themselves arrested, and 200 more were arrested on February 4. Blacks responded with a boycott of downtown Marion merchants, and many black teenagers began boycotting classes as well. On the morning of February 18, as a part of an effort by officials to end the school boycott, James Orange was arrested for contributing to the delinquency of minors. That night, about 500 blacks attempted to march from a black church across the town square to the county jail to protest Orange's arrest. Local law enforcement personnel were reinforced by twenty-one squad cars of state troopers. As the blacks emerged from the church, the streetlights were turned off, plunging the square suddenly into darkness. Troopers, police, and deputies then charged into the assemblage of blacks, beating and arresting them. Later that night a trooper shot Jimmie Lee Jackson, a young black laborer, twice in the stomach—in self-defense, as the trooper stated; in cold blood, as black witnesses reported. Eight other persons—five blacks and three white reporters—were hospitalized for various injuries. And 826 blacks, demonstrators and onlookers, were charged with unlawful assembly. Governor Wallace stated that the riot had been caused by "career and professional agitators with pro-Communist affiliations." Jimmie Lee Jackson died in a Selma hospital on February 26.

Jackson's shooting—his murder, as civil rights workers believed—led SCLC to call on the blacks of the Black Belt counties to march on the capitol at Montgomery, where the legislature was in special session, to demand reforms in the voter registration process. The idea for a march of blacks to Montgomery had been one that SCLC had been suggesting for some time. In the fall of 1963 the organization had announced that it would stage a march from Birmingham to Montgomery, and in the spring of 1964 it had renewed the pledge to undertake it. In his address to the initial mass meeting of the Selma campaign on January 2, Martin Luther King had told the assemblage that if the voter registration drive encountered resistance in Selma, blacks would appeal to Governor Wallace, and if that appeal failed, they would march on Washington again. Throughout the demonstrations, black leaders had continued to discuss the idea among themselves. The proposal thus was not really new. But in the heated atmosphere following Jackson's death, it seemed to many blacks an inspiring gesture and to many whites a menacing one.

Emotions in Selma were running high. On February 25 a fire broke out in the building housing the offices of SNCC. On the same night a group of forty segregationists met to form a National Great Society of White People. On February 27, two blacks were arrested for advocating a boycott of Selma's merchants. On March 1, King led a march of 350 blacks to the county courthouse, and the board of registrars processed a record 266 applications. On March 2, some 2,000 blacks attended Jimmie Lee Jackson's funeral in Selma, and another 700 attended a separate service in Marion. King announced that the march to Montgomery would take place on March 7. On March 6, Governor Wallace forbade the march and ordered state troopers to prevent it. On the same day, Selma came closer to mob violence than it had at any time during the campaign when the Reverend Joseph Ellwanger, a liberal Birmingham Lutheran minister, led a group of sixty white Alabamians in a march to the Dallas County courthouse to show their support for the black cause. Ellwanger, a native of Selma, was a son of the white former president of the black Alabama Lutheran Academy. Segregationists, who could barely tolerate black demonstrations, were particularly enraged at what they saw as white treason. The Citizens' Council doctrine that only white desertions would permit black victory emphasized the threat posed by this protest. Only police intervention at the last minute prevented a furious crowd of 500 whites from attacking the integrationists. It was in this context of extraordinary tension that the march of some 600 blacks stepped off at midday on Sunday, March 7, under the leadership of SNCC's John Lewis and SCLC's Hosea Williams.

The events of March 7 provided the climactic collision between the attitudes of Wilson Baker and Jim Clark. Governor Wallace assured his young admirer Mayor Smitherman that, though the state troopers intended to prevent the march, they would do so calmly and prudently. Smitherman thereupon ordered Baker and the Selma police to assist the troopers at their blockade. Baker, especially in the light of the troopers' actions in Marion two weeks earlier, was convinced that the scene was likely to become a slaughter. He considered the troopers' commandant, Albert J. Lingo, even more injudicious than the fiery Sheriff Clark. Baker therefore flatly refused to obey Smitherman's directive. He suggested instead that the police arrest the marchers immediately as they were leaving the church at which the march was to begin in order to protect them from the wrath of the troopers and of Clark's deputies and posse, who were to aid the state's forces. But Smitherman rejected this plan, and as a result Baker tendered his resignation. After the intercession of several members of the city council, however, Baker and Smitherman were persuaded to accept as a compromise that the police would abstain from any action in the affair at all.

Just as Baker had expected, the troopers and the posse, once unleashed, turned into an undisciplined mob. Trooper major John Cloud, who was in command, later testified that Sheriff Clark had accidentally discharged a spray can on his belt and that there followed such confusion among the troopers that, on Director Lingo's order, he had signaled troopers to discharge their tear-gas canisters. Forty canisters of tear gas, twelve canisters of smoke, and eight canisters of nausea gas were used. Amidst the billowing gas, the sixty-five troopers and ten or more sheriff's deputies charged the demonstrators, and the fifteen mounted possemen spurred their horses forward behind the troopers' flying wedge. Making no attempt to arrest the marchers, the officers instead beat the fleeing blacks back toward Selma's black section. There, after thirty minutes of confusion and violence, Baker and his police were finally able to separate the two sides. Fifty-six blacks were hospitalized with a variety of injuries, though only eighteen of them were hurt seriously enough to be kept overnight. John Lewis, one of the worst injured, remained in the hospital for two days.

Martin Luther King, who was in Atlanta at the time of this melee, issued a call for sympathetic Americans to join him in Selma to renew the march. At the same time, civil rights lawyers, suing in the name of Hosea Williams, filed a petition in Montgomery federal court for an injunction to bar the state from preventing the demonstration. District Judge Frank Johnson scheduled a hearing on this suit, and in the meantime he issued a temporary restraining order forbidding the march until the hearing could be convened. A vast throng had come to Selma at King's summons, and on March 9, rather than disappoint them, King led twenty-five hundred people across the Pettus Bridge to the point at which the March 7 attack had begun, and then back to the church. Segregationists charged King with having contravened Judge Johnson's restraining order by doing so, though Johnson later ruled that the demonstration had not constituted a violation. Meanwhile, SNCC workers and other militants charged King with cowardice for having failed to defy the restraining order; they had wished him to lead the march on to Montgomery despite it.

That night, three white ministers who had come to participate in this march, as they walked along a Selma sidewalk, were set upon by segregationists who had been angered by seeing them eating in a black restaurant. One of the ministers, the Reverend James Reeb of Boston, was seriously injured, and on March 11 he died in the University of Alabama Hospital in Birmingham. In the meantime, Selma police had already apprehended four men and charged them with the offense. Elmer L. Cook, the manager of a novelty company, had seventeen previous arrests for assault and battery. R. B. Kelley, a television repairman, had pleaded guilty to grand larceny in 1961. W. Stanley Hoggle, a salesman, and his brother N. O'Neal Hoggle, an automobile mechanic, were the other two. In April the grand jury indicted Cook and the Hoggles for murder, but in December an all-white jury acquitted them.

On March 11, shortly before Reeb's death, Judge Johnson began the hearing on the petition to permit the march to Montgomery. After five days of testimony, Johnson on March 17 granted an injunction authorizing the march and ordering the state to protect it. On March 21 some 8,000 demonstrators, guarded by 2,000 troops and marshals, left Selma. The march arrived in Montgomery on March 25, and King addressed a crowd of perhaps 25,000 from the capitol steps. That evening, after an automobile chase along the highway between Selma and Montgomery, four Birmingham Ku Klux Klansmen murdered a white Detroit housewife, Mrs. Viola G. Liuzzo, who had come to Selma to participate in the march. It was the third life claimed by the Selma campaign, and that summer there would be a fourth, that of Episcopal seminarian Jonathan Daniels, killed in Hayneville, the county seat of Lowndes County—the county in which Mrs. Liuzzo died, as well. Trials in Hayneville produced acquittals of men indicted in the Liuzzo and Daniels killings, and the Perry County Grand Jury refused to indict the state trooper who had shot Jimmie Lee Jackson. A federal grand jury in Mobile investigated both the Marion riot and the melee at the Pettus Bridge, but it failed to return any indictments at all. But in a trial in federal court in Montgomery, three of the Klansmen accused of murdering Mrs. Liuzzo were convicted of the offense of conspiring to deprive her of her civil right to life and were given ten-year prison sentences by Judge Johnson.

In the meantime, on April 18, Judges Johnson, Thomas, and Rives ruled on the federal suit to enjoin Sheriff Clark's harassment of blacks. They found Clark and his deputies and posse guilty of attempting to interfere with the rights of blacks to register to vote and to use public accommodations. They therefore granted a permanent injunction prohibiting all such conduct. And they also found the posse illegally constituted and ordered it disbanded. And on April 16, Judge Thomas dissolved Judge Hare's injunction of July 1964, which had prohibited civil rights demonstrations, and he also dismissed most of the state prosecutions of demonstrators that had been removed to federal court. On March 25, Judge Thomas, at the request of civil rights lawyers, had issued a show-cause order against Sheriff Clark, charging him with having violated Thomas's January 23 restraining order by having conducted the forced march of the high school students on February 10. Clark was brought to trial on this allegation during late April and May, and on September 2, Thomas found him guilty and fined him fifteen hundred dollars. On March 15, Thomas found the Perry County Board of Registrars in contempt of his nondiscrimination injunction of November 1962, and he amended the injunction to include in it all of the detailed procedures and safeguards that he had added to the Dallas County injunction on February 4. And on April 21, the Fifth Circuit reversed Thomas's March 1964 decision that the Wilcox County board was not discriminating and ordered Thomas to forbid the use of the voucher system and other discriminatory devices in the county. As a result of these and parallel decisions, the federal courts by the late spring of 1965—three months before the Voting Rights Act became law—had for all practical purposes succeeded in subduing the recalcitrance of the boards of registrars in the western Black Belt.[150]

But in Selma itself, though voter registration was now at last proceeding smoothly, the progress had come at great cost to the community. One principal source of the internal turmoil in the city was the black boycott of white merchants. The boycott that black activists had launched in December 1963 had never been fully effective, and it seems to have fizzled out by the summer of 1964. But SCLC had started a new one on February 22, and this one initially proved very powerful indeed. By late March, the increasingly desperate members of the Selma Retail Merchants Association had formed a caravan of trucks, led by a sound truck, to tour all towns within a forty-mile radius of Selma to urge their residents to shop in Selma. The boycott of the city's bus company was so complete that the company went out of business on April 30; it had sharply curtailed its service as early as March 13. Black negotiators, including Frederick Reese and Edwin Moss, had offered to end the bus boycott if the company would agree to hire blacks as bus drivers. The company apparently offered to guarantee that the next vacancy would go to a black but said that it could not hire blacks immediately unless it fired some of the whites who already worked for it. The discussions thereupon reached a stalemate. The company sued the Voters League, which had been transporting boycotting blacks to work in vans, and in mid-April state Circuit Judge L. S. Moore granted an injunction forbidding the league from operating the vans, on the ground that they constituted an infringement of the bus company's franchise. At the same time, the company and the city sued King and the SCLC in state court for almost $110,000 in damages from the boycott and the demonstrations. But on motion of King's attorneys, Judge Thomas agreed to take jurisdiction of the damage suit in federal court, and the company was unable to survive the resultant delay and legal expenses. At the end of April, all bus service ceased in the city; it was never to resume.

The effectiveness of the boycotts proceeded in part from blacks' devotion to King and enthusiasm for the cause that he led. But they were also enforced by what Selma's only black attorney, J. L. Chestnut, Jr., calls

"SCLC's answer to the White Citizens' Council, its gangster element threatening to start a black boycott of black businessmen who didn't line up
with the movement. One or two SCLC workers weren't above going into
homes and embarrassing men in front of their wives and children by
calling them cowards or telling an Uncle Tom, 'If you don't knock off
that crap, you're gonna wish you had, and I'm not kidding.' I saw this and
had mixed feelings. How much were Selma people going to be asked to
sacrifice?" On March 22, the Reverend Clifton C. Hunter, the conservative Methodist minister who had been one of the organizers of the Improvement Association, paid to have his statement rejecting such tactics
printed in the *Times-Journal*. He had advocated increased black voter registration ever since his arrival in Selma in 1957, he wrote, and he continued to support the DCIA's program adopted in 1963. But the only real
paths to progress in the city were negotiations with the "better class white
people of Selma" or action in the courts. To boycott all white businesses
simply because of the race of the business's owner, and despite the fact that
the businessman may have demonstrated sympathy for black aspirations
in the past, was un-Christian and wrong, he concluded. By midsummer,
growing black discontent with it had caused the boycott to collapse.

At the beginning of June, the school board fired Frederick Reese for excessive absenteeism during the preceding semester. Though there can be
no doubt that Reese had in fact devoted much of his attention to directing
the demonstrations, it is not inconceivable that segregationist hostility lay
behind the decision, at least in part. Without any salary other than the
small one that he was paid as a minister, Reese began relying to meet his
personal expenses on the contributions the Voters League had received
from around the nation. Other black leaders quietly complained about
this situation to the FBI, and its agents referred the matter to Wilson
Baker, who undertook an investigation. Early in July, Baker arrested Reese
for embezzlement. Suspicions that Reese might be guilty were increased,
among both white and black Selmians, by the fact that during the spring
the Voters League had turned the administration of the food, clothing,
and other relief supplies that had poured into the city from charitable
northerners over to a black charlatan and confidence man who had suddenly appeared in the city in March, Elder William Ezra Greer. Only two
weeks before Reese's arrest, Greer had also been arrested and, after being
convicted of a sex offense, had agreed to leave the city. In truth, Reese's
behavior was not at all parallel to Greer's; Greer seems to have been engaged in a substantial swindle, while Reese was merely struggling to pay
his immediate bills; the indictment charged Reese with embezzling a total
of $1,850. The coincidence of the two affairs, however, and the observa-
tion that Reese had earlier done little to restrain Greer contributed to the
mistrust of Reese himself. The divisions between the Voters League and
the SCLC staff in Selma, a product of their rather different goals in the

community, had been growing deeper and deeper for months, and a number of the SCLC field-workers were thus easily convinced to believe the worst of Reese. When Reese finally came to trial in March 1966, Ernest Doyle testified that the Voters League's steering committee had authorized Reese to cover his personal expenses from league funds, and Solicitor McLeod thereupon dismissed the prosecution. Reese was eventually re-hired by the school board, but in the meantime the unity of purpose that had characterized black Selma early in 1965 had been irretrievably shattered. Blacks had again returned to the factionalism, jealous rivalries, and shortsightedness that had been all too common among their leadership before the beginning of the demonstrations.[151]

The pervasive demand for unity, on the other hand, had been the bane of Selma's white moderates. Citizens' Council chairman Chris Heinz had commented in mid-February that the demonstrations "afford the white community a timely opportunity to express its unity and stubborn resistance during this period of crisis." And at a Citizens' Council rally toward the end of the month he had proclaimed, "The time of decision is at hand. . . . We must lay aside personal differences and stand united as one unbreakable unit." Nor did the council hesitate to seek to compel the white unity that it sought. In retaliation for what council members regarded as the *Selma Times-Journal*'s excessively moderate editorial policy during the demonstrations, segregationists had pressed a white boycott of the newspaper throughout the spring. The council induced Robert Armstrong, the stationery store manager who was the president of the Retail Merchants Association, to summon a meeting of the association for February 8 to debate a proposal for a concerted withdrawal of all local advertising from the *Times-Journal*. In this case the council's emphasis on racial cohesion ironically was turned against its goals. On February 6, Jewish business-man Seymour Palmer sought a meeting with Mayor Smitherman and city councilman George "Cap" Swift and prevailed upon them to intervene to prevent the association meeting. "I don't want to have to sit in a meeting and vote 'yes' or 'no' on boycotting the paper," Palmer argued. "We have enough dividing us. We need something to unite us." Despite the segregationists' failure to get the merchants' formal endorsement of their plan, however, the council's boycott succeeded in doing the *Times-Journal* considerable damage. The influence of white supremacist hard-liners among the merchants, indeed, lay behind the decision of black leaders to launch their boycott of the merchants on February 22. At the same time, the Citizens' Council also seriously discussed the possibility of sponsoring a petition drive to abolish the mayor-council form of municipal government in favor of a city commission, in the hope that they could thus rid themselves of Joe Smitherman. The council considered dangerously and unacceptably temperate both the newspaper and the city administration, each of which Selma's blacks regarded instead as infected with white supremacist attitudes.

In this context, moderates remained exceedingly reluctant to express their views publicly. At the beginning of February the Edmundite Fathers had paid to place an advertisement in the *Times-Journal* announcing their unequivocal support for the goals of the black demonstrations. Indeed, the order's principal figure in Selma, Father Maurice Ouellet, had been a founding member of the Improvement Association and spoke on several occasions to the black mass meetings. But the Edmundites were essentially the only whites in the city who espoused genuine integration. Most moderates seem to have wished instead for increased goodwill between the races and the more rapid progress of blacks toward economic equality, but within a continuation of separate racial spheres. On February 18, as we have seen, the *Times-Journal* had pleaded editorially for moderates to speak out. And one lonely letter to the editor, that of Eleanor Hammett on March 1, had echoed the call. But when Arthur and Muriel Lewis had ventured to express moderate sentiments privately to their friends at the end of the month, they had become subject to unrelenting harassment from segregationists who learned of it, and other moderates quickly retreated into fearful silence. There matters rested until mid-April.

The issue that finally brought the moderates out into the open was the one question about which they cared most deeply: industrial development. After its formation in the autumn of 1962, the Committee of 100 Plus had labored tirelessly to attract new industry to the area. And at last its efforts had begun to pay off. In September 1964, after a lengthy courtship, Selma managed to persuade Dan River Mills to construct a large new textile factory to the east of town. And in February 1965, after equally lengthy negotiations, Hammermill Paper Company agreed to build an extensive paper mill near the city. Primarily as a result of these two acquisitions, between 1963 and 1967, Dallas County's annual industrial payroll more than doubled, from $7.2 million to $14.6 million. This, as the moderates conceived of things, was the true path to resolving the community's social problems.

But the timing of the announcement of the new industries, and particularly of the Hammermill factory, had been unusually unfortunate in public relations terms. After two years of study and consideration, Hammermill had revealed its selection of the Selma site on February 3, in the very midst of the week of mass arrests from February 1 to February 5, on the day that Judge Hare enjoined all demonstrations at the courthouse and on the day before Judge Thomas's sweeping voter registration injunction. As a result, Hammermill, and to a lesser extent Dan River Mills, had fallen under intense pressure from sympathizers with the civil rights movement. SNCC attempted to organize picketing at every Hammermill office in the

United States. And Martin Luther King went even further, calling at the end of March for a national boycott of all Alabama-made products. He urged labor unions to refuse to transport them. He also sought the end of federal funding for any project in the state and the withdrawal of all federal deposits from Alabama banks.

By April 1965, the title of the Civil Rights Act of 1964 that prohibited businesses from practicing racial discrimination in the hiring or promotion of workers was about to take effect. In response to this fact, and probably in part as an answer to King's plan to boycott the state, the Alabama Chamber of Commerce undertook to print a large advertisement in twenty-one Alabama newspapers and in the *Wall Street Journal* urging all businesses in the state to abide by the new hiring discrimination regulations. It also advocated the opening of new avenues of interracial communication and called for business leadership in doing so. The state chamber asked its local affiliates if they would like to co-sponsor the advertisement, and seventeen municipal chambers, together with four other business groups, agreed. But on April 12, the board of directors of the Selma chamber voted thirteen to five to refuse. The advertisement appeared on April 15, and the absence of the Selma chamber from the list of sponsors provoked comment throughout the nation. On April 16 the executive committee of the Alabama White Citizens' Councils issued a statement congratulating all business groups that had resisted the state chamber's pressure to sign the advertisement. But the Selma chamber's president, moderate grocery executive James Gaston, expressed great sorrow at his board's action. Given the difficulties that Hammermill and Dan River were having with civil rights activists, they needed the support that signing would have provided, he said. Gaston and like-minded Selma businessmen —in particular, Jerome Siegel of the Committee of 100 Plus, People's Bank vice-president Frank Wilson, cotton broker Charles Hohenberg, and the *Times-Journal's* Roswell Falkenberry—therefore launched a campaign to outflank the board by reprinting the advertisement over their personal signatures. It was this campaign that brought matters to a head.

By April 16 Gaston and his associates had collected the support of a thousand white Selmians, and that afternoon they approached the city council and the county board of revenue for endorsements as well. After a lengthy debate among its members, the board of revenue postponed making any decision. But the discussion during the public comments period before the city council meeting went on for two hours and "amounted to the first public debate over a specific issue in Selma's long siege of racial trouble," according to the *Times-Journal*. "Names were called, tempers flared, and voices became impassioned," the newspaper reported.

The moderates had cleverly obtained the services of the new city attorney, McLean Pitts, to present their position; Pitts was well known for having argued the segregationist case during the many federal court suits against local officials over the preceding decade. But the segregationists had been equally clever in arranging for Joe Pilcher, a young attorney who was a close friend of Mayor Smitherman's and had been his campaign manager in the race against Chris Heinz, to argue for the opposition. Pitts rested his plea on the fact that both Hammermill Paper and Dan River Mills were embarrassed and upset by the Selma chamber's refusal to endorse the statement; the two firms felt that the chamber "is letting them down in some of the troubles they are having by being so conspicuously absent from the advertisement," he said. And City National Bank president William B. Craig reported that executives of both companies had called him personally to urge that the chamber alter its position. Pitts added that attracting industry to Selma, and the new white voters who would follow it, was the most effective way of dealing with the threat of black registration. And he said that now that the Civil Rights Act was law, given that the federal courts would not declare it unconstitutional, all citizens would have to obey it, though he assured the gathering that he personally detested the law's provisions. Pitts's call for the city council to sign the advertisement was echoed by members of the circle of moderate businessmen who had been meeting during the past eighteen months—bankers William Craig, Frank Wilson, and Roger Jones, attorney Edgar Stewart, and the YMCA's Paul Grist—as well as by Jerome Siegel, who operated a small loan company and was the president of the Committee of 100 Plus, and by Hugh Bostick, executive of a clothing store. Bostick denounced the White Citizens' Council's propaganda campaigns, which he said had confused and inflamed the public mind.

The segregationists, however, rejected the moderates' arguments completely. "To yield is a sign of weakness," Pilcher thundered. A willing submission to civil rights would open the floodgates to mass integration, even if the immediate concession was small, Pilcher and his allies warned. And Pilcher startled the gathering by revealing, for the first time in public, the existence of the moderate businessmen's group and their efforts to promote racial compromise. His speech implied that these men were traitors to their community. If whites would only unite behind the tough law enforcement exemplified by Sheriff Clark during the demonstrations, then by stalling in the courts they would be able to hold integration to a minimum, he argued. He forced his friend Mayor Smitherman to confess that the mayor and other city officials had been meeting privately with a black delegation headed by the Voters League's Frederick Reese; the first meeting had taken place on April 7. Smitherman rushed to reaffirm his opposition to a biracial committee but said that he nevertheless would continue to meet with black leaders to seek solutions to Selma's racial problems.

Pilcher was joined in denouncing the search for compromise by industrialist Leon Jones, who was a former Citizens' Council chairman; the extremist former assistant state highway director Walter Craig; Citizens'

Bank president J. Bruce Pardue; realtor and amateur historian Sol Tepper, a member of Sheriff Clark's posse; and certified public accountant Lee Calame. Walter Craig expressed the suspicion that Hammermill Paper might have been promised total integration in order to get it to locate in Selma. Jerome Siegel denied it and said that the chamber's failure to sign the statement had given Martin Luther King exactly the weapon he needed in his campaign against the city. Of the moderates' claim that the triumph of integration was inevitable, Sol Tepper said that death was equally inevitable but was not therefore to be embraced. Edward McBride, the dairy executive whose firing of Joseph Holmes in 1955 had marked the Citizens' Council's first flexing of its muscle, warned, with the segregationists' typically twisted logic, that endorsing the advertisement might reignite the blacks' street demonstrations. Edgar Stewart and William Craig defended the moderates' efforts from Pilcher's attacks on them. And, in perhaps the most significant statement of the afternoon, William Craig actually called into question the Citizens' Council's emphasis on white unity, observing that responsible leaders "should not lower ourselves to achieve this unity."

In a stunning repudiation of the Citizens' Council at the conclusion of this emotional debate, the city council voted unanimously to sign the advertisement. Armed with this decision, James Gaston called the Selma chamber's board of directors back into session on April 17, and it reversed itself, now voting twenty-one to eight to endorse the statement. And with the printing of the advertisement now a certainty, the county board of revenue held a special, closed-door meeting that night and agreed to sign also. On April 18 the advertisement appeared in the *Times-Journal,* together with the endorsements of the chamber, the city and county governments, and 1,280 individual white Selmians. The chamber also paid to reprint the advertisement in the *Wall Street Journal.*[152]

These developments unquestionably marked a significant moment in the life of the community. For the first time, moderate whites had abandoned secrecy and anonymity and had revealed their identities openly. But though noteworthy, the events most definitely did not represent the advent of a new era in Selma. There was not the slightest hint in the moderates' arguments that they sensed the moral dimensions of the questions at issue in their town. They had been moved finally to take a public stand by the same consideration that, more than any other, underlay their moderation itself, the desire for industrial development. Their commitments to abide by the Civil Rights Act's job discrimination provisions and to seek to open new channels of interracial communication—the two pledges in the advertisement—were strategic ones rather than engagements of the heart, as their statements make clear. The fact that they were more open to accommodating blacks' hopes than were most of Selma's whites proceeded principally from their greater desire to see the city grow. But this very same set of attitudes made them profoundly hostile to any actions that might give Selma a negative national image. Thus, for exactly the same reasons that they disapproved of Sheriff Clark's strong-arm tactics, they disapproved, and with equal intensity, of the demonstrations conducted by the Voters League and SCLC. Indeed, as the moderates saw the world, there was very little difference at all between the White Citizens' Council and the civil rights organizations; both were enemies of orderly progress.

Given the depth of the moderates' faith in industrial development, Martin Luther King could not possibly have taken any action more likely to alienate and infuriate them than to have advocated a boycott of all Alabama-made products. Insensitive to the black perspective, they continued to believe that if black Selmians had just shown a modicum of patience with the new Smitherman administration, blacks would very shortly have begun to see steady movement toward the peaceful realization of their legitimate goals. Moreover, moderates saw the launching of demonstrations as destructive of the long-term best interests of blacks themselves, because the demonstrations were likely to discourage the new investment in Selma that would bring greater opportunity to black workers and greater prosperity to black professionals and businessmen. Moderates were convinced that, in this sense, the best interests of blacks and whites were identical and that the radical activists of each race were the true enemies of both. And with a confidence in the decisions of Judge Thomas that could not have been expected of any black person, moderates saw no reason for demonstrations when essentially all of the matters at issue were pending before the federal courts. Thus, as the moderates saw things, the demonstrations had given Selma highly detrimental publicity that would damage the campaign to attract new industry, King's boycott of the state held even greater danger of doing so, and all of it was really for nothing, as the blacks' gains could have been obtained without such direct action, either from the new city administration or from the courts. As a result, the moderates were as angry with King and with local black leaders as they were with the intransigent segregationists.

For these reasons, the open break between the white moderates and the adherents of the Citizens' Council did not in fact portend any real improvement in Selma's racial climate. While the blacks returned to their internal divisions, the shared hostility of the whites to the demonstrations and their shared fear of black militancy kept white Selmians essentially united in their dealings with their black fellow townsmen. The negotiations between the Voters League and the Smitherman administration foundered in mid-May on the refusal of the black leaders to endorse the construction of the Hammermill plant in Selma unless Hammermill would undertake to support the general dismantling of the structures of white supremacy in the city. Despite the black boycott of the downtown merchants, the Merchants Association would not agree to direct discussions with the Voters League, and when the boycott collapsed during the summer, the blacks were left to look only to their rapidly increasing voting strength. The number of black registered voters grew steadily through the spring and early summer, with the registrars operating under the terms of Judge Thomas's injunction, and once the Voting Rights Act became law in early August and federal voting examiners were appointed in Dallas County, the number exploded upward. Judge Hare held the Voting Rights Act unconstitutional in October and enjoined Judge Reynolds from placing on the voting rolls the names of any of the people registered by the federal examiners, but in November a three-judge federal court including Judge Thomas unanimously held Judge Hare without jurisdiction in the case and ordered his injunction dissolved. By the fall of 1967, the number of black voters in Dallas County had passed ten thousand—about half of the county's electorate.

In the meantime, in order to avoid the loss of federal financial assistance (as required by the Civil Rights Act of 1964 if a program practiced racial discrimination), Selma's public schools in September 1965 took their first small step toward accepting integration; they adopted a freedom-of-choice plan for the first four elementary grades that resulted in the admission of a total of twenty blacks to three formerly white schools. But even this modest integration was unacceptable to the Citizens' Council. Segregationists at the same time established the private, white John T. Morgan Academy. In 1970 the federal courts compelled the adoption of a plan for broad-scale integration, to be implemented in September 1971. At this point, a second white private school was established, by Meadowview Christian Church, and white desertions of the public school system became a flood. Soon enrollment in the public schools was 70 percent black, while the private schools had become a rival, essentially all-white system.

In 1966, Wilson Baker defeated Jim Clark for sheriff—both in May, in the Democratic primary, and in November, in the general election, in which Clark ran again as an independent. But Baker's primary victory had required Judge Thomas's intervention. The county Democratic Executive Committee, dominated by segregationists and chaired by Selma White Citizens' Council founder M. Alston Keith, had ordered the exclusion of the returns from the black precincts because of various technical errors committed by the returning officers. The Justice Department had sued under the Voting Rights Act, and Judge Thomas had decided that the black ballots had to be counted, thereby delivering the nomination to Baker. It was clear, however, that the majority of Dallas County's whites continued to prefer Clark.

In the four years that separated the municipal elections of 1964 and 1968, Selma's electorate had been transformed. The number of registered voters had risen from 6,000 to 13,500; the number of blacks registered had grown from 250 to 5,000. Flushed with new optimism because of these numbers and because of Clark's defeat, black candidates filed for the mayoralty and for six of the ten city council seats. But the realities of life in Selma were far more intractable than the alteration of the registration figures would indicate. Dissension within the black community deprived Joe Smitherman's mayoral opponent, the Reverend Louis L. Anderson, of solid black support. Voters League president Frederick Reese publicly criticized Anderson for running against a progressive mayor who had shown himself willing to negotiate with blacks. About 250 blacks voted for Smitherman, and approximately 250 more who voted in the council elections abstained in the mayoral race; Smitherman took two-thirds of the total poll. The at-large method of electing council members similarly doomed the black candidates for that body. Some 125 whites were willing to vote for the black moderate leader Edwin Moss, but otherwise the balloting fell entirely along racial lines. About 62 percent of registered blacks and 69 percent of registered whites actually voted, and with an electorate still 63 percent white, only substantial white support of a black candidate or substantially greater white apathy could make any black victory possible. The city government therefore remained all white.[153]

The 500 blacks who would not oppose Smitherman's reelection and the 125 whites who determined to support Moss—perhaps 7 percent of the city's electorate in 1968—essentially defined the extent of Selma's racial middle ground. Following the municipal election of 1968 and most whites' abandonment of the public schools in 1971, it was doubtless clear to all observers that a great deal more than black reenfranchisement would be required for Selma to have any hope of achieving an interracial future.

Aftermath

5

I. Introduction

The seeming end of the national civil rights movement at about the time of the death of Martin Luther King in 1968—at any rate, the rather rapid decline thereafter in the ability of local direct-action efforts to arouse nationwide white sympathy and concern, and the consequent diminution in the influence of the national civil rights organizations—is a historical problem quite as significant as the question on which we have been focusing thus far, of why certain southern cities turned to direct action when others similarly situated did not. Neither puzzle has heretofore received the full consideration it deserves,[1] but the recognition of the crucial role played by municipal politics in generating local demonstrations allows us insight as well into this related enigma.

In truth, an examination of the southern communities that generated the direct-action campaigns reveals that the presumed decline of the civil rights movement is far more an artifact of the recounting of history from a national perspective than it is an accurate portrayal of the experience of southerners during the twentieth century's final three decades. At the level of southern municipalities, the struggle for civil rights continued to play itself out in numerous electoral contests for town councils, county commissions, and state legislative office and in the debates over measures in those and comparable bodies. In that sense, the death of the civil rights movement has been greatly exaggerated. While the national movement's influence was being curtailed, at this local level the movement remained as significant as ever. It is just that, with reenfranchisement and, frequently, after court-ordered redistricting, direct action took on a less recognizable, more ordinarily American form.

In 1994, a northern journalist toured Alabama. After cataloging the shortcomings of various communities, he remarked of Selma, "Perhaps worst of all, it is a place where blacks and whites, like punch-drunk boxers, are still fighting the same old battles of race."[2] It was an observation that clearly reflected the understanding of the civil rights movement as an episode in the history of the nation, one that culminated in the transformation of national policy. Whether it ended with the triumphant statutory vindication of America's faith in individual liberty or merely transmuted itself into rancorous disputes over the racial definition of privileges, the civil rights movement in this conception existed within a clearly defined historical moment, marked off by reasonably precise chronological boundaries: when the problem of southern segregation began to trouble the white national conscience significantly, at one end, and when the white national conscience could consider the problem no longer really a discrete one, at the other. For the journalist, therefore, to encounter communities in which these battles were still being fought, in all their stark ferocity, was to discover people who were almost willfully living in the past. It was a trifle ludicrous; it was as if they were still fighting the American Civil War, or some other event long past, such as Nat Turner's insurrection. Why did they not put such matters behind them?

The answer is, of course, that the civil rights movement will appear very different when viewed from the perspective of the southern towns in which it primarily happened. During the first half of the twentieth century, white supremacy had manifested itself in the form of legally required segregation. But the enactment of segregation laws and ordinances was a political event, one for which the establishment of white political domination was an essential prerequisite. It is hardly surprising, therefore, that local politics looms so large in the emergence of a sufficiently strong black belief that conditions might now permit the amelioration of the practices that these laws and ordinances had imposed. At the national level such an effort would perhaps inevitably seem to be about individual rights, but at the local level it would decisively concern the distribution of power and influence. The modification of conduct that is codified in statutes requires political leverage. Now, legal segregation is, quite obviously, only one possible manifestation of white supremacy; historically, white supremacy has appeared in a great many guises. The disestablishment of the legal requirements of segregation would represent the completion of a struggle conceived primarily in terms of individual rights, but a struggle primarily conceived in terms of the distribution of local power and influence, and rooted in perpetually evolving political competition, would be seamless; it would have no terminus because changing circumstance would constantly redefine its objective expression. Thus the discussion of why and how the civil rights movement ended—which appears to raise such compelling questions for accounts framed in national terms—is revealed to be entirely beside the point when considered from the local perspective. Even the most cursory glance at the history in more recent decades of the three cities with which we have been dealing establishes at once that the civil rights movement never ended at all. It merely, as we have said, took on a more ordinarily American form, because reenfranchisement permitted blacks to begin seeking to influence the political process through electoral competition rather than, as previously, through boycotts and marches in the streets.

The northern journalist's frustration is understandable. Reared on a version of American history that depicted the civil rights movement as an effort to end racial segregation, and racial segregation as a legal system forbidden by federal courts and Congress in the course of the three decades following World War II, he could only find the conflicts he discovered in Alabama's cities and towns anachronistic. This misunderstanding proceeds, it is clear, from twin historical confusions: of segregation, the historically transient manifestation of a racially inequitable distribution of political and social power, represented by enforced racial boundaries, with the inequitable power distribution itself; and of direct action, the most effective form of political participation available under disfranchisement, with the civil rights movement, the extended struggle to compel the larger community to take account of black aspirations. The civil rights movements in southern towns did enter a new phase with the full realization of direct action's utility, and a newer phase still with the destruction of legal segregation. But the recognition that, at the local level, the sudden outbursts of direct action were in their very essence political—prompted by developments in municipal politics, and intended in formal terms to gain particular changes in the administration of municipal affairs—allows us to see why the movement's victory in the setting of general national policy would not have created a similar culmination in the efforts at the local level. The national movement was focused upon the transformation of laws and the vindication of rights; the local movements were bound up with the continuing process of compelling authority to hear one's voice. A brief account of political events after 1965 in the three cities that we have been discussing will help to clarify this point.

II. Montgomery

The election of Earl James as mayor of Montgomery in 1959, and L. B. Sullivan's defeat of Clyde Sellers at the same time, marked the beginning of a dozen years during which the dominion of blue-collar whites at the polls was absolute. But the reacceptance of civic responsibility by white business progressives following the Freedom Rider riots of 1961, aided subsequently by the growing reenfranchisement of black voters as a result of the federal court injunction of 1962 against the county board of registrars, placed the city commissioners under escalating pressure to adopt more moderate positions on racial questions. Initially behind the scenes, but after their reelection in 1963 more and more often publicly, both Mayor

James and Commissioner Sullivan began to do so. The appointment of the biracial committee at the beginning of 1964, the resumption of the hiring of black police officers that spring, and the reopening of the parks at the beginning of 1965 were all voluntary actions of the city government that reinforced those taken under federal compulsion at the same time—the integration of theaters, restaurants, and hotels and the initial integration of the schools. And following the negotiations between civil rights organizations and law enforcement agencies at the time of the Selma-to-Montgomery march, Montgomery police during the latter part of 1965 and 1966 moved to a stance toward demonstrations so tolerant that by 1967 Governor George C. Wallace and his political associates were said to be quite "unhappy with what is considered the city's permissive attitude toward civil rights protests."[3]

These actions focused segregationist resentment upon Commissioner Sullivan. The fact that he had falsely accused Clyde Sellers of holding the very moderate views that Sullivan himself had now embraced marked the commissioner as a traitor in the eyes of many white supremacists, and Sullivan's decision during his second term to move his family into a well-to-do south Montgomery neighborhood did not help matters with his east Montgomery constituency. In 1967, former police captain John B. "Jack" Rucker, an ally of the department's racial extremists, made another attempt to unseat the commissioner. Rucker had resigned from the force in 1963 to challenge Sullivan when Sullivan's moderate tendencies had first begun to reveal themselves. This time Sullivan's evolution had become so clear that Rucker was successful. Sullivan held south Montgomery, but Rucker swept east Montgomery, and the black vote divided between those who appreciated Sullivan's recent actions and those who could not forgive his earlier hostility. Rucker's first action on taking office was to force into retirement the police chief who had guided the department through its late forbearance, W. Marvin Stanley, and to replace him with Drue H. Lackey, an officer who had apparently been a close personal friend of the Klansman who had led the bus station Freedom Rider riot, Claude V. Henley. Rucker also set out to forge an alliance with the third commission member, Cliff Evans, who had been elected to succeed Frank Parks when Parks died in 1966. Both Rucker and Evans resided in east Montgomery—Rucker in the Dalraida area, Evans in Chisholm—and both men resented the influence of the wealthy south Montgomery business progressives.

But Mayor James, of course, also lived in east Montgomery, in the Capitol Heights section, and he had built his entire career upon his ability to reconcile antagonistic forces and people. He therefore devoted his very considerable powers of persuasion over the next few years to finding common ground between the business community and his new commission colleagues, and more generally between the rival geographical and social divisions of the city. James was sufficiently successful with Rucker that

Chief Lackey resigned in disgust in 1970 and, with segregationist backing, announced his candidacy against Rucker in 1971. The principal project with which James sought to conciliate business leaders was the construction of a large new convention center downtown. James eventually won Evans over to the idea, and planning for the center was authorized. But Rucker drew the line here, voted against the project, and began warning his east Montgomery following that the center was an extravagant payoff to business interests, one whose construction would force the city deep into debt. Thus as the election of 1971 approached, James had managed to secure the support of the business progressives and of some blacks who approved of the quiet moderation he had exhibited in more recent years. But as had been the case with Sullivan in 1967, a great many more blacks could not forget the events of his first term. And Lackey's resignation had rendered both James and Rucker rather suspicious characters in the eyes of the extreme segregationists, while Rucker's warnings about the convention center had damaged James's standing with a portion of his traditional east Montgomery following, and others were offended by the mayor's emerging friendship with the businessmen.

A young insurance agent, Lamar Wagner, sensed James's new vulnerability and entered the race against him. Wagner, who had grown up in the city's poorest white area, West End, and had gained some recognition as a sports star while in high school, emphasized his humble origins and vigorously attacked the convention center proposal. In the initial voting, James took the south Montgomery precincts by substantial margins and divided the east Montgomery vote with Wagner; the black precincts went to a black candidate, A.M.E.Z. minister Percy Smith, who finished third. Having received more than 46 percent of the vote to Wagner's 26 percent, James entered the runoff with great confidence. But during the runoff campaign, Wagner secretly effected an alliance with black leaders. The result was a stunning upset. James carried south Montgomery by two to one and held his own Capitol Heights, but Wagner took the remaining east Montgomery precincts and swept the black areas to secure a narrow victory. Meanwhile, Rucker came from behind in the initial voting and defeated Lackey in the runoff by an equally narrow margin.

Wagner's triumph stunned the city's business community, who now saw their cherished dream of a convention center slipping away. But business interests still had one remaining possibility of staving off disaster. Throughout the twentieth century, the municipal general election had been a mere formality; the nominees of the Democratic primaries had always run unopposed. The law, nevertheless, contained a provision permitting an independent candidate to have his name placed on the general election ballot by petition. The chamber of commerce and other business organizations therefore commenced urgent consultations in search of a candidate whom they could run against Wagner. They settled upon the executive of a paper products company, C. James Robinson. Robinson commended himself because, though a resident of the well-to-do south Montgomery McGehee Estates area and a firm ally of the chamber of commerce forces, he nevertheless could claim a background quite as deprived as Wagner's. He had grown up in a Columbus, Georgia, public housing project, had been unable to afford college, and had worked his way up to executive status from an initial position as a delivery truck driver. Robinson launched a well-financed campaign, emphasizing these qualifications and warning against Wagner's lack of maturity. Wagner fought back with the allegation—by no means fanciful—that Robinson was supported by "the rich power politicians who want to operate the City Hall from the Country Club." And black leaders, under the direction of Rufus Lewis, threw themselves into the Wagner effort with the motto "Keep the Victory." But in an upset even more stunning than Wagner's own, Robinson was elected, with a bit more than 51 percent of the vote. Wagner carried the black precincts by enormous margins, taking Hamner Hall by five to one, and he held onto Chisholm in east Montgomery. But Robinson swept south Montgomery, carrying Cloverdale by four to one, and took most of east Montgomery by margins nearly as large—by two to one in Capitol Heights, for instance. In effect, then, Robinson was elected by uniting the white vote against the black. But that unity rested on the anomalous basis of south Montgomery whites' fear of the domination of east Montgomery whites, and east Montgomery whites' fear of the new power of the city's blacks.[4]

As soon as Robinson took office, Commissioners Rucker and Evans, threatened by the alliance between south Montgomery and east Montgomery that Robinson had created, closed ranks against him. When Robinson announced that the city's financial situation required the postponement of building the convention center, Rucker and Evans suddenly embraced the project and agreed to incur a deficit in its behalf. In the spring of 1972 the two men joined to vote city employees a 12.5 percent pay raise, and when Robinson protested that revenues were insufficient to meet the cost, they proposed financing the raises by taking out a loan. In the fall, regaining fiscal responsibility if not political wisdom, they imposed, without Robinson's approval, a 1 percent "occupational tax," in effect a city income tax on wages. The storm of protest was so great that a month later they were compelled to repeal the measure. But by this time their blunders had delivered Robinson virtually complete control of city politics. In the summer of 1973, Robinson persuaded Montgomery's state legislators to introduce legislation authorizing the city to vote upon abolishing the commission form of government in favor of the mayor-council form. The proposal was enacted at the end of August, and that fall Robinson's allies launched the petition campaign necessary to require the holding of the referendum. Rucker and Evans actively opposed the petition drive, warning among other things that the new council would necessarily have black members; and black leaders meanwhile urged the Justice Department to reject the proposed council districts under the terms of the Voting Rights Act, on the ground that they would not guarantee sufficient black representation. It was true that the boundaries specified in the legislative act had divided the Alabama State University campus between two council districts, in an effort to dilute the area's influence. Legislators apparently had believed that, because under the commission, elected at large, blacks could have no members at all, they would be grateful for some representation, and the number of black members under the legislative plan would be small enough not to frighten segregationists sufficiently to produce the council's defeat. But black spokesmen, no friends of Robinson's, insisted on four prospective council members in keeping with their percentage of the city's population, even if it meant the referendum's failure. When the Justice Department refused to approve the council districts, Robinson sued the department in federal court to gain validation of the plan. U.S. District Judge Robert Varner thereupon ruled that the legislature had actually had no power to define the council districts by statute and that the responsibility for doing so properly rested with the city commission. The commissioners promptly adopted the district boundaries proposed by black leaders Joe Reed and John Buskey—Mayor Robinson voting for them because he could not otherwise get federal approval for the council proposal, and Commissioners Rucker and Evans supporting them because the districting greatly strengthened the case of the proposal's opponents. On this basis, the Justice Department withdrew its objections and the question went to the voters in November 1974.

The referendum campaign was a heated one. Rucker and Evans led the effort to reject the change, but Robinson had the vigorous support of the chamber of commerce and the *Montgomery Advertiser.* And black leaders, now content with the council districting if still suspicious of Robinson, refrained from public involvement. The result was a narrow victory for the mayor-council form, by a margin of 52 to 48 percent. The change was rejected in the east Montgomery precincts by enormous margins—two to one in Capitol Heights, three to one in Highland Gardens, and five to one in Chisholm. But the reform carried south Montgomery solidly, and the black vote was closely divided. It seems clear that a principal factor in the acceptance of the alteration was Mayor Robinson's own prestige. In September 1975, the new mayor and council were chosen. Commissioner Evans opposed Robinson for the mayoralty, but Robinson swept the city, taking almost 70 percent of the vote and carrying all but two of the precincts. By 1976, Robinson was widely mentioned as a gubernatorial prospect.[5]

But the introduction of black representation into city government, which had been a by-product of Robinson's feud with his commission colleagues, was about to interact with a police department whose sharp divisions over racial attitudes Robinson had inherited from Rucker. The result of this collision would be the destruction of the mayor's political career. On the night of December 2, 1975, police responded to a report of a burglary in progress at a small grocery store, and in the resultant chase a young patrolman, Donald Foster, shot and killed a black man, Bernard Whitehurst. Subsequent investigations established that Whitehurst merely happened to be passing the scene; the following April, the actual culprit was apprehended. But police scurried to make Whitehurst appear guilty. They erased the tape recording of police radio messages which, a witness reported, had contained the statement that Foster had shot the wrong man. They then took from the police evidence locker a revolver confiscated during a drug raid the year before, placed it next to Whitehurst's body, photographed the scene as thus recast, and issued a statement that Foster had shot Whitehurst in the chest during an exchange of gunfire. Later that night, even before notifying Whitehurst's family of his death, they took the body to be embalmed, in an effort to forestall an autopsy. When the body was exhumed some months later, it was revealed that Whitehurst had been shot in the back.

There had been a time in Montgomery, of course, when such steps would have been sufficient to close the case, but the black members on the new city council were not so easily satisfied. Whitehurst's mother, represented by the young black attorney Donald Watkins, filed a suit in federal court charging police with the wrongful death of her son. As the discovery proceedings in this case gradually revealed the true facts about the killing, the city was very soon in an uproar. Black council members proposed the creation of a civilian board to investigate any allegations of police misconduct, but the idea was rejected on a race-line vote. The federal court jury found for the defendant policemen. But by this time the *Montgomery Advertiser*, under its crusading publisher-editor Harold Martin, and the county's politically ambitious district attorney, James Evans, had taken up the cause. Evans's efforts produced the indictment of three officers in June 1976 for perjury for having denied to the investigating grand jury that the gun photographed next to Whitehurst was the one they had confiscated in the 1974 drug raid. The trial of the first of these three men produced a hung jury, but Alabama attorney general William Baxley initially insisted that he would press ahead with the prosecutions. Throughout these events Mayor Robinson had stood staunchly by the police, even supporting the three indicted policemen in their refusal to submit to lie-detector tests. But when charges began to circulate that Robinson and his director of public safety, Edward L. Wright, had known of the planting of the gun and other official malfeasance and had sought to cover it up, the mayor had had enough. He took a lie-detector test that established his innocence of these allegations, and then on March 3, 1977, he resigned and was succeeded in office by city council president Emory Folmar. Public Safety Director Wright resigned at the same time, and subsequently, though Attorney General Baxley dropped the perjury prosecutions, four police officers were dismissed from the force.

The resignation of Mayor Robinson—unfairly hounded into retirement by political opponents, as his supporters saw it—produced a storm of protest among white Montgomerians. The hostility to *Advertiser* publisher Martin became so great that in June 1978 he turned the paper over to his brother and moved to Texas. The new mayor, Emory Folmar, had formerly been the secretary-treasurer of the city's Democratic Executive Committee, and in that capacity he had campaigned actively against Robinson in 1971. But in the meantime he had become a Republican, and throughout the Whitehurst affair he had strongly supported both Robinson and the police. Elected in April to fill out Robinson's term, he now plunged into rebuilding the police department's shattered morale. So aggressive was his management of the department that he took to riding with officers on their rounds and commanding them personally at crime and accident scenes. This energetic involvement with law enforcement gathered to him the white public sentiment that had been outraged by the attacks on the police during the Whitehurst affair, and soon his popularity in the city fully equaled that of his predecessor.

But Folmar's acquisition of popularity on this basis dictated as well, of course, the acquisition of a ready-made body of enemies. Foremost among them was Councilman Joe L. Reed, who had been the principal voice of black anger on the council during the Whitehurst investigation. Reed was one of the Alabama State University students who had been suspended by the state board of education in 1960 for participating in the sit-in at the snack bar in the county courthouse. In later years he had become executive secretary of the Alabama State Teachers Association (ASTA), the association of the state's black public school teachers. And when ASTA had merged with its white counterpart, the Alabama Education Association (AEA), in response to the racial integration of the public schools, Reed had become associate executive secretary of the united organization. In the meanwhile he had also become the state chairman of the Alabama Democratic Conference (ADC), the principal organization of Alabama's black Democrats, and because ADC endorsement could make or break candidates in black areas in much of the state, he had thus become a power in state politics. As the number of black state legislators grew after the federal courts compelled the legislature's conversion to single-member districts in 1972, Reed was able to use the threat of the withdrawal of ADC support to deliver these legislators' votes for whatever positions his employer, the AEA, favored; thus both the AEA and Reed himself rapidly became the state's most influential legislative lobbyists. Though the leader of a minority on the city council, then, Reed was often able to use his position as a major power broker in state government to counterbalance Folmar's increasingly secure municipal majority.

The one division that could forestall Montgomery's politics from descending into the racial stalemate that the rivalry between Folmar and Reed clearly portended was the longstanding class-based antipathy between the whites of the city's eastern and southern sections. Folmar, a wealthy real estate developer who had represented the Cloverdale area on the city council, was a former president of the Montgomery Country Club. Not since the days of the Gunter machine had such a man been able to hold the mayoralty without serious challenge. But the introduction of blacks into active participation in city affairs by the adoption of mayor-council government in 1975, and the racial antagonism emphasized by the Whitehurst affair in 1976, had had the effect of driving whites together across class lines. The mayoral candidacy of Franklin James in 1983 represented the final attempt to alter this situation. James was a younger brother of former mayor Earl James and, like the former mayor, was a resident of east Montgomery, with a background steeped in the class enmities that formerly had characterized local politics. He set out to build an electoral coalition between black and east Montgomery blue-collar white voters. Folmar fought back by alleging that James was a mere puppet of Joe Reed and his associates and that once James was in power he would turn city hall over to black radical leaders. And the bitter canvass became inextricably involved with another emotional engagement between the police and the black community, the Todd Road incident.

The Todd Road incident occurred on the evening of February 27, 1983. Two white plainclothes police officers, Les Brown and Ed Spivey, driving an unmarked car, happened past a small, dilapidated home on the northeastern edge of the city and had their suspicions aroused by the fact that several large, expensive automobiles were parked in front of it. Inside the house were eleven blacks, relatives of the late Annie Bell Taylor, all of whom had come to Montgomery from cities in Michigan and Ohio to attend Mrs. Taylor's funeral, which had taken place that morning. Just as Officers Brown and Spivey drove past, Christopher Taylor emerged from the house in order to move one of the cars to another parking place. The officers, apparently without identifying themselves as policemen, drew their guns and ordered Taylor to lean over his car to be searched. Instead, the frightened young man fled back into the house, and the two officers pursued, their guns still drawn. As Brown and Spivey burst into the house, not yet having identified themselves as officers, the terrified family believed itself under attack. The male members of the family tried to subdue the two armed invaders, while the females rushed to the rear of the house to telephone police for assistance. Because the women were from out of town and were hysterical, it took the emergency operator some time to obtain clear directions to the house. In the meantime, in the front of the house, the Taylors had succeeded in overpowering the officers and had taken their guns. The officers now, evidently for the first time, revealed that they were policemen. But rather than release them, the enraged Taylors proceeded to threaten and assault them. At this point the personnel dispatched by the emergency operator arrived. One of them kicked in the door, and in the resultant melee Officer Brown was shot and wounded, whether accidentally or intentionally is unclear. The male Taylor family members were then arrested and taken to police headquarters.

In coming months, members of the more moderate wing of the police force, who were disturbed by the subsequent events, secretly informed council members and *Montgomery Advertiser* reporters that, once at headquarters, the Taylors were severely beaten to compel them to sign confessions. And other officers, it appears from later testimony, proceeded at the same time to erase the tape recording of the Taylors' call to the emergency operator. Donald Watkins, the black attorney who had represented Mrs. Whitehurst in her suit against the police in 1976, was now a city councilman, and he used this position to launch an investigation of the affair. As a result of his findings, and additional revelations in the *Advertiser,* the city was plunged once again into bitter recriminations, and the controversy built throughout 1983. Five of the Taylor family eventually were indicted for the attempted murder of Officer Brown and for kidnapping and assaulting both Brown and Spivey. The very week of the election between Mayor Folmar and Franklin James, a hearing was in process before Judge Randall Thomas on the defendants' motion to suppress their confessions, on the ground that they had been coerced. Judge Thomas would grant this motion as to four of the five statements, following appalling testimony by various witnesses; and his doing so would play a significant role in producing a hung jury when the first of the Taylors was brought to trial at the end of the year.

The Todd Road incident rendered Franklin James's effort to create an interracial electoral alliance quixotic. The voting revealed a virtually complete racial polarization. Folmar carried the five white council districts by 82 percent to James's 18 percent. James carried the four black council districts by 84.5 percent to Folmar's 15.5 percent. Nor did James do much better in east Montgomery than in south Montgomery. Folmar received 80 percent of the vote in the eastern districts and 83 percent in the southern ones. Indeed, the election actually worked to give Folmar and Reed more thorough political control of their respective racial groups. Following the 1980 census, Folmar had attempted to use the necessary redistricting to diminish the overwhelming black majority in Reed's district. Reed had then filed suit against Folmar's plan, and Montgomery's new black federal district judge, Myron Thompson, had enjoined it as a violation of the Voting Rights Act. As a result, Folmar had been forced to accept the permanency of Reed's presence on the council. Now, the one black council member who had supported Folmar on some occasions—the member who represented the section of the city formerly the stronghold of Edgar Nixon—was defeated by a candidate endorsed by Reed's ADC. Reed, who represented the Alabama State University area and chaired the university's board of trustees, thus used his conflict with Folmar to enforce the middle-class professional domination of black Montgomery initially engineered by Rufus Lewis. But at the same time, the white councilmen who had cooperated with Donald Watkins in exposing the police misconduct in the Todd Road incident lost to supporters of the mayor. It appears that white observers of the incident tended to discount the clear evidence of official malfeasance because of the equally convincing evidence of the Taylors' assault on the officers, while black observers found the Taylors' actions justified by those of the police. From the black perspective, the central question was of the unfairness of white authorities, but from the white perspective, it was of black enmity to the social order.

Franklin James's challenge to Emory Folmar was the last serious one the mayor would receive for sixteen years. In 1987 and 1991 he was opposed by black attorney James E. Wilson, Jr., a grandson of Solomon Seay, Sr., whose support did not extend beyond the members of his own race. In 1995, Folmar drew no opponent at all. By that year he had created a formal organization, which he called "Montgomery's Team," to endorse and campaign for a slate of council candidates in the white districts. Throughout this period, as well, in an effort to ensure that the municipal racial balance would remain stable at approximately 55 percent white and 45 percent black, Folmar pressed an aggressive program of annexing the new white subdivisions springing up on the city's eastern and southeastern edges. Joe Reed's mastery of the black wards, exercised through the ADC, continued just as absolute as Folmar's of the white in these years. In a sense, Folmar and Reed constituted two halves of a single phenomenon. Each man depended upon the loathing of the other to hold his racial constituency in line, across the internal divisions of class that had played so prominent a role in the city's history earlier in the century.

In the meantime, the Whitehurst affair of 1976 and the Todd Road incident of 1983 seem to have had an effect upon the police department very similar to that of the beating of Robert Felder in 1947 and the rape of Gertrude Perkins in 1949. The extraordinary public scrutiny that surrounded all of these events acted to chasten more extreme elements within the force. The upper hand gained by the moderates in the department after the Felder and Perkins episodes was lost as a result of the intense hostilities aroused by the civil rights movement. But following the Whitehurst and Todd Road investigations, the position of the moderates among the officers was steadily reinforced by the progress of the racial and sexual integration of the department ordered by the federal courts. This integration was quite reluctantly undertaken, but the vigorous supervision of Judge Myron Thompson permitted no backsliding. Within a decade, therefore, the prospect of a repetition of the gross malfeasance that had accompanied the Whitehurst and Todd Road affairs had come to seem relatively remote. Though allegations of police misconduct continued to be made, the department increasingly proved willing to investigate and discipline officers involved. The result was that, with the decline of the police behavior that had lent the racial voting blocs such powerful substance in the late 1970s and early 1980s but with Reed and Folmar now in effect serving as patronage bosses of the two racial groups, race more and more functioned essentially as a political party in Montgomery's municipal life.

It was the growing recognition in the city of the hollowness of the rival racial leaders' charges and countercharges that formed the background to the political upheaval of November 1999—an upheaval that swept away both Mayor Folmar and Councilman Reed in a single mighty repudiation of the municipal political culture that they jointly had created. Folmar drew three serious challengers. Attorney Bobby N. Bright, a successful trial lawyer, prominent Baptist layman, and husband of one of Montgomery's state district judges, received the endorsement of both Reed's ADC and of its adversary as the spokesman for black Alabamians, the New South Coalition, despite the presence in the race of a well-known black candidate, Dorothy Frazier, a former administrative assistant to Governor Don Siegelman. Folmar's predecessor, James Robinson, also sought to return to the mayoralty, and three minor candidates filed for the office as well. Bright's endorsements allowed him to sweep the black precincts, leaving Frazier with less than 3 percent of the poll. Bright finished in second place in the initial round of voting, with a third of the total. Folmar led, with 46 percent of the vote, and former mayor Robinson ran third, with 16.5 percent. In the runoff election, Robinson's voters—representing as they did a crucial minority of whites at last prepared to desert Folmar's cause—proved decisive. Bright again took some 90 percent of the vote in the black districts. But essential to the outcome was the fact that he also received about a third of the vote in the white districts. He was therefore able to defeat Folmar by 54 percent to 46 percent. And though the incumbent allies of Folmar were reelected in four of the five white city council districts, in the fifth the elderly incumbent fell to a political newcomer.

But if the defeat of Mayor Folmar made the election a significant turning point in Montgomery's history, the outcome in the four black council districts marked it as momentous. Joe Reed, in addition to his council and AEA positions, also served, as we have said, as the chairman of Alabama State University's board of trustees, and his authoritarian conduct in that position had made him increasingly unpopular with the university's faculty and staff, who were a prominent element in his council district's electorate. After a bitter canvass, Reed was defeated by a former television news commentator, Tracy Larkin, whom Reed had defeated four years before; Larkin took 55 percent of the poll to Reed's 45 percent. And at the same time, all three of the incumbent Reed allies in the other black districts went down to defeat as well, in two cases by decisive margins. Thus, not only was a third of the white electorate now prepared to repudiate Folmar's divisive leadership, but a clear majority of the black electorate had at the same time had enough of Reed's previously invincible organization, too. And with the defeat of one of Folmar's allies in a white district, and of Reed and all of his allies in the black districts, the new Mayor Bright had a council majority that was not tied to either of the factions whose antagonism had defined city politics for more than two decades.

This astonishing outcome seemed to indicate a willingness on the part of important segments of the electorate to rise above the racial demagogy that had earlier plagued their community. On the other hand, two-thirds of white voters and more than 40 percent of black voters apparently remained wedded to the old order. And its ghosts were not long in materializing. Within months of his inauguration, Mayor Bright was plunged into a controversy reminiscent of former days. On July 11, 2000, a young white policeman, Officer Jesse F. Dodd, beat a handcuffed black schizophrenic, Samuel Day, with a nightstick, breaking Day's skull. The police department at once initiated disciplinary proceedings against the officer; a police hearing board recommended his dismissal from the force for having lied about the incident, and Bright accepted the recommendation. But the Southern Christian Leadership Conference seized on the encounter to demand that Bright also fire Police Chief John H. Wilson, an appointee of former mayor Folmar; and when Bright refused, the SCLC—understanding itself to be speaking for a large portion of the constituency that had put Bright into office—declared its determination to compel him to do so. Once a substantial number of black community leaders, Joe Reed most prominent among them, rallied to Bright's support, the SCLC demonstrations collapsed.[6] Nevertheless, the entire episode demonstrated how very difficult it would necessarily be for Montgomery to transcend its tormented past. And the results of the 2000 census emphasized this conclusion. In the late 1990s, Mayor Folmar's annexation efforts had begun to encounter increasing resistance, particularly in the rapidly developing eastern Pike Road area. As a result, in 2000, for the first time since 1900, black Montgomerians gained a slight numerical majority over whites, by about 4,000 out of the city's total population of more than 200,000. This development portended inevitable future struggles for racial dominance.

III. Birmingham

Albert Boutwell's vacillations during his term in office had managed to alienate Birmingham's rapidly growing black electorate—34 percent of the city's registered voters by 1967—without succeeding in holding the allegiance of the white working class. Racial antagonism had been heightened in July 1967, when an encounter between a policeman and a black robbery suspect produced a riot in which eleven persons were injured and the National Guard was mobilized. In the municipal election of October 1967, Boutwell held the well-to-do white Southside boxes but lost the rest of the city. The black vote divided. The political voice of the black establishment, the Progressive Democratic Council, endorsed former municipal judge Earl Langner, and he carried the black middle-class north Birmingham precincts. But the generally newly enfranchised poorer blacks of west Birmingham followed organized labor's endorsement of attorney George Young. Young, who had been a protégé of the state's white supremacist former attorney general MacDonald Gallion, also carried the white working-class areas and thus won one of the places in the runoff. The other place went to Councilman George Seibels, an insurance agent and the field's only Republican. Seibels took the city's white lower-middle- and middle-class areas, particularly in east Birmingham, where Republicans had begun to develop considerable strength.

In the runoff, the Progressive Democratic Council moved its endorsement to Young, and he of course retained the support of the labor unions. But the Southside well-to-do white vote that had gone to Boutwell now rallied to the business progressive Seibels. Despite the Progressive Democrats' support for Young, Seibels also obtained the endorsement of the president of Birmingham's NAACP branch, dentist John W. Nixon, who actively campaigned for the councilman. And even though Young had been associated with the segregationist Gallion, Seibels's firm defiance of Martin Luther King's demand for the immediate integration of the police force in the fall of 1963 seems to have drawn a portion of the white union vote to him. The result was that Young failed to carry the black and the white labor precincts by a large enough margin to offset Seibels's substantial victories in the upper-middle- and middle-class white areas of south and east Birmingham. Seibels was therefore elected by a narrow margin of 52 to 48 percent.

As mayor, Seibels devoted much of his energy to racial reconciliation. His business progressive vision of an interracial coalition united behind municipal economic development, on the model of Atlanta, made him the first mayor in Birmingham's history actively to solicit black advice and approbation. He made a practice of visiting black restaurants and clubs to socialize and discuss issues with his black constituents. He vigorously pushed city programs to extend sewer lines and street paving into neglected black areas. He joined with a variety of other white business leaders and organizations in supporting the appointment of Arthur Shores to a city council vacancy in 1968. And after the formation of the biracial

Community Affairs Committee of Operation New Birmingham in the spring of 1969, he frequently adopted and championed CAC proposals.

The result of these actions was that, when Seibels sought reelection in 1971, he received the Progressive Democrats' endorsement and swept the black precincts. George Young once again opposed him. Young held the white organized labor support that had been his base four years earlier and made large gains among Seibels's former enthusiasts in lower-middle-class white east Birmingham, many of whom had become disillusioned by Seibels's sympathy for black aspirations. But Seibels retained sufficient support in east Birmingham so that, with solid backing from the well-to-do Southside and the virtually unanimous black vote, he was able to win without a runoff, receiving 60 percent of the poll against four rivals, to Young's 34 percent. The council election was equally encouraging for opponents of white supremacy. In the midterm council election in 1969, a segregationist slate had run against the four incumbents, including the newly appointed Arthur Shores, and had attacked them for building racially integrated swimming pools in white neighborhoods. But all of the incumbents had won, and Shores had finished second in the field of twenty candidates, receiving substantial white support. In the 1971 election this trend had continued. A second black, CAC member Richard Arrington, was elected to join Shores on the council. And chosen with him were white racial liberals David Vann, the principal white negotiator during the 1963 demonstrations, and Angi Grooms Proctor, daughter of U.S. District Judge Hobart Grooms. The result was a solid council majority in favor of racial reform. Seibels's second term therefore saw further significant advances. The city board of education gained its first black member, Ossie Ware Mitchell. Civil rights attorney Peter Hall was appointed Birmingham's first black municipal judge. And Seibels energetically sought to increase the number of black police officers and to improve police relations with black residents of the city. In attempting to hire more black officers, Seibels was constrained both by Birmingham's quite inflexible civil service laws, to which the mayor was in fact deeply committed, and also, it was said, by the reluctance of Police Chief Jamie Moore. But when Moore retired in 1972, Seibels appointed an officer regarded as an ally of the department's reformist wing, James C. Parsons, to succeed him. The number of black policemen increased from twenty-four at the end of 1972 to seventy a year later. By that time, some 750 blacks were working for the city.

Despite the ease with which Seibels had obtained reelection in 1971, it was clear to liberal Democrats, who resented the strongly pro-business attitudes of the Republican mayor, that Seibels's majority was not at all a solid one. Though blacks had responded warmly to Seibels's overtures to them, this allegiance derived more from the mayor's personal conduct than from his usual policy positions. It appeared likely that a candidate who combined Seibels's congeniality with an advocacy of governmental activism more in keeping with blacks' general political convictions would be able to take the black vote away from him. And if that candidate could also obtain the support of blue-collar whites in the union neighborhoods, he had a genuine chance to win. Among the city politicians who found this analysis most convincing were the newly elected councilmen David Vann and Richard Arrington. Vann, a committed Democrat, found Seibels offensive both because of the mayor's party affiliation and because of his insistent collaboration with chamber of commerce forces. And Arrington, as soon as he joined the council, began having squabbles with Seibels. Arrington sponsored an ordinance in late 1973 providing for the employment of blacks and women by the city in the same proportion as their numbers in the general workforce, and requiring private firms who wished to do business with the city to adopt similar goals. Seibels vetoed this proposal and forced the adoption instead of a measure lacking firm numerical quotas. During the same years, Arrington repeatedly attacked police conduct in a series of incidents with black suspects, and he was sharply critical of both the department and Seibels for what he considered inadequate disciplinary actions against the offending officers. Arrington's actions began to solidify black opposition to the mayor. In the summer of 1975, a month-long strike involving about a third of city employees, who were seeking higher pay and pensions for non–civil service workers, exacerbated organized labor's hostility to Seibels. Against this background, David Vann announced his candidacy for mayor.

The election of 1975 was closely contested. With Arrington's support, Vann received the endorsement of the Progressive Democratic Council, which had gone to Seibels four years earlier. But Seibels won the endorsement of the black *Birmingham World* and retained substantial popularity in the black community. In the first round of voting, Vann obtained large majorities in the black boxes, but Seibels nevertheless was able to take 28 percent of the black vote. Seibels also carried the white precincts in south and east Birmingham, but a third candidate, state representative Richard Andrews, cut into his vote in the eastern area and Vann received the support of the white union boxes, obtaining 28 percent of the overall white vote. The result was that Vann led the poll with 46 percent to Seibels's 38 percent, but the presence of Andrews required a runoff. The runoff campaign became quite heated, and some of the charges took on a racial cast. Seibels warned that Vann, Arrington, and the Progressive Democrats were seeking to create a black bloc vote against him. Vann replied that the term "bloc vote" was coded racist language. It was true, of course, that Seibels had been completely unperturbed by the unanimity of the black vote that he had himself received in 1971, but it was equally true that Vann's electoral strategy required as few black defections as possible. The exchange in the end only energized black resentment without correspondingly energizing white fears. Turnout increased in all areas of the city in the second round of voting, but it increased more in black precincts, where 61 percent of those registered voted, than in white, where the turnout was 53 percent. This fact proved the key to Vann's victory. Seibels held the allegiance of the blacks who had voted for him in the first round, but his proportion of the black vote fell from 28 to 24 percent. He received virtually all of Andrews's vote and finished with 70 percent of the white poll. Vann retained the allegiance of the blue-collar union precincts, but his success in inducing blacks who had not participated in the first round to vote now delivered the councilman his narrow edge in the totals, 51 to 49 percent. In the council election, Arrington won a second term easily, and a third black, retired school principal Bessie Sears Estelle, was chosen to join Arrington and Shores on the nine-member body.[7]

Arrington's support for Vann had been active and essential, and in the early years of Vann's term their cooperation remained vigorous. But the administration of the police department soon began to damage it. Police Chief James Parsons resigned in order to accept the comparable position in New Orleans, and Vann appointed William Myers to succeed him. But the Fraternal Order of Police, the powerful police union that appears to have been dominated by the department's least progressive elements, distrusted Vann—in no small part because of his association with Arrington —and was therefore constantly prepared to judge whether Myers's loyalty lay primarily with the mayor or the force. The department's doubts about its leadership climaxed when Vann, in an attempt to punish the Blue Cross medical insurance company for having moved its headquarters outside the city limits, in 1979 canceled the group insurance policy that city employees had with the organization. The police at once went on strike, and soon they were joined by the fire department and street and sanitation workers. After nearly a week of crisis, Governor Fob James intervened to arrange a mediation, as a result of which Vann agreed to back down. But the episode left relations between the mayor and city workers, and particularly with policemen, in shambles. In the meantime, as Vann was struggling to convince officers of his goodwill, Arrington had more and more come to believe that the mayor was no longer sufficiently committed to disciplining errant members of the force. This suspicion received what appeared to be tragic substantiation less than two months after the end of the police strike in one of the most controversial incidents in modern Birmingham history, the death of Bonita Carter.

The affair had its origin in a quarrel between a white service station attendant, Michael J. Avery, and a black customer, Alger Pickett, on the evening of June 22, 1979. Pickett had been angered when Avery asked him to pay for his gasoline before pumping it. Pickett left the station, but he returned some time later with a rifle. Leaping from his car, he began to shoot into the building and succeeded in wounding Avery in the shoulder.

As he fell to the floor, Avery managed to pull the station's burglar alarm. When the alarm began to sound, Pickett fled across the street and concealed himself in some shrubbery, leaving his automobile parked by the gasoline pumps. Just at this juncture, two young black women, Bonita Carter and Louise Daniels, happened by on their bicycles. Pickett called to them from his hiding place and asked them to retrieve his car. Quite foolishly, Bonita Carter agreed to do so; she got into the car, started it, and began to drive away. In the meantime, the commotion had summoned station manager Ray Jenkins from the rear of the establishment. As he entered the front room, he found his employee bleeding on the floor, the burglar alarm ringing, and a car driving away. At the same moment, two white policemen, Officers Richard Hollingsworth and G. Michael Sands, arrived in a patrol car. Rushing to the door, Jenkins shouted to the officers what he deduced to be the case, that a gunman had just shot the attendant and was now escaping in his car, which by this time was in the street. The policemen called to the driver of the car to halt. Miss Carter at once stopped the car and, apparently frightened by the turmoil, lay down on the front seat. The officers nervously approached the automobile, their guns drawn. Just as Officer Sands drew abreast of the car's front door, Miss Carter, who had theretofore been prone on the seat and thus invisible through the windows, suddenly sat up, presumably preparing to explain the situation to the approaching policemen. Sands, who believed that the car was occupied by an armed felon who was now about to shoot him, immediately fired four times, killing Miss Carter instantly. Meanwhile, the actual culprit in this sad episode, Pickett, successfully made his escape on foot.

Bonita Carter's death plunged Birmingham into the most acrimonious recriminations. It seems clear that Miss Carter was an innocent passerby who paid with her life for a mere error of judgment. It seems equally clear that Officer Sands allowed his fears to betray him into an overly hasty response to Miss Carter's sudden appearance. On the other hand, the officer's apprehension is surely understandable under the circumstances, and his actions, however precipitate and undisciplined, certainly cannot be considered malicious. But blacks, with their long and bitter experience of police mistreatment and frequent extrajudicial punishment of members of their race, tended to emphasize the former truths about this complicated sequence of events, while whites, for whom officers more readily appeared to be well-intentioned protectors, emphasized the latter ones. Vann appointed an independent committee to investigate the incident, and it returned a report unanimously finding Sands's behavior unjustified. Vann, however, was convinced that the shooting proceeded from faulty training procedures for the police and an inadequate departmental policy on the use of deadly force; he believed that it would be unfair to punish Sands for doing what he had been taught to do. Rather than ordering Sands disciplined, therefore, Vann instead ordered police training changed and the use of weapons considerably restricted. This decision pleased no one. Black leaders, with Richard Arrington their most vehement spokesman, demanded that Sands be punished, and the FOP, which had threatened to renew its strike of the preceding spring if Sands were dismissed, denounced the new training standards as misguided limitations that would place officers' lives in danger. It was against this background that the 1979 mayoral campaign commenced.

Vann's effort to obtain a second term drew four principal opponents and two minor candidates. Councilman Arrington had the support of most black leaders, but Councilman Larry Langford, who had succeeded Arthur Shores as the body's third black member in 1977, threatened to fragment the black vote, by this time a bit less than 45 percent of the electorate. Councilman John Katopodis, like Arrington the holder of a Ph.D., was an administrator at the University of Alabama at Birmingham and a thoughtful but vigorous champion of the police. Frank Parsons, an attorney and owner of a travel agency who had never held public office, was a less reflective and even more fervent advocate of pro-police positions. Also in the race were Ku Klux Klan grand dragon Don Black and Socialist Workers Party nominee Mohammed Oliver.

In the midterm council elections of 1977, Arrington had broken with the Progressive Democratic Council, the voice of Arthur Shores and the well-to-do black establishment, in anger over its refusal to endorse his protégé Jeff Germany, one of Mayor Vann's aides, for a council seat. Arrington had then organized his own rival political organization, the Jefferson County Citizens Coalition. This breach was in part responsible for the candidacy of Larry Langford. But the Progressive Democrats in fact endorsed David Vann. Vann as mayor had been the principal promoter of a new city program that reserved 15 percent of all city contracts for black-owned enterprises, and he had taken many other steps to improve the lot of blacks in Birmingham. The mayor therefore had every reason to believe that he would receive a respectable portion of the black vote. Langford, a former television reporter and local celebrity, also expected significant black support. If Parsons and Katopodis divided the conservative white vote and Arrington and Langford divided the bulk of the black vote, while Vann retained the support of white liberals and the Progressive Democrats delivered to him an adequate minority of the black vote, Vann could expect to be one of the two candidates in the runoff. At that point, if his runoff rival were one of the black candidates, he would obtain the conservative white vote on racial grounds; if his opponent were one of the conservative whites, he would surely seem the preferable candidate to black voters. Vann therefore could approach the election confidently.

But the mayor's strategy failed to reckon with the ability of his former friend Arrington to exploit black indignation at the death of Bonita Carter. Arrington's new Citizens Coalition established neighborhood head-quarters, appointed block captains in every part of the black community, and proved phenomenally successful at uniting Birmingham's blacks behind its crusade. The result was that Arrington completely swept the black precincts and led the field in the first round of voting, with a bit less than 44 percent of the poll. Langford received virtually no support, finishing with less than 4 percent of the vote, only slightly ahead of Grand Dragon Black's 2.5 percent. And Vann was left to divide the white vote with Parsons and Katopodis. The three major white candidates each took about a third of the whites and finished within 700 votes of each other, Parsons and Katopodis with 17 percent of the total and Vann with 16 percent. Vann carried the well-to-do Southside, Katopodis the blue-collar Ensley and Roebuck areas, and Parsons the lower-middle-class eastern precincts. Parsons edged Katopodis by 97 votes for the second runoff spot.

Those 97 votes may well have determined the future of Birmingham. The white candidates had received a total of 52 percent of the votes in the initial primary, the black candidates 48 percent. In the runoff, a white candidate who could unite the white electorate would certainly win; Arrington had to receive some 3 to 10 percent of the white vote—depending on turnout levels—and a united black vote to emerge victorious. The urbane and intelligent Katopodis might have been able to draw liberal whites to his candidacy, but Parsons's appeals lacked the subtlety necessary for the task. Parsons received the endorsement of former mayor George Seibels, who said that Arrington on the council had judged every proposal by how much blacks would get out of it. Using just such arguments, Parsons sought vigorously to rally whites to his banner. But these efforts only convinced Mayor Vann that Parsons was "waving the bloody shirt of racism." Vann therefore endorsed Arrington. He was joined in this analysis by a small group of white liberals, often associated with the University of Alabama at Birmingham, and by an influential group of business progressives who had worked with Arrington on the CAC and who believed that the election of a black mayor would go far toward altering the negative national image of the city that had been formed by the events of the civil rights years. Arrington thus received the endorsements of both the *Birmingham News* and the *Birmingham Post-Herald*. And the support of these elements proved crucial. In the election Arrington received 51 percent of the poll to Parsons's 49 percent, with more than two-thirds of registered voters—and 72 percent of black voters—participating. Arrington took all of the black vote and Parsons 90 percent of the white vote, but Arrington received the essential support of 10 percent of the white electorate, virtually all of whom lived in the well-to-do Southside area that had been carried by Vann in the initial round. This election proved a turning point in the city's history.[8]

That the city had undergone a permanent political transformation was not, however, at first completely apparent. The racial division on the council continued to be six whites and three blacks. Whites were still a majority of registered voters, and blacks did not appear to be as fully united as the vote for Arrington indicated. The Progressive Democratic Council had shifted its endorsement to Arrington in the runoff, when his opponent proved to be Parsons, but Arrington's anger at the initial endorsement of Vann was not thereby assuaged. In the midterm council election of 1981, Arrington's Citizens Coalition struck back by refusing to endorse Arthur Shores's daughter Helen Shores Lee, who was seeking a council seat. The breach between the coalition and the Progressive Democrats thus became permanent. And the coalition went further, ignoring the crucial support that white liberals had supplied in Arrington's mayoral victory and nominating instead an all-black slate of council candidates, as indeed it had done also in 1979. This refusal to acknowledge the biracial nature of Arrington's backing convinced many skittish white moderates of the accuracy of conservative white warnings that Arrington and his Citizens Coalition allies were seeking absolute black rule rather than interracial partnership. And these fears were lent special urgency by a battle for control of the police department that dominated the first two years of Arrington's administration.

Police Chief William Myers, who had had difficulty in dealing with the FOP's distrust of Vann, was reduced to near-total impotence by the deep enmity between the FOP and Arrington. Caught between Arrington's insistence on reform and the FOP's repeated threats of another strike, Myers finally resigned in frustration at the end of 1980. Arrington and the Jefferson County Personnel Board thereupon commenced a battle that rapidly descended into something akin to total war over the mayor's efforts to find a new chief who shared his views. Former chief James Parsons, unhappy with his new job in New Orleans, applied for the vacancy, and the personnel board ranked him first on the list of three names it submitted to Arrington. The mayor, who had been sharply critical of Parsons during the Seibels years, at once rejected him and asked the board for a new list. Under the law, the board was to supply a new name when the appointing authority rejected one of its nominees for good cause. The board rather reluctantly added a new nominee on this first occasion, but when Arrington returned the list a second time they demanded that the mayor prove that the causes for rejecting the nominees were good ones. In the meantime, former chief Parsons filed suit in state court over the same question. Arrington and the board went through several more such exchanges, amid increasing acrimony. Finally, the board itself filed suit for an order compelling the mayor to choose one of the names from its most recent submission. And Arrington issued a statement attacking both the board's procedures and the civil service law itself, which he depicted as an antiquated obstacle to his reform of the city administration. Just as this lengthy battle was reaching a climax, the midterm council election took place.

The all-black council slate endorsed by the Citizens Coalition was committed to supporting Arrington in his conflict with the personnel board. And this open hostility on the part of the mayor and the coalition to the civil service system further reinforced white suspicions—high in any case because of the coalition's refusal to endorse any white council candidates—that Arrington and his associates were scheming to obtain an exclusively black city government. Former police chiefs Parsons and Myers joined with Councilman John Katopodis to assemble an anti-Arrington, pro-FOP, pro–civil service slate of candidates, and the campaign quickly became a racially polarized contest between these two alliances, marginalizing the candidacies of moderate independents. The alarms sounded by the Katopodis slate drew to it even the white liberals who had voted for Arrington two years earlier, but now felt biracialism threatened. The result was a near-total defeat for the Citizens Coalition. Only one of the coalition candidates, Arrington's close friend William Bell, managed to survive, and only because he alone of the coalition slate succeeded in retaining 9 percent of the white vote. Incumbent white liberal Nina Miglionico also was reelected, with 94 percent of the white vote and 29 percent of the black; she was the sole candidate who obtained genuine biracial backing. The remaining three council seats all went to anti-Arrington whites—incumbent John Katopodis, former police chief William Myers, and outspoken Republican leader Bettye Fine Collins; each received overwhelming white support and tiny support among blacks. William Bell and Jeff Germany—who held one of the four continuing seats—now were the only black council members; white conservatives held a five-to-four majority on the body. John Katopodis was chosen the new council president.

Arrington's considerable political skills were revealed in his response to this electoral rout. He learned from it a lesson that he would not forget. Never again would he neglect his band of white liberal and business progressive allies. Never again, before the conversion to ward election of the council, would the Citizens Coalition fail to endorse a biracial council slate. The final two years of his first term Arrington devoted in great part to currying the business progressives' and liberals' favor. And the mayoral election of 1983 showed the result. John Katopodis, after the triumph of his ticket in 1981, must have thought his victory in 1983 nearly assured. He conducted a commendably positive campaign, carefully avoiding racial questions, confident that Arrington's widely publicized administrative errors during the preceding four years and the momentum of the white mobilization that had occurred in the previous council election would together be sufficient to defeat the incumbent. But Arrington could rely on the desire of blacks not to return to conservative white leadership, and he could hope that his efforts with whites had assuaged the fears of a sufficient number of them. Katopodis might have won in 1979, but now he faced an Arrington fortified with the advantages of incumbency and patronage. And Arrington did not need many white supporters this time, because blacks now held a narrow lead over whites in the number of registered voters. He got far more than he required. He received unanimous black support and a black turnout of 76 percent. And he secured 12 percent of the white vote, the most he would ever obtain. He thus defeated Katopodis by 60 percent to 40 percent of the total poll. In the council election, all five victors—the two black incumbents, two of the white incumbents, and a black newcomer—were endorsed by the Citizens Coalition. In the midterm council election two years later, one anti-Arrington white incumbent, Bettye Fine Collins, was narrowly reelected, but the other four victors—one white and one black incumbent and two black newcomers—were members of the Citizens Coalition slate. The three blacks thus elected joined the two blacks who held continuing seats to give blacks a five-to-four council majority, for the first time in Birmingham's history. By this time, 53 percent of registered voters were black. Retiring council members Nina Miglionico and John Katopodis, though of quite different political outlooks, agreed in believing that the Citizens Coalition now held complete control of city politics. It was certainly an extraordinary reversal, from a council of seven whites and two blacks in 1981 to one with a black majority in 1985. And the turnabout unquestionably was a result in no small part of Mayor Arrington's own remarkable strategic and diplomatic abilities.

Nevertheless, underlying the emergence of the Citizens Coalition's rule of the city were significant alterations in Birmingham's economy and population. At the height of the civil rights movement in the early 1960s, the vast U.S. Steel complex of mines and mills in Birmingham had had a workforce of 22,000, or 38 percent of the area's workers, and other iron and steel enterprises had employed many thousands more. Even at the time of Arrington's initial election as mayor in 1979, U.S. Steel had still employed almost 10,000. But during Arrington's first term this number had fallen precipitously. In June 1982, at which time it employed only 3,500, including management, U.S. Steel closed the Birmingham works for good and abandoned the city that had been so largely its creation. During the same years, the University of Alabama at Birmingham, with its sprawling medical school and hospitals and its workforce of 9,000, emerged as the city's largest employer, and the headquarters of the regional division of American Telephone, South Central Bell, employing 8,200, became the second largest. But the work done for the university and the telephone company was hardly of the dirty and intensely physical variety that had characterized the Magic City's blast furnaces and mines; hence increasingly—and with startling rapidity—the area began to lose the industrial ethos that had marked it for a century. Also, with the closure of the factories and mines and the consequent geographical dispersion of job opportunities, and with improvements in the area's highways thanks to the interstate highway program, commuting became more and more both necessary and practical for blue-collar as well as white-collar residents. Concurrently, the rise of black political power in Birmingham made whites eager to seek suburban white refuges. The result was that the city's population, and especially its white population, began to decline, even as the population of the metropolitan area grew. The population recorded for Birmingham in the census of 1960, more than 340,000, was the largest figure it would ever attain. It fell to 300,000 in 1970, to 284,000 in 1980, to 266,000 in 1990, and to 243,000 in 2000—a figure substantially less than that of 1930. At the same time, the proportion of residents who were black, less than 40 percent in 1960 and 42 percent in 1970, soared with the emergence of black political control, to 56 percent in 1980, 64 percent in 1990, and 75 percent in 2000. Meanwhile, the population of the metropolitan area rose from 635,000 in 1960, to 739,000 in 1970, to 847,000 in 1980, to 908,000 in 1990, and to 921,000 in 2000; and the proportion that was black, more than a third in 1960, fell to a bit more than a quarter by 1990. It is therefore clear that the Citizens Coalition's hegemony derived at least as much from white Birminghamians' abandonment of their city as it derived from Arrington's leadership.

In the meantime, as the coalition was gaining mastery of city politics, the Arrington administration, with the assistance of the federal government, was overcoming the barriers that the civil service system posed to its control of the municipal bureaucracy. The mayor's war with the personnel board over the appointment of a police chief to succeed William Myers had been an element of this larger struggle. Immediately after the coalition slate's disastrous defeat in the council election of 1981, Arrington, determined now to win back the favor of his white supporters, had capitulated to the personnel board and appointed one of its nominees, New York City police captain Arthur V. Deutcsh, as the new chief. But the mayor's surrender in this particular battle, though very public and apparently a genuine concession to the advocates of civil service's sanctity, was actually merely a tactical maneuver, made palatable to Arrington by developments in the federal courts. In 1974 the Ensley branch of the NAACP had sued the personnel board, alleging that the civil service system operated to inhibit the appointment of blacks to government jobs. The Justice Department had joined the suit in 1975, on the side of the black plaintiffs. U.S. District Judge Sam Pointer had ruled the board's entry-level tests racially discriminatory, and the Fifth Circuit affirmed this holding on appeal in May 1980. The plaintiffs pressed now to void the board's promotion examinations as well. In the meantime, Arrington had become mayor in 1979, and at his direction the city had entered negotiations with the plaintiffs and federal officials and reached agreement on a consent decree imposing upon the city the obligation to hire and promote strictly specified percentages of blacks and women in all categories of city employment. Judge Pointer accepted the consent decree in August 1981, just as Arrington's conflict with the personnel board over the new police chief was reaching its climax. Arrington's agreement in November 1981 to appoint Deutcsh was therefore easier for him to make because he could now be confident that, over time, the consent decree would force the board to allow the racial and sexual transformation of the municipal bureaucracy, whatever might be the results of the civil service tests.

During the next several years the consent decree worked just as Arrington and his advisors hoped it would, but in doing so it increasingly angered white and male applicants for employment and promotion whose success on the examinations was disregarded because of their race or sex. The Birmingham Firefighters Association and the FOP had opposed the consent decree from the outset, and in 1984 they filed suit against the city, alleging that the operation of the decree produced racial and sexual discrimination. The Justice Department, whose lawyers had initially designed the decree, now joined with the white employees in arguing that it was illegal. And the city in reply argued that its own guilt in discriminating against blacks in past years was so great that it deserved to be punished with the restrictions on its employment practices that the decree imposed. This odd suit came to trial in 1985, and Judge Pointer summarily rejected the challenges to his 1981 order. The employees and the Justice Department appealed. The Fifth Circuit initially sustained Judge Pointer's belief that the consent decree insulated Birmingham authorities from these allegations, but in 1989 the U.S. Supreme Court held that because the Birmingham Firefighters Association and the FOP had not been parties to the original suit that had produced the consent decree, they should be allowed to challenge it. In the meantime, the Supreme Court in 1987 ruled that decrees requiring such blatant racial and sexual discrimination could be sustained only if they constituted a narrowly limited device specifically to overcome the results of an earlier discrimination made in favor of the groups now discriminated against. The Court returned the suit to Judge Pointer with orders that he retry it to be certain that the 1981 decree met this standard. At the end of 1991 the suit again came to trial, and in August 1992 Judge Pointer ruled that the city had fully proven its own guilt and that the original numerical quotas were absolutely necessary to remedy the persisting effects. He therefore reaffirmed the consent decree in every particular. With this decision, the civil service statute that had done so much to establish the careers of James A. Simpson and Eugene "Bull" Connor in 1935 essentially ceased to represent a barrier to the advancing black domination of Birmingham's government.

Meanwhile, Arrington and his allies had been consolidating their power. Their Citizens Coalition had already succeeded in completely eliminating the Progressive Democratic Council—the Birmingham affiliate of Joe Reed's Alabama Democratic Conference—from any local significance by the time the coalition took control of the city council in 1985. At the end of that year, Arrington reached out for statewide influence. He joined with state senators Hank Sanders of Selma and Michael Figures of Mobile—both also municipal black leaders who resented the extent of Reed's power in their own localities—to form the New South Coalition as a rival to the ADC. Arrington was chosen the new organization's first state president, and thereafter the two federations commenced an acrimonious struggle for control of black politics in many counties around the state. In 1987, Arrington won a third term easily against white conservative Robert McKee; Arrington received his usual 12 percent of the white vote, but that was now enough to give him almost two-thirds of the total poll. In the council election, the last two anti-Arrington whites were eliminated from the body. All nine council members—six blacks and three whites—now owed their positions to Citizens Coalition endorsement.

Just three weeks after the coalition completed its sweep of the council seats, a group of white and anti-Arrington black voters, represented among others by white liberal former councilwoman Nina Miglionico, filed suit in federal court challenging, under the terms of the 1965 Voting Rights Act, the at-large election of Birmingham council members. It was the first attempt by whites to make use of the act's provisions. The Citizens Coalition, through its organization of black bloc voting, was effectively depriving the white minority of representatives who spoke for its views, the plaintiffs maintained. The city replied that the fact that the coalition since 1981 had always endorsed biracial slates and that three of the nine council members were at that time white rendered the plaintiffs' argument manifestly false. But the tiny proportion of the white vote that the coalition slate obtained surely demonstrated that the whites whom the coalition selected held opinions far from typical of the city's white citizens. In truth the white council members were, as everyone in Birmingham knew, in Arrington's pocket. More persuasive was the mayor's warning that the conversion to ward election might exacerbate racial tensions in the city; at-large voting compelled candidates to moderate their views, but districts would encourage extremism among candidates of both races, he said. It was unquestionably correct that the creation of white-majority council districts would allow white conservatives, who detested Arrington and his beliefs, to return to the council; indeed, that was the principal purpose of the suit. But such political considerations, however valid, were irrelevant to the Voting Rights Act claims. In June 1988, U.S. District Judge Robert B. Propst rejected the city's motion to dismiss the suit, ruling that the Voting Rights Act did indeed protect white minorities on the same basis as black ones, and docketed the case for trial. The city thereupon surrendered. In March 1989 the council adopted an ordinance creating six black and three white council districts, and in August, Judge Propst accepted the districting and ordered it into effect for the fall council election. In future years, Citizens Coalition endorsement, which had once been a prerequisite for election to the council, became the kiss of death in the white wards, and the coalition therefore ceased endorsing white council candidates altogether.

If the Citizens Coalition had thus lost its control of the white representatives, however, its hegemony in the black community remained almost absolute. A disgruntled element of blacks who were shut out of coalition leadership began to grow in the 1990s. In 1991 and again in 1995, black Municipal Court Judge Emory Anthony opposed Arrington, but Anthony's support remained limited essentially to white voters. In 1993, Anthony joined Bernard Kincaid to create People's Choice, an organization intended as a rival to the coalition in the black wards. But People's Choice made very little progress in winning the allegiance of the black masses. In 1997, Kincaid succeeded in defeating the incumbent coalition councilman Roosevelt Bell, thus becoming the first non-coalition black to be elected to the council since the coalition's formation. But the same election demonstrated that Arrington's authority remained virtually dictatorial. He had become dissatisfied with two of his council allies, Linda Coleman and Antris Hinton—the council's only black females, two of the coalition's most devoted and long-standing workers, and very popular in their districts, but women whom Arrington had come to regard as disloyal and excessively independent in their attitudes. At his behest, therefore, they were deprived of coalition endorsement, and though they ran anyway, each was defeated by a previously little-known coalition candidate. The coalition seemed so nearly invincible in the 1990s, indeed, that turnout fell to quite a low level. From turnout rates of more than two-thirds in the 1980s, participation declined to half that in mayoral elections, and to just over a fourth of the electorate in council elections.

Arrington's popularity and the power of his coalition persisted despite—and to some degree because of—continuing public reports of widespread corruption in the Arrington administration. In late 1990, U.S. Attorney Frank Donaldson used a federal grand jury to begin an investigation of these stories. In July 1991 the grand jury indicted Marjorie Peters, the city's consultant in the building of the opulent new Civil Rights Institute, a museum that was being erected on the site of the 1963 encounters between black demonstrators and city police under "Bull" Connor. Miss Peters was charged with fraud and income tax evasion in pocketing more than $220,000 intended for the museum's design and construction. Mayor Arrington, assistant city finance director Leonard Adams, an architect, and a contractor were identified in the indictment as her co-conspirators. In September, the architect involved, Tarlee Brown of Atlanta, pleaded guilty to giving Arrington a $5,000 kickback in order to obtain the museum contract. Marjorie Peters came to trial at the beginning of October, and the trial was actually in progress, with daily testimony of the most unabashed venality, when Arrington's candidacy for a fourth term was submitted to the voters. Arrington had loudly protested that the allegations against him represented nothing more than a racist effort on the part of Donaldson and his Republican masters in Washington to destroy the mayor and his allies because they were black; he thus succeeded in arousing intense anger among the city's black citizens. Riding a wave of their indignation, Arrington swept to victory with nearly 63 percent of the vote against five opponents. Nine days later, Marjorie Peters was convicted on all twenty-six of the counts against her, and she thereupon appears to have agreed to join Tarlee Brown in testifying against the mayor. In January 1992 the grand jury subpoenaed Arrington's appointment logs, and he refused to surrender them. U.S. District Judge Edwin L. Nelson therefore held him in contempt. After an emotional rally at the Sixteenth Street Baptist Church, the headquarters of the 1963 civil rights demonstrations, Arrington led a march of more than seven hundred supporters from the church to the U.S. Courthouse, where he surrendered to federal marshals. After one night in jail, however, he relented, paid a $7,000 fine and turned over the logs. Residents quite generally expected that his indictment would quickly follow, but in March, Frank Donaldson was succeeded as U.S. attorney by Jack Selden, and Selden apparently concluded that the evidence against Arrington was insufficient to ensure a conviction. The grand jury did return additional indictments for corruption in the operation of the municipal bus line. In November, however, the grand jury's term expired and it was dismissed, without ever having taken any action against the mayor other than to identify him as Marjorie Peters's co-conspirator. In early 1993, the Circuit Court of Appeals reversed Miss Peters's conviction, but in June of that year she agreed to plead guilty to the various charges against her. Shortly thereafter, in a settlement between the Justice Department and Arrington's attorneys, the allegation that the mayor was her co-conspirator was stricken from court documents. But in August, in sentencing Tarlee Brown on his 1991 guilty plea, U.S. District Judge James Hancock announced from the bench that Brown's testimony that Arrington had accepted his bribe was convincing.

Meanwhile, Police Chief Arthur Deutcsh had been convicted in state court of tampering with official records in connection with an attempt to conceal the arrest of the mayor's daughter. In the wake of this succession of events, and of Judge Pointer's decision at almost the same time sustaining the consent decree's limitations on the civil service system, morale in the police department began a sharp decline. By 1996 the situation had become so grave that the area's white economic powers—virtually all of whom by this time resided in the sprawling suburbs to the south of the city—bestirred themselves to assist the urban center whose difficulties they ordinarily did their very best to ignore. With private donations they commissioned an investigation of the state of the department, to be conducted by former New York City police commissioner William Bratton. Bratton's report, when it was submitted in the fall of 1997, found deep-seated problems with the force's temper and confidence in its leadership; officers quite generally believed that their commanders cared primarily about keeping city politicians happy. The report urged a thorough reorganization of the entire department. Arrington insisted that he too was concerned about this situation, but he dealt with it in typical fashion: he let a city contract to Willie Huff, the chairman of his political organization, the Citizens Coalition, to conduct a separate investigation of the police and anti-crime strategies—an action hardly calculated to calm officers' fears of municipal political interference with law enforcement.

The developments of the 1990s further hardened white hostility to Arrington. The leading spokesman for this anger became white physician Dr. Jimmy D. Blake. Dr. Blake had run against Arrington for mayor in 1991 but had received only 4 percent of the vote. However, he had managed to obtain election to the council in 1993, and once in office Blake had quickly marked himself as the administration's most outspoken critic. In 1997—in the same council election in which Arrington successfully purged Linda Coleman and Antris Hinton for disloyalty—Blake organized an anti-Arrington slate of white candidates that succeeded in sweeping the three white districts. Arrington himself announced that the election represented a pivotal contest between his forces and Blake's, and used the threat which he depicted Blake as representing to rally black voters behind the coalition candidates against Hinton and Coleman. When Blake proved able to unite the white wards against Arrington at the same time, therefore, the city's politics seemed on the verge of a formal racial polarization. But Arrington was not a man to tolerate an organized opposition. The spring of 1998 found Blake, now near bankruptcy, filing suit in state court against Arrington; the mayor and his allies, the complaint alleged, had used political pressure to compel health maintenance organizations in the area to eliminate Blake from their lists of primary physicians, thereby ruining the doctor financially.

By the end of the century, then, Arrington had completed his transition from idealistic academic and reformer to vengeful boss of an imperious and too often corrupt urban machine. His actions would have been sufficient to destroy many another politician, but Arrington wore the armor of history. The repeated revelations and charges of the Citizens Coalition's enemies could not harm him with his black constituency because the city's blacks still saw him as the man who had delivered them from generations of subordination into at least reflected power. The use of that power was far less important to them than the fact of it. Arrington was thus essentially insulated from the discipline of the electoral process by the ghosts of Birmingham's violent past. He prepared to pass on to his chosen successor, city council president William Bell, a political organization that was bound together and seemingly rendered virtually indestructible by the experience of race.

But history's spell, it finally became clear, can guard only those who have cast it. Arrington resigned three months before the mayoral election to allow Bell to run with the advantages of incumbency. Arrington and Bell squeezed a million dollars in campaign contributions from businesses who were under obligation to the administration. The Citizens Coalition cranked its formidable machinery into gear in the black precincts, and Bell loudly proclaimed himself the heir of Arrington's legacy. But as the weeks of the campaign passed in the fall of 1999, it gradually began to dawn on observers that Arrington actually was having difficulty in transferring his magic to his protégé. Bell drew four serious competitors and no less than nine minor candidates into the field against him. Bernard Kincaid, the retired University of Alabama at Birmingham faculty member who had been one of the organizers of People's Choice and who two years earlier had become the only non-coalition black city councilman, received the endorsement of the Progressive Democratic Council—though as we have seen, in the Arrington era the council had been reduced to essential impotence. William Johnson, one of the white city councilmen elected on Dr. Blake's slate in 1997, was the candidate of the white east Birmingham precincts. The presence in the race of University of Alabama at Birmingham history professor Horace Huntley and state representative George Perdue, both prominent figures in black Birmingham, was further evidence of the increasing black discontent with Citizens Coalition rule. But black opposition to Arrington and Bell soon coalesced around Kincaid, and in the end Huntley and Perdue each received less than 4 percent of the poll.

Kincaid focused much of his campaign on denunciations of the Arrington administration's venality. He pledged that his first action as mayor would be to order an independent audit of Birmingham's accounts. In the initial round of voting these attacks gathered him 27 percent of the vote. On the strength of the white vote, Councilman Johnson ran third, with 12.5 percent. But William Bell took more than 49 percent of the poll, missing an outright victory by a mere 479 votes. Kincaid's prospects for defeating Bell in the runoff were not bright. Johnson and Dr. Blake quickly endorsed Kincaid, however, and Johnson created a sophisticated telephone operation for Kincaid to contact undecided voters. In the returns, Kincaid came from behind to edge past Bell by just 1,136 votes.

The pattern of voting in the runoff was an ironic mirror image of the pattern by which Bobby Bright was elected in Montgomery on the same day. As Bright had swept the black minority's precincts, so Kincaid swept the white minority's precincts, with some 86 percent of the vote in the white areas. And as Bright had won by holding a third of the vote in the white districts, so Kincaid achieved victory by holding 36 percent of the vote in the black districts. Though the Citizens Coalition succeeded in delivering almost two-thirds of the vote in its strongholds to Bell, this proportion was far less than the huge margins that Arrington had always received there in previous years. The concurrent victories of Bright and Kincaid in Montgomery and Birmingham, with their virtually identical patterns of support, caused many observers to believe that a new day of biracial politics might be dawning in Alabama. But the city council with which Kincaid had to deal remained firmly in coalition hands, and a clear majority of Birmingham's black voters remained loyal to the coalition's leadership. The vision of an interracial political order would, therefore, require much additional effort before it could become a functioning reality. Indeed, the dawn of the new century found Arrington contemplating a race against Kincaid in an attempt to regain municipal power.[9]

IV. Selma

The defeat of all black candidates in race-line voting in Selma's municipal election of 1968 and the widespread white abandonment of the city's public schools following the federal courts' decree of a general plan for their racial integration two years later made obvious to any who had doubted it the extent of the racial polarization there. The building of an interracial middle ground would clearly be a lengthy and difficult process. There were nevertheless a few signs of progress. By 1970 some eight or ten blacks had been hired as clerks in downtown Selma stores. The accessible young Mayor Smitherman had hired six black city policemen. And his associate the new sheriff Wilson Baker had appointed two black deputies. But from the perspective of the black moderates who had been associated with the Dallas County Improvement Association, led by businessman Edwin Moss, the crucial next step forward—the one upon which all other advances would depend—had to be the admission of blacks into shared governance of the community. In 1971, as another municipal election approached, therefore, these leaders petitioned the city council to consider converting from at-large to ward election of its members. As Moss told them, "We would like to participate with you in operating the city, and if councilmen are elected at large, it would be almost impossible for us to have representation." City Attorney McLean Pitts was assigned to look into the legal aspects of this request, and the result of his inquiry undoubtedly left him flabbergasted. In the autumn of 1971 he returned to the council with the startling news that the method by which Selma elected its governing body was in violation of state law, and moreover that the council had actually been illegally constituted ever since the census of 1950. Under the terms of the Code of Alabama, when the population of Selma had passed twenty thousand in 1950, the council had been required to abandon at-large elections in favor of elections by ward, unless the council by two-thirds vote had agreed to reduce its membership to five; only in that case could it retain at-large selection. The provisions of the code were mandatory, and Selma's default was clear; a suit in state court by black leaders—or by anyone else—would certainly produce an immediate holding to that effect and might well also call into question all of the council's actions over the past twenty-one years.

This information produced a sharp division within the council. The existing method of choosing council members, under which two members were obliged to reside in each of Selma's five wards but all ten were elected by all of the city's voters, could not be continued, but neither of the two prescribed new methods appeared entirely satisfactory. The conversion to ward elections would almost unquestionably lead to the election of black council members in the two wards in which blacks had substantial voting majorities. And though whites would still have a seven-to-four majority— the six members from the three majority-white wards, together with the council president, elected from the city at large—four of the incumbent members would therefore lose their seats. On the other hand, the reduction of the council to five meant that six of the incumbents—five of the ward councilmen and the council president, whose position would be abolished—would necessarily be displaced. And because there would no longer be wards, all five of the new councilmen could live in the same area of the city. For that reason, the council elected at large seemed a less representative body even to some councilmen who had no strong sense that excluding blacks posed any particular problem of representativeness. But other councilmen thought that the inclusion of blacks on the council when they were a minority of the citizenry offended the principle of majority rule; Councilman R. E. Krebs said that the ward election plan "discards democracy," and Councilman Luther Pepper, who lived in one of the majority-black wards, stated, "The minority of whites in my ward have been deprived, not of their right to vote but their voting power [by changing to ward election], and I'm going to fight for them." Councilman Grady Adams, however, believed that permitting the election of black councilmen might allow black Selmians to develop leaders alternative to the radical preacher-politicians who, he thought, too often spoke for them.

Amidst these muddled efforts to discern the true meaning of democracy, the proper theory of representation and the plan most likely to produce their own reelection, the council members lurched toward a decision through a series of acrimonious meetings, public hearings, and preliminary votes in early 1972. Finally, at a tension-filled special meeting on February 7, the council voted six to five to choose the five-member, at-large election plan. But because the state code specified that this structure could be adopted only by a two-thirds vote, the result was to leave Selma with the ward-election arrangement which the code prescribed for all cities of Selma's population class that did not avail themselves of the five-member, at-large exception. It was hardly an unqualified acceptance of black inclusion in the city's governance. Nevertheless, Edwin Moss expressed black Selma's "deep and profound gratitude" for the outcome. And the *Selma Times-Journal* commented editorially that though ward election "has drawn some criticism from predictable sources," yet "the general reaction has been gratification," because "conscience[s] in the white community have been troubled by election set-ups which deprived half of Selma's citizens of direct representation on the Council. The white community knew, though loath at times to voice or to act on that knowledge, that in all fairness the black community should have voting members in city government. . . . A City Council representing all the people of Selma should unite us in the support of programs designed to make this a better home town for us all."

Such were the moderates' hopes as Selma prepared in August to elect its first biracial governing body in a century. Blacks offered no opponents either to Mayor Smitherman or to council president Carl Morgan; Morgan had been a principal champion of ward election on the council, and Smitherman, as we have seen, had been taking vigorous steps to integrate the police force and other city agencies. The new government, nevertheless, proved even more of a partnership than municipal leaders had expected, because of an accidental circumstance. In the majority-white third ward, black carpenter and Voters League activist Ernest Doyle filed to run against the white incumbent Martin Coon, but race-line voting in the ward would of course have doomed his candidacy. After the close of qualification but before the election, however, Coon suddenly died, leaving Doyle unopposed. This happenstance meant that five of the ten ward councilmen, rather than four as everyone had expected, were black. Only the at-large election of President Morgan allowed whites to retain a six-to-five majority. The council that took office in the fall of 1972 thus represented a truly extraordinary departure for the Queen City of the Black Belt.[10]

This council, nearly equally divided between the races, squabbled its way through the next four years. In 1976 Ernest Doyle was defeated by white Billy Driggers, and the council then gained the seven-to-four racial division that had generally been expected when ward election had initially been adopted. But at the same time, the city pressed ahead—if often reluctantly—with the integration of its governmental institutions. In the spring of 1977, under the threat of a federal court order, the state legislature passed a local act abolishing the self-perpetuating feature of the Selma school board, making it instead subject to appointment by the city council. Thereafter, two members of the eleven-member board were to be appointed to five-year terms each year, and three in the fifth year. An agreement among council members led to the appointment of a member from each race, so that at the end of the initial five-year process the board contained six white and five black members.

In the meantime, however, the city's economy had suffered a blow from which it would never fully recover. In March 1976 the Defense Department announced its intention to close Craig Air Force Base, and the process was completed at the beginning of 1977. Craig had been the backbone of municipal prosperity ever since its establishment in 1940. In 1976 it had 1,900 military and 770 civilian personnel; its monthly payroll sustained Selma's retail sector, and the constant rotation of servicemen and their families was essential to the local real estate market. Moreover, the installation's presence had critical implications for the city's balance of racial power. In the 1950s, in great part because of the base and its economic effects, whites had come to outnumber blacks in Selma's population, for the first time in municipal history. They retained this advantage throughout the 1960s and 1970s. But following Craig's closure in 1977, the white population began to decline. In the 1980 census, for the first time in three decades, blacks regained numerical superiority, 14,000 to 12,500.[11]

The changes in Selma's population form an essential part of the background to the initiation at this time of one of the most characteristic, and one of the most debilitating, features of Selma's life over the next twenty years: the persistent resort to the federal courts to determine the structure of the community's political institutions. The first of these suits, filed in October 1978, reflected the frustration of blacks in rural Dallas County at their continuing exclusion from any share in the county's governance. Though blacks had always represented a majority of the county's population—55 percent of it in 1980—the fact that both the county commission and the county board of education were elected at large, and that white turnout rates were always significantly greater than those of blacks, meant that both bodies continued to have only white members. It was clear that if the county were divided into districts, the result would be exactly what it had been for Selma's city council in 1972. But unlike black residents of the city, their counterparts in the county did not have a state law on their side. County officials therefore had nothing to induce them to give up their seats voluntarily, and every inducement not to; they ignored repeated black requests that they move to district election. Black leaders turned to the Justice Department and persuaded it to file suit challenging the at-large election system. But it would be more than a decade before this controversy reached a resolution.

In the meantime, rising black registration and changing white residential patterns had delivered blacks a majority in the third of Selma's five wards and thus the possibility of increasing their numbers from four to six of the eleven-member council. In May 1980, as the municipal election of that year approached, frightened west Selma whites filed suit, claiming formally that the growth of their first ward required a readjustment of its boundaries, though their true aim, of course, was to force the consequent readjustment of the third ward. In order to give himself time to hear the case, U.S. District Judge W. Brevard Hand—who had succeeded Daniel H. Thomas in 1971—dissevered the at-large mayoral and council president election from the election of the ward council members, permitting the former to go forward in July but postponing the latter to September. Subsequently, as a temporary measure pending the redistricting that would be necessary once the final results of the 1980 census were known, Judge Hand altered the boundaries of the five wards, divided them into northern and southern halves, and ordered all ten ward councilmen to run from what were now actually single-member districts. The white plaintiffs were delighted because the effect of this decree was to create a white majority in the northern half of ward three and a black majority in the southern half. The resultant council would have five white and five black ward members, together with the white council president, whereas under the malapportioned existing wards and the traditional arrangement of two members per ward, blacks would have had a majority. Black councilmen Frederick D. Reese and John D. Hunter—respectively, the president of the Voters League during the 1965 demonstrations and the president of the NAACP at the time of the 1955 school integration petition—announced that they would appeal the order to the Fifth Circuit, but the effort proved unsuccessful. The council election in September produced the predicted division of six whites and five blacks. However, Judge Hand retained jurisdiction of the case to pass upon the redistricting plan that this council was to enact under the new census. The stage was thus set for renewed racial conflict during the coming four years.

These two suits—the one filed in response to the pleas of the scorned blacks in the county, the other filed by the apprehensive whites in the city—define the community's dilemma. The issues they raised, of county commission and city council districting, would remain constantly before the federal courts for the remainder of the twentieth century. Districting, though the quintessential political question, is never one that political institutions can easily solve, because the boundaries imposed will determine personal and partisan fortunes. Nevertheless, politicians' common commitment to a practical, negotiated settlement of the dispute that can seek to take account of the wishes and needs of the myriad economic and social factions and interest groups of which the community is composed, in contrast to the abstract mathematical solution likely to be imposed by the courts, will in most areas permit representative bodies, with however much ill will, to argue their way to a compromise. But in Selma, as in other southern communities like it, the historical division of race can seem so completely to submerge other distinctions, and the fears and re-sentiments surrounding race can remain so powerful and so obdurate, that the capacity of political institutions to locate an acceptable accommodation is severely diminished. The situation in Selma throughout this period was, moreover, greatly exacerbated by the fact that the two races were so nearly equal in numbers. Every outcome of every disagreement was measured by the bulk of the community with one standard: when the white half benefited, the black half lost, and vice versa. For this reason, the grudging agreement of Selma's city council to move to ward elections in 1972—a concession in considerable measure coerced by state law—remained a unique event in the community's annals. Subsequently, redistricting virtually always had to be dictated by the federal courts.

The availability of the courts for this purpose proved both a blessing in the immediate term and a curse in the longer term. If the courts had been unwilling to intervene, these significant alterations in the distribution of racial power in the community almost certainly could not have been accomplished without the fiercest acrimony, and public demonstrations on a scale at least equal to those of 1965. Legal proceedings thus permitted the later transitions in race relations to take place more pacifically than had that initial one. On the other hand, if the community had been permitted to work out its own fate through internal conflict, with federal intervention preserved for only the most extreme circumstances, the residents of the area could thus eventually have begun to develop a sense of the all too often obscure and all too fragile common interests on the basis of which they could perhaps have composed their differences. The immediate resort to the courts whenever racial quarrels arose, and the resultant imposition of a settlement from an authority extrinsic to the community, left whites to nourish the perception, so apparent to visitors during these years, that federal power was engaged in an essentially vindictive persecution of their region and city, requiring a series of revolutions in social and political practice that were both punitive and unfair. Concurrently, younger blacks more and more forfeited the understanding that had been the civil rights generation's supreme intellectual achievement, that their world could be changed by their own actions. The majority of both groups joined in the deep conviction that their destiny was not really theirs to determine. Because, in the final analysis, most of the community always expected the terms of resolution for its conflicts to be defined by alien mandate, the community very soon lost the will to fashion an internal compromise. And eventually it lost even the recognition that it had a responsibility to try.

In the meantime, in 1979 the mercurial Mayor Smitherman, evidently exhausted by the strains of the council's constant racial bickering and the city's declining economic fortunes following the closure of Craig, suddenly resigned; he was succeeded in office by council president Carl Morgan. Morgan at once announced his candidacy for a full term in the 1980 elections. Selma's Republicans decided that the moment was opportune to attempt to gain the mayoralty for their party, and the state's Republican National Committeewoman, Mrs. Jean Sullivan, the wife of a Selma businessman, therefore filed to oppose Morgan. During his brief tenure, the frugal Morgan annoyed many city employees by depriving them of a number of perquisites. And black Selmians became increasingly fearful at the prospect of a Republican municipal executive. These two groups joined to convince Smitherman to attempt to regain the office he had just vacated. The result was the most heated mayoral election since 1964 and a smashing triumph for Smitherman. He swept the black precincts, taking three-fourths of the black vote, and thanks primarily to this backing, he was reelected with 56 percent of the poll, to 26 percent for Mrs. Sullivan and 17 percent for Morgan. Councilman William Porter was chosen to succeed Morgan as council president, also on the strength of black support.[12]

The municipal administration elected in 1980 thus had the ten ward council members divided equally between the races and a mayor and council president who had each been elected in great part because of black votes. Black Selma could therefore reasonably look forward to a council redistricting, once the final census returns had been received, that would reflect its new numerical superiority. The actual result was very different. White and black council members proved utterly incapable of reaching a compromise on the redistricting, and the dispute soon again ended up before Judge Hand. The judge too sought to encourage a settlement, but racial fears and animosities prevented any agreement. Finally, in June 1984, a frustrated Hand startled both races by entering an order reducing the council from eleven members to six, with five of the members to be chosen from wards and the council president at large. The first and second wards were, respectively, 89 percent and 67 percent white; the fourth and fifth wards were 77 percent and 91 percent black. The third ward was 45 percent white and 55 percent black. Hand stated that the districting gave blacks an "excellent opportunity" to gain control of the council. Optimistic blacks and pessimistic whites in Selma agreed. But the city's racial divisions would prove more intractable than these observers suspected. Counting on the city's new black majority, black councilman Frederick Reese entered the mayoral contest against the incumbent Joe Smitherman, while black councilman Raymond Major opposed three white councilmen and former council president Carl Morgan for the council presidency. In the crucial third ward, conservative black leader Edwin Moss ran against white incumbent George "Cap" Swift. The result was an overwhelming white victory. Smitherman defeated Reese by 61 percent to 38 percent, and Morgan defeated Major in a runoff by 59 percent to 41 percent. Only about half of registered blacks actually voted, and of those who did, nearly a fifth voted for Smitherman. In the third ward, Swift took 52 percent of the poll to Moss's 44 percent. The council thus had four white to two black members, a disastrous decline for blacks from the near-equal division they had previously held.

Major said that as a result of this election, blacks now found themselves in deep political trouble. And Reese said that blacks would have to reassess their situation in the city; he was particularly distressed by the extent of the black desertion from his own candidacy. But it was the reaction of another black leader to this defeat that would turn it in the longer term into a Pyrrhic victory for Selma's whites. Black attorney J. L. Chestnut told a reporter immediately after the counting of the votes that Reese had been foolish to have used temperate rhetoric in an attempt to gain the votes of white moderates, rather than having tried to galvanize the black community with a stridently racial appeal. Southern whites would rarely vote for a black candidate, no matter how able, if blacks were a majority of the population, he said, because of whites' immense dread of black domination. In a contest of this character, therefore, the real key to black success had to be engendering sufficient anger among black voters to raise their turnout rate above that of whites, rather than a mild approach that would seek to calm whites' fears. Chestnut's analysis of the source of Reese's defeat in 1984 would rule his conduct for the remainder of the century. He would reiterate it frequently and act upon it persistently.

In 1972, Chestnut had formed a law partnership with Hank and Rose Sanders, young black attorneys who had recently arrived in the city. Hank Sanders, a native of Baldwin County on Alabama's Gulf coast, had met his future wife while both were students in the Harvard Law School. They had chosen to settle in Selma because of their passionate mutual desire to eliminate the various racial injustices that persisted especially in the Black Belt. Rose Sanders brought with her to the South a deep conviction that the region's whites were quite generally and implacably inimical to her race—a conviction that her experiences in Selma served only to sharpen. Her husband, more prudent by nature and considerably more inclined to seek compromise, was nevertheless equally committed to racial reform and was therefore easily subject to being stirred by Rose's intensity. At just the time that the municipal election of 1984 was convincing Chestnut of the political necessity of aggressively invoking racially divisive themes, legislative reapportionment was delivering substantial local influence to his law firm. The apportionment that the legislature had initially enacted after the census of 1980 had produced the election in 1982 of the Selma area's first black legislator, state representative James L. Thomas. He joined the white incumbent, William F. "Noopie" Cosby, Jr., in the lower house. But Hank Sanders had been narrowly defeated in a race for the state senate. However, statewide black leaders associated with Joe Reed's Alabama Democratic Conference, dissatisfied with the number of black districts that the new apportionment had created, filed suit against it in federal court. The legislature, meeting in special session early in 1983, responded by enacting a revised apportionment that significantly increased black member-ship, and the federal court thereupon ordered the changes into immediate effect. One of the alterations divided Selma, placing the black eastside and the white westside in different senatorial districts. The state Democratic Executive Committee selected Hank Sanders to represent the new black district; he joined in the Senate the white incumbent who had defeated him the year before, ardent Wallaceite and former White Citizens' Coun-cil chairman Earl Goodwin, provoking the local witticism that Selma now had separate but equal state senators. Two years later, in late 1985, Sanders and Chestnut joined Birmingham mayor Richard Arrington and state senator Michael Figures of Mobile to create the New South Coalition as a rival to Reed's ADC. This maneuver resulted in delivering to Chestnut's law firm a pivotal role in black politics in the Dallas County area. Chest-nut's now clearly defined strategic convictions, Hank Sanders's growing influence in state politics, Rose Sanders's fervent desire to vanquish the white oppressor, and their firm's increasing ability to dictate the identity of many black officeholders all combined with whites' anxiety about their declining proportion of the population to render the racial middle ground in Selma—never very firm in any case—more and more tenuous after 1985.[13]

In the near term, however, the cause of interracial amity continued to look reasonably hopeful. During the summer of 1985, moderates of both races joined to create a biracial monthly meeting over dinner, the Salt and Pepper Club. At the same time, black Randall Miller, a longtime ally of Smitherman's who had headed Selma's urban renewal program since 1972, was named the city's personnel director. The Salt and Pepper Club's meet-ings were discontinued because of declining attendance in 1986, but in that year attorney Nathaniel Walker became the region's first black mem-ber of the judiciary when he was chosen as one of Dallas County's two state district judges. In 1987 the city school board appointed Selma's first black superintendent of education, Dr. Norward Roussell of New Orleans. In the same year, one of the white councilmen elected in 1984 resigned, and two white council members—over the protests of the third—joined the two black ones to appoint the black moderate leader Edwin Moss to the vacancy. Moss's inauguration at the end of July gave the six-member council an equal racial division as it prepared to attempt to arrive at a redistricting in preparation for the municipal election of 1988.

Leaders of both races agreed that a council of only six members was too small to be representative of a city of Selma's size. This fact, along with the goad of the ever-pending federal court suit, pushed the council members and the parties to the litigation to an agreement on a council with four black and four white wards, together with a president elected at large. This arrangement would, of course, restore a one-vote white majority, rather than the existing equal division, and so represented a concession from the blacks. On the other hand, a decision to retain Judge Hand's five wards had already proven its likelihood of giving whites a four-to-two majority at the next election, so the redistricting also represented a concession from the whites. At almost the same time, the decade-old federal court challenge to the at-large election of the county commission and board of education at last achieved its goal. In 1982 Judge Hand had decided this case in favor of the commission and the board, but in 1984, the Court of Appeals had reversed his decision. Judge Hand had therefore reluctantly proceeded to design a district plan for the two bodies, and in 1987, over the objection of the Justice Department, he ordered into effect a proposal for both of them under which two black-majority and two white-majority districts would be created, and a fifth member would be elected from the county at large. The Justice Department appealed, maintaining that Judge Hand had in effect left whites in control of each body. In an opinion issued in July 1988, the new Eleventh Circuit let its frustration with Judge Hand's recalcitrance show. Rather than return the case to the district court for further proceedings, the majority of the circuit court panel issued their own decree creating three majority-black and two majority-white districts for the school board, in accordance with the Justice Department's desires. Judge Hand then capitulated and accepted the same districts for the county commission as well. The result was the election at the end of the year of two whites and three blacks—one of them, Perry Varner, the brother-in-law of Rose Sanders and the office manager for Chestnut's and the Sanderses' law firm—to the county commission. At the same time, three whites and two blacks were chosen to the board of education; a white incumbent succeeded in being reelected in one of the new majority-black districts.

The newly constituted county commission immediately proceeded to replace whites with blacks throughout the county bureaucracy. Bruce Boynton—William and Amelia Boynton's son, and the appellant in the 1960 U.S. Supreme Court decision that had produced the Freedom Rides—became the county attorney. The commission and the county school board were the last of the area's governing bodies to be integrated. All of Selma's various municipal boards had long since had black members. By 1990, more than a third of the police force, a quarter of the fire department, and a majority of city employees overall were black. In addition to the personnel director, the head of the sanitation department was also black. With the addition of black officials at the county courthouse, therefore, the government of the area was now at last thoroughly biracial.

But J. L. Chestnut and the Sanderses by no means greeted this progress with unalloyed satisfaction. Chestnut and his partners fumed at the credit Mayor Smitherman was accorded for much of it in parts of the black community. In his newspaper column, in radio appearances, and in speeches to black organizations and churches, Chestnut repeatedly emphasized—and of course correctly—that the presence of blacks on the boards that governed federally funded programs was required by federal regulation, that the better part of the city's hiring of blacks had resulted from court action or the threat of it, and that the city's new public works projects in black neighborhoods were paid for with federal aid earmarked specifically for that purpose. Smitherman was engaged, he asserted—considerably more controversially—in a sort of public relations confidence game, taking credit for things he had been forced to do to benefit blacks while in fact ensuring that all real power remained in white hands. And most controversially of all, he asserted that Smitherman—through flattery, and through according them the semblance, though not the substance, of authority—had managed to place many of the city's black officeholders in his pocket and that Smitherman's black appointees to city boards were almost uniformly timid moderates who were reluctant to stand up for blacks' true interests. Chestnut was unsparing in his criticism of black councilmen such as Frederick Reese, Edwin Moss, and Lorenzo Harrison, city board of education members such as Marshall Cleveland and Charles Lett, and other moderate black leaders. And he searched constantly for an issue that would demonstrate the truth of his claims and unite the black community in support of his attitudes and allies.

Smitherman soon was responding in kind. Chestnut, unlike Reese, had played only the most peripheral role in the civil rights movement, Smitherman correctly noted, and having missed the opportunity to cut a significant figure in the events that had revolutionized his community, he sought now to generate a sort of junior civil rights movement, of which he could be a leader. Selma already had achieved extraordinary changes, but as proven by the actions of the new black-majority county commission in immediately replacing all of the white officials with blacks, Chestnut and his associates would be satisfied only when whites had been completely eliminated from local authority, Smitherman claimed. Such heated rhetoric further assisted the process of polarization that Chestnut sought. The 1988 mayoral election made an additional contribution to the developing conflict. Black councilman Cleophus Mann opposed Smitherman and a minor white candidate, Coy Darby. Mann conducted a quiet campaign, and many confident whites therefore failed to vote; turnout fell from more than 10,700 in 1984 to fewer than 7,000. The result was that Mann ran a much closer race than Reese had. Smitherman finished with some 54 percent of the vote, to 40 percent for Mann and 6 percent for Darby. Mann at once announced that the official returns did not coincide with the figures compiled by his supporters; his own totals indicated the necessity of a runoff, he said, and the official returns appeared to be based on fraud. The other two black councilmen joined his accusations, and when the council met for the formal canvass of the poll, the members, on a race-line vote of three to three, refused to certify the results. Acrimony and disorder reigned at the meeting; two black spectators were arrested for threatening to assault the mayor. Mann eventually abandoned his contest, but the episode left a heritage of bitterness in the black community. The next year Smitherman appointed a committee to plan an official commemoration of the twenty-fifth anniversary of the 1965 demonstrations, with Frederick Reese and white moderate banker Rex Morthland serving as co-chairmen. Moderates of both races regarded this action as a public recognition of the fact that the movement had emancipated white Selmians quite as much as black and had made the city a more just and better place for them all. The initiative drew warm praise from national commentators. But Chestnut and his associates stridently proclaimed that they would disrupt any ceremonies the city sought to stage with aggressive protests. Senator Sanders asserted that the mayor was seeking to take over the anniversary merely to benefit Selma's public relations; blacks must insist on the ownership of their own history, he said—clearly implying a denial of the moderates' belief that the movement had equally transformed the lives of whites. As a result of these clamorous threats, the city at last dissolved its biracial committee and left the commemoration to an all-black group headed by the Sanderses.[14]

It was against this background of rising racial mistrust that Selma moved toward the convulsion of 1990. Shortly after Norward Roussell, the new black school superintendent, took office in June 1987, a group of black parents led by Alice Boynton, wife of attorney Bruce Boynton, and Ronald Peoples, dean of students at Selma University, formed the Best Education Support Team (BEST) to press for improvements in public education. One of BEST's first actions was to urge Roussell to look into the system of grouping students according to their intellectual abilities that was in effect in core academic subjects in the high school and middle schools. This tracking system had been instituted in 1970, in preparation for the general integration of the schools in 1971. The integration plan ordered by the federal courts to begin in September 1971 provided for the city's eight neighborhood elementary schools to feed into two middle schools, Eastside and Westside. The middle schools fed into a single high school, the formerly white Parrish High, which was renamed Selma High; the black Hudson High was eliminated. Under this plan, because of neighborhood segregation, most of the integration would take place in the high school and in Westside Middle School; Eastside Middle would be virtually all black, and the elementary schools would generally retain clear racial identities. Despite the quite modest nature of the integration thus decreed, it was sufficient, as we have seen, to lead to a massive white desertion of the public schools for the segregated Morgan Academy and another white private school created at this time, Meadowview Christian. In an effort to stem this tide, the principal of Parrish High suggested the assignment of students in the new Selma High to three ability levels in English, mathematics, science, and social studies classes. The school board never formally approved the idea, but it was implemented at the high school and subsequently was extended as well to English and mathematics classes in the middle schools. This arrangement remained in effect for the next two decades, and it did in fact succeed in stabilizing the system's enrollment at 70 percent black and 30 percent white.

BEST's leaders denounced the tracking system in inflammatory terms. Chestnut and Rose Sanders asserted that at Selma High, 90 percent of white students and only 3 percent of black ones were placed in the honors classes, level one—a claim that, as it appears from a subsequent statistical analysis, did not even approximate the truth. A principal source of Rose Sanders's anger is not at all difficult to discern; the Sanderses' daughter Malika had been placed in level two, and Mrs. Sanders repeatedly referred to this fact as clear proof of the system's injustice. Nevertheless, Roussell's study of the system did convince him that it was poorly administered. The difficulty stemmed, he thought, from the fact that the criteria for placing students contained such subjective standards as motivation to learn, which left great scope for the exercise of teachers' judgments. In the meantime, Selma had begun to administer standardized achievement tests to all its public school students, and Roussell discovered that students' scores on these tests frequently did not reflect their class placements. He therefore proposed to the school board that all obviously subjective criteria be eliminated from the placement standards and that students be assigned to levels solely on the basis of grades and test scores. This plan produced vigorous debate, but in January 1989 a closely divided board voted—largely along racial lines—to apply the new standards to the two middle schools and the ninth grade at Selma High beginning the following September, and then to let the standards rise through the high school by a grade a year until they became general in September 1992.

An examination of the level assignments in the ninth-grade English classes in September 1989, in contrast with those in the tenth, eleventh, and twelfth grades, reveals that the real impact of the reform was upon the remedial track, level three. Only two whites and between forty and fifty blacks were assigned to level three in each of the three upper grades. But in the ninth grade, the number of students in the remedial classes soared; the number of blacks doubled, to ninety-two, and the number of whites rose sevenfold, to fourteen. These increases, of course, correspondingly diminished the proportion of students in level two. It is clear that teachers had previously been quite reluctant to assign students to the remedial level—and especially reluctant to assign white ones to it—and that the inclusion of subjective criteria in the assignment standards had given them justification for avoiding this unpleasant decision. BEST, on the other hand, had expected the principal changes to occur at the other end of the scale in the division between levels two and one. But here the new standards made much less significant difference. In the upper three grades, operating under the more subjective standards, the honors classes were 53 percent white and 47 percent black, whereas in the ninth grade, under the new criteria, they were 48 percent white and 52 percent black. There thus may well have been a slight tendency under the older system for teachers to concede the ability of white children, but it was by no means a marked one. In the ninth grade, 37 percent of white students were in level one, 50 percent in level two, and 13 percent in level three, while in the upper grades, 34 percent of whites were in level one, 64 percent in level two, and 2 percent in level three. The corresponding figures for blacks in the ninth grade were 16 percent in level one, 51 percent in level two, and 33 percent in level three, whereas in the upper grades, 15 percent were in level one, 66 percent in level two, and 19 percent in level three.[15]

The outcome of Superintendent Roussell's reform, therefore, was not at all what BEST had imagined it would be. But if the black parents in BEST were surprised, it appears that many whites were equally so. Most of the white members of the school board had been dubious of the new criteria, and substantial numbers of white parents were apprehensive about their potential effects. This white anxiety was doubtless exacerbated by the decision of the board in July 1989 to promote Frederick Reese—still regarded by some whites as a radical because of his leadership of the 1965 demonstrations—from his position as principal of Eastside Middle School to become Selma High's first black principal. There is every reason to believe that white parents' misgivings about Roussell's actions, and their quiet pressure on white board members to resist his plans, played a role in the decision of the white board members to unite to send Roussell a letter—at the same time that they voted to promote Reese, and before the actual results of the new tracking standards had become fully known—warning him of their assessment that he made program changes too hastily and without clear objectives and that his relations with his staff were poor. Roussell's contract, which would expire in June 1990, required that the board notify him by the end of December 1989 whether or not they intended to renew it. This letter from a majority of the board in July 1989 therefore boded ill for his employment prospects. Though the letter was confidential, knowledge of it soon became widespread in the black community, and blacks across the ideological spectrum began to rally to the superintendent's cause—in large measure, it seems, on racial grounds.

Although it appears quite probable that the controversy over tracking crucially influenced Roussell's fate, the subsequent insistence of Chestnut, Rose Sanders, and their BEST allies that the board fired Roussell solely because he had paid attention to BEST's complaints about the tracking system is misleading in important respects. In the first place, the white board members' repeated assertion that they had well-founded doubts about Roussell's administrative skills is by no means unbelievable; in later years, as superintendent of Macon County schools, Roussell presided over a series of actions that drove that system into bankruptcy and receivership. In the second place, Roussell and BEST held very different views about the value of grouping students according to ability. Chestnut, the Sanderses, and the rest of the BEST leadership regarded tracking as a remnant of white supremacy—an attitude fortified by the fact that the plan had been initially adopted in response to the general integration of the schools—and they wished to see it eliminated altogether. Roussell, however, insisted that grouping by ability was absolutely indispensable to effective education. While he had been willing to reexamine the criteria for placement, he wanted if anything to extend and strengthen the tracking system; indeed, he favored the creation of a separate high school open only to honors students. As we have seen, if anyone involved in the controversy had bothered to examine the real effects of Roussell's reform, it would have been apparent at once that, far from dismantling tracking, he had actually made it a good deal more demanding. Finally, BEST strenuously proclaimed that the goal of the board members who terminated Roussell was to replace him with a white person who would restore the former placement standards. But in fact, the same whites who voted not to renew Roussell's contract voted subsequently to appoint another black—Roussell's chief assistant, James Carter—as his successor, and the new superintendent left the revised criteria untouched.

If the situation was more complicated than BEST's description of it, however, there can be no doubt that the BEST membership was sincere in believing that Roussell was simply the victim of white racial prejudice. And the foundation for this conviction was, of course, the historical experience of racial discrimination and conflict in Selma and the vast mutual distrust that this history had bequeathed to the city's residents. Chestnut reports that, without ever having met Roussell, he had initially suspected that Roussell represented a Trojan horse through whom whites intended to betray black interests, simply because the board that appointed Roussell had a white majority. Later, when that white majority refused to renew Roussell's contract, Chestnut at once took up Roussell's cause, even though, as we have seen, the two men's views on educational matters differed sharply. Similarly, it appears that many whites were suspicious of Roussell's reform of the placement criteria merely because he was black. And the white board members and other white city officials passed up numerous opportunities for compromise during the crisis that resulted from Roussell's termination seemingly principally—perhaps entirely—because the affair had become for them a racial confrontation. Such racial assumptions doubtless underlay, as well, the almost universal black certitude that Mayor Smitherman was behind Roussell's termination, even though there was no actual evidence for the notion and the mayor himself strongly and repeatedly denied it. Chestnut is frank in his acknowledgment of the city's situation: "Everyone in Selma is warped by race in some way. The white people who run the town see themselves as superior and uniquely suited to rule. While they view . . . black officials as representing the black community, they see themselves as representing the whole community. . . . [On the other hand, it is] hard to persuade me that any white person in power wants to be fair and work on an equal basis with black people. I assume otherwise."[16]

Just as he had done in the summer of 1963, Edwin Moss, the leader of Selma's black moderates, sought in the fall of 1989 to awaken whites to the cataclysm that was rapidly approaching and to push them into some sort of compromise before it was too late. And just as in 1963, white leaders remained utterly deaf to Moss's warnings. In September the school board's president, white banker Carl Barker, had announced his intention to resign from the board. Subsequently, Mayor Smitherman had persuaded him to withdraw the resignation, because the school system was about to sell a large bond issue and Smitherman felt that Barker's technical expertise in this area was essential to the success of the project. But at the end of November, Moss, on behalf of all four black city council members, wrote to Barker to urge him to go ahead with his resignation at once; at the same time, Moss provided a copy of his letter to the press. If Barker would resign, Moss explained, and the council would delay filling the vacancy, it would leave the board with five black and five white members when the question of the renewal of Roussell's contract came up. The result would be that no action could be taken on the question that did not have biracial approval. And only a decision that was biracial would convince blacks that Roussell had not been railroaded out of office by whites. As we shall see, the solution Moss proposed as a temporary measure in November 1989 was essentially the same one the city would adopt as a permanent solution nearly a year later, after months of upheaval. Moss had explicitly warned in his letter that the termination of Roussell without biracial support was certain to lead to demonstrations, boycotts, and racial recrimination, but all he got for his efforts on this occasion was a sharp rebuke from Mayor Smitherman and the rejection of his request by Barker. Smitherman said that Moss's letter was highly improper and reflected intimidation of the councilman by Chestnut and Rose Sanders. He added that Rose Sanders's real goal was to gain for her law firm the representation of the Selma school system that it already had for the schools and county commissions of the surrounding Black Belt counties; she used this position in the other counties to control black teachers and officeholders and to reap retainers of perhaps $350,000 a year, Smitherman said, and Moss was assisting her, whether he knew it or not, in gaining similar power in Selma. White leaders' hostility to the black militants was so great that the whites were unable to distinguish the cautions of the black moderates from the militants' threats.

At its meeting on December 21, the school board proceeded to act just as Moss had feared it would. The senior black member, the moderate Reverend Charles A. Lett, moved that Roussell's contract be extended for an additional three years, and the motion failed on a race-line tie vote of five to five, with President Barker abstaining. All five black board members thereupon walked out; they would not return for eight months. The remaining whites then voted unanimously to terminate the superintendent's employment when his contract expired in June. Before the vote, Selma High guidance counselor Mrs. Otelia Moss told the board that blacks would picket, boycott, and close Selma down if Roussell's contract were not renewed. After the vote, Chestnut announced that he and Senator Sanders would now press for a legislative act to make the board elective. The next day, picketing began at city hall and at two banks with which white board members had connections. Rose Sanders said that the black community was more completely united than at any time since 1965. She called the decision clearly racially motivated, and a direct response to Roussell's efforts to base assignment to honors courses on academic ability rather than, as formerly, on who the students' parents were.

The board's decision had taken place during the schools' Christmas vacation. When classes resumed at the beginning of January, the black protests escalated. On the first day of school, January 3, BEST organized a boycott by black students. Roussell strenuously opposed the boycott, but about a fourth of the system's students, and about a third of those at Selma High, participated anyway. BEST called for a second one-day boycott for January 17, and in the meantime the Sanderses' daughter Malika and Fatima Salaam, the daughter of activist black attorney Yusuf Abdus-Salaam, began leading student demonstrations. Chestnut filed suit in federal court seeking a declaration that the 1977 legislative act that had converted the Selma school board from self-perpetuating to appointive by the city council, even though it had been passed in response to a federal court order, was nevertheless void because it had not been submitted to the Justice Department for clearance under the Voting Rights Act. Roussell retained attorneys and threatened to sue on the ground that the vote by the white half of the board to terminate him had been illegal. Three white city council members, in a search for a compromise, joined with the four black ones to expess support for a legislative proposal that would authorize a referendum to see if Selmians wished to change to an elective school board. But this gesture came far too late. On January 17, more than 2,200 of the system's 6,000 students and 123 of its 368 employees joined BEST's boycott. Thereafter, many teachers stopped speaking to each other, and enmities among students in the secondary schools led to a rapidly increasing number of incidents in the halls and on the playing fields.

As the school system slipped toward chaos, Selma's leaders at last began negotiations. Roussell stated his willingness to accept a two-year terminal extension of his contract, but efforts to effect a settlement on this basis collapsed when black school board members refused to meet with white ones unless the whites would agree to the extension in advance and the whites refused to take such a vote without the presence of the blacks. On January 22, Councilman Edwin Moss offered the very plan that seven months later essentially would become the compromise that would end the crisis: that the city council agree to use its statutory authority to appoint two school board members each year in such a way that the board's racial majority would alternate annually. But when the proposal came up for a vote on February 19, City Attorney Henry Pitts—the son of the late McLean Pitts, who had succeeded his father in the post—advised the council that Moss's idea would change the tenor of the 1977 act creating the appointive school board by adding a new qualification not contained in the act, and that because BEST had filed suit challenging the legality of the act in any case, the council should take no action affecting the board until the suit had been decided. On the basis of this advice, the white council members joined to reject the plan on a race-line vote, five to four. It is very difficult to believe that Pitts's opinion could have resulted from dispassionate legal analysis. Ever since the enactment of the statute creating the appointive board, as we have seen, the council had been appointing one black and one white in each year that two vacancies occurred, and one black and two whites in the fifth year, when there were three vacancies. If this procedure, which perpetually maintained a board with six whites and five blacks, was thought entirely permissible under the statute, the notion that merely for the council to decide to appoint two blacks or two whites in a given year would add a new qualification to the act is surely a singular conclusion. And if the parties to the BEST litigation had agreed upon a settlement to the suit, the federal court would unquestionably have accepted it. Indeed, the agreement of the following August embodies both of these outcomes. It would seem clear, therefore, that Pitts's counsel, which for the present effectively precluded the acceptance of Moss's compromise, could only have proceeded from the attorney's anger at the black protesters and his determination that they gain no advantage from their actions. His personal rage condemned the community to months of additional turmoil.

In the meantime, the situation had greatly deteriorated. At the now all-white school board's meeting of February 1, Rose Sanders, Perry Varner, and their supporters attempted to disrupt the proceedings with singing and clapping. When the board members tried to conduct business over the noise, Mrs. Sanders threatened to sue them for acting without due deliberation. Smitherman thereupon issued a statement saying that Superintendent Roussell was working in collusion with her because he had failed to control her behavior. Following this spectacle, the school board at a special meeting on February 4 relieved Roussell of all duties—as punishment, it said, for the disruptions perpetrated by his supporters—and appointed

Frederick Reese as interim superintendent in his stead. Roussell called this action proof that whites did not believe blacks capable of educating their own children. Mrs. Sanders pronounced it a declaration of all-out war, and added that the appointment of Reese was merely a ruse by the white board members to conceal their actual goal of appointing a white as Roussell's permanent successor. The next day twenty BEST supporters led by Mrs. Sanders went to Smitherman's office, and when she and associates in her law firm Perry Varner and Carlos Williams attempted to force their way in, a melee ensued, at the end of which they were arrested and carried bodily from the building. Mrs. Sanders was hospitalized for abrasions, muscle hyperextension, and hoarseness and alleged that she had suffered these injuries because of the brutality of the arresting white policeman, Officer Ronnie Rushing. Intense black pressure on Reese compelled him to resign as interim superintendent on February 6. The board then reluctantly reinstated Roussell, but voted at the same time to close down the entire system until the safety of the students could be assured. Earlier in the day, Selma High had been closed because of a number of disorders there, but this action had proven a tactical error when the students thus released, led by adults from BEST, had gone to Westside Middle and run through the school, disrupting classes and badly frightening many of the younger children.

The schools remained closed from February 7 through February 12. During this week a surge of white withdrawals from the system commenced. Chestnut had repeatedly asserted that all white students whose parents could afford private education had long since withdrawn from the public schools and that the white moderates' fear of a further decline in white enrollment was chimerical, but events demonstrated that, as was so often the case, he had exaggerated to himself the extent of Selma's existing racial polarization. By the end of the month the number of white children in the system had fallen by more than a third, and the number at Selma High by more than 40 percent. Only about a third of the nearly two hundred white students who withdrew from the high school had been assigned to level one, indicating that it was primarily the turmoil and fear of violence, rather than any anticipated alteration in educational policy, that drove their decision. The immediate beneficiaries of the withdrawals were, of course, the city's two private schools. But over the coming months an even more alarming development manifested itself: a large number of young white parents began to abandon the city altogether, many of them moving to the nearby but overwhelmingly white town of Prattville. The near anarchy in the public schools clearly was dealing a powerful blow to the dream—never very widely shared, in any case—of an integrated Selma.

Meanwhile, the situation continued to degenerate. On February 8 a group of about three hundred students, led by several BEST adults, got into the closed high school and began an occupation of the school cafeteria.

At the same time, a group of one hundred led by Senator Sanders, Perry Varner, and Ronald Peoples began an occupation of city hall, effectively shutting city government down. The city petitioned the federal court for an injunction against these demonstrations, but U.S. District Judge Charles R. Butler refused to grant it when Chestnut assured him that interference with city and school functions would cease. On February 12, the students occupying the high school cafeteria therefore left the school, and the occupiers at city hall were reduced to twenty-five and began allowing city employees back into their offices. On February 13, Governor Guy Hunt called out the National Guard to preserve order at the schools, and with their protection and that of a state trooper contingent, the schools reopened. Demonstrators led by Rose Sanders and Perry Varner rushed the cordon of troopers and guardsmen at Selma High; several managed to get inside, and those who remained outside devoted themselves to personal denunciations of the blacks among the troopers and guardsmen as traitors. Inside, about a third of the students at both the high school and Westside Middle were too frightened to attend, and clashes continued through the day. The following day black protesters targeted white students in an incident in the high school lunchroom; National Guardsmen broke up the melee, and eighty-seven students were suspended. On February 15 the occupation of city hall was resumed. At the same time, Roussell filed suit against the school board, alleging that his termination had violated the Civil Rights Act of 1977 and requesting ten million dollars in damages. And white parents formed the Public Education Support Team (PEST) to demand the firing of teachers who were supporting BEST's activities. It was against this background that City Attorney Pitts convinced white councilmen to reject Edwin Moss's proposal for alternating racial majorities on the school board at the council's meeting of February 19. After the vote, all four black councilmen walked out in disgust.

On February 23, the city filed suit in state court seeking an injunction against the BEST disruptions. At the same time, it filed a counterclaim in BEST's federal court suit against the act creating an appointive school board, alleging that BEST was actually seeking to drive all whites from the public schools and thus to resegregate the system. In the state court suit, both of Selma's circuit judges recused themselves, and the state supreme court assigned Judge Leslie Johnson of Florence to hear it. Judge Johnson undertook active steps to force the parties to a settlement. Between March 16 and March 26 he presided over talks that appeared to have reached a final agreement. But the vast legacy of racial mistrust in Selma caused the negotiations to collapse, and Judge Johnson at last issued the restraining order the city had sought and began fining protesters for contempt. Johnson reported that full agreements had been reached on three occasions but that elements on both sides who did not really want a settlement kept interfering to prevent the implementation of the terms. The city council apparently agreed to create racial balance on the school board, and the board agreed to pay Roussell a substantial sum as severance compensation. But Roussell declined the offer. BEST thereupon filed suit against the school board for having permitted the adoption of the tracking system in 1970 and asked for ten billion dollars in damages. And Chestnut petitioned the state supreme court to remove Judge Johnson from the Selma proceedings—alleging, among other things, that he had a white man's mentality. At about the same time, BEST's opponents filed complaints with the state bar association seeking the disbarment of the various black attorneys who had been involved in the demonstrations, because of their conduct during them; these complaints led eventually to reprimands for Rose Sanders and Yusuf Abdus-Salaam.

After the failure of Judge Johnson's mediation, the conflict gradually settled into a series of acrimonious confrontations in various federal and state courts. By March the actual situation in the schools had begun to calm somewhat, though as we have seen, white withdrawals had reduced the system's white enrollment by that time from 30 percent to 20 percent of the total. But demonstrations at city hall continued on a daily basis. Blacks had been focusing much of their hope on the local bill that Senator Sanders had offered in the state legislature to transform the school board into a popularly elected eight-member body chosen from four majority-black and four majority-white districts. A deal that Sanders had made with his white colleague Earl Goodwin allowed the bill to pass the Senate. But, as local legislation, it required the support of the entire local delegation, and in the House, white representative "Noopie" Cosby, who considered the proposal motivated by political rather than educational considerations, had it buried in committee, where it died when the legislature adjourned at the end of April. Roussell then agreed to resign and drop his lawsuit against the school board in return for a lump-sum payment of $150,000. The board named Roussell's chief assistant, James Carter, as his interim successor. But BEST was not mollified. Just before the end of the school year in May, BEST supporters signed warrants for the arrest of the six white school board members for the alleged criminal offense of having met secretly on February 4 to deliberate upon the temporary appointment of Frederick Reese.

After school ended, the parties to the dispute made another effort to reach a settlement. On June 22 an agreement was concluded under which board president Carl Barker would resign and the city council would leave his position vacant, thus creating an equal racial division on the board. But on June 25, Barker withdrew his consent to do so when his attorneys pointed out to him that he would then cease to be covered by the school system's insurance against legal claims and would be personally liable for any damages BEST succeeded in winning in its various suits. Rather than seek an accommodation with the insurance carrier, city authorities then announced that the agreement could not go forward unless BEST dismissed all of the court actions. "BEST wouldn't drop those lawsuits if the fate of Selma hung in the balance," Chestnut thundered. The settlement therefore collapsed.

On August 16, a three-judge federal court in Mobile heard oral arguments in the BEST suit claiming that the 1977 statute that had created an appointive school board was void because it had not been cleared by the Justice Department under the Voting Rights Act. On August 17, school resumed and Rose Sanders sought to renew the demonstrations. The protests remained small, but they were enough to push moderate black parents into approaching city authorities and BEST leaders on August 22 about the possibility of again trying to conclude a settlement. The city replied that BEST's dismissal of its suits remained a prerequisite to an agreement. But at this point, at the request of white Selma industrialist Larry Striplin, Birmingham mayor Richard Arrington consented to intervene with his New South Coalition colleague Hank Sanders and persuade him to drop the suits. Once Sanders agreed to do so, on August 27, the terms of the settlement that had already been reached on June 22 as to the structure of the school board again became available. Indeed, the terms were essentially those that had been reached during Judge Johnson's mediation on March 23—and, for that matter, that had been offered to the council by Edwin Moss on January 22 and urged in his letter to Carl Barker of November 1989, before the demonstrations had even begun. Barker would resign as soon as BEST had completed dismissing its suits, and he would be succeeded by the senior black board member, Charles Lett. Thereafter the racial identity of the board's president would alternate annually. The president would vote only in case of a tie, and the city council would always maintain an equal racial division among the board's other ten members. On August 28, the council, with one white dissent, accepted this agreement and instructed its attorney to drop all pending charges against protesters. On August 30, the federal court approved the settlement as well. The long crisis was over.[17]

It is understandable that general happiness and considerable optimism attended the council's formal acceptance of the agreement on August 28; it was, after all, the very first time that Selmians had ever managed to settle a racial dispute by themselves, through negotiation. Moderates of both races were bold enough to think that it might represent a new departure. But Selma's demons were not so easily exorcised. Just as the city's economy never fully recovered from the closure of Craig Air Force Base in 1977, so the bitterness engendered by the encounters of 1990 appears to have left permanent social scars. Because neither Chestnut nor Smitherman emerged from the episode the clear victor, neither man saw his vision for the future of the city fully realized; but their collision had so polarized the community that the moderates' vision too was rendered perhaps perpetually quixotic. In a sense, the outcome was the worst of all three worlds. Chestnut had precisely hoped to polarize the city along racial lines, in order to unite blacks behind his leadership in an anti-Smitherman crusade. In large measure he had succeeded in doing so during the protests, but because the crusade had eventuated in a reasonable compromise, the anger on which Chestnut had counted to increase black electoral turnouts was not thereafter present. Smitherman clearly had hoped that his constructive efforts to ameliorate conditions and open opportunities for blacks would over time gather sufficient support from black moderates and politically or economically ambitious black residents to isolate Chestnut, the Sanderses, and their militant supporters permanently into a minority position within the black community. Before 1990 he had had reasonable prospects of doing so, but his passionate hostility toward Chestnut and Rose Sanders in particular and their allies in general had betrayed him into such a vitriolic and inflexible response during the 1990 demonstrations that it completely stripped him, in the eyes of most blacks, of his earlier progressive image. The result of these parallel developments was that Smitherman forfeited the substantial black electoral support that he had earlier had and was left with only white voters, while black turnout nevertheless remained too small to unseat him. And the essentially racial electoral contests that resulted made the moderate dream of interracial cooperation exceedingly difficult to implement.

The moderates' optimism flowing from the successful negotiation of the 1990 settlement was not long in being disappointed. As we have seen, the chaos in the schools had greatly accelerated the tendency of white parents to abandon the city—a tendency that had already been well established in any case because of Selma's faltering economy. The census of 1990, taken in the midst of the crisis, revealed a precipitous decline in Selma's white population, and the decline unquestionably continued over the next several years. By 1990 the white population had fallen to about 9,700, down from some 12,500 in 1980. The portion of the total population that was white—41 percent—was the lowest in all of Selma's history. This result would, of course, require the redrawing of the city council districts to reflect the new black predominance. And the prospect of black control of the city council plunged Selma into a bitter new racial conflict almost as soon as the one over the school board had been settled. The four black council members claimed that City Attorney Henry Pitts concealed from them the preliminary census results and duped them into joining their white colleagues in approving a redistricting ordinance that perpetuated the existing racial division. Pitts denied the charge, but the black council members pronounced him untrustworthy and retained Chestnut to advise them. Their objections caused the Justice Department to deny the ordinance clearance under the Voting Rights Act. At the same time, they filed suit in federal court for an order to compel a fairer reapportionment. And independently, Chestnut's office manager, county commissioner Perry Varner, filed suit to have the at-large election of the council president declared an illegal dilution of the black vote. In response, Judge Brevard Hand dissevered the election of the mayor and council president from that of the eight ward council members, permitting the former to proceed on schedule in August 1992 but postponing the latter until the districting controversy could be decided.

The continuing dispute over the council districts made the mayoral and council president campaigns even more racially charged than they would have been anyway. Smitherman's apparent vulnerability in the black community drew three black opponents into the field against him: former councilman Cleophus Mann, whom Smitherman had defeated in 1988; Councilman Lorenzo Harrison, who had been Smitherman's most dependable black ally on the council; and James Perkins, a businessman who had served as campaign manager for Frederick Reese in 1984. The Reverend Alvin A. Cleveland of the black First Baptist Church opposed council president Carl Morgan, as did white former councilman J. B. Peeke and a minor candidate, Ernest Swift. Voter registration records at this time were inaccurate because of a failure to remove the names of persons who had died or moved. However, a thorough purge of the rolls produced a total of 7,349 black and 5,768 white voters in the city in 1996, figures that are probably also reasonably representative of 1992. But even though the electorate was approximately 56 percent black, the greater white turnout more than balanced this margin. Smitherman took nearly 54 percent of the poll, to 30 percent for Perkins, 10 percent for Mann, and 6 percent for Harrison. Morgan and Cleveland faced each other in a runoff, but in the second round of voting Morgan won handily, by 59 to 41 percent. Nevertheless, there were aspects of the mayoral results that appeared questionable. The total vote polled for mayor was more than 20 percent greater than it had been in 1988, and almost 10 percent greater than the poll in the race for the council presidency held at the same time. Almost 13 percent of the mayoral ballots were absentee, and Smitherman swept the absentee returns, taking nearly 80 percent of these votes. Without the absentee support he would have been forced into a runoff, though very narrowly so. These facts led Perkins to denounce the results as a product of wholesale fraud and to file a contest of them in state court. The proceedings dragged on for more than a year before Circuit Judge Jack Meigs and were eventually settled only when city authorities accepted a consent decree establishing elaborate new ballot security procedures that placed special constraints in future elections on absentee voting.

While the rancorous hearings in Perkins's contest progressed, the council struggled to reach an agreement on the boundaries of its districts. Councilman John Ingram, the white council member whose district was at the heart of the dispute, produced a plan in the fall of 1992 that changed the racial composition of his ward from 60 percent white to 60 percent black, but the black councilmen rejected the proposal because they believed that, given the smaller black turnout, the percentage was insufficient to get a black member elected. They urged instead a plan drawn up by Perry Varner that would place Ingram in a district that was 70 percent black and was also the home of one of the black incumbents. At the end of December, after much contention, the white council members drove the Ingram plan through on a race-line vote, but in March 1993 the Justice Department denied the ordinance Voting Rights Act clearance. At this point a biracial group of moderate citizens, doubtless hoping to build upon the spirit of cooperation that the 1990 school board agreement seemed to have evinced, drew up a compromise proposal that increased the black population of Ingram's ward to 65 percent but avoided placing any two incumbent council members in the same district. Ingram agreed to sponsor this proposal, which became known as the "citizens' plan," and at the beginning of April he and council president Morgan joined the four black councilmen to adopt it, six to three. But at midmonth Mayor Smitherman surprised observers by vetoing the ordinance. "I'm not giving this city to them without a fight," he told the press, in reference to his black opponents. Black leaders, he added, "don't want to share power. All you've got to do is look at the county commission and see what happened when blacks took over there. They got rid of all the whites in key positions almost overnight." The six-member majority that had voted for the citizens' plan was sufficient to override Smitherman's veto, if they all held together, but as soon as Smitherman had publicly opposed the plan, the two whites who had voted with the blacks began to back away from it. They had been willing to accept the proposal as a biracial compromise, but their white constituents would not tolerate their desertion of their race once the color line had been drawn. Four days later, all five white council members joined to sustain the veto, on a race-line vote.

In late May, even though the plan, because of the mayor's veto, now had no official standing, U.S. District Judge Brevard Hand nevertheless ordered it submitted to the Justice Department for approval. In mid-June the Justice Department cleared the proposal. Judge Hand at once ordered it into effect and scheduled a special council election for August, exactly a year after the regular election would have been held. The election produced the expected racial result. For the first time in its history, Selma had a governing body with a black majority. The new council took office at the beginning of October. In December, Judge Hand dismissed Perry Varner's suit against the at-large election of the council president and ordered Varner to pay all court costs.

A longer-term result of the new black power was perhaps more surprising, however: because blacks now controlled the council, they no longer so frequently felt the necessity to vote as a bloc, and whites therefore began at last to make distinctions among blacks' political views. Two former BEST leaders won election to the council. Mrs. Nancy G. Sewell, the Selma High School librarian and the president of Selma's teachers' union, defeated the white incumbent John Ingram. And Yusuf Abdus-Salaam defeated the black incumbent ally of Mayor Smitherman, Lorenzo Harrison; Abdus-Salaam was the militant attorney whom the state bar had reprimanded together with Rose Sanders, and he was the brother of the young civil rights activist Ruby Sales, whose life Jonathan Daniels had saved in Lowndes County in 1965 when Daniels had stepped in front of her and taken the fatal shotgun blast fired by Thomas Coleman. But on the endorsement of Smitherman, the solid support of the white minority in their districts had elected two more moderate blacks as well; Mark West had defeated incumbent Herman Watts, and McArthur Williams, a former city fireman, was chosen to an open seat over BEST activist Bennie Ruth Crenshaw. The fifth black member was Councilman William C. King, the only black incumbent to survive; he defeated former SNCC field secretary Benny L. Tucker, a leader of the 1965 demonstrations. The races between King and Tucker and between Williams and Mrs. Crenshaw would be refought in 1996, with exactly the opposite result in each case, but for the present the election had produced a council of two black activists, three black moderates, and four whites allied with Smitherman. Because six votes were needed to override a veto from the mayor, cooperation among these elements would be necessary if anything were to be accomplished. The outgoing white-majority council had further strengthened Smitherman's hand by adopting an ordinance that transferred the authority to appoint city department heads from the council to the mayor. Any effort by the new council to reverse this action would certainly meet a mayoral veto. Under these circumstances, the council members—tentatively at first, but with increasing goodwill as time passed—began to work together. Smitherman's conviction that the black majority would attempt at once to replace all white city officials proved false. In 1996, as we have just said, an additional two black activists were added to the council, but in the meantime Mrs. Sewell had proven a more moderate figure than some observers had initially expected, and the mayor had further solidified Mark West's friendship by arranging the appointment of West's sister Rachel West Nelson to a position with the municipal court. The result was that the balance of power on the council was not effectively disturbed.

At about the same time, black moderates, with white support, began to emerge both in the area's legislative delegation and on the county commission. In the legislative reapportionment that became effective in 1994, Dallas County's representation became all black. Hank Sanders's senatorial district was extended to encompass the entire area, and the white-majority district that had formerly been represented by Earl Goodwin was eliminated. James L. Thomas retained his seat in the lower house. But the seat that had been held by white representative "Noopie" Cosby passed to black Selmian Edward Maull. Maull, a retired air force sergeant, was the city's single most outspoken black opponent of Chestnut and the Sanderses, and in 1990 he had filed one of the complaints with the state bar that had sought disciplinary action against the senator. He was elected to the House with strong white backing. In 1998 he was reelected, by a substantial margin, over former BEST leader Ronald Peoples. Similarly on the county commission, the black commission chairman Erskine Minor repeatedly allied himself with the two white commissioners against Perry Varner, Rose Sanders's brother-in-law and the office manager of the Chestnut law firm, during the 1990 demonstrations. In 1992, after the third black commissioner, D. L. Pope, was caught using county equipment to improve his own property, a large part of the black electorate joined with the district's whites to give the Democratic nomination to white farmer John Lide over Pope. Black Orrville teacher Curtis Williams then entered the general election against Lide as an independent, and the result was a virtual tie. After lengthy court proceedings, the seat was awarded to Lide, and whites thus regained control of the commission. In 1996, Williams again opposed Lide and this time beat him handily, by 57 to 43 percent. But Erskine Minor was also returned, in a close election in the Democratic primary, largely on the strength of absentee ballots. By this time, whites had finally begun to learn that the mere racial identity of officeholders was less important than how they would vote once in power. With Minor on the commission, the ostensible return to a black majority was more a matter of appearance than of substance. And black voters, too, occasionally proved willing to ignore race. On the Dallas County Board of Education, which governed the schools outside Selma, white member Elton Ralston won reelection throughout this period from an overwhelmingly black district, thus allowing whites to retain a three-to-two majority on this five-member body.

Such evidence of the emergence of a moderate force in the community's political life was balanced, however, by equally convincing indications of escalating racial polarization. By 1994, Selma High's white enrollment had fallen to just 60 students out of 1,173, down from 463 at the beginning of 1990. Of those whites who remained, about three-quarters were inmates of the city's Methodist orphanage, who lacked the financial resources to go anywhere else. Only 44 of Westside Middle School's 516 students were white, down from more than 300 in 1990. And Eastside Middle was entirely black. In the system as a whole, there were 839 white and 4,484 black students. But virtually all of the whites attended just two of the city's eight elementary schools, located in largely white neighborhoods. White parents in those two sections allowed their children to attend public schools until the time came for transfer to middle school, and then they moved the students to the private schools; in all other neighborhoods, whites attended the private schools from the outset. At the secondary school level, resegregation was essentially complete.

Similarly, the voting in the mayoral and council president elections of 1996 produced the starkest racial division since black reenfranchisement. James Perkins—confident that the ballot reforms that his contesting of the 1992 results had created, coupled with an electorate now 56 percent black, would at last produce a black victory—entered the mayoral race against Smitherman once again. And Alvin Cleveland also once more opposed Carl Morgan. Despite the fact that the city had had no difficulty in surviving a black-majority council, and despite whites' growing familiarity with voting for such black moderates as Edward Maull, the elevation of a black mayor seemed certain to much of white Selma to bring on the deluge. And this intense white terror provided Smitherman and Morgan with the one thing that could permit them to turn back the black challenge: an enormous white turnout. Smitherman was elected with 52 percent of the poll, to Perkins's 48 percent. When the result became clear, late on election night, Smitherman collapsed into sobs of joy. Morgan won a bit more easily, with 54 percent to Cleveland's 46 percent. About 75 percent of registered whites actually voted, to about 64 percent of registered blacks. But Smitherman managed to attract only some 8 percent of the black vote. Though this support was crucial, it represented a remarkable decline from the three-fourths of the black vote that he had received against his two white opponents in 1980 and the nearly 20 percent of it that he had gotten against Frederick Reese in 1984. Nor is the reason for the decline difficult to discern. Smitherman's own deep antagonism toward Chestnut and the Sanderses, and his tendency to respond in kind to their attacks, played directly into Chestnut's hands in the attorney's persistent efforts to unite the black community against the mayor. The openness of Smitherman's hostility made him appear to be just what Chestnut claimed him to be, a white supremacist champion of his race, inimical to the aspirations of blacks. The memory of the young, progressive reformer who had ended the rule of the Burns-Heinz machine had thus long since faded from public consciousness—thanks in part to Chestnut's manipulations, and in particular to the bitter heritage of the 1990 demonstrations, but thanks as well to Smitherman's repeated willingness to play the role Chestnut assigned to him, as in his veto of the citizens' plan for redistricting the council in 1993. When the white electorate united behind the mayor in response to its profound racial fears, as it did in 1996, then, there can be little wonder that even the most moderate blacks felt themselves pushed into uniting on the other side.

Thus Selma struggled toward the end of the twentieth century. The presence of such black moderate leaders as Edwin Moss, Edward Maull, Mark West, and Erskine Minor made it clear that the city's future need not be defined in the polarized terms espoused by J. L. Chestnut and too often accepted by Joe Smitherman. But white apprehension and ancient black distrust and anger made it exceedingly difficult for any substantial part of the community to discern the middle ground. And so the man who had been elected mayor in 1964 on the motto "Thirty Years is Long Enough" continued to preside over a city whose public life constituted a mirror to its inner torment. During Smitherman's ninth term, the inevitable corruptions of extended power began to manifest themselves. In November 1997, Smitherman was forced to dismiss his police chief, Randy Lewellen, and the city clerk, Mary Ramsey, when it was discovered, according to press reports, that they had for years been conspiring together in a false invoice scheme that had cost Selma hundreds of thousands of dollars. And in the spring of 1998, Smitherman himself had to confess to the Alabama Ethics Commission that he had been using a city-owned automobile to commute to his Gulf coast condominium. Such revelations would have been sufficient to bring down many a municipal administration, but Selma's racial division gave Smitherman, as Birmingham's gave Richard Arrington, a strength with his constituency that transcended the usual indicia of character and leadership. The contest in which Selmians were engaged was an attempt to master their destiny. That fact was evident to all of them, whatever their perspective, and it engaged their emotions so fully that concerns which elsewhere would have appeared significant could be made to seem mundane.

All of these lamentable tendencies in Selma's municipal life came together in the city elections of 2000. By this time Selma's electorate was almost 65 percent black, up from 56 percent only four years before. Seeing the handwriting on the wall in this statistic, city council president Carl Morgan declined to seek another term. But when James Perkins announced in December 1999 his intention to make a third attempt to gain the mayoralty, Smitherman's volatile emotions overwhelmed his common sense. In April he announced his candidacy for a tenth term. He had handled the dismissal of Chief Lewellen with considerable discretion, appointing to succeed him the first black police chief in Selma's history, Earnest L. Tate. And now he could note proudly that ten of the fifteen department heads in his administration were black. But he also could not resist an appeal to his white electoral base, warning Selmians that if he did not win, "you're looking at your last white mayor."

Perkins—whose sister was married to one of Chestnut's and the Sanderses' law partners, Collins Pettaway—had the active support of the Chestnut-Sanders law firm. This fact drew into the race also two black Selmians who deeply resented the extent of the law firm's power, city councilman Yusuf Abdus-Salaam and state representative Edward Maull. Abdus-Salaam had worked closely with Rose Sanders during the 1990 school demonstrations and had been censured along with her by the state bar for their activities. But in the intervening decade, a deep gulf of personal hostility had opened between them. And Maull's enmity to the Sanderses had of course been the foundation of his political career. Smitherman apparently hoped that the candidacies of these two men would sufficiently divide the black vote that, with solid white support and the support as well of those blacks grateful for the patronage that he had spread among them, he would be able to win in the first round of voting. Perkins's supporters, led by Rose Sanders and using the slogan "Joe Gotta Go," worked tirelessly, on the other hand, to unite the black electorate in an anti-Smitherman crusade. And, in a supreme historical irony, Perkins himself devoted his campaign to condemning Smitherman for insufficiently aggressive efforts to attract new industries to the city.

In the initial election, Smitherman led with 46 percent of the vote, to 43 percent for Perkins and 11 percent for Abdus-Salaam. Representative Maull, virtually all of whose constituency voted for Smitherman, was therefore unable to attract significant support. The depth of Abdus-Salaam's animosity toward the Sanderses gave Smitherman some hope in the runoff that he might attract Abdus-Salaam's voters to his banner, but the events of the runoff campaign left the electorate almost completely polarized along racial lines. It began with the firebombing of an automobile parked at the Chestnut-Sanders law firm, and from there it managed to degenerate even further. The result was an enormous turnout—more than 17 percent greater than in the first round—and consequently a relatively easy victory for Perkins. Smitherman took some 98 percent of the white vote and held onto his usual 9 percent or so of the black vote, but Perkins received the overwhelming majority of Abdus-Salaam's support and succeeded in drawing to the polls as well probably more than twelve hundred voters who had not participated in the initial election. Perkins thus defeated Smitherman by 56 percent to 44 percent. Meanwhile, a black candidate, Dallas County superintendent of education George P. Evans, had been chosen to succeed Carl Morgan as council president, thereby increasing the black council majority to six to three just as that body prepared to redraw the council district lines in response to the 2000 census, which demonstrated that blacks were now 70 percent of the city's population. These results therefore effectively delivered black Selmians political control of the city.

Nevertheless, the deep divisions among Selma's blacks, which the city's whites had been so very slow to recognize, at once exploded into open confrontation. At his inauguration on October 2, Mayor Perkins had indicated his intention to replace Earnest Tate, the black police chief appointed by Smitherman, with Assistant Chief Robert Green. But Tate had a great many friends of both races, and at its first regular meeting a week later the new city council voted unanimously to retain Tate in his job indefinitely. In the following weeks, Perkins's efforts to shape the city bureaucracy to his liking met increasing resistance. Early in his tenure, thirty years before, former mayor Smitherman had arranged to supplement his mayoral salary by having the ostensibly independent municipal water works board appoint him to the additional position of superintendent of the water works. With Perkins's assumption of the mayoralty, the five-member water works board—three of whom were also city council members—had dutifully named Perkins as superintendent as well. But when Perkins began giving water works personnel orders that differed from the board's own directives, the board at the end of November reconvened and fired Perkins from the superintendency, by a vote of four to one. Joining the majority in this action was black councilman and former SNCC field secretary Benny Tucker. There ensued a series of acrimonious legal encounters, but the board eventually made its dismissal stick. In the meantime, Perkins had submitted his first budget to the city council, and the new black council president, George Evans, had led three other black council members—Benny Tucker, Selma High School librarian Nancy Sewell, and James Durry—into an alliance with the three white council members to draft a significantly revised version of it. Evans had been elected to the council presidency with strong support in Selma's white precincts, over a black attorney who appears to have had the backing of the Chestnut-Sanders law firm, Michael Jackson. Only a week after the water works board's firing of Perkins, the council met to consider the two rival budgets. A raucous crowd of Perkins supporters, led by Rose Sanders, disrupted the meeting; three of them, including Mrs. Sanders, were arrested. The next morning the council tried again. The Perkins supporters once more sought to prevent the body from acting, but this time Evans managed to gavel the rival budget through. The Dallas County Southern Christian Leadership Conference then attempted to organize demonstrations against the four black council members who had voted against the Perkins administration, but the demonstrations soon collapsed. However, the Dallas County Board of Education retaliated against Evans by voting three to two not to renew his contract as the county superintendent of schools. And this dismissal, like that of Perkins by the water works, was eventually made to stick.

In the meantime, the movement of legal precedent had returned the law in the long-running Dallas County Commission case to a version of the position initially urged by Judge Hand in 1987 and reversed by the Eleventh Circuit in 1988. The federal courts therefore ordered in 2000 the restoration of the probate judge, elected from the county at large, to his historical position as the commission's chairman, and the division of the county into four commissioner's districts, two of them overwhelmingly black and two capable of electing whites. The result of this decision was that, at the same time that blacks gained control at last of Selma's city government, whites regained a three-to-two majority on the county commission.

It seemed quite certain that Perkins's defeat of Smitherman in 2000 would come to represent as important a watershed in Selma's history as

Smitherman's own defeat of Chris Heinz in 1964 had been. Selma thus joined Montgomery and Birmingham, whose municipal elections the year before had also marked significant transitions in the patterns of local power. But Perkins's victory was by no means the unalloyed triumph that observers outside the region were likely to think it. Rather, Perkins's alliance with the Chestnut-Sanders faction inevitably aroused the opposition of its opponents and left the city's white minority to hold the balance of power. The county's white minority, too, once more controlled the commission. The advent of Selma's first black municipal administration consequently left the little city's citizens still groping as desperately as ever to comprehend a world in effect created by their nightmares.[18]

V. Reflections

If appreciating the extent of the local movements' connection with municipal politics permits the observer who had expected that their force would have declined with the elimination of legal segregation to understand why the conflicts persist, however, it has as well something to teach the rather subtler observer for whom the constant national debates over racial preferences make the persistent divisions in these three cities seem entirely unsurprising. The direct-action movements had had significant policy content: the adoption of the Mobile bus seating plan in the Montgomery bus boycott, the integration of the lunch counters in the downtown department stores in Birmingham, the fair administration of the voter qualification test in Selma. But in later years, the racial divisions that continued in the three cities—quite unlike those at the national level—were less and less focused on policies. The Arrington administration in Birmingham did adopt racial set-aside programs for city contractors and, under federal court order, racial quotas in city employment. And the result was incessant squabbles there about the equity of such practices that closely paralleled the national arguments about them. But even in Birmingham, and certainly in Montgomery and Selma, the heart of the racial disputes in the final decades of the century was not policy proposals but politics and power; the essential point at issue was who would govern whom. The local divisions were not, therefore, a function of the national ones. Rather, they represented the working out of the new political relationships initiated by the direct-action efforts and by reenfranchisement. They were not, even though they were often taken to be, merely local manifestations of pervasive American differences. They were, instead, manifestations in the present of the dissension created by the experience of local history.

Indeed, looking back from a knowledge of the consequences, we may well wonder how important the policy content of the direct-action movements had been at the time, as opposed to their political content. There can be no doubt, of course, that black resentment of segregation was very real, but that resentment had been intense for many decades and was to be found throughout the South. We have already demonstrated that these three cities developed direct-action movements when so many others similarly situated did not because of particular developments in municipal political life. But if the movements' generative events are to be sought in politics, to what extent may their substance be found there as well? The conscious object of the bus boycotters in Montgomery was certainly the alteration of seating segregation practices on the busses, but it would seem very likely that an equal motive—if one doubtless less clearly articulated to themselves—was the desire to strike back at Clyde Sellers's racially charged electoral appeals of the preceding spring. And boycott leaders themselves acknowledge that one reason for the boycott's early success was the exhilaration that blacks experienced in being able at last to force white authorities to pay attention to their complaints. Similarly in Birmingham, Fred Shuttlesworth's desire to serve as the principal black spokesman in negotiations with the emerging white moderate political leadership, to the exclusion of Shores, Gaston, and his other black moderate rivals, was unquestionably his own central goal in organizing the 1963 demonstrations, and the integration of the department store lunch counters represented simply a way to prove his greater effectiveness. And in Selma, the connection between blacks' vexation at the recalcitrance of the board of voting registrars and their desire to participate in politics is explicit. There can be little doubt, if any at all, that blacks' eagerness to register proceeded in very great part from their desire to participate in the overthrow of the Burns-Heinz machine, initially, and their desire to sustain the new progressive Smitherman administration, and to extend Smitherman's triumph from the city hall to the county courthouse, thereafter. The conduct of the board of registrars, moreover, is doubtless bound up with its members' loyalty to the Burns-Heinz organization and to county officials, as well as the registrars' knowledge that the addition of any substantial number of blacks to the rolls would threaten incumbents' reelection. Thus, even though the movements were certainly aimed at effecting changes in the practice of segregation, it seems very likely, too, that they sought, quite as much, to influence the shape of local politics. Both the movements' origins and their content were products of municipal political competition. It is a very natural development, therefore, that the later racial divisions in the cities retained this political focus.

In sum, then, the essentially universal black aspiration for civil rights expressed itself through direct action in the three cities because of particular developments in municipal politics. The movements remained intensely local in their causes and their concerns. They sought primarily to manipulate power to the benefit of black residents at a time when those residents in great part lacked the ballot, but of course by no means lacked an understanding of how the structure of community power had formed their lives. In our own day, when politics has too often come to seem to very many Americans an irrelevant exercise, it is perhaps difficult to recapture the centrality of municipal political affairs in the black citizenry's conception of its world. But that is simply because most Americans have never been subject to pervasive power without any genuine capacity to make oneself felt within it. In such a situation, politics must seem essential to mastery, and political events the key to one's fate.

Conclusion

6

I. The Movements and the Movement

The argument thus far has sought to explain the profoundly local and political nature of the civil rights movements in Montgomery, Birmingham, and Selma. They were, I have claimed, products of specific municipal political developments, and their goals, though in part to gain alterations in particular local policies, were just as importantly to influence the structure of municipal political life. But if the movements were so intimately involved with such distinctly parochial political affairs, how did they come to have so significant an impact upon the South and the nation? It is to that question that we now turn our attention.

It is not at all unusual, of course, for great historical consequences to flow from events with quite local origins. Many a revolution has sprung from some particular act of resistance to limited local authority. The question must always be why a specific event is perceived elsewhere to hold important general implications. The answer, in this case as in most analogous ones, is to be found at the juncture of power and liberty. The principal strength of the civil rights movement at the national level proceeded from the increasingly widespread popular identification of its claims with the ideals of individual liberty: equality of rights, equal opportunity, equal justice under law. This perception was strongly reinforced by the fact that the movement usually—though certainly not uniformly—was simply seeking to obtain in practice rights that, according to Supreme Court decisions, were guaranteed to all citizens by the Constitution. We have observed, on the other hand, that the civil rights movement at the local level was primarily about the distribution of power and influence, the continuing process of compelling authority to hear one's voice. But it must be obvious that when the inequitable distribution of local power produced an evident breach of the national norms of justice, then the national and local understandings of the movement would become, if only for a historical instant, two sides of the same coin.

This union of national ideals and local political and social rivalry in the decade from 1955 to 1965 was a result, not of alterations in the structure of local power in southern towns, but of the evolution of the national ideals during and just after World War II—and in no small part, indeed, because of World War II—more commonly to embrace a nonracial understanding of their implications. Power was inequitably distributed in all American communities, had always been, and very likely must necessarily be. Blacks had never been content with the discrimination to which they were subject, and they had deeply resented the imposition of legal segregation and disfranchisement from the outset. They had, moreover, utilized direct action from time to time in earlier decades. It was not the tactic that was new; the tactic, in fact, was a quite logical consequence of the conjunction of disfranchisement and the desire to influence the political process. It was the white national response, rather than the tactic, that had changed. The lengthy streetcar boycotts in Montgomery and Mobile at the beginning of the twentieth century, for instance, had provoked little national notice; one would hardly expect that they would have at a time when the federal courts had just accepted the constitutional validity of the segregation ordinances they were protesting. And the bus boycott in Baton Rouge, Louisiana, in 1953, also received little attention—in part, no doubt, because it was so brief, but in part too, very probably, because even though the Supreme Court's school segregation decision was only a year away, municipal bus segregation ordinances were in 1953 still generally considered constitutionally permissible. Even the Montgomery bus boycott, as we have seen, was very slow to gain national sympathy. At the beginning of the boycott in 1955, the unconstitutionality of bus segregation was still not established, and the Montgomery Improvement Association was not attacking the segregation itself, in any case; the connection between the direct-action effort and national ideals of liberty and justice therefore remained obscure. It was only when King and the other boycott leaders were indicted for violation of the Anti-Boycott Act that white national sentiment was decisively aroused in the boycotters' behalf, because the indictments were so widely seen as a perversion of the justice system in an effort to suppress peaceful protest. Similarly, in Birmingham and Selma it was not until "Bull" Connor and Sheriff Clark resorted to force against the demonstrators that sympathy for blacks' cause became overwhelming among whites throughout the nation—and for the same reason: these seemed not to be legitimate law enforcement techniques, but an unjust effort to eliminate the expression of opposition.

The black demonstrators, in seeking to compel local political institutions to take their complaints seriously, were presenting a fundamental challenge to the structure of local power because, as a result of disfranchisement, it was erected on the assumption of black exclusion. When white authorities responded to the demonstrations with indictments, injunctions, and force, it seemed to them that they were taking strictly defensive measures, necessary to preserve the social order. Their actions were a response to what they believed to be—and, surely, correctly believed to be—the will of the electorate that had placed them in office. Black demonstrators, who understood full well that their efforts affronted the existing community power relationships, expected just such a forceful response; indeed, in Birmingham and Selma, SCLC strategists were counting on it. But to observers in the nation at large, the actions of local authorities appeared to be aggressive attacks upon the most essential American values of justice and democracy, the perversion to illegitimate ends of the power with which these officials had been entrusted. Thus the local struggle for access to power and political influence became an expression of the national ideals of liberty and individual rights. However parochial may have been their origins and aims, the direct-action movements in these three cities became connected in the minds of Americans elsewhere with the elemental commitments of their Constitution.

The point is not, of course, that local blacks did not also assert the principles of democracy and individual rights in support of their particular claims; on the contrary, they did so persistently, and quite sincerely. Before reenfranchisement, as we have said, the distinction between the assertion of the rights of a citizen and the desire to be able to influence political power was exceedingly difficult to discern; a government sensitive to the needs and wishes of its citizens is at the core of popular liberty, and it was precisely such a government that disfranchised blacks did not have. Only when blacks had regained the ballot did the difference between the two conceptions of the direct-action campaigns' meaning begin to become clear.

The point, rather, is about emphases. An observer from elsewhere in the nation could not have been expected to know very much, if anything at all, about the subtleties of the community's local political and social rivalries. And even if he had had the time and ability to inform himself on such matters, without having truly experienced them as an essential part of daily reality, he would have found his appreciation of their emotional force inescapably limited. Instead of seeing such obscure political considerations as fundamental, therefore, the distant observer was far more likely to turn to the general explanatory categories he shared with local participants, categories of constitutional rights, and to understand the failure of white officials to respond to black citizens' predicament as both a product and a proof of the deprivation of black citizens' liberties. Correspondingly, when the black residents of a municipality considered their personal condition, they did not first think in abstract terms of constitutional guarantees, but of the immediate necessities and daily affronts that surrounded them. Their too frequent powerlessness before authority and their inability effectively to shape their own lives loomed largest in their view of things, and the fact that this situation reflected an absence of rights and privileges that ought to have been theirs was a derivative inspiration that simply reinforced and defined their grievances.

This explanation for the wider impact of the movements in the three cities holds important implications for our understanding of the pattern of cause and effect in these years. The story of the civil rights movement as an episode in the history of the nation often attributes a causative role to the decade of Supreme Court decisions beginning with the proscription of the white primary in 1944 and ending with the declaration in 1954 that the racial segregation of public schools is unconstitutional. The movement thus seems to represent the struggle by southern blacks to gain in substance the rights that the Supreme Court had said were theirs; blacks began to respond in numerous southern towns and cities to the clarion sounded from Washington. But in truth, as we have said, blacks had been resisting racial discrimination in many places and in many ways for a very long while before the federal courts became their allies. The actual role of the Supreme Court's decisions was not to arouse southern blacks to a sudden new defiance, but to prepare a greater number of other Americans in other parts of the country to regard their struggle as just, and to give particular black protests a greater chance of ending in success, because of the intervention of federal judicial mandates. It is not wrong, in other words, to think of the Supreme Court's reversal of American constitutional doctrine on racial segregation in the years after World War II as having ushered in the civil rights era. But it is wrong to think of the decisions as having done so by generating the black direct-action movements in the South. Rather, they did so by powerfully assisting in the creation of a general intellectual framework that conceived the individual direct-action efforts as components of humanity's great historical struggle for freedom and democracy and of America's endeavor to live up to its noble creed. This perspective on the local movements tended to strip them of their essential localism precisely because it fit them into such a compelling larger drama. It therefore distorted the national understanding of the local movements in ways that it has been the goal of the present investigation to clarify. But this perspective also immensely strengthened the hand of the local demonstrators, by giving them—for the first time in American history, other than in the brief few years immediately following the Civil War—both the sympathy of a vast national audience and the assistance of at least parts of the federal government. This national engagement with conflicts so very local was, indeed, the defining feature of the civil rights era in national history.

The national understanding of the municipal movements in terms of the ideals of liberty and democracy and the basically political content of these movements as efforts to gain access to power were, then, not at all obviously differentiated at the time; in an era of disfranchisement, to reiterate the point, they actually were two sides of the same coin. But the distinction was nonetheless real, and after reenfranchisement it became increasingly consequential. Much of the animosity that came to characterize race relations in the United States in later years seems to have proceeded from the widespread white belief that, federal law having now fully established blacks' claim to equal rights, additional black demands represented an insistence upon special privileges; and the corresponding belief among those blacks who remained loyal to the promise of the statutes that, the new laws not yet having produced the sort of equality that their most passionate advocates had initially expected, the answer must lie in ever more rigorous and racially conscious enforcement of the statutory provisions, based upon ever more explicit insistence on specific numerical outcomes. But both of these sets of attitudes derived from the conception of the earlier movement as a struggle for rights rather than for political influence. It was precisely the conviction that the movement was—as the name that had been fixed upon it asserted it was—about the acquisition of civil rights that had allowed the local direct-action campaigns to elicit the white national attention and sympathy that they had. And so with reenfranchisement, the national argument about the almost medieval question of the extent to which individual and racial identities could properly cohere blustered on, while the political contests in southern communities increasingly were dismissed as of merely provincial interest. Outside Alabama, almost no Americans knew who Joe Reed, Rose Sanders, and Dr. Jimmy Blake were, and even within the state, very few understood the real significance of such figures. In this sense, the very means by which the local direct-action movements had at first been able to have so powerful an impact upon the nation doomed them also to subsequent national irrelevance.

In the earlier period, the principal figure in the knitting together of what we have called the national and the local understandings of the movements had, of course, been Martin Luther King. The conjunction of the national and local was no mere strategy for him; it was an ardent faith. In fact, it had been precisely his ability to see the connection between the immediate frustration at authorities' refusal to spell out the bus company's seating requirements and the resultant arrest of Rosa Parks on the one hand, and the general claims of justice and democracy on the other, and to express that connection so powerfully, that had quickly elevated him beyond the other boycott leaders in Montgomery to such unchallenged preeminence. He had displayed that ability from the very outset. At the initial mass meeting on the night of the boycott's first day, he had insisted, "Now the press would have us believe that [Mrs. Parks] refused to leave a reserved section. . . . [B]ut I want you to know this evening that there is no reserved section. . . . I think I speak with legal authority behind me that the law, the ordinance, the city ordinance has never been totally clarified." And he had added, "We are not afraid of what we are doing, because we are doing it within the law. . . . When labor all over this nation came to see that it would be trampled over by capitalistic power, it was nothing wrong with labor getting together and organizing and protesting for its rights. . . . Not only are we using the tools of persuasion, but we've come to see that we've got to use the tools of coercion. Not only is this thing a process of education, but it is also a process of legislation." However, he had also thundered, "If we are wrong, the Supreme Court of this nation is wrong. If we are wrong, the Constitution of the United States is wrong. If we are wrong, God Almighty is wrong. . . . If we are wrong, justice is a lie. . . . We, the disinherited of this land, we who have been oppressed so long, are tired of going through the long night of captivity. And now we are reaching out for the daybreak of freedom and justice and equality."[1]

The disposition King evidenced in this, his very first movement speech, to identify the particular and the political with the emphatically moral and eternal would be characteristic of his conception of all his other movement activities for the remainder of his life. It would fundamentally shape the way that many other Americans, of all races, would understand the movement. And it would prove crucial, as we have said, to making the local direct-action campaigns components of a national crusade. Exactly because King so readily and so honestly transmuted questions of power into questions of morality, he succeeded from the beginning in permitting the local campaigns to speak to a broader audience. Observers who came to Montgomery virtually uniformly concluded that King, much more profoundly than most of his colleagues, understood the boycott's larger significance. In fact, it was simply that King, more often than his colleagues, tended to talk about the boycott in terms of fundamental principles rather than in terms of its specific origins and goals. And this pattern of thought and expression proved entirely typical of him in his future battles. He therefore continually depicted the local campaigns in just the form in which observers elsewhere also conceived them. It is almost certainly for that reason that Americans so generally came to regard King—far more than other, equally important national black leaders such as Roy Wilkins, Thurgood Marshall, James Farmer, Whitney Young, or John Lewis; and infinitely more than the local leaders who were arguably the movement's heart and soul, such as C. Kenzie Steele, Fred Shuttlesworth, Dr. William G. Anderson, Amelia Boynton, Amzie Moore, or Aaron Henry—as the great expositor of the movement's principles.[2]

King's pivotal importance derives as well, however, from another, perhaps less readily apparent means by which the direct-action campaigns in the three cities had an impact beyond the municipal boundaries. The sources of broader influence that we have just been discussing aid us in understanding the response of observers living elsewhere in the United States. But the response of other southerners is possibly an even more significant element in the general reaction. And that response was in large measure created by the social drama of the demonstrations King led.

The power of the demonstrations in the cities in which they occurred derived chiefly from their capacity to speak to the deeply debilitating assumptions that often guided and restricted the actions of the various segments of the community. Poorer blacks, too frequently inured to poverty and impotence, in many cases by generations-old legacies in their families of essential social immobility, might easily surrender to apathy or despair. The demonstrations could serve to convince them that change was really possible. Middle-class black moderates, on the other hand, were conscious of the rapid improvements in the public institutions and material conditions in black areas in the years after World War II, and they often also were flushed with a new sense of importance because of increasing, if actually still quite limited, influence with leading whites. These blacks had to be shown how starkly circumscribed was the progress they could hope to achieve under segregation. White moderates were filled with false confidence from an even stronger conviction that the conditions of blacks, and race relations in general, were achieving marked advances and that over time the South gradually would see all of its racial problems solved. They had to be taught that segregation possessed the power to render efforts at amelioration within its structures vain. The characteristic that bound moderates of both races together was the belief—by no means false, of course—that substantial strides were in fact being made, though quietly. But when open black demands succeeded in placing segregation under pressure, and segregation roused itself to defend its requirements, moderates learned to their sorrow how pervasive and uncompromising the system actually was. White moderates' own anger at the threat posed by the demonstrators to the community's reputation, or segregationists' coercion exerted through the moderates' jobs or against their families and social position, forced the moderates into silence, or even into making common cause with white supremacy. Black moderates found their access to white leaders eliminated as politicians scurried to put themselves right with the white electorate, and even the most uncontroversial projects in the black sections of town suddenly became suspect. Both groups discovered that their world was far less malleable than they had thought. Finally, the demonstrations challenged segregationist whites' certainty that they held the social initiative. By proving that local blacks could invoke sufficient force—whether from the federal courts or bureaucracy, individual and institutional northern supporters, sympathetic national press accounts, economic pressure on local merchants, or a combination of all of these things—to outmatch the various sources of community control, political, social, and economic, that had sustained white supremacy for more than half a century, the demonstrations could work to convince the segregationists, however grudgingly, that continued resistance was futile.

The social order in the three cities had been preserved by the despondent cynicism of poorer blacks and by the arrogance, in different ways, of black moderates, white moderates, and segregationists. The direct-action movements in all three places compelled the contending elements of the community to begin to reconsider the attitudes that had effectively inhibited genuine renewal. Blacks had to learn both how fully they were enmeshed in the web of segregation and how much power they actually possessed to extricate themselves. Whites had to learn both how very limited was the possibility of reform if the presumption of white supremacy were not questioned and how tenuous was white supremacy's real hold upon the community if the forces that dissented from the orthodoxy were ever successfully mobilized. In a sense, King, having first observed this process at work among the people of Montgomery, spent the rest of his career arranging further proofs of it for other southerners in other towns. In these efforts, the medium was the message; the immediate goals of a campaign in a particular city, the local circumstances that had made the campaign possible, were less important to King and his associates on the SCLC staff than the procedure of placing segregation under stress in order to reveal the nature of its dominion in society. The result was that King inevitably had interests somewhat different from those of Shuttlesworth and the Christian Movement in Birmingham or Frederick Reese and the Dallas County Voters League in Selma, as well as from the other local organizations with which he worked. Just as King tended to talk about the movements in terms of moral and constitutional principles and to neglect the immediate issues of relative community power, so he tended to emphasize in his thinking the social process rather than the declared aims of the demonstrations. And once again, his perspective facilitated the campaigns' having a broader significance than they would otherwise have possessed.

It is perhaps unnecessary to emphasize that the demonstrations by no means succeeded in teaching their lessons to all the elements of the communities in which they occurred. On the contrary, large numbers of residents—especially white ones—continued strongly to resist the social implications of the campaigns. The white attitudes whose errors the campaigns ought to have revealed, indeed, were actually usually hardened by them, both among segregationists and among moderates. And even black attitudes were not altered easily. Moreover, it is probable that King, and even more his SCLC associates, did not themselves understand quite as explicitly as we have just stated them the ways in which the campaigns could address the communities' intellectual limitations. We are aided in our analysis by hindsight, while King was struggling to make sense of a reality that both his own actions and those taken in response to his were in the midst of transforming. Nevertheless, it does seem clear from various observations throughout King's speeches and writings that he was, probably more than most of his contemporaries, moving steadily in these years toward a reasonably accurate conception of the constraints that the interplay of social forces in southern towns imposed upon racial progress. For instance, King spoke in essentially these terms, as we have seen, to both the white and the black moderates during the Birmingham demonstrations.

It is important to note, as well, that the realization that segregation's power depended upon such an interplay of social forces was itself an exceedingly significant achievement. Many commentators outside the South tended to think of the ability of white supremacists to compel submission to segregation within the region as evidence of a strongly hierarchical social structure in which power rested in the hands of a small and virtually omnipotent ruling class. King himself sometimes depicted the struggle in this way as well, as he did, for instance, in his speech at the conclusion of the Selma-to-Montgomery march. And it is precisely this tendency that made it so difficult for observers at the time to appreciate the implications of his other, substantially subtler understanding of the southern communities' dilemma. Indeed, it appears that the more monolithic conception of social power actually worked to obscure the full significance of the demonstrations' various lessons even from King. Nor have more recent students always been clear on the point. But in Selma, easily the least heterogeneous of our three cities, where the White Citizens' Council did indeed labor mightily to ensure total conformity in the community, power in the end proved more widely dispersed than the council's leaders had comprehended, and their efforts failed. In Montgomery and Birmingham, deep social divisions were manifest from the outset. Segregation in fact drew much of its ability to endure precisely from the South's diversity and complexity, since any fundamental reform of society would necessarily affect an almost infinite variety of interests. Each of the segments of community life that we have mentioned—poorer blacks, middle-class black moderates, white moderates and business progressives, segregationist true believers—contributed in its own way to the perpetuation of segregation's hold on them all. Only if the direct-action campaigns could transform the thinking of significant numbers of each group would the demonstrations be able to effect the overthrow of segregation from within the community.

From that perspective, it becomes clear why the civil rights movement required outside support to succeed. Direct action had its desired effect on the residents of the cities in which it was tried, if it did so at all, only at the level of each individual's personal assumptions and beliefs. It is hardly surprising, therefore, that the demonstrations' lessons were frequently doubted, more often than not rebuffed, and very slow to gain social purchase; in effect, they were challenging people's ability to be honest with themselves. But what we have called the national, as opposed to the local, demand of the direct-action campaigns—that is, not the transformation of private convictions and community power relationships, but the alteration of regional practices to conform to emerging constitutional requirements and ethical understandings—could permit the campaigns to end with a semblance of triumph because it was capable of enlisting the aid of the federal courts, the media, the broader white American electorate, and therefore eventually the federal executive and Congress. If the ability of the demonstrations to appeal to national principles had not existed, direct action alone almost certainly could not have brought any immediate change, and probably very little even in the way of long-term change, to the communities. The failure of virtually all such efforts in the region in earlier decades establishes this point decisively. On the other hand, the sort of transformation of personal attitudes among the towns' residents that the demonstrations had the potential to accomplish, when it did happen, was a breakthrough far more significant both for the individual citizen and for the life of the community than any modification of particular practices or policies could possibly be.

These observations allow us to return to the question of the direct-action campaigns' influence within the South. At the beginning of this book I quoted J. L. Chestnut's description of Selma in 1962; the civil rights movement had had virtually no impact upon the city at all, he said, before local circumstances began to prepare some of the community's black leaders to take a more aggressive stance in the fall of that year. Nevertheless, Chestnut himself is an example, along with a handful of other Selmians, white and black—particularly S. William and Amelia Boynton, of course—of the effect that the movements elsewhere had already succeeded in achieving. The demonstrations' influence proceeded in other southern towns, just as it did in the towns in which the demonstrations occurred, at the level of individual assumptions and beliefs. Only the unusually introspective or sensitive person was likely to respond by examining critically the axioms of a lifetime. But in communities throughout the region, a few people did in fact respond in this way. Such conversions were ordinarily insufficient of themselves to produce new direct-action campaigns. It has been the central claim of this investigation that broad-based direct-action campaigns emerged, when they did, only when the particular events of municipal politics and local life converged to convince significant segments of the black community that they were already in the midst of an epochal transition in the existing power relationships, and that it was essential to seize this crucial moment to compel the emerging new order to take account of their theretofore neglected concerns. In most towns, no such convergence of events took place. Nevertheless, observing the demonstrations and similar developments from elsewhere in the

South, some people—comparatively few of them white, many more of them black—found themselves moved to reevaluate their social and strategic commitments. Sometimes, but quite rarely, this process could itself lead to direct-action efforts. The clearest example of this outcome occurred on black college campuses; it produced the explosion of sit-ins in the spring of 1960, on the model of CORE's Miami ones of 1959, and the renewal of the Freedom Rides in the late spring and summer of 1961, when the initial group of CORE riders was unable to continue, following the Birmingham and Anniston assaults. It is hardly surprising, of course, that college students should have been especially receptive to such influences, given both that they were generally more attentive to public affairs than was the mass of the citizenry and that they were less subject than were working adults to the countervailing pressures of jobs and families. Far more often, however, even among students, the response was individual. After the Freedom Rides, it generally produced on the black campuses a steady stream—though certainly not a flood—of SNCC volunteers, rather than additional direct-action initiatives. And in the cities and towns of the South, it produced particular residents who were willing, more directly than ever before, to defy the social and racial orthodoxies with which they had grown up. Unassisted by the more extensive sense of urgency that an apparent revolution in municipal politics could generate in a community, these residents were left to challenge the existing order in ways that seldom gained much notice beyond their own town or county. But such challenges laid the foundation for the future persistent struggles to transform the structures of community power, primarily at the ballot box, following reenfranchisement.

There were thus two separate sorts of impact that the direct-action movements were able to have on the world beyond the limits of the particular cities in which they occurred: one upon the nation and therefore the federal government, and the other upon the continuing life of the region. The former effects proceeded from the widespread, if only partially accurate, understanding of the movements as efforts to realize the ideals of equal justice embodied in the American Constitution, and they eventually expressed themselves in statutory law, especially the Civil Rights Act of 1964 and the Voting Rights Act of 1965. This stream of influences brought enormous changes to the South, and quite significant changes to the rest of the nation as well, but it also prepared the ground for a future muddled by acrimonious divisions over affirmative action in hiring and admissions, busing to achieve racial balance in schools, racially defined electoral districts, and similar policies that could appear to bring rival claims to equal justice into collision. Meanwhile, the latter set of effects on the attitudes and commitments of individual southerners—what at the time was frequently, if not especially felicitously, called the "raising of consciousness"—permitted the residents of the region's communities to begin to appreciate the extent and nature of segregation's hold upon them. Moderates of both races could learn that their society was less malleable, less subject to being reformed from within, than they had believed; the despondent mass of blacks and the white segregationists could learn, in contrast, that forces outside the region were both able and, if only eventually, willing to lend decisive assistance to local black efforts to transform southern racial mores. This stream of influences persuaded far fewer people than the former one, of course, but at least in the South, it proved equally important. Just as the laws and judicial decisions that were products of the former set of influences established the new political framework within which the races would commence to fight out their revised sharing of power in southern communities in future years, so the attitudes introduced by the latter set of influences would shape the intellectual and social context that gave form to those struggles—and in particular, what could often seem to outsiders the quite surprisingly honest appreciation of the deep divisions of race and power that made the struggles necessary. It was the directness of this appreciation that, perhaps more than any other thing, distinguished the continuing civil rights engagements in towns and cities throughout the South at the end of the twentieth century from the confused discussions of analogous questions elsewhere in the nation.

II. The Beloved Community

On the final night of his life, Martin Luther King told a cheering black congregation in Memphis that, like Moses, he had been able to go to the mountaintop and look over into the promised land. "I may not get there with you," he said, continuing the Mosaic allusion, "but I want you to know tonight that we as a people will get to the promised land." It was the tenacious conviction that had sustained his career; he had dedicated his last book, *Where Do We Go from Here: Chaos or Community?* (1967), to "the committed supporters of the civil rights movement, Negro and white, whose steadfastness amid confusions and setbacks gives assurance that brotherhood will be the condition of man, not the dream of man." He called the promised land toward which he believed himself to be leading both his race and his nation "the beloved community," and he meant by the phrase the creation of a brotherhood so comprehensive that, when he spoke of it, the vast majority of his listeners could only dismiss it as a pipe dream. But he himself clearly thought it not only achievable, but achievable in the not-too-distant future as well. It included the elimination of the last vestiges of racism, of course. But the defeat of southern segregation seemed to him to have made that goal attainable. Civil rights leaders had earlier underestimated the extent of racism in the North, he conceded, and racist thought did have firm foundations in Euro-American intellectual history. Nevertheless, the "South was the stronghold of racism. In the white migrations through history from the South to the North and West, racism was carried to poison the rest of the nation. Prejudice, discrimination and bigotry had been intricately imbedded in all institutions of Southern life, political, social and economic. There could be no possibility of life-transforming change anywhere so long as the vast and solid influence of Southern segregation remained unchallenged and unhurt." The demonstrations in southern communities over the preceding decade had thus "constituted the first frontal attack on racism at its heart," and the remainder of the task would go much more quickly now that the roots of racism had been removed.

The excision of racism was only the first step, however. The eradication of want was the second, and an even more important one. "The time has come for us to civilize ourselves by the total, direct and immediate abolition of poverty," through the adoption of a governmentally guaranteed annual income. The third step must be the end of warfare, which could be accomplished if the United Nations would simply begin using nonviolent direct-action campaigns, instead of force, to defeat international aggression and despotism. At that point there could, and would, emerge the fraternity that was humanity's goal: "a world-wide fellowship that lifts neighborly concern beyond one's tribe, race, class and nation . . . in . . . an all-embracing and unconditional love for all men." Civil rights supporters had come together at the conclusion of the Selma-to-Montgomery march in a "moment of luminous and genuine brotherhood." Now southern desegregation would initiate the process whereby the "dark and demonic responses will be removed" from human relations "as men are possessed by the invisible inner law which etches on their hearts the conviction that all men are brothers and that love is mankind's most potent weapon for personal and social transformation." Given these expectations for the concluding decades of the twentieth century, one can hardly doubt that King, had he survived, would have found the reality profoundly disillusioning. Indeed, we know that many of his followers did in fact find it so.[3]

As disappointed as any disciple of King's with the fruits of the direct-action movements in southern communities were the white business progressives. They had always believed that race was a problem secondary to, and in large measure derivative from, economic expansion. They had expected, after desegregation and reenfranchisement, that the entire community would unite enthusiastically in the cause of attracting northern industry. The continued deep racial divisions and frequently bitter political competition in the struggle to redefine the distribution of power within their cities and towns, they could only regard as immensely frustrating shortsightedness. They blamed the failure to cooperate in equal measure on the remaining white supremacists and the black political leadership, and they regarded each group as irrationally racist, willfully blinding itself to the fact of the community's common interests. It was a bewildering outcome for the businessmen. The White Citizens' Councils' members, as we have seen, had universally blamed the defeat of segregation on the desertion of the white business moderates—people who were more interested in money than in principle, as the Citizens' Councils' adherents saw it. If whites had only remained unified, segregationists were convinced, blacks could never have achieved their objectives. The business progressives had been able to stand up to the enormous hostility that the white supremacists had directed at them chiefly because the businessmen were so convinced that black animosity toward what the businessmen regarded as petty and often foolish manifestations of segregation could be, and should be, met with a genuinely forthcoming willingness to compromise. They did not generally view themselves as permitting the fundamental alteration of the social structure, as the segregationists saw the concessions, but rather only as removing what frequently seemed trivial sources of social friction, so as not to divert municipal attention from the really important task of convincing industrialists that theirs was a pleasant and harmonious place in which to locate. If they had understood themselves as breaking down the truly significant barriers that separated the races, as both the white supremacists and the black integrationists did, doubtless they would have been more hesitant. But they understood themselves, instead, as seeking reasonable accommodations to eliminate unnecessary community discord. And now, with the requirements of segregation removed and the franchise restored to black citizens, far from being satisfied with these very considerable ameliorations and prepared at last to join hands in civic partnership, blacks continued to carp and complain, demanding more and more, never contented with any gains; meanwhile, the white supremacists' tenacious prejudices egged the blacks on, preventing them from realizing that their battles had been won. The result, as the businessmen saw matters, was that, though the grounds for community cooperation on the questions of economic development that were actually of consequence had now been created, the community remained fixated on what they were inclined to consider the stale questions of race relations.

From this perspective, the profoundly ironic way in which the frustrations of King's followers and those of the white business progressives paralleled each other becomes apparent. Both groups had sincerely expected that desegregation would initiate a historical process whereby racial issues would cease to be of central importance, and eventually might vanish altogether. Each had thought—the businessmen from the very outset, and King and his allies at least by the mid-1960s—that the region's most significant problems actually stemmed from a lack of jobs and industrial development, rather than from its racial divisions. While King's solution for these problems was essentially a socialist one and the businessmen's was capitalist, nevertheless both had come to believe that, with the prohibition of racial discrimination, the focus of social concerns would inevitably and naturally shift to economic matters. The business progressives had thought that the result would be a recognition of common interests and consequent general community cooperation in the cause of economic expansion, while King and his followers had believed that a nonracial alliance of all the poor and working class would emerge to demand true economic justice, a sort of labor union on a grand social scale that would presage the creation of the beloved community. But both had expected racial questions increasingly to become subordinate to economic ones. The deep disappointment that King's followers felt in future years at the persistent inability of needy whites and blacks to rise above race in order to unite effectively, particularly in the political arena, had its source in King's earlier assumptions, and it was precisely analogous to the business progressives' frustration at the continued racial animosities and disputes in their communities.

It is worth noting, too, that the aspect of King's beliefs that we have been discussing underlay his difficulty in appreciating the appeal of the black power movement, once it emerged in 1966. As we have seen, King tended to understand the goals of the civil rights movement more in terms of equal justice and the attainment of full freedom than in terms of the contest for the redistribution of community power. Indeed, he subsumed power in his thinking under moral categories. "Power," he insisted, "at its best is love implementing the demands of justice." Black extremists, he feared, were advocating "for Negroes the same destructive and conscienceless power that they have justly abhorred in whites. It is precisely this collision of immoral power with powerless morality which constitutes the major crisis of our times." The rhetorical stance adopted by Stokely Carmichael and the new leadership of SNCC that appeared to reject the movement's commitment to nonviolence deeply offended King, of course. But even black power's call for a united black voting bloc in support solely of black candidates he found repugnant. He recognized that race-line voting might be acceptable as a temporary tactic, dictated by the stark realities of a particular community, but as a general determination he found it morally odious. The doctrine of black power, he concluded, "is a nihilistic philosophy born out of the conviction that the Negro can't win. It is, at bottom, the view that American society is so hopelessly corrupt and enmeshed in evil that there is no possibility of salvation from within." The acceptance of such a notion would require the rejection of the dream that had animated King's career. As race-line voting hardened into increasingly inflexible practice in the politics of counties and towns across the South in the years after King's death, his followers could only despair for their integrationist vision.[4]

Younger residents of these communities, white but especially black, who had come to maturity after the direct-action campaigns but who found themselves still surrounded by ubiquitous and frequently acrimonious racial conflict, came easily to believe that the civil rights movement had failed to bring any genuine change to the region. It is indeed true, as we have said, that with reenfranchisement the effort to alter the structures of community power began to be fought out principally in the forum of electoral politics but otherwise continued entirely unabated. It is therefore not at all difficult to understand why young southerners too seldom appreciated the extent of the transformation that the movement had wrought. With the struggle to achieve the movement's most consequential goals still going on all around them, they could hardly have reached any conclusion other than that the movement's earlier accomplishments had been partial, and perhaps even trivial. Older citizens of both races knew well, of course, how vastly more equitable the racial conflicts were. The franchise was now general, and blacks were represented at every level of government; moreover, black rights were buttressed by generations of far-reaching legal precedent and by mandatory Justice Department review of every aspect of southern political relations. In the economic and social arenas, opportunities were now open to blacks that would have been utterly undreamt of at midcentury. Nevertheless, the attitudes of the young did point to a truth, if not the one that they believed.

Community had been intractable for whites under segregation. It had now proven intractable for blacks under integration. White supremacists had been unable to impose conformity upon whites, much less upon both races, because the diversity of social viewpoints and the economic and intellectual independence necessary to withstand segregationist pressure had been too widespread. White moderates and liberals, on the other hand, had found it impossible to effect fundamental reforms in race relations without the assistance of outside forces, because, as we have already observed, the diversity and complexity of southern society meant that any genuine reform would necessarily affect an almost infinite variety of interests. Now black leaders who sought racial unity found that the great differences in perspective and concern within their race made true solidarity exceedingly difficult to attain. And those who sought to reform race relations through effecting interracial alliances discovered the heterogeneity of social interests as great a barrier as ever to basic change. Virtually every election, and indeed nearly every proposal to alter existing practice, whether in education or taxation or law enforcement or the regulation of medical care or the provision of city services or almost any other public function, was likely to raise questions that emphasized the persistent disparities in racial status and the tensions that surrounded them. And though modest measures to ameliorate aspects of the region's various social problems were certainly not impossible to obtain, the seemingly perpetual struggle over efforts to do so remained a constant feature of political, and therefore emotional, life. Even in areas in which adjustments were absolutely required, such as the redistricting of legislative or city council seats to reflect population growth, and even on matters already covered by general statute, such as the prohibition of employment discrimination, every individual dispute was almost certain to provoke a new racial encounter. And the fact that such diverse elements with distinct and often discrepant interests were bound together into a community meant that for all practical purposes, there was no possibility that the strife would ever end. Ensuring that the contests were equitable was all that the society could reasonably expect to achieve. The civil rights movement had made very significant strides toward that goal, but it had believed that it could effect a great deal more. It is for that reason at bottom—because the civil rights movement had seemed to promise, but could not deliver, fraternity—that so many younger southerners came to believe that it had in fact changed nothing.

These comments bring us at last to an explanation for the failure of desegregation not merely to produce anything like the beloved community, but even to yield an end to the conflicts over desegregation itself. The easy answer is that law can change only behavior, not attitudes—that conflict persisted because racial prejudice persisted. The claim is by no means without merit, of course; but racism alone cannot nearly explain the complex outcome of these historical developments. Communitarian visions—whether informed, as was King's, by poignant Christian romanticism or by the chamber of commerce boosterism that lay at the heart of the white business progressives' or by some other consideration—too often share a misleading notion of the nature of community. At the beginning of this investigation, I suggested that a community is marked above all by its capacity to shape beliefs and aspirations. It creates, for virtually all its members, the limits in their minds of what seems possible and what appears to be beyond attainment; it binds them together with the implications of their mutual experiences. This ability is its greatest power. But shared assumption is by no means common interest. Community does not, except in extraordinary circumstances such as foreign attack, generate cooperation; rather, it defines the terms of struggle. The disappointment—whether at the continuation of bitter interracial conflict or at the absence of intraracial solidarity—that so many southerners have felt as the desegregated world has gradually revealed its reality is merely evidence, however painful, of this truth.

Southerners of goodwill have persisted in the illusion that racial animus is a remnant of the era of white supremacy that will slowly give way to harmony if the various sources of tension can be removed. It is certainly correct, of course, that the elimination of social factors that have exacerbated racial antagonism may allow the expression of racial rivalries without quite so hard an edge as that to which we are accustomed. But at the local level, as we have seen, the civil rights movements represented, in very great measure, efforts to compel the redistribution of power, particularly political power, within the community. Because expressions of power are protean, and both the persons who hold power and the situations that emphasize it will necessarily change over time, this endeavor must essentially be perpetual, even though its salience may wax and wane. More than that, however, the illusion reckons without the fact that historic conflicts within a community may be one of its fundamental constitutive elements, a part of the structure of reality for its members and therefore something which the very authenticity of the community itself would inhibit their transcending. Certainly that is true of southern communities; racial conflict has been so much a focal point of their existence that to eradicate it would be in a sense to deprive the communities' residents of their unity with their past. Such an outcome is no more to be imagined than we could imagine a self-conscious people without a history. We can demand that the contest be fought out openly and fairly; we can oppose the maintenance or adoption of practices that deliver victory artificially to one of the various contending parties; but the life of such conflicts must be coextensive with that of the community that defines them—and that concomitantly in so large a part obtains its meaning from them. Visions of communal harmony thus in fact defy the substance of the communities they celebrate, for actual communities must be built upon the aspirations and passions of human beings.

Martin Luther King, we have said, perhaps proceeded further than most of his contemporaries in understanding the complex interplay of social forces in southern towns during the civil rights era. Nevertheless, it is also clear that he profoundly misjudged the events of which he was a part. For the immediate cause of black rights, it is probably a good thing that he did so, since he was therefore able in deepest sincerity to clothe the direct-action campaigns with ennobling constitutional and moral ideals. But in the longer term, his expectation that he and his followers could by their efforts initiate the beloved community could only condemn his enterprise forever to appear to have fallen short of its promise. The truth is otherwise; direct action conceived in terms of its local goals succeeded in placing the contests of blacks and whites on an immeasurably more equitable footing. And yet it is a fact that the political leaders who too often have most benefited from this achievement are the racial polarizers whose community power depends upon the exploitation of racial antagonisms, because it is these leaders who have founded their appeals upon social realities rather than upon dreams of fraternity. It is an ironic outcome indeed, but one very likely dictated by the nature of community itself.

On the other hand, the realism of the racial polarizers need not therefore be regarded as meritorious, and certainly not as noble. Nobility often—perhaps more often than not—lies precisely in the refusal to admit reality. The quest for harmony must perhaps forever be doomed by the structure of community to no greater than partial success. But the community that contained no one dedicated to seeking this goal would surely be a place too abominable to contemplate.

Notes

Chapter 1. Introduction

1. C. Vann Woodward, *The Strange Career of Jim Crow*, 3rd ed., rev. (New York: Oxford University Press, 1974), and his *Origins of the New South, 1877–1913* (Baton Rouge: Louisiana State University Press, 1951). On the controversy over the "Jim Crow thesis," see Joel Williamson, ed., *The Origins of Segregation* (Boston: D.C. Heath, 1968), and his *After Slavery: The Negro in South Carolina during Reconstruction, 1861–1877* (Chapel Hill: University of North Carolina Press, 1965) and his *The Crucible of Race: Black-White Relations in the American South since Emancipation* (New York: Oxford University Press, 1984); Howard N. Rabinowitz, *Race Relations in the Urban South, 1865–1890* (New York: Oxford University Press, 1978); John W. Cell, *The Highest Stage of White Supremacy: The Origins of Segregation in South Africa and the American South* (Cambridge: Cambridge University Press, 1982); and Stephen Kantrowitz, *Ben Tillman and the Reconstruction of White Supremacy* (Chapel Hill: University of North Carolina Press, 2000). Woodward's own reflections on this controversy are in his *American Counterpoint: Slavery and Racism in the North-South Dialogue* (Boston: Little, Brown, 1971), 234–60, and his *Thinking Back: The Perils of Writing History* (Baton Rouge: Louisiana State University Press, 1986), 81–99.

2. An excellent recent survey of the historiography of the civil rights movement is Charles W. Eagles, "Toward New Histories of the Civil Rights Era," *Journal of Southern History* 66 (November 2000): 815–48; see also Steven F. Lawson, "Freedom Then, Freedom Now: The Historiography of the Civil Rights Movement," *American Historical Review* 96 (April 1991): 456–71.

3. E.g., Aldon D. Morris, *The Origins of the Civil Rights Movement: Black Communities Organizing for Change* (New York: Free Press, 1984), 17–25, 40–63, 295. After the Montgomery boycott had begun, Montgomery Improvement Association leaders did contact T. J. Jemison in Baton Rouge to seek his advice on the organization of the car-pool operation, but the Baton Rouge precedent played no more role in generating the Montgomery protest than did the streetcar boycott in Montgomery itself at the beginning of the century. All three of them, rather, reflect independently the general and persistent black resentment against racial discrimination. Professor Morris himself is a bit equivocal on the point. In his text he states flatly that King and Abernathy "were well aware of the Baton Rouge movement and consulted closely with Reverend Jemison when the famous Montgomery boycott

was launched in 1955" (25). But in his notes, though rejecting the contrary assertion of August Meier and Elliott Rudwick in their *Along the Color Line,* he nevertheless retreats to the far more defensible position, "This is not to say that the Baton Rouge movement caused the later movements, but it did play a role in their subsequent development" (295).

4. J. L. Chestnut, Jr., and Julia Cass, *Black in Selma: The Uncommon Life of J. L. Chestnut, Jr.* (New York: Farrar, Straus and Giroux, 1990), 127–30.

5. *Birmingham World,* July 27, 1963.

6. On Mobile in these years, see Bruce Nelson, "Organized Labor and the Struggle for Black Equality in Mobile during World War II," *Journal of American History* 80 (December 1993): 952–88; and Nahfiza Ahmed, "A City Too Respectable to Hate: Mobile during the Era of Desegregation, 1961–1965," *Gulf South Historical Review* 15 (Fall 1999): 49–67. But the full story of Mobile's civil rights struggles still has not been told.

7. Portions of the preceding several pages are adapted from my article "Municipal Politics and the Course of the Movement," in Armstead L. Robinson and Patricia Sullivan, eds., *New Directions in Civil Rights Studies* (Charlottesville: University Press of Virginia, 1991), 42–44, and they are reprinted here with the permission of the University Press of Virginia.

Chapter 2. Montgomery

1. On the background of the bus boycott, see my article "Challenge and Response in the Montgomery Bus Boycott of 1955–1956," *Alabama Review* 33 (July 1980): 163–235, from which a substantial part of this chapter is drawn. Accounts of the boycott by participants, of varying accuracy and usefulness, include Martin Luther King, Jr., *Stride toward Freedom: The Montgomery Story* (New York: Harper and Brothers, 1958); Ralph D. Abernathy, "The Natural History of a Social Movement: The Montgomery Improvement Association" (M.A. thesis, Atlanta University, 1958), and his *And the Walls Came Tumbling Down: An Autobiography* (New York: Harper and Row, 1989), 112–88; Lawrence D. Reddick, *Crusader without Violence: A Biography of Martin Luther King, Jr.* (New York: Harper and Brothers, 1959); Uriah J. Fields, *The Montgomery Story: The Unhappy Effects of the Montgomery Bus Boycott* (New York: Exposition Press, 1959); Hollinger F. Barnard, ed., *Outside the Magic Circle: The Autobiography of Virginia Foster Durr* (University: University of Alabama Press, 1985); Jo Ann Gibson Robinson, *The Montgomery Bus Boycott and the Women Who Started It: The Memoir of Jo Ann Gibson Robinson* (Knoxville: University of Tennessee Press, 1987); S. S. Seay, Sr., *I Was There by the Grace of God* (Montgomery: S. S. Seay, Sr., Educational Foundation, 1990); Robert S. Graetz, *Montgomery: A White Preacher's Memoir* (Minneapolis: Fortress Press, 1991); Rosa Parks with Jim Haskins, *Rosa Parks: My Story* (New York: Dial Books, 1992) [significant portions of which are drawn from my own work]; Fred D. Gray, *Bus Ride to Justice: Changing the System by the System* (Montgomery: Black Belt Press, 1995); Thomas R. Thrasher, "Alabama's Bus Boycott," *Reporter,* March 8, 1956, 13–16; Norman W. Walton, "The Walking City: A History of the Montgomery Boycott," *Negro History Bulletin* 20 (October 1956, November 1956, February 1957, April 1957) and 21 (January 1958); and Edgar N. French, "Beginnings of a New Age," in Glenford E. Mitchell and William H. Pearce III, eds., *The Angry Black South* (New York: Corinth Books, 1962), 30–51. Important original sources relating to the boycott are gathered in Stewart Burns, ed., *Daybreak of Freedom: The Montgomery Bus Boycott* (Chapel Hill:

University of North Carolina Press, 1997). King's speeches and writings from the period are contained in Clayborne Carson et al., eds., *The Papers of Martin Luther King, Jr.*, vol. 3 (Berkeley: University of California Press, 1997). See also David J. Garrow, "The Origins of the Montgomery Bus Boycott," *Southern Changes* 7 (October–December 1985): 21–27; Thomas J. Gilliam, "The Montgomery Bus Boycott of 1955–1956" (M.A. thesis, Auburn University, 1968); Lamont H. Yeakey, "The Montgomery, Alabama, Bus Boycott, 1955–1956" (Ph.D. diss., Columbia University, 1979); Steven M. Millner, "The Montgomery Bus Boycott: A Case Study in the Emergence and Career of a Social Movement" (Ph.D. diss., University of California at Berkeley, 1981); and Douglas Brinkley, *Rosa Parks* (New York: Penguin, 2000). The accounts by Walton, Thrasher, and French, the Abernathy and Gilliam theses, the Millner dissertation, and the articles by Garrow and by me are all conveniently printed, along with a new introduction I prepared, in *The Walking City: The Montgomery Bus Boycott, 1955–1956*, vol. 7 of David J. Garrow, ed., *Martin Luther King, Jr., and the Civil Rights Movement* (Brooklyn: Carlson Publishing, 1989); see also Willy S. Leventhal, ed., *The Children Coming On: A Retrospective of the Montgomery Bus Boycott* (Montgomery: Black Belt Press, 1998).

2. On the early battles between the Hills and Gunter and his associates, and the creation of the city commission, see the *Montgomery Advertiser*, January 12, July 25, 26, 1901, April 1, 2, 1911, May 18, 20, 1919; *Acts of Alabama*, 1911, pp. 289–315, 1915, pp. 52–76, 1919, pp. 97–102; *House Journal*, 1915, pp. 1461–66; *Senate Journal*, 1915, pp. 1144–49, 1170–71, 1173–75. On the Hill cousinry, see Virginia Van der Veer Hamilton, *Lister Hill: Statesman from the South* (Chapel Hill: University of North Carolina Press, 1987). On Hall and the *Advertiser*, see Daniel Webster Hollis III, *An Alabama Newspaper Tradition: Grover C. Hall and the Hall Family* (University: University of Alabama Press, 1983).

3. Montgomery's fascinating politics in the 1920s and 1930s is largely beyond the scope of this book and has not as yet been well studied. It is particularly difficult to decide whether Gunter or his opponents should be regarded as the city's liberal leaders. Hamilton, *Lister Hill*, and Hollis, *Alabama Newspaper Tradition*, both cited above, imply different answers to this question. Certainly the attacks of Gunter and Hall upon the Klan and religious bigotry are admirable. On the other hand, the machine profited handsomely from bootleggers and gamblers in return. (On this point, see Hugh Sparrow in the *Birmingham News*, March 17, 1946, though his account is not reliable in all its details.) And the Klan, despite its highly unpleasant tactics and beliefs, often attracted to it the support of politicians who may be said to have been of a liberal persuasion. (On this point, see my "Alabama Politics, J. Thomas Heflin, and the Expulsion Movement of 1929," *Alabama Review* 21 (April 1968): 83–112, and my "Hugo Black and the Golden Age," in Tony Freyer, ed., *Justice Hugo Black and Modern America* [Tuscaloosa: University of Alabama Press, 1990], 139–55.) Gunter's concern for the destitute during the Depression may appear to mark him as something of a New Dealer, but there is no question that his motives—perhaps rather like those of Franklin Roosevelt himself—were paternalist. And he has no claim to a monopoly on New Dealish actions; if anything, the claims of his rivals Lister Hill and Bibb Graves are superior to his. Finally, as to racial attitudes, both Gunter and his opponents the Hills were paternalist segregationists —not aggressive racists, to be sure, but by no means racial liberals. (For a revealing pseudonymous portrait of the Hill family's racial attitudes, see Charles Denby [Matthew Ward], *Indignant Heart: A Black Worker's Journal* [Boston: South End Press, 1978], 54–86. Interesting insight into Gunter's racial attitudes may be gained

from William A. Gunter, Jr., to J. Lister Hill and J. Lister Hill to William A. Gunter Jr., enclosed in W. A. Murphy to Walter White, January 20, 1930, NAACP Papers, Library of Congress, Washington, D.C.) Perhaps it is best to answer the question of who Montgomery's liberals were in these years simply by observing that the term as it was understood in national politics was inapplicable to the city's political culture. Only much later, after the civil rights movement had passed over the city, would the term genuinely become relevant to Montgomery's community life.

4. *Montgomery Advertiser,* March 15, 16, 1943, August 9, 12, September 5, 6, 1944, March 8, May 5, 9, 1946, March 18, 1947, March 19, 20, 1951; (Montgomery) *Alabama Journal,* May 9, 1946, March 18, 1947. Dunn had resigned in order to permit returning soldiers to participate in the choice of their mayor—one of his campaign pledges in 1944—but had declined to become a candidate in the special election "as I am entering private business here in Montgomery."

5. These figures were developed from Montgomery city directories. After 1952, city directories ceased to designate their entries by race, so the figures cannot be extended beyond that year. Dalraida and Chisholm were not yet entirely within the city limits at this period. Dalraida was annexed in four separate actions, in 1951, 1953, 1955, and 1956. The bulk of Chisholm was not annexed until 1961.

6. On the growth of east Montgomery, see *Montgomery Examiner,* December 12, 1946, January 23, February 20, March 6, July 3, August 21, December 4, 1947, January 22, 29, March 11, 1948, February 24, April 7, June 9, 1949, March 2, 9, August 10, 1950, July 26, August 2, October 18, 1951, April 3, 10, July 3, August 28, October 9, 1952; *Montgomery Advertiser,* March 12, 17, 19, May 10, 15, June 17, 1954, April 12, 21, June 7, July 8, 1956; *East Montgomery Home News,* June 27, July 5, 11, 25, August 18, 22, 29, September 5, 19, 26, October 10, 31, November 14, 21, December 26, 1957, January 2, 9, March 21, 28, May 16, 1958. In this work, I use the terms "lower middle class," "blue collar," and "working class" rather interchangeably; and I wish to avoid giving either them or other comparable socioeconomic descriptions, such as "white collar" and "upper middle class," too precise a definition. Rather, I intend all of these terms simply to reflect the broad, commonsensical perceptions of social division that all Alabamians of the time, of both races, would have recognized in their daily interactions with the world around them.

7. *Montgomery Advertiser,* February 20, March 15, 1955.

8. *Acts of Alabama,* 1949, pp. 819–27.

9. On the Robison-Stakely election and the subsequent personnel board hearing, see *Montgomery Examiner,* December 29, 1949, January 5, February 9, March 9, April 20, 27, May 11, June 1, October 5, 12, November 2, 9, 1950.

10. (Montgomery) *Alabama Journal,* March 18, 1947; *Montgomery Advertiser,* August 28, 1953, October 28, 1955.

11. *Montgomery Advertiser,* September 15, October 3, 4, 18, 24, 27 (third quotation), November 1 (first and second quotations), 3, 4 (fourth quotation), 1953.

12. Ibid., March 27, 1955; see also May 12, 1954.

13. *Smith* v. *Allwright,* 321 U.S. 649; *Montgomery Advertiser,* December 28, 1943, April 4, 1944, May 8, 1946; *Birmingham World,* January 11, 18, 1946.

14. *Davis* v. *Schnell,* 81 F.Supp. 872, 336 U.S. 933; *Alabama Official and Statistical Register,* 1947, pp. 535–39, 1951, pp. 607, 615–17, 1965, pp. 707–9.

15. *Madison* v. *State,* 31 Ala. App. 602; *Madison* v. *Nunnelee,* 246 Ala. 325; Trial Transcript, *Arthur A. Madison* v. *State of Alabama* (Records of the Alabama Court of Criminal Appeals, Office of the Clerk, Supreme Court Building, Montgomery), esp.

32–43; *Montgomery Advertiser,* December 31, 1943, January 15, February 9, April 9, 15, 20, May 24, 1944, January 17, 19, 1945; Edgar Nixon, interview by author, August 2, 1977; *Birmingham World,* June 11, 1948. On Arthur Madison and the Madison family, see Seay, *I Was There,* 56–65, 109–11 et passim. Unfortunately for Madison, his efforts to appeal the decisions of the board of registrars to the circuit court coincided with a heated primary election campaign in which U.S. senator Lister Hill was being challenged for reelection by state senator James A. Simpson of Birmingham. Simpson was eagerly attempting to arouse racial antipathies in the Black Belt and to use these fears to attack Hill, a New Dealer. Hill evidently became convinced that Simpson had put Madison up to the registration appeals in an effort to frighten segregationists. Hill therefore asked future U.S. Circuit judge Richard Rives (one of Hill's principal political operatives) and his first cousin John Blue Hill to stifle Madison's "agitation." Rives and John Blue Hill responded, it appears, by organizing Madison's prosecution (*Montgomery Advertiser,* April 9, 15, 16, 18, 1944).

16. *Montgomery Examiner,* March 16, 1950; *Montgomery Advertiser,* March 25, 1955; Records of the Montgomery County Board of Voting Registrars, Alabama Department of Archives and History, Montgomery. The registrars, indeed, were so willing to register well-educated blacks that they sometimes even failed to enforce against them clear and nonracial requirements. Martin Luther King, Jr., and his wife, Coretta, for instance, moved to Montgomery on September 1, 1954, and both were registered on December 20, 1954, despite the fact that the constitution required applicants to have resided in the state for two years and in the county for one year (Records of the Montgomery County Board of Voting Registrars). It is also worth noting that, despite the rapid increase in the white electorate during the 1940s, in the five years from 1950 to 1955 the number of whites who were registered actually declined slightly. The term "beat" is the designation in Alabama of the civil division that in most states is called a "precinct."

17. On Birmingham's racial attitudes, see Dave Birmingham to James E. Folsom, October 28, 1955, James E. Folsom Personal Papers, Alabama Department of Archives and History, Montgomery, in which Birmingham seeks appointment to the Montgomery County Board of Voting Registrars for himself and his friend Harold McGlynn so that they can undertake a wholesale registration of Montgomery's black citizenry. Historians who emphasize Governor Folsom's relative racial moderation should note that he appointed instead registrars who substantially restricted the pace of black registration in the county.

18. There was also a third area of black residence, as I have said, in Beat 6, in the industrial section of north Montgomery. Blacks in this area were the city's poorest, and relatively few of these residents were politically active. Virtually all black leaders came either from west Montgomery or from the Alabama State area.

19. This account of Lewis's early career is based primarily on a survey of Montgomery city directories; see also Seay, *I Was There,* 161–63.

20. Rufus A. Lewis, interview by author, July 27, 1977; *Montgomery Examiner,* February 15, 22, March 1, May 24, June 7, 1951. As early as 1949, Lewis had appeared at a public hearing conducted by Governor Folsom to denounce the discriminatory conduct of the Montgomery County Board of Voting Registrars (*Montgomery Examiner,* December 22, 1949). In later years, Lewis would serve as one of Montgomery's representatives in the state legislature.

21. This account is based on correspondence in the NAACP Papers. See especially Edgar Nixon to Walter White, December 14, 1944; Donald Jones to Ella J.

Baker, memorandum, September 14, 1945; Edgar Nixon to Ella J. Baker, October 10, 1945, November 8, 1945, November 25, 1945, December 26, 1945; Ella J. Baker to Robert L. Matthews, November 15, 1945; Ella J. Baker to Edgar Nixon, November 16, 1945; William G. Porter to Ella J. Baker, December 9, 1945; Horace G. Bell to Ella J. Baker, December 25, 1945; Edgar Nixon to Members of NAACP Montgomery Branch, pamphlet [November 1945]; Edgar Nixon to Ella J. Baker, May 20, 1946; Horace G. Bell to William G. Porter, May 20, 1946; E. W. Taggart to William G. Porter, June 8, 1946; Edgar Nixon to Emory O. Jackson, July 3, 1946; Emory O. Jackson to Edgar Nixon, July 8, 29, 1946; Edgar Nixon to William G. Porter, August 11, 1946; Willard Upshaw to Ella J. Baker, August 18, 1946; Horace G. Bell to Gloster B. Current, October 28, 1946; Horace G. Bell to E. W. Taggart, November 4, 1946; William G. Porter to Lucille Black, November 12, 1946; Gloster B. Current to Horace G. Bell, December 6, 1946; Edgar Nixon to Gloster B. Current, December 8, 1946; Pamphlet, "Is Hitler Dead?" by Edgar Nixon, October 29, 1946; clippings from (Montgomery) *Alabama Tribune,* November 22, 1946; Minutes of the Convention of the Alabama State Conference of NAACP Branches, Montgomery, October 3–5, 1947, p. 7; Edgar Nixon to Lucille Black, May 1, 23, 1949; Lucille Black to Edgar Nixon, May 10, 1949; Lucille Black to Daniel Byrd, May 26, 1949. On Nixon's background, see my sketches of him in John A. Garraty and Mark C. Carnes, *American National Biography* (New York: Oxford University Press, 1999), 16:454–55, and in Jack Salzman et al., eds., *Encyclopedia of African-American Culture and History* (New York: Macmillan, 1996), 4:2020–21.

22. *Birmingham World,* August 18, 1950, April 29, August 26, 1952; *Montgomery Advertiser,* February 6, March 21, April 20, May 6, 1954, September 23, 30, 1955; (Montgomery) *Alabama Tribune,* September 30, October 14, 1955; (Montgomery) *Alabama Journal,* February 2, 1956; Clifford J. Durr to Hubert T. Delany, September 4, 1955, Durr to Herbert H. Lehman, March 25, 1957, both in Clifford J. Durr Papers, Alabama Department of Archives and History, Montgomery. In later years Nixon believed that he may have been counted out in the executive committee race (interview, August 2, 1977). Following Nixon's defeat of Ronald Young for the presidency of the Progressive Democratic Association, Young was appointed the organization's executive secretary (*Montgomery Advertiser,* July 11, 1953).

23. *Montgomery Examiner,* December 4, 1947, May 12, 1949, June 21, 1951, October 30, 1952; Steven Millner, interview with Erna Dungee Allen, in Garrow, ed., *The Walking City,* 521; Jo Ann G. Robinson, interview by author, January 27, 1978; Trial Transcript, *M. L. King Jr.* v. *State of Alabama* (Records of the Alabama Court of Criminal Appeals), 256–57, 349–59. In her memoirs (*Montgomery Bus Boycott,* 22, 24), Mrs. Robinson gives the date of the council's formation as 1946 and that of her own assumption of the presidency as 1950. Both of these dates are erroneous. In general, Mrs. Robinson's memoir, though an enormously valuable document, is not always factually reliable. For sketches of Mrs. West, Mrs. Burks, and Mrs. Robinson, see Seay, *I Was There,* 160–61, 164–67.

24. This is Mrs. Robinson's own explanation (interview, January 27, 1978). A sociological phenomenon which perhaps enhanced the self-reliance of black women in Montgomery, as in most southern cities, was the gender ratio among adult blacks. The migration of blacks to northern cities, particularly during World Wars I and II, was disproportionately a male phenomenon. Thus in Montgomery in 1950, only 42 percent of adult blacks were male, while 58 percent were female (census of 1950).

25. On Mrs. Robinson's background see her *Montgomery Bus Boycott,* 9–10; Robinson, interview, January 27, 1978.

26. On King, see *Montgomery Examiner,* October 9, 1947. On the Felder affair, see *Montgomery Advertiser,* September 29, 30, 1947; *Montgomery Examiner,* October 2, 9, 23, 30, November 20, 27, December 4, 1947, February 26, 1948. In later years, Robert Felder became the nextdoor neighbor of Rosa and Raymond Parks.

27. *Montgomery Examiner,* February 26, March 4, 11, August 5, 1948, January 13, March 24, 31, April 7, June 30, November 17, 24, 1949, April 12, 19, 1951; Jack D. Shows, interview by author, June 20, 1984.

28. *Montgomery Examiner,* April 7, 14, 21, 28, May 5, 12, 19, 26, November 17, 24, 1949; Joe Azbell, interview by author, September 2, 1982; Seay, *I Was There,* 130–41. Police evidently had been accustomed to receiving the services of black prostitutes for free in return for permitting the bordellos to operate. One observer stated that, for this reason, police refused to take Miss Perkins's complaint seriously. A beating incident led to the indictment of two Montgomery policemen by a federal grand jury at about the same time as the Perkins affair (*Montgomery Examiner,* January 13, 1949; *Birmingham World,* November 1, 1949).

29. *Montgomery Examiner,* December 29, 1949. On James's and Birmingham's relations with the department, see ibid., September 7, 14, 28, October 5, 19, December 21, 28, 1950, January 18, 1951, April 17, May 8, 29, 1952; *Montgomery Advertiser,* January 16, 19, 20, February 19, March 24, 1954.

30. *Montgomery Examiner,* August 17, 24, 31, 1950; *Birmingham World,* August 18, 29, 1950.

31. *Montgomery Examiner,* June 7, July 26, 1951; *Birmingham World,* August 21, 1951.

32. On Williams, see John A. Salmond, *A Southern Rebel: The Life and Times of Aubrey Willis Williams, 1890–1965* (Chapel Hill: University of North Carolina Press, 1983), esp. 198–284.

33. E.g., *Montgomery Examiner,* May 20, 1948, March 24, 1949. On Montgomery's white racial liberals, I have profited from interviews with Virginia F. Durr, May 2, 1979, Clara H. Rutledge, August 13 and 18, 1982, and Andrew S. Turnipseed, July 25, 1989. See also Barnard, ed., *Outside the Magic Circle,* 210–337, and John A. Salmond, *The Conscience of a Lawyer: Clifford J. Durr and American Civil Liberties* (Tuscaloosa: University of Alabama Press, 1990). My use of the terms "liberal" and "moderate" in this context perhaps requires a word of definition. I have classified as racial liberals those whites who sought rapid movement toward the elimination of the legal requirements for racial segregation. Moderates held a spectrum of views between the liberals and uncompromising white supremacists, but all of them opposed arbitrary and highhanded actions directed toward blacks by white authorities, and most sought steady progress toward the elimination of inferior black institutions, within the context of continued segregation.

34. *Montgomery Examiner,* May 22, 1952; *Montgomery Advertiser,* November 7, December 19, 1953, April 17, 1954; *Birmingham World,* August 9, 1949, October 2, 16, 1951, May 27, 1952, December 18, 25, 1953. In addition to Dothan and Talladega, the all-black town of Hobson City, near Anniston, also employed black officers.

35. *Montgomery Advertiser,* December 17, 1953, February 21, March 18, April 15, 21, 23, June 20, 1954; (Montgomery) *Alabama Tribune,* December 18, 1953, April 23, 1954; *Birmingham World,* December 18, 1953, January 22, February 2,

12, April 20, 23, July 2, August 3, September 24, 28, 1954; *Birmingham News*, September 23, 1954. Birmingham's predecessor Earl James had opposed the hiring of black police (*Montgomery Examiner*, August 23, 1951), and Birmingham's attitude thus represented clear evidence of the new power of black voters to influence policy.

36. *Montgomery Examiner*, March 18, August 19, 1948, February 10, May 12, August 18, 1949, February 9, 1950; *Montgomery Advertiser*, October 30, 1966; YWCA Report on Race Relations in Montgomery, 1938, in possession of Mrs. Clara H. Rutledge, Lillian, Alabama; U.S. Censuses of 1940, 1950, 1960. It is difficult to tell from the figures reported in the 1940 census how many black young people were actually in high school classes, and it is impossible to know the number in public schools. The figure reported in the text is the number of blacks of high school age who were attending school. Between 1889 and 1921, Alabama State had offered only elementary and high school classes. It added a junior college program in 1921 and awarded its first bachelor's degrees in 1931. As Alabama State turned its attention increasingly toward collegiate education, leaving only its laboratory school as a remnant of its former mission, the need for public high schools for blacks became increasingly acute in the city. It hardly needs saying that the expansion of black educational opportunities in these years did not indicate any significant white acceptance of racial integration. Indeed, one motive for the expansion was precisely to forestall black demands for integration. When the Alabama Division of the Southern Regional Council, meeting in Montgomery in 1951, adopted a resolution urging the admission of blacks to Alabama's white colleges, the Montgomery County Grand Jury denounced the idea. The jurors said they were confident that the proposal "does not carry the approval of the better group of our colored citizens who carry some part of the burden of community and state life" (*Birmingham News*, February 17, 1951).

37. *Montgomery Examiner*, May 12, October 27, 1949, July 12, 1951, April 17, October 30, 1952; *Birmingham World*, November 5, 1948. Before the construction of Saint Jude's, Montgomery's blacks had been compelled to use Hale Infirmary, a wooden structure containing thirty-five beds that was condemned and closed by the state health department in 1953 (*Montgomery Advertiser*, December 23, 1953; *Birmingham World*, December 29, 1953).

38. *Montgomery Examiner*, October 20, 1949, December 14, 1950, November 15, 1951, March 27, June 19, 1952; *Montgomery Advertiser*, January 31, February 21, May 9, 1954, February 1, 9, 1955. The initial sections of Paterson Courts (for blacks) and Riverside Heights (for whites) were constructed in 1937. Cleveland Courts (black) was built and Riverside Heights much expanded in 1941. Paterson Courts was greatly expanded in 1946. Victor Tulane Courts (black) was completed in 1951, and Trenholm Courts (black) was opened in 1954.

39. *Montgomery Examiner*, May 29, 1947, October 20, 1949, January 5, April 13, 1950, July 26, September 27, 1951, January 10, February 14, August 28, December 18, 1952; (Montgomery) *Alabama Tribune*, December 18, 1953. The leading black proponent of the black farmers' market in the city was Vernon Johns, minister of the Dexter Avenue Baptist Church from 1948 to 1952 (*Montgomery Examiner*, May 8, 1952; interviews by Norman Lumpkin with Rufus Lewis and Eugene Ligon, June 25, 1973, pp. 1–3, and with Mrs. Thelma Rice, August 22, 1973, pp. 1–4, in Alabama Center for Higher Education Statewide Oral History Project Transcripts, Special Collections, Alabama State University Library). Seeking to create a cooperative marketing arrangement for black farmers, Johns opened the basement of his

church to allow them to sell produce from the church facilities. The hostility of his congregation to these activities on church property eventually forced Johns to resign his pulpit, and he was succeeded by Martin Luther King, Jr.

The influence of radio station WRMA spread far beyond the black residents of Montgomery. John Lewis tells in his autobiography of the effect of its programming upon him as he was growing up as a teenager in rural Pike County, near Banks (John Lewis with Michael D'Orso, *Walking with the Wind: A Memoir of the Movement* [New York: Simon and Schuster, 1998], 56).

40. *Montgomery Examiner,* June 26, November 20, 1952; (Montgomery) *Alabama Tribune,* December 11, 1953; *Montgomery Advertiser,* December 2, 3, 4, 1953, March 23, 28, April 13, 1954; *Birmingham World,* December 8, 1953.

41. *Birmingham World,* December 8, 1953, June 15, September 17, 28, 1954; *Montgomery Advertiser,* September 3, 7, 10, October 31, 1954; *Selma Times-Journal,* July 11, 1954, August 21, 1955.

42. *Montgomery Advertiser,* December 20, 1953, January 19, July 20, August 10, September 14, 1955; (Montgomery) *Alabama Tribune,* January 28, August 19, 1955; *Birmingham World,* January 25, July 26, 1955; Yeakey, "Montgomery, Alabama, Bus Boycott," 164–65. The *Advertiser* alleged editorially that Birmingham's August resolution was merely the opening salvo in his rumored race for a seat on the county board of revenue. At the July meeting with the blacks, Cleere and Birmingham almost came to blows and had to be separated by the mayor. The land that was promised as the site of a large new park for blacks at the September meeting ultimately became a parking lot for a white football stadium.

43. The seating policy described in the text was the company's official one. In practice the policy seems to have varied considerably from route to route and from driver to driver. See Trial Transcript, *King v. State,* 360–486, 510–47; Trial Transcript, *Browder v. Gayle,* 58–69.

44. Montgomery City Code of 1952, Chapter 6, Sections 10–11; Code of Alabama, 1940, Recompiled, Title 48, Section 301 (31a, b, and c); *Acts of Alabama,* 1939, pp. 1064–90, 1945, p. 731, 1947, pp. 40–41; Case File, *Aurelia S. Browder v. William A. Gayle,* Exhibit A: "Legal Requirements Concerning the Segregation of Races on City Buses," in Southeastern Regional Federal Records Center, East Point, Georgia (hereinafter cited as FRC East Point); *Montgomery Advertiser,* July 3, 10, 24, August 4, 7, 16, 18, 1900, October 2, 9, 16, 18, 23, November 22, 23, 24, 25, 29, December 1, 23, 1906, January 2, 3, 4, 5, 8, 13, 14, 22, 1907, January 6, 1957; *Montgomery Journal,* July 3, 10, August 7, 13, 14, 15, 16, 18, 1900; *Huntsville Republican,* September 22, 1900; August Meier and Elliott Rudwick, "The Boycott Movement against Jim Crow Streetcars in the South, 1900–1906," *Journal of American History* 55 (March 1969): 756–75.

45. *Mobile Daily Register,* October 16, 17, November 4, 5, 11, December 2, 12, 1902; Mobile City Code of 1907, Chapter 76, Article 2, Sections 773–79; 1921 Supplement to the Mobile City Code of 1907, pp. 280–81; Mobile City Code of 1947, Chapter 20, Article 1; Mobile City Code of 1955, Chapter 10, Sections 4–9. Apparently the ordinance of 1917 merely codified the actual practice that had evolved on the streetcars in the intervening years. At any rate, a careful survey of Mobile newspapers, both black and white, from the period of the ordinance's adoption failed to reveal any comment on the city commission's action.

46. *Montgomery Examiner,* October 30, 1952 (quotation); (Montgomery) *Alabama Journal,* October 28, 1952. Solomon Seay reports that delegations from the Negro Civic and Improvement League had met with bus company manager James H.

Bagley as early as 1949 and 1950 to complain about drivers' lack of courtesy to blacks (*I Was There*, 147–48). The league had been organized by black physician Roman T. Adair in 1936 and had actively sought black advancement during the 1940s (ibid., 117).

47. Trial Transcript, *King* v. *State*, 141, 256–57 (first quotation), 349–59; *Montgomery Advertiser*, April 6, 1954; (Montgomery) *Alabama Tribune*, April 2, 1954; Jo Ann G. Robinson to William A. Gayle, May 21, 1954, in File 2279, Records of the Solicitor's Office, Fifteenth Circuit, Montgomery County Courthouse, Montgomery (second quotation).

48. *Montgomery Advertiser*, February 1, 6, 9, 13, 16, 20, 27, 28, March 10, 13, 16, 20, 23, 24, 27, 1955.

49. Ibid., February 9, 16, March 16, 1955, January 13, 1956.

50. Ibid., February 18, 24, 25, March 1, 16, 20 (quotations), 1955. Ralph Abernathy gives the membership of the committee that drafted the questionnaire as including himself, Nixon, Lewis, Mrs. Robinson, Mrs. Irene West, and Alabama State political science professor James E. Pierce (interview by author, February 28, 1979). Nixon, who presided at the meeting, says that all of the candidates chose to duck the bus seating question (interview, August 2, 1977).

51. *Montgomery Advertiser*, March 16, 20 (quotation), 1955.

52. Ibid., February 9, 13, March 16, 20, 22, 24 (quotation), 25, 29, 1955. Because of the presence on the ballot of a minor candidate, George J. Rivers, the race between Parks and Cleere was forced into a runoff, but the geographical distribution of the vote was identical in both elections.

53. Ibid., March 30, 1955.

54. (Montgomery) *Alabama Journal*, January 13, 1956.

55. *Montgomery Advertiser*, October 28, 1953 (first quotation), January 15, 1954, February 20, 24, March 7, 10, October 19, December 11, 1955, January 17 (third quotation), March 4, 1956; (Montgomery) *Alabama Journal*, November 3, December 9, 1955, January 10, 1956 (second quotation).

56. *Montgomery Advertiser*, December 11, 1955.

57. Ibid., March 6, 1955; (Montgomery) *Alabama Journal*, March 18, 19, 1955; *Birmingham World*, March 22, May 6, 10, 1955; *USA Today*, November 28, 1995; *Washington Post*, April 12, 1998; Durr, interview, May 2, 1979; Trial Transcript, *Browder* v. *Gayle*, 17–20, and Colvin arrest warrant and complaint contained in the case file; Yeakey, "Montgomery, Alabama, Bus Boycott," 231–45. Dr. Yeakey's account of this episode is based on documents not publicly available. On Fred Gray's background, see *Montgomery Examiner*, May 17, 1951; *Montgomery Advertiser*, June 17, 1954, September 14, 1955; *Birmingham World*, August 31, 1954; Gray, *Bus Ride to Justice*, 3–37; for Gray's own account of the Colvin case see ibid., 37, 47–49. Edgar Nixon states that a number of black leaders had pressed for a bus boycott in support of Miss Colvin but that he stifled the idea because he did not think the Colvin family strong enough to withstand the pressure to which they would be subjected (interview, August 2, 1977). Miss Colvin's father, Quintus Publius Colvin, worked as a yardman, and her mother was a maid. On the arrest and trial of the New Jersey teenagers, see *Birmingham World*, July 5, 1949; Seay, *I Was There*, 156–58; and Parks with Haskins, *Rosa Parks*, 93.

58. Trial Transcript, *King* v. *State*, 240, 256–57, 344–46, 357–59, 539–40; King, *Stride toward Freedom*, 41–42. Crenshaw and his brother had handled Governor Folsom's suit in 1948 to compel the Dixiecrat presidential electors to vote for Harry Truman: *Folsom* v. *Albritton*, 335 U.S. 882; *State* v. *Albritton*, 251 Ala. 422. Crenshaw

had also been deeply involved in the Lime-Cola scandal that had rocked Montgomery in 1946 and 1947. The Securities and Exchange Commission found that Crenshaw had instructed Lime-Cola on how to evade the legal requirement that its stock be registered before any sales were made (*Montgomery Examiner,* March 27, April 3, 10, 1947). Crenshaw's father, the president of the Alabama Bar Association in 1936, was the coauthor of a book alleging that the defense of the Scottsboro Boys was a Communist plot (Files Crenshaw and Kenneth A. Miller, *Scottsboro: The Firebrand of Communism* [Montgomery: Brown Printing Co., 1936]).

To the very end of his life, Crenshaw continued to believe that the Montgomery City Code required in detail the specific seating arrangement that the bus company used. When I told him that the code in fact merely required that the seating be separate and equal, he replied energetically and emphatically that he was positive that I was wrong. He was also under the impression that Mobile had adopted its seating plan only a few months before the outbreak of the boycott, though it actually dates, as we have seen, from 1917. He stated that the Montgomery bus company had always been willing to accept the Mobile plan if the city commission would amend the ordinance to permit the arrangement, but that the commission adamantly refused to do so (interview, July 15, 1977). On the other hand, Knabe, who like Crenshaw had been trained in law at Harvard, told me that he never really doubted the legality of the blacks' seating proposal. He said that he opposed granting the concession only because he was convinced that doing so would not produce an end to the boycott (interview, August 5, 1977). Of course, that explanation cannot account for his having said that the proposal was illegal before the boycott had begun. At the time, at any rate, Knabe gave no hint that he doubted the illegality of the blacks' plan. Crenshaw stated to me that Knabe supported his position.

59. *Flemming* v. *South Carolina Electric and Gas Co.,* 128 F.Supp. 469, 224 F.2d 752; *Montgomery Advertiser,* July 15, 1955; (Montgomery) *Alabama Tribune,* July 22, 29, 1955; *Birmingham World,* July 19, September 2, 1955, May 1, 1956; Trial Transcript, *Browder* v. *Gayle,* 10–12; *USA Today,* November 28, 1995; *Washington Post,* April 12, 1998.

60. *Montgomery Advertiser,* December 12–16, 1953, October 25, 27, December 7, 20, 1955, January 25, February 16, 1956.

61. The Selma firings and boycott will receive a fuller discussion in chapter 4; see my "Selma's Smitherman Affair of 1955," *Alabama Review* 44 (April 1991): 112–31.

62. *Montgomery Advertiser,* November 6, 1955 (quotation); Edgar D. Nixon, interview by author, August 2, 1977. On the New York bus boycott of 1941, see Dominic J. Capeci, Jr., "From Harlem to Montgomery: The Bus Boycotts and Leadership of Adam Clayton Powell, Jr. and Martin Luther King, Jr.," *Historian* 41, no. 4 (1979): 721–37. On Powell's drink with Folsom and its devastating effect on Folsom's career, see George E. Sims, *The Little Man's Big Friend: James E. Folsom in Alabama Politics, 1946–1958* (University: University of Alabama Press, 1985), 174–77, 186, 190, 220; and Carl Grafton and Anne Permaloff, *Big Mules and Branchheads: James E. Folsom and Political Power in Alabama* (Athens: University of Georgia Press, 1985), 192–201.

63. *Montgomery Advertiser,* December 2, 1955; (Montgomery) *Alabama Journal,* December 5, 1955; Trial Transcript, *Rosa Parks* v. *City of Montgomery* (Records of the Alabama Court of Criminal Appeals, Office of the Clerk, Supreme Court Building, Montgomery), 7–9. Prosecutors located a white passenger who was prepared to testify that there was indeed a vacant seat in the rear, but the driver, Blake, who had

a better view of the seating situation, testified that all seats were taken. And since all the testimony agreed that several blacks were standing, one would wonder why none of the standees would have taken an available seat.

64. Durr, interview, May 2, 1979; Montgomery County, Colored Marriages, Book 33, p. 16; U.S. Manuscript Census of 1910, Montgomery County, Enumeration District 109, sheet 10; U.S. Manuscript Census of 1900, Henry County, Enumeration District 92, sheet 11; Parks with Haskins, *Rosa Parks*, 2–37. On Miss White and her school's curriculum, see U.S. Department of the Interior, Bureau of Education, *Negro Education: A Study of the Private and Higher Schools for Colored People in the United States*, prepared under the direction of Thomas Jesse Jones, 2 vols. (Washington, D.C.: Government Printing Office, 1917), 2:77–78; and Helen Christine Bennett, "Two Practicing Christians," *American Magazine* 77, no. 5 (1914): 61, 63.

65. Durr, interview, May 2, 1979; Montgomery County, Colored Marriages, Book 48, p. 327; Parks with Haskins, *Rosa Parks*, 38–64. On Raymond Parks's background, see the transcript of the interview with Virginia F. Durr by Stanley H. Smith, pp. 58–59, in the Civil Rights Documentation Project Manuscripts, Howard University Library, Washington, D.C. Parks, a native of Wedowee, had come to Montgomery from Columbus, Georgia, in 1928.

66. U.S. Census of 1940; Montgomery City Directories, 1937, 1946, 1954, 1956; Parks with Haskins, *Rosa Parks*, 65–66, 86, 101.

67. Durr, interview, May 2, 1979; Montgomery Branch, List of New Members, 1934; Rosa L. Parks to Mary White Ovington, March 8, 1944; Edgar Nixon to Walter White, December 14, 1944; Rosa L. Parks to Lucille Black, March 11, 1946 (first quotation); Minutes of the Convention of the Alabama Conference of NAACP Branches, October 3–5, 1947, pp. 4, 7, 10; Minutes of the Convention of the Alabama Conference of NAACP Branches, October 8–10, 1948, pp. 2, 10 (second quotation); Edgar Nixon to Lucille Black, May 1, 1949; Lucille Black to Edgar Nixon, May 10, 1949; Gloster B. Current to John L. LeFlore, December 7, 1951; Newsletter of Southeastern Regional Office of NAACP, August 10, 1953; *Southeastern Youth Reporter*, "official organ of the regional youth conference, NAACP," vol. 1, no. 2 [Spring 1955]: 1; Ruby Hurley to Gloster B. Current, December 28, 1955, all in NAACP Papers; *Birmingham World*, July 27, 1954; Candace Stone, "Community Prayer Service, May 3, 1956, Central Christian Church, Anderson, Indiana," p. 9, in Hazel Gregory Papers, Martin Luther King Center for Social Change, Atlanta; Twenty-third Annual Report of the Highlander Folk School (October 1, 1954–September 30, 1955), p. 1, in Labadie Collection, University of Michigan Library, Ann Arbor; Barnard, ed., *Outside the Magic Circle*, 278–79; Parks with Haskins, *Rosa Parks*, 71–113. The Highlander conference which Mrs. Parks attended was held from July 24 through August 8, 1955. Myles Horton, Septima Clark, and other staff members led it, and participants included Irene Osborne of the American Friends Service Committee, Dr. Herman Long of Fisk University, Dean Charles Gomillion of Tuskegee Institute, Dr. Frederick D. Patterson of the Phelps-Stokes Foundation (a former president of Tuskegee Institute), Fred Routh of the Southern Regional Council, and the liberal South Carolina attorney John Bolt Culbertson. Virginia Durr was a longtime friend of Highlander's founder, Myles Horton, and she served with him on the board of directors of the Southern Conference Educational Fund.

68. This sketch of Blake is derived from a survey of Montgomery City Directories and from Blake's U.S. Army service record. On Mrs. Parks's 1943 encounter

with Blake, see Parks with Haskins, *Rosa Parks,* 77–79, also 133. Blake declined to be interviewed for this study, but see *Washington Post,* July 24, 1989.

69. Interviews with Nixon, August 2, 1977, Durr, May 2, 1979, and Robinson, January 27, 1978; *Montgomery Advertiser,* December 4, 1955; Robinson, *Montgomery Bus Boycott,* 43–52; Parks with Haskins, *Rosa Parks,* 112–28; Barnard, ed., *Outside the Magic Circle,* 279–81. The text of the leaflet given in Mrs. Robinson's and Mrs. Parks's memoirs differs slightly from that given in the newspaper. Alabama State's president, H. Councill Trenholm, furious at Mrs. Robinson for having placed the college in danger of white retaliation by her actions, threatened to dismiss her. She retained her job only by swearing to keep her role secret. In this she was eminently successful; Solicitor Thetford stated to me that despite his most diligent efforts, he was never able to discover the origin of the handbills (interview, September 4, 1976). Rufus Lewis believed that the real source of the boycott was the prominence and popularity of Mrs. Parks, which moved the city's black women to take action (interview, July 27, 1977).

70. King, *Stride toward Freedom,* 43–49; Trial Transcript, *King* v. *State,* 446–48; (Montgomery) *Alabama Tribune,* December 9, 16, 1955; Abernathy, interview, February 28, 1979; Abernathy, "Natural History," in Garrow, ed., *The Walking City,* 117–19; Parks with Haskins, *Rosa Parks,* 129–30. Abernathy states that of the seventy-five people who attended the meeting, about sixty were ministers and eight were women. The idea of holding the meeting under the auspices of the Interdenominational Ministerial Alliance seems to have been Abernathy's own. The people Nixon called after Mrs. Parks's arrest were largely those who had been active in the NAACP and thus had known Mrs. Parks. But Nixon evidently recognized that this group of activists was unlikely to be successful in involving the black masses without the support of the clergy. Nixon had very little contact with the black clergy, but he did know Abernathy well. Abernathy was one of the few ministers who was also a significant figure in the NAACP branch. He was therefore the ideal bridge between the two groups. Nixon asked Abernathy to arrange for the attendance of the leading black ministers, and Abernathy did so, in the process seeking the assistance of Bennett, who was his personal friend, and a Methodist, while Abernathy was a Baptist.

Additional copies of Mrs. Robinson's handbill were run off by Abernathy and King in the Dexter Avenue Church office after the meeting that night, and they were distributed on December 3 and 4. The text of the handbill also was printed on the front page of the *Montgomery Advertiser* on December 4 and was read from the pulpits of most black churches that day, a Sunday. Abernathy states that King offered Nixon his church as the site of the meeting in the hope that he would not be asked to do anything further for the cause. Nixon confirms King's reluctance. But because the church was King's, he necessarily was appointed along with Abernathy to prepare the additional copies of the handbills that night, thus involving King rather against his own inclination in the organizing of the boycott (interviews with Abernathy, February 28, 1979, and Nixon, August 2, 1977).

71. (Montgomery) *Alabama Journal,* December 5, 1955; *Montgomery Advertiser,* December 6, 1955; Gray, *Bus Ride to Justice,* 55–56; Parks with Haskins, *Rosa Parks,* 132–34. On Judge Scott, see *Montgomery Advertiser,* September 25, 1955; Scott was also the great-great-grandson and namesake of one of Montgomery's two founders. Gray has stated that whether the prosecution was carried out under the state law or the city ordinance seemed a matter of no real importance to him (interview by author, October 17, 1978). His statement in his memoirs that Mrs. Parks was

charged with disorderly conduct rather than with violating the segregation laws (50, 56) is erroneous.

72. Nixon says that when he called his old rival Robert L. Matthews, the president of the Montgomery NAACP chapter, to report Mrs. Parks's arrest, Matthews refused to allow the branch to become involved in a boycott without the approval of the NAACP national headquarters. Nixon states that it was this attitude of Matthews's which forced the creation of a separate organization to run the boycott (interview, August 2, 1977). But Abernathy reports that he and King had been discussing for months the need for an umbrella organization to bind Montgomery's blacks together and that he seized the opportunity afforded by the boycott to suggest the creation of one (interview, February 28, 1979). He also states that none of the boycott's leaders had ever dreamed that the boycott could last longer than four days (ibid.). Matthews's hesitancy about the reaction of NAACP headquarters was well founded. Because the boycott was not seeking integration but only an amelioration of segregation, the national NAACP refused to support that aspect of the protest, though it did agree to assist Mrs. Parks's legal challenge to segregation itself. The NAACP was at this very time financing the *Flemming* suit from Columbia, South Carolina, in an effort to have all bus segregation declared unconstitutional by the U.S. Supreme Court. "Obviously," Roy Wilkins wrote, "when our national program calls for abolishing segregation and our lawyers are fighting on that basis in South Carolina, we could not enter an Alabama case asking merely for more polite segregation" (W. C. Patton to Roy Wilkins and Gloster B. Current, December 19, 1955, Roy Wilkins to W. C. Patton, December 27, 1955, NAACP Papers).

73. Trial Transcript, *King v. State*, 106–28, 334; King, *Stride toward Freedom*, 30, 46–58, 72–74; Abernathy, "Natural History," in Garrow, ed., *The Walking City*, 128–31; Burns, ed., *Daybreak of Freedom*, 88–89. Lewis states that in suggesting King, he was merely searching for another name as an alternative to Bennett's; he calls the nomination the luckiest accident of his life. Abernathy is certain that Lewis suggested King's name as a way of preventing Nixon's election; see also Gray, *Bus Ride to Justice*, 53–54 (though Gray's account contains factual errors). Nixon himself claims that he had early recognized King's talents and was planning to nominate him if Lewis had not done so. But Abernathy says that Nixon barely knew King at the outbreak of the boycott; he says that when Nixon telephoned him on December 2, he himself suggested King's name to Nixon as a minister who might be cooperative (interviews with Abernathy, February 28, 1979, Lewis, July 27, 1977, and Nixon, August 2, 1977). I am inclined to believe that Nixon's memory of his early appreciation of King's talents is influenced by the acrimonious struggle for King's mantle of leadership in which Nixon and Lewis engaged in the years after King and Abernathy left Montgomery—a struggle that eventually culminated in Lewis's victory and left Nixon deeply embittered. Bennett had come to Montgomery in June 1952 from Lynch, Kentucky, to succeed Solomon Seay as the pastor of the Mount Zion A.M.E.Z. Church (*Montgomery Examiner*, June 26, 1952). He left in the midst of the boycott to accept a pastorate in San Francisco. On Bennett, see Seay, *I Was There*, 170–73, 183. On King's early life, see David J. Garrow, *Bearing the Cross: Martin Luther King, Jr., and the Southern Christian Leadership Conference* (New York: William Morrow, 1986), 32–51.

74. Trial Transcript, *King v. State*, 59–61, 344–46; (Montgomery) *Alabama Tribune*, December 16, 1955 (quotations); Burns, ed., *Daybreak of Freedom*, 92–93. It is probable that Fred Gray was the author of these resolutions; see French, "Begin-

nings of a New Age," in Garrow, ed., *The Walking City,* 179; and Gray, *Bus Ride to Justice,* 57.

75. *Montgomery Advertiser,* February 1, December 7, 1955; (Montgomery) *Alabama Journal,* December 7, 1955; Abernathy, "Natural History," in Garrow, ed., *The Walking City,* 132; Burns, ed., *Daybreak of Freedom,* 97.

76. French, "Beginnings of a New Age," in Garrow, ed., *The Walking City,* 178–79; Abernathy, *And the Walls Came Tumbling Down,* 142–49, and his "Natural History," in Garrow, ed., *The Walking City,* 128–30; interviews with Abernathy, February 28, 1979, and Nixon, August 2, 1977. Abernathy in his autobiography (144) and French in his memoir (179) each implies that he was the true author of the three demands, but their content convinces me that they actually owe much more to Nixon than to the other two men. King (*Stride toward Freedom,* 63–64, 108–9) states that the demands were adopted by the mass meeting on the night of December 5, and that claim has been echoed by virtually all subsequent commentators. But it is erroneous. The demands were adopted by the executive board on the afternoon of December 5, and they made their first public appearance when King read them to the city commission on December 8. Abernathy (*And the Walls Came Tumbling Down,* 144–45) says that, unlike Nixon, he never regarded the demand for black drivers as a serious one, but rather thought it a negotiating point that could be conceded to whites later. It seems reasonable to me that Nixon, as the president of a union local, may have cared more deeply about this demand than did other black leaders. Abernathy is correct in noting that, under the city and state segregation laws, the hiring of black drivers would have meant that a black man would thus have gained police power to instruct white passengers where to sit. As a result, this would seem to have been the demand that segregationists would have been least likely to accept. It is a fact, at any rate, that once seating segregation was forbidden in December of 1956, Montgomery's blacks ended the boycott without insisting also on the hiring of black drivers. As we shall see, the bus company did not finally hire its first black drivers—Allen Pierce and Thomas Jackson—until July 6, 1962 (Montgomery Improvement Association to James H. Bagley, April 9, 1962, Solomon S. Seay, Sr., to Bernard W. Franklin, July 9, 1962, both in Gregory Papers; Seay, *I Was There,* 234–35, 241).

77. King, *Stride toward Freedom,* 108–13 (third set of quotations); Trial Transcript, *King* v. *State,* 239, 248–50, 336, 346–47; *Montgomery Advertiser,* December 9 (second quotation), 10 (fourth quotation), 11 (first quotation), 1955; (Montgomery) *Alabama Journal,* December 8, 9, 1955; *Browder* v. *Gayle* case file, Exhibit A: "Legal Requirements Concerning the Segregation of Races on City Buses"; Abernathy, "Natural History," in Garrow, ed., *The Walking City,* 132–33; Robinson, *Montgomery Bus Boycott,* 78–81; Gray, *Bus Ride to Justice,* 60–62. Durr stated in a later interview that he provided King with the memorandum that underlay the statement issued on December 10 (Clifford Durr, interview by Stanley Smith, pp. 31–32, Civil Rights Documentation Project Manuscripts, Howard University Library, Washington, D.C.); the same arguments appear in Gray's brief, presumably written in consultation with Durr. Crenshaw did not in later years recall the interchange with Parks that King reports, but he did confirm that Parks was more amenable to accepting the MIA's demands than were the other two commissioners, particularly Sellers. As Gayle and the reporters left the meeting, Gayle told those remaining that he wanted them to find a settlement as quickly as possible. Crenshaw to the end of his life strongly resented that remark, feeling that it was an

effort on the mayor's part to pass the buck to the bus company, which Crenshaw always regarded as an innocent third party in the dispute (interview, July 15, 1977).

78. Trial Transcript, *King* v. *State*, 539–41 (quotation); *Montgomery Advertiser*, March 20, December 31, 1955; King, *Stride toward Freedom*, 110; Mobile City Code of 1947, Chapter 20, Article 1; Mobile City Code of 1955, Chapter 10, Sections 4–9; Montgomery City Code of 1952, Chapter 6, Sections 10–11. As we have seen (note 58), Crenshaw continued until his death to believe, erroneously, that the Montgomery ordinance required the specific details of the bus company's practice.

79. Trial Transcript, *Browder* v. *Gayle*, 46–48 (quotations); Motion of Public Service Commission for Dismissal of Complaint, in *Browder* v. *Gayle* case file. This reversal of positions was so complete that it left Crenshaw confused about what his position had been on the issue earlier in the boycott. He believed in later years that he had argued to the city commission that the state statutes were not applicable and that Gray had maintained that they were (interview, July 15, 1977).

80. Trial Transcript, *King* v. *State*, 346 (quotation); *Montgomery Advertiser*, December 13, 1953, October 3, 4, 1955; (Montgomery) *Alabama Journal*, December 16, 1955; King, *Stride toward Freedom*, 117–18; Robinson, *Montgomery Bus Boycott*, 84–90. Just as the commission apparently thought of the MIA and the bus company as the principal disputants, so the bus company thought of the MIA and the commission as the principal disputants. This odd situation tended to inhibit both the company and the city in the negotiations with the blacks.

It is an interesting index to the extent of the gulf between Montgomery's white and black communities that the *Advertiser*, in editorially congratulating the commission in 1953 for having included a black man on the mediating panel, got Blair's name wrong, calling him T. M. Blain. Blair was Rosa Parks's predecessor as secretary of the Montgomery branch of the NAACP.

81. *Montgomery Advertiser*, December 20, 1955 (quotation); King, *Stride toward Freedom*, 118–19; *Who's Who in America* (Chicago: Marquis–Who's Who, 1967), vol. 34 (1966–67), 717; *Who's Who in Chicago and Illinois* (Chicago: A. N. Marquis Co., 1950), 9th ed. (1950), 196. On Fitzgerald's creation of National City Lines, see *Chicago Sun*, July 21, 1946. The company's determinedly noncommittal position on the boycott is well illustrated by Bernard W. Franklin to Wilhelmina D. Long, March 20, 1956 (enclosed in Wilhelmina D. Long to James E. Folsom, May 9, 1956, in Governors' Correspondence: Folsom II, Alabama Department of Archives and History, Montgomery), and *Montgomery Advertiser*, April 2, 1956. Crenshaw states that National City Lines hoped that by refusing to get involved, it could avoid making anyone mad (interview, July 15, 1977). I have been unable to locate any biographical information on Totten. In 1987, the owner of National City Lines, Harold C. Simmons of Dallas, Texas, informed me that all of the company's records from the period of the boycott were discarded at some time in the past (J. Mills Thornton III to Harold C. Simmons, June 29, 1987, Steven L. Watson to J. Mills Thornton III, July 15, 1987, in author's possession).

82. King, *Stride toward Freedom*, 114–21; *Montgomery Advertiser*, December 18, 20, 1955; (Montgomery) *Alabama Journal*, December 17, 19, 20 (quotation), 1955, January 18, 1956; Trial Transcript, *King* v. *State*, 233–36, 248–50, 336, 539–41.

83. This account relies primarily on Yeakey, who had access to the documents in Gray's legal files upon which it is based; see Yeakey, "Montgomery, Alabama, Bus Boycott," 469–70 (quotation, 470 n), 496–97, 501–4. For the state appeals court's dismissal of Mrs. Parks's case on strictly technical grounds, see *Parks* v. *City of Montgomery*, 38 Ala. App. 681; on Clyde Sellers and the city's negotiations with the

MIA, see *Montgomery Advertiser,* January 7, 10, 1956, and (Montgomery) *Alabama Journal,* January 18, 1956; on attitudes within the MIA, see (Montgomery) *Alabama Tribune,* December 23, 30, 1955, January 6, 13, 20, 27, 1956. Gray states that he had favored filing a federal suit from the outset but had been unable to convince the MIA's executive board to authorize the action, both because the strategy was new and untried for Montgomery blacks and because many MIA leaders had high hopes for negotiations in the early weeks (interview by author, October 17, 1978; cf. Gray, *Bus Ride to Justice,* 68–69). Clifford Durr stated that he urged Gray to press for the filing of the federal court suit because he was certain that the state courts would dispose of Mrs. Parks's case on technical grounds in order to keep the constitutional issues from getting before the U.S. Supreme Court. Durr reported that he drafted a proposed federal court petition and that Gray took it to New York to obtain the advice of NAACP Legal Defense Fund attorneys. It became, Durr said, the basis for the petition that Gray actually later filed (Durr, interview by Stanley Smith, pp. 38–41). Mrs. Durr says that her husband helped Gray with all the briefs and submissions in the boycott suit and that she personally typed them (interview, May 2, 1979). A version of the federal court petition giving Rosa Parks and Claudette Colvin as the plaintiffs was submitted to Robert Carter by Gray and Durr for Carter's suggestions, and it remains in the NAACP Papers; it can be internally dated to mid-January. In the end, as we shall see, Gray became concerned, he says, that the fact that Mrs. Parks's criminal conviction was on appeal in the state courts might create unnecessary legal complications in the federal suit. He therefore deleted her name as a plaintiff and located other women who agreed to serve in her stead (see Norman Lumpkin's interview with Fred Gray, September 1, 1973, p. 4, in Alabama Center for Higher Education Statewide Oral History Project Transcripts, Special Collections, Alabama State University Library, and Gray, *Bus Ride to Justice,* 69–72).

84. Trial Transcript, *King* v. *State,* 252–53; (Montgomery) *Alabama Tribune,* January 20, 27, 1956; *Montgomery Advertiser,* October 3, 4, 1955, January 7, 18, 19, 22, 24, February 5, 28, 1956; (Montgomery) *Alabama Journal,* January 23, 24, 1956; Burns, ed., *Daybreak of Freedom,* 121–24, 128–30. My account of this episode differs considerably from King's in *Stride toward Freedom,* 124–26. King publicly accepted the three ministers' explanation at face value (though privately he had his doubts; see Burns, ed., *Daybreak of Freedom,* 122). I am led to reject it and to credit Gayle's testimony at King's trial on the point for two reasons. Most importantly, King's version does not adequately account for the nature and content of Gayle's statement of January 23. Secondly, an attempt by the city to perpetrate a hoax is inconsistent with Thrasher's presence at the meeting. On J. Michael Nicrosi, see *Montgomery Advertiser,* November 16, 1962.

85. *Montgomery Advertiser,* January 24 (first quotations), 25 (third and fourth quotations), 26 (fifth quotation), February 10, 14, 1956; (Montgomery) *Alabama Journal,* January 24, 1956 (second quotation).

86. *Montgomery Advertiser,* January 31, February 2, 1956; (Montgomery) *Alabama Journal,* January 31, 1956; *Birmingham World,* February 3, 1956; Minutes of the MIA Strategy Committee Meeting, January 21, 1956, in Martin Luther King, Jr., Papers, Boston University Archives; Burns, ed., *Daybreak of Freedom,* 94, 128–30, 133–35; Gray, *Bus Ride to Justice,* 68–72; Azbell, interview, September 2, 1982; Gray, interview, October 17, 1978. Gray confirms that the bombing united the MIA's leadership behind the filing of the federal suit. Cf. also Felix E. James to Martin Luther King, Jr., March 8, 1956, King to Joffre Stewart, August 21, 1956, William

Cooper Cumming to King, July 31, 1956, and King to Cumming, September 18, 1956, all in King Papers. The members of the MIA's strategy committee, in addition to Mrs. Robinson, Powell, and Langford, were Ralph Abernathy, Solomon Seay, Mrs. Roman T. Adair (the wife of a black physician), James E. Pierce (a professor of political science at Alabama State College), and A. W. Wilson of the Holt Street Baptist Church. On Alford, Pierce, Powell, and Wilson, see Seay, *I Was There*, 133, 173, 178, 180.

Between January 26 and January 29, with the situation obviously deteriorating rapidly, Governor Folsom attempted a secret mediation. Abernathy states that Folsom intervened after a delegation of blacks asked him to do so. But the governor's efforts proved fruitless (Abernathy, interview, February 28, 1979; William V. Lyerly, interview by author, September 2, 1976; Trial Transcript, *King v. State*, 254–55, 496–97). The suggestion by Professor George E. Sims that the MIA's federal suit may have been filed as a result, at least in part, of Folsom's personal urging is certainly erroneous (Sims, *The Little Man's Big Friend*, 178). It does not accord with the chronological sequence of the events. Nor is it in keeping with Folsom's own attitudes; after the federal court's declaration in June that bus segregation was unconstitutional, Folsom sought privately to persuade the MIA's leaders to abandon the boycott, and when they failed to do so he attacked them publicly at a news conference, saying that they were hurting their own cause by pushing too hard (Robinson, *Montgomery Bus Boycott*, 129–30; *Montgomery Advertiser*, June 13, 1956).

87. *Montgomery Advertiser*, February 3, 1956.

88. W. C. Patton to Roy Wilkins and Gloster B. Current, December 19, 1955, NAACP Papers. Mrs. Robinson makes a similar point in her memoirs (*Montgomery Bus Boycott*, 78).

89. *Montgomery Advertiser*, January 27, 1956 (quotation), January 12, 14, 26, 27, March 19, 1957. See also (Montgomery) *Alabama Tribune*, January 27, 1956, in which the editor, E. G. Jackson, commented, "There is not one of our leaders who want[s] to mingle with the white people on the buses and no other place on a public carrier and they are not asking for that at all. We are asking for first come, first served basis"; see also (Montgomery) *Alabama Tribune*, January 13, 1956. As late as March 14, less than a week before King's trial for violation of the Anti-Boycott Act was to begin, the MIA's strategy committee voted to recommend that the boycott be terminated if the city and bus company would accept the Mobile seating plan and the request for greater courtesy by drivers, would promise to consider hiring black drivers at some future date, and would agree to return to the lower fare in use when the boycott commenced (Minutes of the MIA Strategy Committee Meeting, March 14, 1956, in King Papers). It is worth noting, as well, that following the integration of the buses, a group of blacks renewed the effort to establish an all-black jitney service, though King managed to kill the movement (*Montgomery Advertiser*, January 29, 1957).

90. *Montgomery Advertiser*, December 5, 1955, January 18, 22 (second quotation), 26, 28, 1956; (Montgomery) *Alabama Journal*, January 24 (first quotation), 27, 1956; Trial Transcript, *King v. State*, 213–27; Trial Transcript, *Browder v. Gayle*, 32–36; King, *Stride toward Freedom*, 115, 118, 120. Beatrice Jackson swore out a warrant against a black man, Thomas Carter, alleging that he had beaten her in the face and thrown a steel chair at her for riding a bus. But at his trial in Recorder's Court, Carter insisted that the boycott had had nothing to do with the assault; he was mad with her, he said, because of a dispute over some furniture (*Montgomery Advertiser*, January 26, 28, 1956). White Montgomerians repeatedly told me that they knew

that there had been intimidation of many blacks to keep them off the buses be-cause they had been told so by their servants or other employees. I am inclined to believe that these stories were usually told to employers in an effort to offer accept-able explanations for cooperation with the boycott. But the tales, while protecting the individual black worker from reprisal, had the harmful effect of preventing whites from recognizing the extent of black support for the MIA. Abernathy reports that the commissioners made repeated efforts to divide King from the remainder of the MIA leadership, as well (interview, February 28, 1979; see also [Montgomery] *Alabama Tribune,* December 30, 1955).

91. *Montgomery Advertiser,* February 2, August 26, 1956; Clifford J. Durr to Corliss Lamont, February 7, 1957, Durr Papers; Gilliam, "Montgomery Bus Boy-cott," 114. Jack Crenshaw believed to the time of his death that rivalries among various factions within the MIA leadership produced the bombings (interview, July 15, 1977). At the other extreme, Fred Gray suspected in later years that the city commission had ordered the bombings (interview, October 17, 1978). Many of the whites whom I interviewed believed that the boycott was prolonged unnecessarily as a sort of confidence game through which sympathetic northerners were being rooked for contributions.

92. It is worth noting in this regard that stories about the boycott had at this time not yet reached the front page of the *New York Times,* and would not do so until the indictment of MIA leaders for violation of the Anti-Boycott Act on Feb-ruary 21, except for one article on the White Citizens' Council's rally at the state coliseum on February 10.

93. King, *Stride toward Freedom,* 121–22 (quotation); *Montgomery Advertiser,* Feb-ruary 11, 1956. A considerable number of businessmen participated in the negotia-tions at one stage or another, but the principal business negotiators appear to have been Joe F. Bear, the owner of a lumber and construction firm; C. T. Fitzpatrick, the owner of a laundry and dry-cleaning business; James G. Pruett, the president of the local division of the Trailways bus system; and Mark W. Johnston, a vice-president of a bank. Bear was the chairman of the Men of Montgomery for February; the organization's chairmanship rotated monthly, on an alphabetical basis. Fitzpatrick, Pruett, and Johnston were the presidents of the chamber of commerce for, respec-tively, 1954, 1955, and 1956. The inopportune timing of the Men of Montgomery's intervention was to some extent dictated by the organization's structure. The group met once a month, near the beginning of each month. When it met on De-cember 6, the boycott was only one day old. When it met at the beginning of January, the city commission still appeared to be negotiating with the MIA. By the time it met about February 8, however, the impasse between the commission and the MIA was apparent and the organization therefore felt compelled to act. On the Men of Montgomery, see *Montgomery Advertiser,* October 19, November 3, Decem-ber 11, 1955; (Montgomery) *Alabama Journal,* February 8, 1956.

94. *Montgomery Advertiser,* January 19 (quotation), February 8, 9, 1956. Despite the statement by King quoted above from *Stride toward Freedom,* most of the sur-viving black leaders agree with my assessment that by this point the prospect for a negotiated settlement was exceedingly dim (interviews with Abernathy, Febru-ary 28, 1979, Gray, October 17, 1978, and Robinson, January 27, 1978). Rufus Lewis adds the interesting point that because white leaders, after years of ignoring blacks, were at last taking them seriously, the MIA was rendered quite reluctant to end the boycott that had finally given its members access to power (interview, July 27, 1977). And A. W. Wilson of the Holt Street Baptist Church reported that the

boycott had unified the black community and significantly increased attendance at church services (interview in [Montgomery] *Alabama Tribune,* March 2, 1956). The business negotiators are unanimous in stating that, though they approached the negotiations with high hopes, convinced that a settlement could be found, they quickly came to see that the blacks were unwilling to make any concessions (author interviews with Joe Bear, March 9, 1979, C. T. Fitzpatrick, January 11, 1979, Mark Johnston, July 19, 1977). I should also note Gray's statement that after February 1, all elements of the white community expressed to him privately a willingness to accept the MIA's original proposals if he would withdraw the federal suit (interview, October 17, 1978). The sequence of events during February and early March makes this particular assertion seem implausible to me, though I do certainly accept the accuracy of his report in his memoirs (*Bus Ride to Justice,* 72–73) that white officials both pressured him and offered him bribes if he would agree to dismiss or carry over the case.

95. *Montgomery Advertiser,* December 8, 1955 (first quotation), January 9 (second quotation), 11 (third quotation), 12 (fourth quotation), 15 (fifth quotation), 17 (sixth quotation), 19, February 15, 1956; Code of Alabama, 1940, Recompiled, Title 14, Section 54. Fred Ball's father, one of Alabama's most distinguished attorneys, had induced the U.S. Supreme Court to declare peonage a violation of the Thirteenth Amendment, in the famous Alonzo Bailey case (Pete Daniel, *The Shadow of Slavery: Peonage in the South, 1901–1969* [New York: Oxford University Press, 1973], 65–81).

96. Trial Transcript, *King* v. *State,* 161–62, 186–87, 190; (Montgomery) *Alabama Journal,* February 13, 1956; *Montgomery Advertiser,* February 14, 1956. Thetford stated to me that he was deeply dubious of indictments under the Anti-Boycott Act as a tactic; he felt that, after a series of lengthy and emotional trials, the prosecutions would result only in small fines for the boycotters or at most brief jail terms, without doing any real damage to the boycott itself. His own preference was for the bus company to seek a broad injunction against the MIA on the ground that its car-pool operation was violating the company's exclusive franchise. If the MIA then disobeyed the injunction, its leaders could be jailed indefinitely for contempt. This strategy, he believed, would have broken the boycott, but he was unable to convince Crenshaw to adopt it. Crenshaw stated that he was equally dubious of prosecuting under the Anti-Boycott Act, but that the company was unwilling to sue for an injunction because doing so would have involved abandoning its position as an innocent, neutral third party and allying itself publicly with the city's effort to preserve segregation. He added that such an injunction was not, he thought, likely to have ended the boycott in any case. Thetford said that his hand was finally forced on the anti-boycott law when, as a result of the Ball letter, Judge Carter became convinced of the necessity to enforce the statute and came to him with the information that he intended to charge the next grand jury on the subject. Judge Carter does not recall the Ball letter, but he confirms that he decided to charge the grand jury about the act and thereupon informed Thetford of his intention (interviews with Thetford, September 4, 1976, Crenshaw, July 15, 1977, and Carter, October 16, 1978).

97. *Montgomery Advertiser,* February 6, 21, 22, 28, 1956; (Montgomery) *Alabama Journal,* February 8, 20, 21, 1956; Trial Transcript, *King* v. *State,* 486–92. The complete text of the Men of Montgomery's proposals, dated February 13, 1956, is enclosed with Joe F. Bear to William F. Thetford, February 15, 1956, in File 2279, Records of the Solicitor's Office, Fifteenth Circuit, Montgomery County Court-

house; a condensed version was printed in the *Montgomery Advertiser*, March 16, 1956; for the MIA's reply, see Ralph D. Abernathy to Men of Montgomery, February 20, 1956, in File 2279. The proposals also involved all-black buses during rush hours on predominantly black routes and a pledge to return the bus fare, in stages, to a lower level; the fare had been increased by the commission to compensate the company for the losses that the boycott had produced. Bennett told a reporter that the assistant pastor of Bennett's church had favored accepting the compromise as well, but I am inclined to believe that this statement was an evasion, meant to avoid giving the reporter Alford's name. Lynn reports that the Men of Montgomery did not receive a single suggestion as a result of its appeal (interview by author, December 29, 1976). Thetford stated that he was convinced that the Men of Montgomery's mediation would fail, but that if the blacks had accepted the compromise he would then have entered a *nolle prosequi* as to the indictments (interview, September 4, 1976).

98. *Montgomery Advertiser*, December 9, 1956.

99. On Judge Johnson, see Tinsley J. Yarbrough, *Judge Frank Johnson and Human Rights in Alabama* (University: University of Alabama Press, 1981); Frank Sikora, *The Judge: The Life and Opinions of Alabama's Frank M. Johnson, Jr.* (Montgomery: Black Belt Press, 1992); Jack Bass, *Taming the Storm: The Life and Times of Judge Frank M. Johnson, Jr., and the South's Fight over Civil Rights* (New York: Doubleday, 1993); and *Montgomery Advertiser*, October 23, 25, November 6, 1955, February 4, May 31, December 9, 1956, (Montgomery) *Alabama Journal*, October 24, 1955, January 31, 1956. On Judge Rives, see Jack Bass, *Unlikely Heroes: The Dramatic Story of the Southern Judges of the Fifth Circuit Who Translated the Supreme Court's* Brown *Decision into a Revolution for Equality* (New York: Simon and Schuster, 1981), passim; (Montgomery) *Alabama Journal*, August 30, November 6, 1934, March 13, 1935, July 5, 1949, May 8, 9, 10, 1961; and *Montgomery Advertiser*, March 13, 1942, April 20, September 3, 1946, August 1, 1947, March 11, 1951, May 31, 1956. On the Madison affair, see note 15 above; on the Tuskegee registration case, see Robert J. Norrell, *Reaping the Whirlwind: The Civil Rights Movement in Tuskegee* (New York: Knopf, 1985), 55–68. On Judge Lynne's segregationist sympathies, see Seybourn H. Lynne to James A. Hare, March 15, 1965, in James A. Hare Papers, University of Alabama Library, Tuscaloosa. Of the four federal district judges in Alabama in these years—Seybourn Lynne and Hobart Grooms of Birmingham, Daniel Thomas of Mobile, and Frank Johnson of Montgomery—only Johnson, a hill-country Republican from Winston County, could be called a racial liberal.

100. (Montgomery) *Alabama Tribune*, December 16, 1955 (first quotation); *Montgomery Advertiser*, January 27, 1956 (second quotation); see also *Alabama Tribune*, December 23, 30, 1955, January 13, 1956.

101. The purpose of the boycott is a matter of some dispute among the MIA leaders I interviewed. Mrs. Robinson stated that, because of the progress the Women's Political Council had already been able to secure, particularly in getting buses to stop at each corner in black areas, she was initially quite optimistic about the prospects for negotiations. Gray said that he never had any hopes for the negotiations and favored a federal suit from the beginning, but he also said that most of the members of the MIA's executive board believed that the negotiations would produce a settlement. Abernathy said that because the city and bus company officials had seemed willing to listen at the earlier meetings and because the black proposals seemed to him so modest, he expected the whites quickly to accept the MIA's position. Lewis stated that at the outset no one really thought about whether

or not the boycott was likely to produce concessions; he said that the boycott was born in the anger over Mrs. Parks's arrest and that its initial purpose was not to gain alterations in the bus seating policy but to demonstrate forcefully the extent of black resentment. Nixon said that the exchanges at the time of the Colvin arrest had convinced him of the futility of negotiating, and that he supported the boycott not because he thought it likely to produce concessions but because he thought that by making Mrs. Parks's case a cause célèbre, blacks would be able to prevent the white courts from shunting her case aside. He feared, he said, that white judges would never consider a test of the segregation laws seriously unless the test was so surrounded with publicity that they were compelled to do so (interviews, January 27, October 17, 1978, February 28, 1979, July 27, August 2, 1977). Each of these positions is entirely plausible, and very probably each reflects some aspect of the historical reality. At the same time, the memory of each participant has necessarily been shaped to some extent by his or her knowledge of and reaction to subsequent events. In the final analysis the historian must ground his or her judgment in the sense one derives from the contemporary documents.

102. *Montgomery Advertiser,* December 8, 1955.

103. *Acts of Alabama,* Special Session of 1921, pp. xxii–xxiii (first quotation), 31–33 (second quotation); House Journal, Special Session of 1921, pp. 183, 200–201, 260–62, 268–70; Senate Journal, Special Session of 1921, pp. 33, 143, 185, 218–21, 233–34; Code of Alabama, 1940, Recompiled, Title 14, Section 54. The act passed the House 48–22 and the Senate 19–5. Alabama had already had an anti-boycott law on the books, enacted in 1903. The 1921 act, however, greatly strengthened the provisions of the earlier one. On the origins of the 1903 act, see Henry M. McKiven, Jr., *Iron and Steel: Class, Race and Community in Birmingham, Alabama, 1875–1920* (Chapel Hill: University of North Carolina Press, 1955), 99–105. On the 1921 strike, see Daniel Letwin, *The Challenge of Interracial Unionism: Alabama Coal Miners, 1878–1921* (Chapel Hill: University of North Carolina Press, 1998), 184–88.

104. *Thornhill* v. *Alabama,* 310 U.S. 88; *Lash* v. *State,* 244 Ala. 48; *Lash* v. *Alabama,* 320 U.S. 784, 814. Justice Thomas's opinion relied primarily upon Justice Felix Frankfurter's decision in *Milk Wagon Drivers Union of Chicago* v. *Meadowmoor Dairies Inc.,* 312 U.S. 287. But Justice Thomas's reading of section one of the act, while saving it from unconstitutionality, had its own problem. It had the effect of making section one essentially identical in meaning to section four, which read, "Any person, firm, corporation or association of persons who uses force, threats, intimidation or other unlawful means to prevent any other person, firm, corporation or association of persons from engaging in any lawful occupation or business shall be guilty of a misdemeanor." In fact, section four differed from section one, at least as Justice Thomas interpreted it, only in that section one forbade hindering or delaying, as well as preventing, the business. However, as the MIA had only hindered, and not prevented, the bus company's business, section four did not apply to its efforts. Abernathy's claim in his memoirs that the statute prohibited only secondary boycotts, incidentally, is certainly erroneous (*And the Walls Came Tumbling Down,* 165).

105. Trial Transcript, *King* v. *State,* 193–227, 360–445; *Montgomery Advertiser,* March 20, 21, 22, 23, 1956, August 16, 21, 24, September 7, 13, 1957; *Selma Times-Journal,* January 22, 23, April 18, September 17, 1958. Assistant Solicitor Stewart was also the county Democratic Party chairman ([Montgomery] *Alabama Journal,* February 4, 1956). Though Judge Carter was perhaps not so aggressive a segrega-

tionist as was Montgomery's other circuit judge, Walter B. Jones, Carter's own attitudes nevertheless were themselves the principal reason for the prosecution's success at King's trial. As we have seen, Carter had personally precipitated King's indictment, in response to Fred Ball's letter (note 96, above). And Carter told me in an interview that he had done so because of the violence and intimidation surrounding the boycott. He said that the intimidation of the city's blacks to compel them to abide by the boycott was common knowledge, noting that his sister's maid and a janitor at the courthouse had both been threatened, though in each case unsuccessfully. (The courthouse janitor whom Carter mentioned was also one of the state's three black witnesses to prove the allegation of violence; Trial Transcript, 216–22.) Carter emphasized to me that he did not think King was to blame for such intimidation; he believed that irresponsible elements among the blacks were the perpetrators. But he felt that King's trial was necessary to end the boycott, and thus the violence; and he felt that his conviction of King had in fact had the salutary effect of calming the situation in the city and of placing the boycott on its course toward being ended (interview, October 16, 1978). Carter's comments would seem to imply that he found King guilty not so much because he was actually convinced of King's own culpability, but primarily because he considered the verdict socially useful.

Randall Kennedy, "Martin Luther King's Constitution: A Legal History of the Montgomery Bus Boycott," *Yale Law Journal* 98, no. 6 (1989): 999–1067, though marred both by factual errors and by interpretive misconceptions, contains an excellent discussion of the legal significance of this prosecution; see esp. 1034–43. See also Robert Jerome Glennon, "The Role of Law in the Civil Rights Movement: The Montgomery Bus Boycott, 1955–1957," *Law and History Review* 9, no. 1 (1991): 59–112.

106. *King* v. *State*, 39 Ala. App. 167; *Montgomery Advertiser*, August 5, 1956, January 19, May 1, May 15, 1957. Rosa Parks's appeal was similarly mishandled. Because Gray had failed to create a bill of exceptions during Mrs. Parks's trial in Recorder's Court, the Court of Appeals ruled in February 1957 that there was nothing before it to review and therefore similarly affirmed the conviction without reaching the merits of the appeal (*Parks* v. *City of Montgomery*, 38 Ala. App. 681).

107. *Montgomery Advertiser*, March 20, May 11, 12, 31, June 1, 6, 20, 21, 22, 23, 26, 29, 1956; *Browder* v. *Gayle*, 142 F.Supp. 707; *Holmes* v. *City of Atlanta*, 350 U.S. 879; *Mayor of Baltimore* v. *Dawson*, 350 U.S. 877; *Flemming* v. *South Carolina Electric and Gas Co.*, 224 F.2d 752. Judge Hutcheson had been very reluctant to appoint the three-judge court to hear the Browder suit, and had done so only after Judge Johnson's strenuous insistence (Sikora, *The Judge*, 14–15). The *Flemming* decision of the Fourth Circuit was appealed to the U.S. Supreme Court, but the Court dismissed the appeal as premature; the Fourth Circuit had merely ordered the district court to proceed to trial on Miss Flemming's complaint, and the Supreme Court thus refused to consider the appeal until a jury had actually decided to award her damages. The district judge who was handling the case, George Bell Timmerman, an ardent segregationist and father of South Carolina's governor, had initially ruled bus segregation constitutional. When the Fourth Circuit reversed this finding and returned the suit to him for trial, he then ruled that though bus segregation was now unconstitutional, it had been constitutional at the time of the bus incident that had led Miss Flemming to file suit, and the bus company was therefore not liable for enforcing it. The Fourth Circuit reversed this holding, too, and once again ordered the case to trial. In June 1957 the suit finally went to a jury, and the jury

promptly found for the defendant bus company. That decision ended the case. Thus, ironically, the challenge to bus segregation upon which the NAACP had been depending would never, in fact, have produced a Supreme Court ruling on the matter, while the suit that grew out of the boycott succeeded in obtaining one (351 U.S. 901, 128 F.Supp. 469, 239 F.2d 277; *Montgomery Advertiser,* June 14, August 5, November 16, December 1, 1956, June 11, 1957). The Supreme Court's dismissal of the appeal in the *Flemming* case, in April 1956, produced one of the oddest episodes of the boycott. The Court's action was erroneously reported in the press as representing a declaration that bus segregation was unconstitutional. National City Lines in Chicago had been expecting that outcome, and it planned to use the decision to extricate itself from the dispute in Montgomery. It therefore at once ordered its Montgomery affiliate to cease enforcing the segregation law. Within days, however, the press corrected its account to reflect what the Court had actually done. The city of Montgomery then sued in state court and obtained an injunction from Judge Walter B. Jones ordering the bus company to abide by the segregation statutes. That injunction remained in force until the Supreme Court's ruling in *Browder* v. *Gayle,* when on motion of the bus company, Judge Jones reluctantly dissolved it. The erroneous press report about the *Flemming* decision also led to the abandonment of bus segregation in quite a number of other southern cities, and in many of them the abandonment proved a permanent one (*Montgomery Advertiser,* April 24, 25, 26, 27, 28, 30, May 1, 2, 3, 4, 8, 10, December 21, 1956).

108. *Montgomery Advertiser,* June 2, 4, 5, 12, 27, July 6, 10, 12, 21, 24, 25, 26, 30, 31, August 1, 2, 14, 21, December 7, 1956. In view of the antagonism that both the national NAACP and its Montgomery branch had shown to the boycott during its first three months, this allegation of Patterson's must have seemed cruelly ironic to the MIA's leaders. But despite its falsity, the allegation appears to have been widely believed in segregationist circles (e.g., ibid., April 8, 1956). Patterson also claimed that the NAACP had paid Autherine Lucy and Polly Ann Myers Hudson to undertake their abortive effort to integrate the University of Alabama. The pretext for Patterson's suit was the failure of the NAACP to register with Alabama's secretary of state as an out-of-state corporation, but Patterson asked for a permanent injunction forbidding the NAACP from registering in the future, on the ground that the organization was a threat to the public welfare. At Patterson's request, Judge Walter B. Jones granted a temporary restraining order forbidding the NAACP to operate in the state without registering, and also forbidding it from attempting to register while the court action was pending. Judge Jones also ordered the organization to produce various documents and files of correspondence, including its Alabama membership lists. The temporary injunction remained in effect for the next five and a half years, while attorneys struggled over this production order. In December 1961, Judge Jones replaced the temporary injunction with a permanent one. That injunction remained in effect until October 1964, when the NAACP at last regained the right to exist in the state.

109. *Montgomery Advertiser,* August 26, 1956. Graetz and his family were attending a workshop at the Highlander Folk School in Tennessee at the time of the bombing, and the house was unoccupied. Graetz, though white, was the minister of a black Lutheran church. He had come to Montgomery in June 1955 and remained until August 1958, when he moved to Columbus, Ohio. Graetz's race had attracted much attention to him from the outset of the boycott; he was a special object of harassment from segregationists, who found the idea of a white's cooperating actively with the MIA astonishing and outrageous. On Graetz, see the *Mont-*

gomery Advertiser, January 10, 12, August 24, September 17, 18, 19, November 1, 1956, January 2, February 20, 1957, *Birmingham World,* August 9, 1958; on his church, see the *Montgomery Examiner,* December 18, 1953. His own account of this bombing is in his *Montgomery,* 81–84.

110. *Montgomery Advertiser,* August 6, October 7, 17, 1956.

111. Ibid., September 7, 9, November 22, 24, 25, 27, 1956.

112. Ibid., April 5, 12, 27, July 25, August 3, September 2, 5, 12, 13, 15, 20, 25, 26, 27, 28, 29, 30, October 2, 3, 4, 5, 7, 10, 11, 14, 16, 19, 21, 1956. Commissioner Sellers's wife launched this movement. It lost its force when the National Congress bowed to the segregationist pressure and repealed its endorsement of integration, but the PTAs that had withdrawn in the meantime remained independent despite the repeal.

113. Ibid., April 1, June 29, 30, 1956. On Dr. Dannelly, see ibid., November 11, 1956.

114. Ibid., May 29, 30, 31, June 1, 3, 6, 16, 19, 26, 29, 30, July 1, 2, 9, 10, 12, 13, 18, 20, August 2, 3, 4, 24, September 5, October 4, 18, 20, 21, 23, December 9, 1956.

115. Ibid., February 19, March 11, July 22, August 10, 24, 1956. On Jack Brock, see ibid., April 15, 1954; on the racial attitudes of Brock and his associates, see ibid., August 5, 6, 1956, February 11, 1957; *Birmingham World,* July 15, 1949, April 18, 1950; *Selma Times-Journal,* October 25, 1957; and (Montgomery) *Alabama Labor News,* February 14, May 22, June 19, July 3, 17, October 23, November 6, 1956, January 11, March 15, 29, July 30, 1957. Brock's brother Elmer B. Brock, the chairman of the secessionist Southern Federation of Labor, was an active member of the painters' union and apparently had been the grand dragon of the Ku Klux Klan in Birmingham before his removal to Montgomery. In 1950 he had been indicted in connection with a wave of Klan violence in the Birmingham area. Brock's close friend and fellow *Alabama Journal* printer Eugene S. Hall was the editor of the White Citizens' Council's Montgomery newspaper, the *States' Rights Advocate,* until he was dismissed by the Citizens' Council in November 1956. In 1957, as we shall see, he would be charged with complicity in the bombings that followed the integration of the buses. Though Jack Brock denied that he himself was a Klansman, I believe that a number of the men associated with him were the organizers of the Montgomery Klan klavern in September 1956; and the men arrested for the January 1957 bombings were, according to the police, all connected with that klavern. Brock was the editor and publisher of the *Alabama Labor News,* a strongly segregationist journal opposed to the national AFL-CIO.

116. (Montgomery) *Alabama Labor News,* October 23, 1956; *Montgomery Advertiser,* January 27, February 1, April 3, October 27 (quotations), 1956; John P. Kohn, interview by author, September 2, 1982; Edward J. Hill to John P. Kohn, October 25, 1956, and John P. Kohn to Edward J. Hill, October 31, 1956, in author's possession.

117. *Montgomery Advertiser,* October 31, November 1, 3, 1956.

118. Ibid., October 28, 29, 30, 31, November 2, 3, 13, 14, 15, 16, 18, 20, December 4, 6, 18, 20, 21, 22, 1956; *Gayle* v. *Browder,* 352 U.S. 903; Clifford J. Durr to Carey McWilliams, November 16, 1956, Durr Papers; King, *Stride toward Freedom,* 158–74. Gray's statement in his memoirs (*Bus Ride to Justice,* 93) that Judge Carter continued the injunction hearing without rendering a decision is erroneous. The Supreme Court's decision to dispose of the Montgomery bus segregation case with a single uninstructive sentence was a part of a pattern of such behavior. It had done

the same with the earlier cases involving public parks and golf courses, for instance. Apparently the Court wished to leave the impression that its *Brown* v. *Board of Education* opinion of 1954 had already dealt with all such questions. But the logic of *Brown* v. *Board* does not apply to the other situations. In *Brown* the Court held that, regardless of the equality or inequality of the physical facilities, separate schools were inherently unequal because the simple fact of separation of schoolchildren by race had been shown to harm black children psychologically. However, there were no comparable studies demonstrating that blacks were psychologically harmed by the requirement that they play golf on certain courses or that they sit in certain bus seats rather than other ones. And in the absence of such studies, the logic of *Brown* is inapposite. The Court did not at the time provide, nor has it ever provided since, any clear rationale for its elimination of segregation from areas other than education. Moreover, the *Browder* decision perhaps deserved fuller comment from the Court because it was the first of the segregation cases that the Court had considered to address the sort of segregation that had originally produced its validation of the "separate but equal" doctrine in *Plessy* v. *Ferguson,* segregation in public transportation. Unlike *Brown,* therefore, *Browder* directly confronted the *Plessy* holding.

119. *Montgomery Advertiser,* December 11, 13, 19, 20, 1956; Robinson, interview, January 27, 1978.

120. *Montgomery Advertiser,* December 27, 28, 29, 30, 1956, January 1, 2, 3, 6, 9, 10, 1957. The operation on Mrs. Jordan's leg was eventually completed successfully, and she was released from the hospital on January 27. That the snipers in the four shootings in December 1955 were black is simply my assumption; the culprits were never apprehended. One white man, Henry Alexander, a plumber, confessed at the end of January 1957 to the bus shooting of December 31, 1956, but the snipers in the five other shootings of the latter period are also unknown.

121. Ibid., January 11, 12, 13, 16, 17, 18, 28, 29, 1957, February 21, 22, 24, 27, March 2, 6, 15, 16, April 14, 15, May 13, 18, June 2, 1976; *Birmingham World,* March 23, 1957. Evening bus runs were not resumed until March. The murder of Willie Edwards did not become public knowledge until 1976, when one of the Klansmen confessed to the crime; at the time it was thought to have been an accidental drowning. It is conceivable that the bombing of Allen Robertson's house was intended to draw the Kings out onto their porch, to ensure that they would be killed by the second bomb, timed to go off shortly after the first one. The bomb that destroyed Robertson's house also damaged a black taxi stand next door.

122. *Montgomery Advertiser,* January 11 (quotations), 12, 31, 1957; Shows, interview, June 20, 1984.

123. (Montgomery) *Alabama Labor News,* November 6, 1956, January 11, February 15, March 15, 29, July 30, 1957; *Montgomery Advertiser,* January 31, February 1, 2, 4, 5, 11, 1957; *Selma Times-Journal,* February 20, 1957.

The charges were as follows: (1) planting bomb at Robert Graetz's house—Eugene S. Hall, a printer, and Charles Bodiford, foreman at a furniture factory; (2) planting bomb at Martin Luther King's house—Donald Dunlop, an ex-convict and a plumber, and Raymond C. Britt, Jr., a flooring company employee; (3) bombing home of Allen Robertson—Raymond Britt and Henry Alexander, a plumber; (4) bombing home of Ralph Abernathy—Henry Alexander, Raymond Britt and James D. York, a road scraper operator for the city; (5) bombing First Baptist Church (black)—Raymond Britt; (6) bombing Hutchinson Street Baptist Church—Raymond

Britt and "Sonny" Kyle Livingston, an employee of a construction machinery company; (7) sniper shooting at a bus—Henry Alexander.

In addition, in 1976, Raymond Britt confessed to, and Henry Alexander, "Sonny" Kyle Livingston, and James York were indicted for, the murder of Willie Edwards, Jr. (note 121 above). But lie-detector tests appeared to clear Livingston of this charge, and all of the indictments were subsequently quashed as legally defective, ending the case. No charges were laid in connection with the bombing of the Bell Street Baptist Church or the Mount Olive Baptist Church, nor was anyone charged with the actual bombing of Robert Graetz's home, as opposed to the planting at the same time of a second bomb that failed to explode.

124. *Montgomery Advertiser,* February 1, 4, 5, 6, 7, 11, 12, 17, 1957; (Montgomery) *Alabama Labor News,* February 15, 1957; (Montgomery) *States' Rights Advocate,* February 7, 25, 1957.

125. *Montgomery Advertiser,* February 6, May 28, 29, 30, 31 (quotations), 1957; *Selma Times-Journal,* May 31, 1957. The acquittal was lent special weight by the fact that the jurors included a number of men very prominent in the community, in particular John H. Haardt, a wealthy realtor and brother-in-law of H. L. Mencken; Peter B. Mastin III, the foreman, scion of a well-known family; tire salesman Robert W. Woolfolk; and lumber executive David F. Gorrie. The defense also offered witnesses who provided the defendants alibis. Livingston's wife testified that she and her husband had been in bed asleep at the time of the explosions, and Britt's wife and her niece testified that they had been playing cards with him when the bombs went off. The state, however, offered the testimony of a fellow Klansman, Walter L. King, who swore that he had attended the meeting at Britt's home at which the bombings had been planned.

126. *Montgomery Advertiser,* November 27, 1957.

127. *Selma Times-Journal,* January 21, 1959 (quotations); *Montgomery Home News,* February 5, 1959.

128. *Montgomery Advertiser,* April 29, 1947, March 9, 16, 1956, March 22, July 18, 1957, September 9, 13, 1959, January 15, February 16, April 27, May 30, 31, June 1, December 15 (quotations), 1960, November 16, December 19, 20, 1962; *Montgomery Home* News, November 20, 27, December 4, 11, 1958, February 5, 12, 1959; *Selma Times-Journal,* May 29, August 14, 19, September 17, 1959; Newsletter of the Alabama Council on Human Relations, August 1955, Montgomery Improvement Association Newsletter, January 15, 1959, both in King Papers; Newsletter of the Montgomery Chapter of the Alabama Council on Human Relations, July 25, 1957, Thomas R. Thrasher to the Congregation of the Church of the Ascension, December 1, 1957, Thrasher to Frederick B. Routh, March 27, 1958, Minutes of the Executive Committee, Alabama Council on Human Relations, July 10, 1956, Robert E. Hughes to Frederick B. Routh, September 8, 1956, Hughes to ACHR Board of Directors, July 19, 1956, Report of Robert E. Hughes to the Southern Regional Council for Period December, 1958 through February, 1959, all in Southern Regional Council Papers, Atlanta University Library; FBI Case Files, Freedom Rider Investigation, January 28, 1961, Birmingham Public Library; Barnard, ed., *Outside the Magic Circle,* 245, 276–77, 308–9.

129. *Montgomery Advertiser,* June 12 (first quotations), 13, 14, 18, 19, 26, July 14, 1956; Statement of Disbursements for February, March, April, and May 1956, Report of the MIA Committee on Salaries and Office Personnel, April 18, 1957, Edgar D. Nixon to Martin Luther King, Jr., June 3, 1957 (second quotations), Nixon

to King, November 4, 1957, all in King Papers; Nixon, interview, August 2, 1977; Burns, ed., *Daybreak of Freedom,* 273–79; Graetz, *Montgomery,* 86–87; Fields, *The Montgomery Story,* 29–53 et passim.

130. *Montgomery Advertiser,* February 24, 1957; Recommendations Made to the Executive Board of the Montgomery Improvement Association, by the President, May 24, 1956, Minutes of the Executive Board of the MIA, meetings of January 20, January 31, 1958, MIA Newsletter, April 30, 1959, all in King Papers; Burns, ed., *Daybreak of Freedom,* 279.

131. *Montgomery Advertiser,* June 5, August 3, 4, 5, 6, October 15, 1957; MIA Newsletter, November 18, 1957, King Papers.

132. *Montgomery Advertiser,* August 26, 27, September 18, December 23, 31, 1958, January 1, 2, February 5, 11, July 22, September 8, 9, 10, 1959, April 16, 1960; *Selma Times-Journal,* August 26, 27, December 30, 31, 1958, July 22, September 8, 9, 10, 11, 1959, February 25, 1965; "Information obtained in conversation with Commissioner L. B. Sullivan and Chief of Police G. J. Ruppenthal, November 14, 1961," memorandum in James T. "Jabo" Waggoner Papers, Birmingham Public Library; MIA Newsletters, September 27, 1958, January 15, 1959, Fred D. Gray to Executive Board of the Montgomery Improvement Association, July 10, 1958, all in King Papers; *Gilmore* v. *City of Montgomery,* 176 F.Supp. 776, 277 F.2d 364.

133. Fields, *The Montgomery Story,* quotation on 87; *Montgomery Advertiser,* August 1, 11, 13, 1957, February 18, 1960; *Selma Times-Journal,* April 28, 1959, February 18, 1960.

134. (Montgomery) *Alabama Journal,* September 22, 1959; *Birmingham News,* February 18, 1960; *Montgomery Advertiser,* December 31, 1958, January 3, 4, 20 (first quotation), 30, February 10 (second quotation), 13, 19, March 16, 22, August 30, 31, September 6 (fourth quotation), November 30, December 4, 1959; *Montgomery Home News,* September 10, 1959; *Selma Times-Journal,* January 19, 27, February 20, August 30, 31, September 6, December 4, 1959; Executive Committee of Montgomery Improvement Association to Harold Harris, August 28, 1959 (third quotation), and Annual Address by President Martin Luther King, Jr., on the Fourth Anniversary of the Montgomery Improvement Association, at the Bethel Baptist Church, December 3, 1959 (fifth set of quotations), both in King Papers; remarks of Robert D. Nesbitt to History 371, Huntingdon College, June 24, 1987; *Acts of Alabama,* Regular Session of 1957, pp. 483–88; *Shuttlesworth* v. *Birmingham Board of Education,* 162 F.Supp. 372, 358 U.S. 101. King's decision to leave Montgomery for Atlanta has not to my mind been well explained in the literature. King himself publicly attributed it to Atlanta's superior access to transportation facilities. Biographers have emphasized King's growing national stature and the resultant need for him to be free of parochial responsibilities in order to take direct charge of the Southern Christian Leadership Conference's floundering Atlanta headquarters (e.g., Garrow, *Bearing the Cross,* 118–25; Adam Fairclough, *To Redeem the Soul of America: The Southern Christian Leadership Conference and Martin Luther King, Jr.* [Athens: University of Georgia Press, 1987], 47–51; Stephen B. Oates, *Let the Trumpet Sound: The Life of Martin Luther King, Jr.* [New York: Harper and Row, 1982], 145–46). I have no doubt at all that these factors did weigh heavily with King, but the push internal to the Montgomery situation seems to me at least as significant in moving King to the choice as was the external pull from Atlanta and the SCLC. Garrow does allude correctly to the strains within both the MIA's leadership and the Dexter Avenue congregation and to the MIA's increasing difficulty in sustaining

the enthusiasm of Montgomery's black masses (*Bearing the Cross,* 88–89, 94–97, 99, 101–2, 107, 113, 122–23). But his account, like the others, tends to stress the external factors. I am convinced, however, by Robert Nesbitt's report that King privately gave the resistance of Montgomery's black teachers to the filing of the school integration suit as the principal factor behind his determination. Nesbitt states that Dexter had offered to let King preach only once a month if he would agree to stay. And given the church's willingness to dispense with the bulk of King's pastoral duties, the need for him to give greater attention to SCLC affairs could just as easily have been met by moving the SCLC's headquarters to Montgomery as by moving King to Atlanta. Moreover, Nesbitt's account simply seems to me to reflect more persuasively the true reality of King's situation in the city as I understand it.

135. On Alabama's suit against the NAACP, see *NAACP* v. *State ex rel. Attorney General,* 265 Ala. 356, 699, 349; 268 Ala. 531; 271 Ala. 33; 274 Ala. 544; 277 Ala. 89; *NAACP* v. *Jones,* 268 Ala. 504; *NAACP* v. *Alabama,* 357 U.S. 449, 360 U.S. 240, 377 U.S. 288; *NAACP* v. *Gallion,* 190 F.Supp. 583, 290 F.2d 337, 368 U.S. 16; *NAACP* v. *Flowers,* 217 F.Supp. 70. On the extreme segregationist support for Patterson, see *Montgomery Advertiser,* May 12, 15, 16, 17, 18, 21, 22, 23, 24, 27, June 1, 1958, *Montgomery Home News,* May 16, 23, 1958. On black trepidation about the Patterson administration, see MIA Newsletter, June 28, 1958, in King Papers. On Engelhardt's appointments, see *Montgomery Advertiser,* September 4, December 4, 18, 20, 23, 28, 30, 31, 1958, January 5, 17, 18, 20, March 21, 1959, and *Montgomery Home News,* January 1, 1959. For the gubernatorial votes, see *Alabama Official and Statistical Register* for 1959. The position of state highway director was entirely within Patterson's gift. The party chairman, however, was actually elected by the state Democratic Executive Committee. In the election of 1958, the party's states' rights faction had recaptured control of the committee from the loyalists, for the first time in eight years, by a margin of thirty-nine to thirty-three. At a caucus of the states' rights members on September 13, they had pledged themselves to support Montgomery attorney Frank Mizell for the chairmanship. Patterson, however, considered Mizell an ally of the forces that had been involved in the murder of his father, and he therefore decided to engineer the selection of his own man, Engelhardt, in Mizell's place. Turning, quite ironically, to the committee's loyalist minority, he obtained their united support, because they detested Mizell even more than Engelhardt. And through the exercise of all the pressure at the administration's command, he persuaded a handful of states' rights men to desert their caucus's nominee. Engelhardt was thus elected, thirty-six to thirty-five.

136. *Montgomery Advertiser,* August 30, 31, September 4, 5, 6 (quotation), 7, 11, 1958; MIA Newsletter, September 27, 1958, in King Papers. Davis, a junior high school physical education teacher, was tried in circuit court in November, but it took an all-white jury less than fifteen minutes to acquit him (*Montgomery Advertiser,* November 22, 1958). Subsequently Davis sued *Jet* magazine for libel for its account of these events, and recovered $45,000 (*Johnson Publishing Co.* v. *Davis,* 271 Ala. 474).

137. *Montgomery Advertiser,* January 4 (first and second quotations), 11, February 18, 23, 24, 25, 28, March 2, 4, 6, 7, 9, 10, 11, 12, 13, 14, 17, 19, 20, 1959; (Montgomery) *States' Rights Advocate,* March, 1959; *Montgomery Home News,* January 22, February 19 (third quotation), 26, March 5, 12, 19, 1959; Shows, interview, June 20, 1984. On Sullivan's background, see *Montgomery Examiner,* April 5, 1951. On his Klan connections, see FBI Case Files, Freedom Rider Investigation,

November 10, 11, December 1, 1960; *Montgomery Home News,* September 17, 1959; (Montgomery) *Alabama Journal,* May 30, 1961; *Selma Times-Journal,* May 28, 1961; *Montgomery Advertiser,* September 9, 1961; Shows, interview, June 20, 1984.

138. *Montgomery Advertiser,* January 15 (first and second quotations), 16, February 15, 25, March 1, 6, 7, 8, 10, 12, 13, 14, 15, 16, 17, 19, 20, 21 (third quotation), 22, 24, 25, 1959; (Montgomery) *States' Rights Advocate,* March, 1959; *Montgomery Home News,* January 15, 22, February 5, 12, 19, March 5, 12, 19, 26, April 2, 1959; MIA Newsletter, April 30, 1959 (fourth quotation), and Annual Address by President Martin Luther King, Jr., on the Fourth Anniversary of the Montgomery Improvement Association, at the Bethel Baptist Church, December 3, 1959, both in King Papers. On the conflict over the city sales tax, see *Al Means, Inc.* v. *City of Montgomery,* 268 Ala. 31. On "Red" James, see Barnard, ed., *Outside the Magic Circle,* 139, 224, 241.

139. *Selma Times-Journal,* January 21, 1959.

140. Ibid., June 14, 16, 1959; August Meier and Elliott Rudwick, *CORE: A Study in the Civil Rights Movement* (Urbana: University of Illinois Press, 1975), 91, 102. The apparent connection between the Miami sit-ins in the summer of 1959 and the wave of sit-ins throughout the South seven months later has not been generally noted in the literature. In fact, the Miami demonstrators evidently were acting on precedents stretching back to the Congress of Racial Equality's founding in Chicago in 1942; see Meier and Rudwick, *CORE,* 13–15. On the Greensboro sit-in, see William H. Chafe, *Civilities and Civil Rights: Greensboro, North Carolina, and the Black Struggle for Freedom* (New York: Oxford University Press, 1980).

141. *Montgomery Home News,* March 3, 1960 (quotation); *Montgomery Advertiser,* February 26, 27, 28, 29, 1960; Trial Transcript, *Dixon* v. *Alabama State Board of Education,* 67–68, FRC East Point. It is worth noting that the extreme white supremacists and the black civil rights leaders were each equally eager to identify their causes with the battle against Communism at this period.

142. *Montgomery Advertiser,* March 1, 2 (quotation), 3, 4, 5, 6, 7, 8, 1960; Seay, *I Was There,* 217–22; George McMillan, *Racial Violence and Law Enforcement* (Atlanta: Southern Regional Council, 1960), 18–23; Bernard Lee to John M. Patterson, February 27, 1960, H. Councill Trenholm to Robert C. Bradley, February 29, 1960, Affidavit of John M. Patterson, July 26, 1960, all in Case File, *Dixon* v. *Alabama State Board of Education,* FRC East Point. One of the twenty students placed on probation was future Montgomery city councilman and black political leader Joe L. Reed. Associate Public Service Commissioner Ralph Smith later stated that the March 1 demonstration had been in large part staged by a reporter for the National Broadcasting Company, Sander Vanocur (*Selma Times-Journal,* May 26, 1960).

143. *Montgomery Advertiser,* March 9, 10, 11, 12, 13, 17, 29, 30, 31, June 15, 16, July 10, 21, October 4, 1960, November 29, 1961; *Birmingham World,* October 10, 1962; Martin Luther King, Jr., to Dwight D. Eisenhower, telegram, March 9, 1960 (quotation), in King Papers; Robinson, interview, January 27, 1978; Levi Watkins, *Fighting Hard: The Alabama State Experience* (Detroit: Harlo Press, 1987), 26–55; Robinson, *Montgomery Bus Boycott,* 168–70.

144. *DuBose* v. *City of Montgomery,* 41 Ala. App. 233; *King* v. *City of Montgomery,* 41 Ala. App. 260, *Embry* v. *City of Montgomery,* 41 Ala. App. 568, *King* v. *City of Montgomery,* 42 Ala. App. 462; Seay, *I Was There,* 222–23; Barnard, ed., *Outside the Magic Circle,* 289–92; Gray, *Bus Ride to Justice,* 177–80.

145. On the *Times* libel cases, see *Montgomery Advertiser,* April 7, 8, 9, 16, 19, 21, 28, May 16, 31, July 26, 27, August 2, 6, October 29, November 1, 2, 3, 4, 5,

December 2, 1960, January 30, 31, February 1, 2, 3, 4, 5, 7, 8, 10, 11, 16, 22, 23, March 3, 4, 18, 21, 28, April 14, 26, 27, June 27, September 9, 10, 1961, August 31, September 19, 1962, January 7, March 10, June 9, 10, 1964; *Selma Times-Journal,* November 1, 1961; *New York Times* v. *Sullivan,* 273 Ala. 656, 376 U.S. 254; *Abernathy* v. *Patterson,* 295 F.2d 452; *Parks* v. *New York Times,* 195 F.Supp. 919, 308 F.2d 474, 376 U.S. 949. On the Alabama State expulsion case, see *Montgomery Advertiser,* July 15, August 22, 23, 27, September 23, 1960, August 5, 1961; *Dixon* v. *Alabama State Board of Education,* 186 F.Supp. 945, 294 F.2d 150, 368 U.S. 930. On both topics, see also Bass, *Taming the Storm,* 156–62. On the Regal Café cases, see *Nesmith* v. *Alford,* 318 F.2d 110, 319 F.2d 859, and note 144, above.

146. McMillan, *Racial Violence and Law Enforcement,* 18, 21, 23 (quotations); FBI Case Files, Freedom Rider Investigation, October 8, 1960.

147. *Montgomery Advertiser,* February 18, 28, March 1, 4, May 16, 17, 18, 19, 20, 21, 25, 26, 27, 28, 29, 31, 1960; *Selma Times-Journal,* February 18, 22, 28, March 1, 4, May 16, 17, 18, 19, 25, 26, 27, 29, August 2, 1960; Gray, *Bus Ride to Justice,* 150–59. Circuit Solicitor William Thetford told me that he had gone into this prosecution of King much against his will. In the first place, he noted, no one in the history of Alabama had ever before been charged with state income tax evasion. And in the second place, King had just moved to Atlanta only weeks before the indictment was returned, and Thetford very much wanted to let this sleeping dog lie. But John Patterson, he said, had become convinced that the prosecution would be an effective strategy against the civil rights movement. Governor Patterson summoned Thetford to the capitol and demanded that he present the state's evidence to the county grand jury. Thetford did his best to dissuade Patterson, he reported, but the governor remained unmoved and Thetford finally yielded to his insistence. Thetford said, however, that he was secretly pleased by King's acquittal, because he viewed it as finally ridding his jurisdiction of the troublesome minister (interview, September 4, 1976).

148. On the background of the Freedom Rides, see Meier and Rudwick, *CORE,* 33–39, 135–38; a fuller account of this subject is to be found in the discussion of Birmingham in the next chapter. The U.S. Supreme Court had ruled in December 1960 that segregation in bus terminal facilities violated the nondiscrimination provision of the National Motor Carrier Act of 1935 (*Boynton* v. *Virginia,* 364 U.S. 454), but the decision had simply been ignored throughout the South. CORE undertook the Freedom Ride to demonstrate this fact.

149. (Montgomery) *Alabama Journal,* May 15, 16, 17, 18, 19, 1961; *Montgomery Advertiser,* May 20, 28, June 1, 1961; C. A. Evans to Mr. Parsons, May 15, 1961, Director FBI to Attorney General, May 16, 1961, Alex Rosen to Mr. Parsons, May 16, 1961, SA Barrett Kemp to SAC Thomas Jenkins, May 18, 20, 1961, all in FBI Case Files, Freedom Rider Investigation; Jayne Lahey to Robert F. Kennedy, May 17, 1961 (telephone messages from Fred Shuttlesworth and Floyd Mann), Robert F. Kennedy to John M. Patterson, telegram, May 20, 1961, transcript of telephone conversation between Robert F. Kennedy and George E. Cruit, May 17, 1961, Robert F. Kennedy memorandum to files, May 20, 1961, all in Robert F. Kennedy Papers, Kennedy Presidential Library, transcripts in Birmingham Public Library; Detective Marcus A. Jones to Chief Jamie Moore, May 16, 24, 1961, in Eugene "Bull" Connor Papers, Birmingham Public Library; Excerpt Transcripts, *U.S.* v. *U.S. Klans,* vol. 1, pp. 144–53, vol. 5, pp. 36–39, vol. 8, pp. 268–76, FRC East Point; Lewis with D'Orso, *Walking with the Wind,* 29–64, 121–58; remarks of John M. Patterson to History 371, Huntingdon College, July 8, 1987; interview with John M. Patterson by Norman

Lumpkin, May 22, 1973, pp. 15–20, in Alabama Center for Higher Education State-wide Oral History Project Transcripts, Special Collections, Alabama State University Library. Patterson states that both he and Floyd Mann had received a firm commitment from Sullivan to protect the Freedom Riders in Montgomery, but that they subsequently found out that Sullivan had at the same time secretly promised the leaders of the mob to leave them a free hand.

Montgomery officials had expected the initial group of CORE Freedom Riders to continue from Birmingham to Montgomery on May 15, and in anticipation of their arrival they had staged surprise fire inspections of the restaurants at both the Greyhound and the Trailways terminals and ordered both restaurants closed for alleged fire code violations. By the time the second group of Freedom Riders actually arrived on May 20, however, the alleged violations had been corrected, and officials were thus deprived of this tactic. See Trial Transcript, *Lewis* v. *Greyhound Corp.*, 329–57, FRC East Point. On the Nashville students, see also David Halberstam, *The Children* (New York: Random House, 1998).

150. *Montgomery Advertiser,* May 20, 21 (quotations), 23, 24, 26, 27, 28, 30, June 1, 2, 3, 1961; (Montgomery) *Alabama Journal,* May 20, 23, 25, 26, 27, 29, 30, 31, 1961; *U.S.* v. *U.S. Klans,* 194 F.Supp. 897; *Lewis* v. *Greyhound Corp.,* 199 F.Supp. 210; Excerpt Transcripts, *U.S.* v. *U.S. Klans,* vol. 1, pp. 8–60, 71–108, 144–45, vol. 4, pp. 3–30, vol. 5, pp. 26–39, vol. 8, pp. 3–14, 18–45, 46–56, 65–105, 187–229, 252–77, and Trial Transcript, *Lewis* v. *Greyhound Corp.,* 23–33, 186–209, all in FRC East Point. On James Zwerg, see Mary R. Zwerg to Robert F. Kennedy, May 20, 1961, Kennedy Papers, and Affidavit of James William Zwerg, May 27, 1961, in *U.S.* v. *U.S. Klans* Case File. John Lewis told Diane Nash that when he regained consciousness after having been knocked out, he asked a policeman for protection, and the policeman replied, "Ask Abernathy" (telephone message from Diane Nash to Robert F. Kennedy, Kennedy Papers). Lewis's own account of the riot is in Lewis with D'Orso, *Walking with the Wind,* 158–61. The evidence is clear that Montgomery police had abundant advance notice of the arrival of the Freedom Riders' bus. Sullivan admitted in testimony in federal district court that Floyd Mann came personally to police headquarters and told him that the bus was twelve miles from Montgomery and would arrive imminently. And Special Agent Spencer Robb of the FBI's Montgomery office testified at the same hearing that he had talked to Acting Police Chief W. Marvin Stanley about an hour before the bus arrived and that Stanley had assured him that both regular and reserve police were alerted and that there would be no trouble; Stanley told Robb that the Freedom Riders would be allowed to use the bus station's facilities on an integrated basis, in accordance with court decisions, but would not be allowed to integrate facilities elsewhere in the city. *Advertiser* reporter Stuart Culpepper testified that Detective Sergeant Jack Shows had told him at the police station a few minutes before the bus's arrival that police would not lift a finger to protect the Freedom Riders. Culpepper also testified that when the initial call came in that there was trouble at the Greyhound station, the dispatcher refused to send a car, but said he would wait to see what happened. In an interview with me, Shows said that Police Captain—and future chief—Drue H. Lackey, the commander of the department's patrol division, was an intimate friend of Claude V. Henley, the automobile service manager whom news accounts identify as a leader of the mob. Shows suggested that this relationship might have caused Lackey to be reluctant to dispatch officers to the bus station (interview, June 20, 1984). Sullivan testified that he himself had made the decision not to station officers at the terminal in anticipation of the arrival of the bus; he said that he feared that doing so

might attract a crowd. News accounts, however, state that members of the mob, awaiting the bus, had kept vigil at the bus station all of the night preceding the riot; they sat in cars parked near the terminal and stood in small groups around the station. At the conclusion of the testimony in the Justice Department's suit seeking to enjoin the Klan from interfering with the Freedom Rides, U.S. District Judge Frank Johnson formally found that Montgomery police had willfully and deliberately failed to take measures to ensure the Freedom Riders' safety.

Mrs. Frederick Gach, a native of Phenix City, ironically had been a high school classmate of Governor Patterson's. Mr. Gach, a native of Detroit, Michigan, was studying pharmacology at Auburn University. On the Gaches, see also Barnard, ed., *Outside the Magic Circle,* 289, 298; on the riot in general, see 296–99. The other arrests besides the Gaches were of brothers William F. and Eiland Cranmore and juvenile Eulis Taylor, all for failure to obey an officer (Excerpt Transcripts, *U.S.* v. *U.S. Klans,* vol. 8, p. 84).

Deputy Assistant Attorney General John Doar, who had come to Montgomery with John Seigenthaler, watched the entire riot from a third-floor window in the post office, next door to the bus station, along with Alcohol and Tobacco Tax agent Louis Fisher.

Some fifteen to twenty-five Montgomery Klansmen had been among the eighty Klansmen involved in the Birmingham riot on May 14, as well (SA Barrett Kemp to SAC Thomas Jenkins, May 15, 1961, FBI Case Files, Freedom Rider Investigation).

151. On the president's reluctance to intervene, see *New York Times,* May 24, 1961; (Montgomery) *Alabama Journal,* May 23, 1961; draft of wire from John F. Kennedy to Alabama congressional delegation, May 22, 1961, Kennedy Papers. Abernathy accused the president of playing politics during the episode (*Montgomery Advertiser,* May 23, 1961). On Patterson's endorsement of Kennedy and its consequences for the governor, see *Selma Times-Journal,* June 17, 29, July 2, 15, August 10, 1959, October 19, 1960; *Montgomery Home News,* June 18, July 23, August 13, December 24, 1959, January 14, 1960. On the Alabama Air National Guard's role in the Bay of Pigs invasion, see *Montgomery Advertiser,* March 17, 1998. On Patterson's reluctance to cooperate with Kennedy and the dispatch of the marshals, see (Montgomery) *Alabama Journal,* May 17, 19, 1961; *Montgomery Advertiser,* May 20, 21, 22, 1961; transcripts of telephone conversations between Robert F. Kennedy and John M. Patterson, May 20 and 21, 1961, Robert F. Kennedy to John M. Patterson, telegram, May 20, 1961, and memorandum to Robert F. Kennedy, n.d. [May 20, 1961], all in Kennedy Papers. L. B. Sullivan similarly refused to receive a telephone call from Robert Kennedy on May 15 (*Alabama Journal,* May 19, 1961).

152. *Montgomery Advertiser,* May 22, 23, 24, 1961; (Montgomery) *Alabama Journal,* May 22, 23, 24, 25, 1961; Robert F. Kennedy to Floyd Mann, telegram, May 21, 1961, transcript of telephone conversation between Robert F. Kennedy and Assistant Police Chief E. P. "Tiny" Brown, May 21, 1961, Robert F. Kennedy to John M. Patterson, telegram, May 21, 1961, William Geoghegan to Robert F. Kennedy, May 22, 1961, all in Kennedy Papers; Excerpt Transcript, *U.S.* v. *U.S. Klans,* vol. 8, pp. 43–44, FRC East Point. Kennedy also wired Mayor Earl James on the night of May 20, 1961, presumably to inform him of the dispatch of the marshals, but I have been unable to locate the text of this telegram. Jessica Mitford's own account of her visit to Montgomery is in her *Poison Penmanship: The Gentle Art of Muckraking* (New York: Vintage Books, 1980), 70–78; see also Barnard, ed., *Outside the Magic Circle,* 299–302. Fred Shuttlesworth's account of these events is in Detective Marcus A.

Jones to Chief Jamie Moore, May 24, 1961, in Connor Papers. John Lewis's is in Lewis with D'Orso, *Walking with the Wind,* 161–68. Solomon Seay's is in his *I Was There,* 223–25. On the role of Meriwether, see *New York Times,* May 24, 1961, and *Montgomery Advertiser,* May 22, 1961; on Meriwether's appointment to federal office, see *Montgomery Advertiser,* February 1, 16, March 3, 5, 6, 8, 9, 15, 1961. The two homes firebombed were those of James Peek, Jr., the white restaurant owner and former Klansman, and Harry Blanche, a black laborer at a lumber company. After this second riot, the number of marshals in the city was increased from 400 to 666, but on May 25 all but 100 were sent home (U.S. Justice Department Press Statement, May 25, 1961, Kennedy Papers).

Judge Walter B. Jones ordered the arrest of the Freedom Riders for violating his injunction of May 19. The two white female Freedom Riders were allowed to return to Nashville by train on the day following the initial riot, and Barbee and Zwerg, the two badly injured Riders, were hospitalized. The remaining Riders went into hiding in Abernathy's church and in various black homes around Montgomery to avoid Judge Jones's arrest order. Governor Patterson's declaration of martial law late on May 21, however, had the ironic effect of saving the Riders from arrest because it compelled the suspension of civil process in the city. Thirteen of the original Freedom Riders thereupon returned to Nashville to take final examinations at Tennessee A. and I. College, where they were students. Four others, including John Lewis, traveled on to Jackson on May 24, along with twenty-four new Freedom Riders who had come to Montgomery for the purpose. Apparently through the intervention of Senator James Eastland, initially belligerent officials in Mississippi agreed to guarantee the safety of the Riders there in return for an agreement from the Kennedy administration not to interfere with the Riders' arrest and punishment. Freedom Riders continued to pour into Jackson throughout the summer of 1961; all were imprisoned as soon as they arrived, and many spent months in jail. On the hiding of the Freedom Riders in Abernathy's church, see notes of telephone conversation between Burke Marshall and Ralph D. Abernathy, May 23, 1961, Kennedy Papers. On the reception of the Freedom Riders in Mississippi, see William Orrick to Robert F. Kennedy, May 24, 1961, Robert F. Kennedy to James G. Pruett, May 24, 1961, transcript of telephone conversations between Burke Marshall and Mississippi Attorney General Robert Patterson, May 22, 1961, and between Robert F. Kennedy and Mississippi Governor Ross Barnett, May 23, 1961, and log of telephone calls of Attorney General, May 15–26, 1961, all in ibid. See also Lewis with D'Orso, *Walking with the Wind,* 169–74. On May 26, a group of eleven new Freedom Riders led by Yale University chaplain William Sloan Coffin was arrested by martial law troops in Montgomery for violating Judge Jones's injunction, just as they were attempting to leave the city for Jackson. On this episode, see Trial Transcript, *Lewis v. Greyhound Corp.,* 44–109, 212–86, FRC East Point; and Gray, *Bus Ride to Justice,* 180–85.

153. *Montgomery Advertiser,* May 21 (first quotation), 23 (fourth quotation), 24 (second quotation), 26 (third quotation), 28 (fifth quotation), 31 (sixth quotation), 1961; (Montgomery) *Alabama Journal,* May 23, 25, 26, 1961. On T. B. Hill, see *Montgomery Advertiser,* May 5, 1982. Winton Blount gives his own account of these events in Winton M. "Red" Blount with Richard Blodgett, *Doing It My Way* (Lyme, Conn.: Greenwich Publishing Group, 1996), 88–90.

154. (Montgomery) *Alabama Journal,* May 22 (first and third quotations), 23, 24, 25, 26 (second set of quotations), 27, 1961. On Stanley, see *Selma Times-Journal,* November 5, 1964.

155. *U.S.* v. *U.S. Klans,* 194 F.Supp. 897; *Montgomery Advertiser,* June 1, 3, 4, 1961; Bass, *Taming the Storm,* 173–83.

156. *Montgomery Advertiser,* May 5, 1956, May 30, September 23, October 31, November 1, 2, 1961, January 4, 5, 6, 7, 1962; *Selma Times-Journal,* July 26, September 24, November 1, 1961, January 5, 1962; *Discrimination in Operations of Interstate Motor Carriers of Passengers,* 86 MCC 743; *Lewis* v. *Greyhound Corp.,* 199 F.Supp. 210; *U.S.* v. *City of Montgomery,* 201 F.Supp. 590.

157. *Selma Times-Journal,* August 10, 19, 1960, November 14, 1961; Seay, *I Was There,* 225–31 (quotations). Seay prints the full text of his letter in his autobiography.

158. Montgomery Improvement Association to James H. Bagley, April 9, 1962, Solomon S. Seay, Sr., to Bernard W. Franklin, July 9, 1962, both in Gregory Papers; *Selma Times-Journal,* September 26, 28, October 16, 1962, November 2, 3, 1964; Seay, *I Was There,* 234–35, 241.

159. *Montgomery Advertiser,* April 23, May 18, 1960, March 16, April 28, June 22, July 25, August 8, 9, 10, 11, 12, 13, 14, 16, 17, 18, 19, 21, 23, 1962; *Cobb* v. *Montgomery Library Board,* 207 F.Supp. 880. The city commission's decision to leave the library open but to remove the tables and chairs had been taken after private discussions with the moderate business leaders, before the emergence of the public debate about the action. But the moderates' public defense of the acceptance of the library's integration was essential to preserving the commissioners' willingness to resist the segregationist pressure to reverse the action.

160. On the long battle over discrimination in voting registration in Montgomery, see *Alabama ex rel. Gallion* v. *Rogers,* 187 F.Supp. 848, 285 F.2d 430, 366 U.S. 913; *U.S.* v. *Penton,* 212 F.Supp. 193; *U.S.* v. *Parker,* 236 F.Supp. 511; *Montgomery Advertiser,* May 24, June 7, 14, July 2, 14, August 12, 19, 25, September 21, 22, 30, October 1, 5, 6, 7, 1960, January 17, 25, August 4, November 3, 4, 1961, January 4, 5, 6, 8, 9, 10, 11, 31, November 21, 1962, June 19, August 13, 1963, August 13, December 18, 1964, February 7, 1965; (Montgomery) *Alabama Journal,* May 1, 1961; *Selma Times-Journal,* June 6, 9, July 1, 13, August 12, 25, September 21, 30, October 2, 1960, January 17, May 2, August 4, November 3, 1961, January 3, 4, 5, 10, 31, November 21, 1962, June 19, August 13, 1963, January 15, August 13, 1964, February 7, 9, 1965.

161. On Judge Johnson, see Yarbrough, *Judge Frank Johnson,* Sikora, *The Judge,* and Bass, *Taming the Storm;* but none of these biographers emphasizes the significant transition in Johnson's attitudes in the early 1960s that is asserted in the text. Cf. also Gray's assessment of the judge in *Bus Ride to Justice,* 177. One white liberal's poignant and profound reaction to witnessing the initial Montgomery Freedom Rider riot—very similar to the one I suspect Judge Johnson also experienced—is in Barnard, ed., *Outside the Magic Circle,* 296–97: "I felt absolute stark terror," Virginia F. Durr reports. "It destroyed the confidence I'd been building up for ten years. . . . I'd begun defending the South, and Montgomery in particular, because of the many kindnesses we had received. We had met with unkindnesses, too, but we had met with enough kindness that I was beginning to feel that Montgomery was my home. . . . But all of a sudden I was terrified. These were the people I was living among and they were really crazy. They were full of hatred and they were full of bigotry and meanness."

162. On the 1963 municipal elections, see *Montgomery Advertiser,* January 1, 5, 6, 9, 10, 31, February 1, 10, 17, 20, 21, 24, 28, March 1, 3, 4, 10, 12, 13, 14, 15, 16, 17, 18, 19, May 18, 20, 21, 1963.

163. Paul J. Dumas to E. P. "Tiny" Brown, August 30, 1964 (third quotation), in Paul J. Dumas Papers, Duke University Library; *Birmingham World,* April 25, 1959, August 17, December 11, 1963; *Montgomery Advertiser,* August 4, November 30, December 5, 6, 7, 9, 1963, January 16, March 4, 5, May 13, 1964; *Selma Times-Journal,* October 21, 1962, December 6, 1963, March 4, 5 (first and second quotations), May 12, 1964; Gray, *Bus Ride to Justice,* 205–8; Seay, *I Was There,* 248; Fairclough, *To Redeem the Soul of America,* 179–80; Garrow, *Bearing the Cross,* 314–16. Seay's own account in his autobiography confuses the events of 1964 with those of 1965. Garrow refers to the MIA's opposition to the Alabama Project as "idiosyncratic," and Fairclough attributes it to a growing conservatism within the organization. In fact, of course, it derived from the confidence that Seay and his associates had developed in the city's white business progressive leadership; they simply did not accept that further direct action was necessary to obtain progress in Montgomery, whatever might be the situation elsewhere in the state.

164. Paul J. Dumas to E. P. "Tiny" Brown, August 30, 1964 (quotation), Dumas Papers; Fairclough, *To Redeem the Soul of America,* 260–61.

165. *Montgomery Advertiser,* July 2, 4, 29, 30, August 4, 27, September 2, 6, 9, 1964, January 28, February 25, 28, 1965; *Selma Times-Journal,* August 4, 27, September 2, 6, 11, 1964, January 28, February 25, 26, 1965; *Carr* v. *Montgomery County Board of Education,* 232 F.Supp. 705; *NAACP* v. *Alabama,* 377 U.S. 288; Paul J. Dumas to E. P. "Tiny" Brown, May 24, 31, 1964, Dumas to file 245, June 6, 1964, Dumas to Brown, June 7, 1964, Dumas to file 249, June 14, 16, 17, 1964, Dumas to file 250, June 18, 20, 23, 1964, Dumas to Brown, July 2, 1964, Dumas to file 255, July 3, 1964, C. E. Grider and Dumas to file 255, July 6, 1964, Grider and Dumas to file 256, July 13, 14, 1964, Grider to file, July 18, 21, 1964, Dumas to Brown, July 21, 22, 1964, Dumas to W. Marvin Stanley, July 28, 1964, Dumas to file, August 4, 8, 9, 11, 17, 21, 24, September 26, October 25, 1964, all in Dumas Papers; Seay, *I Was There,* 243–47. On the future of Montgomery's school desegregation case, see Bass, *Taming the Storm,* 262–73.

166. *Montgomery Advertiser,* March 16, 17, 18, 1965; *Selma Times-Journal,* March 16, 17, 1965; Paul J. Dumas to file, January 31, February 1, 2, 1965, Dumas and W. M. Craft to file, February 7, 1965, Dumas to E. P. "Tiny" Brown, February 7, 1965, Dumas to file, February 8, 10, 13, 18, 22, 23, March 3, 1965, J. W. Foster to file, March 7, 9, 1965, Dumas to file, March 8, 10, 13, 14, 15, 1965, J. W. Foster and W. M. Craft to file, March 15, 16, 1965, Dumas to file, March 16, 17, 18, 19, 1965, J. W. Foster to file, March 19, 20, 1965, Dumas to file, March 20, 21, 22, 26, 1965, Dumas to Brown, March 26, 1965, Dumas to file, April 2, 4, 5, 6, 7, 8, 9, 12, 1965, J. W. Foster to file, April 9, 11, 1965, Dumas and Foster to file, April 12, 1965, Dumas to file, April 13, 14, 15, 1965, J. W. Foster to file, April 16, 17, 1965, Dumas to file, April 18, 19, 1965, J. W. Foster to file, April 21, 23, 1965, Dumas to file, April 25, May 6, 12, 19, June 8, 26, 1965, and Dumas, Summary of Racial Events of 1965, January 9, 1966, all in Dumas Papers. On the afternoon of the same day as the March 16 melee, a much larger demonstration that had applied for and received a parade permit marched to the capitol with a police escort and held a rally without incident. The demonstrators involved in the melee took the question of the constitutionality of the use of the permit ordinance in these circumstances to federal court. In August, Judge Johnson refused to take jurisdiction of the demonstrators' cases (*Forman* v. *City of Montgomery,* 245 F.Supp. 17, *Johnson* v. *City of Montgomery,* 245 F.Supp. 25), but in February 1966 he in effect agreed with

their contention, in forbidding the use of the parade permit to inhibit picketing (*Smith* v. *City of Montgomery,* 251 F.Supp. 849).

167. On the rival Democratic electoral slates in 1968, see *Alabama Official and Statistical Register* for 1971, pp. 396–410; *Montgomery Advertiser,* September 13, October 23, November 4, 7, December 18, 1968. On enforcement of the ICC order, see Catherine A. Barnes, *Journey from Jim Crow: The Desegregation of Southern Transit* (New York: Columbia University Press, 1983), 168–73, 176–84, 200–201.

Chapter 3. Birmingham

1. Though the civil rights collisions in Montgomery, and to a lesser extent Selma, have produced substantial memoirs, the events in Birmingham have for some reason failed to do so. Martin Luther King provides his own, in large part ghostwritten, account in Martin Luther King, Jr., *Why We Can't Wait* (New York: Harper and Row, 1963). The only other immediate participants to publish their recollections are Charles Morgan, Jr., and G. Thomas Rowe, Jr.; see Morgan's *A Time to Speak* (New York: Harper and Row, 1964) and his *One Man, One Voice* (New York: Holt, Rinehart and Winston, 1979), and Rowe's *My Undercover Years with the Ku Klux Klan* (New York: Bantam Books, 1976). For somewhat earlier periods, see too Nell Irvin Painter, *The Narrative of Hosea Hudson: The Life and Times of a Black Radical* (Cambridge: Harvard University Press, 1979), and Paul Hemphill, *Leaving Birmingham: Notes of a Native Son* (New York: Viking Penguin, 1993). Useful contemporary sources are Geraldine Moore, *Behind the Ebony Mask* (Birmingham: Southern University Press, 1961), and Jacquelyne Johnson Clarke, *These Rights They Seek* (Washington, D.C.: Public Affairs Press, 1962).

But if memoirs are few, Birmingham has, far more than the other two cities, been the object of scholarly investigations, and my account has much profited from many of them. The best of the general studies is Leah Rawls Atkins, *The Valley and the Hills: An Illustrated History of Birmingham and Jefferson County* (Woodland Hills, Calif.: Windsor Publications, 1981). On the city's first half century, two works were especially valuable to me, Carl V. Harris, *Political Power in Birmingham, 1871–1921* (Knoxville: University of Tennessee Press, 1977), and Henry M. McKiven, Jr., *Iron and Steel: Class, Race, and Community in Birmingham, Alabama, 1875–1920* (Chapel Hill: University of North Carolina Press, 1995). Also quite useful were Justin Fuller, "History of the Tennessee Coal, Iron and Railroad Company, 1852–1907" (unpublished Ph.D. diss., University of North Carolina, Chapel Hill, 1966); Marlene Hunt Rikard, "An Experiment in Welfare Capitalism: The Health Care Services of the Tennessee Coal, Iron and Railroad Company" (unpublished Ph.D. diss., University of Alabama, 1983); William W. Rogers and Robert D. Ward, *Labor Revolt in Alabama: The Great Strike of 1894* (University: University of Alabama Press, 1965); and Daniel Letwin, *The Challenge of Interracial Unionism: Alabama Coal Miners, 1878–1921* (Chapel Hill: University of North Carolina Press, 1998).

On the years before and just after World War II, I have been particularly influenced by R. J. Norrell, "Caste in Steel: Jim Crow Careers in Birmingham, Alabama," *Journal of American History* 73 (December 1986): 669–94, and his "Labor at the Ballot Box: Alabama Politics from the New Deal to the Dixiecrat Movement," *Journal of Southern History* 57 (May 1991): 201–34. Also important in shaping my thinking were William D. Barnard, "George Huddleston, Sr., and the Political Tradition of Birmingham," *Alabama Review* 36 (October 1983): 243–58; Wayne Flynt,

"Organized Labor, Reform, and Alabama Politics, 1920," *Alabama Review* 23 (July 1970): 163–80, and his "Religion in the Urban South: The Divided Religious Mind of Birmingham, 1900–1930," *Alabama Review* 30 (April 1977): 108–34; Glenn T. Eskew, "Demagoguery in Birmingham and the Building of Vestavia," *Alabama Review* 42 (July 1989): 192–217; Leah Rawls Atkins, "Senator James A. Simpson and Birmingham Politics of the 1930s: His Fight against the Spoilsmen and the Pie-Men," *Alabama Review* 41 (January 1988): 3–29; Blaine A. Brownell, "Birmingham, Alabama: New South City in the 1920s," *Journal of Southern History* 38 (February 1972): 21–48; Robert P. Ingalls, "Antiradical Violence in Birmingham during the 1930s," *Journal of Southern History* 47 (November 1981): 521–44; William R. Snell, "Fiery Crosses in the Roaring Twenties: Activities of the Revised Klan in Alabama, 1915–1930," *Alabama Review* 23 (October 1970): 256–76, and his "Masked Men in the Magic City: Activities of the Revised Klan in Birmingham, 1916–1930," *Alabama Historical Quarterly* 34 (Fall–Winter 1972): 206–27; Richard A. Straw, "The United Mine Workers of America and the 1920 Coal Strike in Alabama," *Alabama Review* 28 (April 1975): 104–28; Virginia Van der Veer Hamilton, *Hugo Black: The Alabama Years* (Baton Rouge: Louisiana State University Press, 1972); Evans C. Johnson, *Oscar W. Underwood: A Political Biography* (Baton Rouge: Louisiana State University Press, 1980); Robin D. G. Kelley, *Hammer and Hoe: Alabama Communists during the Great Depression* (Chapel Hill: University of North Carolina Press, 1990); Michael A. Breedlove, "Donald Comer: New Southerner, New Dealer" (unpublished Ph.D. diss., American University, 1990); Glenn Feldman, *Politics, Society, and the Klan in Alabama, 1915–1949* (Tuscaloosa: University of Alabama Press, 1999); and Judith Stein, "Southern Workers in National Unions: Birmingham Steelworkers, 1936–1951," in Robert H. Zieger, ed., *Organized Labor in the Twentieth-Century South* (Knoxville: University of Tennessee Press, 1991), 183–222.

For the civil rights years themselves, three works dominate the historiography. Edward Shannon LaMonte, *Politics and Welfare in Birmingham, 1900–1975* (Tuscaloosa: University of Alabama Press, 1995), a doctoral dissertation completed at the University of Chicago in 1976, is a careful study by a political scientist of the sources of public policy formation in the city in four periods: the years just before World War I; the Depression; 1954; and the 1960s and early 1970s. These chronological comparisons permit many instructive generalizations, but they also lead to the sacrifice of much significant detail. As I hope my account demonstrates, the inclusion of these details in the story of Birmingham's racial crisis makes it quite a different one from the version that LaMonte offers; in particular, it reveals more fully the complexity of the city's internal social conflicts and the depth of their historical roots. Robert G. Corley, "The Quest for Racial Harmony: Race Relations in Birmingham, Alabama, 1947–1963" (unpublished Ph.D. diss., University of Virginia, 1979), and Glenn T. Eskew, *But for Birmingham: The Local and National Movements in the Civil Rights Struggle* (Chapel Hill: University of North Carolina Press, 1997), are both studies of the same period by historians who are Birmingham natives, but their interpretations differ so sharply that they might as well be studying different towns. The arch-segregationists in Eskew's Birmingham are the absentee capitalists who control its heavy industry; "Bull" Connor in Corley's Birmingham speaks for the working-class whites whose votes keep him in office, but in Eskew's Birmingham both Connor and his constituency are the industrialists' dupes. Each historian creates a story with a clear dramatic structure, but for Corley the tragically missed opportunity is the white business moderates' failed initiative in creating the Interracial Committee in the early 1950s, while Eskew gives the committee barely a glance. For him the tragedy—as is clearer in the unpublished Ph.D. dissertation (University of Georgia, 1993) than in the published version—is the failure of the CIO's biracial organizing efforts of the 1930s to survive the decade. I myself—possibly because I was not shaped by Birmingham's deep divisions—occupy the perhaps tenuous middle ground between the pro-business and pro-labor interpretive extremes that Corley and Eskew have defined. But I wish to emphasize that I have learned a great deal from each of them. Also instructive for this period were Andrew M. Manis, *A Fire You Can't Put Out: The Civil Rights Life of Birmingham's Reverend Fred Shuttlesworth* (Tuscaloosa: University of Alabama Press, 1999); Jimmie Lewis Franklin, *Back to Birmingham: Richard Arrington, Jr., and His Times* (Tuscaloosa: University of Alabama Press, 1989); Frank Sikora, *Until Justice Rolls Down: The Birmingham Church Bombing Case* (Tuscaloosa: University of Alabama Press, 1991); William A. Nunnelley, *Bull Connor* (Tuscaloosa: University of Alabama Press, 1991); S. Jonathan Bass, "Bishop C. C. J. Carpenter: From Segregation to Integration," *Alabama Review* 45 (July 1992): 184–215; and the three investigations reprinted in David J. Garrow, ed., *Birmingham, Alabama, 1956–1963: The Black Struggle for Civil Rights* (Brooklyn: Carlson Publishing, 1989): Glenn T. Eskew, "The Alabama Christian Movement for Human Rights and the Birmingham Struggle for Civil Rights, 1956–1963," 5–114; Lewis W. Jones, "Fred L. Shuttlesworth, Indigenous Leader," 115–50; and Lee E. Bains, Jr., "Birmingham 1963: Confrontation over Civil Rights," 155–289.

Three works became available after the completion of the present study. S. Jonathan Bass, *Blessed Are the Peacemakers: Martin Luther King, Jr., Eight White Religious Leaders, and the "Letter from Birmingham Jail"* (Baton Rouge: Louisiana State University Press, 2001), is a quite instructive, if rather defensive, account of the moderate recipients of King's castigation. Louise Passey Maxwell, "Remaking Jim Crow: Segregation and Urban Change in Birmingham, Alabama, 1938–1963" (unpublished Ph.D. diss., New York University, 1999), usefully describes the institutional evolution of segregation in various contexts, but it lacks a clear sense of Birmingham's deep social and political divisions. Diane McWhorter, *Carry Me Home: Birmingham, Alabama, the Climactic Battle of the Civil Rights Revolution* (New York: Simon and Schuster, 2001), has a subtle understanding of local conflicts, but it is marred by an excessive trust of interview materials.

2. This account of Connor's background is derived from Nunnelley, *Bull Connor*, 9–23; see also *Alabama Official and Statistical Register* for 1967, p. 234. It was at this time, too, that Connor gained the affectionate nickname "Bull," after a popular cartoon character featured on the front page of the *Birmingham Post,* "Dr. B. U. L. Conner." It is worth noting that Birmingham also had a black professional baseball team, the Black Barons; but despite the many talented players on its rosters, it of course received no radio coverage, and most whites were barely aware of its existence.

3. *Birmingham News,* August 2, 9, 24, September 8, 23, 24, October 2, 3, 4, 13, 17, 18, 20, 1925, September 3, 4, 14, 16, 17, 18, 29, October 4, 5, 6, 13, 15, 1929, August 1, 2, 5, 19, 20, 22, 24, 25, 26, 30, 31, September 1, 2, 7, 8, 9, 10, 11, 12, 13, 1933; (Birmingham) *Labor Advocate,* August 12, 26, September 2, 9, 16, 1933; *Birmingham Age-Herald,* February 5, 27, April 21, 22, 26, 29, May 1, 2, 3 (quotation), 5, 6, 19, 1937; Nunnelley, *Bull Connor,* 9–23; Eskew, "But for Birmingham" (Ph.D. diss.), 29–74; McKiven, *Iron and Steel,* 153–65; LaMonte, *Politics and Welfare in Birmingham,* 15–39, 69–87; Harris, *Political Power in Birmingham,* 57–95; Atkins, "Senator James A. Simpson and Birmingham Politics of the 1930s"; Eskew, "Dema-

goguery in Birmingham and the Building of Vestavia"; Brownell, "Birmingham, Alabama: New South City in the 1920s"; Barnard, "George Huddleston, Sr., and the Political Tradition of Birmingham"; Flynt, "Organized Labor, Reform, and Alabama Politics, 1920"; Flynt, "Religion in the Urban South"; Snell, "Fiery Crosses in the Roaring Twenties"; Snell, "Masked Men in the Magic City." In the 1917 election, Nathaniel Barrett's principal support had come from the True American Society, an anti-Catholic organization in which James Jones was a leading figure, whose membership was soon absorbed by the rising Ku Klux Klan. On the decline of the Klan after 1928, see my "Alabama Politics, Senator J. Thomas Heflin, and the Expulsion Movement of 1929," *Alabama Review* 21 (April 1968): 83–112. On Horace Wilkinson, see Glenn Feldman, *From Demagogue to Dixiecrat: Horace Wilkinson and the Politics of Race* (Lanham, Md.: University Press of America, 1995). The city commission was established in 1911 as a three-member body. In 1915 it was increased to five members, but in 1923 it was returned to three members again, and it remained at that number until its abolition in 1963. The mayor—the president of the commission, who supervised the city's finances—was elected separately from the two associate commissioners. Until 1957, the two associates—the commissioner of public safety, who supervised the police and fire departments, and the commissioner of public improvements, who supervised street maintenance, garbage collection, building inspections, and like functions—were elected in a free-for-all campaign, and the commission itself, at its first meeting after the winners took office, decided by vote which of the positions the two would occupy. Therefore, if no candidate received a majority of the votes cast in the first round of voting, the runoff included the top four candidates. In the municipal elections of 1957 and 1961 the system was changed so that the two associate commissionships were filled in separate races, just as the mayoralty had always been.

The reader will note the introduction in this account of terminology such as "industrialists" and "corporate interests," alien to our examination of Montgomery above. By these terms I mean to refer, of course, to the owners and executives of the heavy industry—mines, mills, and factories—which were the backbone of Birmingham's economy. Elsewhere in this chapter I refer also to "business interests," by which I mean to include commercial, professional, mercantile, and financial in addition to industrial elements. I need hardly say, however, that the objectives of the city's heavy industry were by no means always coincident with those of its bankers, brokers, realtors, contractors, merchants, or professionals. It was from the latter groups, far more often than the former, that the figures whom I designate "business progressives" or "business moderates" were drawn.

4. These paragraphs are derived from McKiven, *Iron and Steel,* 7–53, 89–131. In areas of the economy outside heavy industry, such as the building trades, printing, and the railroads, however, the craft unions affiliated with the American Federation of Labor held their own and continued to be the principal defenders of racial exclusivity in these job categories. On the national context of these developments, see David Montgomery, *Workers' Control in America: Studies in the History of Work, Technology, and Labor Struggles* (Cambridge: Cambridge University Press, 1979), and his *The Fall of the House of Labor: The Workplace, the State, and American Labor Activism, 1865–1925* (Cambridge: Cambridge University Press, 1987).

5. On these events, see Norrell, "Caste in Steel" and "Labor at the Ballot Box"; Ingalls, "Antiradical Violence in Birmingham during the 1930s"; Eskew, "But for Birmingham" (Ph.D. diss.), 29–39; and Kelley, *Hammer and Hoe,* 57–77, 138–51.

The argument in the next several paragraphs is influenced principally by the two very fine articles by Professor Norrell.

6. Kelley, *Hammer and Hoe,* contains a full account of the Communists' activities in Birmingham in these years; see also Painter, *The Narrative of Hosea Hudson.*

7. On these programs, see Rikard, "An Experiment in Welfare Capitalism."

8. On the decline of the company welfare programs, see Eskew, "But for Birmingham" (Ph.D. diss.), 23–27; on the quite inadequate public efforts to replace the corporate programs, see LaMonte, *Politics and Welfare in Birmingham,* 88–132.

9. Norrell, "Caste in Steel," figures from 676. Stein, "Southern Workers in National Unions," and Letwin, *The Challenge of Interracial Unionism,* while by no means denying the impact of Birmingham's white supremacist social order upon the United Steelworkers and the United Mine Workers, respectively, nevertheless tend to see both the ideology of unionism and the unions as institutions as being significantly subversive of white supremacy's domination in the community. Eskew ("But for Birmingham" [Ph.D. diss.], 29–65) joins Stein and Letwin in this emphasis, at least as to the Depression years. On the other hand, Norrell, "Caste in Steel" and "Labor at the Ballot Box," and McKiven, *Iron and Steel,* while not denying the existence of biracialism within the district's labor movement, place much greater stress upon the capacity of the larger society's racism to mold and use the unions to reinforce the destructive implications of segregation. (On the historiographical context of this debate, see Eric Arnesen, "Up from Exclusion: Black and White Workers, Race, and the State of Labor History," *Reviews in American History* 26 (1988): 146–74.)

My own sympathies rest in greater measure with Norrell and McKiven. It is true that, particularly in the midst of the desperation wrought by hard times or the enthusiasm of organizing campaigns, white workers were sometimes willing to accept a degree of collective action with blacks that at other times they resisted. And it is equally true that the industrialists' strident denunciations of this collaboration at all times was a principal source of the social authority of such attitudes. But beginning with the institutionalization of collective bargaining in the 1930s, the unions rarely hesitated to join in writing into their labor agreements the same sort of racial discrimination that the industrialists had generally practiced on their own in the open-shop era. And such contracts merely reconfirmed racially exclusionary practices that skilled workers had themselves sought, and the mills had enforced, for half a century. The notion that the ideology of unionism had any real hope of making much headway against such practices can only derive, I think, from insensitivity to the power of the historical traditions at work in Birmingham. Moreover, as I shall shortly attempt to demonstrate, the acceptance of such an argument would deprive the political events of the late 1930s and 1940s of the internal consistency that they otherwise possess. In fact, the remnants of the racial seniority lines and the racially coded job classifications were finally eliminated from the Birmingham mills of U.S. Steel only under the compulsion of a federal court order issued in December 1973—by which time the corporation's operations in the city were less than a decade from final liquidation (*U.S.* v. *U.S. Steel Corp.,* 371 F.Supp. 1045; see also *Birmingham World,* November 6, 1963, and John Martin to Burke Marshall, December 2, 1963, in Burke Marshall Papers, Kennedy Presidential Library, transcripts in Birmingham Public Library).

10. My understanding of Birmingham's political culture in the early decades of the twentieth century is influenced by Barnard, "George Huddleston, Sr., and the

Political Tradition of Birmingham"; Flynt, "Organized Labor, Reform, and Alabama Politics, 1920," and Flynt, "Religion in the Urban South"; see also my "Hugo Black and the Golden Age" in Tony L. Freyer, ed., *Justice Hugo Black and Modern America* (Tuscaloosa: University of Alabama Press, 1990), 139–55, and my "Alabama Politics, Senator J. Thomas Heflin, and the Expulsion Movement of 1929." I do not mean to imply that this political culture was unique to the city. In its general outlines, it was common to Alabama, and indeed the South, in this period. On the other hand, the industrial character of Birmingham, and the centrality of race to the employment structure there, lent it a particular intensity in the city. I should emphasize, as well, that my characterizations of the differing attitudes here are the broadest of generalizations and are subject to numerous specific exceptions.

11. On the annexation, see LaMonte, *Politics and Welfare in Birmingham,* 29–31. City boosters in the Commercial Club, the predecessor of the chamber of commerce, had campaigned for the annexation, apparently with little fear of its political implications. Very likely they assumed that the recently adopted poll tax would effectively keep the blue-collar vote in check. And indeed, as Norrell demonstrates, the poll tax did hold the white working-class electorate far below its potential numbers throughout the first half of the twentieth century ("Labor at the Ballot Box," 207–8).

12. On the election of 1917, see Eskew, "Demagoguery in Birmingham and the Building of Vestavia."

13. On this election, see Norrell, "Labor at the Ballot Box," 213 (quotation); Barnard, "George Huddleston, Sr., and the Political Tradition of Birmingham"; and Eskew, "But for Birmingham" (Ph.D. diss.), 39. The next year John Altman ran for the city commission against "Bull" Connor but finished seventh in the field of eight (*Birmingham Age-Herald,* February 28, May 5, 1937). The extent of Altman's influence on Commissioner William Harrison had been a principal issue in the mayoral election of 1925 (*Birmingham News,* September 23, October 3, 1925).

14. E.g., James H. Willis to James A. Simpson, August 16, 1949, and James A. Simpson to James H. Willis, August 18, 1949, in Eugene "Bull" Connor Papers, Birmingham Public Library.

15. Eskew, "But for Birmingham" (Ph.D. diss.), 73; LaMonte, *Politics and Welfare in Birmingham,* 69–132.

16. *Birmingham Post-Herald,* February 8, 1952; *Birmingham News,* February 8, 1952 (quotations). The circumstances of Connor's impeachment will be discussed below.

17. Eugene "Bull" Connor to Franklin D. Roosevelt, August 6, 1942 (first quotation), and August 30, 1944 (second quotation), both enclosed with Connor to Governor Chauncey Sparks, September 1, 1944, in file folder "Race-military order, Maxwell Field," in Governors' Correspondence: Sparks, SG12491, Alabama Department of Archives and History, Montgomery; see also Connor to James A. Simpson, May 17, 1945, in James A. Simpson Papers, Alabama Department of Archives and History, Montgomery. On the installation of the "race boards," see Connor to C. L. Harris, June 29, 1944, Connor Papers; see also O. P. Young, minutes of meeting with James O. Henry et al., January 6, 1943, and N. H. Hawkins, Jr., "Comments," n.d. [May 1944], both in ibid. On the large number of racial incidents on Birmingham buses during World War II, see the file folder containing racial complaints aboard buses for the years 1942 and 1943, in W. Cooper Green Papers, Birmingham Public Library; see also, more generally, Eugene "Bull" Connor to Major General Edward H. Brooks, February 14, 1946, ibid. Much of this evidence is summarized in Robin

D. G. Kelley, "The Black Poor and the Politics of Opposition in a New South City, 1929–1970," in Michael B. Katz, ed., *The "Underclass" Debate: Views from History* (Princeton: Princeton University Press, 1993), 304–9. On Connor's first decade in power, see Nunnelley, *Bull Connor,* 15–40; Eskew, "But for Birmingham" (Ph.D. diss.), 38–87; Eskew, *But for Birmingham,* 53–102; Corley, "Quest for Racial Harmony," 34–78; Kelley, *Hammer and Hoe,* 176–229; and Norrell, "Labor at the Ballot Box." Nunnelley emphasizes that Connor's popularity in the early years rested primarily on his reputation as an opponent of professional gambling and vice, and he argues that the commissioner did not begin to rely upon the race issue until 1948. But Nunnelley constructs this case by focusing his attention essentially entirely on Connor's campaigns for reelection in 1941 and 1945, to the exclusion of his actions in office. It is true that, amidst the comparative political calm that had settled over the city after 1937, none of Connor's opponents differed with him on his enforcement of segregation in these elections, and therefore the race question never arose in them. And there can be no question that Connor's quite public crusades against gambling and vice were powerful components of his popularity. But it seems equally clear that throughout this period, Connor's vigorous efforts to maintain white supremacy and to eliminate "outside agitators" were very much a part of his public image and an important source of the electorate's enthusiasm for him.

18. *Boswell* v. *Bethea,* 242 Ala. 292; *Hawkins* v. *Vines,* 249 Ala. 165; *Steele* v. *Louisville and Nashville Railroad,* 245 Ala. 113, 323 U.S. 192; *Davis* v. *Schnell,* 81 F.Supp. 872, 336 U.S. 933; *Birmingham World,* January 1, 11, July 5, August 9, October 15, November 26, 29, 1946, June 17, 1947, June 8, August 13, October 12, 15, 29, November 23, December 21, 24, 1948, January 11, April 1, 1949, March 2, 1951, February 9, 1954; Norrell, "Labor at the Ballot Box," 224–25; Kelley, *Hammer and Hoe,* 182–84; G. Moore, *Behind the Ebony Mask,* 195–96.

19. In 1938, in a sort of aftershock of the 1937 municipal election, the former Klansman and labor ally Ben F. Ray, who had been a leader of the revolt against the presidential candidacy of Alfred Smith in 1928 and would be a leader of the loyalists' attempt to suppress the Dixiecrat revolt of 1948, ran against James Simpson for the state senate. Ray, a close associate of Bibb Graves and Horace Wilkinson, charged—with much justice—that Simpson sought corporate control of Jefferson County. He demanded a public referendum on Simpson's civil service bill. Simpson's substantial victory offered clear confirmation of the emergence of Birmingham's new political order. On this election, see Atkins, "Senator James A. Simpson and Birmingham Politics of the 1930s," 21–24.

20. On these elections, see Eskew, "But for Birmingham" (Ph.D. diss.), 52–53, 79–81; Norrell, "Labor at the Ballot Box," 222–23, 228–29.

21. Nunnelley, *Bull Connor,* 65–66.

22. *Buchanan* v. *Warley,* 165 Ky. 559, 245 U.S. 60, *Harmon* v. *Tyler,* 158 La. 439, 273 U.S. 668, *Monk* v. *City of Birmingham,* 87 F.Supp. 538, 185 F.2d 859, 341 U.S. 940; *Birmingham World,* June 7, July 29, August 5, 1949, July 18, 1950.

23. *Birmingham World,* February 5, April 12, May 21, July 2, 23, August 2, 9, 20, September 10, October 18, November 5, 1946, January 10, 14, 17, June 17, 1947, June 8, 1948, May 29, 1951; *Monk* v. *City of Birmingham,* 87 F.Supp. 538; Corley, "Quest for Racial Harmony," 35–38; Eskew, *But for Birmingham,* 53–57. On the early history of Smithfield, see Lynne B. Feldman, *A Sense of Place: Birmingham's Black Middle-Class Community, 1890–1930* (Tuscaloosa: University of Alabama Press, 1999).

24. *Davis* v. *Schnell,* 81 F.Supp. 872, 336 U.S. 933; *Alabama Official and Statistical Register* for 1947, pp. 535–39; *Alabama Official and Statistical Register* for 1951, pp. 607, 615–17. A full discussion of this subject appears in the next chapter.

25. On the struggles, see William D. Barnard, *Dixiecrats and Democrats: Alabama Politics, 1942–1950* (University: University of Alabama Press, 1974).

26. *Birmingham World,* August 2, 1946, June 15, 22, July 2, 1948, June 14, 17, 21, July 15, August 2, 12, September 13, 23, 1949; statement of W. Hugh Morris, June 22, 1948, Connor Papers; Abraham Berkowitz to W. Cooper Green, June 15, 1948, James H. Willis to Green, June 17, 1948, Ed Stack, executive secretary of the Young Men's Business Club, to Green, June 21, 1948, all in Green Papers. A detailed account of the Klan's June 1949 assault on the white restaurant owner, Steve Marshlar, is in Staci S. Simon, "A Study of the Slovak Community at Brookside, Alabama" (unpublished M.A. thesis, University of Alabama at Birmingham, 1997), 28–32. Brookside police chief Elmer B. Brock, who was indicted for complicity in this assault, in later years joined his brother Jack in Montgomery, where both were deeply involved in the efforts to prevent the integration of the buses, as we have seen. On the Klan's activities in this period, see also G. Feldman, *Politics, Society, and the Klan,* 285–324.

27. *Birmingham World,* March 29, April 1, 26, 29, May 10, 20, 24, 27, June 3 (first quotation), 7, July 1, 8, 19, 22, 26, 29 (second quotation), August 2, 5, 9, 12, 19, 23, 26, September 6, 9, 13, 16, 30, November 11, 1949; James H. Willis to James A. Simpson, August 16, 1949, and Simpson to Willis, August 18, 1949, Connor Papers; Sidney W. Smyer to City Commission, November 16, 1948, Mrs. M. E. Haney to W. Cooper Green, March 30, 1949, Emory O. Jackson to W. Cooper Green, April 4, 1949, Statement of R. E. Chambliss, white male, to Detective Paul E. McMahon, May 23, 1949, Emory O. Jackson to James W. Morgan, wire, June 3, 1949, James W. Morgan to W. Cooper Green, June 17, 1949, J. J. Green to W. Cooper Green, August 13, 1949, Statement of James W. Morgan, August 13, 1949, all in Green Papers; Trial Transcript, *Monk* v. *City of Birmingham,* 29–33, 67–70, 92–93, 118–28, 133–39, 164–66, 173–74, 183, in Southeastern Regional Federal Records Center, East Point, Georgia (hereinafter cited as FRC East Point). Mayor Green, a former resident of the area, had taken a leading role in defining the initial racial boundary in 1923. Commissioner Connor also had earlier lived in the area. See also Stephen G. Meyer, "Doing the Master's Business in Alabama: The First Dynamite Hill Bombings and the Fight against Residential Segregation in Birmingham, 1947–1954" (unpublished graduate seminar paper, University of Alabama, Tuscaloosa, copy in possession of the author).

28. *Birmingham World,* September 30, November 11, 29, December 9 (quotation), 16, 1949, January 20, 1950; Horace C. Wilkinson to James H. Willis, November 14, 1949, Wilkinson to Willis, November 30, 1949, and Wilkinson to Willis, December 28, 1949, all in Connor Papers; *Monk* v. *City of Birmingham,* 87 F.Supp. 538. On Wilkinson's arguments, see his brief requesting a rehearing by the Fifth Circuit and his application to the U.S. Supreme Court for certiorari, both in the James W. Morgan Papers, Birmingham Public Library. On Wilkinson's background, see G. Feldman, *From Demagogue to Dixiecrat.* Wilkinson denied to Judge Mullins that the Birmingham zoning ordinance prevented blacks from living in white areas solely because of their race or color. Rather, he said, it did so because of the real differences between the races. The ordinance, he argued, made each race feel more at ease, "the white because it has a distaste for the colored, and the colored because

it would feel less imposed upon and more independent" (Answer of Defendants, December 12, 1949, in Case File, *Monk* v. *City of Birmingham,* in FRC East Point).

29. *City of Birmingham* v. *Monk,* 185 F.2d 859, cert. denied 341 U.S. 940; *Birmingham World,* April 18, 25, May 2, 5, 30, October 17, December 22, 26, 1950, January 9, May 8, 11, 22, 29, 1951. Police stated that they did not believe the May 1950 bombing of the office building was racially motivated, though its location appeared to indicate otherwise.

30. *Birmingham World,* August 5, 1949, January 9, 1951, January 8, 1952; Nunnelley, *Bull Connor,* 36–37.

31. *Birmingham World,* August 26, 1949, April 25, May 12, June 27, 1950, January 9, February 27, July 24, 1951, December 23, 1959, December 27, 1961, August 7, 1963; James E. Lay to Whom It May Concern, October 3, 1963, and Abraham Berkowitz to Burke Marshall, October 22, 1963, Marshall Papers. Captain Lay in his statement gives the date of organization of the unit as February 1957, but I believe this is a typographical error for February 1951. At any rate, there can be no question that the unit was in operation by the summer of 1951, because there are references to it in the press by that time.

32. On the Cater and Wallace Acts, see *Acts of Alabama,* Session of 1949, pp. 991–98, and Session of 1951, pp. 1307–12; on the Committee of 100, see Clarence Lloyd to W. Cooper Green, January 14, 1950, Clarence B. Hanson, Jr., to Green, March 14, 1950, Hanson to Committee of 100, memorandum, April 25, 1950, Green to Thomas W. Martin, December 14, 1950, all in Green Papers; on the Young Men's Business Club, see Anthony Paul Underwood, "A Progressive History of the Young Men's Business Club of Birmingham, Alabama, 1946–1970" (unpublished M.A. thesis, Samford University, 1980), and esp. 14–18 on the YMBC's relations with the chamber of commerce; on established industries' surreptitious opposition to industrial expansion, see W. Cooper Green to Henry Ford II, August 17, 1949, in Green Papers, Kenneth H. Bradshaw to Charles H. Stant, Jr., April 20, 1962, in Arthur J. Hanes Papers, Birmingham Public Library, and Eskew, *But for Birmingham,* 167–70. On the centrality of low wage rates in the industrial ideology of the Birmingham district, see W. David Lewis, *Sloss Furnaces and the Rise of the Birmingham District: An Industrial Epic* (Tuscaloosa: University of Alabama Press, 1994). My generalization about the primary sources of support for the efforts of the Committee of 100 derives from the committee's membership; for the committee's full membership in 1950 see Clarence B. Hanson, Jr., to Committee of 100, memorandum, April 25, 1950, and for the full membership in 1959 see P. A. Sieverling, undated cover letter for booklet on resources of the Birmingham area [1959], both in Green Papers. The chairmen of the committee from 1950 to 1963 were Clarence B. Hanson, Jr., the publisher of the *Birmingham News;* Edward L. Norton, the chairman of Royal Crown Cola; Joseph N. Greene, the chairman of Alabama Gas; George A. Mattison, Jr., the president of a building materials company; William P. Engel, a realtor, insurance agent, and mortgage banker; James A. Head, the president of a business supply company; and Caldwell Marks, the chairman of a manufacturer of bearings and mechanical power transmission equipment. See Sidney W. Smyer to City Commission, November 16, 1948, Green Papers, for an example of a segregationist business leader whose attitudes nevertheless resulted in a racially moderate policy recommendation.

33. Donald Comer to W. Cooper Green, July 7, 1949, Green Papers; for additional goading by whites, see Abraham Berkowitz to Green, June 15, 1948, Ed

Stack, executive secretary of Young Men's Business Club, to Green, June 21, 1948, Frank B. Yielding, Jr., to Green, June 23, 1949, Green to Mrs. Anne M. Parker, June 28, 1949, Edna M. Levenson to Green, April 20, 1950, Ida D. Rosenthal to Green, April 21, 1950, Mrs. T. D. Abernathy to Green, April 24, 1950, and clipping from *Birmingham Post,* April 24, 1950, all in Green Papers. On Comer, see Breedlove, "Donald Comer."

34. *Birmingham World,* June 14, 17, 21, July 12, 15, 1949; *Birmingham Age-Herald,* May 1, 1950; Mrs. John Keith to W. Cooper Green, telephone message, September 27, 1949, Ray Mullins to C. E. Armstrong, November 2, 1949, and C. E. Armstrong to Robert E. Chambliss, November 3, 1949, all in Green Papers. Police Chief Elmer Brock was a brother of Jack Brock, the immediate past state president of the AFL, who, as we have seen, was later deeply involved in the events surrounding the bombing of the black churches and homes in Montgomery in January 1957, at the conclusion of the bus boycott. It is also worth noting that the statute which the Klansmen were indicted for violating in connection with the boycott of the restaurant that served both races was the same Alabama Anti-Boycott Act of 1921 that Martin Luther King and the other leaders of the bus boycott would be indicted for violating in Montgomery in February 1956.

35. *Birmingham Age-Herald,* May 1, 1950; *Birmingham World,* July 15, August 2, September 23, 1949, July 31, 1951; *Montgomery Advertiser,* April 23, June 2, 4, 10, 11, 1957; *Selma Times-Journal,* June 10, 11, 12, 14, September 2, 1957; *Ex parte Morris,* 252 Ala. 551. Ironically, it was the precedent of *Ex parte Morris* that in 1956 would allow Attorney General John Patterson to request, and Judge Walter B. Jones to order, the production of the membership lists of the state's NAACP branches. The state supreme court relied upon its decision in the *Morris* case in affirming Judge Jones's holding of the NAACP in contempt for failure to comply (*Ex parte NAACP,* 265 Ala. 349). The U.S. Supreme Court in June 1958 reversed this decision and ruled—just as Morris's attorney had argued in 1949—that production of the membership lists was a threat to the First Amendment freedoms of speech and association (*NAACP* v. *Alabama,* 357 U.S. 449). If this doctrine had been accepted a decade earlier, the almost certain result would have been the continuation of the Klan's reign of terror in Birmingham through the early 1950s. A more detailed account of the Klan in these years is in G. Feldman, *Politics, Society, and the Klan,* 285–324.

36. *Birmingham World,* June 17, 21, July 1, 1949, July 13, 1951.

37. On the background of the Interracial Committee, see *Birmingham World,* July 30, 1948, July 25, 28, August 4, 18, September 29, October 3, 24, 27, November 3, 1950; Corley, "Quest for Racial Harmony," 43–67; and LaMonte, *Politics and Welfare in Birmingham,* 148–53. On Zukoski, see Eskew, "But for Birmingham" (Ph.D. diss.), 66–76; Eskew, *But for Birmingham,* 81, 369–70; and *Birmingham World,* March 8, 1946. In addition to Patton and Shores, the blacks at the May meeting were S. J. Bennett, A. B. White, Carol W. Hayes, Paul L. Ware, and J. Clyde Perry.

38. *Birmingham World,* March 22, 1946, January 31, 1947, July 25 (first set of quotations), 28, August 4, September 29 (third quotation), October 3 (second quotation), 24, 27, November 3, 1950; May 15, 1951; Minutes of Interracial Steering Committee, October 18, 1950, Interracial Committee Papers, Birmingham Public Library; LaMonte, *Politics and Welfare in Birmingham,* 144–48. Emory Jackson was not above the use of distortion in his campaign to discourage black participation in the Interracial Committee. The committee was evenly divided between the races, with twenty-five white and twenty-five black members, and each of its subcommittees was constituted with equal care, as we shall see. But Jackson referred

to the committee's black members as its "nonpolicy making, all-black advisory committee" (*Birmingham World,* October 24, 1950).

39. Membership List of the Interracial Committee, 1951, Crawford Johnson, Jr., et al. to potential committee members, January 24, 1951, and Organization and Rules of Procedure of the Interracial Committee, April 24, 1951, all in Interracial Committee Papers. The four black members of the nominating committee were A. B. White, the manager of one of the city's black public housing projects; Robert C. Johnson, the principal of Parker High School, who would become the father-in-law of future secretary of state Colin Powell; Ensley mortician W. E. Shortridge; and Negro Tuberculosis Association executive secretary Robert Coar. Shortridge was a relatively independent member. Coar had been a leader in the Smithfield resistance, but his organization depended in part on white charity. And Johnson and White held jobs that were quite vulnerable to white pressure. In the fall of 1949, investment banker Mervyn Sterne had told black advocates of an Urban League chapter that he and his white associates were unwilling to work with blacks who belonged to militant organizations and that they would not discuss controversial matters (Corley, "Quest for Racial Harmony," 56–57). Since Crawford Johnson and Clarence Hanson joined with Sterne in deciding, only months later, to replace the Urban League chapter with a local committee, largely because of these and similar concerns, I assume they shared Sterne's desire to appoint black moderates to the committee. And of course, the blacks who were nominated for membership generally fell into this category. On the other hand, the willingness of white leaders to include such activists as Patton and Taggart in the organizational meeting indicates that they were open to a committee membership rather less accommodationist than they actually got. I therefore attribute equal weight in producing this outcome to the campaign of intimidation launched by militants such as Emory Jackson and Cornelius Maiden. The nominating committee was initially intended to contain four whites as well as four blacks, but the fourth white member, Richard J. Stockham of Stockham Valves and Fittings, apparently was not active in its deliberations.

40. *Birmingham World,* July 25, 1950 (quotation), May 20, November 14, December 2, 1952; January 29, 1954; *Birmingham Post-Herald,* November 29, 1952; Minutes of the Organizational Meeting of the Interracial Committee, April 24, 1951, Minutes of Interracial Committee Meeting of June 15, 1951, Minutes of I.C. Executive Committee Meetings, June 22, July 10, 1951, Minutes of I.C. Personnel Committee Meetings, October 31, 1951, April 14, October 10, 1952, December 28, 1953, L. N. Shannon to Roberta Morgan, September 28, 1951, and attached job description for executive secretary, September 26, 1951, all in Interracial Committee Papers. On Bishop Carpenter, see Bass, "Bishop C. C. J. Carpenter" and *Blessed Are the Peacemakers,* 29–38, 167–73. The personnel committee's initial choice for executive secretary, Samuel F. Adams, Jr., was appointed in June 1952, but he declined in order to accept a post with the State Department.

41. Minutes of the I.C. Day Care Committee Meetings, March 24, May 6, 20, 1953, January 26, May 4, August 2, 17, 1954, June 13, October 12, 1955; and Minutes of Interracial Committee Meetings, September 18, 1951, June 18, 1953, February 22, May 17, December 20, 1955; all in Interracial Committee Papers.

42. Minutes of the I.C. Recreation Committee Meetings, September 18, 25, 1951, June 17, 1952, March 17, 1953, April 7, September 8, 1954, August 11, 1955; Lucille Douglass to Recreation Committee, memorandum, June 17, 1953, Paul R. Jones to Roberta Morgan, memorandum, May 13, 1954; Minutes of Interracial Committee Meetings, September 18, 1951, January 10, December 18, 1952, June 1,

October 20, 1954, May 17, September 21, 1955; Report of the Executive Secretary, January 1953; Report of the Recreation Committee to the Annual Meeting of the Interracial Committee, January 26, 1954; all in Interracial Committee Papers; *Birmingham World,* August 3, 1948, February 26, 29, March 7, 1952, July 31, September 8, 1953, November 22, 1955.

43. Minutes of the I.C. Housing Committee Meetings, July 31, 1951, August 30, September 9, 1954, January 31, May 13, September 15, 1955; Minutes of the Interracial Committee Meetings, January 10, 1952, June 1, October 20, 1954, May 17, 1955; Roberta Morgan to A. Key Foster, memorandum, November 5, 1951; Report of the Executive Secretary, January 1953; all in Interracial Committee Papers.

44. Minutes of the Interracial Committee Meetings, September 18, 1951, January 10, December 18, 1952, January 27, June 18, December 9, 1953, January 26, June 1, October 20, 1954, May 17, 1955; Minutes of the I.C. Executive Committee, March 25, 1952; Report of the Executive Secretary, January 1953; Report of the Interracial Committee to the Annual Meeting of the Jefferson County Coordinating Council of Social Forces, June 23, 1953; Minutes of the I.C. Hospital Facilities Committee Meetings, February 5, 1952, May 13, October 7, 1954, November 9, 1955; Roberta Morgan to Merrill F. Krughoff, March 2, 1956; all in Interracial Committee Papers; E. M. Friend, Jr., to W. Cooper Green, January 28, 1950, and Statement of W. Cooper Green on the Construction of the Negro Hospital, February 1, 1950 (quotation), Green Papers; *Birmingham World,* July 12, 1946, June 25, 1948, June 6, 13, 23, 1950, April 10, 1951, February 29, September 23, 26, 1952, April 21, June 16, 1953; G. Moore, *Behind the Ebony Mask,* 156–58. Dr. Brannon Hubbard of Montgomery, who led the fight to permit black doctors to join the Alabama Medical Association, was the father of Dr. Brannon Hubbard, Jr., whose efforts, as we saw in the preceding chapter, helped prevent the Montgomery city government from closing the public library to avoid integration in 1962.

45. Minutes of the Interracial Committee Meetings, May 16, 1952, December 20, 1955; Annual Report of the Executive Secretary, January 1953; Minutes of the I.C. Executive Committee, September 21, 1954; Minutes of the I.C. Transportation Committee Meetings, May 28, September 23, 1954; Paul R. Jones to Lester N. Shannon, memorandum, June 17, 1954, Paul R. Jones to Transportation Committee, memorandum, June 24, 1955, Lester N. Shannon to Transportation Committee, memorandum, December 20, 1955; all in Interracial Committee Papers; *Birmingham World,* August 13, 1954, October 20, 27, 1956. On racial friction on city buses, see the folder of complaints for 1942–43 in the Green Papers, and *Birmingham World,* December 2, 6, 1949, July 31, 1957. On Orzell Billingsley, see *Birmingham World,* September 7, 1951. A survey of thirty Birmingham buildings with elevators, located throughout the city, conducted by the Alabama Council on Human Relations in 1957 found four of them still practicing elevator segregation (memorandum attached to Robert E. Hughes to Harrison E. Salisbury, April 25, 1960, in Southern Regional Council Papers, Atlanta University Library).

46. *Birmingham World,* August 3, 1948, August 2, 12, December 13, 1949, February 28, August 25, November 24, December 19, 1950, March 2, September 7, October 16, 1951, November 8, 1953, July 2, 1954, December 13, 1955, June 23, September 22, October 6, 10, November 14, December 15, 19, 1956, March 2, 1957, April 12, 23, June 11, July 2, 1958, April 25, November 14, 1959, February 24, May 25, 1960, January 4, 28, September 9, 1961; G. Moore, *Behind the Ebony Mask,* 33–34, 63–66, 71–86, 95–97, 110–23, 156–58, 169–71. For a full account of the activities of the Interracial Committee, see Corley, "Quest for Racial Harmony," 43–114.

47. Nunnelley, *Bull Connor,* 4–5, 25–29, 45–49, 65–66; *Selma Times-Journal,* August 16, 17, September 9, 1954.

48. Minutes of the Interracial Committee Meeting, June 15, 1951; Minutes of the I.C. Executive Committee Meetings, June 22, July 10, August 10 (quotation), 1951, January 3, 1952; Minutes of the I.C. Negro Police Committee Meetings, January 17, May 27, June 17, 1952; I.C. Negro Police Committee to I.C. Executive Committee, memorandum, February 18, 1952; Mervyn H. Sterne to Douglas Arant, February 23, 1952, and February 25, 1952; all in Interracial Committee Papers; *Birmingham World,* July 24, July 31, August 24, 1951.

49. *Birmingham Post-Herald,* December 22, 24, 25, 26, 27, 28, 1951, January 1, 4, 5, 7, 8 (first quotation), 10, 11, 15, 16, 19, 23, 25, 26, February 8 (third quotation), 9, 14, 20 (fourth quotations), 21, March 21, 26, 27, 28, 29, 31, April 7, 11, 12, 15, 16, 1952; *Birmingham News,* February 8, 1952 (second quotation); *Birmingham World,* December 25, 28, 1951, January 8, 11, 22, 25, 29, August 15, 1952, February 3, 13, 20, March 3, 1953; James W. Morgan to W. Cooper Green, January 16, 1952, W. Cooper Green to Milton Fegenbush, January 18, 1952, and Report of the Citizens' Committee on the Birmingham Police Department, February 19, 1952, all in Morgan Papers; I.C. Negro Police Committee to I.C. Executive Committee, memorandum, February 18, 1952, Mervyn H. Sterne to Douglas Arant, February 23, 1952, and February 25, 1952, I.C. Committee on Negro Police minutes, May 27, 1952, all in Interracial Committee Papers; *Connor v. City of Birmingham,* 36 Ala. App. 494, 257 Ala. 588; Eskew, *But for Birmingham,* 89–102; Nunnelley, *Bull Connor,* 40–47. Connor's persecution of Detective Darnell began when *Birmingham News* columnist Walling Keith mentioned the possibility that Darnell might oppose Connor in the 1953 municipal election (Nunnelley, *Bull Connor,* 41). The willingness of the *News* thus to publicize Darnell's potential candidacy seems to me to indicate that business progressive elements may have been encouraging his political aspirations. I suspect that such confidential backing may have emboldened him to seize the opportunity to embarrass the commissioner when it presented itself, but on that point evidence is lacking. It is also worth noting that, at his hearing before the personnel board at which he unsuccessfully appealed Connor's dismissal of him, Darnell testified that Connor was personally responsible for the police department's failure to pursue the investigations of the Smithfield bombings (*Birmingham World,* February 3, 1953).

50. *Birmingham World,* August 8, 1950, September 11, 1951, May 13, 1952, May 8, 12, June 5, 9, September 18, 22, 1953, January 29, February 19 (quotation), March 19, May 7, 18, 28, June 1, 4, 1954; (Montgomery) *Alabama Tribune,* January 29, February 19, March 26, June 11, 1954; *Selma Times-Journal,* March 16, 23, 1954.

51. *Birmingham World,* December 28, 31 (quotation), 1954, January 4, 7, 14, 18, 21, February 1, 11, 25, July 5, 26, 1955. In September 1955, Patrolman Lynch filed a civil suit against the NAACP. He sought $100,000 in damages on the allegation that the organization had persuaded Patrick to file his complaint against Lynch and had paid Patrick's legal fees, thereby depriving Lynch of his job (*Selma Times-Journal,* September 25, 1955).

52. Minutes of Interracial Committee Meetings, January 10, May 16, October 13, 1952; Minutes of I.C. Negro Police Committee Meetings, January 17, May 27, June 17, 1952; I.C. Committee on Negro Police to I.C. Executive Committee, memorandum, February 18, 1952; Mervyn Sterne to Douglas Arant, February 23 and February 25, 1952; Questionnaire sent to southern community leaders on use of Negro police, n.d. [April 1952]; Report of the Committee on Negro Police, n.d.

[c. May 16, 1952]; Report of the Committee on Negro Police, n.d. [c. June 10, 1952]; "Report on a Study of Negro Police Made by the Jefferson County Coordinating Council of Social Forces, Spring, 1953"; Report of the Interracial Committee Executive Secretary, January 1953, June 18, 1953; Report of the Interracial Committee to the Jefferson County Coordinating Council of Social Forces, June 23, 1953; all in Interracial Committee Papers.

53. Minutes of the Meetings of the Interracial Committee, June 18, December 9, 1953, January 26, February 25, June 1, 1954; Minutes of the I.C. Nominating Committee Meetings, December 28, 1953, January 12, 1954; Roberta Morgan to Merrill F. Krughoff, March 2, 1956; all in Interracial Committee Papers.

54. Minutes of the Meetings of the Interracial Committee, June 1, October 20, 1954, May 17, 1955, and Minutes of I.C. Negro Police Committee Meeting, July 28, 1954, all in Interracial Committee Papers; *Birmingham World,* September 10, October 1 (first quotation), 5, 1954, June 24 (second quotations), 28, 1955.

55. Minutes of the Meetings of the Interracial Committee, June 1, 1954, May 17, September 21, 1955, Minutes of the Meeting of the I.C. Negro Police Committee, July 18, 1955, and Paul R. Jones to Subcommittee on Police, June 29, 1955, memorandum, all in Interracial Committee Papers; *Birmingham World,* June 24, 28, July 19, 29, August 2, 16, 26, September 6, October 4, 18, November 1, 1955.

56. Fred L. Shuttlesworth, interview by author, May 18, 1989; *Birmingham World,* January 20, 1956; Manis, *A Fire You Can't Put Out,* 10–67; Jones, "Fred L. Shuttlesworth," esp. 117–33; *Selma Times-Journal,* October 17, 1958.

57. Shuttlesworth, interview, May 18, 1989; *Birmingham World,* June 7, 1949, July 29, August 2, 16, 26, September 6, October 4, 18, November 1, 1955, January 10, 20, 1956; F. L. Shuttlesworth et al. to City Commissioners and Citizens of Birmingham, July 25, 1955, in Albert Boutwell Papers, Birmingham Public Library. The long-standing enmity between Shuttlesworth and Ware appears to date from their argument at the July 9 Ministers Conference meeting.

58. Minutes of the Meetings of the Interracial Committee, May 17, September 21, 1955, Interracial Committee Papers; *Birmingham World,* March 19, April 6, December 7, 17, 1954, January 11, March 29, 1955; *Selma Times-Journal,* November 28, December 12, 15, 1954, May 13, June 3, 19, October 4, 30, November 17, 22, 1955, February 12, 19, March 1, 1956; Corley, "Quest for Racial Harmony," 89–94; Eskew, *But for Birmingham,* 105–14. On Asa Carter, see Dan T. Carter, *The Politics of Rage: George Wallace, the Origins of the New Conservatism, and the Transformation of American Politics* (New York: Simon and Schuster, 1995), passim.

59. Minutes of the Meetings of the Interracial Committee, May 17, September 21, December 20, 1955, March 2 (second quotation), April 13 (seventh, eighth and ninth quotations), 1956; Minutes of the Meetings of the I.C. Committee on Negro Police, July 18, 1955, January 6, 1956, Minutes of the I.C. Executive Committee Meeting, February 2, 1956; Minutes of the Joint Meeting of the Red Cross and Community Chest Executive Committees, April 2, 1956 (third and fourth quotations); Minutes of the Meeting of the Board of Directors of the Birmingham Community Chest, April 6, 1956 (fifth and sixth quotations); Draft Statement of Interracial Committee, March 1, 1956 (first quotation); Roberta Morgan to Merrill F. Krughoff, March 2, 1956; all in Interracial Committee Papers; *Birmingham World,* January 11, 1955, March 9, July 7, 1956; *Selma Times-Journal,* February 26, March 1, 6, 7, 9, 12, 16, 22, 1956; Corley, "Quest for Racial Harmony," 96–114; LaMonte, *Politics and Welfare in Birmingham,* 151–57. On the Lucy riots, see E. Culpepper Clark, *The Schoolhouse Door: Segregation's Last Stand at the University of Alabama* (New York:

Oxford University Press, 1993), 14–113, esp. 57–109. The white supremacists' campaign against the Interracial Committee had begun to have an effect even before the Lucy riots. In December 1955 the Coordinating Council rejected the committee's formal request for authorization to hold a second Race Relations Institute during the coming spring. Henry Johnston sought to resign as the committee's chairman and was forced reluctantly to accept another term only because Stockham Valves executive Lester N. Shannon and Coca-Cola bottling executive Sanders Rowland both refused to take the position (Minutes of the Meeting of the Interracial Committee, December 20, 1955, and Minutes of the I.C. Nominating Committee Meetings, October 20, December 19, 1955, all in Interracial Committee Papers).

60. *Birmingham World,* October 1, 1954.

61. Ibid., May 29, June 12, July 31, August 11, 14, October 23, November 20, December 8, 1953, October 19, 1954, February 4, May 10, 1955, December 5, 1956. A thorough account of the NAACP's battle against the Birmingham Housing Authority, though one that rather understates its negative implications for the branch, is Christopher MacGregor Scribner, "Federal Funding, Urban Renewal, and Race Relations: Birmingham in Transition, 1945–1955," *Alabama Review* 48 (October 1995): 269–95.

62. *Birmingham World,* January 10, June 8, 1956; Shuttlesworth, interview, May 18, 1989; Corley, "Quest for Racial Harmony," 124–32; Eskew, *But for Birmingham,* 124–28.

63. Shuttlesworth, interview, May 18, 1989.

64. *Birmingham World,* July 7, 14, August 1, 8, 22, 25, September 7, October 20, November 10, December 26, 1956.

65. Ibid., November 29, 1955, April 13, 20, May 4, 8, 22, September 19, December 26, 29, 1956, January 2, 5, 16, February 2, April 17, May 1, June 15, July 31, October 26, November 2, 6, December 11, 1957; Shuttlesworth, interview, May 18, 1989; on the constant police harassment to which Shuttlesworth was subject in these years, see F. L. Shuttlesworth to Eugene Connor, August 9, 1958, Boutwell Papers. Four of Cole's assaulters were convicted in Recorder's Court of disorderly conduct and conspiracy to breach the peace, but they appealed to Circuit Court and sought jury trials. The two ringleaders were indicted by the county grand jury for attempted murder, but apparently the charges against all six men were eventually settled with the payment of small fines (*Selma Times-Journal,* June 7, 1963).

66. *Birmingham World,* June 1, 1956, January 2 (first quotation), May 4, 8, 25, 29 (second quotation), June 1 (third quotation), 8, 1957; Eskew, *But for Birmingham,* 118–19; Nunnelley, *Bull Connor,* 49–62. The *World* reported that Connor received a total of about 350 black votes; it attributed them to the fact that Connor had received the endorsement of organized labor in the election (*Birmingham World,* July 30, 1958.)

67. Statement of the Interracial Committee, draft, March 1, 1956 (first quotations), Interracial Committee Papers; *Birmingham News,* April 13, 1963 (second quotations).

68. Clarke, *These Rights They Seek,* 71.

69. *Decatur Daily,* October 5, 1945; *Alabama* News Magazine, October 12, 1945; Albert B. Moore, *History of Alabama and Her People* (Chicago: American Historical Society, 1927), 3:222–23; *Alabama Official and Statistical Register* for 1943, pp. 201, 659. On Seybourn A. Lynne's role in the expulsion movement, see my "Alabama Politics, J. Thomas Heflin, and the Expulsion Movement of 1929," esp. 109–10. On Seybourn H. Lynne's racial attitudes, see, e.g., Seybourn H. Lynne to James A. Hare,

March 15, 1965, James A. Hare Papers, University of Alabama Library, Tuscaloosa. In 1951 Governor Gordon Persons appointed Seybourn A. Lynne to the Decatur circuit judgeship formerly held by his son; the elder Lynne served in this office until 1958, when he was defeated for reelection by future state supreme court justice James N. Bloodworth.

70. *Who's Who in Alabama* for 1972, p. 147; *Selma Times-Journal,* May 10, 11, July 24, 1953, June 12, 1955, May 22, 1963; *Birmingham World,* October 13, November 3, 1953, June 25, 1954. On Judge Grooms's strong belief in states' rights, see *Perry* v. *Folsom,* 144 F.Supp. 874. In May 1961, President Kennedy appointed a third federal judge in Birmingham, Clarence W. Allgood. Allgood, for many years a close political associate of Senator Lister Hill, was one of the district's referees in bankruptcy from 1938 until his appointment to the bench. He had earned a night-school law degree from the Birmingham School of Law and in the 1950s had actively assisted University of Alabama officials in their efforts to discourage black applicants to the school (*Selma Times-Journal,* May 7, 1961; Clark, *The Schoolhouse Door,* 19–20, 116–18). But by the time of Allgood's appointment, the Christian Movement's principal challenges to segregation were already far advanced, and he therefore did not have the influence on the development of Birmingham's racial crisis that Lynne and Grooms had.

71. *Johnson* v. *Yielding,* 267 Ala. 108, 165 F.Supp. 76; Case File, *Johnson* v. *Yielding,* in FRC East Point; F. L. Shuttlesworth to City Commissioners, June 2, 1958, Boutwell Papers; *Birmingham World,* August 15, 1952, August 7, 22, 25, September 7, October 20, 1956, February 27, April 24, 1957, January 29, April 26, May 24, June 7, 21, July 5, 26, August 2, 6, 9, 1958, February 10, 17, 1962, April 2, 1966; *Birmingham News,* January 31, 1965. The agreement of the personnel board in July 1958 to drop its whites-only rule appears to have resulted in part from the fact that in May, Howard Yielding had resigned as the personnel board's chairman, and he had been succeeded by the racially moderate Henry P. Johnston, the broadcasting executive who had headed the Interracial Committee. The other two personnel board members were Charles A. Long and Dan R. Hudson.

72. *Baldwin* v. *Morgan,* 149 F.Supp. 224 (first quotation), 251 F.2d 780, 287 F.2d 750; Trial Transcript and Case File, *Baldwin* v. *Morgan,* in FRC East Point; *Birmingham World,* November 29, 1955, December 26, 29, 1956, February 2, 27, March 9 (second quotation), July 3, October 23, 1957, March 1, 29, 1958, October 28, 31, November 4, 28, 1959, January 2, December 10, 1960, February 22, April 29, 1961, August 11, 1962; *Selma Times-Journal,* October 17, 1957, October 28, 1959, February 19, 1961.

73. *U.S.* v. *City of Birmingham,* complaint and temporary injunction, and J. M. Breckenridge to Jamie Moore, June 18, 1962, all in James T. "Jabo" Waggoner Papers, Birmingham Public Library; *Birmingham World,* November 29, 1955, December 10, 1960, May 17, December 20, 1961; *Boynton* v. *Virginia,* 364 U.S. 454; *Discrimination in Operations of Interstate Motor Carriers of Passengers,* 86 MCC 743; Nunnelley, *Bull Connor,* 118–20; Catherine A. Barnes, *Journey from Jim Crow: The Desegregation of Southern Transit* (New York: Columbia University Press, 1983), 132–37, 142–84; *Selma Times-Journal,* December 5, 1960, December 14, 20, 1961.

74. *Shuttlesworth* v. *Dobbs Houses, Inc.,* original complaint, first amended complaint, second amended complaint and injunction, and Burke Marshall to Arthur J. Hanes, April 30, 1962, Marshall to Hanes, May 29, 1962, and J. M. Breckenridge to Burke Marshall, June 11, 1962, all in Waggoner Papers; *Smith* v. *City of Birmingham,* 226 F.Supp. 838; Case File, *Smith* v. *City of Birmingham,* in FRC East Point; *Birming-*

ham World, September 24, 1960, August 23, 1961, February 7, 14, April 14, June 6, 9, July 18, 25, 1962, December 28, 1963; Barnes, *Journey from Jim Crow,* 137–42, 182–83; *Selma Times-Journal,* June 20, July 11, 17, 1962, December 6, 1963. The *Smith* suit had originally sought the integration of the Birmingham Public Library and of facilities in the city hall as well as of the airport motel, but the former institutions had desegregated voluntarily before the case finally came to trial.

75. *City of Birmingham* v. *Baylor,* unpublished opinion of Recorder's Court Judge Ralph E. Parker (first quotation), Morgan Papers; *Cherry* v. *Morgan,* 267 F.2d 305; *Boman* v. *Birmingham Transit Co.,* 280 F.2d 531; *Woods* v. *State,* 40 Ala. App. 532; *Kelly* v. *State,* 273 Ala. 240; *White* v. *City of Birmingham,* 41 Ala. App. 181, 272 Ala. 301; *Shuttlesworth* v. *City of Birmingham,* 41 Ala. App. 697, 272 Ala. 708, 368 U.S. 959; *In re Shuttlesworth,* 369 U.S. 35; *Ex parte Shuttlesworth,* 41 Ala. App. 543, 273 Ala. 228; *Shuttlesworth* v. *State,* 42 Ala. App. 34; *Birmingham World,* July 14, August 8, December 29, 1956, January 2, 16, February 27, March 20, 23, April 6, 17, July 31, October 26, November 2, 1957, February 26, March 1, October 18, 22, 25, 29, November 1, 5, 8, 15, 29, December 6, 20, 1958, January 21, 24, April 29, June 3, August 5, 22, October 28, November 28, December 12, 1959, January 2, May 7, December 17, 1960, November 15, 1961, January 13, 31, February 7, 10, 14, 24, March 3, 7, 28, July 4, 7, 18, 28, 1962; *Selma Times-Journal,* December 28, 1956, March 18, 21, 29, 1957, October 14, 17, 22, 26, 28, 30, November 13, December 2, 9, 1958, January 16, 22, February 10, April 24, June 1, 1959, January 28, December 14, 1960, January 8, February 28, March 2, June 15, 29, July 13, 1962, December 13, 1963; on Judge Parker, see ibid., February 10, 1958. See also James W. Morgan to Edmund Orgill, June 19, 1956, Earle Newman to Birmingham City Commission, June 23, 1956, James W. Morgan to Earle Newman, draft, June 26, 1956, F. M. Jessup to James W. Morgan, June 26, 1956, Ordinance 1487-F adopted October 14, 1958 (second quotation), Statement of the City Commission on the Adoption of Ordinance 1487-F, Statement of Mayor James W. Morgan on the Bus Protests, October 22, 1958, James W. Morgan to Howard D. Willits, November 17, 1958, Resolutions Concerning Public Transportation Adopted at a Mass Meeting of the Alabama Christian Movement for Human Rights, December 14, 1959, John Foster to Birmingham Transit Company, January 16, 1960, all in Morgan Papers; and Defendants' Brief and Argument, *Boman* v. *Birmingham Transit Co.,* U.S. District Court, Northern District of Alabama, October 1959, and Decree and Permanent Injunction of H. H. Grooms, District Judge, *Boman* v. *Birmingham Transit Co.,* June 28, 1962, both in Waggoner Papers. More than a year after Judge Grooms's final order in the bus segregation case, a white resident wrote in consternation to Mayor Albert Boutwell, "It was my understanding that you were elected to keep this city segregated. Yet I am constantly hereing [*sic*] reports that our city transit buses are in fact intergrated [*sic*]. That Negroes are setting throughout these buses is shocking. Many white people are standing rather than sit by these impudent Negroes. This must stop. It should not be allowed. People should not have to call the police and complain about such incidents. White people are stricken with fear. They are being upset by these bold Negroes. This sort of tactic by Negroes works against the health of white people that have to ride the buses. Namely old people, women and children who may not have the use of an automobile as would be the case of well to do people who have even gone so far as to advocate intergration. What is the policy of the Police Department and the city government as regards segregation for transit buses operating in Birmingham? Is it to allow Negroes to have the run of the buses? Is there a way for bus patrons to have the bus driver stop the bus and

call the police if Negroes fail to move to the rear of the bus? Its [*sic*] my under-standing that bus drivers no longer will direct Negroes to the rear of the bus."

This revelation of the interplay among racial prejudice, class resentments, and lack of information that lay at the heart of Birmingham's segregationist commit-ments concluded, "I don't intend to be intergrated with the Negro and will not personally until Kennedy and his dam family and all Dam Yankees and turncoats themselves intergrate fully with the savages. After all you politicians, professional people, and others of wealth and high influence do not have to intergrate socially or otherwise because of your station regardless of any act by the United States gov-ernment to force intergration of the races by whatever degree. If you and the pre-sent administration are not going to keep this city 100% segregated then in the name of White Supremacy quit your office so that the citizens may select those who will" (S. F. Moody, Jr., to Albert Boutwell, July 3, 1963, Boutwell Papers; see also F. L. Shuttlesworth to Albert Boutwell, wire, October 14, 1963, ibid.).

76. *Acts of Alabama*, Regular Session of 1955, pp. 492–96. Regular Session of 1957, pp. 483–88; *Montgomery Advertiser*, March 20, 21, June 2, 1954; *Selma Times-Journal*, June 24, August 3, September 22, 1955, August 25, 1957; on Engelhardt, see *Montgomery Advertiser*, July 25, 1956; on the initial efforts of the Boutwell and Johnston committees, see Edward R. Crowther, "Alabama's Fight to Maintain Seg-regated Schools, 1953–1956," *Alabama Review* 43 (July 1990): 206–25. In later years the authorship of the Pupil Placement Act was often attributed to Boutwell—and he himself publicly claimed credit for it—because he had chaired the committee that subsequently amended it. In fact, however, his role in its creation was very small. He did, though, play a leading part in obtaining the adoption of the 1956 constitutional amendment that relieved the state of the duty to furnish public schools, in preparation for the possibility of closing them. (For Boutwell's claim to have originated the Pupil Placement Act, see "Statement by Mayor of Birmingham Albert Boutwell, former State Senator and Lieutenant Governor of Alabama, on the Decision of Judge Seybourn Lynne of the United States District Court in the Bir-mingham School Case, May 28, 1963," Boutwell Papers.) It seems probable that Bobby Wood, unlike Senator Engelhardt, had intended his proposal as a sincere effort to facilitate the gradual integration of the state's schools.

77. *Shuttlesworth* v. *Birmingham Board of Education*, 162 F.Supp. 372, 358 U.S. 101; Hearing Transcript, *Shuttlesworth* v. *Birmingham Board of Education*, in FRC East Point; *Birmingham World*, August 9, 16, 1955, August 24, 28 (second quota-tion), 31, September 4, 7, 11, 14, 21, 25, December 28, 1957, March 8, April 9, September 17, November 26, 1958, January 30, 1960; *Selma Times-Journal*, August 21, 1955, August 22, 23, 25, September 3, 6, 8, 9, 10, 11, October 31, November 1, 8, 21, December 18, 1957, January 7, 21, March 5, April 3, 4 (first quotation), June 3 (third quotation), August 24, November 24, 1958, August 7, 1963, January 21, 22, 1964, January 21, 1965.

78. *Armstrong* v. *Board of Education*, 220 F.Supp. 217 (second quotations), 323 F.2d 333; *Nelson* v. *Grooms*, 307 F.2d 76; Trial Transcript, *Armstrong* v. *Birmingham Board of Education*, in FRC East Point; *Birmingham World*, September 3, 1958, June 25, July 13, 1960, June 16, 30, July 11, August 1, 22, 25, 1962, June 1, July 17, August 24, September 7, 11, 14, 18, 28, 1963; *Selma Times-Journal*, February 12, 13, 24 (first quotations), March 2, May 12, 1959, June 19, July 10, 1960, June 13, 22, July 11, August 19, October 3, 4, 5, 1962, May 28, June 18, 26, 27, July 2, August 19, 21, 22, 30, September 1, 4, 5, 11, 12, 16, 1963.

79. *Shuttlesworth* v. *Connor*, 291 F.2d 217; *Birmingham World*, March 29, 1958,

February 24, 1960, February 28, March 14, 24, 28, April 11, May 16, 23, June 9, July 18, December 15, 1962, January 26, March 27, August 3, September 11, December 28, 1963; *Selma Times-Journal,* May 24, December 6, 1960, March 21, 22, 25, April 4, May 17, 18, July 11, 1962, July 31, 1963; Jones, "Fred L. Shuttlesworth," 116.

80. *Birmingham World,* September 7, 1951, September 8, 1953, November 22, 1955, August 14, 17, November 6, 1957, January 18, July 2, August 30, 1958, January 3, April 25, June 10 (first quotations), 13, 17 (second set of quotations), 20 (third quotation), 24, September 12, 26, October 28, 31, December 23, 1959, February 24, June 25, July 13, 1960, February 16, April 24, 1963; F. L. Shuttlesworth et al. to James W. Morgan, petition, October 8, 1958, Morgan Papers; Shuttlesworth, interview, May 18, 1989. Some details of the Birmingham stalemate, especially as to the precise roles of Arthur Shores and Seybourn Lynne, are not part of the public record, and my account of them represents a deduction from those aspects that are. That Judge Lynne was not above such machinations is established, however, by his conduct in the Roosevelt Tatum case in 1963 (see John Doar to Nicholas Katzenbach, January 24, 1964, Marshall Papers). J. L. Chestnut no longer recalls his part in the stalemate (J. L. Chestnut, Jr., interview by author, July 29, 1991). It is worth noting, as well, that in her speech to the Christian Movement on June 5, 1959, Ella Baker called for a reexamination of Martin Luther King's doctrine of nonviolence and a recognition of the right of blacks to use force in self-defense. It is clear that, even though she was serving as the Southern Christian Leadership Conference's executive director at this time, the elements of her later sharp disagreements with King were already present, foreshadowing her subsequent role in the creation of the Student Non-violent Coordinating Committee.

81. *Birmingham World,* November 10, 1956 (third quotation), June 20, 24, 1959, April 13, June 8 (first quotations), December 31 (second quotation), 1960, April 10, 13, 17, June 5, 1963.

82. Clarke, *These Rights They Seek,* 25, 27, 37, 56, 58, 71; G. Moore, *Behind the Ebony Mask,* 33–34. Clarke, a graduate student in sociology, conducted this useful survey of the members of the Christian Movement, together with members of the Montgomery Improvement Association and of the Tuskegee Civic Association, as a part of her research for a doctoral dissertation in 1959.

83. *Birmingham World,* March 19, 26, April 2, 6, 9, 1960; Eskew, *But for Birmingham,* 148–50. Eskew reports that Shuttlesworth had personally witnessed one of the early sit-ins (in High Point, North Carolina) at the beginning of February and had become very enthusiastic about the tactic, but it is not clear whether he broached the idea with the Birmingham students or if they independently came to him. At the same time Shuttlesworth was convicted in the sit-in case, he was also convicted of giving police false information and was sentenced to an additional six months in jail and a fine of one hundred dollars on that charge. It had originated when a black man named James Mallory was sexually injured by his wife, Mildred, with a potato knife during an argument over money. Mallory subsequently told a pawnbroker, and then investigators from the Christian Movement who were called by the pawnbroker, that he had been injured by a group of white men. Shuttlesworth thereupon sent police a telegram requesting an investigation. He got no reply, but two months later police suddenly charged him with giving them false information. Even though Mallory testified that he had in fact told the Christian Movement investigators what Shuttlesworth had said he had, Shuttlesworth was convicted anyway.

84. *Gober* v. *City of Birmingham,* 41 Ala. App. 313, 272 Ala. 704, 373 U.S. 374; *Shuttlesworth* v. *City of Birmingham,* 41 Ala. App. 319, 273 Ala. 713, 373 U.S. 262; *Billups* v. *City of Birmingham,* 41 Ala. App. 318, 273 Ala. 704; *Birmingham World,* April 2, 9, 1960, June 3, 1961, February 7, 1962, May 22, 1963; *Selma Times-Journal,* March 31, April 1, 5, June 7, 1960, May 31, 1961, May 20, 21, June 19, 1963. The sentences of Billups and the ten students had already been reduced from six months to one month as a result of their circuit court trials, but Shuttlesworth's six-month sentence had been reimposed.

85. *Birmingham World,* June 7, 1949, April 13, May 18, June 8, August 3, 20, 27, September 3, 1960, September 16, 30, 1961; J. L. Ware and C. H. Oliver to James W. Morgan, May 7, 1960, Student Non-Violent Coordinating Committee to James W. Morgan, August 10, 1960, both in Morgan Papers; LeRoy B. Oliver to James W. Morgan, April 13, 1960, Macon L. Weaver to Arthur J. Hanes, January 24, 1962, both in Connor Papers; Eskew, *But for Birmingham,* 144, 146, 363; Nunnelley, *Bull Connor,* 32–34, 82–85. On Clyde Carter, see Trial Transcript, *Lewis* v. *Greyhound Corp.,* 101–9, in FRC East Point.

86. *Birmingham World,* June 8, 1960.

87. Minutes of the Southern Regional Council, Alabama Division, Executive Committee, September 17, 1954; Minutes of the Alabama Council on Human Relations Executive Committee, July 10, 1956; Robert E. Hughes to ACHR Board of Directors, memorandum, July 19, 1956; Robert E. Hughes to Frederick B. Routh, September 8, 1956; Robert E. Hughes to district officers, memorandum, January 23, 1957; *curriculum vitae* of Robert E. Hughes; all in Southern Regional Council Papers; Corley, "Quest for Racial Harmony," 182–86. Tuscaloosa Klan leader Roy Hartley was convicted of intercepting Hughes's mail during this period and was placed on probation for five years (Robert E. Hughes to Harold Fleming, August 18, 1959, Southern Regional Council Papers).

88. *Time,* December 15, 1958 (first quotation); *New York Times,* April 12 (second quotation), 13 (third quotation), 27, May 4, 1960; Robert E. Hughes to Frederick B. Routh, September 25, 1958, Robert E. Hughes to Harrison E. Salisbury, April 25, 1960, Harrison E. Salisbury to Robert E. Hughes, April 28, 1960, Robert E. Hughes to Paul M. Rilling, August 19, 1960, all in Southern Regional Council Papers; *NAACP* v. *Alabama,* 357 U.S. 449; *Selma Times-Journal,* July 12, 13, August 16, 1956, July 27, 1959, April 27, May 4, September 2, 4, 6, 7, 9, 1960, January 5, 20, 1961, July 16, 17, 1964; Corley, "Quest for Racial Harmony," 186–90, 197–210. On the hope that Hughes had for access to the mass media at this period, see also his funding proposal for an Emergency Project in Education for Democracy, n.d. [internally dated to late 1959], in David J. Vann Papers, Birmingham Public Library. The story of the commissioners' libel suits against the *New York Times* is a complicated one. The effort to sue the *Times* in Alabama—rather than in New York, where its principal business offices were—presented substantial legal difficulties. Judge Grooms initially held that since Salisbury had prepared the articles in Birmingham, he and the newspaper could be sued there. But the *Times* appealed this ruling to the Fifth Circuit, and in June 1961, in an opinion by Chief Judge Elbert Tuttle, that court held unanimously that an early decision of the Alabama Supreme Court had required libel suits to be filed where the newspaper was published. The Court of Appeals therefore ordered Judge Grooms to quash service of process in all seven pending libel cases, and in March 1962, after the plaintiffs had sought repeatedly to amend their complaints to an acceptable form, Grooms dismissed all of the actions.

At this point the Bessemer city commissioners dropped their suits, but the Birmingham city commissioners appealed the dismissals to the Fifth Circuit. While this appeal was still pending before the Fifth Circuit, the Alabama Supreme Court in August 1962 decided Montgomery commissioner L. B. Sullivan's libel suit against the *Times,* which had been filed in state court at almost the same time that the Birmingham commissioners had sued in federal court. The opinion in that case held that the earlier Alabama Supreme Court decision had not in fact meant to require suit only where the newspaper was published, as Judge Tuttle had believed; the state supreme court now upheld the validity of suing the *Times* in Alabama. Because the Fifth Circuit's initial ruling in the Birmingham case had rested on this point of Alabama law, the court was now bound by the Alabama Supreme Court's clarification of its holdings. And so, in November 1962, the Fifth Circuit vacated its earlier decision and ordered the city commissioners' suits reinstated. In the meantime, however, the *Times* had appealed the Alabama Supreme Court's *Sullivan* decision to the U.S. Supreme Court, and Judge Grooms decided to hold the Birmingham suits to await the U.S. Supreme Court's ruling. In March 1964, the U.S. Supreme Court reversed the Alabama Supreme Court's *Sullivan* decision on First Amendment grounds but made no comment on the question of where the suit ought to have been filed. In April, therefore, Judge Grooms ordered the Birmingham suits reactivated in accordance with the Fifth Circuit's November 1962 ruling. In September 1964 the suits finally came to trial. Judge Grooms dismissed the suits of Mayor Morgan and Commissioner Waggoner, neither of whom was mentioned in the Salisbury articles, on the basis of the U.S. Supreme Court's new *Sullivan* standard, requiring the plaintiffs to demonstrate actual malice on Salisbury's part or his reckless disregard of the truth. But Grooms held that the evidence indicated that Salisbury did indeed feel actual malice toward Connor, and he therefore allowed Connor's suit to go to the jury. At the trial, former *Birmingham News* city editor Fred Taylor testified under oath that he did not believe that either fear or racial conflict had existed in Birmingham in 1960. After four days of deliberation, the jury awarded Connor $40,000 in damages. The *Times* once again appealed to the Fifth Circuit, and in August 1966, by a vote of two to one, the Court of Appeals ordered the *Connor* suit dismissed on the grounds both that the *Times's* contacts with Alabama were insufficient to claim that it did business there and that the malice toward Connor had not been adequately proven. Seybourn Lynne, sitting with the Fifth Circuit panel by designation, dissented. Connor chose not to attempt to appeal to the U.S. Supreme Court, and the long struggle thus came to an end. The grand jury's indictment of Salisbury for criminal libel was never tried because New York refused extradition in the case (*Connor* v. *New York Times,* 291 F.2d 492, 310 F.2d 133, 365 F.2d 567; *New York Times* v. *Sullivan,* 273 Ala. 656, 376 U.S. 254).

89. *New York Times,* April 27, May 4 (quotations), 1960; *Washington Post,* October 23, 1960; *Selma Times-Journal,* July 19, August 2, 1962.

90. *Birmingham News,* December 20, 1960; Resolution of the Board of Directors of the Birmingham Chamber of Commerce, May 18, 1961, Morgan Papers. On Mortimer Jordan, see the clipping files of the Alabama Department of Archives and History, Montgomery; on Sidney Smyer, see Eskew, *But for Birmingham,* 109–12. The records of the Birmingham Chamber of Commerce from this period are not open to researchers, and therefore the earliest origins of the change-of-government movement remain somewhat obscure. In particular, the precise date of the establishment

of the study committee and the full content of its deliberations are unknown. The account in the text represents what are, I trust, reasonable deductions from the facts that are in the public domain.

91. *Birmingham World,* March 3, March 6, 1953; David J. Vann, "The Change from Commission to Mayor-Council Government and the Racial Desegregation Agreements in Birmingham, Alabama, 1961–1963," rev. ed. (Birmingham: Center for Urban Affairs, University of Alabama at Birmingham, 1988), 4–6; *Reid* v. *City of Birmingham,* 274 Ala. 629.

92. On the long and ultimately unsuccessful annexation struggle, see Eskew, *But for Birmingham,* 182–83; Underwood, "A Progressive History of the Young Mens Business Club of Birmingham, Alabama," 32, 33, 36–37, 45–46, 96–98, 145–47.

93. "Report of a Committee of the Birmingham Bar Association on the Subject of the Form of Municipal Government Best Suited for a Greater and Better Birmingham," February 23, 1962, p. 3 (copy in Vann Papers). Smyer had first publicly suggested that the bar appoint a committee to study the proposal to change the form of city government at a joint meeting of the Rotary and Kiwanis Clubs, apparently held shortly after the first of the year (*Birmingham News,* April 11, 1961).

94. "Report of a Committee of the Birmingham Bar Association on the Subject of the Form of Municipal Government Best Suited for a Greater and Better Birmingham," February 23, 1962, p. 28; Leigh M. Clark to Herbert Peterson, February 26, 1962, Vann Papers. Committee members other than those mentioned in the text were Samuel H. Burr, the son of a former president of the state bar association, who had also been a leading figure in the Democratic Party and an outspoken opponent of federal civil rights legislation; Mayer U. Newfield, son of a longtime Birmingham rabbi and a former Securities and Exchange Commission attorney; Douglass P. Wingo, a former president of the Birmingham Bar Association; and Malcolm L. Wheeler, the son of a recently deceased Birmingham circuit judge. On the Birmingham bar, see Pat Boyd Rumore, *Lawyers in a New South City: A History of the Legal Profession in Birmingham* (Birmingham: Association Publishing Co., 2000).

95. *Morgan* v. *Virginia,* 184 Va. 24, 328 U.S. 373; *State* v. *Johnson,* 229 N.C. 701; August Meier and Elliott Rudwick, *CORE: A Study in the Civil Rights Movement* (Urbana: University of Illinois Press, 1975), 3–21, 33–39; Barnes, *Journey from Jim Crow,* 44–48, 58–60.

96. *Boynton* v. *Virginia,* 364 U.S. 454; Barnes, *Journey from Jim Crow,* 87, 144–51.

97. Memoranda on information obtained from G. Thomas Rowe, Jr., September 19, October 7, November 5, 16, December 15, 16, 1960, January 3, 26 (first quotation), April 24, 1961; SAC Birmingham to FBI Director, April 19, 1961 (third quotation), Director FBI to SAC Atlanta, April 24, 1961, SAC Birmingham to FBI Director, April 24, 1961, SAC Birmingham to FBI Director, May 5, 1961, SAC Birmingham to FBI Director and SAC Mobile, May 14, 1961; all in FBI Case Files, Freedom Rider Investigation, Birmingham Public Library; Barnes, *Journey from Jim Crow,* 157–61; Meier and Rudwick, *CORE,* 135–38; Nunnelley, *Bull Connor,* 91 (second quotation). The precise date that Cook contacted Page to tell him about the Freedom Ride is unclear, but it was definitely between April 27 and May 3.

98. *Birmingham World,* April 29, May 6, 1961; *Birmingham News,* May 3, 1961; Officers J. C. Wilson and J. W. Watkins to Chief Jamie Moore, May 4, 1961, Connor Papers; Nunnelley, *Bull Connor,* 91–93.

99. Arthur Hanes campaign circular, Vann Papers; *Birmingham Post-Herald,* September 24, 1954, December 14, 1960, April 4, 1983; Nunnelley, *Bull Connor,* 91–94 (quotation, 93). Diane McWhorter reports (*Carry Me Home,* 215) that the picture

was taken by *Birmingham News* photographer Thomas Lankford at the request of a city official, Clint Bishop.

100. Memoranda on information obtained from G. Thomas Rowe, Jr., May 4 (first quotations), 10, 12, 1961; SAC Birmingham to FBI Director, May 5, 9, 10, 12 (second quotation), 13, 1961, FBI Director to SAC Birmingham, May 10, 1961, C. J. McGowan to Alex Rosen, May 12, 1961, SAC Birmingham to FBI Director and SAC Mobile, May 14, 1961, SA Barrett G. Kemp to SAC Thomas Jenkins, May 15, 1961; all in FBI Case Files, Freedom Rider Investigation; Nunnelley, *Bull Connor*, 62–66.

101. SAC Birmingham to FBI Director, May 9, 13, 15, 16, 17, 18, 23, 29, July 7, August 3, 31, September 2, November 3, October [misdated; actually November] 6, November 9, 1961, January 5, January 8, 11, 15, 16, 1962; SAC Birmingham to FBI Director and SAC Mobile, May 14, 15, 1961; C. L. McGowan to Alex Rosen, May 14, November 2, 1961, SAC Miami to FBI Director, June 22, 1961; SA Clay Slate to SAC Thomas Jenkins, October 18, 1961; Statement of Millard A. Nunnelley, August 24, 1961; Justice Department press release on the Anniston arrests, May 22, 1961; all in FBI Case Files, Freedom Rider Investigation; Officers R. R. Long and J. B. Jones to Chief Jamie Moore, May 11, 1961, Connor Papers; Meier and Rudwick, *CORE*, 135–38; Barnes, *Journey from Jim Crow*, 157–61.

102. SAC Birmingham to FBI Director, May 15, 16, 17, 18, 20, 21, 24, 25, June 1, July 14, 25, November 29, 1961, SAC Birmingham to FBI Director and SAC Mobile, May 14, 15, 1961, SAC New Orleans to FBI Director and SAC Birmingham, May 18, 1961 (quotation), SAC Detroit to FBI Director, September 18, 1961, C. L. McGowan to Alex Rosen, May 14, 1961, J. Edgar Hoover to Robert F. Kennedy, May 16, 1961, Alex Rosen to Mr. Parsons, May 18, 1961, SA Barrett G. Kemp to SAC Thomas Jenkins, May 15, 17, 24, 1961, SA Barrett G. Kemp to file, May 17, 1961, SA Barrett G. Kemp and SA Byron McFall to SAC Thomas Jenkins, June 1, 1961, Statements of James D. Peck, Herman K. Harris, Isaac Reynolds, Charles A. Person and Dr. Walter Bergman to SA Vernon G. Smith and SA Eugene B. Culberson, New Orleans, May 18, 1961, all in FBI Case Files, Freedom Rider Investigation; Officer Marcus A. Jones to Chief Jamie Moore, May 16, May 24, 1961, Connor Papers; *Shuttlesworth* v. *State*, 42 Ala. App. 19, 275 Ala. 698 (cert. denied); *Shuttlesworth* v. *City of Birmingham*, 42 Ala. App. 1, 274 Ala. 613, 376 U.S. 339, 42 Ala. App. 675; Corley, "Quest for Racial Harmony," 214–17; Eskew, *But for Birmingham*, 153–62. In the Anniston trial, the government proved unable to connect Exalted Cyclops Kenneth Adams to the riot, and Judge Grooms therefore dismissed all charges against him. Adams, who had been a leader of the assault on Nat "King" Cole in 1956, would be convicted in state court in 1963 for a series of assaults on blacks in Anniston that followed the black riot of May 11–12 of that year in Birmingham (*Selma Times-Journal*, June 7, 1963). Nunnelley (*Bull Connor*, 94–110) creates a portrait of the Freedom Rider riot that tends to exculpate Connor from direct complicity, but the evidence seems to me quite clearly to indicate the contrary.

In 1983, Dr. Bergman and James Peck separately sued the FBI for damages on the claim that the bureau, with its prior knowledge of the likely violence, could—and should—have prevented their injuries. Both men won substantial judgments. But the claims of the plaintiffs in these suits were, to my mind, erroneous. The FBI agents did everything they could have done to protect the Freedom Riders, within the limits imposed by the necessity to protect Rowe's identity. Anything more, while it might have prevented the injury to Bergman and Peck, might very well also have cost Rowe his life. Moreover, Bergman, who was the most seriously injured of the demonstrators, was not hurt in the riot at all, but rather in the attack on him by his frightened fellow bus passengers in Anniston. This assault was one of which the bureau had absolutely no prior warning and which agents were in no position to have prevented. The assault was an outgrowth of the earlier attack on the Greyhound bus, to be sure, but even that attack was one of which agents did not know in advance. What agents had been told—and what, in fact, Klan officers had planned—was merely that Klansmen in Anniston would make sure that the demonstrators were aboard the bus and would then send them on to Birmingham to be beaten. And as to the injury to Peck, though the bureau did indeed know that the assault on the Freedom Riders in Birmingham was quite probable, Shuttlesworth had told Peck personally of the likelihood of such an attack as the demonstrators were preparing to leave Atlanta, and Peck had nevertheless rejected Shuttlesworth's recommendation that the demonstrators alter their plans. In addition, until the night before the riot, Birmingham agents continued to hope that Chief Moore would seek to protect the Freedom Riders. Finally, it is beyond doubt that both Peck and Bergman, in deciding to participate in the Freedom Ride, understood that they were placing themselves in danger. That they should then blame the FBI for events whose true roots are in the Klan's malevolence and Commissioner Connor's callous demagogy seems to me distinctly unfair (*New York Times,* January 23, March 8, June 1, December 10, 1983, February 8, 1984; *Peck* v. *U.S.,* 470 F.Supp. 1003, 514 F.Supp. 210, 522 F.Supp. 245; *Bergman* v. *U.S.,* 551 F.Supp. 407, 565 F.Supp. 1353, 579 F.Supp. 911).

103. *Birmingham World,* December 29, 1956, January 2, 5, April 17, May 1, July 31, October 26, November 2, 6, December 11, 1957, April 16, May 17, 31, July 2, 9, 12, 23, December 10, 1958; David L. Boozer to Jamie Moore, March 27, 1963, bombing case number C-25388 and attachments, and *Birmingham Post-Herald,* March 28, 1963, clipping, all in Connor Papers. In 1977, Robert E. Chambliss was convicted of the September 1963 bombing of the Sixteenth Street Baptist Church, in which, as we shall see, four children died. In 1980, attorney and National States' Rights Party leader Jesse B. Stoner was convicted of the June 1958 bombing of Fred Shuttlesworth's church. This bombing, the second of the three bombings of the church, did little damage, thanks to the heroism of church watchman Will Hall, who picked up the smoldering explosive and moved it into the street just before it detonated. In April 2001, Thomas E. Blanton, Jr., was convicted of the September 1963 bombing of which Chambliss earlier had also been convicted. And in May 2002, Bobby Frank Cherry was convicted of the same crime. Wilcutt, Chambliss, Stoner, Blanton, and Cherry are, to date, the only five people who have been convicted for any of the numerous racial bombings in Birmingham from 1947 to 1965.

104. *Birmingham World,* January 20, 24, April 4, December 19, 1962, January 16, March 27, May 15, 18, August 24, September 7, 11, 18, 28, December 14, 1963; Birmingham Police Department, summary of investigation of bombings of three Negro churches on January 16, 1962, dated January 19, 1962, Summary of Facts Regarding the Bombing in Front of Bethel Baptist Church, dated December 17, 1962, and Re.: Bombing in front of Bethel Baptist Church, December 14, 1962, dated December 19, 1962, all in Connor Papers; SA Barrett G. Kemp to SAC Thomas Jenkins, May 24, 1961, and SAC Birmingham to FBI Director, June 9, 1961, both in FBI Case Files, Freedom Rider Investigation.

105. Resolution Approved by the Board of Directors of the Birmingham Chamber of Commerce, May 18, 1961 (first quotation), and Resolution of the Junior

Chamber of Commerce of Birmingham, Alabama, n.d. [May 1961] (second quotation), both in Morgan Papers; Sidney W. Smyer to Dr. L. Wilkie Collins, November 30, 1961, Connor Papers; Corley, "Quest for Racial Harmony," 217–21; Eskew, *But for Birmingham,* 170–74. For other local reaction to the Freedom Rider riot, see John E. Murray to Eugene "Bull" Connor, May 16, 1961, James K. Beard to Connor, May 16, 1961, and Emory O. Jackson to James W. Morgan, May 18, 1961, all in Morgan Papers.

106. "Report of a Committee of the Birmingham Bar Association on the Subject of the Form of Municipal Government Best Suited for a Greater and Better Birmingham," February 23, 1962; David Brook to Municipal Government Committee of the Birmingham Bar Association, memorandum, July 14, 1961; Erle Pettus, Jr., to Douglas Arant et al., August 24, 1961 (quotations); Leigh M. Clark to Herbert Peterson, February 26, 1962; Abraham Berkowitz to Douglas Arant et al., March 1, 1962; Don M. Jones to Abraham Berkowitz, memorandum, February 15, 1962; all in Vann Papers. The account of these events in Vann, "The Change from Commission to Mayor-Council," 11–14, is erroneous.

107. *Shuttlesworth* v. *Gaylord,* 202 F.Supp. 59; *Hanes* v. *Shuttlesworth,* 310 F.2d 303; Case File and Trial Transcript, *Shuttlesworth* v. *Gaylord,* in FRC East Point; *Birmingham World,* October 28, 1959, June 25, July 13, 1960, August 23, 26, October 28, 1961, January 17, 1962; Arthur Hanes to Mrs. J. H. Berry, January 2, February 5, 1962, and Minutes of the Park and Recreation Board, December 8, 15, 28, 1961, January 12, 1962, all in Hanes Papers; *Shuttlesworth* v. *City of Birmingham,* complaint, dated March 2, 1959, filed October 19, 1959, *Shuttlesworth* v. *Gaylord,* order, August 21, 1961, and declaratory judgment and permanent injunction, November 8, 1961, and J. M. Breckenridge to Arthur J. Hanes, November 27, 1962, all in Waggoner Papers; statement of Commissioner Eugene "Bull" Connor, October 25, 1961, Connor Papers; Corley, "Quest for Racial Harmony," 223–25; Eskew, *But for Birmingham,* 178–80.

108. Birmingham Downtown Improvement Association to Mayor Arthur J. Hanes et al., December 12, 1961 (third quotation), Statement by the Board of Directors, Birmingham Chamber of Commerce, December 15, 1961 (first and second quotations), Resolution of the North Birmingham Chamber of Commerce, adopted December 12, 1961, Resolution of the Birmingham District Methodist Ministerial Association, December 11, 1961, Dr. L. Wilkie Collins to Sidney W. Smyer, November 29, 1961 (sixth quotation), and Sidney W. Smyer to Dr. L. Wilkie Collins, November 30, 1961, Thomas W. Martin to Eugene "Bull" Connor, December 27, 1961, Dr. Arthur K. Black to Mayor Arthur J. Hanes, December 29, 1961 (fourth quotation), Officers J. W. Holland and J. E. Lambert to Chief Jamie Moore, January 18, 1962 (seventh quotation), all in Connor Papers; Dr. L. Wilkie Collins to Mayor Arthur J. Hanes, December 7, 1961, Henry C. Barton et al. to Arthur Hanes et al., December 27, 1961, both in Hanes Papers; Vera G. Bruhn to Birmingham City Commission, December 4, 1961 (fifth quotation), Waggoner Papers; *Birmingham News,* January 10, 1962; *Wall Street Journal,* March 12, 1962, quoted in Corley, "Quest for Racial Harmony," 223 (eighth quotation); Eskew, *But for Birmingham,* 180. See also C. C. J. Carpenter to Eugene "Bull" Connor, December 26, 1961, Connor Papers; and T. R. Banks to Arthur J. Hanes, June 18, 1962, and Minutes of the Open House Discussion of the Parks Situation, December 11, 1961, City Hall Council Chamber, both in Hanes Papers.

109. R. J. Bell to Arthur J. Hanes, December 16, 1961 (third quotation), W. B. Houseal to Board of Directors, Birmingham Downtown Improvement Association,

December 18, 1961 (first quotation), Joint Statement Issued by the City Commission on January 17, 1962 (sixth quotation), all in Hanes Papers; T. W. Aitken, Jr., to Arthur J. Hanes, December 23, 1961 (fifth quotation), and Resolution of the Jefferson County Citizens Council, adopted December 8, 1961 (second quotation), both in Waggoner Papers; Kirkman O'Neal to Eugene "Bull" Connor, December 11, 1961, Earl C. Morgan to Eugene "Bull" Connor, December 18, 1961, Lieutenant E. E. Loveless to Chief Jamie Moore, December 18, 1961, A. Bakane to Eugene "Bull" Connor, July 24, 1962 (fourth quotation), all in Connor Papers. See also Leonard R. Wilson to Eugene "Bull" Connor, December 11, 1961, William S. Pritchard, Jr., to Arthur J. Hanes, December 15, 1961, Resolution of the Birmingham Baptist Pastors' Conference, December 18, 1961, W. T. Crosby to Arthur J. Hanes, February 22, 1962, all in Connor Papers; C. J. Cochran to Arthur J. Hanes et al., January 4, 1962, Waggoner Papers; Alice Moore to Arthur J. Hanes, February 16, 1962, May Holden to Arthur J. Hanes, May 10, 1962, and Resolution of the Jefferson County Citizens Council, adopted November 10, 1961, all in Hanes Papers. On William B. Houseal, see also *Birmingham World,* October 15, 1946.

110. Eskew, *But for Birmingham,* 180. The other members of the delegation were Committee of 100 chairman James A. Head, Vulcan Materials president Bernard "Barney" Monaghan, and Episcopal priest David C. Wright.

111. *Birmingham World,* September 16, 30, 1961.

112. Ibid., August 23, October 28, November 25, December 16, 20, 23, 30, 1961, January 3, 6 (second and third quotations), 1962; Resolution of the Young Men's Business Club of Birmingham, January 8, 1962, Officer J. W. LeGrand to Eugene "Bull" Connor, November 1, 1961, Officer J. W. Holland to Connor, November 14, 1961, Officers J. W. Holland and J. E. Lambert to Chief Jamie Moore, January 18, 1962, all in Connor Papers; "This We Believe," statement adopted by the student body of Miles College, December 29, 1961, and David Vann, "Outline of Possible Suggestion for Park Desegregation Plan," and "A Plea for Courage and Common Sense," petition of group of white business leaders, adopted January 3, 1962, all in Marshall Papers; Vann, "Change from Commission to Mayor-Council," 11 (first quotation). Edward Gardner refused to sign the December 14 statement, and Lucius Pitts and Herbert Oliver also did not sign it. But Christian Movement treasurer William Shortridge, who was by far the most moderate of Shuttlesworth's associates, did sign.

113. Officer J. W. LeGrand to Eugene "Bull" Connor, November 1, 1961, Connor Papers.

114. Shuttlesworth vigorously imposed his conviction of white negotiators' untrustworthiness on his subordinates, whom he was empowered to remove from their Christian Movement offices at will. At the first negotiating session after the beginning of the 1963 demonstrations, Episcopal bishop C. C. J. Carpenter, the moderate who had been the first chairman of the Interracial Committee, was present, and he much impressed Shuttlesworth's associate John Porter with his apparent sincerity and goodwill. As they emerged from the meeting, Shuttlesworth reports, he denounced Porter for being soap in the hands of whites, for having been taken in by Carpenter, as Shuttlesworth saw it. If Porter failed to adopt a tougher stance, Shuttlesworth told him, this would be the last negotiating session he would be permitted to attend. A liberal white ceases to be liberal the moment a black seeks his rights, Shuttlesworth said in his interview with me. Whites smile as if they mean yes, but their smile really means no. In Birmingham, he maintained, not a

single advance had been a product of interracial cooperation; all of them were the work of blacks alone (interview, May 18, 1989).

115. *Birmingham World,* January 31, 1962 (quotation); Corley, "Quest for Racial Harmony," 230–32.

116. Officer J. B. Jones to Chief Jamie Moore, January 24, 1962 (quotation), Officer R. R. Long to Chief Moore, February 20, 1962, both in Connor Papers.

117. Officer R. R. Long to Chief Jamie Moore, February 20, 1962 (second quotation), Officer Marcus A. Jones to Chief Moore, February 27, 1962 (first quotation), Officer L. H. Kirk to Chief Moore, November 7, 1962, all in Connor Papers; *Birmingham World,* September 1, 1962.

118. Officer J. W. Holland to Chief Jamie Moore, February 22, 1962, Officer Marcus A. Jones to Chief Moore, February 27, 1962, Officers J. E. Lambert and J. C. Wilson to Chief Moore, March 21, 1962, Detective Marcus A. Jones to Chief Moore, March 28, 1962, Officer R. R. Long to Chief Moore, April 9, 1962, Officer L. H. Kirk to Chief Moore, April 11, 1962, Officer J. B. Jones to Chief Moore, April 25, 1962, Officer A. Wallace to Inspector W. J. Haley, May 5, 1962, Officer J. E. LeGrand to Inspector Haley, May 15, 1962, Officers C. L. Edmondson and J. B. Jones to Chief Moore, June 13, 1962 (third quotation), S. L. Matthews to Eugene "Bull" Connor, April 4, 1962, C. J. Cochran to City Commission, April 5, 1962, W. D. Kendrick to Arthur J. Hanes, June 29, 1962, Kendrick to Connor, September 6, 1962, Felix Snow to Connor, September 7, 1962, Connor to Snow, September 10, 1962, Snow to Connor, September 15, 1962, Connor to Snow, September 17, 1962, and Resolution of the Downtown Action Committee, November 13, 1962, all in Connor Papers; Statement of Arthur J. Hanes, April 4, 1962 (first quotation), L. G. Waldrop to Hanes, April 6, 1962, Roy Wilkins to Hanes, wire, April 5, 1962, Jennie Berman et al. to Hanes, wire, April 5, 1962, Bishop Charles E. Golden to Hanes, wire, April 7, 1962, Rufus T. Washington III to Hanes, April 6, 1962, all in Hanes Papers; *Birmingham World,* April 4, 7, 11, 14, September 1, November 21, 1962; Corley, "Quest for Racial Harmony," 232–35 (second quotation, 234).

119. Officer J. E. LeGrand to Inspector W. J. Haley, May 15, 1962, Officers O. V. Vance and J. E. Lambert to Haley, June 27, 1962, both in Connor Papers. The Christian Movement had informed its members of the forthcoming SCLC convention in Birmingham as early as November 6, 1961 (Officers J. E. Lambert and J. B. Jones to Chief Jamie Moore, November 8, 1961, Connor Papers).

120. *Birmingham World,* December 16, 1961, January 27, 1962.

121. Officers C. L. Edmondson and J. B. Jones to Chief Jamie Moore, June 13, 1962, Connor Papers; see also Officer C. R. Jones to Moore, March 12, 1963, and Officers R. S. Whitehouse and R. A. Watkins to Moore, April 18, 1963, ibid.

122. On the conflicts, see *Reid* v. *City of Birmingham,* 274 Ala. 629; *Connor* v. *State on the Information of Boutwell,* 275 Ala. 230; and Don M. Jones to Abraham Berkowitz, memorandum, February 15, 1962, Vann Papers.

123. *Sims* v. *Frink,* 205 F.Supp. 245, 208 F.Supp. 431.

124. Powers McLeod to David Vann, June 4, 1962, Abraham Berkowitz to Sidney Smyer et al., August 15, 1962, and attached memorandum re. petition, August 15, 1962, and suggested basic content of statement to be issued by citizens' committee, n.d., Berkowitz to Vann, August 20, 1962, and attached memorandum re. suggested statement of Birmingham Citizens for Progress, August 20, 1962, Erskine Smith, memorandum re. election of change form and city government [*sic*], August 29, 1962, Berkowitz to Allen Rushton et al., October 19, 1962, S. M. Walker to

Birmingham Citizens for Progress, October 25, 1962, Speech prepared for Erskine Smith and David Vann by Crim-Thomas, Inc., Advertising and Public Relations, October 29, 1962, Berkowitz to Vann et al., November 7, 1962, Vann to Ivan Swift, November 9, 1962, Memorandum to Birmingham Citizens for Progress re. campaign pointers, n.d., Memorandum to Birmingham Citizens for Progress re. questions and answers on mayor-council, n.d., Forms of Government in Major Cities of America, 1962, and seventeen reasons to retain city commission form of government, n.d., all in Vann Papers; *Birmingham World,* October 24, 31, November 10, December 19, 1962; *Birmingham News,* August 26, 27, 29, September 2, 28, October 11 (quotation), 16, 17, 20, November 2, 8, 1962; *Birmingham Post-Herald,* August 17, 20, 29, September 5, 29, October 12, 17, 19, 24, 25, 31, November 1, 2, 8, 1962; Vann, "The Change from Commission to Mayor-Council," 6–7, 13–28; Corley, "Quest for Racial Harmony," 225–30; Eskew, *But for Birmingham,* 180–88; LaMonte, *Politics and Welfare in Birmingham,* 164–71; Nunnelley, *Bull Connor,* 125–28. Emory Jackson, whose information on the point is to be trusted, put the number of black voters in Birmingham in December 1962 at 8,246 and in Jefferson County as a whole at 12,369 (*Birmingham World,* December 19, 1962). In the initial election for the new city council the following March, the two black candidates received 9,339 and 8,772 votes, returns that seem to confirm the accuracy of Jackson's figure (ibid., March 9, 1963).

125. *Birmingham Post-Herald,* October 31, 1962.

126. Officer O. C. Ellard to Inspector W. J. Haley, May 23, 1962 (quotation), Officers O. V. Vance and J. E. Lambert to Haley, June 27, 1962, both in Connor Papers; *Birmingham News,* July 3, 1962.

127. *Birmingham News,* August 28, 1962 (first and third quotations); *Birmingham Post-Herald,* August 29, 1962 (second quotation); *Birmingham World,* September 1, 1962.

128. *Birmingham Post-Herald,* October 19, 1962; *Birmingham News,* May 16, 1963 (quotation); Corley, "Quest for Racial Harmony," 235–36; Nunnelley, *Bull Connor,* 130–31, 136. The other four subcommittees of the Senior Citizens Committee dealt with inadequate school financing, insufficient medical facilities for the poor, the city budget deficit, and expressway construction. Though no subcommittee was appointed for this purpose, it seems almost a certainty, particularly in view of the timing of the committee's organization, that it also lent support to the change-of-government campaign. That support, indeed, very likely strengthened the three commissioners' obduracy. The twelve black negotiators are in some accounts called members of the committee, bringing its membership to eighty-nine, but the committee itself listed only the seventy-seven whites as members. Moreover, the list of seventy-seven includes all who were invited to join, though some of them did not actually do so and others attended irregularly. It appears that the active membership numbered about sixty. The committee's chairman seems to have been Thomas W. Martin, chairman of the Alabama Power Company.

129. Memorandum re. telephone call from Powers McCloud [*sic*], president of the Alabama Council on Human Relations, September 18, 1962 (first quotations), Alabama Advisory Committee, U.S. Civil Rights Commission to U.S. Civil Rights Commission and Civil Rights Division, U.S. Department of Justice, special memorandum, n.d. [September 19, 1962], both in Marshall Papers; Richard A. Puryear, Jr., to members of the Birmingham Chamber of Commerce, September 19, 1962, and attachment (second quotation), in William C. Hamilton Papers, Birmingham Public Library; Corley, "Quest for Racial Harmony," 236.

130. Lucius H. Pitts to Burke Marshall, telegram, September 17, 1962, Pitts to Robert F. Kennedy, October 11, 1962, Oscar W. Adams, Jr., to Kennedy, January 5, 1963, all in Marshall Papers; Newsletter of the Alabama Council of Human Relations, May 1963, p. 2, Hamilton Papers; *Birmingham News,* September 20, 1962; *Birmingham Post-Herald,* September 21, 1962; *Birmingham World,* September 26, 1962; on white businessmen's reaction to the boycott of the preceding spring, see E. L. "Red" Holland, Jr., to Burke Marshall, April 30, 1962, Marshall Papers. The other blacks who were to see the attorney general were William E. Shortridge, Leroy S. Gaillard, Jr., Dr. James T. Montgomery, and C. E. Thomas. However, only ten men actually attended the meeting in the end, and there is no way to determine which two of the twelve listed here were unable to go. Kennedy and Marshall also met during the same period with Mayor Hanes and apparently obtained from him a commitment to maintain law and order (*Birmingham News,* October 17, 1962).

131. Shuttlesworth, interview, May 18, 1989; Howell Raines, ed., *My Soul Is Rested: Movement Days in the Deep South, Remembered* (New York: Putnam, 1977), 155–57; Corley, "Quest for Racial Harmony," 236–37; Eskew, *But for Birmingham,* 202–5. This account of the meeting rests simply on Shuttlesworth's own memory of it, but I accept the accuracy of the details he reports because they seem to me entirely consistent with both his and the other participants' general attitudes and conduct. At the concluding session of the SCLC convention, on September 28, Martin Luther King was assaulted by a member of the American Nazi Party, but Birmingham authorities handled the incident efficiently (*Birmingham World,* October 3, 1962).

132. Indeed, Shuttlesworth emphasized this point to me when I talked with him (interview, May 18, 1989).

133. Officers J. E. LeGrand and C. C. Ray to Chief Jamie Moore, September 12, 1962, Detective Marcus A. Jones to Moore, October 2, 1962, Jones to Moore, November 13, 1962 (quotation), Officers C. L. Edmondson and R. J. Hooper to Moore, November 20, 1962, all in Connor Papers; Fred L. Shuttlesworth, "Why We Must Demonstrate," March 19, 1964, Boutwell Papers; Norman C. Jimerson to Burke Marshall, October 19, 1962, Marshall Papers; *Birmingham Post-Herald,* October 19, 1962; Corley, "Quest for Racial Harmony," 238–40; Eskew, *But for Birmingham,* 205. The chronology offered in the text differs somewhat from that to be found in standard accounts. The restoration of the segregation signs is usually placed in mid-October, and the action of Connor and his fire inspectors is cited as the principal cause. But the documentary evidence seems to me clearly to indicate that the signs went back up in mid-November, and I believe that the failure of the biracial negotiations and the consequent renewal of the downtown boycott were at least as important as Connor's threats in producing this outcome. In the first place, Edward Gardner's statement of November 12 is explicit that the signs were still down on that date. And in the second place, if Connor had been aware that the signs had been taken down at the time of his speech of October 18, he would certainly have said so. The entire purpose of the speech had been to prove that the leaders of the chamber of commerce and the change-of-government campaign were preparing an end to segregation. To this end, Connor produced the evidence that he had: that the merchants were considering hiring black clerks. But if he had known about the integration of the department store facilities, his case would have been very much stronger than it was. I conclude that Connor first learned of the integration on November 13, and that the fire inspectors' intimidation which then resulted merely served to reinforce for the merchants attitudes actually rooted primarily in their

hostility to the new boycott. Because of their predilection to blame politics for racial problems, however, the merchants quickly came to think of Connor's intervention as having forced their retreat from the September agreement. It is also worth noting that our only evidence of the supposed actions of the fire inspectors is the merchants' own subsequent claims, made to explain to the moderates their decision to restore the signs. My examination of the records of both the fire inspectors (who were under Connor's jurisdiction) and the building inspectors (who were under Waggoner) failed to disclose any unusual activity during this period. Nevertheless, I do accept that the intimidation by the fire inspectors that the merchants later alleged actually did take place. The story seems persuasive to me primarily because it was very much in keeping with Connor's beliefs, his past practices, and particularly his immediate political interests to have taken some such action. Because he had just lost the change-of-government referendum through a combination against him of blacks and white businessmen, he needed, if he were to survive politically, to drive a wedge between these forces. And anything he could do to create recriminations between Shuttlesworth and the downtown merchants would therefore have seemed highly desirable to him.

134. Officer R. A. Watkins to Chief Jamie Moore, April 15, 1963 (quotation), Connor Papers; Officers Watkins and R. S. Whitehouse to Moore, October 16, 1963, Hamilton Papers; *Birmingham World,* December 8, 1962; *Montgomery Advertiser,* June 2, 1963; David J. Garrow, *Bearing the Cross; Martin Luther King, Jr., and the Southern Christian Leadership Conference* (New York: William Morrow, 1986), 220–30. I should say as to the preceding paragraphs that I lack direct evidence of the reactions of the white business progressives to these events. Nevertheless, I believe that the statements in the text represent reasonable deductions from the businessmen's general attitudes and their actions during this period.

135. *Birmingham News,* January 4, 5 (first quotation), 1963; *Birmingham Post-Herald,* March 2, 1963; *Reid* v. *City of Birmingham,* 274 Ala. 629 (second quotation); *Tucker* v. *McLendon,* 210 Ala. 562; *Connor* v. *State on the Information of Boutwell,* 275 Ala. 230. The attorney for the city in the *Reid* case, John S. Foster, was a law partner of Douglass P. Wingo, who had been a member of the bar association's change-of-government committee. Justice Coleman, a former state senator from Greene County, had been the chairman of the Greene County White Citizens' Council before his election to the state supreme court; his grandfather, Thomas Wilkes Coleman, had been the chairman of the suffrage committee at the 1901 Constitutional Convention and had been principally responsible for drafting the constitution's disfranchising provisions. Equally unwavering in his white supremacist views was Chief Justice J. Edwin Livingston, a former adjunct law professor at the University of Alabama, whose brother was the chairman of the Macon County White Citizens' Council. Usually agreeing with them was Justice Robert T. Simpson, a former Florence prosecutor and judge of the state court of appeals. But these three more conservative justices were balanced by a more liberal group, led by Justice Lawson, a former state attorney general. Ordinarily joining him were Justice Merrill, a former state senator from Anniston, and Justice John L. Goodwyn, a former mayor of Montgomery, who, as we have seen, had been responsible for initiating the reform of the Montgomery Police Department. The seventh justice, Robert Harwood, a former presiding judge of the state court of appeals, usually could be counted as a member of this group as well, though in racial cases he often sought to avoid the substance of the questions presented by taking refuge in procedural

matters. In the *Reid* case, however, Harwood stood with Lawson and Goodwyn in dissent, while Merrill joined Livingston and Simpson to give Coleman his majority.

136. *Birmingham Post-Herald,* November 2, 1962, January 5, February 9, 12, 20, 21, 25, 26, 27, March 2, 6, 13, 19, 27, 28, April 1, 2, 3, 1963; *Birmingham News,* January 18, 22, 24, February 1, 4, 12, 24, March 3, 4, 5, 12, 27, 28, April 1, 1963; *Birmingham World,* January 5, February 6, 13, 16, March 2, 9, April 6, 1963; Mervyn H. Sterne to Louis Oberdorfer, March 7, 1963, and E. L. "Red" Holland, Jr., to Burke Marshall, March 12, 1963, both in Marshall Papers; Corley, "Quest for Racial Harmony," 244–49 (quotation, 247–48); Eskew, *But for Birmingham,* 188–91; LaMonte, *Politics and Welfare in Birmingham,* 171–76.

137. Detective Marcus A. Jones to Chief Jamie Moore, November 13, 1962, Officers J. B. Jones and J. E. LeGrand to Moore, January 24, 1963, Officers C. L. Edmondson and J. B. Jones to Moore, February 26, 1963, Officer J. C. Wilson to Moore, March 6, 1963, Officer C. R. Jones to Moore, March 12, 1963 (first quotation), Officer W. E. Chilcoat to Moore, March 20, 1963 (second quotation), Officers C. L. Edmondson and J. B. Jones to Moore, April 3, 1963 (third quotation), Officers R. S. Whitehouse and R. A. Watkins to Moore, April 5, 1963 (fourth quotation), all in Connor Papers. Following the change-of-government referendum, Gardner had told the Christian Movement membership that the results proved that "There are lots of white people in Birmingham that are glad that 'Old Bull' is almost gone."

138. The one contemporary account of which I am aware that seems to me to capture at least elements of this aspect of the events is that of George M. Murray, the Episcopal bishop coadjutor of Alabama, an active participant in the negotiations between the business progressives and the black moderates in 1962 and 1963; originally published in the *Living Church* magazine, it was reprinted in the *Montgomery Advertiser,* June 2, 1963. But Bishop Murray's hostility to Shuttlesworth is so great that he is unable to comprehend Shuttlesworth's motives, and he merely attributes Shuttlesworth's actions to a lust for power. See also Emory Jackson's reply in the *Birmingham World,* June 5, 1963. For the black moderates' initial estimation of Boutwell, see, e.g., E. W. Taggart to Albert Boutwell, March 28, 1963, Arthur G. Gaston to Boutwell, April 16, 1963, H. H. Perritt to Boutwell, April 18, 1963, and attached statement signed by A. P. Allen et al., all in Boutwell Papers.

139. Burke Marshall to E. L. "Red" Holland, Jr., March 8, 1963, Marshall to A. L. Feldman, March 8, 1963, Holland to Marshall, March 12, 1963, all in Marshall Papers; *Birmingham News,* April 5, 14, 1963; *Birmingham World,* April 10, 13, 17, May 8, 1963; *Birmingham Post-Herald,* April 9, May 4, 6, 1963; *Montgomery Advertiser,* May 4, 1963; Eskew, *But for Birmingham,* 205–8, 211–16, 291–95; Garrow, *Bearing the Cross,* 669 n. 4. Garrow reports Addine Drew's account of her conversation with King as follows: "I remember saying to Mike—Dr. King—'For our sake, please wait.' And he said, 'Deenie, do you think it's going to make a difference whether it's Bull Connor or Boutwell or whomever?' I said, 'It will make a difference to us psychologically. I don't think Boutwell will have any kind of feelings toward us, but we have been mistreated so badly by Bull Connor all these years that black people will feel better with him out of office. I will.'" King, she added, "never felt that that was too important, but if we wanted it so much, he waited." Corley states ("Quest for Racial Harmony," 249) that Gaston and Pitts also pressured King to postpone the demonstrations until after the elections, but other evidence indicates that they had not known about the planned demonstrations in advance.

140. *Birmingham News,* April 3, 1963; *Birmingham Post-Herald,* April 3, 4, 1963;

Birmingham World, April 6, October 5, 1963, January 2, 1965; Corley, "Quest for Racial Harmony," 248–49; Eskew, *But for Birmingham,* 190–91, 371; LaMonte, *Politics and Welfare in Birmingham,* 173–75. Subsequently, roll-call votes appeared to indicate that the council contained five moderate members and four generally more segregationist. The moderates were council president M. Edwin Wiggins, a retired executive of the Alabama Power Company; Dr. John Bryan, the executive vice-president of the chamber of commerce and a former Jefferson County school superintendent; Nina Miglionico, an attorney and the council's only female member; George Seibels, the insurance agent who would succeed Boutwell as mayor in 1967; and Alan T. Drennen, also an insurance agent. The segregationists were optician E. C. Overton, attorney John Golden, Woodlawn merchant Tom Woods, and Don Hawkins, a salesman for a national glass company.

141. On the reaction to the Albany precedent in Birmingham, see *Birmingham News,* July 13, 26, 30, September 7, 1962; *Birmingham World,* April 10, 1963.

142. *Birmingham Post-Herald,* April 9, 1963; Eskew, *But for Birmingham,* 226–27, 246–47. Eskew (217–309) contains an excellent day-by-day account of the demonstrations; see also Corley, "Quest for Racial Harmony," 249–75.

143. *City of Birmingham* v. *Croskey,* 217 F.Supp. 947; *Shuttlesworth* v. *City of Birmingham,* 43 Ala. App. 68, 281 Ala. 542, 394 U.S. 147; *Walker* v. *City of Birmingham,* 279 Ala. 53, 388 U.S. 307; Fred L. Shuttlesworth to Eugene "Bull" Connor, telegram, April 5, 1963, Connor to Shuttlesworth, telegram, April 5, 1963, Shuttlesworth to Connor, telegram, May 2, 1963, Connor to Shuttlesworth, telegram, May 2, 1963, all in Connor Papers; Eskew, *But for Birmingham,* 237–43, 252–54, 256 (quotation, 237). The eight who served the sentences in the fall of 1967 were King, Abernathy, and Wyatt T. Walker of the SCLC, and Shuttlesworth, King's brother A. D. Williams King, John T. Porter, J. W. Hayes, and T. L. Fisher of Birmingham. Judge Jenkins had acquitted Edward Gardner, Abraham and Calvin Woods, and Johnny L. Palmer. Justice Coleman dismissed the convictions of Andrew Young, James Bevel, and Nelson H. Smith.

144. Shuttlesworth, interview, May 18, 1989; David J. Vann, interview by author, August 16, 1991; "Outline of Negotiations" (quotations), unsigned, undated memorandum in Vann Papers [this memorandum, presumably by David Vann, apparently was written in late May 1963]; *Birmingham Post-Herald,* April 9, May 4, 1963; Corley, "Quest for Racial Harmony," 254–55; Eskew, *But for Birmingham,* 235–36. Father Foley stated that on April 8 he informed King that he had received firm assurances from the incoming city council that it would create an official biracial commission, and that these assurances were the basis of the two sides' agreement to meet the next day. Foley hoped that council's willingness to establish a biracial commission would persuade King to suspend the demonstrations in order to allow the commission to negotiate reforms. But of course King regarded the mere formation of a group to discuss possible changes as an entirely inadequate concession.

145. Eskew, *But for Birmingham,* 214 (first quotation); *Birmingham World,* October 31, 1962 (second quotation), April 10 (third, fourth, fifth, sixth, seventh, and ninth quotations), 13, 17 (eighth, tenth, and eleventh quotations), 20, 24, May 8, June 1, 5, 1963. On John Drew's earlier refusal to accept community leadership, see ibid., January 28, February 4, 1949.

146. Vann, interview, August 16, 1991; Officers B. A. Allison and R. A. Watkins to Chief Jamie Moore, April 10, 1963, Officers R. S. Whitehouse and B. A. Allison to Moore, April 11, 1963, Officers R. S. Whitehouse and R. A. Watkins to Moore, April 12, 1963, all in Connor Papers; *Birmingham World,* April 13, 24, May 8, 1963;

Birmingham Post-Herald, April 10, 1963 (first quotations); *Birmingham News,* April 12, 1963 (second quotations); Eskew, *But for Birmingham,* 229–35. The SCLC representatives on the central committee were King, Abernathy, Young, Wyatt T. Walker, James Lawson, and Dorothy Cotton. The Christian Movement was represented by Shuttlesworth, Shortridge, Edward Gardner, Nelson H. Smith, Lola Hendricks, John T. Porter, and King's brother A. D. Williams King. The moderate members were Gaston, Pitts, Shores, Long, Oliver, Drew, and Drew's wife, Addine (Eskew, 233). For a white moderate's effort to use Gaston's April 9 statement to prevent a rapprochement between Gaston and King, see George E. Trawick to Arthur G. Gaston, April 10, 1963, Boutwell Papers.

147. "Outline of Negotiations," Vann Papers.

148. Powers McLeod to Burke Marshall, October 28, 1962, McLeod to Marshall, January 17, 1963, Martin Luther King, Jr., to C. C. J. Carpenter et al., April 16, 1963 (fifth set of quotations), statement of six members of Harmon group, undated, unsigned [internally dated to c. September 20, 1963] (sixth set of quotations), all in Marshall Papers; Officer R. A. Watkins to Chief Jamie Moore, April 15, 1963 (third and fourth quotations), Connor Papers; *Birmingham Post-Herald,* January 17, 1963 (first set of quotations); *Birmingham News,* April 13, 1963 (second set of quotations). King reprinted his letter to the Harmon group, slightly revised, in Martin Luther King, Jr., *Why We Can't Wait* (New York: Harper and Row, 1963), 76–95; see also King's statement to the movement mass meeting following his release from jail, in Officers R. S. Whitehouse and R. A. Watkins to Chief Jamie Moore, April 23, 1963, Connor Papers. The eleven initial members of the Harmon group were Alabama's Methodist bishops, Nolan B. Harmon and Paul Hardin; its Episcopal bishops, C. C. J. Carpenter and George M. Murray; Birmingham's Roman Catholic bishop, Joseph A. Durick; the moderator of the Presbyterian synod of Alabama, Edward V. Ramage; J. T. Beale, secretary-director of the state's association of Disciples of Christ; Greek Orthodox priest Soterios D. Gouvellis of Birmingham; Birmingham First Baptist Church's pastor, Earl Stallings; and Jewish rabbis Milton L. Grafman of Birmingham and Eugene Blackschleger of Montgomery. Beale, Gouvellis, and Blackschleger did not sign the April 12 statement. On the background of these clergymen and the composition of King's reply, see Bass, *Blessed Are the Peacemakers.*

On April 11 a biracial group of nine ministers, led by the white liberal Lutheran Joseph Ellwanger and the black moderate Congregationalist Harold Long, issued a call for negotiations between blacks "representative of the entire Negro community" and "all elected officials and other persons of influence in our city." But unlike the Harmon group, they affirmed the right of citizens to demonstrate and endorsed blacks' desire for equal opportunity and equal access to public facilities. Emory Jackson of the *Birmingham World* editorially applauded this statement. However, it proved no more successful in bringing the parties together than was the statement of the Harmon group (*Birmingham World,* April 17, 20, 1963).

149. Martin Luther King, Jr., to C. C. J. Carpenter et al., April 16, 1963 (third quotations), Marshall Papers; Vann, "The Change from Commission to Mayor-Council," 29–30; *Birmingham News,* April 3, 4, 13 (second quotation), 1963; *Birmingham Post-Herald,* April 5, 9, 15, 18, 24 (first quotation), 25, 1963; Corley, "Quest for Racial Harmony," 251–54; Eskew, *But for Birmingham,* 247, 253. A local witticism during this period reported that Birmingham was the only city with a King, two mayors, and a parade every day.

150. Officer R. A. Watkins to Chief Jamie Moore, April 15, 1963, Officers R. S. Whitehouse and R. A. Watkins to Moore, April 23, 1963, Officers B. A. Allison, R. A.

Watkins, and R. S. Whitehouse to Moore, April 30, 1963, Officers R. S. Whitehouse and R. A. Watkins to Moore, April 30, 1963, Lieutenant Maurice H. House to Moore, April 30, 1963, Officers B. A. Allison and R. S. Whitehouse to Moore, May 2, 1963, Lieutenant Thomas H. Cook and Officers R. A. Watkins and R. S. Whitehouse to Moore, May 3, 1963, all in Connor Papers; Corley, "Quest for Racial Harmony," 255–62; Eskew, *But for Birmingham,* 240–69; Garrow, *Bearing the Cross,* 242–51.

151. *Selma Times-Journal,* April 15, 1960 (first quotation), April 1, 1962 (second quotation).

152. Officer B. A. Allison to Chief Jamie Moore, May 9, 1963, Allison to Moore, May 9, 1963 (second report), Officers B. A. Allison, R. S. Whitehouse, and R. A. Watkins to Moore, May 14, 1963, Allison to Moore, May 16, 1963, all in Connor Papers; *Montgomery Advertiser,* May 4, 1963 (quotation); *Birmingham World,* May 8, 1963; Corley, "Quest for Racial Harmony," 262–64; Eskew, *But for Birmingham,* 266, 269. On the evolution of the Kennedy administration's civil rights policy, see the excellent account in David L. Chappell, *Inside Agitators: White Southerners in the Civil Rights Movement* (Baltimore: Johns Hopkins University Press, 1994), 147–211.

153. "Outline of Negotiations" (quotations), Vann Papers. The specific chronology of these events is a matter of some dispute. Eskew (*But for Birmingham,* 269–70), following the account given by Vann in 1978, places the initial negotiating session on the evening of May 3. On the face of it this is a trifle improbable, and Vann himself is less than positive of the assertion: "About May 3, I believe, it was the head of Sears and Roebuck, Roper Dial, who called and asked me if I would undertake negotiations on behalf of the downtown businessmen. . . . And that very evening we met for the first time in the back room of Birmingham Realty Company, again under Mr. Smyer's auspices" (Vann, "The Change from Commission to Mayor-Council," 30–31). Corley, on the other hand, follows the "Outline of Negotiations" in placing the first session on May 5 ("Quest for Racial Harmony," 263–64). The "Outline" appears to have been written much closer to the events than was Vann's 1978 speech, and its detailed description of the meetings of the white businessmen on May 4 and May 5 lends it additional authority. I join Corley in finding it the more persuasive evidence, despite the fact that its provenance is unclear. Vann's own considerable hostility to the demonstrations is apparent in his comments in the Minutes of the Meeting of the Alabama Advisory Committee of the United States Civil Rights Commission, Birmingham, May 22, 1963, Marshall Papers.

154. Kelley, "The Black Poor and the Politics of Opposition," 318–20; undated, unsigned statement of six members of the Harmon group [internally dated to c. September 20, 1963] (quotation), Marshall Papers.

155. Officers R. S. Whitehouse and R. A. Watkins to Chief Jamie Moore, May 7, 1963, Watkins and Whitehouse to Moore, May 7, 1963 (second report), both in Connor Papers; Corley, "Quest for Racial Harmony," 259–60; Eskew, *But for Birmingham,* 268–69, 271–73. The crowd would again turn to violence following the demonstrations of May 6 (Eskew, 275) and May 7 (Officer B. A. Allison to Chief Jamie Moore, May 9, 1963, Connor Papers); Eskew, *But for Birmingham,* 280–82).

156. "Outline of Negotiations," and "Points for Progress, Birmingham, Alabama," annotated in David Vann's hand, both in Vann Papers.

157. "Outline of Negotiations," Vann Papers.

158. Ibid. (quotations); Henry S. Jones to Albert Boutwell, May 7, 1963, Kirkman O'Neal to Albert Boutwell, May 8, 1963, Herbert Qualls, Jr., to Albert Boutwell, May 9, 1963, all in Boutwell Papers; *Birmingham Post-Herald,* May 8, 9, 10, 11, 14, 16,

1963; *Selma Times-Journal,* May 12, 1963; *Birmingham News,* May 16, 17, 1963; Vincent Harding, "A Beginning in Birmingham," *The Reporter,* June 6, 1963, 13–19; Raines, ed., *My Soul Is Rested,* 162–66; Corley, "Quest for Racial Harmony," 267–69; Eskew, "But for Birmingham" (Ph.D. diss.), 74–79; Eskew, *But for Birmingham,* 275–83. Among the Senior Citizens who joined Governor Dixon in opposing the negotiations, it appears, were Lewis Jeffers of Hayes Aircraft and William J. Rushton of Protective Life Insurance; see comments by Winton M. Blount on Alabama business leaders to be contacted in regard to the integration of the University of Alabama, undated [c. May 22, 1963], Marshall Papers. Other prominent Birmingham businessmen who were reported to be strong segregationists or supporters of Governor Wallace were Craig Smith of Avondale Mills, Milton Andrews of the Bank for Savings, publishing executive Elton B. Stephens, construction executive R. Hugh Daniel, Robert E. Garrett and Claude S. Lawson of U.S. Pipe and Foundry, John A. Hand of the First National Bank, Arthur Weibel of U.S. Steel, Richard A. Puryear of Alabama Gas, and Frank Samford of Liberty National Life Insurance (ibid. and covering note, in ibid.)

159. Vann, interview, August 16, 1991; "Outline of Negotiations" and text of settlement (quotations), both in Vann Papers; Joseph Dolan to Burke Marshall, undated memorandum and attachment [internally dated to c. May 10, 1963], Statement of Sidney W. Smyer, undated [internally dated to c. May 14, 1963], Fred L. Shuttlesworth et al. to Sidney Smyer et al., memorandum, May 17, 1963, and Memorandum on conditions in Birmingham, unsigned, December 17, 1963, all in Marshall Papers; Officers J. B. Williams and J. N. Spivey to Chief Jamie Moore, October 1, 1963, Alabama Christian Movement for Human Rights flier, October 1, 1963, and Fred L. Shuttlesworth to Kenneth Royall and Earl Blaik, October 2, 1963, all in Hamilton Papers; *Wall Street Journal,* July 16, 1963; *New York Times,* March 16, 1964; Eskew, *But for Birmingham,* 282–83; Corley, "Quest for Racial Harmony," 269–70; Garrow, *Bearing the Cross,* 252–55, 463–65. The facts that the white negotiators had earlier told their black counterparts that they had located five or six black employees who could be quickly promoted, and that there were five stores involved in the negotiations, lend strong support to the blacks' interpretation of this aspect of the agreement.

160. Eskew, *But for Birmingham,* 283–86; Ralph D. Abernathy, *And the Walls Came Tumbling Down: An Autobiography* (New York: Harper and Row, 1989), 267–68; Garrow, *Bearing the Cross,* 255–56.

161. Shuttlesworth, interview, May 18, 1989; Officers R. S. Whitehouse and R. A. Watkins to Chief Jamie Moore, April 5, 1963, Whitehouse and Watkins to Moore, April 10, 1963, Officers B. A. Allison and R. A. Watkins to Moore, April 10, 1963, Whitehouse and Watkins to Moore, April 23, 1963, Allison to Moore, April 30, 1963, Information on Press Conference of M. L. King, May 3, 1963, 10 A.M., all in Connor Papers; Raines, ed., *My Soul Is Rested,* 171–74; Eskew, *But for Birmingham,* 286–89 (quotations on 287, 288); Garrow, *Bearing the Cross,* 256–57.

162. Officers J. E. LeGrand and M. A. Jones to Chief Jamie Moore, May 16, 1961, Officer B. A. Allison to Moore, May 9, 1963, Officers R. S. Whitehouse, R. A. Watkins and B. A. Allison to Moore, May 17, 1963, all in Connor Papers; *Birmingham Post-Herald,* May 9, 1963 (quotation); Eskew, *But for Birmingham,* 289–90; Garrow, *Bearing the Cross,* 257–58.

163. Officer R. S. Whitehouse to Chief Jamie Moore, May 10, 1963, Officer R. A. Watkins to Moore, May 15, 1963, both in Connor Papers; *Birmingham Post-Herald,* May 10, 11, 14, 1963; *Birmingham News,* May 16, 17, 1963; Eskew, *But for Birming-*

ham, 291–96; Garrow, *Bearing the Cross,* 258–60. Shuttlesworth's need to avoid acknowledging to himself the extent to which he compromised his convictions in agreeing to the Birmingham settlement seems to have distorted his memory of the events. As he recounted to me the meeting with King, Abernathy, and Burke Marshall on the morning of May 8, once he compelled King to say to Marshall that the movement had to retain unity, Marshall then reluctantly said to Shuttlesworth that Shuttlesworth could have everything he wanted. Marshall thus revealed, Shuttlesworth asserts, that he was acting in the interests of the white businessmen and was attempting to get them the best deal possible; when King agreed to stand with Shuttlesworth, Marshall then and only then made the further concessions that Shuttlesworth was demanding. The terms of settlement that Shuttlesworth announced on May 10, he claims, were his own demands, and much stronger than the ones which King had earlier approved, at Marshall's urging (interview, May 18, 1989). The evidence does not confirm Shuttlesworth's recollection of this episode. But the fact that he remembers it this way suggests his reluctance to admit to himself how much the settlement actually reflects the triumph of his black moderate rivals.

In a statement issued to the press on March 19, 1964, in preparation for the renewal of downtown picketing, Shuttlesworth provided a lengthy summary of the events from the fall of 1962 to the date of the statement. Though exaggerating the terms of the September 1962 agreement, the statement did formally acknowledge the linkage in the May 1963 agreement between the desegregation and the state court suit to validate the change of government. The statement also emphasized Shuttlesworth's distrust of the white negotiators, both local and federal: "Not one promise made in good faith [in September 1962] was fulfilled. . . . It is tragic that it took 3400 people in jail, widespread use of dogs and fire hoses, and many other indignities, for the Statesmen of Birmingham to pledge again in May the promises broken and unkept in September. The negotiations were far from ideal. Our insistence upon face to face meetings was fruitful only in one or two instance[s] with a few Merchants, with Messers Smyer and Vann discussing behind the scenes essential points with first one side and then the other. Representations of the Federal Government, zealous in their hopes for peace and quiet, must not have understood that these gentlemen were more concerned with stopping demonstrations than advancing the cause of Negroes." The statement went on to emphasize the presence of Executive Secretary William Hamilton in the talks, despite the Boutwell administration's subsequent lack of commitment to the agreement's terms ("Why We Must Demonstrate," Special News Bulletin from Alabama Christian Movement for Human Rights, by F. L. Shuttlesworth, President, March 19, 1964, Boutwell Papers).

164. Text of Press Conference by Mayor Albert Boutwell, undated [internally dated to c. May 3, 1963], Boutwell Papers.

165. Officers R. A. Watkins and R. S. Whitehouse to Chief Jamie Moore, October 16, 1963, Hamilton Papers; *Birmingham News,* May 11, 1963 (second set of quotations); *Birmingham Post-Herald,* May 10, 11, 12, 14, 16, 1963; Corley, "Quest for Racial Harmony," 273 (first quotations). Segregationists demanded to know the names of the white negotiators, but evidently because Hamilton was one of them, and because to have revealed that fact would have impugned Mayor Boutwell's veracity, the Senior Citizens declined to reveal their representatives' identities. To blunt the segregationists' furious inquiry the Senior Citizens eventually announced their entire membership, but other than its chairman, Sidney Smyer, they never made public who was on their race relations subcommittee. It was not until the

following October that Shuttlesworth, at a Christian Movement mass meeting, finally identified Hamilton as one of the negotiators.

166. John L. Swindle, memorandum on bombing damage, n.d. [September 1963], Boutwell Papers; *Birmingham Post-Herald,* May 12, 1963; *Birmingham News,* May 12, 26, 1963; *Birmingham World,* May 15, 18, 22, 1963; Corley, "Quest for Racial Harmony," 274–75; Eskew, *But for Birmingham,* 300–304. At the Christian Movement mass meeting just before the Klan rally on May 11, James Bevel had announced that the rally was about to take place and had suggested that blacks go out to Bessemer and investigate it. But at the mass meeting of May 13, Edward Gardner insisted, and apparently accurately, "The row we had the other night wasn't our folks. It was wineheads. It was Saturday; it was their night" (Officer R. S. Whitehouse to Chief Jamie Moore, May 13, 1963, Officers B. A. Allison, R. S. Whitehouse and R. A. Watkins to Moore, May 14, 1963, both in Connor Papers). The heroism of the Smithfield civil defense unit unfortunately brought it to the attention of the regional civil defense director in Thomasville, Georgia, who promptly ordered the unit to cease using civil defense insignia and equipment in connection with the quasi-police activities that had done so much to protect black Birmingham from the Klan's malice during the past decade (Dial F. Sweeny, Region III Director, to All State Directors, Region III, June 21, 1963, Lt. Col. H. K. Harris, Chief of Reserve Police, Jefferson County, Ala., to All Unit Commanders of Civil Defense Reserve Police, Jefferson County, undated, Abraham Berkowitz to Burke Marshall, October 22, 1963, James E. Lay to Whom It May Concern, October 3, 1963, all in Marshall Papers). Apparently thanks to the efforts of white moderates and liberals, however, the prohibition was rescinded after three months. Klan pressure eventually cowed James Lay, though, and he subsequently refused to cooperate with the investigations of the September bombing of the Sixteenth Street Baptist Church (see *Montgomery Advertiser,* July 28, 1997).

167. *Connor* v. *State on Information of Boutwell,* 275 Ala. 230; *Armstrong* v. *Board of Education,* 220 F.Supp. 217, 323 F.2d 333.

168. Louis F. Oberdorfer to Robert F. Kennedy, June 5, 19, 28, December 26, 1963, memoranda, in Robert F. Kennedy Papers, Kennedy Presidential Library, transcripts in Birmingham Public Library; John W. Macy, Jr., to George Huddleston, Jr., June 6, 1963, John W. Macy, Jr., to Robert F. Kennedy, memorandum, July 15, 1963, Don M. Jones to Abraham Berkowitz and C. H. Erskine Smith, May 15, 1963, memorandum, all in Marshall Papers; Officers R. A. Watkins and C. L. Borders and Sergeant C. D. Guy to Chief Jamie Moore, July 19, 1963, and Detective Marcus A. Jones, memorandum of activities, August 7, 1963, Hamilton Papers; J. M. Breckenridge to Albert Boutwell, May 23, 1963, Newman H. Waters, Sr., to Boutwell, May 31, June 14, 1963, Boutwell to Waters, June 11, 1963, Malcolm Bethea to Boutwell, July 11, 1963, J. M. Breckenridge to John S. Foster, July 16, 1963, Jamie Moore, record of telephone conversations with George W. Barron and Marvin Stanley, July 22, 1963, and Edward Mullins, July 23, 1963, Statement of the Mayor and City Council, July 23, 1963, and J. M. Breckenridge to Ann Ingram, November 20, 1963, all in Boutwell Papers; Case File, *Smith* v. *City of Birmingham,* in FRC East Point; *Birmingham World,* May 22, 29, June 1, 26, 1963; *Selma Times-Journal,* May 20, 21, 23, 24, June 6, July 24, 25, 31, August 4, 1963; Report of the Community Affairs Committee, in *Birmingham News,* March 22, 1964; Nunnelley, *Bull Connor,* 165–67.

169. Officers R. S. Whitehouse, R. A. Watkins, and B. A. Allison to Chief Jamie Moore, May 27, 1963, Hamilton Papers; William L. Batt, Jr., to Burke Marshall, July 30, 1963, E. L. "Red" Holland, Jr., to [Edwin O. Guthman], undated memorandum

[June 1963], both in Marshall Papers; Abraham Berkowitz to Albert Boutwell, July 2, 1963, Berkowitz to William C. Hamilton, September 23, 1963, Lieutenant Thomas H. Cook to Chief Jamie Moore, July 18, 1963, all in Boutwell Papers; E. W. Taggart et al. to Albert Boutwell, August 2, 29, 1963 (third quotation), both in Vann Papers; *Birmingham World,* June 1 (first quotation), 5, 12, July 20 (second quotation), 24, 31, 1963; *Birmingham Post-Herald,* June 12, July 9, 12, 24, 1963; *Selma Times-Journal,* July 14, 17, 1963; Corley, "Quest for Racial Harmony," 280–82; Eskew, *But for Birmingham,* 312–17.

170. William A. Morgan, United Americans for Conservative Government, statement, January 9, 1963, Don M. Jones to Abraham Berkowitz and C. H. Erskine Smith, May 15, 1963, both in Marshall Papers; Lieutenant Thomas H. Cook to Chief Jamie Moore, July 3, 1963, Jamie Moore, memorandum to file, July 19, 1963, Birmingham "Daily Bulletin," National States Rights Party mimeograph, August 1, 1963, United Americans for Conservative Government, flyer announcing meeting of August 16, 1963, Continuing Growth of the Ku Klux Klans, memorandum, October 5, 1965, all in Hamilton Papers; Detective Marcus A. Jones, report on Loveman's tear-gas bomb investigation, August 19, 1963, Statement of Albert Boutwell and M. E. Wiggins on Loveman's tear-gas bombing, n.d. [August 15, 1963], Dr. Edward R. Fields, Report on the Seventh Annual Convention of the National States Rights Party, Birmingham, September 1, 1963, Lieutenant Thomas H. Cook to Chief Jamie Moore, memorandum, July 18, 1963, and W. A. Morgan to George C. Wallace, wire, September 3, 1963, all in Boutwell Papers; *Birmingham Post-Herald,* August 9, 10, 16, 1963. The memorandum of October 5, 1965, on the Ku Klux Klan puts its strength in Alabama at 11,600, and there is every reason to believe that the Klan had been as large two years earlier. Almost all of the klaverns were concentrated in the band of industrial cities across the north center of the state, from Tuscaloosa through Bessemer and Birmingham to Anniston and Gadsden, though there were also klaverns in the Decatur, Montgomery, Selma, and Mobile areas.

171. *Armstrong* v. *Board of Education:* Order of District Court, July 19, 1963, Plan Submitted by Board of Education Pursuant to Order, August 19, 1963, Order Approving Plan, August 19, 1963, and John L. Swindle, memorandum on bombing damage, n.d. [September 1963], all in Boutwell Papers; *Birmingham Post-Herald,* August 21, 1963; *Birmingham World,* August 24, 1963; *Birmingham News,* September 9, 1963. When the board of education submitted its integration plan on August 19, Mayor Boutwell issued a public statement reflecting his consistent effort to retain the support of both segregationists and moderates: "I share, fully and personally, the deep and widespread resentment against this intrusion of the federal judiciary into the lives of parents and children in this city. . . . The Board of Education and its attorneys fought courageously to postpone this tragic hour as long as they could. I have supported the board and its attorneys all the way. They deserve the thanks of the people of Birmingham. . . . Whatever the effects may be of the plan and the court's decision, and however sick at heart they may make us, I know the good, responsible people of Birmingham will meet this hour with dignity and in an atmosphere of law and order, which we intend to maintain. We will not endanger our children or imperil the system of public education by turning our bitter resentment into words or actions that might incite violence of any kind. . . . Any person or group, regardless of motive, who would incite actions that would endanger the schools and imperil the safety of children, would be compounding this tragedy inexcusably. Any such person or group will deserve and receive the same bitter

resentment that we now level at federal intervention" (Statement of Albert Boutwell, August 19, 1963, Boutwell Papers).

172. *Birmingham Post-Herald,* June 8 (second quotation), July 9, 12, August 9, 10 (first quotation), 30, 1963; *Birmingham World,* July 17, August 21, 28, September 4, 1963; *Birmingham News,* September 1, 2, 3, 1963; *Selma Times-Journal,* August 4, 22, 30, September 1, 2, 1963; LaMonte, *Politics and Welfare in Birmingham,* 186–87. The *Birmingham News* put the size of the NSRP motorcade first at forty and later at sixty cars, but the Associated Press put it at one hundred. When the United Americans filed their school closure petition, Mayor Boutwell responded in his usual conciliatory fashion. The mayoral election in the spring had in effect been a referendum on the question of closing the schools, he asserted, and his election had constituted a mandate to keep them open. Moreover, "Private schools for a city this size would be utterly impractical. To close the schools would be to close out the futures for thousands of our children." But he also emphasized, "I commend and congratulate [the petitioners] for their good citizenship. They have responsibly refused to allow their emotions to turn them into rabble-rousers. They have turned to the due processes of law. The law guarantees them a full hearing on their petition. . . . Those who wish to protest the open-schools policy adopted by the school board should use this forum provided by law—not the streets, as advocated by some extremists in the various [private school] fund-raising meetings which they have been sponsoring around the city" (Statement of Albert Boutwell, September 1, 1963, Boutwell Papers).

173. *Birmingham News,* September 1, 2, 3, 4, 1963; *In re Wallace,* 170 F.Supp. 63; Detective Marcus A. Jones, report of activities, September 6, 1963, Boutwell Papers. Detective Jones identifies the Bessemer Klansman as "B. C. Creel," but I believe he means Robert Creel, the exalted cyclops of the Bessemer klavern; there is no B. C. Creel listed in the Bessemer city directories of the period. The belief of Wallace and his advisers that the general police power, the state constitution's requirement that the governor take care that the laws be faithfully executed, and a state code provision making the governor the head of the state's law enforcement agencies were sufficient grounds to justify Wallace in ordering the closure of schools threatened with disorder was questioned by at least one legal authority at the time (*Birmingham News,* September 2, 1963). In an advisory opinion requested by Wallace at the end of September, indeed, the state supreme court held that the governor had no power to open or close a school unless his doing so was "the actual and incidental result of keeping the peace" (*Opinion of the Justices,* 275 Ala. 547). But Wallace's conviction that his exercise of the police power in the face of violence would insulate him from contempt proceedings in the federal courts is essential to understanding his actions in the school integration crisis. In addition to his own encounter with the contempt proceeding of 1958, Wallace also doubtless had had his fears reinforced by the contempt citations that had been entered against Mississippi governor Ross Barnett and lieutenant governor Paul Johnson in connection with the integration of the University of Mississippi in 1962. Ironically, Wallace's attempts to close the schools in Tuskegee, and a few days later in Birmingham, Mobile, and Huntsville as well, became the basis for the federal court finding that the local schools were under state control, thereby permitting the issuance of the nation's only statewide integration decree in 1967 (*Lee* v. *Macon County Board of Education,* 231 F.Supp. 743, 267 F.Supp. 458). On the closure of the Tuskegee schools, see Robert J. Norrell, *Reaping the Whirlwind: The Civil Rights Movement in Tuskegee* (New

York: Knopf, 1985), 128–63. On the 1958 contempt proceedings against Wallace, see also Jack Bass, *Taming the Storm: The Life and Times of Judge Frank M. Johnson, Jr., and the South's Fight over Civil Rights* (New York: Doubleday, 1993), 184–96, and Carter, *Politics of Rage,* 96–104. On Wallace and the Birmingham school desegregation crisis, see Carter, *Politics of Rage,* 162–94.

174. Transcript of telephone conversation between George C. Wallace and Albert Boutwell, September 3, 1963, 10 A.M. (second quotation), and advice of Reid Barnes, dictated September 3, 1963, W. A. Morgan to George C. Wallace, September 3, 1963, telegram (first quotation), all in Boutwell Papers; *Birmingham News,* September 3, 1963.

175. *Birmingham News,* September 4, 5, 6 (quotation), 7, 8, 9, 10, 11, 1963; *Birmingham World,* September 7, 11, 14, 1963; Detective Marcus A. Jones, report of activities, September 6, 1963, John L. Swindle, memorandum on bombing damage, n.d. [September 1963], Statement of Chief Jamie Moore, September 5, 1963, 8:15 A.M., Police memorandum on meeting of Jefferson County Citizens Council, September 7, 1963, Resolution of the Young Men's Business Club, September 9, 1963, Resolution of the Business and Professional Men's Association, September 10, 1963, Memorandum of telephone conversation between Jamie Moore and Joseph Dolan, September 10, 1963, Memorandum of telephone conversation between Jamie Moore and Oscar Adams, September 10, 1963, Memorandum of telephone conversation among Jamie Moore, Burke Marshall and Robert F. Kennedy, September 10, 1963, all in Boutwell Papers; Statements of Jamie Moore, September 5, 1963, 9:55 A.M. and 12:30 P.M., Memorandum of telephone conversation between Jamie Moore and Joseph F. Johnston, September 5, 1963, 3:40 P.M., Statement of Eddie J. Coleman, September 14, 1963, Statement of Thomas Lyman, September 28, 1963, all in Hamilton Papers; Carter, *Politics of Rage,* 172–74. The members of the Birmingham school board at this time, in addition to its president, steelworker Robert C. Arthur—who had run for the city commission with black endorsement in 1953, as we have seen—were its vice-president, Liston A. Corcoran, an East End insurance agent and future city councilman; wealthy industrialist Herbert Stockham of Stockham Valves and Fittings; and physician Dr. Charles W. Neville. The fifth seat on the board was vacant because of the resignation of its former president, Mrs. Adelia Troxell. The course of these events differed slightly in Huntsville. Wallace had closed the schools initially there, as in the other three cities, but that community's disapproval of his action had been so emphatic and unanimous that when he permitted the schools to reopen on September 9, he also allowed the state trooper contingent in Huntsville to permit the registration of the black students. Thus integration actually came to Huntsville a day earlier than to Birmingham, Mobile, and Tuskegee. After a lengthy hearing on September 24—at which the governor's attorney, John P. Kohn, urged the en banc U.S. district court to declare the Fourteenth Amendment unconstitutionally ratified—the five federal judges replaced their September 9 restraining order with a temporary injunction to the same effect (*U.S.* v. *Wallace,* 222 F.Supp. 485; Case File and Hearing Transcript, *U.S.* v. *Wallace,* in FRC East Point). On the integration of the Birmingham schools, see *Montgomery Advertiser,* March 6, 1985.

176. *Birmingham News,* September 10, 11, 12, 13, 14, 1963; *Selma Times-Journal,* September 10, 11, 12, 1963; Detective Marcus A. Jones, report of activities, n.d. [September 14, 1963], Florence H. Bayer to Albert Boutwell, September 17, 1963, Albert Boutwell to Mervyn H. Sterne, September 17, 1963, Clancy Lake, text of

broadcast, November 26, 1963 (quotation), all in Boutwell Papers. Boutwell was in fact a Methodist. A boycott also developed at Graymont Elementary, but this one appears to have been more a product of parents' fears for the safety of their young children than of a desire to protest integration. By the end of the week, Graymont attendance had returned to normal levels. Elsewhere in the state, a boycott was attempted at Mobile's Murphy High School, but it soon collapsed. In Tuskegee, however—probably because Tuskegee was a very small town, with an even smaller and quite cohesive white community—the boycott proved completely successful. Very shortly, Macon County's public schools had been entirely abandoned to black students, and all white children were in private schools. This outcome was precisely the one the Wallace administration had desired for all of Alabama.

177. *Birmingham World,* September 18, October 16, 1963; *Selma Times-Journal,* September 16, 17, 18, 20, 27, October 30, 1963, June 1, September 1, 1964; *Washington Evening Star,* September 19, 21, 23, 1963; Statement of Albert Boutwell, September 15, 1963 (first quotation), Statement of George G. Seibels, Jr., September 15, 1963 (second quotation), Police memorandum, report of meeting at church of Joseph Ellwanger, unsigned [internally attributable to Detective Marcus A. Jones], July 15, 1965, John L. Swindle, memorandum on bombing damage, undated [September 1963], all in Boutwell Papers. The subsequent FBI investigation of the church bombing indicated the likelihood that Chambliss's accomplices had included fellow Klansmen Thomas E. Blanton, Jr., Troy Ingram, Bobby Frank Cherry, John Wesley Hall, Charles Cagle, Ross Keith, Jack Cash, his brother Herman Cash, Earl Thompson, and Arthur White; the state troopers' investigation had focused on Klansmen Chambliss, Hall, Cagle, Keith, and Levi Yarbrough. Chambliss was brought to trial and convicted of the bombing in 1977, but he refused to reveal the identity of his associates and eventually died in prison, without breaking his silence, in 1985. See Sikora, *Until Justice Rolls Down,* passim, esp. 69; see also undated police memorandum on meeting in Colonel Albert Lingo's motel room, September 29, 1963, Boutwell Papers. In the spring of 2000, however, Cherry and Blanton were indicted for complicity in the crime, and both were subsequently convicted of it. Sims and Farley were convicted of second-degree manslaughter in the death of Virgil Ware and received suspended sentences of seven months. An internal police review cleared Officer Parker of any wrongdoing in the death of Johnnie Robinson, and the county grand jury declined to indict him. Officer Parker stated that he had fired his shotgun over Robinson's head and that, as had happened in the Coley incident, Robinson was struck accidentally by a stray pellet from the shell.

178. *Birmingham World,* September 10, 1946, September 25, October 2, 5, 1963; *New York Times,* September 18, 1963; Officers R. S. Whitehouse and R. A. Watkins to Chief Jamie Moore, September 20, 1963, Joseph N. Langan to Nina Miglionico, October 14, 1963, both in Hamilton Papers; J. L. Ware and C. H. Oliver to Mayor and City Council, September 28, 1963, Boutwell Papers; Burke Marshall and Louis F. Oberdorfer to Robert F. Kennedy, memorandum, September 19, 1963 (quotations), Orzell Billingsley, Jr., to Robert F. Kennedy, October 5, 1963, and attached Statement of Alabama Democratic Conference to Birmingham City Council, October 1, 1963, all in Marshall Papers; on Oberdorfer's efforts to mobilize southern white business progressives, see Oberdorfer to Robert Kennedy, June 5, 6, 7, 19, 28, July 10, 18, November 13, December 26, 27, 1963, February 17, 18, 1964, memoranda, Kennedy Papers. Arthur Shores and his Smithfield neighbors suffered an ad-

ditional blow at this time when, as a result of the two bombings of Shores's home, insurance companies began refusing to write homeowners' policies in the area; see John J. Drew to Burke Marshall, September 20, 1963, Marshall Papers.

179. *Birmingham World,* September 25, 28, October 2, 5, 9 (third quotation), 12, 16, 1963; *Birmingham News,* September 6, 29, 1963; *Selma Times-Journal,* October 7, 11, 1963, February 28, 1964; *New York Times,* September 25, 1963 (first quotation); draft of statement of Young Men's Business Club to *Birmingham News,* undated [September 27, 1963] (second quotation), Vann Papers; Burke Marshall to Pierre Salinger, memorandum, October 9, 1963, and Marshall to Orzell Billingsley, Jr., October 9, 1963, both in Marshall Papers; Statement of Birmingham religious leaders, September 17, 1963, and draft second statement of religious leaders, undated [c. September 17, 1963], George M. Murray to Albert Boutwell, wire, September 5, 1963, Statement of Earl H. Blaik and Kenneth C. Royall, September 24, 1963, Alan W. Heldman to Albert Boutwell, September 25, 1963, all in Boutwell Papers; Norman C. Jimerson to C. C. J. Carpenter, October 3, 1963, Jimerson to Albert Boutwell, October 10, 1963, both in Hamilton Papers; LaMonte, *Politics and Welfare in Birmingham,* 187–89. The full texts of the statements of the white Birmingham delegation to President Kennedy are attached to Albert Boutwell to John F. Kennedy, September 21, 1963, Kennedy Papers. In addition to Hawkins and Hamilton, the delegation included Baptist minister W. Landon Miller, Committee of 100 chairman Caldwell Marks, CAC chairman Frank Newton, and Police Chief Jamie Moore. A brilliantly accurate satirical account of what might have been a typical conversation between Royall and Blaik and Birmingham's white leaders, by reporter Mary McGrory, is in the *Washington Star,* September 22, 1963. Boutwell's staff went so far as to draft for the emissaries proposed findings about their mission: "We suggest that the President use the entire weight of his office to keep the radical negroes and whites out of Birmingham. The city needs more time. . . . Any attempts at integration should not be made in the presence of television and newspaper reporters in that this has generated considerable animosity and a feeling that many attempts at integration were not truly for that purpose but to gain prestige and publicity to attract nation-wide contributions. . . . It is imperative that the radical elements of both sides who are not native to the community be kept away and out of the picture" (Suggested draft of contents of report to the President by General Royall and Colonel Blaik, n.d. [c. October 4, 1963], Boutwell Papers). Royall, at least, was not taken in by the white Birminghamians' claims; see Kenneth C. Royall to Robert F. Kennedy, March 16, 1964, Marshall Papers. The black members of the group relations subcommittee, in addition to Ware, Gardner, and Woods, were attorneys Oscar Adams and Peter Hall, physician James T. Montgomery, dentist E. W. Taggart, Congregationalist minister Harold Long, Miles College president Lucius H. Pitts, and Mrs. Ruth Jackson, the operator of a school for beauticians.

180. *Birmingham World,* October 2, 5, 12, 19, 1963; *Selma Times-Journal,* September 17, 26, 30, October 1, 7, 1963; Officers R. S. Whitehouse and R. A. Watkins to Chief Jamie Moore, September 20, 1963 (quotation), Officers J. B. Williams and J. N. Spivey to Moore, October 1, 1963, Detective Marcus A. Jones, report, October 2, 1963, Officers R. A. Watkins and R. S. Whitehouse to Moore, October 16, 1963, Alabama Christian Movement for Human Rights flyer, signed by Martin Luther King, Jr., and Fred L. Shuttlesworth, undated [September 25, 1963], Fred L. Shuttlesworth to Kenneth C. Royall and Earl H. Blaik, October 2, 1963, Shuttlesworth to C. C. J. Carpenter, October 2, 1963, Shuttlesworth to Albert Boutwell and

M. Edwin Wiggins, October 10, 1963, all in Hamilton Papers; J. L. Ware and C. H. Oliver to Mayor and City Council, September 28, 1963, Orzell Billingsley, Jr., and Emory O. Jackson, Position Statement, Alabama Democratic Conference, September 25, 1963, Fred L. Shuttlesworth to Albert Boutwell and M. Edwin Wiggins, October 4, 1963, and Shuttlesworth to Wiggins, telegram, October 8, 1963, all in Boutwell Papers; Orzell Billingsley, Jr., to Robert F. Kennedy, October 5, 1963, and attached Statement of Alabama Democratic Conference to Birmingham City Council, October 1, 1963, both in Marshall Papers; LaMonte, *Politics and Welfare in Birmingham,* 188. In obvious reference to Gaston and Shores, Shuttlesworth wrote Blaik and Royall that "the positions of several highly respectable citizens have been compromised in the eyes of the Negro Community by" their having charged King and Shuttlesworth with outside interference.

181. Alan W. Heldman to Albert Boutwell, September 25, 1963, Preliminary Report from the Council and Mayor Regarding the Hiring of Negro Policemen in Negro Areas, October 22, 1963 (first, thirteenth and fifteenth quotations), Statement of Albert Boutwell, October 22, 1963 (fourteenth quotation), Resolution of the Association of City Employees, J. C. Cornelius, president, October 11, 1963 (eighth set of quotations), M. G. Walker, Jr., president of United Protestants, Inc., to Birmingham City Council, October 14, 1963 (fourth quotation), Mrs. Mary Lou Holt to Mayor and City Council of Birmingham, October 16, 1963 (third quotation), Resolution of the West End Civitan Club Adopted October 17, 1963, R. B. Gibson, president (seventh set of quotations), Resolution of the Business and Professional Men's Association, H. E. Archer, president, adopted September 10, 1963 (eleventh quotation), Louis O'Conner to Albert Boutwell, September 11, 1963 (twelfth quotation), Miles College Student Body, Shelly Millender, chairman, to Albert Boutwell, telegram, September 16, 1963 (tenth quotation), Robert C. Ward to Albert Boutwell and *Birmingham News,* September 28, 1963 (fifth and sixth quotations), all in Boutwell Papers; Statement of Albert Boutwell, October 14, 1963 (second quotation), Hamilton Papers; Statement of the Birmingham Fraternal Order of Police, Lodge Number 1, Jack Parker, president, newspaper clipping dated October 20, 1963 (ninth set of quotations), Vann Papers; *Birmingham World,* September 28, October 19, 26, 1963; *Selma Times-Journal,* September 25, 26, 1963. See also Thomas H. Jackson to John Golden, September 4, 1963, Mrs. L. J. Pillow to Albert Boutwell, September 13, 1963, and Mrs. Elsie E. Brittain to Boutwell, October 9, 1963, Boutwell Papers. The segregationists' sense of the passivity of the police and the aggressiveness of the demonstrators during the spring had doubtless been exaggerated by the distinctly partial and defensive reporting of the events in the *Birmingham News* and *Post-Herald.* But when the newspapers covered the church bombing fully and accurately in the fall, it was precisely this new fullness and accuracy that many segregationists found offensive. One of them, Vestavia Hills food broker Roy A. Boggs, wrote *News* publisher Clarence B. Hanson, Jr., "You as a Southern man should know the temperment [*sic*] and personality of our southern negro. He does not possess reasoning and judgment compared with the average white man. There are elements among both the colored and white population that are just trying to find an excuse to cause trouble and what will give them better reason than a newspaper with blaring headlines and pictures telling the stories [of the deaths] over and over again[?] It just makes you sick to think about it, and your papers are nauseating to me for the same reason. Why don't you wake up and help your city? And do everything possible to keep trouble down instead of helping it

grow[?] It is time you people on the newspaper grew up and realize some of your responsibilities" (Roy A. Boggs to Clarence B. Hanson, Jr., September 16, 1963, Boutwell Papers).

182. *Birmingham World,* October 12, 19, 26 1963; *Birmingham News,* October 20, 1963 (first set of quotations); *Selma Times-Journal,* October 14, 1963; Memorandum to Mayor Albert Boutwell, unsigned, October 17, 1963, Memorandum, Detective Marcus A. Jones, October 23, 1963, Officers R. S. Whitehouse and R. A. Watkins to Chief Jamie Moore, October 28, 1963 (second quotation), Officers F. L. Sartain, E. E. Hayes, R. A. Watkins, Sergeant C. D. Guy to Moore, November 5, 1963 (third quotation), all in Hamilton Papers; cf. LaMonte, *Politics and Welfare in Birmingham,* 188–89. Committed segregationists, of course, saw no real difference between men such as Shores and Shuttlesworth, because both were for integration. For that reason, segregationists could explain King's action to thèmselves only as the result of a secret agreement between King and Boutwell for the city quietly to yield to King's demand at a later date—a notion that King's October 22 statement encouraged. See, e.g., Mrs. Thelma Smith to *Birmingham Post-Herald,* October 23, 1963, and Smith to Albert Boutwell, October 30, 1963, both in Boutwell Papers.

183. Memorandum, Statement of Chief Jamie Moore at Meeting with Representatives of Inter-Citizens Committee, November 13, 1963 (quotations), Officers F. L. Sartain, E. E. Hayes, R. A. Watkins, and Sergeant C. D. Guy to Chief Jamie Moore, November 5, 1963, Officers W. A. Noles and E. E. Hayes to Moore, November 27, 1963, Noles and Hayes to Moore, December 10, 1963, Officers F. L. Sartain and R. A. Watkins to Moore, December 16, 1963, all in Hamilton Papers. C. Herbert Oliver was one of Birmingham's most conservative black leaders, but Chief Moore seems to have considered him a dangerous radical, primarily, it appears, because Oliver's church had been the site of the Southern Negro Youth Congress rally at which Progressive Party vice-presidential candidate Senator Glen Taylor had been arrested in 1948; see memorandum, C. Herbert Oliver, Black Male, October 2, 1963, in ibid. The calm at the end of 1963 moved at least one business progressive to cautious optimism; see [David J. Vann?] to Louis Oberdorfer, December 11, 1963, Marshall Papers.

184. *Birmingham World,* October 9, 16, 23, 26, 30, November 13, December 7, 14, 1963, June 17, 1964; Report of the Public Safety Committee, Birmingham City Council, February 13, 1964, Statement [of the Birmingham City Council], February 18, 1964 (first quotation), both in Boutwell Papers; Captain Jack A. Warren to Chief Jamie Moore, memoranda, both dated January 15, 1965, Hamilton Papers; Minutes of Fourth Meeting of Group Relations Committee, October 25, 1963, Minutes of Fifth Meeting of Group Relations Committee, October 31, 1963, C. C. J. Carpenter to Thomas E. Bradford, November 1, 1963, Report of Subcommittee on Ways to Improve the Participation in Community of all its Citizens to Community Affairs Committee on Group Relations, December 30, 1963, Minutes of Executive Committee Meeting, [Community Affairs Committee] January 2, 1964, John C. Barnette to C. C. J. Carpenter, report of Subcommittee Group 1, January 6, 1964, Report of Group Relations Subcommittee on Communications, George G. Brownell, chairman, [February 4, 1964], Tom E. Bradford, Sr., to Executive Committee of Community Affairs Committee, memorandum, February 12, 1964, Executive Committee to Mayor and Council of City of Birmingham, report on Group Relations and Citizen Participation in Birmingham, n.d., Albert Boutwell to Executive and Group Relations Committees of Community Affairs Committee, April 27, 1964, and attached statement, April 27, 1964 (third set of quotations), all in Vann Papers;

First Report of Executive Committee of the Community Affairs Committee, in *Birmingham News*, March 22, 1964 (second set of quotations); LaMonte, *Politics and Welfare in Birmingham*, 189–93. Mayor Boutwell, in his reply to the group relations subcommittee's recommendations, also implied that Hayden and McPherson might have purposely avoided being offered a position on the force, in order, presumably, to keep the issue alive.

185. *Wall Street Journal*, February 5, 1964; Officers F. L. Sartain and R. A. Watkins, memorandum on Mass Meeting of Alabama Christian Movement for Human Rights, January 29, 1964 (first quotations), Officers W. A. Noles and E. E. Hayes to Moore, March 9, 1964, Officers F. L. Sartain and H. M. Hayes to Moore, March 26, 1964 (fourth quotations), [Detective Marcus A. Jones,] report on demonstrations workshop, March 16, 1964, unsigned memorandum, March 20, 1964, unsigned memorandum, March 26, 1964 [both probably from Detective Jones], Fred L. Shuttlesworth to Loveman's Department Store, March 5, 1964 (second quotation), Shuttlesworth to "Dear Friend of Freedom," March 6, 1964, Milton R. Durrett to "Dear Restaurateur," March 6, 1964, Shuttlesworth to Manager, New Williams Department Store, March 16, 1964, and undated Christian Movement flyer for Selective Buying Campaign, all in Hamilton Papers; Fred L. Shuttlesworth, "Why We Must Demonstrate," March 19, 1964, Shuttlesworth to Albert Boutwell, telegram, March 21, 1964, and Shuttlesworth to Boutwell, telegram, March 24, 1964, all in Boutwell Papers; Kenneth C. Royall to Robert F. Kennedy, March 16, 1964 (third quotations), Marshall Papers.

186. Minutes of Fourth Meeting, Community Affairs Committee on Group Relations, October 25, 1963, Vann Papers. It is worth noting that this statement of Councilman Seibels, together with Mayor Boutwell's reported earlier statement to a delegation from the Young Men's Business Club "that you had determined such action not to be in the best interest of the City at this time," must call sharply into question both men's public position that they were ready to hire any blacks who met the various civil service requirements (Alan W. Heldman to Albert Boutwell, September 25, 1963, Boutwell Papers). Moreover, the fact that Boutwell had privately given so firm a rejection as early as September 25 would clearly indicate that King's and Shuttlesworth's actions were not responsible alone for the reform's failure.

187. *Birmingham News*, September 10, 1963, August 11, 12, 25, 26, December 1, 2 (quotation), 1964; *Birmingham World*, July 27, August 3, September 11, December 14, 1963; *Selma Times-Journal*, February 28, September 16, 25, 27, October 4, 19, 1964; "Birmingham Truth," issues dated January 7, March 23, 1964, and undated flyer, "Commission Form is Best!" [internally dated to late January 1964], all in Hamilton Papers; *Longshore* v. *City of Homewood*, 277 Ala. 444, *Bouldin* v. *City of Homewood*, 277 Ala. 665; LaMonte, *Politics and Welfare in Birmingham*, 164–67, 191. On the moderates' conviction that the annexation of the southern suburbs was essential to victory in the change-of-government referendum, witness the *Birmingham News*'s editorial reaction to Mountain Brook's rejection of merger: "Everyone knows that an attempt is going to be made to change the form of Birmingham's government—a government which, though new, even many merger opponents agree has done much to get this city moving ahead. If the progress we have made— progress in which Mountain Brook shares—is not to be sacrificed, full citizenship of Mountain Brook residents in the mother city is vital" (*Birmingham News*, August 26, 1964). Fairfield, Midfield, and Irondale all voted on August 11, as did Homewood. The results were: for 572, against 1,796 in Fairfield; for 175, against 821 in

Midfield; for 146, against 418 in Irondale; for 2,423, against 2,417 in Homewood. In Mountain Brook on August 25, the result was, for 2,923, against 3,177. In Tarrant City on September 15, the result was, for 196, against 1,322. In the change-of-government referendum on December 1, the vote in Birmingham proper was, for mayor-council, 27,075, for commission, 15,029, for city manager, 489; the vote in Homewood was, for mayor-council, 2,374, for commission, 545, for city manager, 68. In the second Homewood annexation referendum, on December 13, 1966, annexation was defeated 2,149 to 4,015. At the same time, annexation was rejected in an eastern unincorporated area, Center Point, 1,274 to 1,713.

My estimate of the increase in the black vote in Birmingham between the two change-of-government referenda was derived as follows. We know that there were 8,246 black voters in Birmingham, and 12,369 in Jefferson County as a whole, in December 1962 (*Birmingham World,* December 19, 1962). And we know that the registered black vote in Jefferson County at the beginning of December 1965 was approximately 38,000 (*New York Times,* January 16, 21, 1966). The increase in the county's total of 25,631 in this interval would indicate an average growth of 712 black voters a month. However, the board of registrars ceased using the Alabama voter qualification test as soon as the Voting Rights Act was signed into law on August 6, 1965, and it would seem certain that the number of blacks registered after the abandonment of the test was much greater than it had been earlier. We know that the board registered almost 4,000 blacks during the month of December 1965 (*New York Times,* January 21, 1966). If the black registration averaged 3,500 a month in the four months from August through November 1965, then the total growth of the county's black vote between December 1962 and July 1965 was 11,631, or about 363 new registrants a month. Undoubtedly, the number of registrations would have varied during this period; it seems to have been substantially greater from October through December 1963, for instance. But this average figure should produce a reasonably accurate estimate if applied to a significant number of months. It would seem, then, that on the date of the second change-of-government referendum, December 1, 1964, there would perhaps have been 21,000 black voters in the county. If the proportion of black city voters to county that existed in December 1962—two-thirds—held constant in the interim, then there were about 14,000 black voters in the city. I need hardly say, however, that this figure, though I believe it is a reasonable approximation, is certainly no more than that.

188. *Birmingham World,* October 12, 16, 1963; *Selma Times-Journal,* October 2, 1963, January 15, 16, 19, March 10, May 6, 7, June 3, 18, 23, July 3, 6, 8, August 30, September 1, 17, 25, October 2, 6, December 14, 1964, January 10, 12 (quotation), 1965; Memoranda dated February 9, 17, 1961, FBI Case Files, Freedom Rider Investigation; Memorandum on meeting in Colonel Al Lingo's room at St. Francis Motel, September 29, 1963, Boutwell Papers; *Alabama Official and Statistical Register* for 1967, pp. 487–548; *McClung* v. *Katzenbach,* 233 F.Supp. 815, 379 U.S. 294; Nunnelley, *Bull Connor,* 167–80. Arrested along with Chambliss, Hall, and Cagle, but not charged, were Ross Keith and Levi Yarbrough. In 1977, as we have seen, Chambliss would be convicted of murder in connection with the bombing. He would die in prison in 1985. In 2000, Thomas E. Blanton, Jr., and Bobby Frank Cherry would be indicted for participating in the bombing with Chambliss, and both would eventually be convicted. The United Americans' secretary and spokeswoman was Mary Lou Holt, the wife of Klansman William A. Holt, Jr., and Donald E. Luna's wife, Sherry, was one of the United Americans' most active members; see Don M. Jones

to Abraham Berkowitz and Erskine Smith, memorandum, May 15, 1963, Marshall Papers. For a white liberal expressing just such despair about the Birmingham situation at this period as the text surmises, see Leslie W. Dunbar to David J. Vann, September 8, November 6, 1964, both in Vann Papers. For comparable black frustration, see John Doar to Burke Marshall, memorandum on conference with Dr. Lucius Pitts, January 15, 1964, Marshall Papers. On Congressman Huddleston's attitudes, see George Huddleston, Jr., to Abraham Berkowitz, March 30, 1964, and Berkowitz to Huddleston, April 3, 1964, both in Vann Papers.

189. Arthur G. Gaston to Albert Boutwell, May 2, 1964, Boutwell to Gaston, May 6, 1964, Sidney W. Smyer to Boutwell, May 21, 1965 (quotations), W. C. Patton to Boutwell, December 14, 1965, Mrs. Verdelle D. Martin to Boutwell, December 23, 1965, all in Boutwell Papers; *Birmingham World,* January 2, October 20, November 27, 1965; LaMonte, *Politics and Welfare in Birmingham,* 200–237.

190. Edward Gardner and Mrs. Georgia Price to Deacons and Trustees Board, Revelation Baptist Church, October 2, 1965, Statement of Alabama Christian Movement for Human Rights, October 4, 1965, Statement of Fred L. Shuttlesworth, October 8, 1965, Statement of Fred L. Shuttlesworth and Mr. Hosea Williams, January 11, 1966, Sidney W. Smyer to Albert Boutwell et al., January 12, 1966, Fred L. Shuttlesworth and Edward Gardner to Albert Boutwell, January 15, 1966, *Board of Education* v. *Williams,* H. Hobart Grooms, Opinion in Lieu of Formal Findings of Fact and Temporary Injunction, January 26, 1966, all in Boutwell Papers; *Cleveland Call and Post,* October 23, 1965, clipping in Hamilton Papers; *Birmingham World,* January 30, February 6, 24, 1965, January 12, 22, 29, February 2, 23, 1966, March 11, 1967; *New York Times,* January 5, 6, 7, 11, 13, 14, 15, 16, 17, 19, 20, 21, 23, 24, 25, 26, 27, 30, 1966. It is worth noting, however, that if the board of registrars maintained the rate of registrations that it had achieved during December 1965, the black electorate could easily have reached 63,000 by March 1967 even if the federal examiners had never been appointed. Once the January demonstrations had ended, John Nixon apparently quietly withdrew his resignation and resumed the NAACP branch's presidency.

191. Alan T. Drennen, Jr., to Albert Boutwell, memorandum, February 8, 1966 (second quotation), Statement of Alabama Christian Movement for Human Rights, Interdenominational Ministerial Alliance, Birmingham Baptist Ministers Conference, et al., March 22, 1966 (fourth quotation), Ferd F. Weil, Sr., to Albert Boutwell, April 4, 1966, John W. Nixon to Boutwell, July 14, 1966, undated press release of Birmingham NAACP [July 1966], all in Boutwell Papers; *Birmingham World,* January 26 (first quotation), February 9, April 2, 1966; *New York Times,* February 23, 25, March 13 (third quotation), 1966.

192. LaMonte, *Politics and Welfare in Birmingham,* 193–99, 231–37; Franklin, *Back to Birmingham,* 54–174, esp. 61–62, 102–5; on Pitts's great influence upon Arrington, see 247–48. In 1977, Arrington broke with Shores's Progressive Democratic Council in anger over its refusal to endorse his close friend Jeff Germany for the city council and formed the rival Jefferson County Citizens Coalition. In 1979 the Progressive Democratic Council therefore endorsed the incumbent, David Vann, rather than Arrington, for mayor. In 1981 the Citizens Coalition responded by refusing to endorse Shores's daughter, Helen Shores Lee, for the city council. These actions created a permanent breach between Arrington and Shores. Franklin's account reflects the quite bad blood between the two men by depicting Arrington as a younger, more militant leader eager to push aside hesitant older

spokesmen such as Shores (e.g., 60–61, 68–69). And this portrait appears to some degree buttressed by the fact that Arrington, like his mentor Pitts, was indeed always eager to espouse in public a medial position between the black moderates and activists. The evidence seems to me convincing, however, that despite the enmity between Arrington and Shores, in practice Arrington remained firmly allied with the black middle class throughout his career—just as had Pitts before him.

Chapter 4. Selma

1. On the history of Selma in general, see Alston Fitts III, *Selma: Queen City of the Black Belt* (Selma: Clairmont Press, 1989). Accounts by participants in the civil rights collisions include James G. Clark, Jr., *The Jim Clark Story: I Saw Selma Raped* (Birmingham: Selma Enterprises, 1966); Charles E. Fager, *Selma, 1965* (New York: Scribner, 1974); Amelia Platts Boynton Robinson, *Bridge across Jordan,* 2nd ed., rev. and enl. (1979; Washington, D.C.: Schiller Institute, 1991); Sheyann Webb [Christburg] and Rachel West Nelson, as told to Frank Sikora, *Selma, Lord, Selma: Girlhood Memories of the Civil-Rights Days* (University: University of Alabama Press, 1980); Ralph David Abernathy, *And the Walls Came Tumbling Down: An Autobiography* (New York: Harper and Row, 1989), 297–361; and J. L. Chestnut, Jr., and Julia Cass, *Black in Selma: The Uncommon Life of J. L. Chestnut, Jr.* (New York: Farrar, Straus and Giroux, 1990). Sheriff Clark's account is highly defensive but not unrevealing. Fager, a white SCLC field-worker, reflects in his narrative the tension that arose between the SCLC and the local black leadership, particularly Frederick Reese, but is not uncritical as well of SCLC's tactics and is quite detailed; as his title implies, however, Fager focuses only on 1965. Mrs. Boynton is strident in her outrage, but she tells a good deal about herself. Abernathy's autobiography, in the Selma chapter as elsewhere, is lively but not always reliable. Chestnut's memoir is interesting and frequently informative, but, perhaps inevitably, it magnifies his own role.

Fager's book reflects substantial later research and is almost as much a secondary source as a primary one. Among the strictly secondary accounts, by far the most useful is Stephen L. Longenecker, *Selma's Peacemaker: Ralph Smeltzer and Civil Rights Mediation* (Philadelphia: Temple University Press, 1987); drawing as did Fager upon the important body of Smeltzer Papers at the Church of the Brethren Archives in Elgin, Illinois, Longenecker reveals a great deal particularly about the negotiations that preceded King's arrival in the city. Much less instructive is David J. Garrow, *Protest at Selma: Martin Luther King, Jr., and the Voting Rights Act of 1965* (New Haven: Yale University Press, 1978), which is inadequately researched in local sources. Considerably superior is Garrow's own subsequent account in *Bearing the Cross: Martin Luther King, Jr., and the Southern Christian Leadership Conference* (New York: William Morrow, 1986), 357–430 et passim. Also commendable is Adam Fairclough, *To Redeem the Soul of America: The Southern Christian Leadership Conference and Martin Luther King, Jr.* (Athens: University of Georgia Press, 1987), 209–14, 225–51, 260–62. But the focus of each of these studies upon King necessarily has the effect of lifting the Selma story to some degree out of the municipal context which I have sought to emphasize here. An interesting account of the background and efforts of one of the white civil rights workers who came to Selma is Charles Eagles, *Outside Agitator: Jonathan Daniels and Civil Rights in Alabama* (Chapel Hill: University of North Carolina Press, 1993).

2. *Selma Times-Journal,* October 11, 1964; Fitts, *Selma,* 4, 31, and appendix.

Prior to 1852, Selma's executive, called the intendant, was one of the five city councilmen and was chosen by the council for a one-year term. John M. Strong, the town's postmaster, also served for four years (1847–50) as intendant, giving him a total of a decade in municipal authority.

3. *Selma Times-Journal,* January 20, February 16, March 8, 11, 13, 24, April 3, 7, 1932. On Burns's background and career, see ibid., May 27, 1959.

4. *Birmingham News,* September 21, 1948; *Montgomery Advertiser,* May 21, 1949, March 13, 1952; *Birmingham Post-Herald,* March 12, 1952.

5. On Heinz's background and career, see *Selma Times-Journal,* September 11, 1955, June 9, 1957, December 4, 1958; *Montgomery Advertiser,* August 8, 1951, October 1, 1957; *Birmingham News,* February 14, 1960; cf. Ralph Smeltzer's interview with Claude C. Brown, July 20, 1964, Smeltzer Papers.

6. *Selma Times-Journal,* April 26, September 28, October 11, 1953, May 5, 16, June 2, 1954; *Montgomery Advertiser,* October 1, 1957, September 20, 1963.

7. *Selma Times-Journal,* August 8, September 11, 1955, August 13, 22, 27, 1956, January 14, 1957, April 15, July 1, 14, 1958, August 10, November 23, 1959, January 14, 1964. A protest candidate who filed to run against Mayor Heinz in 1960 observed correctly that virtually all of the incumbent council members "were either appointed to their office by his predecessor or the political machine that is in control. There are new faces occasionally, but never any new factions" (ibid., February 21, 1960).

8. Ibid., March 23, 1960. In 1958 there were 164 black registered voters in Selma (ibid., April 1, 1958), and though no racial breakdown is available for 1960, it is highly unlikely that this figure had changed appreciably in the intervening two years; only 14 blacks were registered in the entire county from June 1954 to December 1960. Thus the electorate was about 97 percent white at this period.

9. Ibid., January 14, 1958. Burns served as City National president from 1949 to his retirement in 1959. He was succeeded by Recorder's Court Judge William B. Craig, a past president both of the Dallas County Bar Association and of the chamber of commerce (ibid., May 27, 1959). Rex Morthland, the president of the rival People's Bank, said that the organization's opponents considered municipal politics essentially to be controlled from City National's boardroom. Burns's predecessor as City National's president, H. Glenn Boyd, had been very close to Burns during Burns's time as mayor, and under both Burns and Heinz all city deposits were held at City National and the town's other banks were excluded from city business. The city and the chamber of commerce always steered new industries to City National, as well, according to Morthland (Dr. Rex. J. Morthland, interview by author, July 10, 1990). Harmon Carter, a drugstore owner and City National's largest stockholder, was widely regarded as the principal power behind the local machine; see Ralph Smeltzer's interview with Vernol R. "Bob" Jansen, July 16, 1964, Smeltzer Papers.

10. *Selma Times-Journal,* February 27, 1956, January 14, 1957, January 24, 1960; *Steele* v. *Louisville and Nashville Railroad Co.,* 245 Ala. 113, 323 U.S. 192; Harris Wofford, "A Preliminary Report on the Status of the Negro in Dallas County, Alabama" (Yale Law School paper, January, 1953; copy in possession of Dr. Alston Fitts III and kindly made available to me by him), 42–43. Employment statistics are from the U.S. Censuses.

11. Morthland, interview, July 10, 1990; *Selma Times-Journal,* August 13, 1958; agricultural statistics from the U.S. Censuses.

12. *Selma Times-Journal,* September 11, 1955, August 13, 1958, April 19, 1959, March 11, 1960, May 4, 6, 1962, February 5, 7, 8, 1965; *U.S.* v. *Atkins,* 210 F.Supp. 441, 323 F.2d 733, 10 Race Relations Law Reporter 209.

13. *Montgomery Advertiser,* August 8, 1951; Wofford, "Status of the Negro," 45 (quotation).

14. *Fikes* v. *State,* 263 Ala. 89 (fourth quotation); *Fikes* v. *Alabama,* 352 U.S. 191; *Fikes* v. *Long,* 388 F.Supp. 418; *Selma Times-Journal,* March 19, April 26, May 3 (first quotation), 4, 5, 6, 12, 18, 19, 24, June 2 (second quotation), 21, 22, 23, 24, 25, September 23, October 1, 2, 4, 5, 6, 7, 9, November 30, December 1, 3, 4, 6, 7, 8, 9 (third quotation), 1953, January 15, 28, 29, July 20, 25, August 8, 24, 25, October 10, November 15, December 10, 1954, May 12, June 23, 26, August 25, November 23, 1955, March 27, December 7, 1956, January 15, February 26, March 6, 10 (fifth quotations), May 28, 1957, December 1, 1959 (sixth quotations); *Birmingham World,* October 13, November 24, 27, December 22, 1953, January 19, 29, 1954, May 20, 1955; Robinson, *Bridge across Jordan,* 111, 173–75, 218; Chestnut and Cass, *Black in Selma,* 72–78, 401; Wofford, "Status of the Negro," 46; author interviews with Edwin Moss, July 11, 1991, Amelia P. Boynton Robinson, July 26, 1991, J. L. Chestnut, Jr., July 29, 1991, John D. Hunter, August 9, 1991, and Arthur Capell, August 22, 1991. Hunter, the president of the Selma branch of the NAACP during this period, knew Fikes's family in Marion through his insurance business and was convinced of Fikes's innocence. It was he who persuaded the NAACP to take up Fikes's cause—over the objection, he reports, of several members of the branch's board of directors (interview, August 9, 1991). The NAACP sent black Birmingham attorney Arthur Shores to defend Fikes in the Stinson trial in June, but when Judge Callen refused to grant a continuance to allow Shores to prepare the case, Shores withdrew and the case went to trial with the court-appointed white attorneys, Hobbs and Mallory (*Selma Times-Journal,* June 21, 1953). Judge Callen had also ap-pointed white attorneys for Fikes's trial in the Rockwell case, John H. Blanton and Tarver Rountree, Jr., but when Hall and Billingsley took over the defense, Blanton and Rountree asked to be relieved (*Selma Times-Journal,* September 23, 1953). As a direct result of the revision of the jury rolls ordered in the Fikes case, Dallas County had its first black grand juror of the twentieth century in January 1954: Roosevelt Dawson, a farmer (*Birmingham World,* January 29, 1954). But at least by the end of 1961, no other black had served on a grand or petit jury. On Hobbs and Mallory, see *Selma Times-Journal,* October 4, 1953, October 9, 18, 1957, July 1, 1958; on Billingsley, see *Birmingham World,* September 7, 1951; on the impact of the Fikes case on Heinz, see Smeltzer's interviews with Claude C. Brown, January 15, 1964, and Mrs. John Joyce, January 15, 1964, Smeltzer Papers.

15. On the origins of the White Citizens' Councils, see John Bartlow Martin, *The Deep South Says "Never"* (New York: Ballantine Books, 1957), and Neil R. McMillen, *The Citizens' Council: Organized Resistance to the Second Reconstruction, 1954–1964* (Urbana: University of Illinois Press, 1971).

16. McMillen, *Citizens' Council,* 16–28; *Selma Times-Journal,* November 21, 30, 1954, February 1, 1955.

17. *Brown* v. *Board of Education of Topeka,* 347 U.S. 483; *Selma Times-Journal,* May 24, July 11, September 2, 3, 12, 24, October 31, 1954; *Birmingham World,* June 15, September 17, 1954; *Montgomery Advertiser,* September 3, 7, 10, October 31, 1954.

18. *Selma Times-Journal,* October 3, 1954.

19. Ibid., November 28 (quotation), 30, 1954, June 22, September 18, October

16, 30, 1955. The quotation in the text is attributed in the newspaper to a Selma attorney who served as a spokesman for the White Citizens' Council; the reference is unquestionably to Keith. On the salience of white economic domination in Selma, see Smeltzer's interviews with Edwin L. D. Moss, February 1, March 20, 1964, Smeltzer Papers.

20. *Selma Times-Journal*, July 18, 28, August 11, 15, 21, 24, 25, 30, September 1, 1955; *Birmingham World*, July 29, August 2, 9, 16, 23, 1955; *Brown* v. *Board of Education of Topeka*, 349 U.S. 294 (quotation). The systems receiving petitions were Jefferson County, Birmingham, Bessemer, Etowah County, Gadsden, Attalla, Mobile, Montgomery, Macon County, Bullock County, Butler County, Russell County, Roanoke, Anniston, Tuscaloosa, and Selma. On the events that resulted from the Selma petition, see my "Selma's Smitherman Affair of 1955," *Alabama Review* 44 (April 1991): 112–31, from which much of the following discussion is drawn.

21. *Selma Times-Journal*, August 30, 1955. The petitioners were John D. Hunter (the president of Selma's NAACP branch), Seaborn Acoff, Otis and Sadie Mae Washington, Oliver W. Bryant, L. S. Smith, Lucinda Steele, A. D. Bush, Ethel Griffin, H. S. Jones, H. W. Shannon, Minnie Bell Harris, Joseph Holmes, Lottie B. Bridges, Elcania Page, Isaac Rhodes, Kemp S. Stallworth, J. H. Scott, Romie Small, Velberta Chestnut, Elizabeth D. Smith, Ada Jackson, Joe Vann, Sr., Daisy Phillips, Lela B. Suttles, Ernest L. Doyle, Richard Winston, Daniel Stevenson, and Rosa Purifoy.

22. Ibid., September 8, 1955. Those fired were J. H. Scott, Otis Washington, Lucinda Steele, Joseph Holmes, Elcania B. Page, Romie Small, Richard Winston, and Daniel Stevenson. Those removing their names were J. H. Scott, Sadie Mae Washington, Kemp S. Stallworth, Minnie Bell Harris, and Rosa Purifoy. The five claimed that they had not understood that the petition sought integration.

23. Ibid., September 8 (quotations), 9, 1955. Similar firings of petitioners also occurred in Bullock and Butler Counties.

24. Ibid., September 11 (quotations), 16, 1955. The committee consisted of Rex J. Morthland, Sam Earle Hobbs, Green Suttles, Morris Barton, Harry W. Gamble, and A. D. Wilkinson. When I interviewed him thirty-five years after these events, Morthland said he did not recall the petition or the firings (interview, July 10, 1990).

25. Selma City Directories, 1945, 1947, 1950, 1954, 1955.

26. *Selma Times-Journal*, September 21, 1956, March 31, June 5, October 11, 1957, October 9, 1959, October 21, 1960, October 24, 1961, March 3, 1964. After 1961, the *Times-Journal* ceased printing the names of all White Citizens' Council officers elected at the annual meeting. Probably McBride continued as a member of the executive committee for some additional years.

27. Ibid., September 8, 1955. At about the same time as the firing of the petitioners, the *Selma Times-Journal* had dismissed Tommie L. Johnson, the secretary of Selma's NAACP branch, from her position as the paper's black news correspondent. As a result, many blacks also canceled their subscriptions to the *Times-Journal* (*Birmingham World*, November 12, 1954, October 21, 1955).

28. *Birmingham World*, October 21, 1955; *Selma Times-Journal*, April 10, 1956; Selma City Directories, 1939, 1945, 1947, 1950, 1954, 1955.

29. This account is based largely upon the *Birmingham World*, October 21, 1955, supplemented by Robinson, *Bridge across Jordan*, 171–73, *Selma Times-Journal*, November 15, 1955, and *Montgomery Advertiser*, October 22, 23, 1955. Mrs. Robinson reports that the Birmingham milk company's representative was "a Mrs. Hancock" (p. 172), but no such person appears in the Selma City Directories of the

period. She also states that Mrs. Hancock telephoned Smitherman from police headquarters, with police listening to the conversation.

30. *Birmingham World,* October 21, 25, 1955; *Selma Times-Journal,* October 20, 21, 1955; *Montgomery Advertiser,* October 22, 23, 1955; Selma City Directories, 1954, 1955.

31. *Selma Times-Journal,* October 20, 27, 1955; Selma City Directories, 1950, 1954, 1955, 1957.

32. *Selma Times-Journal,* October 21, 1955; Selma City Directories, 1947, 1950, 1954, 1955, 1957, 1959. I deduce the Butlers' estrangement from the nature of their entries in the city directories. They arrived in Selma about 1949; Mrs. Butler's husband, Jack, left town in 1956; and Mrs. Butler herself moved away in 1958.

33. *Selma Times-Journal,* October 19, 20, 1955; *Birmingham World,* October 21, 1955; Selma City Directories, 1939, 1945, 1947, 1950, 1954, 1955.

34. *Selma Times-Journal,* October 20, 21, 1955; *Birmingham World,* October 25, 1955; *Montgomery Advertiser,* October 22, 23, 1955.

35. *Selma Times-Journal,* October 21, 1955.

36. Robert E. Hughes to George C. Wallace, November 7, 1955, Southern Regional Council Papers, Woodruff Library, Atlanta University, Atlanta.

37. *Selma Times-Journal,* October 27, 1955; *Birmingham World,* October 28, 1955; *Montgomery Advertiser,* October 26, 1955.

38. *Selma Times-Journal,* November 15, 1955.

39. Robinson, *Bridge across Jordan,* 173; Selma City Directory, 1957; Louis L. Anderson, interview by author, July 23, 1991. Mrs. Butler, now apparently separated from her husband, left Selma in 1958 (note 32 above), and Officer Bailey's widow, Mildred, after working for a time as a civilian employee at Craig Air Force Base, eventually left Selma as well.

40. *Birmingham World,* December 14 (quotation), 17, 1954.

41. *Selma Times-Journal,* October 18, 29, November 5, 1953, May 22, November 1, 17, December 29, 1955, January 6, February 7, 12, 15, September 21, October 24, 1956, August 28, October 1, 6, 11, 1957, April 24, May 13, June 18, 27, October 2, 1958, March 6, 10, April 26, May 27, August 18, September 9, October 9, November 13, December 1, 6, 1959, January 20, March 14, 17, April 15, October 16, 21 (quotation), November 2, 1960, April 9, 28, October 15, 24, December 6, 1961, April 10, September 30, October 11, 18, December 2, 1962, March 27, 28, April 2, May 19, August 28, 30, September 15, October 30, November 5, 10, 13, December 15, 1963, April 15, 28, October 2, 1964, April 18, 1965; Robinson, *Bridge across Jordan,* 85–86, 163–70, 176–82, 186–88, 213–14, 223–25, 229–31, 233–34; Longenecker, *Selma's Peacemaker,* 26–28, 35–36, 46–47, 52–53, 66, 146; Chestnut and Cass, *Black in Selma,* 81–85, 127, 156, 162–63, 219–24; author interviews with Rex J. Morthland, July 10, 1990, Roswell Falkenberry, July 18, 1991, Frederick D. Reese, August 9, 1991, Mrs. Marie Foster, August 13, 1991, and Arthur Capell, August 22, 1991. On Aubrey C. Allen's views, see Smeltzer's interview with him, January 4, 1964, Smeltzer Papers. On the blacklisting of blacks who attempted to register, see Smeltzer to Emergency Committee on Race Relations, December 10, 1963, ibid. On the power of the segregationists on the various banks' boards of directors, see Smeltzer's interview with Arthur Lewis, February 13, 1965, ibid. The activities of the Citizens' Council were, of course, ordinarily carried out in the shadows and, except for its occasional public rallies, went unreported in the press. This fact appears to have betrayed Fager into the quite erroneous belief that the council in

Selma was marked by "inactivity and irrelevance," and indeed, that it was primarily a device intended by "the whites of breeding and influence in the city" to draw the less "refined" white masses away from the more violent resistance of the Ku Klux Klan (*Selma, 1965,* 19–20). This singularly benign interpretation is of a piece with Fager's general portrait of the community (ibid., 13–21 et passim), one that strikes me as distinctly romantic.

42. *Selma Times-Journal,* May 18, 1956 (first quotation), December 7, 1954 (second quotations), April 8 (third quotations), 10 (fourth quotations), 1957. The notion that segregation was required by God was, however, widespread among Selma's whites; see, e.g., optometrist Sidney L. Wright's letter to David Vann, March 16, 1959, in David J. Vann Papers, Birmingham Public Library.

43. *Selma Times-Journal,* June 12, 1957 (first quotation), April 3, 1964 (second quotation), March 29, 1957 (third quotation), August 30, 1963 (fourth quotation), March 3, 1965 (fifth quotation); see also, e.g., December 7, 1954, January 17, 1958, April 21, 1963, March 19, 1965.

44. Ibid., October 2, 1958 (first and fourteenth quotations), December 1, 1959 (second and fifteenth quotations), October 16, 1960 (third quotations), October 6, 1957 (fourth quotation), October 21, 1960 (fifth quotations), October 11, 1962, October 24, 1961 (sixth and eleventh quotations), August 18 (eighth quotation), 28 (seventh quotations), 1963, November 1, 1962 (ninth quotations), October 9, 1959 (tenth quotations), January 17, 1958 (twelfth quotations), June 27, 1958 (thirteenth quotation), August 30, 1963 (sixteenth quotation), June 9, 1964.

45. Ibid., February 7, 15, March 9, 1956, June 18, 1958, April 9, 1961.

46. Ibid., February 1, 1955 (quotation), February 7, 1956.

47. Ibid., September 29 (second quotation), October 6 (first and third quotations), 1963. On the other hand, Selma's white moderates were themselves so conservative in comparison to the sentiments of similar elements in other southern cities that it was very easy for Hare and Reynolds to mistake them for supporters. Mrs. John Joyce, for instance, was one of the city's leading racial progressives, a strong supporter of the liberal Presbyterian minister John Newton and a sister of the prominent moderate attorneys Sam Earle and Truman Hobbs. And yet, when Ralph Smeltzer questioned her about the White Citizens' Council, she told him, according to his notes of the conversation, that without it "Negroes would take over city, run things by force, live in whites' houses, etc. Would be real, terrible, unbearable terror to live under control of uneducated, uncultured, radical Negroes. Must prevent this, gain time to educate and develop Negroes." Under the circumstances, she concluded, the Citizens' Council had served a purpose. It is clear that Mrs. Joyce, unlike the council's members themselves, envisioned a day when racial integration would become possible, but it is equally clear why the council's leadership might not very readily have become aware of that distinction (Smeltzer's interview with Mrs. John Joyce, January 15, 1964, Smeltzer Papers; see also his interviews with Sam Earle Hobbs, June 4, 1964, with Arthur Capell, July 24, 1964, and with Arthur Lewis, June 4, July 7, 8, 1964, ibid.). For the conclusions of the National Council of Churches investigators, see John M. Pratt, "Report of Fact-Finding Trip to Selma, Alabama," October 1, 1963, ibid.; see also Smeltzer's interview with John Newton, November 26, 1963, ibid.

48. *Selma Times-Journal,* February 23, 1965.

49. Ibid., November 15, December 1, 1957, February 16, March 16, August 27 (quotation), 1958, July 17, 1959, April 24, August 31, 1960; *Birmingham World,* Au-

gust 6, 30, 1958. The Alabama Klans formally thanked Governor Patterson for his support of them in this matter. (FBI Case Files, Freedom Rider Investigation, October 13, 1960, Birmingham Public Library.)

50. *Selma Times-Journal,* January 25, 26, 1959, February 1, 1960, September 15, 1958, May 25, 29, 31 (quotation), June 1, 29, August 26, 1959. On the fishing lake incidents, cf. Robinson, *Bridge across Jordan,* 144–45.

51. *Selma Times-Journal,* December 3, 1959, June 25, 1962; cf. Wofford, "Status of the Negro," 35.

52. *Selma Times-Journal,* July 12, 13, 1960.

53. Ibid., February 24 (quotation), 26, 27, March 1, November 11, 27, 1959, February 24, April 5, November 8, 1960, April 27, May 2, December 6, 7, 1961; *Birmingham World,* December 30, 1959, January 6, 1960, May 6, 1961; *Anderson* v. *State,* 40 Ala. App. 509, 270 Ala. 575; *Anderson* v. *Alabama,* 366 U.S. 208; Anderson, interview, July 23, 1991. Anderson reports that Hall and Billingsley had relied on Gray to prepare the case but that Gray had done nothing. At the outset of the trial, therefore, the defense was not ready. In December 1961, black attorney J. L. Chestnut, Jr., actually did raise the Anderson precedent during a murder trial. The *Times-Journal* reported that as a result the proceedings "gripped the courtroom with near-explosive tension" (*Selma Times-Journal,* December 7, 1961).

54. *Birmingham World,* July 4, 1962; *Selma Times-Journal,* May 2, 3, 4, 6, 1962; Smeltzer's interviews with Claude C. Brown, January 15, February 1, 1964, Smeltzer Papers.

55. *Selma Times-Journal,* March 13 (quotation), 14, 23, May 9, 1960, December 11, 1964. Clark's statement that he organized the posse in 1958 to deal with threatened labor-management conflict (*Jim Clark Story,* 22) is misleading. Clark did undertake to protect strikebreakers during a labor dispute at the Ziegler Meat Packing Company in the fall of 1958, and he may well have assembled a posse to assist him (see Walter C. Givhan to James G. Clark, October 10, 1958, in James A. Hare Papers, University of Alabama Library, Tuscaloosa), but the genesis of the posse as a continuing, formally organized body is clearly in the sit-in crisis of the spring of 1960. On William M. Agee, see *Selma Times-Journal,* September 15, 1965; on Jim Risher, see ibid., April 9, 1961. Arthur Lewis reported that Clark had accepted the Klan into the posse (Smeltzer's interview with Lewis, February 13, 1965, Smeltzer Papers). By 1961, klaverns throughout Alabama were getting surplus U.S. Army revolvers from the Selma ordnance depot for twenty-five dollars per gun (FBI Case Files, Freedom Rider Investigation, February 9, 17, 1961).

56. *Selma Times-Journal,* September 28, 30 (first and second quotations), October 1 (third and fourth quotations), 2, 1962; Capell, interview, August 22, 1991.

57. *Selma Times-Journal,* August 2, 4 (quotation), 1959. Both Episcopalians and a group apparently with ties to the Klan, the Soca Club (Sons of the Confederacy of Alabama), also explored the possibility of establishing a private school at this time (ibid., October 20, 1957, October 19, 1959, September 4, 1960).

58. *Acts of Alabama,* Session of 1890–91, pp. 150–51, see also *Acts of Alabama,* Session of 1844–45, pp. 120–21; *Birmingham World,* April 23, 1958; Fitts, *Selma,* 92–93, 118–19. It is unclear whether or not white Selmians' unhappiness at the county board's creation of a black public school in October 1890 contributed to the establishment of an independent school district for the city in December 1890, but it is by no means inconceivable. Before the creation of Clark School in 1890, the school board had had a rather ill-defined and quite uneasy connection with Burrell Academy, a school for blacks established by the American Missionary Asso-

ciation in 1869 and operated by the association until the facility burned down in 1900 (Fitts, *Selma,* 72–73).

59. *Selma Times-Journal,* September 19, 22, December 3, 1954, August 24, 1956, October 28, 1958, December 6, 1960, September 20, 1964; *Birmingham World,* March 27, 1951, April 10, 1956, February 9, 13, 1957, April 23, 1958; *Selma Sentinel,* August 21, 1965; Wofford, "Status of the Negro," 25–34; Robinson, *Bridge across Jordan,* 51, 136–38, 151–55; Fitts, *Selma,* 91–93, 118–21, 126–27. Selma University, however, continued to offer classes generally unequal to its new junior college aspirations; see "Facts About Selma University," April 1965, in Smeltzer Papers.

60. Wofford ("Status of the Negro," 7–8) encountered this gap between black reality and white awareness of it on his visit to the county in 1952. He found that most whites still thought their county was three-fourths black when in fact by that time it was less than two-thirds black; few whites seemed to realize the extent of the black exodus from the area. On the changes in the economic status of blacks discussed here, see also ibid., 35–44.

61. *Selma Times-Journal,* January 12, 1958, August 26, 1962, July 28, 1963, December 10, 1964; *Selma Sentinel,* August 21, 1965; Fitts, *Selma,* 103, 118, 120.

62. *Selma Times-Journal,* February 18, 1955; *Birmingham World,* March 27, 1951; Fitts, *Selma,* 125–26; Chestnut and Cass, *Black in Selma,* 40–45.

63. On Chestnut, see *Birmingham World,* June 11, 1958, April 25, June 13, 1959; Chestnut and Cass, *Black in Selma,* 3–143.

64. On Craig Air Force Base, see Carl C. Morgan, Jr., "Craig Air Force Base: Its Effect on Selma, 1940–1977," *Alabama Review* 42 (April 1989): 83–96; Wofford, "Status of the Negro," 68–73; Longenecker, *Selma's Peacemaker,* 47–50, 60–65, 96–98. Morgan, the president of Selma's city council for more than thirty years after 1964, was a resident of the city throughout Craig's existence; the base was abolished in 1977. It is noteworthy that in his account of Craig's influence upon Selma, Morgan makes no mention at all of race relations. Wofford is an example of Selma's influence on the young men from elsewhere who were sent to Craig. Stationed there during 1944 and 1945, Wofford developed from his experiences in Dallas County a lifelong, passionate concern for the civil rights of blacks. He returned to Selma in 1952 to prepare the Yale Law School paper about the area's race relations cited here. His involvement with the civil rights movement would lead him into political activity, and eventually to his election to the U.S. Senate from Pennsylvania.

65. *Selma Times-Journal,* November 6, 8, 9, 1955, April 27, 1958.

66. Ibid., October 27, 1955, February 3, May 5, July 16, 1958, October 12, 1964.

67. Ibid., March 16, 17, April 1, 27 (second quotation), May 4, 5, 7, 18 (first and third quotations), June 1 (fourth quotation), 4, 1958. Fager (*Selma, 1965,* 17) and Longenecker (*Selma's Peacemaker,* 18) both erroneously place Baker's appearance at the Klan rally during the runoff campaign and imply that it was a significant factor in Clark's victory. My own investigation of the sources convinces me otherwise.

68. *Selma Times-Journal,* May 19, 1953 (first quotation), May 18, 22 (third quotation), 23 (fourth quotation), 25, 26 (second set of quotations), 27, June 1 (fifth quotations), 1958, January 18, 1959, August 21, 1960.

69. Ibid., June 4, 1958 (quotation); Ralph Smeltzer's interview with Claude C. Brown, January 15, 1964, Smeltzer Papers.

70. *Selma Times-Journal,* March 15, 1962.

71. Ibid., July 25, August 8, 24, 25, 1954, March 10, April 8, 10, September 9, 1957, January 27, December 7, 1958, February 6, 12, March 13, 17, November 9,

December 1, 1959, January 25, April 15, May 20, 22, 1960, January 22, December 18, 1962, February 4, September 9, 20, 22, 29, October 6, November 12, December 17, 1963, July 10, September 6, December 22, 1964, February 3, 4, 9, March 3, 16, April 13, 1965, May 20, 1969; *Montgomery Advertiser,* August 18, 1938; (Montgomery) *Alabama Journal,* April 14, 1953, August 24, 1954, October 19, 1965; *Alabama Official and Statistical Register* for 1939, p. 284; Chestnut and Cass, *Black in Selma,* 172–86; Longenecker, *Selma's Peacemaker,* 86–88.

72. *Selma Times-Journal,* August 8, 24, 25, 1954, August 28, 1957, March 23, August 20, 1958, March 17, 1959, March 13, May 20, September 9, 1960, June 14, 1961 (quotation), September 7, December 18, 1962, September 19, 20, November 7, December 15, 1963, July 6, September 3, 24, December 9, 10, 13, 22, 1964. J. L. Chestnut, who knew both Hare and McLeod, makes an interesting distinction between their respective conceptions of segregation. He says that Hare thought of segregation as a sort of vertical division between the races; Hare was delighted when a black person achieved economic or intellectual advancement, so long as the person's advancement occurred exclusively within the context of the black community. McLeod, on the other hand, thought of segregation as a horizontal line dividing a dominant white race from a subordinate black one; McLeod therefore found any advancement in the status of any individual black person threatening. Chestnut reports also that McLeod regularly wore a pistol in court (Chestnut, interview, July 29, 1991).

73. *Selma Times-Journal,* August 7, 1963 (first quotations), January 12, February 28 (second quotation), December 22, 1964; cf. Ralph Smeltzer's interview with Kathryn Tucker Windham, July 14, 1964, Smeltzer Papers.

74. George E. Sims, *The Little Man's Big Friend: James E. Folsom in Alabama Politics, 1946–1958* (University: University of Alabama Press, 1985), 89; see also 66, 134.

75. *Selma Times-Journal,* January 18 (first quotation), 19, 25, 26, 27, 28, 29 (second quotations), February 1, 6, 10, 19, May 10, 1959, April 20, 1960, August 7, 1962. Deputy Billy Mac Bobo subsequently joined the Selma police force. Deputy Martin Williamson became the manager of the Dallas County public fishing lake and was thus a figure in the series of incidents directed against black use of the lake, discussed earlier in this chapter.

76. *Birmingham News,* January 16, 1971, September 11, 1975, July 8, December 3, 1978; *Montgomery Advertiser,* July 18, 1978, January 3, 1979, September 28, 1980; Athens *News-Courier,* December 27, 1978; see also Ralph Smeltzer's interview with Lewis, December 9, 1964, Smeltzer Papers.

77. *Selma Times-Journal,* December 10, 1964.

78. Ibid., January 7, February 2, 1964; *Montgomery Advertiser,* February 22, 1976; Selma City Directories, 1939, 1942, 1950, 1952, 1954, 1955; *Who's Who in Alabama* for 1972–73, p. 381. Mr. Smitherman was unable to find the time to be interviewed for this work.

79. *Selma Times-Journal,* January 31, 1960; Selma City Directories, 1954, 1955, 1957, 1959, 1960. On Smitherman's childhood and early career, see *Montgomery Advertiser,* September 13, 2000.

80. *Selma Times-Journal,* March 23, 1960.

81. Ibid., January 9, May 14, October 22, December 30, 1956, February 11, August 12, September 30, November 25, 1957, March 10, April 2, 10, 11, May 6, June 9, September 2, 1958.

82. Ibid., February 7, 27, June 12, July 10, 1961, February 27, June 11, July 24,

August 13, September 10, 1962, May 13, 27 (quotation), June 24, 28, July 8, 1963. Fortunately for Smitherman, the bills to pay for the sewer assessments were not sent out until after the mayoral election in the spring of 1964. Furious residents threatened legal action once they received the notices (ibid., June 9, 1964).

83. Ibid., January 31, 1960; Morthland, interview, July 10, 1990; "History of the People's Bank and Trust Company," a folder available at the bank. On the centrality of City National to the machine, see Smeltzer's interview with Arthur Lewis, October 30, 1964, Smeltzer Papers.

84. *Selma Times-Journal,* October 28, 1962. Nor were the young businessmen wrong that the chamber of commerce was unenthusiastic about industries that might upset the status quo; see Smeltzer's interviews with M. L. "Jack" Miles, January 16, 1964, John Newton, January 15, 1964, and T. Frank Mathews, November 27, 1963, Smeltzer Papers; see also his interview with Vernol R. "Bob" Jansen, July 16, 1964, ibid. Mayor Heinz brought strong personal pressure on the young businessmen not to create the Committee of One Hundred Plus; see Smeltzer's interview with Arthur Lewis, February 13, 1965, ibid.

85. *Selma Times-Journal,* November 25 (quotation), December 2, 6, 1962.

86. Ibid., September 11, 1955, January 9, 1961, December 15, 1963 (quotation), January 5, 7, February 2, 1964.

87. Ibid., February 23, 26 (first quotation), 27 (second quotation), March 4, 5, 6 (third and fourth quotations), 8, 10, 11, 12, 15, 16 (fifth quotations), 1964.

88. Ibid., March 13, 1964. It appears that the machine had sought to win Smitherman's allegiance immediately after his surprise election to the city council in March 1960. He had been placed on the board of the chamber of commerce in December 1960 and on the board of the White Citizens' Council in October 1961 (ibid., December 13, 1960, October 24, 1961). But the ploy had, of course, been unsuccessful.

89. Ibid., February 26, March 1, 11, 12, 13, 18, 19, 1964; Smeltzer's interviews with Edwin L. D. Moss, March 20, 1964, Mrs. Amelia P. Boynton, March 21, 1964, Worth Long, March 25, 1964, Arthur Lewis, September 24, 1964, Claude C. Brown, March 23, 1964, and Chris B. Heinz, May 16, 1964, and Smeltzer's notes of meeting of Steering Committee of Dallas County Voters League, January 16, 1964, all in Smeltzer Papers. Claude Brown told Smeltzer that Brown himself and perhaps fifteen other blacks did vote for Heinz, but it seems likely that Brown was exaggerating this number to convince himself that he was not so alone as in fact he was. Edwin Moss was not aware of a single black who voted for Heinz. In the black "mock election" for mayor, the victor was Louis L. Anderson, with 2,506 votes (*Selma Times-Journal,* March 19, 1964; Smeltzer's interview with Mrs. Boynton, March 21, 1964, Smeltzer Papers).

The number of black voters in Selma at this time is not entirely clear. Until 1958, officials had published biennially a complete list of registered voters, with the race of each voter specified. In 1958 there were 164 black voters in Selma and 180 in the county as a whole (*Selma Times-Journal,* April 1, 1958), but thereafter the practice of designating the race of voters was discontinued (ibid., March 9, 24, 1960). However, federal court records tell us the number of each race registered at every session of the board of registrars from June 1961 through February 1965 (*U.S.* v. *Clark,* 249 F.Supp. 720, 731–33). And the board of registrars did not function from November 1959 to March 1960, and again from December 1960 to June 1961 (*Selma Times-Journal,* November 18, 19, 1959, March 11, November 21, 1960, June 14, 1961, May 2, 1962). Judge Daniel Thomas states that as of May 2, 1962, there were 8,597 white and 242 black voters in the county (*U.S.* v. *Atkins,* 210 F.Supp. 441). Therefore, if there were no deletions in the intervening period, then at the time of the municipal election in March 1964 the county rolls carried the names of 315 blacks. It is impossible to tell how many of these voters resided in Selma. However, Frederick D. Reese, who knew the black voting situation well, said that the rolls carried the names of a number of blacks who had in fact moved away— something quite likely, given the size of the black emigration from the county. Reese put the actual number of black voters in Selma at 205 and in the county at 250 (*Selma Times-Journal,* March 19, 1964). But Reese may well have been underestimating the black vote a bit, because he wished to claim that all three of the black candidates for the city council had received some white support. Edwin Moss, who was as well informed about the matter as was Reese, put the number of black voters in the city at "nearer 260" (Smeltzer's interview with Moss, March 20, 1964, Smeltzer Papers). In the election, Reese received 260 votes, Gildersleeve 234, and Doyle 210 (*Selma Times-Journal,* March 18, 1964). I conclude, therefore, that an estimate of about 250 black voters in Selma in 1964 is probably accurate.

90. *Selma Times-Journal,* January 14, March 18, 22, October 2, 1964, February 17, 23, March 19, April 9, 11, 16, 1965.

91. Ibid., November 5, 10, 1963, March 20, 1964 (quotation).

92. On Adams, see *Birmingham World,* August 27, 1946, September 21, 1948, June 30, 1956; Chestnut and Cass, *Black in Selma,* 51–54. On Boynton, see *Birmingham World,* July 20, November 12, 1954, July 4, 1962, September 7, 1963; Robinson, *Bridge across Jordan,* 50–55, 109–14 et passim.

93. Robinson, *Bridge across Jordan,* 136–38; *Birmingham World,* August 27, 1946, May 26, 1953, July 4, 1962; *Selma Times-Journal,* April 10, 11, 1956, April 1, 1958; *Alabama Official and Statistical Register* for 1907, pp. 230–31, and for 1911, pp. 262– 63. Fairclough's statement that the Voters League was founded in 1963, at the urging of the Student Non-violent Coordinating Committee (*To Redeem the Soul of America,* 210), is erroneous. The same error is to be found in the opinion in *U.S.* v. *Clark,* 249 F.Supp. 720.

94. Alabama Constitution of 1901, Article VIII, Section 181; *Giles* v. *Harris,* 189 U.S. 475, 478–79; *Giles* v. *Teasley,* 193 U.S. 146, 147–49; *Montgomery Advertiser,* December 5, 1940.

95. Robert J. Norrell, *Reaping the Whirlwind: The Civil Rights Movement in Tuskegee* (New York: Knopf, 1985), 39–40, 44–46.

96. The Alabama Democratic Executive Committee formally opened the party's primaries to blacks on January 12, 1946 (*Birmingham World,* January 11, 18, 1946), in obedience to the U.S. Supreme Court's decision in *Smith* v. *Allwright* in April 1944 (321 U.S. 649).

97. A particularly clear example of the sort of harassment to which advocates of black voter registration were subject occurred in Wilcox County in the spring of 1963. When the *Selma Times-Journal* reported that black insurance agent Lonnie Brown was urging black residents there to seek to register, the county's white landowners banded together to bar him from coming onto their land to collect insurance premiums from their tenants. As a result, Brown was driven out of business and forced to move out of the county (*U.S.* v. *Bruce,* 353 F.2d 474; cf. *Selma Times-Journal,* May 15, 1963, July 10, 1964, and Frank Holloway, field reports, February 15 and [March 19,] 1963, in Student Non-violent Coordinating Committee Papers, microfilm edition, University of Michigan Library, Ann Arbor [hereinafter cited as SNCC Papers]). Cf. also Robinson, *Bridge across Jordan,* 186–88 (though the harass-

ment in this instance resulted from the Montgomery sit-in rather than from an attempt to register).

98. *Boswell* v. *Bethea,* 242 Ala. 292; *Madison* v. *Nunnelee,* 246 Ala. 325; *Hawkins* v. *Vines,* 249 Ala. 165.

99. *Alabama Official and Statistical Register* for 1947, pp. 535–39; *Acts of Alabama,* Regular Session of 1945, pp. 551–52; *Birmingham World,* January 11, March 8, April 23, October 15, November 8, December 3, 1946, June 4, August 3, 13, October 12, 15, 29, November 23, December 10, 21, 24, 1948, January 11, April 1, 1949; *Davis* v. *Schnell,* 81 F.Supp. 872, 336 U.S. 933; Case File and Trial Transcript, *Davis* v. *Schnell,* in Southeastern Regional Federal Records Center, East Point, Georgia (hereinafter cited as FRC East Point). The amendment was adopted 89,163 to 76,843; it carried forty-one counties and lost in twenty-six. The Jefferson County Board of Registrars used the amendment as authority to examine applicants on the provisions of the United Nations Charter, the duties of ambassadors, the identity of the five Great Powers, the process by which a bill becomes a law, and the origins of the United States, among other things (*Birmingham World,* December 3, 1946). The Mobile County Board of Registrars, with only a handful of exceptions, asked only blacks to prove an understanding of the Constitution, even though the amendment required such knowledge of all applicants. Registrars testified that most whites could be presumed to possess it (Trial Transcript, *Davis* v. *Schnell*). Wofford observes ("Status of the Negro," 52), "The mystery is why the Amendment was proposed in the first place," as it "only formalized what was already being done, and *what is generally still being done.*" But while it is true that the boards indulged in oral questioning both before and after the Boswell Amendment, nevertheless the amendment's creation of a standard of understanding rather than literacy would have permitted the boards more readily to justify the questioning to the courts. On oral questioning under the 1951 amendment that succeeded Boswell, see *U.S.* v. *Atkins,* 323 F.2d 733.

100. *Mitchell* v. *Wright,* 69 F.Supp. 698; *Williams* v. *Wright,* 249 Ala. 9; *Selma Times-Journal,* February 16, March 2, 1965; Robinson, *Bridge across Jordan,* 178–79. The boards also limited registration by various other administrative and procedural devices. State law confined the boards' meetings to two a month, unless they requested special sessions. Boards restricted the number of applicants whom they would see at any one time, sometimes to a single person, and began their sessions late, took long lunch breaks, and recessed early. Some boards had no regular meeting room, so that applicants had to search the courthouse for the place to apply. And if the number of black applicants became too great, the board members could simply resign, leaving the county with no registration machinery at all until a new board could be appointed—an action that state officials could be quite slow to take (see Norrell, *Reaping the Whirlwind,* 65–66, 69–73, 83–84, 89–90, 116–27).

101. *Alabama Official and Statistical Register* for 1951, pp. 607, 615–17, and for 1965, pp. 707–9; *Montgomery Examiner,* December 13, 20, 1951; *Birmingham World,* April 3, September 21, December 18, 28, 1951, January 29, March 25, May 6, August 26, September 12, 1952. The amendment was adopted 60,357 to 59,988. It carried thirty-four counties, including Dallas and the rest of the Black Belt counties, but it lost in thirty-three counties, including both Jefferson and Montgomery.

At the same time that the legislature was strengthening the disfranchising provisions directed against blacks, it was significantly weakening the one disfranchising provision that operated primarily against whites—that is, against persons who were already registered voters—the poll tax. In the same election that voters narrowly approved the new voter qualification amendment, in December 1951, they overwhelmingly approved an amendment to exempt all past or future veterans from the poll tax; this exemption was extended in 1954 to all deaf and blind persons. And in December 1953 they limited the accumulation of unpaid poll taxes to two years, or a total of three dollars. It is probably not too much to say that, from 1954, the poll tax ceased to be a significant barrier to voting. It limped on, however, until March 1966, when a three-judge federal court in Montgomery declared it unconstitutional (*U.S.* v. *Alabama*, 252 F.Supp. 95).

102. *Acts of Alabama*, Regular Session of 1951, vol. 1, pp. 760–61.

103. The entire text of the questionnaire is printed as an appendix to *U.S.* v. *Penton*, 212 F.Supp. 193, 205–8.

104. *U.S.* v. *Atkins*, 323 F.2d 733; *Selma Times-Journal*, May 2, 3, 4, 6, 1962.

105. *U.S.* v. *Atkins*, 210 F.Supp. 441; *Selma Times-Journal*, November 18, 19, 1959, March 11, November 21, 1960, June 14, 1961, May 2, 1962. The text implies, and I believe correctly, a connection between the developing civil rights movement and the variation in the numbers of blacks registered. But I should note that an equally persuasive explanation is political. The application of the new suffrage amendment was initially handled by the board of registrars appointed by state authorities headed by Governor Gordon Persons, governor from 1951 through 1954. This board was succeeded in November 1955 by a board appointed by the second administration of Governor James E. Folsom, which extended from 1955 through 1958. When the administration of Governor John Patterson took office in 1959, it initially failed to constitute a board of registrars in Dallas, and it did not find three people who would serve until June 1961, though a two-member board sat from March through November 1960. Thus the variance in black registration is almost entirely a product of the practices of the board appointed under Folsom.

Boards of registrars are appointed by the governor, who names the chairman, and the state auditor and the commissioner of agriculture and industries, each of whom names an associate member. The board serves for four years, from the October 1 following the governor's inauguration to the September 30 after the next governor takes office.

106. Chestnut and Cass, *Black in Selma*, 51–54.

107. Robinson, *Bridge across Jordan*, 50, 76, 163–70, 181 et passim; Amelia P. Boynton Robinson, interview, July 26, 1991.

108. Chestnut, interview, July 29, 1991. The members of the league in 1936, in addition to Adams and Boynton, were Henry Boyd, Pleasant L. Lindsey, Dommie Gaines, and A. G. Carroll (Robinson, *Bridge across Jordan*, 137).

109. Robinson, *Bridge across Jordan*, 112; *Selma Times-Journal*, December 9, 10, 1958; Fitts, *Selma*, 118. The *Times-Journal* erroneously refers to Minnie Anderson as Jennie Anderson.

110. *Selma Times-Journal*, March 29 (third quotation), April 10 (second quotation), September 9 (first quotation), 1957, December 10, 1958.

111. Ibid., October 21, December 3, 4, 7, 1958, February 6, 12, March 10, 13, 17, August 2, September 9, October 30, November 9, 15, 18, 19, 1959, January 25, May 10, 11, 20, 22, September 9, 1960, January 17, April 13, 14, May 12, 18, 19, 25, June 13, 14, 1961, February 6, 20, September 7, October 18, December 18, 1962, September 29, December 1, 1963; *Kennedy* v. *Bruce*, 298 F.2d 860 (quotation); *U.S.* v. *Majors*, 7 Race Relations Law Reporter 463; *Alabama ex rel. Gallion* v. *Rogers*, *Dinkins* v. *Attorney General*, 187 F.Supp. 848, 285 F.2d 430. The idea to have the county grand jury impound the registration records was Judge George C. Wallace's.

He took that action in Barbour County in October 1958, and Judge Hare merely followed his precedent in Dallas and Wilcox in December. Wallace was subjected to a federal contempt proceeding for his order (*In re Wallace*, 170 F.Supp. 63). While the efforts to see the Dallas and Wilcox records were slowly wending their way through the courts, similar petitions were being heard against many other Black Belt counties, including Macon, Bullock, Barbour, Sumter, Perry, and Marengo.

112. *Selma Times-Journal*, May 2, 3, 4, 6, 1962, October 4, 6, 1963; *U.S.* v. *Atkins*, 210 F.Supp. 441 (quotations), 323 F.2d 733; Trial Transcript, *U.S.* v. *Atkins*, esp. 9–11, 38, 75–80.

113. *Selma Times-Journal*, June 12, 1955, August 25, 1971. For a sketch of Judge Thomas's father, see *Alabama Official and Statistical Register* for 1927, p. 29.

114. *Selma Times-Journal*, October 1, 1959, August 3, December 14, 1960, March 14, April 26, June 27, 1961, August 9, 28, October 16, 24, 1962, January 9, February 21, May 10, September 29, December 1, 17, 18, 1963, March 8, 31, April 14, 23, 24, 26, July 10, September 4, December 18, 30, 1964, February 5, March 16, 1965; *Birmingham World*, April 16, November 29, 1958, March 4, October 10, 1959, August 13, 1960, January 28, March 22, October 18, 1961; *Sawyer* v. *City of Mobile*, 208 F.Supp. 548 (quotation); *Davis* v. *Board of School Commissioners*, 219 F.Supp. 542; *U.S.* v. *Mayton*, 335 F.2d 153; *U.S.* v. *Logue*, 344 F.2d 290. Cf. *Birmingham World*, March 23, July 3, 1951, January 8, October 21, 1952, on Thomas's dismissal, almost as soon as he assumed the bench, of a suit by blacks seeking to be able to take Mobile city civil service examinations; Thomas held that the plaintiffs had failed to exhaust all their administrative remedies. On Thomas's reputation, see Smeltzer's interview with Vernol R. "Bob" Jansen, July 16, 1964, Smeltzer Papers; on O. S. Burke, see Smeltzer's interview with Jansen, February 10, 1965, ibid.

115. *Selma Times-Journal*, January 25, February 8, 1965.

116. *Davis* v. *Board of School Commissioners*, 219 F.Supp. 542. This ruling had itself come only after strong prompting by the Fifth Circuit, and it was reversed just two weeks after it was made (*Davis* v. *Board of School Commissioners*, 318 F.2d 63, 322 F.2d 356).

117. On Thomas's relationships with Dallas County leaders, see James Hare to Daniel H. Thomas, January 6, 1958, August 16, 1962, Daniel H. Thomas to James Hare, July 26, 1962, all in Hare Papers; cf. Smeltzer's interviews with Vernol R. "Bob" Jansen, July 16, 18, August 27, September 24, 30, November 16, 1964, March 13, April 6, 1965, Edgar Stewart, July 17, 21, 25, 1964, B. Frank Wilson, September 25, October 2, 1964, Arthur Lewis, January 21, 1965, and Arthur Capell, October 3, 1964, all in Smeltzer Papers.

118. E.g., *U.S.* v. *McLeod*, 229 F.Supp. 383, *U.S.* v. *Dallas County*, 229 F.Supp. 1014. It is surely no accident that Judge Thomas's rulings in these cases, exonerating Sheriff Clark and Solicitor McLeod of any impropriety in their actions during the 1963 demonstrations, were issued just two days following Joe Smitherman's defeat of Chris Heinz in the 1964 Selma mayoral election. With this evidence of the Selma electorate's repudiation of the hard-line past, Thomas immediately moved, I think, to eliminate a source of segregationist recrimination so that the community's new moderate leadership could, as he saw it, seek rapprochement unhindered by grievances. Thomas's rulings in both of these cases were reversed by the Fifth Circuit (385 F.2d 734), but the reversal did not come until October 1967.

119. *U.S.* v. *Clark*, 249 F.Supp. 720, 731–33. The table of registrations printed in the *Clark* appendix differs a bit from the figures given in Judge Thomas's *Atkins* opinion. The *Clark* table shows that between June 1961 and May 1962 the board

registered 70 blacks and rejected 45 while registering 425 whites and rejecting 43. Despite the board's egregiously discriminatory conduct in these years, praise of it by such figures as Judge Thomas seems to have convinced even Selma's most moderate whites of the board's impartiality; see, e.g., Smeltzer's interviews with Arthur Lewis, June 4, September 16, October 9, November 25, 1964, January 27, 1965, and Arthur Capell, November 29, 1964, Smeltzer Papers.

120. *Selma Times-Journal,* March 4, 5, 1964; Fairclough, *To Redeem the Soul of America,* 179–80.

121. *Selma Times-Journal,* February 4, 1965.

122. Amelia P. Boynton Robinson, interview, July 26, 1991; Robinson, *Bridge across Jordan,* 111–12, 165–67, 189; *Birmingham World,* July 20, 1954, July 4, 1962; Trial Transcript, *U.S.* v. *Dallas County,* 86–87, and Affidavits of Bernard Lafayette and James Gildersleeve in Case File, all in FRC East Point; Reginald J. Robinson, field report, May 25, 1962, Frank Holloway, field report, February 8–15, 1963, James Forman to James Dombrowski, September 20, 1962, Dombrowski to Forman, September 25, 1962, James Forman to Leslie A. Dunbar, April 26, 1963, Wiley A. Branton to Forman, February 5, 1963, March 22, 1963, May 10, 1963, Julian Bond to Branton, May 1, 1963, Survey of Current Field Work, Spring, 1963, SNCC Press Release, April 24, 1963, all in SNCC Papers. The intense harassment of S. W. Boynton, though almost certainly arranged by the White Citizens' Council, nevertheless had succeeded in damaging his reputation even among moderate whites; see, e.g., Smeltzer's interview with Mrs. John Joyce, November 26, 1963, Smeltzer Papers.

123. Author interviews with Ernest L. Doyle, July 23, 1991, James E. Gildersleeve, July 22, 1991, Amelia P. Boynton Robinson, July 26, 1991, John D. Hunter, August 9, 1991, J. L. Chestnut, Jr., July 29, 1991, and Frederick D. Reese, August 9, 1991. On the impact upon black leaders of the emerging division between the young white businessmen and the older members of the political establishment, see Smeltzer's interview with Edwin L. D. Moss, February 1, 1964, Smeltzer Papers, and Frank R. Parker, field report on Selma, Alabama, June 27–July 4, 1963, SNCC Papers.

124. Mrs. Marie Foster, interview, August 13, 1991; Affidavit of Bernard Lafayette, in Case File, *U.S.* v. *Dallas County,* in FRC East Point; Frank Holloway, field report, February 8–15, 1963, Survey of Current Field Work, Spring 1963, both in SNCC Papers; Chestnut and Cass, *Black in Selma,* 132–38.

125. *U.S.* v. *Clark,* 249 F.Supp. 720, 732–33.

126. Anderson, interview, July 23, 1991; *Selma Times-Journal,* May 15, 1963 (quotation).

127. *Selma Times-Journal,* May 21, June 20, 21, 25, 27, 30, July 2, 12, 25, August 2 (quotation), September 24, 1963; *Birmingham World,* June 26, September 7, 1963; *U.S.* v. *McLeod* and *U.S.* v. *Dallas County,* 229 F.Supp. 383, 1014, 385 F.2d 734; Case Files and Trial Transcripts, *U.S.* v. *McLeod, U.S.* v. *Dallas County,* in FRC East Point. Alexander Brown, who was just sixteen, had only gotten his driver's license four months earlier. He was an illegitimate child and used his mother's name, but officials had insisted that the driver's license had to be issued under his father's name because that was the name shown on his birth certificate. Both Lafayette and Brown were acquitted when they came to trial.

128. *Selma Times-Journal,* August 7, 11, 30, September 1, 16, 22, 23, 1963; Frank R. Parker, field report, Selma, Alabama, June 27–July 4, 1963, Amelia P. Boynton to James Forman, September 4, 10, 1963, SNCC Papers; Trial Transcript, *U.S.* v. *McLeod,* 764, in FRC East Point; Smeltzer's interviews with Morris Barton, June 2, 1964, Charles Hohenberg, July 14, 1964, Julien H. Lilienthal, July 22, 1964, Edwin

L. D. Moss, February 1, March 20, July 7, 1964, Maurice Ouellet, November 27, 1963, Edgar Stewart, July 17, 1964, and Edwin L. D. Moss to Dallas County Improvement Association, July 19, 1963, Dallas County Improvement Association to Police Chief Ed Mullen, August 8, 1963, Dallas County Improvement Association to Selma Retail Merchants Association, August 29, 1963 (quotation), and enclosed circular letter to Selma retail businesses, Dallas County Improvement Association to *Selma Times-Journal*, August 29, 1963, Dallas County Improvement Association to Swift Drug Store, August 30, 1963, Dallas County Improvement Association to Alabama Power Co., Coca-Cola Bottling Co., beer distributors, undated, all in Smeltzer Papers; Longenecker, *Selma's Peacemaker*, 85–86. Hohenberg was so disconcerted by the failure of his initiative that he evidently completely refused to assist the moderates' efforts for several months thereafter. Claude C. Brown told Ralph Smeltzer that despite the lack of a formal response from the Retail Merchants Association, the efforts of Morris Barton, James Gaston, and their associates had been sufficiently encouraging to cause him and C. C. Hunter to oppose beginning demonstrations. But Edwin Moss, Brown said, had prevailed on the rest of the DCIA to endorse the demonstrations, by a vote of eleven to five (Smeltzer's interviews with Brown, January 15, February 1, 1964, Smeltzer Papers). However, the president of the Merchants Association, Julien H. Lilienthal, told Smeltzer that the association felt that the DCIA's leadership, though more conservative than that of SNCC, had in fact sold out to SNCC, because the DCIA's demands and those made by SNCC—by which he undoubtedly meant those of Wilson Brown and his two associates—were identical. Lilienthal acknowledged to Smeltzer that the Merchants Association felt that, for fear of a white boycott of the various mercantile establishments, it could take no action without the White Citizens' Council's approval (Smeltzer's interview with Lilienthal, July 22, 1964, ibid.; see also Smeltzer's interviews with B. Frank Wilson, August 23, September 10, 1964, ibid.). Frederick Reese told Smeltzer that Claude Brown's opposition to the demonstrations had badly damaged his standing in the black community. On the relationship of Brown, Reese, and Moss, see Smeltzer's interviews with Reese, June 4, July 16, 18, 1964, and Smeltzer to Arthur Lewis, October 9, 1964, ibid.

Edwin Moss denied to me that there were any differences between the DCIA and the Voters League; he emphasized that they shared the same goals. And as to the action of the SNCC workers in anticipating, and thus undercutting, the DCIA's petition, he said that the three SNCC workers were merely young men trying to become known in the community (interview, July 11, 1991). But both news accounts at the time and the DCIA's own statements are explicit about the association's desire to forestall demonstrations, and the exacerbation of racial tensions that would very likely result. I believe, therefore, that my account of these events is consistent with the contemporary evidence.

The city council took no action on Wilson Brown's September 13 application for a parade permit until its meeting of September 23, when on motion of Councilman Joe Smitherman, the application was formally denied. Black attorney J. L. Chestnut, Jr., had pleaded with a black mass meeting not to begin the demonstrations until the council had had time to consider the permit application, but SNCC and Voters League leaders had united to oppose any delay (Police notes of mass meeting, September 13, 1963, in Case File, *U.S. v. Dallas County*, in FRC East Point). On September 22 the entire white business and professional leadership of the city had united to print a full-page advertisement in the *Selma Times-Journal* repudiating the demonstrations and calling on "our more intelligent and responsible Negro leadership" to "take immediate steps to put down agitation among their people," lest "a two-edged sword [be] unsheathed to shear apart the white and Negro races." See also SNCC's point-by-point reply to this advertisement, in Smeltzer Papers; cf. Smeltzer's interview with Rex Morthland, July 9, 1964, ibid.

129. *Birmingham World,* October 9, 1963.

130. *Selma Times-Journal,* August 27, 1958, September 16, 17, 18, 19, 20, 22, 23, 24, 25, 26, 27, 29, 30, October 1, 2, 3, 4, 6, 7, 8, 9, 10, 11, 15, 16, 25 (quotation), 27, 1963, February 14, March 6, May 27, December 9, 11, 1964, January 18, February 1, 2, 1965; *Long* v. *State,* 42 Ala. App. 476; *Tucker* v. *State,* 42 Ala. App. 477; cert. denied by Alabama Supreme Court, 277 Ala. 700, 702. In a case that grew out of the Birmingham demonstrations of April 1963, as we have seen, the U.S. Supreme Court ruled in March 1969—sustaining a decision of the Alabama Court of Appeals—that a use of a parade permit ordinance such as that approved by Judge Russell represented an unconstitutional infringement on freedom of speech (*Shuttlesworth* v. *City of Birmingham,* 43 Ala. App. 68, 281 Ala. 542, 394 U.S. 147).

131. *Birmingham World,* July 31, 1963; *Selma Times-Journal,* September 18, 20, October 2, 1963; Smeltzer's interviews with Col. Richard Ault, November 26, 1963, March 21, 1964, and Sgt. Joe C. Black et al. to U.S. Senate Armed Services Committee and U.S. Justice Department, Civil Rights Division, January 7, 1964, Smeltzer Papers; Norman S. Paul to Julian Bond, June 24, 1963, Julian Bond to Bernard Lafayette, June 27, 1963, and James Forman to Eugene M. Zuckert, September 25, 1963, SNCC Papers. On Colonel Ault, see *Selma Times-Journal,* March 6, 1966.

132. *Selma Times-Journal,* September 20, 1963 (quotations); Claude C. Brown, interview by Smeltzer, February 1, 1964, Smeltzer Papers.

133. *U.S.* v. *Atkins,* 323 F.2d 733, 10 Race Relations Law Reporter 209; *Selma Times-Journal,* October 4, 6, 7, 8, 9, 1963, October 6, 8, 9, 1964; *U.S.* v. *Clark,* 249 F.Supp. 720, 732.

134. *U.S.* v. *McLeod* and *U.S.* v. *Dallas County,* 229 F.Supp. 383, 1014, 385 F.2d 734; *Selma Times-Journal,* July 25, October 15, 16, November 12, 13, 14, December 1, 6, 15, 16, 17, 18, 19, 1963, March 19, 26, 31, 1964. In September 1964, the Dallas County Bar Association adopted a formal resolution assuring citizens that they did not have to answer FBI agents' questions about voter registration discrimination (ibid., September 24, 1964). On the gulf separating SNCC's perception of these events from the Justice Department's, see Burke Marshall to Gilbert Harrison, October 30, 1963, in Smeltzer Papers, and Julian Bond to Burke Marshall, October 2, 1963, David H. Marlin to Julian Bond, October 11, 1963, Julian Bond to Burke Marshall, October 26, 1963, David H. Marlin to Julian Bond, June 17, 1964, Julian Bond to David H. Marlin, July 1, 1964, all in SNCC Papers.

135. *U.S.* v. *Atkins,* 10 Race Relations Law Reporter 209; *Selma Times-Journal,* August 13, October 4, 6, 8, 9, 1964, January 7, February 3, 5, 1965. Cf. Clark, *Jim Clark Story,* 93, 95–96. The entire text of the voter qualification test adopted by the state supreme court on January 14, 1964, including all twelve of the four-question sets, is printed as an appendix to *U.S.* v. *Parker,* 236 F.Supp. 511, 519–29. The entire text of the test adopted August 24 may be found in Brief of the United States for Supplemental Relief, November 23, 1964, in Case File, *U.S.* v. *Atkins,* in FRC East Point. Though the state supreme court promulgated the tests of both January and August 1964, the questions on them actually were formulated by Mrs. Martha Jo Smith of Huntsville, under contract with the State Sovereignty Commission.

136. *New York Times,* January 31, April 8, 1965; *U.S.* v. *Clark,* 249 F.Supp. 720, 731–33. The figures given in the text exclude the month of October 1963; the Fifth

Circuit U.S. Court of Appeals reversed Judge Thomas on October 3, but he did not enter the injunction against the board until November 1; hence it is difficult to know whether the board would have been operating in accordance with the Fifth Circuit's requirements during October. In that month the board registered 73 percent of white applicants and 5 percent of black ones. In October 1964, federal investigators failed to note how many blacks were registered, but they did note that five blacks were rejected. I have assumed that the five rejected were the only ones who applied during the month, but if the board registered as many as two blacks in October, it would raise the percentage for the final period from 10 percent to 11 percent, the same as for the preceding period.

The board's recalcitrance proceeded, of course, from the attitudes of its members. Throughout these years, the three board members remained the same; appointed by the Patterson administration, they were reappointed by the first Wallace administration. The chairman was Victor B. Atkins, the well-to-do planter, former wholesale grocer, and Burns-Heinz organization stalwart whose career we noticed near the beginning of this chapter. Aubrey C. Allen was an active member of the White Citizens' Council and served as the council's chairman in 1956–57 and its secretary-treasurer from 1957 to 1961, when he was appointed to the board of registrars. He was the agricultural loan officer of the City National Bank, the institution intimately allied with the Burns-Heinz organization and of which Atkins was a director; in that position, Allen worked closely with the county's planters and wholesale grocers. Colonel Joseph R. Bibb, a retired army officer and Citizens' Council member, was a leading figure in the county's Republican Party and served as a delegate from the county to the 1964 Republican state convention (*Selma Times-Journal,* September 21, 1956, October 11, 1957, August 13, October 2, 1958, April 19, October 9, 1959, October 21, 1960, May 6, 1964; Smeltzer's interviews with Aubrey C. Allen, January 4, 1964, and John Doar, July 9, 1964, Smeltzer Papers; Trial Transcript, May 3–4, 1962, *U.S.* v. *Atkins,* 35–38, in FRC East Point).

137. *Alabama Official and Statistical Register* for 1963, pp. 728–29, 756–57; *Alabama Official and Statistical Register* for 1967, pp. 664–65, 675–77.

138. *U.S.* v. *Clark,* 249 F.Supp. 720, 732; Case File, *U.S.* v. *Clark,* in FRC East Point; *Selma Times-Journal,* July 2, 3, 5, 6, 7, 8, 9, 10, August 7, December 8, 9, 10, 11, 13, 21, 22, 23, 1964. On the recalcitrance of the restaurants, see Smeltzer's interviews with Otis "Red" Adams, July 11, 1964, Arthur Lewis, July 11, 12, 20, 22, September 3, October 1, 1964, January 1, 21, 27, 1965, Arthur Capell, July 24, August 8, 15, October 3, 17, 1964, January 7, 15, 19, 1965, and Wilson Baker, December 31, 1964, Smeltzer Papers. The complete text of Judge Hare's injunction, and the state's complaint that produced it, are in the Smeltzer Papers and in the *U.S.* v. *Clark* Case File. On the effect of the injunction, see Smeltzer's interviews with Thomas Brown, July 11, 1964, John A. Love, July 12, 15, August 14, 1964, Arthur Lewis, July 22, 1964, and Morris Barton, July 22, 1964, Smeltzer Papers. SNCC began planning the July demonstrations at the beginning of June, and replaced Worth Long with John A. Love to conduct them (Smeltzer's interview with Long, June 3, 1964; see also Smeltzer's notes of meeting of Steering Committee of the Dallas County Voters League, June 2, 1964). The moderate business leader Charles Hohenberg did his best to persuade like-minded associates to form a committee of ten to negotiate with blacks at the beginning of the demonstrations in July, but without success; see Smeltzer's interview with John Newton, July 6, 1964, and cf. his interview with John A. Love, July 12, 1964. Edwin Moss at the same time sought repeatedly to arrange meetings with public officials to discuss the situation, but he

was unable to do so until after Sheriff Clark's raid on Moss's Elks Club, when the discussions necessarily focused on the raid itself; see Smeltzer's interviews with Moss, July 8, 13, 16, 20, 21, 22, 23, August 11, 1964, and with Arthur Lewis, July 20, 22, 1964.

139. *Selma Times-Journal,* July 12, 13, 20, September 3, 6 (quotation), 10, 24, October 6, 8, 9. November 6, 20, 25, December 6, 7, 8, 9, 10, 11, 13, 20, 21, 22, 23, 1964; *U.S.* v. *Clark,* 249 F.Supp. 720; *U.S.* v. *Atkins,* 10 Race Relations Law Reporter 209; Case File, *U.S.* v. *Clark,* Case File and Trial Transcripts, *U.S.* v. *Atkins,* both in FRC East Point; *Dallas County* v. *Student Non-Violent Coordinating Committee,* 10 Race Relations Law Reporter 234; *State of Alabama* v. *Allen,* 10 Race Relations Law Reporter 234. Smeltzer's interviews with Vernol R. "Bob" Jansen, December 7–12, 23, 30, 1964, Smeltzer Papers, contain Jansen's interesting comments on the hearings before the three-judge court.

140. On Smeltzer's background, see Longenecker, *Selma's Peacemaker,* 2–13. On the genesis of his Selma mediation, see Dallas County Voters League to Willard Wirtz, January 9, 1964, Smeltzer to Emergency Committee on Race Relations, December 10, 1963, Smeltzer to James Forman, December 16, 1963, Chris B. Heinz to Norman J. Baugher, July 16, 1964, and Smeltzer's interview with John Newton, November 26, 1963, Smeltzer Papers. On the Dunn affair, see also Amelia P. Boynton to James Forman, November 30, 1963, Ernest L. Doyle to Forman, undated, Ralph E. Smeltzer to Forman, November 18, 1963, Smeltzer to Forman, December 16, 1963, Forman to Smeltzer, January 12, 1964, and Amelia P. Boynton to W. Ray Kyle, January 23, 1964, all in SNCC Papers. Charles Dunn, the nursing home operator whose firing of his black employees brought Smeltzer to Selma, succeeded Chris Heinz as the chairman of the White Citizens' Council in the fall of 1965 (*Selma Times-Journal,* November 30, 1965). Ralph Smeltzer and Amelia Boynton sought to establish Dunn's discharged employees in a sewing business, but the venture does not appear to have been successful.

141. *Selma Times-Journal,* July 16, 1958, May 27, December 6, 1959, June 11, July 6, 1961, May 31, June 7, November 10, 1963, June 24, July 26, October 5 (first quotations), 12, 14 (second quotation), 16, November 2, December 7, 8, 10, 13, 14, 21, 22, 1964, January 1 (third quotation), 3, 6, 10 (fifth quotation), 18, 19 (fourth quotations), February 4 (sixth quotation), 28, April 18, 1965; Morthland, interview, July 10, 1990; Falkenberry, interview, July 18, 1991; Longenecker, *Selma's Peacemaker,* 24–151, 194–97; Chestnut and Cass, *Black in Selma,* 220–24; Fitts, *Selma,* 140–42; Fager, *Selma, 1965,* 179–84; Garrow, *Bearing the Cross,* 369–70; Fairclough, *To Redeem the Soul of America,* 211–12. On the identity of Selma's white moderates, see Smeltzer's interviews with Walter and David Ellwanger, February 1, 1964, John Doar, February 3, 1964, and Arthur Lewis, June 4, July 10, 1964, Smeltzer Papers. On the black leaders' meetings with the white moderates and Mayor Smitherman, see Smeltzer's interviews with Claude C. Brown, September 10, 16, October 16, 22, 30, November 6, 10, December 6, 1964, B. Frank Wilson, September 9, 10, 25, October 2, 16, 1964, January 1, 1965, Frederick D. Reese, September 3, 10, 24, October 10, 22, November 10, December 31, 1964, Edwin L. D. Moss, September 16, 22, October 1, 9, 16, 22, December 8, 1964, Arthur Lewis, July 22, 29, 31, August 6, September 3, 11, 16, 24, October 1, 9, 16, 22, 30, November 11, 1964, Arthur Capell, August 8, 15, 23, September 11, October 17, November 11, 29, 1964, and Joe T. Smitherman, January 4, 1965; see also Smeltzer to Annalee Stewart, September 24, 1964, Smeltzer Papers, and John A. Love, field report, September 14, 1964, SNCC Papers. On the role of Judge Thomas in generating the white moderates'

initiatives, see Smeltzer's interviews with Edgar Stewart, July 17, 25, 1964. On the white moderates' initial sense of helplessness and their desire for delay, see Smeltzer's interviews with Harry Gamble, July 22, 1964, Paul Grist, July 10, 22, 1964, Sam Earle Hobbs, June 4, 1964, Roger ap C. Jones, August 15, 1964, Julien H. Lilienthal, July 22, 1964, Rex Morthland, July 24, August 20, 1964, and John Newton, July 6, 1964. On Wilson Baker's efforts in the period before the demonstrations, see Smeltzer's interviews with John Newton, December 12, 1964, January 1, 14, 1965, Arthur Lewis, August 27, 1964, Edwin L. D. Moss, March 20, August 30, 1964, and Arthur Capell, October 17, December 23, 1964, January 4, 1965. On Baker's dispute of Clark's jurisdiction, see Smeltzer's interviews with Wilson Baker, December 30, 1964, January 4, 1965, Vernol R. "Bob" Jansen, December 31, 1964, Arthur Lewis, October 22, November 11, 1964, January 1, 21, 1965, and Arthur Capell, August 23, 28, October 17, December 31, 1964, January 7, 9, 15, 19, 21, 31, 1965. On Smitherman's inaugural address, see Smeltzer's interviews with Claude C. Brown, October 9, 1964, Frederick D. Reese, October 9, 1964, Edwin L. D. Moss, October 9, 1964, Arthur Lewis, October 9, 1964, and Arthur Capell, August 23, October 17, 1964. On Sergeant Burke's altercation at the Roman Catholic church, see Smeltzer's interviews with Claude C. Brown, October 16, 1964, Arthur Lewis, October 16, 22, November 25, 1964, January 1, 1965, Edwin L. D. Moss, October 16, 22, 1964, Vernol R. "Bob" Jansen, October 21, November 16, 1964, January 1, 1965, Frederick D. Reese, November 6, 1964, Arthur Capell, October 17, November 11, December 23, 31, 1964, and Wilson Baker, April 18, 1965. On the integration at Craig Air Force Base, see Smeltzer's interviews with Colonel Richard Ault, November 26, 1963, March 21, May 15, July 11, September 30, 1964, Sam Earle Hobbs, June 4, 1964, John A. Love, January 3, 4, 7, 1965, Sergeant Joe C. Black, March 20, 24, May 13, 14, 15, June 1, 1964, Edwin L. D. Moss, February 1, 1964, and Arthur Lewis, July 12, 20, 22, 29, 31, August 6, September 3, 1964, February 13, 1965; and John M. Pratt to Robert W. Spike and James C. Moore, November 14, 1963, Sgt. Joe C. Black et al. to U.S. Senate Armed Services Committee and U.S. Justice Department, Civil Rights Division, January 7, 1964, Col. Carl V. Schott to Sen. Hubert H. Humphrey, January 31, 1964, James P. Goode to Rep. Charles C. Diggs, March 23, 1964, Alfred B. Fitt to Diggs, May 11, 1964, John A. Love to Robert S. McNamara, December 23, 1964, Ralph E. Smeltzer to Howard Bennett, January 12, 1965, and "City Officials Strategy Meeting" notes, January 6, 1965, all in ibid. On J. J. Israel, see Arthur Lewis to Ralph Smeltzer, September 4, 1964, and Smeltzer's interviews with Claude C. Brown, August 13, September 3, 10, 1964, Vernol R. "Bob" Jansen, August 27, 1964, Edgar Stewart, August 13, 1964, B. Frank Wilson, August 23, 1964, Frederick D. Reese, August 11, 18, 27, September 3, 10, 24, 1964, January 18, 1965, Edwin L. D. Moss, August 13 [?], 22, September 16, 1964, Arthur Lewis, August 14, 20, 27, September 3, 11, 16, 24, October 1, 9, 22, 30, November 11, 1964, April 12, 1965, and Arthur Capell, August 23, September 11, 1964, ibid. Judge Reynolds's sudden openness to the white moderates' request that he eliminate the segregation of the courthouse drinking fountains appears to have proceeded from the emergence of some political animosity between Reynolds and Sheriff Clark; see Smeltzer's interviews with Claude C. Brown, March 23, June 2, 3, August 15, 1964, but cf. his interview with Arthur Capell, August 15, 1964. In addition, as we have seen, Reynolds was merely following the precedent set by Mayor Heinz at the city hall during the election of the preceding spring. On the integration of the drinking fountains, see Smeltzer's interviews with Bernard Reynolds, July 21, 1964, Chris Heinz, May 16, 1964, Sam Earle Hobbs, June 4, 1964, Roger ap C. Jones, August 15,

1964, Arthur Lewis, September 3, 1964, Frederick D. Reese, June 4, August 18, 1964, and Arthur Capell, August 23, 1964, in Smeltzer Papers, and John A. Love, field report, September 14, 1964, in SNCC Papers. A general discussion of the white moderates' view of the situation in Selma at the outset of the demonstrations is "City Officials Strategy Meeting" notes, January 6, 1965, Smeltzer Papers; see also Smeltzer's list of integrated sites in Selma as of December 6, 1964.

142. Smeltzer's interviews with Arthur Lewis, September 3, October 9, 1964, Smeltzer Papers; *Selma Times-Journal*, October 16, 20, 28, November 7, 8, 12, 13, 14, 15, 18, 21, 22, December 1, 6, 15, 16, 17, 18, 19, 1963, March 10, April 13, December 22, 1964; *U.S. v. McLeod*, 229 F.Supp. 383, 385 F.2d 734; Clark, *Jim Clark Story*, 64–78. Clark states (p. 74) that he learned of the Fort Campbell briefings in the last week of September 1963, but Judge Hare testified in federal court that he learned of the briefings in the early part of the month (*Selma Times-Journal*, December 22, 1964), and the sequence of events leads me to credit Hare on this point. Thelton Henderson was appointed a federal district judge in San Francisco, California, by President Carter in 1980. Apparently, his having been dismissed from the Justice Department for lying did not become an issue in the confirmation proceedings.

143. *Selma Times-Journal*, November 12, 1963 (first quotations), September 6 (second quotations), December 22, 1964; James A. Hare to Mary Ruth Sevier, March 22, 1965, Hare Papers. Cf. Hare to James D. Martin, August 24, 1965, ibid. Hare at this period also appears to have been unsettled by personal problems; see Smeltzer's interview with Amelia P. Boynton, December 8, 1964, Smeltzer Papers; cf. Smeltzer's interview with Edgar Stewart, July 25, 1964, ibid. Hare's reference to "organizers with police records of ten years or more" was directed particularly against Chicago ex-convict Wolf Dawson, who had come to Selma with Lillian Gregory, the wife of black comedian Dick Gregory. Clark and Hare believed that Dawson, who had just been released from the Illinois penitentiary, had been sent to Selma to organize mayhem in the city (Clark, *Jim Clark Story*, 73–74).

The answer to Hare's central query—how the Defense Department had known of the impending Selma demonstrations in early September—is not at all difficult. The letter sent to the Selma Merchants Association by Edwin Moss and the Improvement Association on August 29 had specifically said that the deadline for the merchants to reply was September 15. Though, as we have seen, Selma's white authorities had paid no attention to the deadline, and seem to have been taken by surprise when the demonstrations began on September 16, apparently the Justice Department took the letter quite seriously and asked the army to make preparations in case troops were needed. In addition, in the intervening two weeks SNCC's Worth Long had made inquiries at the Pentagon about the possibility of declaring Selma off-limits to Craig servicemen. Thus there was in reality no mystery at all to the army's actions. On these conspiracy theories, see also Smeltzer's interview with Arthur Lewis, July 24, 1964, Smeltzer Papers.

144. *Selma Times-Journal*, September 21, 1956, November 13, 1959, December 22, 1963, January 31, December 10, 22, 1964, April 18, 1965; James A. Hare to George C. Wallace, March 19, 1965 (quotation), Hare Papers; Amelia P. Boynton to Ralph E. Smeltzer, February 12, 1964, mimeographed circular "To All of the Churches of Selma and Dallas County," December 21, 1963, Smeltzer to Col. Richard Ault, July 30, 1964, and Smeltzer's interviews with Col. Ault, July 29, 1964, Vernol R. "Bob" Jansen, July 29, August 5, 1964, Edwin L. D. Moss, August 13 [?], 22, 30, December 9, 1964, and Arthur Lewis, July 29, 1964, Smeltzer Papers; Longenecker,

Selma's Peacemaker, 51, 98–100. Serving on the Citizens' Bank board of directors with J. Bruce Pardue were the industrialist Leon Jones, a former chairman of the White Citizens' Council, and druggist Joe Pilcher, Sr., whose son, the segregationist attorney Joe Pilcher, Jr., first publicly revealed the existence of the moderate circle and identified its members—a revelation that took place at an angry public meeting at which Bruce Pardue and Leon Jones both delivered segregationist speeches (*Selma Times-Journal*, April 18, 1965, March 24, 1966).

145. Quoted in Garrow, *Bearing the Cross*, 380; cf. Smeltzer's interview with Frederick D. Reese, December 31, 1964, and "City Officials Strategy Meeting" notes, January 6, 1965, Smeltzer Papers.

146. *Selma Times-Journal*, April 24, June 3, 1958, March 14, 1960, February 16, 24, 26, 27, March 16, October 12, 1964; Smeltzer's interviews with Wilson Baker, January 2, 4, 6, 1965, and Smeltzer's notes of "City Officials Strategy Meeting," January 6, 1965, Smeltzer Papers. Following Craig's acquittal, Flowers dropped the prosecution of Engelhardt. On McLean Pitts, see Smeltzer's interviews with Claude C. Brown, October 9, 1964, Arthur Lewis, September 3, October 9, 1964, February 13, 1965, Arthur Capell, October 17, December 31, 1964, and Vernol R. "Bob" Jansen, October 21, 1964, ibid.

147. Amelia P. Boynton Robinson, interview, July 26, 1991; Reese, interview, August 9, 1991; Smeltzer's interviews with Reese, November 25, December 9, 1964, and Claude C. Brown, February 1, 1964, Smeltzer Papers; Garrow, *Bearing the Cross*, 302, 358–60 (quotation, 359). On the faltering of SNCC's efforts, see John A. Love, field reports, August 13, September 14, 1964, and Frank Soracco to Marion Barry, December 26, 1964, in SNCC Papers. One of Mrs. Boynton's sisters-in-law had been a member of Dexter Avenue Baptist Church during Martin Luther King's pastorate, and she had first introduced Mrs. Boynton to King in the years that he had resided in Montgomery (interview, July 26, 1991).

148. On white Selmians' puzzlement at King's selection of their city, see "City Officials Strategy Meeting" notes, January 6, 1965, Smeltzer Papers; cf. Fitts, *Selma*, 143. On black leaders' enthusiastic response to the white moderates' initiatives in the late summer and fall of 1964, see Smeltzer's interviews with Amelia P. Boynton, August 9, September 16, 1964, Claude C. Brown, September 16, 1964, Edwin L. D. Moss, September 16, December 8, 1964, and Frederick D. Reese, November 25, 1964, Smeltzer Papers; see also his interviews with Arthur Capell, September 11, November 11, 1964, ibid.

149. A full account of the demonstrations is in Fager, *Selma, 1965*, 22–165; see also Longenecker, *Selma's Peacemaker*, 154–90, Abernathy, *And the Walls Came Tumbling Down*, 297–361, Garrow, *Bearing the Cross*, 378–415, and Fairclough, *To Redeem the Soul of America*, 225–51. On the background of the demonstrations, see Smeltzer's interviews with Claude C. Brown, November 25, December 11, 1964, January 1, 26, 31, 1965, C. T. Vivian, December 10, 23, 1964, Harry Boyte, December 14, 1964, January 6, 7, 1965, B. Frank Wilson, January 7, 9, 1965, Frederick D. Reese, November 25, December 9, 11, 17, 23, 30, 31, 1964, January 1, 2, 3, 4, 5, 7, 9, 14, 15, 16, 18, 19, 1965, John Newton, December 12, 1964, January 1, 2, 4, 6, 10, 14, 1965, John A. Love, December 9, 11, 24, 30, 1964, January 4, 6, 7, 1965, James Bevel, January 2, 5, 1965, Edwin L. D. Moss, January 2, 1965, Arthur Lewis, December 12, 1964, January 1, 1965, and Arthur Capell, December 23, 31, 1964, January 4, 5, 6, 7, 15, 1965, and Smeltzer's notes of meeting of Steering Committee of Dallas County Voters League, December 11, 1964, and of "City Officials Strategy Meeting," January 6, 1965, all in Smeltzer Papers.

150. *Selma Times-Journal,* December 6, 1963, January 12, February 28, March 5, 1964, January 3 (first quotation), 6, 10, 15, 18, 19, 20, 21 (second quotation), 22, 24 (third quotation), 25, 26, 27, 28, 31, February 1, 2, 3, 4, 5 (fourth quotation), 7, 8, 9, 10, 11, 12, 14, 15, 16, 17, 18 (sixth quotations), 19, 21 (seventh quotation), 22, 23, 24, 25, 26, 28, March 1, 2, 3, 4, 5, 7, 8, 9, 10, 11, 12, 14, 15, 16, 18, 19, 21, 22, 23, 24, 25, 26, 28, 29, 30, April 5, 6, 11, 12, 13, 14, 19, 20, 23, 25, 28, July 4, 11, 21, September 12, 13, 14, 17, 21, 29, November 29, 30, December 1, 2, 3, 5, 7, 8, 9, 10, 12, 1965; *U.S.* v. *Clark,* 249 F.Supp. 720; *Williams* v. *Wallace,* 10 Race Relations Law Reporter 218, 240 F.Supp. 100; *U.S.* v. *Atkins,* 10 Race Relations Law Reporter 209; *Boynton* v. *Clark,* 10 Race Relations Law Reporter 215, 218, 1472, 362 F.2d 992, 12 Race Relations Law Reporter 620; *U.S.* v. *Logue,* 344 F.2d 290; *Dallas County* v. *Student Non-Violent Coordinating Committee,* 10 Race Relations Law Reporter 234; *State of Alabama* v. *Allen,* 10 Race Relations Law Reporter 234; Trial Transcript, *Williams* v. *Wallace,* in FRC East Point; author interviews with Rex J. Morthland, July 10, 1990, Edwin Moss, July 11, 1991, Roswell Falkenberry, July 18, 1991, James E. Gildersleeve, July 22, 1991, Louis L. Anderson, July 23, 1991, Ernest L. Doyle, July 23, 1991, Amelia P. Boynton Robinson, July 26, 1991, J. L. Chestnut, Jr., July 29, 1991, John D. Hunter, August 9, 1991, Frederick D. Reese, August 9, 1991, Marie Foster, August 13, 1991, and Arthur Capell, August 22, 1991; Smeltzer's interviews with Harry Boyte, January 30, March 10, 12, 1965, Vernol R. "Bob" Jansen, January 21, 27, 30, February 3, 9, 10, 12, March 13, April 6, 1965, Frederick D. Reese, January 18, 19, 20, 21, 22, 23, 25, 26, 27, 28, 30, 31, February 1, 2, 3, 4, 5, 7, 9, 11, 12, 15, 16, 17, 20, 22, 23, 25, March 2, 8, 9, 10, 12, 15, 16, 19, April 3, 6, 7, 1965, John Newton, January 22, February 7, 12, 13, March 11, 16, April 7, 9, 13, 19, 1965, John A. Love, February 8, 1965, James Bevel, January 20, 1965, Arthur Lewis, January 21, 27, February 4, 13, March 8, 11, 12, 14, 17, April 4, 1965, and Arthur Capell, January 15, 19, 21, 22, 31, February 7, 9, 1965, and Margaret Hatch, "Report on Burwell Infirmary, Selma, Alabama," May 11, 1965, all in Smeltzer Papers; Chestnut and Cass, *Black in Selma,* 193–94; Longenecker, *Selma's Peacemaker,* 165–67; Garrow, *Bearing the Cross,* 381 (fifth quotation). On the Marion demonstrations, see Trial Transcript, *Williams* v. *Wallace,* vol. 1, pp. 397–420, vol. 3, pp. 549–81, in FRC East Point, and George Bess, field report, Perry County, Alabama, January 16–25, 1965, Press Release, special report, February 5, 1965, and memorandum, "to all friends of SNCC," February 26, 1965, all in SNCC Papers. On the "Bloody Sunday" encounter, see *Williams* v. *Wallace* Trial Transcript, esp. vol. 1, pp. 129–40, 187–265, vol. 2, pp. 268–367, 472–82, 490–97, 525, and excerpt transcripts of Frederick D. Reese, Albert J. Lingo, Asbury Middlebrooks, and John Cloud.

When the Perry County grand jury declined in September 1965 to indict the trooper who had killed Jimmie Lee Jackson, Solicitor McLeod stated that the trooper's surname was Fowler, though he would not give the man's first name. H. Roy Smith, ed., *Alabama Department of Public Safety, 1935–1975* (Montgomery: Department of Public Safety, 1975), contains a complete roster of all active and living retired troopers as of 1975. Only two Fowlers appear on the list: Johnny C. Fowler, stationed at Evergreen, and James L. Fowler, stationed at Hamilton. It would seem essentially certain that one of these two is the trooper in question. In 1965, Johnny C. Fowler was stationed in Montgomery, and because of the proximity of that posting to Selma and Marion, I suspect that he is the man.

At the trial of Cook and the Hoggles for the murder of James Reeb, the state's case was weakened by a series of developments. The two ministers who were with Reeb, Clark Olson and Orloff Miller, both positively identified Cook, but neither could be certain that the Hoggles were among the attackers. And Miller testified that Cook was pursuing him down the street at the time Reeb was struck, thus making it impossible that Cook could have been responsible for the fatal blow. R. B. Kelley, the unindicted co-conspirator, was called to the stand by the prosecution. But Kelley had been indicted in the federal courts along with the three defendants for violating Reeb's civil rights, and for that reason he invoked his right not to have to incriminate himself and refused to testify. There were two eyewitnesses, but one had moved to Mississippi and refused to return, while the testimony of the other was excluded by Judge L. S. Moore when Veterans Administration medical records established that the witness was schizophrenic. Defense attorney Joe Pilcher, a strong segregationist and a close friend of Mayor Smitherman's, alleged that blacks in Selma had deliberately arranged for poor care in Selma and a series of mishaps that delayed Reeb's transfer to Birmingham for hours, because they wished him to die in order to create a martyr for the civil rights cause. And indeed one of the University of Alabama doctors did think that the delays had contributed to Reeb's death, though two others denied it and a fourth was equivocal. Finally, police had been unable to locate another possible participant in the beating, Floyd Grooms, and Pilcher implied that Grooms may actually have struck the fatal blow. O'Neal Hoggle's business partner Edgar B. Vardaman, who testified that O'Neal Hoggle had been with him at the time of the attack, turned out to be a brother of one of the jurors, Harry C. Vardaman. The jurors deliberated for an hour and thirty-five minutes before acquitting all three defendants.

151. *Selma Times-Journal,* March 1, 22 (second quotation), 31, April 14, 25, 27, July 6, 8, 13, October 4, 1965, March 29, 30, 1966; author interviews with Edwin Moss, July 11, 1991, James E. Gildersleeve, July 22, 1991, Ernest L. Doyle, July 23, 1991, J. L. Chestnut, Jr., July 29, 1991, Frederick D. Reese, August 9, 1991; David Smith to Ralph Smeltzer, May 19, 25, 27, June 3, 4, 9, 15, 28, July 7, August 1, 16, 1965, Smeltzer to Smith, May 24, 27, June 10, 16, August 4, 1965, Smeltzer's interviews with Smith, July 7, 8, 21, August 24, 1965, Kathryn Tucker Windham, June 10, 1965, Frederick D. Reese, February 3, 7, 11, 17, 22, 23, 25, March 2, 8, April 3, 7, 12, 13, 14, 16, 17, 22, 26, 30, May 4, 7, 13, 19, 26, June 5, 10, 14, 16, July 8, 1965, Edwin L. D. Moss, April 6, 7, 14, 1965, Arthur Lewis, March 8, April 4, 15, 18, 1965, and Arthur Capell, April 13, 18, 19, May 4, 1965, and M. L. Miles, statement of Chamber of Commerce on bus boycott, undated [April 14, 1965], all in Smeltzer Papers; Chestnut and Cass, *Black in Selma,* 199 (first quotation), 225–33; Longenecker, *Selma's Peacemaker,* 40–46, 203–12; Fager, *Selma, 1965,* 188–204, 208–11. In his account of these events, Fager, a white former SCLC staff member, scarcely bothers to conceal his belief that Reese was guilty as charged. Indeed, so intent is he on placing events in the worst light for Reese that he does not even report the fact that Reese had been discharged from his teaching position. The source of Fager's resentment of Reese and the Voters League appears to be that the league's leadership was drawn from Selma's black middle class, while Fager, like many SCLC workers, wished to transfer black community leadership to the poor. Fager and his associates played a role in forming a rival association to the Voters League, the Dallas County Independent Free Voters Organization.

152. *Selma Times-Journal,* April 17, 26, May 8, July 8, September 20, 1964, February 3, 7, 17 (first quotation), 18, 23 (second quotation), March 1, April 6, 11, 15, 16, 18 (fourth, fifth, sixth, seventh quotations), 20, 1965; U.S. Census of Manufactures, 1963, 1967; Fager, *Selma, 1965,* 179–87; Smeltzer's interviews with Wilson Baker, April 7, 18, 1965, Arthur Lewis, February 13, March 8, 11, 12, 14, 17, April

4, 7, 8, 12, 13, 15, 18, 19, 26, June 2, 3, 1965, George A. "Cap" Swift and Arthur Lewis, April 16, 1965, John Newton, April 7, 9, 13, 19, 1965, and Arthur Capell, April 13, 18, 19, May 4, 1965, Smeltzer Papers; Longenecker, *Selma's Peacemaker*, 192–98. A third major new industry was announced for the area in July 1965, a paper mill to be built in Wilcox County by McMillan Bloudell, a Canadian company (*Selma Times-Journal*, July 9, 1965). The 13–5 vote by which the chamber's board initially rejected an endorsement of the state chamber's advertisement is the vote reported in the press, but Arthur Lewis told Ralph Smeltzer that the vote was actually 12–7 (interview, April 13, 1965). The account of Seymour Palmer's meeting with Mayor Smitherman and Councilman Swift is from Nat Welch to Leroy Collins, February 8, 1965 (third quotation), Vann Papers. On the increasing bitterness and divisions within Selma's business leadership, see Smeltzer's interviews with B. Frank Wilson, January 22, 26, February 12, April 7, 1965, Arthur Lewis, February 4, 13, March 8, 11, April 4, 8, 12, 13, 15, 19, 26, 1965, and Arthur Capell, January 21, 22, February 9, 1965, Smeltzer Papers. On the Lewises' views, see *Time*, April 2, 1965, 11.

153. *Selma Times-Journal*, July 4, 11, 21, 27, August 2, 11, 12, 16, 17, 22, 29, 31, September 2, 3, 7, October 19, 1965, March 4, 6, April 3, 1968; *U.S.* v. *McLeod*, 385 F.2d 734; *Reynolds* v. *Katzenbach*, 248 F.Supp. 593; *U.S.* v. *Executive Committee of the Democratic Party of Dallas County, Alabama*, 254 F.Supp. 537; James A. Hare to Charles Capps, May 3, 1965, Hare to Joseph Forney Johnston, May 5, 1965, Hare to Jake Timmerson, June 10, 1965, Hare to James D. Martin, August 24, 1965, Hare to Bagby Hall, November 4, 1965, Hare to Charles B. Arendall, Jr., January 25, 1966, Hare to Walter C. Givhan, February 18, 1966, Hare to T. Werth Thagard, April 28, 1966, all in Hare Papers; Chestnut and Cass, *Black in Selma*, 219–418; Smeltzer's interviews with Frederick D. Reese, May 7, 13, 19, 26, June 5, 10, 1965, and Arthur Lewis, May 26, June 2, 3, 1965, Smeltzer Papers; author interviews with Edwin Moss, July 11, 1991, Louis L. Anderson, July 23, 1991, and J. L. Chestnut, Jr., July 29, 1991; Fager, *Selma, 1965*, 208–11; Longenecker, *Selma's Peacemaker*, 216–19; Fitts, *Selma*, 155–70. A freedom-of-choice plan authorized parents of each child to apply to place the child in any school in the system offering the appropriate grade. Both Selma and Dallas County opened the first four grades to freedom of choice in 1965, the middle four in 1966, and the final four in 1967. By 1970, when freedom of choice was succeeded by court-ordered general integration, the plan had managed to place about 15 percent of Selma's black students in school with whites (*New York Times*, May 22, 1970). The organization of Morgan Academy received the strong support of the White Citizens' Council, and council chairman Chris Heinz played an important role in the effort. The president of the Dallas County Private School Foundation, which created the school, was Robert D. Wilkinson, the county Republican Party chairman, a member of the Citizens' Council's executive committee, and the foreman of the grand jury that investigated Thelton Henderson's providing of rental cars to Martin Luther King. In the fall and winter of 1965 the Voters League had attempted to renew the black boycott of Selma's white merchants, but without much success (Frederick D. Reese to James Forman, November 9, 1965, SNCC Papers).

Chapter 5. Aftermath

1. I have commented elsewhere on the question of the national civil rights movement's decline; see Charles W. Eagles, ed., *The Civil Rights Movement in Amer-*

ica (Jackson: University Press of Mississippi, 1986), 148–55. The two chapters that follow are in effect a reconsideration of those earlier remarks.

2. *New York Times,* August 2, 1994 (quotation); cf. *Montgomery Advertiser,* August 8, 1994.

3. *New York Times,* June 15, 1967.

4. Jack D. Shows, interview by author, June 20, 1984; *Montgomery Independent,* November 2, 1967; *Montgomery Advertiser,* March 19, 1963, March 12, 13, 21, 22, 1967, March 11, 12, 13, 14, 16, 23, 24, 31, May 5 (first quotation), 16 (second quotation), 18, 19, 1971; (Montgomery) *Alabama Journal,* June 7, 1971; *New York Times,* January 20, 1964, June 15, 16, 19, 21, 1967, January 5, March 23, May 18, 1971. Rucker's defeat of Sullivan in 1967 had also turned in part on public criticism of the fire department's handling of a disastrous blaze in a downtown restaurant.

5. *Montgomery Advertiser,* April 12, 26, September 27, 1972, October 19, 1973, September 11, 19, 25, 28, October 27, November 1, 3, 6, 1974, May 21, September 1, 3, 27, 1975, December 3, 1983; (Montgomery) *Alabama Journal,* November 6, 1972, October 12, 1973, April 11, 1974; *New York Times,* January 4, 1977; *Acts of Alabama,* Regular Session of 1973, Act of August 28, 1973, pp. 879–923; *Robinson* v. *Pottinger,* 376 F.Supp. 615 (second opinion unpublished).

6. *Montgomery Advertiser,* May 14, 1971, September 3, 1975, June 22, 1978, December 30, 1979, October 3, 4, 7, 8, 12, 13, 14, 15, 16, 18, 26, November 15, 16, 17, 18, 19, 22, 23, 24, 25, 26, 27, 28, 1983, October 14, 1987, October 9, 1991, October 11, 1995, October 11, 13, November 3, 1999, July 15, 18, 20, 21, 22, 23, 24, 25, 26, 27, 29, 30, 31, August 1, 2, 4, 5, 6, 7, 8, 9, 10, 11, 12, 13, 18, 24, 30, October 31, November 1, 8, 2000; *New York Times,* August 8, 1972, September 7, 1976, January 4, March 4, 13, 1977, April 4, 1978, June 11, October 9, 11, 12, 13, 1983; *Smiley* v. *City of Montgomery,* 350 F.Supp. 451, *Jordan* v. *Wright,* 417 F.Supp. 42, *Jordan* v. *Wilson,* 649 F.Supp. 1038, 667 F.Supp. 772, *U.S.* v. *City of Montgomery,* 686 F.Supp. 878, 744 F.Supp. 1074, 911 F.2d 741, 755 F.Supp. 1522, 934 F.2d 1265, 770 F.Supp. 1523, 775 F.Supp. 1450, 788 F.Supp. 1563, *Eiland* v. *City of Montgomery,* 797 F.2d 953, *Green* v. *City of Montgomery,* 792 F.Supp. 1238, *Benjamin* v. *City of Montgomery,* 785 F.2d 959, *Buskey* v. *Oliver,* 565 F.Supp. 1473. On the power of Reed's Alabama Democratic Conference within the state Democratic Party, see *Montgomery Advertiser,* December 27, 28, 1990.

7. *Birmingham News,* October 1, 11, November 1, 1967, October 13, 1971, October 8, 15, November 5, 1975; *New York Times,* July 23, 24, November 4, 1967, December 5, 1968, October 16, 1969, March 28, August 17, 1972, July 15, August 13, November 6, 1975; Jimmie Lewis Franklin, *Back to Birmingham: Richard Arrington, Jr., and His Times* (Tuscaloosa: University of Alabama Press, 1989), 56–108.

8. *Birmingham News,* October 10, 11, 31, 1979; *New York Times,* May 2, 3, 4, 5, June 26, July 7, 18, 21, 29, September 7, October 10, 11, 30 (quotation), 31, November 1, 11, 14, 1979; Franklin, *Back to Birmingham,* 108–74.

9. *Birmingham News,* October 14, November 4, 1981, October 12, 1983, October 9, 1985, October 14, 1987, October 11, 1989, October 9, 18, 1991, November 12, 1992, August 21, October 13, 1993, October 11, 1995, October 15, 16, November 5, 1997, October 11, 13, November 1, 2, 3, 1999; *Montgomery Advertiser,* July 20, 1991, November 13, 1992, March 8, 1998; *New York Times,* October 27, November 5, 9, 10, 1981, January 5, May 24, 1982, October 9, 10, 11, 12, 13, 1983, August 4, 1985, October 10, 1986, October 15, November 10, 1987, June 20, 1988, August 8, 28, 1989, August 10, 1990, January 18, 20, 23, 24, 25, 26, February 28, August 18, November 14, 1992, August 3, 1994; Franklin, *Back to Birmingham,* 175–331;

Ensley Branch of NAACP v. *Seibels,* 616 F.2d 812, *U.S.* v. *Jefferson County,* 720 F.2d 1511, *In re Birmingham Reverse Discrimination Employment Litigation,* 833 F.2d 1492, *Martin* v. *Wilks,* 490 U.S. 755, *Johnson* v. *Transportation Agency,* 480 U.S. 616, *Bennett* v. *Arrington,* 806 F.Supp. 926. Chief Deutcsh was convicted of the misdemeanor in 1991, but the state court of criminal appeals reversed the conviction in 1992. In the meantime, the chief had suffered a brain injury in a fall and was compelled to retire from the force (*Montgomery Advertiser,* January 17, 1994). From 1963 to 1989, when the council was elected at large, five of the nine council members were elected every second year. The four candidates who received the most votes got a four-year term. The candidate who came in fifth got a two-year term and had to run in the next election along with the remaining four council members. After the adoption of districts in 1989, all nine council members were elected to four-year terms at once. They were chosen at a midterm election halfway through the mayor's term so that the tenure of the mayor and the council would overlap.

10. *New York Times,* May 22, 1970; *Selma Times-Journal,* March 4, 6, April 3, 1968, October 26, 1971, January 2, 11 (first and second quotations), 18, 24, 25 (fourth quotation), 28 (third quotation), 30 (fifth quotation), 31, February 1, 7, August 1, 6, 9, 1972; *Code of Alabama,* 1940, Recompiled 1958, Title 37, Section 426; *Acts of Alabama,* Special Session of 1909, pp. 100–102, Regular Session of 1927, pp. 706–8, Regular Session of 1931, pp. 436–38, Regular Session of 1961, pp. 910–15; J. L. Chestnut, Jr., and Julia Cass, *Black in Selma: The Uncommon Life of J. L. Chestnut, Jr.* (New York: Farrar, Straus and Giroux, 1990), 259–61. Not only had Selma been illegally electing its council at large, but it had been holding the elections in March, though the code specified that they should be in August. In 1971 the legislature had abolished party primaries in all municipal elections, and that change too was incorporated in the 1972 Selma election (*Acts of Alabama,* Regular Session of 1971, p. 3592).

11. *Selma Times-Journal,* August 8, 11, September 15, 1976; *Montgomery Advertiser,* October 22, 1975, March 13, 1976; *Acts of Alabama,* Session of 1844–45, pp. 120–21, Session of 1890–91, pp. 150–51, Session of 1977, pp. 678–79; Chestnut and Cass, *Black in Selma,* 260–76, 290–91. The majority gained by whites in the 1950s proceeded largely from the annexation of the new subdivisions surrounding the city in May 1956, but the construction of these subdivisions was, of course, itself a product in considerable part of the prosperity that Craig had brought to the area. On the importance of the base, see Carl C. Morgan, Jr., "Craig Air Force Base: Its Effect on Selma, 1940–1977," *Alabama Review* 42 (April 1989): 83–96.

12. *Selma Times-Journal,* July 4, 6, 9, 30, September 3, 24, 1980; Chestnut and Cass, *Black in Selma,* 409–10. The turn to the federal courts derived in part from the fact that it was only at this time that judges began accepting the arguments both that local at-large election diluted the black vote and that the Voting Rights Act's pre-clearance provisions applied to counties and cities (*Brown* v. *Moore,* 428 F.Supp. 1123; *U.S.* v. *County Commission of Hale County,* 425 F.Supp. 433, 430 U.S. 924; *U.S.* v. *Board of Commissioners of Sheffield,* 430 F.Supp. 786, 435 U.S. 110; *Bolden* v. *City of Mobile,* 423 F.Supp. 384, 571 F.2d 238, 446 U.S. 55). Given how crucially the absolutist "one person, one vote" standard of legislative apportionment influenced the subsequent history of Selma, it is especially ironic that it was the insistence of Dallas County's own Probate Judge "Babe" Reynolds and his local legal advisers McLean Pitts, Joseph E. Wilkinson, Jr., Thomas G. Gayle, and Edgar Russell that had compelled the appeal to the U.S. Supreme Court, over the state's objection,

of the much more modest holding of the lower court (*Sims* v. *Frink,* 205 F.Supp. 245, 208 F.Supp. 431, *Reynolds* v. *Sims,* 377 U.S. 533).

13. *Selma Times-Journal,* June 4, July 9, 11, August 1, 1984; *Montgomery Advertiser,* July 11, 1984; *New York Times,* June 7 (quotation), July 10, 11, 15, August 1, 1984, March 1, 1985; *Acts of Alabama,* First Special Session of 1983, pp. 163–264; Chestnut and Cass, *Black in Selma,* 249–58, 335–44, 401–2; on Chestnut's strategic assumptions, see ibid., 365–67, 407, and *New York Times,* July 15, 1984; on Rose Sanders's attitudes, see also Tony Horwitz, *Confederates in the Attic: Dispatches from the Unfinished Civil War* (New York: Pantheon, 1998), 363–69.

14. *Selma Times-Journal,* July 14, August 24, 25, September 13, 14, November 23, December 14, 28, 1988, December 1, 5, 1989; *Montgomery Advertiser,* July 15, August 28, December 28, 1988, August 31, 1989; *New York Times,* March 1, 4, September 24, 1985, December 25, 1986, July 31, 1987, January 17, 1989, February 20, March 5, 7, 1990; Chestnut and Cass, *Black in Selma,* 259–95, 333–44, 348–50, 359–73, 391–416; *U.S.* v. *Dallas County Commission,* 548 F.Supp. 794, 875, 739 F.2d 1529, 791 F.2d 831, 636 F.Supp. 704, 661 F.Supp. 955, 1337, 850 F.2d 1433. Judge Hand's reluctance to order electoral arrangements that would effectively deliver control of the Black Belt counties to blacks quickly became well known. In 1979, for instance, in a suit challenging the at-large election of the Marengo County Commission, Hand had held that, where blacks constituted a voting majority, even though a narrow one, at-large elections logically could not have the effect of diluting their votes (*Clark* v. *Marengo County,* 469 F.Supp. 1150, *U.S.* v. *Marengo County Commission,* 731 F.2d 1546). On Chestnut's inglorious role in the civil rights demonstrations, see, e.g., Ralph Smeltzer's interviews with John A. Love, July 12, 1964, and Edwin L. D. Moss, July 20, 1964, in Smeltzer Papers, Brethren Archives, Elgin, Illinois; cf. also Smeltzer's interview with Chestnut, July 20, 1964, ibid.

15. The figures in the text are derived from a study conducted by Alston Fitts in early May 1990 and printed in the *Selma Times-Journal,* May 13, 1990. In order to determine the situation at the start of school in September 1989, I have added to Fitts's totals the 196 whites who withdrew from the high school during February 1990. One-third of the 196 were in level one. I have assumed that the remainder were all assigned to level two. Rather more arbitrarily, I have also assumed that equal numbers of the 196 were in each of the four grades, though in fact it seems likely that somewhat fewer twelfth graders withdrew. The figures are therefore only approximations, but they are, I am confident, reasonably accurate ones. It is to be emphasized, however, that the figures are derived from English classes; the situation in mathematics, science, or social studies could well be different.

16. Chestnut and Cass, *Black in Selma,* 402, 416; see in general 391–416.

17. *Selma Times-Journal,* November 13, 14, 17, 19, 22, 24, December 1, 3, 5, 15, 17, 21, 22, 24, 27, 29, 31, 1989, January 1, 3, 4, 5, 9, 10, 11, 14, 15, 16, 17, 18, 19, 21, 22, 23, 24, 25, 26, 28, February 2, 4, 5, 7, 8, 9, 11, 12, 13, 14, 15, 16, 18, 20, 21, 22, 23, 25, 27, March 1, 2, 7, 9, 11, 12, 13, 14, 15, 16, 18, 20, 23, 25, 26, 28, 29, 30, April 1, 11, 12, 13, 15, 17, 18, 19, 20, 22, 25, 26, May 1, 2, 3, 6, 8, 9, 13, 16, 17, 18, 23, 25, 27, 29, June 1, 7, 8, 10, 12, 13, 14, 20, 21, 22, 25, 26, 27, July 1 (quotation), 5, 6, 13, 24, 31, August 3, 5, 8, 15, 16, 17, 19, 21, 22, 23, 24, 26, 27, 28, 29, 30, 31, 1990; *Montgomery Advertiser,* August 31, 1989, August 19, November 1, 25, December 16, 28, 1990, July 7, 1991, February 16, 1992, February 6, 1994; *New York Times,* February 20, March 5, 7, 1990. The white members of the school board were Carl Barker, Mrs. Edith M. Jones, former superintendent Joseph Pickard,

Mrs. Martha Reeves, Clint Wilkinson, and Richard Bean. The black members were Charles Lett, Mrs. Sheila Okoye, James Spicer, Dr. Julius Jenkins, and Freeman Waller.

18. *Selma Times-Journal,* January 19, 1990, August 26, 27, September 16, 1992, June 5, August 26, 27, 28, 29, November 1, 3, 6, 1996, December 28, 1999, January 18, 30, April 5 (second quotation), 30, May 30, 31, July 10, 18, 24, August 1, 8, 9, 10, 21, 23, 24, 26, 27, September 6, 7, 9, 13, 16, 18, 2000; *Montgomery Advertiser,* September 22, 1991, August 26, October 6, December 15, 29, 1992, March 17, April 6, 15, 16 (first quotation), 20, May 21, 24, June 4, 15, 20, 26, August 24, 25, 26, September 6, 7, 15, October 6, 7, December 11, 1993, February 6, 1994, August 27, 29, October 10, 1996, January 17, November 24, 1997, February 25, June 23, 1998, June 5, August 1, 5, 6, 16, 20, 21, 23, 29, 30, September 3, 7, 8, 9, 13, 14, October 2, 3, 11, 23, November 21, 22, 28, 29, December 1, 5, 6, 11, 22, 2000, January 2, 2001; *New York Times,* September 10, 2000. It is worth noting that the outcome of the 1996 municipal election would appear to vindicate the 1992 returns fully from the charges of Perkins and his supporters, despite the existence of the objective evidence cited in the text for the earlier black doubts. In 1998, as well, voters of the judicial circuit that included Selma chose their first black circuit judge, the moderate Marvin Wiggins, who won with some white support in a close contest with a white woman prosecutor (*Montgomery Advertiser,* July 2, 1998).

Chapter 6. Conclusion

1. Clayborne Carson et al., eds., *The Papers of Martin Luther King, Jr.,* vol. 3 (Berkeley: University of California Press, 1997), 71–74.

2. The limitations on King's understanding of the events in which he was involved were only just beginning to be apparent to observers near the end of his life; see, e.g., August Meier, "On the Role of Martin Luther King," *New Politics* 4, no. 1 (1965): 52–59.

3. Martin Luther King, Jr., *Where Do We Go from Here: Chaos or Community?* (Boston: Beacon Press, 1967), iii, 9, 13–14, 100–101, 166, 190 et passim.

4. Ibid., 37, 44; see generally 23–66.

Index

52, 87, 141, 509; Hill family in, 20, 25, 27, 53, 85, 95, 96, 124, 474; Ku Klux Klan in, 22, 76–78, 80, 87, 91–97, 99, 104, 110–13, 117–20, 122, 126, 133, 139, 140, 474, 503, 504, 587n. 3, 609n. 115, 610n. 123, 611n. 125, 616n. 149, 617n. 150, 618n. 152, 628n. 26, 630n. 34, 658n. 170; march from Selma to, 137, 138, 486–89, 503, 573, 577, 620n. 166; municipal election of 1947 in, 25; municipal election of 1953 in, 25, 26, 111; municipal election of 1955 in, 47–51, 563; municipal election of 1959 in, 101, 109–12, 502; municipal election of 1963 in, 133, 502, 503; municipal election of 1967 in, 503, 504, 693n. 4; municipal election of 1971 in, 504, 505; municipal election of 1983 in, 509–11; municipal election of 1999 in, 512, 513, 530, 531; parks in, 41, 49, 50, 54, 101–3, 105, 107, 112, 129, 131, 134, 135, 137, 223, 258, 503; police department of, 10, 11, 18, 22, 33–37, 41, 93, 95, 110, 114–17, 119–22, 126, 131, 133–37, 249, 332, 503, 507–13, 616n. 150, 650n. 135; postwar growth of, 23, 24, 26, 27, 38–40, 51, 52; public accommodations integration in, 136, 137, 503; public housing in, 39, 59, 592n. 38; public library of, 39, 113, 129, 130, 132, 133, 452, 619n. 159, 632n. 44; public schools of, 38, 40, 57, 91, 103–7, 112, 134–37, 393, 503, 592n. 36, 613n. 134, 671n. 20; sectional rivalries in, 9, 10, 23–26, 29–32, 49–51, 110, 111, 503–6, 509; sit-in crisis in, 113–18, 129, 131, 411, 425, 508, 674n. 55, 679n. 97; terminal integration in, 52, 113, 127, 128, 132, 139, 616nn. 149, 150, 618n. 152; Todd Road incident in, 509–12; White Citizens' Council in, 6, 57, 68, 70, 73, 74, 80, 82, 83, 91, 95, 97–99, 107, 110–12, 118, 124, 129, 133, 139, 140, 231, 402, 404, 503, 504, 573, 603n. 92, 609n. 115; Whitehurst af-

fair in, 507–12; white liberals in, 36, 39, 88, 97–99, 107, 126, 131
Montgomery, James T., 336, 357, 649n. 130, 662n. 179
Montgomery Academy, 104
Montgomery Advertiser, 20, 26, 36, 42, 47, 51, 52, 56, 66, 82, 83, 85, 87, 92–95, 97, 99, 100, 120, 125, 506–8, 510, 593n. 42, 597n. 70, 600n. 80, 616n. 150
Montgomery Board of Education, 38, 40, 104, 106, 137, 393, 671n. 20
Montgomery Chamber of Commerce. *See* Chamber of Commerce, Montgomery
Montgomery City Lines. *See* National City Lines
Montgomery Country Club, 505, 509
Montgomery County Board of Revenue, 22, 25, 74, 593n. 42
Montgomery County Courthouse, 113, 138, 508
Montgomery Examiner, 36
Montgomery Fair department store, 43, 59
Montgomery Furniture Dealers Association, 68
Montgomery Home News, 97, 99, 113, 114
Montgomery Improvement Association (MIA), 17, 62, 64, 65, 67, 68, 70–72, 74–81, 84, 86, 87, 89, 91–93, 95, 98–107, 109, 111, 112, 115, 123, 128, 131–36, 138, 140, 191, 198, 204, 212, 227, 445, 566, 585n. 3, 598n. 72, 599n. 77, 600n. 80, 601nn. 83, 86, 602n. 89, 603nn. 90, 93, 94, 604n. 96, 605n. 101, 606n. 104, 608nn. 108, 109, 612n. 134, 620n. 163, 639n. 82
Montgomery Industrial School for Negro Girls (Miss White's School), 58
Montgomery Interdenominational Ministerial Alliance, 34, 62, 125, 136, 597n. 70
Montgomery Junior Chamber of Commerce (Jaycees), 39, 48, 49, 124
Montgomery Labor Council, 92, 95
Montgomery Ministerial Association, 67, 124, 136
Montgomery Parent-Teacher Association, 67, 68, 91

677nn. 82, 88, 681n. 118, 683n. 128, 691n. 150, 692n. 152

Smitherman, John U., 395–98, 421, 426, 672n. 29

Smitherman, Minnie, 428

Smitherman, Thomas, 428

Smithfield (section of Birmingham), 158–64, 166, 171, 174, 178–80, 182–84, 190, 191, 194, 198, 200, 202, 207, 217, 223, 250, 267, 321, 337, 342, 346, 352, 631n. 39, 633n. 49, 661n. 178

Smithfield District Civil Defense Reserve Police, 164, 180, 250, 331, 332, 629n. 31, 657n. 166

Smyer, Sidney W., 190, 195, 235, 238, 251, 252, 254, 265, 275–78, 282, 288, 293, 294, 313, 314, 317–19, 321, 327, 330, 372, 373, 642n. 93, 654n. 153, 656nn. 163, 165

Snuggs, W. Elbert, 394

Socialist Workers Party, 519

South (magazine), 474

South Carolina, 210, 403, 421, 596n. 67

Southern Bell Telephone Company, 165, 335, 452, 523

Southern Christian Leadership Conference (SCLC), 3, 4, 10, 14–17, 134–38, 204, 224, 269, 270, 273, 277, 278, 282, 288, 289, 292–94, 297, 299–301, 310, 312, 314, 317, 320, 325, 327, 352, 373, 374, 445, 455, 462, 463, 473, 475–77, 479, 483–87, 490–92, 497, 513, 561, 567, 572, 612n. 134, 639n. 80, 647n. 119, 649n. 131, 652nn. 143, 146, 691n. 151

Southern Conference Educational Fund (SCEF), 447, 448, 596n. 67

Southern Conference for Human Welfare, 153, 154, 166

Southern Federation of Labor, 609n. 115

Southern Institute of Management, 232, 235

Southern Natural Gas Company (Sonat), 235

Southern Negro Youth Congress, 153, 229, 664n. 183

Southern Railway, 397

Southern Regional Council, 14, 64, 117,

228, 272, 447, 448, 463, 592n. 36, 596n. 67

Southside (section of Birmingham), 201, 202, 273, 369, 514, 515, 520

Sparkman, John J., 160, 443

Sparks, Chauncey, 48, 424

Spicer, James, 696n. 17

Spicer, Mary, 248

Spivey, Ed, 509, 510

Sporting News, 143

Spring Hill College, 277

Stakely, Charles A., 25

Stallings, Earl, 304, 653n. 148

Stallworth, Kemp S., 671nn. 21, 22

Stanford, Henry King, 259

Stanley, Cassius M., 98, 99, 125, 126

Stanley, W. Marvin, 503, 616n. 150

State Sovereignty Commission, Alabama, 239, 340, 684n. 135

States Rights Advocate, 95

Stearns, Sam B., 47–50

Steele, C. Kenzie, 91, 570

Steele, Lucinda, 671nn. 21, 22

Steele, William, 462

Stein, Judith, 625n. 9

Stephens, Elton B., 655n. 158

Sterne, Mervyn, 168, 170, 175, 182, 185, 187, 191–93, 631n. 39

Stevenson, Daniel, 671nn. 21, 22

Stewart, Edgar A., 465, 466, 470, 482, 495, 496

Stewart, Marguerite W., 192

Stewart, Potter, 292, 293

Stewart, Robert, 89, 606n. 105

Stewart, Robert C., 192

Stinson, Dolores, 387–91, 670n. 14

Stockham, Herbert, 660n. 175

Stockham, Richard J., 631n. 39

Stockham Valves and Fittings Co., 170, 173, 176, 631n. 39, 635n. 59, 660n. 175

Stone, Herman, 261

Stone, Lloyd, 244

Stoner, Jesse B., 248, 644n. 103

store facilities, integration of, 7, 17, 136, 140, 228, 230, 263–70, 273, 274, 276–82, 287, 288, 294, 306, 310, 312–34, 336, 337, 348, 359, 361, 363, 371, 453, 455, 456, 486, 562, 563, 649n. 133, 655n. 159, 656n. 163

677n. 89, 681nn. 114, 116, 118,
682n. 119, 685n. 136
Thomas, Henry, 245
Thomas, James L., 538, 556
Thomas, Randall, 510
Thomas, Robert S., 242, 243, 248
Thomas, William H., 89, 606n. 104
Thomasville, Georgia, 657n. 166
Thompson, Earl, 244, 661n. 177
Thompson, Myron, 510, 512
Thompson, R. DuPont, 182
Thrasher, Thomas R., 36, 64, 72, 98,
601n. 84
Till, Emmett, 188
Time (magazine), 232, 235, 257
Timmerman, George Bell, 607n. 107
Titusville (section of Birmingham),
159, 174
Tokyo, Japan, 252
Totten, Kenneth E., 67–70
Townsend, S. Vincent, 378
Trailways Bus Lines, 118, 119, 123, 127,
209, 240, 245–47, 251, 603n. 93,
616n. 149
Trammell, Seymour, 339, 403
Trenholm, H. Councill, 46, 115, 597n. 69
Trinity Baptist Church (Birming-
ham), 189
Trinity Presbyterian Church (Mont-
gomery), 68
Troopers, Alabama State. *See* Highway
Patrol, Alabama
Troxell, Adelia, 219, 660n. 175
True American Society, 624n. 3
Truman, Harry S., 163, 205, 235, 443
Tucker, Benny L., 452, 455, 457, 556, 561
Tucker, Jack P., 399
Tupelo, Mississippi, 412
Turnipseed, Andrew, 36
Turner, Albert, 486
Turner, Charles C., Jr., 98
Turner, John C., 350
Turner, Richard, 463
Tuscaloosa, Alabama, 104, 161, 167,
191, 192, 203, 205, 208, 215, 220,
242, 276, 342, 371, 398, 425, 468,
640n. 87, 658n. 170, 671n. 20
Tuskegee, Alabama, 58, 85, 89, 107, 131,
134, 136, 339, 340, 343, 344, 425,
659n. 173, 660n. 175, 661n. 176

Tuskegee Civic Association, 90, 204,
227, 639n. 82
Tuskegee Institute, 435, 439, 443,
596n. 67
Tuskegee Veterans Administration Hospi-
tal, 388, 389
Tuttle, Elbert, 214, 220, 333, 640n. 88
Tutwiler Hotel (Birmingham), 180, 333
Tuxedo Junction (section of Birming-
ham), 175
Typographical Union, Birmingham local
of, 153

Unitarian-Universalist Fellowship of
Montgomery, 98
United Americans for Conservative Gov-
ernment, 337–40, 345, 353, 370,
659n. 172, 666n. 188
United Automobile Workers, 327
United Mine Workers, 147–51, 162, 169,
239, 625n. 9
United Nations, 577
United Protestants, 353
United States Pipe and Foundry Com-
pany, 190, 235, 655n. 158
United States Steel Corporation, 148,
165, 170, 187, 192, 235, 343, 349,
353, 523, 625n. 9, 655n. 158
United Steelworkers, 147–50, 183, 343,
625n. 9, 660n. 175
Urban League, National, 4, 167–69,
631n. 39

Vacca, Paschal P., 239
Valdosta, Georgia, 3, 7
Vann, David J., 271, 272, 274, 296, 302,
312, 313, 316–19, 330, 350, 362, 368,
370, 515–21, 654n. 153, 656n. 163,
667n. 192
Vann, Joe, Sr., 671n. 21
Vanocur, Sander, 614n. 142
Vardaman, Claude, 205
Vardaman, Edgar B., 691n. 150
Vardaman, Harry C., 691n. 150
Varner, Perry, 540, 548–50, 554, 555, 557
Varner, Robert, 506
Vaughan Memorial Hospital (Selma), 418
Vaughn, W. Prince, 170
Vestavia Hills, Alabama, 202, 237,
663n. 181

West Hills Lions Club (Birmingham), 255
West Point, United States Military
  Academy at, 349
Westside Middle School (Selma), 542,
  543, 549, 550, 557
Wetumpka, Alabama, 189
Wheeler, Malcolm L., 642n. 94
*Where Do We Go from Here: Chaos or
  Community?* 576, 577
White, A. B., 630n. 37, 631n. 39
White, Alice L., 58
White, Arthur, 661n. 177
White, Byron R., 122
White Citizens' Council, Dallas
  County, 6, 10, 14, 15, 57, 97, 108,
  190, 311, 384, 391–406, 411–13, 421,
  422, 425, 432–34, 449, 453, 454, 459,
  464–67, 470, 472, 474, 475, 477–79,
  485, 491, 492, 495–98, 539, 573,
  671nn. 19, 26, 672n. 41, 673n. 47,
  677n. 88, 682n. 122, 683n. 128,
  685n. 136, 686n. 140, 689n. 144,
  692n. 153
White Citizens' Council, Greene
  County, 650n. 135
White Citizens' Council, Jefferson
  County, 190–92, 195, 196, 200,
  201, 231, 256, 304, 319, 337,
  635n. 59
White Citizens' Council, Macon County,
  650n. 135
White Citizens' Council, Montgomery,
  6, 57, 68, 70, 73, 74, 80, 82, 83, 91,
  95, 97–99, 108, 110–12, 118, 139,
  140, 404, 603n. 92, 609n. 115
White Citizens' Council, Tarrant City,
  190, 196
White Citizens' Councils, Alabama,
  97, 98, 108, 109, 190, 191, 215,
  304, 392, 400–405, 412, 474, 477,
  494, 578
Whitehurst, Bernard, 507, 508, 510
White People, National Great Society
  of, 487
Whitesell, Calvin, 122, 127, 128
white supremacy and segregation,
  1–3, 78, 87, 88, 103, 345, 346, 354,
  405, 500–502, 562–64, 602n. 89,
  676n. 72
Whitt, M. W., 197

Wiggins, M. Edwin, 364, 365, 376,
  652n. 140
Wiggins, Marvin, 696n. 18
Wilbur, Susan, 120, 618n. 152
Wilcox County, Alabama, 425, 437,
  440–43, 490, 678n. 97, 681n. 111,
  692n. 152
Wilcutt, Herbert E., 250, 644n. 103
Wilkins, Roy, 570, 598n. 72
Wilkinson, A.D., 671n. 24
Wilkinson, Clint, 696n. 17
Wilkinson, Horace, 144, 163, 627n. 19,
  628n. 28
Wilkinson, Joseph E., Jr., 694n. 12
Wilkinson, Robert D., Jr., 471, 692n. 153
Williams, Alvery, 462, 463
Williams, Aubrey W., Jr., 40
Williams, Aubrey W., Sr., 36
Williams, Carlos, 549
Williams, Curtis, 557
Williams, G. Mennen, 32, 188
Williams, Hosea, 373–76, 487, 488
Williams, J. H., 408
Williams, James "Ace," 242, 248
Williams, Joseph, 356
Williams, McArthur, 556
Williams, Robert L., 162
Williams, Mrs. Roscoe, 77
Williams, Willie L., 225, 285
Williamson, Martin, 408, 426, 427,
  676n. 75
Willie, Louis J., 372
Willis, James H. "Bep," 211
Wilson, A. W., 602n. 86, 603n. 94
Wilson, B. Franklin, 399, 431, 432, 465–
  67, 470, 494, 495
Wilson, James E., Jr., 511
Wilson, John H., 513
Wiman, Martin J., 98
Windham, Waldrop, 239
Windham, Whitten M., 233, 239
Wingo, Douglass P., 642n. 94, 650n. 135
Winnsboro, South Carolina, 245
Winston, Richard, 671nn. 21, 22
Winston County, Alabama, 605n. 99
Wisconsin, 404, 475
Wisdom, John Minor, 208, 218, 343
WMGY (Montgomery), 95
Wofford, Harris, 675nn. 60, 64, 679n. 99
Women's Political Council (Montgom-

ery), 32, 33, 40, 41, 46, 47, 56, 61, 605n. 101
Wood, Bobby, 215, 638n. 76
Woodlawn (section of Birmingham), 153, 201, 652n. 140
Woodlawn High School (Birmingham), 345
Woods, Abraham L., 267, 282, 303, 335, 350, 357, 375, 652n. 143, 662n. 179
Woods, Calvin, 212, 213, 363, 375, 376, 652n. 143
Woods, Tom, 652n. 140
Woodward, C. Vann, 1–3
Woodward, Joe H., 170
Woodward Iron Company, 168, 170, 182
Woolfolk, Robert W., 611n. 125
Woolworth's, F. W., variety store (Birmingham), 328, 359
Works Progress Administration, United States, 38
Wright, David C., 646n. 110
Wright, Edward L., 507, 508
Wright, Theo R., 218, 219, 339, 343
WRMA (Montgomery), 33, 39, 102, 593n. 39

WSLA-TV (Selma), 401
Wylam (section of Birmingham), 368

Yale University, 386, 618n. 152, 675n. 64
Yarbrough, Levi, 661n. 177, 666n. 188
Yielding, F. B., Jr., 190
Yielding, Howard, 636n. 71
York, James D., 610n. 123
Young, Andrew, 293, 301, 304, 314, 320, 482, 652n. 143, 653n. 146
Young, George, 514, 515
Young, Ronald R., 31, 35, 590n. 22
Young, Whitney, 570
Young Men's Business Club (YMBC), Birmingham, 165, 188, 235, 237, 239, 259, 260, 271, 350, 665n. 186
Young Men's Christian Association (YMCA), 39, 177, 215, 395, 419, 447, 466, 495
Youth Legislature, Alabama YMCA, 215

Zellner, J. Robert, 98, 123
Ziegler Meat Packing Company, 674n. 55
Zukoski, Charles F., 168, 187, 192, 193, 255
Zwerg, James, 119, 120, 126, 618n. 152

About the Author

J. Mills Thornton III is a professor of history at the University of Michigan, Ann Arbor. His previous publications include *Politics and Power in a Slave Society: Alabama, 1800–1860* (Louisiana State University Press).